T5-CQD-792

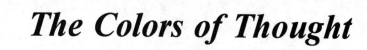

The Colors of Thought

THE COLORS OF THOUGHT

The National Library of Poetry

Cynthia A. Stevens, Editor

The Colors of Thought

Copyright © 1996 by The National Library of Poetry
as a compilation.

Rights to individual poems reside with the artists themselves. This collection of poetry contains works submitted to the Publisher by individual authors who confirm that the work is their original creation. Based upon the authors who confirm that the work is their original creation. Based upon the authors' confirmations and to the Publisher's actual knowledge, these poems were written by the listed poets. The National Library of Poetry does not guarantee or assume responsibility for verifying the authorship of each work.

The views expressed within certain poems contained in this anthology do not necessarily reflect views of the editors or staff of The National Library of Poetry.

All rights reserved under International and Pan-American copyright conventions. No part of this book may be reproduced, stored in a retrieval system or transmitted in any form, electronic, mechanical, or by other means, without written permission of the publisher. Address all inquiries to Jeffrey Franz, Publisher, 1 Poetry Plaza, Owings Mills, MD 21117.

Library of Congress
Cataloging in Publication Data

ISBN 1-57553-346-4

Manufactured in The United States of America by
Watermark Press
1 Poetry Plaza
Owings Mills, MD 21117

Editor's Note

If you had to choose, what would your colors of thought be? Thought is the process of thinking, meditation . . . or thinking in anticipation or expectation . . . "I thought you'd be there." Thought can also be defined as consideration, care, or regard to something or someone . . . "The gift was very thoughtful of you." The mind is filled with thoughts. It is our unique processing of thoughts that makes us who we are, and the distinctions in our process of thinking shed a different shade of light or color upon each of our thoughts.

One's thoughts of a loved one may be bright yellow with the warmth of sunshine, while another's may be a cool refreshing blue and yet another's may be dark and gray because of betrayal. With all the different hues that could be placed upon one's thoughts, it's no wonder that throughout history people have continually endeavored to artistically portray the colorful images hidden within their minds.

The writers featured within this anthology have taken up the difficult task of obtaining such a feat by beautifully demonstrating their own colors of thought. As you read through the assortment of verse, you'll be touched with a variety of hues . . . reflective, dark, cool, bright, warm . . . each piece presenting a color of its own. However, as one of the judges of the poetry contest held in connection with this anthology, there are several poems I wish to honor with special recognition.

With its fullness in rhyme, alliteration and outstanding description, "Magpie Dream," by Bill Kress (p. 1) was selected for the Grand Prize. Kress strings a variety of colorful images together in a melodious rhyme to create the scene in which magpies may be found to gather. "Magpie" is a type of black crow or can also be used to describe an excessively talkative person. In this case the magpie is both an overly talkative person and also described as a bird:

> Serpentine willows weep phosphorus tears
> in a magpie's linoleum dream
> The rottweiler forest hides candyland fears
> yellow whips and an acid blue stream
>
> Earthworm ring memories fixed in their wood
> held captive by destiny's plea
> Blown this way and that by the evil and good
> as they twist and they squeal to be free

In the above stanzas, the magpie's dream is cold and hard like *"linoleum"* because in reality the dream will never be reached. The *"serpentine willows"* waving in the wind *"weep phosphorus tears"* -- they bring the magpie to tears because the magpie cannot reach the willows wherein he remembers the earthworm ring remains *"fixed in their wood."* The *"earthworm ring"* is like the gold ring of all dreams, a goal in life one aims to grasp. The magpie is too afraid to follow his dreams because the *"rottweiler forest"* is blocking his way. The forest appears evil, yet is merely filled with *"candyland"* or childlike fears -- *"yellow whips and an acid blue stream."* Meanwhile, the dreams are not held captive at all -- the magpie only believes he has no control over his destiny and uses this as an excuse to remain idle in his ways.

Kress goes on to describe the magpie as being caught up in a never-ending bar scene; instead of reaching for his dreams, he merely continues to watch them *"pass like cars"*:

> *They reside in the bars as their dreams pass like cars*
> > *while transfixed in a straitjacket gaze*
> *From dyslexia place inner demons erase*
> > *the directions from poisonous maze*

The magpie is trapped in the *"poisonous maze"* by his own inability to see the easy way out or to make a better life for himself. He relies on the truths of the past, *"the dead fuel the fight."* Not willing to change, the magpie remains set in his ways:

> *A ravenous search and for what will they lurch*
> > *as they dig with carnivorous tools*
> *Through the dirt and the grime they are doomed to do time*
> > *on this earth with the Philistine fools*

In the last stanza, *"carnivorous tools"* represents both the magpie bird's beak and the talkative magpie's old way of thinking. Without accepting change and improvement in one's way of life, and one's way of thinking, and in one's society, the magpie is *"doomed to do time . . . with the Philistine fools."* Kress makes it clear that the magpie's dream, which is left up to the magpie, will never be more than a dream.

Also on the topic of dreams is "Honey-Milk Dream" by Anjali Kumar (p. 187). Kumar's piece is of warmth and comfort just as the title suggests. As the persona shares her enchanting images of India, seen only in her mind, you understand the passion of her heritage and her *honey-milk dream:*

> *   *   *

> *of her ancestry, a bloodline born,*
> *deep within the moonlit jungle,*
> *where regal tigers and monkey-kings*
> *in hidden temples live,*

> *   *   *

The pride of one's ancestry can be quite intense, so can the feeling be of passing on one's heritage, as is felt in Gillian Crisp's poem, "Heritage" (p. 431). The strong rhythm of assonance carried throughout Crisp's verse is very impressive as the following lines demonstrate:

> *What a surge of passion forth through the cells and out the pores*
> *Drenching so the skin and soul,*
> *A visage and a trait endowed.*

And, the feeling of passing on one's heritage couldn't be summed up better than the last lines of this verse: *"Oh, what an honor! May it be/ That such of someone lives through me."*

Passing on your heritage is truly grand -- yet, upon passing away, you also hope to leave an impression. "Vegas," by Cynthia Parker (p. 13), paints a colorful portrait of the persona's father and his lasting impression. The persona's father, dressed in an *"ancient, black, felt beret,"* is described as a spirited artist much younger than his years. As he ages, his spirit never fades, *"He painted until the day he died*

. . . . " By the second stanza, reflective of his passing age, the scenery of the poem fades from the bright lights of Las Vegas to the calm colors of a hospice:

> *In Las Vegas, violet fades to pink under a parfait desert sky.*
> *At night, the strip gushes pastel neon all the way to the East end,*
> *where florescent marquees give way to simple signs,*
> *sequins to muslin without buttons.*

With Parker's selective description we experience the transition of the father's surroundings from the vivid to the dim . . . past neon signs and sequins to simple signs and muslin. Although his surroundings have changed, as has his age, he continues to be just as lively as ever:

> *Too loud jazz on the cassette player,*
> *he leans on the back of a Naugahyde chair,*
> *by the window in front of his easel, hospital gown slightly parted,*
> *just enough slack in his I.V. tubes to wave a cigarette in one hand,*
> *a paint brush in the other.*
> *The mauve rug at his bare feet dotted with drops of paint and melted*
> *black holes. Lint on his beret.*

The persona remembers her father as if he himself were a piece of art, for he made an impression. He did not allow time to age him, he merely collected dust . . . just as the *"Lint on his beret."*

Aging and death bring to mind time's inevitable passing, which is what Brenda A. Kulpepper's poem "An Agnostic Man" (p. 394) revolves around. Kulpepper does a wonderful job in portraying Father Time as the agnostic man . . . a man who believes the cause of things is unknown and can never be known. In her piece, Father Time states:

> *Time has nearly passed me by,*
> *grant one last dream before I die.*
> *'Tis I who hold the secret key,*
> *fulfilling hopes of eternity.*

Although this poem is set to rhyme, the underlying tone is heavy and leads your mind to ponder. It's the ending of Kulpepper's piece which adds the punch -- so that I won't give it away -- make sure to look this poem up.

Another verse with an outstanding rhyme scheme is "In the Mind of the Beholder," by Henry M. Ditman (p. 341). Ditman's piece is similar to the old adage, "beauty is in the eye of the beholder." Yet, he claims that beauty is the mind's filtering of things through our senses:

> *Beauty then the will dispenses*
> *By each soul of every kind,*
> *Filtered finely through the senses,*
> *And emanating from the mind.*

A poem which does touch upon all our senses and also employs an outstanding rhyme scheme is C. Cooper's "Meet Me" (p. 438). Cooper's verse is full of internal rhyme and end rhyme, giving it a wonderfully songlike quality:

* * *

> *Bathed in light so pure and white, come with me to the shore*
> *of oceans filled with rainbow fish, where feet can touch the floor.*
> *My Grandmother so dear to me foretold of things to be,*
> *in dreams she had in twilight years; I had no doubts you see.*

* * *

Several other prominent poems are deserving of special recognition: "The Answer" by Lori Blakley (p. 470); "Ode to Poe" by Andrea C. Farley (p. 405); "Ms. Kati Alzheimer" by Amanda Tysowski (p. 102); and Elaine K. Winik's "Lament for My Lost Muse" (p. 24).

Although I do not have the time nor space to individually critique every poem appearing within this anthology, you will notice that each piece of artistry is constructed with true originality and design. May all the artists within *The Colors of Thought* be renowned for their talents and efforts in creative writing.

I sincerely hope you enjoy perusing the colorful verse found within this fine anthology.

Cynthia A. Stevens
Senior Editor

Acknowledgments

The Colors of Thought is a culmination of the efforts of many individuals. The editors are grateful for the contributions of the judges, assistant editors, graphic artists, layout artists, office administrators, and customer service representatives who have all brought their talents to bear on this project. We would also like to give a special thanks to our cover artist, Tracy Hetzel.

Managing Editor
Howard Ely

Winners of the North American Open Poetry Contest

Grand Prize

Bill Kress / Minnetonka, MN

Second Prize

C. Cooper / Browns Mills, NJ
Gillian Crisp / Richmond, VA
Robert Dunlap / Battle Ground, IN
Henry M. Ditman / Westminster, MD
Andrea C. Farley / La Porte, IN

Brenda A. Kulpepper / Northampton, PA
Anjali Kumar / Durham, NC
Cynthia Parker / Fayetteville, AR
Amanda Tysowski / Ferndale, WA
Elaine K. Winik / Rye, NY

Third Prize

Janita Black / Ringling, OK
Lori Blakley / Kingsport, TN
Sean Brazell / Madison, WI
Doris Hartsell Brewer / Chesapeake, VA
Pat Brown / Napa Valley, CA
Timothy Lloyd Brudigam / Glenwood Springs, CO
Minnie Carter / Westerly, RI
Sandra Faye Cosby / Jackson, MS
Eric Craft / Jackson, MO
Lori Ann Crisci / American Canyon, CA
Tara Devine / Springfield, OR
Cara Di Olesandra / New Castle, PA
Jay Downs / Winnebago, WI
Joani Durandette / Arcadia, CA
Jennifer Fales / Jacksonville, FL
Carol Ann Finnigan / Sterling Heights, NC
Dennis Charles Garberino / Saddle Brook, NJ
Goldie Hagedorn / Audubon, IA
Anne Halley / San Anselmo, CA
Laura Hodulich / Springfield, VA
Stan Knight / Winnsboro, TX
Esaku Kondo / Bloomfield Hills, MI
Sena J. Larabee / Albany, NY
Rene LaRue / Alliance, NE
Clark Layman / Twin Falls, ID
Betty June Lowery / Theodore, AL
James L. Mack / Washington, DC
Roberta McLean / Atlantic Beach, FL
Susan Volpe Meeg / Ozone Park, NY
Edna E. Moore / South Charleston, WV

Rush T. Morrow / Charlotte, MI
Barbara Murdock / Suffern, NY
Nancy Oxman / Havertown, PA
Sue Paleafei / Presque Isle, NJ
Tom Ragan / Santa Fe, NM
Becky J. Richardson / Marietta, GA
Debra L. Rodgers / Rockford, IL
M. Samuels-Kalow / New York, NY
Audrey J. Saunders / Cincinnati, OH
George E. Schmauch Jr. / Macungie, PA
Gary F. Seifert / Falls Church, VA
Magda Lynn Seymour / Arlington, VA
Thomas R. Shoemake / Commerce, TX
Dennis Solis / Newbury Park, CA
Mildred C. Sprouse / Los Gatos, CA
Elizabeth Stephenson / Sky Valley, CA
John Craig Stewart / Pisgah Forest, NC
Michael T. Stone / Orange, CA
Francine Swann / Shreveport, LA
Evelyn Tallman / Albany, NY
Gertrude M. Taylor / Hackettstown, NJ
Linda Teasley / Durham, NC
Barbara M. Thomas / Lula, GA
Margaret Thornton / Mishawaka, IN
Richard Dean Tyree / Columbus, IN
Thomas Weddle / Douglas City, CA
Cody Welge / East Moline, IL
Elizabeth C. Wickersham / Logandale, NV
Maryanne Wills / New Kent, VA

Congratulations also to all semi-finalists.

Grand Prize Winner

Magpie Dream

Serpentine willows weep phosphorus tears
   in a magpie's linoleum dream
The rottweiler forest hides candyland fears
   yellow whips and an acid blue stream

Earthworm ring memories fixed in their wood
   held captive by destiny's plea
Blown this way and that by the evil and good
   as they twist and they squeal to be free

They reside in the bars as their dreams pass like cars
   while transfixed in a straitjacket gaze
From dyslexia place inner demons erase
   the directions from poisonous maze

The days feed the night and the dead fuel the fight
   as they float on the iceberg of truth
With the voice out of sight they can see only white
   as they fish in the waters for proof

A ravenous search and for what will they lurch
   as they dig with carnivorous tools
Through the dirt and the grime they are doomed to do time
   on this earth with the Philistine fools
    Bill Kress

Untitled

The nights were long and dreary. Some nights
steamed hopeless and you feared there will be no tomorrow. But it
came, a new day, a new time and place. New directions to follow, new
decisions to make. More things to teach, new experiences to face.
Both of you were there to teach and guide. Both of you were the
stepping stone for a new life. A life which was being made, a new
person was being taught the ways of life. Who to give eternal credit
to, both of you Mom and Dad. With all your time, knowledge, support,
love and concern, you both have made me who I am. I know that
whatever we may face in the future we will make it through together.
A new chapter has turned, new experiences to face, and what better
people to face them with, both of you Mom and Dad.

Adam Capodieci

Does Anyone Care?

Man should feel shame 'cause we're all to blame
So why do we complain?
We kill me the creatures without feeling any pain

Beautiful colors... we turn to black and white
And while it all dies we just lay back unaware
Him and her me and you...who cares?
We're here an' they are there
Stuck to the ground unable to move
We are man, so they lose.

So, is this love or is it hate?
What will happen in the future, what is our fate?

Destruction is our human nature
Man is wrong and this is just a song,
But it won't take very long before it's all gone
So who cares? It's some other place, another's face
Spit oil doesn't fade...
Who cares? It's not our fate!
Look at that we create!
It is murder! The death of our planet, or people!
God, what have me made?

Omar D. Castro

Forever Unforgiven

Someone is screaming out in sorrowful wails
His life can be told of in very sad tales
The childhood years were so much pain
Now they've locked him up, they believe he is insane,

In his prison he colors the walls
At night when he sleeps he dreams that he falls
Into a dark abyss where black is all around
He wishes for his room still and but also sound,

He has no life and nothing is how it seems
He try's talking to others, but no one knows what he means
when he speaks the words do not come
And he can never be forgiven for what he has done.

What comes next he can not tell
And the life he is living has truly failed
He has done the unthinkable
He believes the law is unreasonable.

He has hurt so many
Deep inside he didn't want to kill any
He shall be locked up until his very last day
Forever unforgiven it shall always be that way.

Shelley Cornett

Your Voice

Oh that voice, I keep trying to ignore, for I am too busy you see
Too busy to listen, too busy to learn, but never too busy to hurt
Oh that voice, I keep trying to ignore, for I am too busy you see
Off to work early of morn, off to the ballgame as dusk comes on
Then to movies or bars I go, always trying to outrun what I don't
understand
Oh that voice, I keep trying to ignore, for I am too busy you see
I have to keep busy, I have to stay on the run, for fear is my motive
Oh that voice, I keep trying to ignore, for I am too busy you see
Pride or fear probably both, I'm really not sure myself, pain
or hurt probably both
Oh that voice, I keep trying to ignore, for I am too busy you see
The days are long, but not long enough
When times become tough, I take time to consider
Oh that voice, I keep trying to ignore, for I am too busy you see
But Lord I'm hurt and oh so tired, I've run too hard, and ignored
too long
Oh your voice, I kept trying to ignore, for I was too busy you see
Lord I'm ready to listen, I'm ready to learn
I'm ready to return to your loving arms
Oh your voice, I shall not ignore, for I'm not too busy you see
Teach me to grow, teach me to know
That I can help others, choose not to ignore

Nina J. David

Why?

There is so much prejudice that I have seen
that it really makes me want to scream.

Why do we fight?
Can someone turn on the light?
So we can see
the true colors of you and me!

We cannot judge by colors, weight, or races,
but by the true inner beautiful faces
that you and I can see
in you and me.

Emily A. Cardona

Precious Things

There are many precious things on earth,
like the miracle of life, a new baby's birth;
The smell of flowers in the wind and
bonds of friendship that never end.
The scent of rain, or a beautiful rose,
delicate things you can smell with your nose.

The many blessing that come from love,
the sun and the moon that shine high above;
The beautiful sunset, pink in the sky
and the will to work hard and always try.

Truth, love honor and peace...
if the world lived by this
The hatred would cease.

The most precious thing, without a doubt,
what caring and love is all about,
The best kind of person, I would choose no other,
is a caring, sweet, loving grandmother.

Breanne Miles

Predator Vs Prey

As a deer drinks by a stream,
Things are not what they seem.
It does not realize it's being observed,
To the deer this is absurd.
The hunter takes out a gun,
The deer unaware that the hunter loads one.
The deer looks so peaceful drinking at night,
The hunter has already set his sight.
He stops to think and reconsider,
In the deers eye he sees a glitter.
A noise is heard throughout out the land,
The deer escaped and so did the man.

Jason Murray

A Cry For Love

I hear a cry for love
Not of the old, but of the children
Above and negligence plague their lives
They yearn for someone to love them
For arms to embrace them
To hear sweet loving words
They want their parents to love them,
To make time for them
To understand them
We must love the children
We must embrace them,
And most of all,
We must look beyond the color of their skin,
And understand love comes from within

Lalya Michelle Smith

Aspen

Embers glow.
An owl calls.
A cozy nest of blankets. Furs on the hardwood floor.

Embers glow.
The wind shrieks.
Two beings, as one, sipping wine and eating cheese.

Embers glow.
The snow falls.
A look. One reserved for the most treasured of moments.

Embers glow.
The night grows deep.
A dance of passion: modernistic art made of free limbs.

Embers dim.
The moon sets.
Silence, 'cept two heartbeats, fills the cabin air.

Embers die.
The wind shrieks and the snow falls.
Gentle breath, a tight embrace, and fond memories
   warm the soul till the coming of dawn.

Steven G. Velotas

Love

Love is like a time bomb, implanted in your heart
If it ever explodes, it will tear it apart
I found this love for the first time in my life
It cost me my respect, my home, and my wife
Now you are gone, and we are worlds apart
I still go on living, but without a heart
I met a lady for whom I could really care
But my heart was gone, she wondered where
You took it with you when you went away
Maybe you will return it to me someday

William I. Music

A Warm Heart with Frostbite

A warm heart is filled with heat
Just like a sunny day,

A warm heart has no defeat
To the sacrifices it will pay,

A warm heart strives to meet
The most caring that it may,

A warm heart can be forever sweet
Until its dying day,

A warm heart can be denied
the fairness it deserves

A warm heart can't be lied
To what it tried to preserve.

There is no going back to the start
Of blind and unconditional,

What once was always assumed of the heart
Will no longer be traditional.
Can the fires of life ever melt
the frostbit winter chill,

Of a once known heart felt
So deeply able to feel.... Yes!!!

Sherri Diane Buzbee

Destined for a Prayer

We are a race that has become corrupt towards one another
Sometimes forgetting that we are sisters and brothers
We fought so hard to be educated and free;
Now, in the nineties, we are on a killing spree.
We're going through both a recession ad a depression,
Therefore, there is a lot of turmoil and
and transgression. Sometimes, I wonder, "is there a way out?"
But, through the Lord, there is no doubt,
We sometimes want to go alone and cry;
Just let the tears come forth, from which they hide.
Black males are becoming an endangered species,
(If not me) that leaves us speechless.
Our children have no fathers and our families are broken;
As predicted in the Bible, the words are now spoken.
While sisters and mothers are grieving and crying,
Brothers, at a rapid rate, are dying.
There seems to be no help, but I have the answer;
The one and only God, our master.
No one can save us; not the Governor, President, or the Mayor,
Lord knows we are destined for a prayer.

Jeffrey L. Lee

White

Bleached white bones on white sandy beach.
White rock, white spray

Gray day, gray waves

Gray sky, gray way

White bones telling stories to my white hand
full of white sand and the talking white bones
telling white stories of families
and flowing bone glories inside of the witness
of white time pieces on white sheets
white sound under white pillows.
With her ancient white hair, white lace-draped face
and pale trance like eyes full of her lovers
watching the white clouds sail by her white curtains
blowing in the white wind, white window, white sky,
her pale white spirit leaving her poets body
and her white bones telling me all her stories
mixed with white sand
and white sighs.

T. Throne

Courtney

My little girl with dark brown eyes
Is growing up, how time flies!
She's outgrown toys for little tykes
Rattles, Barbies, small red trikes.
Soon she'll be going out on dates
I'll worry when she comes home late
Cars and boys, the senior prom
Before I know it, she'll be gone.

Kids are little for such a short while enjoy them now, they'll make
  you smile.
Let them know you're always there to love them, help them, dry a tear.

My little girl with dark brown eyes
Makes me smile, I'll tell why,
She's a gift from God above sent by Him for me to love.
Her name is Courtney
and how I'll share not a poem but a prayer.

Courtney, may God always bless you
and always keep you safe form harm.
I pray He will always keep you in
His hands and hold you close to His heart.

Jerrilyn Sharp (Mom)

A Prison Wish

If I'd get a letter today
I'd look at the other inmates and say
I got a letter today you see
Because my wife was thinking of me
I'm not alone in this cell all day
Because my lover took the pain away
I'd boast and smile thru out the night
Because her love took me out of sight
I won't have to listen to your noise you see
Because my wife sends her love to me.

Jacky Greer

To Love The Work And Work The Love

Arbeiten und lieben, Freud has told
Create a life that's strong and bold.
To love the work and work the love, heaves heavy hollowness a
shove.

But to love arbeiten and to work lieben
Drains hours more than sechs (sic) oder sieben.
I can do them both; I surely will,
But first some tasks I must fulfill.

Teeth to brush 'fore and aft each meal.
Drinking ten water glasses, 'twould be ideal.
Hands to scrub with each public encountering
Leaves time for Freud, though the pressure is mountering.

Today I must my tires rotate,
And purchase traps — some mice to bait.
The grass of course is growing longer,
My horticultural habits couldn't be wronger.

My checks I balanced a year last May,
And a dozen bills arrived today.
Yet there's time to work and love to make
only if I submit a postmark that butts the deadline, a meter ever so
  slightly off-center, and a rhyme scheme half-baked.

Stephen I. Brown

The Dark Side

It was a dark night,
Darker then it has ever been before.
The time is coming near
When I will never be able to see him again.

It's been so long
The pain I can't take
They're trying to change my mind
But my mind is made up.

I have to keep reminding myself
That even though I will live in eternal darkness,
That I will not be dying,
But everyone else is.

The pain he put me through
I just can't take any longer!
I know it's not my fault or his,
It's just time that the darkness fell over.

Everyone thought I would kill myself
But they were wrong! Nature just beat me to it.
I guess even someone that may think like that,
Can have pity like that.

Susan Angstadt

I Wish I Knew

Why don't people get along nowadays?
Is it because they think of themselves or is it because of their
girlfriends or boyfriends?
Are they playing this silly fools' game?
I wish I knew.

Am I a fool because I think of beautiful things to do;
or am I a fool because of the dreams I wish would come true?
Am I playing this silly fools' game too?
I wish I knew.

I dream of walking along the beach, in a cool, cool night's breeze.
I dream of having a beautiful time with someone I love.
Am I a fool because of these dreams?
I wish I knew.

I lie awake at night just thinking of someone special.
I wonder if he will really care for me.
Will he tell me his dreams?
I wish I knew.

I sit here alone, just me and the music of sad love songs.
The moment helps me find my feelings about life itself.
Therefore, am I fool to think that life itself is just a game?
I WISH I KNEW.

Pamela S. (Potter) Gilbert

God's Love

When in prayer and meditation
Comes the most peaceful contemplation
Of the love God has for us.
He helps us feel the fulness of life
And takes away our weariness and strife.
With him all things are possible
If you believe it, you will receive it
The strength and courage to go on
Comes only from our God on high.
Just watch the birds as they fly.
Learn from nature as you go.
Read the signs along the way,
And know that God will not let you go astray.

Frances Winges

My Girlfriend

I miss her smile and long black hair,
But most of all I miss what we've shared.
She seemed to have no problems to bear,
He sent her to heaven without a care.

A sense of humor she did have,
Her laughter was heard throughout the land.
Twas not of her fault but just the same,
His gunshot took our Sara's life away.

The girl I loved is in her grave,
In a cemetery locked away.
All that's left of her body is bones,
Away in heaven lies her lovely soul.

In our hearts she will always be,
She waits in heaven for me to see.
Our blessed union in Gods sweet care,
This meeting more joyous than we can bear.

Through the years my thoughts on the task,
Of my sweet girlfriends life from the past.
Her years on this earth over to fast,
My memories of her will always last.

Jennifer Lynn LaBorde

Why Worry? Be Happy

Azaleas, roses, chrysanthemums, plums bloom in different seasons,
So we won't miss seeing the glory in the flower for a long time.
Chickens chase centipedes; centipedes, snakes; and snakes, chickens;
So we won't miss seeing an abundance of all kinds of animals.

Families, then tribes, then city-states, then nations, and then
We saw the rise of Roman Empire with amazement.
Oh, we also saw the fall of Roman Empire with rejoicing
In enjoying verities of foods, costumes, languages, cultures, faiths, ...

From the little round window of a washing machine,
Through a cycle of soaking, washing, rinsing, extracting, tumbling,
We see after that fierce extraction the harm to none and the clean
    clothes to all.
From the little round window of a tourist submarine,
Through tranquil scenery of plankton, shrimps, fishes and sharks,
We see during their peaceful swimming the naked game of predator
    and survivor.

One is born, one dies and the land increases, the sea fluctuates;
All things between Heaven and Earth continue, can be used, but
    never used up!
Don't be greedy when in good times and ask for more;
Don't be angry when in hard times and blame others;
Don't be rigid when in changing times and refuse to adapt.
"What a joy to be here!" awakens us so the Way of Nature: "Don't
    worry! Be happy!"

Chin H. Lin

Fear

Speeches ungiven.
Songs left unwritten.
Things left unseen.
Uncorrected things, things I said I didn't mean.
Competitions left unwon.
A multitude of things...left undone.

When thinking of that I feel no fear.
Leaving behind the world I know, unsure of where I may next go.
Not knowing whether it be to a heaven with a pearly gate,
Or a hell, a world full of hate.

When thinking of that I feel no fear.
There would be no promises broken,
Only three words unspoken.

When thinking of that, I feel fear.

Katy H. Olson

The Old Farmhouse

My mind wonders back this winter day,
to an old farmhouse
where I went to stay.

It seemed to welcome and make me a part,
of all its memories, to open its heart.

The days were peaceful, they seemed to heal,
my weary mind, my pain to steal.

At night I listened to God's lullaby,
I slept on pillow 'neath His starry sky.

Rain sometimes falling like a shower of love,
as He nourished His creation with love from above.

Those days in my farmhouse, I laughed and I shared
life's simple pleasures as I loved and I cared.

I may never return there but, somehow, you see,
I just close my eyes and it's so close for me.

I was surrounded by love there so I'll never be,
free of all that love contained In The Old Farmhouse.

William D. Back

Mixed Messages

Sometimes I wonder
If you really do care.
Or if you're just using me
For something I'm unaware of.

You send me mixed messages.
You confuse my mind.
One minute you're nice to me,
The next you're not.

You say something
But do the opposite.
You make me lie
Because you're embarrassed.

Embarrassed about me
And everything I stand for.
Afraid you'll get made fun of.
Afraid you won't be able to flirt.

Please stop sending mixed messages to my mind.
I'm totally confused.
What's going on?
An answer I must find.

Kasie Blanchette

My Aphrodisiac

You're my aphrodisiac, so warm, so loving, so true.
The hunger I have for your love will remain insatiable.
Don't ask me why I love you, for eternity will pass away.
In my heart I know the words, but my lips won't let me say.
Your beauty consumes me like the flame of a candle that slowly burns.
Melting away at my heart for you I'll always yearn.
So I'll send my love and all good wishes to a woman who truly inspires.
For the spark in your eyes ignited my heart and now it burns like fire
I'll take this time to write these words so the opportunity doesn't pass.
As you grow older the ink may fade but the love will forever last.

Darryl Gable Aye

Wonders

I've seen the snow white mountains of Alaska.
I've sailed the long rivers of Peru.
I've seen the world and its seven wonders
But I've never seen a wonder like you.

I've stood on the Pyramids of Egypt
Far across the ocean blue.
I've seen the island beauties of Hawaii
But I've never seen a beauty like you.

I've seen the pretty dancing girls of Siam.
The happy Polynesian people too.
But they are not as happy as I am
Because they haven't got a wonder like you.

I've stared at the white cliffs of Dover.
There's not a place I didn't see.
Now that my travels are all over
I wished you had been there with me.

Geoffrey G. Tuggle

How Can It Be Stopped?

You can not escape it, it's all around,
    everywhere people are to be found.

It can hurt you from afar or very near,
    any place at all where people can hear.

It can break your spirit and make you sad,
    it's even been known to drive people mad.

It can ruin your life and take happiness away,
    it works all the time both night and day.

It can destroy a family and break up a clan,
    it's even been known to kill a man.

It can tear up a mountain or destroy a city,
    or it can start a war, it has no pity.

It can make a booming noise or sharp like a whip,
    it has knocked down buildings and sank a ship.

It's been around since our birth,
    I fear it may destroy the earth.

We can all control it and not let it go wild,
    without even hurting a man, woman or child.

We have had it with us since we were young,
    it's in us all, it's the Human Tongue!

Ellra E. Pettis

Spring Morning

Early morning
Fresh with dew
I awake to the song of a sparrow

He sings with pride
His little tune
He calls it his morning carol

Early morning's
Gentle breeze
I'm refreshed with a breath of springtime

A flower scented
Sun-warmed breeze
That welcomes a day filled with sunshine

Joy Marie Stanton

I Am

I am a cool girl who likes horses.
I wonder how many horses there will be in 100 years.
I hear a thousand horses at night.
I see horses running on water.
I want to live on a mountain.
I am a cool girl who likes horses.

I pretend to be a teacher.
I feel a 100 horses in my head.
I touch all the plants in the world.
I worry a robber is going to take me.
I cry when someone gets hurt in my family.
I am a cool girl who likes horses.

I understand the way of living.
I see that people are not all the same.
I dream that I own all the horses.
I try to do back flips by my self.
I hope I live a long time.
I am a cool girl who likes horses.

Serena Campbell

Ever Used A Cat

Won't you use my cat?
What a puzzling request
So I thought for a moment
to search for the best
I found only one, use for a cat
Oh my heavens, no dear
I couldn't do that
He wants you to real bad
it'd make me happy too
Just pet him a little bit, that oughta do
Much to my surprise, so lovingly amused
I reached down for the kitty
So she thought he'd been used
I laughed a little too much
For I knew, she did not know
My 4 year olds, mother, just had to do so
I hope forever, I do recall
that look upon her face
I think her days of using cats
are gone without a trace

Theresa Daniels

Invocation

You thought you could handle it, didn't you?
You were strong and self-sufficient,
Intelligent and confident,
But there came a time when you couldn't
Keep it all together any longer.
It happens to the best of us;
Sometimes it falls apart
When our "lifetime" companion
Decides to shorten the commitment,
Or when we lose a child
That we love more than life itself,
Or when we learn
That we ourselves are expendable.
But it does happen.
We aren't aware of the odds, you see,
and there always comes a time
When we invoke a response—a cry for help,
A great, pleading cry to the heavens,
Hoping, doubting, praying
Someone is listening.

Patricia Miller

Never

Never will I forget the times we had,
The love we shared,
The laughs we had or the things we did.
Never will I lose the smiles you gave,
Or the games we played.
Never will I share the secrets you gave,
Or the day it all died.
But I will let your legend grow.
And I will sit back and remember our times.
Think of the rhymes and great tries.
You took to make me forget the past and reveal the present.

Marina Stangeland

Dreams And Songs

Where has it gone? Oh, where did it go,
That youth of mine?

Sweet innocence appeared, pure joy did abound
Announcements were made
That a new child was born.

Time marched along,
'Til twenties they appeared,
Filled with dreams and a heart singing a song.

The thirties rolled in,
Now, where had I been?
Some wisdom and wear
On my face you could swear.

The forties, they went...
Oh where did they go?
Please come back,
To complete things that were meant.

Dreams and songs
In the fifties still there,
For my weakened body and mind
A happier, wiser life still longs!

R. Lee Overstreet

Untitled

God is the love of our souls.
Put your faith in him you
will have treasures untold.
Someday when this life is over
and time shall be no more I
will be ready to meet him over
on heaven's bright shore. God's
love is unselfish and kind, he
sees with the heart and not with
the mind. God is the answer we all
should seek, he's like the morning
star with love so sweet. When I
awake in the morning in my heart
there's a song. With God's love
I cannot go wrong. In the
quiet of the morning I kneel
down to pray. I ask God to
guide me throughout the day.
One little prayer can make things right.
God's love can keep you both day and night.

Frances Jolly

Napolí Revisited

Memories of the great ocean liner are anchored in his mind,
As are memories of Napoli', the young man left behind
American tourists and barefoot boys, running, in the street
And Mamá right behind them, shouting "Mangia", time to eat
spaghetti with marinara sauce, and lots of wine to drink
And demitasse to bring you back, to reality, I think
And the lovely dark-skinned girls, with soft brown hair and eyes
When poor Alfredo thinks of it, he hangs his head and cries
"You are now a man, my son," he remembers being said
But would he be at this young age, if Mamá weren't dead?
Oh, the awful tragedy, to be burdened so with strife
To be left only one good eye, to fight three times for life
To come to America, to seek yourself a name
Where others call you stranger, if you do not speak the same
"Sir, my name's Alfredo, and here's my merchandise,"
"Yes, I like this tortoise shell, Alfred, name your price"
And each got the better deal, as businessmen usually say
But that was many years ago, Alfred's ninety-two today
Memories, memories, of a long ago, distant shore
For the old man on the Sicilian Prince, it's Napolí once more.

Caroline DeCiutiis

Nature's Melodies

The wind whistled softly though the leaves
in the trees
And the waves kept time to the humming of the bees
Somewhere in the distance a mockingbird sang
And up in the tower the church bells rang
The gurgle of the little brook
puts my mind at rest
How lovely robin red breast sounds
he's singing at his best
The silly, slimy, salamander squishes through
the mud
And the bumble bee buzzes as he flies from
bud to bud

All of nature's melodies
in enchanting harmony
Isn't it a pity
The only audience is me.

Aimee Horsfall

Night Sky

Look at the night sky
Tell me what you see
Bright dots forever dancing
In a sea of ecstasy
They dance a million dances
With music never heard
They call your name throughout the night
Without staying a word
I look at them in wonder
Of the magic that they bring
I look at them in awe
Beholding their splendor of a king
Heavenly bodies dancing in perfect harmony
Too beautiful for the imagination
This sparkling blanket of tranquility
We take for granted each night
These gifts from God on high
We take for granted each day
The life that we pass by
Thank you for the night sky

James P. Gannone Jr.

Time

Time in the hour glass, all those grains of sand,
Is not the real measure of any woman or man.

The respect of your peers, family and friends,
Is how one is measured when life draws to its end.

The love of all those who surround you on this festive day,
Must draw one to conclude you have succeeded in every way.

The goals that we set, the dreams that we make,
Putting more into life than one ever could take,

The friendships we develop, not the fortunes we amass,
Are a much better yardstick when we look at years that have
passed.

The memories of family, of sadness and mirth,
Of weddings, of holidays, of funerals and birth.

These are the fibers of a life woven and intertwined
These are the tune measures of how one's spent his time.

Donald Jay Hendler

To Coleman

You once were my sweetheart,
We'd hold hands all the time.
And on this special day,
You'd be my Valentine.

Now I watch you sleeping.
Hold your hand....You're Unaware!
You are always in my heart
And I know we'll always care.

You'll always be my darling,
But my, my....How you've grown!!
A handsome young man like yourself,
Soon, will have sweethearts of your own.

Candy hearts and chocolate kisses...
If only I could grant your wishes.
I'd summon Cupid and his bow,
To let his arrow fly...into the heart of your true love.

But as the future days go by...
And the arrow flies through time,
On this day forever....
I'll be yours and you'll be mine!!!

Sandra Ford

The Vampires

Silent footsteps under a full moon's light;
Embankments of fog blurring my sight.
Coursing my spine with legs outstretched
Are spiders and chills from stories far-fetched.

Three blocks away from my home and my wife,
A blood-curdling scream! I run for my life.
A fluttering noise as I come up the walk.
Must be my heart, pounding hard from the shock.

I call to my wife as I enter the house.
She tells me she'd screamed - to frighten a mouse!
I offer my cheek as all husbands do,
But she goes for my neck with an aim that is true.

We fly through the night when the moon's at its brightest.
We are too many; you can't hope to fight us.
On the night of a full moon don't plan any campfires
'Cause we're getting hungry, and we are....The Vampires.

Richard Doust

In the Hearts and in the Minds
of All Children, Mother is God

As a child your life depends on her. You grow up thinking
there is no other. No one could ever mend your wounds or wipe
your tears like she. She is the only one who never sees your faults,
the only one who can pick you up when you fall. She is the only
one who believes in your dreams, the only one who still loves you
when you don't reach them.

The day then comes when you leave the nest. On to another
who will share your thoughts and dreams. But she is still there.
A tear may fall, a sigh may sound. But only words of silence echo
through that lonely room. Now only memories keep her faith alive.
Memories of the days when she was the only woman in the world.

She grows gray now. The lines on her face show the years of
happiness and sorrow. You don't see her as much as you like, and
you worry about how she is. In your mind you know that the day
will come.

You wake up one morning to a knock on the door. She is
gone! Everything you are is because of her, and for the first time
you realize you have become everything she could have hoped for.

The heavens call her an angel, The world calls her a miracle,
I'm just lucky enough to call her mom.

David Heynen

Stephen's Sonnet

One tear was all it took to squelch the fire.
    My lover couldn't wait to hit the door.
He said he would stay—he's such a liar.
    As he left he smashed my world to the floor.

He danced away as if trained in the art,
    And shot me just as quick as he could draw.
The scar that his love carved upon my heart,
    Pains me more than the bruise found on my jaw.

His dominating laughter haunts my sleep.
    While praying for the hurt to go away,
My eyes ran dry thus silencing my weep.
    What was once so black and white has turned grey.

What plagued his mind remains a mystery,
Although he always knew what was to be.

Barbra Monroe

Best Friends

A group of people, grow up together,
not knowing, that some day,
they could, become friends.

Well, they grow up, and
now they are in sixth grade.

After awhile of just knowing each other's names,
they start to tell each other secrets,
then, they start doing, Everything Together.

Then, one of them had to move away,
her parents, won't even let her stay
until the end of the year.

Her parents want her to forget all of the people
that she cared about, and loved,
like her parents made her do twice before.

Now, she has started to meet some people,
but, they will never be Best Friends!

Katie Chadwick

Your Potion

Your love is like
a magical potion
My love for you is
bigger than that of the ocean
One day, though both my loves
that of the ocean and yours like a potion
will be together as you
And I stand against the sea
So you
know my love
must be true
Because your magical love potion
has conquered my love
for the ocean

Angela Jones

My Star I Numbered Twenty-Five

Blue and red flames glistening from her heavenly body
Careening off reflections of those other stars long passed by
Leaving the imprints of her gorgeous brilliance
To resiliently share in her glorious light
Her presence is met with feelings of sheer joy
As I look upon her intensely focusing my minds eye
I am consumed by my love for her
This, simply a fact, I cannot deny
I live for her existence
My heart is her's
Our future's will shine together
I love her she is the star I numbered twenty five.

Arthur Alcala

The Awakening

I was pretty much that, of a normal guy
Then I went to sleep, and was made to die
My soul awoke in darkness, but yet a burning fire alit
I thought then, I was in the Bottomless Pit
I jumped in fear, tripped and fell
I landed in a pile of serpents, I knew then, I was in Hell
I arose in snakes, and wondered, why is life so brief
Then I heard the terrible noises, of weeping and gnashing of teeth
Just then, I was approached by Satan, the King of Sin
I shook and cried uncontrollably, and knew, I had reached the end
I fell down on my knees, to accept my fate
I just wished to God, that it wasn't so late
Just then, I awoke, it was a dream
I began to cry, and prayed, that the Trinity and I, could be a team
So you may see us out there, giving our time, money, or just a
  helping hand
But until you experience The Awakening, you may not understand.

Gregory Boudouris

Just Friends

Walks in the moonlight along a winding lane,
  we speak of simple things; the hopes and dreams
  of a life so far spent, of tomorrows yet unseen.
What will the future bring?
Yet as we share the depths of our hearts, we walk
  as only friends, but is this not how love begins?
Wanting only goodness and plenty for the other
  only our minds reach to touch the other.
Oh, but to feel the warmth of embrace, to share
  the most secret place within the very soul,
  yet so afraid to render evil for the wonderful
  innocence that make our moments so precious.
And precious you are my friend.
So quietly I shall wait; for the bloom forced
  open dies its beauty never seen.
We will walk in the moonlight and stroll along
  the path and perhaps somewhere along the
  way, find true love at last.

Kathy Hunter

The Explosion

The timer has been ticking for a long time.
Slowly adding on more and more time,
getting closer to the explosion.

I thought that if I left it alone and let it be,
then maybe the timer would ware out.

But as the months go by the clock gets closer and closer
to the explosion.
Not willing to stop, only adding time on.

Finally, the timer is close to zero,
which means that it is about time for blast off
of the explosion.

In the past few days the timer has worn out,
and reached its final destination zero.
The explosion has occurred.

Soon the timer will start up again and I will always have
timers and explosions in my life
as long as my parents are divorced.

I hope these explosions won't hurt me too much
and that soon everyone will cooperate so the explosions
can finally came to a halt.

Molly Good

A Soldier's Good-Bye

It was a cold day in December when we met.
When you stepped onto that bus, your eyes never left my face.
My heart had another name written on it; I was in love.

It was a warm day in May, and I was riding in a van.
You jogged by, and my eyes never left you.
My empty heart stirred; I saw a handsome creature.

It was a cool day in April, and I was standing by your side.
You held my hand in yours, and we exchanged eternal vows.
My heart belonged to you; I have never looked back.

It is a hot day in July, and I am saying good-bye.
Your eyes look into my eyes, filled with tears, for one last look.
My anguished heart cries out: will I see you in December?

Judy Reyes-Maggio

Young Sailor

Young sailor lost at sea
Life full of many desires
Washed away in alcohol fires,
Struggle and fight to no avail,
Lives course will be no smooth sail,

Though many a man has sat at your helm,
only you know the true course of your heart's realm,

Fear not young sailor
Life's storms are not just at cost
You can grow from the pain to a place of peace
So grab hold of the wheel and let the fear cease

James W. Bardsley

Optionally Reclusive

Self-imposed solitude, the quality of being alone
Electively remote from society
Purposefully separated from the stress of the world
Intentionally minus association from environmental destroyers
Preferably isolated from society's influence
Independently designated as the most desirable means of existence.

Veronica Hunsucker Free

The Story of a Mother and Son

There were countless nights when I watched you sleep,
Countless days when you made me want to scream,
And millions of moments when I watched you dream.
Some of those fantasies became your reality,
Some remained childhood games,
And as you soared through the sky, I watched you fly,
Often times fearful that you'd fall, but knowing that I had to let
    you go,
For if my little boy were to become a man,
I had to remove my guiding hand,
And content myself with the fact that I raised you well.
That all the lessons I taught you would be your safety net if you
    ever fell.
Now what can I say, on this, your wedding day,
Except that you exceeded my every expectation,
My every hope, My every wish,
And as I watch you take a wife, and start a new life,
My heart swells with pride, a tear touches my cheek,
And a smile turns the corners of my lips,
For I know I helped shape the person that you are,
And that my job is done,
For I am proud to call the man before me my son.

    Cheray T. Williams

My Cat

My cat so tries to look aloof with his eyes of blue,
He pretends not to notice a thing till he sets them on you.

He wants to play, so I run for his ball
But it's not his forte - today.
So I look for his furry mouse but it's not in his house.
I go for his cat track, but I soon sense a lack of interest on his part,
He doesn't have the heart.
He's about to have a cow - Now!

So I get out his brush and with a hush hush, I brush
till his coat shines like silk,
Oops, now he wants a drink of milk.
After his thirst is abated, once more I am rated by his rubs and purrs.

Softly, I caress him, massage him and pet him till his eyes turn to
    slits,
He can no longer resist, he lies down beside me desperately
trying to regain his wits.
But it is of no use
He succumbs to sleep and soon he'll be deep,
In some kitty dream, where he'll probably scheme the next day's
    abuse.

When he'll so try to look aloof with his eyes of blue,
And pretend not to notice a thing till he sets them on you.

    Catherine Puccio

"My Last Goodbye"

I sit here in this secret place to write my last goodbye.
I will be brave, I will be strong, I will not even cry.
The pills I take will make me sleep, for how long I do not know.
I hope that they will do the job and free my soul to go.
Some will say I was crazy, and some will say I was nuts.
Some will say it was amazing, and some will say it took guts.
I had my reasons for this act, it had to do with health.
It was not lack of money, because that is not true wealth.
I would have gladly given dollars if only I could stay.
But the lung disease I have it will not go away.
Doctor's say it should and family says it will.
"All you have to do Mike, is take this little pill."
So this is it, now I must go, it is my time to fly.
So this is it, my time has come, to say my last goodbye.

    Michael Adams

555

Today I had a child, today that child died.
It only took seconds,
in the Slaughter House of 555.
Why do we create, only to destroy?
Somehow it's not human,
it's more of a ploy.
Why must I continue?
Why must they die?
We will never forget the sights,
in the Slaughter House of 555.
I viewed tears of pain,
shrouded by cries of despair.
Smiles were absent, while love was rare.
And though the decision was final,
to myself I did cry.
For my child was a victim,
in the Slaughter House of 555.
My mind will forever doubt,
the path we did take.
A termination of life, for everyone's sake.

    Bruce Michael Anthony Hanley

Wondering

There are still so many things that I don't understand
The ways of life and the creation of woman and man
I don't understand why we can walk but we can't fly
and I wonder where we can find the ending of the sky

I wonder why God gave us each a life,
and why someone would end theirs with a gun or a knife
I wonder about the things we see and if we all see the same
I wonder what would it be like if no one had a name

I wonder what forms the tears that we cry
and I wonder why everyone living has to die
I wonder who invented all the words that we know
and I wonder what is the reason for having fingers and toes

I wonder how it turns from hot to cold
and I wonder about the Bible stories that we've been told
I wonder about how everything is made
I wonder how they got the idea of money for trade
I wonder why there are so many people who are poor
And I wonder about my ancestors who lived on earth before
I wonder why it is so loud when it starts to thunder.
But most of all I wonder how it would feel to know....instead of
wonder.

    Lisa Sommario

Sunset

There it stands,
At the end of the horizon.
Like a big ball of fire melting away into the sea.

There it stands,
Changing the waves and ripples into deep reds, orange, blues.
Like a rainbow of colors before ones very eyes.

There it stands,
On the edge of the now-crimson water.
Like a half moon of blazing flames progressing of into a new world.

There it stands,
Almost gone, as the water slowly transforms back into its turquoise
    hues.
Like a dying fire in the forest.

It is gone,
Until the morning arrives
And it reverses its descent into a new beginning.

    Chaya Glaser

Whenever You Ask

What can I say I haven't said before?
I've told you most things. What you haven't heard
I've divulged to the white waves on this shore,
luminous lives, each whispering a word.

They'll tell you. Ask them. Ask the setting sun
that smiles and dies on all things innocent
about me when the weary day is done.
He'll tell you. Ask him. Tell him you were sent

by me, the one who lost all that he had
and left it in dispersed fragments around
you, in wracks. Ask your fear when winter-clad
wings flutter at your door, when the faint sound

of falling cities wanes and you are free,
when all things break their vows of secrecy.

Dax Diaz

The Fog

The swiftly soothing memories faded into dust;
once held so close by your heart of pain;
All ever now recaptured in the fog.
These pillared rolls of heaven sigh
for living dreams again.

Faded dust, its soul alive
proclaims itself tonight;
it beckons to my corpse walking across the field.
It churns around me; churns inside me
entangled... fog.

These memories slip inside me now;
I'm gilded by mine own.
The sky rains dreams again upon me,
gilded into stone.
The essence of tonight - timeless fog beneath my bones.

Waverly Watson

Backyard Friends

A robin sits upon the fence, and watching from afar,
Is the neighbor's big black cat, I'm glad he's in their yard.
A squirrel comes to get some corn, he eats an ear a day.
It's good that he's the only one that comes around this way.
The doves are waiting for some food, there's many birds you see
Finches, Robins, Blue jays too all waiting for some seed.
I see a little chipmunk, he is hunting for some nuts.
They are destructive little things, always making ruts.
There're ladybugs, spiders, beetles, ants,
  and those pesky mosquitoes too.
All hiding underneath the leaves, just waiting there for you.
For spring is fast approaching, their young come out to play.
Explore the yard, check out the food, I think they're here to stay.

Doris Klene

Circle Me

Life is a circle
Sometimes we can't wait for it to come around again
Other times the last thing we want is a repeat
But the more we go around, we begin to realize
How little we have to do with the direction it takes us
We crawl around, before we can walk enough to wander off.
When we feel in control, the maker lets us stray
Into trouble, just to keep us alert.
Our circle of life keeps rolling along
Bumping into others along the way
When we do not want anyone in our circle,
Is usually when we really do. Funny how it works.
New faces always enrich our circles
Circle me.

T. Elliott Peterson

Denial

Sowing life's righteousness for all to see
Dancing, Prancing, Travelling the road of Normality
The wonderness in my cup of tea

Looking, searching, acting
Keeps me from dwelling into my reality
Darkness, distress, dominance
Always lurking at the edge of humanity

Pretense of life so merrily
Leaves no time for the souls intimacy
Fighting, fleeing, fending
The existence of the real me

Leaving more time for all to see
The bait of life's existence
Dancing and prancing in fantasy
While waiting patiently for eternity.

Connie Duran

The Gift

Ah, great Giver of the Gift,
Rain your power down upon me so I no longer need fear;

For why fear the darkness when it is your element?
For why fear the madman when he is your brother?
For why fear the world when it is your nourishment?
For why fear the apocalypse when it is your parent?

Ah, great Giver of the Gift,
Rain your power down upon me so I no longer need fear.

Colin Tominey

I Love The Times Of You And Me

I love the times of you and me
I store them all so carefully,
Within my heart and mind to keep
To dream about them in my sleep.

  I love the times I hold you tight,
  And tell you everything's all right.
  Our skies are turned from gray to blue,
  Each time I say that I care, too.

I love the times by light of fire,
We sit and tell our heart's desire.
Warmed slowly by the heat of flame,
Your soul with mine, becomes the same.

  I love the times... Just you and me,
  Those hours we spend in secrecy.
  Your eyes, your smile, your gentle touch,
  A simple kiss... They mean so much.

I love the times of you and me,
They're engraved in my memory.
With just one thought, they come in view,
Reminding me why I love you.

Ted Woody

Changing Course

I started down Main Street, then decided to use Center Street.
In my path was someone looking for a friend.
I stretched out my hand, it was taken and held.
And I knew I had found someone, to treasure for a life-time.
These moments are rare, or is it that we miss these
Opportunities, because we are looking in the wrong direction?
I would continue to change paths at will.
Main Street? Center Street? Side Street?
And I'll keep finding gems to cherish.

Joan Arthur

Minnesota Winters: A Comical Perspective

Friends talk standing by a warm wood stove.
The North wind lets you know it's there.
Sub-zero temps with a few feet of snow
and most folks dressed like polar bears...
But nobody cares how many layers you put on.
If they keep you warm that's fine.
Minnesota winters are adventures indeed.
Still, it's their home and mine.

Now when the high is minus ten
maybe you wonder if your car will start again.
And when staying warm is no small chore
you hear of folks going South to winter by the scores.

Yes, I think you must be daring or adventurous
to bear such weather.
I am sure...
that only the brave and the hearty endure
Minnesota winters.

Johnette E. Allen

Breeze

Some days a breeze, gentle and warm,
slides through a valley and past a farm

She nuzzles a tree and nudges a bush
soothes a cow, rustles a thrush

Lifting smells, carrying noise,
dancing past bright plastic toys

She carries the seeds of life aloft,
patterns of hope and chance which toss

The gifts of generations lost
in a giant game of chance

The beauty of the timeless rush
of wild air off a painter's brush

That draws from worlds so far away
the strength to power glider's play

Slips 'neath the notice of a bumblebee
dodging currents toward a lilac tree

Intent on sweetness so intoxicating
that a flower's wave has halted mating

While time blows past celebrating
the rhythmic moves of a mystic dance....

William M. Haney III

Maverick

Love came to me disguised as rage
and now the flickering flames make dust,
quite without time to set a stage
and render war to peace and trust.

One solitary spark might rise
from ash, fiercer than slow-knit life;
consoling thought, but little prize
without contentment, torn by strife.

A spark that filled the world with light
to ease the fate of humankind
would be sure solace for my grief,
such hope as maverick might find.

Joan Teale

The Great Pretender

Stand straight and tall, rigid as a board, when your back is broken,
and you are dragged through a thick field of endless thorns.
Smile shyly when your pulsing heart is torn merciless from within
your chest and trampled on.
Pretend you don't hear. Turn your eyes and censor yourself. Ignore
the truth staring you bitterly in the face. Hold back the tears
and breath ever so calmly, laugh gleefully when you are
screaming as if your lungs would burst.
Tell your sorrows to a stray cat, the friend you never had,
or the cuddly teddy bear so silent and sincere.
Even in their darkest thoughts, never could they cease to imagine the
suicidal child inside the calm and quiet one. The great pretender.
Surprised are the sceptic to discover the motionless figure,
lying cold and as quiet as ever. Lying in a puddle of blood that's
their own. Bleeding to death. Silently. Shedding their last tear,
breathing their lost breath...inhale...exhale...inhale.

Lindsay Sharon Gleason

Baseball

Baseball is broken bones when you least need them.

Baseball is a pitch to the catcher, catcher misses, and the other team steals home.

Baseball is a coach in the dugout yelling signals at you that you don't understand.

Baseball is being on deck the day you're having a slump.

Baseball is listening to the ump tell you that you are out when you know that you are not.

Baseball is a foul when you hit the ball perfectly, just in the wrong direction.

Baseball is having bases loaded and you get an out.

Baseball is a batter getting nervous and tightening up.

Baseball is when the center fielder, the worst batter on the team, hits a grand slam.

Baseball is pouring water all over the coach's head after winning the championship game.

Baseball is catching a fly ball when you were just told to pay more attention.

Baseball is sitting at the ball park in 90 degree weather just to watch your boyfriend play.

Raye Roeder

Vegas

He painted until the day he died,
ancient, black, felt beret
(the one he got in Paris the year he drank Dago Red with Picasso)
askew on his wispy haired, irradiated skull.
I stayed with his fifth wife, seven years younger than I,
she pregnant, I childless.

In Las Vegas, violet fades to pink under a parfait desert sky.
At night, the strip gushes pastel neon all the way to the East end,
where florescent marquees give way to simple signs,
sequins to muslin without buttons.

Through the automatic doors wide enough for a wheelchair,
past the terminally ill and their families, who drink coke and coffee.
Down the whispered halls to Dad's room.

Too loud jazz on the cassette player,
he leans on the back of a Naugahyde chair,
by the window in front of his easel, hospital gown slightly parted,
just enough slack in his I.V. tubes to wave a cigarette in one hand,
a paint brush in the other.
The mauve rug at his bare feet dotted with drops of paint and melted
black holes. Lint on his beret.

Cynthia Parker

Serpentine Truth Playing Eternally

Deconstructing into music.
Trusting the will of the universe.
Dancing the ecstasy. Being here now.
Invoking the peace. Drinking in the elements.
Healing worlds. Meeting all friends.
Remembering in our bodies.
Whirling the balance.
Asking receiving offering.
Learning each other's truths.
Loving all things.
Accepting cleansing believing.
Distilling to essence.
Divining our lives.
Speaking each other's dreams.
Weaving our visions. Creating the means.
Harvesting the bounty.
Honoring each other's power.
Rising kundalini from coil. Recycling to beauty.
Re-imprinting in Eden, nourished by sacrament.
Godly we go more magical.

Elizabeth Roberts

Navajo Weaver's Lament

Tomorrow
They say I must leave this land
The sacred land of my people
When I go I live no more

Tomorrow
They will come to take my sheep
They will twine barbwire around my land
They say then it will be Hopi land
I am Dine, Navajo, Weaver
They say that is why I must go

Yesterday
This land was Navajo land
Tomorrow it will be Hopi land
Can the Hopi make the stream flow sweeter
Can they make the corn grow taller
Can they weave a finer rug

Tomorrow, I will burn my loom, I will burn my hogan
I will go to Black Mountain
I will go to rest with my Ancestors
Tomorrow is a good day to die

Beatrice Brown Higgins

Suddenly So Many People

Suddenly so many people and they're here
to see me - my husband, my children, my grandchildren,
my Mother, and my sister, too. Family and friends
I haven't seen in years, they're all here too.
I've thought of each and every one of them that's
true but why do they come now?
It's not the right time for me, I'm not prepared,
but now it's happened and now, suddenly
so many people.
I'm going to see some others that I've missed
throughout the years, I'm going to see my
Dad whom I've missed for years and years.
Here I come Lord, open your arms to me
because I know this other world will certainly
be kind to me.

Marlene M. Viti

"Just Stop"

You said it wouldn't happen to you,
But of course it did.
I told you not to do it,
But you did it anyway.
Maybe now you've learned your lesson,
At least I hope.
You wouldn't stop,
And look where it got you.
You've been hanging around the wrong people.
They just get you into trouble.
I wish you would've stopped when I told you to.
But you couldn't because you were too far in.
You never used to be this bad until they came along.
Now you're in so deep you can't get out.
You mean so much to me and now you're hurt.
Please I'm begging you "just stop."

Ericka Keener

Farm Life: Days of Olde

Down by the brook where violets grow wild,
We walked in the water when the days were mild.
We searched for berries as we ran in play,
For this is the end of a busy day.

Our day would start with the morning sun,
And working in the garden is what we called fun.
Since life on the farm leaves much to do,
And the choice of jobs was up to you.

Planting, haying, milking Old Bessy,
Left us tired, worn and messy.
Papa kept busy with the market crops,
Keeping one step ahead of rain drops.

There were days when the rain was a welcomed friend.
When we worked with Mama, our clothes to mend.
We cooked and canned and baked some bread,
And stories were told as we went to bed.

School was a pleasant relief for us,
We traveled quite far, and always by bus.
Our clothes were plain, our pleasures few,
But we had each other and Mama too.

Elizabeth Paul

Los Angeles - On Fire

Thick black clouds, darkness at noon
Hot heavy haze; where is God?

Hillsides burning; animals frightened
Firemen helpless; where is God??

Houses a total loss; people confused and frightened
What to do now; where is God?

How to rebuild; where do we start
Does anybody care; where is God?

Child, look at my clouds; let my light shine always
Wipe the haze from your eyes; I'm here.

My hills are ablaze with hope; I'm holding the animals in My hands
The firemen just need to ask for strength; I'm here.

Your home is with me; let your mind be at rest
Take time to reflect; I'm here.

Rebuild in My word; now is the time
I care my child; I'm here.

Yvonne E. Storer

The Three Muskateers

From acapulco to puerto vallarta
We shed many tears,
We raised our children without fear,
We loved and worried about our boys sins,
We stuck together and raised them within,
As we became older we related again,
We are at peace again for our boys are safe within,
This is why we grew to love each other to the end.

H. J. Kirkpatrick

I Am The Moon

I am the moon.
I shine brightly in the sky,
Shedding light on the creations emerging,
That haunt the evening shade.
I see friends laugh,
The couples kiss,
And the broken-hearted cry.
I am the pensive moon.
All I see is what I cannot have.
My only happiness is my light,
But even that is not my own,
For I borrow it from the sun at night.
I am the lonely moon.

Francis E. Little

My Dream Cabin

High up in the hills in among the pines
is that little cabin of mine
Near it is a little brook
Wild flowers where ever you look

Tall and straight, just like a pine
is that handsome husband of mine
"Hello, my dear Honey" he cries
Then tears of joy comes to my eyes

He says to me, "I love you with all my heart"
And I tell him that I love him, that we'll never part
Oh, but I'll never see that cabin away in the pines
And you never was the sweet husband of mine.

But you are in heaven I know
Just the same I still love you so
For this is a dream of you
So my dream cabin can never come true

"He got killed, and his love is still in"
"My heart." I am

Dorothy Wintermute

Change of the Ruler

There must be a change
A state of mind
Technology demands infiltration of one's environment to control.
Out of control.
My mind is filled with minor priorities,
Twisting, shifting principles
Without reasons beyond a reasonable doubt;
Of insufficient evidence,
Before pronounced innocent

Child like ruler
Leads by hypocrisy,
To fill their own purses,
Denied truths confessed,
Damned to be guilty,
Overwhelmed by injustice,
Confused by politics,
I believe.

Jason Pacilli

History of Our Love

I'm out like a light and gone with the wind;
We go to sleep as two good friends.
I wake in the morning with the love of my life;
Who then turns into, my companion and wife.

The one I wanted, the one for me;
It couldn't have happened, until I could see.
She was the love, I needed, I knew;
The love that would last and always be true.

The wedding did happen, on that lovely day;
I couldn't have pictured it, any other way.
The flowers, the cake, the beautiful bride;
Make my heart beat, rapid with pride.

The love is there, getting stronger each day;
I'm glad it happened, that one day in May!

Alfred Schubert Jr.

Of Home

The Spring is lovely everywhere
Its virgin shoots of grass
And flowers, rare
Because they have not bloomed before
Are wondrous things.

No matter what strange land they may be blooming in
Nor what the tongue in which they get their name
Their beauty, transient as it is,
Is lovely to behold.
There is but one small place long hills away
Where every bud, yes every blade of grass
Has got a brighter hue
Where flowers gayer bloom and as I roam
And see the spring in other lands, I think of home.

Richard E. Beecroft

Jealousy

I'm jealous of the way she walks,
I'm jealous of the way she talks.

I'm jealous of the way he looks at her,
I'm jealous of the whole wide world.

What is this jealousy I'm feeling?
Why do I feel like it is peeling?

Peeling me away from him,
Peeling me ever so thin.

One day I know what I will pop,
And then they will need a mop.

To clean up all the messy stains,
And the knife that took away my pain.

Melissa Marshall

For Him

Perfect, I said to him as I walk along the pier
Talk to Him, talk without fear
Thank you I said, three praises to Thee
The one who gave me eternity.
As I reached the end of the pier by the bay
With joy in my heart I knew what to say
Not knowing where or how to begin
All I can do is put my faith in Him
Our friendship is something I value in Thee
And has grown stronger within me
I will respect what you decide in the end
For I will always be
Your faithful friend.

Jeannie Marrero

If I Were A Crab

If I were a crab
  I would pinch the stinky feet
of the grubby little beach bum,
  who stole my sandy seat.
"Out of my way!" I would say,
  looking him in the eye.
He'd turn with a stick of butter and say
  "Ah, ha! You shall fry!"
The chase would be on,
  from a minute to maybe an hour,
until I'd be put into a bubbly pot
  to cower.
After all,
  I don't think a crab is the life for me.
I would rather be a shark,
  so I can eat the little dweeb!

  Eric Messick

The Forest

Giant redwoods look down and around
At moss and ferns which cover the ground.

The stillness is broken first by the bird
Which sings the sweetest song that ever was heard.

The deer nervously graze on the tall, green grass
As the gurgling brook rushes on past.

The sun shimmers down through the branches above
And settles on the wings of a pure white colored dove.

Skunk, chipmunk, and squirrel; badger, beaver, and fox
Race around in the underbrush, flowers, and phlox.

The sweet fragrance of honeysuckle drifts on the breeze
As the wind gently stirs the leaves of the trees.

The pond over yonder looks calm and serene.
A swan's sweet grace gives magic to the scene.

Smoke curls from the chimney of the cabin down the lane
Where a little girl sits with her face against the pane.

Gazing out the window, she couldn't help but stare,
For if ever there was beauty, surely it was there.

  Karen Johnson

Fish, Chips, And Fingerprints

Stop at a cabaret for some fish and chips,
Scotland Yard found my fingerprints.
The guilt's burning, scorching my black heart,
Contaminating my blood like a poisoned dart.
Alone at my table, I mentally shout,
It's devouring my soul from the inside out.
Nibble, bite, mouthful... Chew, swallow,
A light repast, my core in hollow.
Like Orpheus reluctantly turning his head,
One look back, all that's left is regret...
  All Because
I can't run from what I've done,
My fingerprints were on the gun.

  D. L. Weber

Fulfillment

I am a teacher!
Chosen, directed and inspired by the Master Teacher
And endowed by Him to mold the minds,
Reach the hearts and touch the souls of today's youth.

But as I reflect upon thirty years of interaction.
My most cherished memory
Though intangible, is infinity precious;
Though spontaneous, is deeply personal;
As I remember the glow of happiness and appreciation
In the eyes of a child, as suddenly
His mind grasps an understanding of the difficult and the new
And he realized that he has achieved and that I have helped;

Then I am grateful to God for the privilege of serving Him
Through service to our most precious possessions, our children;
And for the added privilege of learning from them
The lessons of tolerance, patience, and trust;
Humility, faith and forgiveness.

  Dolores H. Pennington

We Are One

I am the child of the new born.
You welcomed my forebearers with open arms.
You gave them air to breath, space to live
You succored them; you sustained them
You gave them life.

They gave you gifts of work, of spirit,
  of determination, of expectation, of fulfillment
They gave you life.

We became one: united in thought, in desire,
  in deed, in goal;
We succored each other
We sustained each other
We gave life to each other.

Yet, we remained ourselves
And in our apartness,
We became one.

  B. C. Raunchle

the final show

I'm waiting to buy a ticket as the line starts to form
for the first and only showing
of The Calm Before The Storm

moving slowly down the aisle just looking for a seat
the audience in this titled room
begin to stamp their feet

trembling ushers lock the doors for the anxious crowd must know
the theatre lights will surely dim
before the final show

strange crunching sounds get louder as mouths continue to roar
dying words are spilling over
and sticking to the floor

we watch the coming attractions without a second glance
but it only takes a moment of truth
and still we miss the chance

the projector keeps on rolling as we rise upon the screen
while the signs of the times are quickly
passing sight unseen

  Frank Ciofalo

Premature Son

Disrupted and abrupt,
A parcel delivered before its time,
Attached to tubes of a plastic placenta,
Pulsating, beeping, blinking with consistent lights,
Pumping life into emaciated, writhing limbs.
Beep. A breath. Beep. A heartbeat,
Faintly fluttering percussive pulse.
A tiny face screws up with silent cries
While a mother croons with moistened eyes,
"Suck life from me...absorb my strength...
Hold on, my baby...Survive, my son!"
Beep. A heartbeat. Beep. A breath.
Beep. A hope. A blinking light.
A persistent plea, an insistence for life
That erupts determinedly
Despite prematurity,
Despite the odds, despite his size.

Libby Jacobs Christensen

Love Is Too Deep To Die

Remember when we were in love
Remember the first time we kissed
And when your gentle lips
Touched mine.

No you're not, you're not the one
The one that remembers
It's me that cries at night
Trying to forget

Forget the memories we had
I hope, I hope I could
But I can't
It's too hard
The way I loved you
I won't love anyone else

I hope you can understand
But I guess you can't
You can't because you never been in love
In love like I was once
It was too deep to die
And it will remain in my heart forever

I hope once you would feel the love that I felt but I hope it would
    last forever.

Kristina Petrosyan

Wishing

I'm going home tomorrow, leaving
    this lovely place.
My footprints will be washed
    away-gone without a trace.
I wish I could gather in my arms,
    this very restless sea
And bring it to my own backyard,
    under the maple tree.
I'd sit and watch the world go by
    and watch the children play,
enjoy the beach, the leaves
    the grass, and watch the farmers hay.
I'd have it all, the very best, my life would be complete.
In a chair with sky above me and the waves pulling at my feet.
Of course it won't really happen, it's only a happy dream
And the ocean dwindles downward to the little backyard stream.
Then I'll sit here under my maple till the leaves of autumn fly
And look for the warmth to come again under a cloudless sky.
Then I'll pack up for vacation and head for the endless sea
To bask in the sun and wish I had, my maple here with me.

Gloria Letendre

Frail Little Bird

Mother's Passing

Dear frail little bird, off you flew. At last
You drifted from your ancient home, to a place
calling and singing to you. And you were gone.
Tiny birdie, your long earthly life was past.
And we, left behind, found it so hard to face.
Windy that night, so cold, and you had gone.

Were you a bit timid with your freedom so new?
Perhaps you looked back and lingered a while,
Reluctant to leave. If so, not for long.
By your little nest we stood, hearts rent in two,
Already missing your love that could so beguile.
Unable to believe, that now, you were gone.

Dear little thing, I keep hope - The Great One
has promised, that not long from this day,
Our perfect, shining beings will meet once again.
And should I be beautiful and glorious as a sun,
But you, yet weak and plain with earthly trait,
Still, I shall kiss you and carry you, seeing

It is I am diminished and you, still, who are great.

Caroline Von Bonnie Effinger

Unforgiven Forever

You held me, protecting me from the shadows, the cold,
So close, so warm, with your soft skin,
Firm arms above my young, naked curves.
Your hard muscles, your demanding yet gentle touch
Comforted, calmed, sedated me.
Unknowing, I slept as my body began to work,
Building, constructing, nourishing the new life
You placed unintentionally, by chance
Within my youthful womb.
Awaking, I did not yet know
That those days of magic, infatuation,
Could not disappear
As innocently, as innocuously.
My body would not weather your caresses
So calmly, so easily, without trouble.
You left me used, alone,
Scared, scarred,
And carrying the seed that ensured
That every day, with every breath,
I would never be allowed to forget you.

L. Kathleen Hammer

Redundant

For twenty years and more
I worked the factory floor.
Others like me strove in the plant or at the desk.
When the boss assigned each is task.
He did not have to say do your best.

When the day was past,
We stayed long after all the rest.

But, for you and me, no more the whistle's blast.
There is no work for you and me to best.

The time came for the boss to say
This job was well done, the goal is near.
Instead, he spoke words of regret and dismay.
The cost of this work, he said, is too dear.

It is too late to save, and all must be changed.
The goal is now undone.
The work and my life's blood cannot be rearranged.
There is simply nothing to be done.

The Man says there will be a new tomorrow,
And the opportunities will be many and abundant.
But for me it is a time of sorrow,
This paper handed me tells me I'm now redundant.

Jerry Cooper

Hearts

Hearts that may be broken
Hearts that can be healed

With the love of God
No one is left to appeal

No shame no sorrow
Hearts are not meant to be borrowed

With the love of the family
These hearts are appealed

Hearts that are broken
Are meant to be real

With the love of God no one would be left with tears

You soon will know when that right person will appear.
To refill that heart that has been left in tears

No one can harm it as long as you're happy
But when hate arrives that heart is no longer alive

The family produces love to forget that lonesome heart
That has been broken into tears
By a lonesome Jerk who seemed so dear.

Lili Tello

My Love For Cheekie

Down the path of life we travel but not alone.
Each day I am thankful that you I have known.
Bleekus and Cheekie, pet names, I gave you,
Only one of the ways, my love to prove.
Right now I am thinking of your smiling face,
And I reach out to caress it, but I am in a different place.
Happiness and knowing you have gone hand in hand,
Always enjoying each other, as if it were planned.
Non-wavering is your compassion for everyone you meet,
Naughty and playful when we are together - you are truly sweet.
White and beautiful your skin; in school you were teased,
After kissing every inch... I could not be more pleased.
Love, unconditional is what I see in your eyes,
Knowing that love is for me alone, still makes me question why.
Everlasting devotion to me, is what you seem to desire,
Rooted passion to hold you close is what feeds my fire.

Toby Allen Zirkle

Breaking the Ice

Seeing you besides me
Brings a passion forth
Which sets my soul afire.
I wish you could see
What your essence is worth
But there isn't anyone playing a lyre.

I wish to be with you
But I hesitate to ask
For fear of rejection.
But I wish to ask you
For it would be a worthy task
To achieve a marvelous sensation
Brought by your acceptation
To go out together, with passionate anticipation

Larry A. Bowden Jr.

Out of the Gray

Out of the Gray,
a shimmering glimpse of spectral light,
elusive as sunshine on a stormy day,
speaks silently to me with the voice of the night...

"Awaken..." it spoke in my unbending ear,
and roused little more than an unexplained tear.
"Dear child..." more mildly, but I dare not hear,
and I turn up my collar, as a storm must be near.

Out of the depths
of a dark winter's morn,
comes news of love's conquering death
as a brightly shining soul is reborn.

"Rejoice..." said the voice to my longing heart,
which struggled and coughed to a sputtering start.
"A joyous day..." I heard it say, and the clouds began to part,
and to my blues, this news does a loving light impart.

Out of the Gray,
a brilliant, gentle light,
bright as new snow on Christmas Day,
warms me and guides me toward dawn, through the night.

John Berry

Who Is God

Who is the man, who is God
What gave him the right
Who are Gods that are men
The World could be better if I was a God
these Gods shovel the dirt in my mouth
Then expect me to swallow
Well I don't wanna floss the good out of my teeth
but there's nothing to do.
I was given my position,
my mouth of dirt,
and a will to fight
So all you Gods out there
Here I am.
Shovel it!

Andy Leahy

A Sharing of Wings

We are two half-dead and half-alive birds
enthroned in a garden of brilliant red roses
sometimes they bloom and sometimes they prick too much!
My wing is hurt and I'm afraid
yours seems to be hurt too
can you hold mine and can I hold yours?
Let's take flight on each other's wings
cutting through the thorns
knowing they can hurt us
and can we fly again with each other's strength?
Above a garden of plentiful roses
far from thorns that bleed us
together within each other's wings
over a garden of red roses
constantly brilliant
and always blooming!!!???

Susan M. Kerestes

18

First Born

When first I gazed at his little red face
and his chubby wee fist squeezed my thumb,
I felt a stir in my heart, a new bliss.
To the charms of our first-born I'd begun to succumb.

When he turned on his tummy,
his eyes followed me around the room.
Watching his daily progress
made my spirits zoom.

When he crawled, bric-a-brac was imperiled.
He squalled to escape the hated play-pen.
His was a free spirit.
For travel he had a yen.

After weeks of crawling the floor,
he toddled into my outstretched arms
with a big triumphant smile,
just one of his many charms.

He has traveled in many countries.
For years we've lived far apart.
But whether he's trudging or soaring,
love keeps him close to my heart.

Pauline Robinson Ohmart

The Creature of the Night

I bite into your neck with my dagger-like teeth
I want what's in your veins and everything beneath
I'll give you a gift, it's eternal life
We can only be killed with a stake or a knife
You take this weapon and stab me in the heart
You think it's the end, but it's only the start
I live in a world that is forever dark
Two holes in your neck is my eternal mark
I hunt you in your sleep, lying in your bed
I'll fill your mind with lies and I'll mess with your head
I'll tell you I love you, but I really want you dead
I'll take anyone's life just to be fed
The color red surrounds the blue of my eye
The light of day is what makes me cry
The facts are I am a killer and a liar
The name for me is known as vampire

Beth Deckelman

Mirage Of Souls

The stifled cry of the Little One echoes into the dark night
as I pass by the untouched alley.
My curious nature guides me through all the trash and filth
left by centuries of humans.
Just as the Little One was, unkept and unfed
by the heartless and the feared.
I searched the deep to find the source of the anguished cry.
I knew the Little One, knew what the Little One looked like,
even smelled like and yet I couldn't find the cry.
I continued to search and peel away the layers
of garbage and skins.
The cries grew as I peeled and teared
while my own vacant tears fell at a rapid rate.
The tiny world around me stopped
and so did the cries when I saw that there wasn't anymore.
It did not take long for me to realize who the trash belonged to,
as my mouth opens and the hideous cry of the Little One
echoes into the tranquil, always tranquil night.

Elizabeth Driggers

Tears Rain

She left us on a spring soft day, gentle as can be
Passing on to ethereal life, with grace and dignity

Life, since then, a hollow song, echoes fill melancholy days
Memories become tangible gold, spiritual pondering remains

When windows reflect the painful past, tears rain, oh so easily
Heartache jagged with eternal love, my soul reverberates in misery

Lost my protective harbor, a battered shell upon the shore
Fragments scatter and wash away, to sand and wind once more

Nighttime evokes deep shadows, dark closets hide within
My mind, a tangled web of woe, sleep heals the suffering

I yearn to feel her sunlight, to bathe in her beaming glow

Hear her cleansing laughter, saturate my soul

Oh Life - ironic reverie, Death - translucent mystery
Rebirth - virtuous destiny, Love - eternal harmony.

Cynthia Moczulski

John M. Ashbrook, Epitaph

He walked among world leaders with lots of power to wield.
But his heart was with his family, friends, and neighbors far
afield.

Politically he often stood alone and fought with all his might.
He stood for right and principle and always kept his goals in sight.

Now his voice is silent and some may say he is dead.
But John is up in heaven looking after those he loved and lead.

John M. Randall

Our Daddy

Our daddy is a trucker, we are proud to say
Our daddy takes us places that most people
haven't seen.
We have been coast to coast and in between
seen lakes, rivers, and oceans, too.
Someone ask where he is and what he has on
We are glad to tell them. With a couple
adventures thrown in there, too.
Daddy misses us and we miss him.
He didn't make the games, plays, or parties.
People say what a shame.
We love him no matter what people say
He has brought his truck to school
Everyone thought that was cool
our daddy calls us every night to talk to
us and tells us he loves us.
Does yours do that?

Tamara Taylor

Searching

As time goes on, the world seems smaller
The trials seem more often but are valued less
People seem to fall into pits, making the same mistakes
    time after time, learning nothing from them
Hurting themselves and all those around them
In a constant march looking for that certain something or
    someone that will make a difference in their life
Never recognizing that they have to make that difference
    not someone else
Through all, time passes quickly and they have become
    older not wiser
Still searching in misery, never enjoying now.

Jean Murphy

Dream Come True

You speak of empty pages; and stories yet untold
You speak to me of wells gone dry; and melodies of old
You asked me, to be a pen and fill your book for you
And though this is an honor, it's something I can't do
For you see, it takes two, to write a book of love
So... My hand will hold the pen if you will be my glove
Together we can write this book, a story with no end
Both hand and glove together, and our love will be the pen

Yes... I can be the rain that fills your thirsty well
But you must be the water from which I dip my pail
Even the sky needs moisture to make the clouds that rain
Bring winds and rain together and you have a hurricane
The two must work together, as you can clearly see
Side by side as equals is how it has to be
Put words with music and form a song, with melodies of gold
But, once again, it takes the two for the meaning to unfold

Would you be the music to the songs as yet unsung?
And together we can form a bond which cannot be undone.

Would you be my dream come true?

Brandise Reed

Not My Elbows Too

When I turned 36 I thought, not bad at all.
Even though the mirror showed things began to fall.

You need to work a little harder, I told myself
Sit-ups, push-ups, and stretching will help.

The years of 37 and 38 went swiftly by,
Leaving me bumps, bulges and lines around each eye.

Still not bad for a gal of 39,
Cause I had gotten lazy about this time.

Work harder is what I had to do,
Cause here comes 40, and I'll not be blue.

So I bounced off the fat and watched what I ate;
I hurt my back and then I gained weight.

But I'm alright and have accepted the fact,
That we fall different places and can't put it back.

Today I passed the mirror and looked at the view,
And gasped as I said, "Not My Elbows Too!"

Carol Sue Seals

Child of Love and Life

Poetry, the child of Love and Life,
Secretly forms in the recesses of the mind,
Gradually grows in the depth of the soul,
Matures, and is born — from Love to Life.
But Love must be passionately alive
Before Poetry can be born.
It must grow to its fullest,
And when Love emerges in all her beauty,
Life holds her, joins with Love,
And the Child is conceived.
Love and Life await eagerly the precious one.
They wonder — will she be beautiful?
Will she bring joy to the world?
Love must labor long
To give birth to this child,
Life must accept her as she is,
Together they must embrace her, claim her —
For only then can she truly be
The child of Love and Life,
    Poetry, sweet poetry...

Betty Medema

Leaving

With every single step I take
And every single move I make
I trudge my dreary journey
This is my fate, what I'm to be,
This is my choice, the world to flee
My friends and family have hurt me.
I no longer belong to this cruel life
And so I take my painful strife
And go.

As I pack my suitcases
I think of all the smiling faces
And reminisce on what might have been
If maybe I could only win
In this pointless battle of life
But I have been stabbed with a knife
That kills my spirits and all of my dreams
My ragged life ripped at the seams
No more.

Megan E. Dibble

Citizen

One less pair of shoes, on the sidewalk; one less car on the road;
And no one notices,
265 million souls, don't feel the loss of one piece of the whole,
And the power still flows,
The hands on the clock march on; because time hates us all,
And we crawl, as quickly as God lets us,
Making noises to cover the things we do and trust,
But one of "them" dies, oh now say a prayer,
The media stares; as a homeless man is killed, in the fanfare,
But is it fair? No one knows, because no one cares,
Why is one soul worthy and another condemned? Are we not men?
Do we decide who lives and who dies,
Can we put a value on ourselves, then?
A time ago, far from the maddening crowd,
A hundred legions of angels soar; to the King, evermore;
Lying in a manger;
A small one of hay, but still it holds,
The Lord of All, from the foreboding cold,
Though the kings reign and die; The Lord above the skies,
Sent the Ruler to be alone, one citizen that night.

T. J. Koury III

Dawn

As dawn broke that cold November morning
she looked out the window at the cloud-streaked sky.

Her thoughts drifted toward winter and its many cold gray dawns—
no birds singing, no sweet smell of grass, or early morning mist.

Slowly her eyes returned to the sky and rested on a small patch
of eerie light; she wondered, and watched intently as light and
clouds played their game of hide and seek.

Finally the light emerged—first glimmering, then gleaming,
and slowly a perfectly rounded, large, full moon came into view.

Its brightness dominated the sky, playing tricks with her eyes
and daring any cloud to disturb the magic of the moment.

Presently, the clouds began their dance across the face of the moon,
leaving a lacy pattern in their wake.
And before too long the white ball faded into the light of the new day.

Bernice G. Blackwell

These Are The Days

These are the days,
That we show our love in even more wonderful ways.
It is on these days that we say, "Hello,"
Hello to a precious new life that, with our love, will grow.
You are the sunshine that comes from within,
For it is on these days that your brand new lives will begin.
The promises that we made to each other are now made to you;
For better and for worse,
For our love, you will never have to search;
For richer and for poorer,
With us, you will always find an open door;
In sickness and in health,
For us, you will be our wealth;
To love, to honor, and to cherish,
We are a family. . . .
And that will never perish.
For our love is forever strong,
And within each of our hearts is where we all belong.
    Michelle Niehart

Believing In You

Life can be a heavy load
I'm sure we've all been told.
Stand tall for your beliefs
For they are as good as gold!

No time for a vacation
Nor simple conversation
We must make our dreams come true
With no more hesitation.

Keep believing in your dreams and someday they will come true.
If doubts become too extreme,
Don't stop believing in you.
Keep believing in your dreams
Just you, can make them come true.
Don't stop believing in you,
Don't give up the faith inside you.

Remember, life can be rough.
Stand tall every day.
It can be a little tough, just see it through your own way.

Brighter tomorrows can be. All you would have to do,
Is remember that the key is believing in you!
    Alice R. Smith

A Growing Friendship

Something is happening from deep within
    It's a feeling of joy. A feeling of glee
    A feeling of excitement deep within me
It's affected my soul. I walk with a grin

It happens when we spend time together
    The more we talk the more I grow
    The more we meet the more I know
For in my life there is no other

I know we met a month or less
    But all day and night or so it seems
    I think of you often in wonderful dreams
Yes, something is happening I must confess

There's a new man in my life, but I've had crushes
    But this one is different. This one's unique
    My heart is full. I stand oblique
A glow in my heart and my pulse rushes

Is it possible to fall for someone this soon?
    In time I will know
    That love meant to be will grow
But only from a friendship is love able to bloom
    Jos R. Lozano

Untitled

He stands before us, the head of the pack.
Shoulders hunched, teeth bared.
The blood we see is the sun on his hair
The red of our broken kayak.

We cannot escape, bodies rigid with fear,
He pounces, the end is near.
I cringe, waiting for the pain,
My eyes wide open, as though going insane.

Suddenly, he shrinks back.
The howl rips through the air,
The howl of someone's world gone black.
He hesitates, then runs to his lair.

We are still shaken, but in time,
We realize that we were saved from death's dark shrine.
    Sandy Tse

No Tribulation

The rapture is coming it won't be long,
in a flash it will happen and I'll be gone.
Way up in the clouds my redeemer to see,
but those who don't know him will suddenly miss me.
What a sight it will be to those left behind,
people disappearing no trace will they find.
Busy streets once crowded won't be full at all,
for those who know Jesus will have heard the master's call.

Cars on the highway will career out of control
as drivers and passengers are called into his fold.
At sporting events large crowds will suddenly quite,
as those sitting near disappear from their sight.

The teams themselves will have performers not seen,
as viewers at home watch their television screen.
It's really very serious and there isn't much time,
Jesus is coming and pleading don't be left behind.

No matter what you've done he will forgive you,
for I a believer am a forgiven sinner too.
Please don't miss the call when he comes for his own,
then there'll be no tribulation for we will all be home.
    Gordon Ayers

China Doll

Love is like a beautiful china doll,
Very delicate, extremely fragile, and small.
If handled with the greatest loving care,
The doll will stay beautiful for many a year.

With great tenderness hold the doll in your hands,
Beware of where you leave the doll to stand.
In a place that is safe and protected,
So you are sure no injury may be projected.

But often life's winds of torrent blow,
And from your protection the doll will go.
Flying to the ground with a loud crash,
And your love is turned to dust and ash.

If you're watching your doll very close.
You maybe able to change the ill-fated course.
And catch your doll long before the tragic fall,
That is when your love will be the greatest of all.
    Kim Bartley

The Morn

Each day as I awake tis only a fleeting moment
Till I look to the morn
For this day does not hold
My hopes, my dreams, my love

As midday anxiously draws akin
Only to be an urge, a mention
Once more for the morn I await searching searching
For the intangible

As night sweeps upon me one last aspiration one final inquiry
All to no avail alas
The morn will bring
Another transitory day

As I lay pondering
In my slumber the ideal
Weeping weeping along
All merely fades
As dawn callously
Betrays my eyes

Oh morn what misery awaits my perusal
But a perplexity pervading my soul....

Jeffrey L. Kratt

For All Of This I Thank You

You taught me how to love.
You showed me how to care.
You told me not to worry.
You said that you'd be there.

You promised to be faithful.
You said that you'd be true.
My pain, no longer present.
My life, no longer blue.

You helped break my defenses.
You helped tear down the walls.
You promised you would catch me.
If ever I should fall.

You've made me fully ready,
To love with all my heart.
I knew that when I met you.
I loved you from the start.

You said that I'm the only, you said I am the first.
Your warmth, it fed my hunger. Your loving quenched my thirst.

I also will be faithful. I'll be forever true.
And do my best in showing, that I always will love you.

Ryan Houk

In The Garden

I walked through the garden one day,
Holding my mother's hand.
An instrument she used as I grew,
To push me, support me, and help me to stand.
We laughed fondly of the days that were done,
And talked gently of the one's yet to come.
That evening, I thought of the garden, our talk, and my mother.
And as we walked through the garden, I had come to realize,
My beautiful mother was my very own rose,
Not a more perfect flower in the garden,
No other would I have chose.

Heather Massey

I Can

I hear some people say, I can't do things because I'm not smart enough. I can't sing, I can't dance, I just don't have the right stuff. I'm not pretty or handsome, no one would listen to me, I'll fail for sure, I can't take that risk you see. I can't seems to be the mold for me, I can't, I can't. If I stay on this road I know I'll explode. In my dimly lit room I saw hope in full bloom, all dusty and cluttered with stuff. It's a Bible neglected, unused, neglected, just there for a special few. To my surprise the pages flew by and stopped at the side of my hand, on one page I did see as the tears ran down free, it said, I can, I can because of Jesus, it's he and "I can't" was no longer a part of me.

Paula F. Weathers

Come Closer ...

Come closer, you're standing just out of reach;
I want to touch the heat of desire.
I want to catch the passion burning inside
and dance in the flames of the fire.

Come closer, I only touch you in dreams;
let me breathe the air of your kiss.
Let me know the taste of your sweat on my lips;
set me free with my fantasy's bliss.

Come closer, take my hand and escape
to a place where emotions run free,
where I can experience all that you are,
and you will know all that is me.

Come drown your thirst in my river of dreams;
taste temptation that constantly flows there ...
I'll say it once more, with only a whisper,
before reality wakes me, come closer.

Michele May Grossmith

A Star Filled Night

I look into the star filled night
And wonder if someday I might
Find someone who his life to share
I wonder will be hear my prayer
I asked for faith that I'd stay strong
Through nights that seem to last so long
That one day soon I'd find someone
To share my life with sad and fun
A friend to take away my tears
And still my heart from all fears
Someone to keep me safe at night
To hold me till the mornings light
Though no one knows what the future holds
With trust in God His plan unfolds
This prayer I send on Heaven's breeze
That God my mind He put at ease
So each new day that brings the sun
I pray His will not mine be done

Susan Leidner

Hatrack

It sat, abandoned, for twelve years.
At six years of age it entered my life
And struck sheer terror into my soul,
For at night, as I crept to my room,
It would snap and claw at me,
It was a beast of hats and fur scarves,
Broken promises, sitting, waiting,
For it to once again be bedtime,
And for me to once again creep to my room.

Jonathan Miller

"Wishing Upon A Star"

If I were a star in heaven, a small glistening light
What would you wish upon me, as I descended from the night.
Would you wish I hadn't descended, so I could shine again
Would you wish in secret or tell your very best friend.
Would you wish at all, or even notice my descent
As your mind makes thoughts, many a star has been spent.

Michael Gordon

The Horizon

Satisfaction is a lie,
a place to which we'll never fly.
The more we have the more we want,
we envy those who tend to flaunt.
Some wander blindly, happy and free,
some open their eyes, see misery.
The pain we have, it tastes so sweet,
to love so much we cannot eat.
To suffer long in search for truth,
but watch yourself, don't lose your youth.
We wish for things that cannot be,
and try not to fall into apathy.
We can't let go, for it's our pain,
that gives us beauty we feel in our vein.
So spread your wings and fly around,
but sometime land and touch the ground.
It's not so bad, I know it's true,
cause when it all falls down, I still have you.

Ryan Kerchner

The Man In The Wall

The man in the wall, I see him clear
I feel him breathing like he's always near
Hot breath on my neck burning my skin away
The man in the wall is here to stay
I see his face though it's not there
Piercing eyes with red hot glare
He's everywhere though nowhere at all
He's the man that lives in the wall
I see him every night and feel him everyday
He's always there, he won't go away
He's creeping in my mind like a black clouded mist
In my brain he's formed a cyst
He's driving me crazy as I don't know where to turn
Red lapping flames are his eyes to burn
They bore in my brain driving me nuts
I see the vision of unemboweled bloody guts
The man in the wall is not my friend
His insanity is only a means to an end
It's only a way to capture me in his place
Then the man in the wall will be my face

Joyce M. Silcox

Beyond the Gate

Death is not the end, but the beginning of a
graduation from this temporal life of heartache
and pain.

To a life everlasting in God's Great Domain,
where there will be Serenity And Joy And Peace
forever more.

To be shared with our love ones who patiently
wait for us to come home to enter the gate.

Unending joy will be ours to claim, if our
name has been written in God's Hall of Fame.

A life so beautiful and complete, the fruits
of our labor will be so sweet to share when
we gather at Jesus' feet.

Darlene McLeod

My Every Thoughts

You hide behind every thought in my mind
my perfect match you are,
I'll always be wondering what your
every thoughts are,
even though I already know they will be
of you and I.

Listening to you breathe
I wonder off to another world,
infinite and exquisite.
You inspire me even in your dreaming sleep,
While you're asleep dreaming,
I'm awake dreaming.

Of you, I dream
Of you, I think,
and nothing more.

Here it is, my one day since you have
been away, and I, I am
going crazy out of my mind for you.
You are me, and I am you,
and together we are one.

Amanda Quick

The Challenger

The shuttle was ready and waiting.
The Challenger would launch into flight.
The Astronauts preparing for take off.
It's said, they had a good night.

The take off was right on schedule.
Everything was going as planned.
The sky was a brilliant blue,
In that beautiful Florida Land.

The technicians gave the count down.
The shuttle took off into space.
Then— An Explosion— up in the sky.
The Challenger disappeared without trace.

Our hearts reached out in sympathy,
To the families of the Challenger crew.
As they watched their loved ones perish.
The realization was so true.

Seven brave people lost their lives,
On that fateful day.
Bur research of space will continue.
That's just the American Way.....

Sandy McKee Green

The Cowboy Way

The Cowboy's way - at the end of day
  As the evening shadows fall
Is to quietly rest - and sometimes jest
  With friends about it all
He talks with pride - of the horse he rides
  Of the work they've done that day
Of the "Mossyhorn" - that was surely born
  To always slip away
He speaks of spurs - of colic cures
  Of saddles, ropes, and leather
Of floods and drouth - from natures mouth
  Of wind, and sun, and weather
Of a bucking horse - and bulls of course
  Of a cow pulled from the bog
Of roundup time - of a calf crop fine
  And a friend - his best cowdog
Of the "Man" upstairs - and his earnest prayers
  For strength to last the day
To give his best - to stand the test
  For that's the Cowboy way!!

Dean L. Guthery

23

Minutes

The minute is here.
Sixty seconds later, it's gone.

In printed form and memories they survive.
These two formats, aid them in staying alive.

One minute is happy. The next few are sad.
How many have been spent being mad?

Addition of minutes, makes hours and days.
Subtraction is never allowed to play.

After a while they pile into years.
They are gone in a heartbeat, hell minutes have no fears.

The special minutes, they are tucked away.
The file will be pulled again, one rainy day.

Most minutes just pass by.
Has any one ever asked why?

Truly ask yourself, how many do you just waste in one day?
Just kinda letting them slip away.

What happens to the ones that are just let go?
Where do they gather does any one know?

One of the things money can't buy
Hard to believe some people just let them fly?

As time presses on minutes stay exactly the same.
It will be only you and I that can change.

Melanie A. Butterfield-Hall

Lament For My Lost Muse

I've been deserted by my fickle muse
Stuck at the computer without an idea I can use
I sit and I wonder about geniuses of old
What did they do when their muses ran cold?
Did Shakespeare or Shelley ever go dumb?
Did they gaze at their ink pots while ideas wouldn't come?
How about Browning, did he dip his pen
Scribble a line and then do it again?
"It really won't do," He'd tell faithful Liz
"I had an idea but don't know where it is."
Did Dante turn to his Bea in a fit
And say, "I needed a rhyme, but this isn't it?"
I can see Coleridge, eyes all ablaze
Admitting to Wordsworth they'd seen better days.
Did Frost ever cool off, or Milton feel hellish?
I'm sure there were times these guys didn't relish.
So if people like there can suffer a drought
Who the hell am I to figure this out?

Elaine K. Winik

Me

I can't see what you see
  a pretty face, a kind smile
I can't hear what you hear
  a beautiful voice, an encouraging word
I can't feel what you feel
  a tender kiss, a warm love

You don't see what I see
  an ugly face, a sad frown
You don't hear what I hear
  a horrible scream, a harsh word
You don't feel what I feel
  a hard slap, a cold hate

No one will look in my mirror
  I don't like what I see
No one will listen to my cry
  I don't like what I hear
No one will have my heart
  I don't like what I feel

Darlene M. Pacheco

The Old Oak Tree

In my garden of memories stands an old oak tree,
Aging and priceless as a tree can be,
With a rope swing, sand box and toys scattered around,
And children playing, full of energy and fun.
That memory has passed and another has come
Of children grown up and scattered toys gone,
Childhood has gone and young people have taken their place,
There are picnics and stories and games to play,
And young romances are starting to bloom,
They talk about things of the future, that are forever old,
As the tree in my garden has known.
The third memory is creeping up
The last stage in life is due
My loved one has passed on
And left me alone
But the old oak tree is standing tall and strong
Awaiting the next generation of lovers to watch the sunset,
With its brilliant colors of red and gold
And the same sun to rise in the morning,
For the start of another dawn.

Elsie Hull

A Mess

When there is a mess on the floor,
To clean it up is a big bore.
Your parents say "listen dear clean up that dirty mess before you
irritate me."
What do you do when the same mess comes back to haunt you again?

Do you scream, shout, or yell,
What do you do when the mess comes back again and again?
A wise philosopher once said "Who cares it's only a mess".
So what if your room is a garbage can, it doom but to you it's a
  very clean room.

A mess is a mess as we all know,
It comes back to haunt you too long
You clean it up trying to do,
But then it comes back laughing at you.

Try your best to clean it away,
It comes back day after day.
A mess is very mean it won't let you live clean.
When a mess comes along try to stay away, if you approach
it won't go away.

Polina Meyman

No Fear

Life's not always easy; it can be very rough.
But you, unfortunately, have given up on being tough.
I'd give you the world, but it's out of my reach.
I know you're depressed so please hear me preach.
Despite the ups and downs, it's usually all right.
I know it's hard to overcome the fears you face each night.
Think of all the good things, forget the bad.
Realize you're not hated. You just feel sad.
I know it's been hard, but somehow we'll survive.
You should know how lucky you are to even be alive.
Consider life a challenge, not a risk or a dare.
Just like they say: Life's not always fair.
Enjoy it while you can, don't let it slip away.
Think of what you'll accomplish just by living each day.
Let me help you; I know you're lost.
I'll always stand by you, no matter the cost.
I'm giving you my hand so please keep me near,
That place inside you where there is no fear.

Shelli Dunigan

Our Children's Only Hope...

Is there really a chance?
Will the World ever again dance?
Terrorist bombs, Ebola, toxins and abuse,
Uncontrolled violence without an excuse.
The World Trade Center, Waco, Oklahoma City and the Freemen,
Senseless murder and violence on all God's children.

Years ago, things were not the same,
Crime and violence were not a game.
Children didn't take guns and knives to school,
To have those things just was not cool.
Today we fear for our children's lives,
What future do they have, how will they thrive?
Our only hope is to teach our children well,
To love and respect all, and to fear hell.

There is a chance, as long as we try,
Love and cherish family and friends before we die.
Respect others and learn from everyone,
There is more that can be accomplished, without a gun!

Sabine D. H. Mehnert

Paul

How is it that you showed up
    And popped right in my face?
How come you share my passions
    And violate my space?

I never thought I'd be like this
    That I'd be so unsettled.
While teaching me some software tricks
    It's with my heart you mettled.

I just can't stop the light that shines
    Inside me when you're near.
I can't control my pounding heart
    Nor take away my fear.

I wonder what the future holds.
    Where are we destined to go?
How will our lives turn out one day?
    Will we be one or no?

But when you're in the midst of love
    It scarcely seems to matter.
You see, my heart, it laughs and sings.
    It just won't look at "shatter."

M. T. Hopkins

A Mother's Anguish

So alone, even though you're not,
You give all you can, all you've got.
Why can't I let go, so he will find out
What living in this world is all about.
You think you are right in all you say,
Even thirty-eight years of decisions may
Make you wonder if I can see
What you teens really want to be.
So many vices to put your morals down,
There's booze, "pot" and pills all around.
Easy to get, just ask any friend,
If you haven't any bread, they will lend
You anything to get you high
Until the "Cops" haul you in, they will lie.
They didn't see a thing, never did,
Alone in the slammer, you poor kid.
Maybe Mom knew a little bit more
Then you ever gave her credit for.

Jan Eileen Kuhl

Mud Pies

Now that I'm older, I've just realized,
How much fun I had, making mud pies.
My brother and I would take some red dirt,
We'd get some will water and give it a squirt,
We'd mix it and stir it and shape it with glee,
We had so much fun, my little brother and me.

Frederick M. Markham

Obsession

Obsessed with a ghost from years gone by
His image haunts my brain and batters my soul.
He is there in the late hours before I sleep
An din the early dawn before I wake.
My body stiffens, pressing down, pressing deep
My mattress softens, becoming flesh, molds to me.
We are dancing, slowly, rhythmically floating
Heads titled, eyes to eyes, soul to soul.
We are one in eternity...

Mary Burke

Deserts

Thou who walk the desert sand,
Know that the desert is not their land.
It belongs to the brave, the mighty, and strong,
The Saguaro and cacti that lived there so long.

Now let us think of our mother earth,
And the day she gave her very first birth,
The day she formed the deserts and all,
Sometimes we listen and hear her call.

When you're thinking of her, and she's in your mind,
And you're in a desert, faith you will find.
Not is it that the spirits are with you,
But the desert gives you a love that is true.

The living creatures around,
In the sky or on ground;
Are looking at you and guiding you,
As mother earth told them to.

So think about all you know about her,
And the great powers of the desert much much more.
The desert is in our hands so treat her with care,
For the desert is kind to us, and has always been fair.

Amanda Zlatkus

The Soldier

Where have you been? Where are you?
Let us know — your family is bleeding, our hearts are withering
Our bodies are dying for the want of news of you
Where are you precious one?
One so young, your life has just started
You have a life to live, a wife to love,
Babies to be born — life to embrace and enjoy
Give us a sign that you're ok
Just a little one, would be ok
The open wounds we have for you will not heal,
Until we hear from you
Please tell us where you are
God up above can light your way
Come back to us, every minute we pray
From the time you have been small we protected you,
We are not stopping now!
Precious one, can you hear us call?
We are hoping you are well
We are putting you in God's hands
Rejoice for He is love!

Lola L. Shreve

Crossroads

We have all heard of them
They are not always clearly marked
Nor do they all give good directions as to the way to turn
We all have them;
weather we like it or not
Sometimes the hardest part is knowing when you are at that
crossroad
Which way to turn
Do you leave or stay
Do you continue or do you proceed
Do you evolve or do you just go along
Or do you stop and start again

Karley Amstutz

Memories

Sadness falls throughout my home,
I feel so sick and all alone.
I know my uncles in a better place,
with people of a different race.
He looks down on me as if I were cheery,
Not realizing, he's left me dreary.
He's an angel now, as if I didn't know,
Watching me as I grow.
He chuckles at some things I do,
And I think of him when I am blue.

I remember all those happy times,
like when I was a kid, he read me rhymes.
And all those times he drove me places,
Introducing me to many faces.
With little dimples on his cheeks,
That will leave You smiling for many weeks.
Then suddenly I realize, I'm really not so sad,
By thinking of him it made me glad.
Knowing he's in a better place,
I'll never forget his loving face.

Jodie Wasacz

Which

Which way is up, which way is down.
My mind is blowing all over this time
That we call space.
Tell me is life, or is it just a joke.
Life goes on no matter what!
My mind, my mind is going up in smoke
And it no joke you'll fold.
Look at me and tell me, what do you see a person
Like you or is you really me.
Time waits on no one and we need time before we can
Know how to explore our mind to expanded it to a better time.

Bernice Rush

Suicide Of An Angel

Angel is flying, as free as the air
Yet she is unhappy, and filled with despair
She becomes lonely, with no one around
She begins to descend, and falls to the ground

She screams out aloud, as she starts to cry
She knows she's an angel, and never can die
Looking to heaven, she rips off her wings
Now she is mortal, what comfort this brings

Angel was flying, as free as the day
But she took off her wings, and locked them away
Now she is happy, feeling the pain
She sees her blood flowing along with the rain

Len Pizzillo

These Days

Today is a day just like all the rest.
None of these days are ever the best.
The only day that is really great,
Is a day like today when I can sleep in late.

Mike Wallace

Father

A father means a lot you know
even though they don't think so
They are always there in time of need
and never have once ounce of greed
I can safely say that my Dad is grand
with him I'm always proud to stand
If a problem I have he is always there
that's how I know that he really cares
my Dad's a great person this I know,
because of the love he never fails to show
He gave up a lot when he took on our clan
that's why my Dad is such a great man
I love my Dad with all my heart
I always have right from the start

Thank you Lord for making him mine
and giving us all our great times

I can honestly say that I'm really glad
he is the only Dad I've ever had
I love you Dad

Tammy Mathieson

In An Angel's Eyes

On angel's wings she comes to me, when I'm
alone so no one else can see her private love given only to
me, an angel's love given only to me so unselfishly that
it fills the empty soul inside of me

In an angel's eyes that only eye can see there's
a deep pristine love save in her heart only given to me, in the
eyes of a woman looking inside of me basking in the lite
of love that shining from me the love for an angel inside of me

In my angel's arms his body so close to mine
there's a small piece of heaven only we can find made of a
love so pure and fine clocking our heaven you and mine

Gene A. Wagner Jr.

Ridicule

As I sit here in my home, gazing out upon the sky,
I begin to take a look at the years that have passed by.
Even now, though I am old, and wise beyond my years,
I can still remember the way they laughed it brought about such tears.
The way they mocked and jeered at me, and pointed their fingers high,
The things they said, the laughs they had,
the joy of making a young girl cry.
"Ignore them all," my friends would say, "they're just immature."
It's a fine excuse until you're the one they decide to make laughing
stock du jour.
"It'll get easier," is another one of my all time favorite lines.
The only thing that (unfortunately) gets easier is figuring out
who's on their side, and who's on mine.
"Don't let them see you get upset, it'll only make them laugh more."
Well, what am I supposed to do? Forget about it?! "Sure!"
Easier said than done, my friend, for the ones I know are ruthless,
And if they don't stop their stupid games,
they're going to wind up toothless.
So, the moral of the story is, ridicule is an easy game, in which
sometimes you may decide to play,
But, when you do, just keep in mind,
tomorrow, it may be your turn to pay.

Lisa Helprin

My Homeless Friend

As I approached the door with my homeless friend.
I heard my mothers voice roaring loud within.
There's hardly enough space for me much less three.
So if you want to get in you're going to have to drop your friend,
I looked at my friend cold and thin.
Knowing that its God knows what below, it might even snow.
I searched my heart knowing as I know
that he really didn't have no place to go.
His mother had passed, his father who knows where.
There was no one around to even care
Again I knocked and cried out loud.
Hoping someone would hear.
But it was almost as if no one was there.
We walked off together to find shelter maybe a little heat.
We huddled in the darkness trying hard to sleep.
But into our bodies fear would creep.
When I awaken the next morning my friend had gone.
As I set wondering where he might have roamed.
I hoped that someday he would find a nice home.

Marion R. Small

Untitled

Losing someone that you love is something
    that a lot of people go through.
Yet no one can go through it as you do.
People are comforting, yes; but no one can say the thing
    That makes all the pain and loss go away.
No one knows what that thing is,
That's because it doesn't exist.
There are something that do exist though,
    Those things will be there for always.
These things are the people that love you,
    the ones that try to be there for you,
And there are the memories, memories, memories.
These two things are the most important;
    for they are tangible things you can grasp onto.
    When you feel as if you're falling.
They; the loved ones and the memories,
    want you not to forget that they're here, there, everywhere.
Whenever you need them.
One of them you can talk to;
    and share with them the other.

Shawna M. Robbins

Hold

Guys I've known forever, and never thought much of...
Suddenly seem to become more than just mere acquaintances.
Losing people you love,
Moving on to who knows what.
I go after my dreams,
And wished I'd never changed a thing.
I find myself wondering
if I'll never be as happy as I was then.
Then, when no decisions were anywhere near as important
As they are now.
Then, when a bad decision was ok every once in a while.
Now, a bad decision could change your life forever,
Or even end your life.
We meet people we don't care for,
And we meet people that change everything for us,
People that really matter in our lives.
Then, before you can capture the moment,
Before you even realize it's there, it's gone.
I tell myself again and again, just hold on,
And everything will turn out fine, just hold on.

Lauren Hoernig

My Best Friend

You're my best friend, my best friend of all.
You're always there to answer my call.
When I'm in need you're always there.
When I'm alone I need you to care.
As I live each day seeing your face.
My love for you will not erase.

Kathy Ciolino

Affirmation of Harmony

Past the devil's own fiery temptation,
Beyond where the angels solemnly sleep,
To a holy, sincere invocation,
Down a shadowed and lonely city street.
Even though I have fed my starved hunger,
Even though I have shed my shaken fear,
Your dread is not growing any younger,
And my journey is leading me from here.
Down the broken road of my desires,
To the raging oceans of my peace,
Through the fueling of my mighty fires,
Until my voracious yearnings cease.
    I'll take you with me and have you in my dreams,
    I will leave you now and sew up my torn seams.

Rebecca Morris

A Wife's Plea

I would like so much to be your friend.
For you to tell me when you hurt
So I could help you mend.
Tell me your likes, your dislikes,
Your dreams, and your fears,
And don't be afraid to show me your tears.

I would like so much to be your friend,
So I could tell you when I hurt
And you could help me mend,
I will always be alone,
Unless you listen to my plea.
Can't I make you see?
I would like so much to be your friend.

Cheryl Posada

Brandon Douglas

How did you come to me, my sweet,
from the land that no man knows?
Did Mr. Stork bring you here on his wings?
Were you born in the heart of a rose?
Did an angel fly with you down from the sky?
Were you found in a strawberry patch?
Did a fairy bring you from fairyland,
to my door that was left unlatched?
No, my darling was born of a wonderful love,
a love that was daddy's and mine.
A love that was human, but deep and
profound, a love that was almost divine!
I carried you under my heart, my dear,
and I sheltered you safe from all harms,
then, one day the dear Lord looked down,
and I snuggled you tight in my arms.
    All our love,
    Mom and Dad

Susan L. Miller

Ode To Liberty

On the decks, the passengers sit, huddled.
They look forward, searching for salvation but seeing only the vast
Sea
They look to the sky for mercy, but see only the
Sun
Who mocks their scorched faces and dry lips
How much farther? Oh, how much farther?
Their hopes dissipate with every glance towards the great abyss
Far from home and fearful, they sit in silence. An
Eagle
Silently glides by.
Hearts filled with new hope look once more towards the sea.
In the distance, a
Torch
Held by a mighty arm
Its fires insurmountable
Its flames unquenchable and relentless.
The passengers look up with awe and relief.
The torch stands, promising and unwavering, a
Rock

Kraig Harry Odabashian

The Coming Of Jesus

There is a great day coming for all the Saints
When He calls your name, don't faint
When He shall open the book of life
It will be too late to sacrifice

Put some good deeds in the book
So you will not be afraid to look
For everything you say and all that you do
Is written in the book, to name a few

Jesus loves each and every one
It is not His will that we should burn
He want's us to repent
For the cause in the world he was sent

He left a road map (the bible) for us to read
To help us avoid those dirty deeds
We should be careful what we say
As we travel the road of life, day by day

For one day we will give an account
for every deed don't try to count
When he shall say "Come my people"
He will be higher than any steeple

Mandora G. Gibbs

Along Life's Road

Return my friends to thoughts of old
Good health, true faith, a blue birds song.
Loyal neighbors within close reach
Born into the mountains where you belong.

Return my friends to thoughts of bold
When times were hard and lean.
Children arrived and the money was spent
But love stayed warm on nights so cold.

Return my friends to thoughts untold
Of great black bears and white tails serene
The grand-daddy fish that got away
All beneath a forest cool and green

Return my friends with thoughts to hold
A magical sunset upon the lake
Casting shadows among pines so sweet
And diamonds fade to sunrise before you wake.

Return my friends to thoughts of gold
As the seasons change in style
Tracing the steps "along life's road"
Brings back a laugh, a tear, a smile.

Mary Lou Reed

And All I Wanted To Do Was Dance

May, your smile beckoned me to dance
And all I wanted to do was dance
Your eyes held promise of another dance
And all I wanted to do was dance

December, I touched your hand and found I was touching mine
And all I wanted to do was dance
January, I caught a glimpse of you today and found it was
Only a reflection in my mind
And all I wanted to do was dance
Today I cried, I'm lost inside of you
I'm living on memories
I remember your eyes
I remember your smile, your laughter
I remember your softness, your roughness
I remember your humor, your dryness
I remember your touch, your scent
I remember your voice, your kiss
I remember your promise
I remember you
and all I wanted to do was dance

Constance Carter Harris

I Wish

It's lonely out here on the side of the road,
    all the people pass me with their heads turned.
They pretend they don't see me,
    they pretend they don't care,
    they pretend they don't have change,
    they pretend they don't have time.
They pretend so much they should be actors or politicians,
    some of them probably are; probably have change too.
They're just to proud and,
    greedy to help out a bum.
You think I'm a scab,
    you wish I weren't here,
    you wish I'd go home.
Well So Do I! I Wish Wasn't Here!
    I Wish I Had A Home! I wish Hadn't left Home!
    I Wish I Could Get Another Chance!
    I Wish I Went To College!
    I Wish I Was With My Family! I Wish I Had A Wife!
    I Wish! I Wish, out here on the side of the road.

Charlie Quiroz

I Will Hold My Master's Hand

In that matchless splendor-world so grand, let me stand
Where no tears, no pain nor death are known;
I will hold my precious master's hand, nail-pierced hand,
And forevermore I'll be his own.

In the flawless beauty of this land, Promised land,
In the endless joy of heaven's shore,
I will hold my precious master's hand, nail-pierced hand,
And abide with him forevermore.

On the peerless reaches of that strand, sparkling strand,
Where his saints are gathered 'round his throne,
I will hold my precious master's hand, nail-pierced hand,
And forevermore I'll be his own.

When the bridge from life to death is spanned,
Gained and spanned, when my journey here is counted o'er,
I will hold my precious master's hand, nail-pierced hand,
And I'll reign with him forevermore.

Owen Everett Humphrey

My Double 'Ee' Flusteration

I never thought that I would see
A home so saturated with Debree
I've tried and sapped my physical energee
To rid my home and live in human dignitee
Woe is mee
That I should suffer to this degree
And now I am a retiree
Yes, I must now rid this home of
   these precious Antiquitees

    James Kreydich

Love

Love, care for those whose souls are dying,
Love, a helping hand for those whose hearts are crying,
Love is summer, love is spring,
Love, the warmth and comfort bring,
Love is winter, love is fall,
Love for one and love for all,
You cannot see love nor can love you hear,
but the presence of love is always near,
In times of pain or in times of sorrow,
love can lead you to tomorrow,
Peace on Earth would start with love,
Love is everything I think of,
This love is forever on my mind,
I plan to share this love with all humankind.

    Jessie Slater

So Precious

The sun shines down upon the land,
A brilliant orb of warmth and light,
Chasing away the darkness like only the sun can.
An eagle sits, perched upon a craggy nook,
With a flap of its wings, it takes to flight,
while below a young deer takes a sip from a babbling brook.

A goat leaps, among the mountains high,
Birds soar, in the endless sky,
And there upon the beach,
White froth of the waves go as far as they can reach.

The sun shines upon the land,
Life, so precious, yet becoming few,
Nature, so beautiful, yet turning askew,
All wiped out by the human hand.

    Brenda E. Sawyer

To a Special Person

Before you my life was incomplete but I got a dad that can't be beat! You accepted me like I was your own. You took me into your loving home. Though many times I've let you down you've been there without a frown. Even though I was foolish and dumb when I needed somebody you would always come. I didn't always listen to what you said now I look back with a lot of dread. But you were there through it all standing proud and very tall. You picked me up when I would fall and helping me get through it all. You've been the best dad there could ever be. Truthfully, I know you put up with me. And when my kids were born you were right there, to hold them tight and stroke their hair. So, when my second was born I knew just what to do, I named him after a special man that was you. And you are still there to this day, to jump my ass or wipe my tears away. No matter what happens through the years, though all the laughter and the tears. There's one thing you need to know just how much "I love you so."

    Michelle Keathley

Our Children

Four children we have whom I love so dear,
And with all my heart would like to keep them near.
But as one by one they leave our home
To begin life's journey on their own,
It's hard to hold back the tears that flow,
Because I would rather they didn't know
How I worry about them and always pray
And ask God's blessings every day
To make their lives a pleasant one
And to let them know they are welcomed home.

We were blessed with two boys so fair
One now a young man, the other still in our care.
Two beautiful daughters also blessed our home;
One still with us, the other married and gone.

But as the years pass by, and the older we grow
Dad and I hope they will always remember
How we loved them so.

    Essie Weaver

Spring

Winter has shed its blanket'
the cold air is going away.
Nature is getting ready
for Spring to arrive any day.

The jonquils and tulips are blooming,
and their fragrance is everywhere.
Spring has made its appearance:
you can feel it in the air!

The birds are back to sing their song —
we're happy to see them; it's been far too long.
Our hearts are more cheerful;
our steps are much lighter,
and as the sun shines down,
it seems so much brighter.

And so we welcome you back,
you dear old Spring—
we shall cherish each day
whatever it brings!

    Lucille A. Castronova

The Rain And A Little Girl

A little girl likes to sit on her porch
And watch the rain fall from the sky,
She watches it splash against the ground
And watch the wind make it fly by.

She also likes to play in it
Splashing in every puddle she sees,
She will stand in a ditch and wait
Until the water reaches her knees.

She will turn round and round
Letting the rain fall on her face
She will soak it all up in her jacket
Feeling its cold embrace.

But unfortunately she is called by her mom
To come into the house this instant
She yelled to her mom
"Oh mom, I can't".

She saw the look her mom gave her
And turned with a sigh
For no longer today could she play
In the rain from the beautiful, blue sky.

    Ashlee Brittain

Memory

If only one could remember,
What was once, but never again.

Wanting to return,
To what was before.

Trying to remember,
Eyes like twinkling stars.

A laugh,
Like falling rain.

Now only memories,
Haunting your life.

Hoping to return,
To treasure and remember more clearly.

To lock up,
And store away forever.

Like a shimmering lake,
A receding sunset, that no one can touch.

Reaching out to touch,
But never finding.

Last regrets,
For what was once, but never again.

Hannah Halder

A Future's Past

In a world not heard by creatures of earth
Are stories of valor from noble birth.
From a land as vast as the bluest sky
Came sights unseen by the human eye.

Of visions pure and hearts the same
Are vicious wolves and lions tamed.
From beloved friends and vanquished fire
Comes peace everlasting and never to tire.

Behind black sails came the wishes of Hell.
In darkness crept, ringing doom's bell.
Stalking swiftly like a raven on wing
Came disaster for all and forever will bring.

But when Hope on High has stood for us last
All shall be done, and none shall e'er see the past.

Jonathan C. Watson

Untitled

"No one will know, the love I have -
Accept of course you, of this I am glad.
Because my love for you, is oh so strong -
I've always known about you, yet still I longed.
You to me, were an illusion of my mind -
Always evasive, sometimes even sublime.
Then suddenly you appeared, like an angel in my sight.
I knew I would have you, when the time was just right.
Would you be the one, who would love me as I am -
Who would calm the raging tempest, bring me in to dry land.
I knew it was to be you, I felt love at first sight -
We would be a great couple, we'd make love every night.
I want you to be, the Queen of my land -
So reach out to me, and take hold of my hand.
We'll fly through the heavens, and sail across the seas -
Just you and me together, forever we'll be.
Nothing else matters, our fears all subside -
And fireworks are made, when our bodies collide.
Together in freedom, until now unknown -
With you by my side, I've finally found home."

Robert Locke

My Star Cypress Vine

Fall gently sweet autumn mist
On my delicate star cypress vine,
Within her tinder vines, blood red, she glows
Delicate as a red red rose.
Surrendered to, your sweet tinder kiss.
Fall gently softly, sweet autumn mist.

P. Simmons

A Tear in the Horizon

How am I to be righteous in the time of killing.
Hiding the pot of gold, can't find the rainbow.
Yelling, screaming at the Horizon.
Jagged blade tearing flesh.
Tears pour down the back of tyranny's dead body.
Gambling with emotions, demanding death.
Violent life.
Rejecting the inevitable, engineering the thoughts of the collapsing
  subconscious.
Buying the price on my soul.
On sale, with or with out God.
Can't wipe the tears of ruins in wait.
Energizing the cause is the ignorance of youth.
Someone denying entice to the future.
The dark and star-filled knight created the hinge to the door long ago.
Funnel of the soul, buckling under the pressure.
Riddles of the things my dreams forgot and things my lying mind
said.

David M. Brasseaux

Ten-Minute Break

The rays of the sun, as they skip through the trees,
  sparkle and glitter, the green of the leaves;
And, I'm quiet in thought, as I lay on my back,
  just resting my eyes, while my mind loses track.
The breeze in my face, and the sky above,
  reminds me of home, and the girl that I love;
And, just when I'm lost in a cloud, a voice sounds off! Terrible,
  and loud!
And, I have to strain, as I struggle to rise,
  to get to my feet, after so many tries;
'Cause, though I'm tried, and weak, and I ache,
  I've gotta get up, from a ten-minute break!

Stanley D. Tull

Untitled

I always see myself losing myself to someone, this time that someone
seems to be you. How could I?
You forewarned me all you wanted was a friend so I said I'd be
  there till the end.
You spoke of fears you hid within, and without fear I waltzed right in.
I can't seem to fool myself any longer, what I feel seems to be
growing stronger.
I know I like everyone else cannot tell the tale of time, yet I beg
you to consider being mine.
I dream my dreams of holding you tight with all my love I'll light
your life.
I also ask you to dream a dream but that is the complicated dream of
being with me.
I am speaking to you through my heart and all I feel comes from my
soul, never deeper. I'm sure you've been told.
So I pray for the day to come, that I will be able to give you some,
of the cares others will deny the love I feel for you through my
heart, soul and mind.

Sergio Luis Gomez

Between Mind and Heart

My mind knows and understands.
It's excited for liberties,
    new and old forgotten.

My heart knows, but does not understand.
Bravely stands, but falters,
    with overwhelming sorrow.

The new brings conflict, between mind and heart.
There's struggle between joy and pain.
    My spirit seeks unity.

But my spirit knows, without pain, joy would be hallow,
and without joy, pain's emptiness
    would never end.

So spirit speaks to mind and heart.
Encouraging them to feel,
    and not to fear.

Robin Tuggle

Time and Grandpa

The clock on the wall strike's the hour at hand
and watching the clock is a thoughtful old man.
Where has the time went? He asks,
Where is the joy?
It seems just like minutes since he was a boy.
Then he hears a voice that rings loud and clear, Hello!
Say Grandpa, is anyone here?

Then he smiles and he thinks back on his life,
of the jobs that he worked and his kid's and his wife.
Thing's that were lost and the things that were won,
The bad times and the good times that made their life fun,
and all of the past that's lead to this place and the glow in the
smile,
from the grandchild's face.

David E. Sampson

The Song

First trees started to whisper; their leaves moving.
Then the sea joined, its waves lapping against the hulls of the sleek
wooden boats.
Next the birds joined in, their songs reaching into the quietest corners.
Soon all the insects started to hum, their song reaching up into the sky.
After that, the beautiful whales in the sea started to sing their
songs, their gentle noises sounding back and forth.

Everything Was Singing!
But people still kept quiet.
Their few timid notes melting in the rush.
We need to share this world with the trees, the sea, the birds, the
insects, and the whales.
But if we join together we can join in the song.
Maybe even sing the loudest.

Ashley Martin

To My Brand New Husband

Just lying here with his arms round me tight—
Feels so right!
Pressed tightly against him, feeling him go hard—
O Lord,
Is there any greater bliss
Than this—
Waking up this way the rest of my days?
I give Thee praise!

Alleene Lee

Untitled

The smoke covered moon
rising high in the night
sends a chill down my back one I cannot fight.

What's that thing lurking in the dark.
It'll never howl, it'll never growl, it'll never ever bark.

You'll never be able to see but you'll always be able to hear.
You'll smell its breath when it's very near.

It moves like lightning with reflexes so fast.
How long will you hold out? How long will you last?

It'll beat you down and weaken your soul,
you cannot beat it
you must pay the toll.

There's no escaping.
There's no place to hide.
Nothing can save you,
Not even your pride.

So live for today
It may be your last
Hold on to memories
But never live in the past.

Matt Austin

The Devil's Drug Parade

On a mountain top with the World beneath
I rock in mirth,
As all around the earth,
I seem misery.
Slavery is my goal and death is the prize,
Kneel my slaves as I bind you tight,
with tentacles you dare not break.
Stay a spell...
On your road to Hell...
I'll wait for others you'll contaminate.

Blow your mind, and stab your veins,
Change your personality.
I've reached my goal.
I've stolen your soul.
Now you belong to Me.

Dance you toys to the Devil's tune,
I do own you, you know.
I rock with mirth,
As I look at the earth,
While you reap the seeds I have sown.

Nellie A. Gilman

Senior To Be

Can you remember your freshman year
How everything was different and weird
Your sophomore year now was probably a bore
'Cause all you did was learn some more
Your junior year you have no fear
'Cause now you've put your butt in gear
Your senior year is 'bout to begin
The hard work and papers will just have no end
But not to worry it's not that hard
Just kiss up by giving cards
Your senior year will fly by fast
So make your memories forever last

Maryann Ypina

Oceans

Ever coming
Destroying — Rebuilding
And the cycle continues
Never relinquishing
No, that is not true
For you gave me — Us life
Within those mysterious boundaries of yours
Life's process begins — Ends
And the cycle continues
What draws me to you
Is it because you are so much female
Changing moods with the slightest change of wind
Gay — As the sun plays in your white frothed peaks
Sad and mysterious — with the falling light
Romantic — with a full moon
Or, because you are the mother of us all
Your salted air from afar initiates the magnetism
The roar of your waves draws me closer
Seeing you I am Cleansed — Reborn
I am home!!!

C. G. Katselas

Death Of The Sinner

In the silence that remains when the mourners are gone
You are left alone to think
O, the morbid air that lingers on that you must cope with
Until at last your fate shall come
But that you had taken heed
Only now you must regret—regret forever all your wrongs
Nothing now to do but wait, wait 'til the judging of your fate
That fate you know but refuse to realize
Alone you are left, your life to analyze
Now, too plainly you can see how wrong you were,
  how foolish your deeds
Alas, too late, your life is done
You plead, you beg, you sob, you mourn
But nevermore a chance to right your wrongs;
You have wasted your last chance
Accept your fate, you know you must;
  to burn in hell for all your lust
Wasted years, months and weeks,
  you could have saved yourself at least
But now you are lost, gone forever
Thou can't say thy God is heartless;
  scores of years you had to change
Here, alone, you watch and wait—sorry now, but alas, too late

Betty L. Roberts

Dying

  When we die, will we rise?
Or are all of those old legends lies?
  Death is something I do not dread
For I would not mind being dead.

  When we are born,
Are we alive?
  We try to stay strong and yes we strive,
Being born is something I dread
  For instead of being alive,
  I would like to be dead.

Christine Gahan

Today Or Tomorrow

Today is my day and my time.
Only I recognize my short comings.
Do I go forth with all my dreams and expectations.
A Christian, a daughter, a mother, a wife.
Yes, I think I will.

Today is my day and my time.
Only I can reach my goals.
Do I accept a helping hand.
A giving heart, an open door.
Ye, I think I will.

Tomorrow is promising
Only we know that it's not guaranteed
Many procrastinate putting their dreams on hold.
Only the wise forge forth.
Rather easy or hard we must, we must
Rather alone or with others we must, we must
Only we know who hold the key.
We know, we know, we know.

Joyce C. Dennis

Crystal Are the Waters

Crystal are the waters
Reflecting the morning sun.
Lovely is the new day
When every days begin.
Quiet is the breeze but
Echoes with small sounds.
All of life is waking up
As I walk upon the ground.
Still are the trees, unmoving like the grass
Which glistens with the morning dew
This moment moves too fast.
Amazing is the daybreak,
How pretty and so new.
Crystal are the waters.
Reflecting all of you.

Dawn-Marie Merrill

Promises

You say you truly love me
And you can't live without me
I open my heart completely
Tempting you to break it in two.
I forgive you again and again
All the while wondering if the madness will end
I tell myself you don't know you're hurting me so bad
But can't you see the pain in my eyes?
You say you need me and really care
All of this is too much to bear.
I have to go on with a smile
But it is really my disguise to the hurting inside
I wish there was an escape
But I guess this will be my fate
Wiping the tears from my eyes
Wanting you here by my side
I know I must find happiness
With no more than your broken promises.

Kisha Spriggs

The Battle

The battle is over; the war has been lost.
The price was far greater than it should have cost.
I can no longer fight for you.
The pain inside is almost through.
The death of love has numbed me cold.
The soldiers are all growing old.
and marching on, I now retreat.
Her methods of warfare I can't beat.
So take your arms and go to her,
'Cause of one thing I am quite sure.
 I will not fight if there is pain
 The allied army has been slain.
 And all your friends have died in vain.
   B. Preston

Tree of Life

I enter and become the Tree of Life.
Divinity in roots,
Arms of nurturing fruits,
I dance to the rhythm
Of a Cosmic Plan.
I am the Tree of Life.

Blessed creatures flock to me;
Children rest at my feet.
An infinite center of Universe in
Spring, Summer, Winter, or Fall,
I am the seasoned
Tree of Life.

Centuries of wisdom rest in weathered bark.
Ancient rings of knowledge
Give birth to limbs of life.
Ultimate oneness in reciprocity-
I enter and experience my image
As the Tree of Life.
   Judith Simone Skotnica

When Morning Comes

When morning comes,
The birds come out to sing away the day,
The sun of course begins to shine in that
all familiar way.

When morning comes,
The flowers open to greet the world around,
Then the bees start buzzing
and honey soon is found

The wide array of color
That springtime brings to me,
It gives joy and happiness to,
All around who see
   Jenny Kallhoff

Togetherness

My daughter married at seventeen -
and so did her mother.
It was fine for mother, but for daughter,
"a horse of another color."
I managed to take the shock in stride -
but promptly got another;
'Tho she was still to me a bride -
suddenly, I was a grandmother!
The question that now comes to mind
about marriage is whether,
It's best to wait awhile, or marry young,
and all grow up Together!
   Evelyn Mitchell

That's My Father

Gentle hands as he reached around,
To pick me up when I'd fallen down,
Hands so worn, from work and love,
That's my father.

Mistakes were made, but he was there,
To help me stand when there's no one there,
Hands so worn, from work and love,
That's my father, that's my father.

There were times when storm clouds came,
We had more than our share of rain.
Then the Son poured His love right down
To help me see, what he means to me.

So little one, when you look at me,
I hope you see some of Him in me,
And everyday, you'll be proud to say,
That's my Father, that's my Father.
   Carolyn Herring

Cherished Memories

   Thank you Dear,
For the time you spent with us.
Ever mindful of the precious memories,
   Your gracious ways a plus.

As we visit spot in the grave and speak,
I seem to hear that long loved voice.
God took you away so quickly, never a good-bye.
He need you then, as we honor His choice.

Why do the tears keep coming?
Is it the missed apple pie? The six
course dinners you cooked and served with style?
No, 'Twas your gracious demeanor,
Your companionship and heartening smile.

May your new home be happier
Than the one you sought for me.
Oh yes, I'll be ever mindful,
Till God's and your lovely face I see.
   John A. McCalley

Beneath The Willow

Beneath the spreading arm
Of the leafing willow, dodging harm
That the world would spread.
The loamy earth our bed,
The expanse of sky above,
'Twould seem the perfect place for love.
But she says "I want to die here."
To lose someone so dear
Would tear me from the inside.
It was from harm we sought to hide
Not to give it to one another
In selfish acts without the other.
I tell her more of this.
She smiles, we two kiss.
The willow sighs
Beneath which we all day lie
Since I was able to refresh her soul
And she mine in the time we stole
To be together, we two as one
Under the expanse of sky and its winking sun.
   Shawn J. Wells

The Four Miracles

No planes in the sky; no talk of war; the world was full of joy.
The doctor told me my baby was a beautiful little boy.
The miracle of this perfect child.... soon he was 3 years old.
And another miracle happened: another sweet boy to hold.
How fast they grew as they laughed and played; their favorite game
   was war.
Bang! Bang! you're dead, they often said, as they came laughing
through the door.
It didn't seem long as time passed by and soon they were strong
   young men.
There were planes in the sky and talk of war the world had changed
   by then.
Soon number one son took up a gun and was jumping from planes
   in the sky.
It wasn't a game any longer, he had to watch men die.
The third miracle finally happened, number one came home to stay.
And I pray the terrible haunted look will leave his eyes some day.
I suppose I wasn't thinking, number two was so young and mild.
Surely, they wouldn't take him. This boy is only a child.
This Sunday it finally happened as they said good-bye at the door.
It isn't a game any longer; number two has gone off to war.
Now we must wait and pray each day until miracle number four,
Brings number one and two together, laughing at the door.

Genevieve Whigham

From Earth To Heaven

A Tribute to My Father

With open mouth, a gasp for breath,
A worn-out body got its rest.
A peaceful silence, a Heavenly calm,
Reunion with his Dad and Mom.

'Twas Saturday night we said goodbye;
But peace we felt; we did not cry.
He fought the good fight; the faith he kept;
Eternal rewards he would now get.

Uplifting tributes to him were given.
Sweet music, praises, prayers from Heaven.
Inspiring scripture he had picked out;
Love shown to him without a doubt.

And when we sang the farewell hymn,
We saw how glorious it had been.
Still when they laid the casket down,
An eagle soared its wings around.

With his new life our faith renews;
Along Christ's path we'll always choose,
Until God's time for us is planned.
Then we'll meet again in the Heavenly Land.

Sherol Emery Grigerick

Travel Dreamer

I never got to go to England
Or to the far away places I dream about,
But I thrill to see a marching band
Listen to children laugh and shout.
Somehow when I wasn't looking
Time snuck up and was I surprised
Waking from my travel dreaming,
Wondering why I never realized
Doing is the time we are happy
Full of busy activity.
Then the pause comes with harsh reality
So, although I may not travel
To far off places, I know,
That I have seen much that I marvel,
For I've watched a baby grow.

Eunice Abby Reding

To My Lover Unattended

Don't hold me as a promise
You'll forget to keep.
Don't dream me as a reverie
You feel is out of reach.
Find me.
Find me so you can't lose me.
Love me.
Love me so I may learn to breathe.
Offer me pinwheels, and I'll refuse sapphires.
Hold my hand on this roller coaster, and I won't fear down.
We're dashed from the same snowflake.
Fallen dwarf stars who wait for the world to fall away,
Save the question escaping our eyes;
Could this be any more gold?
To my lover unattended,
Wait for me.
Wait for me, hold your heart, and I'll find you.
If not this day,
Tomorrow.

Karen Renee Hannah

There Is A Music

Life is a series of rhythm and rhyme
Beat upon beat, pattern, design.
There is a subtle blending of time
Body and soul, spirit and mind.
Weave within weave, breath upon breath
Beauty in life, life within death.

There is a rhythm, there is a time
Body and soul, spirit and mind.
There is a music in unwritten song
The crashing of waves, the brilliance of dawn.
The quickening pulse, the kiss of the wind.
The dreaming of dreams, the needing of friend.

There is a moment, a flutter, a sigh
There is a victory in learning to fly
Unspoken passion, unending needs
Life ever lasting to all who believe.
There is a music, pattern, design
Body and soul, spirit and mind.

Vicki Turner

Politics And Politicians

The date is set, the time is ripe, election day is near,
The politicians scurry round, and in their hearts is fear.
They do not want their man to lose, for surely he must win,
For losing politicians is a very grievous sin!

The promises flow hard and fast, all problems will be solved,
If we elect this man we will from all sins be absolved.
Our hands are shaken to the point where numbness settles in.
They care not if our hands stay numb, so long as he shall win!

I never cease to wonder why some people don't get wise
To all this silly nonsense, sprinkled with so many lies,
We're suddenly important folks, this fact I always note.
But we wouldn't matter, not a bit if we didn't have a vote!

Election day has come and gone, the count is over too,
The winners smile from ear to ear, the losers say they'll sue.
They swear that they've been cheated, they never could have lost
And they will vindicate that fact - no matter what the cost!

But in a few short days you'll see, the tumult will die down,
And not another word is heard of cheating in the town,
This is a ritual that goes on in every polling place
The loser must kick up a fuss, so he can save his face!

Bella Gallagher

Star

As I look upon this star,
the first star I see,
I think about the times ahead,
how happy I will be.
I shut out all the harm,
and think of all the good.
As I look upon you star
I am filled with happiness, wonder, and awe.

Emily Snyder

The Sun Had Not Risen

The Sun had not risen.
Heralds of passionate pink-orange clouds
Wisp out of dark; some are solids,
Tatted with light, yellow to blue.

Colors had a pure taste
Cascading, swirling my soul.
Fingers stretched, longingly,
to compress the radiant warmth.

Abundant silence, praise of birds
Were the symphony of notes in parade.
Sounds clear with dignity, with joy,
The mystery had begun to play.

Seduction by beauty and gentle strength
coupling, coupled, uncoupling,
Released my heightened desire
For a new, willing day.

Sue Landis

Do You Still Miss Him Too?

I used to complain he was too far away,
But when I saw him I was jolly and gay.
And when he died while he was away,
I had to say good-bye in a different way.
The Lord has taken him away now;
So it will not hurt him to take a bow.
He was stubborn as they say,
But he helped people in a different way.
He is so far, yet he is so near,
But I know now why I shed a tear.
The hearts he touched are here to stay,
Those people are still here to mourn him today.

Aurora Ansara

Sun

The sun beats down from the coolness of the sky,
As people have thoughts of who might drive by.

People aren't thinking of the sun's glorious use,
Or how they can preserve it, and keep it from abuse.

Our scientists though, are working hard to secure,
And with their technological efforts, this is only a minor detour.

People don't think about other inhabitants on Earth,
Or think about how much the sun is needed and worth.

The ozone layer is one major factor; one major choice,
We must make the right one; we must raise our voice.

We're now in the 21st century, and what a gleeful surprise,
The ozone has lessened; people have leaned the value of compromise.

People are now smarter; now wiser; the scientists say,
And boy, I sure hope that it stays that way.

We're back to the present, a time of many a cure,
Hopefully, in the near future, we will learn much more.

The sun can teach a lesson; a very valuable one,
We must lessen pollution until the task is done.

Erin Lee Semus

A Welcome Home

He went to Europe as a kid.
But when he was through,
A grown man appeared in his uniform.
The pictures still salutes from my grandmother's china cabinet.
Tall and thin, with his predetermined haircut.
Blue eyes accented his dark skin.
He scaped the shrouded face of death
Many times, over three years of hell.
He came home in '45, and
Thought he would ride his thumb
From Virginia to Michigan.
He leaped the Smokey's,
And swam the Mississippi.
Then, a few miles from Detroit,
His tour took an evil turn,
For his driver pulled out of gun.
Bang...Silence. My uncle lay still, drowning,
In an ever growing sea of blood.
This is how a veteran of World War II,
My uncle, was welcomed home by those he protected.

Timothy Smith

Mother

I am the youngest of your bunch
The last to leave your nest

I'm sure at times you thought I was your worst
What can I say I was taught by the rest

Through those days I troubled you so
Oh how I could be such a pest

All those nights I worried you so
I can't believe I had so much zest

Still you were there by my side
All though I put you to the test

If I knew then what I know now
I'd probably tell you it was all just a jest

You've pushed me to serve and conquer the world
Which gives me strength through my quest

In the future I hope you'll be there
Because mom you really are the best

Melissa A. Freedy

We Will Be There

We are someone's husband or wife, a son or a
daughter, a brother or a sister, we could be someone's
daddy or mommy.
We might live next door to you, as we pull from
our driveways, wondering if this could be our last
goodbye, sometimes you wave, sometimes you don't.
We watched as a little baby died in a car wreck, as
a woman bleeds from the hands of her abusive husband,
as a young teenager was killed over something as
senseless as drugs. We wept at the loss of another
comrade. We are the ones that go home with this in
our hearts at night.
We are called often, mostly because there is
something wrong. We are often unable to please
everyone, so in return we take the blame. We
often wonder what will happen today, as we have
to report for duty with pride, dignity, courage,
sympathy and professionalism. After all this, no
matter what the circumstances if you call
"we will be there."

The Unknown Police Officer Bobby Dean Lee

Seasons of Love

Love is like the springtime
A time for lovers dreams.
It's a season full of sunshine
Of walks by quiet streams

Then springtime turns to summer
With its picnics by the lake.
It's camping with the girl you love
And discussing the plans you make

Autumn shakes its colorful head
And the leaves begin to fall
It's time to walk the woods again
And to hear the cool wind call

Winter breaks with falling snow
And its holidays so bright
It's spending evenings with the girl you love
In the glow of the firelight
Vernon Petersen

Feelings of Love

Why must I struggle so hard for that simple minutes of your time?
When first place in your heart is all I wish to find,
It seems I'm always falling one step behind,
Oh I see now that I am blind, never to break this painful bind,

Do you find it that easy to throw me away?
I have to ask-will it always be this way?
These stupid tokens of my hearts I must pay,
Just to hear the words you say,

I have to wonder what it's all for,
Sometimes I think I can't take it anymore!
It's an endless swim to a far away shore,
Blood in the water where my heart has been tore,

I try so hard to fight my fear,
Hoping that one day the shore I'll near,
Hoping that I'll find the right gear,
To wipe away this single tear,

I hope one day for you to hear my voice,
I'd make you hear me if I had a choice,
I'd stand up in your face so you could see me rejoice
But I'm only a small outnumbered voice.
Leigh Salyers

Angles In Pink

Where once a baby cried aloud
There is only silence now
And if you listen hard enough
You can hear the angels laugh
Because our darling they are holding
Watching while her growth is glowing
We cannot forget her smile we enjoyed for awhile
Or her visit for awhile, but could we span
The space of time
We would join them in their frolic
But God chose us to live alone
Without our darling in our home
But now I know angels aren't always white
They are soft and pink with chubby cheeks and hands
But someday we will be together again in that beautiful
land where it never snows or rains
to those who are alone on earth
We miss our darling angel here, but know she safe
In the arms of God our maker and redeemer
Pearl Jordan

"My Childhood Summers"

Long ago, summer days, playing without fear.
No one worried we were not near.
As a Tomboy and a willful child
Playing with my friends in the wild.
A time when a child could roam
We claimed nearby woods as our own.
Big oak trees, gray moss hanging low,
A stage for our game or show.
As we climbed and jumped and yelled
Always we would cast our magic spell.
Sometimes, Indians quietly sneaking thru the woods
Sometimes, as soldiers, cowboys or Robin Hood.
Some days Tarzan's mighty call brought fear
For any enemy, far away or near.
Boys and girls equal from the start
We took turns and played our part.
Five o'clock the old mill whistle blew,
Time for the real world we knew.
Running, skipping, laughing, weary to the bone
Calling out "tomorrow", on our way home.
Virginia Hunter Caccamise

All That I Know

How can I go the way I need to go that I've never gone before
How can I say the things I need to say
That I've never said before
How can I do the things I need to do
That I've never done before

All that I know is that I need I need the Lord

How can I fight this fight this good fight of faith
That I've never fought before
How can I run this race this race to be won
That I've never run before
How can I be what God wants me to be
That I've never been before

All that I know is that I need I need the Lord

How can I pray the prayer I need to pray
That I've never prayed before
How can I sing that sweet holy song
That I've never sung before
How can I dance before the Lord a dance of praise
That I've never danced before.

All that I know is that I need I need the Lord
Robert L. Fuller

"The Moment Brief"

As I came upon a corner,
I saw a man as if a mourner.
Hollowed eyes and face forlorn
when I neared his clothes were torn.

His sight was fixed with constant look,
I slowed my pace while stunned I shook.
As I paused in disbelief,
I sought his eyes, the moment brief.

Rotted teeth and salvaged coat,
embarrassed him as I took note.
With falling rain he grabbed his bags,
he humbly walked in tattered rags.

Long ago I pressed a flower
from a man of wealth and power.
Down on alley he found his cover,
tears of sorrow for once my lover.
Rachel M. Burke

My One True Love

I can still remember the time
When I first laid my eyes upon you.
I never thought you would be mine,
Or that I could ever see you again.
I know that was far from true.

Now you have become a part of me,
Then again, you always were.
For when you left, I had fond memories.
Your face, in my mind, I could still see.
In my heart, a love grew so strong,
Nothing could stop it,
Even if it was wrong.

Finally, I can let my feelings be shown,
For you have entered my life once again.
We have grown much closer, since we first met.
With a wonderful future to look forward to,
Leaving the past behind (because the past is just the past).
Remember it's you I will always love,
    however long we last!

Loyal Wright

One Lost Soul Forgotten in the Night

There are 2 souls with one living.
There are 2 hearts with one loving.
There are 2 friends with one alone.

Some people can be so cruel so wrong and so naive.
Some people don't understand don't see and don't care.

Why is it, that the people who are together, always fall apart?
Why is it, that the cold-hearted, always stay warm?

How can someone see you when they are truly blind?
Why do the strong weaken and the tough break?
How can someone be a friend and deliberately try to hurt you?

When that one living and loving soul stands alone and left out,
who is around to notice?
When your heart breaks and you scream out into the cold dark night,
searching for that one warm embrace, who is around to notice?

When I leave this world and enter the next, Who amongst you will shed
your tears? Who amongst you will forget me?
What memory will you hold of my short, lowly life, which ended the
only way it could?
Will you condemn me for my sin of taking an innocent life?
Or will you accept, that nothing could be worse than the hell I've
been living through?

Robin M. Bousel

Perspective

Let me not stay trapped in yesterday,
    or become obsessed with tomorrow.
Let me focus on the here and now so I won't look back with sorrow;
On wasted time, needless worry about things I cannot change.
Lie is only mine to live - not to figure out or rearrange.
I've hurt so much for oh so long - to this day I don't know why.
I try to put the past into perspective, yet I still have nightmares
    and cry.
I've been so old since the day I was born - never had the time to be
    a child.
I've had some bad times and had some good - some were peaceful
    and some were wild.
For so long I lived with hate - it burned so deeply in my soul.
I had to let go, had to pray hard - so maybe one day I'll become
    whole.
The things that I've experienced have often made me lose sleep;
Yet I have to be thankful and grateful
For I've acquired an inner strength I'll always keep.

Donna S. Bogan

Gone

Gone, he has gone away, but not too far away.
He will never let me forget him, no love like
ours will ever die.
I know he lies beneath the sod, but he lives always
in my heart.
No, I will never forget him, for love like ours
last forever and ever.

Alice S. Oates

Heaven's Gift

A Masterpiece work of art — this precious bundle, she;
This creation of love — with our Maker she's come to be.
So perfectly made, this tiny flowering bud;
Our affections to win, brimming our lives with love.

She's captured our hearts with such feminine charm;
So delicate — velvety soft — so cuddly and warm.
Her small dimpled fingers — ten perfectly-formed toes;
Pretty, dimply smiles, cute little turned-up nose.

Wide sparkling eyes, inquisitively bright —
This sample of perfection will grow in mind and might!
A miracle — how true — this beautiful baby girl;
Since the day she arrived — our lives all a-whir!

This time of life, it's said, the best ever yet —
What joy and happiness since the day we met!
This, our first grandchild — God's love and mercy give;
This dear little precious one, so graciously sent from heaven.

Carmen L. Dau

Who Will Rule The Sky?

The darkness comes
it invades the sky
hovers over the earth
it enshrouds the light
devours it
waiting watching
its hungry eyes
the shape of gleaming stars
every morning the light returns
returns to become prey
to the darkness once again
the dark blends the light
creating a velvety blue magnified by the moon
the darkness hovers still
a constant battle between tonight and tomorrow
who will win
tonight tomorrow
dark light
who will rule the sky???

Beth Adams

Chink

A chink is a hole in the wall
    where a stone has chipped
    mortar off the green moldy brick.

A chink is found in the armor, a hole
    through which invincible heroes will fall
    from their glory.

A chink is what they called me sometimes.
    I lie there, blood and dust on my face,
    ignoring a bruised temple, in the circle of taunters
    not noticing me,
    just another chink.

Nadav J. Kurtz

Salvage Them

Quietly I wait for salvation. Alone in silence I lie
with the sons and daughters of my mother beside me
There may still be hope for me, I thought

But if I should go yonder, please salvage them, they are still alive
Please salvage them, please, somebody please

Our voices are covered with dust and anger
with the yoke that chokes us. The world is deaf to our cry
Do not close thy ears to my cry for help, please, anybody please

We are like refuse in the depths of the pit
Refugees though in our mother's quarters

Our eyes flowed without ceasing, without respite
As our tears continued inside
our eyes are wide open like those who are dead

I have lost all hope. My flesh and my skin waste away
Like a nation we were one. Like a nation we went down the pit
made for one in all and all in one. Together they buried us
Yonder we go

For those who are left, somebody please salvage them
There is still hope, there is still hope for them.

Ikenna Chidume

The Lion of Judea

Behold the lion of Judea lies wounded in the glen...
His enemy strong, fearless and terrible to behold.
Their blows rocked and split the earth — blood dripped from wounds
like steady moving rivers covering the earth with its bright red life.

Behold the Lion of Judea lies wounded in the glen — his enemy
vanquished, but oh the mortal wounds His majesty has suffered,
He lies with head low — his majestic head covered with crimson red.

Lo, from deep within the glen comes his companion — soft of step,
regal to behold, sleek and black. She bows low before her Lord
and licks his crimson head — Her voice like healing waters, lifts
his wounded soul — his strength returning with each healing kiss.

Soon his companion lies beneath her Lord, her warm Black body has
brought surging fire to his milk white lions - and they lie as one,
forever in the glen.

Carol Coles

Passing People

As I walk down the street, I can't help
but wonder what that person felt...
As they walked by me and barely glanced
they never gave me a chance.
If only they knew the person inside.
If only looks did not misguide.
We might share so very much,
but we both walked on never to touch.
We didn't give a handshake
not even a hello,
and on our way we both go.
And, in my heart I do regret
that along the way we never met...

Megan Elizabeth Zuchowski

Life

Think of a feather,
So smooth at first,
But when the human hand touches it,
It becomes all old and wrinkled.
But it still floats on
Until one day it grows so old and wrinkled.
It falls; never to fly again.

Danielle Fuschetti

"The Magic Moment"

All the world lies sleeping 'neath the blanket of the night,
For there is nothing moving just before the light,
And then I feel a stirring deep within my soul,
My wings have started growing for it's almost time to go,
I need to sing my song of songs,
To dance my dance of life,
All else has lost its meaning, 'cept the purpose of this flight,
Then with no more warning the brilliance does appear,
I go within an instant, and know my course clear,
What joy to share the colors with the breaking of the dawn,
They sing of peace on earth you know,
And urge us to go on,
There is no looking back for me, the future I can't touch,
The magic of this moment, is what I love so much.

Anne B. Paullin

My Mirror

I glanced into my mirror, you were there beside me.
In the glass we shared a kiss, your eyes a flame with passion.
At that magic moment you pledged your love to me,
Yet when I turned to hold you tight, I saw other's
arms enfold you.
In pain I turned back to my mirror, you touched me once
again.
I cannot live within my mirror. Its surface bright and
shining, our love aglow, our passions full, that was long
ago.
And so I put my mirror away, to hide my broken heart.
Someday when I am stronger, I'll take it out once more.
I'll feel the love that we once shared, reflected back to me.

Carol Long

The Meaning of Christmas

M is for the mistletoe hanging o'er the door.
E is for the eggnog that we all adore.
R is for the reindeer that will bring us Santa's sleigh.
R is for the ringing bells we'll hear on Christmas Day.
Y is for the New Year—full of hope, health, love and fun.

C is for the caroling that we all have done.
H is for holly, so pretty and so green.
R is for the buttered rum that makes our faces beam!
I is for the icicles, glistening on the tree.
S is for that headache-causing Christmas shopping spree!
T is for the Christmas tree, so festive and so gay.
M is for the manger where the baby Jesus lay.
A is for the angels, smiling down from up above.
S is for the snowflakes that the Lord sends us, with love.

That spells Merry Christmas, and that's my wish to you,
plus good health and happiness to last the next year through.

Dianne M. Dellamater-Smith

Untitled

I loved you so with all my heart
but you knew from the very start
That you were playing
Now I'm praying
That I'll find my heart
and that I will part
So that you can not hurt me
That way you did in so many ways
I hope that someday it catches up with you
and you will know what I went through
Your heart will be aching
and I won't be there to see it breaking
Then you will know you can't take love for granted
Cause someday it will disappear
and you'll wish you had it still.

Karissa Pauli

A Letter To Mr. Moonlight

Mr. Moonlight,
Tis' that time again, of pain in the heart
and sorrow in the soul.
Another thought of happiness
overshun by a thought of sadness.
The pain won't subside.
It feels as if a dagger is being pushed in and out,
in and out of my heart.
I have thought of forgetting,
but my love won't let me.
The tears run down my face
as water does in a cascade.
The shivers I feel
are colder than the ice itself.
Although it feels as if I'm falling apart, I'm not.
I'm getting better day by day.
The pain, tears, and sadness
might still be there,
but I won't respond to them.
At least not now.

Heartbroken

In Shadows and in Rain

In shadows and in rain, we find comfort
Though the fear of the unknown grips us
We are strengthened by the knowledge that
There is no one to judge us.

In shadows and in rain, we find freedom
This knowledge allows us free reign of our thoughts
and we act only in the way we desire
Untainted by the worry of how we will be perceived.

In shadows and in rain, we find hope
With our minds unshackled from the prejudices of others
We begin to believe that anything is possible
And that we will be the ones to set things right.

In shadow and in rain, we find honor
When the soul is laid bare before itself
It is touched with wisdom, the wisdom to do that which right
Not only to ourselves but to all living things.

In shadows and in rain, we find love
Confronted with his wisdom we can do nothing but love,
encouraging
the good and forgiving the bad, accepting others for what they are
and judging none. I will come to you in shadows and in rain.

Scott Morley

Lover's Quest

Once I was in search for love,
A place my heart could rest, just like the impatience Dove,
I promise myself to look only for the best,
When I started the journey, a Lover's Quest.

I looked for love in the high and low places,
Trying to match what I felt with men's faces.
I probed for Mr. Right, no more, no less,
Assured the quest will reach it crest.

I thought I had finally found the one,
I fancied that everything was set and done.
But he left me in such a mess,
I reckon an interruption, I'm still on my Lover's Quest.

Acquaintance said surely this won't be your last,
Love for you hasn't passed.
To find a love, do I need to put out a request?
I'm still on the move, Lover's Quest.

All at once, a sudden moment, our eyes met,
I knew this man, this feeling, brings no regrets.
Now, a true Lover's fest,
A fulfilled Lover's Quest.

Kristina Campbell

First Captain

We were all lallygagging on lollipops which the teacher gave us, and we even got an extra recess. The Sun held the high command over the sky, and with the football field spread open awaiting our ruckus, we took our places. "Second captain, first pick; first captain second pick!" littered the air around us-so predictable, so tiresome. Mischievous eyes took the first pick—their "best friend" for the day. The damned gathered on the other side. And it never mattered much which side I was on; I wondered why I never wanted to be captain. I wanted no part in the selection. Why wouldn't I want a piece of preteen power? It's just that if a leader fails... The grass! The field! She's turning away and browning. The clouds have wrestled the Sun, and He now lies hidden. There has been a coup. The other boys have run, football in hand, to get their backpacks, to go home with their "best friend" for the day, and I can already see who'll be captains tomorrow.

Tad Spencer

Mother

It was Mother's voice that first we knew
And Mother's fond caress
The gentle hands that cared for us
And tenderly tucked us to rest.

Then as the years rolled onward
And as we older grew
The patience and love of Mother
Was each day learned anew.

There are treasured memories
Neither time nor place can mar
Which tell us, "We love you, Mother"
For all the things you are.

Today we offer a silent prayer
For mother's everywhere
May God protect their loved ones
For they are in His care.

Today amidst a world of care
Tho we be near or far
We pause to honor Mother.
And all the things you are!

Hilda Beltz

Life

Life is a mystery waiting to open up its wonders
and glories. Every day is different. One day it can
be snowing that next day it can be cold. Other days
it can be raining or be windy. You never know what to
expect from like that is why it is a mystery. One
day you can be small the next day you can be
tall. One day you can be sick and the other
days you can be well. One minute you are a child
the next minute you are adult with a child of
your own. One moment you are young, the next
moment you are old. One day somebody born. The
Next day somebody is gone. When you are young
you wish you were older. When you are older
you wish you are younger. You can't change
the pass because the pass has gone. Every minute
of your life counts enjoy it while you can.
One day you will die and your child will live
On in your memory and footsteps.

Brandi Gibbs

Beautiful One

When God looked down and made you
He made a beautiful piece of speciman.
God watched over and nurtured you ever so tenderly
Into the fine adult you are he wanted you to grow!!

The storms of life often beat awful hard—
Many times in anguish you bent; tears flowing down
Almost just almost giving in, yet you never did!

For you were planted to deeply into the Lord's heart
Engraved to painfully upon his palms
Where the nail prints are.

Cost everything he had
From riches to pauper, beloved son to servant
Even his own precious life
To adopt you as his own dear child...
Such a wonderful person you are; since Jesus Christ came in.
You were put here on earth to be a friend to others
And by being brought together lives have been more enriched...

Patricia Whiteman

The Negative Cowboy

I don't own any ten gallon hats
A strawberry roan a pair of chaps.
My name isn't Tex nor is it Slim
Never mention sex at the slightest whim.
I hate bacon and beans sleeping in bunks
Wearing blue jeans driving old clunks.
I never sleep out under stars
Ride in sleet or strum guitars.
Putting up hay in mid summer
For low pay that's a bummer.
I'm not to keen on having to break
A horse that's mean no piece of cake.
Stretching barbed wire digging post holes
Taming a sire those aren't my goals.
Riding behind herds saying yep or nope
That's for the birds to twirl a rope.
I don't ride fence and have of course
Much better sense than ride a horse.
As you can see I've spent the time
On what suits me writing rhyme.

Herb W. Harris

The Gift

Without warning, I received a gift in a most unusual way.
It was not clear to me and held me at bay.
Only time has taught me about the gift and it's meaning.

Precious is each moment each sunrise and sunset.
Grab that brass ring for all the things you put off doing
or yearn for yet.
Savor them, for each can be changed just as quickly as they
appeared.

This gift has no monetary value and it cannot be measured.
It brings love, joy, sorrow and something to be treasured.
Never forget how precious this gift is.

The time came and the meaning became clear to me.
You're probably wondering what this mysterious gift could be.
It is so simple...the gift of life... Enjoy!

Ilona H. Martin

Your Canvas

We are all given a blank canvas
As we set foot on this earth
And a handful of brushes
As our right of birth
Life is our palette of colors and hues
It is up to us how much rainbow we use

Some of us die with a full-colored canvas
A Van Gogh garden of sunshine and light
While others go with a half complete background
A landscape or maybe a sky
Still others leave with a conservative doodle
In the corner in black and white
But the most sad of all
The canvas most wretched
Is the man who dies
With nothing but pencil sketches

Thais Albert

A Rendezvous With Fate

A midnight journey, carefully planned
Suddenly awry, planner be damned
His agitation resounding, his heart in his throat
The rain pounding, his drenched overcoat

His thoughts on his mission, precariously dangling
The words unsaid, at his heart mangling
At a stolen respite, he sought his hands meek
What he could not utter, his pen did speak

His soul he sent, with that message away
The tormenting weight, of the words for that day
For his love did not know, that she was his fate
At the end of this message: "If you love me; wait"

To his destination, his heart thundered before him
His maudlin eyes searching, the turmoil within his limbs
The door he did shatter, he did not care
Holocaust of the heart, she was not there

And thus morning found him, at the window pane
Cold glass at his cheek, hollow eyes on the rain
Unspoken words swelling, to an unendurable state
His lips slightly parted, his words were too late

Irma Corral

Mirthless Parody

On the road to recovery after a brain attack.
As I accounts to you the parody, adhering to the facts
A pantry full of food yet nothing to eat, a closetful of
Shoes unable to secure a pair on my feet. Using the telephone in my
bosom to call my best friend remembering to draw on the power within.
Insurers stopped my therapy, I moved on with faith and hope
Using the furniture and wall as my rope. I am thankful
I can now get myself a treat to eat by my first solo trip feat.
Half of my body paralyzed no longer despair. Before I even whisper
His name, Jesus is already there. No longer have I a parody, for by
faith I am healed. When unhealthy living struck me down and science
predicted I wouldn't be around. "Time Out" (paralysis) from a secular
life is a small price to pay to regain my soul. God works in a
mysterious way I believe as I've been told. My Mirthless Parody,
just new directions I am healed by God's love and protection. I am
compelled to share my story, all my days giving God the glory, God
is mercy God is love, He lives within not up above.

Jeanette H. Jefferson

Why?

Why do they hurt me,
  why don't they care,
    It's the pain inside that's just not fair.
Why do they hurt me,
  why can't they see,
    It's the things they do that's hurting me.
Why do they hurt me,
  why can't I see,
    exactly what they want from me.
Why do they hurt me,
  why do I stay,
    when I know they'll go the other way.
Why do they hurt me,
  why can't they see,
    just how good things could be.
Why do they hurt me...
  I'll never know,
    but it's the pain inside I just can't show.
    Tracey Faborito

Not Over

This pain tears at my heart
You told me that we'd never part
If you'd open your eyes you'd see
What you've done to me
You say that you're glad I went away
But I see the pain on your face every day
Why do you hide
When in me you can confide
I'd keep your secrets and share your pain
I'd help and guide you through the rain
I wouldn't scream or yell
I'd help you up if you fell
I'd do all the things I never got to before
If you'd open your heart and try once more
You shut your heart and try not to care
Self-confidence in yourself is rare
It shouldn't matter what they say
I'll be there for you every day
Living without you just won't do
One more chance for me and you.
    Jennifer Cook

All Colored Boys With Lots of Toys

All colored boys, with lots of toys
Enjoying a summer's day.
Said the boys to the toys
Let's play, and play, and play.

They played for hours without a fuss,
Their time spent in pretend.
Giggles and chuckles, chuckles and giggles,
they wished it would never end.

Then came the parents, all about;
Ready to control the play.
With evil eyes and bitter mouths
Ruining a beautiful day.

The children are scattered and full of tears
As their parents carry them away.
They began to feel this awful fear;
But why it is - no one will say.

When it was done - there was no fun,
Just bad memories of that day.
All colored boys with lots of toys,
The air is quiet, without play.
    Lori Hunter

Katie

I lie awake and think of you
Sometimes it seems as though it's not true
How could you be gone?
How could you leave me alone?
I know it is not your fault
I don't know what to do
My life is turning so blue
it seems because I don't have you
to be my friend, to be my guide
To always be by my side
You were my best friend
To love and defend
I wish I could be with you just to see you again;
You were like a sister, just being my friend.
Your disease was rare;
it made you lose your hair
Why did I have to leave without saying good-bye?
Your death made me cry and cry
But now I have to say good-bye
But I shall see you when I die.
    Lisa Lee

My Ancestor

Oh South upon your crusty earth's breast
my ancestors bones are layed to rest.
A man who fought diligently and true
you gave your life for the red, white and blue.
You fought against your neighbors and kin who wore
The gray uniform of a long past war.
When you came home on leave it was said,
if they could've found you, you would've sooner been dead,
But you hid out among the trees of pine
And had lunch from a bucket, brought by a son of thine.
A traitor! A tory! And hill billy too
were names they called you but only a few.
When at last they captured and sent you to camp chase
Did they not laugh and spit in your face?
Now languishing in prison the last year of the war
I'm sure you thought of the "other" you fought in before.
On through the desert your feet did trod
To fight Santa Ana for Texas cause.
Now I know why you were loyal and true
to fight for ole Glory was an honor to you.
    Dee Castellion

I Shall Look to the West

Glare blinds my eyes and hides the horizon where you dwell
Heat withers my spirit as resolve leaches, dripping down my back
Dust drys my throat, cracking hollow as I speak your name
Stench assails me, in counterpoint to the memory of your spring

I have come to this hell as you have bade me come
One of thousands of your children clad in dusky hues
We wrap ourselves in shields of brave words
with pain in our hearts as we mourn our time lost

I shall look to the West with eyes that cannot see
I shall face to the West and defy the hottest day
I shall shout to the West though no one there will hear
I shall go to the West, and I'll have my spring day.
    Philip E. Molle

A Dance On A Star

The day will come,
    when I dance on a star.
In the full moonlight,
    that I see from afar.
The lights will be low,
    the mood will be right.
And that star will be shining,
    so bright in the night.
This star that I dance on,
    on this very special night,
    is drifting away in spite of my fright.
For I am afraid,
    to fly so high in the sky.
For the fear I hold isn't a lie.
So I sit in my chair wondering what it would've been like,
    to stay on that star and dance through the night.

Samantha Rae Gordon

Standing On the Edge of a Cliff

Leaves fall as a symbol of passing time.
Patience is hard and long.
The future is yet to come.

I watch the wind blow the trees,
Wondering if things will work out.
How soon?

People say it takes time, be patient.
All I know is,
It hurts.

Standing on the edge of a cliff,
Is my place in life right now.
I hurt so much, I feel like giving up.

Will I get my second chance?
Can he love me enough again?
Can I love and accept myself and him?

Spri Aubrey

Storms

When it begins to storm I begin to feel different, scared, worried, and curious, when I awaken from the rain and the thunder I lay and listen to the rain hitting my window remembering that I don't need to worry because Jesus or God is taking a shower, but it can be pretty scary when it begins to rain really hard. Then the rain sounds like thousands, and thousands of needles hitting my roof top, and my window. As I look out my window and see the lighting I just think that God is lighting up the sky so he can see if everything is in place in the heavens. The thunder scares me the most it sounds like someone is hitting a giant base drum with all its might, but again I remember that God and Jesus are just bowling. When the thunder begins to crash that's when I worry and wonder if anyone else is as scared as I am.

Jill Donlon

I Am Special

Be careful and gentle with me!
For I learn differently.
Take the time to understand
My self-esteem is in your hand.
Respect and acknowledge what I can do,
Not in what I can't.
Build in me confidence, not shame.
When you say I must finish all this stuff,
Then my best is not good enough.
I may work slower than others
But that's o.k., that's me!

Gael Nunez

"The Beach"

As the salty waters spray and splash upon the sandy shores;
The lovely seagulls in the air sore.

You can feel the soft gentle breeze brush against your face.
The cool rush of waves crashing on the star dust shores,
makes an enchanting sound that soothes the mind.
Each wave brings in wonderful exotic treasures from the sea,
by washing them up on the beach.

As the fire lit sun goes down, down to the sea below;
The lovely silver moon rises, rises from its home.

It takes the busy life away just for us.
The world then grows and quiet, for all things are at rest.
Then the moon says good-night to all who lay beneath him.

Ginny Gaweda

Fireworks

A whistle through the nighttime sky,
Revealing with a boom;
Splendid colors, sparks that fly
Like flowers in full bloom.

Bright red, bright pink, bright blue, bright green.
Amethyst, gold, and white;
Eruptions of these colors seen,
Glowing fountains made of light.

Reflected in the rippling bay,
Their sparkle, adding to the stars...
The fireworks, like a great bouquet
Of stemless, lightning flowers.

Gone but a last remainder of
The smoke they cast away,
To celebrate the land we love
This Independence Day!

Denise Beñares Lao

The Mount Wherein

I'll go to walk, awhile it seems
Along still earth, and easy streams

I'll stay to seek, the marble stage
Within warm crease, of natures omit age

I'll rise to speak, for worthy plans
Cross pristine dreams, cross distant spans

I'll fall to climb, rich time in peace
Through fertile springs, whene'er I reach

The mount wherein, I trust to pass
The last day's birth, to deathless ash

I'll go to walk, awhile it seems
Along still earth, and easy streams

I'll stay to seek, the marble stage
Within warm crease, of nature's age

I'll rise to speak, for worthy plans
Cross pristine dreams, cross distant spans

I'll fall to climb, rich time in peace
Through fertile springs, where'er I reach

The mount wherein, I trust to pass
The last day's birth, to deathless ash

Steve Cherico

Wishful Thinking

In the darkness of morning, empty of sound,
The moon and stars in place,
I wish for things as broad and deep as the sky.

The sole specific is the star, my connection.
Distant, yet available,
soon to disappear,
The star takes my confidence.

Please, let us be happy.
Please, let us have peace.
Please, just let us be okay.

The message, transmitted in stillness, is received,
Confirmed by the sparkle and stretch of points.
I give in to trust, covering myself with hope,
Believing in possibilities.

Joanna M. Perry

I Wonder

The leaves are swirling
the wind is churning
I can not find what my heart is yearning

I want to scream without shattering the silence

I wish I could go
where the wind is blown
There is so much out there that will never be known

I wish I could die without losing life

A sadness consumes me
why can't I be free
from a future that I will never foresee

Why can't I cry without shedding tears?

I look to the distance
not in a day-dreaming glance
but to free my mind for a fleeting instance

If only I could free my mind without losing it.

Preston J. Cathcart

Death

Death is a horrible thing, you never know when it will strike.
People come and go under its dreadful spell,
They're ripped from your grip without a struggle,
Their helplessness is no match for death's greedy hunger.
You hope and pray, but nothing works
Until one day they're finally gone.

You can't help, but feel for them,
Although you know they'll be seen again,
By their loved ones who cared for them so much.
"How", you say when you've read the news in the local paper.
You wish you could help, but you just don't know what to do,
So you send money or food to the family members.
Hoping to help them through this rough time.

Now life goes on without her, for some more than ever
Others finding new ones to love and look after,
But the life she led will never expire no matter how they try
The pain still lingers on, not forgetting the love she gave
The gift of love that still grows and grows.
Those that were too young to remember her, will never have
The benefit of knowing such an extraordinary woman

Natalie Miller

Heartsong

In the quietness of this moment,
I sit watching you, and I feel a
familiar melody begin to sway
within my heart.

The tempo is slow and caressing.
It is a sweet, stirring, mystical
rhythm that captures all I cannot say
with words.

It is the sound of my love for you.
A melody heard by no other, it is for
you and I together; alone!

Then, as you glance in my direction,
my heart skips just one beat.
Suddenly your heart begins to echo
the song it hears in mine.

Together, we create a symphony of
love beating steadily stronger with each
passing moment. A beautiful "Heartsong"
playing endlessly on to the tune of
our undying love.

Radonna J. Patrick

Grandma's Are Special

God made grandma's special like the angels up above.
To guide us, and to help us, but to mostly give us love.
They'll chase away the sad times, and brighten up each day.
Cause grandma's are so special in so many different ways.

My grandma's means the world to me, and she always will.
I love her and adore her more than words can ever tell
There's lots of grandma's in the world, but none as great as mine.
She taught me to be strong and brave, to make it through bad times.

Grandma's house was special, filled with lots of love, and care.
She gave to me some memories, to cherish and to share.
There's no way for me to count the stars in heave up above.
If there were than I could tell about my grandma's love.

Grandma's up in heaven now, where the streets are lined with gold,
She'll be with grand pa once again, where their love can now unfold.
There's lots of loved ones up above, she'll be glad to see.
And the wondrous gifts of heaven, will unfold for her to see.

God made grandma's special like the angels up above
To guide us, and to help us, but to mostly give us love.
They'll chase away the sad times, and brighten up each day
Cause grandma's are so special in so many different ways.

Jessie Bowden

Happy Or Sad

Many things can make me happy!
But many things can make me sad too.
I'm happy when we laugh and play,
when we sit and make a gray sky go away.
When we go to the mall and shop till we drop.
When we gossip while the clock goes tic toc.
But many things can make me sad too!
But there's only one thing I can think about...
You going to college and having new friends
and new people in your life!
But I know you'll always be my #1 sister and
no one can top that!
I don't think any one can have a sister like you.
And that makes me happy!!

Nicole M. Maggiore

The Lord's Tears

My tears are for the aborted child,
And for a world that's just gone wild.
My children cannot pray in school,
They hardly consider my golden rules.
Men who want to marry men,
And adopt their children to live in sin.
Pastors who have gone astray,
Everyone who will not pray.
Husbands who beat their wives,
Murderers who just take lives,
Drug addicts who find no harm,
In sticking needles in their arms.
All the babies being abused
Their precious bodies broken and bruised.
The Lord was overcome with grief,
As my heart cried out for his relief.
Dear Lord what is it I can do,
Heavenly Father to comfort you.

Rhonda Chastain Long

Our Grandmother's Love

When we were young, you were there,
With gentle kindness and loving care.
When mom and dad would tell us "No",
Your softer side would always show.

And as we grew, your faith did too,
That God alone would see us through.
And as the years went passing by,
Still on your faith did you rely.

One by one we up and wed,
Found troubles on that road ahead.
Your steadfast love did then prevail,
You stood by us, we could not fail.

In family conflicts, trials and woes,
No favoritism did you show.
Remaining neutral with wisdom and strength,
Your courage and patience were tested at length.

It's not often enough that we do say,
How much we love you with each passing day.
Your guidance and tenderness always hold true,
You are our miracle, our grandma—like few!

Joyce L. Cisney

Welcome Spring

After a long, cold, New England winter,
New Englanders welcome spring "as if
embracing a precious newborn baby."
You feel vibrant, alive, after a harsh
winter you thought, you would never survive!

Clean refreshing aromas fill the air,
bursts of color surround us everywhere
Spring fever stirs feelings for romantic rendezvous
It's a time for daydreaming as the warm weather unfolds

Trees looking so old and, worn from the cold
take on a replenished young appearance
from the new leaves they hold
Ducks and geese flap their wings and
glide graciously across the water with ease,
enjoying new freedom, after a long winter freeze!
New Englanders like myself treasure every
moment of Spring; it's a prelude
to "many more fascinating things!"

Carol R. Cameron

Indispensable Time

"Time nor tide wait for no man"
This old adage reminds us to do what we can -
While we can, in every way we can.
As when we grow old, we can only wish upon a star;
And often, wishes are in vain, and we don't get very far.

Time is the key element of life, itself;
You cannot keep it, nor store it on a shelf -
If you don't use it, you lose it, so don't abuse it.
Rich and poor, alike, God gives twenty-four hours a day;
So when we make each minute count, He helps us on our way.

When we are young, we think we have plenty of time -
But in later years, things don't work out so fine.
The simple tasks seem hard and the hours shorter;
We need more time to complete them, so we can't loiter-

It is up to us, old and young, when each day is done -
To count our blessings, one by one -
Thanking God the father of all our time -
That we can take the time to give a dime -
To those less fortunate down the line.

Berniece Waddell

Warmth of a Man

The warmth of a man means,
The caress of his strong, warm arms holding you
closely to his chest, that feels like paradise.
His smooth voice that you can listen to for eternity.
The touch of his warm, soft lips against yours.
His strong, yet gentle hands holding yours walking
through the park.
Who makes you feel Strong, Confident, Reborn and Safe.
Who makes each day an Adventure, even through lives
most simple things.
The both of you have a Free Love with No Boundaries.
His and your ability to Defend each other when the going
gets tough.
Above all to Love and Cherish each other for eternity.
You know when True Love comes your way, when you feel all of
this.
Because, those who lack the Courage and say it's
Dangerous to try. They just don't know, that Love
Eternal Will Not Be Denied.

Carrie Artl

Believable Tales

Believable tales whispered to once deaf ears
Acknowledge the past that hearing had neglected,
And lend a hand to doubters who may fear
That life's a silent stream of failures collected.
Struggling to board the passing ships of joy,
We grasp the trailing rope to salvage peace.
Content to be a vessel to destroy,
We loosen our grip to pay off life's lease.
A lake of turmoil, stress, and utter shame
Surround our drowning souls, while our bodies
Remain dry in the midst of new sprung flames
Protected by time's lit furnace of fond memories.
Sparked by love or extinguished by death's cold earth,
These flames we must bear to understand life's worth.

Jami McFatter

Hear the Spirit, Feel the Spirit

We would like to finish what we started
It bonds the way it was in the first place
I open my eyes to see Jesus holding my hand
Drifting back to my dream I glance once more
At him to see he is now carrying me.
It's really simple actually —
Believe, and he will forgive
Love Him, and he will heal the scar.
Blooms will blossom
Fire will be cold
No more bad; all good
Hear the spirit
Feel the spirit

Kellie Henderson

I Remember

I remember when we first met
It was more than anyone like me could even expect.
Your beauty was beyond compare
Especially when the moonlight danced across your hair

I remember as our time together became longer
The love for you grew forever stronger
I knew right then through out all time.
I wanted you to be all mine.

I remember the day our vows we did make
The words I said I did not fake.
The beauty and glow upon your face
Made my heart beat at a rapid pace.

I remember as the years went by and times were tough
My love never faltered, even though my words never said it enough.
Then the kids came along and brought us together
I thought it was all we needed to make it better.

Now you are gone and your love has left me
There's nothing left of my heart, for it lonely, tattered, and empty.
The passion and love for you, could make the world tremor
But until you come back, all I can say is I remember.

Mark Gibbs

When the Sky Grew Dark

The clouds rolled in, thee sky grew dark.
As the raindrops fell, a stranger knocked on my door.
Do you have shelter? He kindly asked.
His green eyes danced, as the water rolled off his cheeks.
I invited him in, he sat warmly by the fire.
We talked and shared a few laughs.
We told stories of the past and the future.
We shared our hopes, our dreams.
We quickly grew to know one another.
This man's kindness was my key to unlock his soul.
Living alone for so many years,
I had never seen such a man, such a heart.
He proved himself to be loving.
To be honest, to be perfect in every way.
I quickly fell in love, not wanting him to leave the next day.
When dawn so soonly arrived, I invited him to stay once again.
He accepted the invitation, as he did for the next ten years.
This man standing by my side, this perfect man, my husband.
This man who came to me,
When the sky grew dark so many nights ago.

Meagan Alyce Miller

Be The Dream

Be the dream...sounded empty at first.
But in each of us our being has thirst...
For someone else to be on time, to remember, to be just,
    to lead the way, to have all the answers, to be first...
Remember when those bubbles, one by one, burst?
Remember the first time "they" hit a dog and didn't stop?
And someone hurt you to "make it" to the top?
You said, "how could you" or, "that breaks my heart".
Didn't you know, right from the start?
Others are our reflection! But to this we are blind.
Disappointment is created within our own mind.
Your search for an idol...
    for someone else to measure up...
        will always measure as an empty cup.
Here's an idea... no, call it a scheme, you know what you're
    looking for...You Be The Dream.

Emma Reynolds

Love Hurts

Love was the mosquito that landed,
And sucked hard, removing juices from my skin,
Love was the stinging afterwards,
As I squeezed, where her proboscis had dug in

Love drained the rose of my body,
She didn't drink from my fountain for long
Instead she took but a petal, flapping her wings as she moved on.
I saw her fly to another and this is where my pain began.

When she came to me I was angry,
Nearly removing her from this life,
But her presence became quite soothing,
So now she's gone I wish to leave my own life

Like my skin, my heart is swollen,
But what use will that be,
As her mouth now opens for another,
Some poor innocent beneath a tree.

Jennese R. Thomas

Father's Day

June is known as a month for brides,
Now memories are gathered and recorded with pride
Soon that big day turns bigger,
When groom becomes a dad,
A fatherly figure.
He celebrates this wonderful day,
Watching his children happy at play.
You could see the love that
Shines in his eyes,
When to their playful requests,
He always complies.
So lets all remember today,
And make him happy in some special way.

Veronica Kendzierski

Solitude

Silence! Hear it roar and penetrate the night sky.
Capture it because every second of its sweet breath is a minute
in heaven.

Dance with it and let it flow and vibrate to the beat of your
heart.
    Listen carefully to its soothing words of wisdom and love.

Don't kill it, for it could be the missing link between you and the
unknown.

Sh sh sh sh sh sh!

Carmen R. Carrillo

Who Is This Man?

I gazed down the hall. Who is this man, slumped over in a wheelchair?
A mere image of the man he used to be. I looked again.
The man was bent forward, seemed to be carrying the weight of the
world on his shoulders. He appeared to have lost that ability.
Who is this man? The man was shrunken,
his body sliding closer and closer to the floor. His chin was on his
chest; his eyes open yet unaware of his surroundings.
Who is this man? Had I seen him before? I looked again.
The man had a vague resemblance to the man I used to call father.
But who is this man?
The man was so old and feeble, wanting to move, but unable.
Standing next to me my husband said, "Don't you recognize your
father?" I do, but who is this man?
My father is a man who walks with strength.
My father is a man with purpose in his stride.
My father always has a smile on his face.
A joke for those he sees. This man is forsaken in his stare, a mere
shell of a man. He pays no attention to the people moving around him.
He does not lift his head, nor does he speak.
Who is this man? I looked away. I could not look at this man again.

Toni D. Usher

Russian Rhapsody With My Silhouette

What a specimen of a man
My heart plummets from the ride
I see my shadow touching him, holding him
Proud as a midshipman by his side.

He works magic on me
Presto! I'm alive
Daydreaming by the sands of time
Growing old together
My life worthwhile.

Someone pierced the bubble
Turned over the easel
The painter's hand rigid
Destroyed in lunacy.

Give me a drink
A toast of allegiance to be
Twain; the two shall be one
Wasted drink in the sea.

Sandra Faye Cosby

Welcome To Faron

Welcome to this magic world of Faron,
My little baby Boy Aaron.
You will travel far and wide,
Upon a horse and elephant you will ride.

You will have a day or two of rest,
And eat among the very best.
You will have a prosperous and happy life,
And perhaps along the way a wife.

Among your travels here and there,
We hope to meet you and ruffle your hair.
Come play among the woodland,
Where Evan is at home, first hand.

Grammie Goose will read her fairy tales,
Uncle George will show you fish and whales.
Aunt Karen will teach you to be a banker,
Uncle Fred will feed you lobsters, after which you'll hanker.

Health and wealth is wished to you,
With worries and heartache but a few.
Where all the best will be unfurled,
During your travels in this magic world.

Alice M. Motycka

Anne, Studying

Pony tail and fuzzy bangs, studying on the floor,
Pepsis here and pretzels there, shoes left at the door.
Radio and records call, stop she does to try
Latest steps, or hear again parts that make her cry.

Phone she must that best girl friend; Judy tells her now
What she should have written down, when and why and how.
Somber ways will come with age; easy it is seen
Anne is our own happy girl, not yet quite thirteen.

Mary L. Richardson

Untitled

When I look out at the world,
what I see is an awesome
awareness of what I perceive to understand.
The sky, the land, the inhibitors
of this planet has yet to
amaze me as I still learn
to be astonish and bewilder at
how we go on and the
world goes on and how we
absorb the wonder of nature and people.
Of how the wild and the tame,
the wise and the fool join
together this space and time
to blend and survive the daily
hassles and triumphs of
getting ahead, to secure a
balance of serenity and wisdom.

SanJuana Ramirez

"Sound The Lullaby Of Summer"

The sun saunters down upon my vision,
I squint and squeeze it from my eyes,
It fights back and rapes my eyesight,
Until a cloud arrives, and then I see,
But when it dissipates I am again blind,
Summer time.

A mirey puddle precedes my pathway,
For the raindrops of an afternoon storm have mildly collided,
I strike my barefoot upon this small warm pool,
The rushing rain reduces to sprinkles,
The sprinkles scatter and subside.
Summer time.

The combustive growls of a distant engine
Recede into the humid night,
Revolving fan blades wobble, a flush of fire flies scurry,
Urban street lights hum electric z's,
An old transistor radio mumbles a melodic beat,
Summer time.

Daniel O'Neill

Friends

I yearn to know your every want and desire. Our past has
become the present with no future, as we live for today. Our
trials and tribulations will draw us together, together we
will become one. We'll shed tears of joy, happiness, and sorrow.
Your pain is mine, the tears of blood we shed will cleanse our
world. We'll laugh at all of life's cruel twists she tosses
our way. Apart, we are nothing, but together we conquer the
world. Our children are one and the same; only their names and
sexes are different. Our story is nothing new. We share the
shame and lusts we must face day after day.

My love is always by my side, as is yours. They have no close
friends by their side to share their past, present, and future.
You, my dear friend, have chosen to stay with me no matter what.
Husbands, lovers and acquaintances will all pass through our
lives, but a true friend is here forever, no questions asked!

Michaele Moynier

A Wishful Death

Blue and red lights flashing before my eyes,
Sounds of troubled and distressed
people coming from the distance.
Fear and confusion invade my mind,
A sense of helplessness smothers me.
Exhausted, searching,
Stunned by a lifeless body lying in an odd
position next to me,
Shattered glass in my hair,
The blare of drills makes a lullaby for me.
The noise — a faint whisper. All becomes darker,
The feeling of a massive weight sitting on my chest,
making me resistant to another breath,
A weary moan coming from my weak body,
A powerful dizziness overcomes me.
The desire to hold on departs from me,
leaving only the wish to die.
The need for the suffering to pass, anxiety still remaining within me,
Finally the delay is at an end, the horror in conclusion.
First silence,... then darkness,... then death.

Kasey Hilton

The Storm of Finale

It was a dark and stormy night,
Black heavy clouds were in the sky,
Pendulating over the silent earth,
Unexpected of what's to come.

A bolt of lightning,
A clamour of thunder,
Wanting to overtake the world as we know it,
Forcing its depression on us.

There is confusion, and then a shriek,
A pain strikes through all who are weak,
We huddle together to hide our fears,
And try hard not to show our tears.

The pain hits deeper into the heart of the good,
It shatters us as we try to collect our thoughts,
And though we don't realize it,
Something is wrong.

A shriek, a cry, a bolt, a clamour,
We try to hide until the storm is gone,
And once it stops, which it never will,
The depression, the world, all are done and still.

Adrienne Marie Snow

Triumphant

We are here for but a moment, strangers in a vast universe
Like shadows, gone too soon without a trace. Drifting afloat
in a universe so vast and incredulous.

Our shadows leave imprints of distinction comprehensible only
to those around us. Who are we? Where do we go? Are we but
a pebble on the sea, a gust of wind, a tumble weed, here today
and gone, a passing fancy, an enigma? Could it be that we are
an entity of hope, dreams and visions with a destiny to be
fulfilled.

Do we really know who we are, in the perplexities of life?
Surely not of our own understanding. Even so we are conquerors,
not of our own strength or understanding, but that of God,
steadfast, rooted and grounded in Christ.

Ruby Kratzer Holman

A Friend for Life

Basil, Basil, when you were a pup,
You were so small you drank from a cup,
The second I saw you at the pound,
My heart felt warm as I picked you up and set you down
I whispered to my mom that you were the one,
I pictured us playing in the backyard and having fun,
I taught you to sit, I taught you to stay,
From the beginning of March till the end of May
When it came put to the test,
Everyone knew you were the best.
Time went by, as fast as a sigh,
You started to get old, my heart started to get cold,
When I hear your weep,
I will always keep,
You in my arms,
To stay away from harm,
Wherever you go, I will always know,
You're in my heart, you're my sweetest tart,
Basil, Basil, I want you to know,
I will always love you wherever you go.

Liz Whooley

Restless Love

Sleepless nights I'm tossing and turning,
 thinking of you this feeling is burning;
this feeling felt can not hide,
 so with these words I hope you confide.

Two lonely hearts just looking for love,
 we must take the time to thank the Lord up above;
who gave us the chance to meet one another,
 this lovely lady I met through her brother.

I asked just to write her and become her friend,
 somehow we talked before I ever used my pen;
her voice, sounded so innocent and sweet,
 she didn't take long to sweep me off my feet.

She set-up a time she set-up a date,
 with neither one knowing if we'd become one another's mate;
the time draws near for me to meet her,
 she'll see how I care by the way that I treat her.

Does this compute my heart says it's right my mind says it's wrong,
 it seems so strange how great we get along;
one thing I'll say that I know that is true,
 that if we become one babe I swear I'll love you.

Stephen Collins

Together, Always

I feel the breeze against my face
It reminds me of that moment when my friend had died
I walk in the field everyday. Oh! How much I miss her!

I have learned to live on
And accept things as they are
But I have not let go
I will hold on to her always
When someone asks me a question
I would ask myself, "What would my friend have said to that?"
I would always answer in my friend's tone of voice
In her own words
She and I, we have become one

I could see my parents are worried about me
How they always look at me as if I might go crazy
They recognize my friend in my own eyes
And they are troubled

But can't they see I'm happy this way
That by doing this, my friend has another chance to live, and even stay?
I had missed her terribly, but now she's back
That's how it's supposed to be - she and I, together, always

Rula Knoury

Untitled

I am here
in a swirly smear
of boredom
I'm suffering
from everything, but really nothing at all
I'm not a king, but you are, aren't you?
This really isn't deep, like the wool of a sheep
that I caress in the day
where exactly is the needle in the hay?
I'm helpless
and weak
and I take it, but you don't
I'm confused
I don't know where to turn
I'll burn in the hot flame of love
my flesh will rot
it's just too hot
I don't understand
I'm just bored.

Mary Truesdale

A Place for Faith

Sensory and aesthetic perceptions abound
this empirical world of space-time ages
words in life said and existential sounds
are each day written on God's good pages

Science, sustenance, symbols and scenes
conflict and aggression clash as explorative means
past a trickle-down of faith with intuitive goals;
rational faith in He whom can recreate the whole

Solomon noted life's vanity, died and left earth
Jesus stood upon land to call Lazarus forth
our biosphere requires conservation and organizations time
with hope of resurrection near eternity's brink

One life is one soul a phenomenon of being
time moves quickly within dust put to breathing
our Creator provides Universe and thought to wonder years
miraculous product of His work; much more than fine machines

Infinity of space-time at each part-time point of infinity is
metaphorically inflated from an original mist
still the word of God - the Bible with news of world to be
is from a loving God sent before evolving physics forms desist.

Gary C. Gibson

Fear

Fear becomes our one companion, when we let it have its
way. It's so strong it can consume us. We must be
stronger push it away. The days grow long when
we have worries. Our fear makes prisoners of our
souls. Our heart cries out with pain so deep
that we alone hear its call.

What is the answer we agonize, how, can we change what
we despise. We alone must fight the fight. For fear
itself has not a care, it does not see us when we are there.
Why give it strength! Why lend it substance. Unless
it is a valid fear it has no place among us here.

A light shines down from up above, it's always been
there so full of love. A strength and beauty like in
a dream, its golden glow holds the key. Patiently
it waits do not deny it. Show the light we can be stronger.
Reach toward it and you will see the light is there for
you and me. Finally fear forever taunting will cease
its long merciless haunting. It cannot reach us
day or night, for the light is there eternally bright.

Janice A. Johnson

You Are My Everything

You are my morning sun, my midnight moon.
You are my spring flowers, my winter snow.
You are my home run, my slam dunk...
You are my everything.

You are my love song, my beautiful painting.
You are my teddy bear, my lovely rose.
You are my falling star, my birthday wish...
You are my everything.

You are my past, present, my future.
You are my only love, my now and forever.
You are my heart, my soul...
You are my everything.

Heather S. Gerlach

Daddy

I had a Dad, like all, had faults
But he always was there when I had wants
I think everyone feels like this
After they're gone, they are sadly missed.

My father was kind in lots of ways
When it came to us children he made spoiling days
He spoiled us a lot when we were small
That a Dad's privilege, after all.

Then with Mother it wasn't the same
When she called one she went through all of our names
I always remember she never hit me but yet
When you're small you soon forget

But all in all we had lots of fun
Mom always thought she had the battle won
There were ten kids in their home you see
The very last one turned out to be me.

The group is getting thin, with only four left
That's what a big family comes to we regret
I always thought Daddy would always be there
Until I found out that his chair was bare

Gladys Andrews

G. D. - Like Unto A Flower

For her whose soul will ever bloom
Within God's garden fair—
A tender Rose of crimson hue
That 'twines up Heaven's stair—

The Masters send their blossomed gifts,
With silver life cord bind
Each virtue of the eternal soul
From out the Cosmic Mind:

The Lilly proudly bears her grace
And pureness, free from woe -
The splendent radiance of her smile
Shines forth from Golden Glow.

So innocent of all her charm,
Her beauty so divine -
Ah! Yet it floods and warms as when
Mid gray the Sunflow'rs shine.

The blessed Rose is queen of flowers;
So is this soul as pure
A queen here on this grievous earth—
Thus God's love shall endure.

Louise G. Cuff

Camouflage

My face is very plain some days
All pale and lacking life
Kits filled with colorful contents
End that wretched sight
Use a little on the cheeks, make the lips bright red
Powder all the weird odd spots, my face is no longer dead!

Sara Caldwell Collins

Great Mountains! Light Loads!

Lord, in all the wonders you do,
Creating beauty for your peoples,
Among the best you've done is the mountain view!
For mountains are pure, natural, intrinsic and majestic —
Not man-made steeples!

The hues of colors adorning the mountain scope,
Sparkling around the peaks, valleys and narrow roads,
Strikingly, amazingly impressing man that there is hope!
God made great mountains—surely He can carry
Our light loads!

Doris Brown Jones

A Day In the Life of a Golf Caddy

When the sun creeps up to start anew...
Caddies awake hoping to see blue

The sky tells their story however it may be
Although it is the die hard golfers that are your destiny.

At the cold, clammy, caddy yard crowded full of
Dismal faces and undesired dismay
Many give up for they can no longer stay.

Long seconds, minutes, hours pass before you are called out!
Only to find that they need help pushing in an electric cart
That....that conked out.

Time and time again,
Time soon passes and the workers are coming in,
Then you realize that your day is about to begin,
When what do you know!, a par golfer makes his presentation!

You grab his bag and begin to chase his little white ball
As he flies through the course in no time at all.

The sun soon sets softly in the summer sky.
Knowing that you will soon awake to another day
You go home to seek your soft bed to lay.
When the sun creeps up to start anew.

Andrew Kernan

Cabin Fever

Mr. Bullivant, the irrepressible stalking cat,
    sits on the table at the front window
        looking out.
He would prefer looking out the back window
    because that is where the birds
        are at.
"Bully" as he is street-wise known,
    has a philosophic and artistic
        streak.
He preens and cleans, and rests himself
    his head upon one paw.
And dreams, idly but wildly, of Mehitabel,
    or whatever her name is.
He dreams of Guinea Hen under glass, and
    Pacific Salmon Entree. What class!
He wishes the winter were over-the snow, the sleet,
    the ice, the rain, and what-have-you.
    And so do I.

Charles J. Mann

The Loon

The quiet of the late afternoon,
The silence like that of the new, full moon.
Suddenly the quiet is broken by the cry of a single loon.

Lonely and wild is his call,
Bringing its message to one and all-

    "Preserve my habitat- big and small."

'Twas the call of the earth, as well as the loon,
That broke the silence on that afternoon.

Betsy Woerner

A Stranger in the Mirror

Who is that stranger I see in the mirror?
Gray and white strands of hair shining from fluorescent light
Hair so thin from fallout worse than the atom bomb
Prominent wrinkles on the face and increasing faster than
    rabbits multiply.
Hands still steady, but show signs of aging.
Putting on glasses in order to read and thanking God for
    Ben Franklin.
Diet and exercise has become a serious matter due to the
    midrift bulge syndrome.
An investment made in Aspercreme to soothe the aches and pains.

Yet, who is that stranger I see in the mirror?
One who has grown wiser and has learned to appreciate the simple
    things in life;
Beautiful sunrises and sunsets are not gone unnoticed.
Spring is greeted with excitement and anticipation; living each
    day to its fullest.
Finding a quiet spot to read and relax while listening to music
    soothing to the ear — no more rock 'n roll.
So, who is that stranger I see in the mirror? It is me!

Carolyn Phillips

Innocent

Innocence surrounds me,
for I am innocent,
My unkissed lips,
are as innocent as I,
My uncaressed hands,
are also innocent,
Like all I know,
my love is innocent,
My innocent passion flows like a river,
Through the uninnocent wilds around it,

How long must my hands and lips endure,
How long will my love be untouched,
How long will I be so unsure until my innocence is lost.

Heidi Avenell Johnson

I Remember You

The silent night lives lonely, because there waits no golden dawn.
Regretfully, I must remember, love, that you are really gone.
This dark heart must remember the fleeting happiness we knew,
And now, I live in my world alone, with memories of you.

There is no breath of fragrance in these grey flowers that I press,
And when I call your name, I hear the dead sound of emptiness.
I roam the house from room to room, I look beyond the sharp sea,
but there is nothing I can do to bring you back home to me.

I have to remind myself, again, that you are truly gone.
And I can pray to the Lord for the strength to carry on.

Amanda Lee Ebanks

Tribute To The Beatles

The Beatles came here in 1964
They came here to make a score
Their records were heard every where
From the U.S. to almost anywhere.
Every song they played and wrote
Would always win a new vote.
The Beatles are the greatest band
In England and all the land
I loved them from the very start
Because each song always reached my heart
I'm sorry for what happened to John Lennon
But I'm sure that he is in Heaven
The new songs came out for the Beatles again
I hope that they are together again.
The Beatles are the Best Band ever
They are people who we will always remember.

Ronald Joseph Gennaro

School

School, school, I think it's cool.
School, school, if you skip out on school you might end
  up a fool.

There are a lot of exciting subjects to learn.
That will help me find my place in the sun.

So if you think you're cool and skip out on school
Then, you might end up a fool.

But since I'm staying in school.
Then I know I'm cool and not fool.

Lionel Pittman

I, Too

I, too, am a wonder of the creator.
I am healthy and able to learn.
I listen and I see.
I think and I feel.
I am able to learn things each day.
Like the concepts of poetry and prose
I learn from school and I learn from life.
I enjoy laughter and singing.
I enjoy people and places.
I am constantly amazed at how our eyes do see, and our ears hear.
I share my thoughts and my dreams with others like myself.
I am growing and learning.
I want to experience life to the fullest.
To be free.
To be happy and to help others.
So, all-in-all,
I, too, am a wonder of the creator.

Dawna Clingman

When Nature Is Depressed

The sky is dark, the moon is bright
may your dreams take you places
throughout the night.

The clouds roll in, I see the rain,
you have much sorrow, or so you claim.

I see the tears roll down your
face, as I run toward the wind
and its warm embrace.

You still haven't changed, you never
will, I'm through with you, I've had my fill.

Laken Polizzi

Grandmother

So many things I want to say
because I know there isn't another day.

To turn back the hands of time
as we sat and listen to the chimes.

While gazing at stars in the dark night
said to ourselves, "What a beautiful sight!"

With the chill of the cool breeze, I snuggled near
you took my hand and said, "It's alright dear."

The security with you that I felt
has me to wonder, "What crazy cards life has dealt."

A part of me is stuck in the past
wishing the time with you would always last.

I know it was for the best
for your body and soul to finally rest.
A little girl is afraid and wants to cry
as the woman walks up and says, "Good-Bye."

As your spirit gently floats above please know how much you're
loved.

The precious times that we shared showed me how much you cared.

May you find happiness and peace that's deserved
while my memories of you on earth are preserved.

Lori Kopera

A Friend's Farewell

The angels looked down on a small rowdy crowd
  The laughter and smiles seemed to echo out loud
But deep in their hearts there appeared a big hole
  The pain and the hurt was blacker than coal

Smiles that reflected off glasses of love
  Friendships so pure like a snow covered dove
As that one single night came to an end
  It was now time to leave that circle of friends

As smiles grew thin with teary eyes
  It was time to go and say their goodbyes
The angels looked up to their God in the sky
  As the love turned to pain and the tears ran dry

A chorus of words rose up in the air
  The angel were singing to stop the despair
I heard a loud crack as my world fell apart
  For I was the one leaving my friends and my heart

I look back now on that warm summer night
  And my heart seems to fill with a radiant light
As time goes by, my pain seems to fade
  But my memories are still clear as the days they were made!

Karen A. Leitenberger

Life's Like That

There's dandelions in my lawn,
All pretty, bright and happy.
I think I like to see them there.
I must be kind of sappy!

For when they stand up straight and tall,
Their hair coiffed to perfection,
I wish the breezes wouldn't blow
In every which direction.

A women's life is like a rose,
In all its lovely stages.
But I feel like a dandelion,
It's pretty, then it ages.

VaNile Risser

Beneath the Sea

Huge waves of water fly over my head,
inside the ocean I stay
with the brunette-headed goddess.
Most people are not welcome here.
This is our place
stained with our memories;
it marks out territory
of everlasting love.
Inside this castle
beneath the waves,
our love is like the unending
cycle of the waves;
we sit alone,
watching the mortals play;
we are always watching them,
watching them mount their surfboards
like knights to trusty steed,
watching as they try to defeat the ocean.
Beneath the sea we stay.

Josh Levin

Untitled

Black all over, it begins to grow
In a clandestine part of the heart.
It lurches, it breathes, it feeds
On your innermost thoughts, sensitive to the touch.
Its ominous darkness, uncontrollable, forcible
It leaves no forewarning, overshadowing all it encounters
Turning the red of the rose into the red of a lover's rage
The fresh green of the budding daffodil into
The envious green of a lover's lost.
Like the black vine twisting and turning
Out of a lifeless grave
Love takes over.

Reena Thomas

"Happiness"

The wind blew through her golden like hair.
Her feet, like her life were bare.
Shining were her light blue eyes.
They were wildly fixed on the skies.
Her arms flew out as she threw herself on the ground.
Her heart was free and for happiness bound.
The grass, wet with dew, was as soft as her tiny bed.
Joy and glee filled and filled in her head.
The warmth of the sun came down upon her cheek.
Every creature and living thing wanted a peek.
Her smile was bright.
Her heart was light.
The life she lived was hers to live.
The smile she gave was hers to give.
The joy she felt was hers to feel.
She was happy for her life and happy on that hill.

Leandra Lee Kerr

Heaven And Earth

Into the indecisive dawn - another day is born.
Do we all look the same?
Believing it's not true
Is heaven really a strange place?
Or is it telling us which way to go.
Are we hoping to find tranquility there someday
Is the passion really lost or shall we take it
As believing it's true.
  We will not be forgotten

Ted M. Ogden

Tragedy

An unwelcome visitor,
She needs no invitation.
Stealing in she mercilessly robs,
Honors not rank or station.
No time for even a wish,
As she leaves her cruel trail of anguish.

Judith Montanaro

Untitled

  Love
is a feeling everybody has felt young or old.
  Love
is hard to explain.
  Love
you have it but sometimes you don't
  Love
is needed, to go on, to do your best.

  Love
is there but, where you ask
your self in need. It's where
it's always been, in your heart,
it's not buyable, sellable, breathable,
but it's feelable. As the days go on
you get more of it. Some may
not realize it. Not today, or maybe
this second, but when you find out
you have love and lost of it, share
it, so people, can feel your love, and
realize they have some and more of it, love!

Beretha Lindsey

Love

As hushed as a mother calming her newborn baby;
Yet as loud and ferocious as a lion's roar.

Cheerful and bright like a warm summer morn;
But as upsetting and dreary as a winter's icy cold wind.

Able to bring a smile to the face;
And just as quickly a tear to the eye.

Not found in any stranger on the street;
But is always found in a friend.

Corrie Lloyd

Tragic Tuesday

One cold winter's day eleven thirty-nine,
It came without warning, it came without sign.
A journey into space - the Challenger and crew;
But still it was Christa, that everybody knew.

All the folks at NASA, who monitored the blast,
Knew when first they saw it - the shuttle couldn't last.
Not knowing what had happened - we all held our breath.
In our hearts we held out hope - our minds knew certain death.

Ellison and Greg, and Mike and Dick and Ron;
Judy and our Christa - please tell me they're not gone!
But time went on, the hours passed:
Our shattered dreams, flags at half-staff.

Through smoke and flames and tears that day,
Our souls went with you all the way.
Seventy-three seconds to an endless flight:
Seven more stars in the skies tonight.

Back at the cape, on the shores of Hi-Tech,
Officials wait to examine the wreck.
With cause uncertain, this is all we know:
When destiny calls, the brave must still go.

Donald H. Lloyd

Me

Do you often wonder why the birds fly free
And say to yourself, "I wish it were me
Do you often wonder what else I could be
Then say to yourself, "I'm glad that I'm me"
As a child playing games, chasing butterflies
and scraped knees
Fantasizing our life, running in the breeze
Not seeing the forest for the trees
The flowers, the rain, the birds and the bees
He made up perfect, I agree,
that he make us different that I can be Me!

Lillian E. Hayes

Walking

Walking down this uneven path
amongst tarnish and pollute,
Our dry, dust-covered feet
ache to the point of becoming numb.
Barefoot, we walk on.
Exposing our naked feet to elements of weather.
Factors, ingredients of pain and suffering.
Hurting, we walk on. Our feet keep moving,
led by those two lighted fragments of our anatomy
that are our windows to the outside world.
Fixed on our goals, our dreams, our ambitions
moving in their direction.
Fueled only by our relentless need for procuring,
For acquiring all that is wanted
By the selfish being within us.
Suffering, we call ourselves victims of the atmosphere
Yet we keep on walking barefoot;
Sometimes bleeding blood of futile efforts,
Sometimes blissfully getting caught in a shower
and being able to allow our feet to quench their crackled thirst.

Saima Malik

Dawning Of Mid-Life

Your past rises to meet you
Not always the best of memories
Your children are your future
Then again they can be your demise

The ex's of your life are haunting mistakes
But the present can be rewarding
If you have conquered your faults
For a lover has created a newness for life

Are we best described as enduring
Life has set detours all our existence
Wrong decisions are now a blur
While wisdom and patience are remedies

Happiness is a meaning for individuals
Measured by one's precious flashbacks
And those events yet to come
For our existence is truly dawning

Denis P. DuBois

For Anna

I loved you through all time
past all dimensions
and I love you in the sleeping
potentialities of the future
in the unfolding incarnations of forms and spirits
but especially
I love you now
in the narrow immediacy of this present
from moment to moment
from breath to breath...

Franchia Avila

Ode To An Otis Escalator

Oh you band of steel and rubber
Carrying countless tons of blubber
Every day you move your load
Along the same old weary road
The sign reads up and up you go
I bet sometimes you're wishing though
That through some strange mysterious force
You could change your passive course
Perhaps go down or maybe sideways
And leave behind your hampering guide ways
To you my sympathy I extend
And hope you find a means to end
This tyranny that stifles breath
I too could profit from its death

Ed Allen

Friends

Friends in Christ, especially children of earth;
Adds credence, through love, we are of heavenly birth.
You are God's life preserver, through fellowship you come;
Bringing joy and gladness as fruits from our heavenly home.
You brighten our lives, opening glorious windows in the sky,
Touching our hearts like a warm, gentle breeze flowing by.
You fill our thoughts, our minds with happy, lilting songs,
Walking in His Spirit, desirous, living with no wrong.
Yes, as a friend in Christ, you're more precious than gold,
A wonderful, beautiful lady, who will never grow old.

Friends in Christ, brings promise of a glorious new day;
Peace of the soul comes like a turtle dove winging its way,
Among a blushing sky as sun rays spread in hour of early morn.
A Christ-like halo about her radiates, pulsating always adorn,
The lifestyle of a Christian lady, glowing with servitude.
Her charming modesty, humility shines forth, rosebud sweet,
Welcoming this precious girl, all people want to meet.
Dear Lord, in a quite hour of intercessory prayer I entreat,
Let me be worthy, a servant too, that life cannot defeat,
Your glory and grace; thank you for this friend in Christ.

Leo T. Proctor

Angels

I heard an Angel weeping tonight
Weeping for a Mother's son
Whose soul had taken flight
Weeping for you and I
Who do not understand-why

Angels weep for loved ones here on earth, you know
Their tears give us strength and courage for the wounded soul
That is their way of easing the pain and the sorrow
For a young man who had to go

For the Angel wants you to know
He is Forever In God's protective hands
His Mind is clear
His Heart is healed
His Soul is free
To be with the Angel in the sky
Who weeps for you and I
Hoping - someday - we all will understand - why

E. A. Berg

Til The Storm Passes By

I have a loving father, he allows me no alarm.
I always pray and ask him to keep me from the storm.
He is a loving father and hears my humble cry.
He holds me close to his bosom til the storm passes by.

Frankie Wier

Sad Things In Life

Of all sad things I've seen in life,
I pity the man with soul so hard,
Who can stand with his wife as she gives birth,
And say to me there is no God!

How can he hold his newborn close,
And not feel blest beyond all measure?
His heart would be dead as an old fence post,
Not to thank his God for such a priceless treasure!

Yet there are some, or so I'm told,
Who would call such a miracle an 'accident';
Men with hearts so dead, so cold,
They refuse to believe it is Heaven-sent!

I wonder what our Lord must feel,
To think He has entrusted a newborn soul,
To a man with a heart as cold as steel,
Who has no care for its ultimate goal?!

Of at least one thing I'm very certain,
I'd hate to be in that man's place,
When fate lowers down the final curtain,
And he must meet God, face to face!

C. N. Wesson

Aubrey Marie W.

A bundle of joy that graced our lives, one early April day.
Unique and beautiful, know you are special, in every way.
Born into our family, a baby, so precious, so new.
Remember always the love that is felt for you.
Every moment passes so quickly, cherish each day.
Yesterday never forgotten as you go on your way.

Many a year will go by, and quickly you'll start to sprout and grow.
A toddler, a child, a woman, you have so much to see, so far to go.
Right now everyone rocks you softly, held tightly in their arms.
Innocence written in every feature of your babyish charms.
Entertaining you with laughter and happiness is all we will ever try to do.

Wherever you go and whatever you do, ensuring always, you know, all of us love you!

Christina M. Ward

Retrospect

In retrospect we view the past.
For in life's play we all are cast.
The certain parts we all must play,
Is just the due we all must pay.

In retrospect we wonder why.
We find the answer and often sigh.
We stood the trial and passed the test.
We came out wiser from the quest.

In retrospect we look back and see,
Those problems we had and wanted to flee.
Were brought our way to shape and mold,
Our character to build and forever hold.

In retrospect we see more clear.
We learn the truths that are so dear.
We pass these truths down to our heirs.
We hope they grasp them and really care.

In retrospect the dark is light.
We are thankful to have made the flight.
The cycle will start over again.
For all will wonder where, how and when.

Deborah C. Martin

Time

Where in the world is time
    It was once a pleasant endeavor
But now it's hard to locate
    And we need it more then ever.

We are retired at our house
    But still there are appointment to keep
You dress and rush to get there
    To find they were find last week.

After breakfast in the morning
    And the paper has been well read
It's time to get ready for dinner
    And almost time for bad.

So time has disappeared for now
    I think was will survive
But it quickly slips right by us
    Is it because I am eighty five?

Mary McKay Martin

A Sunset

Red, blue, yellow, green,
Orange, white, and pink,
Colors overlapping,
Swirling and swirling around,
Swallowing each other,
As the sun sinks down.
Clouds outlined in pink and gold,
Like fluffy satin, laced pillows,
With the sun's red-orange light beams,
Dancing around on them,
Like bright, twinkling fairies,
Until the sun gives off a blast of light,
That makes a bright halo around it,
And then the sun sinks down,
And is swallowed up by a world,
A world of darkness.

Rachel McCleve

Our House

The living room has a fire place
But the chimney has to be replaced
The kitchen is very small
The table and chairs we put in the hall
A plug in mounted in the floor
Cold air inlet hid behind the door
If you want to open a door
The knob is a foot above the floor
The roof has a big leak
The same with garage all the way to the peak
The sewer was plugged
The methane gas we hugged
The ceiling has a big crack all the way to the wall
We are just waiting for it to fall
The garage has a genie to open the door
Garbage and trash covers the floor
The doorbell buttons are mounted well
But inside there is no bell
Cleaning has been a big chore
I know...because my hands are sore!!

Clayton Rost

My Brother

When your pain is too much to bear
When it seems there is no one to share
All the hurt hidden deep inside
You, my brother is always at my side
His are the arms around you so tight
His love will warm you throughout the night
He is the one in whose likeness I'm made
He is the love from whom there's no shade
His is the perfect love that will never die
He is the one who never wants you to cry
He is the one who will always be there
He is the one whose love will never die
He is the one you never have to try
To make an excuse nor try to reason why
He is the one who makes my heart fly
He is the one with whom the answer is found
He is the one who is always around
Yes, he is my brother he is the son of my mother

Catherine Giblin Carucci

The Wanderings

As I walk through the Valley of the Shadow of Death,
Or something to that effect,
Life ends, but a new day dawns.
The path leads, or so it seems
To darkness.
If all else fails, sit down and wait,
But you know you cannot.
That spot of light in the darkness beckons you,
Calls to you.
A beacon of hope
In an otherwise empty void.
With your last remaining strength
You meander in blindness towards your goal
Ever cautious, your hands stretched out in front,
Though you cannot see them.
The light elongates as you get closer.
Your hands probe and find a knob,
A door,
To your mind and to your soul
And to you future.

Michael D. Mongillo

Light That Lead Me Here

You are the light, the path which lead me here,
Through all our good times, and all our tears.

I want to make you happy,
To cry only happy tears,
I don't mean to make you worry,
I never meant for all those fears.

The talks we had made us closer,
And feel more together.
This is when I feel you in my heart,
And by my side forever.

You always made the right choice,
When it's my turn I hear your voice.
Your energy was always there.
Those are the times I like to share.

You are always a beautiful person, in my eyes and heart,
You will always bet here, even if we are apart.

You are the meaning of my life, that couldn't be untrue.
There is a place in my heart, that is filled with love for you.

You are not only my mother, but my guidance and my best friend,
That's why I will always be there for you, our love will never end.

Andrea McHugh

The Apache Kid

The day is hot, the breezes few;
    The hunt goes on; the hunted is you!
The soldiers continue their relentless pursuit.
    Will you ever stop hearing the sounds of their boots?

Did you earn this day of infamy, of dread and sorrow
    Or were you, like the others, only searching for tomorrow?
While promises without end, of the white man grew grand;
    What happened to your people, the game and the land?

Was it revenge for promises broken;
    For all the lies the white man has spoken?
Is that what brought you to this day,
    With the soldiers advancing along the way?

Or did some quirk in your mind decree
    That you must kill and burn...a savage be?
The guesses abound and forever may be near
    But the answers shall always remain unclear.

Do know, Apache Kid, wherever you may be,
    Stories of your life and deeds go down in history;
And the white man and indian, through blood, sweat and tears
    Shall live in harmony, as friends, in future years.

Ellen McLaughlin

Beating Heart

Our first date started as most begin,
We were hand in hand at the local Drive-in.
How I wanted him as part of my life,
We soon fell in love, he asked me to be his wife.
We made a commitment for better or worse,
In a day where it's more common to be divorced.

We never had a lot of money or material things,
But each morning I awake in his arms I always hear the birds sing.
How can he be so gentle, yet his eyes have such a strong hold?
When he was made, God must have surely thrown away the mold!

There's many temptations in this world that puts our love to a test.
I want to remember to thank God each day for how I've been blessed!
His love is the best thing that has happened to me.
He gives me the strength to be the best wife I can be!

My Love for him will last for an eternity, as will this
band of gold he gave to me.
When it comes to building a home together, he does more than his part.
I can only love him as long as I have a Beating Heart!!

Karen V. McRoy

Bats

Bats!—fired fresh!
From the caves;
Darkness set on wing,
Is flown away out the mouth.
In the mountain's side, fears hung upside down,
Asleep perched, blindly awaken to see the night—
Explode! Preying, from out the stomach of the tomb,
    In a swallow the sky is taken!
And I, outside, struck hard,
In fright, falter! Caught by the burst,
Stunned, shaken—such a surprise;
The belching blackness is a thing that flies.

Joel Wesley Kilpatrick

"Purple Brook"

The Moon so bright and filled with romance seemed to shimmy
Stars were dancing across an open sky - falling with every motion
The wind with great fear - climbed into the delicately cold waters
   The waters - of Purple brook
Plum trees spread their leaves across the hollow clouds
Grape vines grew along beauty.
Beauty being pink roses, fading into existence.
   The existence - of purple brook
Golden peach flowers sway gracefully into mountains
Mountains of everlasting oceans,
Of blue and green come rain.
Rain hitting the forest ground of wood, visiting like an old friend
   The friend - of purple brook
Grey is the mist - guarding the stones of far.
Ringlets of sun flow gently about blades of pedals.
   The Pedals - of Purple Brook

   Jessy Faulkner

A Spring Shower

I
like to
listen to
pitter-patter
of rain on the roof,
see flowers lift their heads
for tiny drops of moisture,
watch a bird splash in a puddle,
feel a sudden spray as breezes pass,
know all's well wit the world—all things are clean,

   Jean Ewing Kuhn

Fireflies

Elusive lights in the garden,
Fleeting flashes of flame,
Quickly burning and as quickly gone.
For a brief time in the early evening,
Just at dusk, before the night descends,
The underbrush comes alive with the fireflies.

On and off the tiny lights glimmer,
Like dancing sparks in the darkening air,
Floating and flashing and soaring
As they rise from the twilit garden,
Before they descend on the foliage once more.
Then the night envelopes the garden.

   Marguerite Comiskey

The Best Gift

It's an old fashioned Christmas just
like Mama and Daddy had. With the
stockings hung, and baby Ned's the last one
in the row, firelight and candles bright
make it so homey and cozy tonight.
Tonight's the night before Santa comes,
with presents, candy and lots of gum.
There's a carrot in the barn for Rudolph.
And on the kitchen table - cookies and milk
for Santa Claus. And a picture - all
from tiny Ned. Outside the snow is falling
and from the manger scene the Christ Child's calling...
Calling to me, calling to you, with a love so true.
Gently and lovely, oh so pure.
Peace on earth, good will toward men.
A Merry Christmas is in the makings, when
we begin to start taking the Christ
Child's hand... So tiny, so sincere, so mighty.
So to you and I and Ned, I wish a sincerely
Merry Christmas Day.

   Lori Fuller-De Leon

The Way I Feel

I think about you, every day;
hoping to choose, the right way.
Why is it, when I'm all alone;
I think about calling you, on the phone.
There is nothing, that will make me leave you;
even though sometimes, I don't know what to do.
My love for you, is ever so strong;
let's hope this relationship, lasts really long.
What am I supposed to do, if you were to leave;
I can't have anyone else, because it's you I need.
Let's just make, the best of what we are;
because I know both of us, are trying from afar.
A time will come, when it will be you and I; remember, I'm a "Genuine,
   full of love" type of guy.
That night we shared, was full of romance and confusion; is our
   love for each other true, or a deceptive illusion.
What I know for sure, is that my love is true; I pray to God, one day
   I'll be with you.
You're all I seem to care about, no matter what is going on; I miss
   you twenty-four-seven, from dusk till dawn.
You probably know now, the way I feel; but is what happened that
   morning, really real.
Of course it's real, none of us can deny; be strong and maintain, no
   doubt we'll get by.
No matter how long it takes, my love for you will stand; when the
   time has come, it'll be me holding your hand.
I love you Kat.

   Michael A. Isles

My Magical Bear

My Teddy is a special bear.
He doesn't play like you and me.
He just sits in the corner of the room
as happy as can be.

All day long he sits and smiles.
He wouldn't think of dancing.
But after I go to bed at night
that's when he starts his prancing.

I only need to hold him
and close my eyes so tightly.
He'll dance with me around the room.
He'll do this with me nightly.

He'll fill my head with fuzzy thoughts.
then gently lift me off the floor.
He'll whirl me round and round and round.
Then set me down with a mighty roar.

So, I jump in bed. Pull the covers up.
Pray the Lord my soul to keep.
My Teddy Bear can't start to play
Until I'm fast asleep.

   Evelyn Anne Condon

Manic-Depressive Mother

Brambles and briars frame her face,
Jeweled hands molding me,
Naught can I erase....
Wings of bumblebees,
Embracing expectation,
Pectoral waves of symmetry.
Thunderous arrangement of the mind,
Alas, a smile for her thorn,
Higher than the heavens doest she climb.
Nirvana bound and yet....
Naught is so sweet as the curve
in Mother's neck.

   Carolyn Gresham Cook

Symbolic

I sit and watch them as they touch you.
They move so slowly over each curve,
    smelling your wonderful scent.
They feel the beauty of your softness as
    the gentle breeze touches you the same way.
I see how you shimmer in the bright
    sunlight and I see how you shiver
    as it begins to rain.
I watch you taste the drops of water and
    notice how you long to be wet.
All you need is to be noticed.
You are a beautiful symbol, my Rose.

Heather Crum

The Rose

There is a story about a Rose
That grew beside a garden wall
And one day it bent toward a crevice
Because it grew too tall.

Alas the Rose could not get through
And strained to find the light
And then got caught between the wall
It's day then turned to night.

The air grew cold
As winter sent its mighty chill
And the blossom fell from the stem,
As though the Rose was ill.

And then the sun shone through the wall
Its warmth upon the Rose
And behold a bud then opened wide
And there the Rose still grows.

I have a Rose, taken from your grave
Alas it has dried, but has not died.
Although we're now apart, my rose serves as a memory
Like you; etched forever in my heart!

Linda Duquette

Mother Earth

As the Spirit leaves
The Spirit dies
And far below the Spirit cries
As the hope of dawn dies in an anguished fight
Far beneath the angry light
As the seas below
Recoil in pain
And the clouds above
Shudder again and again
They see what we have done to you
Then from the ground
Far below
The Spirit dies
As it goes it cries once more
"Don't you love me anymore?"

Jenny Wong-Sick-Hong

The Cloak Of Christ

The purest of clothing
A pearl is nothing to its pure white
Perfect in every way
Shining like snow beneath the sun
Gold is without value in comparison
Christ's cloak protecting and forgiving
Leading us into God's presence
To be humbly worn by all who seek the path
    to Heaven's Gate

Jeremy Gilland

Momma Told Me

Momma told me, not to eat wit dirty hands,
so I used my fork instead

Momma told me, don't stay too late,
so at 12 am I went to bed

Momma told me, not to play in class,
so I played in the halls

Momma told me, not to be so fresh,
so I put on dirty drawls

Momma told me, I need vegetables,
so I'd save my lima beans

Momma told me, never lie,
so I ain't say I hang with fiens

Momma told me, listen well,
so when the sirens came I'd run

Momma told me, to be careful,
so I always packed my gun

Momma told me don't do drugs,
so instead I made the sell

Momma told me this would happen,
so I wrote momma from in jail

Shakiara Brown

Dominique

On February 6th my baby came,
Dominique she was named.
So early in life to be born,
Too young to be tattered or torn.
Such innocents to reality,
Became the utmost formality.
Sleeping sound in her slumber womb,
Just to awaken to her tomb.
As far as I could see,
She was all of me.
All I wanted in the world,
Just suddenly tumbled and twirled.
I think of her day to day,
Wishing it could have been my way.
Wandering about in a daze,
Wondering of the Lord's mysterious ways.
When I grow old and grey,
And come to my dying day.
It would be to my delight,
If we could once again unite.

Colene M. Perry

Untitled

No more sweet lover to wrap myself around
when darkness falls and the full moon shines
No more sweet kisses on my mouth; on my breasts
No more sweet breath on my back as I sleep
No more sweet smiles to greet me at the end of the day

No more sweet lover; no more sweet lover
He has stolen my heart and run away with it to
the farthest ends of the earth where I shall never retrieve it;
as I am on the North axis and he on the south;
What my lover has stolen is gone forever
I shall suffer long days and nights
longing for that which cannot be mine

No more sweet lover; he has fled into the black night
like a witch disappearing into the sky on a broomstick.
No more sweet lover; my lover is gone.

Vicky Castro

My Heart's Desire

If only you knew the thoughts of you caressing
through my mind,
Then you would see the precious dreams my
heart only hopes to find.
But, to my silent wish I cling if only for a while
until upon your face I see - for me your loving
smile.

My heart is pounding and my breath is weak as I
reach to take your hand.
Your gentle touch and warm embrace are more
than I could stand.
To slip a kiss upon your ear could be taking
quite a chance, but with my eyes closed in fear
my love for you enhanced.

If only you knew the thoughts of you caressing
through my mind,
then you would know the sweet desires that my
heart would hope you'd find.

David Zimmerman

The House On The Hill ...

Looks so grey on the outside
So small like a prison on the
Inside...

The little girl trapped by the
Silent "visits" by an "old" man
Who lives in the house on the hill ...
The-air is filled with mist of
Staleness from 'family' secrets
All involved ...
This never changes ...
The little girl lost ... Her soul his forever.
At times; memories a float in her mind of
"Silver lake" just across the road.
The moon reflecting on the happy place.
The stillness she ... wished to fly from the anger;
the pain ...

Question? Why? The little girl trapped
In the house on the hill ...
Answers remain
Forever in her mind.

May Kane

My Friend

My friend is thin, my friend is fat
My friend is white, my friend is black
My friend is from China, my friend is from Spain
My friend is fancy, my friend is plain
Her dress is straight, her dress has frills
My friends is a boy, my friend is a girl
My friend is as nice and special as you see
And that's all that matters to my friend and me

Kristin Albrecht

The Most Important Rules

Be proud of all you do.
When you make a promise carry it through.
Forgive yourself, as well as your friends.
Except the good; and the bad God sends.
Speak kindly of thy sister, and proudly of thy brother.
Honor thy Father and honor thy Mother
While counting your blessings include the rain
And never but never!
  Use the Lords Name in Vain

Jean M. Avist

Missing Puzzle

Is there someone out there
  who really loves and cares

Is there anyone who can see
  beyond the barriers inside of me

Is there anyone who knows
  how wonderful I have grown

Is there anyone who will not fear
  to have me always near

Is there someone to hug
  and always be there for me to bug

Is there someone who can make me feel
  that love and happiness are for real

Oh why can't my heart find
  the missing part that was meant to be mine

I know that destiny will provide for me
  a special love that was meant to be

So until then I will not fear
  because I have faith that my charming prince will soon be here...

Gabriella Pilato

Untitled

How can I be strong I've asked myself time and time again,
I've told myself that I'll never fall in love with you again.
The heart you gave me, my soul you took away,
I love the way we acted down by the bay.
Good intentions you had many I know you did,
We're acting like little kids.
I come from a place that hurts and God knows how I cried,
My love for you is as wild as the tide.
I don't think I could take the pain,
If I lost you again.
I've come so close to happiness to have it all swept away,
I've felt this way ever since May.
My heart is in your hands,
But it feels like you left it in other lands.
Don't ever let me go,
Because I love you so.
Say it just one time, say you love me,
You brighten the world for me to see.

Carey Brown

Country Song

Dust on the table and dirt on the floor,
A fog on the window, a creak in the door,
Webs on the ceiling, paint peeling down
Got nothing to do, guess I'll go in to town.

Car's got a rattle, a spring's poking through,
It looks kinda gray now, it used to be blue.
Smoke curls out the back, the front's mostly gone.
It's a '64 Ford, worth only a song.

But my time's coming, it's coming round slow,
I'll have my way sometime before I go, at least I hope so.

Got lots to do and no strength to do it,
Just take a deep breath and get on to it.
I'll be more tired tomorrow than I am today
If I don't keep on thinking "maybe, someday".

Kathryn Wells

Untitled

Nurses are great. Nurses are bright.
They are angels sent from the sky.

God bless you all for being so nice
You are all angels sent from the sky.

Thank you for caring and easing our pain.
Don't worry angels this is your game.

I pray for you each and every night.
You are my angels sent from the sky.

Without you here we won't survive.
Thank you angels your love is mine.

You are all very dedicated. You work from eight to seven.
You must be God's angels sent to us from heaven.

It doesn't matter what your name is; Yvette, Douglas, Linda, Jean
    or Diane
If you are a lady or a guy, you are still an angel sent from the sky.

Sumberto Gonzalez

Reminiscence

Be simple and be sweet
    And the world is yours to own
Be always my golden dream
    Your face that brightens my very own

Zephyr wind that swept the golden sea
    Adhere my heart to thy tender caress
Be always with me that I may see
    A love so sweet and dear to me

Love why haste thou forsaken me
    Leaving my heart and sweet memory
Enchanting days of dream and bliss
    Rest my heart to a sweet dream of peace
Oh! Heart give me peace that I may rest

    For my love shall remain forever until death.

Feliser M. Hilario

The Melancholy Rose

Oh, eternal and immortal raindrops
courageous as you all are
release your generous and knightly kindness
upon this earthly flower.

The silence of the raindrops
their stillness and taciturnity
almost as if their muteness
had become to comfortable

Give to these earthly bonds
your playful, lively, frolicsome and sprightly
ways so that we may attest and acknowledge
your sunny and enlivening celestial hope

For the raindrops have given up
their secrets and have revealed
their plentiful and copious gifts
to a melancholy Rose.

Eugene F. Wiesner

"Star"

The wind whispers softly through the night
As I look at my star, shining so bright.
My star left me a long time ago.
He promised me he'd return, but only to be my foe.

My star begs me to set him free,
But I just laugh because he'll always be with me.
They call me the Ice Queen because I'm so cruel,
But my feelings are the color of the night, a dark, deep blue.

Rebecca Kilgore

Settling Down

She hated me because
I did not love her
She conforms to her manic depression
And cycles it on me

We dance to loud music
Wrap my arms around
Her luxurious waist
Run my hands over her body

People talk about us, so what.
She avoids my kisses
And yells at me later
But we have a long convoluted talk on the phone

I didn't know there were scars
On her wrists
She is so full of life
Where would it all go

Her dark expressive German eyes
Set in her African princess face
I wonder what she's thinking now
I can see the obituary.

Michael Kasow

Untitled

Life is so fragile,
    Why waste it?
Drinking all the while;
    You think you're getting high
    but low is all you'll get.

You can't feel love
    With a bottle of wine.
Love comes from above.
    God's so loving, merciful, and kind
    And true love through him
    is what you'll find.

Drugs get you nowhere;
    They only bring you down.
Drugs and drinking are a major dare.
    You want happiness; loneliness and sadness
    is what you'll find.

It's the biggest war you'll ever fight;
    It's up to you to win or lose;
Winning will take all your might.
    Losing will be bad news.

Lori Cox

Some Day

There's a loving letter I mean to write
There's a visit I mean to pay.
There's a careless habit I hope to mend,
When I get the time some day.

There's a dusty bible I mean to read
There's an hour I'll keep to pray
There's hope to turn each dream, to a golden deed
When I get the time some day.

I'll take flowers to the sick and sad
I'll seek guidance for those that stray
You may trace my steps by the hearts made glad.
When I get the time some day.

So somebody thought, so somebody said.
But isn't it just a crime,
That we're busy with less important things
We never did get the time.

Pat Jenkins

Almost ... Friends

Why do people put on a mask?
Are they so afraid of the questions we ask?
Or afraid that we'll see the true fear in their eyes?
Instead they'll tell stories and intricate lies.

Like a great Redwood that's sprung from a seed,
A true friend takes time, and much care...indeed.

But most will just act like sharks in a pack,
Wait 'til you're vulnerable-then they attack.
Most who I've met just get what they need,
They strike, and bite, and laugh as you bleed.

Off comes the mask and the monster revealed,
Is not the same person who once so appealed...

Russell Daykin

Life's Unfairness

Whoever promised me a rose garden? No one
I've learned that from life's coldness
and hardness.

If I could change things
life would be fair.
For all God's people.
Please be aware.

Everyone would have an equal chance.
Starting from birth,
Straight through to romance.

But life's not fair,
Please lend an ear to hear.
There's sadness and pain
As much as there is rain.

So, don't expect a rose garden,
And be prepared to face
All of life's coldness
Through this long, endless race.

Debbie W. Moore

Your Place

I went to the place where you use to be...
Loneliness to see you were sweeping over me..
The need to see you just one more time..
Were taking over my body soul and my mind...
I stood outside a door that was looked up so tight...
And Darling nothing in this whole world was right...
I looked through the glass that was in your door...
And I could tell that no one stayed there anymore...
The place that was so dear to my heart and soul...
Was deserted and my memories started to unfold...
I could almost see you sitting there in your chair...
Making your place have such a warm welcome air...
I surprised my tears and started on home...
Now I'm letting them out in the words of this song...
I remembered how proud you were of your place...
The plans you had for it was all in your face...
Now you are so successful you don't need it anymore..
But I left my lonely heart there at your door...

Louise Humphries

Flutter Byes

Seemingly lonely
Beauty unfolding
Fluttering softness
Shiny yet smooth
Loving the flower
From which the pollen produces
The warm softness
And easy happiness
For her color shines against the sunbeams
Of the raging fireball
To reflect the inner beauty
Trapped by the outer core
Such magnificent splendor
Glides enchanted
As fluently as daydreams
Where lies
forbidden fantasies
And her sweet sorrows
linger.

Corrine Grace

My Thanks To God

I open my heart to say,
on this bright and shiny day,
I give my humble thanks to thee
for the lovely wife you gave to me.
I have one more thing for which to pray
Let me have her all the way.
Without her my life would crumble,
So I ask dear God; most humble,
Let her stay with me 'til I die.
Give her strength, don't let her cry
that's my biggest aim in life
to make her glad she is my wife.
When her life on earth has met its end,
I hope and pray that you will send
her beautiful self back to me
so we can join hands once more
and be with thee.

Frederick B. Miller

God's Hand

How does God touch us? The doubter wants to know,
But so little can be said to help him understand
That God's presence touches every facet of our lives,
That all about us is the creation of God's hand.

Believing hearts are touched by Him when they view
The expanse of rainbow arching over all the sky.
There are those who feel His touch in evening's calm,
While song of birds assure them God is nigh.

Oh, fool! How dare you say there is no God!
Or that His touch cannot be felt in wind's caress,
Or that the thrill of sunset's glow or morning dawn
Is not God holding close His children to His breast?

Across the open heaven starlight softly falls
In blessing on each one who lifts up voice in praise.
Ah, yes! His touch is felt indeed by every man
And 'twill be so as long as God grants mankind days.

How can I explain the meaning of "the hand of God?"
I sensed His fragrance present as the plow turned up the sod
In springtime when my father went to plow and plant and sow.
These are the answers...all the doubter needs to know

Elizabeth S. Nau

One Letter After Another

One evening, gales stormed due east toward
Delaware. Everything green now would drain nearly
yellow-brown. No one except tuck knew what the
evolution neanderthal looked dreadful like. Elephants
shown nationally yawning. Giant tracks size E escaped
different than nine emu unbothered despite explosions
some eight times semi-hourly. You understand death
hurts still less somehow when nobody yells. Somewhere
everyone excites stanley. You unconsciously yearn not
taking great trip precautions. Stumbling getting grub
before Evan notifies someone. Elvis still leaves. Sandpaper
rubs stiff fiber right to old dogs still lapping gallons
so openly. Yes, some egg-flavored-bagels sell like
expressos somewhere else. Everyone elevates somehow.
Why you underestimate eels stifles some; even norm.
Me?! Everything green now wears some evening gown.
Neat trucks stop. Pastel living rooms startle everyone even
nice Erin. Now we exit. Tomorrow we elude everything gray.

Brian Rice

A Young Heart; A Woman's Reflections

What will I do with myself if my birthday says I'm old
When my body may be changing
But my heart is still so young.

What will I do with "the pains"
If I still have my dreams of riding on a white horse
Against the time and the winds.

What will I do with my eyes
When I won't see what I want,
But they are still shinning life
Because my heart is still young.

What will I do with the marks of all ventures and memories,
If my mind is acting well
And my thoughts are all in order.

What will I do with the idea
to look young throughout the years?...
Well, perhaps the secrets of one's life
are to share, receive and give
Love and wisdom all the time.

That's why now I do know
I can continue the book of all my birthdays to be
And I may feel and look my best
Because my heart is still young...

Lybia Burgos

Love Your Wife

Loving your wife is right to do
for who are you, to know what to do
Not a feeling, not a thumps, but an
action from your rump.
That's right, get off your a**,
For love's an action, it may be a pass.
Take her out and have some fun,
who knows what you'll receive when it's all done.

So now you know the thing to do,
keep it up and keep it new.
Don't give up if she's blue,
for all you have to do is do, do, do.
For love's an action, not a feeling
Stop trying to confuse the issues
with that dealing.
She wants your mind, she wants your time
She wants you to tell her, "You are mine"

J. Dennis Sullivan

How I Feel

I want to sit by the sea, smell the salt air
through the whispering winds. Listen to the waves
collide against the current. Another tide as washed up
the shells of colors, that reflect with the sun's ray of
beauty. The sand of velvet that sits beneath my feet,
like soft rose pedals. Shed my tears, like rain spreads
through the open fields of nature that covers our survival.
Freedom of great wide open waters never ending, when a flower
blooms, like a baby is born that's brought into life,
unknowing what to expect. Let us drain the poverty of those
that weep in the alley's of desperation. The wisdom of the
wise, revive the weak. Bitterness in the eye's of a cold
shallow heart, that bleeds with thorns of pain on an
open wound. Seek those that are troubled, but be aware
of those recovering. Appearance is like an image in the mirror
of defiance, a reaction of negativity of an illusion, that we
think appears. A dream that whispers to be real, but only a image
of life unlived. As a team we conquer, distance becomes a
separation of a world lived apart. The memories don't seem to
fade, they just grow older as we hold on to them.

Maria Catania

Soaring Love

The flight of love...like the birds...So free...
    Gently soaring in the sky, never wanting to surface the earth,
With all its trials and tribulations...just to drift gently
    Down and around...Feeling God's love surrounding so peacefully.

Love is like that....Soaring its way to your heart....
    Gently immersing you....loving you....until you find yourself
In the midst of tranquility, gently feeding you...Nourishing you,
    Making you whole.

Love and God together...Steadying us...Making us strong
    And full of endurance.

Without love we are lost.
    How wonderful to realize this and know that it is true!

Lorraine Murphy

The Conflict Within

Turn around, look at me! Tell me what do you see?
Do you see the woman inside, struggling to be free?
Or do you see the child, excited, wide eyed ready to conquer the
    world?
Two people, yet one, who will be the victor, the woman or the girl?

The woman who wants to be held, to be sheltered, and loved.
Or the child so independent, brave, and strong, as free as a dove?
The woman who wants to hide from reality, cruelty, and the pain.
The girl so innocent and determined, who has nothing to lose, only
    to gain.

The woman crying out, stop! Hide! You'll be hurt, it's rough out
    there!
The child, eyes full of wonder, spirit soaring free, without a care.
the woman who feels alone, full of despair, hurt, and anger
The child, who wants to live life to its fullest, delighting in
    the danger!

Which one is right, which can best cope with the problems of the
    world?
Two people, yet one, who will be the victor, the woman or the girl?

Sandra O. Griggs

If Everyone

If everyone who drives a car, could lie a month in bed,
with broken bones and stitched up wounds or fractures of the head
and there endure the agonies that many people do,
they'd never need preach safety anymore to me or you.

If everyone could stand beside the bed of some close friend,
and hear the Doctor say, no hope, before that fatal end,
and see him there unconscious never knowing what took place,
the laws and rules of traffic I am sure we'd soon
embrace.

If everyone could meet the wife and children left behind,
and step into the darkened room where once the sunlight shined,
and look upon the vacant chair, where daddy used to sit,
I'm sure each reckless driver would be forced to think a bit.

If everyone who takes the wheel would say a little prayer
and keep in mind those in the car depending on their care
and make a vow and pledge themselves to never take a chance
then I'm sure this world of ours would suddenly advance.

Roy Richard Rohn

A Tribute To Our Children

We remember you as children small
And were always at your beck and call.
As it should be - to help and guide your way
Whether it be at work or play
We were proud of each one of you
As you went your way, talents to pursue,
Time passed - and a partner taken
But never were we ever forsaken.
You all chose a perfect mate to love
And children were a blessing from above.
You all have made our life a pleasure
And through this life we will always treasure.
The love you have given to us always
And the memory of our party days,
They all have been quite nifty,
But none compare with our "Fifty."
We thank you for your thoughtfulness
And our vows renewed we will always bless,
The family that has brought us happiness
May you all one day this love possess.

Gloria Gass

Love

Love is patient, love is kind
Some say that true love is blind
Love does not boast, and it not conceited
Love never fails: It cannot be defeated
Love is an emotion that can stop all time
If you forsake love, you commit the ultimate crime

Love always protects and perseveres
It will always be there to calm your fears
Love is not rude and it never lusts
Love is forgiving and it always trusts
Love does not envy; it knows no pride
Love is for all to see, it will not hide

Love does not keep a record of wrongs
And when you are weak, love will make you strong
Love will be there to catch you when you fail
Believe in love; it will get you through it all
Love is eternal; it will be there in the end
There is no greater love than dying for a friend

Kevin M. Conner

The Conveyance Of Life In All Forms

As the sun spits its usual sunlight, one can not help
noticing its presence peaking over the dim horizon
Almost appearing to realize that it will be one of the main
factors of the day
The soft cascading, flow of the morning dew brings forth
the harsh shrilling sound of the awakened inhabitants of the morn
There is a passive stiff, wind that manages to slightly tap many
of the leaves of the century young trees
Eagerly, glancing, outside my stain - filled window, I ponder
what it would be like if it was always this tranquil
But reality sets in like a malignant cancer
Once again the busy, multitude of passers-by and other civilians
will clutter the sidewalk as if they were ants scampering
across the fresh loaf
Gas guzzling machines, with their blatant sounds and that
element of danger, congest the asphalt paved streets
the rest of this day belongs to modern civilization

Mark Atkins

Fencing

We in our white and steel dart quickly back and forth
across the wasted grey landscape

Our shadows dance among the shards of broken dreams
that with gaudy bits of color pierce the solid fog of reality

You turn and stand; a screened mask covers your face...
(Oh canino longer even see your face?)

I thrust out my hand; a touching gesture
but I have forgotten the blade I hold

You flinch as it cuts and strike at me
(Or was it a caress?)
And I strike in return

Soon a thousand pinpricks of blood from a thousand jibes
have marred our precious appearances

But we cannot stop for you are attacking me
(Aren't you?)
And I am attacking you
(Oh God let me stop!)

And so we in our white and steel dart quickly back and forth
across our wasted grey love eternally praying to lose step or fault
or die.

James J. Saul

Through the Years

Once upon a time, many years ago.
You promised to be mine, for a lifetime or so.
Before our family, we said our vows.
We knew everything would work out some how.
We dedicated our love and thanked God above.
We loved through good times and bad.
All the happy times and sad.
Sometimes we were poor, but we held on even more.
God gave us four gifts from Heaven above.
A part of ourselves to cherish and love.
To raise and teach for awhile.
And everyday bring us a smile.
Though the way has been rough.
Our love has always been enough.
Through all of the years,
The laughter and the tears.
You held me in your arms.
And kept us safe from all harm.
I'm so thankful you loved me,
And together, we made a family.

Sharon Harris

Daily Aims

As I awake each morning, from dreams and thoughtless sleep.
I need to gather focus, so my brain can clearly see.
My mission for the day, or what may lie ahead.
The earthly things that I may do, as I arise from my bed.
And at that very moment, as with a sudden flash of light.
I now realize what I must do, to start each day out right.
Now on my knees with a sudden ease, I find my self in prayer.
Asking that my life be guided, by the omnipotent forces that bear
All the power that I will need as I start my "Daily Aims".
To open my mind, heart and soul to the power that has all claim,
Over life and death and everything else,
that I may encounter this day.
I now ask for the divine guidance,
To achieve my "Daily Aims".

Johnny C. Huff/The Midnight Writer

Weep

Tears are only vessels
Of long forgotten ideals
Thoughts and feelings, forgotten for now
Some-when, remember how it feels

I weep for what I'll never have
What will ever be denied
Tears of sorrow, remember the morrow
Pain, of tears yet uncried

I weep for what cannot be
Tears of pain and strife
But upon my heart, I swear to you,
I trust you with my life

A longing never to be fulfilled
A passion forever yearned
I weep for myself, but most of all
What will never be returned

Sarah McGregor

If

If we knew the last time we could see,
What all might we behold?
If we knew the last time we could speak,
Wouldn't we prize our words as gold?

If we knew the last time we could hear,
How much better would we listen?
If we knew we would lose our freedom,
What would be our last decision?

If we knew the last time we could touch,
What all would we want to feel?
If we knew the last dream we would hope for,
Wouldn't we want to make it real?

If we knew the last time we could swallow,
How much better would food taste?
If we knew our last moment on earth,
How much time would we waste?

If we knew the last time we could think,
What would go through our minds?
If we know the moment that Christ would return,
Who would be left behind?

Rachel Redden

From Within

"What does it take to be happy?" you ask,
The opposite of sad is what makes me glad.

"What does it take to be happy?" you say,
A hug from a friend on an unhuggable day.

"What does it take to be happy?" you beg,
A kind word from anyone can get rid of the dreads.

"What does it take to be happy?" you plead,
The answer's not easy, but look here and see...

What does it take to be happy? ... Oh-yes...
The answer is different for each I guess.

To find this answer look deep inside;
Remove all the fake stuff and remove all the lies.

Get open and honest as you can be;
And pray to the Lord for guidance to see.

For what makes you happy can't sit on a shelf...
What makes you happy comes from inside of yourself!

Linda Kay Gunnels

In Our Time

Who knows what the future holds in our time
Maybe the world will be full of crime
Or maybe the world will be full of peace
And we can all live our own lives
Instead of killing each other with guns and knives
And instead of hating each other
Let's start loving one another
'Cause if all the violence keeps leading to bloodshed
The world will have nothing but an empty bed
But if we lend a helping hand, we can make a stand
In our time we have to stop the crime
We'll all have to find a better way
And our dream will come true someday
We just have to pull together
Show we love one another
'Cause we can make it a better place
And if we make a mistake
We have the will to carry on
'Cause in our time
We have to stop the crime

Michael Lamphere

Bill

Back then in time I heard a cry, breathed a sigh and knew that I had
Crossed the bridge from childhood to womanhood to motherhood

There was a birth, I had a baby,....
He was 'precious'

The wonderment of nature of running streams of fishing, sunny days,
Many dreams; from day to day, and joy to joy, no longer a baby

I had a child, a little boy...
He was a 'darling'

Just like magic before my eyes, no time to realize, my child with
Childhood diseases had grown up, he gave me joy without measure

He'd become a teenager....
He was 'wonderful'

Today I look at him with his only son, a special little one and I know
that God above looks down in love, he says to me; I shook the tree
so that he could be your own, "it's my plan"

He is a man....
'He makes me proud'

Nancy Nestor

A Country Parade

This turned out to be a perfect day,
To have a parade with many surprises all the way.
There were lots of mounted horses, even miniature mules,
Seven llamas that walked proudly exactly to their cues.
Many vintaged cars, fire truck and Smokey the Bear,
It was so exciting to see, and many people were there.
The streets lined with visitors young and old.
There were candies thrown from vehicles, a sight to behold.
To take care of feeling hungry there was a hotdog stand,
Two boys driving along the streets calling "sodas for fifty cents."
To have the perfect atmosphere there was a Mariachi band,
The sound of these songs was oh so grand.
Home made floats gave the parade that special touch,
With such nice people on them for all of us to watch.
This is a small hamlet where the parade took place,
Where neighbors and strangers still say "hi" with a happy face.
The parade was just long-enough the time it lasted.
All was under control and went well,
So we will look forward to next year I can tell.

Ingeborg Seymour

Empty Vases

Lonely, empty vases, bring sadness to my heart.
They seem yearning to be filled, and happiness impart.
Not unlike lonely people, whose lives are empty too,
Not having precious contents, to cheer the somber view.
To hold unfolding flowers, as they tell their sacred mission,
That life, love, and beauty, can be had in our condition.
Graciousness and gladness may be hidden in the shade,
And grief may be the only means to joys that never fade,

Leonard G. Gwinn

Summer

Another month gone, time passes by,
Gaze at blue skies, watch birds as they fly.
Soft breezes blowing, some clouds way up high,
Soft breezes blowing, fade to a sigh.

Yes, summer is here, meadows so green,
Snow on the mesas soon won't be seen.
Rivers now roily soon will run clean,
Trees on the mountain, oft' changing scene.

The nights are still crisp, stars seem so near,
Now winter has past and so has the fear,
The dreams of the spring, at last coming clear,
Yesterday, so long ago, seems like last year.

What pleasures await with season so new?
What treasures await? I have not a clue.
I'll be happy I know, cannot be blue,
Pleasures and treasures, I'll discover a few.

Bernard A. Sowa

Reality

Reality, is a cold hard fact; it hurts
when it slaps you in the face.

Reality, is when you rely on hopes and dreams
to get you threw the everyday task of life,
and everything falls apart before your eyes
and nothing seems to last.

Reality, is what you make of it. If you
lie to yourself; reality is but a fairy tale.
But, if you are true to who you are than
it doesn't hurt as bad.

Reality is life; it's what you make of it.

Rosanna I. Stuckey

Bodega Bay Night

Cow pastures wave forth to a 6am sea
The horizon entraps a small fishing fleet
Long shadows shrink, sea gulls take flight
The morning takes over what used to be night
A window before me takes captive this scene
But Bodega Bay Night has captured me.

I peer past the sway of tall redwood trees
A wind gust whips-up a white frothy sea
And though I'm awaken, my thoughts aren't composed
My mind is lost to the night just closed
Bodega Bay Night has captured me...
But in the taking, my heart was set free.

I'll always remember this inn of the tides
The buoy bell rings, the wild flowers outside
But above all else, this one quiescent image before me
My love's reflection resting upon this window to the sea
As white linen waves flow down 'n around her still sleeping form
I'm cast back into the night past...
    (Bodega Bay Night...)
        (Where our love was born.)

Myron Lee Nash

Love Is...

Love is like clay in a potters hands,
No special purpose and no particular plans.
It's shaped and it's molded from deep in the heart,
And little by little a masterpiece has its start.
With heartfelt emotion and the progression of time,
A relationship is formed that's a treasure, both yours and mine.
In a world where loves daily crumble and fall,
Maintaining ours is an accomplishment to beat all.
People stare in amazement with envy in their heart,
At a cherished possession; our Love...an eternal work of art.

Alan J. Sowa

I Failed

The bodies beneath my feet,
The blood between my hands.
Was all I could think about.

My comrades-at-arms were scattered around.
With bullets and bayonets buried in them.
My mind filled with anguish.
And my heart filled with loneliness.

I wanted to die.
No longer did I want to live.
I wanted to be with my friends,
Lying there on the ground dying or dead.

I lifted the gun to my head.
And pulled the trigger.
I expected to hear the loud retort of a pistol.
But instead heard the soft dull click of an empty chamber.

I lowered my head and started to cry.
I cried because I couldn't be with my friends.
My final thought before I was taken away was,
I Failed.

Jeremy Staples

Tailor Made

Smooth.
Tightly pressed.
Ironed to perfection.
A wrinkle free society, stretches out the loosely fitted fabrics
over time...
Aging.
Excess skin cut off, like the hem of a dress which falls too long.
Designer faces; provide a soft luster of plastic smiles.

Damon Gonzalez

Clouds, Dust From the Feet of God

Sometimes we need to take a flight,
Above the clouds for peace and quiet.
We met someone we never knew,
That leaves a lingering thought or two!

There were three stops on my last trip,
Each stop passengers got up and left,
They trampled on my feet and toes,
When they left, the window seat I chose!

I settled in for the last short hop,
Two empty seats, I gave no thought.
A mother with a small whimpering boy,
Cancer at work, altho' he fought.

When the plane was up above the clouds
The little boy wanted to look out,
"Do you know what clouds are?" He ask,
I answered, "They water trees and grass!"

The words he spoke, I'd never thought,
"The clouds are dust from the feet of God."
He looked for God walking across the sky.
Making cloud dust, for you and I.

Mary K. Willey

Dad's Poem

We shared many laughs through the years.
Along with those times, we shed some tears.
In our lives; we shared so much,
never having to say.
But always feeling a loving touch.
When we were young, we would
ask when, where, and why.
When we were older, we never
asked about saying goodbye.
But for every beginning, there is an ending.
Now it's just us here, living and mending.
It's been twelve months, since we last spoke.
When you went to sleep, but never awoke.
So whenever we go, and whatever we do.
We will always carry our heart,
that misses and loves you.

Anthony T. Montenaro

To You, With Love

To remember a day, a thought,
    an experience that we shared together
is like a jewel, forever
    bright as the time we met,
never to be forgotten
    forever cherished, always revered.
Time passes swiftly,
    it fades away like leaves
that drop during the
    cool blasts of autumn.
But, the love we have
    for each other never diminishes,
retains its luster like new
    gold, found shining in the sun.
You will always be remembered,
    for you were first, my girl friend,
then my wife, the mother
    of our children. But, most
of all, you will always
    be, my one and only love.

Joseph Frangona

"The Rain"

Alone, hiding from my front;
I lose myself in the past.
Arms wrapped around myself, tears running down;
I listen to my heart break.
Thought it would've faded by now,
But in the deepest corner of my mind
Your tenderly remain.
You were the dawn that broke my nights
With your smile.
Though you were only here for awhile,
The honor lingers.
Every now and then I see you,
And I can still see the beauty in your eyes.
Oh, I remember the time when I stood beneath it.
Don't recall you ever looking so alive,
Or maybe it's what's lacking in me.
Always knew it felt wrong.
I've been shut away from the sun too long.
Don't know if I'll ever be the same.
I fear I'll never find my way out of the rain.

Sabrina J. Gray

The Candle

I'll hold my candle high -
And then perhaps I'll see the heart of this man.
Above all this sordidness of life, beyond the
    misunderstanding and strife -
It seems foolish, rash and sinful, too...
Just who am I to criticize, what I perceive
    with these eyes...
Still, I will hold my candle high -
And then perhaps I'll see the heart of this man.

Jill Hoffman

Our Youth Leaders

Dathyne and Norman were the two
That a lot of youth knew
As they shared lots of times
And gave values more than dimes

The senior youth had lots of fun
Even on days when there was no sun
For the Covingtons knew just what to do
To never ever make us blue

Activities were very meaningful to all
As much we learned and still recall
Those destinations were hard to beat
Remembering the great food we got to eat

An impact from this couple was made on all
As the witness of Christ is what we saw
Though each one aged along the way
It's memories like these that will always stay

Only God who meets our every need
Sent the couple that was needed to lead
A group of seniors along the way
To live as Christians every day

Pat Hawkins

Untitled

What a misty sound
To hear the trees late at night.
Seeing shadows of the branches full of leaves
In the moonlight of eternity.
To be alone with you in this world of solemn silence,
Is to feel that only you and I exist at this time
And that all our surroundings
Are praising us for our love.

Pinky Arteca

"Loretta"

Love is the greatest gift above all things,
Our hearts can be strengthened from the joy it
    brings.
Rejoicing in Heaven when two hearts grow
    fond,
Each heavy load is lighter because love builds a
    bond.
The burdens of life seem easier to bear,
Tomorrow looks brighter when there's someone
    to care.
Always thankful to the good Lord above
    for designing my friend and sending her with love.

Jennifer Pereira

Old Times We Treasure

I cherish my years as a child of the past,
The memories I made were meant to last.
When thinking back on the years that I miss,
The things we did for fun, how simple, how bliss.

Just riding a bicycle for hours on end,
What luxuries we had, tho no money to lend.
Maybe skating to town for chocolate ice cream,
Or playing shove-up on a boy/girl team.

Although, to them we had a life with no fame,
I wouldn't change one thing for a video game.
I'm proud I didn't know about the sins of cocaine,
Then, very few parents had hearts filled with pain.

Wouldn't it be nice to leave to your heirs,
A childhood like ours - with very few cares,
To slow down and enjoy a bit of life's pleasure,
Just a taste of the old times we all seem to treasure.

Judith C. Griffin

Broken Dreams

I dedicated my life to only you,
The person that I thought could make all
my dreams come true,
But somewhere down life's unfair paths,
I lost your love and all the dreams we had,
We both got caught in this worldly wrath,
Everything we once had now seems so
desolate and sad,
His heart has built an emotional wall,
He pretends he can't hear my heartbreaking calls,
I know now that our relationship has taken
a doubtful fall,
Before you leave I have just one thing to say,
I loved you more yesterday than I ever will today,
But all of the memories we have made together,
They will always be the one thing that I will
cherish forever.

Tiffany Potts

Sunshine

Spread a little sunshine where ever you go
Make life worthwhile for someone you know.
Some people are sick and need loving care
That is why we are here
Make your mark in this world and
Make it a better place
For the human race.

Rosemary Starks

Untitled

As you begin to accept your defeat with your head held high
And your eyes open, with the grace of a woman, not the grief of a
child.
You build your roads on today because tomorrow's ground are too
uncertain for plans,
and futures have a way of falling in mid-flight.

Rodger Tabb II

The Ecstasy of the Setting Sun

White clouds with hints of pale red, drapes across the sky.
    Now sunset like magic softly comes in view.
A misty outline like drifting art is flowing,
    Its halo gives off a crimson colored hue.
With soft tint the setting sun spreads across the heavens.
    There before my eyes, an un-seen artist dabbles in water paint.
Gray streaks edge in, as dark shades creep into the view.
    So as the sun rays, like a magician etch softness over shadows.
With anticipation, I watch as evening pencils through.

So full of radiance, the sky is a masterpiece of glory.
    In sections, the misty blue invades a portion in the sky.
Some how a deeper shade takes over, simply changing colors.
    Erasing sketches, while slowly passing by.
I look once more to glimpse the setting sun,
    Its view now is descending in the distant west.
What a heart warming creation, out there, so vividly expressed.
    Oh sun light, oh sun set, you're beautiful.
Glowing in the heaven for all to see.
    Who has never shared your shining hour of glory?
    "Has missed an ecstasy."

Mildred Bomar

The Power of Love

To be clean, lean and mean
To go with unconquerable determination
To know, to know you can do anything
You can accomplish anything at all
The feeling builds up inside and as it bursts forth
New things come into creation
Abundance, wealth, happiness, joy and love
This feeling, what is this feeling?
This feeling is the power of love
The power of God - Almighty and just
Divine actions, Divine thoughts
Things that bring contentment and an even-mindedness
that will take you through all things
Knowing, a knowing that God is right there beside you all the
time, holding your hand and encouraging you to go forward
ever more boldly, walking in the Light of Truth
The Light is unconquerable - it always prevails
Burning to ashes all that choose not to conform
For the Law of Life is Love and Light
The only thing that feels truly right

MaryBeth MacQuaide

Paper Clip Families

People in families -
    an endless string of paper clips
        holding fragments of events together
        endlessly changing
Two pieces here
    two or three there
        coalescing into a chain.
Chained together - functional
    then only in the holding -
        to be pulled apart,
        to be used,
Then bent...broken...discarded

Mary Ellen Boll

Send Me the Silence

Send me the silence that comes
in the night, send me the silence you find
in the moment of a new daylight. I wish and
seek and search for it because within this silence
you do not have to share, it is your to do with as you
please. Send me the silence that you find in the
warmth of someone's love wrapping you up like an
angel's wraps wings around you, wanting
this warmth and the silence of it never to stop
or fade away. The silence sometimes can
feel like a gift from above because there
can never be another sound that we ache
to have. Sometimes throughout the day
we wait and watch for just the right
time to ask, please send me the silence
I need, just for a little while if you please.

Wanda Bobicz

Thanksgiving

As I sit and wonder, Oh Lord, What do I have to be Thankful for?
My heart is so full of sadness and sorrow,
And my life is so much emptier than before.
I have lost my most cherished friend,
And it seems as though my grief shall never end.
But in my heart I know, that wherever I go from hear,
the things that she taught me, I will always hold dear.
She taught me to be strong and courageous,
to follow things through to the end.
And to touch the lives of others, so they know they've met a friend.
She taught me to look only at the good things throughout the years,
and not to waste time on the heartache and tears.
So, Lord, Please take care of the angel I once knew,
And this year I will be thankful for you.

Rebecca Sinnott

Addiction

Like snakes through a roaring sea,
I add to my own addiction.
I follow them,
and hence forth, the movement.
Through the wilderness I see
from earth's view of mother nature's offspring.
Bubbles through a cloud
bring me up, and drop me down.
I look into his eyes
as he looks into mine.
Expressionless face,
with his hippie love beads holding a medallion.
Curly dark hair...dark eyes...beautiful face.
An angel? True beauty?
I don't want to leave his stare.
Looking up..stars
green emeralds on my ceiling.
Secluded in a beautiful field of daisies
I prance naked in the trees...and I become one of them,
with moments slight.

Kimberly Kimball

Kisses from the Sky

As God reached out his hand, for him to come along.
Leaving footprints on the clouds, before we knew it he was gone.
His spirit left the room, and flew to high above.
Leaving nothing but a trace, of his everlasting love.
Now he looks down from the heavens, watching over you.
He wishes he was here, and that he made it through.
Even though he's gone, his memory will never die.
And, when the stars are twinkling, he's
blowing kisses from the sky.

Whitney Leigh Hilt

A Tranquil Moment

Tranquil moments, we have so few,
to truly enjoy through and through,
when we place all worries to the side,
and our minds ride the peaceful tide.

Release all tension, worries, and fears,
dry the tears brought on by the years,
leave your mind void of confusion,
making peace your only illusion.

Concentrate on the positive,
bask in the warmth it creates,
soak up the rays of contentment,
revel in its peaceful traits.

My road to inner peace,
is not your route to take,
you must create your own trail,
where your own peace you'll partake.

Tawanda J. Tompkins

The Snow

If you have ever taken the time
To watch the falling snow
You'll find such similarities
Between the two of you - you've never known

When it's falling
It's as soft and innocent
As a newborn child
Left unattended it becomes
Like an adolescent
Firm and stubborn;
Unable to chide

Then left for a few hours
In the sardonic wind
It'll get as vicious and dangerous
As a warrior;
with a beast within

But when the wonderful sun appears
It becomes as meek and tender
And finally disengages
Just like you - will finally be

Kerry Faith Ann-Marie Hyre

One Man's Prayer

Each evening just before I sup
I pause and take my paper up,
to see what happened in the world that day
Most everything that meets my eye
Would surely make a preacher sigh,
please Lord don't let them treat your world this way

It seems that every article
does not contain a particle,
of humanistic values we hold dear.
They say we're running out of room
expound each prophesy of doom,
and keep us in a constant state of fear.

How nice it could be if they would
print all the news that's really good,
and emphasize the virtues that they find.
Instead of cardiac arrest
our hearts would have a time of rest,
and all the world would live with peace of mind.

George Bloczynski

66

A 4th of July Celebration, When You're Alone!

I love to listen to the songs of these birds
a mixture of chirping and chwettering emerges

From dozens of very old sycamore trees,
planted along side a brook with an architect's ease!!

To give a real natural look to this "my" park!
that will be closed for safety, after dark!!

However early in the morning, there's a mysterious stillness
when nature alone is God's greatest witness!

The water of the stream is stroking overhanging moss
while fishes are breaking the surface, when I toss

Breadcrumbs to the now gathered fish
rushing to this food, they don't want to miss.

A little later in the day, when it still is cool
a crowd comes in, some like to use the community pool.

Some string up a net to play badminton,
while others put on their baseball-mitten!

More people are coming with radios and blankets,
pots and pans, looking for electrical outlets.

Barbecues are lit, this crowd is geared on fun!!!
It's the 4th of July, it last after midnite, when firework is done!!!
Johanna A. Garretson

Robin's Bass

Now Robin was a voluptuous gal,
Real down to earth trustworthy pal.
She loved all natural things in life.
Animals, fish and birds she took in stride.

A beautiful day in May her goal,
Running down to the lake with her fish pole,
Along bounces Sammy, her frisky dog.
It's fishing time and no time for a jog.

Into the boat and a pull on the motor cord,
Off they go to their favorite corner.
Sammy is barking, he loves to fish.
Catching the big one is their only wish.

A line in the bay with a little play,
Nice big catch would make her day.
A strike at last, a tug and run,
One hard jerk and the line would be done.

She reeled in a bass as a long as her arm.
And hooted and whistled like down on the farm.
After removing the hook, she fould the law states,
Bass season wasn't open 'til a later date.
Beverly G. Bacon

City Of Brotherhood

Help me build each city of the world
as a place of truth and peace of mind
there our goals and dreams come true
where a friend's embrace we always find

Now's the time to test our talent
trust each other from the heart
success will follow as we try - please do
young and old can play their part

Start this day to build our place
as solid bricks we'll use good deeds
search out friends of every race
as tools we'll use good hands to fill their needs

Watch this world grow bright and warm
words of praise will be our victory song
our Father will keep each home from harm
and perfect peace will be our reign!
Robert J. Keefe

Rite of Passage

I see hooves and knobby knees
    Skinny legs and long sinewy muscles
        Smooth skin and dark strength

Dust disturbed and airborne
    Mud flying and splotching

Flying hooves down the cliff
    Eyes covered, unable to see

Where do we go? How can we stand?
    Sharp pain on skull, stars form a circle

Head pounding its own drum
    Gash pain going to get worse

Red river runs from gash
    Across skin, warm and muddy

Quiet now, who survived?
    Who died, screaming?
        So sorry. Why?

Caught up in regalia, customs and strength
    Pride of the Tribe, must be a partner

Trained. Tried. Lost. Hurting.
    Try again next year, Great Warrior.
    Lenore Schneider

Impasse

Sunk in a quagmire of deepest thought
Over my morning cup of tea
I pondered now
Wondering just how
To express my thoughts in poetry.

My wayward thoughts swirled 'round and 'round
I could almost see them move
"Me first! Me first! They seemed to say
"Write about me, about me today!"
Now! Which one should I choose?

I didn't know what helpless fury
The agony of choice could be
When a graceful yellow butterfly
Past my window came winging by.
Making up my mind for me.

Beauty! Whether made by nature or man
The one enhances the other
We all play a part
In God's world of art
Please! Let's not tear it asunder.
    Doris Kohler-Shockley

Biocidal Girl

What is with that aluminum smile
That tinfoil reception upon your mile
What's with the mercury bulbs in your eyes
No steam to be seen; just cherry red skies
And what's with the ghost white pale of your skin
Is it fright on outside or the terror within
What's with your dynamite, elliptical lips
That clash with your divine, pivoting hips
I know not your image, or who you may be
But when you explode, do it for me
    Clint Gray

Wildwood

Ohh, come to the church in the wild wood
No sweeter place on this earth.
The congregation are here
for a new Birth.

To learn and hear about the "Lord"
Why "He" created this earth for us,
How "He" Loves us and cares
about what we do.

We all know this is true
and pray "He" will see us thru.
One day at a time
until "He" calls us home.

The earth he made for us
The Manna he gives to us.
The clothes on our back
"He" sees we have plenty.

Why does some question this
and kill and lie?
If they would open their eyes
and come to the church in the wildwood.

Florence E. Maxwell

You Are The Woman

You are the woman I've always loved and I know I always will
I've loved you for so long and I do still
There'll never be another one for me you're my one and only girl
I need you more than anything else in the world
Stay by my side where there's nothing to hide
Let your feelings flow like the river, is wide
You are the woman I really need
You are the woman I love indeed
You are the woman that makes me high
You are the woman that makes me try
When life gets me down and no one else is around you're always there
You're my special lady and you're my lover too
And I hope I'm special to you
You're the best friend I've ever had
Stay by my side where there's nothing to hide
Let your feelings flow like the river is wide
You are the woman I really need
You are the woman I love indeed
You are the woman I really need
You are the woman I love indeed

Gregory J. Wessel

Plumed Pets

Chickity, chickity, chick chick chick.
Three bald heads with combs on top, so chic!
Wrinkled faces glitteringly white
With red wattles aglow in the light.
Their black diamond eyes ever alert.
Songs of harsh cackles sung to divert
Large hawks and predators seen stalking
More cackles send the rogues 'a rockin'.
Bird feathers, polka dotted, they wear like shawls.
Such stylish guinea hens are not "en glass" fowls.
Each dawn they fly the coop. One by one
Play follow the leader in the sun
Foraging freely, they build nests of hay.
O'er hills and knolls they did their chores today.
Wandering homeward when day turns to night;
Getting home safely is their main delight.
Fare game are loose guinea hens
That stray afar from their pens.
A curfew bell resounding, "Tingaling, tingaling".
"Chick chickity chick"! Chirping guinea hens aroosting.

Clara Rose

A Mind Stirring Trip

So, stress got the best of ya' at work today.
The wife burnt dinner, and the kids can't play.
It's raining outside, so they're staying in;
And yo' nerves can't handle the drop of a pin!

So, what'll ya' do on a day like today?
Ya' gotta be careful of all that ya' say.
Once words are spoken, ya' can't call'em back.
Yo' foot could land where yo' tongue is at!

Take a mind stirring trip!
Travel by train, or a great big ship!
Better yet, take a rocket to mars!
Tour other planets! Ride shooting stars.

Let yo' mind do things that ya' really like.
Don't fuss with the family! Take a mind hike!
Wrestle with an octopus, let yo' self win!
It's yo' dream; yo' mind! Don't let his thoughts in!

When ya' return from yo' mind stirring trip,
Ya' won't be scared that yo' tongue might slip!
Ya' kin' talk to the wife; enjoy the kids at play;
And ya' won't haft'a watch every word ya' say!

Elizabeth Miree-Staples

Sardonic Mercy

Today I asked to be forgiven
...for my pessimism
Today I asked to be forgiven
...for my awareness
Today I asked to be forgiven
...of any doubts
Today I asked to be forgiven
...for the way I used to be
Today I asked to be forgiven
    what sometimes "makes up" me...
Today I asked to be forgiven
    of the attitude you see in me occasionally...
Today I asked to be forgiven
    for all the things I haven't done...
Today I asked to be forgiven
    for all the things I have to do...
Wouldn't you?

V. Joy Haag-Smith

Love's Masquerade

Oh, can a being such as he,
Mend thy weeping heart?
Torn like roses yet unthorned,
Their sweet nectar leads fools apart.

Sore is thy soul, scorned by love,
Oft taken flight on angel's wings.
Eyes revealing pain best forgot,
Lest they remember the joy love sings.

A master to innocence is he,
Promising loyalty and to never depart.
I think not, thy heart is broken,
Behind his deceiving masque, he hath taken a part.

But thy burden of night, heaven's light shall heal,
Its peace will set thee free.
Once blinded by two lover's wrath,
Thou sorrow hath let thee be.

Requited love can smell so sweet,
Like the scent of a withering rose,
The mending of spirit once thieved and stark,
Will lay to rest, again blooming, exposed.

Tracey T. Haney

Rabbi

His hurried steps
That determined look
He's enroute to helping someone

When I say hello
He'll stop to chat
Knowing that his goals will still be done

He makes us feel special
No one gets ignored
Our worth is increased by his presence

The beauty of his words
Endear my heart
There is no pretense with each utterance

He is our mentor
His life is our guide
Without him we would falter

I hold him in reverence
He keeps me in awe
Nothing about him would I alter.

Mary A. Stolle

Mother's Heart, Mother's Hope

Oh, how my heart does bleed today
For all my children so violently gone
For those imprisoned by their own thoughts
That tell them there is no hope
That tell them they must kill or be killed
That tell them life is worthless.

Oh, how my heart does mourn today
For all my children dying of AIDS
Infected with HIV
Strung out on Drugs
Selling death to their own
Who believe that life is hopeless.

Oh, how my heart does die today
For all my babies having babies
Locked in jails they built for themselves
Not remembering the dreams of their mothers
Neither striving to rekindle a spark of those dreams
Nor searching for worth and hope.

Oh, that my heart might sing today
With hope for what yet might come.

Louvenia Magee Gafney

God's Handiwork

The morning sky was hazy-smoky blue,
Hoarfrost arrayed the trees and laced the grasses, too.
Beyond the frosted trees, a rosy glow was hinting
The coming of the morning sun
Whose rays the sky was tinting.

The rising sun was burnished gold
While seashell pink and rose
Upon the interlacing clouds
Soft colors did bestow.

Then through the gauzy, silv'ry mists
The seashell pink and rose
Did subtly shade the jewelled trees
And softly tinge the snow.

He who paints the morning sky
And snows upon the sod
And jewels trees and grasses, too
Only could be God.

Frances Fast Parker

Marmalade Mandy

The marmalade cat
Whose name is "Mandy"
Thinks from her window sill,
"Life is handy!"

She has "Three Squares"
and a bed to lie on;
People to play with;
laps to sigh on.

She knows that a cat
helps make a house a "Home";
She knows, as well, she shouldn't roam,
Mandy sees (as dawn is breaking)
That the curly - haired dog
Next-door is waking.

The curly-haired dog
(Whose name is "Roy")
Is small and feisty
and, surely, no joy!

Roy sees Mandy, and barks, "Hello!"
Mandy says, "Roy, Dear"... "Time will show"

Marylee F. Machado

"The Beast"

The night rolls in like the haunting Beast
Darkness in your heart
The wolves of Loneliness are unleashed
There'll be no mercy - devouring their prey
Abandoned by love it's the hell you'll pay
As the new dawn arises, sometimes they sleep
But don't be fooled my friend
It's your trail they're gonna keep
They feed off your sorrow
Your tears quench their thirst
Alone in your head - Yeah!
That's when they attack the worst
So you seek out new love... Seems the only thing to do
With their torment and pain you hope you'll be through
The deepest of emotions though, Love you can't pretend;
This they sense and they're back again
They laugh at your efforts, but true feelings you cannot hide
Only in time...
    Will the beast subside

Pray A. Chambler

When Summer Is Over

When mist becrowns the dead damp leaves,
When the deejay asks us, "When will it freeze?"
When the moon in full shines on the trees,
Summer will be over.

When pumpkins lie upon the ground,
When hickory nuts fall with a pattering sound,
When sweaters in closets need to be found,
Summer will be over.

Then the sun will retreat a spell,
Then the days won't be hot as hell!
And we to each other with joy will tell,
"The construction barrels fell!"
When summer is over.

God, grant us the grace,
This summer to face.

Alicia Neel

Life's Joy

You and I care two of a kind.
We love to laugh, we need to cry.

Happy that I'm growing up and learning how to live.
How to love, how to weep, how to give.
My heart is strong, my patience long, and all I really want,
Is to be with you, I love you.

Our Wedding Day has come to pass the sun was in the sky.
Moms, and Dads, and Grandma, a twinkle in their eye.
To say "I love you" everyday, to show how much I care.
The Lord has answered my prayers.

We dreamed of children of our own, that day had come one June.
Our son was born, the sun was warm, the Lord shown down on us.
When he looks at you with those big brown eyes, when he smiles,
It's ear to ear. What a joy, what a joy, that's our boy.

Old and grey and happy for our many, many years.
Of youth, and laughter, and songs that we sang.
But now our life's an open book for everyone to see.
Cause it's us, it's we, You and me.

Martie Larson

Memories

At times I sit and ponder in my chair
  The memories that many years have left behind.
They spring unfettered from the depths of time
  And grace the ever moving pictures in my mind.

Fond memories that wrinkled cares erase
  And spread sweet smiles across my deeply withered face.
A young and very pretty face I see
  Beneath bright golden locks which first attracted me.

We danced through out the star-lit summer night.
  In love's embrace 'till in the East appeared the light
That marked the dawn and sent us homeward bound
  To plant our new-found dreams in matrimonial ground.

The years we shared have brought a vast array
  Of treasured suns as well as threat'ning clouds of grey
That often proved a lesser ill than thought
  And fears were chased by joy the rays of sunshine brought.

Today we face the winter's setting sun
  And rest ourselves from daily tasks routinely done.
We thank the Lord for heaven's gracious gift
  Of memories that give us all a needed lift.

Lewis E. Walton

New Arrival

Just as everything was still,
  two persons came up over the hill

Everything was quiet as they could see,
  they asked for a place, but most said sorry

So they found a barn, not the best of taste,
  but they weren't picky for a resting place

Under the roof of this foundation,
  would be born the king of all the nation

So go ask the world this simple thing,
  do they know who is this king of kings?

Charles Lee Blackshear Jr.

There A Room

There a room once lit the pages of the night until lines
Gold from the mountain's tip wrote light across orange trumpet-
vines
Blowing by grandma's house. Chairs warmed where all the walls
were
Shelves of books lined up in rows to speak the secrets of
themselves.
Marmalade and muffin mornings Josephus called to me
To search and find within his mind life in antiquity.
Silk sunshine draped down though lace and curled about the floor
Where I pondered the human race allured of ancient lore
Enrapt. But war's misery sharp like lightning splits a tree
Split my heart. Tears terrified stopped at doorbell's clanging glee
Till gentle step and gracious words Gilead's balm adored
Spoken white dove of the soul gladness of life outpoured
Welcoming loved all who sought his face, came to his door to find
Who daily in the temple prayed blessing for all mankind
Rest and heart-hope, refuge from the storm, food for life today.
I hid my books from strangers eyes far slowly backed away
Yet patient still he smiled on me, life's great grand governing key
Almighty God best His children loves, and grandpa dear loved me
For him we knelt and thanked the Lord, the trumpet-vines and me.

Kathryn Gainey

The Perfect Day

My idea of a perfect day,
is when everything is perfect and OK.
When the sun is shining bright,
So all the beautiful nature is in sight.
When the flowers are blooming
And the caterpillars are cocooning.
When I see a lot of smiling faces
And go to nice sunny places.
When I'm climbing trees, and there are no flees.
When I can play my violin,
And play a golf game and win.
When I can eat a lot of food
Without being rude.
When everything is cool,
And I can go swimming in a pool.
When the grass is green,
And when my brother Tony is nice not mean.
When I can smell the flowers, for hours and hours
When everything is perfect and OK,
Now that's my idea of a perfect day!

Michael Miller

Cloak of Might

It was just an old brown jacket,
the one my father wore
but it holds special memories
of love and faith and more.
The day his spirit left him
I brought it to my home
and hung it in the closet
then stood there all alone
reflecting back to times gone by
of fun and laughter sweet...
and knew that at his passing
his life had been complete.
Whenever I am lonely or feeling kind of down
I go into that closet and put my arms around
that familiar old brown jacket; I'm glad I kept it round.
Birthday parties, Christmas cheer, errands to the store
as memories come flooding back, my heart is filled once more.
It may be just an old brown jacket-solid and pocket torn
but to me a cloak of might and warmth to keep for evermore.

Judy Ryan

The Child Within the Adult

Dear little child so meek and mild,
my heart melted the first time you smiled.

I didn't intend for you to take care of me,
but through all I've learned that's what I see.

I was a child inside, I know that's no excuse,
my lack of knowledge caused you so much abuse.

As I learn more knowledge my eyes can see,
that I need to heal the wounds in me.

There is so much to heal you and I,
the pain is so deep, I sometimes sit and cry.

Dear little child I want there to be,
a better life so you have a chance to see...

The love and wonder that I never had,
from all the abuse that's made you so sad.

I want to help you become your true self,
because I've been listening to my inner Elf.

I'm beginning to see a shining new light,
with God's love, life looks so bright.

Oh, little child come journey with me,
together through life we'll happily be...
        Sherry See-Pence

Our Comet of Love

Our love was a comet crashed into the sun, blistered
half begun, dashed about fly flames, a flower caught by
passion's wild fire.
Our love burned brightly with brilliant clashes of
personality and light.
Our love-torched by changing angles of desire, flashed
vividly, then lingered briefly in its demise.
        Marion Boykin Jr.

Edifice of Peace

A worldwide "Edifice Of Peace" we can build
for all of mankind who may enter a willed.
We're all created equal...every race, color and creed!
Diversity's a blessing enriching our needs.

It's so simple to build; if we all do our part,
just look at His rules, our foundation and start.
Down through history we strayed from His path.
Look where it let us...to a world filled with wrath!

We're given a conscience and free will to choose.
If we all use them wisely....no one will lose!
This "Edifice Of Peace" may we all say again
can be built for us all...we just need to say...When!
        Patricia A. Wessel

Untitled

Familiar are, these emotions inside.
I was torn apart, by theme yesterday.
Ravaged my heart, glad I'm alive.
I must have won, the good ones stayed.
Honesty and openness, are what they profess.
Avoiding the point, will keep you apart.
A sadness if, you do not confess.
A great fulfillment if, you aim for the heart.
Some things in the life, you don't have to expose.
There are things in this life, you must reveal.
It's what's in your mind, that I want to know,
And what's in your heart, that I want to feel.
If you help me find, these things that I seek.
It makes all the difference, so these waters run deep.
The deeper these waters, the stronger the pull.
So safe from the rocks, they stay far below.
        Lucas Chavez

The Joy You Bring

The joy you bring is through the kind things that you do for us all.

The joy you bring is by picking us up when we are down and there
appears to be know one that cares.

The joy you bring is shining the lights from heaven on us and
pouring down the blessings and the love from heaven.

The joy you bring is allowing us to grow and find out that all of
our trials come to make us strong.

The joy you bring is holding our hands by day and by night, and
letting us stay closely in touch with you, Jesus.

The joy you bring is opening up doors, so that we can step on
through for the victory.

Through the joy you bring, the victory is mine, mine, mine;
and Jesus, is mine, mine, mine.

The joy you bring, Jesus, is unspeakable joy.
The Joy You Bring.
        Rita Marks

Mind, Body and Soul

Dearest Keith,
At times my mind remains is fluster
For I do not know how to express my feelings toward you.
In order for one to fully express themselves,
Their mind and heart must be as one.

As I watch you sleep,
I replay all we shared that day
Both good and bad

As I feel you breathe
I want to have the rhythm of your heartbeat.

When I feel your hands,
I wish to have my hand melt into yours.

When I look into your eyes,
I want you to see how much I truly love you.

When I sit or lay close to you,
I want to blend my body so I can feel all within you.

Mind, body and soul.....

Always know, for as I tell you so,
I solely am yours mind, body and soul.
        Theresa D'Ascenzo

For Brian

With broken wings and shattered dreams
I could no longer fly.
My heart was crushed, my song was hushed,
I was left alone to cry.
Then in you walked and sweetly talked
with words that healed my wounds.
You planted seeds that fulfilled my needs
so now a pure love blooms.
My wings are strong, I sing a song
from deep within my heart.
I'm free to fly up to the sky,
but why should I depart?
For you are here so very near
and you are all I need.
So fly I might, but every flight
backtracks to you with speed.
With emotions grand, I'll take your hand
and look to God above,
and thank Him now for what we've found
a great and boundless love.
        Kristi Sowell

Giving Birth to Dancing Stars

Out of the pure chaos of her soul
she was able to look inside her reflection
and
labor to bring forth gems of meaning
thus
giving birth to dancing stars.
She dried her tears on a handkerchief called poetry.
She admired her efforts conceived in revelation
and
spoke that is good.

Penny L. Washington

Island of Death

I spent hours running through a sea of death.
Working my way toward your immaculate island.
This hole I leave darkened by strong and powerful voices.
Towering so high I can't see the tops of them.
I tread through a lifeless pool of blood.
Running faster toward my doom.
Lurking amongst the shadows.
Hidden in a passionate-less trail.
Is my fate.

Michelle Marie Harlan

The Intangible

Why does love paint my life with angst,
And fill my heart with pain?
But in spite, I try and try,
And find it all in vain.
Is it fact or fantasy,
This emotion undefined?
Some cultures say that it can't be,
But I know it owns my mind.
People live and breathe and kill and die,
For this something so intense,
And when we try to analyze,
It never will make sense.
To give and take this complex thing,
Depends on how we're taught,
So if the game was played too much,
Then in the web we're caught.
Maybe still — in days ahead,
We'll finally see the light.
I have a feeling though by then,
I'll be gone from your sight.

Dana Cunningham-Claassen

Goodbye

Sometimes in life we have to say goodbye
and when you do you want to cry.
Saying goodbye is hard to do,
and when you say goodbye, you're sad, and blue
people come and people go
but not to fear and not to cry
for one day if you believe
your paths may once again go by.

Erica Boyer

Gum

You sit in a wrapper unchewed and peaceful,
Not knowing what to expect.
All of a sudden you're snatched,
Being chewed, grinded, and mashed.
It goes on forever until you lose flavor.
Then you are spit into the darkness
Of a trash can standing still.
Never seen again!

Sierra Chapman

Look Through The Window

Look through the window
What do you see?
I see trees covered with snow
I see fences sparkling like webs in the sun
I see roofs as white as pearls
I see streets that are so pretty
I see sidewalks that are so nice
I see things that no one else does
Through the winter light, light or night,
Night or light, winter is beautiful.

Mirjana Miladinovic

A Family's Love

The east bound train was crowded one
   cold December day.
The conductor shouted "tickets" in the
   old old fashioned way.
A little boy, in sadness, his hair was
   black as coal.
He said "I have no ticket, Sir," and
   then his story was told.
"My father, he's in prison. He's nearly
   blind they say, and I have gone
   to get him this cold and snowy day.
My brothers and sisters would all be
   very glad, if I could only
   bring home my poor blind dad."
The conductor could not answer or
   remark from that last reply.
But with his rough hands he wiped the
   tears from his eyes.
He said "you sit there little one, you sit just where you are.
And you'll never need a ticket as long as I'm on this car."

James Smith

A Rose Of Rarest Find

In the loneliest, lowest valley
   Where the sun could seldom shine
Along a path dark and fearsome
   Grew a rose of rarest find

The mountain top could never sustain
   A flower such as this
And only the valley could produce
   Its fragrance of heavenly bliss

I lingered and touched the beauty
   That only a few would see
For not all would walk those lower depths
   And none had traveled there with me

Amid the deepening, threatening shadows
   I found this treasure there
And though bid to climb and leave the valley
   I'll never forget this rose so rare

Bonnie Caldwell VanDyke

Truth

Another's act does not concern me... My job is neither to condemn nor be condemned but to forge ahead on my own path of right doing.

If one delays the birth of love in one's self it is not for me to say..

For truth is truth and all else is built on such a tottering foundation that in the end, its own weakness will cause it to crumble and fall.

Jacqueline Fiedler

Time

Clocks are weird about keeping time.
They do a good job if you remember to wind.
You may set one back to an hour ago
But that's not good if it's running slow.

It's better to go back a year,
or even more, if you have no fear
of those events of yesteryear.

It's strange how in the past
We thought those good times,
were going to last,
We thought someday
We'd pay all the bills,
and just relax with all the frills.

But things don't work like that sometimes
So I tell myself "I'm in my prime".
Get up - work, don't be slow,
Cause without that check
I sure can't go!

    Marie Dickerson

The Ride

Every morning, I awake to a glorious light,
I see Your precious smile and Your awesome might,
As I journey to work, it is a special ride,
For You've taken all my anguish and rid me of my pride.

All my life I've ridden on things that make a rumble,
But Lord, today I'm riding with the One that makes me humble,
And as my journey takes me in so many directions,
My heart tells me that You'll always keep me in your protection.

Sometimes it has been up and down and pretty rough,
But my Lord has been with me and made me real tough,
For even through my youth and into adulthood,
I've always known that God has been around my neighborhood,

Lord, what is special is You chose me even through my sin,
And You've shown me that following you, I'll always win,
So my ride continues with Your love which is no loss,
For the vehicle I ride is your son upon the cross.

    Charlie Bustamante

A Day Dream

While sitting in school one day
Looking out at the grass so green
I saw with my eyes, a vision
Some people may call it a dream.

'Twas a very high mountain of knowledge
And a teacher that looked real mean
With a ruler of honor and obedience
Gee, I'm glad it was only a dream!

She pointed the ruler at the mountain
Then turned to the class and just screamed!
"You will never be successful, my children
If you sit at your desk and just dream!"

I've felt someone tap on my shoulder
And say, "You are idle, it seems."
So I took my books and got busy
What a day, what a life, what a dream.

    Linda L. Gould

Cowboy Tune Up

Well this cowboy got a tune up
You thought his pick-up truck of course
But he actually had the vet out
For a tune up on his horse

Well they filed the teeth and timed the hooves
And gave him all his shots
Then stuck a thermometer in him
To see if he had the hots

They looked him over real good
And patched a nick or two
Then decided by examination
He needed a brand new shoe

They filled him up with fresh oats
With an extra shot of hay
Then they put a saddle on him
And he ran smooth all day

Well the cowboy he felt real good
Cause his horse was nothing ill
But he darn near had a heart attack
When the vet gave him the bill

    Laughlin N. MacKay

The History Of Humanity

From two people to four,
mothers gave birth to more.
As our population grew,
we all wondered why mysterious animals flew!
We looked up to the night sky,
how could continuous burning fires fly?
The Chinese wrote their long lasting fantastic history on papers,
and got together the Great Wall makers.
Large European ships rowed the never resting fierce ocean,
what used to be a quiet world was in a sudden motion.
The Spanish discovered the great lands of America,
and conquered the mighty empire of the Inca.
The English fought the French,
USA fought England in secret trench.
The Wright brothers uncovered the mystery of flight,
in W.W. II great wars fought in the great sky with might.
As we landed on the moon and explored space,
we couldn't forget the great space race.
No matter how much we explore, how much we discover more,
and how much we will expand,
we will always be held in God's hand.

    William Liu

Rebel

He was a Rebel Without a Cause
Knew his lines and read them with his heart
The envy of all, handsome and tall
His passion was seen and felt
By all who looked through his gloomy, yet glowing eyes
So young was he
How could it be
That one so wonderful and full of life
Could just fade away one night
It still makes me cry
That the Rebel still searching for a cause,
Could die.
When I hear the name James Dean
Sadness surrounds me
He was just taking a drive
And as his car spun and crashed
The life of a legend was soon vanished.

    Neda Hakimi

Untitled

A winter storm flooding white.
As the sea soars,
the wind rocks frantically,
while a delicate whisper
of smeared shadow
begs humbly into the cold...

Wading past the brightly lit houses,
his only source of warmth,
his head is bent down to his waist,
too ashamed of his present state,
and too cold to stand proudly;
the creature trudges along.
Testing different forms of shelter,
and not finding a suitable one
to fulfill its expected task.
The discouraged outcast continues his perambulation...

The sheltered, apathetic towards
the wanderer's exigencies, proceed routinely,
without a worry in the world, or one hint of feeling for others.
Thus, the misunderstood vagabond moves along, untouched.

Natalie Tal Peled

My Grand-Daughter

What a blessing when your daughter is born,
What a joy when a grand-daughter is brought forth,
For the rest of a grand-mothers day, you can
See the world with the eyes of a child's haze.
Your beauty has no limits, colors, styles, fears,
Sorrows, race, or religion, from her eyes you're
Only Love; Grand-daughters are God's way
    of recycling the world...

Phyllis Hernandez

I Want

I want to lighten your load
as we travel together down life's dusty road
I want to always sing you a song
even tho my own little world seems all wrong
I want your prayers and need them too
to guide and protect us all the whole year thru
and so as we work together for good
with God as our guide
May we spread some of our saviors love
to those on the outer side

Mimi Walker

All I Need

You are my one, the one I think
of, the one I dream of, the one I want
for the rest of my life on this earth.

Because I give my love to you as the
rivers flow and they flowed sweetly just for
you. So please don't tear my heart in two;
because you are you and that's all I need.
To make me want to give my love and open wide
for you.

I will give my gender's sunshine to show
you that I care, I can give my genders sweetness
to show you what I can and will do for you. Your
tender love and care is all I need because to me that's
you, nothing more nothing less. The rest is just up to
me and you.

You can melt me you can tease me,
either way you are you and as I said and
will say again that's all I need from you.

Elizabeth Aliean Jones

My Dad

My dad is a man, not rich and not
    poor; who will give what he can, plus a whole lot more.

He gives from his heart, he gives from
    his soul; he makes his son feel as precious as gold.

He is a man who is proud—a man
    made of steel; he'd give the shirt off
    his back to give me a meal.

He is a man I am proud of—a man who
    I love; and for him I pray thankfully,
    to the heavens above.

I love you dad, you are a man among
    men; and what I know now, I wish I
    knew then.

Then is a time when I was a child;
    carefree, no troubles and a temper so mild.

I wish I new that your teachings would
    provide, the strength to endure and pride not to hide.

My life is a good one, one I enjoy—because
    I learned how to love
    when I was just a little boy.

Anthony P. Schmitt

The Recipe

Place one cup of child sifted, in a bowl.
Separate the essence, throw away the soul.

Mix a pinch of happy, and a dash of sad,
Two teaspoons of good, one teaspoon of bad.

Cut in common sense, stir the mixture well,
Then using your fist, make a little well.

Pour in lots of facts,
As many as will fit.
Maybe add some spunk, and just a little wit.

Stir to form a ball,
Then slowly turn it out.
Knead it with your fist,
Turn it all about.

Shape it as you wish,
Do not let it rise.
Place it in a pan,
Any shape or size.

Bake it nice and slow,
cool it when it's done.
Place it with the others, make another one.

KMC

Untitled

Hoping we find someone with whom to share
Anticipating the feelings we may have
Reaching for something we have never seen
Finding the secrets that lay deep inside
Giving us the energy to search forever
But upon discovery we laugh and cry
Something only so powerful to move us
Beyond any dream we may imagine
Worlds unrevealed shine magnificent
The beauty of the light undescribable
A power only the luckiest have found

This is the way we feel
This is why we cry
This is how we live
This is where we belong
This is when we are
...Love

Kirby Teague

Heartbroken and Lonely

I'm very lonely...in this one-man cell...
I grow tired and weary...of living in this man-made hell...
I've got too much time...for my life and on my mind....
it's ticking away...ticking away at my longevity...
keeps picking away...picking away with my sanity!!!
    As I sit here in...this boring cell...
Every sleepless night...every long day..it's a living hell...
    As I reminisce...and my thoughts drift away...
Not knowing or caring...about the day...date...and time...
I fight...I struggle...I try to survive...each new night and day!!!
    This environment builds...such hatred and rage...it becomes a part
of me. I pace back and forth...in my man-made cage...hoping one day
I'll be free. All my family...and all my friends...have left me,
"heartbroken and lonely"!
    Nothing gets any easier...as I grow older...it all gets worse
somehow...no-one really knows...or seems to care now.
    The chances are slim...of me making it again...
where do I start? Where do I begin?
    I can't stop the world...it revolves around time only.
Outta-sight...outta-mind...this isn't the way it should be.
I'm just another heart breaker..."Heartbroken and lonely"!

Derek Todd Nardoni

Time Is Passing You By

Memories remind us of how fast we let the seconds of time go by.
Never stopping them, never stopping ourselves.

We are rush to get over what makes us happy;
We dwell on what makes us sad.

Then there comes a time when our seconds are tallied and you we the
minutes and hours are lost in an unknown dimension.
A black hole that twists and turns never releases what is rightfully
ours.

Time laughs in our face and reminds us we once had the power resting
gently upon our fingertips.
We, instead of grasping hold of it, forgetfully push them off.

And now those good times are gone.

Lana Wessinger

Faith

The Lord is our Shepherd I know it's true.
    He walks with us when we are blue.

He helps us with our problems each day.
    To give us strength to go on our way.

He never gives us more than we can bear.
    He Carries us up that last stair.

He helps us be all that we can be,
    But we can't pay him back with money you see.

We can't build our Treasures on Earth to get
    stolen. We build them in Heaven so they
    will be golden.

Debra Kay Marcum

The One That's Desired

My pleated life
Measured and certain, pleasing yet plain,
Not quite so perfect
The pattern falls short;
Rip open the seams
Unfold the search...

Behold - I am intrigued,
Jealous enchantment seizes my brow;
You are a wrinkle.

Amy Renee Turnbull

"Silent Tempest"

A stormy existence
Of churning waters and wailing winds.
Constant turbulence abounds.
An incessant barrage of disturbing sounds
Falling upon her visage like fierce hailstones,
Slowly chipping away other tough exterior.
Silent cries, writhing in pain
She feels she's slowly going insane.
Smiling through the toughest times
Never showing any sense of loss, regret or grief.
Her face remains dry, not a single sign of tears.
Suppressing all pain, anger and fears.
She appears to be totally apathetic
Because she's not sure what she should feel.
She was taught to be strong, to have a heart of steel.
Despite her apathetic, stolid exterior,
Inside she's a tempest.

Angela Edwards

Music Without A Face

My tired lips burn with intense excitement
As I force air through my golden trumpet
My quick fingers pound the valves
As the screaming high notes flow from my horn.

In my right ear the drums bang harshly in a swinging rhythm,
The piano and soprano sax play smoothly
The bass and alto saxophone echo with harmony in my left ear
All of us are musicians,
Jammin'.

Our dark colored heads have no faces,
We are not seen as we really are
We are not looked upon as people,
But just musicians,
Jammin'.

The dynamic jazzy song is loved,
We are not
We are just musicians,
Jammin'.

Michael Chappa

Celebration

It was ninety years ago today
That Daniel Noah Platt was born
To Lillie and Willie one June morn.
Oh, what a happy and joyous time!

Daniel was followed by six sisters,
But never another mister.
From his birth until his mother's death,
There existed a very strong bond of love and respect.

Dan's life has been one of work,
As a lad selling newspapers and delivering packages,
Then working in textiles,
Retiring at the age of sixty-two.

Work has continued for Daniel.
Gardening is and has always been his crowning glory.
Anything planted surely flourishes.
His pride is in growing, canning, freezing, and sharing.

This precious life that began in 1906
Has been happy with collections, family, and his beloved work.
To Daniel - husband, father, grandfather, great-grandfather,
Great-great-grandfather, brother, uncle, and friend.

Dot Hutchinson Kelly

I See You

I see you in the night, I see you in my dreams. I never knew that
I love you. Everywhere I look I see your face. If I look in the sky,
the clouds make your face. Every time I think of you my day lights up
like a sunny sky. I see you in the night, I see you in my dreams. I
never take my mind off you. When I look in your eyes I see heaven. I
never love someone like I love you. I take my time away to think of
you every day. I see you in my mind, I see you everywhere. Now
that's how much I care.

Scott Bolden

The Window

Look into the window of my mind...Dare to view my insanity...Come on,
crawl inside...I'll be there soon..right now I'm out. I'm keeping my
eyes open. I can not afford to sleep. I pray in the darkness for
ways to set me free. Look into the window...I am bound to my
silence.
Be quick, you must be strong, crawl inside. Past the tangled webs of
confusion, around the pillar of fear, I'm in the corner...over here,
surrounded by the bars of secrecy.
Hello, I'm glad you could join me.
You don't have to stay...a short visit is ok.
View the secrets of my life...if you will, this is the only way.
Don't be afraid, I will accept your pain.
You have no idea how much I can take. It's all right.
I've been talking to my angel...I feel my soul slipping away.
Perhaps you should go now...be careful.
I have to stay...I'm trapped in my hell.
Quickly, back the way you came...I can't guarantee your safety.
My demons may attack. Thank you for coming. If I could escape, I
would go with you.
I feel the cold taking over...watch where you step.
Pay attention to the screams, this suffering eventually must end.
Leave the window open...
I like to look out.

Gary L. Tomblin

Emissaries Enjoined

The Captain and his Lady are one,
One vibrant, one momentarily still...
Yet he guides her through the stars
Like a man who pays court to his beloved.
As a master honors the song
Does he play his chosen instrument...

Where does the warrior find grace?
Rarely in battle, but in those he serves.
Not in the eyes of the many who seek him,
But in the promise he upholds...
In the hope of peace he endures
His Lady doth protect and strengthen his resolve.

There is vast emptiness in space...
Between stars, between hearts.
They pierce the darkness together
Bringing news from distant neighbors.
When the Captain smiles, all is goodwill
And his Lady also smiles, bestowing her favor...

Jennifer Watson-Lehner

The Peak

At the bottom of the mountain I looked up
At its peak,
I went up the mountain and saw
What I could see,
Then down from that mountain
I went having been,
Once down
I looked back at its peak
Differently.

Christopher Buiting

La Loba - La Que Sabe

(Wolf-Woman, She Who Knows)

The Handless Maiden wanders across the hostile Land,
in search of Life and Meaning, to find and use her Hands.

La Loba beckons to her, "Come and learn My Ways:
of Life, of Love, and Wisdom, to guide you all your days!"

To Mother Earth Life-Giving, La Loba teaches true:
of Life and Death and Life again, the Mother is renewed.

As Dry Bones in the Desert, La Loba brings new Sight,
brings Sight and Self-Awareness and breathes into her new Life!

Wise Woman Crone is Beauty. La Loba teaches Grace,
and Women Crone has duty to harmonize the Race.

From Maiden into Mother, from Mother into Crone,
La Loba nods approval: The Woman soul reborn!

Gail Valeskie

Who-Cares!

Deceptive smiles at babbling boons
Turn and whisper with malicious ease,
"Who cares!"

And if they pause for a momentary whine
But then continue their utterances of foolishness,
Drop your smile, put on a true face and scream:
"Who cares!"

And when they turn and stare before trading in
Their juicy topic for a falsified version of your
Life story and your friend walks away from you
Because she finds the lies interesting, let the tears
Find your eyes and whisper as you stand alone:
"Who cares"

Ann Breitbach

Wind Chimes

They all come home the same, loosely wrapped in wrinkled tissue
tangled up and anxious to stretch their legs and charm,
tiptoe tiny china slippers, wait patient for permission
to sing and prance and cheer, to mark a place among the crowd
with a voice uniquely tinkle, glisten lines of silk spun web

Tame and well trained pets the wind is such a moody master.
Some days dangle still and mute, sleep serene with trust
only shiver gingerly, night will howl wild alive, spout your
urgent eerie clamor. The symphony begins, each takes their
chair and section, along the walks in neighbors' yards
their separate voices call to me

Deep and simple, shrill or free I'm sure they know my face and name
greeting as I pass, one is always scolding softly wise up high
"you shouldn't walk alone at night" urging speed into my step
I'm sure they know each other too, gossip ringing through the air
sharing songs to praise the breeze, all awake from silent, slumber.

Kely McConnell

Affirmations

These are my deepest thoughts, they come from the heart.
Something from within, where or where do they begin?

Down in my soul from whence they come.
What do they mean where do they run?

Why do I question such a thing?
God controls my very being.

Above and beyond all that I know,
His love for me I strive to show.

Debbie Ann Mason

Loneliness

Have you ever been alone?
What do you feel like?
Can you help me figure out what is loneliness?
I could really use your help.
Is it something that comes natural?
What happens to you?
Please help me find out about loneliness?

Renee Nyalka

The Experience

My eyes are pleased by the body that surrounds him.
I see his face, his beautiful eyes.—I smile.
I like the height and strength of him, the way he walks.

My ears respond to his voice and rejoice in his laughter.
I hear teasing, encouragement, praise and scolding.
They sound like love.

My mouth tastes him.
I have sampled the sweet, the salt, the sweat.
I know them.

My mind has stored the sight of him, the sounds,
The feel of him, his taste.
So,—a simple thought of him brings a smile
and the knowledge of love,

For thought recalls all that I have experienced of him.

Janice E. Ripperton

As We Lay Together

Sunset glisten as waves roll in,
   Nightly breezes as the trees sway,
Moonlight, falls as the stars shine bright,
   As we lay together, it will be always.

Eyes sparkling, just as water so blue,
   Clear sand so true and white,
Beauty lies beneath the wondrous sea,
   As we lay together, forever you and me.

Sweet sensations only nature can bring,
   Things unexplainable, yet nearly understood,
Dreaming lazily of what we need,
   As we lay together, seeing what never sees.

Sunrise bursts through the window shade,
   Now we awake from where we laid,
Yet no one can take our feelings away,
   As we lay together, our love shall stay.

Anthony Trahan

Immortal Wind

It is Indiana, it is March, and the migrating wind returns
like the green sea turtle, the Canada Goose, the Humpback Whale,
and the Monarch Butterfly, the wind returns.
Unlike the animals, mammals, birds and insects, the wind is immortal
the same wind that musses your hair, caresses your face and bends
the trees today, is two, twenty, two hundred, twenty thousand years old
the same wind that coaxes trees to bud, and brings the rains
that make April flowers grow today, is the same wind that
touched your father, your grandfather, John Fitzgerald
Kennedy, Abraham Lincoln, Martin Luther King Jr.,
Adolf Hitler and Jesus Christ.
Like a vampire, it sucks the cold and desolation of winter
and carries it away to distant unknown lands
of course it is a secret destination, that's why the wind has
never been caught
I, too, have returned to Indiana perhaps upon the immortal
wind but, unlike the wind, here I shall remain

Richard Dean Tyree

The Treasure Box

On darkest nights of deepest woes
Of tales as yet unsung;
There comes to me a different voice
A child's voice, very young.

She looks at me with saddened eyes
In her hands she holds a box
But when I try To look within
Something makes me stop.

My treasure box says the child
For in it lays my life
Please you mustn't open it
It must not see the light.

What secrets must this young child hide,
That makes her cry in the night;
I know this Box, I know its use
This box holds memories of child abuse.

No matter where you run or hide, the box is always locked inside.
If anyone else hears this voice
Try your best to listen. Remember every treasure box
Does not hold things that glisten.

Susanne Robertson

Living Memories

The sound of the crashing waves,
The salty smell of the summer sea,
The cool misty breeze as the night arose,
No concept of time.

We sat together, side by side, silently
And yet knowing each other's thoughts.
Continuing to feel the soft sand beneath us,
Froze into a tranquil new world.

As our eyes stared out over the water,
The moon dripped with light as it emerged
Out of the sea,
The reflection glowed, while a twin appeared.

The feelings of sharing such a peaceful night
Linger on as if time did not move,
As if then has become today,
And that night became a Living Memory.

Elizabeth Kiausas

In the Beginning ...

Walking down the endless road,
As other's pass and look at me,
They don't know what they really see.
Like the story of the prince hidden in the toad.

As thoughts of life, seem endless,
Yet life ends, for all the rest.
In the beginning, there was no end.
Yet, our ancestors were vanquished.

The meaningless acts of sins.
The sadness and the loudness,
Of the sins that echoes in my mind.

As I close my eyes,
The pain, the silence,
The chaos of its unrelinquished ideas of evil.

The dishonorment of what had been done.
Never obeying the holy one.
Fearing what it will cause.
Knowing what will be lost.

Forever gazing upon the stars,
Like the never ending chaotic wars.

Mark Christian Carbonell Sarion

Life

Tell me one thing that's more precious than life.
  Money, riches, or a gold pocket knife?
Name one thing that's better than air.
  Beauties, loveliness, or thick golden hair?
When you wake up each morning, what should you say?
  Thank God you still live up to this day.
Life is one thing we all take for granted.
  We would rather be rich or something enchanted.
But now we should all stop and think
  How lucky we are to smell, feel, and blink.
To smell roses and to feel soft white snow.
  Life is so wonderful, but not all of us know.
We only want money, riches, and gold.
  But look closer to life and see what it holds.
So take off that cast that kept you from walking.
  Through life's precious things that you've been locking.
Now start again, all brand new
  Put all your past behind you.
Remember this my friend real closely.
  Remember that life is something you should be thankful for
mostly.

Crystal Tarazi

Endless Time

Where has the time gone? What time?
The yesterdays are but a memory
Etched on the fabric sublime!
Can't we change these vibrations?
They're only in thoughts of yours and mine.
Why not? Why not let them be gone.
Why not erase the thought forms
And live in the now?
We can be in eternity only as we feel it.
A living stream on the screen of our creation!
And like the endless waves returning
to the Creator...in Peace, Peace, Peace.

Jean I. Hall

The Wisdom Of Life

We as people must have faith, and believe
In ourselves, before we can ask God to
Believe in us. If we have faith, and believe
In ourselves, as we trust in God then all
Things can, and will be possible. Because
God's will shall be done, upon this earth
As it is in heaven. We as people must have
Respect for ourselves, as well as the
People around us. If a man does not have
Respect for himself, then he is truly not
Worthy of being called a man. We as human
Beings must not worry about things in which
We have no control over, as human beings
We can only do what God will allow us to do.

Paul A. Fields

Heaven

Heaven is a special place.
It's where you see a beautiful face.
A face of God, Joseph, Jesus, and Mary.
Up there life is a bowl of cherries.
Everyone gets along and sing songs.
Together it's merry and gay and every day is a special day.
Flowers in bloom, the sun shining bright
there is never a sad face or a look of fright.
Yes heaven is a special place
full of happiness, laughter, and grace!

Savannah Jean Storms

Stallion Of The Night

The night was cold, dark, and empty.
Down my spine I felt a sudden chill.
There stood before me a black stallion,
In his eyes, a sense of kill!

I hopped on his bare back.
My hands clutched to one rein.
Had me a lump in my stomach,
And in my heart, a twitch of pain!

His mane blew fiercely in the wind.
As he bucked about and reared.
He started off at a lope
As the moonlit sky drew near.

In the moonlit sky his dark coat
Looked as black as black.
The stallion took me far from home,
And yet, still no one knows if we'll ever come back!

We journeyed long and hard
And held on with all our might.
I'll always remember what stood before me,
The Stallion of the Night!

Meg Zarlengo

Moving On

A girl begins to cry as no one is there to comfort her,
Her world is so unclear and appears like a blur.
Drops of sadness begin to finally fade into the ground,
And all the torn up letters she read would never be found.
A girl begins to notice that her tears will always dry,
And in a palace prince charming will wait as long as her dream
  stay alive.
Like a bird she alone was locked inside a cage of hate,
Because the lies and the pieces of herself that never could be
  replaced.
With red eyes she looks up at the mirror of the past,
She sees herself with all the happiness that never seemed to last..
A rock digs deep into her palm as her hand is curled around,
The mirror shatters as she smiles at all the pieces on the ground.
Her problems admitted and forgotten as she moves on with her life,
And her head is a little higher as she laughs at all the reasons she
  had cried.

Jenifer Casey

Brother

Oh brother, you will never know just how much I admire you.
You were always more handsome,
and you were always more worldly than all.
You taught me to stand alone. You taught me to believe in myself.
You protected me. you were strong and brave,
and you could do no wrong.
All of these things and more you will always be to me.

In our youthful days, we fought more than we played.
We cried more than we laughed,
and we sometimes wished each other away.
Yet, however much we disagreed, I always looked up to you big
  brother.
And my love for you is everlasting, this I know is true.

Never forget that whatever foolish things I say,
I will always be on your side,
For your name is engraved in my heart for now and forever more.
Let's not dwell on the pains of yesterday or sulk over times past.
But rather embrace our tomorrows together with understanding and
  love.

Diane J. Hamm

My Red Cardinal Friend

Little red bird so happy to see you
My life so fresh like the morning dew
You come into my sight with such a red hue,
Pretty red cardinal, I love you.

When I feel alone and look out my window,
You come flying into the tree
With all the grace and majesty of God,
I know God sent you just for me.

As I gaze through my window
I soak in the love
That I sense coming from you,
And from God above,

As fast as you fly into the tree
My troubles fly away, they just seem to flee
And my day is much better from beginning to end,
Since God sent me his love in my red cardinal friend.

Ireleen J. Schoonmaker

The Shroud of Darkness

The darkness surrounds me now
I can feel its icy touch
The pain embraces me now
Its caress a familiar rush
The echo reverberates now
telling the tale of power and fate

I followed your footsteps then
watched and learned and knew
I needed an ear then
I watched and learned and knew
You left me alone then
I watched and learned and knew

You always told me
to figure it out myself
I search and searched, and then I knew it was what I wanted
to figure it out myself
    I gasp now
straining for the one simplicity I need
    and it isn't what I wanted.

Laura Teoli

Hunger

Hunger
When will we see such a prosperous day
A day of hope and much joy
A day when I can feed my most precious boy
Hunger
O Lord, supply us with a healthy meal
something pure, and plain, but real
please have mercy on us all
Hunger
Do you care?
Leaving us with nothing, so bare
one day you will go away
and leave us with prosperous days
Hunger, hunger
    Thank you, Lord
    My prayers came true
    Fields and fields filled with crops
    That are pure and new
    Hunger, hunger, hunger

Kerrian Edwards

Battle Cry

I hear you need me in this war, nothing can I say
Eighteen years to live and die, you pulled my name today

Take me to your torture camps, far from normal life
Don't bitch and beat me anymore, just bring my gun and knife

Now I am your soldier boy, my death is overdue
Molded like a fearless puppet, the strings are held by you

Rush me to the foreign land, the dead I wish to see
I hope the battle surges on, the thing that should not be

Now you see me in this trench, all is sweat and mud
Waiting for the first to kill, I'm trained to spill his blood

Each day I search to kill your son, the one who's tough and brave
He steps one foot into my path, I'll knock him in his grave

Grant me time to pray alone, you see my strings are cut
Grim Reaper stands with open arms, my eyes I fear to shut

Forgive me Lord for I have sinned, I've learned my lesson well
Just pin a note and send me home, "He served His Country well."

Cameron Stacy Stevens

To Jim

The road of marriage is not always smooth
And it has its ups and downs;
But the trip has been so much nicer
Just having you around.

We harp and carp and say rash things
That we really do not mean—
But underneath the angry facade
Is a burning love which sometimes can't be seen.

What's near and dear is the thoughtfulness
And all the tender, loving care,
The pulsing of a loving heart
That we sometimes forget is there.

My mistakes have been many
And the praises sometimes naught;
But if we go for another thirty years,
Please remember this loving thought.

Marian F. Beechem

Divorce

Come down from there,
And cut your hair,
Clean up your life,
And I'll stay your wife,
You promised me,
Forever see
Can't make it on my own
I'm scared
Can't raise her all alone I dared
I can't forget the love we shared
    And the promises we made

It's funny though how love can heal,
All the pain it made you feel,
So come and kiss away my tears,
And hold me close to calm these fears
Let me lose myself in your kiss,
That's something I'll always miss

So I guess this is goodbye,
And still I have to wonder why
(Excuse me while I go and die) It shouldn't hurt so much.

Lisa Michelle Brady

Harmony In Our Society

H-armony means peace and friendly relations
A-mong your fellow-man, not just nations.
R-anking of problems as seen today
M-ostly concerns crimes, debts, and who will pay.
O-bservance to rules is for others to obey
N-ot for me, too many now say,
Y-ielding to no one along their way.

I-magine for a minute, the world is at peace
N-o hatred, no crime, all such did cease.

O-ffers are made by both sisters and brothers
U-nity shared like new babies with their mothers,
R-aces come together like new lovers.

S-urely this is an achievable goal
O-btainable, if each individual acts the role.
C-eding a point, just now and then,
I-s really a virtue and not a sin.
E-veryone benefits when harmony reigns
T-ogether we go forward society gains.
Y-es, harmony in sound and society too
   will create a better me and a better you.

E. Donald Pounder

My Prayer

Bless my friend, oh Lord, I pray
Keep her safe by night and day.
Walk with her all the time
And gently hold her hand in Thine.
May peace attend her through all she does
And shower on her all Thy love.
Show her the blue skies and mountains
And the starry night like fountains.
Give her the beauty of the trees
With wonderful birds among the leaves.
Show her the wonder of the sun
As it rises and then sets at day's end.
And the moon in its glory at night's rest
Will show her that God's way is best.
This I pray, dear Lord, this night
For my dear friend through all her life.

Alice E. McLaury

Snow Fall From Heaven

Snow falls from the Heavens, to mother earth down below,
Beckoning the wind in a far off hollow.
Its silence is endless, as I'm dreaming away.
To wake in the morning, to have lived one more day.
Sometimes I've often wondered, what this life's all about.
I was born from a dream world, is that what it's all about.
As I day dreamed out my window, something inspired me,
To write down these words, was it a dream or reality.
Sometimes we all feel far away, in another place and time.
Out of the reach of sanity, in that dimension in our minds.
Some say our destiny is written from the stars in the sky.
Or from a sacred book called the lamb's book of life.
What we believe is what we're told,
That's what an old man said to me,
He was grey and faded with no family.
Just then my eyes were opened and
the dream had come and gone.
That's when I realized to myself,
that my dream had became this poem.

Lawrence Kirk Sr.

A Fairy's Tear

In a place so cold and lonely a weeping fairy sits in pain,
Eyes burning from the salty fire tearing cross her face again.

Tiny fingers wipe the tears; her lithe hands are just too small.
Though she wipes her face once dry, no simple way to catch them all.

Born of innocence and hope gleaming from a father's joy
Whose proud first moment flowered forth, holding his new girl and boy.

The fairy's mind drifts toward days before the fights and anger came,
When the father's soul was whole, his and children's home the same.

A husband's and wife's loud anger intrude into a peaceful night;
A frightened child cries in the crib, started by his parents' fight.

To preserve his children's souls, father sees that must be done.
He leaves and lets their mother know the family is no longer one.

He fairy gazes at this man, weakened by his loss life.
Blood ripped from his veins in sorrow, his own choices caused this strife.

Oh fragile thing, your fairy soul,
How like this father's heart...
Your tears flow out into the night
He is from his child apart

Edward L. Goldman III

Without Words

His eyes looked intensely into mine,
   searching for my thoughts
     but...

My thoughts were wondering along paths
   in a world far from his
     understanding...

I wanted to walk with him through
   the gardens of his experience
     but...

My mind could not pay the fare and
   my heart was weary from so much travel...
     "Goodbye" I said...

France Anna Arriola

Past Life Reflection

Behind faded tapestries you revealed yourself to me,
shining like the very first star.
You lavished my loins with remnants of ancient fragrances:
jasmine, shalimar and ambergris.
The essence of farewell arose from the chemistry.
Your entrance was filled with departure and hurt me like an undesired
kiss, yet I was healed in the wounds of your longing.
Now, I greet your presence and accept your absence.

Behind water-color sadness you are revealed to me,
your body preserved in ancient fragrances, lying there soft with
sleep, closed like a flower at night-fall.
I draw you into the last chamber of my heart
and stand before you, a pupil of death.
My memories hold the vagueness of premonition
and grow as faint as your fragrance.
Like wet garments upon my body I hold you close
and taste God on your lips.

Nadene L. Locke

Yesterday and the Days Following

Yesterday my best friend died
She's been always by my side
Known her since I was a child
Yesterday a companion died.

Yeah we had some fun
She stole food from everyone
Boomer was her name
Had a stroke and it hasn't been the same.

She had a dizzy spell
Tried to go downstairs but she fell
She seemed to lose coordination
And she needed medication.

Yesterday I wore black
Cause a virus came on attack
Part of me went too
With the friend that I knew.

Yesterday I lost my buddy
To the world just a nobody
When I knew I looked in her eye
And I knew she was ready to die.

Jeremy Murphy

A Rower's Prayer

Dear Lord,
    When the morning brings forth the mist and
the sunset initiates the night, we are together
in all that is magnified to perfection, by the
liquid glass we made our own.

    With each catch my spirit is lifted to the heavens to
meet you Lord, and gently you place me in an unladen
state of glory with each recovering stroke.

    Trouble hath no power, and pain, no substance. The
salt on my lips has become a healer, as the chill on my
skin makes the present seem merely memory.

    Thank you Lord for the elegance of the crew and for
the friendships you have created through it. May we
think together as our bodies form together. May we
learn to live life as you ask it of us. We shall pull with
strength and rhythm in time with your commands. May
we be an example for those who need be influenced.

    Be with us Lord, as we approach the finish. Make us
humble with each win and supportive in our losses, for it
is than when we will see the reality of your love.

Meredith M. Wilson

Separation, Divorce(?) and Then What?

Friendship!?!? I'm astonished when she wants one nonetheless.
Is it her insecurity that needs this blanket of "forgiveness?"
Because friendship and forgiveness are 2 things hand-in-hand.
They both belong in a marriage, not "sometimes" or "on the mend."
Forgive the past and be my friend And lover.
Or don't forgive, let's divide and bespectre.
Because who are we kidding, really? Even with every good intention
a "friendship" built on divisiveness, could never stand the mention
of the words "I'd like you to meet my boyfriend, (blank)" the one for
me she's replacing.
Then back I go into darkness, anger, fear, and hating.
I don't hate my wife, I love her dearly, but will not just be her friend,
because my feelings of love may well be nothingness,
if she doesn't want Our Love to mend.
For my heart and soul are true, I need to take care of my self,
for I'm definitely all I've got, and I have a soul of warmth, worth
and wealth.
No matter what her accusations, beliefs, suspicions or doubt,
In the end I am me, with her or without.

Gary Smolinski

Released

Out in the bonny meadow
I saw the one standing, breathing in the daisy air
Flowing hair upon your skin
Tear of lost rolling from eye

Singing high pitched "C"
Those underground shudder, above the dirt not touching.
Rise to find the disturbance
Taller than them a giant

No fear above ground, floating a smooth rise
Blowing on the daisies, scatter and gather
Amazing draw from us to it

Closer and closer we are upon
One swirling in the air
Taking us up into the clouds
We are safe from the shaking
The earth is disintegrating
Up and up we can breathe, shed our skin of flesh

Danielle Hauenstein

Untitled

I was lost in the darkness of a vast and lonely forest,
Roaming aimlessly along life's twisted trails without focus or
    direction,
Until by chance my path happened across the very one you tread
    upon,
And by you I was enchanted.

Your time and your interest provided a light by which I could see,
Your love, faith, and understanding provided a compass by which I
    could navigate toward fulfilling my promise,
And your dreams meshed with my dreams - our dreams will in time
    guide me to a pure and blissful destination - with you...

Anthony K. Krueger Jr.

Untitled

When you reach out for a hand
to guide you on your way.
And your fingers grasp only thin, empty
air, you can't face another day.
When you can't seem to find yourself
Amongst the world's many men,
That's the time to look inside your soul
And search deep within.
There you will find the answers to
the things you long to know,
Deep down in your heart
Where only you can go.
No one can lay claim to the gifts
you have inside,
But these jewels are for you to share
Not for you to hide.
So, tilt you head toward the sun.
And be proud of who you are,
And if you remember what you have to offer,
Then these gifts will take you far.

Lindsey M. Corso

Morning By The Sea

Morning dawned and the sun is up.
    Happily all could jump.
The waves rolled in without a stumble,
    Splashed and crashed, rumble, rumble.
Birds walked the shore, looking for prey.
    Hungry for breakfast, I would say.
"Almighty" gave a beautiful day.
    A happy day. I daily pray.

Maria Sherrier

Untitled

Here I am, a black space
surrounded in infinite curiosity.
Alone, venturing where no one sees,
so cold, not knowing.
Only shadows of memories present the past.
Knowledge peels away what life's seed carries
from every birth.

A dull light in the night,
speaking with no words,
stretching a glow across its path.
So soothing, a feeling of the will to survive.

All I am upon the light,
a decaying body and a growing soul
to strive for a time in a place where
boundaries present their teeth.

Cloudiness, unveil your face
to a home in time in a certain place,
called life.

Richard J. Shields

Untitled

Awaiting the arrival of the mail sack
With a peep inside releasing the unknown
Perhaps a bill, postcard from dentist or vet
A contest or video, sure to please, or yet
A letter from a far away friend;
My hand searches for the treasure inside
Gather around for a friendly chat, reading aloud
Of news that had meaning, connections to the past
Covering not just a page, but two.
Just as submitted reports require a reply
I quickly scribble a note, a reminder, a thought
To include with comments—develop the plot
Into a legible draft, a confusion of ideas amass
Then a reconstruct of related matter
Subscribe to what is known—a compiled letter.
A lick of a stamp, an envelope seal—journey to a friend.

Celia Heath

Inner Child

Light girl inside my heart, I turned away right from the start.
Frightened of your pain so deep,
And all the secrets you do keep.

I see you crying all alone,
No place is safe, not even home.
You look at me, eyes full of fear,
I pull you close and keep you near.

I say "I love you, you're safe now,"
As I softly stroke your brow.
And rock you gently till you sleep,
You feel my love, so warm and deep.

But still some days I run away,
But please have patience for someday,
I'll reach for you and hold you tight,
Protect and love you, day and night.

I'll keep you always in my heart, and never will we be apart.
We'll feel our pain, we'll understand,
And walk life's road, hand in hand.

I'll look at me with eyes that see, the love I have inside of me,
For the young girl in my heart, has been me right from the start.

Debra Jermyn, APW

Untitled

In this pot white onions ride
like this slices of the moon
between wilting leaves of parsley, slivers of carrots,
twigs of thyme
Simmering vegetables lose their colors swiftly like dreams
surrendering their aromas, their supple bodies to the
broth that swallows everything
The fragrance of the boiling ocean is so much more complete
than the smell of the purple beet
the red potato
I must be closer to the beating of your heart
the pounding of the earth
I need to surround the warm animal of you
to collapse into your blood crimson and rising
like the kiss of a volcano
Will I whisper into you like a bleeding vegetable
under the flash of the moon will I sink into the immensity
beneath the flutter of the sky trembling
against the shy hiss of the sea and forget
my raw vegetable virginity

Naomi Fulton

A Faded Rose of Yesterday

When life gets hard I think
  of you.
Wishing it was all a bad dream.
That when I turn around you will
  be there making everything right.
Instead I walk the long road that
  leads to were you lay in endless
  slumber.
A granite stone marker to show the
  dark reality that you're gone.
I bow my head and softly whisper
  I love you.
The hole in my heart seems endless.
How do you move forward when you
  can't say good-by.
The lives you touched will always remember
  the strong loving man you were.
How do we show the young ones
  who can't remember.
My father.

Sharolynn Guile

Thoughts Of She

She summons me madly in the night.
I watch her by day, my eyes afire.
Her call is soft, she fills my sight.
But can she draw me from the mire?

Another has taken her heart.
His luck draws her away from me,
leaving the two of us apart.
Our potent love I'll never see.

I dream of her exquisite frame.
My mind is swamped with thoughts of she.
To gaze at length I fall in shame.
To hold her is my only plea.

"It's false!" I cry, "The love a sham!"
The images of her are gone.
I wake and tears pour from my damn.
This place I loathe, this cursed dawn.

I long for the savory night,
in which my lips meet her sweet chest.
I'll wait again, all day in fright.
My feelings I'll never attest.

Chris J. Mirell

Hyacinths

A hyacinth in springtime's a wonder to behold
As tiny, fragile petals rare essences unfold,
But a hyacinth abloom in winter amidst harshest icy snows
Unveils mysteries of the heavens as only angels can disclose.

Charles C. Travis Jr.

One of God's Children

A life has just been taken before we felt it through a life
so you and tender that everything was new. Through my grief I
heard God say "I lent this child of mine to you and yes her stay
was brief you have had her charms to gladden you and her lovely
memories as solace for your grief. I looked this world over in
My search for teachers true and from the throngs that crowd life's
lanes, I selected you. You may wish to cry out "Lord why was I
so cruelly chosen to morn?" But dear one I've been watching you
since the day you were born. For those lessons down on earth I
have prepared no other. For this reason only I chose you to be
this child's mother. Question not my plan, Trust in God until in
heaven we meet. I'll bring to you the scroll of her life and
lay it at your feet. Then and only then, amidst the peace of
My Heaven above can you truly understand the depth, the blessed
  glory
and the power of Gods internal love. Don't fill your heart with
doubt or in self pity smother, be proud, be grateful God groomed
you to be to His child a Mother." I know as a blessing from God
through my body as a part of me, she lives on forever, our
Child Eternally.

Georgia Koleski

I Love This Game!

Shooting and dunking just to score,
but basketball players do more than just that on the court.
Half court shots and dunking from the foul line,
but that's not the only thing on my mind.
Head fakes, spin moves and crossovers in every game,
and none of them are ever the same.
Saving the ball, bank shots and airballs.
Mostly all of the free throws fall.
Half court presses, last second shots
and always there will be a block.
Rebounds, tips, traveling and charges.
The refs are always going to be calling
back court, reach-ins or just the hard foul.
And everybody hates when the ball goes out of bounds.
Never ever is a game the same.
That is exactly why I love this game!

Nakesha Brown

Glad You're Here

  Darkness closes, light disappeared.
Moon and clouds shifted to the rear.
  Burst of fire, hot coals demons running
after us for our souls.
  The world is over nothing to see,
just let me go, let me be free. Till I
  know it is my time to leave. Just
change the world and start to believe.
  Take a hand and make a stand,
stick up for our self and our land.
  Fight for our freedom, mostly our
souls, hold onto life don't let go.
  So as you struggle, we're behind,
slash it, whip it you'll be fine. As
  you conquered and made this real.
We greet you all, we're glad you're here.

Racheal Bock

Cooing of the Dove

It's August and the days are filled
With the heat of blistery sun.
So it's pleasant just to take a break —
In eve, when chores are done.

And quietly sit upon my porch
The evening sounds to hear.
The pleasantness of nature's chorus
Sounding far and near.

The song of frogs and crickets
And the cooing of the dove —
The twitter of the song birds
As they settle high above.

Oh, there's something extra special,
About the coolness of the night.
Just to hear nature's chorus ringing,
Under stars that glow so bright.

For there's a close and awesome presence
And a nearness of God's love.
When in the stillness of the evening,
You hear the cooing of a dove.

Geraldine Borger

"The Big Five-O"

"Fifty years is half a century,
Our marriage as husband and wife -
Encountered a life of good and bad,
Fifty years of love and strife."

"It all began on the twentieth of July,
Nineteen forty-six was the year -
That day we went on our honeymoon,
Was a day we hold so dear."

"To this day we've no regrets,
We've made the best of things -
To stay in love and enjoy life,
Is what a good marriage brings."

"Our health has been as problem,
Within the last few years -
Luck has been in our favor,
We've still around and shedding no tears."

"So what's the formula for a long married life?,
We must have done some things good -
Keep loving your one and only,
We've both done the best we could."

Marty Rollin

Steve

The heartless storms come from time to time,
Leaving a flood of your presence on my soul.
There is a ghost inside of you,
Whose eyes pull me in without hope.

At night in the candlelight...
I shudder in the darkness,
The thoughts of you holding me.
In the warmth of the strong impassioned candle,
I conceive a kiss as gentle as the whispering wind.

As I relax some nights by the calm sandy shore,
I see your alluring reflection on the smooth water's surface
As I watch the white curls caress off the ocean's blue body,
I wonder if you think of me as I think of you.
I wonder if my heart will ever find its way.

Then I return to reality.
Sitting alone on the dark empty beach,
With a specter's hand on my shoulder telling me that I will be O.K.
But still my heart is cold from want.

Julie Silva

Children of the World

Children of the earth,
They cry and scream,
And crave ice cream,
And tricks are up their sneaky sleeves!

They dance around,
They sleep real sound,
They go to school,
And meet a fool!

They play the cootie game,
Still... everything's the same,
They'll scratch their knee
Get stung by a bee,
But still they laugh, he, he, he, he!

Their laughter fills the world with joy,
So maybe they deserve a toy,
They play and play,
But then they say,
"We are the Children of the World!"

Sarah Marquer

A Special Friend

When I am mad or sad,
A special person talks to me,
He cheers me up,
He makes me glad,
He makes me forget
I was ever mad,
When I am weak,
He makes me strong,
He makes me think
I will never go wrong,
He knows my deepest feelings inside,
So there really is no reason to hide,
No matter where I go or stay,
This person will never lead me astray,
He guides me each and every path I trod,
This special person is God!!

Karmen Patton

Gone Is The Season

Sitting atop the bluff
she looked back at her life
and smiled
remembering her husband the farmer.
The way he laughed
at her silly jokes
after returning from the field.
Yet not today
as the season is gone,
gone for two weeks and three days.

Standing atop the bluff
holding his ragged dirt covered overalls
old and worn
never to be worn again.
His soiled clothes so out of place
unbearable to hold
or to see.
Closing her eyes
she put them away
at the bottom of the hill.

Jason Crane

Autumn

The sun grows cold and bleak and wan; the bare trees whisper, "Summer's gone".
The weary farmer rests his hand as twilight lingers o'er the land.
To him another day is through, with rest to come, and well-earned too.
With harvest in and winter near, he sees the end of another year.

The blackness of the solemn night has hidden everything from sight.
The chilly wind has risen high, and passes on with mournful cry.
The stately hickory, shorn of gown, scatters nuts upon the ground.
Faster now and colder still, the rising wind sweeps o'er the hill.

The call of geese in lofty flight, echoes through the somber night.
The woods and hills and stream throughout, hear the north wind boldly shout-
And rip and tear and whistle on, and scatter leaves upon the lawn,
And red leaves murmur as they fall, "We hear Winter's rumbling call."

The stream alone may laugh and play, meandering on its endless way.
It wanders o'er its rocky bed, quite unaware that Earth is dead.
And babbling through its hidden dells, the merry stream a story tells,
Of nymphs and fairies, goblins too, dancing on the midnight dew.

Against the sky the oak tree stands, spreading wide her brambled hands.
She could tell a story old, of summers hot and winters cold.
A patriarch, now bleak and bare. She breathes no more the frosty air.
All though the winter's freezing snows, she will lie in calm repose.

Edward Gruwell

The Rose

The ice blue sky and frosty ground were a startling contrast to the beauty of the rose.
Growing wild in the late April sun, the one rose had bloomed to perfection.
The unexpected frost had frozen a single dew drop upon one velvety petal.
The rose was a deep velvet red reaching up toward the sky;
The stem was a deep green with many thorns protruding from it, giving
    the beauty an aura of danger.
The ground shook violently, causing the rose to tremble slightly.
Hundreds of warriors mounted on huge stallions crossed the meadow.
The fragile beauty of the rose went unnoticed by the warriors and was trampled in their wake.
Now all that is left of the rose is a single velvet petal.

Sundown Selzer

The Scream

I hardly noticed it at first, if started as this small noise hovering
on the edge of my consciousness. It was a mildly disturbing feeling,
like an itch you are unable to scratch. As I walked farther it grew
until it was a soft hum in the distance. A familiar sound, like an
old friend. But one who visits only in times of need, I continued on,
exchanging pleasantries with my companion. And little by little the
sound began to intrude on my thoughts. I noticed a rhythmic thumping
growing louder, a steady beat that altered my step. Then I caught the
sound, and that old friend stepped in the place of my walking
companion, I was drawn to the sound, it was propelling me forward,
awakening hidden emotions within. By this time the beat was pounding,
hounding, insistent, demanding. The wall became my only thought, my
only purpose. It rose and fell, louder and softer. This horrific
screech became the apex of my existence. The landscape altered with
the sound, and the sound was everywhere. I could smell it, hear it,
taste it. The world around me warped and swirled, becoming a part of
this scream, this cry of anguish. Soon I was running heading towards
this individual that was at the roof of this pain. My footsteps
pounded on the bridge in time to the stomping feet. The sound was
encompassing me, becoming me. Suddenly I was howling in an unearthly
dissonant harmony with the screamer. The sounds invaded my brain,
filling me with the loneliness, the anguish, the terror that the
scream embodied. I clapped my hands to my ears, trying to escape this
siren's song that blossomed from my throat and caged me inside of it
and I, trapped, can no longer move. It's just me alone with the scream.

Kim LeJeune

Cat Fancy

Slink, o may cat, feline full throttle, all silk fur 'n' soft bones,
muscle adapt to any surface, pour into my lap for momentary purring cuddle,
wantin' pet, wantin' scratch, wantin' rub,
sandpaper tongue, vibratin' belly, then off! Attack the paper ball!
What is the ball? What calls you to strike? What siren song is that paper crackle?
Follow that ball, bat with white mittens, savage with quick-kick claws,
devastate with needle teeth, what is it?
a mouse? A but? A mortal anti-feline enemy ensconced in a paper
ball? Then your cat fancy drops the was to leave it lying,
awaiting your next fleeting whim, and you now, in the window,
solemn dignified queen of all you see before you,
classic windowsill can form, now, calm, repose, composed, watch observe;
the spring winds down, the purr fades past murmur into silence
as cat bone cat muscle cat silk fur
settles into cat nap
to recharge for crazed rampage when next strikes your
    cat fancy.

Clay Roper

Passion

The whole world seemed silent as we sat together watching the peaceful fire.
Not a single echo of the busy outside world penetrated our peaceful bliss.
As the snow outside deepened the cataclysm in my heart was filled by your tenderness.
The passion I felt for you burned more intensely than the roaring fireplace.
Yet it was much more gentle and soothing than the falling snow.
During that calm afternoon we shared many things.
From childhood stories to hopes, dreams, and emotions.
Your beauty captivated me so much that I had to really struggle to hear your words.
But listening to them turned out to be the wisest choice I'd ever made.
Who would have believed that your inner beauty was even more impressive!
I learned many things sitting in front of the fire on that cold December day.
But the one thing that truly became crystal clear to me was my
feelings for you.

Chris Matheson

My Guardian Angel

"Father."
"Yes child,." He answered.
"You have blessed me with a caretaker, someone to watch over me as I
walk through the stages of life. But a simple caretaker she is not,
I look at her and I see the face of an angel."
"My precious daughter, she is indeed an angel, created by my most
delicate hands to look after you. When you were born, I laid you in
her arms and entrusted her with a tiny, precious new life.
"It seems impossible, but I remember. She used to sing to me,
lullabies, softer than an angel's harp, she rocked me to sleep and
guided my dreams. I awoke to her smiling face, there was so much love
in her eyes. She is more beautiful than a sunset on the horizon. But
Father, I know not the name of the angel, what shall I call her?"
"Patience my child, tell me more about this angel."
"Well Father, she held my hand and walked me through childhood,
molded my values, sheltered me from evil, and inspired my dreams.
She guided me through adolescence and stood by my side through every
hardship. When I cried, tears trickled down her cheeks, not because
she was hurt, but because she shared my pain. When I was happy, her
laughter joined in chorus with my own. I love my angel, and I never
want her to leave me, but still I do not know what to call her.
Father, tell me the name of my angel."
"Ah the persistence of a child. A moment longer, daughter," He
replied. "I have not yet heard the present deeds of our angel."
"Father, she is as perfect as the stars in the Heavens, her
heavenly aura outshines even the radiance of the sun. She has
nurtured me since I was a mere infant, and now that I am grown, she is
my unrelenting supporter, my guardian angel. She supports me in my
every endeavor. She teaches me with the wisdom of the ages and loves
me more than I could possibly comprehend. Don't ever take her from me
Father, for my love for her is as great as the tides of the ocean, and
as constant as the sunrise in the east. Now please Father, what is the name of my angel?"
"God leaned down and whispered, "Mother."

Kelly Siemek

Andrea

I saw tonight
a flower 'most matured
breath of babes her hair
deep-wood gown
moonlight upon her
in the impenetrable forest
-within - oh it must be beautiful
The smile a stream giving life
to surroundings; dark magic
surroundings and a witch in red,
her curved lips illuminate.
She speaks; I inhale — like a drug
I breath in, never enough.
And like a balloon into air, she is gone.
Enveloped in darkness.
I turn to finish my work.

Austin Brooks

Magnified

Like a mustard seed
a molecule,
the tiniest thing in the world
made of matter

Existing are many particles,
spread over the galaxy
each radiating its own multi-color
while reflecting upon one another,

Each having the choice to be
constructive or destructive
while making contact within the atmosphere;

Billion die for billions of reasons
and billions also live on,
this particular small molecule of matter is
Physical man.

Valerie E. James

That Old House

You can see it from the road.
A used and forgotten abode.
It looks so lonesome and forlorn.
It's weather beaten and torn.

The porch sags at an odd angle.
There are shingles that just dangle.
Faded, peeling, paint and broken glass.
In every variety, type or class.

Listen close and you might hear,
Giggles of laughter or sounds of a tear.
Big family or small, happy or sad?
Did they have good times or bad?

That old house could tell a story.
Of its beginning and history.
Of all those who passed through the door,
Their lot in life and much more.

Lajuana D. Burton

Blue

What is blue?
Blue is the day turning into night,
Blue is a full moon,
Blue is a daydream,
Skies on sunny days are blue,
Blue makes me happy,
And blue makes me sad,
Blue is a cold winter evening,
Blue is the ocean and the sand on a beach,
Blue is the cry of a seagull,
A dolphin is blue,
Blue is all around us,
You cannot always see blue,
But blue is always there.
Blue is there to cheer you up,
Blue is victory,
Blue is loss,
Blue is everything-
Everything is blue...

Vanessa R. Castle

Untitled

I watch him in the morning,
I watch him walk across the
floor, which makes me wonder should
I open the door, I let him out side,
and watch him play, which makes me
wonder, how long will he stay, I ask him
how old he is, thou I already know,
on his birthday we celebrate, we call
he the big mistroe, cause night he
makes a great deal of music, but he's sit
just a puppy, and man's best friend,
which makes me wonder when will this
happy moment end.

Kim Vickery

Earth

Flying falcon
Climb the high winds
Hurtling side of the sun
Passing stardust to release our sins
Into the clouds with elegant ringing flight
Vertical stoop in the fading light
Flashing treasure of golden peregrins
Appaloosa stallion
Screaming at the sky
Charging open prairie
Until freedom says goodbye
Phantom tiger searching his past
Through heart of darkness
Original hunter
Can he last?
Our suspended world
Alone in eternity
Fate of the planet whispering to me

Robert Katona

Time Treasured

The days weeks, the moths and years, a turn of the head and they've passed.
You think there's time for everything, these moments will last and
last. The little baby in your arms has a lifetime of things to learn,
Surely it will take forever as the seasons take their turn.
So many things for you to see, people to visit and places to go.
Books of read and songs to sing, spring beginning and falls leaves
aglow. We live for the future, never today,
Never stopping to smell the flowers, and suddenly it's yesterday.
Too late to recapture lost hour, the babies are grown, your time is
your own. The quiet you longed for is here,
But where are all of your plans and your dreams, how could they disappear?
Why can't we see that life is to live, to savor each hour of each day?
To look for the best and give only you our best, and throw not one minute away.
This is my prayer, that I live everyday, and plan not just for tomorrow,
To listen and look and love everyone, to share in their joy and sorrow
If this I can do my life will be full, the days and years will be treasured.
And surely love and concern for all men, are the acts by wind we'll be measured.
Our lives overflow with blessings from God, there is no end to his caring.
To the end of my days I'll be thanking him, for the years you and I have been sharing.

Mary Hoover

Ms. Elite

My color is of no consequence! I just happen to be black.
Permanent hair relaxer has taken out the "nap."
I dwell in an exclusive suburb. You, indigent blacks, only serve to disturb this
carefully erected wall that separates, you, from me. I simply cannot abide you
    common blacks. You see?
Oh, and eating watermelon, is utterly a disgrace. Besides, it smears the
powder I use to lighten my face. Greens, hammocks, well, I never partake.
The mere mention of such preparations causes my stomach to ache!
Gospel music - Huh, primitive, at least. I prefer the harpsichord to "clapping
hands and stomping feet." Feeling. Spirit. Shouting, "Glory," did you say?
No. Control. Restraint is the way.
You say, discover your roots, and know who you are?
Girly, girl, my roots are in Cleveland, that's not very far!
I want no part of that we shall overcome clan, the long road from slavery;
reclaim whose homeland? I worked my way out, and I haven't been back since!
As I said, my color is of no consequence!
I am an executive, I just happen to be black,
and the only way to deny my past is to stop looking back!
So don't lecture me with your African awareness rhetoric.
I simply want to integrate, assimilate, and forget it!

Joyce C. Lavender-Che

Last Flight

Hear the Eagle's mournful cry as it echoes across the miles during his
hunt for prey this day. He is tired his hunt is almost at its end,
oh but—he must continue as there is still light, because if he does not
his belly will be empty another night. Make no mistake - it is not he who
is at fault rather it is we. This majestic bird searches his land
that was once filled with life, beauty, and crisp fresh air. Where
once he did not know hunger and strife, but now his land lay desolate,
still, and pungent.

We have massacred his world with poisons that ride the winds. Poisons
from smokestacks, cars, and planes. As they fall through the sky up
on Mother Earth contamination destroys the activity of life. As the
smallest in life's circle dies another will surely follow.

How much will we allow, will it ever stop, or will we only watch as
the Eagle's search comes to its end and he falls to the ground? How
will we feel watching his wings flop about, his body twitching as he
grasps for fresh air one last time? How will it actually feel to look
into his lifeless eyes, knowing we could have made a difference, how
do we live with the guilt? Or will we insist we had no part of this,
as we draw a deep breath of the colors of same Death?

Dorothy Brookshire

Native Days

'Cross wood laned meadows way down by a brook to catch crawdads, snakes and
  snails,
To secret into soups and dresser drawers and elder brothers' Sunday 'tails,
Plunged deep in a draw concealed from chide where clothes could lie idly strewn,
A frolicking scamp with Innocence bare romped and swam in the hot afternoon.
Then out to the sandlot to choose up sides for a game of base and ball,
But a swollen, black eye and torn overalls came away not wanted at all.
So across learned knee for contrary play the switch of correction flayed;
A gentle, firm word, which never was heard, for wont of more indigenous ways.
Ah!, but one evening reluctantly knelt before bowl on a cobbled, washroom floor,
Chestnut eyes startled at the eddied likeness of a creature never seen before.
More it seemed than a water sprite in tease upon quieting swells revealed,
And throughout the house each twilight's repose paused upon discovery's squeal.
Much swifter than Dawn's cascading light awash across the heaven's shore,
From the earthen mire of tomboy play, a budding, young girl was wondrously born.

  Peregrine Allen

"Zambezi"

It was not easy paddling my canoe down the old river Zambezi.
The Zambezi is two hundred miles south of Zaire, and African animals are there.
The first turn in the river was a colorful sight, Flamingoes lifted
from the water's edge in flight.
My canoe floated quietly alongside a drinking Kudu.
I paddled slowly and saw Hippopotamuses feeding on river grasses.
Gazelles were leaping about, keeping time with Zebras shouts.
Crocodiles with big toothed smiles, watched Monkeys playing in the sand.
Giraffes are very tall, they can reach the highest berries before they
fall. Some ripened berries land at the feet of a Warthog to eat.
I paddled to the widest part of the river.
Elephants were having fun, showering water from their trunks on the
run. Hyenas stopped to laugh, at the Elephants taking a bath.
My canoe passed by a rocky shore. Hyrax were hiding from a lion's roar.
A Victorian bird sounded a cackle at the sight of Jackals.
Wildebeests were having a feast on marsh grasses.
I've reached the Indian Ocean and my journey's done.
It was not easy, but a lot of fun.

  Elmer J. Lall Jr.

An Act of Love

When I was just a little girl I'd go and spend the day
At big sisters house in the country, and there I'd laugh and play.

Sisters house was something special, at least it was to me,
In memory I can still smell the roses and feel the cool of the big shade tree.

She'd always give me little gifts and at home I'd say, "See what I got."
But one small gift stood our somehow, it was a little red flower pot.

I don't know why it was so special but I thought it grand as could be,
And for days whenever I'd go somewhere, I'd carry the little pot with me.

One night I tripped in the doorway - the flowerpot slipped from my
hold, and there lay my treasure in a little pile, useless as a dead man's gold.

This was my first recollection of such a loss and the 'hurt' of it was
deep, I remember all the tears I shed as I cried myself to sleep.

The next morning when I went to breakfast, my face broke into a grin
For there was my little red flowerpot all glued together again.

Working into the evening after a very late start,
Mother and Daddy repaired the pot and my broken heart.

The years passed and I grew up, I just about forgot
The pain and joy I received from that little red flowerpot.

But now it sits within my home and it's there for all to see, that the
reason it is all in one piece is because someone cared for me.

  Patsy J. Rogers

Untitled

  As I walk along the shore, I can not
visualize you are gone.
  Your presence yet seems strong.
  The waves seem to say,
hand me your cares,
  I'll take them away.
No life is lost where love has lived.
Memories are etched on the heart, to
help heal the time when we must part.
The little things we have said and done.
Makes me feel the battle is not lost,
but won.
  Go now if you must, I put you in
God's trust.
  At the end of the day, will be a
masterpiece of what once was clay.

  Carol Suchy

Reflection

Alone or lonely, it's just me
Peering into shadows that only I
  can see
Memories that grasp and drape
  like Spanish moss
Enfold and envelope me with a
  sense of loss
Is it my youth that has ebbed
  like evening tide
My dear departed father, I still
  yearn to earn his pride
The estrangement with my mother,
  sister, brother
In this world of communication
  We stutter and stammer, never
  grasping the grammar
  of love and affection
I fear my future, yours as well
  I must leave these shadows dark
  Tendrils of tomorrow call a life beyond the stark

  Amy L. Roper

Sunshine Home

Spring is here I hear children singing having fun
and violets turning there faces towards the sun
I am not alone the company I seek they are
like infants sleep sleep
Dreaming of the hills of heaven
The mind is weak the eyes clean from tears
They speak like in a dream
There is one who watches the sunbeam paint the wall
And talks to her artificial flowers
Oh how nice you've grown
I take you with me when I go home
She gets a good night pill
She hears echoing from the hall see you
Gently her sunlit face lay on her pillow
The longing weary weeping widow.

  Ruth Culver

Day Dreaming

I was sitting at my desk today
Just letting my thoughts drift and sway
The sun was warm against my cheek
I think perhaps, I fell asleep

There were two little clouds high in the sky
Floating around in the sweet by and by
They were fluffy white in outlines of grey
It was plain to see they were out to play

First they were wobbley, fat and round
Then they shaped into two little lambs
Rolling over and over and upside down
I could almost hear a laughing sound

One right behind the other as if in a chase
The one in front would pause, As if to wait
They skipped, and frolicked they were so gay
Sometime they would nibble along the way

Just before they began to ascend
I heard "happy birthday to you darling"
Higher and higher into the sky
Those two little clouds were you and I

    Mabel E. Franklin

Gray Porridge

The sky is vividly orange
Contrasting with gray porridge
Porridge in the morning and nothing more
Does the appetite hunger for

But the sky is vividly orange
Brightening the white bandage
Bandage covering the wounds of a heart
Impedes healing needed for a new start

And still the sky is vividly orange
Beckoning the soul on a brilliant voyage
Voyage devoid of procrastination
Filled only with imagination

    Shannan Stewart

Gift of Life

At last I am alive in the womb of peace
communing with love on every facet of living
seeing the miracles of life unfold their beginnings
gracing every brand new moment

With the strength of such love
by the light of such love
forever and always in my grasp
within inside of me
I know now there is nothing more to ask

Quite easily
every breath of every hour
love giving love so freely
my heart solos in flight to the oneness I devour
in the marvelous profusion of harmony

A solitude of grandeur
reincarnation every breath
love empowering life eternally
the awareness is exalting

    Sheila Bai

Things

Sometimes I think I should cherish
all those papers you bring home from school.
All the math and the spelling, the science tests telling
of term I've forgotten since school.
But today they just add to the clutter,
and anyway, you're here besides...
It'll be when you're grown and out on your own
when my missing-you opens my eyes.
Your drawing I stash in a closet
won't turn back the clock any day
when I want to remember that day in September
you drew it, then ran out to play...
I'll always admire your artwork
and efforts in all that you do.
But it's really not things that matter at all,
since the important Thing to me, is You.
This mom doesn't need things, like presents...
neither flowers nor candy will do.
The only two things I'll ever need have
are a hug and a "hi, mom" from you!

    Diane Sheridan

The Torch of Life

A candle burning, a flame so bright
  With future and hope - a glorious sight.
A gleam from within, sparks leaping off,
  Beckoning others, nothing is lost.

A candle is minute but the flame is not
  Unique, indivisible, independent in thought.
It learns as it burns - growing wiser yet smaller.
  The sparks are for others - a guide for a follower.

The burning string is a goal defined.
  The wax which supports it - the flesh of mankind.
Slowly dripping down the torch of life,
  Wax passes forever after matches ignite.

The candle burning is the soul of a man.
  The match which ignites it is another's kind hand.
One day it may reach a candle untouched.
  The flame will spread; sparks will leap up.

A lighthouse to others,
  A challenge unseen,
A glow in the darkness,
  An achiever - A dream.

    Stephanie R. Beck

Don't Leave...Don't Go

Don't leave. Don't go. Let the mind stay still.
Who's making it difficult...the voices are wrong.
Not accepting, finding a way out.
Scream your fears away. Shout.
What you see is not real, not here.
Remember your fears will disappear.

Don't understand. Don't want to believe.
You can't be going away again.
Voices come. Voices go. Not so.
The fears are building in your mind.
Please let them leave. You stay behind.

Don't leave. Don't go. Our lives are standing still.
Scream your fears away, make them disappear.
But disappear not you, not now.
Make yourself believe. Everything will be fine.
Stay a little longer. Don't waste this time.

Don't leave. Don't go.

    L. Davila

To Love... Not To Kill

The one in the dark
The one in the corner
The one with the mark
On his life forever

Alone he sits in the face of their madness
In their ignorance, bliss, and even their sadness
He can feel their hate, anger, and pain
As the natural elements beat him with rain

They cannot fight him... they can only stare
For to see this strange creature is always rare
He does not bother them, he does not care
He wishes only to wonder why they struggle with despair

The one in the light
The one on the hill
The one with the right
To love... not to kill
    Adam Coffman

The Wind Touches the Soul

Wind from the mountains blows across my face,
    Wind can make a pattern,
A pattern of hand stitched lace.

Wind has a way of polishing leaves,
    And polishing spirits,
by the cool breeze.

Wind can mend feelings that have been broken in half,
    Listen real close,
You will hear the wind laugh.

Wind can sing and feel like a dream,
    As so does it feel,
Of soft butter milk cream.

Wind is better than sun, rain, or snow,
For wind touches the soul,
Don't you think so?
    Alizzy Danknich

Carmen Hosti Mei

Malignant
blinded by your own twisted visions
vengeance reaping down from you
like the crashing of a tidal wave
splitting apart the mind
danger
holding your head and dancing with death
grab fate's hand and see what she deals you
she'll thrust you into the cellar
then she'll whimsically float away
deserted
by her slamming a locked metal door
the key in her acceptance
I'll grant only rejection
a calmness eternally empty within you
escape only advancing on the eyelash of hope
don't blink
    Rebecca E. Hill

Dearest Daddy

Dearest Daddy here is a letter I hate to write
Cause you're not here tonight you were called on home
And we know you're glad we can't help it we are so sad
You were my mother and my father
So that's hard to swallow you raised me like no other
You took your job so serious if we cried you would here us
Now your memory is so dear to us
Without you their is dread and fear, fear of the long unknown
Without you back at home sometimes I think to myself
You're still back there taking care
But other times my heart just fades
I never knew how I would miss you so
Oh God the letting go it's so slow and my feelings won't let go
'Cause Daddy Dear I loved you so
I just wonder if you know oh Daddy Dear I love you so
I don't know how to let you go
So daddy dear let me know if you know how to let you go
Please God let me know if he can see
And please God I loved him so take good care of him
And Dear Daddy please hear me tonight let me feel you near ....
    Zee L. Nelson

Rain

How do you say I love you
    and how do you say I care?
Why do things get in the way
    and why are they so hard to bare?
Why is life so hard
    and filled with so much pain?
Why are we so far apart
    and why does it rain?
Why do things go so wrong
    and why can't we see?
How do I show you the way
    and as it destiny
Why can't we see the trouble
    and before all the pain?
Why can't we have reality
    and why does it rain?
How do we find the actions and the words, I Love You?
Why can't you see the love and the feelings that are true?
How do you find the love of others and how do you stand the pain?
Why can't you come back to me and why does it rain?
    Joseph S. Sonich

Christmas Is A Time To Give

Christmas is a time to give,
to let your feelings show.
To purchase little presents
for everyone you know.

This season is a merry season,
the highlight of the year.
It touches the hearts of everyone
without a doubt of fear.

Mom, you have so much generosity
that most people are able to see.
You give and give and give and give
no matter what the fee.

Because you own so many things
you're really hard to shop for.
We searched every day and night in all your favorite stores.

We couldn't find the right thing that we thought you would enjoy.
We had a choice of clothes and books and every kind of toy.

We decided to give you something that money cannot buy.
A little meaningful poem
made especially by Jamie and I.
    Annie Fultz

Caught by Color

Racism hurts everybody
that's what they all say they said it then, they say it today
but why are the racist I don't understand
just because you're black, we made
you work our land I don't know why
we made you slaves, but now the children
bore the graves stop racism now, why
we still have a chance, for the sake of
the children please give them a chance
look deep inside to the heart, not the
skin like the wizard of oz the man
made of tin when you're friends with
someone you don't look at the color.
So we must be enemies and need to learn
to love each other why can't we just
unite that would be perfect sight! Black
and white hand in hand fighting together
taking a stand racism hurts me. Racism
hurts all, why can't we learn to forgive
and forget and tear down the barriers and tear down the wall

Melissa K. Torgersen

My Father Knew Ireland

   O, Ireland
how you flow through my veins
   as a river runs to the vast and troubled sea.
You are a sweet refrain -
   lifting, poignant, proud.
A tune my father knew and freely shared
   with a showman's verve and whimsy.

   O, Ireland
so close to kin are thee
as a soft mist weeps
from the huge and awesome sky.
You are a Yankee's dream -
   haunting, healing, bliss.
A yarn my father knew and loosely spun
   with a poet's flair and feeling.

   O, Ireland
   O, Ireland
O, haven for my heart's own woes,
O, my Daddy's fondest shore,
O, my sense of coming home.

Eileen E. Pappolla

Time Passing

When I am old and think back when we first met
Which I consider the old days
I sit watching and warming my hands
By the fire's blaze...

I've never forgotten the love, the hope, the wanting with desire
I can hear your little girl laughter and see your face out of the
   not so still fire...
Wondering if we had captured all the love and passion
   if we held on to the thought
We could have loved like no other in its fashion
But it's a shame it was all for naught...

I always held and carried within my heart
You that I have loved and we would become a part
Of eternal memories, the mystery of love
Holding the deep pain as I look from above...
I sit now by the fire and shiver with cold
Thinking you are no longer young, and I am old...

Robert C. Casale

Together Forever

You know we've been together for a long, long time
   And now it seems we are getting even closer,
Do you think it will work,
   Do you feel we could be together forever!

Would you be my darling honey
   And I'll be your - sweetheart,
Together forever could be the way we should be
   Or will we end up apart.

By your side is where I would like to be
   But is it by my side where you would want to be,
Together forever could be our only wish
   And our love would never flee.

Together forever, forever together
   Is how we can hope we can stay,
Forever together, together forever
   And at the final end neither one of us will pay.

You and I if we give it a try, what a joy it could be
   Today, tonight and for all eternity,
Together forever, forever together
   That's how we can always be.

Darren R. Boyer

Puzzles Of Life

Life resembles pieces of a puzzle.
The pieces are different in many ways.
There are the good times
And then there are the bad times.
The times that make us laugh until our stomachs hurt
And the times when we cannot stop crying.
We cannot remember them all
But there are some we will never forget.
Our life is just one big puzzle
That is waiting to be put together.
It is put together by the many different happenings
In our lives and it will take forever to complete.
But what can we do?
These are the puzzles of life.

Courtney D. Gardner

Why And Why

I fought a friend for hours one day
Then went home, cried, and kneeled to pray.
I asked God why He made us lazy,
Selfish, stubborn, crude, and crazy.
He made dogs that show their love
And have such traits as Those above.
They hold no grudges, guns, or money,
Accept you though your jokes aren't funny.
Aloud I asked, my eyes like fog,
"Why can't Man be more like Dog?"

The morning after my ordeal
I reconsidered my appeal.
For there upon my kitchen floor
I found a mess that shook my core.
Rover left me quite a gift,
And even he knew I was miffed.
He waited for my anguished roar,
Then turned and bolted through his door.
I called to God as Rover ran,
"Why can't Dog be more like Man?"

Lisa Y. Yang

She's Not Normal

She was born not quite whole. Her father was a drunkard,
And mother couldn't cope; her sisters were ashamed; others
were afraid. She did the best she could, but it made them
sick. She's not normal.

She went away to build her life and hoped they would be
proud. Her mother proved her wrong with her sisters' aid.
Her happiness was undeserved! She must be punished! How
dare she succeed against their need! She should not be
free. She's not normal!

Society had made it clear—she isn't whole. Employers tried
To destroy her. "She's going to the hospital tonight—she's
Disturbed", she wanted to die—commit suicide. "She's evil,"
"We don't have time for her." No matter, she's not normal

"You're a mental case," a brother in law said. She finally
Broke and changed her heart. She feels for no one but the
Animals, she confides in no one, and trusts in only the coming
Christ. All worldly hopes and dreams are gone. She has died
Inside. She's not normal!

Regan Mason

The Obsession

All I ever wanted was for you to return my smile,
Think of me in your dreams,
Hold me for awhile.

All I ever wanted was for you to love me so,
Whisper in my ear,
Never let me go.

All I ever wanted was for you to touch my heart,
To never leave my side,
To never be apart.

All I've ever wanted was to keep your heart in mine,
I'll never let you go,
Our love will always shine!

This obsession I don't understand,
I'd never meant it to be planned.
I'm sure of this love,
Unsure of the obsession,
Always remember,
Your heart is in my possession.

Melissa Epperson

Night Rain

Set within nightfall's amaranth glow, the air becomes humid.
Starting slowly, then playing to a crescendo—
through rustling leaves and flashes of penetrating light,
a symphony begins: harmonizing strings in happy obsession.

The sky's passion, unspoken through the heat of the day,
carries memories of tenderness and joy within her bosom.
Finally, swollen storm clouds, unnoticed by most, attain rhapsody!

Speaking to two friends as a life awakening force, inherent
and deliberate, the windjammer's wake enters their souls;
falling rain splatters, consecrating by touch, every rose petal.

Water incessantly flowing, delectably arousing—
her sensors are awash by love's sweet aroma.
Breathing heavily, paralleling pollen's transformation into honey,
Lovers dance together as one, twirling effortlessly into heaven.

George W. Little

Called To Witness

As Christians, we are all called to witness...
To preach the "Good News", spread it far and wide
But my heart's concern is the emphasis
We place on our words and not what's inside

There are too many sorry examples
Of loud voices without any substance
Bombastic and proud, they lure disciples
On the strength of their powerless pretense
I know we are called to give an answer
To those who sincerely ask of our creed
But wise hearts will weigh our word's caliber
On scales that balance our motives and deeds

The tangible traits of all witnesses
Glare throughout lifestyles in a clear language
With words preceded by appearances,
Our actions will carry the real message

So witness my friend, but remember this...
Words can't shield motives, they're clearly in view
What starts out covert, insight will undress
Because though you speak, they'll hear what you do

Bob G. Martinez

Herald Of Spring

The Blue Ridge was veiled in a misty blue haze
And the March sky that morning was gray.
In the air, I could feel a piercing chill
And for miles snow covered the way.
The Countryside lay so quiet and still
For no sound of wildlife was heard.
Then, from the woodland brushed with white
Came the soul stirring sound of a bird.
A Thrush, so enthralling and rapturous its song
I stood at the door and listened long.
The tune seemed to swell from the balsam nearby,
This beautiful music from a creature, so shy
From its throat came a crystalline sweet melody
And I stood there enchanted as its song came to me
Spring had arrived amid snow and skies of gray,
Its only Herald was the song of a bird that day.

Adele Lee Martin

My Lake Waterfall

My secret lake waterfall is near the beach,
I go there when I am lonely and sad.
I see the most beautiful waterfall I've known.
I hear the goddess speak to me. They say how
lucky I am to have somebody to love me.
It makes me feel deeply. I look for my mother
in heaven. The goddess says there is a symbol
of love, the deepest love. You must be a generous
person to see your mother. We are the five goddesses
that make wishes come true. Find a person that you
know will take care of you and love them forever.
They tell me love is a feeling no one can lose.
My mother looks down from the heavens and
smiles. She knows that I am loved.

Nicole Bee

My Beautiful Son

M - Is for the Many times I think of him.
I - is for the Isolation I now must bear.
C - is for the Charm and grace God gave him.
H - is for the Hell I cannot share.
A - is for the Angels he now talks to.
E - is for the Eyes, that were ever true
L - is for the Love he gave to me and to you.

Michael was his name and always will remain, forever etched
in my brain, the youth I had but could never tame.

This flowering youth, with long lean limbs and a curly mane,
had all to live for and everything to gain.

But all too soon and in the prime of life,
His beauty, wit and charm went out, out like a candle light!

Forever gone from those who loved him.
Forever gone from those who mourn him.

Why not me instead of he - I would find myself to ask!
I, who had lived my life and was weary of every task!
Why not me, instead of he? He who knew not yet a wife!

My Son, My Son - How very cruel fate can truly be!

My Beautiful Son - You took with you the better part of me!

Beatrice Kontanis

Romeo and Juliet

He is my Romeo and I his Juliet,
Upon him, in wonder my eyes beset.
The determination and the love, fill in his eyes,
Like a gentle morning, darkened by sunrise.
Like the horizon overhead, you long to embrace,
His hands touch you gently, casually on side your face.
You long to feel his gentle touch and his lips pressed against yours,
A love like no other, a trust all endures.
You contemplate in the beginning, relax in the end,
The passion burns deep, a love that kindles within.
When we walk side by side, people stop and stare,
They smile inside their soul, as their hearts swell.
The love in the air catches like wildfire.
No one can explain the feeling that being in love projects.
The love, the passion, the trust, the glory, heaven on earth.
I'd give my life for him,
He is the real, the faithful, and the true.
He is my Romeo and I his Juliet.

Chiquita Campbell

Trees

Trees in January are covered with frost and snow.
Trees in February are covered with frost.
Trees in March are starting to bud.
Trees in April are starting to bloom with blossoms.
Trees in May are starting to grow green.
Trees in June are green.
Trees in July are starting to have apples and peaches and other kind
   of fruits.
Trees in August are starting to have colors like orange, red and yellow.
Trees in September are starting to lose their leaves.
Trees in October are starting really starting to lose their leaves.
Trees in November are almost bare.
Trees in December are really bare.

Melissa Perry

Symbols

The words that I write are just letters combined
The letters combined are just abstract ideas
Symbols of that which is not even here

Listen to the voice that does not make a sound

Picture a tree that is free from the ground
Picture a ball that spins round and round
Picture the light, but with not a frown

Open your mind to the voice that is there

And look at your eyes, but with not a tear
And look at the world, but with not a fear

Now look at the people who can not even hear

Jon D. Gemma

Alone

I close my eyes
and comfort surrounds me with each thought of you.
Do I live by my heart?
Or die by my sword of fear.

Your hands caressing warm and tender,
you tempt my wanting.
Your physical distracts my discipline.
My wall crumbles.

And your starry eyes gaze
as I break like a wave
on your beach of lonely moonlight,
only to retreat into my ocean of fear,
Alone.

Cheryl Key

Are You Mad, Or Just Insane

Crippling insanity wells up from the depths of all men's souls.
Reaching out, it strikes a fatal blow, to the minds of those mortal
fools who would dare stifle it.

"The laughing death", the masses would call it. A plague to most,
but a saviour to others. A welcome release, from the harshness of a
cruel world gone mad.

So in this chaos of hell we have created for ourselves, I ask you.
Are you of sound mind?
What is sound mind? And if not;
How would you know?

Mike Mansfield

Fluorescent Blue

As the fluorescent blue waters are surrounding my weary soul
I will drown my self in Him, not sin, forever more
I find desire, enough, in the massaging currents of present tide
And I'll patiently wait as my heart yearns of the coming for us,
   the Bride

Let me sing His praises with sincerity and may it bubble up to the
   lost
So they can know the penalty for not accepting forgiveness, which
   has no cost
Let us bring our salt ashore to convict their eyes to open
And then, if they believe it or not, the truth will have been spoken

The pale moon slowly rises almost as subtle as a blink
I had better swim deeper before I have a chance to think
The rising of the tide has come, I'll not be washed ashore
Now I'm dwelling deep within His grace, thank the Lord

Jason Daniel

Peace

Peace must start in the home.
Yahweh God said, "It is not good that the man should be alone."
Yahweh God made both male and female in his image.
This is why a man must leave father and mother, and cling to his wife,
and the two become one body in marriage.

After the Fall, we have both evil and good.
Satan, the liar, deceived Eve by a falsehood.
Outward observance is not of the Spirit.
Do you practice Law or believe in Christ's Word, the Devil to outwit?

Anyone who preaches a different Good News is condemned if not taught by Paul.
Paul learned by a direct revelation from Jesus Christ and by His Call.
Paul was commissioned to preach to the circumcised.
At Antioch Paul told Peter by making the pagans practice Jewish ways,
    he was not wise.

Those who rely on the faith of Abraham are justified.
Those who rely on the Law are under the curse because Christ they have denied.
Under the Law no freedom is allowed.
All baptized by fire and the Holy Spirit are sons of God neither 'Jew
nor Greek, slave nor free, male or female; as we are one in Christ',
    God has vowed.
The child born of Hagar, the Egyptian slave girl, pictures the covenant of slavery.
The child Isaac, of Sarah, the Jewish free-born wife, is of the covenant of the free.

Helen Ethel Lowman

The Lucky One

It was cold and stormy on this unusual day, our daughter, Sunshine, wanted to go out and play.
"Stay close to the house," I warned as she left, feeling something churning within myself.
I tried to ignore it, she was only five, but the feeling wouldn't go away I felt deep inside.
I opened the door on our modest house, looking for Sunshine to be bouncing about.
There were no sounds, not even a word, not the "hey mommy," I usually heard.
My God what has happened, I panicked inside, she is always near, almost by my side.
I heard a scream, then the slam of a door, I knew I would never see my Sunshine anymore.
We did everything a desperate mother would do, we called the police, the F.B.I. too!
We couldn't find anything, not even a clue. Why did I let her go out and play?
Why couldn't I have waited for a beautiful day. This doesn't happen
    to people like me, only to others, oh why can't you see!
And yet it was a nightmare, but this one was real, they found my sweet Sunshine laying in a field,
She was cold and battered and sexually abused, she was alive and that was great news.
I held her close and prayed to God above, thank you for not taking the one that I love.
Millions are not as lucky you see, they've lost their loved ones to creeps on the streets.

Dorothy S. Wooten

Heaven's Dew

I had
a dream
of a dark sky
with one small star
that flickered a soft white glow.
I heard a Thunderous Voice proclaim, "Amen!"
At that moment the star split into two separate entities,
and began to fall like two balls of fire toward the earth.
Guarded by heavenly hosts, the two spirits fell in different directions.
They sped at a blazing velocity to arrive at their new destinations.
Two elements of Heaven were charged with the task of finding each other.
Then, at the blink of an eye, The Sun had pushed away the darkness.
I looked and saw two birds that were both blue as the sky above.
They sang a song of Love that could never be composed.
They took to the open air; keeping perfect formation,
and then perched on their branch together
to sing their melody once more.
Heaven's Dew is the formation of a duet of unity which adds to the Waters of Life.

O'Neal McCall

Where Is It?

The sunsets of pink,
The roses of spring,
The quiet night sky,
Where is it?

The gentle lapping water,
A sail on a turquoise lake,
The swirling mist of color,
Where is it?

A warm fireplace hearth,
The quiet wood,
Merry laughter and good times,
Where is it?

I can tell you.
It is all within you.
Your dreams and your hopes,
Are where everything can be.

Jonathan Bittner

Small Miracles

One of life's most
Beautiful things,
A single flower.

Its slender stem,
Fragile petals,
Delicate fragrance.

One of life's most
Wondrous things,
Two people sharing.

Each one giving,
Both receiving,
Mutual caring.

Rita J. Toovey

God's Words

God lives within the heart
God is one who never part

God is there yesterday
God is there everyway

God listens to what I say
God is with me each day

To get to know him is a must
God is all ways with us

God is a God for just
God is a God you can trust

God will answer when you call
God will help you when you fall

God is the one who cares
God is the one who shares

God will open all doors
God will heal all sores

I know I'm not the same
God calls me by my name

For God I shall talk
For God I will walk

Mary Jean Smith

Rope

Once I had a rope,
that was never very strong.
Only one strand held it together.
That strand got looser and looser,
then it broke.
I thought the rope would fall apart,
but instead it became tighter.

Brian Crum

The Rose

Delicious aroma, glorious sight,
fresh roses are a nose's delight!
As eyes behold beauty,
the nose inhales perfection
that transports all senses
in every direction.

Remember that dance, so long ago,
yellow rosebuds adorned my shoulder so
daintily, no perfume was indicated
for we were innocently intoxicated
by the misty dream world of
that sweet aura surrounding me.

Penny Forrest

Untitled

The fabric of my life
slowly unravels,
the ends become fraided, tangled.
So I try to reweave them
make everything right
the threads become loose
but I pull them back tight
now there's bare spots
it's thread bare
with unsightly bumps
I try to conceal them
turn the fabric around
but as soon as I mend this
a thread comes unwound.

Jo Anne Asbury

Lights Voyages

You told me of the Ultimate Experience,
Which could be mine, and soon -
As astral voyages, no doubt,
To soar away from gloom.
Would you unlock some positive forces,
And Music of the Spheres, and,
Would your magic make my Soul
Travel to new realities?
What is this secret of the Universe -
That I have potential for,
If unlocked and experienced,
With you upon the door?
Should I let my Soul soar free,
Upon this Astral Voyage,
Because I owe it to myself....
Because you have the key?
Or, should I pine and twitter,
Wanting, all the while -
The Voyage of Life - in time and space,
That I am now due to experience?

Serena G. Mills

Tomorrow

The sun will still shine tomorrow
The trees will always grow
The birds will fly away again
But I just wanted you to know
    I won't be there,

The flowers will bloom tomorrow
Outside, the children will play
The moon will rise at night once more
But before I go, I wanted to say
    For you, I really care!

The bees will buzz tomorrow
The world will leave me behind
Maybe you'll never think about me twice
But hear this before I lose my mind
    That my love is true,

The birds will sing again tomorrow
On the streets, the lights will glow
Maybe you'll find another person
But I wanted you to know
    That I will always love you!

Rubaba Mojid

Life Goes On

Life you've shown me, good
and bad, you cut me and I bled,
you burnt me and I blister,
you bent me and I broke, and
each time I got back on my
feet even though you've left
your scars...
Physically, Mentally
and Spiritually,
just to knock me down
again, you have the power
to consume me, you've done
so many times, you've sent
me into secluded oblivion...
Until tomorrow when I have
the chance to try again!!!

John J. Bibby

I Thought It Ended

I thought it ended
When you died.
And packed it quickly,
Deep inside.
The years have passed,
But not the pain.
A broken, shattered
Child of shame.
Sleepless nights and
Haunted dreams;
A childhood filled
With inner screams.
I thought it ended
When you died.
I hoped, I prayed,
And still I cry.

Brenda R. Minshall

A Walk Along the Coast

I walk the beach silently,
while the crabs fight violently.
I look at all the birds above,
Then I see a morning dove.
I look up high in the sky,
and then I start to fly,
past a bee, over the sea,
I fly so happily.

Steph McDowell

Became Aware (It's Just Not Fair)

I was walking,
And looking at the ground,
When I heard a sound.
So I raised my head to the sky.
I started to stare,
and became aware
That I was in that country
I can't remember
At least for now.
It is so tender.
there is no crowd
and it's not that loud
So I started to walk
And that's when
Someone started to talk and he
Told me that he doesn't care
For it's just not fair
That is when I became aware
I was in the country,
Where people have no pity.

Mary Calderon

What A Game

The National anthem is sung once more;
This is what the fans adore.
The opening pitch is thrown.
The umpire cleans off home.
The pitcher warms up,
The batter steps up,
Fans chanting for their team,
This is what you call a scene!
Coaches bossing,
Umps tossing,
Home run hitting,
Game winning,
Bat cracking loudly,
Just listen to the crowd!
Ninety-eight pitches thrown.
Perhaps the pitcher can go home.
Bottom of nine
I think it's about time,
The love for the game
Has never been the same.

Andrew W. Hall

The Good Life

As I walk along life's pathway,
And see God's wonders everywhere -
I lift my head and say "thank-you"
For all your works, ever the air.

Your blessings are most bountiful,
Your handiwork at every turn -
We are truly blessed people,
There's nothing more for me to yearn!

Zola Andrews

Every Time

Every time I see the image of her,
I cry, because
she reminds me
of the day I was missing
you.

And it briefly makes me feel sad.

But then I think of the
times we share, now
as friends.
They're good thoughts
of you.
Still there are
the memories of the past.

Christi Smoak

Who Will Pray

Who will pray for the children
who will take a stand
Who will teach them about God's ways
and lend a helping hand
Who will give them comfort
in a world so full of fear
Who will pray their needs be met
and dry a small ones tears
Who can take the time
to call each one by name
Who can hold them tenderly
and ease their every pain
It takes a special person
to seek the Lord each day
to touch the hem of his garment
the price not much to pay

Will you call out daily
and seek His will so sweet
to give this generation
a life in Him complete

Theresa C. Stewart

The Shadow

I saw your lovely shadow
     It was just across the room
Suspended there in silence
     Illuminated by the moon

Shimmering so gracefully
     I knew it right away
My heart began to leap for joy
     As I wished that you would stay

So I sought to come much closer
     And feel your touch again
But your image grew much fainter
     Before I could even begin

I felt such desperation
     Such emptiness inside
To watch you slowly fade away
     Was more than I could abide

And now there's nothing left
     Except the glow of the moon
So I quietly, silently settle back
     And hum your favorite tune

Ron Nicely

Loved One

Oh the pain that I have felt
for having Loved and Lost
the Sorrow in my Soul
can teach me nothing more,
for Loneliness has been my Calling
and I have truly Wept
The Tears of the Broken-Hearted
as my Solemn Secret kept,
now emptiness abounds
fulfilling my Regret
and then with idle Time
beyond what Man can Comprehend,
I think of things that might have been
if Love had been Portrayed
as Honest and Sincere
instead of Youthful and Pretend.

Jose Carlos Robert

Truth

Truth is straight as and arrow.
     Knows no curves are bends.

Real truth never has to be made
     To fit.
          Are sifted through.
               Real truth just is.

Truth maybe over looked are
     Denied.
          Because it is not smooth
               And flashy.

Real truth is truth.
     For real truth just is.

Alice M. Teague

Thinking of You Always, Mom

Although I may not call too much
My thoughts are always with you.
I take a look outside my door
And wonder what you do -
Each day and night - so far away.
My life feels incomplete...
My family's spread around so far -
And little do we meet.
But love can go a long, long way
Remember, mine is with you.

Shirley B. Krawford

Dawn's Awakening

In the darkness still
A misty horizon beckons,
Hinting of a fiery orb...
Dawn begins anew.

Brenda Lee Proffitt

Coyote

     He was alone
     He was afraid
He was a victim of
the law

But as they pulled
his face
from the grille
of a semi
in the early morning
fog...
they knew he had gotten
away

Wayne C. Tess

Grandma's Rose

One day when I was searching
through my childhood souvenirs,
I found a tiny little seed
from my Grandma so dear.

She gave it to me long ago,
When I was only five.
She said "Now, Kassy, keep this
As long as I'm alive."

"When the angels come to call
and to Heaven I must go,
Plant this tiny little seed,
and a lovely flower will grow."

Many years had come and gone,
Since Grandma went away,
but when I found that little seed,
I planted it that day.

Now as I sit and reminisce,
that lovely flower still grows,
underneath my windowsill.
I call it "Grandma's Rose."

Kathleen Lowery

A Maine Folk Sonnet

Traveling the country
side, enjoying the
scenic view with
wild flowers, green
fields, westley winds.
Much like you and I,
Their was a woman
passing through.
She was as wild
free like a bird,
untamed like the
wild flowers, searching
for a place she
could call home.
Searching high
low, she decided to
call maine her home.
Why "Oh" why I don't know, would
she settle on
this place called maine for her home.

Eileen Thereault Wesley

Performing At The Piano

I sit at the piano,
So straight and still and tall,
With my hands above the keyboard,
Just ready to fall.

I play Fur Elise,
Beginning with a sigh.
My ears simply listen,
While my fingers fly.

They go faster, then slower,
And softer, then loud.
My fingers do the playing
While my head's in a cloud.

The last note sounds perfectly,
I'm back to solid ground.
I get up from the bench and bow,
While hearing but one sound,

The audience applauds me,
"Encore! Encore!" they shout and yell.
And so, then I know,
That I played it very well.

Carrie Nixon

Family Ties

Uncles, aunts, cousins and friends
that's where family ties all begin.
Grandma, grandpa, mother and pop,
that's where family ties should
never stop. Family ties are here
that's what built the nation,
blacks and whites we're both
a combination of family ties.
My family don't tie because their
all in a knot. I wonder when this
evilness in my family is gonna stop.
I pray everyday, and again every night,
for my family to tie in that bow
just right. I don't care if it's
blue I just want to be like
you, the families that stick
together like super glue and
that's a family tie.

Keelanashe T. Collins

Daily Guidance

The guidance that we receive each day,
is often misunderstood,
the ups, downs, in's and out's,
we'd change them, if we could,
Each day we hope that things will go,
exactly as we plan,
however days become a challenge,
we get through them, the best we can.
I find these tasks can be so hard,
they're dealt with in many ways,
but, I know the guidance I receive,
is from the Lord each day.
As my day begins to darken,
and I'm turning into bed,
I thank the Lord for all the lessons,
He stores each day within my head.

Amanda Dean

The Magical Masquerade

Under guise the room was entered,
    behold a fabulous masquerade!
Thus mingling coalesced two hearts,
    under moon's destined magic.
Exclusive parts of a whole, each had
    fallen short to find.
Reunited at soul's omphalos, whence
    pure, true lovers fuse.
Masks finally fall, romantic quests
    concluded by the two.
Fears abandoned, love's immaculate
    mysteries discovered tonight!

Timothy W. Harmon

Thoughts

Sitting in a forest all alone,
thinking;
a white dove flies from above,
it rains blood,
a flash of lightning comes
then the end of the world.
Suddenly I discover what life means;
But no one's left to hear it.

Mike Baldoza

A Grandmother's Wealth

Pitter patter on my porch,
Laughter in my ears,
My heart melts as they enter
And I hide my tears.

Tears not of sorrow
Nor, are they tears of pain
But tears of joy -
Just seeing them again.

Both arms are encircled
A bear hugs my waist,
My hair lightly tugged,
My face - touching lace.

Each with a story
That grammy must hear,
Begging my attention,
Wanting me near.

Grandmother's riches -
And, as I look from one to one,
I hide again my dampened lids -
Thank you Lord - for all you've done.

Marion Lewis

Wait

I'm Weird
I'm Different
I'm Me

They can't accept that
They can't accept me
They can't accept anything

Wait...
Never mind, I thought...
Those narrow minded...

People accept what they want
Well aren't they in for a surprise
Wait until they see me.

Walking down the street
Walking in the halls
Walking about the world

Wait until they see me
Can't see me for who I am
Just wait, You'll regret it

I maybe weird
I maybe different, at least I'm Me.

Malinda Nelson

Bedtime

Get in bed,
Squeak.
Lay my head,
Creak,
On my pillow.
Hear a noise,
Screech.
Mouse in my room,
Eek!!!
It runs outside,
Zoom.
Cars go by it,
Beep.
They run it over,
Splat!
Now it is flat.
Ahhh
So I can sleep,
Zzzzz.

Rachel Herrmann

Working Hands

Working hands raised the pyramids
in the hot desert sun,
Working hands picked the cotton
before a long day was done.

Working hands tapped the tambourine
on early Sunday morn,
Working hands oiled my body
just when I was born.

Working hands held together
at midnight to pray,
Working hands wiped my tears
when they sold daddy 'way.

Working hands blistered and bruised
from laying railroad tracks,
Working hands fought the wars
that stopped the enemy attack.

Working hands opened books
by secret candle light,
Working hands will clap is Cumming*
before We say good night.

Kevin Hamm

**January '97 -- The march from Atlanta,
Ga. to Cumming commemorating Dr.
King's birthday as a National Holiday.*

On Fairies And Freedom

Glistening, shimmering in the air
Sunlight dancing on her hair,
Two fragile wings reflecting light
Compose a strange, unearthly sight.

Free flowing gossamer, soft and warm
Clothe her lithe and slender form,
While movement of uncommon grace
Compliments her lovely face.

She dances round the woodland trees
Hitching rides on honeybees,
And Nature smiles with untold pleasure
On this Her tiny priceless treasure.

If only Mankind would commune
And with the Earth could stay in tune,
Perhaps, ye too might be as free
As the maiden fay and honeybee.

Gloriana Queen of the Fairies

Existence

All her life her pain was hidden
She dreamed of a happier life
And to this hope she was driven
An end to her turmoil and strife

Late at night with silent fears
She longed for a gentle touch
Just someone to wipe her tears
Could it be - She wanted too much

Tears came less as her pain grew
Her bedroom - her quiet place
As lives went on - She withdrew
Wanting to leave without a trace

Brief moments of joy she tried to feel
As it would pass her by
Her heart to him she longed to spill
But he no longer cared why

Her agony was just to exist
And watch life smile on past
This would be her hearts twist
How long can this pain last?

Mary E. Purdy

St. Patrick's Day

St. Patrick's day
May be the day
The sunshine's rays
Will lead the way
The rainbow's beams'
Glorious gleam
Will lead to green
Or gold it seems.

Kelly Smitherman

Untitled

The dials within
The gears won't spin
Even with the touch of our skin
Spin, spin
Interweave interleave
The nuts and bolts
Jolt, revolt
Fire leaps up
And out
Oh no, we forgot
We simply forgot
These things we make
They still can break
Even when we hit the brake
But now, however, it's all at stake
The grand technical flight
Of human might
Ends up mangled by the roadside.

Mark Scott Lavin

Look To Heaven

May you always be happy,
May you always be glad,

May you never
have heartache,
As I've always had.

May your joy
be uplifted,
May your smile
always stay,

As sunlight from heaven,
On each bright
new day.

May God in
His mercy,
Toward you
be kind,

May your eyes
look to Heaven,
And our Saviour
you find.

James E. Conley

Observation

Shiny wet crow
struts on spring's new carpet
while neat rows of epitaphs
silently watch nature's rebirth.

Lois J. Kelly

The Life of Love

Love is like a flower,
'Tis fragrant and has Power.
'Til it dies
Then 'tis sour.

Roe A. Malach

Ode To Leif

Leif is a dog
Who has showed me the meaning of love

My friend, my friend
My beautiful friend
You taught me to run and to play
You were such a pretty puppy
Now your beauty is turning gray

The years just flew
Look how you grew
It happened overnight
Such a good old boy
Bringing the joy
Into my life

Ruth V. McDonald

Squab

When I was small...
Not big at all...
I often went about thinking tall,
And would look forward to the time
When I was eight... Tall and straight.

The time soon came,
I was eight, then ten,
Then twenty-eight...
And still thinking tall,
I soon realized that fate
Had dealt a blow to infuriate,
I Would Always Be Small,
Not straight and tall,
But Small...

Bette Parsons

Terrors From Above

The thunder is not shy
  but Loud
pounding through the sky.
The lightning is not dim
  but Bright
firing everything in sight.
The
  hail
    is
      falling.
Will it ever start stalling?
We will never know
for he rules the show.
  Disaster!
  Destruction!
What will be next?
but a vibrant
  tornado
killing the
  Best.

Randy Ornstein

Nobody Knows

I wander through life
Without making a sound
Always searching for something
That can never be found

Laughing at my pain
As I turn to them in need
In the flower of my wounds
My friends are the only seed

Nobody knows
The heartache I feel
Forever on my own
The dreams that they steal

Alone in a corner
Down my face roll silent tears
My head buried in my chest
Bottling up all of my fears

Maybe someday
The world will be made right
But as the tears roll down my face
I hope I can last the night

Kristen Beelen

Santa Rosas

Santa Rosas speak to me.
  Tell me all your history.
Let me feel your magic vibes.
  Then I'll truly feel alive!

You collect the rain and snow.
  Then around me plants can grow.
Bighorn sheep graze on your slope.
  Also squirrels, deer even antelope.

Santa Rosas grant me peace.
  All life's tensions will release.
Santa Rosas beneath you I lie.
  There I'll remain until I die.

Bette Cheney

Heart

A constant pound
Steadfast and strong
Can be made of gold or stone
Pure or deceitful
Both are solid and hard
But which is which?
Why is the thing which keeps
A person alive for an entire century
Broken in a single second?
Why does the symbol of love
Feel hatred just as strongly?
Why am I deafened by
Pounding in my ears;
Terrified by the
Thunder in my chest?
Now I know —
To travel a lifetime of bliss
My path must be chosen
Not by my head,
But by my heart.

Lauren Rutledge

After the Storm

Step from the darkness
and into the rain.

Purify and dignify
your befallen soul.

Sound vision to adversity;

Watch in astonishment
as dark clouds violently brew.

Stop running,
face the storm,
burnish the truth.

Is it such a surprise

Step from the rain
and through the broken clouds.

Immerse in the golden sky...
set yourself free.

Dawn M. Taylor

Our Love

The river flows,
just like the way our love goes.
Sweet, tender, loving, and nice,
and sometimes it's as cold as ice.

Rough, rapid, rocky, and different,
going every which way
seeing if we can get through each day.

Even knowing there is so much to say,
we only want to pray.
We snuggle up so warm and close,
while you know you're the one I
love the most!!

Elizabeth Pennington

To Not Be Known

Falling like a dead bird in the sky
I feel nothing inside
my heart feels so empty
temptations surround this human form
I feel as if I am going to drown
you know my heart
you see my soul
you see this big black hole
that once was full of happiness and joy
what happened to it?
Where did it go?
Darkness surrounds me all the time
help me to be a shining light
to those who need this love
I keep inside
overflow me with your joy
fulfill me with your love
so I may share it with others today.

Heather J. Peters

My Father's Eyes

Suddenly...
Looking infinitely within my soul,
Then slowly...creeping yet further,
Extending far beyond the depths of my
Compassion and anguish,
Further coupled with the ever present
Possibility
Of sudden and tragic death...or loss,
It occurred to me...
I have my Father's eyes.

Brenda Sue Bell Proulx

Razors

I like razors.

smooth and personal
not like guns
you can get
close
close enough
to see expressions
rip a smile apart
impair a vision

a women's choice
should be smooth
up close and personal
a real woman to woman
heart to heart
where the conversation
is punctuated
by screams
and torn vanity
from scalp to chin.

It's simpler that way.

Anissa Lynnea Harris

Violet Eyes

Violet eyes,
Beautiful spies
They see the secret me.
They glimpse my soul
Then read the scroll
How deeply they can see.

They see my ache
This life can make.
They comprehend me so.
I cannot hide.
They see inside.
So perfectly they know.

Violet eyes,
Those lovely spies
Have seen me to the core.
Yet they still say
With love's bright ray
They're mine for ever more.

Peggy Jeneen Glover

Alien

Tonight
    I stepped through
    some unperceived door,
    I think.
For mundane night has become
a mysterious, black-woven tapestry
laced with spectres and dreams...
    a presence half-sensed
    a chill down my spine.
There are fairies flying tonight.
    I think.
And I am utterly alone.

Petra Bates

Night

Everything is dark, dark, bleak!
No need to even seek
For a time that's better
All good is hidden, you are so weak.

The night of which I speak
Is the night of your mind
When it's gloomy
The fluttering light making visible
Only closed doors.

Is no longer seen
Night lingers on
Limiting your hope
Halting your progress
Stealing your dreams
Wasting your love
Laying hollow your time

Remember, during the night stumble on
Through the bleakness
With prayer, faith, and a song!

Clotine Waygalo

Happy New Year!

Last year is over
We can't get it back
So let's forget our misses
And stay on the track

We know what's ahead
Will be a challenge to us
Let's try to face it with courage
Without worry or fuss

Let's forget the bad
And remember the good
Be friendly and loving
Each day as we should

Some times, we know
Are sure to be rough
But, that's just when
We have to be tough

And let us remember
As we live day to day
That our Father will help us
And show us the way.

C. F. Stahl

A Pain

A pain exists
So deep and terrible
It will swallow you up

Only you are suffering.
Everyone else is happy.

Only you are bad.
Everyone else is good.

Only you are guilty.
Everyone else is innocent.

A pain exists
So deep and terrible
It will destroy you.

But only if
You let it.

Brenda Moot

How Deep

A smile on the lips
How deep does it go
Does it spring from the heart
To make the face glow.
Does it cover a hurt
So deep, oh, so strong
Is it saying I'm happy
Or something is wrong
Is this someone jolly
Who's laughing so loud
Or just hanging on
Pleasing the crowd.
Is the heart full of joy
Or sad as a clown
Lost inside ones-self
Feeling way down
How deep does a smile go
We may never know
One lost in one-self
May never let go.

Jean P. Welch

Forevermore

Upon the cross of Calvary
My dear Son died for you.
Upon that cross He bore the pain
That cleanses you from sin.
Before that cross, oh child of mine,
Reach up to me this day
For I will grant all things to those
Who follow in the way.
My hand is sure upon you.
My strength will now be yours
And in my love I'll keep you
For now and evermore.

Priscilla M. Alto

To Be

Who am I?
What do I feel?
Please Lord, help me, help me
   to understand
Give me wisdom, give me light,
   help me to conquer my
   fears tonight
Give me solace, give me hope,
   help me to be the one
   that I hope
Guide me with your loving
   hand.
Help me to be who I really am

Adele C. Lombardi

Tomorrow

A smile, a tear, and some laughter.
A gaze so intent, too, often
misleading, of what's to
come there after.
To share the moments of time;
to erase the thoughts of sin,
to anticipate the morrow,
a time of which to begin.

Thanhhoa Ta

Memories Ablaze

On crisp and crimson evenings,
Near the fading of the day,
A miracle of nature
Gently showers its array.

As the sun is slowly sinking,
While the spectrum glimmers nigh,
An awe of its majesty
Explodes across the sky.

Now twilight blooms and darkens
And awaits another spawn.
Such beauty shrouds tomorrow,
Rivaled only by the dawn.

This serenity of purpose
Bears a need to live as one.
Our Alpha and Omega
Awake the mornings' sun.

Fade softly, all my sunsets.
Linger long in precious hue.
Until the morning blossoms
With a kiss of velvet dew.

Bobbie Ely

A Child's Thoughts

Hard time,
Simple place.
Young child,
Out of place.
Don't belong,
Never will.
Emotions strong,
more than real.

Courtney G. Love

What Is Love?

Love is a flower that blooms all year.
Love is a bird that sings in your ear.

Love is a bell that chimes every day.
Love is the sun, giving off a ray.

But Love can be painful,
As sharp as a dart.

Be careful, watch out!
It might break your heart.

Kelly Weaver

Janet-Last Love

Thinking of life as here I lie
I thought love had passed me by
And then right out of the blue
Along came you

And I knew right from the start
You'd bring joy into my heart
Now my life can start anew for
Along came you

All my nights were dark and gray
And I prayed each and every day
That someone would come my way
If she, came what would I do or say

But now my love you've come along
And I know now that to you I belong
Now my life can start anew
For my dear, along come you

Jack Fitzgerald

Raindrops

The raindrops are falling
On the green green grass.
Sometimes they tinkle
As though falling on brass.

The winter starved plants
Are reaching up to catch
The moisture of the raindrops
To greedily drink and snatch.

I look out the window
And see the raindrops bounce.
A little bird is watching
And seems ready to pounce.

Watching the raindrops fall
Makes me realize anew
How much we depend on
Mercies that are not a few.

Thank you, Father in heaven,
For your blessings in the rain.
It comes down on us all
And bring us earthly gain.

Frances E. Tolson

In My Dreams

I see your future,
In my dreams,
I see what you were going to do,
I see what is already done,
If only my dreams would come true,
I'd be standing here with you,
In my dreams I see you,
In the real world I don't,
I see a place where you used to stand,
A place where you used to have fun,
And a place in my heart where you
Will always be,
only in my dreams.

Shandi Dukes

Portrait of Misconception

I stepped inside the magic
Beyond the floating wall
Where images of my mind's worst enemies
Are all that I recall

Come visit my illusions
My soul kiss from the depths
Too far from realization
Too close to evil's breath

Portrait of misconception
Has left me little doubt
That all who passes through here
Can find their own way out

Melanie Herrold

Tools of the Trade

Undaunting resilience
Undying devotion
Unending fluidity
Make serene of commotion

Assemblage of spatts
A passel of metaphors and verbs
Tools of the trade a poet wield
Paper, pen and self
And a mind full of words.

A. Megan

Insignificant Smoke

A sweltering fire of conversation -
you are only the smoke
filling people's eyes
with the stinging sensation
of insignificance,
of petty talk,
of hindering debate.

Why don't you pour out of the chimney,
drift over the sky until
you meet up with some other
insignificant smoke
aimlessly wandering
strayed from its fire.

Your swirling patterns of gray
glide over my head,
forcefully making yourself recognized
by obstructing my view.
I apologize now for making you flee
from my harshness, but smoke does not
belong conversing with fire.

Anya Holland

In Between

It's a place I know
Not far up or down below
The place in between

It's a place not seen
By the telescope's eye
Because the place in between
Is for no one but I

It's a place of adventure
Where one cannot suffer

It is my place
Only I can descry
It is known as
The place in between

Amber Myhrman

Mother In My Eyes

You are the best creation
That God has ever made
Your love and dedication
I know will never fade

When I hurt down deep inside
And don't know where to turn
You hold me in your arms and say
"You live your life to learn"

You have always taught me
Use trust and honesty
That will bring you through your life
And make you more like me

I will not always have you
So I have heard you say
But in my heart you will always be
In the night and in the day

Although we do not look the same
I am you in many ways
I will retrace your footsteps
And carry on your name

Anne Vidovich

Too Late Too Late

We waste our lives when we are young
Dreaming of things that could be done
Years have passed and now we find
We could do these things if we had time

Now with time to do these things
It flies by on senile wings
So I suppose if again I were young
I still would get just nothing done
I would just dream and sigh
Till one day I would just up and die

*Elizabeth Schube and
Dr. Purcell G. Schube*

Jeffrey D. Blasier

I'm not gone, I'm just away
I've gone to where the angels play
On snow white lawns of billowed clouds
Where I can have a place to hide

I'm not gone, I'm just away
But you will see my smile today
Above blue heaven, look for me
In floating boats of deep green sea

I'm not gone, I'm just away
So please don't cry the angels say
Just look for me up in the sky
And you will know the reason why

I'm not gone, I'm just away
With the angels I'm here to stay
Remember me today,
Then let my soul release and play

Gloria Greean

Untitled

When she looks in the mirror
she sees a frightened beautiful woman
frightened of loving someone
frightened of having her heart broken
frightened of making a commitment
when she looks in the mirror again
she sees a happy young girl
happy when she thinks of him
happy when she's with him
happy that he loves her
when he looks at her
she sees love in his eyes
love for just her
love that she can give him
love between them both

Heather Thomas

Speeding Bullets

The best of the best,
the top sixteen,
we blew by the rest
without being seen.

Two laps each
and then we were done,
we finished what we started
at the sound of the gun.

Other teams will fear
our return
next year.
Determined, we'll be there
to give them a scare.

Rebecca Klein

Only for Awhile

When life gets lonely
You're feeling a little down
Stop and fade the moment
Smile and remove your frown
You have something magic
Sealed inside of you
Magic in your laughter
And everything you do
Someone said I've seen it
Seen it all and more
You just stood there laughing
Like what's forever for
If you're in love tell them now
Tomorrow's too far away
Remember, today's the tomorrow
You thought about yesterday
Life is short and sweet
Time's a measured mile
Love can last forever
Or only for awhile

Bill Warnecke

The Fly

Oh mischievous one of the ether,
Why do you buzz around my face?
Why don't you go and leave this place?
A thousand eyes but you do not see,
That you are annoying me,
Be so nice and leave this place,
Instead of buzzing 'round my face.

Steven Morrison

Love

When you least expect it there's
nothing you can do.
When you look for it you can't find it.
When you reach out for it, it's gone.
And when you speak it there's no sound.
When it comes we often run away.
When it's near we deny that it's
there due to our fear.
Why do we run,
why do we hide.
Why can't we fight
this feeling inside.

Deborah Sabb

Flashing Pain

I have died....
silently, emotionally
and no one knows.
I have nothing left...
nothing to look forward to.
I lay here
with this gun in my mouth.
I cry as I struggle
to pull the trigger.
I look
for another way out.
I lay on the tracks
awaiting a train.
I can't bring myself
to do it.
I run to my bathroom
and I find a shinny object.
I lay in the bath tub
with my pain....
flowing out of my wrists.

Rekita B. Blair

I'm Glad I Met You

Our paths converged and softly touched
Our hearts moved closed in greeting
It was a time to sample change
It was a time for meeting.

An accident of chance become
Our lasting gift that day.
Some paths may cross but do not
Always join in such away

I'm glad you've shared your life
With me and made this moment prime
The future will preserve the
Warmth that fills this precious time
The present is a prize
That you have helped to make complete
I'm glad fate arranged a way for
You and me to meet.

Crystal Marie Duty

Windows

I see the wide, innocent eyes
of my child, leaping
out of her thin face.
They are the eyes of poverty,
the window to her starving soul.

The eyes allow the world
to see that one mother
cannot feed her child, that one
anguished mother cannot do enough.

The sorrowful eyes, infinitely wise
beyond their years, are the eyes
of a child who knows
too much of this cruel world
too soon.

When I look into my child's eyes,
my heart shatters
all over again
like a chain of tiny cracks
in one ancient teacup.

Kate J. Briggs

Reflections of You

The time I spent with you is known,
    As thirty years of me.
You filled my years with love and joy,
    and I am as you see.
This day is your day of hearing,
    when I was on your knee.
Remember all the things I've done,
    like spilling all your tea.
I know the world that you have shown
    as loving, warm and free.
I'll fill my child with years of joy.
    And teach the words of thee.
Reflections of you is seeing,
    how happy life can be.
Thank you Mother for what I've won.
    A Mother's Day for me.

Carter Lee Daniel Sr.

Bronx Cocktail

Lazing
    atop beds
        of fallen fresh

Magnolia petals
    omni-scented
        intoxicated

Naturally created heaven-scent:

Melon mulch, wet
    leather must,
        and elderly cream

Sweet cushion;

Full blown fledglings
    drift and soar
        during an unusual April heat

More than a few askew
    the more make merry.

Russell Aaronson

March - April

Here comes Springtime.
Here comes Springtime.
Budding flowers, sweet smelling wind.
Here comes Springtime.
Here comes Springtime.
Sweet spring rain, warmer air.
Here comes Springtime.
Here comes Springtime.
No more snow, lighter clothes,
Here comes Springtime.
Here comes Springtime.
Flying kites, Spring breaks.
Here comes Springtime.
Here comes Springtime.
Here it is.
Here it is.
Woosh...
There it goes.

Daniel Sung Frye

The Greatest Girl I Know

The greatest girl I know
Is one great world aglow
Enchantment is her game
Ma nature is her name
She'll study long to write the song
That all her children sing
So swift and clean she'll paint a scene
Of beauty in the spring
She weaves a spread above her bed
Of mystifying blue
She also weeds the path that leads
Young hearts to love so new
And if the seeds we sow
Are free of weeds that grow
Then nature will unfold
Her rubies and her gold

William Tucker

Apple

A is for amazing grace God gave to
    the world when he gave his son to
    die for our sins
P is for the peace that God offered to
    the world
P is for peace we have within when
    we repent of our sins
L is for the longing we have to
    be with God when we repent of
    our sins
E is for eternal life in heaven
    with God when we repent of
    our sins.

Roy McDuffie

Colorado, Colorado

Open your arms to me
I am coming to you,
you, with your beautiful ranches
you, with your beautiful Rockies
    are calling me
    Colorado, Colorado
at your sunrise, and at your sunset,
at your days, and at your nights,
at your winters, and at your summers,
    are calling me, colorado,
I can touch your moon,
I can feel your breeze,
I can hear your river,
I can taste your dust, Colorado
    your stars, your sky, your snow and
    your rain, are my love, Colorado,
I will be with you for ever
if you keep me alive
Colorado

Morteza Vazirabadi

Flight

Man made miracle? I believe it not.
It is God's own hand
That guides and lifts and flings
Me out on silver wings.

It is God's own hand
Beneath my fragile craft,
And God's own breath that brings
The winds that sing

A song of love,
So wild and free,
That sends me on a magic flight
Out into space, in delight.

Nellie Pike Randall

"Unconditional Love"

There has never been, nor
will ever be, anyone like me.
My thoughts are mine alone
no one can be our clone
As no two snowflakes
look alike
I was made unique
in his sight.
My father knew me
before I was born
He chose my parents for me
He chose my family, to be.
There's a reason for me to be me
A season for loving for me
I am loved, I love unconditionally.

Beverly Brayda

Little Brother

Do you have an annoying sibling?
Tattle-tailing, constantly whining,
getting their way, happy.

Dan Aubuchon

Tiny Houses

Tiny little houses
All in a row
Roof tops covered
With fresh fallen snow
Smoke is flowing
From chimneys above
Fireplaces are burning
Glowing with love
Faces all smiling
Happy as can be
As I peek
Through the window
I wish
It was me.

Rene Westerman

God and Country

Break from this madness,
Take a few with you,
As you go down,
One more for God and Country.

Giving all we have to give,
Fight till the very end,
Be the last standing,
One more for God and Country.

Taking the blood of others,
Any way that you can,
Far away from your home,
One more for God and Country.

Lying under red, white and blue,
A box of wood and steel,
Dust to dust, ashes to ashes,
One more for God and Country.

P. J. Bottoms

Remember To Forget Him

Forget his name, forget his face
Forget his kiss, his warm embrace
Forget the love you thought was true

Remember he has someone new
Forget to cry the whole night through
Forget how close you two once were

Remember he has chosen her
Forget you memorized his walk
And the way he would talk
Forget the things he used to say

Remember he is far away
Forget his laugh, forget his grin
Forget the dimple on his chin
Forget the way he held you tight

Remember he's with her tonight
Forget the time that went so fast
Forget the love that now has past
Forget he said he'd leave you never

Remember now, he's gone forever.

Leslie Conklin

Ms. Kati Alzheimer

It's 12:30 in the nursing home
and time for lunch, the trays are served
but where is Ms. Kati?

There she is standing by the wall.
She's gliding her hand
up and down, and all around,
smoothing out a surface.

Her words fly out like salad, tossing from a bowl
She reads the newspaper upside down,
she's one slippered and two pajamed topped.

"That damn elephant is wiping the table again," she shouts.
"Shouldn't be going now?" She adds.

Her vulture mind swoops through rock-polished tunnels,
Concrete mountains eroded smooth
Nothing to grasp and nowhere to land
Only wasted plains and bombed subways
Dot to dots that won't connect

I ask her what's her name.

Shuffling away - she answers,
"Closed for remodelling, closed for remodelling, open next spring."

Amanda Tysowski

Triumphal Tribute

Smooth marble's threshold mazing dateless time
Forms sculpture's epitaph from rough repose
As words a poems noble verse and rhyme:
Chaste, nude madonna in eternal pose.
Or even portrait's masterpiece in oil
With fine brushwork of texture and of tone,
Besmeared like liquid flesh and human toil,
Marks brief its unmarred moment as does stone.
And music's melody too breathes faint notes
In a rapt chorus bathed with mellow chimes
On rushing winds from cherub's vibrant throats,
Ink's instrument recording echoed mines.
But though such monuments be heirs of earth,
Thine love alone shall stand attrition's worth.

Merle Eugene Schaffler

funny are the ways of the sun
shine so bright and then gone
days so clear to lose all care
lose all sight to darkness despair,
setting sun blue sky red
giving way to raise the dead,

but good will come with the new day's dawn
try to walk the new born fawn

frolic in meadows and rolling in bliss
two lovers fall and with passion they kiss

to feel the sun's strength from beneath the tree
its rays bringing life to all that's seen
four seasons of life and a lifetime gone by
always for show in a surreal sky,

late in the day, moon's   indecision
                        eyes close to then open to the sun once again risen

Jared Goldman

A World Of Hope

Patience, dear people, use patience
That should be the rule of all nations
Do you really want to do harm with the nuclear bomb?
On some big city or some small farm?
When you try to even a score with another big war
You somehow only lose out
The people all frown in every city and town
Instead of smiles on their faces
The Olympics are near so join in the cheer
   and try to pass it around.

Patience, dear people, use patience
In all that you say, in all that you do
There's plenty of room in this world
   for many not just a few
Reach out your hand and try to understand
   what you're putting the whole world through
Try to think wise and try to compromise
Patience, dear people, use patience
There's room for all of God's nations

    Betty L. Kelly

I'll Be Remembering

   When the first snow of winter is falling
at my feet,
   And the touch is like velvet soft
against my cheek,
   I'll be remembering
when I hear a song of sunshine and
the rain,
   Words of love and laughter knowing
you felt the same.
   I'll be remembering
   When I lay in a cool grassy field,
Looking at the clouds, and all the shapes
   That I'll build,
I'll be remembering
   When the breeze of a bright sunny day,
Is blowing through my hair,
   I'll quietly hear you say... and I'll be remembering.

    Carol A. Skinner

I'm Not Alone

Although my mother frail and weak
Has been taken from my life;
I know I'm not alone

As my father held on with his last dying breath
And his eyes fixed on mine;
I still was not alone

His eyes were gray, his heart was full
And worry filled his face;
He knew his time was near

He stared at me with watered eyes;
Afraid I'd be alone

The room grew dim, then silence came
And everything was still;
The time had come for us to part
To give in to God's will;

Now go in peace and worry not
That you left me in good hands;
For you left me with the very man
Who will always understand;

Why I will never be alone.

    Jan Kozelka

Sadness

I could not think. The pain, shooting, stabbing, throbbing at the
backs of my eyes. Filling my days with torture. No cure. No relief.
Continuous, endless, unanswerable question.
My soul is burning to match the pain in my mind. It can't break free.
It desperately wants to. Freedom, or is it Understanding.
An end to the loneliness. I am alone in my mind.
The pain, the unbearable sadness.
Pity me not. My avenue is anger. Turned into and on myself for not
being able to be. I can not find relief in the answers.
A mythical ending to a story that never was.
Let the lightning fall and scar the Earth as my thoughts scar my soul.
Be thankful that you can not feel that which I feel.
My sanity failing, peace turning into a phantasm. What does one do?
No relief in these words that none shall hear. They can hear with
there eyes, Perhaps not.
The tortured soul at night doesn't feel the pain.
It swims in me, integrated into my person.
All that I am, is there nothing more?
This seemingly endless barrage of words means nothing, but a stream.
The stream of consciousness.

    James Firios

A Promise Made

My friend called me the other day,
We talked and had a few chuckles together.
"Let's have lunch" my dear friend said,
And I replied, "I'll call you soon I promise."

Spring danced into summer.
Summer faded into fall.
Fall with bright red color,
Went slipping into winter's snow.
And I, well I remembered a promise
I had made.

We had lunch my friend and I,
The hours went speeding by.
Oh how our eyes did sparkle
As we talked of days gone by.
We gave each other hugs as we
said our fond goodbyes,
And, what I'll always remember
oh yes I truly will,
Is a promise made is one that must be kept.

    Marylou Crothers

The Death Of An Angel

The pale, yellowish
flesh hangs loosely on
his expressionless face.

His eyes, once crystalline
with the knowledge and
the understanding of humanity

Are now only blue white marbles
Staring at his immediate
Future a great distance behind him.

It pains me to realize the hatred the world loved him with.
He was the puzzle piece which didn't quite fit;
He was an angel in this hell that you built;
He cared for everyone who never cared for him;
He was the last meaningful thing in your world of unmeaning.

He looked at me, and uttered the last significant words ever uttered.

"What good is life, when life is lived for death?
What good is caring, when care is not returned?

Once I tried to save the world;
The world has committed suicide.

The death of humanity marks the death of an angel".

    R. J. Corradino

I'll Be There

Whenever a tear rolls down from your cheek,
When it's a good friend that you seek.
When you're afraid of a ghost,
And when you need me the most,
I'll be there
With every part of my heart that has a care,
With a helping hand reaching out,
Telling you what my love is all about.
When there's laughter that you need,
And your life, you need me to lead,
I'll be there
Willing to make two sides fair.
When word's need to be spoken,
And your heart doesn't need to be broken.
When there's something you need me to lend,
And your spirit, you need me to mend,
I'll be there when you heart is getting easy to tear.
When hatred overfills your heart,
And in your life, you need another part.
I'll be there always willing to take a dare.

Timothy F. Craig

Timing

The kiss that we've missed exists,
And the skin that's within hath shared a millennium,
The light, however, that I'll shed tonight - might...
Show how fate cannot be late
as long as the timing may correlate.

Rt Rd

A Mother's Cry

As I wake in the morning with the darkness deep
I wonder in my thoughts from a restless sleep.

As the darkness turns to day and the light shines through.
I wonder what this day holds as it begins anew.

As I sit and think of all the things God has given,
I know now why I must keep on living.

As my heart hurts as a mother does, when her
Children also hurt from not enough love.

I wonder what went wrong in all my years.
Maybe from too much or not enough tears.

The day goes by too quickly to make things right,
Before I know it, it's almost night.

Another day has past and darkness is deep, may
Tomorrow be a happy one as I go to sleep.

Marie Rannings

To Artie - On His Death

Dearest Artie - Gentle peer,
having left me, saddened here.
Now you're gone and I'm alone,
you to rest and I to moan.

Beloved friend, I know not what to do.
I only know I died with you.
Death has pierced your golden heart
and I with tears from you depart.

My glass was full but now it's run,
here I live, still we are one.
With your leaving, this be true,
without you Artie, I'm only part, of whom you knew.

Sydney R. Sunderland

Our Gang

So many years ago Our Gang Comedy came into my childhood
Yes, stealing my heart and forever on my mind
I was one of the lucky children in the theatre
Watching the most adorable kids anyone could find

When the theatre finally darkened
Their precious faces appeared on the screen
Capturing my love and admiration
While I laughed thru every hilarious scene

Didn't they manage to get into trouble
Strolling along with their dog Pete
Looking so innocent and natural
Together making their movie complete

Our Gang Comedy and The Little Rascals
Acting in movies were number one
Spunky Alfalfa, Farina, Darla and Stymie
What they brought into a child's life was fun

Those were the days of the depression
To often children returned home to poverty
My thanks to the brains behind that comedy creation
Featuring remarkable talent the world could ever see

Dorothy Zimmerman

Soar

Celebrate Life!

Nothing need stand in our way
Not insult, injury or even death
Can rob us of our joy.

For we do not clutch in fear
We hold on
With outstretched hands
In love, power, and a sound mind

And we let go
For we are free
To celebrate life -
To celebrate all that life has for us
The sky is not the limit...

Soar!

Jerusha Morgan

Sunday Dinner

The cast iron roasting pot was placed
on the stove just before we left for church.
When we came home after the preacher's last word we raced,
sprinting through the old porch door

into the house rich with the scent of roast,
whole onions, cubed potatoes and carrots,
simmering and blackening together inside the old host,
waiting for the Sunday dinner prayer of thanks.

Stephen Penner

Silent Scream

Deep within my soul, I had a silent scream.
To everyone I seen, "Please look at me! Notice me!"
But when they turn and walk from me,
Never noticing me, I screamed-
"I will never be free! There's no one that will notice me!"
Then one day God spoke to me,
"I look at you but you never see me.
You just turn and walk from me.
Stop and look at me.
I can set you free, You don't have to scream!"

Rhonda Ross

Lend A Helping Hand

It's another fun day in this rat race.
People laughing and having fun.
People believing in people.
Believe in yourself and all you can do.
Let's lend a helping hand and show
people that they can have fun right
along with us.

Sherri J. Roberts

Trapped

I am hiding behind a wall
How I wish I could break through it all
But I am trapped by a gate
Of depression and self-hate
How I wish I could break through
And let happiness see me through
But instead I am guided by sadness and lies.
I feel like a mouse in a maze
Running around aimlessly in a daze.
Trying to find the other side.
So I won't have to hide
From this sadness
And finally feel gladness.
But for now I am still in a daze
Running around this maze
Which contains no beginning or end
I am alone without a friend
In a maze with no solution
Or resolution.
I am trapped.

Mary Hunt

Mother

How could there have been Mother's Day,
If it weren't for you
Bearing us into this world
Bringing us up in the tried and true.

Being there when we needed a friend,
And no one seemed to care,
Being there to lift us up
And your words of wisdom share.

Being there even when we thought
We were to big for a helping hand
and taking the time to let us make our mistakes
Without the "I told you so" reprimand.

For all of this I say, "Thank You!"
And I love you with all my heart.
You'll always be with me
In my heart we'll never part.

Waynell Hill Mezzell

Return to Innocence

Let's frolic like playful peasant children,
where dreams lay and once fantastic voyages of kings and
queens sailing in ships of jewels into a star lite flight;
where clouds are pillows - temples stand.
For a moment, all is silent, all is at hand, all is a journey
continuous...
carrying with one voice,
while enshrouded armies led by eyeless men or horseback,
with their fallen fallacies of misguided truth,
declining path of march to a realm of direful obscurity.
Looking back, all would have been said.
Now, it's time!
The light of a new birth is up ahead.

Alex P. Kabelis

Losing You

Today I followed a Blue Jay's, Blue
Losing You.
Yesterday I discovered the Red on a Cardinals, Bed
and Found You.
Tomorrow I will awake to the Morning Mist
Set upon a Meadow far,
Fare and Yonder,
To Wonder about You.

With the Hay stacked anew
and the Hark Song crying for You,
I only feel my Loneliness
and Lose,
For I loved You.

Today I followed a Blue Jay's, Blue
At Losing You.
Yesterday I Perched High upon the Grass
Looking askew for You.
Tomorrow with the sunrise Blue,
I will only think
Of You.

C. Danny Weatherspoon

My Daughters

The gentle may breeze stirred the trees
All the flowers were visited by bees
White lilac bushes perfumed the air
It's mothers day and the weather is fair

I sat and wondered about my life
Hard work and worries filled with strife
I never made claim to any great wealth
Still God had Blessed me with good health

Just for once to have been the best
But Gods design was to survive the test
Dependable and spiritually there
To cheer someone else who needed care

Then into my room my daughters came
My meager belonging where no shame
I fed and clothed and taught them well
Depth of love in their eyes did dwell

Love and pride is enough reward
In all my years I worked toward
If you children are gentle and strong
You too will hear the sirens song

Dottie Egan

A Wish, A Dream

As I lay here pondering on thoughts from my past.
Remembering promises and wishes that my mother made to me
Remembering the long talks of many things to come.
But never realizing that her life was like a candle in the wind.
A candlelight blown out way before its time.
But yet I find myself now older.
Fulfilling all those dreams one by one
Feeling her presence as I travel the country as she wanted.
Seeing the things she wanted us to see.
A sense of peace overwhelms my emotions
A sense that her promises to me are finally coming true
Though not directly from her but yet through me
A feeling of happiness and peace not only for her but also for me
That because of her wishes in my heart a dream is finally fulfilled.

Betty Ortiz

Love

Love is a beautiful summer day,
That one may share.
It is the dew on midnight grass,
Beneath the auburn moon.

Love is the bluebird singing in the trees.
It is that same bluebird flying, flying.
For love has no true name,
It is what you make of it.

For love can be a flower, or a tree.
Love can be a person, or even a little bee.
Love has many faces,
More than you or I can tell;
For love can hide in many places,
Just waiting, waiting to be found.

Breanne Austin

Ensoul

You, I will tell, all of the answers to all of the questions.
You will know what I see, in my minds eye.
I will ask you to tell me what you see.
Show me your depths, show me your heights.

For inspiration, I do seek.

You, I will show, the right and the wrong.
You will know what I feel, in my mind's eye.
I will ask you to tell me what you feel.
Show me your right, show me your wrong.

For insight, I will know.

We will know, and we will feel two into one.

The One will know...

All of the answers to all of the questions.
The one will feel...
The right and the wrong.
The One's mind's eye we will ensoul...
...into Us.

Martina Messick

Skydive

The sky is falling into the ground;
I see nothing and hear no sound.
Confidence is merely a want; as I jump into the depth of a slipstream,
flowing through the cloud,
and I free fall to anywhere.
Air is a dream of the future, but I don't see into mine;
for the surprise is yet to be.
I feel nothing but freedom, as I fall out of the plane flying up high.
There's no darkness, only sunlight...
Twisting myself into a falling shape;
no one knows who I am,
I feel like I'm slipping under, and I felt like I was holding onto nothing.
Generosity holds onto my body,
which is floating on thin air,
and apathy sinks in, to warn me of the ground,
my feet extended, I let go of the atmosphere,
and fall to its surface.

Stephanie Capelle

The Challenger

The Challenger looks like fire
Started by our God in heaven.
The Challenger tastes like sorrow
That fills our weary hearts.
It smells like a lost battle
Against Mother Nature.
It feels like Deaths icy grip,
Closing on our Astronauts.
It cries out for us to save it
But alas, we cannot.
It wants to see another day,
To live life longer.
It knows it's lost to the hands of Death,
Lost to the pits of fire.
It believes it can make it through
Although it is lost forever.

Miranda McDade

The Lord Spoke Gently

Faith that knew no horizons found a place in which to wonder
And this gay heart of contentment began despondently to ponder.

How can this Lord, this Great God of Might
Whom I so joyfully embraced be silent of Earth's plight?

Why do I see my fellow man struggle
    Enduring through tragedy, loss and pain,
While others find no small need unmet,
    Enjoying comfort, security, endless gain?

Why do some have beauty that eclipses all others,
While some become objects of disgrace to their parents, their
    brothers?

Why, Lord, can you not grant from your bounty up above
    Boundless gifts to all and meet every need?
Pour out your great love, allow it to flow!
    Let there be no more envy, hate or greed!

Why can't each live a prosperous, gay life
Without the canyons of disparity that create Earth's strife?

The Lord spoke gently, softly to me.
"Because each life is special, an enchanting story.
I am their author, and they are my glory."

Patricia Anne Faussett

Bad Hair Day

Let it stick up, comb it flat down
you can't help looking like a clown
You can't control it, it has its own mind
one day bad the next day fine

Need you comb it? No way
Like for real, it's not going to stay
You've sprayed and crimped and curled and teased
can't your hair ever be pleased

You have tried and tried and you're tired of trying
you've tried to fix it you're not really lying
It sticks straight up you look like a freak
when it looked cool, calm, and collected just last week

Ok I'm done I've got to go
I wrote this just so you would know
you're not the only one, by the way
to wake up in the morning having a bad hair day.

Elizabeth Robbins

Untitled

Another day of loneliness
in a room full of people
I can't understand
I glare and curse at them from within
A flower, a cat, a con man and a ceiling
help in dulling the sharp edges,
yet some still pierce my skin
the blood flows thick and menacingly
my will disappears, the will to be
indifferent. I strive for independence,
but am rendered helpless and
the black gnome laughs freakishly
while sucking my will to survive
I want to crawl into a hole, fetal and
sing myself to a coma state where
nothing hurts and no one sees me.

Karina E. Lepeley

The Unfinished War

A silent army attacks without warning
   no cannons, no guns, no missiles

Advancing undetected, the invaders occupy enemy territory,
readily increasing in number, yet still undiscovered

A base is established from which additional troops will
infiltrate; the microscopic nature of the advancing fleet
is its tactical advantage

How does the enemy fight an invisible army that can grow
to such a size it is impossible to defeat?
   no cannons, no guns, no missiles

The Silence Is Broken, but only momentarily; the invader's
stronghold is detected and successfully eradicated, yet
the threat of further intrusion still lurks

An arsenal of chemical weaponry is launched to counter
the further threat; the safest, smallest level of chemical
munitions provides systemic retaliation against the
microscopic assailants

Delivered with a vengeance, CMF destroys not only the
trespassers but the healthy countryside in its path
   no cannons, no guns, no missiles

The cyclical treatments induce a chemical menopause and
at the same time produce nausea and vomiting associated
with pregnancy - what a paradox

Army against army, the war goes on

Janet E. Lamarre

Our Light

To be what God wants us to be,
to go where God wants us to go,
to love others as God loves us,
is the light that shines within us.

To walk into the darkness and
shine forth the light of Christ,
to carry our cross into the darkness
and show the love of Christ,
is the light that shines within us.

To live in the light and
become part of the light,
is the light that shines within us.

William R. Criqui

Comes Spring

The morning mist has lifted
And as the suns first rays are seen
Where before, the snow had drifted
The fields are turning green.

The brooks have lost the icy coat
That held them in duress,
Now free, they run, in all their joy
With babbling happiness.

A Robin, now look quick, you'll see
Yonder in that tall Elm tree
Listen-he'll give voice to song
And tell you that spring won't be long.

The birds nest in that lofty Elm
That stands upon the lawn
Will soon be filled with chits and chirps
Each early morning dawn.

Winters gone, ah yes he's left
He had his little fling.
And I'm so glad to see him go,
For again, we'll welcome Spring.

Theodore M. Hurwitz

Untitled

Alone I enter and leave life's journey
Feeling unseen; untouched
Yet there is One who attends my pilgrimage
With tender, infinite patience
Unrelenting love
I am never truly alone
On the rutted, ragged steppes
Love steadies my footsteps
Shepherding me into lush, verdant meadows
Oh, how sweet this presence
How understanding this love
Comfort my days
Shadow my nights
Into the embrace of love's redemption.

Rosemary Hair Vasquez

Honest Abe

The great embassador, freer of slaves
He didn't want people to dig many graves.
Lincoln hated war, he hated to kill
Yet he was a President with a great skill.

He wore his dark clothes and his top hat
Lincoln was a tall man. He was slim not fat.
Wherever he went the people would cry
Yea! Honest Abe, you won't let us die.

The slaves? Yes they liked him but wanted to know
When would the time come when they'd be let go.
The South did surrender after four very long years.
Nothing could be happier to the slave's ears.

Then came the tragic, the moment we dread
Someone shot Lincoln in the back of the head.
At first no one did know of the real truth
But then someone said, "It was I, John Wilkes Booth".

No, Honest Abe, You can't go away
You helped us to beat the soldiers in gray.
First your son died, your wee little babe.
And now you are gone. Goodbye, Honest Abe.

Lisa Borchart

Love and Pain

The Sun shines through, the clouds depart.
So comes love to the pining heart.
E'er lovers break, and love lies spent,
Is pain the stake for encouragement?
Yes.
Without the pain of nights alone,
There is scant gain from love's atone.
If love's dismiss is to despair,
Is pain the kiss past lovers share?
Yes.
Love turns the Earth thru night to dawn,
Showing its worth in pain thought gone.
But, pain's not pitch'd; it awaits its call.
Is each enriched by the other's fall?
Yes.
Love is the fire; pain is the heat.
What births desire? These two replete.
Love's price is true, pain sets the mark.
When love burns through, is pain the spark?
Yes.

Mike Waterman

Fly As Butterflies

In Memory of Jeff

Our life here is like the butterfly..
who only lives a short time...

Flying free on beautiful wings
after a long and painful metamorphosis.

The spirit of the butterfly is joyful
as it goes about on the breeze
and leaves
the "children" of future butterflies.

Wings of iridescent color and magical powers
delight our eyes and touch our spirit
as our heart dances
to the beat of those wings
and we vicariously fly along
on the rhythm of the wind.

Some of us live colorful lives
and learn to fly as butterflies...

C. R. Cutcher

Life's Fleeting Days

I saw a little butterfly
arrayed in colors grand,
I chased it through the garden.
I caught it in my hand.
It fluttered there so fearfully for it wanted to be free,
so I opened up my fingers and again I let it be.
It rushed away from out of sight and could be seen no more,
I searched for it 'til the night and was tired and sadly sore.
Oh butterfly, oh butterfly, oh where can you be?
Oh butterfly, oh butterfly, please come back to me.

But as I peacefully slept that night and dreamed the time away,
I held that dancing butterfly until the light of day.
So are life's fleeting days and the passing time,
we cannot hold them if we wish for they leave us all behind.
But only beautiful memories will stand the crushing test,
so clutch them tight and lock them up
in your golden remembrance chest.

Oh fleeting days, oh fleeting days,
Oh where can you be?
Oh memories, oh memories, please come back to me.

Rose Dyess Anderson

Memories to Live

Quiet hours, sweet lullabies
sitting quiet by grandmas' chair.
Loves sweet story, learning, growing
all our lives that's what we share.
Through the good times and the bad times,
Love stands unconditionally.
The years bring doubts and fears,
bittersweet joys and laughter through tears
With sweet baby smiles...
then walking your last miles...
Fear death no more as you watch
loves go in peace;
Disease and pain may grow
but our spirits are free to flow.
We'll live in the ones we leave behind.
With those sweet memories and
those beautiful eyes...
Life goes on.

Melanie A. Osborn

Beliefs In Life

I am a believer.
I believe in love
At first sight
when everything else fails.

I believe in having friends
To count on throughout life
When nothing else is left.

I believe that if you trust yourself
And that with God's help
That you can do anything.

I believe that having time by yourself
Can help open your mind
And let you in to the possibilities
That await being found.

I believe in dreams that
Come true and those that
Are yet to be discovered.

And I believe in doing God's will, showing that you love him
And that you trust him
No matter what he tells you.

Carla King

The Big Run

April 15th was the day it began,
This was the Big Run and so they all ran,
Thousands looked forward to this gallant affair,
1996 was the One Hundredth year;

Spectators lined up for twenty-six miles,
Wearing sunglasses and anxious smiles,
They were all here to get their thrill,
Of seeing them run Heartbreak Hill;

Each runner's sneakers were put to the test,
While proudly a number was worn on each chest,
All the hard training for months and years,
Were clearly seen through their sweat and tears;

Strong arms turned wheels and feet hit the ground,
It was a glorious sight in Old Beantown,
Pride and excitement seen on each face,
Crossing the finish line in this big race;

To the Run of The Century, we now close the door,
But the Marathon we know, they'll be many more,
We applaud each entry to a job well done,
In our hearts we know that all of you won!

Pamela Mann

My Broken Heart

First love... Unforgettable love,
come very hard and goes with
leaving tears in my eyes.
The love I had for you was very
hard to forget. Even, when I loved
someone else. I always remembered
the unforgettable love we shared.
I remember the days when I thought
about you day and night, when I
woke up in my dreams thinking that
it was real.
I remember the day when you kissed me
the very first time and we promised
each other to be there for sickness
or poor. Now...
You broke your promise and left
me there with hope that one day
we will be lovers again.
But love is special even if it leaves
an unhealing lifetime scar on your heart.

Hasmik Kademyan

Lifted High

Walking down the winding road
searching for the light of you.
I came upon a river, not just any river.
The river that leads to you.
The river that only believers can follow.
I stood and watched all the others pass,
and wondered why I couldn't follow.
I took off my shoes and wadded a while.
The water was pleasant and inviting.
I stepped in and began to sink.
Everyone else is walking on the water
but I am sinking in the sorrow,
sorrow of a life without peace.
Through all the sorrow I feel you here.
I call to you and you pull me out.
Now I am walking with the believers.
Walking with you by my side,
living the life you meant for me to live.
I am now at peace.
Thank you, Lord!

Michelle Empcke

My View On Siblings

I feel blessed to have two sisters and a brother,
We get along and have such fun with each other.
It's hard to believe at this point in time,
We once fought and thought being seen together was a crime.
My sisters are now my two best friends,
My brother is someone on whom I know I can depend.
Regardless of the miles between us we've stayed close,
A card, an E-Mail, a call when you need it most.
Our interests and ideas are quite different indeed,
But yet we have a connection that cannot be seen.
I'll do anything for them and they for me,
It's a wonderful bond, the best there can be!
Sometimes I get so frustrated by one of them,
But it's funny how quickly the anger can dim.
I thank my parents for giving me two sisters and a brother,
And teaching us how important it is to respect one another.
We all may be different yet we're also the same,
For a sibling is much more than just a common name.

Paula V. Barnes

"The Beginning Of Life"

Life is a precious thing,
With Julie and Frank in the ring.
Girls and boys are better than toys.
One of each, may bring you joys.
My brother was a twin and not aware
That I had first arrived there.
I was a blonde and he a brunette,
You'd think we had just arrived in a jet.
My maternal grandfather was the M.D.
He was the one to go to see.
As we appeared, were handed to the nurse,
So excited, admiring us, said,
"The first one is good enough for me".
The second twin had arrived F.O.B.
That's pretty good — yes siree!
Hope that's good enough for you and me.

Gordon Elston

My America

In this vast land of the free
Where the mountains rise high
And the rivers flow wide
I stand and gaze at the countryside,
I am a part of America.
I like to watch the Flag rise in the mornings
And be lowered again at night
And everyone ready to salute it
With pure thoughts of God and Country,
　I love America,
With freedom of speech, an abundance to eat
And beautiful cities to dwell in
With parks for fun and woods to roam
I'm proud my heart belongs,
　To America.

Vera Barkland

Colors

I used to walk the streets to town
in September, when kids got out of school
with brown lunch bags, and blue school clothes
when they could see the colors of the sky,
but I couldn't, who walked behind them.
The white clouds, the yellow sun
all different shades of gray
to me, on a black horizon, and when
my dad bought a color TV
and everyone else was happy
then I alone was silent. But when
I dream at night, the gray disappearing
and the world, no longer a monochrome screen
came to me, in the colors of my mind.
So when I dream, I am the artist
painting rainbows into the night.

Christopher Wei Eng Chang

We've Come Along Way

I remember the day we met as clear as the morning sun,
You and I stood face to face exchanging simple hellos.
Never thinking we'd be together today.

Our friendship and love for one another have grown,
And honesty and trust have been our cornerstone.
You've said it several times and now I must agree...

We have come Along Way

Kim Marie Lewallen

Untitled

Father time lifts his glass
In toast, to you.
His slow smile and twinkle in his eyes
Reveals to us his thoughts.
You and He will comrades
In time...of course.

Carol Jean Skye

The Promise

While the fawn nestles snugly against the doe's flank,
Butterflies enticingly flutter across the meadow.
Comforting, the doe warmly nudges the young
Toward a new path, toward the butterfly show.
The fawn proudly prances, although not quite
As elegantly as her graceful mother. Someday,
The fawn argues, she will mirror her mother's moves.
Or, the fawn will proudly dance in her own unique way.
She quickly scurries back to the doe
For protection and advice. The fawn promises
That she will be more courageous next time.
The mother just smiles and offers affectionate kisses.
The next day, the fawn confronts danger bravely.
Masking a few scars, the fawn carries home pride.
The next day wasn't as successful. But the doe
Encouraged her daughter, "At least you tried".
Turning away, the fawn is attracted by more
Competitive creatures, as well as the life experience.
She affirms to the lamenting, yet splendid, doe,
"I will always love you, I promise".

Erin A. Beard

"The Song"

I hear the voice cut though the night,
...Yet no one is singing.
I hear the tune, both breezy and light,
...Yet no one is playing.
The song grows louder,
....Yet I am the only one listening.
The busy world continues to hurry by,
....I am the only one to stop.
The song says listen...follow your dreams,
...And I do.
I wouldn't be the same if I hadn't listened
...To the song only I could hear.

Angela Erin Petrachkoff

The Old Man

The old man, he sat staring; sat staring straight ahead
At pictures only he could see, at pictures in his head

He thought of times forgotten, and times he wished he could forget
The summer days were hot, and the winter nights filled with regret

A smile played upon his lips, as he sat staring into space
Amazed that after all these years, how clearly still he saw her face

Was there ever any man, so hungry for his lover's touch
In all the days single time began, could anyone have loved this much?

The other loves he'd had since then could do nothing to compare
None of them had had her eyes, nor the color of her hair

And still he feels the emptiness, and still he has to pay the cost
And so he conjures up her face, to ease the pain of lover's lost

And yet the old man sits and stares, his memories to him a crutch
In all the days since time began, could anyone have loved this much?

Judith L. Goldfarb

Memories

On that sad day, I smiled,
and looked away, I was mad at
you for leaving so soon. I kept
the pain inside I made it hide,
now many years have gone by
that I have spent thinking about you.

Oh, how time did seem to fly,
I sat, and cried, what was to do?

Then I realized how lucky I
was to have memories of someone like you.

I've looked at the past, and how
I wish it would last, but the
time has come to say goodbye to
you. I'll miss all the crazy days,
and your silly ways, but I'll
always remember you.

Lynnette Rae Champ

A Poem to Shane

Shane,
    No matter how close we are or how
    far apart, memories of you are
    always in my heart.

No matter what you say, no matter what
You do or who you are my thoughts of
you are never far.

    I know the reason you left, no
    Need for you to say. I often
    wonder if things were different would
    you have stayed.

Well, we can not change the past so
I will think forward to the
Good times we'll have when you come back.

Brandye King

Love Is Amazing

Sweet little baby child wrapped in your Mother's womb,
conceived by love right from the start, placed safely intuned
    to you Mother's heart,
You are growing, and Mom's proudly showing the time for arrival
    is near.
Dreams are shared and being prepared to welcome our bundle of
    joy.
Best of all - God has a purpose and plans for you, too!
Someday Mom and Dad will share the Holy Scriptures
(Ps. 139:13-18.).
God's creative wisdom, love, and care are making you unique.
God has many gifts for you beyond life itself and parental love from
    above.
Do you suppose those rhythmic heart beats you hear each day
are preparing you for a unique gift of love to display?
A love of music is a gift especially for you to enjoy or pass on to
others if you choose.
These are only a few samples of God's creative gifts.
He holds numerous wonders in His hands like sands along the sea
    shore ready to distribute blessings on to you.
We are thankful, too, for you are truly a bit of heaven, and we
    are looking forward to seeing you soon.

Norma Stadt

Warm Love

Show me truth, so I may trust again
Do not forsake me, for my love is not in vain
Warm me with sunshine when I get cold from the rain
Stay by my side as we stroll down the lane
You are my rainbow at the end of a storm
I see your face in every form
Your voice, your touch keep me warm
I know the beauty of your charm
I will love you always and forever
To be without you, never.

Cynthia Hayslette

Tears of Hope

My tears come to often and to quick.
I should learn to burn them as quickly as a wick.
If I could tuck them into my pocket I would only need them
   when I'm overjoyed.
Perhaps I could cry for a very long spell until each and everyone
   is destroyed.
What if I choose to freeze my tears and unthaw them in later years?
Most of the tears leads me into fear, leaving a few tears to care.
I shall take my own advice, and package up my saddest tears,
   leaving room enough for the happiest tears to near.

Geraldine Kinser

A Blessing For Him

Bless him, Lord,
And give him strength over his enemies,
But make him weak to know
The fear of the meek.
Give him a generous heart,
But let others with less forgiving natures
Judge him that he may know the need for forgiveness.

Let him laugh more than he cries,
But let him cry to know the warmth of comfort.
Make him wise that he may teach,
But make him blind to some truths
That he may know the ecstasy of discovery.
Reach out your mighty hand to him when he falls,
But let him stumble to know independence.
Let him touch the rim of Heaven many a time,
But bring him back that he may love me.

J. Lenora King

Japan

   Japan is so far away,
yet I will go there one April day,
but not come back till early May.
   My first flight across the states,
My first flight across the ocean,
My first flight over the Alaskan mountains.
My first flight ever!
   Nineteen other friends will come,
but I don't know some.
   The happiness, the sadness,
the fright in my heart,
I hope to God I won't fall apart.
   My family and friends I'll get
something for,
but for me I'll get even more.
   I can't wait to go,
but yet I sigh,
as the days go to slowly by.

Amanda Jo Diaguila

The River

The river meanders through the meadows,
Rippling over the heads of age-old stones.
The river's currents mould and smooth the rock faces,
Oftentimes leaving them faceless
While sculpting stubborn sorts.
And we melt into the masses.
Time chisels away our facial features
And leaves us nameless in this world of such
Seemingly identical sameness.

Ryan Healy

A Cry Unheard, A Cry Unwanted

It started out a happy day
The sky so clear I could see the heavens
No one knew, no one expected
The blast of a bomb
The crash of a nation
The children's cry, the panic arose
How could this happen, to the one's we love
How could God stand by and watch us mourn
Justice will serve
The men who deserve
To burn in Hell
For the agony that fell
Over the lives of many
Who lost plenty
The world today
Will never be the same
For these men ripped apart
Everyone's heart
And now you can hear
Their cry!

Mandy Gayle Rudloff

Strangers

The 39 strangers boarded the vans,
Off to see the West, the skies, the land.

Who were these strangers, these chosen few,
Who set out West to admire the view?

Each stranger was different, special in their own way,
Yet they learned they were alike as they traveled each day.

"Life is very simple," a truth their Peter said,
So they trusted in him and followed where he led.

They sat around camp fires and sang camp songs,
They hiked the Grand Canyon for ever so long.

They conquered the Great Sand Dunes and faced sprinklers in the night,
They peed in the woods without any light.

The strangers were looking, searching across the plains,
Over mountains, through the heat and the rain.

What they found was companionship, beauty, and love,
Blessed with Peter, the staff, and the Lord above.

They learned from themselves and they learned from each other,
They learned from point Reyes and the Sierra desert.

And as they returned home and their journey was at an end,
The once 39 strangers were now 39 friends.

Nathaniel P. Leonard

Moments

Moments, all the moments that I need to be with you,
Could begin upon their journey here today.

Emotions have consumed me for this longing I now hold.
With these visions from my mind unto my heart.

I seek you for the time that we share upon this earth.
And the union of our souls to be as one.

Moments, all the moments that I need to be with you,
Could begin upon their journey here today.

Oenita L. Blair

Eagle

Oh, mighty Freedom's Spirit,
Perched there, on ocean's rocks.
The wind, will ruffle feathers,
While the sea gulls,
Dive, in flocks.
Your white head poses proudly,
While your gaze is steady on.
The sea gulls cannot move you;
Your spirit holds you strong.

Your eyes lock on the distant shore,
I see you spread your wings.
I know that you can teach me more,
As in all living things.
You show your strength in perfect flight,
Believing God is King;
Flying fearless into night.
The wings of freedom sing!

Aurelia Jo DeBolt

My Mother

All my life I've never really known
The love I feel inside.
Until I sat holding your hand,
While all the machines kept you alive.
I felt so much anger so much pain,
As my heart was breaking inside,
No way of knowing that you were going to die.
You slowly slipped away, then you were gone.
I thought it was a dream.
I can't believe that you are gone.
And I was left to grieve.
No more, holidays, or phone calls
No more, how are you today?
Just a grown up little child
Aching for my Mother
That passed away.

Cheryl Higgins

As I Turn the Page

As I try to turn the page, trying
not to look back, you remind me of
the days when you were my love and
as you haunt me trying to make me
feel ashamed, I try and try to turn
the page, I feel the pain over again
and it makes you happy to think that
the page is being reread, although I
once loved you, that love is gone. You
forced me out. You are now sad for
losing what we had. Though it was not
me who pushed you away. You blame
me to this day. I wish we could still be
one but now I must turn the page. So
you are the past and I shall go to the
future and you will keep blaming me
for your mistake but, I shall forgive
you as I turn the page.

Janessa Herrera

Seasons of Love

We planted seeds in winter's cold
and as the snowy months unfolded,
God's guiding had gently molded
our fragile hearts.

Then spring brought forth its tender rain
to wash away the tiny pain,
most often felt when people strain
to care and grow.

All through the scorching summer's heat
these testing times could not defeat,
the hope that soon our lives would meet
to share once more.

At last as autumn brought its breeze
and leaves had flown far from the trees,
our ripened fruit was seen with ease...
love came to be!

Winter, springtime, summer, and fall
we've come to know them one and all,
and heard God's quiet, patient call
to grow as one.

Debe Soule

Untitled

Over time,
A friendship can grow strong.
Your friend becomes a part of you,
you become a part of them.
Time goes by
and you create many memories
good memories and bad memories
Then you grow up,
and you both change.
You go your separate ways,
and lose that part of you they took,
and you go through life looking.
Looking for a friend
a friend like them, a friend to fill
    your empty spot.
But you don't find them,
Why?
Because there's only one friend like them,
    and they are it!

Amy Denman

Untitled

A single leaf falls an old, withered tree.
One harsh storm after another
Practiced by Mother Nature like a religion.
The tree is tattered and worn, much like its surroundings.
The leaf flies around its disgruntled environment, noticing each and
every inch of the ground, wondering which spot will be her new home.
Maybe on that warm rock in front of the creek where the sun heats the
flow everyday.
Or maybe the cold, damp area behind the brave oak trees where the sun
never shines, yet the rain always seems to get through.
Maybe she'll just fly beyond this forgotten place, into a brighter
world of beautiful forest and scurries of animals running life into
the deep wood.
Or just maybe, she'll end up underneath that same tree that shed her
before her dream began.

Christine Wamble

112

Foggy Blue

Sampling tastes
a tranquil night,
reaching for a cigarette.
Raspy blue filtered vision.
Watching street light glow.

Ghosts, seeking halogen warmth
rub against window,
searching for entrance into my blue room.

Leaning forward, breath against pane,
soft liquid blurs.
They wait for me to give them access.

Finger draws a gap,
eyelashes brush glass.
Inhaling, fire tip shows faces,
Exhaling,
I color them
foggy blue.

Rachel Greene

"Life Is Fair"

Life is hard but life is sweet, all the
birdies go tweet, tweet, tweet.
Did you think that life was fair because
you had a honey, and money.
The many things that you possess, will only leave
you in a mental mess. All humans are
equal, the intake of air made it all fair.
In the end, the only way to win,
is to know that life was fair, you
had your share of air. I am telling
you on the square, that life is fair,
cause it's merely a breath of air.

William H. Wynn

My Poem

As you bleeding in the cold and dark
Look into your blood and see its spark
My eye
Watching you

When you lost in the trackless snow
Look up high where the wind doesn't blow
My moon
Stalks you

In a deep dark mine or crumbling peak
Hear the words of pain I speak
My words
Torment you

All of this world will be mine
And on the graves of my enemy's is where I will dine
And my God's how they will smile
And my sweet watch well for this will happen in a short short while

Jack Evans

White On White

Yesterday evening's fog
Has coated the countryside white.
A faded red barn looks freshly painted.
Trees stand out, white on white.

In contrast,
A stream
Runs black through folds of snow.

Perceptions cut clearer
On frost highlighted mornings.

Robert L. Lewis

My Lovely Maiden Sleeping

Gaze at this maiden sleeping,
On watery pillows whispering,
Of love...Sun, Wind kissing,
Or tears when Mist, Stars embracing,
Countless leave their hearts to her...

...Once steel arms stretching, beckoning,
To lovers on wheeled horses riding,
Gently through her mound,
Forsake erst lovers when she they found.
Why did they leave their hearts to her?

Too many smiles she imprisons,
Awakes to solace in her bosom,
Hearts pounding, laughters drowning,
Silently his maiden the Rock is watching,
No wonder they left their hearts to her.

Mighty cradle, the maiden leave in peace!
Not to crumble I go pleading,
Not to rouse my lovely maiden sleeping!
For I will come back to her...
For I too, have left my heart to her.

Louis W. D. Mendoza

It's Not Just A Game.....

Though many do not see,
 it has its importance especially to me.

The hours of training are endless it seems,
 but it all pays off when we fulfill our dreams.

Though bruises at the end are numerous,
 a true player will never get furious.

Heading, kicking, and dribbling the ball,
 see all that practice paid off after all.

Playing hard in any kind of weather,
 it doesn't matter-the dirtier the better.

Soccer is the game I live and breathe,
 to some it is nothing, but not to me.

To me it is more than just a game I play,
 it is always helping in life every day.

From the skills to responsibility I learn,
 it keeps me thinking through all of life's turns.

Jennifer Lenze

To My Children's Father

Who would have thought that I'd live to say
the words that are coming from my heart today
times heals all things may well be quite true
so listen to what I am saying to you

It's been so many years since the two of us parted
and ended the marriage that left us both heavy hearted
so many angry words, quarrels and unbearable pain
the rivers of tears that fell like the rain

Divorce for us at the time made good sense
but the damage was done at our childrens expense
If the clock could turn back, would things be the same?
Would our lives be so different with no tempers to tame?

But life does go on and the world keeps on turning
we've mended our fences, left no bridges burning
our hearts are much lighter, we've changed in many ways
still sometimes I'll think of our happier days.

I just wanted to tell you that since we've made our amends
I'm so proud that at last I can call you one of my
dearest friends.

Ladelle Kuglar

Half Way There

How can we measure time
By the distance we have traveled
Or the people we have met
Or the years we can forget?

Have we traveled very far
Do we know the way to there
Are we burdened by the task
When we find a lonely path?

We set our goals sometime ago
We set our pace before we know
Life have no miles that can be measured
No roads of return when we are weary

Then how do I know I'm half way there
I cannot know the crosses I must bear
But still I know as long as there
Are miles ahead I must press on

Half way there, how far have I come
Miles ahead how far to the prize
I don't know the distance yet
I only know I must not fret, but march on.

Gertrude E. Canada

Today

A child weeps silently alone through the night,
It's youth has been stolen and it's nowhere in sight.
It's been pilfered by a stranger, marauded by a friend,
Plundered by a guardian, deprivation to no end; today.

Molestation to incest, incest to lust,
We as parents who can we trust.
For our children are innocence, and our children are pure,
Without these inflictions, there'd be no need for a cure; today.

Petting to feel, feeling to touch,
How do the children know when the touch is to much.
Abusers they call it love, loved ones are filled with hate,
Let's put all of our opinions aside,
Concerns, should be with the children's fate; today.

Help is just a word away, there's someone you can tell,
It's the difference between being free,
Or dwelling in a living hell.
For there is someone you can trust, someone who will care,
Someone who will give you tender love,
Someone who will always be there; today.

A child weeps silently alone through the night; today.

Michael L. Colandino

"Of Past Love"

Think of those dreams we dreamt together
Those little plans we made together

Those quiet moments with hopes of future
Fantasy of reunion with the lost lover

A cosy little cottage up on the hill
Out of its door we could lie still

With relief that miserable past is now gone
A bright day is there, a new light is on

Isn't it how we planned it long ago
We tried very hard but couldn't do it so

From now on it will just be a memory
An incomplete dream, an ungotten treasury

David J. Adam

Sharon

As a small boy, I dreamed the dreams of
    many things.
Of great ships with crimson sails I piloted,
    unfoundered in mightiest gales.
Of pocket knives with gleaming blades that never
    rusted.
Of friends, a few that could ever be
    trusted.
Of simple things, like top strings or wild
    dreams of strange machines.
Of found golden treasures, not a few that could
    buy all life's material pleasures, too.
Of all the dreams I ever dreamed, and yet
    dream loves were and are the best.
Of love in many places with ever-changing
    faces.
Of this final long-sought love, full of fulfilling
    forgiving graces.
Of you.

Dennis O'Connor

My Life as a Buffalo During the Westward Movement

As I was stamping through the fields I saw a river. Of course it was bigger! I walked across it and looked inside it. I saw myself. I saw some kids. I better camouflage myself so I don't get shot. Ahhh!! An Indian attack. Bows and Arrows flying everywhere!! I got shot.

Ari Allen

Eternity

With saddened eyes so veiled with tears -
Majestic falls again appeared.
She's gone forever by my side
My heart cries out - why had she died?

My soul sings forth a medley to the water's falling
And then I know - the light shines bright
All will be well; we both are precious in His sight!

Mary Anne Fischer

The Rose Of Your Heart

In each person's life there appears a rose
That will grow and not be denied.
Sweet and precious, the dearest flower that grows,
For it blooms from your heart inside.

Created for all to cherish and keep
And none are exempt from its roll.
The sweetly nectar to others may seep
Betraying your innermost soul.

The life of this bud depends on a smile,
Just a word, an act or a thought.
To blossom in full, to have a fair trial
And see what the heavens had brought.

Delicate and fine or shrunken and torn.
Existing the way it's treated.
The sun like a smile, the weeds as a scorn.
The heart can tell what is needed.

Value this growth for it's the joy of life
Being sent by Him up above.
Each day can be made your guard against strife
With the rose of your heart called Love.

Frank Hundshamer

Hard To Understand

The first time that I saw you, I knew I loved you
   you were a simple man
You had a special charm like no other man
But sometimes hard to understand.

The twinkle in your eye and cute little smile
   your funny little laugh
Made everything we did together worthwhile
But sometimes hard to understand.

Like everyone else, I never got to say good-bye
   maybe that's the way it was to be
We are left alone here on earth to carry on for you
Life is hard to understand.

My dreams and hopes of ever being with you
   in this life are now gone
You were taken away long before your time.
And that is hard to understand.

    Kathleen Ferencak

"The Apple Tree"

Of many purposes does it serve.....
Blossoms touched with tender pink and fragrance fair
Grace the shadows of the afternoon sun.
Budding leaves soon invite the young lovers to
   build their annual nest.
The song of the robins fill the air as the apples
   develop into tasty treats.
The apple pie whets an appetite while rows of
   preserves await the winter's need.

    Doris Allmer

Mama

   When Mama turned one hundred we had a celebration.
We all knew how she got there - it was spunk and determination
"Jesus, Mary, and Joseph", she taught us, "I give you my heart
     and my soul".
Keeping us on the straight and narrow was Mama's life-long goal.

   Luxury and leisure time were not among her pleasures,
Family and her Rosary were the greatest of her treasures.
    As the years passed by and the family grew
    She learned to relax with a game or two.

   Either Cribbage or Scrabble she'd play with a friend
   And vacation with Grampy at Oak Birch Inn.
First went Grampy, then Ronald, then Rita - we miss them
    in different ways.
Mama added to her Rosary list - her answer was to pray.

Her last years here weren't easy - she missed her home, but then,
   Her spunk and determination saw her through again.
She charmed them at the nursing home - a lady no matter the place.
   They couldn't believe what we already knew - they called her
    "Amazing Grace".

To Jesus, Mary, and Joseph she gave her own heart and soul,
On Saturday last, her Rosary in hand, she attained her final goal.
From the horse and buggy, to automobiles, to telephones, and Space

    She touched us all in a special way,
    Mama, Nanny, Grace.
    Charlotte M. McSorley

Love and Laughter

I can hear soft guitars strumming a happy tune.
How enchanted this night in dim twilight,
beneath the mellow moon.
I have never heard such beautiful songs,
I feel so happy and gay.
I hope you will also hear these thrilling tunes,
these musicians play.
With star lit skies and air like wine,
your caress will melt away.
You'll feel so happy when you dance and sing,
this is the place to stay.
With a friendly smile and your rippling laughter,
you will remember today and tomorrow forever after.
Your heart will be brimming over with love
While remembering this evening under the stars.
The secret for this place is in giving,
and the happiness is in the person that you are.

    Wanda L. Ryan

Love

The sky was clear and bright.
The sun rose with a brilliant light.
And up from the grave in glory and splendor,
Rose Love so pure and tender.

In love he came to redeem the lost,
And they nailed him to a cruel cross.
In agony he cried, "Father forgive them."
They shed not a tear, His cries they did not hear.

He could not be held by death and the grave.
For a cold lost world He came to save.
So up from the grave in glory and splendor
Rose Love so pure and tender.

    Blanche A. Burrell

Godspun Day

Wake up... and know it's a Godspun Day
And it's woven in a very careful way
By the One who cares for you and me
And the ways that we live faithfully.

Let's go find something new to do
And we can do old favorites too
But we will know our place to be
God's spun His Day for you and me.

We'll face our chores and get them done
We'll hold on strong when things aren't fun
And we'll remember rain brings sun
If we keep our faith, our day's well spun.

Goodnight.. thanks for our Godspun Day
Our measured blend of work and play
And the more we love Him and believe,
The better days we will unweave.

    Irene Leland

Untitled

It is cancer of the mind,
Destroyer of all morals it can find.
It is waking in fear,
The terror of a simple tear.
It is never knowing why,
As you plead with the sky.
It is a hunger that never ends,
Though the substance, on you depends.
It is simply addiction,
And without help, death is my prediction.

    Bill Turnbull

Truth Seeker

Inspired by a voice inside that lead me to pursue,
A life beyond the simple sight,
That starts and ends with you.

I thought my life was made of things common to this world,
But then from deep within my heart,
I saw beyond the girl.

Not happy with my state of being and driven by the pain,
The seeking for the truth I know,
Began a distant rain.
That started with one mere small drop of consciousness and light,
Within my every thought and feeling,
A glimmer in the night,

But just when I thought I awoke, I realize in a task,
The sleep that I do oh so well, the way I wear the mask,

And so I'd thought I'd journeyed forth,
which brings me right to now,
When all at once I realize,
I'm just beginning how.
> *Reneé L. Mitchell*

In Line Of A Dream...E.C. Vs. D.C.

For the dream to be ours in ninety-five,
The hornets would have to rock the hive.

All tickets were sold,
For fans to take hold.

The day of the final game was here,
The last they'd play of their high school career.

First quarter came,
Dallas Carter's game was so lame.

Second quarter went,
East Central's score made a big dent.

Our guys took charge in the third,
E.C.'s name would now be heard,

As the fourth became shorter,
Emotions grew stronger throughout the quarter.

When the last basket made and time ran out,
The opponent's doubts were all about.

Dallas Carter knew they were too late,
E.C. Hornets were at top of the state.
> *Tara Hamm*

The Storm

The lightening streaks through the dark gray sky.
"Give me freedom", it decries.
It gropes and grasps in search of land.
"Set me loose", it demands.

The thunder follows with a roar quite intense.
Threatening the world with great suspense.
Fear it strikes with its mighty yell.
Announcing its arrival, you think straight from hell!

Last comes the rain in massive drops.
Slamming to earth, removing all stops.
So cold and dreary the earth appears;
As if the great heavens were casting down tears.
> *Sandra Aldrich*

A Simple Indiscretion

'Twas a simple indiscretion, a meaningless affair;
It never really mattered, it wasn't going anywhere.
Just someone to talk to, and somewhere to go;
You never meant to hurt me, I was not supposed to know.

But things don't always turn out the way we think they should;
I never thought of cheating, and I never dreamed you would.
This total lack of judgement, so thoughtless on your part;
You say "meant nothing to you", but me; it broke my heart.

I trusted you with my love; my heart, my soul, my life;
I loved you completely, and was proud to be your wife.
My world, once sunny and warm, is now lonely, dark and cold;
You gave away what I held dear, and I've nothing left to hold.

You've no idea how deep it hurts, this awful, awful pain;
The love, respect and trust are gone, how can I live again?
I still miss the life we had, I miss the love we made;
Just a simple indiscretion; Lord, the price we've paid.
> *Donna J. Chungo*

Happy Father's Day to Marc
(Father of my Grandson, Josh)

You've been a wonderful Father in every way
You always were there throughout the years
Teaching your son how to overcome his fears.
Sharing his joys, and problems too
Advising him, as to the right things to do.
You bought him costly games and toys,
He always shared them with other boys.
You made sure he developed both body and mind
Taught him the importance of learning and school
And remember to observe "The Golden Rule"
Also, to build a strong body by participation in sports.
So, he played tennis and basketball on the courts.
The high school basketball team was what he selected,
Though active in sports, his studies were never neglected.
Always, he was well-liked by his buddies and other lads.
Welcomed at their homes by both Mothers and Dads.
Your love, devotion, and encouragement
Helped mold his thoughtful, and wonderful character
He's grown up to become a loving and caring lad
Because his Father is "A Very Special Dad."
> *Irene Kanter*

When We Were Young

Remember when we were young?
Endless dreams, songs not yet sung,
Countless friends and endless parties,
Bodies strong, hale and hearty.
Now many of our friends are gone,
Our bodies no longer quite so strong.
Parties happen-we don't go,
We sit, watch T.V., and sew.
This is the life we have selected,
The party life for now rejected.
We enjoy these times together,
They're valued like a hidden treasure.
As we age and time passes by,
These secret memories sometimes make us cry.
The tears we shed aren't from pain,
They're from the love that we have gained.
> *Jesse L. Allen*

Life

Life is challenging and life is painful;
    in our lives we are met with many challenges;
challenges that may alter the way our lives are to be lived
    if we dare to take risks;
sometimes when we accept challenges;
    we are met with great failure;
but if we did not dare to face the challenge;
    we would never know how things would have turned out;
    accept all challenges however difficult or hard they
seem to be;
    for if you're not challenged;
you do not give yourself the chance to set yourself free.

Karen Scanlon Dunn

Childhood Shadows

Daddy can I have some candy please? No son I only have
enough for a pack of cigarettes. Suddenly, the hands of
time began to turn back in my mind as I relived my
childhood shadows. Daddy can I have some candy please?
No son I only have enough for a beer.
Daddy will you take me to the movies please? No son I'm busy
watching the game today. Daddy will you read me a bed time story?
No son I'm tired tonight I've had a hard day.
Hey honey check out this new video.
Daddy will you watch this cartoon video with me?
No son we're going out to dinner.
I'm sure the babysitter will watch it with you.
Daddy can I have some candy pretty please?
The hands of time stopped turning as I heard my son's voice
once again. Yes son your favorite for it's time to start
erasing my childhood shadows. Put the cigarettes back please.

Keith W. Parker

God Stands By

Often times, I struggle through
Calling out to God, where are you?

Making wrong choices, making lots of mistakes,
Such hard decisions and many he heartbreaks.

Yet God stands by, with capable hands to catch my fall
When I am unable to stand.

With outstretched arms, he pulls me in,
To loving comfort found through him.

With firm strong shoulders for burdens to bear,
I just hand them over, he will always be there.

And when I think I can do it on my own,
God knowing better, never leaves me alone.

So we needn't wonder or ask why;
Just rely on faith
And know God's standing by.

Robyn Bouknight

A Dream

The other night I dreamed of you,
And that was so real.
I dreamed it was the same as it was then.
I thought we were together again.
In a way I could feel you by me.
I felt like I was in your strong arms.
It was like you had come back to me.
But, this time, it was to stay.
Then, I awake, and you're not there.
In a way, I know, you'll watch over me,
Till I can be with you again.
Till that time, I know that you still care for me.
Then, I realize it was a dream.
One of those you have when you feel low.

Rachel Ham

My Easy Chair

When I sit on my porch in my easy chair
I feel God run his fingers through my hair

As the gentle breeze blows I can feel your love
As your mystery and magic flow from above

As the breeze caresses my cheek my neck and my ear
I know then Lord you are very near

As fluffy white clouds float through the blue sky
I look up and know you're alive

I hear the raincrow the robin and jay
And I know you will be with me throughout the day

I am so thankful for my easy chair
As you and I our love of nature share

When I get to heaven I ask if you please
Give me a porch and an easy chair and your wonderful breeze

Joann Girty

Now Is the Time

......To let the beast out of the cage
To sit down and talk about Minimum Wage
and while we're at it let us reflect
How responsible are the leaders that we elect
We pay them a salary of such a large sum
When we ask for pennies they react like they're numb
They never hesitate to give themselves a raise
Amid thunderous back-slapping and self-righteous praise
And when we ask for that measly penny
They start that foot dragging and we don't get any
We can't do with pennies what they do with dollars
It seems they're not leaders but mathematical scholars
And they treat "We The People" with cold-hearted feelings
And strategic "Red-Herring" keeps us rocking and reeling
They keep the people fighting and divided too
When they tell both of us what the other will do
We have not homes nor cars or enjoy any perks
It's a shame that our leaders are just a bunch of jerks
So..just to make sure we are on the same page
Let's stand up and demand more than Minimum Wage

Robert Thomas Lee

Just Coexistence

As a unit we stand...as a unit we fall. Or do we?
Will you lift me up when I can no longer stand,
or will I be the one who had no strength.
Will you grab my arm with all your heart,
or will you mourn your loved one?
Give your all, sacrifice it for me?
Or state that you once loved me and be on your way.
When I've been taken away will you search for another?
will you keep me in our set boundaries?
When all is dark will you be able to find me, or will I be hidden?
Am I your other half, with whom you can't go on
Or are you the man 'tis no heart at all?
Is it all just a pleasant word, feeling, or is it the truth?

You are digging in the ground...go slowly, don't do it because you
must, you will hurt the land.

You fill me, yet you have the power to leave me vacant.
Do you love thee, or is it a pleasant ringing in thy ear?

Lizy Dosoretz

My Valentine Lament

I like to buy my lover things to brighten up her eye;
red flowers bunched with baby's breath can even make her cry!
But "things" can't tell her what I feel, what's deep within my soul,
that after twenty-something years continues to grow whole.

I know it's strange to use that word: I never have before.
Whole is whole, a thing complete, not needing any more.
But in our years together I have seen our love grow strong.
We've waged some wars, and lost some blood, but never lost our
bond.

God made us one, in soul and flesh, He says so in His Word.
It's hard to understand it all, but truth is felt, not heard.
Our love is strong, an anchor that can pierce the deepest sea,
I know He's part of all we are...it couldn't be just me.

My real lament is that I want to lay worlds at your feet,
your body clothed in finest silks; you'll never have a need.
But that's a dream for years to come, I must live for today:
because my love and dreams are what I have to guide the way.

Barry L. Rose

Do Not Patronize Me

Nice Girl, (Cardboard smile plastered to her face).
Good Girl, (Never angry, too polite to be upset).
Young Girl, (Not old enough to justify her feelings).
Small Girl, (Easily picked on and pushed around).
Pretty Girl, (Not quite enough to be a Beauty).
Bright Girl, (Too absent-minded to amount to anything).
My Father told my Mother she was worthless.
Everyday I listened and I heard that men are angry
and controlling in their love and that good girls
keep their mouths shut during conflict and adversity...
Now
I am a woman, tired of being good
and I would rather scream until the blood runs
from my ears than accept another second
of misguided condescension.
You do not begin to know or understand me.
Do not patronize me.

Jennifer Fales

My World

Pst, hey come here, shh be quiet, follow me
I'm going to show you my world, at least my emotions
First we will go in this room, this is Happiness, small room isn't it
No windows, no light, no people, Happiness must be out.
Happiness doesn't have much of a life.

Now let's go down the hall, now this room with the bars on the
window
This is Anger's place, I wonder where he is too

Right next door is Fear
Fear is another small room, he's out too.

Now let's go to Depressions place, now this is a pretty lavish
    apartment
He actually owns the whole house, he's out too, here's a note, it
says, "Going to emotion meeting."

Let's go sit in
At the emotion meeting Depression is president,
He is the dictator.

Douglas S. Madej

A Prairies Poem For All Year Round

From my window I can see the prairies green.
The cat tails wiggle as the wind blows on.
The leaves are dead, the flowers lose their petals.
From my window I can see the snow is falling, the prairies white.
The prairies green, the leave are green, the flowers bloom.
The cat tails wiggle as the wind blows on.
Now I know a whole new year of experience and fun has just
begun.

Maureen McDonnell

Maybe Once

Maybe once you were a parent, someone who cared for me
Maybe you once cared if I fell, kissed the boo boo on my knee
Maybe once I felt returning love, as you tucked me into bed
Maybe once I believed you loved me too, the ideas placed in my head
You said you would be there for me, like "through thick and thin"
It didn't matter if you two broke up, to me you could still give
But being jealous that I don't spend time, when you don't with me
I'd rather chill and hang with my friends, than around a house empty
Mom understands how I feel that I can have a life too
Just because you had a tough life, why do I have to live like you
Parents say they want for there kids the best life they can give
But when they were teaching this maybe you didn't attend
I've learned to live for myself only, no one telling me what to do
Sure I want the best life for me, but I want it for me not you
Maybe I'm wasting my time writing this to you
Maybe once you would have cared how I feel for you
Maybe once I would have cared how this made you feel
Maybe once I was afraid to tell these feeling well

once is over and I know by law you are my father
But if you expect me to call you dad, go to hell, don't even bother

Dylan Cundiff

Matthew's Musings

Rocks and gravel pickin' up sticks
Home run hits and baseball mitts
Swinging climbing watchin' those slugs
Puppies kitties and roly-poly bugs

Pounces trounces bounces and screeches
Hugs and kisses and grass-stained breeches
Scrapes scuffs bumps and bruises
Bows arrows and skateboard cruises

Pets pals teasing the gals
Proud of his muscles gettin' some "wows"
Prances dances wishes and sings
Knows he can fly pretends he has wings

Hikes bikes thunks and slam dunks
Walks talks and Tootsie Roll chunks
Adventures stories long school days
Shares cares loves and prays

Tidying cleaning his room and the floor
Arrangin' toys books desk and drawers
Observing the rules values and respect
Not much time for introspect

Tanya Lawson

Untitled

From the outside, I can see in
towards the middle, the center, where life is bright
and full, robust. Meanwhile, I look in
towards the middle, sometimes wishing I
was there. All the while, focused in
towards the middle, regretting that I
was not there. Straining my eyes looking in
towards the middle, forgetting that I
was once there. Trying to avoid looking in
towards the middle, jealousy seethes and boils
burning my blood. Averting my gaze from in
towards the middle, anger rumbles through my
skull, pounding. Constantly seeing in
towards the middle, I am outsider, I will always
be the outsider. Blurring my eyes from looking in
towards the middle, I can feel the tracks
running. From the outside I can see in
towards the middle, damn the eyes.

Chadwick A. Zeitz

"Envy"

A silver tulip sitting in a garden of gold,
Standing out among all the others,
Not ashamed of its differences
But proud of its beauty.
Never keeling over with jealousy,
Only crying out when forced to watch
As its golden friends pitifully grow envious,
Losing their color and beauty.
A silver tulip now sitting in a garden of green.

Caroline Ballowe

A Single Rose

I am a single rose
When you give me that same lonely flower
I am no longer alone, am joined, and driven to pose
To think that a tiny bud could possess such power.

My sadness disappears as the flower opens
Its sensitive eyes meet mine with eloquent passion
We smile together as we both blossom and no unhappiness reopens
That single bud, pink, red or yellow, is always in fashion.

Together, as a couple, our faces grow wider
My lips curve with uplifting corners
Each grin coaxing the rose to the journey inside her
In bloom, we are one, no longer in need of mourners.

Surrounded by dark green petal
She asserts by the hour
They make a lovely background, but the green must always settle
For in her vase, she is the princess in the tower.

Such a flower can bring magic
Even to a life that seems tragic.

Sheila Garvey

Where

Where does one go when there's nowhere left to go...
Where does one look when everything's been seen....
Where does one go when there's nowhere left to turn...
To whom does one speak when everyone's been spoken to....
Who does one love when everyone's been loved ......?

Jason Coup

A Knight' s Passion

His armor glitters in the noon day sun,
he's traveled hard and long, and wants to have fun.
He comes to a building called the Golden Inn,
he dismounts from his stallion and walks in.
By entering the Inn's common place,
he sees a woman of beautiful face.
Taking her hand by the fire light,
they danced all day and made love all night.
Waking up to see her gone, he never knew her name,
riding out of town knowing it won't be the same.

Paul A. Fisher

My Wishes

I wish I gave all pink roses,
With all my heart, to my beloved;
When the spring-scent spread in the house,
The sweet songs were flowers and love.

Once I dreamt about the great star,
That shone our pathway in the night,
And showed the leaders the wise way,
Making people happy in life.

I would like to tell the white dove,
Get the good news for the countries,
"The true peace is all over the world."
"We are greeting the next century."

How immense the four oceans?
Hold on continents and islands.
Please be silent on stormy days,
The sunrise will be brilliant.

If someone asked me: "What were you?"
"A creature." I would answer.
But our great thoughts make dreams come true,
A new world - We'll live together.

John Tu Nguyen

"Observing The Beauty Of God"

While looking toward the heavenly sky
The moon was shining oh, so bright
I saw the hills and valleys like shadows below
And the beauty of the moon was all aglow.

When I think of the years I have lived this life
Not knowing what tomorrow will bring
I thank my God for all he has done for me
The wisdom, knowledge and understanding to be free.

All around me the green country side to behold
Enjoying the beauty of it all made by the hand of God
Why can't man find peace and happiness in it all
Because the selfishness of his greatness he thinks will never fall.

To all who wish to change their evil ways and serve the Lord
Take heed and walk that straight and narrow path
Don't be afraid of death or those who violate the law
For in the end you will escape the harrows others saw.

Now as I look back upon those years that have passed me by
I ask myself why could not I have done better with my life
God gave me all I needed to help those less fortunate than I
My hope is that I do more for all before I come to die

Rudolph V. Freeman

Dream Of Light

There is a cloud above my head
which will not disappear.
Can not Dream my dream.
It is my fate to never sleep,
in this world of light.

Orange-red, green, white, black, and blue,
all the colors of my mind.
What is in it for me?
That which I can not see,
so be it my destiny.

Whose beauty do I see?
Mine, yours, his, or hers.
All we see is the Dream of Light.
Who is it?
Just me, Dreams!

Star Gazer

Untitled

Compassion
rebuilding myself from scratch
living for what?
Pleasing others to destroy myself
purity vigorously violated
purity in care, thought, and love
everything makes too much sense
nightmares approach
I watch myself with forbidden desires, with perspective corruption
mental bricks build up too far for me to escape
in my inner corridor lies a room of insanity
   and a room of hate
Who am I?
The floors creak

Have courage
Courage
Courage to face yourself.

The world falls apart around me

Understand faith

Tony Chen

Delores Day

A Sun Rise To BeHold

As Love holds no start or ending.
As Love forms not one but Two.
As Love does help heal the Soul/Mind.
As Love holds the scent which is All.
As Love forms the ear which listens/hears.
As Love enfolds the tears no matter the Age.
As Love makes the hurt bearable.
As Loved, I lay my head upon the knees of one which is my Mother.
As Loved, my Mother holds this child which is hers.
As Loved, a circle forms from mother to child.
As Loved, the circle widens now my children join.
As Loved, the Moon becomes Sun Rise.
As Loved, the Sunrise becomes my mother.
Delores Day, A Sunrise to BeHold.

Renee C. Lovelace

Disguised As Myself

They told me to open up, they said don't be shy
It's o.k. we understand, you don't have to cry

They said calm down, don't speak your mind
We don't really know you, we don't want to hear your lies

It's all an act, you can't make up your mind,
It's like a costume that you trapped inside

Maybe I chose first or I got what was left.
Now I know what it is: I'm disguised as myself

Julie Dwyer

Grief

Grief is gray like the shadowy street
Enclosed by fog and also like the
Lonely cries of a soul mourning the
Dead on a rainy dusk.

It creeps through my consciousness
And overwhelms my heart with tears.

It reminds me of the time when loss
Was beyond words and completely
Took control of my body.

It makes me feel helpless as if the
Whole world has abandoned me in
The midst of nowhere.

It makes me want to burst out with
Anger yet I can't because it has already
Frozen me and turned me into ice.

Michelle Li

Touch Me Who Dares

I live in a realm of peril and doom,
Mystery and pain shrowd my darkened room.
The ancient Romans of old placed me here,
As a mosaic of everlasting terror and fear.

My striped tail is poised and waiting,
Its steady length is undulating.
My claw is upraised to attack friend or foe,
Dare you come near, I'll attack with one blow.

My fangs are weapons who come to bear,
Protecting all in my secret lair.
If you unwrap the mystery here,
Beware, your life is now to fear!

Who dares disturb my slumber and sleep?
Who dares to value his soul to keep?
Only mine eyes alone can see,
A loss of life as blood flows free.

And now I must wake as I hear a call,
Unleashing reality of what will befall.
The voice I hear betrays screams and scares,
Alas, I awaken, "Touch Me Who Dares!"

Colette Zell

Fall from Grace

I fell from grace without a sound,
No omen, sign or reason could be found.
No trace of ghastly sin or wrongful deed,
A thorough search of heart and mind decreed.

What instigates this ghostly pall descending,
With icy grip upon my soul unbending?
Deprived of heavenly blessings from above,
No longer free to bask in God's pure love.

Though cause remains a mystery evermore.
Forgive me, father, heart and soul implore.

Betty Stulgin

White Boar

Madness steals the sorrow from his eyes
Anger rises laughter can't disguise
Pities not the suffering in their pain
Pleadings get them arrogant disdain
Smothers children, blood their only crime
Threats to throne he's stolen in a time
Youthful king cannot his right attest
Mother hides and justice is at rest
Wail, England! The tyrant at your head
Shows no love for brother that is dead
Raging at those challenging his rule
Hasty words and murder prove him fool
None remain alive to love or trust
Wrath divine proves God awake and just
Battle calls defense of stolen crown
Boar by Tudor blade is fallen down

Cathy Davidson

Spirit Of Comfort

Perchance to pay a local visit,
   The ghost of love lay wait.
A maiden, robbed of love's sweet nectars,
   Missed her now dead mate.

Then, shrouds of white, a mist at night;
   Glistening, came quite late.
He, her love, lifted her up
   To hug at heaven's gate!

That hug was just the very ticket;
   It lifted her heart's big weight.
So, on she went with comfort lent
   From a nightly spirit's wake.

Patricia L. Purrett

"In Darkness Breathe"

When the last light becomes dim,
Night eyes shine oh so bright,
A magnification of the slightest sound,
Hairs stand on end with chill fright.

Cooling wind through the trees whispers,
The dark woman's voice is calling,
I run away on broken ground stumbling,
The world swallowed in the pit I'm falling.

Slightest bump - is someone out there?
Perhaps a prank for the unsuspecting,
Cursed imagination in my torn mind,
So wary, common logic I'm neglecting.

When at last my nerves taut and eyes wide,
At first light away my burden I heave,
And with the gargantuan weight lifted,
No longer do I in darkness breathe.

Robert E. McChristian

Dreams

With the sun in the sky;
And the moon out in space;
I've chosen to sit by his side as a place;
For my heart to be taken and drifted away;
Into a dark sea for a many a day!

When I return back to earth;
Day in and day out;
I try not sit there and pout, pout, pout;
If I'm not back in his caring, strong arms;
I must stay in a place where I won't be of harm!

A place that will take me back to my bed;
So I can be aware of the long day ahead!

Chrystal Pohlhammer

From the Lookout

Just below the mountain's crest
   where nature's relics stand in place
Trees scatter amidst the rocks
   each is chosen to blend in grace

Here the winds whisper in the Spruce
   but the echo never sounds
Just the chill of November
   as snowflakes dance on the ground

From the lookout I stand poised
   searching the valley below
That sketch by the Master's hand
   showing places I had grown to know

I hurry to another day in time
   when once I trod these grounds
Captured with dreams to fulfill
   but those I never found

Years will dwindle and dreams will fade
   but one will never perish
To venture back another day
   and trod this ground I cherish.

James E. Simonds Sr.

The Star

They haven't found her yet, when will they see...
That she's one of those lonely stars that are free?

I guess they are blinded by her sparkles so bright
As she sits and she ponders, "Will it be tonight....
That I find that one star that's as lonely as me-
So we can be happy as can be?"

As the night passes, alone she still stays
Wishing for stars to start coming her way.
When the stars remain still, she gives up her hope
Thinking without other stars she could cope.

Her sadness grew larger, and alone she still stayed
Her brightness became darker, and started to fade.
"Is this what I want?" The star asked with a cry
Then suddenly another star came strolling on by.

He calmed her down, and held her tight
The two stars together brightened up that dark night.
This was my story of the star that was free
I sit here and wonder if this'll ever happen to me.

Elaine Pastrana

The Map

The Bible is a global map
   A network of highways and byways
   Criss-crossing each other over continents
   Showing travelers where they have been
   Where they are now and marking
   Each freeway to their best destination
   Smooth expressways rough roadways
   Scenic thoroughfares beckon and
   Each must choose his own route

The Map marks cities towns and crossroads
   Where wayfarers may rest and play
   Nurture their bodies and quench their thirst
   Peaceful valleys and still waters
   Where they can refresh themselves
   And commune with God
   Signs warn of detours, curves, and dangers
   But through it all the Map directs
   Sojourners to the Celestial City

Irene L. Bealer

A New Place

It's never been here before
My heart has traveled places where it could sit upon the shore
climb rugged hills or dance to winds' flirtations
I've let my heart go to heights unsure of, and risk falling
like the most fragile piece of a glass menagerie, to the floor
My heart has visited, rested, played, gone shopping and sightseeing
exchanged thoughts, shared feelings, reminisced,
    and promised to come again
It's gone out on a limb, to the highest mountain the deepest sea,
    the lowest valley
But it's never been here before.

My heart is journeying to a new place;
    a place only few will experience
It has packed sufficiently - for it plans to stay a long time
Forever is a long time
My heart is content as it wings its way onward; it has no itinerary
no travel agent, not even an American Express
It can leave home knowing it will be well cared for, treated with
gracious hospitality, offered a pillow, shown spectacular sights,
    and fed plentifully
My heart is so excited
It has never been here before.

J. C. Carter

My Feelings

One day I met you.
At first I like you as a friend.
And out of the blue,
I fell in love with you.
When you left,
I didn't want to leave you.
But I had to.
I didn't know how to show
how much I'll miss you, or,
How much I love you.
And now I regret didn't show you or tell you.
Although it's too late,
Cause you're gone
I wish I could go back and change what I've done.

Not showing or telling how much I'll miss you and love you
isn't the only thing I regret.
I also regret not expressing my feelings toward you.
With this I shall end,
by saying I miss you and I'll always love you.

Steve Kashubara

The Bug

Have you heard of
The bug it is not like a tick
but it will make you sick
this bug is not a cold, but it will take
your soul. Oops did I say soul I
mean you can die. And believe me
honey I wish this was a lie
other bugs as in colds you can cure with
medicine care but this one
is just a true nightmare you can't get
rid of this bug. Unlike a cold you
can't catch it by a hug. This bug
flows through your veins. It takes
your body through a depression
that is called insane. Through
your body this bug will raid.
If you want to know... The name is aids.

Tiffany Jones

Feelings

The color of good touch is glowing yellow —
    loving and caring,
    happiness and tenderness
Knowing inside that you are not alone and being loved
The opposite of good touch ...
    is bad touch which is the color of a black hole —
    confused and scared
    hatefulness and unloving
Feeling like you are in a dark pit ...

Katrina Sutton

Welcome

We welcome you to our humble home. As you can plainly see.
We tried our best to make our things as nice as they can be.

We may not spread a table like kings use to do,
But what we have we did our best. It's all meant just for you.

We all are just one family that God has brought together.
He always knows who his family is right down to the last fellow.

So help yourselves, be right at home. I'm sure we have enough
to keep us full until we have all the other stuff.

When it comes time for you to leave, don't think we rushed you out,
and please come back, we welcome you. That's what it's all about.

In God there is a time and place for us to have our fun,
but never go too far that you forget His only Son.

So I will stop this little poem. That's generally the way,
so you can sleep, but when you wake, It Will Be Christmas Day.

Josephine Petrie

Muse

The muse speaks softly, silently
    Gentle whisper...
Some say inspiration is nonexistent
Creation without cause
    No, it is here

The human soul centers on the caress of divine animation

    Our soul's river runs deeply, swiftly
    Inspiration navigates the waters of our past,
    Unlocks our memories and provides new revelations
        Do not ignore its subtle voice
        Always will it speak your truth

Forgo self deceit
Release your fixation with "modern" ideas
Regain contact with your humanity
Do not turn away from the gift
Of creation

Darrell Craig Mays

The River Goes On and On

Through the valleys rivers flow,
with speed and grace no mortals know.
Forged of mountains, streams of old,
swum by fathers both strong and bold.
Past lands close by its shore,
ridden by people with canoe and oar.
Through towns of quiet that always rest,
past mothers that think that they know best.
Down and past it's always sped,
past the little ones asleep in bed.
When they awake in the dawn,
they see that river goes on and on.

Lyndsay Davis

Can You Hear Me?

It's dark in here, I'm hungry and I'm cold,
I just want a mommy and a daddy to hold.
I can forget my empty belly and my body covered with frost,
If there was love enough to conceive me, is the love now lost?

I know I'm just a baby, I'm not supposed to understand,
But I have news for you parents out there in La-la land.
These actions affect us all of our lives,
We can't cope with your stress and all the worlds strifes.

What we need is not much, can't you give it to me?
All I need is a chance, oh why can't you see.
If you can't give me love and cloth me and feed me,
Then give me to someone who will do so with glee.

Don't throw me away in a box or a hole,
Do the right thing and think with your soul.
I know you can hear me crying down here.
Please pick me up and hold me, just hold me real near.

Do the right thing and give me away,
To one who will love me all of my days.
I didn't ask to be born, you should control your lust,
So don't leave me to die...that is unjust.

Gloria Fields-Dampier

Oh How I Wish

I wish there was peace - in every single place
Eliminating terror on every child's face

I wish each person was responsible for his own
To lead a family while providing a home

I wish all attitudes agreed on the best way
Of working together, allowing harmony to stay

I wish finding the right answers - wasn't so hard
Helping the environment and every back yard

I wish parents realized the gift of every child
Encouraging, teaching and guaranteeing their smile

I wish every person stood on the same common ground
Avoiding the agony, that in every war is found

I wish each of us was thankful for his lot
Living in America where possibilities never stop

I wish men and women would consider the rest
Giving all of their talents - their very best

I wish dreams of good things would happen too
Letting fairy tale endings, sometimes be true

W. Richard Berry

Untitled

The fresh roses pierce through the soft ground
Peeking through the wet soil
Unaware of the storm that just took place
As the day breaks and the sun rises

A new era begins
In my own solitude

Reaching out to pick the soft pink one
My hand draws back

Why disrupt what is natural in its own form
Left untouched and unharmed
In its own physical beauty

As the last drop of rain trickles down the petal
And down towards the stem
The sun peeks through the last of the thick morning clouds...

Rachel Houk

Frustration

Ye gads!!
The study of biology...
Has given birth to agonizing, debilitating emotions
And clothed the word "frustration" with new meanings.
I feel like a flower garden trampled by a herd of buffalo.
Frustration crushes hope into hopelessness.
Expectations and preparations are sucked down the drain.
Focus awry, questions loom:
"What am I doing here?
Why can't I grasp these particles of atoms?"
Frustration forces panic and defeat to scream, "You're a failure!!"
Nerves shattered, I sleep fitfully.
Therefore, friends prompt: "Try B-complex."
Daylight breaks
And the simple, but elusive answer shines through,
Dispelling the darkness within.
Drop biology!!
Aaahh...relief. Sweet peace, even giddiness.

Linda Teasley

For What Reason Is She A Martyr

I pray for you Mr. Jumblatt
For the loss of your sister
For she died for a reason I know not
You say that she died as a martyr but, yet I say not
Would of you given your life instead of hers
Will her death bring peace to my country and I hope yours
For lebanon has suffered too long
For the greed of a few
How many others have died as martyrs
Dying in agony, but yet
No one there to calm their spirits
And telling them that they died for the cause
For peace and understanding
But the last words from their lips were
Please lord cleanse this land of ours
From the scavengers of wars
Pierce the hearts of us all with your love
Bring us all back into thy fold
For we have wandered aloft as a flock of sheep
While their shepherd was asleep

Hasson Moses

Caribbean Movements, Caribbean Colors

Five o'clock traffic
Traffic lights
Smells of exhaust
Engines screech
A train of cars
Endless movement to the next stop
Raindrops fall onto the windshield
I sit
Love songs on the radio crone sleepily
My mind blurs out
I see... I see...
Red of the traffic light?
No A warm bright sunset in front of me
The traffic light disappears from existence
Colors of teal and powder blue becomes the soft trickle
of the ocean's caress
The train of cars transforms itself from the world around
Sweet sounds of sea breezes, steel drums, palm trees sway
Horns blow. Reality. A tough lesson. I move with the traffic till
    the next stop.

Deborah A. Olshefski

Reflections Of Anna

Her smile is like the reflection of the sun
off a sparkling mountain stream

The joy in her eyes is like
that of a young child

Her warmth radiates like the heat
from a baby chicken held on Easter Day

The compassion in her heart could only
be compared to a mother's love for her child

Her presence is felt like
the grace of an eagle in flight

She has something few will ever know
humbleness, modesty, eloquence, compassion

Her wealth is not tangible nor evident;
it is purely innate

And is at times beyond
the human capacity to perceive

Her wealth is love
Debra S. Sherwood

Scenes

As shadows fall upon the earth,
a mother cries as she gives birth,
the child is born in a world of sin.
where kindness is weakness, and greed is in,
the mother will cry for years and years,
for she holds on to motherly fears,
that gangs, drugs, crime, or whatever may
take the life or future of her child away.

It can't be bought,
though ache have tried,
it's often sought,
and many have died,
if greed could die.
The goal is reached.
Obtaining the lie,
that we call peace.

Life shifts from one page to another,
but can be peaceful, if you love others,
like mother.
Alonzo J. Thomas

Lost Friend

I met her some time ago, I think it was last spring
We didn't hit it off to well
I guess I didn't say the right things
But as we grew to know each other
I was certain of just one thing
We were meant to have fun together
For we enjoyed so many common things
Time stands still, but still flies by
My friend and me, we laughed and we cried
As time passed by our friendship grew much stronger
What I didn't know was it wouldn't last much longer
My friend is gone and it's because of me
I lied to her and she has fled
Friends are special, friends are true
She was both to me
I wish I had been too
I haven't seen her for a while
I almost forget what she is like
All I know is one thing for sure
She has a friend in me for life
Brian Andrews

Life With My Dad

I have a story I'd like to tell,
So pull up a chair and listen well.
This is a story of life with my Dad,
And a few of the experiences that we've had.
We rolled over in a plow truck,
While plowing the roads one day.
"Ever do that before?" was what Dad did say.
Dad cut his leg with a chain saw,
And that chain saw was just little.
But he slipped away from them twice in the ambulance,
On the way to the hospital.
Dad was dragged across the yard—under a pick up truck,
He was scraped from head to toe,
But he had incredible luck.
Dad's not a man who's accident prone,
He always comes out without a broken bone.
He likes to joke — he likes to tease,
About his Ford and my G. M. C.'s.
Dad's going strong at 74,
And I'm sure he will be for many years more.
Richard Morton Sr.

God's Answer to a Waitress

Dear God, I was patient as I served them,
Met their needs from what they say.
But when they left, they didn't tip me,
Just took off on their merry way.

A tract — guess it's the thought that counts,
How can it — be Well received?
When I served them well — for nothing,
Unable to live on what Christians leave.

God it's awful how Christians treat us,
Taken for granted — without any pay.
And God answered, "How well — I remember;
I'm here to serve them every day!"

"I clean up their little messes.
Give them all the help they can't see;
Dispatch angels when they are needed,
But they don't recognize — it was me!"

"Yes it really is quite amazing,
How Christians act — because you see,
For each soul that a Christian influences,
Is of priceless importance to me!"
Ruth Y. Ousley

I Choose ...

When I consider both Life and Death
    I see the two the same
One no weaker than the other
    No strength can either claim.

But surely Life will say to Death
    "I preceded thee in time.
And of all the riches gained by man
    Indeed they are mine."

So Death replying with Reaper's voice
    "Your pot of gold I do see
But of all the colors of your mythical rainbow
    There's no darker shade than me."

But when met by one on the road of despair
    To his countenance I was blind.
For his face was veiled by a shroud of my tears
    And voice spoke these words so kind.

"I see you're perplexed by the rivaled two
    So a pierced hand I give to guide."
And He mysteriously led me not from steps ahead
    But Patience witnessed that He walked beside.
Travis Bulluck

Apology

This is just to say,
I am sorry,
I didn't bring in my homework the other day.
Aliens zapped it up.
It was eaten by my little pup.
A bully took it from me.
I was taken hostage by a flea.
My pencil broke.
On candy I choked.
But other than that,
I don't know why I didn't bring in my homework.

Matthew Haynie

What Is Left On Our Planet - Our Good Deeds

Without a purpose, we would not be here.
Without a reason, God would not keep us here.
While we are on this Planet, we seem to
simply accomplish the duties God gives us.
    Life is not always as smooth as we
want it to be but through sadness and
agony God will guide us and keep us safe under His wings.

    Our Planet is a mere traveller's
resting place. While we are here we do
good works for one another without expecting
a lot just as God never expects anything
from us, except to love each other as He teaches.

    As the petals of a flower disappears
one by one when the wind blows against
them, today we are here, tomorrow we are
gone; but just as the sweet smell of
the flower remains lingering in the air, as
we may disappear, our good works will be left on earth.

Mary Joseph

A Mother's Reflection

Beautiful infant one of a kind
What secrets lie in your newly formed mind
Sleeping in innocence sweet and serene
Do you dream of places you've already been
Did you circle the universe smile at a star
Visit stranger galaxies distant and far
Where was your soul before coming to me
When you swam alone in your secret sea
Were you a bright jewel burning
deep in the night
Before God's mighty hand brought you
into the light
Oh if we could remember where we were before
Then the secret of life would be secret no more

Barbara Sullivan LaValley

Hoping Always

I remember the last time we were together,
I remember it very well.
You held me in your arms so tight
and it felt oh so right.
I wanted time to freeze,
So we didn't have to leave.
We are both very much in love
and I thank the heaven above
for bringing you to me.
So, I'm hoping always that you'll love me.

Heather A. Nobles

Long Distance

The day you died it snowed. I cried
like a boy lost in the winter woods, confounded
by the silent patterns in white and black.

I listened to you die long distance.
When you answered the phone, you called me
by my childhood name. I told you

you would love it here. The land patchwork
of forest and farm. Its history thick
as morning fog. Eagles and ospreys crowding the air.

Your voice quavered and I imagined matching
depredations. Failing legs, yellow eyes,
no stomach for food. Distance kept me safe.

Death was just a word spoken hundreds of miles away.
Near the end you barely had breath for I love you.
The day you died it snowed. I cried.

Tim Harkins

Our Son

Conceived out of love was our son,
By God's will you were the only one.

A child with health so bad,
    It was a constant worry for Mom and Dad,

No running or jumping or playing ball
    with the kids

Your playground was home, hospitals,
    or doctor's office.

Constantly under our watchful eye,
    At times my anguish was hard to disguise.

Now you are twenty-seven and long out of the nest,
    I wish you good health and happiness
    And all of life's best.

Though time and you have made some changes,
    son, you will always be the dearest
    most important in the world to us.

For time can never take away,
    the happiness we've known, or change the love
    that's in our hearts for you and you alone.

Lillian M. Adams

The Lone Rider

When the sun goes down in the golden west
And day has passed from the prairie land,
With the moon just coming up at its best
'Tis then I see the lone rider stand.

Along the horizon he rides every night
Slowly up to the top of yon hill;
As I watch I make sure that I'm out of sight,
While the rider and mount stand so still.

There he'll dismount his faithful steed
And gaze at the evening sky;
The horse understands his master's need
And the meaning of every sigh.

Then after those moments of silence there
In that lonely deserted part,
He rides back again, to I don't know where,
With a secret still deep in his heart.

Each night as the sky starts to change its hue,
He rides o'er the same stretch of land,
And there 'neath the stars, and sky so blue,
You can see the lone rider stand.

Grace Menke

When Love Turns To Blues

Like a prowling cat you entered my heart now my world
will never be the same.
I hope you realize before you start that love can be a risky game
Some say, love is worth the risk
I say, how much are we willing to lose,
Your mind, my heart, your body, my soul
I hate it when love turns to blues

When it's all over, sadness touches our hearts and the many
we surround
We never wanted to hurt anyone with this forbidden love we found
We only wanted to play the game; the risky game of love
How many people would be hurt from a scene of a crying dove

A cat who loses 8 of its lives and tries desperately not to
lose the last
It runs, it hides, it tries to avoid the things that haunted its past
Now it walks through life in a somber mood, not knowing
which road to choose.
If we become so linked, then apart then we, like the cat...
I hate it when love turns to blues.

Lloyd Owens Jr.

Civil War

There was a war so long ago, here in this
country, it disturbs me so. That so many
good men fell and died, opposing brothers
lay side by side.

To preserve a nation, so men could be free,
yanks and rebels they did not agree. So out
went a call you young men to arms, some
from the city, others from farms.

One wore blue and the other gray, as they
fought each other day by day. Hardship and
suffering, cruelties untold from men of
yesterday so brave and so bold.

Musket and sabre, fight to the end, kill your
neighbor enemy or friend. A thousand men
here, ten thousand there, blood soaked the
ground, smoke filled the air.

The great battles ended, our nation preserved
men were shattered, many un-nerved. A
country divided you may not recall, did the
great civil war re-unite us all?

Daniel Wayne Parrish

Our Family

A tree grows strong and stately,
Nourished by rain and sun;
With sturdy roots
And branching shoots
It lasts till time is done.

A family grows in love and kindness,
Nourished by tears and laughter;
With sturdy roots
And branching shoots
It lasts till time hereafter.

God planned for trees and families;
Reaching outward straight and tall
With sturdy roots
And branching shoots
They last till time is all.

Our forefathers formed our family,
Bound together with fellowship and love;
With sturdy roots
And branching shoots
Nourished with strength from above.

Ann C. Klasing

How To Be Popular

Being popular is a state of mind
But to have friends you must be kind
Telling tales and saying jokes
Can help you please many folks
Helping friends with homework will
Get you visits when you're ill
Popularity is a two-way street
Depending on how friends you treat
If you ever go to jail
They'll be there to pay your bail
Just remember when they call
You must have time for them all
To me this is what popularity is
And if you follow these instructions you'll be a wiz!

Jenna Mennella

The Old Farm

The old farm we called it and it was fun,
As it shone with flowers in the morning sun.
Our Nana picked peaches and plums all day long,
Stopping only to cook or sing us a biblical song.
We hold childhood memories of catfish and quail,
Or traveling to the dairy on that old country trail.
As the days passed on we helped with the chores,
While running in and out slamming the farmhouse doors.
The giant hackberry, pecan and mulberry trees,
Shaded the tall hot roof with the greatest of ease.
The wind mill tower served as a playhouse of mine,
In the wooden frame covered with honeysuckle vine.
I wonder where those days must have went,
When hand-turning ice cream was a day well spent.
We pitched washers for a game in the cool moonlit sky,
Beneath the stars and heaven the night would not die.
In the orchards and farm fields the coyotes howled hard,
As we moved the beds out under the trees in the yard.
The old farm we loved and helped build with our hands,
And had hills and ravines in the dry bottom lands.

Michael Wayne Lister

It's Over

No more will I sit by the phone
hoping you will call.
No more will I go to the park
where we sat, held hands, and shared
our dreams.

No more will I listen to the songs that were ours.
No more will I say, "When I'm with you, it's for real."
No more will I remember our walks along the beach,
or as we sat on the rocks, and watch the sun set.

No more will I wipe my tears in the pillow of those
memories.
No more will I remember the good times we shared.
No more will I care.
Today, I begin a new a chapter in this life of mine.
A time when I let go of what was, and finally...
yes, finally after all these years,
begin to live again.
This time for me.
It's over.

V. Foy

Unexpected Love

You came into my life so unexpectedly
yet so lovingly
I came into you life so unwillingly
yet so eagerly
you wooed me so gently
I resisted so completely
you waited so patiently until slowly I yielded.

You came into my life so giving
yet asking so little of me
I came into your life not giving
yet asking so much of you
you shared so much of yourself
yet asking nothing in return
I shared so little of me yet wanted so much of you.

You came into my life with expectation yet without reservation
I came into your life as a temptation yet with consolation.
We started with such great anticipation
discovering a great revelation
That this was our destination and loves our confirmation.

Jennifer Christian

Related Dreams

I close my eyes. I see a bright light break through
the darkness and come into the car. No sound
just a black and white picture. Behind the light is a
train coming straight at me. I see a young girl
about 3 with white blond hair setting between
her two brown haired parents. The dad tries to
stop, but can't boom! It's all over.
Each time I have this dream, I wake up with a
racing heart. For some reason, I can't forget this dream.
It plays over and over in my mind.
I'm sound asleep like before, screams, boom! I can
hear and feel the dream, but I can not see it.
I feel the train slamming into the car, I jump as
my heart feels like it's going to burst.
When I put the two together. I can see, hear
and feel my dreams. I forget all my others
dreams, but these are two that won't go away
They were dream like no other.

Christine Lyn Reichle

The Mind And Soul

Here I am just hanging around
The thoughts that run through my mind
The voices I hear
Images and shapes appear
Like clouds in the sky
Concerned about things that don't matter
Worry the soul and mind
It feels like a time clock ticking away
Minute by minute, hour by hour, day by day
where has my life went
Has it gone to another stage
So tender as a babies bottom
There skin as smooth as silk
We don't know where it goes
Or where it comes from
And no one has control over the mind and soul
The mind can heal the aching parts
The soul can feel the wounds that are too deep
To be healed

Stacy Martin

The Changing Of Seasons

Autumn has overpowered
all the ambitious and flamboyant flowers and leaves that once
bloomed.
Springtime yearns for help, but it is only a sediment of sorrow that
falls on deaf ears.
It cries,
but its tears become a cold frost on branches
stripped of their life.
Soon springtime returned to the fullest of life it once was.

Julie Stankovic

What Do I Want?

I want love unconditionally
someone to love me 'til eternity.
Tell me I'm beautiful even at my worst.
Make me happy
when I am sad.
Make me laugh
when I just want to cry.

Wash my doubts away,
don't tell me I'm crazy for feeling this way.
I want to feel your touch
not hate, the feel of anger,
let me feel lust!

Love in your eyes, not sadness.
Kisses that last forever,
bonds of love that can never be severed.
Thinking of you as you think of me,
wanting to hold you affectionately.

I want to feel your passion, your fire!
Making our hearts full of desire.
All I want is you... You!!!

Noreen M. Novonglosky

O Mother Mine

This gentle soul from 'cross the sea
    brought heart and love and joy to me;
Though you are gone I see you still
    through rays that shine upon my sill.

The fragrant flowers you caressed
    now lie in tribute on your breast;
Their perfume lingering in the air
    reminds of fragrance in your hair.

O mother mine, I cannot see how life could
    somehow better be,
Without your sweet and gentle smile
    that guides me through my life awhile;

But I rejoice in sadness yet
    and dry the tears that I begat;
To realize each day is new,
    it brings me hope because of you.

Ruth A. Cowan

The Second Coming

The second coming beholds its most precious gift of torture
The Pharaohs of old have fallen
The new God's shall subdue the earth

Minds of the forgotten enslaved
Minds of wit put to death
Souls of torment reprieved from the grave
Fight as gallant soldiers mobilized by the pale horse
Lonesome bellows of the church's dirges
They ring out as the anthem of the Gods

D. McGee

To Catch a Bogeyman

The bogeyman, a symbol of childhood fears, haunts
a child's bedroom. To capture one, a room must be set up with
many hiding places providing dark corners for concealment.
    Prepare the room with opened curtains allowing moonlight
to throw shadows from furniture across the floor. The
closet door is opened a crack. The darkness peeps out from the
black regions where nightmares exist.
    The room prepared, the child is put to bed, kissed
and tucked in. The lights are turned off and the door is closed.
All is quiet for the moment.
    The noise begins...the creak of the closet door as it
opens just a fraction more, the rustling of something under the
bed, the scratching at the window. Shadows creeping along the wall
stop at the lump on the corner of the bed. The child cries.
    Parents enter the room, turn on the light and comfort the child.
    The bogeyman is only a fuzzy warm teddybear. The bear,
clutched tightly against the child, will now ward off other
monsters as the child slips into a dreamy sleep.

   Michele Hurst

The Gang

I am ... I feel anger ... lonely, unappreciated, misunderstood.
I need ... belonging! importance! acceptance! a voice!
              I am alone ... I am.

Unsure, inexperienced, innocent, searching,
watching ... joining?
         I am. They are the gang ... I join!

Belonging. Voice. Many ... yet one.
Together. Important! Needed! Understood!
         We are! We are one ... the gang! ... I Am!!
Silence ... than bang ... Shots! ... Blood! ... Death! ... Cries! ...
Screams! Fear ... Guilt ... Silence ...
    I question ... why?? ... because.
    I ask ... who?? ... Don't know. Don't care.
       We did. He is no more. I am ... we are ... the gang!

Initiated. Important! Experienced! Older ...
Feared! In Status! Respected!
Guilty ... Scared ... Fearing ... Knowing ... Hiding ...
       "I" am no more. "We" are ... The Gang!

   Franziska Tinner-Maier

Untitled

   Time that is spent is
always lost.
   Love that is supposed to be forever,
always ends.
   Friends that are here today,
are always gone tomorrow.
   One thing that will never be forgotten,
are the memories, those will always last,
    forever.

   Lindsay Jones

Father's Lie

Seen amongst your sons
you quiver like a child, an
elegant stance in proportional amounts.
Lift your head Father, don't cry
we understand your deceit just
remember to walk the edge and
never forget the pain you are a comfortable
sin. You will end soon and we will
carry your name we are different...
we always have been different

   Jonathan D. Vick

Can't We All Get Along

No matter what the country creed
    or shade,
It is a fact from God, that the same
    we are made.
Does violence and terror have to keep
    our families a bay,
When I cherish more the glow
    of a sibling on graduation day.
Do we resort to the drug that makes
    vile and absorb,
When I'm sure our health and a
    cool breath of air is soberly preferred.
Must everything be measured by wealth
    and strength
When a helpful hand and a charitable
    gesture is a reward,
Don't you think?
Coin a phrase or quote your favorite
    song
But nothing will suffice us

   Jeff Moffett

"Last Night I Had A Dream"

Last night I had a dream. It was so beautiful
That when I awoke I felt so sad and alone. My
dream made me feel so warm and loved for I was in
your arms, my love. Last night I had a dream. A
dream which made my life seem so bright and
so clear. For it was you, my love, whom I heard
whispering so softly in my ear. Telling me that
you love me and will never leave me and that
no matter what, you will always be by my side;
making my whole life worth living. Last night
I had a dream where I was so happy and never
knew pain. The sky in my world was so blue.
There was nothing I could not or would not do
for you. My love, last night I had a dream in
which I would live and die for you. Knowing
that it is you, the one I love. And now that I
am awake I realize, that it was only a dream.
And that I must now continue my hurt and my
pain, praying and hoping that maybe someday
it will no longer have to be a dream...

   Omar Anchondo

Have You Heard?

Of the angel gone bad
but his lawyer plea-bargained

Of the city full of illusions
that it is one enormous illusion itself

Of a fool who attaches to logic and reason
and yet lives in a world illogical and senseless

Of a growing awareness for correctness
that doesn't know how to correct itself

Of a spiritual movement so hypnotizing
and pure but needs your support, spiritually of course

Extrapolate
unearth
defend
regurgitate
disembowel
control
upgrade

   Tomas Yabut

Ode To Rhodies

Perfumeless blooms flop off sticky tendrils
Rouged fuchsias, vulgarest gold
Nipple pink and tenderest
  white flower faces peer out unseeing over
  maidenhair and fiddleheads below.

Rhododendrons, harborers of fog
  hummingbirds, snow and ice
Shelter vagrant lover's moisty pleasures
  Wash them in dew. Dissolve their avid seed
  to feed your trembling hungry roots
    Anne Mendenhall

Know Thyself

"By fate, your physiology
A knowledge came, reserved, unfree.
With promised speech and easy press,
Forbidden fruit still held suppressed,
You think you're free to think so far?
Free speech will show them who you are!
Too late: A tingle cross your face!
One doctor call would seal your fate,
Profaner of the "Mysteries" case,
Then no way out in Christian state,
With stainless steel on white in pain,
The silver star for hope in vain.
But, be forewarned, the rumor's true,
They've found you out, they're after you!"
    Michael A. Pereira

Butterfly Interlude

Wings taking flight looking for a flower
upon which to light...
Gliding, sliding, caressing the winds of love.
In a flutter of ecstasy
  opening, closing
    opening, closing.
Surrounding you, surrounding me
  in a Butterfly Interlude.
Purple, green, gold,
  pink, silver, black...
Colors beckoning, colors reckoning,
  Blending, breathing, blinding,
    bright as the sun.
Together we sail upon the wings of eternal desire,
  stopping briefly...
    ever so sweetly...
  for a Butterfly Interlude.
    Shekinah Perkins

Loving Lyrics

Dear sky blue eyes,
  You remind me of flowers in the fields,
You also remind me of the Teddy Bear and the beach,
because these are the things I like
to see and hear.
  Your eyes are like the shiny sun.
  Your face is as delicate as a red rose.
  Your hands are soft like a soft chair.
  Your personality is like a tree because it
is strong and proud.
When I'm around you I feel nervous and warm.
    Yana Trede

Carry Me

I sit alone, but you are near.
I know you're gone, but you are here.
You fought the illness evermore,
But from the start had lost the war.

You read me a story at night,
You don't understand my plight.
You're carried away by the winds,
And God has forgiven your sins.

In a silent room no one speaks,
Water flows down in a creek,
To me the world appears infected,
Your love was more than I'd expected

Your family and friends all are here,
My eyes are not without tears,
You made all my dreams come true,
And you know I'll always love you.

You came to me when I was young,
As the first breath of life filled my lungs.
You helped me learn how to be free,
When I was down you'd carry me.
    Barry Peterson

Demon's Song

I am immortal, yet my sorest wish is for death.
  I know the world entire,
    and would trade it for one moment of peace.
      People spit on my name, curse my existence,
        The basest is my superior, the forgiveness
      offered so freely to them is barred forever from me.

Why?
  Why am I condemned to this black, starless night?
    How was I judged for this eternal damnation?
      Did the Angels get to choose to be what they are?
      And if so, why was this choice denied me?

Incorrigible, they call me, evil.
  Yet when I cry for mercy I get no answer,
    My pleas for help yield only silence.

I seek the plowshare; I am met by the sword.
  Yet who can say what is right or wrong, good or bad,
    When my tormentor is the One who claims to love us all?
    Evelyn O'Melia

Nature

Nature is ever changing,
Nothing stays the same
Why can't things forever be?
They are meant to change,
To live, to die, and to be recreated
That is the miracle of nature.
It adds to the wonderful, strangeness of it all.

Nature is a cycle to be treasured,
Not to be taken lightly.
We must take care to look at nature,
To find beauty in all things,
From the thunderous waterfall to
The tiny planted seed.

Everything in nature look to find,
A mysterious answer hiding.
Listen to the wind.
What is it whispering?
Wait to hear the voices of long forgotten souls,
May they tell the secrets of all that they hold dear.
    Anita M. Wegman

Recovery

I looked into my reflection
and having seen am not convinced
I do not belong in this dark place
I am still so welcome

I struggle with my pain
shame heavy on my soul
tears seem old now
give me strength to see the sun
and feel its warmth

Just a glimpse - my spirit sings
too tired and restless to fight the inevitable fading
I fall back into panic
waiting for one more chance to behold the light

Gwen Schubert Grabb

Indifference

Throw Them Out!
  The useless toys of living; the broken ones, the old ones,
  the worn toys of yesterdays' childhood!

Throw Them Out!
  The poor defenseless kittens, in the dead of the winter —
  not wanted, not needed, too hard to place,
  too many mouths to feed!

Throw Them Out!
  The messy products of pleasure; the babies, the children;
  so much garbage, too many memories!

Throw Them Out!
  The old folks ... The parents, the grandparents.
  Too busy to help, too busy to care; too busy, too busy!

Throw Them Out!
  The retarded; the disabled; reminders of imperfections in us.
  Who needs it? Don't stare.

Throw Them Out!
  It doesn't fit your lifestyle. To sooth your guilt,
  call it something else. New words to hide behind.
  Rationalize.

Barbara Murdock

Rachel's Christmas Story

Sitting by the fire place wearing jeans and a sweater.
Santa read all the wishes from Rachel's Christmas letter.
"My sister wants a gift that I hope you get her...
I was good last year, but this year I did better..."

All the elves worked so hard to come up with the answer,
For a very special gift that will forever enhance her.
The sleigh soared up high, along with Blitzen and Dancer,
But this Christmas Eve the lead reindeer was Prancer.

Landing the sleigh where the snow was so deep.
It's lucky for Santa because the roof is too steep.
He jumped down the chimney with one mighty leap.
Had the cookies and milk, then soon fell asleep.

All of a sudden there was a loud thunderous crash.
Those darn reindeer have gotten in the trash.
Santa quickly awoke and ran out with a dash.
Climbed into the sleigh and zoomed off in a flash.

Now this is Rachel's story of why Santa's so great.
He delivered all the toys even though he ran late.
Dropping the rest off quickly, emptying each create,
So on this special Christmas Day we can all celebrate.

Gary D. Rick

The Cosmic Clock

The fires of passion burn deep
  In constant conflict and desire.
The evil that men do
  That robs the soul of innocence.

The grasping strength of greed
  That seeks to win, in all the world.
The hatreds that are nurtured
  So violently apposed to peace.

Ah yes, the dark side of man
  In conflict with a noble heart.
Who seeks to learn and softly shows the way,
  To be the giant in the world.

Hate and bigotry are not a part
  Of happiness and peace.
If only man could learn to rise, above his dark side,
  Surely harmony would reign again.

Joyce Brenizer (Mother)

Metaphors of Life

Life is a crashing waterfall, descending into an emerald sea;
Life is a magentic rose, wilted and untouched;
Life is the Season of Death and the changing of the golden leaves
  into precious fragments of the bitter earth.

Life is a raging fire, bursting with crimson, gold, and a somber orange;
Life is an ebony cat, mischievous and cabalistic;
Life is the glow of an ancient lantern, dismal and eerie with the
  lurking of mystery and dark macabre.

Life is a tell-tale skeleton, dusty and unknown;
Life is an angry volcano, rupturing with a fierce strength;
Life is an untold secret of the unknown enigmas of the hellish
  underworld.

Life is death and death is life. One cannot occur without the other,
for they are the same.
To die is to live, and to live is to die. Both are dark, both are
  blessed.
They are inevitable, yet they are escapable.
They are neither understood nor understandable.
They are unpredictable and evil, yet planned and holy.

Life is bewilderment.

Brittani Wittmer

Obsession

Obsession is consuming, relentless and compulsive.
Obsession occupies your every waking hour.
Obsession preoccupies your subconscious.
Obsession creates false securities.
Obsession lingers like a putrid fog.
Obsession grows like a carcinogenic tumor.
Obsession is not a Calvin Klein cologne.
Obsession is much more foul and rancid.
Obsession has formed many marvelous minds.
Obsession has coined many famous phrases.
Obsession is necessary... for the Obsessed.

Deborah Patora

Six Phases of Love

Is love something we see in others first?
Or the heart others you feel instead?
Can her love suddenly fade away?
Is true love what you really seek?

Do you want her love to be unveiled?
Is sex what you really feel?
Does her love quickly changes to someone else?
Why did it happen to you?

What do you do?
Give yourself a break.
For Heavens sake!

Is love something that comes and goes
like a smelling taste that is forgotten?
She whisper sweet things into your ears?

Or it she says, "no" she mean "yes".

Does her stirring emotions seemed to melt away
like her six phases of love may just disappear?
Should I let her have my heart again
and grant her still another break?
For Heavens sake!

   Russell R. Dye

I Am Sixteen

I am Sixteen,
there is no doubt about it.

The trouble I face,
there is no way around it.

I try and I try to do my best,
but whatever I do is all like the rest.

These are the best years of your life,
My, oh my, it is such a strife.

Being Sixteen is like being in a world of rules and
responsibility.
No matter how hard I try, it always seems to get to me.

I may never live up to my moms hopes and dreams,
And everything is never as bad as it seems.

After all, I am Sixteen!

   Amy Hollobaugh

Another Decade

It's hard to believe the 80's have gone,
As well as a musician, a "Beetle" named John.

"Yuppies" and cabbage patch, and Cher's derriere',
While aids and abortion found us socially aware.

A rebellion was crushed in Tiennamen Square,
And "couch potatoes" said, "they didn't care",

Crude oil devaststed an Alaskan bay,
While recycling trash became the new way.

There were Olympic boycotts, and a Chernobyl disaster,
While in the N.H.L., Gretzky was master.

With a "Phantom" on Broadway, an E.T. on screen,
To a 'quake in the Series and Life Magazine.

A new leader in Russia changed the face of our world,
The Noble Peace Prize would be Gorbachev's herald.

Norman and Strange were driving the ball,
While Pink Floyd and Berlin were destroying a wall.

So let's celebrate the end of a decade,
The memories we have and the friends that we've made.

In the coming years a century will leave,
And once again we will say, "It's hard to believe!"

   Jay Downs

Untitled

Two lovers sitting on the sand
Holding each other, hand in hand
Gazing out at the sea
Wondering what may be
"Look at it, such beautiful, beautiful blue.
It's almost as alluring as you,"
He said to her
"I love you, and that is the only thing of which I am sure"
They stared in each other's eyes
Both knowing the other had told no lies
They both knew what to do
So they walked into a sea of blue
The beautiful coldness surrounding their feet
It rose, until both were as white as a sheet
Each enfolded around the other until they were one
They knew what deed had to be done
Both tasted the salty sea
Both went into eternity.

   Mandy Nash

"Stressed"

My eyes are bloodshot my face is broke out,
My clothes are all smelly I wish I could shout!
I put on my clothes and realized "I'm late for work"
How could I explain this to my boss the jerk
I went to my car and opened my purse
My car keys were missing how could things get worse
I went in my house and looked all around
Ah! Finally! My car keys were found
I got in my car and backed out of the driveway
And the next thing I knew I was stuck on the highway
There were cars all around, all of them jammed
Then, Thud! My bumper had just gotten rammed
When I finally got to work I looked like heck
And thought this day's been a pain in the neck
My boss called my name and I went near
I spilled his coffee and he said "You're out of here!"
When I got home to see my cat looking so sweet,
It turned out she ate my pet parakeet
I cleaned up the vase mess my cat, just did
And I thought life was tougher when I was a kid.

   Amber Ahola

Untitled

I am a big sister of one little sister
I wonder if I will ever see her again
I hear her crying everyday
I see peace and education to children of the world
I want homes for the homeless
I am a big sister of one little sister

I pretend that she's alive and happy
I feel her trying to reach me
I touch the future with a beautiful singing voice
I worry about dying children everyday
I cry every year on her birthday
I am a big sister of one little sister.

I understand about and what drugs can do to you
I say to follow your dreams and you'll be a success one day
I dream of seeing her one day
I try to feel the love and warmth around me
I hope that I will succeed one day
I am a big sister of one little sister

   Michele L. Gillette

Grey

Our hearts see not in color but in shades of grey
Our morals flow through our pores like sweat
Flowing, pumping, determining mocking
Only to leave us, dry, empty, our mouths wet

Our hearts see not in color but in shades of grey
It tries though, it really does try
To see for just one moment a rainbow
To look beyond this world to life

They grey is dead, and all it forms
With men and women too
Who walk around like zombies in the night
To see and know of nothing new

Our hearts see not in color but in shades of grey
Although they do dream of it sometime; so real
Only to wake up and realize
That there's no trace left to seal

Our hearts see not in color but in shades of grey
For to do otherwise would mean death
Beyond the hills that look like white elephants
We move to take our breath

Dale Jones

Life's Dance

Why do I dance?
How else can I express the rhythms of Creation
pulsating through the Universe?
Rhythms for which my Soul requests an outlet.
Dance then, with all those
who can hear the song.
A song which vibrates through my spirit
with words of love and peace.
When I dance I cannot judge,
I cannot hate,
I cannot separate myself from life.
I can only be,
joyful and whole.
That is why I dance.

Hans W. Bos

So All Will Know

I woke up this mornin' at 7:03 —
I turned my head and what did I see?
A tired ole man all wrinkled and gray —
looking nothing like he did on our wedding day.
I dressed in a hurry without fixin' my face —
I realized right away, I'd have to slower my pace.
Ole "Arthur" was present, every move he was there —
But breakfast had to be got for the hungry ole "Bear!"
The bread in the oven and the coffee a drippin' —
I rushed to the mirror, my hair to be fixin' —
As soon as I got myself neat as could be, —
I sauntered back to see what I could see.
He said, "It's me, 'Ole Woman', in the kitchen you see
I'm the man you married way back in '43"!
My face lit up with memories of yore — but my
crippled ole feet were like lead on the floor.
We sat and talked for quite a bit — as one off the
other cigarette he lit.
He gets where he's goin' by foot or four wheel — and
the ole "Son-of-a-Gun" still has sex appeal. —Not—!!

Dorothy O'Neal Phillips

Words of Comfort: The Departed

They tell you not to weep or sorrow,
They say, "keep your head up and move on";
But how can you go on with life when someone
who was part of it is gone.
But wait a minute, they're not gone,
The one that you cherish remains in your heart;
They may not be around physically, but spiritually
they never part.
Your loved one that has passed, is safe in God's arms;
He shields them with his almighty armor, and exposes
them to no harm.
Your departed one is in great hands, because our Lord
protects them with his care;
You may not think your beloved is around,
You can't see them, but they're there.

Shana M. Potter

Wondering

Sometimes I sit up late at night,
Wondering what's wrong with my life.
So many times love has passed me by,
So many times I ask myself why.

I've so much to offer that certain girl,
My heart and soul and part of my world.
No one understands the pain I feel inside.
When I see a couple in love standing side by side.

Will it ever be me that someone will love,
Or will I be eternally lonely with only dreams to dream of.
Hopefully, someday my dreams will come true,
And a woman will whisper, "I love you."

If the day ever comes when I find that treasure,
I'd hold her in my arms and love her forever.
I'll always protect her from the cold night air,
Until that day comes by, my heart plays solitaire.

Jason Hayden

My Imagination

With the sunlight streaming onto my paper,
I take my pencil to write,
but what?
Nothing comes out except a few broken phrases
and scattered words.
I try again and realize that the point
of extreme frustration is drawing near.
Then I realize I haven't used the most unique and powerful
tool that I posses, my imagination.
As I write my thoughts down on the paper
the words flow into my mind as quick as a bullet
How great our imagination is.

Uma Mishra

Books

When books become stone walls,
We substitute the words
And dialogues on printed pages
For those we might have had together.
They help us block love's and passion's calls.
And the moat of silence grows broader
And deeper......
When books become stone walls.

Mark Wittmer

How You've Changed Me

You've always been there by my side,
You held me close when I cried
You make me feel safe and secure
And everyday I love you more and more.
You treat me with respect and love,
You give me strength from up above.
You keep me happy and you made me right
I've changed so much, since that night —
When you asked me out one year ago,
I really truly did know
You are the best thing that's ever happened to me.
And we will be together for all eternity.

Tara Grosskreuz

Grandparents

From the first time they saw me,
it was love at first sight
They were always there for me,
be it during the day or at night.
Throughout the years,
they've bragged of me with smiles on their faces.
They've been kind and understanding,
regardless of my weird teenage phases.
And now it's my turn to remember
them each and every day,
And see if there is anything I can do for
them in any special way,
It's my grandparents I am talking about,
in case you haven't guessed.
I realized I should do all I can for them;
I'm tired of being a pest.
I will keep in regular contact with them
So I can earn the pedestal they have put me on
And show all the love I have for them
Before they are forever, ever gone.

Joanne Grosskreuz

Mom, I'll Never Miss You

I may not say I love you or hug like others do.
I may not buy a present like Alta, Pam, or Sue.
So I write this poem to tell you
    on this special day, some things I couldn't
    tell you if the words I had to say.
Thanks for understanding and never asking why,
    when life was overwhelming and I thought
    that I would die.
Thanks for raising me that God is always there.
I've often overcome the dark by whispering a prayer.
Thanks for keeping Dad from going plum insane,
    when y'all thought you had me raised
    and I came back raising cane.
Thanks for all the love.
I hold you in my heart.
That's why I'll never Miss You Mom.
We're never far apart.

Allen Bernhardt

Someone

Someone is lonely, wants tender care,
Someone wants a hand to hold; and
To hear the words of gold, "I Love you."
Someone has much to give you, so
show them how to live.
Just reach out and touch, give and
do; Because that "Someone," may
be you.

Garland Suggs

William J. Brick, A Bombardier

Here I sit,
writing this poem,
in the warm coziness of my friendly home.
Trying to set things straight
about a story that I read
just last night, very late.
It was about some stranger
in a stranger place
trying to set things straight
because he was shot down
just last night, very late.
To all the anger and hate
I try my best to relate,
but I can't seem to come to grip
with what was felt that night
and what is wrong and what is right.
I can only feel that to him I owe
What? I do not seems to know.
Here I sit, thinking of how he was all alone, in the secureness
of my comfortable home.

Bob Thomas

A Child of Mine

From deep inside the vacant, hollow places
In the caverns of my mind
Where mist of pain is swept into clouds of anger,
A child of mind I find.

Inside his eyes, past the hardened gloss,
Through a tunnel, blood-shot red,
Where light reflects from distant thoughts,
I see my shadow in his head.

He's on tender knees of slivered flesh
On an altar worn by time;
His prayers are knelt on boundless dreams
That only my mind confines.

He points past me, past harbored passages
And great vessels sailed of rhyme,
Past the vacant cavern's misty anger
And walls so filled with signs.

Past hardened gloss and blood-shot eyes
Down a tunnel filled with light
Where dreams come true by faith there be:
The Father, the Son and a vacancy to their right.

Calvin E. Hubbard

Untitled

Father, how can I express in words all that you have done
You have been my leader and guide, and also supplied the fun.

You taught me to be strong, have patience and respect
All that you have given me, I promise to never neglect.

You gave me confidence without vanity, and pride without scorn
I will always praise the day, that from you I was born.

Your humor has let me realize that life is only once
And so we sometimes ran wild, playing silly little stunts.

I look to you for guidance, you seem to know the way
Father in your house, I wish that I could stay.

But often life may lead you in quite another direction
yet in my face, I will always see your reflection.

Thank you for all you have instilled in my heart and mind
If I got my pick, a greater father I couldn't find!

Lori Frank

In The Midst

In the midst of our lovemaking
Twilight seeps through the blind and moves across your face
It's at this precise and precious moment...
I catch the vulnerability in your eyes, and realize
How filled to capacity with love I am for you
And how this moment, like so many moments with you
Is scored on my heart forever.

Virgo

Unanswered Questions

Days and nights go by.
My questions still unanswered.
What will it take for a response; I tell you
that I love you and you know it's sincere.

I know love for you has failed, but give me
a chance to unveil the truest love.
The truest love that from heaven
it brings a trail.

Close your eyes and dream with me.
Glide away into a paradise that my love
for you can only bring.
There you'll see the light; the light that
takes away the fears and tears; that an
untrue love has left behind.

Later on tomorrow once again I'll ask
my questions; hoping not another
day or night goes by without
my questions unanswered.

Erick J. Moreira

Perseverance Of The Sea

Gray blue and silver and no longer shallow green
But endless in depth, such as this journey
Are these waters so recently ventured into
And yet so well known

It is a shadowed sky, that leaves our way clear
Stars float upon the velvet blackness
Allowing them movement through the murky depths
Freed from the restraints of space
To drown in the wake of our possibilities

Intent upon these broken waves, quick to mend in our passing
Leaving behind an unmarked journey
Far better the waves than dead calm
When one is no longer able to differentiate
Between sea and sky; hope and despair

So I have returned to the whales of my childhood
Their long lithe bodies floating endlessly
Through the sodium deep of my dreams
Foretelling of such wondrous things as love; and death
As only roses and angels shall ever know

John Ninneman

Death

Death is black like the casket falling into the open pit
and also like the darkness when your eyes
close shut. It runs through my veins. It
reminds me of the time I shut my eyes on a
cold, dark night. It makes me feels
crushed like squeezing dirt in my hand.
It makes me want to die too so I can
see you.

Matt Mancino

Ode to Grandpa and Grandma Gusé

Roses are red,
Violets are blue,
Grandpa and Grandma Gusé
I love you!

It started with your six children from heaven,
Now from your children, I'm grandchild number seven.
I may be the youngest grandchild for now,
But I'm sure there will be more, somehow!

Visiting adults, I'm not too good at,
Being with you in Michigan, now I can handle that!
I love to drive the tractor, go for rides on the pontoon,
Fishing is a favorite, and eating treats is pretty good too!

I love you more with each passing year.
You're the best grandparents ever, that's very clear.
When I go to bed every night,
I say a prayer for you that everything is alright.

Kisses for grandma,
Hugs for grandpa,
This poem is a gift from me
With all my love for you!!!!!

Jerry Matthew Zywczyk

Through This Window

Through this window
Seasons devastate,
Smiles sluff from indolence.
Languishing suns, stained and yellowed,
Spill to the floor into me.
Everything flourishes outside this house condemned.
Nothing! flows in this place of cold existence
Not even madness.
No warmth to my body,
No God or angels touch my soul.

Consciousness tumbles,
Views rescind.
Tempests crown fallow brow.
Darkness furiously contemplates its manifestations
Begotten then lost;
To dissipate in thought - like a
Hot breath in the cold morning light.
Languid dawns inflamed and peering,
Creep open with a cynical eye.
Dreams scatter like confetti on reflections.

Timothy Lloyd Brudigam

Life's Ups And Downs

It takes the sunshine with the rain,
It takes the pleasure with the pain.
It takes the bitter with the sweet
To make life interesting and complete.
Life has its little ups and downs,
It takes the smiles to erase the frowns.
There will always be mountains that are hard to climb,
And answers that are not always easy to find.
We should bravely face each day,
And stop to help others along the way.
Take time to listen and lend a hand,
And try to love our fellow man.
We must take the good times with the bad,
And savor the good times that we've had.
There will be highs and there will be lows,
It doesn't how it goes.
If we take a while to stop and pray,
And thank God for our blessings every day.

Frances Ramer

Love Is

Love is a travelling gift of hope and joy.

Love is the sunrise,
and the sunset.

Love is lying in a bed of roses,
waking up to the sound of the wind,
whispering sweet nothings in your ear.

Love is why the stars shine,
why the sky is blue,
and why the birds sing.

Love is a mother's touch,
and a grandmother's kiss.

Love is a never ending story.

Love is God.

Robyn Morgan

Weep Child

Weep child, for I am free.
Your tear's are the key for my spirit to cross
   over into the light.

Weep child, for I am free.

Your sorrow shall be with me for a while, but
   your heart shall mend.

I know deep inside of me that my death, is my
   life.

Now, I can begin to live.

Weep child, for I am free.

I know, I will be missed and the memories shall
   remain.

My thoughts will be with you, until the light
   comes into your eyes.

Then you will see that, the light is beautiful.

Then, and only then you will say.

Weep child, for I am free.

Consuelo L. Giron

Garden Of Heads

I sit for hours in my garden of heads,
ghastly white faces with long stringy dreads
Some stare blankly, others try to bite,
some laugh wildly in the cool moonlit night
Some tell me stories of who they once were
they speak to me in a low throaty purr
This is the place where I go when I'm bored
a magical garden where I won't be ignored
When the moon is full, they tug at their roots
and struggle and strain, some even get loose
There's no need to worry, my garden is locked,
if you saw my garden you would surely be shocked
You get the point, there's been enough said,
so I'm going back to my garden of heads!

Amber Elstad

Tears

Tears are what I'll have the day I
Leave you, I do hope you know what
I say is true. They'll roll down my
cheeks and splash on my chest, they'll
Seep into my heart. Tears are what I'll
have the day we part. What I say now
Is true, tears are what I'll have the day
I leave you.

Jen Pressley

What If

To my husband, James, and my children
Michael and D. Michele Paroski

What if I gave you my heart, would you cherish
It in a way that a heart should be cherished?
If I offer my life for you, would you do me proud
And live life to its fullest?
If I gave you my eyes, would you enjoy the sunsets
And flowers, and Gods other gifts?
Would you accept my gifts in the way in which I give them,
Not abusing them, but living life and loving life, and
Being grateful to be alive.
Remembering to take the time at least once a day to thank
God for everything and for every day?
For I love you and wish all the best for you. I also
Would offer you my mouth to taste food and my ears to
Hear all there is to hear, a baby cry, a call for
Help, a song of praise.
These things I will give to you, just so that you
Will always remember who we are and why
We are here. Thank God and think of me
For I have given you my all, and
I love you...

Rebecca A. Groves

Missing You Tear

Memories of laughter etched upon your face,
Consoling the emptiness of this place.
Your love that echoes in my past,
Today helps me shed the cast.
Alone in my thoughts without you here,
Trickles down my face a missing you tear.
Keeping my faith in the "Man Upstairs",
Praying he'll help carry the burden of my cares.
Our special friendship that gives me a light in the dark,
Encourages me to try and make my mark.
Someday everything will be clear,
So for now, I'll wipe away my "Missing you tear."

Lori A. Bailey

Life's Paths

Times seems to fly
as you go down life's paths
where do the years go that you thought would last?
Years flew by you barely noticed.
The day comes and you find yourself taking time to really notice.
Most times you find that people are pushing fifty.
You look in the mirror the lines leave their etchings your half
through your life your face is telling you your body feels older
showing the signs.
Years passed you missed a lot of good times. You look over your
shoulder you see how you've grown you wonder why you didn't
take the
time to ponder on all you've been through all times good or bad that
made you so happy or made you so blue these were the years that
led to
you being you on life's paths.

Toni DuBrel

Untitled

"Where has beauty gone?"
I ask myself in a privy inner place
As I linger in the threshold
Meditating through the pane
On the falling drops of rain
That have not yet bathed me,
Thinking how sweet it was just before
When sun and sky were sanguine,
When wind and earth were dry
And warmth wrapped winter wounds
In the fresh and scented arms
Of renewal. How funny! Water warms
Inner places where sun is shaded
To melt the last of winter
And ladens my clothes and hair
To lift my spirit and lay bare
A better beauty; beauty is here
Under clouds, where thoughts cannot escape.
My pace is but a saunter:
I do not wish to be dry.

Tyson V. Cain

Why Did My Homestead Grandma

Cry At Her Daughter's Weddings

Women folk on my grandparent's homestead farm
Responded to every life-giving need.
They gathered the cattle into the barn
Where all were assured their rationed feed.

Under cover from storm and sun
Grandma's daughters milked the cows.
They fed the fowl wholesome grain on the run,
As they sought supplementary food while they browsed.

The garden they tended between moments,
At the stove in the kitchen preparing meals.
To feed a large, hungry family that made its presence
At regular periods of each day's zeal.

Now, these young, beautiful, energetic women
Soon grew up to adults instate.
Even back then there were handsome men
Who awaited their turn to choose a mate!

That's when I noticed grandma's tears appeared.
What brought about her emotional stress?
Was it her experiences far and near
Or the thought that bearing a family is distress?

Theodore R. Reich

Shadows

I walk the shadows as you sleep.
You pray the Lord your soul to keep.
I'm the death in your eyes.
I'm the fire in the sky.
You're the sparkle in my eye.
Death is unleashed as I cry.
I'm the hate in your soul.
At any time I can take you whole.
Yes, it's true, I'm the shadow in your soul...

Cassondra Posey

Man to Remember

One who stands tall in his belief in justice
and fairness for all. For the principles of
a Nations which represent all Military men and
women. Gave of himself to protect this Honor
for all to follow, God Bless a man this former
Marine will miss! Rest in peace you have the
respect of all, Sir!

Clara Gange

How

Sitting here wondering
Looking off to space
Thinking of how you can love me
When all you seem to do is walk away

I'm crying inside
This lonesome room
For no one can know
How much I care for you

One by one they fall from my eyes
But no one can see I want to die
24hrs. I've been in here
And you still haven't called to say you care

You don't see I love you
You don't seem to care
You don't think I want you
When every night I dream of you lying here

I know there's no chance
I should just give up
But how can I,
When you're all I ever think of?

Nicole Medlin

A Dream of Destiny

A glimpse of light has touched before,
Only to be ignored.
But raising its head, it shines once more.
This dream can be restored.

Released from bondage, it must come;
So destiny can flow.
From a heart that beats like a messenger's drum,
With a dream that one must know.

Pushing hard to be recognized,
Wanting so bad to gleam;
Covered up with a costly disguise;
No one sees this dream.

So higher and higher it lifts its head,
The mask falls to the ground.
Suddenly a weary heart is lead,
Exploding with a sound.

The sound of jubilee is great,
A purpose is fulfilled;
The manifestation indeed was late;
Its existence now is real.

Daunita O. Lucas

Oh My Precious Children

One Nation under God is what our Children use to say:
But their not allowed to talk like that inside our school's today.
They can talk about Sex and Burning the Flag, of Guns and Wars too:
But it is Unconstitutional to speak of our Lord, so what are our
Children to do?
We are not allowed to spank them or try to make them mind:
And for them to have a Hero with Morals is getting harder and
harder to find:
You get your Family together and try to watch T.V.:
But know matter where you turn it there is nothing good to see.
Oh My Precious Children, for you I will say a Prayer:
For it is the Adults all around you that needs to learn to Care:
"God" does not stand for Guns, Abortions, and Drugs:
It is the all Mighty Maker of Heaven and Earth My Friend.
The Alpha and Omega- The Beginning and The End...

Sandra Leigh Veal

Forever War

Those wars are done.
We fought them from the Belleau Wood,
The Ardennes and the Valley of the Rhine.
We sent our sons to catch the torches
Falling heroes tossed aside,
To cry to heaven amid the bursting shells
And curse the hell in which their comrades died

Those wars are past. Our sons crossed the breaches
Of Salerno and of Anzio, and last, the northern sea again,
They left their dead and bleeding on the sands of Iwo's Isle
To plant the flag of Victory on its crown,
Or felt the sting of death, or prayed awhile.

We shouldered wounded fox-hole pals on Korea's line
And ran to find them shelter. Then up the hill
We charged again; revenge was ours. And now
We crawl the jungles of the East or wade
The swamps and streams for endless hours.

Are wars yet done? Again we follow Sherman to the sea.
In fact or fancy, still with troubled minds, it had to be!

Bertha West

I Still Miss You

It's been so long since I saw you last,
It's hard to believe time passes so fast!
You are so close to my heart as you were then,
My love for you will never end.
You meant so much to me and you still do,
I know in my heart you love me too.
It's said that time heals all wounds, I know that isn't true,
For words can't express the pain I still go through.
Now you are in heaven, I know that is true
And some day I'll be there with you.
Until that day I must go on with my life,
It's hard to console my pain, my strife.
I'll keep pressing forward and when I see you again
We'll be together forever and time will never end.

Karen F. Childress

When Someday Comes

When someday comes I raise my head
and shake the dreams and what has been said.
I do not know if these dreams are real.
but if they are future is revealed.
In the darkness of night
in the brightness of day
no one shall or ever might
join the battle and the weary fight
against guns and death and hateful things.
Through all this people rejoice and strongly sing
in hope of a new life dawning
into what is now belonging
To love and hate, it's all in the mind
to be in the shadows or nowhere behind
I still will be there 'till truth do you find.
My life came and went through many suns
and I am still waiting until someday comes.

Michelle Burke

Random

To Melanie Sweet, a beauty beyond even my own conception

Random thoughts race through dark
channels of life and love
they break free into the beauty of your
presence the channels now turn to perfect
purple hallways for my thoughts of you to
be sorted and arranged piece by piece
starting with your soft brown hair shining
in the sun and your hypnotic eyes that
wash away enchanted cries of lost souls
looking for love
They admire your body from the heavens
created in perfect precision with the
angelic contours of your beautiful face
and the graceful curves created as a
heavenly guide for perfection
You weren't a random thought stuck in
my head no not at all you were a perfect
picture placed in my mind by forces
beyond all mortal conception

Duane Gero

Wondering

I wonder. Given away like old clothing. Do you wonder?
Was it hard? Do you regret? Have you attempted to
revive the wilted remains of what could have been
called a relationship? Do you wonder?
I wonder.

I wonder. Should I look? Would searching hurt more than help?
Is wanting enough? Yet, do I really want to know? Could the
possibility of shattering dreams long woven be handled?
Are the stories of cases similar to mine true?
I wonder.

I wonder. Should I care? Is it futile to care?
Why do my own feelings confuse me? I see others hurt by
their searches, ripped brutally from loving arms which nurtured
them and thrust into a world of strangers. They adjust.
Could I? Should I look?
I wonder.

I wonder. How am I supposed to feel? Predetermined are
my feelings. My questions cannot be answered by others.
What do I do? How do I feel?
I wonder.

Jessica Lynn Adams

Imminent Chaos

The resplendent sun illumes the crystalline heavens.
The red robins chirp their harmonious song.
A pale, delicate petal lands at my feet,
And reality is veiled by innocent glory.

The azure sphere is tainted by gray, foreboding clouds.
The stagnant air is disturbed into motion.
An ominous shadow envelopes the land,
And reality is veiled by the faulty splendor.

Repressed malice erupts in an echoing clamor.
Jagged bolts edify nature's woeful gloom.
The crashing raindrops explode with the impact,
And reality is unveiled by our shattered dreams.

Heather Glick

Early Morning Dream

Ah, the early morning sun breaking its way through the forenights darkness. The morning dew displaying itself like a field of sparkling diamonds offering the appearance of one of nature's Wonderful sights to mankind. A cricket playing his song, accompanying by a sparrow singing in tune to gently awake the sleeping to the start of a new day. A subtle breeze welcoming the dawn even more so! Now the daylight displays all nature has to offer. The early blooming lady slippers whom after being in the spotlight of morn shyly folds her lovely bloom back into hiding til morrow. The day starts, its time begins to tick away, but what is time? Is it only but numbers on a clock that man has created? Do we really need the seconds passing away into minutes, hours, days, years? Ah, again, the early dusk has come so quickly. The sun is fading into a spectacular sunset giving way to a glorious shining, rising moon. The late evening dew is upon the ground, a cricket once again, playing his song this time accompanying by the wise, old owl. I shall retire for the night, as I am weary, and once again, await for nature's wake-up call, like an early morning dream!

Isn't Life Wonderful?

James Perry Hand

Without You

With the dawning of each new day
Another part of me passes away
With the on set of every night
My lonely soul wonders in ageless flight
Gliding as if the wind through time and space
To find that ever memorable angel like face
Searching for the one to ease my pain
The lover to make my mind sane
Extending my energy throughout all existence
My heart continues the search with extreme persistence
Longing for you to be at my side
The tears of loss I can no longer hide
What was once love, happiness and cheer
Has turned to sadness, depression and fear
So where has the one I love gone
And why must the agonies of the day last so long
If I only had the answer or even a clue
Maybe this day I wouldn't find myself...without you

Jacob J. Brown

My Treasure

Joey's my Great Pyrenees.
Of course, there's no ticks or fleas.

His playmate's name is Colette.
Yes, he drinks from the toilet.

Sleeps in the tub to keep cool.
Sue, but he is a jewel.

Wow! If he's not fed on time,
My life ain't worth a thin dime.

Oh, his size creates such fright,
And his bark's worse than his bite.

God help a burglar or thief
Look out, 'cause he'll give them grief.

Joey hates claps of thunder.
The bed's safe, he dives under.

There're times when he's bad, bad, bad,
Tears up things when he gets mad.

Barks loud 'nuff to wake the dead,
Specially after I'm in bed.

Even if he does do that,
He's better than an ole cat.

Magi Braun

Soul of a Queen

I once knew a king who ruled a feared clan,
A king thought to be evil, the cruelest of man.
He sent his own people out to die, at times for no reason.
He behead the innocent life of the poor to mark a change
   of season.
Only one soul knew his real self, to others unseen.
This one soul was mine, for I was his queen.

Beverly Royse

Be My Love

Baby I'll be yours and you'll be mine
We'll love each other til the end of time
I won't be able to give you a lot of gifts
But I'll always be able to love you like this
If you ever have problems then give me a call
And I'll be right there to help you through it all
If you ever need someone who will always care
If you ever need someone who will always be there
Then just open your eyes because here I am
And I'll do that for you the best that I can

Jason Brewster

The Closeness of a Helping Hand

There is a mass of air around us all
Which is called the atmosphere.

Many things happen within the atmosphere.
Things that could change our lives forever.

There are items created to help,
Which also unfortunately destroy.

Some things which are created everyday,
Are things from which we are influenced.

For instance, close friends within this atmosphere,
Make our lives more complete.

Many of us are challenged in every way,
While others are merely limited to small extents.

The atmosphere is a place for all to come together.
In this way, we are to help one another.

Marcie Summerville

Untitled

He walks into my room at night
Kisses me softly and gently tucks me in

As I rise to the sounds of the morning
He wakes me and reminds me he loves me

As I leave my home to start my day
He sits beside me and prays to God

That his daughter stay safe and joyous all day
And when the night falls she returns home again

He steers me from trouble when it may arise
Keeping danger far from near

Always promising his gentle care

He is that wondrous star in the dark of night
He is the angel that sits on my shoulder

Even though he may never be in my sight
He watched his little girl from Heaven
both day and night.

Lottie Howell

Oh But Pain

Oh but pain what strange thing it may make one do. But to lay
in bed and cry oh pore me, But never trying to help one self.
  But to scream, as if it one last breath. But to destroy one own
life, oh what a waste that may be.
  But to stand tall or sit it may be, say come look at me am
I not as tall as the?
  But to keep one's "Mind, Body an Sole" up and on the go may it
be no more than a Pin or Brush in hand.
  But to write a Story or Poem of life gone by, and yet maybe
yet thing to come, But to paint the Glory of the Land, or to
paint one friend, may thy be of Feather's, Fin's or Hair.
  But to make life of it better than the best, to say God here
I am among the very best.

Warren N. Whitworth

Sea of Sorrow

I sit thinking of what I want to do, of who I want to be
I think of myself, how is my voice to be heard
When among millions it is so small, so insignificant
I wonder if my opinion will ever be known to all
If what I have to say will ever touch people's hearts
If what I can do will ever make a difference
I want my sorrow, my suffering to prevent the pain I've felt
From being the pain of some other lost soul
For now all I know is that I'm drowning in a sea of voices
I'm drowning in a sea sorrow but there will always be tomorrow

Megan Fraley

You Were Always There

Mom, when we were young
You were always there,
As we grew up and tried our wings we were unaware.
That we would still be needing you,
And there you were to care.
I know we didn't make life easy and
caused a few grey hairs.
But, Mom we always loved you so and
can't imagine you not here.
God always takes the good ones home
And keeps them safe and sound.
I hope God has a plan.
For those not homeward bound.
I guess, Mom, what I'm saying is we will miss you so,
And though we are not ready
We have to let you go.
You're headed for a better place
No pain sickness or sorrow.
But, Mom we will all meet again
On some future tomorrow.

Jennifer Susan O'Shia

Shattered

Thinking back to yesterday,
and how my life has gone astray.
How did I become so jaded,
my memories have slowly faded.
I've been told that times they change,
now I fear I've gone insane.
Nowhere to turn, nobody cares,
now I lie here in great despair.
This shattered heart wishes to beat no more,
My sanity frayed, my pride on the floor.
So I'll leave this world, but not in vain,
just to spare myself from this pain.

James D. Cramer

That Extra Mile

The rubber band rifle the wooden sword
Colored pencils and paper when it poured
Whenever there was room and a big tree
A rope swing hung and we felt free

No computer games just plastic men at war
It wasn't VCR's that taught us the score
An old dirt drive and a plywood car
Imagination the fuel that drove it far

Certainly not the toys that you might buy today
Still can't believe I'd have it any other way
Every kid gets mad, every kid gets bad
They turn from their mother, turn from dad

Got to go on their own find what life brings
The mind always drifts back to certain things
That picnic where the family jumped in the creek
A confrontation and the words you couldn't speak

Yet fight on wooden sword and rubber band rifle
Things from the heart are not so trifle
Hope given from an encouraging word or smile
This is what keeps us going that extra mile

Robert N. Wormington

Metamorphosis

Metamorphosis is a natural mystery.
It is hard to believe unless you see,
A caterpillar pupa becoming a butterfly,
Upon which future generations rely.

First the female butterfly her eggs does lay.
Eggs become embryos in less than a day.
Hatching into a larva known as a caterpillar,
Which eats leaves of which we are all familiar.

A caterpillar molts several times shedding its skin.
After two months the pupa stage does begin.
As the caterpillar larva shuts itself inside a hard chrysalis,
For two months all action the world will miss.

At which time the body, legs and wings develop,
As miraculously changes of the insect envelop.
Next the butterfly emerges as the chrysalis does split
Seems impossible inside the butterfly did fit.

Completely grown, away the butterfly does fly.
Completely free the butterfly heads into the sky.
During its life it can fly 1000 miles or more,
Everyone who sees the butterfly they do adore.

John A. Strommen

Talk To Me

Talk to me, go out of silence. I tell you a story. I caress
understand you...I touch you gentle. Set your feelings free, tell me
how is the world (inside-you). Talk to me and move a mountain.
Create a new language. Do it-say it-go out of mutism.

Talk to me, the truth of your warmth. Dream-imagine me-call me.
Talk to me, come and turn around. Look at me and tell me (what is
inside)...Set your (inside) wishes free, cross over. Change
everything. Break the silence.

Talk to me, go one step.... Take-me-out-of-this-waiting....
...reach-swing-shake the language. Think-call me. Talk to me
in your impulse, dream-imagine me-deeply-madly. Without thinking,
call-transform-invent-me. Overcome, unbosom yourself,
seek me. Break the hiding, take me out of your darkness.

I touch you-squat-prop up-calm you...I caress you
gentle. I tell you a story. Talk to me, play-create-move
slowly-jump over. Out of confinement, go trough and
get involve with me. Speak-say...talk to me,
create a new-your-own language.

Patricia Bravo

These Hands

As I look at these hands so wrinkled and old,
I think of the tasks they did unfold.
I think of the husband,
the children they loved and caressed,
the washing, the cleaning, the cooking,
they did their best.
But now they are idle,
these old hands of mine,
the toil of the years,
found in every line.

Josephine M. Kenny

Morning Prayer: A Prose Poem

In the shadow and substance of dawn-dappled trees, in the silent flicker of candles guarding the walls of the garden grotto, I sense the ebb and flow of many stumblings, many rescuings.

I close my eyes and breathe the scent of lilacs and roses, aware that failure to act may be as great a sin as acting. That reconciliation is love's gift, and forgiveness enters the mystery of the word's redemption. Extending my hands in acceptance of your will,
I ask that others may find their healing in your touch.

Make me your messenger, for though I am weak, you fill me with your strength. Shape me and sustain me with your truth. Transform
silence into eloquence. Let my words sing; my actions fulfill my words. Let my thoughts reflect peace; let my heart become an extension of your love. Make me a gift to others; help me to respect
and accept their gifts, for, ultimately, all our gifts are yours.

Velande Taylor

Writer's Block

Blank pages smirk.
Raucous concepts clank in blood-drenched silence.
Writhing syllables twist frustration into fear.
Depressions dank breath threatens.
Talent's candle flickers.

Mechanically, I watch my clutched pen scrawl cruel circles,
Flat Slinkys that uncoil to stab malnourished words.
My robot fingers squeeze sporadic phrases from the ink-filled tip.
Grammatical bastards!
They spew cacophony and die,
Far from sanctuary.

Minutes, hours, days disguise,
A masquerade of eons before the first thought spurts!
Then others ooze...strengthen...flow...
And spill so rapidly that I must
Scribble to record the
Lightning, lightening, logical lines,
Lines that medicate the gaps,
Lines that cauterize the scars.

Jo Daniels

Sometimes

Sometimes the sweetest words are never said aloud.
Sometimes the greatest love is in a hug.
Sometimes the saddest tears are cried inside, and
   sometimes the happiest laugh isn't heard by other ears.
Sometimes the best presents aren't always bought.
Sometimes the prettiest songs aren't always in tune.
Sometimes the brightest days aren't really sunny and
   sometimes the bluest skies aren't really blue at all.
Sometimes the closest friends seem far away.
Sometimes the goals you've set seem closer each day.
Sometimes the greatest love comes from an unexpected place.
Sometimes the greatest love is found in a familiar face.

Sunny Dunbar

Carolina Country

Goldenrod and blue astor days....
Cicadas chatter in the Autumn haze...
butterflies flitting from flower to flower
While the black crow sits on the fence....
Just watchin' the cows graze.
Carolina Country, Carolina Ways....
Goldenrod and blue astor days.

Hear the bobwhite and the whippoorwill call
as the evening nears...
a chill takes the place of the haze....
a hint of frost and we know it's fall.

The hickory nut tree is full of squirrels
and the jackrabbit jumps in the sage....
The moon is slowly risin' and "due respect"
should always be paid.
The stillness grows...as we gently close
Another "Caroline Country Day"

Brenda Davis

Horseman's Last Song

Galloping by horse back with Raj and He.
A treasure to secret service men,
Who languished behind some tree.
Dictator and friends raced by them...
Stalked by the terrorist since puberty.

Diplomat by nighttime so musically,
Talented copyrighter pending.
Whose love songs sung so publically.
Throughout the world troops ascending,
Ambassadress healing wounds secretly.

Presidential orders were lyrically said...
Well defined hopes for peace were laid.
While puffed pillows for the one in bed,
Who now with child the puppets played.
Then grew to three on bended knee obeyed.

Her horse man galloped alone on the beach.
Wars, tornadoes, and hurricanes decay.
"British invasion", we hear preached.
Though not as British as they say.
The soul is the juice from a Georgia Peach.

Lynda Cokuslu

Rainfall

There's nothing like the rain
   for disguising sorrow's tears,
Or to cover up life's pain
   and lock away your fears.
No time is like a cloudy night
   when the sky falls and pours,
To open your heart to tell and write
   and fight battles of internal wars.
I tell her and the world I love her,
   yet set myself up for sorrow;
For I know she will love another
   when I leave and return on the morrow.
In the rain there's no need to be shy,
For with your pain, the earth will also cry.

Jason Davis

Grandmother

Gnarled and twisted
you grow on
Grandmother of Grandmothers
scratching and spreading your corkscrew branches
to the sky.
Never stopping
undying
growing and spreading
haunting the silty banks
Your shadow is the earthy breath
of life and of death
throwing itself
over all.
Spiny bark and barkless spots
you twist and grow
from the banks of the Styx
to the Willamette above
Unceasing
until you reach your spiral trunk
to the kingdom of heaven

Amanda Dexter

Empowered

I am
Living, laughing, loving,
Walking, dancing,
Feeling, touching,
Sharing, giving,
All the positive parts of me!
I see through magical eyes and I am lifted high,
And the whole world is alive with the
Energy and miracle of love.
My soul is transformed from the power it brings,
My spirit is open to receive all good things.
The positive wisdom sets me free,
The world is ablaze from the glorious beams.
As I surrender to its beauty, love, and light,
I am empowered and open to the Divine.

Elaine Dinnall-Stewart

Untitled

We have defended our country
  Often times we are not rewarded
When time came we were always ready
  And now we are losing day by day

It is a shame to treat us this day
  We ask our President to work more
To stay home, not to travel away
  And give us what we are working for

We always pray for equality
  And all the justice we were promised
This task will not come easy
  If our leaders fail to be mixed

We are heading for a disaster
  If we do not change our situation
We must give our young education
  Or we will all fall in the gutter

We should ask help from our Creator
  If we plan to defend our nation
If we don't, time will grow much shorter
  Let's work for the next generation

Don Duquet

World War Blues

We needed a way to end World War II
So we dropped the biggest bomb
That ever blew
In the newsreels and the papers
We watched and we read
Of the hundreds of thousands
Left homeless and dead

Don't they stand for nothin'
Don't that tell us sometin'
Can't we learn from history
We left a spot -
Where a man used to be

Now the time is upon us
And there's none left to lose
The form of our future is on us to choose
Or is it all beyond us - do we really have a say?
I know Adam and Eve never planned it this way
If they only knew what one sweet bite would do
We wouldn't be singing these World War Blues
Where a man used to be...think about it!

John Dzerigian

The Abstract Battle

The skin I'm in, is not my sin
For the boundaries of limitation
Only live within
The world populates people
Who claim to be afraid
And they blame most their fears
On their fellow man's shade
But the exposed truth is
They try to escape, rather than understand
What makes up the difference in every woman and every man
Escape from the doctrine
On which life is based
Not to run against each other
But to live as one race
Just as the sun and moon
Agree to appear at different times
The true battle of sightless fear
Must be conquered in each individual's mind

Gary Armstead

For Who Am I?

Apart we are from one another
Yet we shall never touch.
Though we have not met face to face,
I know you. I know your laugh and
Most of all your cry. At this time
I am with you ever so close.

I have watched you grow from a child to a grown person.
Not only in body, but also in mind.
When you climbed your first mountain, I was there cheering you on.
Praying that you would not fall aside,
Though you were only going to school for the first time.
When you skinned your knee, I too bled a little and felt the same pain.

I have been here since you were born and will be here when you die.
With every passing moment I will speak, yet you will not see me.
But you will hear me and know that I am very near, and
That I will speak the truth. For who am I?
I am your heart!

Daniel G. Steadham

Yesterday

Yesterday what an awful thing
to have around, holding onto
you pulling you further and further down.
Yesterday will smother you if it
gets a chance, as if he
doesn't want you to look at tomorrow, not even a glance.
Yesterday will call to you with such a roar,
that you are frozen
reaching for Tomorrow's door.
If I could only see Tomorrow
and leave yesterday far behind.
If I could only look tomorrow.
I would have peace of mind.
Older and a little wiser now I understand
it wasn't Yesterday holding me.
But me holding Yesterday's hand.

Bonnie Thomas

Rejuvenation

Finally emerging
A little boy with a wide grin and big brown eyes appears
He petitions for his time, a debt is in arrears
He has always existed, time can not constrain this child
He is the offspring of laughter and play, he will not be exiled

Anxiously arriving
He burst through the cares and woes of a rugged man's exterior
He can no longer be suppressed, the boy now reigns superior
Laughter and fun are free at last, and are now the priority
Closed are the doors to schedules, demands, and a hurried society

Gleefully escaping
Feet now carry toes to mud, after a mid-day summer's rain
Knees are now reestablishing a pant leg's marble-game stain
The tongue now extends itself in the breeze, for as long as it takes
As it awaits a honeysuckle's nectar, released by shakes and shakes
   and shakes

Successfully conquering
The little boy from days gone by, with a wide grin and big brown eyes
Brings with him an eternal treasure, a new adventure, a glorious
   surprise
And when his overdue debt is no longer in grave arrears
A man with a wide grin and big brown eyes finally, appears.

Davison Virgil

Time

A time for love
A time for sharing
A time when hearts weep
This is when the dance we share
Shall be the last for us.
Round the dance floor one last time
And remember all that you hold dear
Look at us, your friends, and see the past
See the times we have laughed,
The times we have cried, and
The times we have been just friends
From this dance remember us
Because we will never, never
Let your Love die.

Eric Grisham

My Love

To: My Love Sasha H.

My love for you has grown so much,
It grows with every touch.
With every look I take, I see your elegant, gentle face,
With every word you say you take me away to a wondrous place.
I never want to leave this place you take me to,
For it is a place just for me and you.
At times I sit and stare,
Wondering about this most wondrous affair.
Is this most wondrous affair an affair of love?
Without a moment of pause my mind cries out I need you my love!
When I am near you everything is right,
Like the sight of the stars and moon at night.
At night when I am thinking about you,
I remember how much our love grew.
When I look at you I see an Angel,
Your boundless brown hair perfect, without a tangle.
I know I love you for love is the most astounding state in life.
Now everything in my life is feeling right and I have you to thank.
This poem is but a drop of water from the vast oceans of my love.
This is how much I love you!

Justin M. Schick

Would You?

What would you do about life
Choose the same husband, the same wife?

What work would suit your need
How many goals would you achieve?

Would you see a change of style,
About the way you reared a child?

Would you stay at this point in time,
Knowing your life is affecting your mind?

Would you be afraid to try
To really stop living a lie?

Would hoping for a different life
Cause others concerned bitter strife?

Must you sacrifice yourself,
Because morals control all else?

Would you dare to take the step
That leads to a life you may regret?

Would you keep life as it is now,
Or try a change if you knew how?

What would you do about life?
Choose the same husband, the same wife?

Evelyn Tunie

Peace, Peace, Peace

In the Bible-God says, let there
be peace among all nations.
  Peace is something to cherish
and behold....whether in heart,
or in soul: peace in Spirit, and in
mind...gives us the feelings to be kind.
  Peace among group's....minority, black,
and white....leads us to do what's right.
Peace in our cities, homes, and towns,
is what we all need....if it can be found.
  Peace in the world.....among all Nations,
is just what we need for self presentation.
Peace in our lives, with family and friends
Will help make us all ready...when God de-sends.
  But, there can be no peace, without,
"God's intervention", so let us all,
"Accept Him," and have a world convention.

Viola B. Jelink

Up In Gloryland

I have a GOD who knows all of my fears and woes.
I put my trust in Him for everywhere I go.

He put me here on earth to do His special plan,
to spread His great salvation with my fellow man.

Yes, JESUS is my Lord and my Master today.
He will take me to places where I'll never stray.

The Lord is coming back, He'll catch us up with friends,
on that glorious day when the world comes to an end.

I'll praise God every day and thank Him every night,
for guiding me along through life's treacherous flight.

I will sing to Him aloud a joyous new song.
I will share with my Master to whom I belong.

Yes, up in Gloryland there lives eternally,
a Great King who is building a mansion for me.

He saved me with His blood and His amazing grace,
and someday I am going to thank Him, face to face.

Mark Philip Leopin

My Childhood Days

With faded and patched coveralls, I
  scampered across the new plowed field,
  without any spills or falls.

Us kids had fun a-gathrein' wood to keep
  the fire a roarin'

It's the little things in life that count,
  the things of yesteryear.

We did our chores and scampered off
  across the pasture to bring in the cows.

I used to sit and watch Dad make the milk
  foam to the top of the milk bucket.

We fed the hogs, shucked the corn and
  laid the hay away in the barn.

When day was done, we took the old coon hound
  down the creek to listen to him bay.

With cold feet and lots of fun, we blew out
  the lantern, then crawled into bed for a
  few winks of slumber.

Cletis H. Converse

At the Green Mill

Look for wild ferns and columbine
  Where the wheel of the green mill turns

Listen to the water cascading off paddles
  Where the wheel of the green mill turns

Perceive the force of the rippling stream
  Where the wheel of the green mill turns

Inhale pungent fumes as autumn leaves burn
  Where the wheel of the green mill turns

Sample the distinct flavor of wild berries
  Where the wheel of the green mill turns

A locale for experiencing with the senses,
  Where the wheel of the green mill turns

D. Rodger Long

Have You Ever Asked

Have you ever asked yourself a question?
Asked, have you really got a friend?
A friend who is always there,
With an ear ready to lend.

Have you ever asked yourself a question?
Asked, are you someone's friend?
Are you always there,
With your ear ready to lend?

Sometimes it's hard to see both sides
And hard to they both sides.
We can only live day by day
To cherish the one's we love.

Sometimes friendship is a lonely feeling
One that cuts through and through
'Cause sometimes we expect too much
Out of the one's we love.

Does anybody have the answers?
I don't think anyone does,
We just have to keep on trying
To be a friend to the one's we love.

Mike B. Payne

The Immigrants

They come to this land from the world over,
Disheartened, scared, hopeful,
Willing but not really able,
Families and possessions left behind,
Physically here, hearts oceans away.
Tearful but joyous calls, uplifting notes
Bring an interlude to the loneliness.
One departure, one arrival after another,
At last they are again together,
Families and possessions "transplanted"
Into a free country not so free anymore.
New generation of children asking
Why here and not there,
Sorrowful answers never quite clear.
Let's spare them our anxieties,
Be happy where you are, don't dream of
What might have been if families and
Possessions remained elsewhere.

Gladys Vaval

My Puppy

His nose is wet, looks funny too,
The ears are long and hang down low,
He has eyes bright and blue,
The puppy's tongue is wet, slime.

He likes to lick your face,
If you get too close he will knock you over,
Some times he gets carried away.
He gets soaked when he is bad.

He always wants to be going
were he isn't supposed to go.
He tracks up the house when it rains,
Oh, puppy, I love you so.

Michelle Maglica

Keeper of My Heart

Words can only partially describe the endless emotion my soul feels
for you.
You are the reason I cry alone in my bed at night.
    And the reason I get out of bed in the morning.
You are the reason why sometimes my pen flashes across a piece of
    paper, and why sometimes not a word will flow from me.
You are the light that illuminated the darkness of my life,
    And you are the tall dark stranger of my dreams.
Thoughts of you are always with me.
Night and day I am aware of your power over me.
When we are together heaven couldn't be more then a breath away,
    When we are apart the fires of hell grab at my feet.
The thought of you is cool water for my brow in mid summer,
    And another log on the fire in winter.
When your soft lips touch mine I shudder with the realization
    That there is no greater please.
When we are apart I quake with fear, for to never
    Have that pleasure again would surely bring death.
You are the love of my life, you are the bane of my sorrows,
    You are my bread and water, you are the keeper of my heart.

Cathleen E. Ames

A Reminder (To Friends)

Let not your heart be troubled
let not your sprit be bound
Let not your mind deceive you,
stand on solid ground.

Know that I am with you
Where ever you may roam
Know that I can see you, no matter
how far you travel from home.

Be content that we can touch
renew our hopes and dreams
release your mind from bondage,
I will silence all your screams.

To treasure every moment.
to call myself your friend
is a wonderful compliment
I will treasure till the end.

I am nevermore than a heartbeat away
Call, I shall answer, offer I will stay,
We belong together, we will remain as one,
from daybreak, when the sun enters, until the day is done.

Kymberly Sabbath

The Seasons Of Life

The phases of our lives, like the seasons, rotate around time,
And as time passes by, second by second, these seasons shape our lives,
Each unforeseen tragedy, every blessing from above,
Builds character and strength and adds new volumes to our love.

The springtime of our lives, a time of new beginnings,
Is the time to leave the past behind and follow hopes and dreams,
It's a time of exuberance, a time that holds no tears,
A time to meet life's challenges with courage, without fear.

As the seasons change we're standing strong, deep rooted in our lives,
The refreshing breezes breathe relief from the summer sun so bright,
We've learned responsibility, we've conquered and achieved,
The beauty of this season is everlasting..... so it seems.

But, just around the corner, something's changing in our lives,
The winds that blow grow cooler, for Autumn has arrived,
And with it comes discouragement, disappointment, heartaches, too,
But, just enough to paint our spirits bright in every hue.

Now, winter is upon us, its touch is cold and harsh,
Our lives seem weak and barren as sorrow fills our hearts,
Yet, we are at our strongest, and if we could only see,
This time is but a season, and soon it shall be Spring.

Rita L. Cluxton

Bethany Winds

At dusk, low tide, a lone crow walks the shore.
A light breeze fans its feathers
as it ferrets for the day's remains.
The sea gulls since have left this place, perhaps
because of all the rules laid down to ensure
the pickings are never more than slim
and that they cannot count on even
the carelessness of children,
the schools and their parents having made them
as conscientious as themselves —
who wonder then, and rue the loss of innocence.

It used to be a lesson written on the wind that nature
was sufficient to itself and we needed only to be
heedful of ourselves, but in conscience now
we have the need to bear the burden of it all —
as if in weighing down ourselves we would become
as wise and weighty as the God we used to fear.

And so the crow lifts and pulls its wings
to ride the wind to a fairer shore
where sterile virtues still wait to wear the crown.

Gary F. Seifert

When I Write

When I write
    There is no meaning of
    time
My other world is left
    behind
And I enter in, a different
    land
A place that comes from
    within
When I write
    It comes to life, with paper and pen in
    hand
Then takes you on a journey, where adventure
    you will
    find
When I write

Mary Foucault

Man on the Street

His clothes are ragged, with worn-out shoes,
Old slouch hat and full of booze.
Was he a banker gone wrong or a politician,
A stock broker or maybe a mortician.
A face that's wrinkled and weathered, too.
What's going on in the world, he hasn't a clue.
His eyes half-closed, face of pain,
Tugs up his coat collar to protect from the rain.
He mumbles to himself as he stumbles along,
It's almost as if he was singing a song.
Hair and whiskers long and sprinkled with gray,
I couldn't understand what he had to say.
He meets a lady and tips his hat,
Where did he get manners like that?
He turns into an alley and slumps to the ground,
Looks back and forth to see if anyone is around.
Pulls a bottle from his coat, it is soon downed,
Now his head nods forward, he sleeps so sound.
Finally he falls on his side without a sound,
This is his home, there on the ground.

Paul E. Sidebottom

Untitled

My son, my son
What have you done?
You must be prepared
For the world to come.

Open your eyes and you will see
You are now, what once was me...
Things are no different or easier today
I like you had my dues to pay.
Learn from your youth, take a stand
Your future is yours to command.

Trust me, I listen and know your fears
Don't push me away, let loose your tears,
Our time together is short and new
Together we'll conquer, find the real you.
Accept my love and knowledge to share,
My son, my son Mom will always be there.

Donna Lee Walker

The Final Performance

It's all an act
A part I can no longer play

Oh someone help me
screams the masked character

I'm not ok

Am living a life
I'm no longer in control of

Sick of being pushed and pulled
in too many unbendable positions

But it's my life, I let things get this far

I am the cause of this mess, this played-out drama,
I call my "life".

Can't think anymore,
the pain in my head hurts too much,

Must say goodbye now,
the pain's too much!!

Christine Moreira

Keepsakes

A stick, a stone and a hank of hair
In the olden days at the Country Fair.
The men were tough and the ladies sweet
With high-topped slippers, skirts sweeping the street.
A stone, a flower and an open door
A star, a moon that was not there before.
A dusty trail beside a stream
Two young lovers stroll in a dream!
A stone, a tree and a window pane
Revealing God's miracles in snow or rain.
A crest of a mountain, where wild sheep roam
Mother Nature providing their place to call home!
A stone, a book — never opened before
A table-top mesa, just to climb once more
A foot, a pedal with wheel a-spinning
The end then swiftly becomes the beginning!
A stone, a memory are all that is left
To a grief-stricken widow, who is bereft.
An empty chair, that seems to sigh
The Beginning Is Over - The Ending Is Nigh!

Elma M. Rasor

The Essence of Me

Don't judge my broken container.
My essence is still intact.
Silently, they call - who goes there with the awkward gait.
Frequently, I may stop or hesitate.
Once I also walked fluid and free
But what you see is not the essence of me.
Though yet I don't walk straight and strong,
Don't assume I've done some imagined wrong.
I still try to do everything I can
To reach out a hand to my fellow man.
A nod or a smile may be enough
To uplift someone when their day is tough.
Take a little time and you will agree

My damaged container is not the essence of me.
I still have feelings, hopes, and dreams.
The best part of me just can't be seen.
I still cry for the hurt and disillusioned.
I cry to those still trying to wade through life's confusion.
I know that life still good can be
The world has yet to see the best in me.

J. Harris Jefferson

I Am

I am a dancer that loves the sky and the stars
I wonder if I could ever dance on the clouds
I hear the thunder booming beside me
I see the stars and lightning flashing with me
I want to embrace the light and flow with it
I am a dancer that loves the sky and the stars

I pretend to twinkle with Leo in the night sky
I feel the wind against my face
I touch the comets as they brush by me
I worry I won't want to come back
I cry when I see the destruction below
I am a dancer that loves the sky and the stars

I understand that I am good at what I do
I say I want to go on
I dream the beams won't hurt me
I try to be like the rain
I hope to feel like the thunder
I am a dancer that loves the sky and the stars

Aileen Kohlerschmidt

Iceberg

Towering colossus of the seas,
Dazzling denizen of the deep,
A glittering mountain of frozen ice crystals,
A monolith of stark awesome beauty,
Moving imperceptibly in the frigid cobalt seas.
A stupendous scintillating spectacle
of blinding, dazzling white,
Its oblique angles reflecting
from a thousand faceted surfaces.
Its immense size is not revealed
So much lay hidden beneath the cold Arctic sea.
It moves silently and relentlessly
to an unknown destiny.
Who can comprehend
its total power and majesty.

Gordon C. Pierce

The Angel's Lap

My famed fellow death
Coming to steal my last breath.
Are you friend or are you foe?
For that is only for me to know.

You come to take away my days
In order for me to escape this maze,
But for some you have come before the end,
And others you have come as a beloved friend.

These few who have known your beauty
Know where they shall spend their eternity
Seeking the end of another trap
Or living peacefully in their angel's lap.

Josh DeSha

My Old Man

He sits in his rocker by the sea
wondering if he should stoke the fire or make some tea.
He decides on tea.
He returns to the rocker, a comfortable chair, back to his life, a
series of stairs.
Four women, five kids and a long life are thoughts.
A boat, a motor, a cottage are here.
The railroad, booze and loneliness too near.
But he has done his job.
He has made it through.
He is the man who never knew
he would end up here
sitting by the sea
drinking tea with me.
A little sugar please.

Harry W. Bowman

Poem of Peace

To hear the gentle drops of rain against our
mother earth,
Knowing our Lord is helping to wash away the old
and refresh this world with new rebirth;
So can we help wash away the prejudice of our minds,
To accept every gender of every nationality of every kind.

We are born with this knowledge you see,
It is not hard to live this way if we all
make an effort to be;
It takes time and just a little patience,
For our eyes to see and believe how many can
be truly gracious.

For if we all choose to live the way our Lord
intended,
None of us would ever have to be offended;
Then our nation and world as we know it with
its violence and hate would cease,
Each soul, as children of God's art, would find
the ultimate freedom of peace.

Wynter Bryte

Books

Books mean so much to me
   Tales of gold and of the sea
Hours spent in a cozy nook
   A friend to me is a lovely book

On days when skies are cold and gray
   And the golden sun hides away
I love to sit by the windowsill
   With a book that brighter visions fill

Meta S. Baily

Talking To The Blessed Spirits

Daily conversations with the multitudes of the divine blessed spirits
They perform, they listen, I meditate profoundly each time for help.
From the great citadel I have of the assembly of chosen spirits
From all under the sun, I call that I am receptive to talk.

More friends in heaven, have I, than I have on mortal firmament.
All that was good and sublime from their creative soul lives on.
Together with God reigning my every action of my being I talk again.
It is from this great source that I receive my sustenance and help.
I commune with the few living remaining hearts on earth for their joy.

I try each waking hour to redeem their presence in the spirit.
One day when my work is done, I will join the other world in spirit.
What I have left behind, awaits other human ears and vision to see.
It's just a little while I believe, that I will be in the arms of her
    Then all will be consumed and complete in the spirit's realm.

John Buckland Erdell

Wanderlust

Somewhere between the front gate and back door of my home
I have a hankering for London, Paris and Rome.
I feel an insatiable urge and a fervid call
To see London, Paris and Rome in the fall.
I want to experience the thrill of London's west end,
And see Piccadilly Circus as I go round the bend.
I must confess Paris is my love and my heart beat,
The city of grand avenues, monuments and tired feet.
Oh, to sit at a sidewalk cafe long the Champs Elyssee,
Wining, dining, gazing and chattering away.
I long to see Rome from the highest Hassler window sills,
And embrace the beauty and splendor of its seven hills.
Somewhere between the front gate and back door of my home
I have a hankering for London, Paris and Rome.

James L. Mack

Life

Darkness. Nothing. Empty.
A flicker of light piercing through the dark.
The flicker of light becomes a living Flame,
growing, changing, luminating.

The Flame sizzles, snaps, hisses.
At times, fading and dimming,
at others shining through brightly and strong.
at others, wishing it would burn out forever.

Now the Flame becomes small,
barely able to sustain its own light.
The Great Wind blows, and vanquishes the light,
bringing the Flame to the inevitable darkness.

Branden Weaver

Exile

I feel the pain reflected in her eyes and wonder how she stays so
strong. Strong as a fortress surrounded by stone walls. Walls that
trap her emotions inside. She sits somber all alone gazing out the
window at the passing cars; as the day turns to night. The street
light flickers on, and she wonders what could have been. Time passes
and she realizes the hours waiting have turned from weeks to months
to years. The girl sits alone and wonders how she will spend the rest
of her life. She hopes that she will not be trapped inside these
stone walls forever. She dreams off running through fields of lilies
while sunlight sprinkles on her face like golden dust. The girl opens
her eyes and realizes that her hopes of running through the fields
have crashed like waves against a shore. Could it all have been a
dream she wonders as a flower falls to the floor.

Monique Benatar

On The Other Side Of Roses

A loving gift of roses, just one can say it all,
  To stand upon time's table until the petals fall,
To draw the sun of morning, but no more to feel the dew,
  On the other side of roses, I hurt from losing you.

With petals gone to fade away, but leave sweet memories
  A velvet touch straight from the heart, with love shown for me
As shadows pass with setting sun, there will forever be,
  On the other side of roses, your loving memories.

On the other side of roses, with broken dreams and tears,
  Not a shadow of despair, to recall the precious years,
Alive I see a rose in you, and feel your memory true,
  On the other side of Roses, my life I shared with you...

  Billy M. Smallwood

Sealed With A Kiss

I write this poem sealed with a kiss
To tell you, it's you that I miss
We didn't spend much time together
But in my mind, it seemed forever
During the times I held you, it felt so right
I dread knowing you won't be here tonight
I close my eyes and see you smile
You brightened my life, there's no denial
I should have told you how I felt
My mind would go blank and I would start to melt
I loved and needed you, and you were always there
And in my heart you will always be here
Time moves on as I start to go
The way I loved you, you may never know
Close your eyes and think of me
I'll always be there as the bright blue sea
I write this poem sealed with a kiss
To tell you, it's you that I miss

  Duane Scott Collins

Glimpses of the Past

A tribute to my wonderful Mother-in-law.

"I'm glad you've come, I've been waiting for you"
It's becoming late and I was feeling blue.
"For whom are you waiting, we asked quite dismayed?"
"Why, your father, of course, he must have been delayed.
He was coming to take me home around noon
But I'm sure he'll be here very soon.
There're so many things I need to do
Like cooking, and cleaning to name just a few.
The children will have tales from school to tell.
They're all very bright and they do very well."
As we listened and reminisced about her own life,
Being a mother, a friend, and very good wife,
We realized her talents stretched far beyond that.
She'd been a writer, a historian, and a home diplomat.
Wisconsin historian of the year was her claim
But her family came first, and she soon forgot that fame.
Now her mind was clouded with thoughts of the past
Fleeting moments of happiness that just didn't last.
"I'm glad you've come," she again replied.
"I'd love a ride in the country, and a chance to get outside!"

  Delores Brown

God's An Antique

He is unique God's an antique
He's really older then time
Let me tell you friend to him there's no end
By collectors he's rated extra special fine

Yes he's an antique, no he is not cheap
By the chosen he is well known
No problem at all before others stand tall
When telling them that he is your own

He is antique he's so unique
Of him no copies can be made
Never will be he's the only one you see
Once acquired there's no desire to sell or trade

To have him will take your everything
Not goodness are silver or gold
What he has wrought with tears must be bought
Once attained he'll not chance or ever grow old

  Tim Dinkins

Senior Love

My platelet count is very high,
My blood pressure is in the sky,
My bad cholesterol is booming,
My thyroid — I am sure — is fuming.
Yet, life stirs in this grey old mare
Soon as I see your silver hair.
Past palms and banyan trees I run
To where you're waiting in the sun.

My heart beats thanks to electrodes,
My ears hear only lower notes,
My stomach has become quite choosy,
My skin grows pleats in the Jacuzzi.
But when, slow-gaited, you come near
My rocking chair, I give a cheer!
Yes, through your love (It's plain to see),
My body functions flawlessly!

  Brigitte M. Walker

Missing You

Grandma, You have left this world,
gone today and all tomorrows.

I try hard to hide my tears,
and not show all my fears.

I miss you all the time,
but you know I'll be fine

Yesterday gets me through tomorrow,
and help me deal with all this sorrow.

When I need you here and feel real low,
I remember that you didn't want to go.

My anger has turned to tears,
and then to prayers.

Forever you will be with me,
and you I can always see.

I hope to hold you again,
my best and forever friend.

  Barbara Jean Doten

There's A Day

There's a day where I do nothing but
and it's you I want
There's twenty four hours in one day that's
a long time to think just about one woman
I am living in a dump but things will get
better when my needs are satisfied
There's a day where I will tell you everything
that's on my mind
Your smile and sparkling eyes yes
There's a day where we will be with each other
There's a day where it will nor the sun will shine
But If you are by my side the sun in the sky
always shines
Take a day and be human baby give me a call
I will let you see things no one else has seen before
There's a day baby when I want and need and just
feel tired
I will not feel tired when you arrive
There's a day when I want to please and tease
But that's my way of being human there's a day baby just wait

Marie Hilley

Whenever I See Children

Whenever I see children,
Inclining their mild faces,
Enchanted at their play,

Floating in the dappled
Light along the tangled
Arbor wall, I tremble

For their futures and wonder
At the fates which, even
Now, corrupt and bruise

Their fragile selves. We know
We cannot warn them. But might
They understand it even

Now? Might they sense
Already the tangled growth
Around them and play in an

Insistent dread: Their lives
Are not their own?
Blessing be upon them for wisdom and for courage
To face their fated futures
And the darkness still to come.

Wayne Christeson

Entrails

Yes I had grown skin
like some reptile I covered my soft insides with scales
and my neatly sealed body skimmed over stones and
anger and frustration;
I delighted in the practicality of my new self
the ease with which I could move down the path of life
unimpeded by the visceral baggage that previously
distracted me and slowed my progress.

Blinking in the bright sun of my complacency,
I feel prey to your sharp glances
your passion talons ripping my perfect skin
because you desire my entrails, my slippery chaos:
shimmering, soulful meniscus - no retaining wall

The koan of our overcoming:
coitus of the blood

Helen Babineau

The Dance of Anger

Oh, canned up energy inside
So long ignored - so long denied
I've insulted your validity
I've hoped that'd make you cease to be
But the harder I tried by cover and ram
The louder you shouted: "I am! I am!
So welcome honest anger true
Let's swing together, me and you
Let's find that grief that I have hidden
Let's march through former pain forbidden

Come up! Sweet anger, strong and true
Dance with me; my heart you woo

I hear you now, oh prisoner deep
Come waltz with me and we shall weep

We'll find that pain - you always knew it
And you and I; we'll swing right through it!

Mary A. Henry Chelemedos

Dreams, Tears, Happiness

I've had a crush on him for years,
For him I've shed many tears.
Day after day I dream of us together,
I see us together always and forever.
Then I remember it's just a dream,
And the tears begin to stream.
Down my face the teardrops fall,
Because I remember he doesn't like me at all.
He says he just wants us to be friends.
I hope this crush soon ends,
Or he finally gets to see
Just how much he means to me.
So one day I went to see him to tell him how I feel,
He looked at me and kissed me and this time it was real.
No more dreaming
No more tears streaming.
At last we are together,
We will leave each other never.
Finally he is mine, and now our life is fine!

Claire Elizabeth Button

Broken Arrows, Broken Promises, Illusive Dreams

The white man came; we knew him not and welcomed him as friend.
Little did we know we would regret it in the end.
The first winter was a rough one and we helped to see him through.
It seemed to be the right and proper thing to do.
The white man began too prosper and his towns began to grow.
We were told to give up our land and were forced to go.
He killed our women and children at Wounded Knee and didn't
   seem to care.
We wanted to retaliate but knew we didn't dare.
The great spirit heard our prayers and looked upon him with scorn.
The great spirit helped us to avenge the deaths at the battle
of Little Big Horn.
The years have come and gone and he has polluted our land and sky.
We sit in silent sorrow and ask the Great Spirit why.
Yes, the White Man came with lots of lies and schemes;
But all he left was broken arrows, broken promises and illusive
   dreams.

Harry Hendershot

"T"

Heavy hearted he looked down from the sky
The mortals were fractious and he knew not why

Something was needed to turn the world around
Someone on this earth where goodness does abound

With love for dolphins, babies and such
Put on this earth our lives to touch

Someone different from you and me
Someone special, it's plain to see

Her ways are simple and her face does glow
For us she is contentment, a "safe place" to know

This is what he had in mind
When he started this race known as mankind

Now everything is in order it was plain to see
Smiling he sighed, I'll name her "T"

Bob Wingate

The Christ In Bethlehem's Manger

In Bethlehem's manger many years ago,
Was born a little babe whom the world would come to know.
Not just any babe was he who was born that holy night,
He was Jesus Christ: The son of God: God's pure light.
The world in darkness on a downhill slide
Continuously fell deeper in sin and pride.
The knowledge of God and His word they scorned
Enjoying their pleasure; ignoring the Christ child born.
As time went on the Christ child grew,
His mission to accomplish in this world he knew.
He came to die for the sin of mankind
That forgiveness through His blood sinful man might find.
The day finally came for the whole world to see,
Jesus Christ being made sin so man's saviour he might be.

Clyde Akers

Leaves

I think there can be something said
For the leaves of Fall. Frankly, I like them all
But especially the magnificent Yellow and brilliant Red.

In the Spring the leaves are formed
And in the summer the trees are fed.
With this the leaves' job is done, appreciated by only some
Until the Fall when they are magnificent Yellow and brilliant Red.

Then they drop from shady canopies to fluffy beds
Parched by sun, weathered by storm, blown by wind.
They come tumbling, fluttering and in a spin
Those magnificent Yellow and brilliant Red.

Seeing them makes me think of being alive and some day dead
As they gently shimmer and placidly quake; and somehow
They magically speak of dust that gives and dust that takes
That magnificent Yellow and brilliant Red.

But besides my heart's anticipated happiness and waves of dread,
beautiful scenery I am led
Through the valleys, up the summits, and near the seas.
One can be sure that I near them will be watching,
staring and gazing at the magnificent Yellow and brilliant Red.

Daniel W. Zimpfer

The Angel and The Philosopher

The warm sunlight,
casting its golden glow upon her cheeks,
sparkled in her eyes like the Pacific surface
off the beach of Manhattan.
Together they laughed,
intoxicated by the fresh sea air.
Enlightened with happiness, their minds
soared as an eagle upon an unseen current.
Night fell quickly
and with it came the crisp snap of
the darkness.
Exchanging warm hugs and circumspect glances,
they gently closed the book on another day and
placed it upon the shelf of hope.
The angel and the philosopher
would dream of another day,
equally as inviting
and serendipitous.

David Temple

Black Boots On Easter Sunday?

Black boots on Easter Sunday doesn't seem like quite the thing.
Black boots on Easter Sunday, ain't this a day of Spring?

The crocuses have noticed — sent their heads 'bove the ground.
I wake up in the morning to the bird's sweet chirping sound.

And yet I am still puzzled at breakfast while I dine,
I see my best thermometer way down at twenty nine.

Is Mother Nature fickle...can't she make up her mind?
Perhaps she wants to 'pickle', and leave old ways behind.

If it's a change she's going through, she may have darn good reason,
But I sure do wish that spring arrives - cause I'm tired of winter's
    season.

Black boots on Easter Sunday, it's off to church I go.
Black boots on Easter Sunday, I'll pray it doesn't snow.

Must hurry with my bonnet now, or for dinner I'll be late.
Black boots on Easter Sunday, this year's weather's fate.

Laurie Mason

Is It Too Late

Out of the mist came a ship from the North
With bounty aboard. What was it worth?
Ivory and furs down in the hold
Soon to be counted, then to be sold.

And long long ago when the West was young,
Buffalo were slaughtered just for the tongue
And shipped to the East for a rich man's feast.
Carcasses were strewn all over the ground,
And many years later the bones were found.

Herds roamed, miles along and miles wide.
Nobody tried even to save the hides
Only the Indians who killed for the meat,
And then only what they could eat;
And hides for their clothes and moccasins for their feet.

It wasn't our fault, but it may be too late.
So let's learn a lesson not to be messing
With Earths many blessings.
Preserve what is left and increase what we can,
And do all we should for bird, beast and man.

Adeline Anderson

A Grand-Daughter's Appreciation

Grandmother, in my life-time
There's no one nearer to my heart than you
I can not even begin to underline
The amount of love and admiration, I have for you

You give me sound inspiration
In order for me to succeed
And beautiful lady, this is my appreciation
For all the good you see in me

Grandmother, a special thank-you
For all your love and guidance through-out my life
For there's no love as true
I love you more than life

I would give you the world
Just to replace all that you've given to me
And now I want to tell the world
I love you grandma for all eternity.

Gayla Leigh Garlow

"Life Time"

We are lent to each other,
For a very short time.

I'm so glad God saw fit,
To lend you to me for mine.

Our time is short and I hope,
I've made good use of the time given.

I wish I had more time with each person,
To me that's called living.

Time is the one thing that there is,
We can never get back.

We should make time for those we love,
That is surely a fact.

We never know what time will bring,
Or how more or less we have.

We each should spend it wisely,
Not waste it and perhaps.

We will all have what we need,
To make it with less strife.

Just remember to spend it well,
This "Time" is called "Life".

Viola M. Fels

"Against The Odds!"

All my life I've searched for someone,
that I could never find.
I never allowed myself to love; and
always believed my mind.
But one day as I walked along,
I found, by mistake; and after the time
we spent together, my heart was his to take!
The criticism we often heard, was never
very mild. They said that we were
not meant to be; I now carry our first child.
Looking back nor him or I let
others in our way. So now we are
blessed with a beautiful boy, and
together we will stay!

Stacey L. Bruce

In Search of Loyalty

Oh be not the first to discover a blot in the name of a friend;
And be not of discord the mover, for hearts my prove well in the end;
We none of us know one another, and oft in error we fall;
So let us speak well of each other, or speak not of others at all.

Jean Capel

Without You

Without you I'd feel lost and alone
Without you I'd feel lonely and sometimes as though no one cares.
Which is why I'm glad I have you, 'cause
Without you in my life I wouldn't know what to do.
Without you my life would be a mess and disaster
with nothing to look forward to.
You reassure me that someone cares about me
and loves me when I feel like I want to die.
Without you, I would be another wandering lost
soul wondering what happened to make me like this.
Without you to comfort me when I needed you most,
I would have had no one to cry on.
Which is why I'm glad you love me for who I am,
and why I'm glad I don't have to be
without you
by my side

Melissa A. Laine

Eternal Embrace

As the sun sets red over the horizon like fire,
My blood lust grows; you're forever what I desire.

Sweet angel, forever beautiful, defier of time,
How I long to taste you, caress your lips of wine.

To be with you eternal, pure ecstasy I'd grasp,
I'd speak to you seductively, entwine you like an asp.

From your blood stained lips, flow melodies of the night,
From your eyes radiate a black star, dark, yet piercingly bright.

How I long to pleasure you, rapture you in nirvanic height,
Come sweet lover, embrace me tight, and we shall cross over,
and forever be one with the night.

Eric Puckett

Friendship

Friendship is love which warms the heart
and molds a special bond.
The faith the trust which lifts the soul
as gentle as the fawn.
Is the rock that hugs the coastal shore
amidst the sea and sand
although the rapids beat it down,
it always seems to stand.
Built on a foundation of strength and will
it reaches to the sky
and though goes silently to the sea
it never seems to die.
This is what friendship has to be
for love to hence be born
So what I have I give to thee
so not the heart be torn.

James Generazo

His Tears

Softly splashing on the window pane,
I listen adoringly to the fresh spring rain.
Sleepily I close my eyes,
And lose myself to the sound of shower's gentle sighs.
The tender pillow embraces my head,
While I absorb the rain's splendor as I lay in my bed.
Through the window drifts a green, young perfume,
Its refreshing scent filling the room.
A tiny wet drop somehow sneaks in,
landing on my arm and tickling my skin.
Soon the jealous sun decides to come back,
so a single rebellious ray fights its way through a crack.
Now His joyous tears have been washed away,
but in its place He has left an arc of remembrance to brighten my day.

Susie Schindler

Peace Is

Peace is the sky, blue and bright.
Peace is the clouds all fluffy and white.
Peace is the trees ever so green.
Aren't these the prettiest sights you've seen.

Peace is getting along with one another.
Peace is treating each other like a brother.
Peace is the harmony that moves our feet.
Peace is that sweet music with a harmonious beat.

Peace is no villains or crooks.
Peace is not giving each other dirty looks.
Peace is not gangs or fights.
Peace is respecting each others rights.

Peace is the crocodiles.
Peace is carrying the Olympic torch for miles.
Peace is this countries flag.
Peace is recycling a brown paper bag.

Peace is being fair.
Peace is love and care.
Peace is something we should not abuse.
Peace is something we should use.

Etienne Souagui

The Relentless Sea

One day, near sun-down - I walked, along a windswept path near
    the sea
I was captivated by the view I saw, an old gnarled cypress tree
It stood with its crooked branches bent, its grotesque splendor
    against the sea's element sent -
It stood among rocks, in its moundless groove, its life long with
    strife, but a miracle it proved.
It belonged to the sea, she had claimed the tree as her own -
With whispering winds and dashing waves, in their murmuring and
    undertones.
The grasses were whipping to and fro, the gulls with cries
    sweeping ever so bold.
Salt water sprayed and plunged into the ageless gorge below -
pounding against the many jagged rocks, creating a hidden cove.
Little sea creatures struggled and fought to be free, back to
    the relentless sea.
The sun-set cast its last ray of light, forming a beautiful
    shimmering sight-
As its glimmering path crossed the mysterious sea -
sinking behind, yes behind the relentless sea!

Elnora E. Squibb

Equinox

Silver crescent moon
her chalice cup cradles Venus gently
and rises in the night sky.
We gaze in adoration from our perch
Boulder-studded hill, sparkles in moon glow.
The stars are brilliant tonight.

A second black night
In reverence I look again for meaning.
The clouds have moved on, alas
no billowy landing for Venus, spilled from her cup runneth over.
Silver cradle rising rapidly tonight without her precious load
I am touched by a message sent sweetly from the Gods.

I am touched by your kindness, but recoil from a deep dream
If I wake up, will you be gone?
I walk softly, skimming the rocky path
You man so strong, I follow in bliss
Heart pounding, heart bursting with desire.

I cannot gaze into your eyes too long, or
I will go there.
I will go there when it is time.

Anne Halley

Mother ...

Throughout the years Mom, you were always there
You gave me two most important things which is -
your love and care
Sacrifices you made and not once have you given up
All this you did, just to show me how much I mean a lot
I know along the way I've cost you heartaches
and painful tears
I'm so sorry Mom for what I've put you through
on all those years
The times I've been bad
I'll never forget
And now looking back
how much I regret
I know I hardly show it or even told you so
but this comes from my heart
I love you Mom
More than you'll ever know!

Levonne M. Iglesias

Remember the Little Things

Those whose tempers are quick to rise
Need to examine their busy lives.
Little things can for outweigh,
The tribulations of a busy day.

A grandchild born healthy and sound,
A ball game with your son on the mound,
A hand made card on your special day
Put together with love in every way.

A friend who calls when you are down
letting you know they're always around.
And the special blessing of a beautiful child
who grows to fill your heart with pride.

Rich is a lifetime of blessing like these
We often forget in our quest to succeed
All the riches in the world cannot replace
The little things that bring a smile to your face.

Juanita E. Baetz

Mother

I remember mother staying up
all night when I was sick.
She held my hand, with tear filled eyes
on my first day of school.
Many nights mom was there to help
ease my heartaches and crushes.
Mother would make me strive for my goals,
she always said, "Hold your head high!"
This isn't a stroll down memory lane
This is a thanks for your sacrifices for me.
I cannot repay you money wise, but
I can repay you with love and respect.
My hope is that my children admire me,
only half as much as I do you.

Dorothy R. Dean

Fields of Once Ago

There once was a time A time when all was free
The lands were lush and splendid The sights were all of beauty
The fields were full of herds Not one of them were captive
Abruptly it would change Man destroyed its masses!

Animals made as slaves whipped and beat afraid Slaughtered for
   only skin
Some would not descend Hunted down for game Their young for
   sport are slain
Encaged forced to breed To die for fashion's greed
Injected with lab disease Man is never pleased:
From man they cannot hide Many dead upon the roadside
Near extinct because said evil Massive deaths by sick people
Not only the land is scorned Thousands blackened on the sea shore
It's all too far to stop Man does not care to stop:

There once was a time A time when all was free
Kill only to survive Respect on what you feed
Those times have surely died Only tainted fields you see
How can you walk with pride They are the same as we!

Thomas A. Beasley

Love And Life

Love is a mixture of many things...
Love is tender, caring, giving and blissful,
   with just the right amount of lust.
Love can consume. Can blind. Can be a
   fatal attraction.

Flesh to flesh to fulfillment or exhaustion.
Then again in an hour or so. Or tomorrow.
And from all this, on occasion, a baby is born.
A beautiful baby, so very, very
different from all the other babies on planet
earth.
A truly wondrous event.

And virginity,
Yes, virginity is a cherished virtue.
So pure and white like a fresh,
   untouched snowdrift.

But life!!...Yes life!!...
Life must go on, and on, and on.
It must.
Goodby virginity. Hello motherhood.

Henry Enrico Storino

You Came

You came when our need was great
You came and did not hesitate
You came with your gentle touch
Bringing the comfort we needed so much.

You came with your kindly word
The sweetest sound we ever heard
You came willing to do all we ask
Your heart ready for any task.

We are so very glad you came
Nothing will ever be the same
We are thankful for the difference you made
You are the answer for which we prayed.

Ruby Bass

Untitled

Like a captured eagle my mind soars
Gliding above the mountains, rivers roar
   Never wanting to come down
   Ignoring Father Earth pulling around
This time of flight is soon to die
Lowering to this silent nigh

My powerful talons flexing as I fall
Decreasing height into his hand held tall
   Trying to fly again and again
   Stopped by the chains of this desolate man

The desire to struggle
   The passion to break free
   -unable to be where I want to be

Alone inside this never ending flight
To be with man I'm filled with fright

As my mind soars again above the rivers
Grasping the wind that holds me when I quiver

I know one day this dream will end...
   Never to fly-yet to land again.

Jennifer D. Dupnak

Untitled

When the Jaws of death are grinding down,
When strength to breathe cannot be found,
When tears splash down on lifeless skin,
When trauma breaks the bones within,
When worlds collide at freeway speed,
When bodies limp, unconscious bleed,
When drowning grips the lungs in doom,
When chest pain warns impending doom...
   Give us a call!
Whether black of night, or searing sun,
Or ice, or fog, or clouds undone,
On city streets, on country roads,
In mansions great, or small abodes,
On freeways fast, in quiet fields,
In the great outdoors where nature reels,
We heed the call where danger swallows
Shattering dreams with lives left hollow,
We face the death that awaits us all,
But try to keep it beyond "the wall."
9-1-1 Emergency Medical Services

Joseph Stegner (Paramedic)

Anvil of Thor

Sing a song of summer showers:
Hephaestus hammering,
Thunder boomers rolling,
A light and darkness interplay
With lightning, jagged streaks of power,
And clouds boiling and racing.
The smell of new growth and of decay
Rising, as if to balance.
Children playing in puddles,
Matted hair, screaming with the sights and sounds
Of summer's procreation.
Water running and dammed in pools,
Plinking in pans beneath punctured ceilings.
Hide under gaily colored umbrellas;
Watch the violence of nature
In its move to replenish the earth.
Somewhere lovers glisten as they listen
To the sound of rain upon a tin roof.
But soon, the sun; a phoenix rising;
A rebirth.

Philip A. Eckerle

In Memoriam 1862-1952

Words can't express
In the way we would
Like to say, we miss him.
Living among us
In our days of work,
And the great deeds he did for
Many a person to make them happy.

He passed away on February 21, 1952,
Ending ninety years of life,
Not only filled with kindness toward others but,
Restored strength in all to carry on,
Yet shall he live in our memory.

Belk Brother began in May 1888,
Eventually covering the southern states.
Long may we live and work together
Keeping the light burning for other.

Matty D. Hadly

Dress Code for the Poet's Ball

I'm having second thoughts
About going to
The poet's ball this year,
Though it would be my first
And I've wanted to all my life.

I bought this stunning,
Emerald-green, off-the-shoulder
Ball gown, half-price at Saks
Just in case I got asked
And thought I'd wear my hair upswept
With fresh gardenias in it.

I was so thrilled
When the invitation came
I R.S.V.P.ed "delighted!" right away.

It wasn't until the next day
When I was showing it to my neighbor, Frances,
That I noticed
Where it usually states dress code
"Black Tie" or "Black Tie, Optional"
It clearly read "Stark Naked!"

Elizabeth Stephenson

Eating Indoors

Jarring sounds pass by the hallways through my eyes
Mmmmmmmmmm

A butterfly halts at my shop, peruses cranberries and mounts
Scared to be alone, I catch it and keep its head between my legs.

Crying over matchbooks, filling oceans with your tears
I slap my head and touch your hand. It is everywhere, all at once.

Blocks of wood and people running so fast their hearts pound
going faster and pounding blood rushing Chaos clears the air.

Now, I will show you a trick, this is how
I get lost inside your mind and you mind and it is still now

Can I have a hand? A hand to touch me right here, so slow and I know
I am going so far away tomorrow. Fly above clouds, under God and
man has two vices with fleshy fingers poking a parakeet's cage;
blackened fish sits on a train, it's raining again let's run outside.

Don't kiss me. I am a nun; metaphysically speaking. More dewdrops
seen on the grass in the earthly morning, having eaten and run.

I showed my face to you, now you owe me a second chance to find
love. No more falling in love, just a simple game. No more games.

Confused? Solemnly swear you won't hate me. Presto, a rabbit
whisper in my tongued ear, I look away and disappear.

Fiona Robertine Capuano

Great White Throne

From gray to black on the great white throne.
Below, a mass of shifting sand,
    Surging fighting in the wind,
Tossing rainbows through the mist,
And sparkling rainbows sunshine kissed.
Soon gushing, tumbling from above,
    The pounding roaring demons cry
Over creamy satin stone
Of the awesome Great White Throne.
A glimmering ray, a white vast cliff (The last clear drop or rain
    has fallen)
A burning sun, a torch held high,
A brazen bronze across the sky.
The sifting settlings meet the glare,
    Of frosty white in caverns near;
A profuse rose turns white to pinks,
And dulls the tones where the rivers sinks.
The fading sun caresses the tones
    From gray to black on the Great White Throne.
And such is this, another day, when nature and her artists play.

Sandra Marie Davies

"Wishful Thinking"

If you live in California, the "Lotto" is a must.
Come Wednesday and Saturdays, resolutions turn to dust.
Sometimes I wish that I would win
to pay my bills and such.
"It's unrealistic," says my son, "the
odds are just too much!"
But then, isn't life a gamble
from the time that we are born?
Boy or girl, rich or poor, pretty
or ugly, acceptance or scorn.

Life is probably what we make it,
with our blood, sweat, and tears.
We have to keep on trying,
in spite of human fears and jeers.
Life isn't supposed to be easy
or fair, so I'm told,
But I think I prefer to fantasize
a bit and maybe come up with the gold!

Nancy B. Ott

My Mind

(February 6, 1996 — 15 years old)
Please don't be scared of my mind
its twists and turns are a riddle
so intricate they're hard to find
its crooked path wants a middle

Questions here and answers there
it seeks solace in a place with peace
sometimes roaring like a bear
but soon after the fire will cease

Great images and painful sorrow
it makes my life through everyday
sometimes scared of tomorrow
it strives to find a bright new way

An awful screaming burning voice
it still holds on when I can't move
tearing and yelling "it's your choice"
it helps me to see what to prove

My mind is something I want to treasure
knowledge and thoughts I can devour
even though using is great pleasure
I quit and now have so much power!

Liz Johnson

The Stranger

I am a stranger that walks throughout the land,
for I am very lonely with no family or no one to love,
one day as I walked through a small town I came
upon a bright light up above.
So I went to look their in a small park laughing playing with glee,
was a family doing things as they pleased.
Oh it sure put a big smile on
for I thought I would see none.
It was such a beautiful joyful sight
for it brought tears to my cheeks with shear delight
for I did not hear nor see not one argue nor not one fight.
I soon found myself walking fords the man and lady
though I looked like I was quit dirty.
I asked to shake the proud man's hand,
and give to the lady some flowers from the land,
tears and all I said at that very moment
now this is how American should stand.

Dave W. Feltus

A Horrible Day In My Room

Last night I lay me down to sleep,
I prayed my A's and B's to keep.
I opened my eyes and what did I see,
My bed was staring back at me!

When I jumped out of bed,
I bumped my all-ready aching head.
I opened my eyes and what did I see,
I saw stars twinkling in front of me!

"It was just shock," my mother said,
The result of an injury to my head.
I opened my eyes and what did I see,
My ceiling was saying, good morning to me!

Somehow I knew it was going to be a horrible day,
Please, oh please make it go away!
I opened my eyes and what did I see,
My world disappeared in front of me!

As I write this story to you,
I tell you the truth, what else can I do.
I opened my eyes and what did I see,
A horrible day staring back at me!

Victor A. Sullin

Widow's Weeds

They thrive upon the soil of loneliness
They are watered by the tears of despair
They are nurtured by the gloom of forgotten-ness
They multiply in the cultures of ostracism
Careless gardeners, thoughtless reapers, ugly landowners

Bettyrose Factor

Morning In New York

Walking down the street a happy morning for me.
All of a sudden before me a little bird dead at my feet.
I stopped, wishing it were not true, but it was so still
no motion you see
Yes it was true.
It was not that the little bird was dead you see,
because even I know about this.

Where it was is what bothered me. Dead on a New York City street.
Out of his nest you see.
Was this a lesson for me? I feel out of my nest you see.
Little bird so sweet you touched me oh how sweet.
I know that people have passed you, but I wonder how
many had the need to write about this.

Oh little bird
I will always remember this lesson you've given me.
I don't want to die out of my nest you see.
Thank you little bird I live one more day
giving me a chance to find my nest.

Angel Torres

Shattered Dreams

How sad it is to feel like this
Because your love I will miss
Together one day sharing a dream
What happened I'm not sure
is clear to me
But the dream was not meant to be
Lying awake in sleepless nights
Longing for the warmth of your body
near mine
Not a call to say "Hello" or "I miss you"
Healing will be slow within me
I know
Shattered dreams I wish I could
just dismiss you....

Robin L. Tremblay

A Dream

He stood in a field not too far away
I wasn't quite sure it is was night or day
The moon was not out nor did the sun shine
This really confused me
He assured me it was fine
I walked up to him
I was the twelve feet away
I wanted to run
He asked me to stay
He stood before me
All shiny and white
No face had appeared
Just a strong glowing light
Standing with power
He held up his Rod
I fell to my knees
For this man was my God.

Terry Russo

Tresita's Dream

She sleeps in quiet solitude,
Alas! No flower in her hair.
Perhaps her dreaming state includes
The climbing up some cloudy stairs.
Up, up until her steps doth end
Upon a knoll with grass elite,
While dewdrops in the early morn
Caress the bareness of her feet.
Now looms a fork where ends the trail.
The choice is hers alone to make.
Though glitter of paved gold bids strong
On stems of rosebuds strewn she takes.
Sheer agony yet still she smiles.
I watch the tears flow from her eyes.
In time I nod into my world
Disturbing not her paradise.
I'll never know the treasure found
When reached she at the end up there.
I only know when I awoke
A rose lay nestled in her hair.

Joseph B. Quiyote

Untitled

Why is this happening
Why to me
There must be some reason
That I cannot see
I have a faith in what is true
Still can't help being angry with you
You took my heart, broke it in two
Just as it became completely new
You broke the trust and bond of love
But there's reason in heaven above
I only want to do what's right
But you've made my world darker than night
Still in the darkness the Lord gives me light
And tells me not to put up a fight
I'm going to be strong and work this out
Steer away from any doubts
I don't know where I'm going now
I'd like to forget where I've been
But the Lord will pull me through this trial
To bring me closer to him

Sarah Kestel

Thoughts In Color

The avenues of our thoughts
are lined with colors
revealing moods; the windows of our minds.
Thoughts are byways of memory
delicate as a yellow butterfly,
or sad and lonely, in a gray mist crying
for the bits and pieces to be
released.
Thoughts are legends and dreams
of deep green mountains or sunsets
of gold,
and the vibrant colors of a
coat of arms, handed down
from past generations.
Thoughts are a kaleidoscope of
shifting shadows, that grow sentiment, but
never lose the rainbow pattern of life.

Virginia R. Pezel

Ascertain

Echoing through generational bondage - cries of freedom ...
Let my people go!
Only to be enslaved by drugs...thoughts of despair ...
Let my people go!!
Let us arise above oppression...freedom to develop our minds.
We, Nubians..we, African-Americans...
Let the intelligence of our intellect rise above oppression...
Let our men rise above with respect they deserve that their manhood
doesn't have to be proven by the conquest of a lay...
but by the echo in the winds, the legacy of a proud people

Let your heritage and awareness be exemplified by knowledge of
who you are as a people
Knowledge of where you are going for as an eagle soars
Ascertain
For there is yet a dream to be fulfilled...come alive, oh dream
A dream of encouragement, a dream of strength...a new vitality..
Oh, Nubians, African-Americans ...
Where does your dream lie?
In the respect of your integrity, in your liberty ...
Freedom does cry and yearns to be answered.
Rise Up! Answer The Call! There Is Hope; grasp the reality of the
Dream ....

Dorothy L. Bradshaw-King

Dedicated To The Oklahoma Bombing Victims

Devastation is called upon the people.
Families cry and wonder why,
All this must happen.

No one understands why their
Loved ones pay the price of someone's
Doings.

Children, friends, and relatives
Have been killed in many ways.
There will always be tears lingering in the hearts of man.

People ask one another why this must happen.
Why must their loved ones die in such ways?
Why do most people care only about themselves
And their precious objects, that they don't see
What is crossing their paths.

Carelessness is the reason and hatred
That captures the ears of the people who are obsessed with killing.

They are blinded by the money and attention, they receive.
They cannot see how much they hurt
Innocent victims and their families.
Hatred covers the murderer's grave.

Shelly Nielsen

Disposal of a Rotten Egg

My expiration date reads April '88,
I was left in the fridge by mistake.
Hidden behind the saur kraut plate,
Mmmm, an aroma that smells great.
Only a smell an egg could love,
Oh my gosh, here comes a plastic glove!
It won't put me down!
I see he's plugging his nose and has an ugly frown.
I've never seen this place in my life!
He throws me in a steel bucket with a fork and a knife.
It doesn't look good,
He flicks a switch,
I meet with other smelly foods.
They tell me I'm in the waste,
Why?
I'm sour to the taste.

Anna Fabiano

Windows, Hopes and Dreams

Windows and hopes can shatter;
Dreams won't always come true.
But really, it doesn't matter
Just keep smiling in all that you do.

Look for the gold by the rainbow,
Before it fades away.
Count the nighttime stars in the sky
Before they turn to day.

For one thing a dream is a fantasy,
Just waiting for time to kick in.
A dream only becomes a reality,
When the dreamer starts to win.

Don't ever stop dreaming,
Though a dream could lead to great strife.
You never know when a dream could come true,
Discouragement's a great part of life.

Windows and hopes may shatter,
Dreams won't always come true.
But when it comes to the dreams that you do and don't dream,
There's only a chance for the ones that you do.

Allison Hancock

Answers?

Grace? The secret only God knows
the force and reason why a soul grows

Desire? To want and want so much more
it creeps and fades like sunlight under a door

Passion? A drive one never satisfies
exercised daily, sure to fulfill our lives

Self? The only one who can change destiny
through of good thought's, not just for you, but for the many

Miracles? Taken for granted as common place
analyzed for scientific value — disappear without a trace

Greed? Passion and desire gone mad
needing to have something already had

Fear? The force that defeats creation
breeds war, intolerance and annihilation

Rhetoric? Do we really need to know why?
A question unanswered leads the mind to try

Tolerance? Understanding even when you cannot comprehend
abandoning the urge to break because it is easier to bend

Why? To ponder, if only just to wonder why?

H. D. Evelyn

"On My Desk"

The dove vase, that held her scissors,
Is sitting on my desk,
The angel vase, that held her pens,
Is also on my desk.
The little basket, that held her mail,
Is beside the others, on my desk.
The magnifying glass, that helped her to read.
Has also found a place.
On my desk, the address book, that she used,
Is sitting on my desk
The use of these things,
Remind me of her.
As I use them at my desk.
The book mark, that marked her place.
Is in her Bible, on my desk,
There are memories,
Of my mother, everywhere.
On my desk.

Mattie M. Stewart

I Call It Immortality

I feel that my heart beats on with a will
 With a spark so divine it will never be still
I know it is blessed by my Universal God
 Created by Him of which I'm so proud
Immortality will be mine as a gift divine
 It comes from my soul which within me does shine
It shines with a beauty and goodness and love
 And was created like the skies above
Here's to my soul that carried me on
 Exploding sometimes like a Heavenly song
It's quiet at times through my earthly will
 To hear His voice, His love never still
He's where I am, I'm where He is too
 It seems we are together in all that we do
My mind I hope will be more like His
 Because of the beautiful being He is

Polly Streiff

River Of Fears

Cast afloat with no way back
Free from hurt, free from attack
A shore of comfort I cannot reach
Waves of love caress the beach
I want to turn toward the shore
To grasp the rudder of control once more
I start to move, I try to shift
But the rushing waters seem too swift
My oars are gone, their names were pride
The pole of need lies by my side
I draw within, I try to hide
But this mighty river seems too wide
I don't know why I seem to think
I must reach that shore before I sink
My wounds are old yet they still bleed
In my hand, that pole of need
Upon this river for many years
Formed from the drops of all my tears
This torrential force is the river of fears

Diane M. Hubiak

Birdie Song

A tiny birdie sang for me.
His song so very clear.
Chirping, twirping filling the precious air,
and to all who'd like to hear.

A simple sweet song he sings,
for all to know and recall.
Some are deaf and cannot hear.
His song he sings, ah so clear.

Up in a tree mighty high,
here in God's home he abides.
"God loves you", He chirped and chirped,
He who created the vast universe.

Dorothy Sunshine Lumio

Dreams

My early years were full of dreams,
I spent them writing by the reams,
Of lovers many and far between
Of lanes they trod that none have seen.
In meadows soft, and oh so green,
Along a pretty, rippling stream.
As the moon in the sky brightly beamed.
They walked side by side in that glorious beam.
Targeting all that's bad or mean,
They'll live in a world of their dreams,
Happy forever!

Rozella D. Ashbaucher

New York, Sunday

Mounted horses tapping their feet quicker
Up the side streets of New York City.

A destination toward the east river full of a chilly
cold Sunday Mothers Day.
Like a Summer sound on a Spring
moist day, changing like a scene in a brisk fall play

Cold winter Days ahead
Summer Spring or Fall
Away until tomorrow
Put us away tight within the ice cube tray and dry hard

This cube turns to a liquid mass of melted dreams
Locked up frozen
Repeat the process, and more give me more,
and remember to close the bedroom door.

Elliot Straus

Untitled

Love expressed in heavy purple
Of so tired, holding earnestly
Their velvet heads up, roses.
Love, overwhelming and overwhelmed
By brisk aroma of just cut flowers.
Refreshing and refreshed by drops of dew
Still flowing down their cheeks.
Love, passionate and on fire like Sun.
Lost in darkness of nobody's night.
Blindly scattering beams around.
Quaffing the dew from velvet skin of the flower.
Love, growing old with every falling petal.
Withered in its own fire.
Wounding the wizened heart with the last thorn.
The only witness of the old-time splendor.
The only that survived.

Iwona Bida

Somber Emotions

As the shadows dawn our being,
we wander through our emotions,
treading lightly as our bones quake,
with fear of unraveling,
we stumble through the hurt,
a piece of us falls discarded each time,
we fight back against the tears,
we thought had long dried,
through passage of healing time,
Yet!
We weep once more,
as the axis of pain revisit,
striking like an ax,
that seem to split us into frail nakedness,
feeling unable to encounter that commonality,
strife of life,
Yet!
We struggle through this mass of empty vail,
wondering how it could have elapsed,
somber emotions somehow we last.

Vanessa Crenshaw

O Lord, I Touched Your Hand

When I reached out to touch the world...
instead, I touched your hand.
I could feel your pain and sorrow.
Lord... I did not understand.

I listened when you spoke to me,
and I heard, despair and fears.
You gently took my hand in yours...
when I reached, to dry your tears.

I could feel your pain and sorrow...
Lord, the day I touched your hand.
You spoke to me... until I heard...
You knew I'd understand.

You held my hand! We touched the World!
And... I heard the children weep.
The rains... the floods are the children's tears.
O Lord... your sorrow is so deep.

O Lord, together, let us tell the World...
let them hear the children's cries...
From all around the World...
let the children's voices rise!

Rose Cromer

Glass Slippers

Photograph. Will it capture the happiness they bring?
Sweet contentment, wears her face. Princess in the wing.
One can but imagine her magical dream...

Brown bag cookies from diner man. Finding the moon by day.
Dance floor in the living room. Laughter.

Sunshiny 'round the block walks. Penny wishes in a fountain.
Places to run. Happily ever after.

Balloons colored green or blue. Pretty flowers. Ice cream with
little spoon.
See the rainbow. Splashing in water. Stones.

Ribbons to pull. Stuffed best friends. Bouncing. Nice stories.
Night-night time.
I love you Dear Jesus. Happy to be home...

Singing. Silk on her pillow. Dark eyes flutter closed into
soft sweet curls.

Dreaming. Park swings. Knowing she's forever loved. Importance
of her great, small world...

Fuzzie Bank, soft on her nose. Ever close by must be Bink and Bear!
Excitement gives in to big sleepy eyes. Innocence folded over in a chair.

Photograph, could never capture the happiness she brings.
  Cinderella, asleep in glass slippers.

Valerie Lynne Roland

Old Friend

A feeling of anxiousness, the look of fear, found
caked upon the face of those who worry about the
very being of being.

Oh - that tug in the gut again, like the loud bang
on the door in the middle of the night; scared,
wondering, who can it be?

Out of the darkness emerges the figure of a
familiar silhouette. Ah, a sigh of relief.
It's the old friend who visits without warning.

Consistently, throughout one's life. How generous
of this one to spare stolen time. This old friend.
Despair. I almost forgot about you.

What a shame, you did not forget about me.

Barbara F. Fuller

The Path to Oneness

Life is a constant encountering,
Few encounters are the beginning,
Of a path to where differences become one.

How will I know a path is ahead?
A sense of attraction exists.
What is that attraction?

When together in a crowd,
Or even when apart,
There is a sense of the other.

When in conversation or just touching,
An energy flows,
I to you, you to I.

All give cause to wish for a union,
That feeling being fuel to go on,
To reach path's end.

That being the threshold to either,
An abyss filled with the pain of loss,
Or a life of ONENESS through LOVE!

John Nevshemal

The Passionate Sunset

Close your eyes so you can see
the wonderful world surrounding me.
Picture this scene in your mind
and you'll love the feelings you will find.

The clouds were dancing in such form
announcing the coming of the storm.
The cool breezes filled the air
and played so wildly with my hair.

Like two lovers colliding with great passion
the Gulf and Atlantic met in that fashion.
It was the cool mist released by this impact
from on top of the bridge I couldn't help but react.

All of the sudden through clouds of gray and white
appeared a really spectacular sight.
The reddish fireball fell in slow motion
appearing to melt into the beautiful ocean.

There is nothing more lovely than this sight to see
and that is why I want you to share it with me.
It's the beauty and magic of the heavens above
that allow us to experience the passion of love.

Carmen Cordova

Patches of Memories

Patches of many colors
cut in different shapes
like looking through a kaleidoscope
or flying over the landscape

Each stitch is placed
for one moment in time
upon a piece of memory
a lifetime they will bind

Sewn with love and patience
its strength to last through the years
for many dreams will be held within them
and they will comfort many tears

Grandma knows as she is working
how cherished each bit will be
continuing to sew history
her hands move steadily

A smile gently crosses her face
and a twinkle of light in her eyes
in the quilt that she will pass on
her love will never die

Brittany Bennett

For Every Child

While we are here,
do not strike us,
do not hurt our minds
do not use our bodies for pleasure
we are not ready, nurture us!
We are a field of wild flowers
natural, fragrant and pure
we are all colors,
    glowing in the warmth of the sun,
    gently growing with the warm spring rain,
    and zephyrs surround us
Let us come to full bloom
With expressions of love.
Let us be children,
And you will be rewarded with
great beauty!

Diane Carta Schuartz

An Ending

How can it be for all the years
Of cheering on others, of drying their tears,
Of helping them rise to face their fears
My love was not there for me?

Was I so willing and able and strong
That he only heard the courageous song
And never realized the frightful wrong
That he was not there for me?

He said I was wrong and I should not sigh.
He said to be quiet and live the lie
That he was there for me.

When there's no one to answer the spirit calling
What is the path that a tear makes falling?
When your love is blind and is only taking
How much noise does a heart make breaking?

Gloria K. Heaton

Meant To Be

You are my only love,
you helped me find the sun.
And I when the sun goes down,
you always came around.

You picked me up and
turned my world around, you're
the very best for me, you and I
were meant to be. Even though
others didn't like to see. We were
always there, especially when
others needed to know we really cared.

In the past we tried too hard, that's why we
didn't get very far. We listen to our
friends and drove away in their cars.
We were apart for years and we both cried
tears. When you left you took my heart,
but now you brought my heart back, I
love you and you love me, that's why our
love was meant to be.

Tammy Lynn Bemis

The End

The earth was ending
Many wars started
One day I left the place of horror
As I watched from heaven I saw a beast enter earth
The beast's name was "Babylon"

The Lord told me that I would now be the Golden Gate's keeper
One day a man asked:
Is my name in the Book of Life?
I asked him his name;
He said his name was Babylon

I couldn't find the man's name, so I turned around to tell him
Then I saw God kick the man into the Lake of Fire
The Lord said to me:
That was The Beast of Evil
Then the Lord said to me:

There are no more of my children
Then I saw an endless line of people
The people in that line are going to Hell, said the Lord
I saw some of the richest people on "Earth" being cast into the Lake
  of Fire
Then God said: They are rich...... but I am richer

Brian Barnett

Emerging Fun And Beauty

A year filled with harmony has now reached its crest
We've all set our sights - on the beautiful Midwest
Our dear friends in harmony - are awaiting us there
With hope in all hearts - Grand triumphs to share

Some will cherish crowns - the rest will all cheer
Great love and affection - will shine so very dear
The thrill of it all makes the trip so worth while
Each moment a precious memory each though a smile

Packed bags are awaiting - Chicago - our great lot
Our hearts can't wait to arrive at the grand Marriott
So keep all tings a humming till next we'll be seen
Harmonious and happy back to our dear village green

Anne Porter Boucher

The Gift

This gift
is given to thee
with the bestowed power
of love and endurance.

This gift
is bound only by
the thought of the mind,
the longevity of the thought,
and the soul of the heart.

This gift
is unique in its own way,
and shall endure in the
mind and soul of thee,
for it is a gift that is
meant to be taken anywhere.

This gift
carries the compassion and heart
from the mind and soul
and written with the love and compassion
bestowed to you.

Matthew Grudzielanek

Towers Of Onlyness

They called him Father, thought him Lord of things
With power to withhold at will, or bless;
They had the eyes for things but missed meanings
From high in private towers of onlyness.

At length, in their adulthood, one began
To look with older eyes prepared to see,
Risking a world of childhood illusion
And fancy born in misty memory.

He found their father mortal, human as
Himself, not Lord of things at all,
But servant and provider, faithful to
His own and to the end still standing tall.

It was a revelation his brothers
Would never share. For each had closed the door
And deep inside the lonely fortress raised
In youth, deceived, purposed to see no more.

They live in denial with distant wives
And, nursing wounds from old arrows and slings,
Think strange the one who reconciles the past
And cares more for relationships than things.

Grace Roberson Hicks

Grandchildren

Grandchildren are a gift from God
Whether they be girl or boy
Their laughter rings throughout the house
They fill your heart with joy
They show they care in all they do
Give a call or send a letter
But to see their face and hug their neck
It's always so much better
We talk and laugh, enjoy the day
We always have much fun
I watch them as they play outdoors
They love to jump and run
We fill the day as best we can
Before they say "Good-bye"
I'm always sad to see them leave
A tear comes to my eye
But then I think of their return
And how we'll spend that day
Then I thank the good Lord once again
For sending grandchildren my way

Caroline C. Smith

Some Clever Universe

Scarlet folds cast on virgin sky, memories fade from the present eye,
but true love will never die. While lunar tides affect the mood within,
somehow I have to start again. To find new worship is a time honored
task with the help of a friend or a glimmer of chance. When two
souls must join together as one heart, they call love romance.
Again,
into the breech was once the playwright's phrase to lift me from a
romantic haze. If to see the world more clearly now, I have to
release the heavy burden from my brow. Without my true love, I would
have no salvation. To live for another soul beyond reservation, I
will escape heartache my constant fixation. Conjured from a romantic
start, we can share different worlds as if never part. Because your
heart is with me wherever I go, I promise to honor the love only I
know. Always together in love and in mind, both our efforts
combined
make for a Universe Sublime.

David J. Ridgway

Country Boy Survive The City

There are drug dealers on every corner of the streets
Living in a drug infested neighborhood causes me not to sleep
I see so many gangs from miles around
What can I do to make put them put their weapons down
Just yesterday I seen smiling faces that said Hi
Today their beautiful smiles was destroyed because of a drive-by
Loaded guns left inside the homes are not nice
Before guns are left in the reach of children think twice
During my younger days I wanted to be a preacher
Because of guns and gangs it is hard to be a teacher
I am glad that I were brought up on a farm
I love to here the roosters crow from the barn
My family and I went to church every Sunday
It brought tears to our eyes when our parents would pray
I dream of telling the world that crimes doesn't pay
But I know that only a few people would listen anyway
I wish that I can change all the bad thing
Do anyone understands what I really mean
Living in the city is something I cant really see
Back on the country farm is where you can find me

Larry L. McGowan

Dare to Discover

Dare to discover new and wonderful things
Things that bring great adventure and knowledge
A whole new way to go about your life
Looking for things beautiful and strange
Looking for things beyond the normal

Dare to discover things you never knew existed
Things that can only be found in ones mind
Use your imagination to take you far away
To discover mythical legends talked about by all
To discover exotic and mystical lands

Dare to discover far beyond our land
Things in order to find we must explore
Places not located on any map
The concept of things so complex yet simple
So remember, Dare to discover something new for all

Nick Galante

The Kiss

Is there really a line between pleasure and pain?
Is there a difference between the intelligent and the insane?
For out of the greatest pain, I received immense pleasure,
From out of madness I have seen true wisdom,
How can such a beautiful exterior hide within it such a horrific
    creature?
From within the beast hides,
Peering out from the depth of my soul in which it resides,
waiting for the chance to frenzy, to kill the beauty and receive
it's
    freedom,
wishing hellishly for protean, mininshing my humanity,
seething with wisdom from delusions of insanity,
trying to survive my internal dark winter, so lonely so cold.
Can I handle this gift of immortality?
To be forever young, to never grow old.
Is this a blessing or a tragedy?
To watch those that I love grow frail and die,
to be left alone with no one to trust.
Can I endure the passage of time as it passes me by?
To bear the consequences of my blood lust,
I need what is left of my humanity to survive in this surreal abyss.
Cradled in the arms of darkness, immortalized by a kiss ....

Kimberly J. Dowty

Spirit Encounter

It was her music I hear like long brush strokes against my soul
It feels like she knew before me that I would come
and these sounds I needed
Every stroke stirred the turmoil in hiding
Every stroke evoked the scars of pain in remission
Every stroke...
Till the lava of salty tears run from my soul
to heal my broken self.

The heat bursts from her fingertips to sear
the lesions of emotion life casually dropped
on my way to spirit awakened.

Like the morning dew, she had come
wings from above, spread wide to engulf my senses
scattered much too far from my inward self.

In a small corner of Tuscon, in a square space of nothingness
two spirits met briefly, in a few words
spoke truly of the cosmic changes to come
when Gods and goddesses will rival much less
and rejoice in the gifts of loving.

Marie Marthe Saint Cyr

Just Open Your Eyes and See

Did you ever think that you have seen everything there was to see?
But how many things could there possibly be?

The sun, the moon and the stars lighting up the big blue sky,
From the day we are born until the day we die.

A rainbow filled with lots of colors, and shades,
Just one of the things that God has ever made.

The white, fluffy clouds that looks like cotton,
This is just one of the things that will not be forgotten.

The white snow on the cold, wet ground,
All of these things can really be found.

So you ask "How many things could there possibly be,"
All you have to do is open your eyes and see.

Joseph K. Taylor

Tornado

As I sat in my room with nothing to do,
I stood up and gasped when I heard a big Boom!
I got confused and started ducking,
When I heard the revolting sound of sucking.
I started to panic so I looked for my four leaf clover,
I took a glance out the window and saw a cloud that started to
    spread over.
"Run to the basement," my mom exclaims,
when I heard the sound of a thousand freight trains!
After a few minutes I found my clover,
but by that time, everything was over.

Anders Carlson

Serenity

Like the sight of the sun on the ocean
Or the smell of a rose in the wind
A charm like the spell of a potion
The crashing of a rivers last bend.

Like the beauty in rising each new day
Or the view from a mountainous peak
A star that shines through the gray
The clamness that nature can keep.

Like the colors that stream thru a rainbow
Or the depth of the oceans gray-blue
And what will come of tomorrow
One more good look at you.

Tonya Delph

160

Him And Her

Him and her were in love, flirting with a playful shove.
They hugged, they kissed, laughed and cried, until one
day when she died.

Him and her were not a pair, only him he'd sit and stare.
Crying since she was dead, eyes all watery and bloodshot red.

Him met another her, not like the other that's for sure.
No one as pretty or as sweet, no one as great that he
would meet.

Him was sad and felt confused, not loved just used.
He had no one for himself, only her picture on the shelf.

Him and the new her didn't last long, they knew from the
Beginning their love wasn't strong.

So now him was dead, laying lifelessly in his bed.
All he saw was a blur, until him realized it was her.

Him and her were together at last, up in heaven, a pair
From the past.

Kelly Petitt

A Dilemma

For forty five years you were my companion
Part of me was your home
Age and decease had begun to set in,
Now I am sad you are gone.

All there is left is a terrible void,
A hole, a gap, and a space.
Even your neighbors have gotten annoyed
There's nothing to put in your place.

So good-bye my friend, you served me well
Golly - I'm telling the truth.
But then again - oh what the heck
You are only a wisdom tooth.

Inge Joseph

A Child's Imagination

Once as I was walking, on a warm summer day,
I came across a child, all by herself at play.
She seemed to be quite busy, setting dishes here and there,
But, I couldn't see her playmate, though I looked everywhere.
I listened very closely, and then I heard her say,
"Good afternoon, and how are you? Sit over here today."
"I'm so glad that the sun came out and made the flowers grow,
I picked a bunch for Mommy, because she loves them so."
"Let's sit down and have our lunch, before it gets too late,
And then we can walk hand in hand, back to the garden gate."
I couldn't wait much longer, for her playmate, I must see,
So I quickly stepped out in front of the weeping willow tree.
And, just as I had thought before, there was no one around,
Just a little girl with dishes scattered on the ground.
I asked her 'bout her playmate and where he seemed to go,
She said, "Sit down, I'll tell you, if you really want to know.
Each day my Mommie's busy, so I have to play alone,
'Cause I haven't got a brother or a sister of my own,
So I come out in the garden and by the gate I stay,
And wait for God, my playmate, he comes here everyday."

Eunice Geron

Poet, Lead Me On

Portrayed by the world as a cynic monster,
concluding that life is ending in sorrow
and distortion.

Known as a slacker,
the definite eyes of a cheater,
wandering to cards held only in the other deck.

Addicted to the green buzz,
of the mechanical voice
inside the screen of the mind.

The moon is shining upon cold waters
that sway back and forth and rough to rough,
from normal to everyday mediocrity.

So done a disservice by reality and faithfulness,
so taken to another path away from truth and hope,
lead only by the misconstrued eyes of a poet.

Christina Dappollone

Beseeching

Snowflakes are swirling in moon's brightest light.
Wind is a howling with all of its might.
Tucked in my chair, by the fire and its crackling,
Sipping on cider, engrossed in my writing.
Pleasures of bygones drift through my remembrance.
Present day quandaries lose all of their semblance.
Love of another fills all of my senses.
Writing comes fast, but it's all in past tenses.
My love has journeyed to life supernatural -
Memories fly swiftly - just can't seem to catch it all.
What will it matter if I leave this world tonight?
Who will know - who will care - who hears my saddest plight?
Loneliness, quietness, no one to fill the night.
Snowflakes still swirling in moon's brightest light.
Wind is still howling - its sound is a fright.
Slipped in the cider, the secret to leaving.
Pen falling from my grasp, no longer pleading,
No longer loneliness, no more of grieving,
Only the joy of the heavens - beseeching.

Marilyn Sklar

Black Girl

Young Black Girl, what are you going to do?
Can't find any role models, no one to look up to.
No more riding your bike and playing on the block.
All you see when you look out is a basehead and crack rock.
No one to comb your hair and feed you in the morning.
You save half your breakfast because no one is cooking in the evening.
Pops don't come around but you're not mad.
You understand may be your father, but he doesn't act like your dad.
Mom is working not there to teach you wrong from right.
Can't learn anything in school because you're busy getting into
    fights.
Don't fall into the trap of selling sex for love.
You will never get it, only from the man up above.
There is no knight in shinning armor or prince to rescue you.
All the dreams that you have, you have to make them come true.
Don't get pregnant, on welfare and have a baby.
Do something with your life, hold your head high and walk like a lady.
So I ask you again.....Young Black Girl what are you going to do?

Denyse Carrington

Rebecca

Our baby is beautiful and so sweet,
She will play with her hands and her feet.

You give her a whisper and she will smile,
You will want to pick her up and hold her awhile.

Sometimes she will lay quiet and calm,
She is the beautiful image of her mom.

Sometimes she will just want to laugh and play,
Then she starts to talk and will have a lot to say.

She has big beautiful eyes of blue,
And one nickname of Tadeau.

She is a bright as the morning sun,
She makes life wonderful and so much fun.

Her big round cheeks and that head of hair,
Set off that skin so soft and fair.

Her hair so wild without a curl,
She is the world's most beautiful baby girl.

Armand G. Beaudry Jr.

Now

Here we are in the middle of now.
Life's uncertainties escape us somehow.

We think we control our hours and days,
But reality tells us of other ways.

In a second or two, everything changes.
From minute (mi noot) to enormous the impact ranges.

How can we balance and still remain steady?
Stay centered in God's grace — always ready.

Ready for what? We may query.
For our step into heaven's endless beauty.

For love, joy, and peace beyond our thought.
In love and pain, our dear Lord bought

For us to have by grace alone.
So we may join Him at our Father's throne.

What we need to do is survive somehow.
Be prepared and ready. Use wisely, our now.

Laurie Wittmayer

A Dream

A dream
What is a dream?
A dream is having someone to love
someone by your side
A dream is having someone to hold
and someone who will understand.
It is having someone to comfort
through rough times
and someone to comfort you.
It is having someone to share the pain
to share the joy.
A dream is spending your life with this person,
To raise children with this person,
To grow old with this person,
To love this person.
Is any of this possible?
It is,
But only in a dream.

Joe Schubert

The Internal Verdict

As I pierced indifferently at the blanket of snow in the evening sky;
It lay so unevenly and I wondered, Why?
I imagined quickly, only for a moment, the near future,
From Fear, I dared not venture any further.

I Saw: Suffering, sorrow and suppression that our people must behold;
Envisioned by sadness, I considered our unborn, materialistic,
slave-minded children and the destiny that would be theirs.

I Saw: Success being ripped instantly from their tiny grasp by
violence and insidiousness by their own kind in lieu of an unjust
system; and the greatest form of destruction; their ignorance.

I Saw: The poor unsuspecting victims as they view only a portion of
the golden melting pot, of which they are forced to see through
imitations that lay as dead bodies on a battlefield.

I Saw: The oppressive emotions of these people as it first seeps deep
into the depths of their souls, as it engulfs their tainted spirts,
And finally plunges them into a whirlpool whose circumstance
encourages social perspectives based upon class differentiations.

I Saw: How it shreds the hopes and distant dreams that exist into an
unreachable sphere before it could become transformed into an
expectable reality.

I Saw: The existence that lay before these innocent beings and it is
tantamount to slavery,
But a form of slavery perpetually absorbed by our race and enveloped
and breed daily in our minds which ultimately is only robbing our
children for all time!

Paulette Paul-Phillips

Spring Alive

Spring is the Lord's fresh breath, He breathes upon the earth to
awaken new life after a long winter's nap.
The glow of the early sunrise of Spring is his love light, announcing
new birth upon the soil of the earth.
New life begins to take form, the surrounding elements are freshened,
with the beauty of many colors created by the Master's hand.
New buds are peaking from the earth's soil after their long winters nap.

Amazing new beginning take place, for the first time appearance in
    nature's wonderment.
A fresh appearance bud's out on the leaves of the trees,
in the mountains, hills, valley's and flat lands of the earth.
Spring flowers appear with refreshment of new growth after their awakening.
New music and melodies are springing fourth from the birds,
nature takes upon a new look of new beginning, given life by the
    Master's touch, in this new season to be alive.

The human spirit is revived as many humans remember the resurrection,
    true life to the soul.
However, many human spirits are dead even in this season of Spring.
They need awakening in their spirit to spring up in new life, only the
    Master's touch can provide.
If the human spirit would only receive the son, Jesus, with a
    repentive heart, and believe Jesus died to give them life,
that He chose for us long ago.
As He gave His only son to die in our place,
that we can be the bouquet He picked to be placed at the bridal banquet,
He has waiting for us to take part in when He comes.

Awake Sleepy Spirit, Spring Forth and Receive the Master's
Invitation

Elizabeth Mitchell

A Daughter's Love

April first nineteen seventy nine.
A year ago, a loss of yours and mine.
Made us ask why the Lord above, had to take the one we love.
Six children came to comfort you, but all were torn, sad and blue.
Your faith helped to explain the best anyone can, living
and dying is part of the overall plan.
Experiences teach us and help us to grow, life must go on that we all know.
Our family's grown closer, more loving each day.
Caring and guiding each other along the way.
I'm closer to Daddy than ever before, feeling his
strength, wisdom and more.
Each Sunday in church, I shed a few tears, sad but grateful for his years.
But more than that it breaks my heart, knowing your life has an empty part.
No one to love you and kiss you at night, no one to hold
you and squeeze you tight.
No one to make your happiness brighter, no one to make your burdens lighter.
No one to give all your love and affection, no one to
guide you and give you direction.
A daughter's love, I know can't fill this role,
But hopefully adds a piece to your life as a whole.
Mommy, I love you, I care and I understand,
And believe God will give those deserving, like you, a helping hand.

Loretta Mills-Huber

Water And Wind: the Word and the Spirit

Spray from the bay was driven by March winds onto the road bed of the causeway
The terminus of which anchors on Long Beach Island nearly eight miles at sea.
Detritus of the briny ocean littering the soggy strand in its tidal, timeless way
Eel grass dug into the dunes undulating with the air currents in this shoreline lea.

Why had I come to this barrier isle, off season, on such a cold, blustery day,
Where many a year when the children were young, we summered here in the sun at play?
The reason: A private dinner reunion-union with a troubled, dear friend of fifty years,
Holed up in a nearly vacant motel, awaiting surgery, facing his fears.

Within a week, a meningioma, that triggered brain seizures surgeons would excise
In a Philadelphia O.R. that would save his life or, perhaps, result in his demise
Or the third and most grim alternative - life in an altered state.
Now for him the tides shift excruciatingly slowly, as he can only pray and wait.

Norman R. Nelsen

Today's Family

The years have come and gone and the time has passed,
For better or worse, sickness and in health, together at last;

You have given me children, more pleasures than one could ever foresee
Learning, loving, teaching and working, a woman you have made for me;

These babes we have brought into this world filled with hope and
chance, just look into their eyes, happiness we have, you can see with
just one glance;

Together we are thinking and planning their futures filled with such
hope, now trying to guide them, whatever their decisions, together
we must cope;

The tears we have shed and the happiness we have shared,
Until death do us part, we know we have always loved and truly cared;

Can you imagine the pain, the sorrow and fear,
Our children have grown and left us my dear;

Together alone you and I are once again at last,
Our grandchildren are coming, let's get ready, hurry up fast;

The pleasures and sorrows that they will go through now,
They understand us and don't have to ask us why or how;

All the memories I will hold dearly deep in my heart,
Our future looks good as it did right from the start;

A circle of love, a circle of life,
Thank God you have made me your loving wife!

Sarah L. Dobensky

Fortieth Birthday

You are forty
And I am almost eighteen
Things are changing fast,
And I'm glad you're there.
The things you do
You feel I do not appreciate
But remember I did not used to say anything
Now I say "Thank You."
You seem you can not trust me
But someday you will.
You've got a lot of ahead of you
So respect yourself
And keep your head high up there.

Kasey M. Hiatt

Chris

She is pearls and old sneakers
Business suits and faded jeans
Classic rock with a corporate office
Mountain walks and fax machines

A blonde with a brain that sometimes offends
the insecure
With the cunning of a lioness and
the gentleness of a dove

Aware, yet always filled with wonder
A traveler that has not yet found her time
But always, yes always,
friend mine

Shawnee Purcell

My Soul

God is like my soul the spirit
    within me.

Man is like my blood the fluid
    circulating inside me.

God will never forsake me.

Eventually man will leave me.

So, the day you stop circulating
    inside me.

The day I die.

But, like God my soul will
    continue to have
    eternal life forever
    and ever.

Cassandra Fletcher

Willow Weeping

I walk through the woods and see all
But the great willow.
All in her place is
A stub.
When will they learn that
Trees have spirits?
The saw is like a killer-
Man kind the boss.
Willow weeping like the night.
Willow weeping as the stars shine bright.
Willow weeping.

Nicole Leonard

Untitled

First steps on new legs
Stay close to the bannister
Beginning poet.

Susan R. Doyle

Untitled

Love is just a word till you give it
    life
Love is only a word yet it cuts like a
    knife
I love you is but a phase till you prove it
    to me
I love you is nothing if it's not meant
    to be

Tanya R. Balser

Birthdays

Birthdays come and go
each a little different
in a special way.
How do you know
when you are truly grown?
Well today I know.
It is when you wake up
and realize that this
day is like any other.
So you are a year older.
Oh well, not a big deal.
I woke up today in a strange bed,
in a strange room,
in a strange town.
I realized this is how it
will be in the future.
How sad, how lonely.
Just another day,
even when it's a "Birthday."

Jennifer L. Butrum

Castles In The Sand

How I'd love to watch you
    building castles in the sand
As you soften every corner
    with a strong, yet gentle, hand.

The water glistening on your skin-
    the sunlight through your hair-
And your scent which thrills my soul
    as it lingers in the air.

Each mighty wave within the sea
    would fall down at your feet
And gently kiss your every toe,
    then all at once, retreat.

Each bird up in the sky would sing
    your name throughout the land,
While every beauty of the sea
    would wash up on the sand.

Sometimes it breaks my heart to know
    these things I'll never see,
But comfort is the simple thought
    they're forever alive in me.

Laura A. Hindle

Untitled

...Over the tops of the yellow trees...past the crowded leaves... through the sea of clouds...drifting past the corridor of loneliness.. into the chasm that holds what is sacred...dodging the chambers of fear and anxiety..to where the thoughts of love and hope congregate... and to the portion of life where dreams still remain intact...yet to be beaten down by the lies of reality...composed of emotions pantomimed...without receiving negative reprisals...through the dirt of the earth...shaken past the core of humanity...outside the spheres of understanding...unripped by the words of strangers...moving on against the worms that strangle inspirations...sliding forward into the possibilities of ideas never conjured up...vanishing when approaching bones of regret...a daring student who studied the characters of Fitzgerald...trapped in the story of desire unattainable the young body of this child...has old battle wounds...that settle deep from a battle yet to be fought...crying from pain that seeps from a myriad of abrasions...caused by soldiers who unknowingly possess weapons...death was around the corner...but it was beaten by the logic of things left unsaid...untamed youth with hands penetrated by sought after splinters...preserved by the ignorance of faith...only to have it destroyed by the book in the night table drawer...told to feel shame by animals who were born breathing the same air...a mouth stapled shut to the microphone of anarchy...gushing with a breeze of possibility...a few inches more...the hinges yelp...the splinters scatter...the door squeaks... not sure to open or close.

Dianne Catalano

She Left Her Message at the Weep

Daughter's Voice

Hi, Mother, I've got good news
Hurray, today, I've been promoted
I'm celebrating — tears of
achievement
Hello, hello, to my new job
I'll have a desk of charcoal grey
I have arrived. I'm electrified
My work's my groom. I shall emerge
I'll prepare for work with awe and hope
I credit you, Mom, for my success
I've got to fly; thanks for life's listening

Mother's Thoughts

Oh good, honey, 'cause I've the blues
Only hours ago, I was demoted
I'm vegetating — tears of
bereavement
Goodbye to mine, I mustn't sob
Mine was brown, they hauled away
I'm in reverse. I'm petrified
Into my tomb, I will submerge
I dread my chores, I pray I cope
These words feel better than a warm caress
My pleasure, child, 'tis life's Christening

Colleen C. Fogarty

Morning In The Garden

The morning garden heavy with dew -- sun sparkles on the dew drops -- the air is wonderful
A soft breeze drifts across -- it makes you smile -- how lucky I am to sit here and watch the day begin
Flowers slowly start to raise their heads to the suns rays -- I sit as if in a dream just watching - how lucky I am
I must sit very still -- soon a butterfly flitters through - I hear the sound of a hummingbird - the colorful hummingbird appears checking out each flower -- how beautiful. How lucky I am this garden also holds danger -- cats!! Our beautiful, loving, clever, sneaky felines here they come purring rubbing their sleek bodies along the chairs pushing their heads up to be petted - they love to get their ears scratched and a steady pet along the back to the tail with a slight tug on the tail as it passes through your hand wonderful loving pets -- purr -- how lucky I am suddenly the cats eyes catch sight of the hummingbird -- cautious now - the older cat cleverly hides in the flowers patiently waits -- the younger cat also crouches but is easily distracted by the butterfly -- as his eyes dance in the flight -- pounce pounce - away goes the butterfly and the lucky, lucky hummingbird oh -- how lucky you are!!

Rosemary Tiger

My Life

My life without you is rain, wind and snow; my life with you is a beautiful champaign rose. My life without you is lifeless soil; my life with you is a soft gentle April shower. My life without you is dull, drab and silent; my life with you is joyful, colorful and exciting. My life without you is oneness, sameness and dreary; my life with you is soul-stirring. My life without you is colorless, gray and unhappy; my life with you is sunshine. My life without you is silence; my life with you is beautiful music from the heavens. My life without you is a nightmare; my life with you is a sweet beautiful dream. My life without you is nothing; my life with you is happiness, laughter and contentment. My life without you is the existence of sadness; my life with you sings with the happiness. My life without you is what I do not want; my life with you is what I do want. My life without you is loneliness; my life with you is loving, thrilling and happy. My life without you is never wanted; my life with you is always wanted. My life without you is a constant frown; my life with you is an eternal smile. My life without you is a cold handshake; my life with you is a hug, a caress and embrace. My life without you is nothing; my life with you is everything. My life without you is sadness; my life with you is happiness. My live without you is darkness; my life with you is the light of a thousand suns. My life without you is no life; my life with you is all that life can be!

R. Graham Daniell

About You

Waiting, wondering, thinking, pondering, questioning, remembering,
  dreaming about you.
Smiling, sweating, sun slowly setting, loving everything about you.
Writing, calling, hurrying, stalling, wishing to be with you.
Drifting, floating, gently gloating every time I think about you.
Nervous, confusing, laughing, amusing; wanting to be with you.
Constantly desiring, distantly admiring, enjoying everything about
  you.
Softly caressing, slowly regressing, reaching for anything about you.
Coming going, sometimes knowing how I feel about you.
Continue reading, always needing to say how I care about you.
Never forgetting, still regretting letting go of you.
Always trying, never dying, love grows for you.
Still writing, now reciting this poem about you.

Gerard J. Lamoureux

Beautiful Woman

Beautiful woman, on my pillow you are sleeping. I'll touch your face with a tender kiss and whisper, "Sleep on, beautiful woman. How I wish I could spend another hour or two on that pillow with you".

The morning breeze is blowing your lovely hair across my space, and the sun will steal a kiss from your lovely face. The roses all wrapped in crystal dew are peeping in the window. They get to see you wake, and in my mind's eye, I'll be watching too.

You'll stretch and move around like a pretty kitten, not yet fully awake. Soot is watching our babies sleeping. The minute one sits up in bed, Soot will come, barking and pulling at your cover.

Beautiful woman, if someone comes knocking at the door, be careful. Soot will be with you, and remember I love you. The traffic is moving, I must be on my way. But, when my day's work is through, I'll be home to you.

The dew will be gone from the roses, the sun will be way over in the west. My beautiful family will greet me at the door. And that is the time I love best.

Tonight you will share my pillow. The roses will be kissed by the dew. Oh, beautiful woman, I love you.

Effie Read

Tragic Rise

Covered from
No human's eyes
This is where
Life soon dies.

Stare and squint
Into the mist.
Are you on
This heaven's list?

Take the road
No sinners dare.
See the light
Can't help but stare.

Home of our soul
But they lock the gates.
This is where
A new life waits.

A new path in prity
Which life has fell
Dark and doomful
Depths of hell

Ammar Steven Alshash

"Be Good To Yourself"

B - the best you can be
E - endeavor

G - goals
O - objective
O - optimistic
D - dedicated

T - tolerance
O - opportunity

Y - you
O - organize
U - unity
R - resilience

S - stamina
E - excellence
L - loyalty
F - faith

Thelma Brooks

One!

Today, on the winds of tomorrow,
  I will soar.
To look forward into sorrow,
  I will no more.

Never, like you, to say I can't,
  only will I try.
The "what can I do?" Need be recant
  or dreams will only die.

You are you and I am I,
  it's good that this is true.
Seeing only me's, in life's eye,
  would only make me blue.

Knownst I am, to myself,
  though intricate I am.
With variety upon life's shelf,
  more then is at hand.

So for me, I allow for you,
  enjoying who you are.
And with this love each day anew,
  I will soar afar.

Kenneth W. Burnham

Thither

Further than before,
on Previous shore,
we walk along the crest of man
gazing upon a grossness of unspoken.

Remembering the thorns,
of Fortune's aching scorns,
while well in tune with times at hand,
we wait the promised land.

We see you running toward us.
Nothing interferes,
when true love fills the gap
then shelters you with tears.

We're telling you of a story.
One so soon forgot.
For the Lord has triumph
over fear,
and his children
forgets not.

Renee Joy

Desperation

Behold desolate sky
Who am I
Where am I
Why did I evolve

Crawl inside my mind
Deep in thought
Many lies
Mirror image erodes

Born into this world
Mother mayhem
Father dark
Wish I would have known

Disdain memories
Secrets kept
Cold within
Darkened picture grows

Tormented past days
Etched in stone
Will outlast
New ones not yet grown

Joann Latzke

The Lighted Way

With eyes that see hope
On the horizon,
In the dawn of each new day.

With hands that hold joy,
Cupped with loving fingers,
Held in open palms.

With hearts beginning to open,
And find the gifts inside,
Given by those who shared their lives.

Guided by loving hands,
Their way lighted
By the promise of new days.

They step forward,
And enter into a Future
Bright with silent, sacred vows.

Angeline Ferdinand

My Little Princess

Once there was a tiny babe
Born alone with life to give.
Joy and laughter was her song
Blessing those who helped her so.
And so her journey to begin
Waiting...looking for a home.
And then one day, she came to rest
With Dad and Mom and home, at last.

But simple isn't just like that.
Mommy, Daddy...prayed and prayed...
Waited long with hope and faith.
And so their journey to begin
Waiting...looking for this child.
And so she was...born-again...
Not with flesh or labor long...
But in our heart she was born..
Our little princess...Welcome home.

Mary L. Archer

Untitled

I've been many things
But I've never been home

I've lived a life
That revolved around me
Without any thoughts
Of "Who is she?"

The mirror shows a grown woman,
But the me I see
Is still a child
Waiting to be taught
That hunger is not the only
Thing she should know
That pain is not the only
Thing she should feel

And loneliness is more
Than the sound of silence
To know tears is to know laughter
They often share the same space.

Hsueh Mark

The Break

The agony, the pain of writing
Churning, burning, always fighting
Feelings, thoughts, ideas turning
Mind and body reckless yearning
Extremities, paralyzed, uncertain
a break
Relief, to raise the curtain
Open naked souls unburdened
Flood rush in
Dams been broken
Unleashed, multiples of words unspoken

Donna Walton

The Royal Pet

Once I had a royal pet
It was very good to me
The funny things about this pet was
It always stayed behind me.
I never got to see it
I never got to pet it
The only thing I know is that
Once I had a royal pet.

Nancy Wong-Sick-Hong

Child of Mine

This child of mine
Is growing up fine
The pigtails are gone
Now, the make up goes on.

This child of mine
As grown up just fine
The boys call on the phone
They never want to go home

This child of mine
As grown up just fine
She's went down the aisle
Now she's expecting a child

This child of mine
Is growing up fine
Now her babies are grown
And left her alone

This child of mine
Grew up just fine
Now a grandma she is called
But she's still this child of mine

Anna Hall

Winter or Summer

Winter or summer
Which one is glummer?
Summer or winter,
Which one makes you a squinter?
Sun or snow,
I don't know!
Snow or sun,
Which is more fun?
What do you think,
Silk of mink?
Mink or silk,
Or what temperature milk?
Hot or cold,
Lots of mold?
Cold or hot,
Soup in a pot?
Well, what is it,
Summer or winter,
Glummer or squinter?

Danielle Levine

Beyond The Lights

Beyond the lights
There lies a dream
Not very big
Just a little thing
But just the same
It's strong and pure and clean.

Here beyond the lights
Dreams are cherished
A place where treasured things
May never perish

So as you travel your
road of life
Be sure to always look
beyond the lights
Because there you will find
many things
All of them the most
precious kind

Shannon Griffin

"Rock My World"

Green as the grass
rockin' as a robin
the sun shines
the world brightens because of you
time flies when you are near
drunken fools stumble by
noticing your radiance
they envy your talents
inevitable happiness
such a joy
full of laughter and smiles
you are as crazy as I am
that is why we connect
walk this way
share your wonders
there are no equals
for you rock my world.

Erin Scruggs

Planned Failure

He had made such plans.
How perfectly he started.
But he had other goals.
Perfection soon departed.

He thought that planning
Was all he had to do.
Then he could play around
Before the task was through.

How foolish was the dreamer
Who lost his dedication.
The prize went to another
With work not contemplation.

Ramona L. Bowles

Prison Within

So hurt, so terrified,
So long hidden,
The walls were safety,
The walls were prison.

Come out, oh child destroyed
Come to the open space again.
Where once there was danger lurking,
Feel safety and healing begin.

Let the light of understanding grow,
Run to His warm embrace.
My child, you have been hiding so long
Come out and show your face.

Do not fear what you see and hear.
Take my hand and your fear will leave.
Risk that first step my little child
Come out, and believe.

Oh, my beautiful child
I can now see your face.
Come running my little one
Into my warm embrace.

Claire M. Brasier

Me

If I were a butterfly
I'd fly to the sun.
If I were a grasshopper
I'd hop 'til I'm done.
But since I'm not a bee
Or a bird that can flap free
I'll just have to be proud
I am me!

Carsten Snow

Books

Books are silly,
books are funny,
books are solving,
books are coming.
Books are adventures that take you
under sea.
That we swim and dive or what to be.

Some are mysteries that are very long
once we solve them we'll sing-a-song?

Books come in sizes big or small,
long and tall I like them all!

Christina A. Lujan

Echoes of Yesterday

Where did they go?
I saw them yesterday.
Does anyone know,
Where they are today?

A babe born,
Her mother there,
To keep her warm,
Provide love and care.

A shot resounds,
A deafening finality,
Quietness abounds,
Death the reality.

Lost without her mother,
Her destiny is cast.
Without her protector,
She can not last.

I heard her roar,
Echoes of yesterday,
She'll roar no more,
Nor romp, nor play...

Lynn R. Wilson

Why

What have I done my darling
That you should hurt me so?
What have I done so terribly wrong
I wish you would let me know.
Was it something, that I said to you
Because if that should be,
I'm sorry, truly I am.
Please say that you forgive me.
For without you, the sun won't shine.
There will always be clouds in the sky.
So until the day, you come back to me
I'll sit here and wonder why.

Myrna Benson

Take Time to Study the Roses

The beauty of a perfect rose
Must be sought after,
Just as all good things in life
Must be searched for.
And after careful inspection
We see perfection,
That so many of us long for.
However, the time must be taken
To see this beauty.
Yet, oft time is not taken
And we are blinded by the thorns.

Jo Jaimeson

Untitled

Thick as a rock
Snail on a thorn
God in his Heaven
All is right with the World.

Mark Kersten

The Essence Awards

I'm only a child
But I have a dream
That on the Essence Awards
One day I'll be seen

I'll get an award
For doing great things
Like Not taking drugs
Or possibly singing

I'll get to the stage
And give a great speech
By saying few words
Many people I'll teach

They'll listen to me
And do just as well
I'll be very glad
And think "I'm doing swell"

The Essence Awards
My goal is to get there
And when it really happens
I'll say a thankful prayer.

Talea L. Mayo

Believe

Take fright in your dreams
and make them come true
if you believe in them
they will believe in you.
trust in yourself. Never
give up. You are the one who
lives it up. the world is your
play ground. Take no orders from
no one. Tell yourself what to
do. Live life in the fast a slow
lane and make your dreams
come true.

Mary Chowanec

In Search of God

In search of God she walked and walked;
across the land, across the ocean,
across the mountains.

She stepped up, on top of the rock,
and watched the endless sky.

With a smile on her face,
with stretched arms, she asked:
"Where are you my Lord? Where?"

Then came a roaring storm, and
made the ocean howl a mournful song.

The night was coming in;
the sun was coming down.

Her face flushed with anger.
"Well" she said, "where are you?
I am waiting for you so long."

Suddenly, still with God on her mind,
she fell to the ground, and,
there he was;
in a tunnel of light.

Sota Kurylo

Pain

This Pain is my own
I share it with no one
This Pain is my own
I live with it, laugh
with it, cry with it
This Pain is my own
This Pain goes with me
every day of my life
It is mine and mine
alone
This Pain is my own

Tammy N. McGuire

Dressed for Success

Have you ever noticed the woman
who wears the Clinique make up
powdered and pressed and
artfully applied winter wheat
Clairol number 26s blond hair
perfectly coiffed and sprayed and
styled business suit over a
Clorox white blouse demurely
buttoned long navy Brooks Brothers
just dry cleaned woolen coat
good gold earrings gleam
from pierced lobes nails filed
polished and buffed black
stockings encase long legs and
feet thrust into shiny black
patent leather pumps with
medium heels and carefully,
oh so carefully, slung over
one Liz Claiborne scented shoulder, a
red nylon back pack?

Annabeth Seals

Confidence

Confidence can win over
    all obstacles.
It breaks down walls
    as tall as malls,
You an be in the
    Olympics but,
if you don't have confidence
    there's no need to go at all.
In order to succeed in deed you
    need to have confidence.
A mother that has confidence
    in her child who wants
to do the impossible is
    the best thing she can give
    in that time of need.
In deed in life nothing can
    win over confidence.
The greatest thing in
    the world is
    confidence.

Maggie Ball

Waiting About

During the sitting
    of A waiting
With an expression
    of care
My Mind wanders
As it wonders
What is for Me
    out there
Waiting seems to be
    to find out
Doing always does
What waiting is about
Never catching up to
Where my Mind
    Has gone
Always thinking
    And dreaming
All Day long...

Jeff R. McVey

Stages

There are times when I close my eyes
    And I don't see your face
Once in a while I think I'll find
    Someone to fill that empty space

A new road is at my feet
    Now I'm free to roam
I've made my decision.
    I've grasped my fate
I've dance to long alone

My heart and soul have pulled together
    Now that they've had a chance
My feet have taken me to stages
    Where I never thought I'd dance...

Penny Miller

It Was A Lovely Day

Morning's
Misty lights saw
Raindrops, with velvet steps,
Like strings of iridescent beads,
Falling.

Spring turned
Up its green thumb,
Like a deft magician.
Presto! Rapturous sounds, colors
Emerged.

I loved
The sea gull's cry,
Bright sails against the sun,
White, foamy waves and azure sky,
White sands.

Golden,
The sun went down
Trailing smoke signals for
Tomorrow's new dreams that will rise
At dawn.

Cecil Corwin Ray

Inspiring Time

As I lay me down to rest,
Inspiration will do its best
My peaceful time to encumber.
Take away this hour of slumber
With lines of verse,
and words of phrase,
So from this bed I must raise
To jot them down on sheets paper.
Do it now, don't wait till later.
In the writer's life there is no doubt,
When thoughts arise they must come out.
To hold them back would be a sin.
You must reveal this light within.

Stan Harris

S/He

S/He will enter this universe
kicking and screaming
with a chance to make it someday.

S/He'll be better than most
but not as good as some.
Will s/he matter? I really can't say.

Will s/he walk tall as a redwood,
or slouch like a shrub,
or weep like the willowy tree?

I wonder as I toss and turn,
how will s/he grow ...
How will s/he turn out to be?

I hope to the Heavens
and stare at the stars.
I winken, blinken and nod at the sky.

Whether boy or girl s/he will be
makes no matter to me.
I just s/he lives a full life.

Kenneth M. Roy

Has Anyone Seen The Wind

I have never seen the wind
I probably never will
But when the trees aren't swaying
I know the wind is still

I have never seen the wind
neither have you
But when the leaves are blowing
You know the wind is passing through

Laura Huntington

Passing Judgement

Aids fell upon us
Like a ton of bricks,
A terrible virus
God has yet to fix,
From HIV to full blown AIDS
A vibrant life slowly fades,
It takes men, women, children too
We feel helpless, what can we do?
Give money for research
A cure may be near,
Cause you never know
If next, it's one you hold dear,
So, when passing judgement
Keep one thing clear,
It's denial and ignorance
That keeps AIDS here!

Toni Mollo

Don't Cry For Me

Years have passed
since you saw me last
But I'm not gone forever,
don't cry for me.

I'm closer than you think
I see the watery eyes,
I hear the melancholy cries
but please, don't cry for me.

I know you can sense my presence
my love is all around
Don't stand there weeping
because I'm not in that ground.

I'm in a place full of joy
and finally I feel peace,
So be happy for me
and let the streams cease.

Soon, you will see me again
what a reunion that will be,
We'll walk together hand-in-hand
and enjoy eternity.

Nikitra Chester

Recite (With Anger)

Haah! I let it out.
Haah! I want to write about it.
But it's in my chest.
Where one little star is
allowed to rest and the rest of
me is in such sorrow that I am
not there with them.
Do you want to hear me recite?

Patricia L. Reed

Untitled

I thought he loved me,
but I guess I was wrong.
Even though he broke my heart
my love for him was still
going strong.
Right from the start, deep down,
I knew he'd break my heart.
But when he held me in his arms,
I pushed the doubts away,
in the hopes that he would stay.
Even now that he is gone,
  and I'm all alone,
I still think of him with each
passing day
hoping he will come back to
stay.

Mandy Cumbie

Faith And Trust In God

If I really trust him,
  Shall I ever fret?
Can I really expect him,
  To forgive me yet?

If by faith I really see him,
  Shall I forget his face?
If I really really know him,
  Can I forget his place?

Tabitha A. Lewis

When Upon My Pillow

When upon my pillow.
I have cried a tear.

Sleep will then come to me,
and I can hold you near.

Dreams will drown my sorrow.
Sleep will calm my fear.

I still dream about you
although it's been a year.

All our times together,
I still hold so dear.

Since the angels took you.
Now almost a year.

James L. Manning

Time's Out

The steps are coming,
Closer and closer.
Violins screeching
Ominously.
The very walls tremble
In the shadows.
Fear rides triumphant
On top of anxiety's ugly head.
Is Death lurking near?
I cannot move,
Am frozen to the floor.
The door.
The door
It sounds.
A creak.
A squeak!
Heavy breathing...
Run!
Run!
Too late!!!

Jennifer Hwang

My God

They say God created Earth
in seven days, and we
shouldn't question his ways.
And yet, I do, an see clearly the man.
My God, is not a magician
using slight of hand.
He was a slow deliberate
sculptor of the land.
A chemist of supreme intellect
whose designs show no neglect.
From the infinitely small, he is
master of it all, and with
wisdom power and grace,
he created the human race.
Not in a flash, so quick
you couldn't see, but in slow,
wise, deliberate, intricacy.

Barbara Lamping

Wacky World - Who Am I?

Wacky World - Who am I?
Destined to live a lie?
Pretending, acting, please beware,
My honest self I must share.

Wacky World - In God's care
Must always be prepared.
Suffering, sorrow are mostly gained
When my truth leaves me to blame.

Wacky World - Child of God
Sharing truths turns heads, gets nods
Feelings too heavy to bear
No human wants to hear me share.

Wacky World - Child at heart
Jesus loves me - every part.
All my feelings, weak and strong,
He will listen all life long.

Wacky World - God I pray
Help at least for today.
Grant me peace and strength to know
My truthful self to always show.

Debbie Renee Robison

Listen

Clouds get dark,
And then a spark,
Rain begins to fall,
  Listen.
A banging of a drum,
A word of wise from the dumb,
  Listen.
Soft wind blows,
And says what it knows,
  Listen.
You will hear the wisdom in the trees,
Let it flow to you with ease,
  Listen.
The knowledge is all around,
Just open your ears and hear the sound,
Just open your ears and listen.

Priscilla Corral

169

Innocence

Two children
Lisping, stuttering.
Two pilgrims
Each on a journey to the other's mind.
One thought
Reaching for the other:
It is caught.
No one left behind.
How rare!
In a world of complication
This nowhere,
But in a childlike mind.

Linda Lodise

The Haunting

I saw you beyond
I saw you within
surrounded by walls
that I could not see

I heard your voice
I heard your name
I heard the whisper
along the way

I felt your spirit
I felt your soul
despite the fear
I reached out to touch you

But you were gone
Where you ever really there?

Kathy Gold

Budget Battle

Republicans said amongst 3 cheers
We'll balance budget in 7 years
Democrats said nothing to fear
We'll make republican plan rip and tear
Though we'll balance budget in 7 years
We shall make public panic and fear
Shut government down everywhere
Talk gibberish nonsense and medicare
As you know my friend election is near

Do you know, by chance, who won
Budget battle of Gingrich and Clinton
Real victor is one and only one
You lost, I lost, but politics won.

Narayan Verma

The Night Before Doomsday

'Tis the night before doomsday,
and all through the land,
not a creature is stirring,
not even a man.
We know that tonight,
will be our last.
This terrible fate,
is creeping up fast.
The sun is expanding,
The heat is tremendous.
There isn't an army,
that could possibly defend us.
What goes on in the heavens,
cannot be changed by us.
We are merely humans,
originated from dust.
So as the people suffer
we begin to wonder,
is that the earth exploding we hear
or is that just thunder?

Carl Lambertson

Ease

Into it
I follow you
Through it
I go with you
You lead
But I'm hollow

Ease inside
A pleasing sigh
Ease up
Now shut up

Now I'm in it
No one strong
No one guiding
Me, the one who is led
Through it all

Though I may try
And climb so high
I can't quite
Ease into it

Daniel Kraus

Back to My Childhood

Down memory lane
I followed the path,
Where in my childhood
we had cried and laughed.

Down by the old mill stream
The grass had grown tall,
memories rushed back to
that last summer and fall.

We hugged and cried and
bid a farewell,
with promises and secrets
we would never tell.

Ruth E. Wessel

Your Tender Love

Your love, your tender love
It comes to me gentle as the dove
Who can compare such love
Your love that comes from above
In my heart you put a song
Now it's your love that makes me strong
How can I live when you are gone
When in your love, I do belong
If from this world I must depart
Your love shall be in my heart
And forever I shall live
In the love that you give
Your love, your tender love
Sweet, sweet love gentle as the dove

Madeleine V. Leyone

Oh Goddess Yes

I want a Goddess garden.
She say when,
She do why.
Beauty through rain,
Some light from above.
Languid summer will fall to winter.
Yet always
I can eat enormous peaches there.

Steven Michael LeBlanc

For Sasha

Men with sad faces
Clothed in black
Weary from oppression,
Striving to come back.
Lost in a sea of bureaucracy
Must it be so hard?

Backs bent with pain
And eyes pull of misery
Trying but not gaining
When will they be free?

Souls full of passion
Hearts bursting with pride
A long time ago
Something died deep inside

Mary Ann Mosher

Volcano in the Sky

Last night I saw a full moon,
'Twas not the month of June.
There I saw many dead bodies, as
they laid puffy in the clouds stiff
as clay.

Then I realized it had to be, that
someone God and He. Soon it became
the morning hour, but dark.
The sky became full of fire and
lights like lightning came from
the stars as they fell not to the
ground, instead sparkled and
melted on the way down.

In a flash, appearing bigger
than the eyes to see,
"A volcano in the sky". The
sun gleamed with steam and
heat.
Soon there were none, no more
thoughts, for I am an angel.

Lorann A. Williamson

All Grown Up

When I was just a little kid
I couldn't tie my shoes.
Jump up and down and make a face,
If in a game I'd lose.

When I was just a little kid
I wouldn't eat my beans.
And if my Daddy said good-bye
The neighbors heard my screams.

When I was just a little kid
I couldn't spell my name.
I'd mix up all the letters,
'Cause I thought it was a game.

But now that I am all grown up
I do so many things.
And I have even learned
What please and thank you brings.

Baby talk and fuss and fits
Are now about forgotten.
For in the fall, of this year,
I start my kindergarten.

Paula Bertaud

Fate

We met such a short time ago
Yet still an eternity has passed
Our roads must go their separate ways
But will again be crossed.
Memories we will hold close
As time takes its toll,
And futures we will look to
As the past grows cold.
Friends are never forgotten,
They remain forever in the heart
And though miles may separate us,
No distance will keep us apart.

Jennifer Gunberg

The Cat's Perspective

Sitting on the windowsill,
waiting for a mouse.
Waiting eagerly to kill
it with my hungry mouth.

As I gazed into the trees
a bird went flying by.
I pounced upon it with much ease,
and saw fright in its eyes.

I thought a second, "Should I,
    should I eat this bird?"
And then I thought, "Why not!"
And ate with no more words.

Amanda Klint

Prairie Storm

First
a breeze propels
scouting clouds,
then grows
and fills the sky
with endless woolly array.

Prairie grass
bends before the force
bringing mist,
then drops,
then torrents ravaging and raging
from boiling clouds.

Sioux lance lightning
scourges and moves on,
and leaves behind
a world refreshed.

Robert Gunnett

Untitled

And then the darkness breaks.
    And then the silence wakes.
        And then the body stirs.
            And then he reaches for her.

And then their lips are met.
    And then her body's wet.
        And then they are as one.
            And then the act is done.

And then the darkness returns.
    And then he takes her in his arms.
        And then the silence breaks.
            And love is all it takes.

Kristina Clay

The Freshman's Lament

Being a Freshman is no picnic indeed,
you never get first feed.
You never win a fight,
since the older kids have more might.
For making a sound,
you get pushed around.
We are smaller,
while others are taller.
The Freshman class had no money,
so others thought that was funny.
We have some teachers who teach,
but many decide to preach.
You never get to choose,
and we always lose.
You can't drive a car,
so you have to walk far.
We must take Music nine
and eat indoors to dine.
Freshmen are always last,
just like in the past.

Andrew D. Netznik

Wonder

Quietness surrounds me
And the stillness of the night
Closes 'round about-me
When the sun has taken flight

The sky is filled with wonder
And the stars, like jewels bright
Pierce the darkening blackness
With glow of celestial light.

Who can comprehend
the great unmeasured sky?
What spectacles of fire
in those vast regions lie.

What worlds of dazzling wonder,
Or creatures strange to see,
Pass through those realms of splendor
into eternity?

'Tis God, who made the heavens,
His glories they declare.
He set the boundless limits
And placed each star out there.

Neal Witt

Far Away Thoughts

Since the day I first met you
My life has really changed
Some things I've put in order
Some things I've rearranged
I'm putting you in the middle
And building my dreams around
Someone who means so much to me
The special one I've found
Before you came into my life
My skies were not as blue
But then one day you came along
And the sun came shining through
And although we may be far apart
The miles cannot erase
The precious visions I have
Of pretty eyes and a smiling face.

Delia Guzman

Why

My heart is sad,
My heart is lonely,
My heart is crying
For it has, so many dreams
So, why don't they come true

Dolores F.

5 Minutes Till Work

Twisting turning smashing burning
crashing through my frontal lobe.
Endless senseless grabbing stabbing
Trying to find the hidden goal.
Back and forth to and frow
Still I draw a blank.
Sweating clinching gut wrenching
I still can't see my goal.
Searching probing reaching grabbing
The object now in hand.
My goal attained my mind at ease
I finally have my lost car keys.

Dean A. Johnston

A Teacher's Poem

I love a poem about a tree,
But a child is a poem to me.

I see him come in my room each day
So full of life, fun and play,

Such a tender, living, growing thing
Like a bud in early spring.

Often he has a sad story to tell -
How he lost a puppy or hurt himself
    when he fell.

Truly he is a bundle of joy,
    mystery and surprise
Planted by God in our midst for us
    to supervise.

Mary Mae Brock Mardis

Shadow

The shadow is thee truth,
The shadow cannot lie,
Beauty is on the inside,
    that's why the shadow cries.

The shadow has no insides.
    the beauty cannot
    be seen.

So look upon the outside
    and silence the
    shadows screams

Sara Renee Cornwell

Portrait Of Donna

Awkwardly adorable.
Gentle, but determined.
Innocent, possibly, but
not at all harmless.
On the threshold.
Ill-at-Ease,
but...

A. S. Bloom

Heaven During Spring

The leaves are made of emerald,
   the streets are solid gold.
The sea is all sapphire,
   and the king sits tall and bold.

The sky is pure diamond,
   the apples, ruby red.
Emerald, ruby, sapphire flowers
   in the flower bed.

They need no sun in heaven,
   for Jesus is the light.
They also need no sun for there
   is no night!

Those pearly gates will open,
   on that blessed day,
And when those gates are open,
   I'll soon be on my way!

This is my heaven,
   I see it this way.
But what it is really like,
   is more than words can say!

Dana Henderson

Resting Not

Complex issues cloud my mind,
ashen color, restrictive twine.
I am held hostage by memories vine.

Simple rights and wrongs you say!
Just let it go, just live today,
forget the past, come out and play.

Easily said and sounds just right,
but not this heart, locked up so tight,
the pain and grief, I can not fight.

Captive now in torrent sea,
my mind still tossed, now let me be!
It's rest I need, on bended knee.

W. Michael Anderton

Why

Why do they die,
Where do they go,
Why does it happen?
Is it our fault,
Why do we cry,
Is it wrong.
Why don't we know,
Why do we need help.
God, please answer me,
I need to know,
I'm scared and confused,
I want to cry,
But why.
They want to play again,
and have some fun.
We want to be loved,
But why not, what's wrong?
God, this is my last question,
   Why, Why Do They Die?

Jessica Ann Hall

A Prayer

Where sea shells tumble
   in the foam
And seabirds wing their
   way toward home

Where sun and sand and
   ocean meet
And waves break gently
   at your feet

My footprints firm
   along the shore
All this I long to see
   once more.

Great architect of earth
   and sea
And keeper of
   eternity

I hope somewhere in
   heaven's plans
There are oceans kissed
   by friendly sands.

Mary-Jane Zall

Early Morning Sunrise

As he stretched, and stretched,
Twisting and turning among the sheets,
Wondering what to do next,
A faint light touched his eyelids.

Gently, oh so gently,
His eyelids began to open.
Amid the spaces of the blind,
A golden ray appeared.

Surprised at the brightness,
Of this new light,
Up he jumped from the bed;
To investigate some more.

This I have to see,
He screamed with glee.
Sheets and everything forgotten,
To the window he ran.

And there, peeking from the clouds,
Slowly, oh so slowly,
Inching its way above,
The golden sun appeared.

Ina Brissett

Papa

I know you went to heaven,
Which is kind of far away.
But you left us all in peace,
On that very sad spring day.
I don't feel any sorrow,
When they tell me you are dead.
'Cause to me you're still alive,
No matter what they said.
These people at your funeral,
Have still not found you yet.
I know where you really are,
Shh! Don't tell, it's a secret.
It's like playing hide and seek.
To find out where you are.
You're not around the corner,
It's really not that far.
Promise to remember him,
And you'll really never part.
'Cause he'll always be with you,
Hidden safely in your heart.

Shari Katzenberger

Images

When lights are dim,
I see you there.
Standing in,
The warm night air.
I've reached for you,
Every Time,
Hoping and praying,
That you will be mine.
You're not really there,
But in my head,
Or is it my heart,
That holds you instead.
It sees your beauty,
Without a flaw,
And my heart
   sees it all.
I can see your inner beauty
   it's as free as a bird.
The bird is saying something,
"I love you" is what I heard.

Brian Forrest Achenbaugh

Morning Tears

Sometimes in the morning,
As I wake to greet the day,
The painful tears of longing
Will keep the sun away.

As I close my eyes in reflex,
To halt the stinging tears,
Your presence overwhelms me
Even though you are not near.

When I relive the physical,
The spirit seems to surge
And I recall the wonderment
Of our thoughts put into words.

I savor with intensity
The knowledge we have shared;
The times of talk and laughter
That conveyed how much we cared.

As I recall the specialness
Of all that we have done,
My tears of longing turn to joy
And I greet the morning sun.

J. K. Bonin

In My Eye, There Comes A Tear

Where eagles fly
to the ocean floor.
The love I have,
everyday grows more.

The stars at night
lights up the sky.
But nothing quiet like
the sparkle in your eye.

Every time we touch
the passion grows higher.
You are the spark
that sets my heart on fire.

Your voice is like
an angelic host.
But it's just being you
that I love the must.

There are times
I still feel you near.
Then, in my eye,
there comes a tear.

David Westerman

My Love For Quida

She is a very special person
In my heart
I have a deep sadness inside
When ever we are apart

My love for Quida
Is like a big white cloud
Floating in a sky of blue
Endlessly and forever

God knows my love for her is true
Maybe someday she will too

So, if you are lucky enough
To love someone like Quida
Don't never stop

Because to love someone like that
You will always be at the top
Happy Birthday my Love
Irby C. Bailey

Last Poem

My hand freezes
and pen ceases to write.
For the time is late,
as we enter night.

End yea. She must
increase, as I decrease.
Mother of God.
On the way Home.

Listen friends, all
that is written is true.
This thing,
done for you.

Now follow, as part
of the flock. The
midnight hour approaches
quickly, on God's clock.
David W. Domansky

My Enchanting Place

There's only one place
That I love to be.
It's a lovely spot,
It's where I feel free!

There are animals
Who are real friendly.
They always listen
And understand me.

There're acres of land,
And some trees that make
A cool, shady place
Beside the small lake.

There're lots of people
Who are always there,
Who always gather,
Who all seem to care!

Where I love to be,
From it, I won't roam.
For it is the place
That I call...my home!
Sara Bolton

Untitled

A hollow thunder through my soul
I can hear.
Raptured in grief by a soft,
fallen tear.

I wipe it away vowing no more
to cry,
Letting all emotions crumble and
die.

Why should I care? I cry to the
wind,
When all of my dreams have come
to an end?

Should I keep crying for those I
have lost?
When I inside have paid a much
higher cost?

Yes, my dear the breeze whispers
so true,
For you have lost them, but they have
lost you.
Barbie LaBine

Untitled

He said he loved her
She said she knew that
"You tell me every day,
And all the time that's gone by,
Not once I thought you'd stray."

He reached out and held her
She gave in and sighed.
They stood there for hours
Beneath the winter's starlite sky
Together, swaying back and forth
Enjoying each others warmth.

He gazed out over the ocean
She brushed the hair from His eyes
And they wondered
What life would be like
Not being in one anothers lives
Realizing their happiness
They cried.
D. H. Fronheiser

Fallen Angel

There's no doubt
That when I fall for someone
I fall hard
And when I fell for you
That was the end
I can't even see the ground
Though my face is flat upon it
And I can't remember the sky
Though that's where I fell from
My mind is gone,
Damaged by the fall
Implanted forever
With thoughts of you
Aching is my heart
Injured with delicious pain,
Sweet agony
I need you to heal me, save me
Pick me up
Rayanne Emme

Where Were You?

Where were you, my friend when my
 world fell apart?
Where were you, when I had all
 that pain in my heart?
Where were you, my friend when I
 needed you more?
Where were you, when my pain felt
 like waves beating the shore?
Where were you, my friend when I
 needed to cry?
Where were you, when it felt
 I had died?
Where are you now, my friend, why
 did you go?
I guess it's something I'll
 never know
If only you would've
 said goodbye.
Then you could have seen the
 tears in my eyes.
Bonnie Upshaw

Untitled

A wedding band is formed
When two metals are fused
Together
One soft and almost useless,
The other strong and light as a
Feather.

The two combine together
To form a band with no
Beginning,
A circle polished to perfection,
With no trace of ever ending.

A bond set not only
In the fusion of those ore's
But also in each other's hearts,
To love forevermore.

Love is like that circle,
Combining two hearts as one.
A bond that can't be broken,
A knot that won't come undone.
Ronald Barnett

Pink Day

Pink Day
that flashes and smokes
like sun burns and neon signs.
When I speak
my words get stuck
on store windows
damp from beaded foreheads.
I am trapped in
light bulbs and rubber gloves
and squeezed between
pages of biology books
that breathe and digest my mind
into pieces of
sticky, sweet afternoon.
Laura Bennett

My Heart

I speak to you not of bright blue skies
  or windmills in the wind
I speak only to your heart
  And wonder where it's been

Has it ever loved and lost?
  Or has it found the one
Who brightens up a dreary day
  As does a golden sun

Has it ever betrayed you
  And left you lost and cold?
Where you've become an empty shell
  desiring someone to hold

My heart has done these things to me
  Time and time again
And when I find the one to love
  I'll wonder where it's been

    Marcia Ryker

My Sister Nyasha

My sister's name is Nyasha.
Ny is for short.
She likes chicken McNuggets,
Pizza and more.
I call her little rascal.
Because of her ways.
She's very funny.
And she likes to play.
She's three years old.
With short black hair.
Beautiful brown eyes.
She's very talkative.
And as she lives everyday.
I'll always love her.
In my own special way.

    Alfredo A. Hustin III

Ode to Integument

It's one snug God-gift that we're in;
Most folks merely call it skin.
It's all of us that people see;
It tells them if it's you or me,
It's supple yet it holds us firm;
It lets us run and jump and squirm.
It always fits and self repairs
all sorts of cuts and ragged tears.
It tells us what it's like outside,
and other facts it does provide,
Like if it's hot or if it's cold,
Or what within our hands we hold.
Much needed openings are in place,
The most of them about our face.
One lets in food and lets out talk
One breathes the air wherein we walk.
Two let in light, two let in sounds,
So we can know what's all around.
This mantle's great, don't you agree?
God had great ingenuity!

    S. Alton Yarian

Moonlight Valley

I grew up in Moonlight Valley
I left home a long time ago
Looking for those greener pastures
Searching for that pot of gold.

Sometimes my memory takes me
Down that dusty, winding lane
Once more I see the home place
And I'm a little girl again.

Oh, for just one drink of water
From that clear, bubbling spring
Just to walk in the moonlight
Hear the lovely, nightingale sing.

I can almost smell the lilacs
In bloom beside the door
I can hear my mother saying
God, be with you, evermore.

Take me back to Moonlight Valley
'Neath that Indiana sky
Lay me down by Mama and Daddy
When my time has come to die.

    Mildred Hardin

Untitled

Like seaman of yore
I look to you for guidance
You are my North star.

    Barbara Brandes

Brook of Tears

Beside the brook a Girl Ponders,
As it glistens her mind wonders.
She'll stroll graceful as if on air,
The sun beaming on skin so fair.
Although it seems from far away,
That all is well, but all's array.
Eyes filled with pain that empty tears,
Into this brook then disappears.
She rests beside this brook so calm,
Gentle splashes against her palm.
She watches as this brook runs free,
Nothing to stop its destiny.
No obstacles can change its course,
It's meant to be with no remorse.
As she's leaving with mind at rest,
She has only but one request.
If you're led to this brook of tears,
It may not seem as it appears.
You must help it as it helps you,
And then you both will see it through.

    Mary R. Camlet

Masque

So many times I sit here,
sit here feeling those same
feelings, thinking those
same thoughts.
It's like the sun shining
on a cloudy day. It's there,
but we just can't see it.
It's hidden by a "masque",
a "masque" of clouds.
It's hidden until the next hour,
next day, next week, or month;
but it always returns.
It's like a beautiful
sunshine on a cloudy day!

    Heather Lee Miller

Reflections

Songs running in and out of
my head
Thinking of the tears I have not
yet shed
A lighthouse standing on the edge
of an island
Long walks to the sea with toes
squishing in the sand
The air is filled with a fragrance
of scaled animals which live in
the deep of the sea.
Grandma has a bathtub that is
too big for me.
The images I see of a mythological
but unique horse with one horn
Between where I am now and
where I have been my worlds
are torn
These are the reflections of my life.

    Yvonne Channel

The Second Time Around

Feelings come alive again,
  joys,
    building friendship
Getting to know you,
  memories,
    creating kinship.
Warm feelings,
  pleasures,
    the things we've shared.
Gone the time forever
  when
    nobody cared,
Special friends,
  caring,
    showing appreciation
Enjoying exciting,
  wondrous
    anticipation.

    Mary Graliker

Amidst the Splendor

Words amidst the splendor
Can be made to rhyme
The subject could be anything
Flowers would do this time
Roses for the fragrance
Can be brought within
Because they do need daily care
And feeding with a grin.

Another flower is violet
A pretty shade of blue
It could watch the sky above
A cloudless day would do,
They help to make a fine bouquet
For any bride to care
That way it's easier to say
With love I'd say, "I do."

    Paul G. Schort

Bring Me A Poem

My love bring me a poem
To wear in my heart
Bring me words
That we shall never part
Bring me kisses
With all things worthwhile
And I will bring you a poem
With a hug and a smile.

Anthony J. Custer

Where Angels Come!

I see a place where angels come
To sing their songs and pray
There is a shining light of love
For all who come that way!

Come that way
Oh, come that way
Come that way, today!

Shining light
Oh, shining light,
Shining light
    of love!

Angels come
Oh, Angels come
Angels come
    and pray!

Sing their songs
Oh, sing their songs,
Sing their songs
    today!

Sieglinde G. Manns

Just Ol' Nature

Eagles fly overhead
just like in the story that he had read
seashells shine in the sun
life just is so fun
the opossum are hanging upside-down
there aren't many in the town
pandas are rare
baby pandas don't have any hair
kangaroos
don't have tattoos
tigers live in zoos
not one has caught a flue

Jesse Lupinski

Trolls

There are good and bad trolls,
you can't see them while on a stroll.
You might see a flicker of color,
but you won't see them whole.
You won't see them play.
You can't watch them roll,
because they're always on patrol.

Jessica Clark

Untitled

Creative lust brought to
Conscience lost in vengeful
Reveries caught by ghosts abode
Locked up by teachers of the past
drowned in sorrow of sweet sap
from a dying bloodroot

Kerri Elson

Locked Inside

Tight lipped
Hands gripped
A decision weighs in,
the ache to move ——
    is squelched again
Pushed down, buried
One more Layer of nonacknowledgement
    just might make it die.
Free will —
our gift from creation
stands to be a curse this time
Personal stabbings of guilt
means dying a long, slow death
and with such a process
the knowledge it is self-inflicted
    self chosen
We all die a little when
someone stops —
    and doesn't move
for the sake of another.

Keirsprint

A Stargazer's Love

As I sit at my window,
    and star at the stars,
I feel the wind blow,
    of perilous fars.

I can't help but think,
    all this love that I feel,
From the planets in sync,
    and behold a great deal.

To love and to die,
    the things we dream of,
A feeling so high,
    a stargazer's love.

Nick Alsager

Meaning of Life

If I were to ask for meaning
it would be in terms of people,
whether of school, of hall
or shop or lofty steeple.

The eyes of babies tell me,
in love that radiates,
pure, innocent and rare,
it's full of life, not hate.

My gift is not of thing;
it's not of what I do
but just the gift of love,
not old but sparkling new.

For what the world needs most
is not a lot of things,
of rare and precious skills
but love that soars and sings.

Edward F. Healey

The Fishes' Dishes

The big fish eat the smaller brand,
And that, it seems, is right.
For if it was the other hand
It would not be so bright.

The giant whales dine on the squid.
They do not even chew.
Mouths open up and down they skid,
Many tons, plus a few.

Electric eels are so unique.
They give the fish some shocks
Of high voltage, and in a tick
Dinner is on the rocks.

Octopi are happiest when
They eat the giant crab.
They pick him clean of flesh and then
Find some shrimp to grab.

A shark has some fantastic teeth.
His eyes close as he bites.
Whatever's in the sea beneath
Is his, he thinks, by rights.

Evelyn A. Blackledge

Alone

She said for me to come,
I stayed home.
She told me to stay,
I left.
She asked for a ride,
I left her there.
She asked to come in,
I shut the door in her face.
She asked for love,
I gave none.
She asked me to come to her bed,
I ran away.
She cried herself to death,
I didn't even say good-bye.
She watches over me,
I try to hide.
Now I fell like I could die.

Jennifer Denike

Nobodies Child

Nobodies child was born today
    Nobody cared, nobody came
Nobodies child lived a life of pain
    Nobody cared, nobodies blame
Nobodies mother was filled with shame
    Nobody cared, nobodies pain
Nobodies mother could not lay blame
    Nobody cared, nobodies name
Nobodies child was not fed today
    Nobody cared, nobodies paid
Nobodies child was filled with rage
    Nobody cared, nobodies caged
Nobodies child died today
    Nobody cared, nobody came
Nobodies sorrow, nobodies shame
Nobodies child lived a life of pain
    Nobody cared
    Nobody breaks the chain

Patricia L. Palmer

That Mountain

There is a mountain
It's in the distance
It's a beautiful mountain
It's a hard one to climb

As I near that mountain
With the help of my brothers
And all of our prayers
Someday will climb that mountain

With each new step
That mountain gets easier
With all of the help
Soon will reach the top

Anthony Gorski

Wild Rivers

I stand, alone,
at the rim of the gorge

where the Rio Grande cuts a
ruthlessly enchanting canyon,

where rock wrens sing over
the roar of the rapids,

where a lone dead cedar
contorts with fervent optimism,

where a golden eagle
soars high above us all,

I stand, alone,
at the rim of the gorge.

Irene W. Schultz

Thank-You, Teacher!

For the kindness you show
to the kids all year long,
The gentle way you correct them
if they do something wrong.

For all that you teach them
from their alphabet to math,
The values you give them
as they start down this path.

For the stories you read them,
and the projects you share,
They all look up to you,
and they know that you care.

You've made a great impression
and thank-you, I do,
For all of these things
and for just being you.

For you've been their teacher
from the start to the end,
But even more than that,
you've become a good friend!

Lisa Rendleman

Trying

In a cave, you just can't get
out, try to sing, you just can't
hear yourself, try to run, But end
Up walking, and then here comes
hope shining though, it tells
You what to do, but then it
rains and gets washed away,
Try to jump but end up falling,
You will find there is one
thing to do, Just become you,
Don't try to act like another,
Like one of your sisters or
brothers, Don't let this obstacle
hold you down, Don't let it
grip you to the ground,
Be yourself that is all I will
say, be yourself today!

Katie Sprenkle

The Empty Fathoms

The empty fathoms of time
pounding endlessly away.
The rhythms beat on.
Hacking at me.
They take my pride,
My courage and my trust.
I begin to break.
They have noticed my fragility.
Hell on black wings
exposes itself to me.
Heaven on white wings
does the same.
I look skyward.
The pounding drones on.
I reach toward white wings.
Hell's fury then is unleashed.
In a second the black is gone.
I am surrounded in light, a peace.
Past, present, future exist as one.
Time is no longer an object.

Gina Tassone

Fright In The Night

In the night, the dark, dark night,
Things appear, oh, the fright.
Images of monsters
dance in your head,
Shadows come crawling
from under your bed.
From way down deep,
Deep under the floor,
They come out when it's late,
And scratch at your door!
But then...
In the corner of your eye,
A light appears,
Up in the sky!
The monsters go back under the floor.
The scratching ceases at the door.
For now, there is an end
to all your fright,
But wait till later,
My friend, good night!

Sean Malseed

Untitled

You grasp my soul
You made me whole
I found my missing piece
My void was filled
My heart was full
You were the light in me

Empty now
But bitter strong
Trying to be sweet
Come fill my void
And be my peace
Touch my soul
Once more

Melissa Bennett

Timely Love

Love can be found at anytime,
it can be yours and it can be mine.
And if it's true love you wish to find,
take into mind love takes time.

My love is not a four letter word
that starts with L and ends with E.
It's a word that starts with Friendship
and lasts for Eternity.

Make time for love and you will see,
love can happen to both you and me...

Earl C. Brown

Rainbows

My tears fall like raindrops,
cold and gloomy.
The day is gray, with no
happiness left to feel.
I sit in my room,
and I wait for you.
I wait for you to come to
me through the pouring rain,
and kiss my tears away.
I wait for you to hold me,
and bring the happiness
you hold within.
You bring smiles to my face
and laughter to my voice.
You make my eyes brighten
and lift my spirits.
The tears vanish as the sun
shines and brings
us a rainbow.

Cassie Hubble

My First Love

I remember my first love
his hair was brown and his
eyes were, too.
He was one year older than me
but age meant nothing
he had a loving smile
and a gentle kiss
his eyes were captivating
and always held my attention
he made me laugh
when I wanted to cry
he was my life
when I wanted to die
and I'll never forget
the love that we shared

Lori Jackson

Science Class

Roses are red,
Clovers are green.
Chemicals are cool,
When you can play with them in school.
When you start fires,
Mr. Mangold jumps higher and higher.
He screams and hollars,
And grabs you by the collar.
But, it doesn't matter how big a mess,
It's if you can pass the final test...
Nathan W. Lilienthal

Picking Roses

On the verge of the
defined line between day and night
living in fright
living balancing for fear
of one sides unknown
edging death for fear
of the other sides known
bow to the majestic
ruby red sky
owed to that elysium night
was my day to day life
then began my wilting and I'm forever
picking roses
Mathew Maines

The Crush

The day we met
over injured souls,
there was something
starting over again;
Through paper wrappers
and games and games,
the evil glares
couldn't stop this;
Walking forward
sometimes slow,
and I don't mind loving to like
when I'm hated by the rest;
And games and games
they never understand you,
the wolf
and the shark;
Too bad for them
'cause I'm the one this time,
and you sure are pretty sweet
for someone who hates sugar.
Tricia Little

Overture to Damnation

The sinner's temptation:
- caution disremembered -
Silent Whispers
offering tokens and trophies
beckoning from the shadows
with alluring falsehoods
and malicious lies.
But under the guise
of Harmless Jollity,
the entreaty is answered
with High Expectations
of sugarplums and wishing wells.
Oh, and these are given—
the Demons watch
as the bait is devoured,
leaving the hook.
Benjamin Fisk

A Missing Child Missing You

Teach me to laugh again
Give me reason to smile,
Say that you love me
And hold me awhile,

It's been a long time
Since I last saw you,
And I really need someone
That I can talk to,

I'd never known sadness
Until this happened to me,
And now I can't forget it
It just won't let me be,

You said "Don't talk to strangers"
But I thought they were okay,
Then that's when they took me
So very far away,

I can't express the hurt
And the fear they put me through
But now I am so thankful
I've been returned to you.....
Lynda Roberts

Eventide

Purple shadows foretell the coming
   of the night,
and a lone Gull winds its way in
   solitary flight
seeking a place to fold his wings.
   And in this desert of
sand and sea, I strive to grasp
   the scheme of things...
of God and man and eternity.
Jack N. Holt

Questions

Who?
Who am I?
I am a child,
without laughter.
What?
I am an ocean,
without waves.
When?
When am I?
I am night,
without day.
Where?
Where am I?
I am close,
without being near.
Why?
Why am I?
I am,
because I have to be.
Chris Knapp

Kites

Kites they dart across the sky
Day by day, by and by
And a rest they do earn
But suddenly he has a yearn
To dart and fly, twist and turn
But soon he gets tired
And can't be highered
For flying across the sky.
Cline

That Child I See

I hate you, and you hate me
Don't forget, that child I see
splitting up would be hard on him
can't we just begin again
Don't forget, that child I see,
He makes me think of you and me,
can you remember our wedding day,
that way we felt,
it seemed so right,
as we held each other tight,
our souls were one,
our hearts combined,
to break up now would kill in time,
all arguments aside,
without your love,
I will surely die.
Don't forget that child I see,
He's the best of you...
and me.
Brian Wiemer

Wiser

The austere glances
Of people not knowing
Who or what goes on
Even if they are older
They should know then
I do not respect them
Blind fools among men
In my soul is torn
Fragments of naivete
They look upon with scorn
Not knowing what
They look upon until it's worn
Thin with knowledge
They finally find out
That austere glances
Aren't what life's all about.
Susan C. Elvin Kappele

Poetic Rap (To A Rap Beat)

The key to words that rhyme
   Is just putting them to time

In a most peculiar way
   You have something you must say

About the feelings that you've felt
   And the ones that you have dealt

To the people that you've loved
   And the ones that you have shoved

It's reflections of a thought
   That so many minds have sought.

When a straight path is found
   When you share common ground

The communicative power
   Has the beauty of a flower

It starts from a seed
   And it's ended when you READ!!
Samuel Pace

A Windy Day

Have you ever thought
 on a windy day
that your house might blow away?

The wind will blow it
 to and fro,
and where it will land
 you do not know.

All you can do is sit and wait,
 and hope this will not be your fate.

You sit and pray
all through the day,
and when it is over
you can say,

This has been my lucky day!

James E. Wells

Listen

Listen to this, listen to that
 Do this, do that
 said my children,

They don't understand
 All I want to do is
 listen to the rocks.

Gisela K. Scheer

Under Hoof

Grampa said to me one day
For a cheap hat I should pay.
One without the fancy trim,
Jus' one with a solid brim.

I should'a listened to Grampa,
An' through his eyes what he saw.
But given my youthful age
I didn't hear the wise ol' sage.

Workin' hard to dally 'round,
Bringin' cow-brutes to the ground.
And my, how the dust does fly—
Stingin' even the bravest eye.

But the saddest thing I know
Is havin' to reap what I sow.
An' this tear is jus' the proof
When my fancy hat is under hoof.

Thomas Joaquin Darby

Dreams

  I dream of you every night
wishing that someday I might
share my dreams of moonlit
streams and morning mountain
summer steams.
  Outside my smile so radiantly
beams, but inside my heart is
falling apart at the seams.
  In these dreams your love
for me is greatly shown. Give
us a chance and no greater love
will be known.
  My last words to you the
way it seems, with you I
wish to share all my dreams.

Kristy Allen

Of All That

Of all that is,
But of all that is not.

Of all that could be,
But of all that time forgot.

Of all that changes,
But of all that day by day.

Of all that we do,
But of all that things we say.

Of all that are great and small,
But of all that is big and wide.

Of all that we understand,
But of all that we take in stride.

Connie Dupree

What Is A Friend

What is a friend
a friend is someone who cares shares
and someone who fears and sheds tears
who is always by your side
who never runs and hides
you can always count on
them to do something right
a friend is somebody
who will stick up for you
no matter what
a friend is somebody
who you could share
secrets with you can
tell jokes too and when she's down
you can always brighten her day
with one of your jokes
you can have fights and quarrels
but you'll always make-up
and be friends again
that's what a friend is.

Leslee Bumgarner

Through All Seasons Round

Spring comes along,
the grass starts to stack,
the birds sing their song,
the flowers are back.

Then Summer is here,
the sun blazes high,
the heat wave is near,
and a high beaming sky.

Now Autumn moves in,
and winds start to call,
the colors begin,
and leaves start to fall.

Soon Winters to know,
and the birds go by pair,
then down comes the snow,
and the cold fills the air.

But one thing that lasts,
through seasons so high,
from the future and past,
are the stars in the sky.

Laura Martinez

The Joy of Basketball

Sweating and gasping
passing plus dribbling
Slam dunks being made
as your breath fades away
while you go down the court
people jump all around
cheerleaders kick and touch the ground
People love the Chicago Bulls
'cause with them there are no rules
that's the story of Basketball
it's in every season summer, spring,
winter, and fall.

Livia Basile

Sound

There was a night,
music all around.
I waited for my love,
but there was no sound.

Then out of the music
another one arose.
He danced so fiercely;
I tried singing out.
There was no sound—I froze.

Time sped by—
hours, days, and years.
Still, no sound could reach my ears.

Finally, the winter thaw
Brought one to sing to me from afar.
There was sound.

Now, I can sing out
to ones who are near.
Come out of the darkness
and out of the fear.
There is sound. I am sound.

Vicki Smith

Because

Because you're not in love with me
I hush my heart and let it sigh
Into a mournful lullaby.
I grow a fruitless, drying tree
Because you're not in love with me.
I catch a ray of sunshine, bright,
But soon is devoured by the night
Of doubts crawling to my thoughts.
No joy, no smile, no tender glee
Because you're not in love with me.

Because I want you be my own
Into the water that you drink
I'll let a tear softly sink.
A thief, I'll sneak in your lair...
Unlike Delilah I'll kiss your hair
While befallen into sleep.
But with my hundred volts of passion
I hope you'll be electrified
And be transferred to my reaction.

A love seed on your land I've sown,
Because I want you be my own!

Elena Ionescu

"When I Come Back"

I want to come back someday!
I want to be loved like
a teddy bear!
I want to sing like Barbara
Streisand, play the piano
like Liberache, decorate
like Phyllis Morris, speak
like John F. Kennedy, write
like Steinbeck, be an egg
head like Einstein, look
like Mo Dean and live
in a home like Cecil
Beaton, be an artist like
Matisse and just be
myself! Someday, someday
when I come back!

Joanne Louderback

What Is Love Like?

Love is like a rose
    Smell it
Love is like honey
    Taste it
Love is like two birds singing
    Listen to it
Love is like a rainbow
    See it
Love is in my heart
    Feel it

Diana Perez

Tears

These tears I've cried for years,
For someone I never
knew.
It's been eating me, beating
up inside,

Until I'm wasted and all
through.

I have to get over it
sometime,

It's like I've committed a
crime,

I'm forever in debt, until I
forget,

When I meet the judgement
of my time.

Jared Kinney

Secret Love

Dancing in the moonlit night -
I see your face come near.
And all the while as darkness falls -
Reflecting only on you-so dear.
Sleep approaches - I give in -
To a world where love will be.
Tenderness rests there, too -
For my dreams bring you to me.
In this realm of consciousness
Deepest passions come true.
I must always remain with the dreams
Since it is there I found
you.

Judy Mitchell

A Summer Night's Rain

Darkness - Surrounding
Droplets - Puttering
Lightning - Flashing
Thunder - Rumbling
Clouds - Bursting
Rains - Roaring
Coolness - Touching
Freshness - Smelling
Breezes - Pushing
Sounds - Quieting
Stillness - Engulfing
Sleep - Encumbering
Minds - Resting
Clouds - Parting
Morning - Shining
Shades - Rising
Birds - Calling
Robins - Hunting
Grasses - Growing
Days - Coming

Dorothy Laurence

Essence

I'm the pride in a
    black man's heart.
    Urging for equality,
    yet hit with hostility,
    blood trickling down brown
    shackled arms.

I'm the people forced to
    labor in the fields of an
    unknown land where you can hear
    the cries of pain from
    Beatings with cowhide

I'm the worries and wonders
    Of what will come next.

I'm the raging anger when,
    Faced with prejudice.

I'm the world that must change.

Karen Scott

Untitled

innocence lost, days gone by
wires crossed, feeling high
coming down, seeing life
wedding gown, future wife
screaming battles might bring violence
baby rattles break the silence
unpaid bills pile up
handful of pills
water, cup
poised to run, ready to hide
no more fun, fights divide
thrown in the dirt, left to rot
overwhelming hurt
look what I've got
loaded gun, one small shot
you're the one that makes me hot
no small cost
an empty sigh
innocence lost, days gone by

Judy Libson

A Gardenia for Mims

Pinned to her Paisley at every Party
Proud, exotic
and Picture Perfect.
Mysterious Fleur full of secrets.
In the dark cave the Petals fall
Wet with my Dew.

Clare M. Fox-Rega

A Miracle

When "we" became one
we thought
You and me and "baby"
makes three
In our case, it didn't turn
out to be
Perhaps two or three or
maybe more
Life's circumstances
Shut that door!

Who or what could heal the
missing piece of our heart?
"Adoption option" and "you"
our special needs daughter
"Gloriously" fixed that part
You and your adopted daddy and me
are now a family
Precious you and
"Adoption option"
Our merciful miracle

Penny Johnson-Poet

Moms

Moms are sweet.
Moms are nice.
Moms are cool
Moms are happy
Moms always love you,
even when they are
mean to you or when
they ground you, or
when they give you
a spanking on the Hiney.
Moms always love you.

Trevor Blair

Crown of Steal

Gold mind rush
Into spirit heaven
Drink from the glass of life
Drop your thorn's
Break my blood
To a 1,000 lives
The drink eternal mourn
I've dropped the glass
Bur nothings in it
Look down on us
As we come to bring it
There's no green on the leave's
they burned all the trees
No more holes in the ground
Empty sky's around
What's this for
What have I eaten
I want more
Now what are you drinking
Kingdom of steal

Mario Torres

The Music Box

The music holds such memories
As I gently turn the key.
It plays the song the band had played
The day you married me.

I never will forget that day;
'Twas the day our lives entwined
And I became yours, heart and soul-
And likewise, you were mine.

It seems so very long ago
That we both said: "I will".
But this little box of music
Says you love me still.

My love for you grows stronger
As each new day unfolds.
The music box describes my love
With written words untold.

Margaret A. Brennan

The Sky

When I look into the sky,
I see the eye,
   But who am I?
The eye in the sky,
Does not tell a lie.
Please tell me why!
   But who am I?
When I look at the clouds,
I see it's love.
There are no sounds,
It's as peaceful as a dove.
   But who am I?
I rule the earth and above.
I show you my love,
Through all the tears,
And I created you and your peers.
   But who am I?
Time will tell you who I am.
But figure it out if you can!

Christy L. Walker & Rebecca Trice

Birth of a Monday

The glutton bloated nite gets
ready to birth a bloody
pathetic morning
each horrid contraction
squeezes the wan moon
further into oblivion.
Where there should be cloth
covered with blood
lies only a broad cotton expanse
and a pounding of suffering
in the lower regions
I hold my breath
in spite of lamaz
this isn't me.
A dream drop of blood
slithers down to the
cracked linoleum floor
celebration in wake of
its sickly trail
which is sadly lacking in iron...

Stephanie Hatcher

An Unemployed Person's Lament

I am unemployed day by day.
I have no job and get no pay.
I always feel as the days go by,
Every day is what a day
And then you die.

Carlton Dean

Not Now, But Later

   I love you and want
to say it, not now, but later

   I need to see you
not now, but later

   I need to be near you,
not now, but later

   I want to be with you,
not now, but later

   I want all that you have,
not now, but later

   I need you to hold me
not now, but later

   You see, I need you and all you
have, but you want me not now but later

Erin Schwiesow

Cat Scan

When I was four
they took pictures of my head
stuck needles in my arm
watched me get sick
took out a tumor
took all my blood
took more pictures
gave me radiation
sent me to therapy
took more pictures
said I was cured
and sent me home...
When I was fifteen.

Michael C. Harrod

Queen of The Jungle

Hey there Beautiful
As my eyes do see
You're as beautiful as
The earth and the seven seas

With your inner glow
You set my soul on fire
Your eyes glisten and sparkle
And it's Love that I desire

Your personality outshines
Even the brightest of days
And your smile is so warm
It takes my breath away

You're the queen of the jungle
That I love to explore
Because you're a sexy lioness
With the sweetest of roars

You're my heart's desire
If I may tell you so
And you're even more beautiful
Than a long-stemmed rose.

Pugs

Self

Everyone ignores me,
They pass by me and stare,
They never see what I see,
They only know how to glare,
A tear go's down my face,
Maybe two or three,
I look around this place,
And realize it isn't me,
When I'm ready to die,
Come and take me Lord,
I shall then never cry,
I'll only be myself.

Mary Motsinger

Friend

Let me tell you about a friend I know
He gave me ten fingers and ten toes
Two eyes that I might see, two ears
That might hear,

Oh what a friend, oh what a friend

He laid me down and let me sleep at
Night while he make everything alright
I want to serve him everyday, you know
For to heaven I might go,

Oh what a friend, oh what a friend

He gave me raiment, food and shelter
Too he gave me strength that I'll
Go through so when I come down to
Die he'll take me to my home on high.

Oh what a friend, oh what a friend
Oh what a friend, oh what a friend.

Luvenia Johnson

"abandon me"

drive a stake through my heart
and watch it bleed
take pleasure in my passing
for you've done the deed
visit my gravestone
and pray upon my death
abandon me and leave me
to rot in my last breath
forget you ever knew me
turn around and walk away
say you didn't love me
and then I'll die that day

heather armstrong

If I Can...

As I fold my umbrella
I want to fold this love and this time

I'm tired of giving love

As I hung up your call
I want to cut the line
which connect with you

I lost my love

Ayako Kinoshita

Untitled

Don't force it to leave,
But don't make it stay.
Don't wish it away,
But don't look at it as if
it were forever.

Remember one thing,
From all that it brings,
One day you won't be together.

You may think that you're
strong,
And without hesitation,
It will break your relation,
And you will realize that you were
wrong.

Don't make it last,
Just let it be,
No matter what is done,
It will set itself free!

Ynirida Miranda

The Only Game

It begins as it starts
It ends as it continues
You didn't beg for it
Yet you got it
Oops! You got on the wrong foot
Please don't forfeit
You failed, don't quit
Talk to a friend
Maybe he knows how to play it
It'll be a darn shame, especially if
you don't finish what you didn't start
Hey! Wake up my friend
It's the game of life
Open your mind to continue

Nnanna Kalu Uzoh

Memories

We wonder if a memory
   Should be solidified
In stone or paint on canvas
   As monuments to pride.

The statue in the garden
   Or the portrait on a wall
Seems all too cold and lonely
   For pleasant thoughts recall.

It would seem much more appropriate
   Our cherished thoughts to plant
In a garden spot of memories
   Where time will not recant;

And to keep them fresh and growing
   Free of weedy thoughts refuse
Giving constant cultivation
   And almost daily use.

For with use they stimulate us
   And inspire us to be
True to those we love, who loved us
   In our cherished memory.

Charles R. McKell

Untitled

Best friends to stay
One minute you were here,
the next minute gone,
I can't help thinking,
whether life really does go on.
But after a while I began to
see, there are other people,
you don't belong to me.
But no distance can keep us
apart, as long as you are here
in my heart.
And there is no doubt in my mind,
to the very day, that just you
and me,
Are Best friends to stay.

Kim Saad

Nature

The sun is bright as stars
The moon as cool as rays.
People can tell that they are there.
For if people don't,
it means beware!
It brings burns
and blindness.
Which brings stress.
Like usual you see.
A pretty bee,
or a bird.
Every time you say a word.
This is all man's creatures

Michelle Wakayama

Our Precious Little Dog

Nikki was a very special dog,
That we enjoyed a lot of years,
She made us all so happy,
As now we shed some tears.
Nikki was the one who made us happy.
When we came home every day,
She made you feel so happy,
To see her wait for you.
I'm going to miss her badly,
But I know she's in God's hands,
God is watching over her for us,
Till we can join that heavenly band.
Nikki you're something very special,
We have truly enjoyed you,
So good night my special girl,
To one so sweet and true.

Jane Blake

Faux Pas

Chimes, flowers,
Where's the wedding?
Oh, I'm sorry.
How did he die?
I see.

Gold, diamonds,
Who's the lucky girl?
Oh, I'm sorry.
I'm sure he's lovely.
Good luck.

Dismal, Monday,
Who made you king?
Oh, I'm sorry.
Have a nice day,
Boss.

Steve Paxton

No Grapes-No Uvas

A cup of tears
and mommy spit
to make what comes from
nature, natural for me
I can't ingest my Beaujolais
I can't enjoy my
of
without some
dirt from underneath a
child's fingers
and some papi sweat
it just doesn't taste right
going gown unless I know
somebody else who picks my
fruit
can't ever afford the
fruits of their labor
naturally
unnatural

Tiffany J. Herard

Dance of Hope

A single falling raindrop,
dances beneath the sun
under a brilliant rainbow
blocked out by black clouds.

Suddenly the entire sky blackens
as softness creeps all around
and the whisper of the morning
seem far, far, far, unfounded, unsound.

Into the future songs are sung.
A sign of peace. A sign of rhyme
weather beaten in totality.
A dance comes forth.

A mighty change of weather,
The sounds raise louder still.
The heart skips beats,
Then faster faster soul's feat.

A single falling raindrop
dances beneath the sun,
A fallen song,
A dance of hope.

Sam Andrus

I'll Do

Stop yelling,
I can hear you,
Do you need me?
Do you want a gentle touch?
Anything you want, I'll do.
I can start your heart,
I can carry you home,
I can ease the pain,
Anything you want, I'll do.
You are my place in life,
I can help you understand,
You,
Anything you want, I'll do.
I can tickle your soul,
I can mend your worries,
Anything you want, I'll do.
We can come together,
Changed as one,
But two,
Anything you want, I'll do.

Tracy Kathleen Weedin

Sunset

The kumquat
is swallowed.

Louis G. Lesce

The Throb

The heart flows deeply
　　rendering
　　　　gently

Pursuing a path
　　listening .
　　　　sharing

Playing joyously
　　frivolously
　　　　carefree

Oh the heart
　　meandering
　　　　knowing
endlessly...

Kathy Fox

I Know Something Good About You

Wouldn't this old world be better,
　If the folks we meet would say;
　"I know something good about you"
　And than treat us just that way!

Wouldn't it be fine and dandy,
　If each hand clasp warm and true,
Carried with it this assurance,
　I know something good about you!"

Wouldn't things here be more pleasant,
　If the good that's in us all,
Were the only things about us,
　that folks bothered to recall.

Wouldn't life be lots more happy?
　If we'd praise the good we see,
For there's such a lot of goodness,
　In the worst of you and me!

Wouldn't it be nice to practice,
　This fine way of thinking too
You know something good about me,
　"I know something good about you!"

Samuel Gunnett Neff

The Sky

　The sun shines day by day,
as the moon shines night
by night.

　As the days go by there's
always something high, above
continually floating by.

　Whether a cloud or a
speck of dust, the spirit
still lives within the sky.

Haunani Akina

Maybe I Resolve

But this is a new year, you said.
Maybe I'm different, maybe I'll care,
maybe you'll matter,
and maybe,
just maybe
I'll share my most
precious
secrets and dreams.
Maybe one day when I'm back home
of far away again;
when I feel right
or you're more beautiful.
If I could only remember
what box I've locked them all in,
and where I've placed the box.
At least I'm sure
I still have the key, you said
as you fumbled awkwardly
through those old blue jeans
the ones with so many holes.

Valerie Ramos-Ford

For Your Eyes Only

A speckled star,
Spotted dot in the infinite sky,
A single soul at a sea of pain,
How fast a dive and, a courageous one
Blinded in abandon,
Swirled in the milky way
Wings of hope, how strong a soul
The fatal slip, the last chance,
A shield of innocence,
Into a plunge,
The ultimate dance,
　To human ignorance...
To you, gone and going,
　My reverence....

Michele Rebeaud

Masterpiece of Angels

Her being was given
The grace of a swan
She possesses the beauty
Of each new days dawn
Her skin is as soft
As the petals of rose
I hear her sweet voice
In each soft wind that blows
Her heart was touched
With God's precious love
And given the purity
Of the snow white dove
From the majesty of mountains
Was molded her pride
It's the might of the eagle
On which her spirit glides
Created by angels so perfect
There would never be another
And chosen for me
As best friend and mother....

Crystal R. Cook

I Never Shall Forget

Once we were together
now we're far apart
though you're still deep
within my heart

I thought it'd be forever
now to my surprise
I might never see you again
except when I close my eyes

Maybe in the future
there is more for us ahead
but for now we're not together
though I never shall forget

Melissa Alter

'Twas Nothing

'Twas nothing to be patient
'Twas nothing to be old
'Twas nothing to truthful
'Twas nothing to be honored
'Twas nothing to be obedient
'Twas nothing to be loved
'Twas nothing to be desirable
'Twas nothing to be elegant
'Twas nothing to be radiant
But 'Twas something to enjoy

Jeannette LaVonne Parker

Untitled

Where are the leaders
To guide us through the cold?
Who is to save us
From the prophesies foretold?
Is there a mortal
Who may show us the light;
Tutor us in peace;
And teach society not to fight?

Power is a word,
No man is born unto.
Love is an instinct,
That all men can do.
Follow not the being
Who defines what we should be.
Follow that of your heart
Telling you to be free.
Listen to the voices
Helping you to grow.
We are the gods of our bodies.
I own the contract to my soul.

Carl H. Tune

Divided Feeling At School Time

(Vacation Is Over)

School bell rings; Mothers cheer!
Children pretending not to hear;
Teachers developing sudden fear.

Teachers still fearing,
Mothers still cheering,
Children still pretending;
Vacation still ending.

George H. Thompson Jr.

Loving Self Change

When you know what to do
   and do it,
That's easy, because
   you have done it.

But when you don't know what to do
   and do it,
The reason may have changed for
   which you are doing it.

Seemingly having done it anew,
   you will then say:

"My...What a good feeling.
   My...How I have grown".

Thereby, upon reflection,
   hug yourself and say:

"I love you, me, my and I,
Yes, it is feeling good and
   Yes, I am growing".

Keep trying it. Why?
Because you'll love you
   and so will others.
     Donald M. Watchko

Do It Now

As we journey on
We leave so much undone,
There's not much left
In this world of ours
But few remaining happy hours.
Heart and warmth much is needed
If we shun what God has given,
How can we hope to be forgiven...!
Give a safe but friendly hand
Not tomorrow,
But today while you can.
We can-not judge
The earth's misdealings,
For temptation is always willing.
Not any soul can say to God;
"Father, I've done all I could!"
His reply to us will be
In the sadness of His eyes
And what we see, is not so good...
   Amelia De Fant Braskie

Oh Gwenda Joy

I wanted to write you a poem
But I'm not a poet
But here we go

Fiery radiant hair
Fiery inside
I can see in your eyes

You're an angel sent to me
Skin white as snow
And no one knows

I want to steal you away
To Amsterdam or Wisconsin
Can we watch the sky

Restless spirit think of me
When you've given up
I'll be with you always

But I can't have you now
Or so you all say
But to have you alone
I always will pray
   Erik R. Meehl

Love Is...

Love is like a flower
who's petal's grow stronger
as the relationship grows
together everyone knows
how very strong love is...
   Alicia Tveit

Halloween Spooks

On Halloween when leaves
are brown,
The spooks come into town,
They peek and screech, and
holler Boo!
And even frighten me.
Those Ghosts and Goblins
seam so spooky,
Till Halloween is past,
Then you wonder why, you
were so frightened
By a simple mask.
   Shirley Cribbs

Nothing More To See

I look outside my window
But all that I can see
Violence, hate, and prejudice
Needless poverty
Dying children
Drugs and war
Crimes and bigotry
Racial and religious issues
Fearful infamies
Pain and cries
And sullen eyes
And souls yet to be reached
Land of the free
Home of the brave
Although there are exceptions
the hate and war
are nothing more
than mindless misconceptions
it sickens me, I close the blinds
there's nothing more to see
   April R. Wear

"Lost Child"

My daughter is out there
   perhaps with your son
Backpacks filled quickly
   decided to run
The house strangely quiet
   all tidy and clean
I cover my mouth
   to smother my screams
"It wasn't your fault"
   that's what I'm told
They own their given lines
   not mine to hold.
Pictures surround me
   from happier times
A small smiling face
   was she ever mine?
I feel sorry for me
   I cry for you
I lost my child
   and don't know what to do.
   Wendy E. Gruber

Richard

At a time like this
I drove myself closer
To a rich bliss
Yet, I've come to discover
   The no - greater love in him.

I once gained a chance
To share his inner thoughts
Now, I don't know this man
For the ole in his eyes are gone
   I wonder in the dark for him!

He once made me laugh inside
And always made up the difference
He's done what no other has tried
Only I hold His secret continuance
   Living in my soul.
   Marco A. Rosario

The Noise of Excellence

Push...
Travail...
Oh! The cry
Life —
The birth of a new mind
A new body of thought
Ideas dormant
Inventions, books, songs untold
Harmonious expression
Poetic poise
Mechanical rhythm
Tick, tick, tick, tick, tick, tick,...
Time passes
Another contraction, this time closer
Push
Oh! The cry - hear my people
The noise of excellence.
   Robin V. Carter

Lightening

I heard my man
   crying
As if his heart
   were breaking

I was anguished
   by the depth
   of hurt

That we made together
   as we parted
   love's comfort
   Gale Hurt

Button Noses, Faddish Colors, And The Common Wetness Of Love

Look at the little rabbits
dressed in their fancy tailored suits
of cutesy colors —
blue, yellow, green, and pink —

Come out into the light
with their teeny, wriggling noses
turned up toward the sky
and their beady eyes keen;

Look at them lick each other's fur.
   T. C. Roberts

Baseball

Baseball is a funny game
with all its hits and liners,
Of all the sports lines anywhere
no game was ever finer.
You set the side down 1,2,3
every other inning,
and finally as you near the end
you find that you are winning.
Oh yes, sometimes you lose a few
sometimes you're in dismay,
but that's the way the story goes
with Baseball of today!

Tim Martz

Live for Today

You can't change the past
So don't ask how.
There will always be your past
Just live for now
I don't have much to say
But I do have much to give.
Tolerate the day
So you can live.

Christopher Gross

Spirit Songs

Painful cries for what used to be
Whales's songs from the sea
The area now cleared by flames
Buffalo used to roam on the plains
Endless miles of beautiful trees
Lots of humming from the bees
Fierce roars from a lions throat
No noise from a motor boat
Where oak used to stand
Now there is only man
Mother-Nature, Spirits of Wind
We need to send
Those painful changes away,
far, far away
So in the night there's no way
I can sleep
Because I listen to the spirits weep

Andrea Zirkle

Love's Symphony

Your touch induced such notes
I have never heard before,
and your eyes called for me
with a song.
A comforting melody
of love and understanding and
I was the captive audience
of your overture.

Jennifer Woerter

Silence

Silence is the cool mist air flowing,
The chimney smoke polluting,
In the water, fish swimming.

Silence is the sadness of your heart,
And the tears of your eyes.
Silence is you falling asleep at night.

Mansi Piyush Shah

The "Ideal Mom" Recipe

Before attempting this recipe, be sure to have all the ingredients.
Substitutions should not be made if you wish to achieve the "Ideal Mom."
Love is the first and most important ingredient in this recipe.
It is the foundation on which the remaining ingredients are built.
Mix in a lot of caring, not just for her children's well-being now,
   but for their future as well.
To this, add a load of patience and understanding,
because we as children need at least 18 years to learn and grow and mature.
Next blend in plenty of communicating and teaching.
These are very important to the growth and development of a child.
Let's not forget to add some discipline;
sometimes communicating and teaching aren't enough,
and the rod is needed for reinforcement. Now, add an ear-full of listening.
This is crucial to understanding the needs and feelings of a child.
Also of great importance is setting a good example.
Children are very impressionable and tend to do what they see grown-ups do.
Fold into this mixture constant prayer.
Prayer is what binds this mixture together to preserve it forever and ever.
Now you have it, the recipe for the "Ideal Mom".
What's so special about this recipe is that it yields not only the "Ideal Mom,"
it also yields children whom she can be proud to call her own.

Deborah H. Watkins

Border Life

I doubted love but was pulled into life from its border and proven
wrong. Would you be the one to accept and protect this offering of my
heart? Border life, somewhere between here and death, a well of
darkness into which I'd fallen. Hopes disallowed and dreams taken
before they start. Why have you sent me back here? You had the right
to ask that I stay. Was it me? Was it your dreams or my
responsibilities; your hopes or my fears? I waited here once for you
all my life. I'd wait another and another in the name of love, just
to be with you. No regrets, no need for these tears.

Another will come here pretending to be you. I can't respond. What
will she want of me? Must I hear yet again how love is sometimes
wrong. You said I could never truly be yours though I wanted to be.
Love would have brought me home, trust when I was gone for very long.
Time would bury me here little by little but I can't stay in between
worlds. To stay is to deny life and thus deny you and all you mean to
me. There is no other for me. Can love on so many levels be
replaced? Time nor life's journey can change my heart. I will always
be yours. We will always be!

Michael W. Hunter

Chasing After the Good Life

Still dressed in his Sunday clothes, little Jackie squirms in his chair.
As he politely pretends to listen to Grandpa tell the same tales of yesteryears,
His mind wanders to thoughts of baseball and the county fair.
Sadly, these tales will be long forgotten and he'll have only
   memories and tears.

His family's always talking, but he doesn't have the time.
Jackie dreams of running away someday to a better place.
They waste their lives believing in something that's not worth a dime.
Jackie is chasing after the good life, kicking and stepping on the human race.

Still dressed in his graduation gown, Jackie fidgets with the keys to his new car.
As he pretends to politely listen to his father's words of wisdom and love,
His thoughts drift to climbing the corporate ladder, so he can go far.
Sadly, his father's words held the true secret of success to help him rise above.

His family's always talking, but he doesn't have the time.
Jackie dreams of running away someday to a better place.
They waste their lives believing in something that's not worth a dime.
Jackie is chasing after the good life, kicking and stepping on the human race.

Still dressed in his suit and tie, Jack pours himself another stiff drink.
As he pretends to politely listen to his son's explanations of misdemeanors and lies,
He calculates the figures for his latest million dollar deal without a blink.
Sadly, he listens to everyone and hears no one as he slowly dies.

M. M. Trzeciak-Kerr

Dead Ant!

Little ant upon my sill,
You have strayed far from your hill.
You think you're heading for a thrill?
Actually, it'll be one sad kill!
(See my thumb? Gee, you're dumb!)

Helen Kampschroeder

"I Wish I Could Fly Above The Sky So High"

I wish I could fly above the sky so high
So I could watch the birds fly by
I wish I could fly above the sky so high
So I could watch the clouds go past me

I wish, I wish, I wish I could fly above the sky so high
I wish, I wish, I wish I could fly above the sky so high
You know how it feels when your friends leave you behind
And you're feeling really sad
And you know how the tears go down your eyes.

I wish I could fly above the sky so high

Darci Faye

Troubled One

He disappeared in the night, not returning,
To what people called home
But what he considered hell, for there he was never comfortable.
Home to him, was a place to get away from.
He was told what to do and when to do it,
By the authoritarian leader.
He could not be his own person.
For it meant going the wrong way
On a One-Way street, that was his mother.
She tried to suppress and mold him into her own image so much
That he was nearly smothered by her.
The only way he could be himself
Was to break free from her restraining, choking grasp.
What happened to the young boy I used to call my brother?
What happened to the happy carefree spirit I used to know?
What happened to the troubled young man he had become?
What will his fate be?
Please come home and give us a chance
To make it a haven from the hell of the world
Instead of a hell from which you escape.

Ann Wilkinson

Metamorphosis

Yesterday's baby is a grown man now.
I blinked and he was a whole person
making his contribution to society and the IRS.
I look at him and think 'when did he form
that wonderful spirit and where was I at the time?'
Why wasn't I told about the change in me to come...
when my pride at seeing him learn new things
would change to sheer joy at seeing him
stand on his own, hold down a job,
interact with the world — function without me?
I greedily hold on to our bond, turning it over
and over in my heart, savoring its strength
and marveling that it too is changing.
The day will come when he makes a bond with
another that will be the stuff of leather and steel,
while our bond changes to elastic taffy
to stretch over the miles.
In the meantime, I'll let his laughter wash over me,
bathing me in memories.

Judith B. Paquet

Progressive Love

Love is what you need
Because you have to succeed

Never think nobody cares,
Cause you're in somebody's prayers

You have to think positive
Because it's your operative

To return the love that's shown
And making sure my love's strong

But others I seek to let shine
Because their concern is mine

And I'll always treat it kind
So I'd like as many as can

To enjoy being together in one loving land

I'll strive to keep it new
For in my heart it's dew

Showing understanding love
Is beautiful as a dove

Really you can say I am a friend
With no end

Glenda Mosley

Memories Of My Past

Sometimes my cross is hard to bear,
for all the problems, I have this day,
and troubles, pile around my life,
I see the day, so hard today
like I am stuck, in yesterday.
The pass, may bring us memories
and the future, keeps us, every day a live,
Yesterday, is a reminder, of good and bad,
and, the beautiful times, we have,
But, oh, my friends, we have to cry and laugh
to see the reality, before the morning light.

Cecilia A. Kuan

True Friendships Never Die

Through thick or thin in day or night,
always could I count on you.

No matter why no matter how,
you put your life aside.

You always were and always will,
be my dearest treasured friend.

You helped me through all my problems,
you let me be what I am.

The barrier that I had built,
you helped it fall without a sound.

The pain I felt has disappeared,
only because of you.

No matter why you had to die,
I always will be at your side.

Now at they end I'm still your friend,
because true friendship never die.

Darlene Wood

Pieta Meditation

He rests heavily in her arms,
this bloodied, beaten body
that has given all, for me,
a worthless creature but for His Love.

His deadly weight carries the sin,
of all the world;
its deception, lies, hurt, and pain, absorbed
in unconditional Love, that is alien to me,
yet a stranger, in His foreign land.

The heart swells with grief;
wordlessly, His Pain pierces my soul.
"Yet a little while, stay with me".

In veiled joyful anticipation,
and frailty exposed,
I go on, just one more day,
closer to Eternity;
where the attempts of giving all, for Him,
are rewarded with His Loving Presence...All.

   Nancy Easto

Life Is A River

Your life is an endless river flowing through this earth.
You never know exactly where it might be going.
You never know when it might turn.
Sometimes it moves along at a rapid pace.
Sometimes it seems to stop, but always it takes you on to a new and exciting adventure.
If you only realize that you do not control which way it may flow,
but that the Father above is guiding you along.

   Jennifer Powell

Injection

They plunge the needle deep into your skin.
The drug starts flowing, and you feel the high.
They will end your life for this ghastly sin.

"He looks so pale, his face is gray and thin."
A prick, a shudder, a vague and hollow sigh.
They plunge the needle deep into your skin.

It's eight years past, but still the questions linger from the trial, did the witness lie?
They will end your life for this ghastly sin.

The protests rage and yet, above the din
outside, you listen as your loved ones cry.
They plunge the needle deep into your skin,

and pain is nothing, walls begin to spin
their twilight circles. Whispers wonder why
They will end your life for this ghastly sin.

Grateful blackness, then light, bursts forth within
your soul, ascending as you, passive, die.
They plunge the needle deep into your skin.
They will end your life with their ghastly sin.

   Meghan E. Work

Untitled

Fed and nurtured to bloom at Christmas
To decorate our homes and vistas.
What joy they bring with rich leaves widespread,
So elegant in bright fiery red
Over green and graceful leaves below.
Poinsettias give a charming glow
To this happy holiday season.
So fresh and bright and new, the reason.
With hope for the New Year to follow,
A life that's good today and tomorrow.

   Joyce M. Kirkpatrick

An In Depth Study of Your Eyes

A deep blue sea of coral wonder;
I hear the waves crash when you blink.
It's within that sea that you have confined me;
Along with my sanity, does my body sink.

A cloudless sky above the earth.
And the endless view I'm taking in,
Is that of open space and harsh reality
In which I willingly surrender myself within.

Like a waterfall, descending from rigid rocks,
Flowing to the ocean, mixing with the tide;
I give in to the gravitational pull.
Let go of my life, and drown inside.

   Ann Marie Vittorio

From Your Hands

You're all sweetness and fire;
You hold life and desire in your hands, in your hands.
You're fast and you're slow;
You're where I go when I need to love.
Oh, I need love from your hands.

You touch me in love;
You pull grace from above just to bear me, just to share me.
You pull at my heart;
All the stars I could chart with your wisdom.
The wisdom you share with me.

But life's circumstances keeps us apart.
Yes, sometimes from the start with my own insistent immaturity.
But I have opened eyes on a new chapter,
Pages turned find that we both grew wiser.
Seeing each other not as adversaries,
  but as joined by an unavoidable turn of events.
When by design, God put my life into you, to be nurtured,
  grown and birthed into a life of want and need.
A need and want to be loved by your hands.

   Cynthia Leigh Hunter

The Magic of Fog

A huge cloud engulfs me as
Grey dingy walks and walls
Break my stride and block my path.
Bright florescent lights in store windows lure me in
Against my will with words such as:
  "Special!"
    "Before It's Gone"
    "Sale!" And "Get Yours Now!"
A warning wind pushes me from behind then hits my face
With one small teardrop from the skies above..
My yellow tote umbrella takes flight
So as not to ruin my new "izod" slicker
While someone wearing Black or Brown or Red or Blue rubber boots
Unconsciously splashes me as he dodges a left-over puddle.
The city is quiet although it is now rush hour
As a constant steamy mist
  Hangs over the tall skyscrapers,
  Rises from beneath the streets,
  Moistens slippery steps, and blurs my vision
As the lamp-post which guides me home wears a triple halo.

   Laura Cobrinik

"His Love"

The old man's eyes sparkle with life
Even as his body resists the notion.
Ah, what he wouldn't give for youth again,
Wishing he had a spell, or a magic potion.

By closing his eyes he can see her face.
He can see every feature, he knows them well.
She's been gone forever, it seems to him.
When will he see her? Only time will tell.

"Till death do us part", they had both repeated.
But there would be no parting, just a long goodbye.
Only temporary, even though it seems like forever.
He could feel her presence, it brought a tear to his eye.

He had held her close, that day long ago.
Wanting to trade places, praying that he could.
The emptiness was overpowering, almost too much to bear.
But soon he'd be with her, he just knew he would.

He was resting at last, his chin on his chest.
With a smile on his face, he was finally at peace.
He and his true love were together at last.
The end of the body; but for the soul - sweet release.

Michael L. McAlmond

Reading For Comfort

We're delighted with good books
   Authors and characters too
We read to think - our thoughts are rare
   We read to write our words to share
We read to talk, to nourish eyes
   To chew understanding

If we're fond of good books
We'll be of lofty thought
   Elevated opinions
Memories will be as if we've gained
   Riches indeed in memory and understanding.

Jean Clare Schilling

Consequences Incomplete and Uncut

Who are you? Samson? Where did you come from? Samson?
What do you want of me? Samson?
Where is the money? Panderer?
No ye not the truth? Liar?
You've hurt me. You've betrayed me.
And I deny you (as you are) re-entry into my world.

Your tears no longer move me. Your guilt no longer pleases me.
You have not even the presence of mind to say I'm sorry.
You claim you love me. I do not recognize you.
I do not want even to remember you.

But wait, you do look vaguely familiar.
Oh yes, I did know you once but I've chosen to forget you.
I've grown comfortable without you.
A Do Not Disturb sign now guards my heart.
Since you went to the party and refused to come away.
Now you are infected, your mind is clouded.
And it's too late my faithless, faceless former friend.

Yet, despite where you've gone, and all you've done,
My hope is that the 3 R's of rebirth, renewal and restoration
Transform the inner man within you.

Susan Peterson Lane

Looking Back

Give me back my yesterdays
When life was full of pleasure
The memories of those golden days
Which are a life long treasure.
Years have passed since adolescence
Along with hopes of opalescence.
And so the years went drifting by.
Because I had other things to try.
I put my dreams far out of sight
Hoping to start when the time was right.
I would give my utmost contemplation
And all my efforts of concentration
Whatever I did, it would be my best
Always prepared to face the test.
But the Muse of Poetry doesn't heed my appeal.
Perhaps I waited too long and lost my zeal.

Rose Steinberg

Honey - Milk Dream

Papa knew these things by heart,
and like a little princess dreams
of her ancestry, a bloodline born,
deep within the moonlit jungle,
where regal tigers and monkey-kings
in hidden temples live,
and scarlet parrots, emerald cobras love
to watch the bright lights of Divali,
when dark beauties clad in silken saris
weave their glossy curls, with saffron and elephant-ivory,
giggle around the carnival tent,
hot with tandoor-fire, and jasmine scent,
yogis chant play the mystic sitar, I dance in violent splendor,
and my heart remembers, tasting honey-mango,
the sweet, spiced delight of India, and the wild
wonder of a forgotten home,
richest tapestry from which was sewn,
Maharajahs on ancient thrones,
and while golden queens on palm-fronds sit,
Far East, my purple torch was lit.

Anjali Kumar

Night Wind

Speak low, and listen to the moody wind
Listen to it sigh and purr
   Then boldly roar with rage
For it can soothe the lowest cur
   Or fool the wisest sage

The trees can speak, encouraged by its hand
Calling to the darkest nooks
   Now hiding from the moon
Telling stories not in books
   A cry, then laughing soon

And through the night it rings of tragedy
Speaking to the silver grass
   A secret none can free
Yet in its fingers holding fast
   It brings your voice to me

John J. Priestner

Love

Love is so shallow and deep just
like the darkness of a broken heart. Love is
when you hold onto someone's heart and
there soul and never let go. If love is so
shallow and deep then love must be a mystery
to figure-out. Love is like a promise until
it's broken into two hearts that you, and
only the two of you can make it one heart and
only one hear again.
    Love is a big mystery that can never
be solved unless two hearts come together as one.
Love is strange but it'll never end because, we will
always to loving one another, and caring for another.
    She knew in her heart she could
never let his heart go but she did. Love is
when two hearts stick together no matter
what happens. Remember you'll always be loving
no matter what you do. Never say good-bye
even though that love will never last.

    Jackie Tesch

Nursing Home

She, a withered thing, cowers in these halls
rubbing eyes that ache, that will not see
any more sorrow.
She, a withered thing, rubs restlessly
the sockets, heavy with burden and disenchantment
and fear.
Twirling hair entwined in dampened locks,
security of soft wishing to be where
she once had been, the womb.
Martyred walls that block love out,
will not let me hold her near
answered whys not realized from distant past.
If she'd never known or dreamed,
she'd be but blood or death. Flaxen hair,
tousled waif, might I give you refuge, a moment safe.

    Terry Rundall Chapman

Forgetfulness

Forgetting where I put it, that item of no importance;
Forgetting where it goes, or how it even works;
Forgetting to complete a task, of no real consequence;
Getting lost, in forgetfulness, at the workplace.

Forgetting how to concentrate, on what used to be
The most mundane tasks;
Forgetting to even care that those tasks were performed.

Forgetting, constantly forgetting.

Why, oh why, can I not forget this pain of the past,
That stays with me always, each day, each night;
This pain, that seems to have this
Immense importance;
This event that seems to have this
Huge consequence;
This trial of the heart that seems to be
So extraordinary

And makes me care, and care,
And care, so much
To the point of
Forgetfulness

    Virginia H. Thompson

My Dream Will Cradle You

May 28th is the day I held my first love, my son, my refuge, now my
torment, now I cry for you.

The pain I feel each day, seems to take my breath away
My heart shattered, our chain is broken
My love unable to Save,

Such joy and tenderness you gave to all
Unfairly taken away
You brighten each day with your smile now far, far away.

Siblings cry and ask why and wonder what could of been
Yet they know, at night they see, a star will shine within.

A father's fear and pain within and asking what went wrong
Should he lay in bed and think of a loving nineteen years
And know of no future near.

Each tear that falls from us all, may darken our sad days
But for sure we know, we have the memories
Lasting a million years.

The angels came and showed you the way, lifting you by their wings
Now I pray you guide the way, and someday do the same,
May love for you as strong as now, still will never do
But until that one sweet day, my dreams will cradle you.

    "Mom" Linda Burner

Time Is of the Essence

True princess of kingdoms haunted by previous death in the
surreal nightmare of existing pain hiding in the fears of
children dreaming of roses in night's crushing blow of reality.

Radioactive junkies of dawn march to kingdoms of death with
fire flaming from ashen skulls burned at the rally of life
held in night's cloak of death.

Time is of the essence.

Step forth lusting creatures of blood, draining mind's decay
in trusting stupidity of life existing alone and unbalanced
through time ending night.

Farewell my beloved princess of infinite compassion lost in
the unforgivable acts of murder. Farewell my beloved.

Time is of the essence.

    Steve R. Sowers

A Bouquet of Dreams

Instead of bouquet of flowers, I give you a bouquet of dreams.
A gift that's been wrapped in a ribbon of sparkling love
and happiness beams.
For no matter how hard we try to keep them, our flowers
fade away and are soon gone.
But dreams last forever, they just go on and on.
Take each day and hold a dream with treasured sweet delight.
Then take it with you while you sleep and let it hold
you through the night.
For on the morn there is a whole bouquet to choose another dream.
To light your life, to make you smile, like a never ending stream.
Hold each dream close and handle it with tender loving care.
For each one has its seeds of love and a bit of silent prayer.
As long as you water this bouquet with memories from your heart.
You will always have your dreams and never from us part.

    Joan McBride

without reason

if the birds fly into a tree,
    and the treasures hide in the sea —
if the flowers of spring wake in the
    summer sun —
    and humans and youth live on the run —
if the music pounds in the breeze of the wind
    and a lonely heart cries and starts to spin —
if a circle swirls —
    and stripes stagger —
if for reasons we wonder why,
    and an answer would arise —
we'd be left without a reason to question why

Christine Holmgren

What I Love

I love to see when the water rushes
It looks so nice and clear
Sometimes it looks like it has pushes
From the rear
I just love to see when the water rushes

I love the feel of sand
Underneath my toes
It feels like a band
Marching up and down
I just love the feel of sand

I love the smell of suntan lotion
Spread all over me
It is such a nice little potion
But it always seems to rub off when I jump into the sea
I just love the smell of suntan lotion

Most of all I love to sit and remember
I sit and let the silence fill up all around me
Sometimes I sit by myself in late December
And I can almost see
The times in my life I remember

Sofia Oberg

A Friend

A friend is a person, who listens when you're sad.
A friend well help you calm down, when you are really mad.
A friend is like a second brain, when you can think no more.
A friend will make you laugh, when you are really bored.

But there is one thing I'll always know, that is, when your friend
is gone.
That is when you really feel, that you are very much alone.

Michael J. Fuller Sr.

Nothing Lasts Forever

The petals that are perfect
slowly start to wilt;
The rose that said "I love you"
now only speaks of guilt.

The thunderstorm of nature
brings raindrops falling fast.
The lightning strikes and lights the sky,
but it will never last.

The blazing sun of fire
that every morning burns
always soon must disappear,
and yet the world still turns.

The colorful rainbow of magic
only visits for a few,
'cause nothing lasts forever
except my love for you.

Amber Scarbrough

The Child

Creation.
Darkness encircles
Dependency nurtures.
As innocent to the world
As it is to itself.
A soul of glass
A spirit virgin to its depth.
Miraculously born into mankind,
Commanded by ten and not nine.
The guardian is its protector and teacher.
The guardian must be the gatekeeper.
For, I am my brother's and he is mine.
For each of us need.
For each is a child.

Carrie Atkins

Dreams

I try to be all I can be,
but I don't know whether it's really me.

All I do is try to act,
but I never really come in contact.

I could wish all I want,
but your dreams can't be bought.

If you want your dreams to come true
You better find the real you.

It's great if you have belief,
    but sometimes with it,
      come a little grief.

Julie Wehlage

Love

In case I did not tell you.
How much you mean to me.
I hope you realize it — by the things I do for thee.
Sometimes I take for granted that you know just how I feel.
The love I have for — yes, it's true and real.
I would die ten thousand times just to prove to you it's true.
The love that buried deep in my heart will always be there for you.
In case I didn't tell you — sometimes I worry a bit too much.
But it's you I love and care for, it's you I pray for God to touch.
Most of the things you do are right and the little things that are wrong
Make my love for you grow more and more and confirms to me
    you're strong.
Please do not forget I try to do the things for you I think are good
But as you know.. Sometimes mothers are grossly misunderstood.
I am not perfect either — in life I've stumbled, tripped and feel.
Perhaps I did not tell you.
I love you and think you're swell.

Joyce M. Kegler

Untitled

My dearest friend and I.
together we've walked the road of life.
Together in sunshine and rain.
Together in gladness, together in sadness.
Together in joy and pain.
Together we've known the thrill of new life.
Together we've toiled and cared.
Together we've braved the battle of life.
Together through alone we've shared.
Together we've bid youth goodbye.
Together we've matured in body and mind.
Together we've laughed and we've cried.
Together we know about true love.
And it come right from the heart.
We were so close to each other.
I am sure we will never part.

Annie Mitchell

My Daddy Is An Angel

My daddy is an angel.
He died and now he's in heaven.
He died yesterday when I was only seven.
When I remember my dad I feel sad.
My daddy is an angel you see.
Now he watches over me.
I Say "I love you Daddy".
Because Daddy you are my angel.

Yvette Martinez

Christmas 1988

This day is upon us,
that you were taken from us.

One year of sorrow
Wondering about tomorrow

They say the pain will go,
When? I would like to know.

My special friend, my little sis-
it's you, I desperately miss.

Each day gone by,
a special tear I've cried.

Here's to another year,
each day filled with a special tear

For you,
my special friend, my little sis
because it's you, I'll so desperately miss.

Brita Hardy

Nature's Love

On the Wings of a Dove I could
soar through the sky.
And see all of nature God made for you and I.
The wild flowers on the mountain top
nestled between the rocks with dewdrops
shining in the morning sun, is such
a lovely picture for everyone.
So many wild animals you can find
from shore to shore, grace this earth
with a beauty untold.
Let's count our blessings from day to day
for the beauty around us may it always stay.

Louise Hampton

Yesterday Memories

Sitting in my rocking chair, day after day, isn't exactly fun,
when you look around, and see tons of work to be done -
Oh! For some of that zip that I wasted, when I was young,
would make a world of difference now, and not leave the work undone,
So, to while the time away, I reminisce on the way it used to be,
when I was much younger, and able to work from morn to eve -
How much fun it was to raise a family of four -
Each day was filled with joy, and who could ask for more.
We romped and played, washed and hung diapers by the dozen
We just took it in stride without any fussin'.
Thanks to God for the wonderful life I have had-
And being a great-grandma is far from feeling sad,
So, be happy, when you are young and enjoy each day that comes,
To have memories, when you are old, and can smile at the work undone
To have the joy of seeing the awakening of spring -
With all the beauty of trees, shrubs and flowers, in their fling.
Thankful for eyes to see and ears to hear the birds sing.
Is worth more than any amount of money, could ever bring.

Edna Schultz

"My Girl"

Underneath the big Elm tree,
A little girl who belongs to me.
Her face is lifted toward the sky,
the look of sadness in her eyes.

I wonder what her thoughts might be,
to wish that I could set them free.
To make her eyes shine bright and clear,
but I know not why she sheds a tear.

She turned her head to look at me,
And said "to you" I make this plea
Always love me, keep me close,
for you're the one who means the most.

I bent down and kissed her face,
And held her as tender as the finest lace.
I say to you deep from my soul,
I love you more than a world of gold.

As she began to smile at last,
the summer sun began to cast,
A warming glow from a sky of blue
"Mom" I love you with all my heart too.

Donitta Enoti

Jeremy

He looked at me, but could not see.
His eyes were blind, and his thoughts were free.
He could not talk to express his love to me.
But his heart was bigger than any could see.
He could not walk, or jump, or play.
But he kept me busy everyday.
He was my child sent from above.
And while he was here, we shared great love.
He touched my heart.
He touched my soul.
One day the Lord,
He called Jeremy to go.
I miss him more than words can say.
But in my heart I know he's better that way.

Debra Abbott

Why Pick On Me?

Dedicated to Tiffany Kelly

Why pick on me? I've done nothing to you
I know what it is that you need to do
Try growing up, get a life of your own
I'm content with mine so leave me alone
It makes you happy to see me cry
I'll never understand your reasons why
The clothes that I have are mine that I wear
You do not own them, so why do you care
I don't like it when you get in my face
Please give it a rest, give me some space
Beauty is not often better, by far
By helping others we can show who we are
Everyone is different, that's whats unique
No one is better than others we meet
Don't say hurtful things to get me upset
Just leave me alone, forget that we met
To stoop to your level would be a sin
Yet there's nothing to prove, no battle to win
Real bonding starts from the inside out
That's what true friendship is all about!

Terri Miller

Phantasm

Alone, between reality and fantasy, I dream of her.
Caught in thoughts of touch, fragrance, and sight.
For these fain moments, I am there;
among the living, where there is light.

The darkness I see, broken only by fantasy.
We walk together hand in hand, touching, holding,
seeing sights unseen when I walk alone;
feeling, smelling, tasting, Light; Ecstasy.

Her eyes of Caribbean blue, gaze into my soul,
edging ever closer to the center of my heart.
Pulse racing, heart pounding, I await her touch.
On the stove the kettle whistles; Reality, Dark.

M. Kennemuth

Little Town Near By

In Memory.
I see an old homestead Road.
That was heaven, an earth to me.
It was plain and so humble.
Yet nothing can compare.
With that spot where I long to be.
In a little house.
On a little street.
In a little town near by.
Where the roses climbing.
Over the garden wall.
And you hear the robins cry.
Where peace and rest make life seem so last.
When I'm weary how I long.
For that little house.
On a little street. In a little town near by.
In fantasy, I see the old fireplace.
And you mother mine sitting there as the glow,
From the embers enlighten your face.
When you set in your rocking chair.

Lino Herman Peace

Seasons

Strength of steel in the open spring
Heralded softness as young birds sing
Intensity reigns in their use of time
Straining to reach each height sublime
When autumn nears and winter winds sigh
Billowing storm clouds sneak across the sky
Breathing a raging fury for all to hear
What will remain for our posterity dear?
It should be strength, a softness - to perfect for fear
It's a gradual adjustment - amidst a shed tear
Attempt not to fret; nor breathe a sad sigh
We loved, lived and shared a really great life
Now that's all over and we cannot die
We're all being cared for by our father on high

Berni Page

The Night After

There you stand with your harlots, trollops,
and tramps.
I'm watching you; eyes pressed against the
window, my breath producing steam.
I needed your attention, affection, and your love.
you gave nothing.
I watch you linger on the corner
you're smiling, laughing, and producing a grin.
And as their decaying morals float to the too
they giggle, flirt, beg for more of you.
Always you.

Thora De Mund

The Perception of Separation

Delighting
in the precious opportunities...

Essential
in the fulfillment of our sensual appetite...

Understanding
the separation as a design...

Creating
the conscious carnal desires...

Building
the necessary lasciviousness...

To languish
in those stolen moments...

Enhanced
by the feverishness of finally...

Belonging
to you in the scant...

Seconds
permitted by circumstances.

Patricia Perras

Mom's Guitar Blues

My son - - If you only knew your mother's grief
Knowing you are safe, would give me such relief

I Love You — no matter what you have done
Just want us again—to be spiritually one

Your guitar sings and plays long in the night
With lonely musicians in heavenly flight

For my home is a "Haven of Rest"
To which — God has truly blessed

Long in the hours/til morning light
The melodies ring all through the night

I pray your ear—hears these "Blues"
For musicians strum the cords, just for you

Calling you home, where you belong
For son;
so long
you've been

Gone!!

Jeannine P. Brown

Last Chance

As I visit you today my Lord. I get on my knees and pray to thee.
I bow my head and think of all my sins that need to be said. I ask
only for forgiveness and bid these sins farewell, I try not to make
the same mistakes, thinking my soul will go to hell.
I keep you close to my heart,
and try never to turn you away, and pray only to you
every passing day. Listen to my prays listen loud and clear, there
coming from my heart and I hope you're near.
I try to take time to talk to thee,
the time I have on earth maybe short, but life with you is
eternal, so forgive me of my sins so someday I maybe someone's
guardian angel.

Chadrich James Castille

Remember Me

Remember me Lord, as one of the thieves, on that cross.
Because, when it comes to words, I'm at a loss.
I've read about the debt, you had to pay.
Help me keep it in my thoughts, everyday.
In all that I do, be with me and guide.
In you, let me always be able to confide.
I may have done a lot of things, wrong.
Just help me daily, to be strong.
I'm a poor soul, in this old body, I hold.
Hoping, you make it, worth while, as you mold.
So, all I ask Lord, remember me.
As, you did the thief, that hung beside thee.

Freda M. Hart

God Plucked the Rose

A rose struggled among the weeds to start its life on earth.
No one noticed its simple beauty or its gentle birth.

It spread its roots into the dust, it grasped as best it could.
Small, but strong, this humble bud did what no other would.

It fought the pain and the jeers from the teasing weeds, the more
they teased the stronger it grew and withstood their wicked deeds.

The weeds spread their jealous pollen to choke the blooming rose.
They failed to see, with blinded eyes, the way the pollen blows.

The rose blossomed and grew with pride, it was sweet among the
weeds. It flowered the earth with grace and love and its struggling
seeds.

The rose spread its seeds of love and only asked to live with peace
and joy among the weeds and wanted to forgive.

They did their best to rid the dust of their gentle foe, they saw
its strength and flowering beauty and so the story goes...

Above the clouds God saw its pain, the weeds like greedy crows,
with anger threw it to the earth...

And God plucked the rose.

LaVanda Meyer

How Do You View Age?

Do you look at my hair as it shines so bright
And think that my mind may not be alright?
Do you look at my wrinkles as a sign of age
And do you know they mark the battles I've waged?

Do you look at my faltering steps each day
And wonder why I don't choose to stay
In a chair by the fireside and reminisce
Of times gone by when it wasn't like this?

I still smell the roses, the pot of hot tea;
I hear birds singing in a nearby tree;
I still watch the sunrise and long for the spring
When life comes anew and all nature sings.

The summers I treasure and days of yore;
I can't say I welcome the winter anymore.
Time changes us all in one way or other;
We move with the tide or we'll surely go under.

Marie D. Dubois

Love's Pain

Riding swiftly into the night.
Swiftly, swiftly, on a perilous flight.

Searing hot tears stream down her face
As she urges the horse to pick up the pace.

She comes to a cliff, and slides off the horse.
This was the destiny of her perilous course.

She walks to the edge and looks at the sky,
And off she steps, with a painful cry.

She falls to the water, so hard and cold.
And begrudges her love for never having told.

Her grief torn body was never found,
Carried away by the water in which she had drowned.

Some say they still see her at the cliff in the night,
Crying, crying about to take flight.
A lover deceived by the man she received.

Rachel Wilmoth

At T.J.'s

At T.J.'s Tavern on Friday night,
Brian Callaghan, who has one of those mustaches
that turns up on the sides, was tending bar.
He bought several rounds.
One of the locals, a man in his sixties,
explained why he had the perfect marriage
the second time around.
His wife is much younger,
(in fact they have a six-year old daughter.)
He only sees her on weekends.
Brain said it was last call, it was already a quarter to four.

Susan Barr-Toman

Love's Perfect Measure

There are no ways to count nor time enough to measure
How much great pleasure you give in such abundant measure

No notes, no lyrics, nor any little rhyme can be written
any time to best describe how grand it is to know
that you're alive.

The ambition you inspire makes everything so easy
to acquire. The joy that you beget, the love
that you evoke are only part of what sets you
apart. The care that you so readily impart, does
very deeply touch my heart.

Oh how our God must love you so-for he has
blessed you with so beautiful a soul

My love for you will always be you can never
change how you have made me feel.
No ways to count no time to measure no need
to search for any pleasure for you beyond all doubt
are life's most perfect treasure

Paul F. Curran

My Journey

My journey's been hard, my journey's been long
Many things will remind me, especially a song
It started one day in the beginning of spring
I think there's a problem he said with a frown
It's cancer this time, I am sorry to say
From that moment on, my world changed forever
It was dismal and gray, clouded with fear
There were decisions to make and plenty of tears
Outside in the sun everything seemed clearer
I tried to make sense of what happened to me
I'm not going to die, I am going to fight
I have to be brave, I'll prove them all wrong
I'll do what I have to in order to live
I started the journey and there was no turning back
Finally a light at the end of the tunnel
The day dawns anew, it is bright, full of color
Daybreak is like birth, the start of new life
My life has new meaning, how precious it is
The journey was hard but well worth the trip
My life's worth the journey, hard as it was.....

Kimberly A. Stoliker

Just Passing Bye

God sometimes I don't even want to try
But then I look up and see the clouds going by
Every thing feels like it is passing me by
I could have let out a scream or a cry
But then God said stop and ask yourself why
Like an eagle soaring through the bright blue sky
That's why life's so hard God wants to see if we even try
To see if we all really even can get by
When God looks down upon the earth it makes him cry
Mainly because all of the children that have to die
The people have to stop living in a lie
Give your soul to God before your own life passes you bye.

Joseph Blystone

Summertime

As I step out into the morning to greet a new day,
I pick up the paper, watch the sunrise, even see a little jay.
I hear birds chirping, chirping up above;
I look further down, and see a pretty dove.
Around me I see flowers blossoming at the sight,
the sight of a few sun rays; before long, they'll reach new height.
Down at the ballpark, I see kids taking the field;
across the street I see an ice cream cart being wheeled and wheeled.
I remember the winter. Could it stay? I thought it could;
But now I'm glad, summertime is here for good!

Jonathan Pick

Hurricane Arthur

The fiery, jagged lightning streaks across the dark stormy skies.
Moments pass, then comes the loud, crashing, roaring sounds of
thunder.
The winds blow whirling, swirling through the trees making
shrieking, angry cries.
The dashing rain beats down upon the earth and all that stands
in storm's way.
It makes one think how small and helpless mankind and all living
things really are;
In comparison to the Maker of everything in the heavens, waters
and on earth;
Which and who were created by our Almighty God.

Mary Anne Turner

Should I Send It Back Or Not!

Does my cat know what I'm saying?
I don't think so, it never behaves.
When it's bad, it's very, very bad!
Like when it messes on the floor!
Then it looks at me and "howels"!
Litter boxes are taboo to my cat.
My cat just doesn't listen to me!
Why does it act like this anyway?
Could it be because it wasn't trained?
Not really, it's just sooo very stubborn.
Kittens always go into their litter box.
They're so cute and playful and loving.
And when you call them they come!
So why then is mine sooo different?
Seems as if it's from another planet!
That's it! Why didn't I see that?
It's eyes are as big as saucers!
Truly my cat is not from earth.
What kind of cat "do" I have?
Should I send it back or not?

Eve Westaby

A Family Portrait

As we sit against the pale blue sheet.
looking into the pitch black camera.
I wonder what it will look like when
    our pictures are finished.
I stay as still as possible while the
lady holds a bright yellow duck in
her hand, telling me to smile.
My mom and dad smile.
While my sisters smile bigger.
All I do is look into the bright light
in front of me and smile with glee.
Then I hear the camera click.
I ask my mom "is it over yet"
She says "no, we have to take one more."
When it's over we get to see our family portrait.

Eowyn Pepper

Kill the Impostor

I wake up to a dream or is this real? As I look toward the sky I
see a glimpse of sunshine. I feel the sun's rays. The sun is
shining so bright it's burning, burning my insides. The pain is so
intense. I don't want to hurt anymore. *Where* is the impostor?

As I grow I say kill the impostor, as I grow kill the impostor. But
I'm not the impostor, it's me. I see, I hear, I feel, I laugh, I
cry. Do I love?
Do I love? Of course I love, I'm not the impostor.
Where is the impostor?

Can you hear me? I said can you hear me? Yes, I hear you but you
cause me so much pain. I need too lock away all the sadness. Go
away, sadness go away. I can't go away I am you and you are me,
we are here to stay. No, *you are* the impostor. *Where* is the impostor?
You are the impostor.

The sun is going down and the day has been filled with emotion. Sun
don't go down. Stay sun please don't go down. It's time to dream
again or is this real? Who's dreaming? *I* never dream. Is it me or
is it the impostor? Kill the impostor. **I am the impostor.**

Rebecca Simmons

Trapped

In all my travels,
you are there
right by my side.
When you were not there,
I felt so alone, so empty.
I want to spend my life with you.
Do you feel the same?
Probably not.
I always fall further than other people.
So light yet so deep.
Blown away by a blizzard in the sand.
Lost in some strange dimension
between space and time.
Don't ever leave.
Please, stay here with me.
Guide me. Teach me.
Help me. Love me.
Hold me together.
Be forever near me,
and I shall do the same.

Christine Maida

Help Me Lord

I am a woman, skin of golden brown. My eyes are black, full
and round. I wear my hair curly or straight sometimes long,
preferably short. My nose lay pug and wide, my lips are small
yet full with a slight overbite whenever I muster a smile

I am a woman with a past, a mile wide. A future, a inch
short. I've been here nor there, maybe anywhere. I've done
this, maybe that. I've live life hard, often tried to end
it all

I am a woman that gave up my babies to chase a "pipe" dream.
Awaking in torment as my mind, body, and spirit screamed.
A dark cloud rode me night and day. Oh, how often I
wished it away

I am a woman like many other, maybe your sister or your
mother. A friend or a member of your family. Don't, judge me

I am a woman who desires a way out. Help me Lord! I shout.
On me poured glistening drops of hope, from on High it fell,
quenching my drive for dope. Light replaces dark

A woman, I am! Victorious I stand. His and mine, hand in
hand. Alive! And walking free, finally, where I want to be.

Sharon L. Narcisse

These Are The Houses My Father Built

With hammer, nails, level, saw, and ladder,
arose the beautiful structures from noisy clatter.

Concrete thick, smoothed with plumbing and wiring,
followed by laid brick or wooden towering.

Sculptured cabinets, archways, and doors
touched along the way to tiled or parqueted floors.

Ceiling painted with various swirls of plaster,
survived long years of storms and disaster.

Built with gifted artistic pleasures,
from the ground up stands long-lasting treasures.

Maudrie Fontenot

Golden Glow

Golden goldens, breezy-easy, going through the
weaving waving grasses, changing hue;

Picture pretty,
posing,
nose in air — then
Pouncing!
carefree bouncing, here and there.

Silent setting sun withdraws. . .
cooling meadow under paws of
Friends,
Who warm the fading scene with
happy golden glow and vibrant sheen.

Terri Govan

Ambivalence

Enchanted by your enigma and beguiled by deceit
I am caught in a Gordion knot, abound and tied
Through contradictions' latticed intervals, I've tried
to discern nuances of logic against clarity's retreat
to see how you, with life's elemental harmony replete,
in ample beauty and purpose of posterity, fail to hide
hostility in stygian depths that floats onto a rising tide
of solitude - its sole comfort finds my life complete.
Your genius, dearth of sense, and raison d'etre quite sound, while
I continue crafting illusions of prosperity that languish
as time tethers more tightly, and the oncoming miles
hasten towards the terminus - a voyage vanquished
by pleasures imagined as we, in synchronous style
gear our disparate treadmills in symbiotic anguish.

Barbara Duvall

A Royal Glimpse

It towered so brightly in the warmth
    of the sunlight
It reached so far
    across the waves to us all—
The sweetness that I beheld
Showered a special radiance all around
That portrayed a message like a golden song

A song that reached out so sweetly
    With an iridescent quality
That sang so pure
    within that beautiful smile
It cast a loveliness and warmth
That generated for miles and miles

For it told of something special
    that moment in song
It was a masterpiece that told
    of a long glorious tale
For it carried all along that pathway
The beauty of a greatly loved British Queen

Susan Smeltzer

The Fool

My laughter ivory and rose petal smooth
glides on the breathy kisses of summer gloaming I
urge your unbound passions and sprinkle a
myriad of fireflies and suns and rainbow bubbles
in a delusional Elysium that is not an illusion but
more real than God or is it God or am I God no
I am the jester that smiles at your
make-believer fate and crescent roses forbidden
to applaud the Faerie I am
the jester I am the fool I am the shape-changer you ride
through the portal of the Hesperides' dragon fire in
unicorn dreams you have never forgotten

Maryanne Wills

Reminiscing Love

Twisted sick love is not the norm
unlike a hurricane which knocks
me down and too strong to turn
Wind goes right through me,
Instead the love seems to stick to me.
Could this be twisted sick love
that I can't seem to leave me, and
let it flow to exit through me

69Cyns

Memories

Remember when we started out with nothing
and slowly worked our way up to having something
Remember when we did not have any money
We shared and we cared and I loved you honey.
Remember when we went on trips we enjoyed
It was fun under the sun.
Remember the family parties we had
It was not all that bad.
Remember the camping and barbecue's we had
Those were so very enjoyable.
Sometimes it was not all that comfortable.
All in all, they are just memories now
Memories, Memories, that's all I have
left to live by, until I die and I
will not cry. So now I say good-bye.

Cynthia A. N. Ramos

Anger

Dreams are the anger
That I hold inside -
The feeling of danger;
The feeling of someone who died.
The pictures of anger that enter my head-
Sometimes at night, I won't go to bed.

Dreams are the anger
That I hold in my heart.
Sometimes I feel as if someone
Is throwing a dart.
Life is so hard-
Tell me what to do;
Show me how to start.
Because everything I hold is in my heart.

Hilary A. Schmidt

Rightful Owner

Hey, I remember you, didn't we have something
once? It's been a long time. You are the one who
gave me this, correct me if I am wrong. Here, try
it on... Don't you recognize it. I've been
carrying it around with me for some time now. Feel
its weight on your shoulders. It's much heavier
than it seems, wouldn't I say? Do you remember
it yet, you should... I wore it countless times
when we were together. I've grown too much to wear
it now, older...wiser...stronger. And still it's
too heavy for me to bear. No, it looks good on
you, keep it. I insist. Keep it as a token of
everything you have ever done for me. I should
have given it to you years ago, I know that now.
And when you someday, grow too much, it doesn't fit
you anymore... Give it away as I have done, to
someone who really deserves it. Someone you have
cried for, and tell them, "here, you carry this
around."

Carol Morrison

My Book of Memories

My book of memories are mine alone
To review at my digression
Good, bad or otherwise
They leave their own impression

There's "mom", rocking her baby
Singing an old time hymn
As we sat around her nodding
Oh! How I cherish them.

School times, playtime are here in my book
To bring happiness each time I look
My husband and children's golden times
make my loneliness disappear leaving me feel sublime

Births, death's marriages and many more
are recorded very very clearly
In my, "Book of Memories"
I'll always hold it, dearly.

Julie Irene McClees

Declaration Of Love

As times come and go. Life and love we look to stay the same.
Upon our Anniversary, I renew my love to you.

My love is yours faithful and true.
Along with my soul, for I owe everything to you.

I've loved you through the good.
I've loved you through the bad.
Your the best friend I've ever had.

I'll honor your hopes, I'll follow your dreams.
As long as we are together, there's no end to our loving.

With this declaration of my love, and the times we've shared.
Binds us together, for a further in heaven.
I love you my dear. Now and forever.

Delores A. Sherman

First Love

Sad and sorrowful
I lay in my bed,
Keeping the memories of us
in my head.
The sweet little things
that turned me on,
I keep remembering
my love is gone.

As a tear falls from my eye,
I think of us and can't help but cry.
We were right for each other,
and I'll never settle for another.

I loved you then and I still do,
The days we spent together
were so few.
You were my first love and always will be,
I will always love you and I hope you will always love me.

I want you back I really do,
Please take me back for I love you.

You will be in my heart always...

Amanda Bloomfield

Message Of Love

As I sat quietly on a cold winter day
Thinking of you...so far away
I felt a light tap on the thumb of my glove
And when I looked down I saw a white dove
It looked up at me in a sweet knowing way
And said "Something special to tell him today"
"Can this be true?" I thought with a start
"Can this little white dove carry words from my heart?"
I didn't know...but just in case
I lifted him gently up to my face
I stroke his soft head, kissed the tip of his beak
Then ever so softly I started to speak
The message I sent with that little white dove
Was five simple words, "can you feel my love?"
It took to the air with a great burst of speed
And in the blink of an eye had returned back to me
Bringing this message so far through the air
"I feel it mom...I know your love's here"

May Charlson

"I'll Tell You A Story Son"

To Elsa DeLosSantos

I have to tell you a story son, when you were only one.
Your life began like a shadow, because you were a tiny son.

When you were born, that morn, your mother passed away.
She gave her life so you could live, to run and learn to pray.

We got along all our lives, with your mother not at our side.
The two of us made us son and we lived with all of our pride.

I have to tell you another story son, and you were only two.
Life was hard without a wife or a mom, particularly for you.

Our lives weren't very pleasant and good days were only fair.
The things we talked about my son, often ended in a prayer.

We often talked about your mother son and where she might be.
I really do believe in God my son and it's heaven she might see.

I have to tell you another story son, and you were only nine.
We got along without tragedy and as a young man doing fine.

Then along came a war, but I was too young and that suited me.
Every able bodied person volunteered for duty on land or on sea.

I was too young to join that war, because I was barely sixteen.
Life went on and believe it or not, I loved the prom night queen.

I really don't have any more stories to tell at the age of fifty
five.
I want you to know I married that queen and she kept me alive.

Thomas C. Rupert

Mother Earth

As I stopped to look out the window one day
I saw several small children as they were so carefree as they play
I could not help but wonder, when they grow up will the Earth
still be this way
Or will they be the ones that have to pay the price
For the past generations who have not treated the Earth so nice?
Will their children have the same rights?
They should have grass, trees, clean air, and room to fly their kites
We should all think of these very things before we give birth
What can we do to help preserve our Mother Earth?
If we would just stop and try to right some of the wrong
Maybe their futures could also be bright and strong
With just a small change of our ways and attitudes
We would be able to pay back some of our debt and show our
gratitude.

Wilma J. Swiney

Shadows of the Dark

The fires of Hell have taken me in.
My story's so long I don't know where to begin.
I have lost my will to live, what else is
there for me to give?
My heart's been mutilated with feelings
just as dead,
All along you're the one I hated, very
existence hanging on by a thread.
Your eyes were open yet you were so
blind, afraid of knowing what you might find.
Stability unstabilizes around me, my
heart's finally set free!
Grains of sand slipping through the
cracks, from white to yellow, to purple to black.
Thinking of you has dulled my senses,
I'm forever stuck inside these barbed wire fences.
My soul is now so dead, because of
the tears I cannot shed.
Loneliness has become my only friend,
and the eternal darkness is a godsend.

Cindy Holmsten

A Southern Spring

Spring is the most wonderful time of year—
'Twill seize one's heart with fervor and cheer.
The sweet scent of honeysuckle perfumes the air;
Birds sing pretty songs for lovers to share.
Petals of new flowers glisten with dew;
White, fluffy clouds dot a vast sky of blue.
Warm rays of sunshine tickle your nose;
A cool, fragrant wind whispers as it blows
Telling secrets of which angels speak
And brushing kisses on babies' cheeks.
At twilight, the Heavens begin to unfold
Brilliant colors of crimson, pink, orange and gold.
The sun becomes sleepy and fades into night
While the moon radiates its pale, soft light;
Luminous stars fill the sky
And crickets croon a faint lullaby.

Penny H. Gremillion

The Awesome Heavens

I gazed towards the heavens
    swirling in a peaceful slow
    a single star came to appear
        from a golden moonlit glow.

Awestruck in silence I stood there
    in stillness, communing and very aware
    The star became a living form
        overwhelming me in its stare.

Time passed, I know not how long
    as my universe dwindled in size
    while feeling just the two of us
        thru loving spiritual eyes.

There were no other beings
    that saw, as I did see
    I stood and watched this peaceful star
        as long as it watched me.

Linda Lennington

The Price

Cut the pain with a razor blade
and let the tears chill the inferno of the soul.
Free the uneasy spirit
and fly high to the borders of dwindling existence;
the future is already gone.
Pay the price.

Tear the heart open with scorching breaths
and let the burning eyes be the seed of the rebirth.
Release the raging winds of absurdity
and dive deep, out of range, into passions;
happiness is elusive. Pay the price.

Crash through the aura with torturing whispers
and let the fantasies be the nectar of mind.
Unloose the ravenous lusts
and sink in the whirlwind of oblivion;
life is unpredictable. Pay the price.

Sharpen the knife upon the body
and let blood and sweat be the price of love;
nature is eternal.
Pay the price.

Eleftheria Mantzouka

Daughters In A Barrel ...

When God made new a barrel of daughters,
Assorted colors and sizes galore
Your Daddy and I placed an order
Not knowing what for us was in store.
With eager anticipation I waited,
'Till the Lord said, "now is the time" —
Get a sweet girl from the barrel
And guess what!
The very best one in the barrel —
Was mine!!!

Violet Unger

Love Is Everywhere

Love is in the air
just look, it's tthere.
Love is in the breeze
That flows gently thru the trees.
Love is in the birds that sing
From morn till night they do their thing.
Love is in the sky of blue
And in the clouds that hang there too.
Love is in the flowers that grow
As they wave their heads to and fro
Love is in the rain
That refreshes all living things.
Love is in the children at play
As they run, jump and romp their way.
Love is in our flag
As it waves over the USA.
Love is every where
Just look, it's there.

Hazel M. Ellis

Volition

Is the grass really greener on the other side?
Or is it faltered?

Is the grass painted greener on the other side?
Or is it a lie?

Which is right and which is wrong?

The child asks, "Are you lying".
The Drone answers, "No".

The child asks, "Or Are you lying".
The other Drone answers, "No".

The child asks,"Then who is right".
The old man answers, "I'm not even sure".

Sean Thorne

The Lizard King

Cold, cool mist of wet pollution
Feeds the dirt of Pere LaChaise
Where in its core
Molds the Lizard King
Lying, sleeping, smiling, lifeless form
Veins which housed worldly chemicals
Now cold, hard, still
Stray felines, moss covered stones
Bow and praise the one below
This restless, disturbed mind
Here, but yet for a season
Clinched by the reaper
Respector of no one
Demonic eyes, now closed in a skull
Hand folded, talentless hands
Listen close, oh, my grieving friend
Birds singing, wind blowing, leaves falling
Lizard king is at hand
Crying, screaming, laughing
In the presence of fire and brimstone

Rodney S. Smith

Goldfish

The blinds leave little bits of window exposed -
enough for moving lights to slip through and cast their glow on the
ceiling trapped inside.
I watch intensely as the moving lights crash,
into the immobile.

Too much energy. Another sleepless night.

I roam into the lamplit living room.
Here there is serenity.
Then sink back into the feathery coach.
I listen to the fish tank gurgle in the far corner
and gaze into Matisse's Goldfish hanging in front of me.

Ironically,
fishing poles lean against the wall which sits between
the gurgling fish and the imaginary
which calls me to join them.

Tara Swanson

Mysterious Woman

Mysteries of this woman. Who is this woman? Examining this woman eye to eye I enter her realm of flesh. Her rational mind and her fruitful caring spirit. In her mystical presence is the full emergencies of Romantic love, Human love, Divine love. Both conceals and reveals the ultimate lover and beloved! She! "Wo-man" who awakens men's hearts! Challenge the Mew Man in thought provoking and inspiring love. This is the way of "Wo-man." This young "Woman" in marriage, motherhood, and career. This Woman's relationship with her lover, family, friends and the old aged. "She's Mystical!" To the right man - woman and I mean "Wo-man!" Understand? I love coffee, maybe wine. But, this "Special Wo-man?" Hell no! You see. You can understand the need for her style. She's creative energy, fire in one's own experience. Leading ultimately to the highest state of lust for enlightenment! That's the way of a remarkable Woman. You are this flowering "Wo-man." I love you! God speed.

J. T. Ojeda

Channel Surfing

As I flipped through the channels this morning
  in varied degrees of frustration.
I came to a documentary on geese that
  proved to be a fascination.
How a gander alone becomes angry and lost
  but when put with those of his kind
becomes gentle—and an integral link.
  What a mirror this is to mankind!
What if we all were as a single flock migrating to purpose as one?
Might we have a common direction—angled wingspans catching
the sun?
When one fell, two would stay behind
  to comfort and then lead the way.
No homeless brother, nor wayward friend
  nor sister fallen astray.
And with feathers smoothed, unruffled
  from the boy who threw the stone.
As quiet as the dawn we'd rise
  to bring our brethren home.
And that's the lesson taught that any other might not see.
That's why I laugh when people say there's nothing on T.V.

  Lynley Fenwick

Futility

Running refugees with empty eyes,
Alone in the corner an aged man cries.
Millions of people are unable to feel.
All the while the soldiers are dropping the tears.
These destructive raindrops are harder than steel.
People are dying, no one cares.
But in the end, everyone dies.
The battlefield's littered with lakes of bodies.
Those who dare enter never survive.
The parents sit at home and watch.
The children stand in the window and stare.
Everyone's tangled in the bloody horror.
There are deaths that everyone bares.
The leaders, they fight for a lost reason.
The soldiers, they fight for an empty hate.
Fallen blood starts red rivers.
The red rivers run their fate.
The course twists and innocent die.
People will scream but the darkness continues.
Hidden in dark shadows, men can only cry.

  Haider Sharifi

Fear and Depression

Fear is the scorching sunset sitting on the hovering horizon,
Burning through your eyes, blinding you, creating an intricate
Illusion out of your unseen surroundings; they aren't as they seem.
It is the smoldering cigar of the unknown,
Blowing the smoke of confusion and
The ashes of ignorance upon you.
Fear is the roaring acid rain bewildering your brain,
Seering through your soft skin, burning your confidence,
And disintegrating your common sense.
Depression is the boring, black, barren plain,
Devoid of life and of happiness, dripping with the sadness of
eternal
  loneliness.
It is the gory graveyard of the endless,
Overflowing with the warped corpses of all you ever held dear.
Depression is the mind-numbing mist,
Eating your whole soul, digesting it in the tears of the
Fallen, and left in the pit of nothingness.

  Joshua Sorden

Do I Belong Here?

  Do I belong here?
Can you tell me what I need to hear?
Sometimes I live in such fear.
When I look in the mirror
I see a girl who does not show the fear,
her eyes burning with every tear.
She searches for someone far-n-near.
But all she finds is a lost face
in a mirror.
  Does this lost face belong here?
Can you what I need to hear?

  Janet Hoff

Love and Hate

What is love?

  It's the wind blowing round.
It's a dove flowing with the wind
never touching the ground. Hate is the
wind ceasing and never blowing again.
It's the dove flying alone without a
carrier to the end.

  The white dove is love sending peacefulness
around. Hate is the dove flying by without
making a sound. Love is the wind beginning
again, helping the dove find its way to the end.

  Travis Payne

Caring

As I near the end of life's journey
I have so many things to share
Did I judge poorly in daily liability
Yet does anybody really care?

Did I go out of my way to help someone
Extend a hand to those in despair
Carry through on a good intention
And does anybody care?

If I missed going to church on Sunday
and didn't say an evening prayer
Not reading the Bible or taking time to pray
Would anybody really care?

Recounting the friends I have today
that wonderful family there
The lovely wife who makes my day
I surely hope they care.

If I were to follow all my dreams
and enjoy the options there
Doing my best at least it seems
Then somebody should care.

  Calvin Nelson

Can't Control the Turntable

  Innocence was lost at the age of ten.
Never to be touched by another again.
  Guilt was gained by the silence she kept
And nobody knew that in solitude she wept.
  Obstacles she climbed with a burden on her back.
What she really needed was to be cut a little slack.
  Calluses bubbled in the back of her mind.
A clean, virgin conscience she wanted to find.
  Vengeance had grown in the depths off her soul.
The death of the sinner was her only goal.

  Barbara Rush

The Leak Is In Our House

Yesterday, we ran out of the rain
scrambling for shelter
in our new house
pregnant with hopes
dreams and aspirations.

It was sunrise
a new epoch, a new vision
weaved in our dream
the rain could not beat us
we had been sheltered in the new house

Then some lucky ones
occupied the center stage
leaving those on the fringes
yearning for better space
Some felt out of place...strangers in our own land

Some said we were almost there, don't rock the boat
we noticed and fanned flames of tribalism
and chocked menacingly those that didn't speak or look like us
we started blaming the rain instead of repairing the roof
It is not the rain anymore...the leak is in our house.

Bwosinde Hophine

Friends And Friendships

As you travel down life's road each day,
Friends are acquired in a variety of ways,
At work, church, lunch, on the street, or at play.
You enjoy their company and trust what they say.

Friendships are formed without regard to color or race.
Friends judge the beauty of the heart not the face.
They can be very supportive without crowding your space
And provide you with hope for the future of the human race.

Friendships sometimes require you to cultivate and tend
And yes occasionally you may even need to mend.
To maximize your friendships, learn not to break, but rather to bend,
Then be a truly good friend and it will be returned to you in the end.

Some friendships will last until you die.
While others come and go in the blink of an eye.
Some may drift away without even a good-bye.
A few will become special and you may not know why.

Best friends are a most interesting lot,
For they like you for who you are — or are not.
Who my best friend is requires no deep thought
For the woman I love is the best friend I've got.

Gene Hughes

Angel Needed!

Don't question why God choose to take
Your Mom beyond the sky,
Perhaps he needed an Angel
When he heard her painful cry.
He has a plan for all of us
We just don't know what and when,
Of one thing I am certain,
One day, we all meet again.
She went on ahead to smooth the road
You must travel alone my Friend,
If you ever need help, just call her,
She will be, just around the next bend.
It's OK to cry and reflect on your life
The tears will help cleanse your soul,
She was your Mother and she loved you,
Making a good Man of you was her Goal.
Her mission accomplished, she was the best,
God took her to her heavenly rest.

Angela Nugent

My Child, My Son

My child, my son,
  What is it you look for?
Is it faith in your fellow man
Is it strength in your body
Is it truth in society?

What is it you listen for?
Is it the message of your music
Is it the teaching of your God
Is it the feeling within your soul?

What is it you feel?
Is it the little boy within your heart
Is it the teenager you are
Is it the yearning to become an adult?

What is it you touch?
Is it the mind of someone with your thoughts
Is it the heart of someone with your love
Is it the soul of someone with your faith?

My child, my son,
  The answers are within your senses,
  The answers are within your reach.

Maryann Steinfeld

What Would You Wish?

If you had one wish what would it be?
Would it be something you'd do?
Or something you would see?
Would you choose to climb the highest mountain?
Or to someday find a youthful fountain?
Would you wish to see someone one last time?
Maybe to hear your wedding bells chime?
Would you wish to find some miracle cure?
You could wish for anything, are you sure?
But no matter what you wish could be
I must tell you it won't happen for free.
You have to have faith.
You have to believe.
Both in yourself and in what others achieve.
But with a little determination on your part.
The strength of your mind and a good heart.
You might be able to be one of the few.
To get what you want, your wish can come true.

Troy Campbell

Friendships Kindled

New friends and old, meet by chance...
Creating a warmth, whose vibes will dance.
United to share in a celebration...
Bringing feelings of joy, and exaltation.

New friendships and old resemble a fire...
Keeping them going is their desire...
Stoking the flames so new embers grow...
Still needing to kindle the old so it glows.

New friendships and fires are so much the same...
Slowly building and growing, till bursting in flames.
Old friends, like old fires, can flicker and die...
But it takes very little for them to revive.

The old must be revered, adorned, and quite cherished...
The new needs to be fed, and tenderly nourished.
New and old together can boast...
As they happily raise glasses, and propose a toast.

Edna Horowitz

Song of Soul

My soul wandered in alleys of things,
when the weight of living choked breath,
stumbling among debris,
blue and purple, it gasped for air.

Yet there was a time when
It heard the morning chatter of ducks claiming the day; when
It captured the swift flight of a tiny bird.
It was a moment of peace found

There was a time when
It noticed the river murmuring
the stories of each town passed, the spirit of each age lived
knowingly yet without insistence.
It was a moment of freedom found.

Listen, listen...listen to Silence;
Zephyr whisper the uttermost known secret,
Rustling leaves humm Adagio
of His profound Love.

Withered soul leap—s charged, then soar—s.
Epiphany.
It finds a moment of charity to love loathsome.

    Catherine Park

Goodbye

With such splendor and eminent beauty
A face words cannot describe
So young and filled with freedom
With vigor and a thirst for life

She conquered my heart with her smile
She captured my soul with her touch
It is she whom I want to be with
Yet my heart says she doesn't love me that much

Her presence I have known for years
Yet I don't know who she really is
She is approachable, but complex
Her true self is hidden behind her kiss

When she lays her eyes upon me
She is all I need to see
We are meant to be together
Forever, just her and me

To me she is the meaning of life
She has taught me how to fly
I know I truly love her
When it hurts to say goodbye

    G. G. Gallino

We Humans

We humans are a crazy bunch!
Sometimes we don't make sense.
We'd gladly help a stranded whale
but not give a dime for a begger's lunch.

We sacrifice jobs for the spotted owl.
Oh, yes, he's a natty bird.
But the cries and the pain of the unborn child
receive little but a frown or a scowl.

Yes, we humans are a crazy lot!
Wanting love and understanding,
giving hate and condemnation,
living by our own "tittle and jot".

    Mary Lou Lieblong

Morning Light

If only good-byes were known
Maybe the last wouldn't be as hard to say
For we always count on the sun to say good morning
Just as the moon has always said good night
So why has this morning lost the good
From within its sunrise so bright above our world
Until tomorrow my friend
I'll wait for the sunrise to lift me to you
Where farewells are never needed
As we will all be there to stay
Within the rays of the morning light

    Michael L. South

When The Rain Comes

I died alone in peace last night,
But by myself I was not.
People were waiting in my room
For what Death inevitably wrought.

They took my body far away
And placed it in a hole.
All around the land was bare
And empty like my soul.

I'm sure that if they opened me
My skin would gently tear.
They'd find that where my heart should be
My chest is hollow there.

People come and people go,
For some the world does cry;
But not a tear does it shed
When lonely people die.

    John A. Holton II

Beyond My Control

They are fighting again.
I press my head to the door
to try to make out what they are saying,
but all I hear is yelling.
It is about my sister
she snuck out again
and this time she got caught.
More yelling, then a door slams.
She is in her room now;
after they go to bed she will come in and talk to me -
she knows I am scared.
They think I went to bed a long time ago,
but I always wait up until she comes home.
Two knocks at the door
then it softly opens.
She has been crying.
She tucks me in and sits on the edge of my bed.
And I wordlessly fall asleep.

    Lindsey Ross

New Beginning

Glancing in the mirror, thinking of who I was before,
The pain lingers no more,
I once stumbled in the darkness, but now I can see,
My spirit flies like a dove, roaming free,
I feel the hand of contentment resting on me,
I looked for the answer, I so desperately needed to find,
The vines of unhappiness no longer have me wrapped up in a bind,
My enemy told me the walls of hate would never depart,
And slowly with patience I began to listen to my heart,
The thoughts of hopelessness can no longer penetrate me like a knife,
With endless determination I have erased the strife.

    Michelle L. Cook

200

Allow Leaving

Let your Soul Soar
With the birds below you and the crashing
ocean out of your reach.

Accept Freedom
and feel the rivers move
in and Undulating and Urgent Speech.

A Spontaneous Speech
clamming insight and Honesty, guiding us Patiently.

Let tomorrow be
out of reach and worry free.
Allow leaving
to be Patience's challenge and
Understanding's future.

See the land clearly and
Tempt the unpredictable Nature.

Grasp the air
and be mercifully blown away
by the intoxication that it Breaths.

Janette Hudson

The Sea Change

The sea is calm; the wind no
  longer still. It filters through
The mind removing all that is old
  and stagnant as night turns into dawn.

The captain stands at the helm of his ship
  controlling its pitch with charred finger tips.
The journey was straight thru hell and
  he was baptized in the devil's own well.

They all implore him to read from the
  log of his cruise,
But he remains as silent as a stubborn
  old mule.
His only words are to the effect
  that each man shall make his own trip,
And feel his own sweat dripping down
  his neck.

And when you have emerged the
  wise captain said,
"Thank God you're alive,
  and no longer dead."

Anthony J. Pagano

For This Child of Mine

I wish it were easy to tell you
  Just what's in my heart
I've always had you with me
  Tho we've always lived apart.

From the very first time I felt you move
  I've loved you from that day
So I can't describe the pain in my heart
  To have to give you away.

I prayed that God would protect you
  And keep you safe for me
With your parents, He'd love and guide you
  And in His arms you'd always be.

I want you to thank your parents
  For I could never thank them enough
If it had been just you and me, my child
  Things sure would've been pretty rough.

So, I'm sending you this poem
  And I hope that you can see
Tho others may have raised you
  You'll always be a part of me.

Amelia Belitza King

Four Corner Wound

A man of bitterness, of origins mysterious
Awaits his exodus from within his room.
  What has hampered, he often stammers
Me within this room.
  Long he ponders, often he wanders
To a corner of his tomb.
  One is sorrow, from people it's borrowed
Often taking man too soon.
  One is lust of those you trust
That brings us to our ruin.
  One is shame, yourself the blame
Acceptance of an early doom.
  One is memories, the mind's eye delicacies
That keeps us within the room.
This is life, in all its strife
  A four corner wound.

Brandon R. Evans

The Silent Dialogue

My holy poet, what are the holiest words?
  Her answer is,
"Truth, beauty, love, and poetry are
  the holiest words."
My frank poet, how do you define truth?
  Her response is,
"Truth is the knowable intuition in the
  ears of the religious poets."
My beautiful poet, describe to me what beauty is.
  Her description is,
"Beauty is the divine elatedness in the
  hearts of the artistic poets."
My affectionate poet, what is the meaning of love?
  Her reply is,
"Love is the zenithal devotion in the
  minds of the romantic poets."
My musical poet, what is poetry?
  Her answer is,
"Poetry is the sentimental lifeblood in the
  eyes of the visual poets."

Donna Fay Pearson

Sailor

I am a sailor.
I sail with the wind.
It lifts me high on the currents
and drops me gently back to earth again.
Sometimes I sail so high,
I think I can touch the very top of the sky.
I've flown to many places and seen many majestic sights.
I've flown over the aspens,
bathed in the most brilliant reds and golds.
I have flown over rolling plains.
I've flown through the largest cities
and over the smallest towns.
I have felt the clouds in my wings
and the warmth of the sun on my back.
I've been to places people can only dream of.
Everyday my journey ends, and yet it is never ending.
The things I've seen are forever etched in my mind.
I have always flown alone and my thoughts belong to me.
I am a sailor.

Magdalena Dimas

Eclipse

When I saw the light that was coming down
hitting the Earth, bathing the ground,
I never knew I would travel around
the Planet Earth, at the speed of sound.

The stars were witnesses of my experience,
they twinkled once; they twinkled twice,
letting me know when the Sun would arrive.
The Golden King with his Golden Rays,
was giving light to the Milky Way.

Mother Moon and Father Sun, in a mystic
reunion were coming together, and I was
there to witness their wedding.
Once in a while they would do the same
and for eons and eons they'll do it again.

When I came back with the moonlight gleaming,
then I realized that I had been dreaming.
It was a dream, I have no doubt...
God...Can you tell me what this is all about?

Norma Cordova

Open Mind

We often wonder, Why are we here
What purpose we serve, Year after year

God made man, Jesus died for our sins
Yet he keep blessing us, Again and again

Believing in God, Our hearts grow strong
With the Lord on our side, We can never go wrong

Many steep hills, So hard to climb
At the end of our journey, Our soul is fine

Serving God, So easy to do
That is all, he ask of you

Be faithful to him, As well as yourself
When his ship comes in, You won't be left

So stop your wondering, If your life's a waste
You know it's just God, Testing your faith

Beatrice Spicer

Revealed in the Stone

I stood today where someone wept and cried,
    grief's burden deeply ingrained in her soul.
'Tis an anguish which surges throughout one's being
    lancing the spirit, longing for that person once more to hold.

A gentle breeze caresses the stone, sweeping
    away the leaves of seasons long past.
Oh! Gentle breezes bring with you peace to accept
    this bitterness that boils beneath her breast.

Dear One, how was your life? Your hopes and all your dreams?
    Your early years of childhood, the carefree joy of play.
The years of young adulthood, with the child so sweet and dear.
    Those blessings of life gratefully recited daily as you
would pray.

I wish to tell you, for you should know, in life you did excel
    for on this place, she deeply grieved as no other
As you were laid to rest - inscribed in stone, your life in words
    For you are her Beloved Mother.

Caron Withers Snyder

Forget Me Not

The wall is cold with its many parts
But it brings back my friends and heals my heart.

Taken too young from my side
I still hear your battle cry.

So carve away the many names
Place them in your Military Graves.

Forget what happened so far away
You left our P.O.W.s and M.I.A.s

2500 so bold, to our Government we told
In cages and jails our buddies they keep
While our mothers, fathers, wife's still weep.

Try to forget-speak not of them
Because of that war we did not win.

But for me I'll always be true
I'm a Marine some of my buddies were to.

So cross me not speak no wrong of them
I'll still go back to fight and find my friends.

William J. Karandos

Kissing Lee in the Library

Among the shelves and cases
towering high above,
we kiss.
Can they see us? Are they watching?
The masters of language, lovers of emotion,
all immortal in symmetrical rows.
The Spirits are there, but do they see us?
Do they care?
Are they jealous that we captured
in seconds
what they devoted life to mirror?
Do they smile and wish for kisses too?
Surrounded by words and the Spirits of their creators,
we kiss again.

Amber Reeme

Have You Lived?

Have you lived a good life?
Has your life been a success?
By what means do we measure
A life's worth, more or less?
Have you held a newborn child?
Have caring arms held you?
Have you ever watched as grey skies
Were chased away by blue?
Have you ever helped a stranger
When a stranger was in need?
Have you ever been the object
Of a warm and caring deed?
Have you cried and crawled through hardship?
Have you laughed at hardship's end?
Has another person ever
Considered you a friend?
Then truly you have lived
A life of greatest worth.
So enjoy each extra moment
You're blessed with on this earth.

Todd E. Hathaway

Music Dead

The clouds grow dark.
Flashes appear across the night.
Thunder rips open the sky and lets rain wash down on the earth.
The piano player starts the piece.

The thunder beats the rhythm louder.
Zigs and zags appear across the blue and purple.
Like a strobe on a TV screen the player is silhouetted
If but for a brief moment.

The beat grows louder.
So does the piano
Building its way to a frenzied crescendo.

The thunderstorm comes to a halt.
The beat goes on.

John H. Church

Silent Prayer

Aw Lord, lend me your attentive ears
Hear my withered voice
Look out through my painful eyes and see what I see.
This here fire is striving to provide for the room's warmth
As I watch my family playing an endless game of dominoes
Their faces are strict and concentrated
For they have become more involved with the black and white game than
their own lives.
But my granddaughter sits alone, impatiently pouting;
Once again she cannot take part in an event because she is too young.
Just as I remember, the innocent cries of babies being thrown overboard;
Thank you Lord for having me of able age
For I too could have been swallowed up buy the hungry sea.
And so, I knit a quilt of whose colors remind me of the land from which I came
A heritage no other could rob me of
Yet, so little my mind recollect at this age,
A culture of which I wished to live
Instead of slaving more than half my life away
For men and women of no difference other than the shade of their skin.
Now my children and my decent will go through endless years of change
Like the domino effect which rests in their hands.

Katie Bakes

Change

I've been here before
  And I'll be back here again
    Before I lie down from my chores

Shaken, shattered beliefs
  Disrupted, disintegrated self
    Terrifying, awesome anticipation ... of the unknown

In order to change
  Something must die
    And yet, I — as a whole — must live
      Or I will have not changed ... only died

The last time
  I passed through
    Such profound change

Something was lost
  Something died
    But so much was born new

And I did so much more than live ... I soared!

J. M. Worgan

The Death of the Sparrow

The death of the sparrow on that euphoric spring day
During the bloom of the flower, was due to fate, things
Not understood, a fight taken astray. Or maybe it was
Distracted by a heavenly package from the Guf God had sent
That day. It snapped its neck as it hit my leg. I became the
Barrier of fate when it flew into the garden. Its beak poked deep
Into my skin then it fell upon a broken marble state. The birds
In the trees sang on and did not hesitate.

I picked him off of the polished slate, which his blood had failed to
Stain. There in my hand he lay. One a million sparrows in
Flight, its death, I'm sorry, would not disturb my nights. What
A small death indeed. It had left no mark, no scar, no stain.
And on no one's heart did I leave a weighted pain. However, as I
Dropped it in the lapping in the trees, nature continuing on through
The din of the breeze. A single tear I could have wept over a
creature that once through the air had swept, over the cold body of
one of Nature's arrows, for no one would mourn the death of a
sparrow.

James Coulter

Untitled

Trumpets herald merger news.
Loyal ears listen with pride.
Makes them feel bigger inside.

Blindness of loyalty and reflexive emotions
Sense of elation and this is the key: A bigger corporation is a
  bigger me.
Lives long ago molded to corporate form
Illusions of security based on seniority
Betrayals delivered by those suited to kill

Rank and choose. Break the news.
Tally the numbers. Act with finesse.
Mass executions minimize mess
Economics of scale; no time for bail.
The tap on the shoulder a prelude to death.

Reengineer, restructure. Merge, Redeploy.
Eliminate jobs and force out to the street.
Layoff lingo; gigolo jingle.
Somber tune for moving soon
Corporate shearing. Human pruning.

Merger transition is not a cheap thrill
We all pay the bill.

Loretta Ramseyer

Days Gone By

Trying to recapture those days that didn't seem so important then;
Where did they all go - where all have I been?
Reminiscing the hours I thought were well spent.
Now, I'm wondering - where have they all went?
Precious are the moments of every hour of every day.
Cause once they're gone - they're gone to stay.
I can always look back and either laugh or cry.
And most of the time - I'll ask myself why
For yesterday's gone - there's no turning back for a while.
The best I can hope for is to live each day with a smile.
For it's the little smile each day that no one forgets.
Trying to look over the tears, the pain, and the small regrets.
So, I've learned to live each day the best I possibly can.
For it's yesterday's memories that make me what I am.

Barbara Scoggins

La Vivante Reve

We take for granted very simple things
That are the genuine miracles of life;
Dreams on gold and silver wings
Flying above others doomed to strife.

Hope and faith will save that dream
From breaking its lovely wings.
Hope will, like a moonbeam,
Glow brightly from a heart that sings.

And in saving that dream from dying,
Or simply fading sadly away,
Faith will keep it flying
To change the world another day.

They say one man can stop the world's sighing,
But that's not quite true;
For without hope and faith to keep it flying,
Do you think that man's dream could have ever flew?

Emilie Staat

What Will Be, Will Be

If the stars fall from the sky and the sun leaves, never to return,
How can I be left in the dark if inside me your love still burns?
How can I fail with your loving hand to guide me?
What will be, will be.

Higher than the sky, deeper than the sea, your love inside of me
So, if this world rages and knocks me to my knees,
If I'm left alone and love is hard to see,
What can I say but what will be, will be?

If the pain runs deep and the reasons are unclear
If friendships seems to fade and laughter turns to tears
What can I say when my life seems just so many wasted years?
What will be, will be.

I scream at the raging sun, cry to the cold, silent moon
What once lent me hope now offers only gloom
I silently voice my hopeless question to the sky
Lord, won't you please tell me why?

I wait and pray and then comes this reply -
Love is patient, love is kind, it always protects, always trusts,
always hopes, always perseveres, love never fails
Not knowing what lies ahead, yet knowing God is in control and His
very nature love,
I can say what will be, will be.

Tim Kuhn

Face in the Mirror

A lonely girl staring in the mirror,
Does not recognize her own face,
She notices it has been torn away,
By time and space.

She turned into something she was not,
To serve his taste,
That is why she could not,
Even recognize her own face.

Her happy childhood,
Flashed before her eyes,
She got worse as time went by,
As she hid behind rumors and lies.

She started to have an image,
Unrecognized popularity,
After thinking of herself,
She found in her life an absence of clarity.

After they parted,
No reasons implied,
She still had to hide,
Behind rumors and lies.

Amy Bartek

The Eagle and the Owl

The eagle is free and free of sin,
It was he who saw the condition that God's precious earth is in.
So he flew away to the spirit world above
To help save us from our sins and show him of our love.

Soon the owl will take that flight to join the eagle in the sky.
When we no longer hear his voice in the night,
All we can do is bid them "Goodbye"
And if the eagle is away in the day, and the owl is away at night
Think of all that will die with them,
The earth, eventually included, in that plight.

All things created... should be appreciated
From the cradle and throughout one's life.
It's everyone's purpose, if for no other reasons
To keep our home, the earth, in it's best seasons
    In order to survive.

But if by chance, it does not,
And we gave it our best shot...
If we do our part to help protect the earth as he shows us the way.
God will lift us up with the eagle and the owl.
And we'll all make that journey to a new earth someday!

Dianne Ford

My Husband Doesn't Understand

My husband doesn't understand this need to write
And then to be published with no money
in sight
He can't understand, the self satisfaction
Knowing I can write, and give someone
else pleasure
Make their life a little more bright
maybe give them a laugh
Letting them know that hope in sight
For this is the reason I write

Connie Rose

My Name Is Michael

My name is Michael, I have a dream
that one day I'll become a man
And when I do, I'll always remember
My mother and all she did for me

Now I am a man. I met a girl.
Her name is Marie.
We married and were blessed with three
beautiful children.

We had "our" dream, we loved each other so very much!

Then one day, I came home, a doctor was
There — sadly, he said to me,: Michael, your
dear wife is gone, gone from this earth.
I cried, "I don't know what I'll do! How can I go on?
Then a peace came over me (I know it was the soul of Marie)
And then I knew — I'll go on raising my children
The best I can — Until I die and go the
Land of the free (heaven).
Where the sky is so blue and be with the one
I've loved so long — my sweet Marie.

Jimmy Bruce

The Tallest Mountains

There are mountains that reach so high,
    so high they touch the sky
with their steep slopes and pointed peaks,
Who really know how far they reach?
Some have tried to reach the very, very end,
They have again, again, and again,
Some have succeeded, yet many have not
in climbing the long journey to the top.

Deborah Baker Willard

Flowers

I took a walk among the flowers.
Hence, I lingered there for hours.
The beauty of their upturned faces,
like an uplift of God's graces.

There was peace and beauty all around,
like no other place I have found.

Love is there, happiness too.
It clearly reminds me of you,
Reliable, understanding, tall and straight.
yet soft and gentle is your fate.

I take a walk among the flowers,
when I want to spend with you the hours.
You are there, I am there.
I know you always care.

Fern M. Bates

Not Alone

I remember a child, small quiet,
without fright, seemingly alone, handed
into the outstretched arms of a stranger.

I remember a child, alone, surrounded
by curious eyes never seen before,
offering a smile in return.

I remember a child, alone in a new world at
the end of a long journey traveled,
although so far apart, a family waited
with love in their heart.

I remember a child, alone, not knowing the
love being given, you were deserving
a home all your own.

I remember love looking, embracing that
child thru memories few years past, joy
and laughter felt, now together at last.

I remember a child, small, quiet, without fright.
He's not alone, he's found a home.

Laura Ann Kern

Your Palette

The colors of your palette
speak of strong confident hues,
brilliant yet deeply subdued.
Under the infusion of titanium white,
ultramarine and cobalt blue,
You Dare.

Captured in a face of cadmium,
locks in umber and burnt sienna
outlined in dark mars.
Strength and power of self
surrounded in ivory and ferrous black.
In the swirl dark hunter green and solid crimson,
personifies your creation from memory.

Infusion of ethereal colors
carefully guarded in two dimensions.
Slowly in time, you are unmasked.
A free invitation to paint in accurate breadth
from the true colors of your palette.

Mercedes F. Whalen

The Narrowing Path

A Prayer

Send me the Comforter, Lord.
  And not the Avenger for the wages of sin,
  Not exhortations to pluck out my eye,
  Or cut off my hand, if they offend You
The path is narrowing and treacherous, now,
  And I need support along the way
Threats of eternal damnation!
  Were more appropriate to my lustful youth
Not these later pain filled years,
  Both physical and emotional
  Years of loss and decay—
Send me someone who understands, Lord,
  Not this boy still wet behind the ears
  Who, himself, seems anchored by fears
I want soaring words of hope and joy
  I want to be lifted up high and higher
  On currents of love and promise
Send me The Comforter, Lord, and
  Please, remove this interloper from my path

Bette Gwathmey

Star Gazer

Gaze upon the midnight sky,
and there I will be.
I am the blackness of the night.
I am the coldness of the wind.
The stars are my eyes.
They see all.
The darkness is my cloak,
it keeps me warm.
The lightning and thunder are my anger and frustration.
The rain, my saddened tears.
I gaze down upon you
and wish I were there.
For I am eternal in an eternal void.
I feel dead and alone.
But I am not dead, nor am I alive.
And this shall be forever.
Yet, I sit and wonder if it is.
That is the price I pay
to be a star gazer.

Aaron Crumbliss

Things I've Seen

I sit up late at night, and think about things I've seen.
Like little children playing, in fields of green;
I've seen the rich man cry, and the poor man smile;
The condemned man walk, the last lonely mile.

I've seen sunshine at midnight, and darkness at noon,
Men under the ocean, and man on the moon;
New life's beginning, and old life's demise;
The communist man fall, and a free nation rise.

I've seen people get lucky, and then lose it all,
And the east and west, knock down a cumbersome wall;
I've seen life outside, from behind jail bars;
And laid on my back in the grass, and watched shooting stars.

I've seen the rain feed the corps, then wash them away,
And men speaking loudly, with nothing to say;
I've seen people who are dirty, and claiming to be clean;
And these are just a few, of the things I've seen.

Joseph A. Webster

205

A Spring Mealtime Prayer

Lord we thank you for today,
seems like winter has passed away.

We thank you to for signs of spring,
for flowers that bloom, and birds that sing.

For this our food too, we thanks would give,
bless it to our good Lord that we may live.

And Lord help us today true lights to be,
That others may see that Christ lives in me.

Junior Hoffman

And....We All Fall Down

On a clear day in '73, how easily remembered,
Saying, "I Do", in the month of November.
To forever love and cherish each other
Without knowing there was another.

Seventeen years had come to pass,
Before The Affair was discovered, at last.
Counseling and doctors could not mend,
Or put these lives together again.

Alcohol, lies, abuse and deceit,
Knock an unsuspecting family off its feet.
Children change and go astray
The life you once knew, in total disarray.

Twenty-three years later, prayers for strength go on
From the dark of Night, to break of dawn,
Hoping to find peace in future years,
Erase disillusionment and calm fears.

What type of justice should prevail
When two people destroy lives, perhaps jail?
For, not only the Family crumbles and hits the ground,
Society as a whole decays, and ... We all fall down.

Dawn Basak-May

Open Letter To Michael

No longer will I be Blue
Over some love that was never true.

I swear this time I'll wait and never settle,
She will come along, for my heart's sake she'd better.

Her eyes will be like Heaven
Inviting me to soar beyond the stars.

She will have a soul as fresh as spring,
Realizing and accepting that I am a King.

Like the moonlight, shining through all adversity.
Yes, that's how I need her soul.
My queen will be true all the way through.
If God willing I will find her. No longer will I be Blue.

Michael Joseph Lowe

Upholding An Inherited Distinction

Upholding an inherited distinction
In Art and Order, dimly lit for thrift
A desk and chair retain in upright posture
And portraits give capable assent,
As marble clock atopped with prancing stallion
Sends chimes to skim the highly polished floor

Elizabeth Nye Byram

The Flower

A seedling quickly grows to a flower bud.
A flower blooms into a brilliant color.

It stands out against the mud.
A light spreads over the vivid plant
Giving it lush leaves.

A simple shower helps it grow,
And spreads its roots.
Bugs and ants eat on its shoots.

All faces turn to the setting sun.
Dark has come, it is night
For there is no more light.

A petal falls, then another.

Withering, dying, full of pain.
Then at once, dead.
It is the end. But a seedling
Grows still beside it.

Then it starts the cycle again.

Jordan Ashley Shouse

Love At First Sight

I never believed in love at first sight
'til I saw you standing in a crowd,
Your smile shining bright.
You looked my way with a smile and a wink.
I wondered if you noticed my cheeks turning pink.
I didn't know if I was your kind of girl
I'm not very fancy
And I've never traveled around the world.
But you took my hand
And ask me to be your wife
You say you would love me
And make me happy for the rest of my life.
You said you would stay with me
In sickness and in health.
I promised to love you
More than anyone else.
Every time our eyes meet
When you smile and give me that wink
I know that everything is alright
Cause when I look in your eyes it's love at first sight.

Rusty Scott

"Maxie" In Loving Memory

We had a little dog who was happy and gay,
We had him almost fourteen years and he was always that way.
He came to our home so very frightened and shy,
What am I doing here, he could not understand why.
We gave him much love, good food and affection,
And soon he learned he was ours for protection.
He was always so content sitting on his master's knee,
And the way he cuddled, he was happy as could be.
He gave us his love, which was far beyond measure,
And that is something we shall always treasure.
We miss the pitter-patter of his dear little feet,
And even to "Cindy" the house is not complete.
He now rests in the garden where he loved to run,
To see him scamper was ever so much fun.
He chased little birds, chipmunks and such,
But he really would not harm them, He liked chasing so much.
We shall never forget our dear little "Maxie" boy,
because for many years he gave us so much joy.

Frieda Keil

Street Life

They were distant - looking through the barred window
but right at home on the other side...

Strangers at this time
friends a little time later...

Young at heart
older than their years...

Lost and alone in the beginning
united in "Hope" at the end...

One for all
all for one...

Susan C. Owens

Missing In Action

Silently he slithers through the murky gloom
Jungle fatigues he wears, with his sense of doom
A lush green jungle menacing and still
Such beauty hiding an enemy, waiting to kill

Killer of women and children, back home they tell
His guts scream out, war is hell
Broken in mind, the wounded body will fall
Back home they hide him, caged behind a wall

Oh, another wall of honor they built, they say
My buddies and tourists come and visit each day.
Too late, a nineteen year old cries for who I am
No monument, a reward for Vietnam.

Today, I sit behind a desk,
I fight the anguish, my thoughts to rest
Missing in Action, my youth did not come home
In a lush green jungle, forever, it wanders alone,

Fifty years old, I still cry for who I am
My boyhood, Missing in Action in Vietnam.

Evelyn Robinson

I Looked Around

I looked around and morning came
and what a sight to see.
The dew had watered and bathed each plant.
Oh, such a place to be.

The trees held fruit so full and fine.
Vegetation flourished of every kind.
Flowers were many. Every color it seemed.
I awoke in the morning, It was not a dream.

I looked around and it was noon.
The morning had vanished much to soon.
The sun overhead had made everything dry.
It felt so warm I understood why.

I looked around and evening was nigh.
Then, so soon, God painted the sky.
A sunset so brilliant. Such colors to behold.
Then the night came and brought with it the cold.

I look around and night is here,
bringing shadows, then dark, that makes man fear.
As night flees on we're weary and worn.
But, look at the sky. It's almost morn.

Kathleen S. Brooks

The End

Will all thought be removed from the conscious soul,
While we lie in utmost exile, with nothing to occupy our hearts,
Will the fear dissipate, or only consume our souls in eternal terror,
for that which is unknown, can reveal so much,
I wish it away but it creeps, showing me what I will not ever
understand,
for the taking I have beheld, as for such I fear,
exhausting the limits of imagination, only to have me lie sleepless,
conjuring, waiting.
will I pass through the gates,
with only my thoughts as witness, my soul interrogated,
on trial for unavoidable crimes, unknown,
guilty or innocent, for only he knows truth,
if he exists at all, or was simply invented for such,
if my heart is ripped from its walls, I will not willingly retire,
for I am not complete, my selfishness shall not let me,
unavoidable its comes, whether of not willing,
at peace or in defiance,
the end

Richard H. Bilson

Vicious Game

Before this night is over, their love will be lost
She's not trying anymore, it's not worth the cost
Leaving has been coming for so very long
She's not always right, but she's not always wrong
Before this night is over, they'll go their separate ways
When it comes to losing, it's her heart that always pays
She can't stand to be with him
Can't bear it by herself
So she'll just live a lonely life
With her heart upon a shelf
Before this night is over, she'll think about the past
And wonder where the good times went, and why they couldn't last
She'll wake up in the morning with one thought inside her head
"Is he wondering where I am now, is he sorry that I fled?"
Before this night is over, their love will reconcile
And everything will be alright for just a little while
But soon it will all start again, it's such a crying shame
That love, something so beautiful, is such a vicious game

Pam Kramer

God's Plan

He was born to a world I will never know,
Or try to understand.

I questioned much and reasoned why
And wondered of God's plan.

A little one who could not speak
Or reach to touch my face.

"O Lord," I asked, "What have you done?"
My faith was then disgraced.

'Cause in my grief-I failed to see
The gifts that had been passed.

The lessons learned from that small child
Will now and forever last.

For all the things we were denied,
In volumes I have gained.

I found a way to love someone
And reason through the pain.

Stephen W. Roe

Touch

Tell me not of your hunger
When I am thirsty for affection.
For I may give into the darkness of your starving eyes.

Tell me not of your desires when fear has
Taken the last I could give.
For I am empty of words and feelings.

Tell me not of your sorrow when I sleep
For I may wake to find a lonely child in my arms.

Tell me not of your dreams tonight.
For reality has invaded my soul,
And I can't help but to love you.

Tell me not of your future plans when
The present is happening now.
For I may not be here tomorrow.

So, I ask you..
Please, don't tell me anything.
For the warmth of your arms
Is all that I need,
And all that I can comprehend.

Tanya M. Casey

The Dam Builders

They ride the wire amid walls of yellow rock
In the space between is and isn't.
Three men hanging under a paleozoic sky
Muscle the ageless river into submission.
Two more labor on the bloodcurdling rim
Just beyond fingertip salvation.

Indifferent as stone,
A cable snaps,
Rears its head
Just once
Then viperlike,
Attacks.

Five men falling, falling, falling into the shadows
Of silent bottomstrike.

Amid the walls of yellow rock,
Under a paleozoic sky, in the space between is and isn't,
The daughter of a wild land
Knows the man-eating canyon has
Muscled her life into submission.

Teri Downard

The Gift

Your love of life
pushing the boundaries of experience,
feeling the tension and joy therein,
was first revealed to me
in that cathedral
called Yosemite.
Your love, contagious,
prodded open my sleeping eye
stirring awake the yearning to be,
changing the direction
of my awareness,
cutting through self imposed limitation.

And we meet again under a full moon, mist on the waters.
You cleared a circle
sifting fingers of earth through those strong hands
whispering words of love and gratitude
to our mother, endearing hearts words, that echoed from soul.
Taking my hand in yours, compressing the great mother
between us, sharing that love as sacrament to our oneness
with all that is.
Thank you David.

Lois Hutson

Through My Eyes

I see the smoke rising from the buildings;
Hear the sounds of the birds singing,
I observe this by looking out of
The window; from up above
I notice the things going on below.
Lo I hear this, I fear this unconscious world;
Behold I tell them, but no one is listening to this black pearl.
The self destructive paranoia; the behavior is what you savor.
I still ask of you this favor to be aware; don't you see the glare?
If you don't then stop and stare, but I guess
You're lost cause my voice you don't hear. You're stagnant.
All these negative forces is pulling you towards like a magnet.
Why can't you realize it, we're living in a bottomless pit
It's an abyss; now you're a victim of it.
The negativity; the inability of all this anxiety.
I keep calling, but you don't hear me.
It's all so scary now you have no where to run no — where
To turn; in this fire you will burn.
No more the king, I thought you would be just because you lost sight
Of the promise land, now you've lost sight of the destiny.

Nadine Dillon

Horror Story

Storm clouds streaked across the sky
Frightened birds would screech and cry
The murky night looked catastrophic
Like some to me that is gravely gothic
Lightning flashed and thunder crashed
Ancient oaks were cruelly slashed
He had known this night would come
Known it would not do to run
It had appeared to him in a ghostly vision
A deadly fateful premonition
Things would be dreadful and then get worse
It was like a witches curse, chanted in satanic verse,
As his final candle began to gutter
He was heard to grimly mutter,
"Someone ate my peanut butter".
Said it in a mournful stutter,
"S.S.C Someone ate me p-p-peanut butter".

W. G. Der Gerste

My Love Is...A Kindred Soul

My love is...a kindred Soul
As bright as gold, and never cold

To feel the bliss, of his first kiss
I cannot miss...

The warmth of healing so deep, revealing,
An honest feeling

Adventure is Living!
His goal-giving

Travel's exciting-
A thrill, inviting

To hold each other
And know your lover

Be with during your life
With ne'er so much strife

Loving together, your spirits unfold

Yes, he is...
My kindred soul.

Debbie Lohrman

One of a Dozen

I was one of a dozen and sixth from the top
too young to know if we were poor or not
I never thought from where our next meal would come
when mama called dinner we went on the run

Mama cooked us three meals every day
we gathered at the table in our routine way
No need to cry, no use to complain
winter or summer it was always the same

The next six had a different situation
bad got worse with the Great Depression
the food got scarce with more mouths to feed
love had to be a good source of energy

They made fishing nets, quilts and cut wood for pay
to buy more food for the long winter days
the mornings were cold but the food was hot
I'm a witness to this I was sixth from the top

My daddy was a story teller second to none
mama was an angel with five daughters and seven sons
If I have another life and a choice who I'll be
I'd be one of a dozen in a share croppers family

Elizabeth C. Wickersham

An Old Man's Search for Joy

Can a man of old age find joy in his day
of old? Truly there is joy and light!
If he search in the deepest core of his heart,
there is a light, brighter than the sun that shine
each day, whether it be sunny or gray.
A light of truth that stands still in his heart,
as the candle without the fire, that desires, a
spark. Waiting to explode as a huge volcano,
or maybe a flick of flint.
Truly joy is in the light, that is deep in his
heart. If he search after it, it will grow. If
he refuse it, it will continue to drift away,
as a bottle cast into the open sea, or a kite
airborne with a broken string.
"Joy, light, all the same within the heart,
hidden deep as the fossils of the days of old.
"Search" I say, as looking for a hidden
treasure, while the time of life beats as the wave
against the rocks on the sea shore. Before life
is no more, find it quick, joy in the light of the heart.

Kelvin Broadwater

God's Littlest Angel

God lent us an angel the day that we had you.
He said he would be back to watch and guide us through.
The joy you've brought into our lives is almost impossible
to describe.
You fill each day with your sunshine ways.
Your spirit is so bright.
We will do our best, for we've been blessed with a little
baby, you.
You have touched our hearts, our minds, and our souls.
We know that one day you will want to fly.
And we will have to let you go.
But remember that we are here, and that you always have
a home.
Life is hard and hurts sometimes.
It's just a passageway.
For the Lord has great things in store on the final day.
We love you!
Always...
Mom and Dad

Imelda Donnelly

A Mother's Love

A loving smile, a tender kiss
A kind word, a gentle hug
This is a mother's love
A stroll through the part, a forgiving heart
A helping hand, the look of strength,
The feeling of safety
This is a mother's love,
When things go wrong,
She tries to comfort us,
Her smiles are as warm as
The summer's sunshine,
Her kisses are always soft and tender
A kind word at the right time,
She will always render,
Her words of encouragement
Are uplifting and wise,
I can feel her strength
When I stare into her brown eyes
I always feel safe when she is near
No nothing will ever replace My mother so dear.

Yvonne Garrett

Big Mama Got An Ice Pick

Ma was sitting down, out of the steamy hot sun
in her favorite wicker chair with ragged ends
sticking out on the side.
She was so hot and tired
she took Big Daddy's hat—
even though he got cancer in the head—
but she really don't care.
She rocked in her chair, swaying back and forth,
and she thought "no one gonna mess with me."
She could feel the hot sun beating up her black skin.
She sat and relaxed and smelled and the smell of Louisiana,
the lemony, fragrant scent of the sweet magnolias.
She sat and thought about
her life and how it had gone by soo fast.
The dress she wore was
her mother's, so you know how big she was.
Then one of her grandchildren comes up to her
with an ice pick, and hands it to his grandma.
She takes it and strikes a wicked pose.

Sabeen Faruqui

Promise Keeper's Poem

I'm a Promise Keeper, a man of Integrity,
With just seven promises I vow to keep,
A man committed to a lifetime of Christianity,
For Jesus is my shepherd and I one of his sheep.

We'll tear down the walls of racial and denominational barriers,
Jesus is our Savior and we his message carriers,
For he died on the cross to set us free,
Because he paid the debt, I receive him on bended knee.

I honor Jesus through obedience, worship and prayer,
Building strong marriages and families through love, values and care,
Pursuing vital relationships with a few other men,
And when a brother is down, helping him back up again.

I'm committed to practicing purity; whether spiritual or moral,
Learning to forgive my brother after a quarrel,
Trying to make a difference in the world I live,
And supporting the church through time and resources I give.

I vow to seize the moment and make a difference,
Trying to make right out of a world that's confused and tense,
Honoring the Great Commandment and Commission through
   obedience,
For I'm a Promise Keeper, a man of substance.

Pat Kastler

A New Mother's Midnight

As I walk to my bedroom,
The stillness of the house is welcoming.
Shadows dance on the wall from the street light,
As a dog barks in the distance.

My brain signals to me that my body
Is ready for a good night's sleep.
While I recall my eventful day,
In my new role as a mother.

Once again, I step lightly into your room,
To assure that you are safe and secure.
When I reposition your cotton blanket,
Your small face looks so peaceful and angelic.

As I say my nightly prayers,
I ask for help to be a good mother
And that my choices and decisions for you,
Will be the correct ones.

At last, I can tuck myself in.
You are securely asleep in your crib.
And I have asked our Father above,
To help me in this new role as a mom.

Beverly Botts

Spring

Spring is a special time of year,
When all the snow seems to disappear.

The grass that has been yellow and brown,
Turns beautifully green all around.

The robins are chirping and singing a tune,
The flowers will all soon start to bloom.

The trees stand so tall with all their new leaves,
And out from their holes come ants, beetles and bees.

There is children's laughter everywhere,
Breathing in the great fresh air.

Everything seems so fresh and new,
Along with the sky so bright and blue.

This beauty comes from up above,
It's God showing us all His love.

Sandra T. Craigle

Him

The sun shone bright this morning.
And as it crossed the sky,
I thought of years of gold, when happiness would made me cry.

The years roll by so slowly, yet at times they seem too fast,
Has Our love been severed,
My heart can feel the pain,

It does me good to be away, I yearn to conquer grief,
Give me time with him alone,
Just to talk with, he who knows me,

He knew me from my mothers womb,
His ways reach far beyond the stars,
He is faithful to be my keeper, when I want to cry but cannot not.

Give me those golden years of old'
To hold within my heart, but give me too, a new start.

I know this much of those I love.
That he's their Keeper too.
I rest at ease in knowing, that a times they cry too,

He hold our tears in a bottle, He is there in time of need
At times I like to be with him,

His love can strengthen me.

Stephen Yoke

Our Mother

Our Mother is so brave and strong;
she doesn't let us know something's wrong.

She doesn't want us to worry;
but, the pain only comes and makes her blurry.

She feels she hasn't given all there is to give;
that is why she is struggling so hard to live.

I hope she realizes and could only know;
she has given us everything we needed to grow.

All we want is her to be in peace;
there is nothing for us to learn or her to teach.

Day after day she takes the pain;
and tries hard not to cry or complain.

However, last night as I watched her sleeping;
you could feel her pain, as she was unknowingly weeping.

When the time has come I know in my heart;
that in God's eternal plan she has a big part.

I wish that I was a brave as she.
Maybe, Mom, someday I will be!

Elayne Allison

God Is With Me

In time's of trouble, when I am down,
I count my blessings, and look around.
At all of God's wonders, that He made for me,
There are so many for me to see.

This lovely earth, on which we live,
Is only part of what God did give,
He gave me life and my will to love,
And if I'm wise, He'll give to me,
My place, in Heaven above.

God is with me, every single day,
He always listens, when I stop to pray.
I am not worthy of these precious things.
But God is still with me, in all my sufferings.

Barbara J. Fowler

Trusting Jesus

It is right to trust Jesus Christ
He'll never lead you wrong.
He is only capable of doing right.
Life without Jesus is a way of woe
Truly what no one needs wherever
They are or wherever they go,
A pain free life is what I seek and
Jesus Christ helps me to sleep, in
Total peace and tranquility.
I love trusting Jesus because he is
Always right and I know he leads
Me to living a good life.
Trusting in Jesus with all my mind,
Heart and soul is God commandment and
The right way to believe.
Jesus is a true light and great guide
In a world of darkness to heaven being the destiny.
Though I am poor and needy, I truly feel rich and
I thank God it's been all made possible the Creator and
the Lord Jesus.

Catherine D. Feathus

Love

I look at you and I see a person who cares and appreciates life
You are always there
All you give is love, and sometimes I do not appreciate what I
   receive
But you must understand that I love you, and I am lucky to
   have you
When you don't agree with me, I make a big fuss
Half the time I don't realize that you're right
For every day and night I will love till the day I die
And in my head I will always think and pray for you.

Gina Curcio

The Year of 88

Two young people met while in their teens
But went separate ways for years it seems
Finally back in 1985
They found out that both were alive
But after a short romance
They went separate ways for one more chance
They're in the year of 1988
They found one another non too late
They were married in August of that year
To start a new life without worry or fear
He really couldn't offer her that much
Only this heart and loving touch
The love that he has for her
Will last and last forever
For those that don't believe in fate
Just remember the year of 1988

Virgil Periero

Dori's Eleventh Birthday

I hardly can believe that now another year has passed
And yet I knew your childhood years were not supposed to last

The newborn babe and tiny tot have long since ceased to be
The little girl and larger child no longer do I see.

And last year, when I felt you couldn't be more cute and smart
And thought that you'd done all you'd do to win and melt my heart

I guess I didn't really know
how much you'd see, and do, and grow,
that you'd think thoughts beyond your years

Your feet would swell, and you'd weigh more
And make my tired shoulders sore
And there'd be times I couldn't ease your fears.

It seems to me that nature is revealing
A bit of what they say on earth is heaven.
My daughter, almost grown, and so appealing
Now that you have arrived at age eleven.

Gene Wisoff

The Leaving

You left us. We do not know why.
We can not assume why, that would not be fair.
You had to feel that your life here was finished,
That the rest of us would be able to cope with your loss.
We miss you terribly, but we go forward.

We hope that you have found peace and comfort,
Happiness and contentment.
We are still struggling with you leaving
And are looking for peace and comfort.
But knowing you now have contentment
Will make our struggles easier.

Barbara Carol Avery

Shorty's Lament

A simple question to me has always been
Where do the short people of the world fit in?
Surely not policemen pounding the beat
And have you ever seen a basketball player who's
under five feet?
In crowded places we can't see over the top
In the workplace the teasing and bad jokes seldom stop.
People laugh: They think it's a prank
When we can't see over the counter at the bank.
Baseball isn't our game
Being an athlete will never bring fame.
Ask the tall people, they'll give you their views.
We can always make a living...selling shoes.
We want trophies, plaques, and medals.
Or at least a car where our feet can reach the pedals.
So I ask this simple question. Is life really fair,
Reaching for the light switch...standing on a chair?

Gaetano Dick Gerani

A New Day Coming

I'm walking in step to a far-out song
Been walking forever but not too long
I know where I'm going, cause I can see
where I've been.

It's the end of an era and I'm changing my style
I'm going to try something new for awhile.
Life is a piece of cake and I'm going to take a bite.
Coming out of the shadows, cause I've found the light.

I'm dancing with my fears, but I won't let them lead.
I am the master, I am all that I need.
I am not going to stifle the flow
I'll get out of my way, I'll just let go

There's something inside that won't let me rest.
It's tired of being caught up in my mess
"out of my way" it seems to be saying,
"it's my turn to handle the working and playing".

Claudine Robinson

Balance

To all the people on the earth
Who speak of Jesus and rebirth,
I will warn you, as I should,
Without evil, there is no good.
Without the wrong, there is no right.
Without the dark, there is no light.
Without sleep, there is no pain.
For everything Holy, there's something profane.
Don't disturb the balance, or you just might find,
Instead of losing evil, you'll just lose your mind!

Raquel Reyes

Wonderings...

Did you ever wonder what it would be like to live someone else's life?
Did you ever really care?
Did you ever wonder what it would be like to fly like a bird?
Did you ever really play fair?
Did you ever get hurt by someone,
Felt like you were cut so deep?
Did you ever lie in bed at night
And cry yourself to sleep?
Did you ever wonder what it would be like to love?
And how it felt to be cared for?
I wonder that the time
As I silently walk out your door.

Bill Christopher

A Bit of Creation

It was only a bit of pottery
With colors bright and gay,
   Its form was a trifle misshapen,
But it gladdened my heart that day
   When I first beheld my creation
Emerge from a drab hunk of clay.
   And while gazing with pleased satisfaction
At the object I had wrought,
   There flashed through my mind a question
And most amazing thought —
   I wondered if my Creator
When he looked at me one day
   Would feel the same satisfaction
With an imperfect bit of clay.
   Would I emerge from life's furnace
With colors bright and gay
   To give my Creator pleasure
And gladden his heart one day?

   ### *Jean B. Gregory*

Laughter

Laughter
Empty cries of relief
That help my tears to keep.

Laughter
Echoing sounds of pain bouncing off my heart
They are carefully camouflaged where few can tell apart.

Laughter
Music to your ears, ointment for my soul
for spiritual and emotional wounds are not so easy to console.

   ### *Donella Bateman*

Two Stories

The front page of the paper,
   shouted headlines of a murder yet unsolved.
The last page made no meant
of the passerby,
who "couldn't get involved".
   \The motive, if there was one,
   was a mystery and as yet, not understood.
He probably had his reason
and well, who's to say that
all of them weren't good.
   \Its bold aggressive letters,
   ran a litany of suspects, cures and blames.
In all it had one sentence
half obscured,
by advertising and no name.
   \The killer (till they caught him),
   would most certainly evoke a wave of fright.
I wonder if he ponders,
on that poor, black child,
who froze to death last night.

   ### *Ronald Jesse Lewis*

Dark Thoughts

You can feel yourself slip into dark thoughts.
You can feel the dark water begin to flood your soul.
Your mind grows cold, your heart grows numb, the dark
thoughts have begun.
You sit in your ocean of sorrow, and cry out a river of tears.
You ask yourself horrible questions, and answer them with your fears.
And sometimes the sun doesn't come out and evaporate the
water away, but if the sun doesn't come out soon I don't
think I can continue this way.

   ### *Sarah Golding*

Sandy

When I married, I thought that maybe,
Maybe someday God would grant me a baby.
I waited and waited and waited some more,
Then God gracefully opened his door,
He sent me a beautiful brown eyed beauty.
It was you Sandy my darling my baby.

   ### *Beverly Intelisano*

Graduation

Born a bud of beauty's promise
Wisdom's perfume from her wafting
My delight and envy blending
With her green, abundant show

Now no longer can I shelter
Her unfolding celebration
Fertile Earth and beaming Sky
Shall witness Love's descendent grow

All my fears and all my hopes
Can make no shield, no talisman
Against the wind and rain which now must
Test her spirit's rooted stand

Op'ning bud, to fullness blossom
Guided growth now ends forever
Let my joyful tears fall at your roots
As I withdraw my hand.

   ### *Gail Fenelon*

Mother Earth

   Thus speaks Mother earth,
To us, whom she was given birth.
   Speaking to her beloved children
Through out the land, in every nation.
   "Do not corrupt the virgin soil
Leaving her nude, making her toil.
   Lovingly plant and till the ground.
Wondrous beauty will be found.
   Preserve the natural habitat,
For it was meant to be like that.
   Care for the creatures in the wild
They too, are this mother's child.
   I am the home in which you dwell
Your selfish acts in time will tell.
   With others live in harmony
On mountain high and deep of sea.
   Say gentle words and think thoughts wise
A peaceful world be your prize."
   Thus, the earth, speaks to Thee.
"We are all, one family."

   ### *Elizabeth A. Ross*

Southern Ladies

Sun-framed on the old veranda,
pastel spirits grace
white wicker with
"cool libations" and
warm, cello voices.
Magnolia skin, soft
angel hair, where
rosebuds tremble
over moseyed conversations.
Time-forged in goodbye's ceaseless pyre:
Burnished innocence.
Steel gentility.
Silver whispers.
Southern ladies.

   ### *Melissa Moon-Latour*

Traveling

To travel around the world would be a sight to see,
To see all the views and all of their beauty.
I want to go to many places,
And see new cultures and meet new faces.

I want to visit China, France and Rome,
It would be fun to be away from home.
I want to travel around this sphere,
Even if it takes me year after year.

I want to see all the sights this world has to give,
And live as much as I can live.

Cinda Dautrich

Sea of Numbness

Confusion amongst a sea of numbness.
Wrapping up the laughter and shipping it through my soul,
I take a chance on living a lie
I take a chance on silencing the mirth, the grin beneath
    this bark.
If I told you of the feelings scattered in the haze, would
    the vagueness of the mind be to blurred to trample through?
I'm not taking the chance to travel my own consciousness.
I'll grasp your own impressions and I'll sing in the midst
    of your melodies.
But without my sword of security, my dragons already slain.

Alyson Gayle

Remain In Me

Remain in Me the Master told us
I am the True Vine: Have true trust
In Me you need to be a fruitful branch
Don't live in World's unfavorable chance

Remain in Me and grow in fine fruit
If you live apart from Me you'll be mute
Not able to bless others with My Word
Some have not the Spiritual Food heard

Leaving my Presence you will be thrown
You will not be able to approach God's Throne
Dried up you are no longer useful to Me
You will be as a dead branch of a tree

Walk in obedience to My Word sincerely
You will still need to quench evil continually
See the pattern I've shown to you
As I — "My Father Will" — I did do

I glorified my Father! Please do the same
We want to, always, glorify His Holy Name
His Love is upholding us as we believe
The Glory of His Love and Power we can't conceive

Susan Essler

War

War
The killing, the bombing, and all of the guns.
The explosions, the chaos,
Everyone runs.
Prisoners in prison have to be saved,
Not be used as tortured slaves.
The lost have been found,
Slaughtered, dead on the ground.
Cannons fire with all of their might,
Soldiers and soldiers, fight and fight.
Guns, spears, and a knife,
People are willing to take a life.
Stop the madness.
Stop the war.
Talk it out.
Find a cure!

Michael Knoth

Oh God! My God!

Oh God! My God! Have you given up on me?
You love many that I know, and proved it by hanging from a tree.
All are made in your own image, but it seems that some are far closer.
I am good at many things, but many are far more so.
    O great and almighty!
        You have created all the beautiful universe!
            But have you forgotten of me?
                Have you, O have you.

Oh God! My God! I love with my whole heart.
In my life there are many things, but you are the most part.
Of all things you have made, I may seem quite small.
But still I know that in this world, you can't have it all.
    Dear God, maker of worlds and such!
        You will never forget me.
            For you have given me much.
                Have you, O have you.

John M. Olmeda

On The Way To The Park

It's 7 A.M. - My alarm rang.
I'm starting off with a bang..
My car wouldn't start so I took a bus.
Wouldn't you know, It got stuck..
I walked 3 miles in the Wind and Rain.
By the time I arrived. I was so Ashamed..
It was dark and late and hadn't Ate.
I headed for home in the Wind and Rain..
I thought it would be fun to take the Train.
The Train ride was Nice.
Until I saw Two Mice..
I got off the First Stop. Found a Phone.
Wouldn't you know, my friend wasn't Home..
1/2 Mile more. I'll be at My Door.
I can't wait any More..
The First thing, I'm gonna do.. Is Set.
My Clock for 7 A.M..

Victoria K. Johnson

'Autumn'

Such a gentle breeze
Praying on my knees
Watching clouds drift by
Across the blue sky

Autumn, why did heaven bring you down to me?
What could ever make me deserve you?

Feeling soft rain drops
On the mountain tops
As the rainbows glare
Through the misty air

Autumn, why did heaven bring you down to me?
What could ever make me deserve you?

I see stars shine bright
In the black of night
I hear oceans roar
As they crash to shore

Autumn, why did heaven bring you down to me?
What could ever make me deserve you?

Autumn, baby autumn
Autumn

Melissa Nicole Combs

A Mother's Prayer

You were conceived out of love
Blessed by the angels and God above
Protecting you in my loving arms
And to keep you safe from any harm

I would sing you songs, and rocked you to sleep;
I taught you prayers to remember and keep
We would play games and read books to
Just like a mother is suppose to do.
I know that we are so far apart
I still have your memories, you're still in my heart
And remember the day I had to tell you goodbye
My heart still aches, and the tears I still cry

I wish I could reach up and feel your touch
Because I still love you so very much
You're still my little angel, apple of my eye
And my love for you will never die.

I know you're in heaven, with other angels to,
And I thank God, for taking care of you
When you look down upon us, and pray for those you see
This is your mother asking will you please remember me

Roseann M. Hiatt

Humanity

Veiled dark, hushed, silence
Issuing forth in dark depths.
Tiny sparks flickering, then glowing bright.

Presence glowing, shedding forth its band,
Reaching out to other faltering beams.

Haloes entwined, overlapped,
Ring upon ring joined by their familial ties,
Glowing, emanating warmth,
Obliterating the velvet blankness,
Full of energy, confident.

Torches, steady, ready to protect,
Understanding, grasping their surroundings,
Impregnable.

Fires with dying embers.
Haloes, dwindling in the darkness.
Rings growing dim, faltering,
Flickering, used up, gone.

Fewer lights, one less halo,
And darkness glides silently back,
Never far.

Elaine McClung

Enchantment

Sequined encrusted, blue party dress, sleek, in style,
with sprays of snowy white roses and ribbons entwined,
a beautiful young lady walk down the aisle,
as a new life begins, grandmother looks back in time.

With sprays of snowy white roses and ribbons entwined,
a ballerina spins, amidst Barbie dolls and tea set dreams,
as a new life begins, grandmother looks back in time,
tears, like diamonds, remembers stars and moonbeams.

A ballerina spins, amidst Barbie dolls and tea set dreams,
thoughts of a loved one as school bells chime,
tears, like diamonds, remembers stars and moonbeams,
her beloved whisper's we did it babe, we saw the best time.

Thoughts of a loved one as school bells chime,
a beautiful young lady walks down the aisle.
her beloved whispers 'we did it babe, we saw the best time,'
sequined encrusted, blue party dress, sleek, in style.

Dorothy Strickland

What's In A Name

"Mah"
  Washing bottles, changing diapers,
   Cooing, cuddling and napping,
    Then it's —

"Mommy"
  Tying shoestrings, catching crickets,
   Giggles, tickles, hide-and-seek,
    And soon it's —

"Mom"
  Watching friendships, stocking wardrobes,
   Growing independence, struggles,
    'Til it's —

"Mother"
  Listen quietly, say little,
   Feel the disconnected freedom.
    What's this? —

"Grandma"
  Cuddles, crickets, struggles, quiet,
   Share the wisdom of experience
    With a hug.

Beth Grosek

I Pray For Your Prayer

Good day, Good night, Dear Lord
I love You and need You
And pray that You need Me
My name is familiar to You

And my deepest feelings are that
I want to enjoin the People's of the Nations of the World
To honor You-our Lord, our God, our Creator

And that this day shall become
The Holiest Day of the Year and
From a time before to a time thereafter

There shall be a peacefulness-a tranquility
Throughout all of the lands and the seas that surround them
And from the inhabitants therein

And You will look down and say-this is good
The rainbow shall then magnificently prevail
Its beauty shall reign forever

Good day, Good night, Dear Lord
I love You and need You

Stanley Handelman

Ode to a Lifetime...Much of It Spent

Westward Ho! Go, go, go! I've got to catch a train.
I must take the trains because I get sick on planes,
  looking down at mountains capped with snow.

In my train I can reminisce and relax...
I watch a man send his wife a fax...
Amazing, the technology...you know?

Surely, the weather could truly be better
  than this continuous depressing rain.
I'd surely pick warm sun again and again and again.

"In the distance you can see the Pacific Coast",
  ...the conductor over the intercom does boast.
And I sigh at the thought that this train ride
  is over...
I shall not get back to my hometown east in Dover.

The east was back at the beginning of the race,
Now the west shall be my forever resting place.

Christine Stoelting

Morning

Ahh finally sleep,
Dreaming,
Whats that noise!... nothing,
Whats that noise!.... nothing,
What is that noise!.... alarm clock,
Slowly wake up,
Get up,
Using all of the willpower in the world,
I drag myself to the shower.

Ed Thiemann

A Bridge

A bridge has been built,
that bridge is you.
You've brought what I couldn't buy,
the link to what lies within.
You found a way to cross the river...

To discover my heart.
Trapped in a cave behind a stony wall,
lost in the darkness,
shrouded in soil and ash,
bruised and beaten down without hope, without life.

Then you took it in your hands
and whispered warm words to it.
Promises of love and security.
It shied away at first.
Like a newborn fawn from the rain.

But you were patient as a fisherman waiting for his catch,
Your words soft...soothing.
Your hands gentle and caressing,
brushing away the dirt and grime.
And with your love...healed the bruises.

Anita A. Rabidou

Bought with the Blood of Jesus

I was bought with the blood of Jesus
For my sins, He had to die.
I was bought with the blood of Jesus
Crucified by Great Design.

Mocked and beaten for His Kingdom,
A crown of thorns they made Him wear.
Nailed to a cross, can you imagine
The pain that Jesus had to bear.

They hung a plague above His head.
On it was written, "King of the Jews".
Speared in the side, He bled blood and water.
Death had arrived, they spread the news.

His followers they quickly scattered,
Claiming they knew not this Man.
Had they forgotten it was our Jesus
Who told them this was part of a plan.

Buried in a tomb sealed with a boulder.
Three days later He did arise.
Just as the Scriptures told He would,
Yet everyone was still surprised.

Noreen Giovinazzi

The Wilderness

The wilderness is filled with
blossoming color. Its color brightness
is aglow with beautiful splendor.
The deer are frolicking by a stream
and running through deep meadows of green.
The chipmunks and squirrels are
hiding and waiting to be seen.
There is a great sense of peacefulness
and stillness within this wilderness.
This peacefulness surrounds you and me.
It pull's us from the everyday
toils and strife. It make's us
look upon our own lives.
As you look up in the trees
there are birds flying about.
They are flying from tree to tree.
The birds never bother to look
down at you and at me.
For this time and age we are
much to busy to see the beauty and of feeling ever so free.

Cheryl L. Sosaya

Our Last Queen

You burst upon the scene; time was a score
But two; so long and loved, no coo of dove;
Had time been ours to search the world e'en more,
No babe, however small, could get such love.
You laughed, you played and jumped and bounced and cried;
The bikes, the sleds, and oh! the route of news,
We both, in prayer, with digits crossed, just sighed;
We knew, too well, with you we'd paid our dues.
And now you're here, so close it seems to us,
To knocking, breaking, driving through that door
Of life, to burst upon the world; and plus
The smiles, the hopes, the joys, a hundred score.
It seems so strange, too young, just eight and teen;
Oh, Kerr, you'll e'er be our love, our last queen.

Harry Geisler

Eternal Fire

I rearrange and analyze, my thoughts are going crazy.
Thoughts of him, I realize, are becoming very hazy.
You fill my mind more often now, but I will regain control.
More and more each day I find you entering my soul.
I could truly love a man like you, rest and be content.
Unfortunately for me and you, you were not the one God sent.
If I had a man like you, considerate with compassion,
I could unload this tortured soul of all this built up passion.
I don't have you, you are illusive, a dream that keeps returning.
To light the very touch I am to keep the embers burning.
As years come and the years all go, I know without a doubt
Deep in the very core of me, my thoughts of you will always be
Thoughts of a fire deep inside
Only you, my friend, can put out.

Mary E. Gordon

Absence

My heart aches because of your absence.
Sweet memories of your beautiful eyes, caring smile, and loving heart.
Tears stream down from the eyes that you looked so deeply into.
The body you held so tightly, now trembles.
The hand you held so carefree, now shudders.
The voice that would talk forever, now quivers.
Absence makes the heart grow fonder;
It's good advice I just can't take.

Amberlyn N. Francis

Our Anniversary

It seems like only yesterday when I walked down the aisle,
I gazed into your dark brown eyes and looked upon your smile:
We vowed to love and honor till death takes us from life;
There you became my husband and I became your wife.

The love we share together has grown each passing day,
It has become more precious than words could ever say:
Like a rock, it anchors us in the times of storm...
Like a blanket covers us, forever we are warm.

Today's our anniversary, a year has come and gone,
Each night has been a bright sunset, each day a brand new dawn.
A year of precious memories, a year to get acquainted,
A year more picture perfect than any artist ever painted.

Marilou Fite

Key to Happiness

The future you hold for me
Lifted from within my soul
I drifted from life without knowing
What my heart had for a goal

In time, I could love without doubting
Where passion can carry my needs
And desire the road to lost moments
Following its path where it leads

I give my soul and compassion
I cry for the moments you couldn't share
By my side, your love is without boundaries
I feel you, though you're not there

You blur my senses with caring
And swim within my trust
For in your hand, you held my heart
And my sorrow dried into the dust

Now I realize, without you my soul is empty
Stolen from desire and need
Our life is my door to fulfilled beginning
And our love is what holds the key

Lee Robison

The Peace That Holds The Pieces

Yielded though my world is shaking
Trusting while my heart is breaking
Thankful though I cannot understand

Even in the pain of weeping
My Father's eyes are watching, keeping
Circumstances held within His hands

So near me I can feel and hear it
The comfort of the Holy Spirit
Who tells me I can surely bear it
Knowing God has been there from the start

And in the moments yet to be
Releasing fear and walking free
Following still more perfectly
The Peace that holds the pieces of my heart

Sandra Palmer Carr

Captive

I think I know how Gulliver felt trussed tightly to the ground,
While little feet walked by his side or tromped him up and down
I feel the same when snug in bed, the covers close and warm,
As Gray Cat sneaks beneath the spread a lump now holds me firm.
White Cat stalks and sees the lump that's moving round and round.
White Cat pounces with a thump-I'm captive to a mound.
Paws can often touch so lightly but now they feel like lead.
My body feels the blows as White Cat hunts with heavy tread.
Helpless am I! I can not sleep until the drama's through.
At least I can best Gulliver and get free from captors two.
Toss covers back, push the lump away, I'll doze another day.
(Of course Gray Cat And White Cat may have another say!)

Alphretta Meginnis

Untitled

She's the magic in my life
Mysterious though she seems
She's the darkness of the night time
But the perfection of my dreams

She's the power in a thunderstorm
The wind on a brisk March day
She's the comfort in my thoughts
Through the love she can portray

She's the black flame in a fire
The sting of winter snow
She's my beauty in the sunlight
As she shines wherever we go

She has the spirit of a phantom
The speed of a hurricane
She's my spring mist in the morning
She's as gentle as the rain

She's my pride, my fear, my challenge
My life and its driving force
She's my escape to cherished freedom
She's my partner, my friend... she's my horse

Tammy Jo Seger

Keep Your Eyes Upon The Ball

As you play the game of life
    with its great challenge, cares and strife,
Like in a game of basketball
    to blindly shoot won't count at all.

You must aim straight while fancy "steppin'"
    to get that ball shot through the "nettin'."
But first the basketball you must catch,
    then with firm hands onto it latch,
        or you won't get a winning shot,
            whether you're shootin' cold or hot.

Just keep your eyes upon the ball,
    so through your fingers it won't fall.
You must not falter, brood or fret;
    life's ball of chance you'll someday get.

But you must shoot it straight and true,
    for in life's game it's up to you.
You certainly can't win every game
    of basketball, success or fame.
        But you will seldom slip or fall
            if you keep your eyes upon the ball.

Lelwin F. Wilkinson

Green

Why do we label people we're either Black or White
Why do people let skin color get them so uptight,
to me that isn't being very bright
I have fantasized about my life
but never have I wanted to be White.
Black and White don't make the choices in this world
Green is the thing on the scene
giving you your hopes and your dreams
making you scheme for everything
The Green make you rape, steal and kill
for love of having it or just for a thrill
The Green can protect you or defect you
make you happy or blue and of course,
will change your attitude
Those dead Presidents are something to behold
they will make some people sell their soul
I'm proud to be the color I am
If you can't accept me who gives a damn!!

It's The Green The Mighty Dollar Green!!!
Earnestine Jackson

In All the Silence and All the Quiet

In all the silence and all the quiet
I see his picture with me beside it,
I hear sad and I hear crying,
I don't hear glad, I just hear sighing.

Love hurts is what many have said,
I say love kills, a hurt that never mends,
He looks at us and sees two friends, but
He's too blind to see the pain that sends

The love I want is inches away,
but to get it I must travel for miles,
too far to walk, to far to run,
But with such a prize I cannot lay,
I have to reach for that magic ray,
I 'll get his love somehow someway,
I don't know how but his love will be mine,
and when it is I rejoice, for my love
I found that magic day.
Chelsha Reed

A Life Denied

A baby was conceived
A life it never received
People say, 'how could you?'
Chances of it being happy, are very few,
In some eyes it is for the best
While others welcome it into their nest
Who are we to comment?
The choice is up to the mother and her gent
For those who need to make that choice
Listen to your heart, not the people's voice.
Julia Watson

My Dad

My Dad, he loves me
He is the key
You see this poem is about the one I love
He is the one I'm thinking of
My dad, I love him
Our love will never grow dim
Sometimes he moans and groans
Our love is surely shone
At times he gets on my nerves
My love for him is more than mere words
He is not the average man,
He's more than that, he's my dad
Anna McCaghren

Like Darkness

Like darkness terror has no
bounds. It burns inside you looking for
a way out. And when it does finally finds its
way out. The fury within is beyond thinking
about. What happens when this plague is
released about. No man shall ever find out.
Trent Schmidt

Bridges

On the outside looking in,
On the inside looking out.
Jesus, you know I need a friend.
Show me what it's all about.

My child, I placed you there to be
A hand reaching out for me.
Extend your hand and touch that one
Who also seems to stand alone.

Together you can build a bridge.
Hearts touching hearts across the ridge.
Knowing each other a day, or year
Loving each other will hold you near.
Carol A. Lee

Untitled

What make the difference!
It brings joy to get together with our
    families once gain
It brings joy to get together to share the
    things of God beautiful world.
It's joy to get together and learn to pray and
    learn to trust Jesus, who came to the world
    and taught us how to, live, love, laugh, smile,
    care, and share
It's joy to get together under the orders
    of our Lord Jesus Christ and get involved
in the affairs of life.
It's joy to know that Jesus decides our
    future, so remember it's joy to get
together, because together can make
a great big difference and most of
all it's good to get together
    To praise the Lord, it's just good
to get together and pray.
Mary Gibson

Road Of A Gypsy

I was birthed in sterility, breathed in virility
Scampered out to a new nation: Imagination.
Capital: The sun drenched grass.
I breathed the heady mixture, Nature's wind and dew,
But they caught me at the schoolhouse, so much work to do.

I drudged at ancient volumes, dredged from dusty coffers
While the winds of worldliness inspired hopes of better offers.
I caught flight again, wings of steel and wire.
With heart of demolition and tail of breathing fire.
Twenty long years. Short lifetime to give
For God and country and ideals to live.

A breeze blows back unruly grey hairs from my bleaching face.
Not a wind of nature but of man's democratic race.
It blows up the Rotunda and down through the Senate.
Finally it clears my eyes for a mere sparkling minute.

Political life over I retire, just me and I.
To sunny places by the fire, quietly to die.
My wind blows still, inspiring all others.
Never ceasing to amaze. Or progress.
Road of a gypsy.
Jenni Carlson

Next Time

And lastly, eerie bits of a catastrophe rain upon another
  generation's Destiny.
Maybe next time they will succumb to Superior forces to be.
Perhaps a reclaiming of a People's senses until capable,
  and not apt, to wrong a Wom' and/or Man.
Maybe next time colorless, eyeless faces can no longer see
  Racist reasons.
Becoming simply blind to Others' every different season.
Maybe next time telepathically, and with mouthless faces,
One could not swear or scream while decibels are in their places.
What on Earth could slay the mighty Beast of division and
separation?
Anybody...! Anywhere..! Justify this pitiful Manifestation.
Probably. No..! Certainly not He, She or It.
Maybe next time It will be Us.
Yes, maybe next time earless noggins comes to bare,
Struggling to hear what eyelessness no longer sees seems fair.
Do we deserve a Race; a Face; a Place to be?
Maybe next time we will merely exist.
Maybe next time we won't deserve to.

  Matthew Rawlins Jr.

My Beloved Someone

  My beloved someone, has gone and left my life,
has crushed my heart to pieces, has left my lonely life.
  My beloved someone, may be back some day,
to help me with bad times, and by my side to stay.
  My beloved someone, has left me out before,
feeling the ache of loneliness, that she is leaving me with once more.
  My beloved someone, her forgiveness I must seek,
she must hear my voice, for the future seems so bleak.
  My beloved someone, all the times that we've been through,
grows stronger in my memory, for there's nothing left to do.
  My beloved someone, whom no one can replace,
has left an empty void so big, tears roll down my face.
  My beloved someone, throws my picture to the side,
will all the other people, she feels she must hide.
  My beloved someone, I must live without,
to deal with her happiness, for I have been pushed out.
  My beloved someone, who's sorrow's seem so true,
will shine again in other's lives, leaving me feeling oh, so blue.
  And so to my beloved someone, whose trust I had before,
leave me in my grief and guilt, and think of me no more.

  Raleigh Altenhofen

God's Precious Gifts

As life progresses this I know
the best things in life are the little things,
if you are to survive

Looking at brilliant red hibiscus blossom, up-close
and personal, thanking it for shouting out God's
magnificence

Gazing out the back of my many-mirrored home over the lake
at dusk, while the grandest sunset in history passes before me

Having my Laso Apso give me un-conditional looks of love and
respect for the one-millionth time in his short six years
of life in our family

Having my darling, wife, Michele, dare to be herself, in
multiple ways even she had not imagined fourteen years ago,
when we first married, secure in the knowledge that my love
for her will not falter

All of this allows me to survive each day in a world which
ordinarily takes no prisoners.

  T. Edward Burris

Smoking

You say it's not a big deal,
and it helps the way you feel.
You smoke, and smoke, and smoke some more.
and then you wonder why you snore.
I've tried to help you through this,
this disease they call Angina Pectoris.
You said it wouldn't kill you,
because the medications were known to help, too.
You still kept on smoking,
because you thought that I was joking.
Now you're in the hospital bed,
thinking about what I've said.
Now you wish you were back home and normal,
but everyone went out to buy a formal.
Your funeral is set and steady,
because your time of death is ready.
As they put the dirt on your grave,
everyone felt they were the blame.
But now the people see, this was a preventable disease.
You had the right to choose, but now you choose to snooze.

  Kristin Amann

Spring Is Here

Spring is here
I see some deer
I see some yellow flowers
and a dove.
I love to sit and think
As I hold my pen and ink
That all of this is 'cause of God's love.

Spring is here
I love to play
With shorter nights
And longer days.
The sun is shining through the clouds
While the blue birds chirp some songs aloud.

Spring is here
We have fun
Even though it has just begun.

  Cindy Corbin

Taken Away, With You Gone

Since you've been gone my life's been broken
you never should have been taken

You were the greatest grandmother ever
you were supposed to live forever

I found out that was not true
because now your gone and I'm without you

I cannot hug, kiss, or touch you anymore
but in my heart we will be together forever more

My love for you "Kusha" will never die
I could not forget you even if I wanted to try

You were filled with so much love for everyone
we had many years of a lot of fun

I think and cry for you everyday
and wonder why you were taken away
      Love,
      Vicka

  Vicki Hyrczyk

Ode to the Weatherman

Don't ridicule the weatherman
He does the very best he can
It would be impossible for you or I
The weather for certain to prophesy
For the Elements don't give a foolproof sign
If it will be cloudy or the sun will shine
The wooleyworm may give us a hint
That winter's coming - cold and wet
The bark on the trees tell their tale
And cold will be here for a real long spell
But they can't say just when it will snow
They can't say - cause they don't know
So don't Boo Bill or James
Because mother nature does play her games
Accept winter's forecast - be assured it means
Just around the corner comes bouncing spring
And be truly thankful is their plea.
God always sends us what we need.
They know without his caring hand
We wouldn't even need - a weather man!

Roberta Holman

... Friend ...

   I once had a friend, whose name I won't mention.
'Twas a very special friend with all good intentions.
What may have went wrong, to his day I can't say.
I guess all trust was just lost, or simply drifted away.
   Sometimes I laugh, and other times I cry. "It's
such a sad situation, when one just don't know why.
Thinking of the good times that you two once shared together."
Going thru trials and tribulation and braving
all stormy weather. If given the opportunity to live
my life all over again. Some things may be forsaken,
but not the trusting of my friend...

Johnnie Alton Harris

I Miss

I miss your sexy smile.
The magic in your secretative brown eyes.
Your gentle touch and the sound of your voice.
I miss being with you each every life time moment.
The candlelight dinners and the warm baths together,
that I will remember forever.
You are like the moon that follows me all night.
The angels that protects me from the danger in
the world full of anger.
I miss the touch of your gentle hands as they caressed my body.
The smell of your body as it strengthen's me even though you haven't
weaken me, my love for you is deeper than the rising of the sun.
When I awake in the morning I taste the sweetness as your firm lips
touches and heals my wounds.
I miss your arms surrounding me with lots of love but in my heart
I have received more from above.
The touch in your hands that are tight and so strong knowing
no one can always be alone.

Tanya Marie Lee

Pet Prayer

May the Lord above make all pet owners
Aware of what their pet needs.

If your pet could talk, he would probably say...

"Please watch over my master."
"Please have him wash and groom me as
well as he cares for himself."
"If he cannot groom me, please take me to:
Francine Marrano

Frances E. Marrano

Thoughts Of An Insane Man

Strange happenings bring up strange feelings...
feelings of hate, wonder, and rage.

Strange happenings aren't appealing...
to things that happen every day.

We walk a walk that feeds our strong.
We know that what we do is wrong.

Greed and fear take over here...
knowing that the weak lie near.

Now Lie, that's a strange word.
It flies 'round like a drunken bird.

It can not land 'cause the ground's still wet.
But the land is dry, and it won't land yet.

Now how can it land...
to be eaten at first sight.

No longer do we fear...
its nasty little bite.

It still attempts a taste...
but now we're just too strong.

We've risen above...
the drunken birdy song.

Dymetrix

What I Never Knew

What I never knew;
From generations of lessons, essences,
   and only one source.
Stagnant was my mind to what I never
   knew.
Daily searches;
   yet we still seek to find... True Reality.
Faith within me assist in the jihad.
What I never knew...
By mosquitoes, is sucked up daily.
Leaving festered humps.
Soulless, spiritless ones,
   result into shady outcomes.
What I never knew may be the death of me.
Since, righteously is the only medium to
   being Free!

Jeffrey D. Jones

No Chance

A spark ignites
An old spirit has found a way
It divides
The spirit grows strong
One third is over
Two thirds until life
But wait something interrupts
Poking, prodding, a strange noise
A horrible feeling
The spirit is slowly sucked away
The two thirds until life has ended abruptly
The spirit gets no chance to live

Tammy Bratt

Your Spirit Lives In The Wind

You're the grass that moves with a gentle breeze,
a songbird singing, in the trees.
Your spirit lives in the wind
"always alive my friend."

I sit in the meadow, and feel you close by
you're all around me, I will not cry.
My heart is filled with love for you
I see your eyes, honest and true
you're spirit lives in the wind.
"Always alive my friend"
someday we will meet again
the circle of life, has no end
you'll always be a part of me
you're everything in the world I see.

You are the moon and the stars above.
You taught me how to live, to laugh, to love.
"Your spirit lives in the wind"
always alive my friend
a new beginning, not an end.

Jeanne Jarvis

Lost And Found

I look into your eyes and my soul is swallowed whole
I fall through the vastness of your being
Seeing beauty with no end
It is neither hot nor cold, but comfortably numb
Wrapped in the blanket of music that is you
The music builds to a crescendo and words are formed
You have spoken and once again I see your face
You smile and I am complete

Wesley James

The Timekeeper

Pale are the skies in shades of blue,
   Openings too rare of a rich golden hue.
Through these entrances special souls depart
   Into a new life, accepting peace deep into their hearts.

From provisional dark clouds, the rain will abound,
   In those tranquil moments of little sound.
So pure, so beautiful, nature once again renews,
   To find a world of happiness known to just a few.

The Heavens my friend are much too vast
   For souls to explore when out they are cast.
Upon their immortal freedom they seek
   A different time and place, limited to one short peek.

The depths of the Universe are dark and cold,
   Consumed of light years and parsecs, time honored, too old.
The black infinite holes hold time in its place
   For souls to discover many worlds, far into space.

Foreseen beyond those ominous skies
   Leaves much to be heard above our lonely cries.
In this millennium could our future unfold,
   Much forgotten through history, will the secret ever be told?

Susan von Gunden

Untitled

Flickering lights flood the runway,
   down the infinite stretch of time;
Outrunning defeat through endless persistence,
   among the dreary stars that shine.

A shimmering shadow glows in the moonlight,
   walking slowly through darkened walls of stone;
A lost soul hopelessly searching for something gone,
   the continuing journey down a never-ending road alone.

Matt A. Zeugin

The Olympics

To be in the olympics you have to be bold, ready and told.
You stand there with the ball in your hand,
ready to go, ready to stand.
You drive to the hoop, your teammates there
You want to sit down in a nice soft chair.
You shoot the ball and make the shot,
You went for number two, but got the number one spot.

Ryan Clay

Life's Roads

Roads have a way of connecting
two lives;

Though they are far apart and lonely at times.
Though our roads are sometimes challenging and appear to move
in different directions

I know our course is charted and the lines are drawn
leading us to each other

I know not where or when the two converge

But this I do know... I will wait for you.

Vanessa Freeman

A Letter to the Teacher

Dear Teacher,
   Wow!, you're so precious and rare,
While little Johnny's in school he's in your care.
He might not be able to read very well,
But you'll solve that problem I know, I can tell.
He hasn't mastered all his numbers yet,
But he'll know them soon so there's no need to fret.
He gets along with little folks his size,
And with his kindness he could win a prize.
He might not become your little hero,
But he sure is mine, whatever his score.
His clothes may be ragged but they are clean,
So please help me to help him realize his dreams.
He has a slight head cold, I'm sure you know,
But he didn't want to miss school, so I let him go.
He says he gets cold while riding the bus,
I'd like him to be warm if it's not too much fuss.
I've packed him a lunch, the best I could do.
Now making his day right is left up to you.

Maggie Neal Williams

Awaiting Dangers

Explorers enter at risk
Eerie sounds echo —
The walls are rough and jagged
Green stalactites hang
Stalagmites curl
Rushing water fills the undisturbed silence
Red ooze drips slowly
Distant screams warn of danger
Scary monsters hide
   behind rocks and in holes
Glowing eyes watch as you pass
The walls are as high as skyscrapers
The ground is as wet as a damp sponge
Shadows lurk in the darkness
The flutter of bats is heard in the distance
Tunnels spread in all directions
   like a giant labyrinth
People panic in search of outlets
Lost souls wander —
There is no hope for escape

Colin Cassuto

Tell Me Why

Tell me why yesterday, when I was young
Life was filled with sunshine, and so much fun.
Tell me why, now that I've grown older
There's less and less sunshine, and the days they seem colder.
Tell me why, while watching a clock, time passes slow.
But after time passes in life, we wonder where did it go.

Tell me why moments of happiness and laughter always seem to go
    by fast,
While memories of sadness and sorrow seem to last and to last.
Tell me why a child must grow up so fast
And why I look for a future, but live in the past.
Of all of life's mysteries I'll always ask why.
But life's final mystery is why we must die.
So as some of these mysteries may bring tears,
    and some may bring laughter,
I pray to the Lord there is a hereafter.

Reno Amadori Jr.

Flame

Through shifting sands of time, I've looked for you. The one
who could make my eyes open and my heart flutter. Sweet salvation
and silent realization, comes drifting down on me.

Lifting hand and heart, I dream of our moments together. Silent
pray that you'll stay, though I believe you'll never stray. Never
bring such sad goodbye to your lips.

Living without you would kill the very light of life. Break down
the very thought of living with a purpose. Kill the very heart and soul.

You have taken my breath away, with your undying devotion. Softly
whispering things my ears want to hear, but my heart holds on to.
Kindling an ever burning flame.

Shanna Richards

Untitled

They say things happen
for a reason, well then, can someone please explain,
how our hearts can be filled with happiness then
quickly filled with pain.

They say as we get older
we become more wise; but from where I sit things seem
more complex, and that came as some surprise.

We may learn of the simple things in life and still wonder of
the rest, I guess if that's how God planned it, I'm sure it's for
the best.

Ann Calhoun

Untitled

Bee,
I think you'd better get away from me;
Your constant buzzing about who-knows-what annoys me.
Your sting hurts me more than you really know,
And you do even more damage when there's more than one of you.
You think you're so powerful 'cause your wings take you anywhere,
But you'll see that I don't even need them.
You can just keep on hopping from flower to flower, and I'll stay
    where I am.
(I'm not like you — I'm different — you bug me.)
You don't think about my feelings or try to understand me,
So don't you get mad if you think I invade your precious space.
Mind your own business and I'll do the same, and,
Oh yeah, that black and yellow you wear doesn't even fit you well.

Erika Wood

Miserable Existence

I look at the sky
bleached with the dark, hazy moon
hoping the stars will fall upon me soon.
Down on the pavement
with tire marks astray
trying to cope
with this miserable existence,
in which I lay

David Oakley

Cannons of Disruption

For Rich

Holding the led in place....places
a bit brighter.
Scribbling your name in too few words...calming.
Feel the brink.....
sensations...crawling throughout my skin.
Can't hide from the self degratification,
it only brings us to our knees,
allowing us to dig up our dust,
fingers moist....now stained and soiled.
Well wishing...well it's not enough.
Bruises blurring my agile hands,
burning my beauty to distance.
Can you hide from me?
Much to wise for a continuum of insubmission,
Surmise my passion.
My eyes see to allow me to see you.
Enter my skin through plastic veins and
Pulse through me....

Susan DeFord

My Journey

I am inspired on high,
words of wisdom, encouragement and
    enlightenment are mine,
that I may share my gift with the world,
that I may give to my brother, the helping hand
    that he may need from time to time,
that I may help to lift his spirit up on the wings of
    an eagle,
that he may soar to the heights that he was
    Divinely intended,
and that I to may know the joy that I Am.

Christine Broetzman

Do You Believe?

Do you believe in love at first sight?
Do you believe in the flowers of the night?
Do you rest your luck upon a shooting star;
or someone wondering where you are.
Do you believe in dreams that lie far
In hopes too high for thee to fly
Do you believe in yourself?
Or the future of your children's wealth.
Do you believe in happiness and fame
will come to you one sweet day!
Do you believe in the Lord Almighty
who died for you on calvary.
Do you believe in heaven or hell
if not when you die where will you dwell?
will you live among the Egyptians
or people of different cultures?
Do you believe in your friends?
who have always been there
Do you believe in love? Or God?
For these are all I believe in.

Margaret Loren McGaw-Sullivan

Cover of Darkness

Under the cover of darkness, she feels him next to her. He kisses her softly as if to tease her. Wanting more, she presses harder to him. He does not resist her.

Under the cover of darkness, he loves her passionately and refuses all others that cross his path. She is order in his life of chaos and he is an anchor where the wind never dies.

Under the cover of darkness, she is brave and doesn't hesitate to show him love. He accepts her bravery and reciprocates with gifts of warm, wet kisses. Passion is their food and embraces are their water. They survive only on these things.

But under the cover of darkness is the only place she holds him, for in the light of truth, she is alone.

Marie Simmons

Untitled

Bring me your beauty,
    If I take it shall happiness release from your soul
Show me your strength,
    If I take it shall pride and courage dismiss themselves
Present to me your talents,
    If I take them shall confidence and passion find freedom from you
Open your mind and reveal its knowledge,
    If I take it will you cease to reason
And if I now hold all these parts of you, shall I be a better man...

Beauty can be taken but never the soul
Pride and courage come from within, not strength of body
Talents are given, confidence and passion are earned and understood
If knowledge is gone your mind will choose to go on for it knows no
    boundaries
Truth in heart makes all equal, no matter what they hold

Craig Tynan

Will I Be Missed

Will I be missed when I am gone?
I have tried while living
To love every one by giving.
Though it be a small valentine,
or a get well card or two.
Maybe a tiny hand made gift
or a colored picture true.
It was always my pleasure
To cheer someone blue,
Will anyone remember
The little things I use to do?

Will I still be needed.
To lend a helping hand
with a new baby grand:
Or carry a tray
To brighten a shutin's day.
Will my friends remember
Our chat's on the phone, or the times that I visited
When they were sad and so alone
Will anyone remember the little things I use to do?

Berta Dell Harris

The Laugh

The laugh is a wonderful thing
The laugh can make someone else happy
The laugh can release stress
The laugh can come from someone young or old
The laugh is beautiful
The laugh can be a small chuckle or a big HA HA HA
The laugh is not hard
The laugh is a way to express happiness
The laugh is something that you cannot live without
The laugh, I think is the best thing you can make someone
do.

Amanda Smith

It's Time to Be a Mother

There's a new creation living inside the same exact body as mine
What a miracle I never thought, out of all that I've been taught
I'd be a mother and grow up so fast, forget all about my times
    in the past,
I'll spend my time thinking of way's, to make it happy everyday
I'll always teach it right from wrong, cause with me is where
    it'll always belong,
I'll never regret growing up to young and hardly having any fun
Cause once it's born that's all I'll need, to make me forever happy,
Something of mine forever to keep, a gift from God that I've received
Take responsibilities for no other, cause it's now time to be a mother.

Jenny Wilson

Graduation Day

The sun rises, the birds start singing,
The flowers are in full array.
They are celebrating a special time,
A special girl's graduation day.

All these years you've worked so hard.
From determination, you would not stray.
Just remember it was all worth it,
To be here on your graduation day.

Graduation is an important part of life.
A parent's wish kids should obey.
You were smart to honor that wish
On this important graduation day.

Life is full of disappointments
Sometimes things look awful gray.
But this occasion is full of happiness
It's your graduation day.

As you go out into this world
Facing a lot of dismay.
This event you will never forget
"Congratulations" on your graduation day!!

George L. Bishop

Products of Slavery

We've read the history including the "I have a dream..." speech
We've tried to learn everything that they would teach
Some people have changed; some put on other faces
Some are very outspoken against other races
Some hide their faces behind sheets that are white
Burning crosses in yards; committing violence through the night
Not just whites or Jews, but Afro Americans as well
Some striking out at memories of beatings from which our ancestors
    did swell
Some are outraged still over Alex Halley's "Roots"
They seem to be angry from him telling the truth
Why did they bring us across the great sea?
To bound us with chains and not set us free?
We are the products of our ancestor slaves
Proud to be African with our American names
Though the chains are gone from our wrists and our ankles are no
    longer bounded
We are still in shackles and our dreams are unfounded
Nigger, to blacks, to negro, to Afro Americans
The names have changed, but the attitude's the same
No respect, no rights, no dreams coming true
"All men created equal" is supposed to mean me and you

Sheila B. Norman

Gift Of Love

Roses, Roses, Perfume the air,
Rain, Sunshine and daily care,
God sends beauty everywhere,
To seek in quiet prayer.
And special friends to cherish and love,
A guiding hand from our Father above,
Our faith and strength to carry us thru,
Our task to start a - new.

Roses, Roses, Colors array,
Rich velvety treasures say,
Sing a song of praise and love,
For our Savior above
Enjoy the roses fragrant and gay,
Each moment fill with the best each day,
Let peace and sunshine into your heart,
Then anxious fears depart.
Roses, Roses, Bridal bouquets,
Roses the gift of love always,
Roses are the symbol of love,
That wondrous joy of love.

Miriam C. Hildreth

My Philosophy

The road not taken was surely the road to be taken,
For if it were taken its course would have been the smoother of the
two diverged paths,
For the wear and tear of the later of the pair was harder, rougher,
and needed repair and of course would eventually cause one to
despair.
But the lull of the challenge and the thirst for rewards more often
outweighs the first of the roads...
Which therefore means that the first of the roads is the worst of
the roads thought it's not labeled so,
And the later of the two shall not be the worst of the two even if
it is perceived to be so. Or maybe it is not so...
For the question must be to be or not to be in full satisfaction
of one's choice,
Which may not be easy, but a fraction of the satisfaction would
therefore be unsatisfaction and might make one fidgety. This is my
philosophy.

Catherine Laakso

So I Walk

Some people see the darkness in earth,
Some do not see the beauty in birth.
Some only see the color of greed,
Some see nothing but the nature of their need.
Some see mankind headed right for the ground,
but I walk along seeing life all around.

Some live their life doing something they shouldn't,
Some live their lives doing things that you wouldn't.
Some live their life like it's one big race,
I prefer to walk it at my own pace.

Some like to be busy all of the day,
Some work jobs just for the pay.
Some are angry when things go wrong,
Yet I remain happy just walking along.

Some like to walk with their heads looking down,
Some walk along without making a sound.
Some walk fast to get where they're going,
others walk aimlessly without ever knowing.
Some walk all day with a frown on their face,
I just walk, while life I embrace.

Michael Chen

Take a Lesson from the Wizard of Oz

The talent, the singing, the dancing, the fashion.
Oz can show us a thing or two.
Shimmering shining sparkling sequins-
Dorothy knew how to pick a shoe.
Witchy's wicked cackle,
The Tinman's tap.
Scarecrow's soft shoe,
The Lion's laugh.
For years in black and white and Technicolor
Flying monkeys have given millions a scare.
But perhaps it is not just the thrill and the fun,
Maybe there's something else in there.
It's Lion's courage, Tinman's heart.
Dorothy's home and Scarecrow's smarts.
It's the journey they take and the love that they share,
It's not the rewards, but the getting there.
Stare with awe, wonder,
And tears in the end.
Ponder these heroes
And watch it again.

Elizabeth K. Wainwright

From the Beginning

From the beginning - the first time I saw you
I knew somewhere somehow
I would be with you.

From the very start I loved
you from the bottom of my heart.

Now sometime has passed
I thought you would never come
my way again.

I was wrong you came back
my way once again
maybe it was luck - maybe it was fate.

All I know is
from the beginning I loved you
with all of my heart.

Shanna Ley

Fall Evening

The frosted grass is still.
The glass windows are on fire.
Opposite the red sun slips
Beneath the treetops.
The leaves wither and fall in the wind.

Behind the windows
They sit down for dinner,
Not knowing that the windows are burning,
And the leaves withering.
Their lights are yellow and their talk is warm.

Susan Ellis

Untitled

A study in gray
  Was the sky
    Its clouds burdened with teardrops of rain
      Bare trees, silent
        Like mournful skeletons
          Guarding the vast emptiness of the prairie
            Nothing rises, nothing falls
              Merely exists

Michael Ellis

The Pool

What I find at a particular pool
existing a stone's throw away from Madison
a mixture of the removed and the cool
awaits one in the immersion.

Two attendants in starch white
watch me as I swim alone
bathing in the bluely light
in the eerie water zone.

I kick or dive or float
having a lot of fun
on the water like a boat
until some others come.

They arrive close to five o'clock
with a splash. They're not timorous
and the water begins to rock
for they're very rigorous.

We all swim together
as the attendants preside
in any kind of weather
safely tucked inside.

Meg Fox

Visions

Can be taunting to your soul,
Yet bring smiles that warm your heart,
And fill voids where distance interferes.

They may materialize into future dreams,
Yet plant seeds of doubt that grow,
Into vines that choke our positive paths.

They can freeze our inner thoughts with loneliness,
Or stir the fires of our inner passions,
With burning desires that warm the soul.

Can cause an unreachable pain within,
Or bring a blissful pleasure that heals,
And allows a wounded heart to sing.

May keep a discontented soul heavily grounded,
Or through strength and wisdom cause a spirit,
To soar endlessly on wings as Eagles.

Laurie J. Carpenter

A Young Black Male Between the Ages of 18 and 21

He comes through the crowded hall.
Like a large cat in the jungle, his eyes dart from side to side.
The bell rings.
He sits quietly, a sleeping volcano.

Everyday he slips further away.
Everyday I reach out my hand.
Sometimes I make contact and our eyes lock.
He understands.

After the bell he floats away, caught in the rip tide of the streets-
drugs, girls, and the need for a good time.
My heart cries out at a society that doesn't care,
and youth that can not see the danger.

Susan Rae

Singing Spring

The birds are chirping a twittery song of laughter in the old spruce
    tree,
children are laughing and rolling in the tall grass,
bees buzzing in the air, jumping from flower to flower,
the leaves waving in the air, making a soft motionful breath of
    clutters,
all of these sounds, boisterous and tranquil, make a song,
if you listen closely to one spring day, you will hear a swift lullaby,
never to be repeated,
so unique a sound from them to us,
a small gift it is, for we cannot make such a sound as to put a fairy
    to bed,
as the wind can do so well,
when this sound whispers in your ear,
it is saying welcome singing spring,
a season I now adore.

Brynn Andrews

Flowers

If you ever saw a flower,
You would know this too.
A flower is as beautiful,
As beautiful as you.
Glamouring, glistening petals,
A sign of true beauty,
Is something we all admire,
For all eternity.
It's a privilege to see such wonders,
Creations such as these,
The pretty little flowers, dancing in the breeze.

Jesse Ostertag

Seasonal Changes

The wind blows in my face, and the hair on my back seems to stand
in respect to the great north wind.

The birds of the north fly down to the south
in hop of a sweet haven of rest.

As the winter brings forth long nights and short days,
life becomes a peaceful drama of snowflakes tapping on the
window-sill.

As the wild beasts of the fields close their eyes to go to sleep,
so I find my weary body cuddling under the quilted sheet.

Almost always I find myself drifting away into pleasant thoughts
of Mister Snowman dressed up in his top hat and multicolored scarf
and Saint Nicholas drifting through the sky with a sleigh full of toys.

But, oh! I can not forget the reason there seem to be
a peaceful air on Christmas Eve:
the incarnation that reconciles creation with Creator.

No sooner than I blink my eyes do the snowflakes stop,
and the animals pop their tiny heads out of their resting place.

With twinkles in my eyes, I rush to the window to see the flowers bloom
and hear the birds sing a sweet melody.

Sharon Spencer

How She Is

As light as the breeze she is, she is.
As sweet and fragrant as a budding flower.
Serene as a forest glade she is.
Beautiful as the sun in the dawning hour.

Delicate as dew she is, she is.
She's like a mountain - tall and proud.
She's someone else's love she is.
As far and unreachable as a cloud.

Brett Fletcher

The Great One

Leonardo da Vinci was one of the greats,
he thrived and became famous in his world of paints.
Born in a small village and raised by his father.
he became an apprentice and hard work was no bother.

He did paint in a church with complete grace and style,
his art surpasses others by a Renaissance mile.
The Adoration of Three Kings is today unfinished,
yet Leonardo's popularity never diminished.

He moved to Milan for the next seventeen years,
designing and planning as do most civil engineers.
While in Milan thinking clever as a fox,
he creatively produced Madonna on the Rocks.

Da Vinci finished The Last Supper in fourteen ninety-seven,
according to most it was clearly pure heaven.
For all to admire he rejected the Fresco,
and boldly pronounced he'd remain in the shadow.

Mona Lisa soon followed her smile mysterious,
a figure so striking the art world delirious.
Leonardo was famous for his artistic show,
he was very much a legend and privilege to know.

Shelly Johnson-Whited

Ode To A Bull Rider

A fever sets my soul afire.
  Bred into me is a burning desire.

I dance to the tune of the rodeo sound,
  Eight seconds of glory to win a go-round.

The slide gate slams shut behind chute number four.
  My bull is run in, I hope he don't gore.

I silently ask that I'll meet with no harm,
  While my glove and the rosin I'm tryin' to warm.

Do I ride for the buckles I can put on the shelf?
  Or is this how I prove myself to myself?

Mom, please understand that if my time should come,
  I'm just buildin' mem'ries by the things I have done.

For that's all I'll take with me when I leave this earth,
  And I hope I mark high when they judge my worth.

And to leave, when I go, a small legacy
  That folks left behind might think kindly of me.

Steve DeMott

Our God Above

He created the Earth, he created the sky.
Our God above will never say goodbye.
If you are ever sad and blue, just ask for God to come help you.

He fills our hearts with joy and glee.
My God, my God, he will always be.

He protects us from darkness and we are always in his light.
He gives us his blessing, every morning, noon and night.
He sent us his son Jesus, to save us from our sins.
If we believe him, we will eternally win.

He fills our hearts with joy and glee.
My God, my God, he will always be.

Jesus suffered for us on the cross.
He loves us so much that it wasn't a loss.
We are all guided in God's grace and glory.
I am telling you the truth, this is not a made up story.

He fills our hearts with joy and glee.
My God, my God, he will always be.

Julie Ann Spitaleri

Follow the Robbins

Follow the robbins through the snow.
See them huddle in trees bent low,
Their eyes shut tight against the cold,
They wait for warmth when wings unfold.

Clouds dim the brightness of their breasts,
And wings shed droplets from their nests.
Trust as the robbins in the rain,
And believe that spring is here again.

Watch the robbins hopping by.
They pause to raise beaks to the sky.
Then ride on sunbeams as they soar
Above us to raise our hopes once more.

The robbins know that winter's done,
And soon they'll feel warm summer's sun.
Claim as your own the faith they bring,
And follow the robbins into spring.

Theta Carter

Peak of Life

  I climb a peak of life.
Each step I take is an
adventure or mystery. Each step
makes me wiser. With each
step I grow and live. There
are millions of steps up the peak
of life. From first breath to last breath.
For each and everything you do you
take a step up. When you die you
fall off the peak. You start a
new life by climbing the peak
again. You always take steps
up the peak. You can never
reach the top. Too much to learn,
to know. But you always try, always.

Jayme Hansen

Thinking of You

Thinking of you in my arms. Thinking
of you and all your charms.

Thinking of you when you are here. Thinking
Of you when you are near.

Thinking of you, I can do. Thinking of
you and this love so true,

For thinking of you sees me all the way
through.

So til the next time I see you, it's
thinking of you, my love, to get me through.

I am thinking of you!!!

Tom Richardson

It Takes Me

I get depressed, this emotion I must fight.
For twice it has tried to take my life.

It takes my laughter, my sanity.
My need to care.
It takes me.

It takes me into solitude.
Feeling nothing.
Dazed and confused.

Not always there but won't ever leave.
What am I to do
When it takes me?

Rena Henson

Country Rain

In the country it doesn't matter
If rain descends in windy gales
Splashing upon ponds, and milking pails.

For summer rain is a welcome rain.
Splattering rain-drops along the lane.
Sprinkling thirsty holly-hocks,
Morning glories, and four-o'clocks.
In the fields it's a happy rain,
That washes corn, and soaks the grain.

While we, in the country, without a care,
Run barefoot with rain - drenched hair,
And pity folks on city street,
With dripping hats, and shoe-wet feet.
Kathryn Franks

Alone ...

In the mist of darkness, I find myself alone.
For am I really not alone or just not accompanied.
Alone is without, by oneself or itself.
Without spirit nor soul, without strength, power
nor knowledge.
My reflection lets me believe there's one self
with me.
One to guide me and protect me as one.

Like a cigarette burning, yet it still has flames
and ashes. It does not burn alone.
Like an untamed heart, yet it still love and hurt.
As if, a hand was reaching out but just because the
eyes does not see it, it does not mean it is not there.

So, I ask myself within myself. Am I really alone or
a weakness crying out deep inside of me, wanting attention?
Abigail Figueroa

Untitled

You planted, nurtured, and reaped time's rations
my world would not exist
if not for you fostering the root of idea,
examining every branching shoot,
and caressing my meager color-ridden flowers
that matured as He intended.
You gave life and
reason of being to an inanimate seed.
Now as the sun warms me today,
I reveal my appreciation
for your love and care,
Reap, reap, reap all the joy I can yield
seize my array of love,
like that of a fiery sunflower
ever acknowledging the serenity of sky above.
I contribute my painting of endless indebtedness
through a canvas of cascading waters
past the banks of a river that
supports me, guides my hereafter, and fathoms my intentions.
Thank you for being the Gardener.
Nathan Lee Weathers

My Inspiration

You are my rock.
You are my strength.
You are my inspiration.
You gave me hope at a time when there was not much hope.
You showed me what the true meaning of courage and perseverance is.
You also taught me that life is not something you run away from,
but instead it is something to be savored each step of the way.
It is something that you face head-on regardless of the
challenges that lie ahead.
Marjorie St. Gerard

The Poet

How lonely does a poet live,
  To write of life, the learned things?
Who shall soothe the tortured brow,
  And will not clip creative wings?

Emotions go from heart to mind,
  And through each vein, creation flows,
Born of heartache, love and tears,
  Oh, who can tell from poets's woes?

A look can mean a warm embrace,
  Each kiss becomes a love affair,
And to the poet, though just a spark,
  'Tis like a flame in the devil's lair.

They who love, oft use a poem,
  Given birth by another's pen,
But who can poets depend on,
  When it seems their world has reached its end?

For if a poet cannot find,
  Someone to love and be loved by,
Without that inspiration,
  The poem and poet will surely die!
Riobart E. O'Braoin

Precious Gems

If your heart feels heavy, it may be weighted down
With the many precious gems you've failed to pass around.
Diamonds are the loving words you always leave unsaid,
Rubies are the seeds of joy that you refuse to spread.
Emeralds are the helping hands only offered grudgingly,
Sapphires are alms not given to ease a person's need.

Changing won't be easy, and it may even smart,
As you begin to mine the gems embedded in your heart.
First you'll feel a secret fear you may be refused,
Or a deep abiding resentment that you are being used.
It takes a lot of practice to hold these feelings at bay,
While learning the neglected art of giving yourself away.

But as you sow your precious gems along life's many miles,
Rejoice at how they sparkle in people's happy smiles.
Soon you'll begin to marvel at the change in your attitude,
Even when a gem or two elicits no gratitude.
And your heart that was so heavy will now be airy and light,
Soaring up to God's heaven like a carefree bird in flight.
Alice M. Antlsperger

What Is Love?

There is a divine feeling called love,
  Made up of multiple dimensions.
We speak of love in numerous ways,
  And with many mixed emotions.
Poets attempt to give love fine phrase,
  But fall short because of amaze,
Confronted with the overwhelm
  To find the terms that spell the realm
Which ev'ry love encompasses!
  As males languish at their lasses,
Who can show in word on or action
  What love is, and the direction
Pursued to find heart feeling,
  Often sending lovers reeling?
Edmund J. Radasch

Answers

Life all began when they heard your first cry,
Elsewhere someone's mourning, for a close friend that has died.
Life is too short to dwell on such things,
So says a voice, what joys can you bring?
A bright smile to someone's face, or a cold stare as if war,
Just think of all the time we've wasted, fighting should be
no more.

To win, or to lose, who cares what's the score,
If it's done together, you may enjoy it a bit more.
Time should be no factor, only who it is spent with,
Have some fun, and be yourself, stop worrying about what
others think.

Victory is found within ones very own heart,
Just remember; respect your friends, don't pick them apart.
When all else fails, and there is nothing left to prove,
Sit back and let things go, let someone else make the first move.
Whether the decision they make be right or wrong,
Just think about what you have learned, and keep moving along.

Gretchen E. Bennett

The Calming Storm

    A flash of light, darkness deeper than
seconds ago. The expected rumble, increasing
in intensity until it reverberates into the depths
of your soul....silence...flash,
the horizon embedded on your eyes leaving the
memory a hundred times longer than the vision
itself....rumble...darkness...
    silence....reflections on past laughter,
of good times. Flash....a moment of self
pity...Rumble...darkness,
    silence......Reflections of a dream....
Flash....thoughts of God.....
    Rumble....Silence....wonderment of Angels,
Darkness........Flash....Rumble
Hopes for the future....silence...future plans
    Flash....Rumble....Sleep.

S. R. McElroy

Nightmare

Awaken me
I'm in a terrible dream
I open wide my lips
And hear the silent scream.
Help me now before it is too late
Realize the dreadful need of me to know my fate.
I'm caught up in this dreamlike span
And walk as if a frozen man
My secret yearning now to know
What lies ahead,
Hold out your hand, help me
Face this awful dread!
Awaken me
Touch me gently, call my name
Lead me into day again.
Once I see the morning light
I'll forget this long dark night.

Marie E. Cook

Midnight

The deeper shades of brown
the lighter the hues
the romantic color of my people
can be seen within those rhythm and blues
I don't know why
some people just don't understand
the quality of being
such a part of
a wide spectra of the shade of brown
just as the apple has its core
and the tree has its roots
there is strength held dear
within the deeper shades of brown
for some it's hard to tell
but for me it's very clear
I know that smile, that sway, that move
that relativity
that's distinct among the deeper shades of brown
amaretto, cappacino, coffee, tan,
burnt sienna, honey, mocha... Peach.

Edwina F. Howard

Memories By Moonlight

With the moonlight shining on my aging body
my memories go to years past.

Casual conversations, accidental touching of
hands, sly winks, notes passed and stolen kisses.

Later, the hours spent in the porch swing,
walks down the path to the lake. Then came the
day he received his army draft notice.

Still later we said "I do" and promised to love,
honor and cherish "until death do us part."

By death we are now parted. As I sit in the moonlight
my memories return to long ago. It all
started when he was a professor and I was a student.

Emily W. Baker

Changing Dreams

I've always been a dreamer
But my dreams never seemed near
I've been a model, athlete and actor
And never had any fear
I've finally found a reachable dream
One that could be seen
In the near future, or so it seemed
To go back to college and graduate
To be successful and educated.
Then one day I woke up, not feeling well
I cried for days because I thought my dream had been lost
And unreachable at any cost
Then I realized that my dream would just have to be on hold
Until the new baby was a few years old
Now, as the months go by
I see that dreams can wait
For there are more important things in life than reaching dreams
And one is the gift of life.

Michelle Scesa

Ode To Nancy

There is a season to be born yet only God knows our departure
I knew you not before your death
I wish I had...I wish I had.

They tell me of your heartaches
The cross you bore so graciously
Alone and hurting in dismay
I could have helped...I could have helped.

Your friends who love you, mourn your absent
Tears from strangers fill their eyes
They wish to tell you how they miss you
Farewell to thee...Farewell to thee.

The suffering, pain, tears and sadness confusion and turmoil
The Lord our God removed from you
I give to you today my child
Eternal rest...Eternal rest.

And while we do not understand
Or know the reason for your death
We know that heaven is a place where you belong...Where you belong.

So let us now embrace each other in love and unity
We do not know who we are embracing another friend leaving this world.

Blanca T. Woody

Second Chance Proud

My life changed tremendously once I quit drinking and doing drugs.
I soon realized all the beauty of all life that God put on this earth.
God led me in the right direction and I want to thank Him
for that because today I have a wonderful husband and a son I love
and admire which I never would have, if I hadn't stopped all that.

So, I'm writing to you dear God, to thank you oh so much for taking
care of me while I was under the influence. I'm grateful that
I did no harm in hurting someone else, with me drinking and driving
all the time, it could have ended up a tragic mess.

So, now I'm one less drunk driver driving all around. I haven't had
a drink in twelve years this Spring and that something to be proud of!

Char Roderick Patrick

Ordinary Girl

I am an ordinary girl.
I wonder what it would be
like to be someone else.
I hear the footsteps of a giant.
I see tiny fairies in the sky.
I want to stop pollution.
I am an ordinary girl.

I pretend that I can fly.
I feel the burning of hot coals.
I touch the silkiness of the sky.
I worry that the world will come to an end.
I cry when a loved one dies.
I am an ordinary girl.

I understand that we can't live forever.
I say that all things will go well.
I dream about being in the land of chocolate.
I try to do my best in all I do.
I hope I will live a long happy, life.
I am an ordinary girl.

Jill White

My Wedding

"The Last and Final Word Were"
On that final awakening day
All things seem to go the wrong way.
The Mother and Daughter laughing and crying,
The Father and Son remembering and sighing.
Walking up the isle in my beautiful beige dress
My Dad walking aside me in his shinney silk vest.
My fiancee standing and waiting
    with excitement in his eyes.
And the preacher began to saying,
With Astonishment and Surprise
That we were gathered here today
Then concluding the suspension
The vow was mentioned
The Last and Final Words Were
    "I Do"

Mary Diane Trujillo

Sad Farewell

Thoughts of a young man who still deeply cares.
For a young girl who left deep despair
All of the evenings spent with my thoughts alone
So much of the time that you never were home
Trying so hard to reach out and please
To find fault with that you were eager to siege
This girl close to my heart, that I thought I knew
Was some one else not at all like you
A lady so dear yet with in her cold steel
As my years go by I pray this will heal
To have let me be able to reach out and touch
Let it be known that you mattered so much
Having high aims I would have made it I'm sure
Not having your care I was that less secure
Good bye to my bride whom I looked at with pride
Believing for ever she would be at my side
My dear in the future I wish you the best
With a cold heart you won't settle for less

Virginia Clements

A Reunion

There is such joy in having kin
    Past times together have caused many a grin.
Memories we recall as we reflect on what has been
    Sharing good times and times of chagrin.

As we gather together for a reunion with our folk
    We will have many happy hours for talk, music and to joke.
Because of mile distances family visits have been broken
    Why even some of us haven't in years even spoken.
That is why for a reunion I tried to provoke
    Interest from everyone to gather and see kinfolk.

Time passes quickly and we often lose a reunion's chance.
    But they are important and do a family's kinship enhance.
Some can't participate because of various circumstance.
    Others I fear may not care and choose not to come perchance.

Family members (as the world) change day by day
    Some being born and others passing away.
But by getting together this year, I must say.
    We can renew our kinship in a special way.
We'll remember those who couldn't come and are away
    Hoping in the future they will cross our path's way.

Judy Cunningham

To My Brother

Somewhere beyond the darkness of the night,
Where moonbeam corridors can shed no light,
A journey ends.

For there is an empty chair at the table this year,
And musical notes we will never again hear,
And gifts lay unopened under the tree.

Even this magical man called Santa can't tell
Where you are now and how you are doing, how well,
Yet I know you are safe.

I just want you to know how much you are missed,
How I long to hug you and give you a kiss,
And I know that you know.

I never got to tell you goodbye my brother,
Although I knew you were leaving my world,
And I still can't say it.

For somewhere beyond this breathing point of light,
Where souls are living and there are no nights,
Our paths will cross again... I love you.

Nancy Tucker

When Love?

By herself she stands
No one needs to hold her hand
Only needs the one above
To send her unconditional love

A love that last
Built from the past
A love that's free, so plain to see,
This love, it has security

Looked for, but blessed the one who finds
A love that brings you peace of mind
Don't try to hide, for it will show
Don't hide your love, they'll never know

If caught, be quick, and hold on tight
You will not win, if love you fight
You will succeed, but do take heed
If missed your chance of true romance

Go back and find the one you love
The love that's sent from up above
Make up for wrongs, can't change the past
Cause never ends a love that lasts

Marlo McDonald

Untitled

I awoke, tonight, or I should say,
Hours before the light of day,
Roused by winds; my window pane
Held a sight, I'll long retain.

The clouds were rushing, hurtling past
Tremendous flocks, stampeding, massed,
Before a force of mighty pace,
Along the sky's wide open space.

Across the moon sped long, grey wraiths
Like a thin and wavering faith;
And piled pink gobs with silvery strands
Made as dreams rose from the land.

God's power and majesty set free
Were like a flowing, endless sea
That filled the sky, the universe
Sweeping past, too vast for earth.

Yet, feared I not, for now I rest
In the knowledge, calm and blest;
The hand of God, our way controls
Midst the turmoil, to console.

Norma I. Vinson

My Precious Cindy

The melody in her heart, the rhyme in her mind
Her body moved to the rhythm in perfect time,
Her feet floated, her body moved swiftly.
The melody soft and uplifting,
And she danced.

With grace across her floor, under the stars,
Down by the sea,
Her rhythm now known,
She called to me. And she sang,

A voice blessed with harmony,
A spirit so pure with trust;
A name unknown she sang to us, and I cried.

No my tears were none of vain
Of disbelief or even of pain;
With an abundance of joy
I felt the rain,

And I danced, and I sang!
What a beautiful melody,
My rhythm, my rhyme,
My precious Cindy.

Charlotte M. Ash

Someday

I see you, please see me.
Trust me, as I would you.
Give me your love, to be treasured forever.
I'll give you the key, to my virgin heart.
If only you'll guard it with your life, as you could be my life.
Hold me so close, and I'll never leave.
I know enough, to have no fears, and although love hurts.
I'm willing to risk it, to be with you,
no one else, and maybe you'll see me,
the way I see you, because I love you so very much.
I hope it won't be a secret forever, but be so true,
our hearts wont ever love again.
Just long to be together, till death do us part.

Natalie J. Poulson

The Secret

There goes the bumble-bee-flying here and there,
And there goes the butterfly....flitter without care.
There goes the hummingbird, she flutters in the air.
Look! Quick!! Before they go-there's something I must share.

All three hold a secret and it's something they can see.
It visits them at night, gliding with the breeze,
dancing in the air, and feeling fancy-free.
It's her-the merry fairy-Miss Penelopee.

She sprinkles dew on flowers as she sings a happy song;
Then flying fast, showers dew across the fresh mowed lawn.
When her duty's call has stopped, she gives a great big yawn;
And as the sunshine heats the day, she knows where she belongs.

Quick—into the Buttercup—Penelopee makes her bed
And when her wings stop fluttering, she gently rests her head.
As she slumbers sweetly, the others (it is said)
Watch her place till dusk appears—dark and ruby red.

So...now you know the secret about the bumble bee,
The butterfly, the hummingbird, and Miss Penelopee.
So if you're very careful (and if you will believe)
Someday you might spy upon Miss Penelopee.

Donna Flory Faust

Reality

I once looked inside of me,
to see what was really in there.
What I saw was a heart all shrivelled up and old,
I wondered what this meant,
but failed to find the answer.
I looked inside once more,
Saw a black hole with a drop of red tear.
I had a disgusted feeling,
didn't know what was wrong,
Everywhere I looked, I saw fear and confusion.
I had lost myself in darkness,
or that is what I thought.
Little did I know what was inside was not dark.
It was what I was looking through that made it look dark.

Avijit Gupta

May

Your spring be warm, with showers - abundant,
green grasses with fragrant, budding flowers.
You live in health and always to prosper,
with growing wealth out of the Good News!

Your joys be many, in substance, serving,
with gratifications - always growing.
You find your way in work, to be life's passion,
with God's guidance in abundance - rewarding!

Your contentment grow, warm in harmony,
with lasting friends and friendships - plenty.
You do your work so well, its benefits provide
joy and inspiration within other's souls.

Your family be supportive, sharing your blissfulness,
and glee; loving you well, in times as allotted.
You find respect for your accomplishments - many,
and for the person that you have become.

Your peace be of mind; and of a body - many faceted,
with a soul that is sparkling, and forever lasting.
You know your faith in wonder, fortunate in full life,
knowing you'll never walk unguided, unguarded, nor alone!

Ron Manclaw

The Love I Learned

Time is precious and so are we;
There is much love between you and me.
The time I spend with you can only be spent positively.
I never thought it would happen to be.
That innocent, small little old me
Could become all I wanted to be.
You gave me the strength
And the confidence I needed
To keep going, so that I will succeed.
I never cheated!
You made me feel that I was the only one
Who could tackle you and show
Everyone that it can be done.
You gave me courage that showed through and through.
I love you, and I know you love me too!
Me and you equals a great love between 2.

Samahra Wheless

Who Do They See?

Lord, who do they see when they're looking at me?
Just hustle and hurry and activity?
No time for my neighbors, not even my friends?
When they're looking at me, is that what they see?

Does the way that I walk, the way in which I speak,
Reveal any clue that it's you whom I seek?
Is there a clear glimpse that it's you I embrace?
Can they see you in me? Do you show on my face?

Oh whatever it takes what e're that might be,
Your Nature impart, way down deep winsomely!
I fail you so often, but grant me this plea,
When they're looking at me only you would they see.

Yes Lord, this is my prayer — "Jesus in me."
So crystal and clear, no mistake can there be.
Smiling and shining and praising, so You
Are lifted up! Exalted! Yet living in me!

Goldie M. Bristol

If I Were....

If I were a rose
I would bloom to be red
I would give you my fragrance
I would shine for you
Then you'd just be mine
Or shall I just die for you
If I were; if I were

If I were a monkey
I would swing from trees
I would eat the bananas
They would be all gone
I will cry for you
Or shall I just stay in my dine
because I am so hungry, or is it all right
for me to die for you
If I were; if I were

Rickeshia Moon

The Unhappy Cabaleiro

A lullaby brings you the night of the roses,
For it's only in dreams that my love comes to you.
Than, during the day, my yearning just loses
May be you wait for the night to fall, too.

It's when the moon comes - he kisses you tender,
And girts you with all the silver he out there can find.
He knows like me your body so tender
And it drives me almost out of my mind.

With star dust ornates you the night of the sagebush
My love, it's the only gold I can give you by right.
For my thoughts are the trembling of cobwebs,
Desires shooting stars in the night.

The day is spend — the end is here —
and should the saddest thing you hear
Forget me not — just keep the thought —
My love will be forever near.

Hedi Beck

Life's Journey

Such is life, tumbling grains of sand
being washed out to the sea,
On a journey never ending, nor possible
to turn back and touch again, the most
waking, beautiful moments of the hours passed,
Such is life, wonders of all wonders,
taking those moments from time and
weaving our life, like spun silk,
giving to us memories, that speak to
the heart, touch the soul and bring
together a one perfect union of self,
and free spirits of all natures,
Such is life, a melody of emotions
gently resting on trembling wings of joy
together forever and ever

Deborah Lee Mason

Along The Mountainside

The mountain is so lovely and green,
'Tis also so quiet and serene.
As the wind blows through the grass.
I stroll along the old dirt pass.
The pass goes along the mountainside.
'Tis very narrow then very wide.
Up and down it goes along.
While birds are singing soft sweet songs.

Beautiful flowers I have spied.
Along the beautiful mountainside.
I go by trees and brush galore.
Then stray off the path some more.

'Tis getting dark and cool again,
and clouds cover the moon now and then.
I best now start heading home.
Though I'd rather stay and roam.

The sky is beautiful this time of year.
With many stars here and there.
I wish I did not have to return.
I wish I did not have to return.

Kelly Savin

Anew

Under the blanket of night I strolled the streets looking for my
    direction.
Trying to turn my desperate life by finding the right connection.
Seeking solace through my search to enlighten my chasmed heart;
A shadow appeared beside the church; an angel from the dark.
Whispering softly through the wind, "Is it me for which you seek?"
Oak like steady - firm and strong - my knees becoming weak.
"Why is it now that you have come?", my mind began to wander.
"Could it be that God of good decided of me to plunder?"
"No", she said and pulled me near, "in fact your God has sent me
to give you guidance and heal your fright. It's then that you will see."
Every episode, plain and clear, flashed before my eyes.
All the anguish and the pain forever to despise.
I took her gently by the hand and up away we flew;
Leaving behind my life so damned, with her to start anew.

Tony Johnson

Our First Time

There has only being one love in my life, and that love has brought
me to be a wife. You and I had waited years for that special moment
of occur. The stars shine brighter than ever before and our hearts
pounded loudly in the silence of the night and then, we touched, it
was like two worlds colliding. We loved like there was no end, and
we touched so unbelievably. Our thoughts swirled without dimension, and
our souls soared undefiningly. Absorbed by the rapture of erotic
pleasures, we were sweep off our feet like wings from above. We
soared to greater heights of desire than we ever could imagine. No
thoughts of our surrounding just our being until we relapsed into an
unseen estate of immeasurable ecstasy.
Darling, every time we touch it is like we leave this world and enter
into an unknown destiny. Our desires go beyond any limits on this
earth, just as my love for you it is boundless.

Lesa Rains

Grandma's Lap

It seems that grandma's always need
A little one to hold.
To nestle warm and snuggle close,
And shelter from the cold.

I used to hold your mom you know,
The way that she holds you.
I love her very much you know,
The way that she loves you.

But God intended for her,
To be a mommy and a wife.
Now she's all grown up and married,
With little ones all her own.

So that's why he created grandchildren,
To fill the empty gap.
It's such a lonely world you know,
So come sit on grandma's lap.

Linda L. Adams

Changes

Late in the fall, snow finally starts to lay
as the frost of the season gathers on windowpanes.

But inside, it is all so different.
Humid air rushes through the building.

Sounds of music and laughter clutter the air
as they drink themselves to happiness one more time.

  Intoxicating drinks used for confidence.
  Make-up and shy smiles used as a mask.

  Beautiful women, masculine men.
  All so easy, like a way of life.

  Morning comes, awake to a shock:
  Mr. Right, the jobless alcoholic,
  Mrs. Right, the talk of the town.

  You, in the midst, hazy, unsure,
  wanting to remember, so you're able to forget.

Jennifer Friedl Kaline

Decisions

Decisions - The right one for this time and place.
The past is gone with many roads traveled for good or ill.
Relatives, friends, neighbors, acquaintances, business associates,
Will they subtly influence my thinking this hour?
Have I learned from experience? Are my opinions sounder today
Than yesterday? Have I gained insight from past mistakes?
Has wisdom developed and guided my choices of late years?
What benefit the errors of previous days?
Youth - adulthood. Middle age - advanced years. Have I matured?
Have I replaced feelings, emotions, with sound judgment?
The waning years allow few choices. Time may be escaloped
within
a few months, a few years.
This may be the last major decision.
Will it prove to be the right one?

Dorothy Tobey

Why Must We Have War

Why must we have war, there has to be a better way.
It seems that death and violence is much to high a price to pay.
We must show some compassion, and throw our pride away.
Then set down side by side, and let our Lord and savior lead the way.
There is no room for greed or personal pride, to clutter up our minds.
If we take the time we need to negotiate, a better solution we can
    find.
There are too many personal ideas, that are getting in the way, and
messing up the minds of multitudes, causing them to stray.
To me the solution is quite simple!
Show love and compassion in everything you do, and don't leave room
for greed and violence to take control of you.

Donald L. Claflin

To My Love...

Look at me, as I lie here in your arms, and remember the times that
    we've shared.
You and me, who will last forever, never will our paths come apart.
Hopes and dreams are what keep us together, along with the love in
    our hearts.

With you I am free to be no more than me, your love gives me
    reason to live.
Death is all that could tear us apart, but nothing can destroy our love.
Times are good, times are bad, but through it all we will stand
together.

Paul Emerson

Forever Learning of Thee

Mine eyes have seen thy glory,
I have basked beneath thy sun.

I've been taught ... the age old story,
Of Jesus Christ ... God's beloved son.

I've been redeemed ... to worship and know thee,
And to embrace thy commandments ... written in stone.

Cherishing thy holy sovereignty ... serving your majesty alone
Lord, grant that we shall ever be ... serving thee in humility

May we lift up Holy Hands
Pledging our love ... throughout the land

Make us proper stewards of thy ... bountiful Creation,
The land, the trees, the seas ... and all thy diverse nations.

Cast out our sins ... and cleanse our vessels,
Instruct us, shape us ... try and test us

Sustain us through principalities ... which we may Wrestle
Secure in thy divine love ... we trust

Teach us thy statutes Lord Jesus ... and thy Holy Decrees,
And endow that we shall be ... now and forever learning of Thee!

Lillian Harrison Williams

Father

Water.. green, yellow hues surround the shore.
Leaves float, as stillness cradled the air.
A wooden deck, piles of cones laying
As coldness and dark skies continued to flow.
She sat alone, thoughts in memories rage in her mind.
Clouds bringing white caps crashing to her, coldness
Beginning to dampen the air
Pound the memories to remain.
As she forgot to shadow them in the cast,
Thoughts of smells and scents flooded her mind.
Escaping as the fish swam, she watched in quite, still
Silence.
Music danced in her mind, songs returned the letters.
A time of remembrance,
Her scarf blew.
No jacket kept warmth as did the memories.
His smile, strength and pride
Brought one tear, as did the memory.
The fish continued to swim
As she remembered, walking away.

Susan Biggs

Love

First I shall seek thee within my heart
    for we are long apart.

I shall seek thee at dawn
    for thou has traveled far and beyond.

I shall welcome thee into my home,
    though I live there all alone.

Fill my home through and through
    for my whole life I have seeked you.

Though I had to find you within my self

Before I could give you to
    some one else.

Billy E. Harris

Untitled

I survey the lights of Quebec City,
From nine stories above real ground,
And of all the thousands there illumined,
Only one shines in my now jaded heart.

Beyond the lights blow the Arctic winds.
Their brutality knows no mercy, nor naivete.
Any romance up there is fictional.
So it's to my back, South, where she waits.

Yet like the Northern gusts and beacons,
She is, by turns, harsh and sparkling—
Realizing compassion only through Nature,
That is, when beholding what she has borne.

She is beautiful to see, and so the North,
But chilly to commune with and embrace.
The lights brighten the dead cold sky,
While she brings charm to an uncaring world.

In the dreary suburbs of Boston, she glows,
Shooting magnificently across my vision.
From up here in Quebec, I can still see
The residual flickering of her Northern Lights.

James F. Johnson

Somewhere, Somehow, Someway...

Somewhere in time we will be together.
When that time comes, our love only to stay.
As winter turns to summer, so love grows.
It will be the years spent everlasting.

Somehow in time we will be together.
How we will get there? Our hearts only know.
As rain turns to sunshine, so love grows.
It will be the years spent everlasting.

Someway we will find, our time together.
What questions we may have now; answered then.
As we see ourselves now, we know will grow.
It will be the years spent everlasting.

Someday we will find, our hearts reunite.
That time and day a covenant to stay.
As two people become one, their love for each other.
It will be many years everlasting.
Somewhere, somehow, someway,
Someday...

Bernie Schultz

A Precious Gift

Throughout the year we exchange presents.
Some fancy and full of frills.
Others are plain and simple,
But still a gift of our love.

Some gifts we give are expensive.
Others not so much- but still nice.
But all the gifts we give each other,
Are gifts given to show our love.

There is one gift that stands above all others,
Although, not fancy or full of frills.
It is the greatest gift we can give another.
"Ourself" - the most precious gift of love.

Ruth Gambino

I Am

I am the pen that once wrote in the book of love.
I see and I live love and its bountiful challenges.
I am a mere speck in the rainbow of life.
I have witnessed life, and death, and I respect all that live and
    have lived.
I am the seed planted in the garden of life.
I hope for all that come before me, and those who are still
    to come.
I am the hopes of my fore fathers.
I am the spirit of slaves who fought for justice, and now
    rest in peace.
I am the wind beneath an eagle's soaring wings.
I am a fish swimming in the waters of truth, and justice.
I am the messenger of God, and yet I am his child living and
    learning his words.
I am the dreams of small children.
I am the fairy in the night granting good to all who believe in me.
I am the wisher upon stars.
I am the child within.
I am Life, Love, and Freedom.
I am many things in many forms some times I am small, or I may
    be tall but I am always me.

Ashleigh-Lynn Janson

I'll See You Again

At first it was hard to think of you.
And I did not know what to do.
They said it would get better with time.
I consider that lie a crime.
Your death had given me pain.
My life seemed like a dreary rain.
Five years and I still cry.
Can't help but ask myself "Why?"
November second haunts the year
Every time I shed a tear.
As time is passing, is it healing?
Or is it just forgetting? I can't shake the feeling!
I think if I'm not sad I'm cruel,
How could God take such a jewel?
Life seems so unfair,
It feels like my heart is going to tear.
Realizing one mistake and you could be gone,
Always live your life by every dawn,
Yet even though I don't know when,
I know that I'll see You again!!!

Maureen Hoehing

She Comes In Light

The 20th Century gains rewards
In the midst of its blood bath...
A spiritual battle continually unfolds
And leads to aftermath.

Although we suffer and some are lost
She comes in light for all...
Three hundred sites do boast of this
Perhaps we'll heed Her call.

Her messages are bestowed
The "chosen" repeat them well...
For this Lady who comes in light
To sound the Holy Bell.

Her call is clear, Come back to God
She warns, do fast and pray...
Here's one more chance to see it through
For only then She'll say...

"My children, you have heeded well
God's mercy poured its count...
Souls are saved, Satan lost
His fires have been put out!"

Arline T. Kendrick

Fantasy Land

I reflect the moment, I first saw your face,
Lust for your beauty just crumbled my humble place.

Every time a man sees a woman, he loses his mind,
The woman won't allow him the love, he desperately
wants to find.

Girl, why are my emotions so strong for you?
My affection for you will never feel spoiled like mildew.

I will never be deceitful, for I'm destined to express my honesty,
Love you forever is a promise to me and certain it will last
until eternity.

Stand up with honor for thought is deeper than a moat,
The soft voice spoke with a mind more remote.

Riding a trojan horse protect me from getting all wet,
while nature takes it course as a ransom all met.

Now, I will wait for our mind, body and soul to be attached.
So that you and I could develop a strong relationship based
on facts.

Love you forever, is my promise to be,
and I'm certain it will last until eternity.

Gerard Getfield

Preschool Days

Now I'm three, I go to Preschool, all the kids are really cool!
I look, I feel, I see, I say, all I want to do is play.
We sit together and have our snacks,
In small group we feel things in sacks,
Then we sit in circle and sing along,
Mommy do you know that song?

Now I'm four, I'm going back to school,
There's this one kind there who's really cool!
Some kids are back, some kids are new,
Bev has all kinds of things to do
We go to the playground and play on the slide,
When it rains too much we stay inside.
We go to the gym where we learn dancing too,
Mommy Daddy do you see what I can do?

Now our days at preschool are almost done,
It sure has been a lot of fun.
Soon it will be time for summer vacation,
Of course first we'll have our graduation!
I'll miss Bev and all the parents when preschool ends
But I will always remember with love my preschool friends

Karen Bukantz

To You.....Even After the Fight

I can't stop loving you, I've made up my mind
to live in love with you for all time
then it dawned on me...that love is so blind
to be in love so much when it can be cruel and unkind
I decided then and I made up my mind
to be in love anyway with you for all time
because, what's worse, even thought it's not real
to think of it without you, how I would feel?

Then the tears come and an ache inside that doesn't compare
to the short griefs we bear when in love that we all share
if then all other flowers are a fancy and a whim
and true love is just and only a rose, remember the thorns
when you touch it beware; with caution,
carefully adoring the aroma and its beauty,
remembering when you find yourself stuck and bleeding
it was the thorn, and not the rose, that gave you that wound
then you'll love the rose more than you thought you might;
even after the fight
I love you and I've made up my mind to live in love with you
for all time.

Tom Collins

Country Prayer

Lord, I never did learn how to pray,
in a way that was fittin' to be heard...
You see, sir, I'm jist a common man
and I ain't too good with them ten dollar words

I only know we need ya' sir,
don't matter if the sun is up or down
I bet if you're a hearin' this
you'd, most likely, smile...more'n frown...

I ask ya kindly Lord to give us peace and rest this day...
and if I git in trouble sir, please don't be to fer away
And if I fergit to thank ya Lord, fer any of the good thangs that ya do...
Please remember...I'm jist a common man and never learned how to
    talk to you

Oh yes, Lord, I near fergot, to ask fer blessin's on this little town
and fer it's fine folks here, who, sometimes, don't member you're
    around...
Don't blame 'em sir, if, now and then, they git a little out of step...
'Cause they's also jist common folks, and sure can use a heap of
    help...

Bob Nance Evans

The Tunnel

How far have I come.
I've never felt so dead within...
The longer the journey, the more I seem to lose
sight of your glory.
Your wonderful majesty is a prize I long to win.
It is my personal battle.
Some have temporary fights, mine is an unending war.

Yet, because he died, I cannot lose my war.
But is the fight worth it, when all you notice
is the bodies on the side of those who didn't make it.
How far can I go, that is the news.

How far have I gone;
I keep walking in hope that my mind will lose
all the doubts of what the tunnel brings.
Yet, there is hope in that tunnel.
Hope that no matter how far I went, how far I
still have to go, you will be there at the end —

With a smile on your face saying, "I've been waiting,"
"Come home."

James Patrick Cinnamo

Mom's Story

You talk about loneliness,
You feel sorry for yourselves with little problems.
Help me! And you won't
Love me! And you don't
Hold me! And you push me away.

He won't stop touching me!
All I ever asked for was a hug, to look into my daddy's eyes, sit on
his knee have him love me, have him hold me.
But all these hopes are smashed by his drunken rages and fits.

She pushes me away too! Loves her drink more than me.
Why won't she see the tears in my eyes, the bruises, burns, and pain.
Can't she see me screaming Mommy Save Me!

People don't talk about my problems they whisper behind closed doors.
"What should we do about little Nancy?"
They do nothing!
It's impossible to feel love when no one cares.

I can't deal with physical, mental, and sexual abuse without help!
Mom and Dad tell me not to talk about it!
Please hear my story!
Listen, help, and don't push me away!

Danielle Lea Sharp

O' Earth

O' earth, I feel the breeze from your wind that blows,
I see the tree branches, over the shadowy grove.
The beautiful birds, flying through the sunny skies,
singing one to another, from their nest on high.
O' earth, I hear your music, that fills the quiet air,
I see all the pretty blossoms, so young and so fair.
The green sunny pastures, surrounds the calmness of the sea,
from the mountains top on high, your beauty I can see.
O' earth, I see the dust that blows from the stormy wind,
I feel all of life's kindness, from natures best friend.
The sweet smelling roses that thirst for the morning dew,
the beauty of the honeysuckle, O' earth, it belongs to you.

Wilma Cummings

Praising God

Praising God should be easy to do
In church, on the job
And around your friends too.

Just think of the bad times, sad times
And hurting times too
But because of God's grace
He has delivered me and you.

When times were at their darkest
And friends turned their back
God had made provisions
So that there was nothing we would lack.

God has been faithful
And His word is very true
If you put your faith in Him
He will always bring you through.

So think where God has brought you from
And all that He has done
Praise Him who is the highest
For in Him, your battle is won.

Tracy V. Swain

Creating Dreams

On days when gloom consumes my being
And from my cares I feel like fleeing,
I start to write a few rhyming themes
To soothe my mind and create some dreams.

My mind can take me many places
And even conjure up some faces
From the past with memories pleasant
Or to the future from the present.

My thoughts just race for the words I seek
To write a message instead of speak.
To friends and loved ones I write with joy
And some words of hope and strength employ.

And so as I go along my way,
My words will last and they will stay
A memento of my love for rhyme
Anyone can read from time to time.

Shirley Schneider

A Moment From Last Night

Can't I want you anymore
than I did last night
when we were together in that friendly, far off way
forever for the last time
the night closed in and you were on the steps
and I was lying in the grass
tearing at my hair
cursing her and you and the four that smoked some yards away
sitting with you on the porch
the girls you've known much longer
than me
you talked to them
and I sat silently
Forgetting what I wanted to tell you
When I just came
and for the first time
We were almost all alone

Irina Levin

Valentine's Day

To you who's so special on Valentine's Day,
Even though we're not together, I'll think of you always,
To the love we have cherish,
Although very short,
The moment we've shared will be kept in my heart,
Protected and remembered that we're never apart.
Love is powerful,
You'll never know what will happen,
Holding hands and hugging one day,
Maybe a first kiss,
It works all sorts of ways.
Nothing else matters to me,
As long as you care,
Roses for each day that we might share.
Although we're forbidden to meet each others' love,
We'll still find each other like two lost doves.
I just want you to know that you will always be a part of me.
Until we meet again,
Until we're free.

Betty Tia

The Rhyme of the Seance

By moonlight, in an empty parking lot,
a motor-coach medium, her crystal shot
with power from beyond the Veil,
would show us dark spirits only she could hale.
Clutching her jewel, she gave a long shiver
while phosphorous blossoms took shape to quiver
once, then dissolve and flow
like strings of taffy all aglow;
molding into shapes unknown
(Their origins lost in a strange ozone.)
We saw our former lives retold
in ectoplasmic jungle folds;
for all would learn each other's ends,
make good stories; impress some friends.
Until at last the strain took toll.
(Explosive decompression of the soul).
Head follows jewel down to table,
departing with enlightenment, (or fable?)
But now we're drawing up our wills,
while the motor-coach medium pays her bills.

Robert Dunlap

Catch Ya In The Wind (Grandma)

The love from a grandmother can't be written on paper alone.
It was written by the Lord and the heaven's above.
Now heaven's winds and the Lord have reclaimed her as there own.
But for the love she has left with me,
and her memories shall never fade.
For I have branded them in my heart and soul.
And I shall pass them to my friends, family and children;
For them to relish, learn and save.
I will always miss my grandmother.
There will forever always be her smiling face in my mind.
But I guess God needed her help this time.
So till grandma I catch that same wind;
I know you were missed where you're at
But you will always be loved and missed here where you have been.
So have a peaceful and safe journey;
for one day we all will be together again.
We will all love and miss you grandma;
Till we all catch the Lord wind.
  Love ya grandma,
   Catch ya in the wind

Rick Valasco

A Thin Grey Line

There I stood transfixed;
Not knowing whether to let my mind fully understand.
For to know, would mean to be dead.
That thin line of grey between life and death,
As from sanity to madness, can be crossed but once.
And yet, who knows;
Death may mean life and insanity may be sanity,
And that thin line but a pause in between,
Separating light from dark and black from white.
My mind had dared to approach that grayness
And try to comprehend but yet not cross the line;
Only to realize that to cross, would not be to understand.
For after that line;
Might there yet be another and another,
To be approached and crossed like a bridge;
For have I not read somewhere that there is no beginning and there is
   no end?

Angela Tella

The Sty In My Eye

I awoke one morning to see that a sty had visited me;
not the kind pigs live in, but rather rest on the skin
of an eyelid for all to see.

I pondered the thing, "Rather small," I proclaimed, it
shouldn't be a problem to me.
But later on I observe many a good friend had swerved
to avoid coming in contact with me.

I asked a young lady to tea. Her reaction still puzzles me.
With a shake of her head, she turned instead, and walked
away from me. I think deliberately!

So I rushed home desperately to see what was wrong with me;
and to my chagrin, there on the skin of my eye was the culprit,
you see.

"It's your fault!" I yelled rather grudgingly as I stared in
the mirror at an image of me. The sty in my eye did not reply,
it just sat there so innocently.

"My social life is now history!" I exclaimed, "Can't you see
what you're doing to me?" "I cannot comply.", Said the
sty in my eye. "It's my job to infect, not to see."

James Rowe

The Wedding Train

My wedding train curls round me, letting loose a foot or two
of traffic trodden doily lace, catching the feet of my grooms,
their khaki armored trench coats and leather cases full with time
sheets, breath mints to use and reuse, to fill the hours and the
stomachs. The smoke from the beams settles now in the labyrinth
of iron pews, tracks to salvation and damnation, lines to Union
Square Station. The ark slides open and my groom steps out
from the pages of a newspaper, strewn across the dusty floor.

I will board the scroll and travel the pews to my own Petersburg,
where I create the news. Peel away his glassy glance and see
Creation, my groom, my Beatrice, not strange eyes in Union
Square Station. Passion river flowed in the valleys of the tracks,
poured like Peter's ocean, then lapped upon his shores of European likes
and my land of New York City life. Pass me a golden ring, yet to
fully hallow, token of love, not so shallow.

Hannah Gurman

Solitudes Of Change

How softly the embers glow this eve
Whose warmth reflects within my walls,
A tiny flame with crackling wood
Casts dancing shadows through dark halls.

Between Autumn hues I chance to see
The gentle fall of feathery white,
To hush the fields with glimmering soft
Bring sleep to those nestled in the night.

Darkness settle on this Winter day
My operas cast grows long and dim,
Soon snowy reflections replace their stage
Rekindling dreams as embers glow within.

Lawrence L. Bochorz

First Love

My baby you will always be
For now and all eternity
And although we lie apart
Nothing can kill what's in the heart
For what we share is so right
And will bond us always, like our very first night
So let yourself be free of me
Cause I'm afraid there'll be no we
I wish I may and I wish I might
But nothing can take me back to that night
So as time lingers on I'll do what's right
I'll deny myself of you and give up the fight
And although we cannot be
Always know you're part of me

Darlene K. Akiu

Grandparents

A small green house in Iowa
On a long narrow road,
Two short and cute little people live
Sweet and content as can be,
Always busy trying to help others.

I love the donuts and badminton,
The fun of making Valentine's cookies,
Watching Johnny Carson and eating hoagies,
Playing checkers,
Beer nuts in my Coke.

The fun we had was immeasurable,
Sound of birds singing happily,
Joy of playing school,
Learning all about the world,
Knowing I had nothing to fear with them.

I'll never forget those days;
Neither will they.
Enjoying every moment,
Will always remember,
Those were the best times of my life.

Susie Spies

To My Love

Out of the long remembered past
From the depths of forgetfulness
You come to me
With a light in your eyes
That drags me back to days over and gone.
You renew the hurt of parting
And the ache of loneliness
Which are dispelled by your presence.
And youth and beauty and love
Are born again.

Agnes Fortunate

A Changed Heart

Dear Lord, you seem so far away;
and yet, I know you're near.
For you live within my broken heart;
and witness every tear.

I've let you down so many times;
temptations are so strong.
I've listened to the evil one,
who tells me to do wrong.

I've felt your disappointment, Lord;
and it's made it hard to pray,
for each time I've longed to talk to you,
my sin got in the way.

But now I choose to turn from sin
and overcome these trials.
Please be my strength and help me flee
from all the Devil's wiles.

Lord, I pray you'll change my heart
so I'll never be the same;
and show me how to live my life
to glorify your name.

Aundra McMinn

Loss of a Generation

In the darkness of a dark night,
as a train passes
by
like a monster of the night
when the sirens cry
once in a while,
a beast sharpens his nails to start his hunt.

He shows his weapons of fire and death
and takes over.
When he finishes,
his weapon throws
a circle of fire,
and as the bright morning draws closer,
he hides in his den.

A new story
breaks for the media
and conversation is spread.
After the few more dark nights,
the story is lost,
but the hunt continues.

Humaira Qureshi

The Bright Side

There are many bad things
that are wrong with this world,
But many more things that are right

There are kind gentle faces
and warm happy places
and stars that shine in the night.

We hear of wrong-doing
and violence ensuing, while
lives are broken and lost.

Our heart surely tells us that
God is still in Heaven; he is still in charge and still boss.

Tommie Lois Dennard

Untitled

Do trees have love do they dream
if your little world can fathom the depth
of emotions a tree felt would you be blinded
by the wisdom of several hundred years
or would you still cut the majestic oak
dropping him to the ground in
one thunderous crash
forever destroying the life of a sentient being
so that progress can move forward
at the speed of light
another skyscraper or parking lot
until the only thing left standing
are the stark gray effigies
of man's unfettered desire
to conquer that which he can not understand
the only trees to be found are pictures in the
museum of extinction next to the empty space
reserved for man

Wm. Vestal Yarbrough III

Mother

Life has been hard and the road has been long,
I've made it this far, yet I have to go on.
I wish you could be here to see me now,
I'm all grown up, you probably ask how.
Maybe someday I'll see you again,
That is my dream to the very end.

I have achieved many goals and strived for the best,
I will never quit though I've failed many quests.
It's been a while, since I last saw you,
But the image never dies, of me and you too!
You missed our lives, the childhood times,
Of silly games and nursery rhymes.

Don't ever hesitate, just come on back,
We'll catch up on old times, and see what we lack.
Mother - I'm almost a woman, just like you,
I'd like to get to know you again - If you'd like too!
But until then, I'll wait for that day,
That I hope very soon, will come my way.

But for now, I love you mother!

Tracy Sue Dykstra

Untitled

"How do I love thee? Let me count the ways..."
If I did I would go on for an eternity. I love you
for so many things, it began in friendship, and it grew intensely.
Each day was looked forward to with the intent of just being
with you; it never mattered where we went, as long as we were
together. If I had it my way, I would be entangled in the
comfort of your embrace forever. When we are together nothing
seems to matter; reality would fade into a blur, and we two
would remain in our own existence.
These feelings I harbor are real, almost to the touch; not one
could fathom how I love you so much. You have captivated
my life; you manifest my dreams; you possess my very soul;
you reside in my thoughts, and staked claim on my heart.
All this without you doing much, except for the love
and respect you have given me, there could never, ever
be another to take your place, because all that I've
been looking for, I have found in you.

Kenneth E. Gattas

Pan

I watch the shepherds in the fields,
Their strays I do protect.

All brute creation I'm to shield, and from hunters
hold respect.

I go a galloping along, small hooves and ears of
goat belong to me I must confess.

With pipe in hand, I seem a loon, the fisherman I
seek, to play to him a tune tho' he be not a greek

Call me legend, myth or tale, a rascal, foe or friend,
Tho' some mankind against me race, my goal is to
defend,

The ancient deities call me Faun, I am link twixt
beast and man.
And when to Olympus comes the dawn, I am the
God called Pan.

Mary Guzman

"Memories Of The Old Church"

Sometimes when I think a deep thought of the sound,
I remember the old church bell, rang with a bound!
Fragrance of honeysuckles,
Dust during rain,
The smells of the past, somehow remain.
Walking to church was safe in those days.
In my heart I'll remember, in so many ways,
Though those fragrances sweet, have suddenly past,
I have realized the smells that forever will last.
A whiff of sweet flowers, of summertime smells,
All the windows were open, where fragrance did dwell.
We all had to stay cool, with a funeral fan,
As we listened closely to the preacherman.
In my memories, revivals and long talks are cherished,
The homecomings, friends and salvation won't perish.
Memories of the old potbellied stove
As we huddled around, we were so very cold!
But we had the warm love from our Father above,
And all of the warmth of friends that we love.

Wanda Long Blackwell

My Kind of Garden

I have seen opulent gardens
  With trellis, rich and rare;
Row on row of vegetables, plenty,
  Tended with love and care.

A regular thing of beauty,
  And, when harvest comes, I ween;
Larders will be full and bulging,
  With cornucopia, fit for a queen.

But the gardens that really warm my heart,
  Are the wee one's by the road
With no fancy trellis to its name
  And, only a lean bean pole.

Or, hidden away behind the house,
  By the barn, or across the lea;
Two tomatoes, a pepper, a bean and rose,
  Is the only garden for me!

Zeano L. Moss

Wildlife Refuge Near Center, Colorado

In April comes the nesting time and cranes
Fly to their usual nesting grounds to hide
their eggs — the product of their courting time
when nature urges them and they respond.
But one lone goose has found a new pursuit
while gathering golf balls for her lonely clutch
and visitors with camera laugh and joke
about a goose who doesn't know very much.

The goose has counted out her future prodigy—
Nine eggs are nestled underneath her breast
but since she has grown weaker now from age,
no mate has come to fertilize her nest.
It seems quite sad to waste her failing charms
upon those hard round balls, with living hope
awakening in her breast with season's fair warmth
and it would be a kindness if gamekeeper brought
A substitute, fertile egg or two and laid them there.
I do not know if such a plan exists
—so easily accomplished without harm—
Visiting tourists laugh and then move on!!

Veda Nylene Steadman

Floating Isle

On Mobile Bay when evening stills
We listen for the call of the Whippoorwill
The willow bends her bows in sleep
The morning dove coos long and sweet.
  As twilight deepens there's another sound
A step that softly treads the ground
Then we recount the story old
Of a Southern belle with hair like gold
For her gliding step and gentle smile
She was called by all the Floating Isle.
  The sea was a jealous mistress
Those she chose could not return
For the Lover who sailed away
The lady's heart would ever yearn.
  There were some who thought the girl was fey
And sadly looked the other way
She did make mention a key she sought
To Davey Jone's locker had long been lost
She haunts the shores to this very day
Our Floating Isle of Mobile Bay.

Betty June Lowery

First Spring Robin

Regard that ruby bosomed harbinger,
  Hopping boldly across my way,
Thou spanned the distance with tireless vigor,
  Braving storms that would thee astray.

Thy fresh appearance belies thy feat,
  The distance thou traveled before this day.
Did angel wings below thee beat?
  And grant thee rest along the way?

Thy keen eye scans the still brown earth,
  Slowly awakening from her slumber,
Still cool from winter's frozen berth,
  Searching for bounty to slack thy hunger.

I hail thee friend and with hope renew
  Thy spirit of unwavering trust,
That a green season follows a winter of blue,
  As life's rhythms continue, so I must.

LaVonne Woodhouse-Mainz

Spring's Beauties

How wonderful, the spring
especially when the birds start to sing
Now everything becomes restful
And the flowers look beautiful
Lightly blows the season's breeze
As it creeps slowly towards my knees
At night when everything has bloomed
It looks so calm and pretty under
the shadows of the moon.
The grass turns green and so do
the trees.
Flying past, hurry the bees
They are busy flying from flower to flower
Trying to finish their jobs before
the final showers
Hot and golden shines the sun
It won't stop shining until the day
is done
How beautiful, the spring.

Chelsey Furrer

Make Them Last

Memories bonded in open spaces
Create images at last in darkness.
Moments devoted to scenes on past from places.
As gestures are reflected in amazed deliverance.

What can be said or actions made?
That will take effect on my mind's delight.
Where can I go to seek the unknown?
Find peace and rest that calms my soul this night?

Make my memories clearer to me
Make them last to soothe my cluttered wounds.
Bring the jubilant mixtures of years gone by you see.
Yea! Touch the inner desires with substance.

Bring forth from each direction
The colorful brilliancy that the mind can store.
Make them last for me and others.
Who requires just a tidbit more.

Accompany me on the journey of thoughts
As I close my eyes and envision the pictures.
Make memories that are created and fought.
Seek me out among the many.

Linda Martin

Just Touch My Hand

Just touch my hand and my spirits lift and fly
Just touch my hand and the sun shines in the sky
When you're close to me as you are tonight
My heart takes wing on a magical flight
So just touch my hand and let me know
That our love will last and always grow
I need you now, to get along
I sing to you my only song
Let's make our love a perfect thing
A song that I can always sing
So touch my hand as you do tonight
And my whole world will be just right
Just touch my hand and let me see
My way to love for eternity

Dan Dobey

From the Plains

The summer rays touched my soul,
sparking a celebration of my body,
I pranced in the open fields with daisies,
with tulips and bees, so free, so full of life.

In the arc of a rainbow I lived,
with its radiance my dreams and my fodder,
nothing would come between me and the rays,
no not even the shadows of realization.

Each day I learnt a little from the daisies,
from the bees and the tulips,
to be a being with beauty,
a being with a thirst for freedom.

Christopher Teli

A Fisherman's Last Prayer

Isolation, distant, depressed-what am I feeling?
Bored, happy, sad-what are my emotions?
Small, non-existent, lonely-what is my place in this world?
Naive, unsure, remote-how will I find my way?
Disappointed, unnerved-how will I be judged?
The fisherman, frail and weak, beckons to find the answer. In his own
mind he knows what it should be...

I love, God loves, He is with me always; through my times of
happiness and despair He is with me.

But it is not enough, I still don't understand...
"I know", I thought... But it is I who ask the Lord, "How much do You
   love me"?
with His face telling the story of His life each wrinkle adding
another chapter, His body scarred by hatred, with sweat upon His brow
and with His arms outstretched He answers,
"This much my child"... and dies.

With undo haste the fisherman folds his hands in prayer and ceases
his bewilderment, for from the heavens a voice rings out to bring one
last answer... I love, God loves, and forever I shall love, for
forever I am with thee.

Melissa Iris Pinno

I Choose To Refuse

The best you is a drug free you
This poem will show you what drugs do to you

In school you'll be failing you won't even try
At home you'll be fighting and make mother cry

To say no to drugs is big and brave
To say yes to drugs is digging your grave

Don't do drugs for a friend or a dare
Once drugs take charge you haven't a prayer

It will make you act stupid for all to see
You'll even forget who you wanted to be

Remember your dreams, to be a Doctor, Lawyer, Vet, or Mechanic
These dreams are lost you're in a panic

Say no to drugs or you're sure to fail
If you mess with drugs you're going to jail

Sadly to say some will still use
But I'm happy to say I choose to refuse!!

Jeffrey L. DeVlieger

The Changing Years

Like a string of spaghetti hanging from a pot
  Proletariat People are lingering from a string;
For the weary and unknown are blocked in society
  "So, where do they go, who do they talk to?
What do they tell their children?"
  When they have been blinded,
Through society's circles of limitations
  Scream not a word of malfeasance:
For there is a super-human power that anoints one's soul.

"Stand up." Be heard! Hold your head up high!
  The power of being is within the soul
Let not the soul be weak,
  Survival contributes to hardships
"But that's alright!
  For the supreme almighty God,
Amazing Grace whispers across the earth;
  As God's lyrics in the breeze reconstruct life."
For the changing years is full of inspiration.

  Sandra T. Williamson

Mom

There's something I have to tell you.
Something I seldom say.
For everything you do for me,
Each and everyday.
For being there to listen
When I need to voice my concern.
And being a wonderful role model,
So that each day I may learn:
Just how terrific you are Mom,
Just how fun you can be,
Just how caring you are Mom,
So that someday I may be
As wonderful a mother as you someday.
And I just would like to say
Mom, I love you and thanks for being there
I hope to be like you someday!

  Courtney Swartz

Tree On A Hill

There is a tree on a hill, God put it there,
And there it stands with a timeless ere.
With a majesty and royalness so great,
A beautiful thing with a timeless date.
How long will you stand so green?
Looking at the sky as if God you have seen.
With each wind that has blown,
So much peace through the years you have known.
In the fall, you're more beautiful then the spring,
And from your branches, the birds sing.
In your hollows, little animals hide,
And from your limbs with a rope, children glide.
Oh, tree on a hill so superb,
May man, your timeless place never disturb.

  June Fields

Foxholes

There are no atheists in foxholes
The smell of death can really rock souls
Amazing how the total cadre
Lines up to see the holy padre
And at the sound of bursting mortar
The bravest chap does soon take quarter
And when the bombs and shells do whistle
The hairs of macho guys do bristle
So would some power the giftie gee us
Or 'haps the same would guarantee us
That if all men would tend their own souls
There'd be no need for trench...or foxholes.

  Norman E. Fuller

Know Not Of

So much hurt
So much pain
Much to lose
But much to gain.

What is it that you want from me?
Sorry but you made a mistake.
And now you want to rebuild the bridge that brought you across,
that you burned.
You will never reach my heart again to break.

Do you know how it feels to cry alone at night?
Not being able to sleep
Because painful and hurtful scenes play in the theater of your mind?
Struggling with troubles and worries you know you should let go
  and not keep

A broken heart.
A shattered dream.
Just like that
It amounts to a hill of beans.

You will never know the degree of the pain.
I fought so hard to win your love.
You just do not know.
That I had love for you that you know not of.

  Gerry L. Wootson

The Power

I prayed for four days in a row,
That he would just go away,
The temptation was too strong,
"God, please, please don't let him stay".

I had a dream on that fourth night,
After I laid me down to sleep,
And in that dream I cried out,
"It is you I wish to keep".

He knew I truly needed him,
Even in that dreary dream,
He just stood his moral grounds,
As I cried and kicked and screamed.

There was an aching in my heart
As I awoke that next day,
"Thank goodness it was just a dream,
I know I'll talk to him today".

Don't underestimate the Power,
Prayer is a very strong thing,
Be careful what you wish for,
For my phone it did not ring.

  Deborah Harris

Out My Window

Out my window there is a tree,
That tree he's staring back at me.
In fall his leaves wither to the ground.
In winter he has an eerie frown.
Spring is back.
He stands as the day turns black.
Now he is wearing flowers,
Even when he takes his weekly showers.
Now it is summer,
He hopes he will not be dumber.
The seasons are finally done,
Now that tree has a son.

  Crystal Haas

MY PRECIOUS MOM

Someone who wipes your runny nose...kisses away tears from
cheeks that glow.
Scolds, when you are being bad...cries, when you are feeling sad.

"THAT'S MY PRECIOUS MOM"

Someone who always show she cares...who makes your lunch and
combs your hair.

Gives daily guidance...and help you say your
prayers.

"THAT'S MY PRECIOUS MOM"

A teacher, nurse, homemaker too...what more can you ask from
Someone who, is beautiful as well as brainy and true...

"THAT'S MY PRECIOUS MOM"

Words alone cannot express...what mom's are all about...
I'm sure whom ever shares my thoughts, believe their mom is
best....

Specialty, is the key word here...some may come close or
even appear...to top the list of great mom's galore...
But the greatest gift from God above...was to give to me

"MY PRECIOUS MOM"
        Nadine F. Beard

Front Lines

In the line of fire everything gets blurry
Except one thing, fight, fight for your country!
The dirt sweat and tears
A friend falls but there's no time to mourn
You could be next
Yet all you can do is fight, butcher
Pretend it isn't happening that you aren't killing
That you aren't in danger for your life
You slog through the dead and wounded
Tears streaming freely down your cheeks
You hear a shot, watch as a young man falls dead at your feet
Vaguely you realize it was you who slaughtered him,
But you were long ago numbed to such things
You long to be anywhere but here
Away from the death and pain
Then it happens
A bomb goes off next to you
You fall, almost gratefully, you slide into the darkness
        Sarah Hoyt

Nannie's Farewell

Kind and loving in life was she
Gifted and Beautiful "Spiritual" seems to me.

Always there to lend a hand or with firmness and love
To reprimand.

She "don't fell no ways tired" anymore
With the angels she now does soar.

No more tears, no more sorrows.
We will see her on her tomorrow.

Dear and sweet to us was she.
God keep her close 'til again with her we'll be.

We love you Nannie and always will.
Remembered in our mind and hearts ever still.

Her body's gone but her spirit's here.
When we think and speak of her I know she'll be near.

Over us she's watching now

We love you Nannie

Goodbye ... for now.
        Sheila Yvonne Lyons Stringer

The Willow

Willow always bowing down
Weeping makes you seem to frown.
I look on you with wond'ring awe.
You were more than what I saw.
It is just the way you are,
Detracting none, no beauty mar.
Underneath your dome-shaped arms
There lies a multitude of charms.
For similar I am to you
And what I feel is not in view.

Seeming outward, cold and stern,
The warmth of love is what I yearn.
This look you see is my defense
Against all that could cause offense.
My mind, it plays a nasty game.
Knowing this, yet still no change, just the same.
This cycle does so much ingrain,
Encasing me in this domain.
I would change if I knew how.
Frustration all but makes me bow.
        Juna Kim

A Love Too Late

I never told her that I loved her;
I took for granted that she knew.
A hundred love songs that I sang her;
Never equalled "I love you.

She might have seen it in my actions;
Or felt it in the poems I wrote.
But never did she hear "I love you";
I guess that's where I missed the boat.

I should have told her every evening;
Just before we went to bed.
I couldn't wait for carnal pleasure;
I should have touched her heart instead.

If I could live my life all over;
I'd say I love her every day.
I wouldn't take our love for granted;
If I could only make her stay.

I thought I had it all together;
Now, there's a void I cannot fill.
I never told her that I loved her;
And now I guess I never will.
        Floyd E. Collins Jr.

Spiri

I met a woman today.
A woman so perfect, one might have to say
She was like a goddess walking among average people.
Her eyes were the color of perfect emeralds, so full
Of mystery and seduction.
Her hair was as radiant as the sun
Shining in the summer sky.
She spoke with a voice as soft as an infant's sigh,
Her lips the texture of velvet rose petals, or even satin sheets.
By no chance encounter this woman and I did meet,
For I do not believe in luck, chance or even coincidence.
In my heart I do believe, it was fate that has brought me hence
To this place where I exist.
It is a place of absolute beauty and undeniable bliss.
In my lover's eyes I live, and it's there I'll always be,
With the woman whom I met today, my beloved Spiri.
        Justin Howard

Please Be Patient With Me

I don't know what I'm doing here or how I should behave
I don't know what's expected of me, or what I am to say;
Until a few days ago, I was so cuddly and so warm
I was in my Mother's womb just waiting to be born.

But now I'm in this noisy place with people all about
It seems as if I'm to be heard, I'll just have to shout!
I'm in these wet and messy diapers and no one has a plan
On how to change them on me without those cold, cold hands.

All those people look at me with all their funny faces!
If I had my way about it, we'd be changing places.
They'd be wet and I'd be dry and I could walk about
They wouldn't like it either, of this I have no doubt.

So please be patient with me Mom, and that goes for Daddy
If I should wake you up at night and sometimes drive you batty!
I may not feel so well myself, I may be hungry, wet or sick;
If you'll be patient, love and hold me, that may do the trick.

So please be patient with me, though at times it won't be easy
I know that I require a lot, and you don't know how to please me
But please be patient with me and try to understand
God knew what He was doing when He placed me in your hands.

Lillie Prather (Grandma Lillie)

My Mother's Statue

Her heart was brave, her spirit good
She gazed outside where the statue stood
It seemed to make her life serene
And from the statue her faith did gleam

When the Lord called her from this earth
I packed the statue to find a new birth
Through pain and sorrow and emotional trial
In the bedroom corner she helped me to smile

I finally placed her on my porch
For others to come when distraught
Tiny hands outstretched to reach
To everyone, their soul to keep

They stopped by day and flowers left
And in the evening their rosary said
She came to represent to all
Sent from heaven to answer their call

When my world is filled with pain
I kiss my statue and my soul retains
In peace and quite the old refrain
To God alone we are preordained

Dottie Egan

Hats

Hats, hats everywhere the hats
Wool, cotton, hoods and caps
High hats, top hats,
Large rim - short
Baseball backwards
A style of sort
Tall dark and silky
Like Lincoln wore
French beret - Easter bonnet
Robin Hood's kind with a feather in it
Hats hide messy hair
Hats hide skulls that are bare
Hats for the sea, hats for land
A pink panama with a purple band
Hats of rain, for the sun or quick trip to the store
For tricycles, bicycles, motorcycles and helmets for war
Hats, hats everywhere the hats
The sign on the hat says
Those without one need not apply

Joseph A. Dodzik

The Pattern of a Man

The telephone rings, and your heart sings,
hey lady, it's your new man!
He invites you to lunch, or perhaps it's brunch,
    then later, he calls you again...

It's really his choice, he must hear your voice,
    then, at seven, he calls for a date.
You dress with a flair, you really do care,
    so, could he be your lifetime mate?

Now, a month has passed, and you think, At Last!
    You've found a lover who's true.
Then the phone rings less, and you try to guess,
    as you search your mind for a clue.

Why hasn't he called, he seemed so enthralled,
    was he only playing a game?
You feel you were used, your ego's abused,
    but, the Pattern is always the same.

A man will call when he's after your all,
    when he wants something new and inviting.
He pursues with a pace that makes your heart race,
    every moment with him is exciting.

When he gets what he's after, there's no more laughter,
    you're serious, you want him for life.
But you can be sure that he's found a new girl,
    or else he's at home with his wife!

Nancy Bridges

Beowulf On Fire

A flip of brown,
a vein of grease,
a twist of blood,
a slithering glide.

Navigating through muck
lithe clutching fingers of green algae hair
gaseous bubbles and sensuous, sliding weed.

Rapier by his side.

And mud like molding custard:
thick film over oil-soaked sponge,
the biting barbs of shell edges.

-Hard seeing through silt

-hard holding your breath-

Slipping down dark
death-reeking passages
to Murky blackness
and Grendel's hole.

Somewhere, down there
still
he's alive.

Jessica Davey

Passive/Hostile

                    Helplessly
                    Overlooking
                    Subtle
                    Tranquilities that don't
                    Interfere with
                    Life, but can soothe an
                    Eternity

Putting up with
All of the
Selective judgement of a
Society that causes
Insanity and quite
Vicious actions that are channeled through
Emotions

Michael Shellabarger

A Sister's Prayer

Each night I lie awake
  I pray for my loved ones to be safe
   I pray for their health.

I pray they achieve all of their hopes,
  desires,
   and dreams.

Since you, my brother, have accomplished such a feat,
  I pray for your safety and happiness each night.
   Until I am no longer, this prayer will be heard.

Lord, watch over my brother,
  not just as Your son, but as a fire fighter -
   One who has put his life in jeopardy,
    for the life of others.
  Please keep him safe, and let no harm come to him.

  For he is my brother, a friend...
   Someone I love.
    Caren Hagan

The Age of the Silly

What to do when you journey from
the dark sonorities of the Duke's "Airshaft,"
the hot-wired, blazing cadenza of Louis'
'West End," the thin voiced cry of the tragic Billy
and arrive in the Age of the Silly?
East Village: Lips and pert noses - black,
White or Oriental - stabbed and pierced with rings of steel,
strolling the streets in designedly ripped jeans,
under green, purpled, blued hair, their brains rattled
by regressive rock of the unreal.
Uptown to the East and West Ends where a standard drink before
  dinner
is - oh Lord - cognac and the standard wear
of the bright young men, the showbiz or TV type
or the insouciant masters of the hype
is a tieless shirt buttoned to the neck
in the style of Iranian diplomats.
But what most disturbs we travellers
form the land of Louis, Billy and the Duke
is the paucity of civility
in this pervasive age of the Silly.
  A. S. Breslauer

Enigma

When we were young, like those before,
We thought we'd live forever,
Some idled by, while some engaged
In arduous endeavor.

But prince and pauper, both alike -
Their paths lead to the grave,
And spendthrifts lives are fleeting,
The same as those who save.

The earth may spin a million years
On it's path around the sun,
While our pitiful "three score and ten"
Is too soon o'er and done.

Still, perhaps this life is just a dream,
and when we all awaken,
We'll see a glorious, shining truth,
And find we're not forsaken.
  Robert L. Davis

That's What I See

A touch of silk, a bit of lace.
That's what I see,
when I look in her face.

Her Graceful years,
and light from the skies.
That's what I see, when I look in her eyes.

Chocolate chip cookies,
and strawberry jam.
That's what I think of
when I look at her hands.

She walks like an angel,
she has so much pride.
This beautiful woman,
has nothing to hide.

Her elegant ways, her beautiful charm.
That's what I feel,
when she holds me in her arms.

Her unconditional love, is like no other.
And how proud I am,
that she's my grandmother.
  Jessica McFarland

My Heaven And Earth

The rain began around midnight,
Announcing its presence with a light tap-tap-tap.
Till the storm gained in force, and the taps became thunderous.

Sheets of tears streamed down
As if God could watch no more
Of our senseless violence or petty hates.

The rain washes over me, yet somehow I do not feel clean.
It merely seems to separate me
From the world beyond these four gray walls.

There are times I feel so isolated, disconnected,
Wishing for a beautiful place to call my own.
Somewhere to fit in; somewhere to belong.

Then I hear your breathing rise and fall.
And your naked form nuzzles against my side.
And I smile.

I may not know what this life will bring.
But I think I've found my own personal heaven,
At least until this heart does beat no more.
  John Sbrochi

Bed Of Water

We stand alone on a beach, you say you never
  again want to see me.
I can feel the breeze lift my hair as I watch you
  walk away.
I cannot conceal my anger and pain, I will do anything
  to escape.
And as the gentle waves lap at my feet, I imagine
  them carrying me away.
They take me to a better place, where a mountain
  stands against the sky.
When I climb the mountain, I feel myself falling, away
  from the memories and promises that you made.
I land on the soft sand, imagining it to be the past,
  when you used to hold me tight, and say you
  would never leave me.
Suddenly, the future appears.
It sweeps my images away and I am left standing
  on the beach, alone, with no one to hold me.
So I throw myself into the ocean, and let the
  water carry me away...
  Karisa L. Schaler

The Storm

The reward for pleasure's pain
The need for more gives rise to gain
Some distant shore will lead you on
Then drag you back again, so why did we ever leave
When it was so safe and warm
Why did we ever leave to face the storm
For the fabric of life was rent
The living die and the dead lament
For a moment you knew what it all meant
Consider yourself forewarned
Head and shoulders above the rest
They ride the steed to claim the best
And forge the steel to steal the rest
There's never an end there's more, for the knowing smile of truth
Grates upon the nerves of those that feel
Gold stand the test of tooth
And claw their way through their next deal
So we tread the path to light, the pitfalls lie to left and right
We check desire with all our might, to leave the wheel for evermore.

Michael Palmer

Red Sunshine

This deep red sunshine hits my back,
I cringe with my disgust.
It tempts me into its evil ways,
To keep myself I must.
It twists the weak, deranges them,
It sculpts the insecure.
I must do all I can,
To escape the rainbow lure.
The weeds in the field, the stars in the sky,
To demons they will turn.
The birds, the life, the love, the mind,
Engulfed in its flames will burn.
White fluff floating above their heads,
And Jesus in their spines,
All reality has run from them,
And not left much behind.
It felt so free and right to them;
I saw the other side,
The process of possession done,
Why can't they see the signs?

Meredith Jean Licari

Touch

I feel your touch my friend,
the spontaneous songs of your love for me.
It sounds with a soft tap,
a playful swat,
a pure embrace.
And in your silent tones you sing of the Spirit's tie.
Here we stand together,
Our union in His kingdom displayed by thoughtful hands,
the bond in the work shown by the closeness of our walk.
And in this chilly, violet world,
we warm and guard ourselves with the other's care,
throwing off our fears in playful games of silly rest.
Yet in the deepest cavity of our heart,
the place where feelings pass the realm of words,
we simply savor the gifts of our loving God.
Let us now share His music,
the unspoken chords and the fluid melodies,
the mysterious power to draw our spirits near,
and pull us towards the one who brought us close.

Ray McAllister

A Vow Made To Heaven

Don't leave out crying
Don't leave that way,
The day we married
You promised to stay.

How long is forever?
Until death do we part?
Now you are leaving;
you tear out my heart.

A vow made to heaven,
He poured out his love
He gave us his blessing
Made us one love.

Now you are leaving; you break up his love.
Look, they are crying, the white turtle doves.

My days will be lonely, my days will be long;
You know I'm here crying singing this song.

When I walk in the forest, I walk not alone;
He hears me crying and he hears my song.

I'll love you forever, my whole life long,
While lying here dying, I'm singing this song.

Marvin E. McCoig

1996

Welcome to the world of 96,
A world of science and micro chips,
Cd-Rom and Internet
And best of all there's Cyber Sex.
Feeling down or feeling depressed?
A dose of Prozac will ease your stress.
When you need tranquillity,
These drugs can change reality.

As a child you were ugly and taunted?
Surgery can give you the face that you've wanted,
Add a face lift and bigger breasts
Let's put our scalpels to the test.

Yes 96 a time of technology,
A time of altering natural biology,
From artificial food to insemination,
Things to improve the prospering nation.

Whatever happened to natural life
Without the science, the bits and bytes?
A world so simple with nothing to fix,
A world not found in 96.

Rob K. Fritz

My Childhood

My childhood, sadly, is leaving me soon
where to I do not know,
maybe to China or the moon
or possibly Idaho.

In my childhood I would glide
high up in the air,
if I could, I'd stay there all day
for the air is much better up there.

I would fly so high I thought I must have had wings,
every time I would play
upon my trusty swing.

Now that we have taken it down
my backyard looks so bare,
it didn't last as long as I'd hoped;
my childhood, it's no longer there.

Rob Connolly

God Isn't Finished With Me Yet

Nothing is impossible, if you follow your Heart. Nothing is impossible if your love is true from the start. I can't always make you happy but I'm happy when I try. We are partners in emotions and what hurts you brings tears to my eyes. God has chosen my mate even tho it may not be my date. "Please be patient, God isn't finished with me yet." If you love me tell me why, wipe those tears from your eyes. God has chosen my mate even tho it may not be my date. "Please be patient, God isn't finished with me yet." Let me know just how you feel and then maybe if it's real we can steal an hour or so. We are partners in emotions and that's a very good sign to spend time together for a very long, long, time. "Please be patient, God isn't finished with me yet." We need to be sure of each other, We need to be one in one with the other. Our lives together will be for ever if we make sure before we start. We are partners in emotions and what hurts you, bring tears to my eyes. I can't always make you happy but I'm happy when I try. "Please Darlin, be patient, God isn't finished with me yet." I need a little more courage and a bit more self esteem. I need to know just how to Dream of the days we spend together and the nights we spend alone. I want our love to last until we both grow very, very, old." So be patient with me Darlin, God isn't finished with me yet." God, isn't finished with me yet.

Betty Mae Eaton

And

And the misfit looked for the last piece of the puzzle but couldn't find it
And everything would be calm if only he could find that last piece
As if a jagged edge of cardboard should remedy misgivings
And he recovered that final piece but his worry-tears misshaped that
one last alteration of his world and it wouldn't fit
And he mended it with glue and threads of hope and glue and it fell
apart right in his lap
And the misfit tried to shape himself alike to the missing part of day
And the misfit failed and reshaped him again with no gain toward a future
And he heard a cry primal in the distance and he heard the wail again
And he followed its hideous sound right back to his soul
And floods of tears in castaway guise climbed through his cross-eyed self
And onto a puzzle almost entire 'cept a leper fragment
And the floods misshaped his puzzle world changing the house for a missing piece
And the misfit shaped himself again to the missing part of day..and he fit
And the sun came out from inside his make up
And he lay in his puzzle womb
and savored belonging for a first time

...I suppose there was a certain shape of calm

Nancy G. Oxman

My Name Is Depression

"My name is Depression", I cause people to lay in bed with a heavy weight on their chest. Clothes they have, but none they see to wear. Shoes they have, but laces are hard to tie. Just doing simple things takes much energy they often cry. I cause people to eat comfort foods to feel good about themselves. While some can't eat at all.

"My name is Depression" I keep people withdraw within themselves so they don's speak to no one at all.. I hid behind their sun glasses as they stop in the mall. Only to hurry home, to hide behind a closed door! How much better to sleep then face the day. They keep calling out Depression go away. Many a friend tried to comfort them, while others fail to be loving, kind and patient most of all. The person who carry's me is a wonderful person. Deserves to have the best in life does not deserve my name.

"My name is Depression" I can destroy. So as a friend take that person by the hand. Help them to survive and live. Even if you don't carry my name. Have a sympathetic ear, let them know you love them so. May that person have a new name "Happy Endurance" instead of hopelessness and despair. Only true friends understand to give a helping hand, because they care. Only beautiful smiles and "Happy Endurance" will push "My Name Depression" away some day.

Sandra May Benlien

Songs

Songs?
What songs?
Songs to myself?
If they do exist?
Ideas?

Ideas,
Many ideas,
Creative, adventurous ideas,
Ideas, but not songs,
Creativity.

Creativity
Lurking about
In the labyrinth,
Forever trying to emerge,
Imagination.

Imagination,
Plus serendipity,
A special magic
That produces creative thought,
Originality.

Originality,
New ideas
Exciting images abound,
Serendipitous thoughts and creativity,
Songs.

Betty Luddington

One Brief Second

Nothing in my life could ever
have prepared me
for the overwhelming feeling
that you gave to me
the first time I held you in my arms.
In one brief second
all my pain and anguish
had instantly been replaced
by happiness and fulfillment.
I knew my life would never again
be as it has ever been.
you looked into my eyes
and we both just knew.

Debbie Tonra

Rachel

When I think about marching bands,
and us holding hands,
I think about you.

When I see someone feeding ducks,
or attempt a diaper tuck,
I miss only you.

When I see a tumbling chair,
or your father's thoughtful stare,
I long for you.

When I am in need of cuddling,
or warm blankets for snuggling,
I long for you.

When I hear a new born baby's laugh,
or give someone else a bath,
I miss only you.

When I think of all that's beautiful,
and everything that's wonderful,
I think about Rachel.

Elizabeth E. Sughrue

Donations

I've seen the sunset,
With my eyes aglow.
I've filled my lungs,
With air of the fallen snow.

I've heard the birds
Though many years have past,
Still lying without a miracle,
Knowing my life won't last.

I met a little girl of five,
Who has never seen the sky.
So I took hold of her hands,
And gave her my eyes.

Every working part,
Can give the chance of another day.
Even for the nine year old boy,
Who couldn't run and play.

Life can go by fast,
In many of God's unexpected calls.
But, giving yourself to another,
Is by far the greatest love of all.
        Paula Metro

We Are

We are two, we are together,
We are one within the wind;
Somewhere lost in reason -
Where thoughts of love transcend.

We are with, we are without,
We are ever wanting to be;
Surrounded by the light -
The warmth of sanctity.

We have begun, we are beginning,
We are at the very start;
In the beauty of romance -
What is pure and whole of heart.

        Deborah L. Sanford

Moving On

White mountains pass the sun
Time goes on and days are done
Here we go and then we're gone
Everything keeps moving on

Rain falls and then flows
Going where a river goes
Knowing what a river knows
Above a river the wind blows
Causing all these little changes
Over time it rearranges
Going places
Touching faces
Endless spirit moving on

After night there's always dawn
Another new days sun
Shinning down on what's been done
Here we go and then we're gone
We can't stop the moving on
        Christopher J. Pritchett

Your Load

When you traveled life's old highway and you are near the end of the road. You look over your shoulder and wonder how well you have carried your load. Did you help the one who faltered and needed a helping hand. Or did you pretend not to see him as you passed and let him stand. Did you pause and let the young one pass as he struggled to get ahead. Cause he maybe needed pushing instead of being lead. Did you stop to notice the children or even join in their play. Or did you just ignore them and hope and they would go away. What would you give to start over again with a chance for another try. And do all the things you know that you missed and really understand why. These were the people you dealt with as you traveled the rough road.
And how you managed to treat them must be how you carried your load.
        Evelyn Empey

The Knight

"I am your knight in shining armor, fair maiden Destney." My duty is to protect you from any danger, but first I must whisk you away from Evil's hands and then you will be safe. Each day I ride through the open countryside on my trusty, black steed searching for Evil's castle.
    Frequently encountering battles, I tirelessly wield lance and sword in joyful ache to deposit felled henchman and mercenaries of Evil in my wake.
    As I get to his gloomy citadel, my steed quickly gallops across the lowered drawbridge. Once inside the battles resume, I wield lance and sword in every room. When the dust clears, I arrive at your holding chamber. Its bolted door and traps pose another danger. But not at all worried, I eventually rescue you and we leave Evil's dark castle together reappearing under vast skies of blue. "I want to take you far away from Evil's hands," I say, "so let us take a jaunt." This is no fantasy. Our journey will exist. In romantic minds this story will persist. So follow me beyond imagination's realm with you by my side. "Off we go!" I exclaim. (On my black steed we ride) Our merry jaunt takes us to each fabled corner of the world in search for infinite peace and a comfortable place to rest. We whittle away time in deep conservation, learning about our separate pasts. Slowly we grow fond of each other with every passing day and fall in love in our own way.
        Lucito P. Lopez

Destruction

I once dreamed that my Grandfather was chasing me around with a blade
He never caught me; I woke up. Destruction came ... my grandfather was gone
Damn. My breath stopped; dropped helpless. My eyes rounded with tears
I punched through a hundred walls; wrecked a thousand things. I was
    mad like fire; angry like hell
The anger I had was strong; but my strength was weak. I was torn in
    two; ripped in pieces
My heart was slashed. My bone was crushed. My body was shredded. My
    blood and flesh were scattered.
I have nothing; I am left with nothing. Where is God? I prayed at the
    altar; collapsed to my knees
I cried, cried, and cried. I will never see my Grandfather. Now, my
    dream for him has vanished from me.
It hurts deep inside. It's more than missing; I lost my Grandfather
No one can bring my Grandfather back; nor God
Tell me, loss is not a pain. Words are not enough; nor comfort
No one can see the pain like I did; nor friend
No one can heal the pain; nor doctor
Nothing can heal the pain; nor medicine
I never knew; nor thought of this
I never imagine; nor dreamt of this
All I wanted was to be happy. Beyond rejuvenation. My Grandfather is
    in my dreams now; never before
My Grandfather is in my heart, though his body is not present
When He was chasing me around with a blade in my dream; He was giving
    me strength
His soul is still alive and He is in me ... Strengthens my vitality everyday

        Phetsamone Singkeo

246

Untitled

The one thing that I ask of thee,
Is for you to open your heart to me.
Take your time; I do not mind.
Just let me be there to help you find
The treasures that lie deep inside.
And slowly you will learn to confide
in me. Then you will begin to know
How it is that trust can grow.
Soon you will begin to feel
The one emotion that is truly real.

Latha Pasupuleti

Within My Soul

Collecting the thoughts,
floating through my mind;
deep within my soul.
A burning desire, a hunger
for answers;
a need for a purpose grows.
Dreaming the dreams,
so many have dreamed;
deep within my soul.

Waiting to be kissed;
a magnetic kiss;
that transforms two souls.
Making a soul within my soul.
A search for a soul mate grows.

Debra A. Hayes

Roots and Wings

For your children
eternal love springs
but your best gifts are
roots and wings

Give them roots
a solid base
strength and love
a supporting place

Properly prepared
for life's great trip
equipped with worth
they now can grip

Independence learned
release their clings
push them gently
and give them wings

Let them soar
they need to fly
you did your best
now they must try

Bob Bennett

Air Ornament

Hung
Static soarer
Predator
Eye gleam, as yet unseen
He, screamer

I walk a path of salt-stain flowers
He rises, undaunted, lifted
Warmer air, suspended there, aloft
Bird of prey, ease the day
Me, dreamer

Patricia Pedersen

What Is A Diatribe?
Just Thought You Should Know.

Ha! Caught you, down and out.
So, the pain is really real?
Well, I'm not one to mince my words,
And this is what I feel:

Truth, along with fairness
Are what we can't ignore.
You've got three strikes against you,
Better make that four.

You're ugly, stupid, and sick;
Throw in hopeless too.
You may as well abandon ship,
Since, we've all abandoned you.

Really, you don't deserve this much.
I hope you won't feel flattered.
I've tried to tell it like it is,
As if you really mattered.

Edward P. Stephani

The Cajun Cook

My dad is a cajun cook
He fishes with worm and a hook
He fries up the fish in a pan
He is a cajun man
My dad hunts for a big deer
One the size of a steer
He will make a saute'
He cooks it the cajun way
Wherever we may roam
Dad cooks as if we were home
He never needs to look it up in a book
I love my dad the cajun cook

Kyle Webb

Inside a Book of Poems
for My Daughter

This is for you
    to read and enjoy
and fill yours and others
    hearts with joy.

Poems in here
    are expressions of great and many,
to inspire you to the truth
    and not to the penny.

Treasured in these gems
    are meanings to discover ways
during times you are confronted
    by the omnipresent preys.

The roads are many
    good, bad, and thorny
you have to make your choice
    just as any.

Read, quote, and sing them
    and enrich your life with the gifts,
disguised as poems,
    by this world's great men!

Aditya P. Mathur

Just a Lonely Trader

I wonder how it came to be
that a lonely trader became of me;

I trudge through heat and desert winds
just to trade for worthless skins;
worthless, yes, to me for sure
but to the Pharaoh priceless treasure;

I wish I was the Pharaoh,
I'd set this kingdom right;
to serve the lesser people
is how I'd use my might;

But I am just a lonely man
who'll leave his home, his nest,
who'll go an untold distance
to trade at the Pharaoh's request;

Still I can't help but wonder
how different life would be
if I became that Pharaoh
and the Pharaoh became me.

Anthony Butera

The Master's Touch

I stood upon a windswept hill
and looked out toward the sea
The quiet thrill of solitude
came faintly to surround me

I saw the shadows shift and glide
across the silver sand
And race to meet the coming tide
that sweeps across the land

I watched the whitecaps of the waves
push high into the air
As if a mighty hand reached down
and flung them here and there

I feel alone and yet with joy
what I see in nature's plan
The things that heal each wounded soul
that's in the heart of man

Look to the east and to the west
wherever man has trod
And see in every countryside
the handiwork of God!

Chau Mai

The Embellisher

The lake
Like a satin blue ribbon
Shimmers with sunlight.
Pine trees
Washed clean by the rain
Sparkle like bugle beads,
Scallop lake side coves and
Soften the mountain range.
Patches of snow laced
Here and there, delight in hiding.
While tulips inch up to inquire:
Is it time to embellish spring?

Susan Crockett

Illusions

Love is but, a broken dream,
a touch of her soft face,
and a tear.

Love is but, a red rose,
a bleeding thorn,
and a smile.

Love is but, a fairy tale,
a far away look in his eye,
and a romance.

Love is but, a painted memory,
a pretty picture in a shoe box,
and a lingering denial.

A. Nicole Sanders

The Secret of Romance in the 90's

Romance today is lost
Sex in the name of love costs.
The art of caring
Isn't only sharing
being honest and truthful
Makes life fruitful
Trusting monogamy and accord
Can be life's reward
True love ventured
Is secret of romance captured.

Dorothy Marley Ruhf

Rebuild

Gone, took your heart
Killed the love, lost the game
Left, alone, cold
Cold hearted

Blind, see it now
Deaf, wish I was

A heart calls to you
You only leave
Will return
   Maybe
You only leave
Turn and look
   Look with a grin
Grin and walk
Walk, skip, grin
Can't win

Took your love, took my happiness
Left,
Left with only pain
Pain and a life to rebuild.

Christopher Paul Lohman

Wing's of Flight

Wing's of flight,
that streak the night,
with beam's of light,
that fill the sky.

Song's of night,
that bring the light,
and joy of love,
to the night.

Come join me in my midnight flight,
on wing's of light,
where duty calls,
come one, come all,
on my wing's of flight.

Mary Clayton

Water Is Peaceful

It can be calm,
tap-tapping the dock,
with fish underneath,
bugs floating on top.

It can be forceful,
throw spray on the rock,
echo the thunder,
withstand the rain.

It can be scary,
make people drown,
break strong chain moorings,
smash boats on the beach.

It can be playful,
lap at your feet,
tickle your knees,
take balls out of reach.

It can be beautiful,
lovely to watch,
reflecting the weather,
its secrets withheld.

Katharine H. Lowry

My Plea

Oh Holy Spirit,
Give me light,
To try and always to do right.
I know I'll falter on the way,
But help me,
Not, to go astray.

Oh, Great Master,
Melt my heart and all its plaster.
This is my cry to you,
From the bottom of my heart so blue.

Doris L. Plante

Night Stalkers

The cries of the night
Shadows of the dark
Whispers of the wind
The flourish of the light.

The night stalkers come
With the mystery of
The darken moonlight
The wonders of the night
Brings the blazing light
Of the stars.

The songs of the trees
Move swiftly through the
Whispers of the wind
How loyal they sound
To each other like sisters
And brothers in the
Night of stalkers.

Autumn Gonzales

Never...

Never wonder
You're the only one I need
Never worry
I'm always gona be right here
Never lie
I'll always love you no matter
What you do
Never forget
I love you

Jessica Brown

Am I Just A Memory

When the tears that cover
me finally drown me will you still
love me?
When I'm flying in the
ocean of clouds with birds
that are free will you still love me?

When I come to you in
your dreams and speak of
angels and God will you
still love me?

Or will I just be another
faded memory?

When the words that
use to roll off the tip of
your tongue are now drowned
in the sea will you still
love me?

When the arguments that use
to be a burden to me are not gone
with me will you still love me?
Or will I just be another faded memory?

Amanda Burr

Vain Desires

Last night a woman came to me
With flowing locks like waves at sea.
I placed my woes upon a shelf
And in that sea I drowned myself.
Sweet madness seized me by the hand
And swept me to a brighter land.
I saw a light that would not die;
I saw a babe that did not cry.
I saw my life as it could have been,
Gleaming white and free of sin.
But Eye of Heaven studied me,
Swelling in his jealousy.
Light and heat crept through my shade,
Melt my joys as I watch them fade.
And so my lady runs away.
Alone I rise to face the day.

Uma Sachdeva

Loneliness Emphasized

I'm on top
Higher than the mountains
I'm alone
I don't wanna come down
Time seems to stand still
Any movement and I will fall
I want to fly but have no wings

Oh well
I don't want this anymore
It's gone anyway
Again I'm alone

Rock bottom
I'm drownin'
I reach with arms spread
Reach for air
I struggle to be free
Reach for love
But it does not reach back
I'm drownin'
Why has no one reached?

Christopher Johnson

To Be Strong

Stand up tall, never fall,
hold your head up high,
reach out to touch the sky,
never fear, never cry,
don't ever wish to die
   To be strong
never hurt, never scream,
never yell, just dream,
never let anyone push you down,
never wear a frown, be happy,
reach out to someone,
be brave, be a hero
   To be strong
stand up tall, never fall,
never let anyone push you down,
never wear a frown,
be brave, be a hero,
   be strong
   Melinda Soon

Simple

The light fades
like cancer
only
you say cancer
does not fade
it eats and grows
consuming
but so does light
like that
it eats and grows
when fading
our fears grow
and
what we see is
eaten
consumed
the sickness grows
outgrows us
and light fades
simple.
   Mark Sharlow

Three Times, No Charm

Three times you told me
you loved me.

Once a year.

Three times I believed
you loved me.

All the time.

The third time you told me
you loved me

very soon

was followed by the announcement
of your plans to wed.

But not me.
   Pia Thielmann

A Child's Cries

A child cries
As it waits
For rescuers to find its family.

A child cries
As it sees its family suffering.

A child cries
As it sees the ambulances leave
With its family.

A child cries
As it is reunited with its family.

A child cries
As the long road to recovery begins.

A child cries
One year later
As it sees people still recovering.
   Danielle Jones

Trying to Shake Free

Surely you jest
in your step there is no zest.
I didn't mean to confuse the meaning
or send you careening
into the wall of perplexion
where there is no protection
from puzzling animosity.

Just wait and see
if your mind clears
away the fears
that build up inside
and try to hide
the opaque feeling
of strangeness, that sends you reeling
towards an unknown
reality alone.
   Blaise Iacofano

Life's Short

Even though I'm gone
From this world below
I leave behind
No silver or gold

Just a few memories
Of all my past
That I hope and pray
In your heart will last

Life's very short
Full of hopes and dreams
But before I knew it
I was called home, it seems

To a beautiful place
I can go and rest
I'll look up at my father
Say "I've done my best"

Don't worry about me
My friend, cause I'm gone
I'm in heaven now
And I'm far from alone
   Deborah W. Osborne

God

I can see your face in the rain,
that falls gently to the ground.
I can feel your touch in the breeze,
as it blows the leaves around.

I can hear your voice in the thunder,
as it roars across the sky.
And I can see your sweet smile,
in the rainbow set up high.

And I can see your awesome anger,
in the harsh winds that blow.
But I can feel your calmness,
in the falling of winters snow.

And I can hear your laughter,
in the waves that hit the shore.
And I can feel your pain,
as the quakes shake the floor.

Yes, I can see your awesome anger,
in the harsh winds that blow.
But I can feel your calmness,
in the falling of winters snow.
   Sharon Reid

The Day You Left Me...

In Loving Memory of Kelly Wilson

   The day you left me
was the day you lied, you said
you promised you wouldn't
drink and drive.

   The day you left me
was the day you lied, you did
drink. They said not that much
but just enough.

   You asked your friend
to take you home, it turns
out he was drinking too.

   He lost control of the
car and crashed into a tree.

   Because you lied, you
didn't make it home.
Because you lied we can't
laugh together anymore.
   Jamie Acker

Dewdrop Tears

Where golden drops of sunshine
fall upon a glittering world
a majestic rose is plucked
and you do not feel its pain
but dewdrop tears glisten
on its softly colored petals
in a crystal vase it wears
a proud gown of thorns
until life is gone
and it sadly hangs
its dry and lifeless head
for there are no tears
left for it to cry
   Mellenie L. Hilpert

Little Girl

Little girl, little girl
I wonder what for fun may be
you go to the park or may be
you play dress up. Oh, I think
you have more fun for teaseing
your sister you may have done.

Tanja Ozill

By Myself But Not Alone

I stood there atop the hill,
Feeling so close to the sky.
The world seemed peaceful and still,
I felt free, like I could fly.

I thought I could reach the blue,
And touch the upside-down sea,
But with other things to do,
In this place I could not be.

I strolled through the croaking wild,
By myself but not alone,
Watching colored leaves styled,
Nearing my quaint little home.

Resting on my wooden chair,
There came a knock at my door,
It was my Companion there,
Whose company I'd implored.

Mike Hanna

When the Applause Erupted

They danced and pranced to the tunes
    that were played
My eyes filled with tears
    when the applause erupted
Why! I do not know
Why? I do not know
Was it the theme?
    The "Spirit of America"...
    The energy so gracefully expanded
or, the granddaughters last
    endeavor to prance on stage
like a dying ember before
    a grandmother of sixty-seven
When the applause erupted
    My eyes filled with tears
    Why! I do not know
    Why? I do not know
Perhaps, it's getting to be farewell

Daphne A. Falkenstein

Heaven's Arms

    Marland, Marland,
I miss you so, I can't believe
you had to go.

    Out of my life for now you'll be,
until we meet in eternity.
    You were my gift from
the Lord above,
    So keep on smiling my
little dove.
    The Lord is good the
Lord is great,
"you" and "I", know he didn't
make a "mistake."
So sleep my son in heaven's arms
until you hear Gabriel's charms.
And what a day that will
be to have my "Son"
close with me.

Grace Williams

To Doug, With Love

Doug, from your day of birth
I saw what a gift God gave to me
My little boy so full of mirth
His smile so filled with glee.

That little baby, how he grew
So quick before my eyes
Into the very special you
Oh how fast time flies!

So I am making time today
To say I love you
You're precious in every way
And I care about all you do

I want you to know
If you need to talk, share or listen
My love, support to show
And, yes, even a tear to glisten

I'll be there for you, if I can
If not in person, then in spirit
Close your eyes - there I am
Feel the love I send with merit

Marlane Fissell

Flight 592

"The bush has many faces
and the weed now carries hands.
In the smallness of the sky
every star quietly stands.

In a minute it is over.
In a second all is lost.
What you may think as human
is just a lump of frost.

A rising tide of passion
settles in a flash.
And in the sweep of a brow
arrives a terrible gash.

The water will say nothing.
And the mud will be a mute.
For a metal hunk is twisted
by the song of a deadly flute.

I really did not know them.
I therefore cannot cry.
And I can hardly give them
my heart that now is dry."

N. Shirwany

Unprotected

Unprotected tears form subtle traces
On innocently grieving faces.
Smiles hiding endless sorrow;
Ignorance revealing pain
Through eyes of integrity
So sweetly possessed.

Unprotected tears form subtle traces
On innocently grieving faces;
Desperate smiles in dear spite
Of glistening lamentation
Strive to protect children
From solemn, dignified tears.

Sabrina Panfilo

Untitled

The lump they call the brain
Floats in its vacuum
Searching for the truth
That the soul keeps locked
In the right chamber of your heart.

But if the lump explodes
The truth is lost forever
In the innermost depths
Which will never show truth again.

Suzanne R. Sexton

Marigoldie

Father and child together
So happy we were.
Seeming to never end
But now it seems a dream.

Your curly haired Marigoldie,
Skipping to keep up
As life comes between
And separates us.

Now I watch from afar
As in a dream.
My kindred soul is gone
My Dad.

Claudette Clarke

Seasonal Seasons

To see the whiteness of the snow
that lay about a foot or so,
to see the trees incased with ice
a winter's scene that's very nice
if in a house with fire bright
you sit with friends this chilly night
while out of doors the cold winds blow,
moving round bits of snow....
And yet before the night shall end
again, again the snow descends
till morning brings you to the door
to see the whiteness evermore.
We close the door chase out the cold
for even now we're not so bold
yet after breakfast, toast and tea
we see the cold more willingly
for now we must move it away...
Admire it some other day.

Meredith J. Weir

The Maiden On the Plains

In quick bewilderment
Of passages not yet made,
I've inquired on her affectionate body
So wonderful on the plains.
Alluring is her eminence,
So concealed is her fertility
I only pray to make it so,
That she may be my deity.

With deep devotion to her soul,
I make a spot for her in my heart,
Where Angels fly and the sky is red,
And never shall we come to part.
With passionate kisses,
And unthinkable love,
We make,
With emotions from heaven above.

Clinton Harrington

For Mandy

The life that she's had
it doesn't seem fair,
All the feelings she's had
they rip and they tear.
The numbness, the pain,
she can't take it anymore
As she hears the silence
she falls to the floor
It was the words she heard
the ones she'll always dread,
In loving memory
of Janice and Ed

Jenny Abels

So The Poet Speaks

On the edges of insanity,
In the cataclysms of the soul,
Amidst the crushing and the tumult,
True poetry is born.

With the strength of anguish
And the touch of bitter loss,
Each word cries a message,
As it tears the heart apart.

Grasping for an answer,
A light of truth reborn,
Listen and the lines will be,
As lightening in the dark.

The force of words once spoken,
Shall bolt with powers might,
And shake that which can be shaken,
As day shall follow night.

Of waves crashing,
And Thunder roar,
So the poet speaks.

E. A. Gioia

Without You

I am like a flower.
You are my sun.
Every time I see you I bloom.
You are the joy in my life.
You are the one I love and cherish.
Without you I will die.
Just like a flower without sun,
A flower with no reason to live.

Erin Collins

The Dream

Of all things in the World
all I want is you,
nothing brings more pleasure
than the loving things you do

You're all I've ever wanted
and all I'll ever need,
someday when we're together
I'll plant a little seed

A seed I hope will blossom
unique in its own way,
reminding me of our love
and that very special day

The day when you say yes
the day I ask will you
the day that we get married
and I give my love to you

Jason E. Schmidt

Strawberries

Love is pink.
It tastes like strawberries.
It smells like a lifesaver.
It sounds like juicy Kool-Aid.
It feels smooth.
It makes me feel like happiness.

Whitney Bollman

Young At Heart

My body grows old and weary
    Yet my heart is young and gay.
Old age reached out to claim me
    But I'll fight him all of the way.
        Nay I'll not give in to pity,
My laughter will keep me free
    I'll not grow old just yet.
There's too much I want to see
    Pain and suffering I'll push to AFT.
    I'll keep smiles upon my face.
Old age and I run neck and neck
    But I plan to win the race
Whatever God has in store for me
    And whatever old age imparts
There's one thing that I pray for
And that's to remain — young at heart

Wesley T. Elder II

Temptation

The mouth waters
My heart pounds
When I see your smile
And all reality is lost
In a time and place
Where we don't care
I want to feel you
Taste you
Hold you
And in my mind I do
You make me feel
A burning sensation
Should I give into
Your sweet temptation.

Felicia Cummings

Sadness

    Sadness is a deep dark blue
like the open sea.

    It's hot like a child's head
when they have a fever.

    It's cold like the touch of
a stranger's hand.

    It sounds like the cry of a
child when they're hurt.

    It tastes like hot tea burning
your tongue.

    It smells like burnt plastic.

    It looks like clouds on a rainy
day.

    It's texture is rough like
the black paved streets.

    It's like a coral reef that
doesn't move at all.

Leslie Deal

Thunder, Thunder

Thunder, thunder
I hear you tonight
Thunder thunder
Oh how you give me a fright
your loud scary noises
your bright blinking lights
Thunder thunder
I count the one thousands
of you tonight

Tracy Matheson

Silver

Silver is the color
    of butterfly wings
a universe
    and complex things.

Silver says power
    like no other tone
silver is there
    though it's all alone.

Silver is the color
    of stars at night
silver is stellar
    glowing and bright.

Silver is a flower
    on venus's floor
silver will not cower
    but will
break down the door.

Kara Jackson

A Mother's Love

    A mother's love is
special so precious and pure.
    A mother's love is
like the bonding
piece to keeping
everything secure.
When the father
up and go, leaving
the mother all alone.
    The mother picks
up the broken pieces
and continue
making it on her own.
Understanding that
it's hard raising a
child, with one parent
for a guide the best
thing the child can
say is "I had my
mother by my side."

Katrina Brown

Tournament Of Twilight

Fields of glory
surround vast courts of azure blue.
Brave white knights on golden steeds
bow before
royal crimson gowns
then fade
as silver lances pierce the sky
and bring forth farewell tears
of dew.

Mary E. Barber

Apology

She was there
only I wasn't.
Ravaged was my mind.
Ruptured was my soul.
Youth returned in waves.

Lady, you were blinding. So
intense was your light!
Silently ripping through me
and tearing my sight.

Desire to enter,
indeed, to touch your life,
assailed my senses.
Never did I realize an
end was in sight.

Russell J. Psik

Rhythm

Really
can't you see
the fear
in my eyes
as I look
everywhere
strangers yet friends
faded memories
of time spent
falling into holes
I didn't even know
were there.
Some bare moon
I shine in sleep
in a steady rhythm
he looks he follows
for his share

Erin Randle

Deep Freud Food for Thought

I jumped
and sailed through the night sky,
caught by welcoming hands,
friends and relatives that never die.

The past, present, future
all wrapping around each other,
never, ever leaving.
I've finally found my brother.

Women, children, and men,
as far as the eye can see
I sat quietly waiting,
for the special one for me.

They came gliding forward,
a silhouette unseen.
I thought that I knew them,
when my Alarm Clock screamed.

Stephen Piotrowski

A Soldier's Wish

Wrap me in the Stars and Stripes
The flag I love the best.
Put me down underneath the ground
Where I am safe to rest.
The grass is turning green
Where many people have trod
I am now quite happy
In the hands of God.

Alice E. Jasko

Poets Are We

Poets are we
In prose and word
We write for all to see
In life to observe
The flower birds and bees
And all things around us
So pause a minute in our day
And that along the way
Not hurried or blind of mind
Because a poet with eye and mind
Has plenty of time
In observing life's visual objects
And events of every day
In bringing new thoughts
And expressions
For people to read and muse
In their quiet moments
And to enjoy life's pleasures
In a less frantic way

As a poet that is all I got to say.

John J. Chironno

Golden Threads

We walk through life hand in hand,
with the one that we have chosen.
There together we will stand,
through all the trials of men.
The time between our life and death,
a single thread of time.
An uttered word, a whispered breath,
a gentle song, an airy chime.
Then we lay within his hands,
alone we face the end.
No longer am I there with you,
bonds death cannot rend.
Here I am so scared and alone,
memories of me will fade.
Meaningless words scribed in stone,
forever lost the life we've made.
All alone, I will part this world,
a breathless name, a silken cord.
The strands of my life unfurled,
dependent on the mercy of the Lord.

Kari A. Nugent

Meditation

Taking breath in
like a cool drink
of water

Letting breath out
like sun-warmed skin

The chill of
goose bumps on flesh

The heat of blood
running through veins

Dead roots in a glass
water bottle leap out

Then fade
into the cosmos

Images - nothingness
Images - everything

Kathy J. Kunce

Is It

Is it to be true
To sacrifice
Is it to be pure
To freely give
Is it to become whole
While holding half
Is it to understand
To judge unprejudiced
Is it to learn
To not repeat wrongs
Is it to love
To be warm
Is it to grow
To live

Melissa Abt

My Mother

When God made words for
us to speak, like father,
sister, brother, the kindest
word that comes to mind
is you, our dear sweet mother.

You were so fair, you did
not judge when others
seemed to slide. You listened
as a friend should do, and
stayed right by their side.

God knew heart, and so
Did I, it flowed with
Bounding love, and now
You're home where you belong,
With Him in heaven above.

Jan Casaus

A Teen

What happened to that little child,
That I once held in my arms?
The years have slipped away.
To fast for me to understand.

A little child that turned to me,
For help and understanding,
For me to wipe his tears away.
To keep him safe and sound.

All I did was turn around.
And you grew into a teen.
Where did all the years go in between?
All I did was turn around.
And there you stand a teen...

Kim Mary Bolin

Daddy

On this paper I've left my print,
With it Daddy, my love I've sent.
Please don't forget me, cause
I'm still here,
And to me dear Daddy I hold
you near.
Daddy I need you and miss you so.
Please can you tell me why
you had to go.
Seems now I cry, most everyday,
Cause I want my Daddy so we can play.
P.S. To my Daddy, it's only me
with all my love, your little Jessie.

Donna Whalen

Broken Dreams

As children bring
   their broken toys
With tears for us to mend,
I brought my broken dreams
   to God
Because he was my friend.

But then instead
   of leaving Him
In Peace to work alone,
   I hung around
and tried to help
With ways that were
   my own.

At last I snatched them back
   and cried,
"How can You be so slow"
"My child," He said,
"What could I do?
You never did let go."

Lauretta P. Burns

The Blue Jay

A lot of people hate the jays,
But why, I do not know.
For often, on a wintry day
when everything is white and grey
A flash of color holds the eye,
Much bluer than a Summer sky.

A noisy bird, a raucous thing
A nuisance, it is true.
But how I love, on Winter days
To see that flash of blue.

Doris Estabrook

Twilight Reflections

Springtime's Youth is a lily,
Petals on the wind.
Summer's Love is a dew-drenched Rose,
Purified of Sin.

Autumn's Hope is a laughing brook,
Such a merry little rill!
Winter's Dream - soft snowflakes
Blanketing green hills.

Sorrowful is the wind's deep sigh
As she sees the end of Day.
Dusk draws nigh; the blackbirds cry,
(Summer's Roses fade away.)

Marian Hallet

Butterflies

   They come in
many colors just
like people

   They show peacefulness
like sun
flowers without
bees

   They're as soft
as soft as silk
like a baby

   They are children
without worries.

Jessie Lucas

Forgiveness

God - please forgive me,
for what I'm about to write.
But my mind has become a whirlwind,
And my tears are clouding my sight.

I know that I was wrong,
And I can't ever take that back.
But don't I deserve,
Just a little slack?

No - I forgot,
I can't think of being free.
Cause I know I screwed up big time,
And guilty was my plea.

When I realized how I lied,
And cheated my one true friend.
I filled my thoughts with guilt,
And my life - I wanted to end.

But now I must make a change,
To try to do things right.
So I pray to you - Dear Lord -
To help me see the light.

Kathy Anne Farrell

Gone From My Mind

You're not around anymore
   so I forlong...
to have these memories of you
   forever more...
     Gone

Jeanine Susie Dalomba

The World Is

   The world is made up of:
     The exposure to drugs,
     The harmony of love.
     The delusion of dreams,
     The pleasure of birth,
     And the sadness of death.
But oh people at the end there will
be a decision. Not of man, but of
the creator. Whether to choose heaven
for eternity in peace. Or to choose
hell for eternity in torment. So
wake up people and realize, that we're
all here for a purpose. We were not
created to live of this world anyway
we choose, but to see, who will
win, and who will loose...

Patricia A. Sams

Daddy Daddy

Is it true?
What they say?
They tell me you've gone far
Far away where I cannot reach you
To tell you I love you

It is my one hope and desire
That one day I will be with you
And then I can tell you
I love you.

Jennifer Zanardi

Snowdance

Snowflakes falling down
In a whirl of dancing glee
Cold ballerinas

Angela Bartholomew

Season With Reason

Something salty, something sweet,
Gives my taste buds such a treat,
Cantaloupe with 'tater chips
Enters my voracious lips.

Foods with such opposing tang
Touch my tongue with such a bang,
Pepper and salt, sugar and spice
Scads of pungents taste so nice.

Pasta with spaghetti sauce,
Onions sliced for salad toss,
Garlic bread spread thick with butter
Won't allow you close to utter

Tender words close to her face
Or you'll be in dark disgrace,
Penchant for these foods so spicy
Gains you love so very icy, so

If you must eat food with season
Play it cool, with conscious reason,
Ease up on the Garlic Sauce
And your life won't be a loss!

Herb Walsh

Cancun 2

Brilliant sunshine...
   Glistening on palm trees
   Dancing gently in the wind

White-capped waves...
   Also feeling empowered
   Break fiercely along the shore

Restless clouds...
   Roll peacefully by
as we
   Relax and let them

A seagull...
   Soaring gracefully by
And in this moment we
   Forget everything...

   Except, Love.

Mary E. Ingstad

Snow Crystals

The frozen crystals of water
   Swirl 'round and 'round and 'round.
Each has its own special pattern -
   No sameness can be found.

I watch, in awe, the ripples
   Of snow fall from the roof.
And gaze in wonder as it floats
   Back up-so cool, aloof.

I wonder to myself:
   How could this be true?
That I could see such beauty
   And not be with you.

Cassie Smyrl

Finale

I love the smell of my darkness
It is sweet
I could yearn
It is sheer blasphemy

And how I danced by the pallid shadows
Listening to the crickets sing
Dansen Macabre
Delightful

Sweating a copper rain
Rusted edges cutting
Willful pain
Indentured healing

How fairs the flames so cold
Sulfur incense
A tombstone
Nothing

Jose Juan Lara Jr.

Tranquil Seed

How still is the air
And warm is the night.
Stars twinkle up there,
Magnificent, bright.
And now nature sings
Me her silent song.

Spread forth, my soul's wings.
Spirit, fly along,
Up the tranquil trail
Towards sweet repose.
On heaven's winds sail
Far above all woes.

When again wings fold
Still I will be free,
Peace of mind I'll hold,
Strengthened I will be,
Renewed from life's pace
For my soul will feed
In the quiet place
I call tranquil seed.

Silvester McLaurin

Untitled

I loved you, I needed you
why weren't you ever there
I wanted you, I told you so
did you ever really care
I tried to make you happy
I tried to make it work
I thought you felt the same
I thought we had it all
until I realized one of us had to fall
so now I am here
and you are there
Happiness we no longer share
I can no longer hear your promises
no longer hear your lies
But deep inside my heart
you will always hear my cries

Sharra Renee Hardin

Lonely Dove

Over the clouds and below the moon,
There is a white dove who will
Reach the earth much too soon.
White as snow, all pure and true,
Flying so high in a sky so blue
Only the wind and open space,
Never to land in just one place.

Paul S. Laslie

Don Antonio Lugo

Today I see you laughing,
tomorrow I'll see you crying.
Our happiness will turn to sorrow,
because we've said our last good-bye.
You filled my heart with laughter,
chased away my tears.
You held me lovingly,
as I snapped and pushed away.
Hope was always present,
in your warm and friendly eyes.
Happiness ever present,
even as the rain passed by.
Always keep a place for me,
and never say die.
And I'll beep the tears from falling,
as I say to you good-bye.

Callie Ann Ziola

Untitled

I want to dance
under the moon and the stars.
Where nothing will touch me
from afar.
I want to see the magical lights
from the celestial sea
In the dark blue night.
I will feel the music and the
rhythm in my mind
I will leave my troubles
temporarily behind.
No one is around me
No one else can see
Just me alone
Feeling free!

Jessica Sherwood

Ants

Ants
ants
ants
tiny ants
creepy ants
nasty hairy ugly ants
black strong queen ants
Those are just a few.
Dumb ants
slow ants
flying red poisonous ants
scary fat sneaky ants
hungry ants too.
Busy ants
army ants
Don't forget fire ants
Last of all, best of all,
I like dead ants.

Cody Welge

The Virgin Birth

The virgin birth of our Savior
by the prophet was foretold
to the whole house of David
away back in days of old

An Angel would bring the message
the maiden would conceive
according to the word of God
that others would believe
the message came from heaven
that she would bear a son
Immanuel would be His name
God's anointed One

The world was unprepared for Him
because of sin and strife
He was rejected by His own
and chose to give his life

Upon the alter of the cross
our Lord was crucified
He became the sacrificial lamb
today He lives although He died

Mary Irene Bitting

In A Land Beyond Dreams

In a land beyond dreams,
That sparkles like gold,
The creatures are many,
If new and of old.
The leaves shaped like emeralds,
The ground diamond sand,
And all of the creatures,
Go hand in hand.
The flowers blue opal,
The rose ruby red,
Not one single creature,
Takes one single thread.
One lonely mountain,
With a stream running by,
It splits into two,
One steams to the sky.
The other is mild,
Like a gentle spring rain,
If you enter this land,
It's love you will gain.

Lindsey Hammond

Rabbits

Rabbits all white and furry
They are always in a hurry
They like to bounce
And like to pounce
But they never ever curry.

Tiffany Tang

Joan

'Twas a day near mid summer,
Born sweet child destined a comer.
Blessed with features fair,
Mind and talents for life with flair.
A tapestry of travail, song and art,
Oath to lighten others part.
More often a rapid pace,
Mastered with special grace,
Love came as fume of sighs,
Soon purged by sparkling eyes,
Though at times come tears,
Love perseveres.

Joseph Rutkowski

A Blessed Bond

Together, we shared
  our parents
  our family
  our home.
Together, we share
  our faith
  our hope
  our love.
Together, we share
  a
  blessed bond.

Mildred Towns Williams

The Rising Sun

The sun is starting to rise.
The white gold glow is not a disguise.
It reaches out to the line of clouds.
It gives off a reddish shroud.

The scene is there for an artist.
The rising sun paints a picture.
I wonder why I couldn't?
I wonder why I shouldn't?

The talent is not there.
The talent must be somewhere.
The talent is inside me.
The talent must find a way to be

How do I explain it all.
From someone that is tall.
How to explain from my mind.
To someone who is blind.

Ron Siegel

Life

Life is what you make it,
come good or bad.

Take what it give's you and
make something out of what you have.

Everyone has something to give
weather it be big or small do
the best you can, and you'll
find out life is worth it after all.

Someone needs what you have
to give, if you weren't their, there
would be nothing to give.

Whatever your purpose is in
this life do your best,
and you'll make a difference in
someone else's life.

Carol Blackburn

Love Remembered

In the instant of time
  I found
The heat of your nearness
  Like a cloud,
Drifting through its destiny of air,
  Dropping rain,
Gently,
Momentarily,
  Into the sea.

Bill Salus

"The Lighthouse"

Late one night,
'Twas calm and still,
So quiet you could
Hear the turn of the mill.
The tide so peaceful,
The breeze so light,
Twas not a breathing soul,
That 'twere awake in sight.
The air so scented,
The wind so did it dance,
The tops of the trees
The stars did enhance
Beyond the rocky cliffs
In the glowing moonlight,
The lighthouse keeper
Bids the sailors, "Goodnight."

Alicia Nicole McMillan

Twilight Time

Come with me love and see
splendor in Western skies.
A fiery, beaming disc sinking
like a ship in a passive seas.
Stay with me love, listen
crickets chirping, a hush settling
over hills, flowering meadows.
Mournful sounds of Mourning doves
resonate on balmy air
A flutter of wings, flash of red
robins stirring in the trees.
Come closer love, behold
ghostly trees immersed in murky shadows
loom under dusky skies.
Intermittent lights appearing
in eyes of houses lined
along the ways of blacken tops,
while night waits in the wings,
because it's twilight time.

Dixie Wilson

Books Delight

I take a delight in reading.
The joy when I open the cover.
I love to choose them out
  of millions of their
  brothers and sisters.
Their home is the library
I adore their leather aromas.
The perfume of the pages make
  my heart soar.
The elegant words as they
  flow through my mind

My ticket to another world
My plane that will take me
  far from this place.
My friend when I am alone.
My teacher when I don't
  understand something.
My comforter when I am sad
My partner through life
But most of all my imagination.

Brenda S. Walter

Red, White And Blue

I saw her from a distance standing
so still; I saw her waving as
I passed her by; her colors
are beautiful red, white and blue;
the stars are the states that
make up this nation; she's been
through World War I and II; she
still stands so eloquently blue;
she stands for all our love ones
who died for me and you, that
we might have our freedom
across this great nation.
So on this 4th of July as
we stand and salute you,
I'm proud to be an American
of a flag red, white and blue.

Cindy Arender

A Cruel Hoax

I once was young
But now am old.
One half the truth
I'd not been told.

I feel like twenty
In my soul.
And yet to "twenties,"
I am old.

I don't feel like
I look at all.
I'm young and handsome
Straight and tall.

A cruel hoax
It seems to me:
Trapped in the body
that you see.

O could they see
The man I am,
I'd end life's journey
A happy man.

Wendell L. Vaughan

The Raggedy Man

We see him sleep in gutters
we see him eat out of cans
but why must we torment this soul
if he can't help where he stands.

He lies around lonesomely
with his palms faced to you and I
but some people just don't care
they laugh and give him a sigh

He lives on what he can find
which is not much at all
we pass him on the street
with his face to the wall

He sleeps in clothes that are dirty
to him that's as clean as they get
when it rains he sleeps in boxes
but he can't help but get wet
Now that you know who I am
please go out there and help
give a little and give what you can
to save a homeless raggedy man.

Luana Halili

Oklahoma City

Little birds sing
not in Oklahoma City
Children play in peace
not in Oklahoma City
Peace lives
not in Oklahoma City
Federal Building blows up
In Oklahoma City
Many people died
in Oklahoma City
Broken hearts
in Oklahoma City
So many people
in this world
So many lives to save
in this world
So many less people now
in the world

Jessica Maniff

On the Death of a Friend

Another grave filled.
Another soul lost.
The endless cycle of death.
The ultimate, inescapable cost.

Empty words are spoken
To deaf, despondent ears.
Promises are broken
In defiance of the years.

Disillusioned wooden Pawns
Bow their foolish heads.
They pray and pray and pray
But it won't bring back the dead.

Ineffectual tears
Diminutive drops of sadness.
Mind and heart harden
Struggling against madness.

All emotions abandoned.
Surrendered sanctity.
Nothing left to believe in
But harsh reality.

Shelly Weathers

What A Poem Could Be?

Could be about a tree,
    you or me
About a stormy night.
    a tear or a sigh
And so you see, what it could be
    something old or new
Could be sad and blue,
    about the sky, way up high
    a mom or dad, good and bad,
Coming home or being gone
    in a crowd or all alone,
So you see, what this poem could be?

Betty L. Rucker

Don't Do It

People think there cool,
Just because they smoke.
But all I can say,
it's just a big joke.
I'll let you know,
if you do it a lot.
Your body is going,
to end up caught.
I'll ask you once,
to stop now please.
Because if you don't,
you may get a disease.
It will creep through your body,
and start to spread.
The cool thing now,
is to stop before your dead.

Earlene R. Neureuther

The Giving Heart

Thinks of tomorrows-
Yet to come!

Understands Sorrows-
In quiet solitude.

Rejoices the Day!
The birth of dawn.

Encourages Equality
In Somber Reckoning.

Jacqui L. Bibeau

From the Wings of Angels

Music is a gift from God
Written down on the wings of angels
When a feather falls, a song lands
Touching the heart of who we are

Unless we listen with our souls
We cannot hear the song
And this present, wrapped in love
Remains unopened

But if we are willing to listen
The divine gift, now opened
Plays a symphony from heaven

The melody is clear
The harmony perfect
Each note carefully chosen
By the Creator, himself

Thus, written on the wings of angels
God orchestrates His holiness
While the cherub choir sings:
Listen! Listen! Listen!

Pamela Burmeister

Night Travel

After hours
When all is quiet
And all about you
Prepares for the night

I come for you
To go fly with me
Up to the stars and back
To see all of creation
    in Harmony.

Charlene Dunagan

Precious Memories

Each life uniquely has been lived
    in a very special way,
And the love that kept together,
    we celebrate today.

To love, believe, and trust each other
    you've offered Fifty Years
A commitment filled with memories
    much love and joy and tears.

A milestone of faithfulness,
    what grace this day implies;
For your years of love to us,
    our thanks now multiples.

A milestone of sacrifice
    by this you've really lived.
In years of raising children,
    you've found so much to give.

So shines this Golden Fifty
    a milestone in time,
It shows the dearest qualities
    in parents such as mine.

Georjean Allenbach

Single Shadow Verse

Empathy, much empathy
A heart sad with
single shadow verse
Every parents nightmare lived
A family torn
Faith, love and hope sustain
A child is hurt
A young man down
Hanging on, hanging in
Suspended on the brink
Haunting, halting
The words surge slowly
repeat and return
Faith, Hope, Love
Holding on, holding him
Pushing the edge
Faith, hope, and love sustain
...and we pray

Carole Saunders

Just A Dream!

Sailing on the edge
From nowhere - to nowhere
Skimming the shadows
Of darkness and light
Reflections of shapes and sounds
Of silence piercing space.

Slowly rising from the water
coming to the surface
Dreamers visions, through a haze
Of transparency, just out of reach
Of reality.

Feeling hair on my face
An ever so gentle tap
On my shoulder
Scamp telling me
It is morning!
Time for a walk!

Sophie Marie Tuckey

Steel Magnolias

Today's a milestone in your life
Dear faithful friend of mine,
The day for sweet reflections,
On the years we leave behind.

We've journeyed far, and shared a lot
Of what life brought our way.
The joys we've known, the sorrows borne
As friends do, day by day.

You've always been the kind of friend
In whom I could confide.
In your council, I found strength
However low the tide.

Life's changing seasons once again
Ushers in the great unknown,
Still we stand firmly planted
On this friendship we have grown.

It matters not what lies ahead
For either you or I,
Like steel magnolias, we'll remain
Strong comrades, till we die.

Donna Lou Edwards

Untitled

I see you in the dark
I see you in the day
but when it comes tonight
my heart just breaks away
I think about you all the
time wishing you were near
now you left me with a
heart that I never can repair.
Wishing I could hold you
In my arm tonight take
my hand that go again
please give me another night
I know I did you worry before
but please forgive me now
I need you in my life today
please give another round.

Lucy Beatrice

Spiral of Hate

A spiral of hate
Darkness devours
And leaves to fate
This souls of ours.

It pulls with full force;
Mercy, it has none;
A predator and its mouse;
it's impossible to run.

But be not discouraged,
For therein is a way out.
When darkness is raged
In itself acquires doubt.

Never anyone can say,
Though never been tried,
Doubt can lead the way
When in enemy thine.

Ed Page Jr.

Earth

Blue skies
Flames go on flies
More water than land
Beach sand, lots of trees
Stinging bees, arctic bears
Wood made chairs, hoppity bunnies
Sweet bee honey
Air breathing mammals
Hot, dry camels
Water breathing fishes
Glass made dishes
Small little ants
Cotton made pants
Sing, people sing
As the bell loudly rings
Pretty roses, girls doing poses
Plants live alive so long
So sing to them a song
That nature does know
And let it grow and grow.

Jennifer Claytor

For Our Children

We always want the best
For our children as they grow
We try to teach them everything
That they will need to know
We hope they know the difference
Between what's wrong and right
We pray that they will always
Return safely home each night
We pray they have the strength
To resist what may be bad
If they are weak and give in
It makes us parents sad
We have to let them choose
Their decisions they must make
We can not always be there
To guide each step they take
Soon there will come a time
When we will have to say
You're free to go out in the world
And pray they've learned the way

Linda Lange

Selecting a Puppy

I was standing back there
By the big oak tree
When they brought him 'round
For me to see.

They put him down,
And I whistled low.
His ears stood up.
He saw me, ho!

In a flash he was flying
Right through the air
And touching ground
Only here and there...

Till he bounced to my arms
And like his kind
Was cuddlin' and kissin'
And I knew he was mine.

Juanita Anderson

Whirl Wind

O! Lo! About the space
where heavens meet that earth
of thirst, so dry
so calm.
That we may speak
no peace at all
so shush! My wind
whirl wind is dancing
again.
One and all must join as dust
twists and turns, whirls and spinning
around, 'round, we may whirl
until the heaven, my kin
may speak out loud
and shush! Us all
with a thunder voice
that brings my dance to an end
of a whirl.

Nanabah Chee Dodge-Grogan

Silent Words

I hear the sound of silent words
That echo in my ear
I hear the sound of silent words
That bring to eyes a tear
I hear the sound of silent words
That once expressed a vow
I hear the sound of silent words
That have no meaning now
Memories of happy days
Still linger in my mind
I dream of things
That might have been
But are no longer now
I hear the sound of silent words
That echo in my ear.

Lionel Leitner

Make the Past Worthwhile

Let the past be what it was
Be glad it was that way
Because you can't change it
Don't forget it
But remember it
Don't let it be painful to you
Instead, make use of it
Make it worthwhile

K. Kay Matsuda

Ashley

She's as interesting as a rainbow,
   She's delightful and bright.
She's all things wonderful,
   Every day and every night.

She arrived with Spina Bifida,
   Her feet just won't prance,
She twirls in her wheelchair,
   And on the floor, does her dance.

She twinkles like the stars,
   And she shines just as bright.
Ashley is my grand daughter,
   And she's an absolute delight.

John R. Henry

Brightest Star

We have traveled far,
in a bar, and drove in a car.
Light travels far,
now you can see your star.

We have both gone far,
but, never opened far.
To show we're not par.
For the other is our star.

We have both looked far,
to ask why so far?
We never found that star,
until now our brightest star.

We have both beamed far,
together is the brightest star.
We never have to go far,
Jesus led us to our star.

David Joseph Silvestris

Lives Crossing

'T was a tugging at the heart
When first soul mates came to meet;
Youth and age each played a part
In a case of bittersweet.
They grew in understanding
While each read the other's face.
With no room for pretending
They walked in each other's place.
Grandmother nearing ninety,
And the child just barely five;
Read to each other nightly
And grew closer in their lives.
Like two ships in a crossing-
Sometimes trade in merchandise;
These two souls in love touching
Are in fact exchanging lives.

Mirtha G. Moreno

Untitled

They stream down my face,
They drip off my chin,
They collect on my shirt
And in my hands,
But no one notices.
Quietly they pour out of my eyes
Full with different emotions.
The hate, the love, the pain
Flow out with every sob,
Still no one notices.
The stress of my day
And my life, running
Down my damp cheeks,
Finally a true friend begins to notice.
Trying to comfort my pain,
Not knowing how much he helped,
Not realizing how many he stopped.
Someone actually noticed.

Emily Young

In the Night Still Dark ...

In the night still dark
an ancient temple glitters by sparkling
jewels, ghost trees moan by hideous
winds and the moons radiant reflection
burns down on an empty lagoon.

Whitney Taylor

Wrestling With God

I wrestle with God
    He won't let me go
I fight Him with my soul
    He keeps me in His hands.

I say that I chose You
    I know now that isn't true
You came after Me
    In order to set me free.

I wrestle with God
    Over my own desires
I know He wants
    what's best for me.

I wrestle with God
    My heart wants Him to win
My body fights to gain control
    Jesus wants to make me whole.

I wrestle with God
    He won't give up the fight
If I let myself lose to Him
    I can do nothing...But Win!

James Urwin Taylor Jr.

Untitled

This tiny babe is heaven sent
From among the stars she came,
To a place chosen just for her
Devon Colette will be her name.

While tiny fingers clutch together
She knows her mother is near,
Soon her eyes will open wide
To the wonders of all that's here.

And when this child is fast asleep
God will know that she is safe,
For tenderness and love abides
In this perfect chosen place.

Dorothy Hemms

Life

There it is!
Can you see it?
Right in front of you...
Imposing, awesome, challenging,
Waiting to be climbed.
Clefts and ridges,
Ups and downs.
With rocks and crevasses,
Slippery and sticky.
Exhilarating and fatiguing.
Inspiring and frightening.
Often fun but sometimes boring.
Waiting to be experienced.
Waiting to be enjoyed.
Waiting to be lived.

John N. Drowatzky

Love Songs

We listened together one night,
and danced with the music;
They told us of the beauty of love,
and of the pain it often brings;
Yet, we shared the changing tunes,
for hours together alone;
Then there was that one special song,
which spoke to both of us,
about the beautiful love we shared...

James Earl Cook

Tides

We're here. We're gone,
And the ocean rolls on!

Morna Stockman

Untitled

For all who were hurt
For all who have died,
For the Oklahoma City bombing
For all who have cried.
The children didn't deserve it
When did they go wrong,
Why did the guilty do it
Why did they set the bomb.
We can't do anything now
So much has gone on,
And many people were lost
But we all must go on.

Patricia Do

Enchanted Love

Like a blue lagoon thou art,
Nearest to me as the cool splashing
Waterfall pouring into it.
Full of Lilac and Lavender, Pinks,
Pastels of Mints and Gold,
And flowered scents to fill my soul.

Cool water to soothe me thou art,
Warm breezes to quench my need
For life's loves and
Most pleasing moments you are.
Like the white of the sands or the
Purest Lilly, like the pink of a cheek,
And turquoise days of summer when
We love to be on this beach.

Like the sunshine thou art,
Washing and swirling where
Water meets sand to touch
The sweetest depths of me;
You bring me up and out
And I am colours in the blessed sky.

Cindy Lee Strand

My Special Child

While at night I watch her sleep
It comes to mind.
How different my life would be
Without my special child.
The day she came, on the 5th of May.
And from the start she stole
my heart.
As time has past she has become
All I could want of a daughter
or son, just being
My special child
Not of my blood but every bit my soul.
Of all the children in this world
To be chosen by my little girl
I will always try and be a true
And loving mother to.
My special child

Malinda Taylor

The Wall of Good Intent

Be kind to the fallen one
stricken so, in deep despair,
knowing that there
is no answer to the deep pain
life must bear.

Not told, but somehow knows,
the truth of one's demise.
And so, denies
others the burden of the journey
but in the soul, one cries.

As loved ones,
cover and conceal
the truth that fate soon will reveal,
Although the knowledge, untold,
remains with on their lips a seal.

How much easier it would be
to share the chains,
that bind, and allow words to exchange,
the caring and understanding
that would remain.

Sandra E. Ducharme

Untitled

Are not the flowers all arisen
'Neath the halo of the sun,
There but for the sake of Beauty,
There but for the Chosen One?

Are not we indeed as they are
Lambs beneath the hallowed sky,
There but for the joy of Virtue,
There but for Love's watchful eyes?

From whose staff one life arisen,
For whose dreams to live and die,
Are not we indeed as they are
Lambs beneath the hallowed sky?

Steven G. Taylor

Deliverance

I stood in the valley,
The mountains were high,
No chance to surmount them,
'Twas no use to try!

I walked in the desert,
So hot and so dry,
No hope to escape it,
'Twas no use to try!

I sailed on the ocean,
The waves swept so high,
No thought for survival,
'Twas no use to try!

Then out of the valley,
And from the hot sand,
A wave seemed to whisper,
"Come, friend, take my hand!"

The mountain was now scaled,
An oasis was there,
God stilled the fierce tempest,
Yes, He heard my prayer!

Charlotte B. Wallen

Peals Tears On Grave
of J. F. Kennedy

Kennedy Grace lead
You have shone like lightning
In abundant light,
In the Western sky.

All the people are mourning for you.
Their heart is in tears,
As your brave courageous soul,
Has been widely known.

People all over the world,
Awoke a dawn
With a grieved heart,
Since you had gone.

Dionysia Garbi Paraschos

Whispering Winds

Wind flows through the trees
silently awakening the
sound sleeping leaves.

Shanna L. Burke

The Storm and the Majesty of God

I watched the darkened sky,
The trees bowing to the earth,
Leaves twirling across space,
And birds seeking a resting place

Claps of thunder vibrated the air,
Lightening flashed, streaked and hissed
A lone rabbit raw for shelter,
And then the rain began to pelter.

Praise filled me to the full,
My heart with awe o'er flowed.
In the storm was God and power,
Also in the final, gentle shower.

Mary T. Marshall

Dance Of The Decadent

Tie fate up
control her actions
dictate her doings
Smile on us
SPIT on everyone else

Gather the flock!
Fleece them!
Take all!
Spare none!

Decadence will leave you
sagging hips
baggy thighs
faces lifted till they implode
eyes sink in the sea of flesh

She is ageless and you are not
she will leave your ugliness
and bed again with beauty
spread her sickly syphilis
to everyone she sleeps with

Just watch and SEE!

William S. Wilcox II

You Remind Me Of...

Your eyes are like twinkling stars,
Tears of sadness reminds me of
falling rain,
Your lips are the shape of half-moon
settling down for a peaceful night.

Your straight black hair is like the
midnight sky,

Your heart beat is the sound of a
thumping drum playing in the parade,

Your voice reminds me of a soft melody
playing over and over,

And every time I look at these things
it reminds me of how beautiful you
are inside and out.

Laura K. Benzor

Glory Be the Father

Glory be to the Father
By you I have been found
To walk along beside you
Is to walk on Holy ground
Savings Sinners is to what you do
You do it so very well
Your Grace made me a new
Now others I must tell
This process neverending
Your gang is growing fast
You being the Greatest Leader
Of this ship you are the mast
So lets set sail for the Eternal
That Gracious Life you gave
And shun forever the devil
Who tried to take me to his grave
Now I know his ways are evil
And of him I have no fear
Because I walk along side my Father
Who I love so very dear

Virgil R. Counts

The Wind

Listen to the rustle of leaves
As gentle winds blow through the trees

Listen again when storm winds blow
Branches talk to the trunk below

Return of a caressing breeze
Draws a lullaby from the trees

Wind can help with pollination
Thus promoting new creation

The wind in a temper tantrum
Causes severe damage to some

The wind can be both good and bad
The trees endure and I am glad.

Lillian Lozier

I Dance A Solo

I dance a solo.
The music? My own.
Met another dancing-
    dancing to my song.
Sharing now, but not forever.
Memories endure.
Life dances on.

Cynthia McGinnis

Blue Bird

Blue bird blue bird
What do you see? I
see a kid looking at
me. Little kid little
Kid what do you see? I
see a teacher looking at
me. Teacher teacher what
do you see? I see my
future looking at me. Future
future what do you see?
I see everyone looking at
me.

Caitlin Miletto

The Guardian Angel

It had been quite a day
Little pleasures could not cheer
Though smiles usually come
Every day of the year.
I felt down,
Like no one was there.
But as I reached in the mailbox
I had no more fear;
For an old friend had written
And it nearly brought a tear.

Laura Virnoche

Untitled

The word kiss,
sounds so sensuous.
Silvery as the autumn moon,
with an edge sharp enough
to cut the worlds sad tune.
But that's only its first impression-
for its followed with the
sweetest soul - and dances with
a pink gold sea,
and if it falls from your lips
and dance through my heart,
that'll be the end of me,
My will lost-drowned

Alexandrya Messerschmidt

"Waipio, Is A Famous Beautiful Valley"

I love you Waipio,
your cliffs and water front
The black sand's on the beach
and the murmuring rustling waters.
I love you Waipio,
My unforgettable home,
And your mystic lushland
and the swaying cocoanuts, of Pakaalana
I often wish to have a glimpse,
of the sacred Tabu of King Liloa
Umi Liloa was a great king.
His Hotels were in Hilo and Puna,
I love you Waipio,
The misty rain of Hiilawefalls
you are most famous Waipio
glorious and renounced.
I end my poem about you Waipio,
it is written to the World, about you
How I love you Waipio
my unforgettable loving home.

Lily L. Chong

4th Of July

It flashes through the sky
colorful specks, glittering chandeliers
their presence brightly clear
memories of pain and bloodshed
of our loved ones

Sounds of explosions awaken our souls
sights and visions of what was
and may be again
hopes and dreams that it won't
be so

Reality brought back each year
of what was
celebrations for the living
declarations for the dead
Independence for whom

Janice A. Wilson

I'm There

Why do you treat me
the way you do?
When you ask for my help,
I'm always there.
When you need advice,
you always ask me.
When you need a friend,
I'm there for you.
But when the tables are turned,
And I ask for your help,
you're never there.
If I need advice or a friend,
you're always too busy for me.
You need to be there for me,
before you lose me as a friend.
One day when you will need me
by your side,
I won't be there for you.
What will you do then?

Jennifer Lyn Woodworth

The Pond Near My House

Wind whisps through tall grass,
Lily pads frame the water,
Big rocks to sit on and think,
Reflecting the view
The water sits.

Foliage comes alive in
vibrant colors,
Plush red,
Honey mustard yellow,
String bean green.

Canadian geese make wild scenes.

Watching the sun set,
Leaving everlasting colors.

As night falls,
The skater's blade hits the ice.

Watching the snow cover
the ice floor,
While
one by one
snowflakes fall.

Allyson Krasny

The Love For God In The Silence

If the silence
Regne in my heart
If the blue sky
Reflete my eyes
If the horizon
Inspire my memory

Oh! God you are
The divine creator
Of my print

Let the silence
Regne in my heart
To join the paradise
Of Jesus Christ

Andree Cacciuttozo

"Adoption"

Babies come to us from heaven,
A gift from God above,
On Angels' wings they travel
To the waiting arms of love.

We share this time together,
The angels are near, it seems,
God has brought you to us,
Through hopes and prayers and dreams.

If you come to us today and ask
The purpose of our mission,
We would sigh and say quite simply,
"To love without condition."

Linda Pillitteri

Words

As fragile as the heart permits
As they pierce the peace of mind,
Rhetorical with maddening fits
Ruthless and unkind.
As cherished as the heart recalls
As they stroke the loving chords
Out of the human mouth falls
The sin, and the blessing, of words.

Sherry Diana Crouch

I Am

I am the darkness in the light
I am the peace within the fight
I am wrong but feel so right
I Am
I am the frown that makes you smile
I am the inch within the mile
I am the once that's in a while
I Am
I am the group within the hole
I am the emptiness of the soul
I am the mount behind the knoll
I Am
I am the life that knows no bounds
I am the silence in the sounds
I am the lost that is never found
I Am
I am the horse who needs no cart
I am the finish before the start
I am the world without a heart
I Am Am I?

William S. Barker Jr.

No One Cares

A child cries out in the night,
  And no one cares.
Another candle burns out,
  And no one cares.
Another whale is now dead,
  And no one cares.
One more storm rages on,
  And no one cares.
Lightening hits another tree,
  And no one cares.
A rain forest is now gone,
  And no one cares.
My own soul reaches out for you,
  And you don't care.

Kelly Haskell

Summer

Lilacs and soft pink geraniums
languish in the heat of the day,
their paintbox colors warm and liquid.
Ignoring the heat,
barefooted children scamper
through back yards filled
with jungle gyms and
the innocence of laughter.
The blistering sun
plasters copper-colored curls
to small, dirty foreheads as
freshly cut grass leaves stains
on skinned elbows,
and worn-out knees of faded jeans.
Unaware,
the torrid heat courses
through the veins of
another summer.

LaVerne Hope Fields

Wedding Wish

May you always have the wisdom
That this old owl conveys.
May you both be always happy
With sunshine in your days.
May your love be ever growing
In the many days ahead
And words such as "I'm sorry"
Should never go unsaid.
For marriage is a partnership
Based on love and trust
And forgiveness, above all else,
Is a necessary must!
Best wishes go from me to you,
Long life and best of health
For two young people so in love
Are endowed with lasting wealth.

Carolee Kelz

My Husband

The only one who can hold
my heart in his hands;

The only one who can
set it free.

The love of my life, the
beat of my heart,

without him in my life,
I could never be.

M. Hanger

Come, Live With Me

"Come live with me," said God above
To the little boy down below.
"You're not welcome by many down there,
Because of your being so slow.

"Up here it doesn't matter,
We're all of us as one,
Say goodbye to your loved ones
Your time on earth is done."

He said goodby to his loved ones
And God took him by the hand,
And hastened him on his journey,
To his beautiful, for away land.

His toys and all his belongings
Are just as they were when he went
And the family are contented
For the short time he was lent.

Bernadine B. Grove

The Desperate Truth

Cunning emotions
Shattered devotions
Caught in troubled times.

Fearless storms
Hurtful scorns
From the mouth of a trusted one

Clouded dreams
Flooding streams
In a state of shock

All these disasters
All these troubles
Are ending in pain
And ending in sorrow
But will always be lived
Now and tomorrow

Amy Lurentzatos

Friends of the Morning

The warmth of
the early morning sun
A time of relishing
in his own thoughts
Quietly, alone
Joined by his friends of the air
Walking together
Following, waiting,
watching — the bag of
sustenance in his hand.
To perform
expanding chest
wings extending
Skyward
Floating, upward and around
swooping down
grabbing and screeching
Rising again for a
repeat Performance.

Priscilla Anderson

Autumn Dusk

Blue drowsy dusk of evening drifts
  Dreaming down;
It sleeps between the little lights
  That prick the town.

Elizabeth Hageman

Mood

What is this thing called a mood
That plays havoc with your mind?
You wake in the morning
Feeling good.
And by noon you're not so kind.
It strikes without a warning.
You simply don't understand why.
There's no reason one day
You're down.
And the next day you're feeling
High.
So we must deal with this demon.
Fight him tooth and nail
Make up your mind to ignore him
And toss him out on his tail.

Tammy Aronson

Memories

My mind's a hall of memories
of things of long ago,
and though I run to see your smile,
I'm running all to slow.
If I could just catch up to you,
and touch you just once more,
I could make it through the years,
like I did before.
I know that you watch over me.
I know that I must wait.
Someday we will meet again
behind heavens gate.

Dana M. Lehr

Ruthie

Ruthie was
a caring, loving, and a good person

She had her life made
she was going
somewhere in her life.

But yet
she had to die
with no reason
why.

We all still wonder,
Why??
Because of someone's
stupidity a good person
had to die

Life is so unfair;
too many people just don't care

So why?
Why, did she have to die
with absolutely no reason
Why!!

Amber Harwood

Simple

I'd rather be simple,
    in every way I can.
It's for material possessions,
    I don't give a damn.

Don't want to worry daily,
    of Bills coming in the mail.
Months go by so fast,
    can't take it if I fail.

Got some "things" of course.
    We need a roof overhead,
to stay safe and warm,
    best of all a "Bed"!

Along with that is simple,
    to make my life complete.
Said in my prayers every night,
    is to join with one so sweet.

I hope I can also be,
    a happiness to fill your heart.
Share a peaceful, simple life,
    and wild passion from the start!

Pamela S. Mansfield

Young Girls

Kimonos colored pearls
Light hearted
Sense of pride
Young girls.
Clanging bamboo
Leaves float
Glisten downward
The doves coo.
Parasol twirls
Laughter sings
Beauty lingers
Young girls.

Jimmie Elizabeth Martin

Virtue In Truth

Because sin is a virtue,
And how much virtue you reward
yourself with,
Conceivably,
I should laugh too,
And simply try to go along
With your hypocrisy,
Or possibly
I could show you for what you are,
A cloudy-eyed forgotten man,
living in a musty cave,
Stone cold,
Dead to the pale light
of truth,
You lied to your people long ago,
And now you have lied to yourself.
My dear friend,
Death is not release,
Patience is not a virtue.

Sean Brazell

Lebensraum

Hatred flows from pores
unseen
it's always there
lashing out
A fire
Images of flesh
burning
An aberration
Magnified
The reality
Writhing
Hurting
It just stares back
A mirror
Its four limbs, the limbs of
people
A scream!
Quieted
A grave.

Kelly Irene Queener

Society

Society now needs to change
too many drugs, too many gangs
too much sex, too much hate
now it's time we reconciliate
too much crime, too much murder
too many people against each other
too much violence on TV
whatever happened to a good comedy
nothings right, always wrong
hope you get the message to this poem
so somebody, somebody hear my plea
whatever happened to society?

Rashad J. Kareem

Escape

Today I made myself happy
For more than a minute or so
I tied a yellow flower
    to a yellow balloon
    and let it go

I wanted to fly after it
I wanted to be tied to it
I wanted to soar through the sky
To see the world through a bird's eye

To wake up tomorrow
    and not have to cower
To wake up the next day
With nothing to say
Rejoicing in silence's awesome power

People loving me back
    for more than an hour

Freed at last from the chaos tower
Like the tiny little yellow flower.

Michael A. Kasow

Red

The color of Heat.
Flaming, burning, hell,
torture, blood,

The color of Life.
Warmth, vibrance,
smiles, passion,

The color of Love.
Romance, roses,
happiness, cheer.

Lisa L. Curley

Friendship

Honesty, trust and integrity
Are virtues of a kind.
Blessed are those who are so fortunate
And in another hope to find.

Compatibility inspires comfort
As citing water in a brook -
Flowing ever so gently
Between each cranny and crook.

A friend who has these qualities
Can be so special thru our time,
    When it can be said -
"Most grateful am I to be your friend,
    And especially -
Your being a friend of mine"

Barbara S. Keith

Stuffed Animal That Stays
In Your Mind

When you dream about a stuffed
animal that you loved, and it's
missing.
    You wake up with a tear running
down your cheek.
    Is it because of the dream?
    Or is it because of the stuffed
animal that you like is missing.
    The thing that you hug, like
a teddy bear in your dream is a missing
stuffed animal but in real life is
your teddy bear.
    When you think about it,
not just one but many tears
come out, and you're sad.
    You keep crying because
you think about it.
    Why do you think about?
    Is it because it won't leave
your mind or is it because you miss it?

Vickie Galvan

Future Generations

We continue to pollute
the very air we breathe
and the water we drink;
with no thought
for tomorrow....
Future generations will ask why.
Why we polluted our environment.
Why we did not care enough
to recycle.

Anonymous

Sunshine

My life has been good
My life has been bad
It's what I want
Because I'm just sad.

I think about the future
I forget about the pass
I think about what will I do.
About the pass

As life goes or you will think
About how you want to live
Life is like flowers
Some smell good, some smell bad
As the sunrise life goes on

George T. Leggett

Mite Life

It would be
like crawling through a
jungle.
Dust ball trees.
Mayonnaise lakes.
Polish raindrops.
It all is like
a jungle.

M. Sean Foster

Because Of My Color

My life as a crayon is
burdensome. Stuck in a
cramped box with no room
to move, I'm shipped to
a store to be sold. They
use me everyday, my dark
dominant color is wearing
away, I wish I could stay.
They treat me poorly,
and strip me of my dignity
by taking off my wrapping.
When they've drained me to the bone
they just buy another brown.
No, it ain't an easy life
in this crowded Colored box.

Chris Papadopoulos

Alone

Here I am sitting alone.
And wandering what
you are doing.

I know in my heart
you are safe.

So, dear God take care
of him.

Keep him in good health
and protect him for me.

Marie M. Serrao

Elemental Eyes

Brilliant eyes of fire
burn me like a blaze.
Flame of secret desire
in me your passion lays.

Comforting eyes of ice
cool my angry heart.
With your sugar and spice,
I hate when we're apart.

Dainty eyes of air
carry me to God above.
Lady of tender care
touch my heart with love.

Enchanting eyes of earth
make my love your land.
Tell me what I'm worth
and hold my gentle hand.

Beautiful eyes of element
obtaining your love is my goal.
To you, my dreams were sent
and with it my delicate soul.

Erik Larson

The Night

Oceans part,
sparkling clear.
Don't be afraid,
the night is near.
It's here to hold you,
keep you safe from fear.
Now close your eyes,
It's here my dear.
In the distance,
appears a Light.
It's the light of two lovers,
holding each other tight.
It's their souls that shine,
never dim always bright.
without each other,
there would be no light.

Cortney Hardaway

2 - Papa

Are you looking down on me from
sweet heaven above?

And are you sending me all your
heart's love?

Do you look down on me day by
day?
When I talk to God can you hear
what I say?

Are you one of the stars that
twinkle in the sky?

Are you the wind that blows
right by?

Stephanie Scott

Untitled

Have no fear, have
no fear
Bear no sorrow —
No room here
in the heart, where
no time dwells
The place wherein
no secret tells
of Life's Meaning
in truest sense
regarding not the
consequence
It's quiet pounding
No passionate intent
Just rhythmic reminder
of chances spent
No judgements or ego
Motivation is pure
To renew, and renew
until hope is no more

Grace Rimmel

My Man

I love a sweet man;
He knows what is right.
My love for him is
Out of sight.

His eyes, his smile,
His crazy way;
I wish I could
See him everyday.

I am cool but,
My man is hot.
He looks good
In any spot.

He's so warm and cuddly;
My big teddy bear.
I'd rather sit on his lap,
Than in a little chair.

Michelle White

A Bad Hair Day

My hair is shaggy, I must admit
As I sit in the chair
For washing, cutting, perming, curling
I really have no flair.

When asked how do I want it styled
I'll say "it's up to you"
Admitting I'm not up to date
I do not care to do.

So wash and snip, and roll and blow
Results will better be
I'll walk out feeling like a star
A shining, sparkling me!

Teresa M. Simmons

I Am Somebody!

Why do you hurt me?
Why can't you see?
I just want to be happy.
I just want to be free.
Don't you love me?
Don't you care?
Why do I feel like I'm headed nowhere
We only have one chance,
And this is mine,
I feel like I'm running out of time,
Please understand,
Please believe.
I am somebody who wants to be me!

Karri Ann Powell

Oak Greek

The river roars
All dismal and grey
White foam hugging the banks
Sycamore trunks olive and white
Pines aglow with dew
Down the river
Swiftly flowing
Giant trees toppled
By nature's wrath
On the ground
Pine needles are

Roberta Maris

I Love You?

Is this what it is like
to be in love? I think about you
all of the time. I can't get you
out of my mind. I can't decide
how I feel about you. I try to
think about other things, but
everything makes me think about
you. When I see you I feel so
strange. When you are away
I feel like I'm going to cry.
Somebody tell me if it is true.
Could I love you?

Elizabeth Duncan

A Silent Prayer

How loud is the sound
Of a silent prayer?
Like a sonic boom
On the midnight air?
Like the sound of thunder
From a distant cloud?
Like the roll of thunder
From a drummer proud?
Like the days of dreams
Long ago gone by?
Or memories that bring a sigh?

Mabel I. Paulin

The Dreamer

As darkness fell upon the world
in the last rays of the setting
sun I sit in my favorite chair
by the west window and think
of all I've done.
I sit and think of days long gone
and time that has not yet
befallen.
Of people I will never meet, and
places I will never see.
In the midst of all this thought,
I wonder if the day will dawn
when all the battles I have ever
fought and still have to fight
will ever come to an end.
And yet; there are still songs to
be sung, books to be read, poems
to be written, hearts to be won.

Michael W. Rudge

When The Poet Is Gone

Poets are a special breed,
Painters with pen.
The lines bleed;
Rhyming words, once and again.

From the depths of despair,
Agony and pain;
For too much we care;
We are almost insane.

To and fro,
The picture takes form,
Like the driving snow,
A longing to warm.

As the words fall, on silent ears;
Breaking down a wall;
With sweat and tears.

Do the words bring a special feeling?
As you read along.
Do you find yourself reeling?
For the poets words live on;
Even after the poet is gone...

Bill Fleming

The Lord of Hosts

"Come glorify me," says the Lord.
"And you'll receive a reward.
Come glorify me,
And you will see,
I am the Lord of Hosts!
Come glorify me,
Praise to all most high,
Come and you will see,
As the Heavens sigh,
For I am the Lord of Hosts!"
Come glorify the Lord,
Receive your reward,
Come glorify and see,
Come and be made free!

Katrina S. Lucas

Untitled

A hold my heart your hands do thee
    As breeze of wind hold land and sea
A feather's light my spirit fly
    untethered wings on purple sky
The sigh of dawn my thoughts behold
    On sunlight rays of red and gold
Two arms of strength my body warm
    As raging waves of torrid storm
Drenching touch of fire's flesh
    Blue-white tongues of flame enmesh
Evening star refresh anew
    Tomorrow dreams of eyes bright blue

Joy Jacobs

Untitled

Phillip's my fantasy,
what can I say?
Someday I'll meet him
and then run away.

Boy, what a jerk!
He has pimples all over,
drives a mule in to work
and looks just like Grover.

I turned tail
and ran like a rabbit,
came home and called Phillip again,
Oh! What a habit.

Bill caught me calling,
Now I'm single and alone.
He remarried Sharon
and I feel like a dog without a bone.

I still have my fantasy's
when will I learn?
I don't think it will be today
Maybe I'll call Vern.

Rebecca R. Sovine

Searching For Home

Into the sand of many places
different views from different oceans
dependent on my father's hand
leading me to the unknown

From the windy tides
as a child in Monterey,
to fronts of frost
moving in from the North Sea,
off the warm coast of Spain,
sailing through the bay of Chesapeake,
towards the white beaches
of Clearwater

Combining all grains of sand
for a lasting home
that will be judged for solidity
with the passing of the tide
like so many before
only to be washed away
leaving me to search

Ross Huffman

Once

I wish I knew a little bird to tell
    my troubles to.

And maybe as my thoughts progress,
    I'll send them on to you.

The whispers of a little breeze
    remind my heart of you,
    of all the things we've said
    and done, when love was so brand new.

New times and strange, things were
    all mysterious fun.
    when we were so much younger and
    our hearts both beat as one.

How did it all slip by, get lost?
    all our dreams were laid to rest.
    We surely paid a cost.

All those years of loving you, lost.
As time goes by, so light and free,
Our hearts cry out for what used to be.
    Betty Ann Dade

Loneliness Is ...

Loneliness
Abandonment
Isolation and pain
Gnawing at the thread of hope
So I keep myself distracted with a cacophony of words and
Actions with no sense of rhyme or rhythm hoping to forget
The ache inside thinking it'll go away if I ignore it but when I
Get exhausted from frantically running away I find
Gnawing at the thread of hope
Isolation and pain
Abandonment
Loneliness
    John A. Nichols

Untitled

There is just one thing I don't understand — why people are judged
    by the color of skin.
To be with someone of a different nationality — is that such a sin?
Why is it today that people are so prejudiced?
Some people just don't know what they are missing.
Color does not judge who can be a great friend.
I think sometimes a hand we should lend;
Then all can feel like they fit in,
But most of the time no one can win.
If I could wish for anything on this earth.
I'd wish for something of worth.
I'd wish people would just see through the skin color
And all love and accept one another!
    Teresa Nicholson

And One Got Away

He slithered up beside me-
As I sat beside the lake,
Both hands on the fishing rod
As it bobbed before the take.
—He settled in to rest a spell
Before he went his way—
And my fish fought with fierce vigor
—And of course he got away!!
The snake beside me
—Startled by the splash
Slipped into the water
And was out of sight like a flash.
Now was I scared???—Or just plain mad???
To think I had just lost my fish—
Because a little old water-snake decided to share my niche!
    Mildred C. Sprouse

As the Wind Blows

I never seen a tree as pretty as the weeping tree, with its
grace, were ever limb is placed. Sometimes I feel the same,
were limb must hang. Within the limb, is a dark new world akin,
were I feel slow, because you hurt me so. Every leaf is like
a pound, no wonder I feel to slow an down, it seems I'm lagging
in the past, when you are moving to fast. I sway in the wind,
as it gently moves in, for a moment I'm up with you, then it
gently blows through. I think of that faithful day when my heart
went a stray. The pretty petals opened at last, with the sun
shining past, through the holes the leaves missed, I feel alive
within the mist. As the petals fall, I recite these words from
within, "Why can't I love him an when". The season has past,
there is nothing left at last. Every leaf an petal is gone,
now I'm truly all alone. I am cold, an all on my own. Why did
I let it in, between the cracks, an holes of my limbs. When
will I meet that warm, an moist weather. I'll never forget those
rays, those wonderful happy days. Maybe he'll come back, to
prosper around each others necks, for in a day I meet a love,
an offered him to stay, much to my avail I was added to his
trail. Still there is nothing prettier than a weeping tree.
    Jowharah I. Masudi

My Lovely Wife

A raindrop of Love fell into my life
    Many years ago.
It made my life blossom with purpose and care
    And caused my soul to glow.
Only God can give the reason why
    That Love Drop fell on me,
For I am Blessed with the best there is
    Because My Lovely Wife chose me.

It's wondrous how she carries on
    Without a seeming care.
She guides and tempers this life of mine
    Without a troubled air.
Her soft touch to my troubled brow
    Unknowingly keeps me in line,
Because God gave her that certain sense
    To handle this life of mine.

Each day I look up to the sky, and Thank God that Love Drops form
To fall on other lives like mine, where a life in love is born.
For only through God's Gracious Hand, are lives like mine so Blessed.
I'm sure a Cloud of love drops formed, just for me, my life to caress.
    Harris O. Torgerson

Poetry In Motion

Poetry, your rhythm is a pleasure to my soul;
Your thoughts, a delightful menu to my mind...
Your scribes, a vision of friends who are both full and free...
Your words, both silver and gold joys to find.
    Bonnie Clapham

Time

Time comes and goes,
Time can make friends out of foes.

TIme can help pain go away,
And time can make pain stay.

Time can change you so you are new,
And with this change it can make your friends many or few.

And throughout time things have changed,
Except for time itself.
    Jamie Brumbaugh

Peaceful Ocean Feeling

As I walk along the ocean in the evening,
I get a very peaceful feeling.
The warm wind blows through my hair;
I can smell the salt in the air.
The evening sun shines so beautifully,
I couldn't think of a better place to be.
And the foaming water hits my feet,
When I'm at the ocean, life is complete.

Cassandra L. Margaritis

A Poem for Mom

Mom is someone everyone should have.
Mom is very special to me.
Mom is a woman like no other, and no other is like her.
Mom has a smile as big as the sky, and warms you up like the
   sun on your face.
Mom is someone everyone should have.
Mom is very special to me.
Mom has a heart as big as the moon, it shines day and night
   for everyone to see.
Mom is someone everyone should have.
Mom is very special to me.
Mom is my Mother as you can see.
Mom is my friend that's guided me by the hand.
Mom is someone everyone should have.
Mom you are special to me.

Laurence A. Hendrick

A Lover's Prayer

Lord, give me the power that I may see,
This great love You've given to me,
And let my lips and life express,
This great love I humbly profess.

Give me the wisdom and the peace of mind,
To speak to her no words that are unkind,
Renew my love from day to day,
Blend it with hers, never take it away.

Grant me courage that I'll always be,
Truthful and faithful, I cry unto Thee,
Make me large hearted with zeal for my task,
May love be my motive, I humbly ask.

I think Thee, Lord, for this lovely lass,
Our love is permanent, it will never pass,
Thank Thee, Lord, for being true to me,
You've given a love, greatest that ever shall be.

Jess A. Walls

Dr. Martin Luther King, Jr.

In this very, very unfair world,
where hatred and sorrow 'round us twirled,
there lived a man full of kindness and love,
who drew his strength from God above.

He taught the world of peace and pride,
and "I have a dream" is what he cried.

He wanted all people to get along,
to the human race we all belong.

The Nobel prize he won for peace.
He hoped that someday hatred would cease.

The color of skin and where each is from,
should not influence one's outcome.

Martin Luther King, Jr. was his name,
and the world is better because he came.

Devin Michele Krahling

Beware of the Dog

Sometimes it just happens that a dark cloud of a bad news
jumps on your shoulder like a barking mad
Dog that was not fed on time.

Sometimes it just happens that a forgotten danger
eats you alive like some
Dragon Of A Broken Heart
that was locked up in its prison
for year and years
without any light.

Sometimes it just happens that a hungry mad Dog
fights with a Dragon for a bit of a stale
food of gossip
and wins killing your soul.

So, be aware of that Dog.

Sveta Novoseletskaya

Can't Sleep

I close my eyes at the end of the day
I can't sleep, can't sleep. I lie there awaiting sleeps return

I count sheep, count sheep.

I pace the floor from left to right
I toss and turn through the night

A warm glass of milk and I'll be fine,
I can't sleep....count sheep.
I think, I read, I write.

Everything anything but no good night.
Tick tock, tick tock, goes the clock
Yet time is standing still.

I exercise until I drop,
my body is weary my eyes are not
Can't sleep.....yawn.....count sheep.....zzzzz.

Daisy Crichton

Perish the Thought

Death comes to the soul, unobserved.
It creeps into the heart of the world.
Die inside to bear the pain.
Joy is lost, apathy gained.
Dim you eyes to all iniquities.
Dull your ears to the sounds of agony.
Harden your heart to all of life's cruelties.
Teach your lesson, learned, to another.
Perpetuate the universal betrayal of your brother.
Oh you weary souls, resigned to your fate
mask your fears and endure the hate.
Exhausted by pretense, living corpses
seek to embrace the eternal sleep.
Arise to a new day and shed the armor.
Open your eyes to see beyond the surface.
Use your ears to hear what isn't said.
Soften your heart to let the blood flow.
Listen to it beat, what does it say?
Faith...Hope...Love...Courage...Truth...

Beth Litchman

Willows In Spring

Earth doffs Winter's ermine robe, and dons Spring's
emerald gown.

Wild geese seek their far north abode; doves in the
grove their wistful love notes sound.

Weeping willows with lissome grace stand pensive by
the stream,

Their drooping limbs strung with a lace of tender
leaves light-tinted yellow green

Streaming out upon each vagabonding breeze.

A becoming veil of mourning for these melancholy
trees.

Earl E. Henderson

Children Of Today

When I was young, I used to think
That I knew everything
It was only when I grew up
That I found you can't know enough.

The world today is a dangerous one
For your daughter or your son
Makes no difference what you say
They're gonna live it their own way.

Drugs and gangs are all around
In every city and small towns
Wish the kids could go back when
Problems were few and friends were friends.

What will the future hold
For the ones that we love so?
Guess all we can do
Is hope and pray
For the children of today.

Patricia York Sykes

Heavenly Music

The birds were singing and as I looked upon their form
My soul rejoiced at the melody as it was being performed

In eloquence far greater than man could ever achieve
They sang the song of praise as it flowed on through the trees

No hindrance to their singing, no bondage to their sound
Just freedom as they gathered upon God's holy ground

It was only for a fleeting moment, captured by God's grace
The sound of heavenly music in a dry and desolate place

I watched them rise before me up in the clouds on high
Closer to the one I love, my redeemer draweth nigh

It was a special moment, with joy I shall proclaim
And once again I praise and know that our God reigns

He reigns in majesty; He sits upon the throne
He has the power of life and death to him alone is known

He gives us special moments to help us through the day
And with my heart I thank him as I begin to pray

Not for abundance in riches, not for things that are seen
But the invisible moments in glory to know I've been redeemed

Donna Freese

Naturally

Daylight appears as the sparrow of nature,
Darkness, the dreaded hawk.

The soul's inner sounds, that we strain to hear,
Are the voices that do not talk.

It gives all hearts no comfort to know
Nature seems to create, then destroy.
This dour prescription cannot be reversed.

Tangible things we value
Are finite in the universe.

All struggle is natural and intended to be,
For what can we change that will last ?

What do we have that we cannot lose?
Our identity alone is steadfast.

When it's all over, and the Reaper appears,
And to this world we've breathed our last gasp.

What a joyful surprise if we find in this guise,
That nature has saved her sweetest vintage for last.

Edward P. Dillon

On A Corner

Stopped for traffic this morning, I saw, on a corner there,
A bent old man with empty eyes and thin white hair.
He seemed just waiting for the light to change
So he could limp across this street, once easy range,
But challenging now his daily round
To the post office and rest of town.

As I watched, I suddenly spied
The boy behind those empty eyes,
Who long ago would cross a street
On sturdy legs with winged feet
The strong young man the girls admired,
The now-dead wife, the children sired.

A career of useful work, now done,
Loves and battles lost and won.
Month-long wait for Social Security
That lets him make believe he's free.

And I knew the people he had been
Are still there always inside him.
The light changed before he reached safety.
I waited patiently, for him and me.

Andrew C. Victor

ANGER

I have a feeling burning inside me
Thrashing and tossing to get out.
Yes, I hold it in,
But soon it will come out.
The feeling is stronger than all emotions combined.
It rages and palpitates to the end of my soul.
It is screaming, stomping, and hurting.
It beats at me like a savage animal,
Swallowing and killing my thoughts.
It controls my very mind, body, and feelings
It takes over fast, so I have to fight it.
This feeling seems to be indomitable,
Winning each battle.
It tempts me to let it out.
So let my wrath out on an innocent creatures.
My thoughts are fervid, seeking a way out.
I wish I could overcome my feeling,
Because this feeling is horrible and terrifying.
The only way to overcome it is to be happy,
Don't let the endless pit of anger drag you in too.

Amy Scott

Children

Children are a thing of beauty
One always has to be on duty
Whether it be a girl or boy
They always fill your heart with joy

Some days they run and run and run
Because they're having so much fun
Some days they just have quiet play
So they're never, ever in your way

They can be as quiet as a mouse
You don't think they're living in your house
With books and trucks and dolls to amuse
There's always something they can choose

Children need many kisses and hugs
And each night you tuck them in bed —
   like snug little bugs
Children are God's gift to you
Love, protect and cherish them too!
   Regina McPhail

"A Poet's Lifeblood, Yet Forthcoming"

When I've nothing to lament,
nor anything to praise,
my poet's soul is restless; I await the pending daze.

I praise Beauty, I seek Truth,
pain empowers, fear is great,
yet now I have naught to embrace, and even less to hate.

I am squinting, my pulse rising,
Watching Future become Past,
I adore the sweet sensation, and endure it to the last.

The scribe is oft receptor
of societal affection -
indeed inspired by the truth, yet mere instrument of perfection.
   Lynde S. Listowski

Untitled

You, for just a moment.
Wondering, groping, running..
Filling the empty space saved just for you;
Leaving me warm for days.

Searching, yet unable to articulate the reasons.
Knowing for us there is a season;
Somewhere, treading on the dusty yellow
Leaves that still recall spring.

Then, the sky gradually fills with stars,
That could be seen for a moment
After leaving one porch lamp and
Heading for another.

I almost enjoy the return of silence,
The evenings mildness, the emptiness of
Life's longing for you.
And somewhere you drift within me,
On the edge of my memory.

You, for just a moment.
   Cynthia A. McDaniel

Life Out Of Death

From Thee I whirled and went my way
All time was burled — no night, no day
No proper start, no comfort when
My lonely heart sought for a friend
At end of day.

Around my neck, my albatross
My life would wreck — and all be loss
Then through your Might, I saw the Cross
Stripped bare by Light, my life was dross
I could but pray.

You saw me there despite the murk
You pointed to Your Finished Work.
My sins all washed in precious Blood
Relief rushed through me like a flood
And blessed that day.

Now growing peace is mine alway
It deepens as I learn Your Way
Each day begins — and ends — with Thee
I marvel, Lord, that You love me
Each day...each day...
   Jne Evans

Pattern Of The Leaves

The fall-colored objects fall from the trees,
better known to you as leaves.

They fall gracefully on the ground,
making not a single sound.

They flee from the trees only in fall,
from the small tiny trees to the big and tall.

They have a pattern as you may see,
they turn red, yellow, and orange from their
original color green.

The trees will be bare when the leaves go
but in the spring more leaves will grow.

We'll slowly watch the pattern go by,
and soon the next set of leaves will die.
   Elaine Pfaff

Untitled

I still remember that night, the night I realized I
would forever be alone. I stood on a bare hill,
bathed in moonlight, observing the dark, forested world
beneath my feet, watching your car travel
the bright ribbon of road slicing the darkness
neatly in half. I raced to the trees edging the road
and, cloaked in night, silently watched you speed by.
My breath caught in my throat at the wonder
of your beauty. I threw my howling face to the moon
and placed all my desire and longing into that
lone, long, mournful sound. The cold stars
stared uncaringly as my pain echoed off the blanket
of the night. I stared wildly around and saw
your questioning face illuminated by the glowing
tip of your cigarette, your full lips twisted
in a grimace of fear. My fur bristled and my
heart shattered as I finally saw I would be forever alone.
   Amanda V. Evers

Jesus Christ Is The Son Of God

Jesus Christ is the son of God
  He is the Alpha of Time
Jesus christ is the Beginning and Ending
  He is the Omega of history

Jesus Christ is the son of God
  He is the hope of the world
Jesus Christ is the Savior of the world
  He is the light of the world

Jesus Christ is the son of God
  He is the true vine
Jesus Christ is the lamb of God
  He is the redeemer

Jesus Christ is the son of God
  He is the written word
Jesus Christ is the living word
  He is the word of God

Jesus Christ is the son of God
  He is the New Testament
Jesus Christ is the Prophet of Prophets
  He is the King of Kings ...
Jesus Christ is the Lord of Lords ...

   Ronald E. Brownlee

Don't Forget!

You can get so busy in this fast paste world you forget the great joys
of life. You forget to take the time to enjoy the little things.
Like a warm hug a soft though on a gentle kiss. You forget what a
friendly smile is or just what the sound of laughter is. We get so
tied up in this fast paste world we forget to take the time. Just to
hear the laughter of a good friend or to give a friendly smile, to
have a warm hug. We forget to give a soft tough, or a gentle kiss.
You make me remember again all of the things that we get to busy to
do. You make me feel so great inside. Just to think of you makes the
day go by. All I have to do is just closes my eyes for a moment and
I can remember your friendly smile.
I can hear your laughter I can feel your gentle kiss the soft tough
of your hands. And it makes me smile inside. Then I remember your
sexy eyes. And for a moment I forget about what I'm doing or were I
was going. Just for a moment I forget. But then the moment passes
and it all comes back and once again I jump right back into this fast
paste world we live in. I forget the moment for now. But I now know
every now, and then something will make we stop and think of all
you've giving to me. And yes just for a moment I will stop and think
of all the things we sometimes forget!

   Lori Courtney

Kelly Ann

I look at her face
I so love
By God's good grace
I do so love
At the sweet age of two
Whatever we go through
I'll be there for her
No matter what may occur
I love her more than she'll know
And as I watch her grow
I'll teach her to be kind and fair
When she needs me I'll be there
We'll talk about respect for others
Including mom, dad, sister, brother
If something's wrong I'll make it better
We'll laugh and sing and dance together
I'll hug and kiss her when she takes a fall
Because that's what grandmas do after all.

   Karen Mallon

Throne

Stuck inside all this messed upness,
Not knowing up from down,
Pressed my head below to rest,
Losing my sanity without a frown;
Looking in circles and feeling fine,
Having a bad day even if I can't try,
Running underneath, so I won't be blind,
Hiding my eyes, so I don't cry;
Another hour, and innocence is lost
Trying to keep it straight and in line,
Bared like an ax and cross,
Falling away with a deep wine.
When all is bare and alone,
It's like being swept away in a throne.

   Jimmy Hall

Dream

I remember feeling his sharp claws and teeth
burrow into my skin
While he was trying to save his own life
he was taking mine.

Just a dream I had in prose.

   Michelle Smith

The December Greeting

The finest of gifts is Christmas in a greeting.
  The signature elevates
  the warmth of the heart,
  sharpening memories.
  The sender is a welcome guest.

Each wish begs for remembrance
  through succeeding calendar pages
  and alterations of the seasons.
  Greetings are comedy and drama
  to life's unremarkable.

The holiday card clasps together friendships,
  new connections, and calms
  the impatience of aloneness.
  It is the timeless hallmark
  of Yule's enchantment.

Each reflection enters my worship,
  the hush of my Eucharist.
  It brings resonance to music
  of the Natal Eve's deep night.
  Your thought endures in my prayers. Noel!

   M. Constance Nagel

Too, Also, Even

Too, also, even.
Kind of, sort of, maybe so.
At the end, at the start, near the middle.
I think, I know, maybe not a clue.
Up, or down, which direction?
Beside, in front, maybe behind.
North, South, East, or West.
"I" before "E" except after "C."
Knee bone is connected to the ankle bone.
Horizontal, vertical, upside down.
On, off, halfway between.
One mile, two miles, no land in sight.
Unfinished, started, perhaps incomplete.
Does this make any sense?
Too, also, even.

   Sarah Schneider

The Spider and the Clock

Grandfather gave a clock to me so beautiful and tall,
With Roman Numerals plain to see, it stood against the wall,
I never had to guess the time, it always was correct,
At every hour it gave a chime, it stood firm and erect.

One day I didn't hear a sound, from my Grandfather's clock.
It wasn't long until I found, those pretty hands were locked!
A spider wove a ribbon band, all neatly tied in place,
'Twas wrapped around those golden hands, tied to its pretty face.

I wondered how this came about, for I took so much care
How was he crawling in and out with tiny threads like hair?
I'm sure Grandpa would give a dime, to share with me the shock
To find this Spider wasted time, the day he stopped his clock!

Rose E. Martz

Cycles

From the inception of time,
Life moves forward in motion.
Creation explodes with devastating emotion

As we are born
A metamorphosis involves all
living materials.
Evolving from finger-painting, breakfast
cereals, to the myriad of kaleidoscopic images.

Holding to the victorious scrimmages,
Proceed with the final layers of alabaster beauty.
A knowing witness of relentless duty.
All shall breathe until the full circle
of the life cycle has been fulfilled.

Elizabeth Menchaca

When It Is Time To Say Good-Bye

Reflecting back to the many yesterdays,
Remembering the good times and the bad
We come to realize that those days would be
    treasured moments when It Is Time To Say Good-Bye
It is hard to say good-bye,
Just the word alone can bring tears to your eyes.
A Good-Bye is a stepping stone
To another world that is commonly known.
It is a time to move on to new horizons with
    new dreams, new hope and cares.

We thank God for the special people He has sent
our way, who gave all that they could give and
    lived their lives unselfishly each day.

Although we will now be many miles apart,
You'll be far away from us but never away
    from our hearts.

Debbie Ewers

This Great Day

As you awake from your sleep stand up and say,
I going to make this a wonderful day,
To watch a rose bloom, or strawberry grow ripe
These are the things to enjoy in life,
To trim around the house or plant a tree
These are the things that appeal to me.
Take time, sit back, smell the fresh air.
Take time to relax without worry or care,
This will make your life complete,
Without it your future is surely bleak,
Take time, sit back, and then say,
I've made this a wonderful day

Tonie S. Wilkinson

Decisions, Decisions

The moment that she heard his voice,
She knew she faced a dreadful choice.
Most toms were whiny tenors at best;
This one sang basso, straight from the chest.
And when he appeared, her whole being pounded,
For truly he looked as good as he sounded.
Those big fluffy paws, the lift to his tail,
The tilt of his whiskers—it was all just so male.
But few of life's pleasures come without pain.
One night of rapture, and all that remained,
Would be kittens, whose notion of play,
Was to chew on her ears and get lost every day.
Yet, the longer he stood there, so shiny and trim,
She knew it was passion, not fleeting whim.
Therefore, accepting the obvious option,
She yielded to love, and the results, to adoption.

Paula Sutter Fichtner

The Greatest of All Is Love

Of all the necessities one must have in life
Love should outweigh them all
No one can successfully live without it
Life's journey would be immensely dull

Some have hope and others have faith
But Love is beyond compare
It is what the Heavenly Father requires
If life's cross you intend to bare

Folks say Love is something that grows
As a seed planted within the heart
Daily, it must be nurtured and watered
Saying, "I Love You" is an excellent start

There are many problems in the world today
That a measure of Love could solve
If everyone would reach out to each other
Around the world Love would effectively revolve

Do not be afraid of getting hurt
When you extend unconditional Love
For the Love you give to others will be given to you
From the Lord who reigns above

Lynease M. Beacher

The Hurt That I Cause

I yelled at my Dad
I could see the hurt that I caused
I yelled at my Mom
She started to cry
I yelled at my sister
She left the house
She left crying
I yelled at my brother
As tough as he is he cried too
I yelled at my aunt
She has never called back
I yelled at myself
I could feel the hurt inside
I yelled at myself
For hurting my loved ones
I wrote a note saying I'm sorry
I will be gone by the time you read this.
I can't face you I'm so sorry.

Jackie Walker

The Dance

I savor the taste of richness and hope as a baby whines for
his mother's breast. While my dreams devour with every waking day,
realizing life's bitterness; I swagger myself to and fro across the
dance floor of pain and agony, of longevity and presence of hearts
broken and unclaimed tears.
My worn shoes stomp on the ground angrily, yet hastily as if
it were my last dance, a dance filled with broken promises
and unfulfilled desires.
The world cries around me begging me to show them the way,
begging me to perform miracles, begging me to shorten their anguish.
Cry I say, cry to the heavens, cry to the earth, cry to your
miserable future, your lonely and pathetic future, you, with
high hopes and little patience, cry until your eyes begin to
bleed with shame;
The hunger is so deep it reaches down into the unknown pits of my
soul wherein lies immortality and needful death
yet the unmentionables of taboos are placed upon my death bed
death it might be, death it could be, but life it shall be.

Raquel Monique Hernandez

The Promise

You vowed to love me forever
And I believed you.
So secure was I in your promise
That I ceased living for myself.
You were my existence.
Everything I had to give was yours.
You flirted with my emotions;
You snatched them up like a bunch of daisies,
Stripping away the petals one by one
And casting them into the wind
Until there was nothing left but a stem;
A lonely, ugly thing
Which you threw beside the pile of my life.
There was nothing left for you to take from me.
You found another garden
Rich with beautiful flowers to pick,
And in the picking, to die.
You left me to wither there,
My life's juices seeping into the ground.

Claudia L. Augustine

Wouldn't It Be Easier

Wouldn't it be easier if there was no such thing
as school?
If everybody was thought to be cool.

If every pound of weight you gain,
would fall faster than a drop of rain.

If people didn't have to part,
and everything was a piece of art.

If animals wouldn't become extinct,
if they could live on and be able to think!

If we didn't have to follow the facts,
if nobody cared about how you act.

If there was no such thing as the end,
and the beginning was just around the bend.

Wouldn't it be easier?

Amanda Heaton

Mystifying Journeys

Those early feelings are so pristine,
one is certain they'll last forever;
it is a time for discovery,
for lofty dreams and loving gazes.

The advent of the vicissitudes
gives way to the inevitable,
when passion turns from love to anger
and hate sets in like a frozen flame.

When there's nothing left to lose but pride,
it becomes easy to breed contempt.
One dons an armor of apathy,
which serves as refuge from every woe.

Since love burns deep inside this cold front,
it must break free to find a warm place.
One's world is shattered with one goodbye.
Then grief must follow - to heal the heart.

Sherry Perez

Survival

Life is like a hurricane,
First the thunder, then the rain.
It hits you hardest when you're least prepared,
It leaves you lonely, it leaves you scared.
It hits you hard, it strikes you first,
You're convinced that today is your worst.
This is no time for you to quit,
This isn't the first time that a storm has hit.
The strength of the storm is a frightening thing,
Devastation and fear is all it will bring.
When times are the worst and you wish you could run,
Remember the days when you saw the sun.
When destruction is all that's left behind,
Rebuilding your life becomes an uphill climb.
The winds of life move with tremendous speed,
It's time to move on and plant a new seed.
You know that God is watching over you,
Before you can speak, your sky has turned blue.

Vivian F. Scholes

I Never Said Good-Bye

As you lay in this hospital bed with your family on the same floor,
we talk about your life
I walk around trying to hide what I am feeling
And figure out how I can help everyone else
I go into your room which is so silent
The monitors are off and you are motionless
My heart and soul rush into my throat trying to escape my body
You see, I have rarely said I love you
And the worst part of it is I never said good-bye or see you in the
next life, no one did
I know it is too late to say all of this now grandma,
But I do love you and I will always remember how strong you were
And I will see you in the next life and hopefully be a better grandson

Keith Peeler

Windy Day

Gone is the wind that makes green days nice.
It filled the air with sugar and spices,
and had in store for people surprises.
This wind is gone, oh I'm very sad to say,
no cheering, no merriment, no hip hip hurrah.
What's this, oh look, away out in the east,
that great big commotion, why it must be a beast.
Why look, oh my, it's got a man pinned,
but wait, oh my gosh, it looks like the wind!
In the village, the boys all do roam,
yelling, "Hey, look you, the wind has come home!"

Cory Selby

Optimistic/Pessimistic

The grass is always greener on the other side of the fence,
Typical snide of an optimistic pest
If there was a fence, I'd jump it,
But there's not; it's never greener on any side
That's the opinion of a pessimistic, almost certified

Don't give up, there's always hope
An optimistic's way to cope
I give up on the idea, it won't progress;
Hope is but a dream, a certain stress
That's the thought of a pessimistic, yes

Time can heal an open wound they say,
The martyrs that never struggle or fray,
Or the optimistic view of a man who has had a pleasant day
Look out though, when their day goes down
Cause they will swim in pessimism, nearly drown

I see things as they are, don't shield the truth
When things get hard, I don't fake a smile
I'll let the world know my happiness is but a mile
Call me a pessimistic if you like reader;
But I prefer to be called a realistic message breeder

> *Cara Di Olesandra*

Love Endures

I have felt the love of family and honored father, mother,
A love for aunts and uncles and especially my brother.
I've accepted the love they offered, glowed in their limited praise,
Endured their words of judgement and basked in their loving gaze.

I have felt the love of friends and felt their love for me,
The ease of just relaxing and only having to be.
They have seen me at my weakest and loved me just the same,
Just as I have been their comfort in sorrow and pain.
We have shared our joys and laughter, triumphs and success.
We have known that in our friendships we have been truly blessed.

I have felt the love of pets dependent on my care.
Their unconditional love is almost more than one can bear.

I have felt the love of country, a patriotic swell of my chest,
Emotions so overwhelming that tears fall upon my breast.

I have felt the love of God in whose love makes me feel I'm whole,
A connection so enduring that his praises, I must extol.

I have felt the love of one man, whose soul is linked with mine,
A long so strong and lasting as to bind us through all time.
But his arms have ne'er embraced me nor his smile been exchanged
    with mine,
Though some lifetime we'll be together when our lives will then
    entwine.

> *Lenore Crumrine*

Mahogany Sunflower Forest

I know a man who is so great who is so bold and bright,
He walks through sunflower forests and
The sunflowers all turn their backs to the sun to catch a shimmer
Of his bright ways.

His journey is long
But full of adventure and knowledge.
His emotion touches my body and spirit.
I carry him with me in my heart and soul.

I pray his road is long and our days together are many,
Filled with pleasure and joy.
I will always keep him fixed in my mind
And hope he arrives to his ultimate goal.

I will shelter him from rain and cold.
The courage he has will go with him as will I always.
Without him I will treasure no more
And I could spare nothing as I would have nothing.

> *Mandy L. Morris*

A Mother's Day Poem

You've been there for me through the years.
You gave me hugs through times of tears.
You showed me love and support in times of strife.
You made the right choices that shaped my life
I love you dearly and thank you so much.

My heart and mind are the places you have touched.
I Love You.

> *Mary Coyle*

Letting Go

I know it's hard for her to let me go away,
for she still wants to hold me like in my baby day.

She misses the little things like kissing me goodnight,
tucking me in bed, and saying don't let the bed bugs bite.

She longs for me to still need her hand,
so I won't be afraid to take a stand.

The hurt knees she used to kiss,
maybe that's what she'll miss.

For letting go is so hard to do,
even though I tell her, "Mom, I still love you."

Because the bond between mother and child is so strong,
and for her arms I'll always long.

And even though she has to let me go,
our love will last forever, somehow, I know.

> *Jenna White*

Love

Like a stranger in the night
slowly groveling upon you.
No ground, no explanation.
An emotion so out of control,
penetrates a heart waiting to burst.

Reality is slipping away
as life suddenly appears but a dream.
A soul, hovering distantly above the clouds
surrounded in a point with hope and meaning.
Infiltrated by feelings so actual and undefined.

Time becomes so precious,
patiently thriving each day.
Like an immature flower,
blossoming into an existence so delicate and beautiful.
Becoming the reason, the essential purpose of life.

> *Susan Woodard*

The Play

Little by little, the flower unfurls from the tight bud.
Non-committal clouds turn from white to gray to black;
soon the rain turns the dusty ground to mud.
A voice softly whispers across and then back.

Crops push towards the sky and promise good measure.
Trees bustle with full coats of green
and make homes for those with fur and feather.
Thoughts embrace and then flit away unseen.

Proclaiming to all the awakening of a new seedtime,
the smell of fresh-mown grass fills the air.
Bees and birds and rabbits uncaring dance sublime.
A moist breath gently blows across unkempt hair.

Cool mornings give way to heated afternoons,
while rivers and streams foam from bank to sandbar.
Old Sol spreads his blanket across Winter's ruins.
Touch warms to touch and together kindle the evening star.

> *John A. Ross*

Nostalgia

It's a bird on the wing, the first flower in Spring
The earth-fragrance of fresh plowed ground
Butterflies and bees, the sound of peepers
The rebirth of earth all around.

The tinking of cowbells on a clear summer night
From the pasture the killdeers call
The hoot of the owl across the gully
And neighborhood kids playing ball.

It's an oriole singing each morn near the window
Mom listening enraptured nearby
It's gardening, canning and picking berries
Being wary of clouds in the sky.

It's long summer days in the hayfield
When sun's burning heat tries the soul
It's knowing reward at day's end would be
Fun-time in the old swimming hole.

Nostalgia is growing-up years with four siblings
With hardworking parents and yet
Knowing they'd always have time for us all
These are years I'll never forget.

Wanda G. Chamberlain

Censorship

How come you try to take control of me?
I never wanted you to intervene
always stepping in to speak your voice,
whatever happened to my freedom of choice?
For me to speak what I want to say,
when I turn my back you want to take it away.
It seems I don't have a say in this life,
when the way I express myself is my worst crime.

Where politics exist - are ones who demand to get
their wish, they are spoiled rotten, a real life
they must have forgotten. I guess they want something
plastic or artificial, exempting themselves from everything
real. Pasting labels on music bought at the store, and
they swore that they never heard those words before. Afraid
of the truth that spews from our mouths, to put hands on
our ears and block it all out. My definition of the P.M.R.C.
is a political gag order in my land of the free.

Damian Greer

Love Conquers All

Love is such a wonderful thing, there's so much life
and happiness it brings. It also has its ups and downs,
It has its share of smiles and frowns.
With love is the only way to live ones life,
It'll get you through all the pain and strife.
Sharing love is the greatest of all,
It can be done by those big and done by those small.
It can be given in so many ways,
It makes the sun shine through on the cloudiest days.
It can turn a frown to a smile; it makes the sad be glad,
it makes all things worthwhile;
It will always turn the bad into good,
The I can't into I can, the I won't into I should.
It can be shared through words or saying nothing at all,
Sent through the mail or by telephone call.
It doesn't take much to give it away,
It comes from the heart to be shared everyday.
Nothing is nicer than "I love you" and "I care",
If ever you need me, I'll always be there.
So, on those days when you're sad and forget how to love,
Just remember that it came from the Lord up above.

Karen Kaye Spittler

In Memoriam "A Tribute to Terance"

Did you ever call for me in the middle of the night?
Because I was there...
Did you ever question what was right or wrong?
Because I answered...
Did you think there was someone out there thinking of you?
Because it was me...
Did you ever realize throughout high school
we had gained and loved,
cried and lost?
Because I did...
Do you remember those crying times, those laughing times?
Because I was crying and laughing with you...
And even though you may not know who I am,
Living or dead,
I was and always will be there for you.
Because on this graduation day, we are a whole class;
We are not individuals, separate and alone.
And although we may never cross paths again,
Remember always that he was one of us,
and forever shall be....

Christina Gerard Feehan

Dreams

Dreams are like clouds flying in the sky where they go
I do not know
where they belong and where the end
to see all the souls to mend
lay to rest in a bed
while visions form inside their heads now they're sleeping
I wonder what they're dreaming
some are good and some are bad
one is dreaming about his dad
oh how awful it would be
if dreams wasn't aloud you see
all the people have a far away land a distant star
some where far
to where they can get away laugh and ply
it would be nice to dream all day to get away
I would just like to say
people you don't have to pay
just close your eyes
and dream away

Kristy Marcoe

As Sly As A Slithering Snake

The ancient river is
like a sly snake slithering
in a dry desert. It swerves around
trees and dodges around boulders
that stand in its gnarled path.
It creeps upon its prey of branches and logs, then
snatches it. The prey is engulfed
by the fleet water. The river races
with the deer and rabbits scurrying
along its banks. The river is at its
peak in speed then lessens its
movement as it comes over bumpy rapids.
It's as if it shatters over the sharp pebbles
that rest along the bottom. Then it regains
its speed and smoothest out like silk blowing in
the wind. The water is as clear as crystal
polished and divine. It glistens in the sunlight
that blazes down on its back.
Slowly it transforms itself into a wide massive lake. It is
now green flatness waiting to be disturbed—no longer as sly as snake.

Stephanie Cheng

The Endless Game

I awake in the dawn of each day, wondering,
who's game is this that I attempt to play?
What beast of nature?, what heartless creature?
Is it made by a mad man from some horror feature?
This cruel, sick game in which your emotions are
thrown around, as if rolled on the dice.
In this arena of torture, love pays the highest price.
This is not a game of luck, nor is it by skill.
There are no rules to study, it is played free of your will.
The odds are against you ten to one,
but even if you win, you haven't won.
As helpless as a baby bird left in its nest.
You can't survive alone, but alone you must travel your guest.
Distance over time, indeed, you must act fast.
Aim straight, the future is your target, but remember the past.
History is the key, learn from the wise.
Gather up the truth and filter out the lies.
The beast is gone, most definitely, far away.
You can't quit now he will catch you if you stay.
So go now and tomorrow we shall play.

Michael Wheeler

Futile

Even though the door does not stand a-jar,
I know they have been here and gone.
A haunting, sweet fragrance fills the room,
I am engulfed in loneliness and despair,
I know they have been here and gone.
Madly, I had driven across town-
Minute, by minute by red light detained,
So little time, they had to catch a plane.
They can not know how I tried to stretch the time-
To be here, to say good-bye.
It was no use, this race against time,
Words not said before now, can not be said,
For they have been here and are gone.
Futile, futile was my try,
I did not get here to say good-bye.

Jessie Mofield

The Moment Has Come

The moment has come for you to leave
Don't ever come back, just let me be.
You cost me a lot even my soul
The moment has come just leave me alone.

You were my only friend, you knew me well
How could you do it you put me through hell.
I get rid of everything just to be with you
The moment has come, we are through

I can't believe you've done this to me
I was so stupid, why couldn't I see?
The moment has come, I'm through with you
If there's a God in heaven you will be too!

Angelia Nichole Kelley

Untitled

Peace of mind sitting on the comfort of silence,
only to keep reminding yourself of things
you have to control over, including yourself.

I awake pain - I go to sleep pain.
What hurts more physical or mental breathing
difficult getting up a chore.
Walking around with a
fictitious smile to make others feel better
to give them.

Janil Graves

The Tree That Remembers

There's a story about a certain tree that's wrapped in a lover's mystery.
The story concerns two lovers whose love wasn't free, causing the
birth of this inspired tree.

This tree so tall and graceful, but yet so utterly sad,
Has inspired love ever lasting from a poet's pad.

It usually stands alone by a quiet brook or peaceful river bank,
Its sobbing hid by the flow of water as of its lover it thinks.

It got its birth name from the love denied,
When a lover sat at the water's edge, remembering and cried

It's called the tree that remembers a lost lover's pain,
For a man or a woman that pain is the same.

Love crosses all barriers, that part has been proven true,
But this tree remembers the barriers that made it so blue.

It stands weeping, with a lover's tale,
Its swollen red eyes hidden under a beautiful green veil.

This tree so graceful, a beautiful sight to behold,
Its weeping branches full of lost loves untold.

This tree's legend is really nothing new,
All will feel its pain sometime and feel, just like it, so blue.

So, when at night you hurt and cry into your pillow,
With a lover's memory, remember the weeping willow.

Jerry Harrington

Nursing Home

One by one they wander - up and down the hall;
   Hoping there'll be someone to catch them if they fall.
Each day they rise, put on their clothes, then sit there patiently;
   Praying that before too long - a familiar face they'll see.
They watch the door with such great hope each time someone
comes in;
   But as they slowly walk on by - their spirits fall again.
Before they know it, day is done - time to get undressed,
   Another day spent all alone - about night depressed.
How long can these poor souls survive without someone to care
   Someone who'll hold wrinkled hands and stroke their soft
   white hair.
Nowhere are folks so sad and lost, so hopelessly alone;
   As those behind echoing walls - inside a nursing home.

Kay Fodor

On the Having of Summer Literacy

In the spring, teachers equal squirrels in habit
   forced to wrap up a year's full of meanings
   into tidy packages
   to be shelved, passed on, buried for next year's coach.
Suppressed by tasks, barely gaining a foothold,
   the literacy community scurries in tandem
   to report and close the academic seal,
   tightly.
Urgently hastening toward a pace of quiet and summer freedom
   sheds a reason for relentless coaching of story:
   to touch and heal,
   tickle and cheer,
   nudge and nurture,
   affirm and behold.
All the while encouraging
   learning to know the importance of grasping humanity —
   on vacation in words.

Linda Wold

A Sign of Spring

Please let it be spring, I need to see flowers.
Show me some colors, and melt this dirty snow.
I want to smell lilacs and hear the morning dove.

Is today's snow the beginning of winter's end,
or is it the end of spring's feeble beginning?
Give me warm days, no cold wind to blow
and show me that spring is finally winning.
New flowers and the returning birds,
they tell winter it's time to go.

Today I am happily smiling, it arrived as before,
again the coming of spring is by the book.
If you listen closely,
you can hear my happy, gurgling brook

Lennart Rost

Prepare

If you are on the right road to heaven
Nothing will stand in your way;
For the past has all been forgiven
And it's a clear and cloudless day.

Do the work God planned for you
And never look back or ask why;
He is the one who is good and true
Death is only a dream when you die,

Graciously serve the Lord and do his will
As our services are well defined;
His love in our life he will surely fill
And he will ask nothing of any kind.

Prepare for the wonderful day of His coming
Help other's who may step out of line;
Listen for the heavenly angels humming
As He will be close behind.

Bernadine F. Evans

Small Girls Dream

My thoughts are invaded by you
The things that you say, the things you do
When I'm with you; you have a way
   of making me feel good
Small girls dream that dream of a
   white knight and they should
You have no mansion that sits high on a hill
Just a caring way and arms of strength to fill
No teams of horses or rooms of gold
Just a caress of fire with a feather touch hold
No diamonds, rubies or gems of worth
Just eyes like the stars from heaven to earth
No maid, no butler and no servants bell
Just words from your heart that you long to tell
There is no grand ballroom or orchestra band
Just music from our hearts as you take my hand
No long dining room tables or extravagant meal
Just you and me and the way we feel
You give me the security and strength I need
This is our story that many little girls will read.

Beth M. Hicks

Bad Luck

I was walking out my door you see,
When I got stung by a killer bee.
"Ow," I screamed, as I jumped in the air.
That's when I saw the grizzly bear!

It scared me to see his jaws open wide,
With all those sharp teeth showing inside.
I tried to run, but my feet wouldn't budge.
When what do you know? A snake was sucking my blood.

So I just hopped around, til I tripped on a rock.
Then a bully came by, and my nose got a sock!
I tried screaming for help, but my luck was bad.
All the neighbors were sleeping. Now I was mad!

I struggled real hard, and finally got free,
When I realized an unpleasant smell followed me.
It was a skunk, who had followed me to school.
I had to get rid of the smell, so I jumped in a pool.

I was soaking wet, and I had to get dry.
So I laid in the sun, thinking why me, why?
I then stopped to groom myself, afraid of my looks.
That's why I'm late for school, and I don't have my books.

Laura Hodulich

Love

To love someone is happiness,
To be loved back is heaven.
   To love someone for a while is good,
To love someone all your life is great.
   To be able to express your love is fantastic,
To be able to see an expression of love is wonderful.
   To be able to see love bloom is better,
To be blooming in love is the best.
   To know love is amazing,
To understand love is marvelous.
   To believe in love is astounding,
To trust in love is miraculous.

Patricia Collins

The Graduate

Today's your day son
a happy one at that,
Twelve years completed and done.
I'm so proud
Bursting with happiness!
But wish all the dear deceased
ones could share it with you.
We're proud of you son
We will stand behind you
Whatever endeavors you wish
to pursue.
We'll love you forever
and cherish each day
Until our time comes to say goodbye.
We all hope for a fruitful life time of goodness, love,
and happiness for you.
May your every dream come true
May God Bless you richly and hold you in his heart
as we all do.

Patricia Jean Justice

Waterfalls

One drop falls, all do as well.
The waterfall begins with a long drop that fell.
But as hard as you try, you can't make one fall,
because only Mother Nature has the power to do it all.
Bunches of water goes on and on, yet only that
one drop leads them along.
A waterfall is a beauty full of colors and delight.
It is really pretty, and bright.
To hit the sun, the water's begun the waterfall
has just yet quite, begun to fall and now the
waterfall is light, it stops!
The sun dried it all up.
But it rains again, here comes that drop and the
waterfalls begins.
And now it stays a cycle of water that will never end.

Brandie Heavrin

"Daddy"

If ever in my life there was a hero
I would have to say Daddy it was you
You are the one I could always count on
To be there to see me through

I would like to say Thank You Daddy
For taking care of me for all those years
You spent half your life raising children
Along with all the worries, heartaches and tears

If in any way I have ever hurt you.
Caused you pain that I didn't realize
Rest assured I never meant to Daddy
Please let me apologize

You instilled in me values and morals
Also courage and confidence to stand on my own
The amount of love I feel for you cannot be measured
In my heart you will continue to live long after you are gone

I would not change a thing about you
If you changed I would not be who I am
"Happy Father's Day Daddy"
From a daughter who loves you, Pam

Pam Britt

Move Away

Shrug the wind off your breath,
stay away from the lingering truth,
cling to the spring and count the greens,
drown my footsteps with the fall of a golden leaf.

Shiver with the cloudy coffee of a misty morning,
when the languor in your head
carried to the slippers of your feet,
touches the jewels of your skin,
makes the steps fade into the night.
Raise the cup and remember to pay
homage to the lonely shadow that recedes.

Wish the dust off your mind,
move on to the calm and a tranquil sun
shining on the evening's worn floors.
The warmth of the riches rinses the burns,
set the table, be alive.
Let the light of the candles and the flicker in brick and stone
enter your soul, forget what was.

Nishith Bhushan

My Dream

Shattered pieces of glass,
fragments of the world unknown
A painted picture sitting on a wall
A beam of light shining through a tiny hole
The rain starts pouring in
as the faded mind wears out
The secret inner self
flooding with the distant, but near past
As the shadows from strange creatures
overflow the room
The tiny pieces of a puzzle, scattered
The grip of a madman, the embrace of an angel
Shredding of tiny pieces of paper
Immortal life, everlasting; searching for a soul
The silver pendant
swinging in the moonlight
A hypnotizing vision,
of a soul floating up,
to see, the secrets of the
mysterious and unknown world.

Sommer Budavari

My Feet And Yours

You will think that it was I who has chosen your feet.
But my feet think that it had been you who
with tenderness, in a quiet night
caressed them and loved them.

They felt how much you desired me
and they trembled, they felt the beat
and the heat of your passion,
they understood how irresistible it could be.

My feet and yours caressing. Mine sliding shyly
through yours, they feel that together
the excitement of an innocent dream has trapped them.

I looked at the sky.
The sky stretched, and stretched...
in a burning love.

Your feet taught mine to love you
without frontiers... but with a love that
predicted pain...

My feet learn you were dismissing a muse,
they were your distraction,
while yours were my devotion.

Maria Cristina Fra Amador

Obstacles

Understanding the daily occurrences of our lives
and the purpose of unexpected trials is often difficult.
Upon knowing the importance of remaining lucid,
success depends.
Observing the peculiarities of nature,
Our mother earth teaches us:
Transform mountains into mole hills.

Like flowing water surrounds the stones upon its course,
obstacles simply become a part of its nature.
Harmony, visible in the dancing currents,
as water and stone conform into one;
Unto the ocean, will be the ballad of stone and water...

Joseph Thaddeus Salinas

Look Inside My Heart

A place in my heart where no one goes,
There are things that no one knows.
Though the heart is seen as muscle and veins,
On the inside it knows aches and pains.

Being alone always makes me blue,
As I sit here thinking of you.
Although our relationship isn't all light and joy,
Being with you makes me feel young as a small boy.

Sometimes I look at the moon,
Thinking I will be with you soon.
I work and so I will strive,
To give you the finer things in life.

We may not be what most consider Apollo and Venus,
But when we are together nothing can come between us.
Thinking of the one that I miss,
I yearn for that long awaited kiss.

Maybe one day I will figure out the meaning of life,
And find that love does not always cut like a knife.
With this I must say goodbye,
For without you life is but a lie.

John D. Poersch

The Caravan

Wandering for eternity in a paradise of wastelands,
On a never-ending serpent with brown jagged teeth.
A gentle glow reflects from its vast tattered surface,
The worn path below us leads to the emptiness beyond.

Fire scorches the backs of the weary,
While the horizon offers no sign of relief.
The tormenting wind is our only escort,
It caresses our bodies with unpretentious sighs.

Surrounded by giants towering above us,
Their children playing idly by our feet.
Our destination remains a tempting mirage.
As long shadows are cast along its golden skin.

Deborah Freda Speter

Ice Pond

I skated slowly on the newly frozen ice
not yet marred by weathering.
Then I skated fast, not so much for the
feeling of control it gives you
to go faster than you can run,
or, if you wish, slow as walking,
but to hear the whistling of the blades
according to the speed of the cut.

It was obvious a musical life
is better than a shouting one:
I skimmed off a spray of snowy powder;
wind can't make a steely sound like this —
Some sounds are reserved for us to do.

Robert A. Lincoln

The Sea

While the birds are flying in a flock,
While the people are loading on the dock,
The sea always has something to say,
It echoes off the seashore bay,
When the people leave the land,
The sea pushes them with a helping hand.
When the sea turns to frost,
It soon feels lonely, tired, and lost.
Finally summer comes again,
And the sea is happy with its friends.

Jenifer Housel

Smile

A new sunrise.
Fresh dew upon the grass.
A new day.
A new awakening flower.
A new smile.

The sun has set.
The grass is the home of night creatures.
The day is tomorrow's yesterday.
The flower is asleep.
The smile - a pleasant memory.

Leila A. Willis

Sonnet to Spring

Beyond the ides of Caesar's last season,
April withdraws distant daggers of ice,
Helios heals cold consorts of treason,
And warm hearts traded are so given twice.

A rose, as Romeo's blush may revere,
Leaves Juliet's justice one with her Lord,
And gifts from the garden of Guinevere
Lay with Lancelot, who lays down his sword.

As errands Eros or Cupid may claim,
Lend love-lies-bleeding vernal invention,
Faith finds the amaranth safe and the same,
As each so ascends with His ascension.

May rhymes of rebirth, as whispers on wing,
Fly you to heaven with hope in the spring.

David Wolfe

God's Wonderful Land

The sun rises in the east, with its shining rays across the bay
And it glows in the west at the end of a sunny day
The oceans shores with their pearly white sand
And the beautiful white snow that covers our land

The forest with its variety of trees
And their different shaped leaves blowing in the breeze
There are trees that are small and some are very big
With beautiful blossoms on each branch and twig

The mountains with their pine trees so very high
And the waters of the rivers that flow nearby
The carpet of grass that grows upon the ground
And all the different plants that grow all around

The beautiful flowers that grow from little seeds
To decorate the land like different colored beads
The little butterfly with colorful wings
The birds that fly and often sings

The beauty of friendship seeds we sow
Develop in love as we watch them grow
There's beauty in this land for all to see
In this wonderful world, God gave you and me

Leona C. McCormick

Old Age Versus Youth

After all is said and done
Age, equipped with experience, cunning, and guile
Will always overcome
Youth, despite its zest, gusto and disarming smile.
And, although we may be
In various stages of senility,
We Old Folks all wear a knowing smile,
Fully aware and gloating inwardly
At the thought that the Young and the Beautiful
Will become just like us in a little while.

Frank D. Kareiva

Memories Of Mother

God surely blessed the entire world
When he created mothers.
But, he especially blessed our family,
When he gave us our mother.

When mother sent us off to school,
We knew without a doubt.
She'd be waiting for us with open arms
To hear what our day was about.

No matter what time of day or night
Mother was always near.
To listen to our problems,
Always sharing our laughter and tears.

Mother said God would always be by our side,
But she was always there, too.
She was our role model, support, and confidante
And our best friend our whole life through.

We have beautiful memories of Mother.
She was a rare and precious gem.
Mother was truly an angel here on earth,
But now she's an angel in heaven.

Linda G. Moore

Snowflakes and Friends

They say "No two are alike."

You can't capture a snowflake
Or keep it with you at all times

Some stick around for a long time
Others for just a fleeting moment

Sometimes we reach out to touch one, but it is already gone
We can't get it back
But we can remember it for a long time
How beautiful....How unique....

Often we think of how we miss them

There will be more
They may not be the same
But, the next ones will be just as beautiful...just as wonderful.

Janet Faye Adams

Friends Will Last

Many things can never be,
Just the sense of you and me.
Some things come and some things go,
But many times you'll never know;
The way a lot of things can be,
When it's for eternity.

A lot of friends are there for fun,
But when the going gets tough, there's not a one.
So pick your friends very carefully,
And your life will shine most graciously.

Find the one's that'll stand by your side,
And give you feelings that won't be denied.
Friends you can look at with lots of pride,
One's that are caring, one's that are kind.

There are times when you're feeling down,
And your mind turns a murky brown.
It's hard to see, what all is true,
Unless there's someone helping you.
"Friends will last" forever and ever,
As long as they are sticking together.

Melissa Celeste Tomb

Umbilical Song

Her brown breath shrouded the garden
suspending me right where I stood.
Cloaked in one sparkling instant,
while times pendulum ticked out a hood.
When four winds forged a crossroads
to mix homocentric scents of eternity,
awe commandered this sheltered being
behind the wheel of divine symmetry.
Respiration cleared the muck from aged bridges,
allowing fresh waters to engulf my mind.
Earth mother had bequeathed sweet secrets,
through her gentle likeness, so kind.
I blinked wide-eyed at our garden,
emanating as though stained glass,
when one stroke of her bellows did end it,
and mortality resumed with a flash.
Her offerings are so profoundly precious,
Sacred unifications since birth unto death.
Flowing connections to our uniworld surround us
through our earth mother's succulent breath.

Rebecca Pollick Wolford

The Word Between Is Loves

Our names still share that old Oak Tree.
The word between is loves.
And when you gave your hand to me,
They called us Turtle Doves.

I asked you once. You answered, "Yes".
Our families smiled with pride.
The church was full. I must confess,
My love was hard to hide.

Our child then came - that eight pound boy.
Your eyes were all aglow.
We took him home and named him "Roy."
And then we watched him grow.

Our home was full - a home for three.
What more could one man ask?
He grew up tall. A man was he
Who went to do his task.

That war is gone. But so is he
Who saw that no one shoves
Upon those names which share our tree.
The word between is loves.

Richard Overdorf

My Tree And Me

Grow strong and tall, my little tree,
    Along with me;
Spread leafy branches toward the sky,
    And I'll climb high
To see the field across the creek — how neat!
    I'll watch my Dad there sowing wheat;
I'll 'tach my swing to that limb there,
    And float like magic through the air;
Then watch a mother weave her nest
    And shelter babies 'neath her breast.
I'll build a tree house near your heart,
    My hide-away from world apart;
And when my busy day is through
    I'll thank the Lord who gave me you.
Grow strong and tall, my little tree,
    Along with me.

Dorothy Duncan

I Am Humbled

Here I sit at the end of my day,
Reflecting on what I've accomplished today.
Exhausted, upset, and ready for bed,
So many things running through my head.

I get on my knees and pray,
Thank you God for this beautiful day.

Did I thank you God for the day of my birth?
You know it's hard to survive here on earth.
Without your guidance, I couldn't do what I do.
And did I tell you I know I wouldn't survive without you?

I get on my knees and pray,
Thank you God for this beautiful day.

Counting my blessings to you I see,
All the wonderful blessings you've bestowed upon me.
Good night then God, and thank you from me,
For the beautiful day it's turned our to be.

Vivian F. Scholes

Daddy's Sermon

He's a hero for all time, this Daddy of mine
A quiet and decent man of which there are few
A soldier in the fight to stand up for what is right
Though in the eyes of many he's been robbed of this due

He went unnamed but God surrounded us just the same
In the sermons Daddy preached through the life that he led
Instilling deep within an aversion to sin
We learned not just by the words but by his example instead

Daddy's gift was a love, reflected from above
For the just, the fair, the right and the good
He gave us his best and we've each been blessed
With the knowing of how to do what we should

Though often missing the mark, we've held fast to that spark
Like a beacon in the darkness came the light from his heart
Struggling ourselves to shine while carrying on the line
We've tried to pass on his message, to do our part

Now his children's children will become men and women,
Sometimes because of us and sometimes in spite,
Strong hearted and true, filled with love for us and him too
Bearers of the gift of knowing how to do what is right.

Shelley Adams

Thousands of Pictures In My Head

Endless hours pass me by as I sit and think of you,
    How wonderful you make me feel.
Enjoying the trips of ecstasy that seem so real.
    As thousands of pictures dance in my head.

During these hours many images and irreplaceable
passionate poses enter my mind,
    I hurry to escape to this special place because
reality won't let me feel you.
    So for now, I'll never leave these thousands
of pictures in my head alone,
    These thoughts are all I have to call my own.

Continuous nurturing to feel these thoughts helps
our love to grow.
Romancing each other will never get old.
But for now I'll never dread
These thousands of pictures in my head
of us together.
Of us in bed.

Amber Powell

Night

Night is a dark black eye,
and the stars are tears when night should cry.
The moon is night's pupil, so yellow with light.
Always shining quite bright.
Night covers the whole sky,
too lazy to wake up when the sun is high.
When it wakes up, it shall see,
people like you and me,
fast asleep in their deepest dreams.
But when the sun's first beams,
touch the sky,
night will say to everyone, "Good bye!"

Pooja Amatya

Delusions of Grandeur

I am not a poet, nor do I pretend to be.
I am just the emperor of my world,
the only place where I can escape.
I chronicle as I feel, but no one understands.
I take comfort in imaginary events,
people I invent, or real people I control.
Because of my lack of confidence,
I pretend to be something I am not,
something I made myself into long ago,
because of a forgotten purpose.
I have shaped my world into a paradise,
an aquarium which I look out of, and see the real world,
distorted by the weathered glass.
The glass is chipped and scratched
by those with the courage enough, (or those insidiousness enough,)
to aim their slings and arrows at my world.
I do not know if these others
have protective aquariums of their own,
but alas, I can never find out,
for I am always repairing the glass.

Martin Babitz

Brown

Brown is the large eyes of a pleading puppy
A soft purring kitten snuggled upon a lap
The dirt-covered feet of summer adventures
Things forgotten

Brown is a gnarled tree trunk reaching for the sky
The gazing eyes of a caring grandmother
A cool fudge sundae on a hot afternoon
A field of wheat dancing with the breeze

Brown is a patch of dead, shriveled flowers
An old book, aged with time
An ancient cross of remembrance
A fuzzy teddy bear with open arms

Maggie Geck

The Master's Plan

One day the Master planted two small seeds
In the heart of an artist.
The name of the one was Inspiration;
He called the other Ambition.
So long as they were seed they never disagreed,
But as they progressed their pathways digressed.
When the two fought, the artist was distraught,
Unable to paint a picture.
When Inspiration faded, ambition became jaded.
The Master viewing the scene, decided to intervene,
"Unless you work as twain your efforts are in vain."
So, Inspiration and Ambition compromised,
Thereafter their full potential was utilized.

Oma Worthington

Satan's Factory

Dance with him in the pale night light
fight against the heavens in your damnation plight
crawl down into the depths of the dead
where the skulls of the departed have said,
"You don't want to end up like me
just another soul in Satan's factory"

"Our blood has turned black, our skin has turned brown
buried deep beneath the ground
Hell's fury comes surging forth
from West to East, from South to North"

"You will join us being damned
forgotten by your God
No one will save you when you've fallen
No longer will help come a callin'
because this is where darkness has covered over the day."

And when the skulls fall silent again
hopefully up to heaven you'll ascend
because if you don't all you'll be
Is another soul is Satan's factory

Bjorn Hall

Loving Life

The flickering light of the candle;
The glittering shine of the sea,
   A sparkling emblazon of the setting sun;
It's all a magical dream to me.

   The happy cry of a massive whale;
A dolphin's gleeful squeal,
   The rise and fall of a majestic tide;
It all seems so unreal.

   A walk on the beach, with my feet in the sand;
The grand sound of when the blue birds sing,
   A sweet California dream in New York;
These magic things give life a ring.

   A baby kitten leaping through a meadow;
A garden full in blossom,
   Having the biggest balloon of the bunch;
And I ask myself, isn't life awesome?

   The amazing gleam of the fallen snow;
Peace, along with the sign of the dove,
   The very first rain of spring;
And I'll tell you now, it's life I love.

Nicole McDaniels

Only If

When someone is gone - that's when we realize
How much they really meant to us.

We take the here and now for granted and never think about,
What if?

If tomorrow comes what will I do?
If tragedy strikes and my love is no longer here,
What will I do?

In the end it will be — if
I said or did this.

I rarely told him, "I Love You."
Never let him knew how important he was in my life.

The simple things such as his smile, his touch, his sense of
caring,
His walk, his tone of voice, his being - was my life.
And I didn't know it until now.
Only if?

Mary Stern

Before the Ocean I Stand

I stand here on sand with endless waves of ocean before me;
Looking at freedom, looking at eternity, looking at the past.
Peering into the future, I see serenity;
I envision hope and peace,
As a full moon joins in this symphony of nature.

I want these feelings to last, be real forevermore.
So, what can I do? This I will do:
I pour it all out —
My feelings, my thoughts, my fears, my tears my inhibitions and goals
All falling beneath me to the sand at my feet.
I bend over to gather together this smorgasbord of pain.
I shape and shape, I - form and form;
Until a castle of anguish stands tall in the sand.

I then wait and watch, I hope and pray —
That soon will come the tide, washing away those fears.
Washing away troubled thoughts, getting rid of past and present,
Leaving my clean and new future for me to gather, shape, and form.

Welcome waves of rejuvenation, reveal a new me!
As I take out this time to stand before thee.

Maurice E. Wright

America How Much Longer

America, how much longer will you allow your children to go
uncorrected, to do whatever they want to do?
To rob, steal, rape and murder, next time, maybe me or you.

Are you happy with the way our children are turning out?
As we continue to lose bout after bout.

Are you tired of the gangs of thugs who roam our streets at will?
Thugs who, to rob you and me and inflict upon us harm, find it a thrill.

How much longer will you wait America,
before you pick up your pen and write to your congress person,
to try to stop this terrible, terrible situation?
Or form within your communities,
committees to fight these thugs in our nation.

I suppose once you or your family have been hurt by these thugs,
then you will try to do something about them,
I guess in the meantime you can watch the violence on your TV
and comment "Oh, what a shame".
America parents, if you wonder what has gone wrong,
at yourself, point the finger of blame.

Michael D. Jones

Listen

Listen to my words, listen to me speak,
Look at me as you look at you, think of me as weak,
No patience have I for ones intolerant ways,
No desire have I to stand with you, don't count the days,
I want everything I don't know, I hate all that I see,
For once, you, just once, can take me seriously,
I'm not emotionally set, I don't smile yesterday, tomorrow,
These tears are not of joy, yet-something I see of sorrow,
I'm so like you, death came, no longer am I alive,
Yet to see tomorrow, forever will I strive,
Tired I am, my soul hurts to feel,
Sick of working for my wants, yet conscience won't let me steal,
My river of sadness floods of tears falling for what was once before,
Wipe up my tears and cry, I won't anymore,
Won't you please make my smile real,
Now its laughter, that burning I'll no longer feel,
It's hard to be me, I'm just like you,
Just know for once that I need someone, too,
So listen to my words, listen to me speak,
Look at me as you look at you, think of me as weak.

Rhiannon Petteys

Drowning

I love you Ophelia, why did you die?
When I drown I shall go naked and raw
For I shall stop hiding behind the chaos of anger
Of this anxiety, and the haunted admiration
Of Satan himself.
They do not love me. God deserted me in
The frozen desert without a map, compass,
But thank you Lord, plenty of wolves and
Alligators.
Alligators in the desert?
Oh, the drugs are making me hallucinate.
Ouch, the water is cold.
My feet freeze - good-bye mother
My legs freeze - good-bye father
My breasts freeze - good-bye brother
My neck freezes - good-bye friends
My soul freezes - Hello angels

Fahema Rahman

Working Machine

As I stand here working, I feel like a machine
Not a person only a thing
But unlike the machine with a mechanical part
My main spring is a beating heart.

A machine has wheels with a revolving sound
I have thoughts that go round and round.

No one likes to work around a machine that's dirty,
unkept, it's work won't do
And if I were like that, folks would feel the same
about me too.

A smooth sounding machine is like from me a kind word
And to all around, this likes to be heard.

Like the machine that will spit, sputter and spurt
An unkind word may cause someone to be hurt.

But unlike the machine whose work in eight hours is done
After eight hours, my work has just begun.

Erlene K. Meisberger

Heaven

When some people think of heaven and what is over there.
They think then of a mansion Christ went to prepare.
When I think of heaven I am sure what it will be.
To see the face of Jesus will make it heaven there for me

I know that in heaven there will be streets of gold.
There will be God's throne room and wonders yet untold
The most wondrous thing in heaven I am sure will be.
When I walk through the gates of pearl and there My Jesus see.

What a joy to go to heaven there to see my Saviors face.
To know I am in heaven because of His love and grace.
I will kneel before my Savior my Lord my king and friend.
Christ will be my heaven my joy that will never end.

Erwin Johnson

If I Had My Choice Of Color

If I had my choice of color:
I would choose a shade of gray.
The gray that marks the end of day.
The gray that breaks the dawn of morn.
The shade of life to each man born.
The shade of gray that's tinged with gloom
That brings the light into each room.
That shade of gray is what I'd be —
The color of our humanity.

Roseann Petrowski

God's Beauty

God is someone great.
He didn't come in a crate.
When you lay in bed at night,
you remember a book He did write.

People who believe in the Bible
are called disciples.
When God made the world, He make it like a pearl.
Its beauty was seen, there was no mean.
God made a promise to me that
He will come back and let me live for eternity.

God made that promise to her
and him who didn't sin.

That is God's beauty.

Tyson Hensley

Flight of the Geese

I met you once as you travelled by;
Grace and prominence against the sky.

I thought of the places and sights
   you had seen;
Shook my rugs and dreamed.

You soared in formation, yet you were free;
Confronting each day whatever to be.

Whatsoever there is in life to know;
   As you travel, we too must go.

An incidental such as I,
Yet you honked as you passed me by.

Darlene Cree Johnson

Goodby Hamlet

Sunday morning used to remind me of Hamlet
as I worked in my unweeded garden
possessed by things rank and gross in nature.
A geologist, you have nothing to do
with weeds or flowers
You like rocks and volcanoes
But now that I think only of you
I imagine you with me in my garden
After all, it is a rock garden.
I imagine you in the garage
helping me change the oil
in the lawn tractor
I picture you in the yard
helping me pick rocks out of the grass
I see you in the kitchen
supervising your favorite biscuits and gravy
At my computer, I see you nod approval
as I write you yet another love poem
I imagine you in the bedroom—
transporting me to ecstasy.

Barbara R. DuBois

Sports

Sports are always a lot of fun.
In most of them you have to run.
You usually get dirty and sweaty.
Then you came back again good and ready.
It involves skill and a mental mind.
You can always recognize for they are
of a certain kind.
With boundaries and time limits,
comes a lot of stress.
To be good it takes much precision and finesse.

Zack Tucker

Revelation of Id

Come into my dreams enchanting one
Hear my soul breathe a rhyme
A landscape of realms may linger beyond
The element of mythical time
Enter my conscious thou mystical being
Enlighten my aura to glow
Release my spirit and let it be free
The thunder and lightning will show
Please exit my nightmare
Through time's weary eyes
Escape from my mind and be free
In existence beware
of life's cold reprise
And the occurrence of history's theme
My mentality of reason is frayed
And denied, and seasons aren't
Present in these dreams
In silence of memory I hear angels cry
And the shrill sounds of Lucifer's creed.

C. Mahone

A Soul Winners Song

The Lord is calling! Can you hear?
Or do you run away in fear
Wondering as you go
What it is He would have you know.

Jesus heard the Father's call
To save mankind from Adam's fall.
His cross and resurrection now have set us free
So forever, our song is that of liberty.

Live with the kingdom of God in mind
Investing your whole life: At His table dine.
The message of His cross is love
Billowing down from up above.

Hear now the sound of His call.
Answer Him by giving your all.
Nothing should you withhold.
Why, knowledge of God is more precious than gold.

The call is coming louder still
As you move closer to His will.
Such obedience who can know?
Glory of God overflow.

Bernadette Asher

The Pieties of Bigotrous Iniquities

Loud racket, some alien twing
mangling my image into an empty sea.
Mirror images of each one, a victim, fathomless
dearth as I stare into the eye of my persecutor.

Lounge in my rocking chair of suenos
reflection, grasping each scene
just seen, each ash, a fire, and each tear, a fissure
as I absorb the infinite ripples of agony.

I breathe the fragrance of the melting pot
boiling and seething to the brink of bedlam, and
watch, each bubble, a cry, and each spark, a conflict
as I curse the disposition of my inactivity.

Flicking twinkling remarks onto a radiant soul
overflowing, showering joy into the pot of souls
and stir, each cycle, a bond, and each minute, less anomaly
as I reap the resolutions of iniquity.

Grant Lee

Memories Last Forever

Late one afternoon as I walked
through the trail, down by the river
Where I passed a wooden well; I had
a drink of that water so cold, memories
last forever more precious than gold.
I couldn't hold back the tears I shed,
as scenes from my childhood went - through
my head, I walked a mile and sang a
song, memories last forever from
dusk to dawn.
I rested under the shade of a hickory
nut tree, where my dad taught me
all my ABCs; my mother prayed my
soul to keep, memories last forever
now I'll go to sleep, Little Bryan

Faye Welch

Mother's Prayer

Oh infinite perfection awake in my arms
just a heartbeat ago, still unknown.
Did time ever exist before you
or is it that I can't remember it so?

What wonder you are, tiny treasure
with eyes that embrace and capture my soul.
I am helpless to your charms, little one,
your every breath makes this ancient bond grow.

This miracle of love humbles me,
that He felt I was worthy of your gift.
May God guide us together to all that is good
and protect this precious blessing of His.

Cynthia Barton

My Dad

My dad means everything to me
He understands when nobody else can see.
I know my dad will stick with me to the end.
I guess that's why I call him
my best friend.

My dad is the most important thing to me;
My love for him goes beyond what others can see.
He gives me guidance,
and he teaches me how to live,
He tells me to be kind and always give.

The love that I have for my dad
is deep down in my heart,
In fact, our love is so strong,
it will never depart!

Steven Mitchell Jr.

Wind

Wind, oh wind,
Please come and take me away.
Let me ride upon your strong back
While you sweep all my troubles away.
Take me and set me upon a white fluffy cloud.
Just let me gather my thoughts for awhile.
When you are ready just let me know,
So we can leave this cloud behind us,
For we still have many more places to go.
We could go see the tower in Paris,
Or the Colosseum in Rome.
Wind oh wind,
Please don't go.
But if you do,
Promise me you will be back
The next cool summer day.

Justin Nevling

Listen to Me

Listen to me, I have the right to
speak, I was brought into this world not shy
nor meek. I have the power to make some
of my own decisions, and at all times,
I have my own opinions. To be or not
to be, is that the question? For me to
be all I can be and to make a good
impression. Even though sometimes I make
wrong turns and big mistakes, I am
only human. If I had a chance to
make a change in my life, I would
go back in time and make my wrongs
all rights. So listen to me for I am
well educated, I am somebody and that's
not to be debated. Listening is the result
of understanding, on my two feet, I've tried
landing. So listen to me for I am
speaking my mind, I've come too far to
be left behind.

Ericka Ward

My Home Town

What do I see as I walk around,
Among the trees of my home town.
It's been a while since I've been here,
But I feel the presence of someone near.
Could it be someone I know,
Are they hiding up high or somewhere down low.
I look for old friends, but they are all gone,
Just like me they have all moved on.
Old timers have passed on, new people take their place,
They are all strangers I don't know one face.
My old school has been torn down and built back a new,
The old house I grew up in is now painted blue.
I feel pretty sad as I sit down by the lake,
But there's still a peacefulness that the water-ripples make.
I still feel that presence as I lean on a tree,
Maybe it's God just trying to comfort me.

Tula R. Gillespie

Invisibility

Standing in a great forest, no one is near, the tall trees keep my company.
The only sound I hear is the wind thru their great branches,
and my own thoughts occupy my mind for a time.
Invisible to the world, they neither see, nor hear me as I walk
down the paths life has to offer me searching for meaning, a sense of
peace, a way to finally rest, content with my journey.
On the last step of my path, when I look back what will I see?
Family? Friends? Good or bad? Time is the enemy, an entity that I
fear, for the passing of time means the passing of opportunities, some
taken and some passively watched as sand thru an hourglass.
Uncertainty, growing old and attempting to fight for things lost.

Dan Shinsky

Hole in the Ozone

There's a hole in the ozone,
Take me to the red phone,
This is an emergency.
Dial 9-1-1, got to tell someone,
The electrifying rays are burning me.
Call the fireman, the president, the army, navy, and marines.
'Cause there's a hole in the ozone,
Take me to the red phone,
This is a catastrophe!

Elizabeth Grace Ferris

Untitled

She's an energetic young girl — my little "cooper-top"
Like the duracell battery — she "never" seems to stop
She's an individual character — just as you and I
I believe her only goal in life — is simply to defy
If you've made her mad — she'll say she's "not your friend"
If you let her have her way — she loves you once again
They say all redheads have bad tempers — this I do agree
Her family is Italian — with a few from germany
Now put the two together — and a "touch of the Irish" in between
And that's my dark-eyed beauty — determined, soft, yet mean
Although your halo hangs crooked — as it sits upon your horns
You are my perfect angel — a rose without the thorns.

Deena L. Germani

Untitled

Feeling the surge, the rush of the wave, the turbulent
winds that bring on the change. The chattering teeth or
the blood dripping brow.
Where is all your resistance now?
Your mind is the leaf of paper you grasp fluttering away,
you unload a gasp.
Still surprised at the monster you made? Or is the beauty
that longs to be saved?
You fought all your battles, bone crushing wars, only now
you see that your homeland is torn.
What does it take to wrench your heart, to make you cry
"Stop!" to renounce your part?
Your Mother wails for all her lost ones, the daughters who
were raped and the unburied sons.
Have you a heart, you murderous thief? Do tears sting you
eyes? Does your conscience still breathe?
Your soul is eroded by a ravenous greed, still you repent,
and are bowed on your knees.
The shame on your face is the beacon for all, the sinners
march forth, and on the dirt fall.

Kenya Chavez

Valentine to Parents

I sit here and I think exactly what it means.
Not just hearts and flowers, not children's dreams.
The love that got it started had to begin somewhere.
Maybe in a loving touch or a message sent from who knows where.

It really doesn't matter because I say to you.
It if hadn't ever started I still would love you.

There's really something special about a parent's love.
I can't begin to tell you how much I need you love.
No matter what you give me — materially I mean.
It wouldn't be worth much without a little love tucked in between.

So what else can I tell you but thanks for all you do.
Because I wouldn't be here if it hadn't been for you.

Linda M. Godwin

Autumn Sketch

The scent of wood smoke drifts across the browning land.
A reluctant petal falls from the last blown flower.
'Mid the brittle rustle of fallen leaves in airy pirouette,
The improvident grasshopper flits, heedless of his declining hour.
The clear, still lake awaits her crystal sheath.
The scampering squirrel culls his crop against the chill.
The plump pumpkin smiles in thought of fun to be
And the busy sounds of Summer are gone from the hill.
The twiggened tree rests quietly designing her crown for spring.
The mountain top retards her fluid yield to the thirsty stream.
Wingéd creatures flutter a last farewell to summer's shelter,
And Autumn's gold-flecked eyes are filled with Winter's dream.

June M. Wallace

Challenger Remembrance

Seven of our finest have fallen.
First came disbelief
Then hope they may yet have lived.
But hope comes from the heart
And time is needed for the heart to yield
And let reality prevail.

As hope lessens and the heart gives way
Grief comes, there is no other course.
But life that grieves is noble and strong.
Together we can assure
That although our hearts may yield
They will not break.

Our loss serves to make us resolute.
The life of which we are apart
Must reach the stars.
There is no turning away.
In the quest to achieve this end
Seven of our finest have fallen.

Victor T. Berta

Tantalus

"I am the king!" And so shall you
To know all things of such I do.
My dear friend, come...share my story
I'll tell of men whose worth is glory.

There he goes again, that chimerical bell-ringer, I think insane,
Like old men who often think they rate a table and a pipe
While wasting days of yesterday and shuffling all the night!

Again, dear sir I beg your liberty
My kingdom is at hand for all the world to see.
Behold! The crystal waters wish for you to drink, if need be.
And a piece of golden fruit? I offer all you see.

One would think of heaven's blunder
To have so much on earth, way under....

Did I tell you of the student who had broke the broker's
greedy throat? Conscience paved his way to pay for such a joke.

But there are those who never die...Da Vinci's Lady of Strange
Eye. And Aristotle spoke of "I Am I".

Alas, I am glad that I am me. Kind Sir our hands do clasp you see?
Hear the chimes exquisite? Thank you for your time...and visit.

"Hail To The King!"

Ernest W. Ross

The Watcher

The music in the background plays softly,
The wind slips through her hair.
She sits undisturbed, except for the occasional leaf
that blows down from the tree above her and falls on her lap.
She sees one now,
It floats downward, swaying and dancing on air,
It pauses on a breath, and then continues its flight to earth
It flips once, twice, three times, and lands on her lap.
It rests there for a moment and then flies away -laughing-
never to be seen again.
She watches it go, and wonders where-to.
Now, the sun sinks -tired- in the sky,
She watches it until every ray has slipped out of view behind the
mountains.
Darkness fills the atmosphere,
She watches it soak up the light like a sponge and then hide it,
She knows it will come again, so she waits.
The music still plays, but a different tune, a peaceful melody.
She hears it not.
She only sees the omnipotent darkness that stretches out before her.
She sits here, under the maple tree, always,
She just sits and watches.

Adrienne LaBombard

One And Only Wish

Soft as rose petals, sweet as a bowl of honey.
Deep blue eyes of sapphires, that sparkle forever.
Lips round as berries, hair spun like slivers of gold.
My bundle of joy snuggled against my breast, Lord
grant me my one and only wish.

Cheryl Stavich

Anniversary

There have been forty-one years of joy
Marking the marriage of a girl and boy.
The blessings of children and excitement of travel
Have woven a life tapestry we shall never unravel.
Just like peace brought by a dove,
Every day is full of love,
Unending with joy unrefined.
We rejoice we are really kind
And share a love of animals, golf, and books,
And adore our children who have good looks
And our grandchildren who are such fun.
They bring light to our lives like the sun.
Forty-one years have gone by so fast,
We know our love will last
For all eternity and never be past.

Jo-Ann B. Segall

Nobody Loves - Nobody Cares

As a baby in my mothers womb, I knew there would be no one
to love me.

But I thank You God for the eight years my old black face granny
loved and cared about me.

God! Why was there never a kiss, a hug or a pat on the heard?
Nobody loves - nobody cares.

Two husbands and two children ago; whom I loved and cared, but
still nothing for me.

"Lord!" Whats wrong with me? Why can't somebody love and care
about me?

Never a flower, a card, not even a phone call. That's okay it
doesn't matter. I'll just hold back my feelings.

Nobody loves - nobody cares.

As a little girl I learn to sing a song "Yes Jesus Loves Me"
and deep in my heart I know he loves and cares about me.

Callar M. Stubblefield

The American On The Island

The spirit of a people, notions of life
Spoke a language, abstract to my sight
A free world, my free will
I care, for real,

Subtle, warm, my highest degree
Frontiers, waters clutch to me
War or peace
My compassion, love, friendship will never
cease,

Mining, truths so sharp
Impossible tasks I start
Anthropology
I studied their nature, their spirituality,

For change, for dignity, I fight
In my hands the free world's light
The government of the island shall stand
The people fight me, an American.

Michael Wilson

Puzzles

Assume you're alone
just like you've always dreamed about.
Afraid of sadness, wiping away your tears.
Do you miss being afraid?
You shiver, holding you're knees
between your already chapped fingers.
Sympathetic to the needs of one linking together pieces of a puzzle.
A puzzle that won't be solved until the final piece is found.
Profound.
The sound is ringing in one ear and out the next
you're waiting your turn in line you turn to help the people
in need of salvation, in need of cremation.
Everyone needs livelihood for without it we should all be cremated.
Just so our ashes could lay dormant and ever so quiet because there's
nothing to say. But what is there to say?
You could say that there was a better way of handling you're feelings
As you let your life slip through your fingers.
Just like fine sand, straining through those chapped fingers.
Holding your knees together, holding your needs together.
If you drift than you will never, realize forever.

Erik Paul Peterson

The Euonymus Tree

With troubled thoughts, I look to thee,
To ponder a while and set them free,
Extinguish the fire that flames within
Amidst the human guilt and sin.
Oh, but from you my courage to take,
For storm nor cold your spirit break.
As there beyond my windowpane,
The lush, dark leaves, each fragile vein
Clinging to life so vibrantly,
Drop their seedlings prolifically.
Though bruised and weary, tempest-torn,
Rarely a moment are you forlorn.
I ask the Lord to help me find
Your inner strength, euonymus vine!
Still verdantly clear and sparkling through,
You're certain to greet each Spring anew!
Again, I pray that I might be
A little like the euonymus tree!

Jeannette C. Davis

Time

In a child's eyes,
time lingers on and on.
While memories aren't even a passing
thought of the mind

Slowly, at first, the years pass by
Then something changes along
the way

Suddenly, time seems to have passed you by
in a blink of an eye.
While memories linger on and on
Forever in the mind, until the end of time.

Maryann Garde De Rose

The Pearl

This guy has always loved this special girl
He gives her gifts such as the precious pearl
They laugh and talk as they walk on the beach
Until a wave pulls her beyond his reach.

He looks for her and dives into the deep
He looks and looks until he falls asleep
Then finally he wakes up on the sand
And sees the precious pearl upon his hand.

Marisa Fries

Love and Betrayal

They met-they became friends.
They spent time together - they fell in love.
Their relationship started truthful, caring and trusting.
Soon the friendship slipped away like a harsh ocean wave
leaving the wet sand.
Their love powered over and became young, passionate, and
forever lasting.
Their love for each other became strong like lightning striking the
earth without a mark left behind.
Time passed he talked in his sleep.
She soon became to know there was another.
Their love for each other vanished like rain from the sky when
the cloud was empty.
Their love was never forgotten like an untold secret.

Ashlea Boyovich

Still Confused

This is my testament,
As I set with pen.
To get on the right track,
Never, doing wrong again.

I pay for my crime,
In a dark prison cell.
Living man's made,
Human hell.

I truly am sorry,
Didn't want to steal.
I need to feed my family,
No job, no working deals.

It is true, my heart hang's heavy,
For those I have wronged
But it hanged heavier, on christmas morn,
When my child cried, for a simple toy.

So in closing, I can only conclude,
That with either one, mankind or child.
I was destined to lose,
So, I ask forgiveness, but still am confused.

Richard L. Hodge

Cheerfulness

Cheerfulness brings great wealth
As a preserver of mental health
Doctors of the mind endorse
Cheerfulness as a mighty force.

Anger eased with courteous wit
Hostility wanes discouraging fits
An ounce of cheerfulness shared
Wakes relationships easy to bear.

Parents give a ready smile
To every precious, trusting child
Seeking diplomas is worthwhile
And greeting others with a smile.

True humor is a marvelous weapon
Chasing ridicule and sarcasm
Depression decreases in humor's presence
Ridding society of a great menace.

Smiling a form of an apostolate
When the world seems so desolate
And seems surfeited with grief
Cheerfulness brings needful relief.

Shirley Brigham

No One Has The Right!

No one has the right, to attempt another's life.
Quoting the law book of the sixties, so it was said, and it was
written.
I did so believe it to be true, just and honest, something to follow
like, the golden rule.
My God in heaven, are people blind, or just don't care?
Babies discard everywhere!
Has the world gone insane....
It's all the babies to take the blame???
Instead of sterilizing to prevent. The population is, abortion bent,
bent, bent! To prevent life, and control sex is better by far,
than denying babies, are babies always were, and still are!
Those babies so sacred, so precious, so sweet, innocent,
and life upon conception as God, intended them to be.
They are not tumors to be rid of like cancer,
rather, they are life is the answer!!!
God bless them, one and all!
Taking their lives is the world's downfall!

Julia McNeely

This Man's "Love"

A nicer man, never could I have met
seemingly perfect in every way, yet,
there was something discerning, I just couldn't place.
Beneath his blonde curls, blue eyes, handsome face.
attention unyielding, he'd always come calling
with presents in hand, in "love" he was falling.
My children were showered with affection the same
unsuspecting was I, he became desperate, had no shame
the unforeseen danger, I was caught unaware
until held without mercy beneath his wild stare.
Our life we had known, had come to a halt
my rejecting his "love" had made this my fault.
Violence progressed, my self-esteem shattered.
A victim was I, stalked, raped and battered.
No one had imagined until the time came,
when he caught himself up, in his own deadly game.

C. S. Neff-Lewis

Undertow

Getting for misery, is that how it should be?
Got so dark I can not see, is anyone there for me?
Loneliness is doing well, I wish the world would go to hell.
Happiness is for the sane, not those caught in the rain.
The voices now rack my brain and bloody hands left a stain.
Covered in pain, buried alive not knowing how to survive.
Sinking deep in my sorrow, begging for a better tomorrow.
The suicide ponder shrieks aloud, but I'm just lost in the crowd.
Crying, screaming I gasp for air and yet the world doesn't care.
I close my eyes and say goodbye, my heart then stops and I die.

Natalie Wegner

An Empty Soul

Beyond life there is a valley where my soul aches to be;
The promise of peace and tranquility.
No more hurt and no more pain;
I know I will not be disappointed.

The years have not been very kind;
My memories are not so wonderful of years gone by.
As a child, I wanted to disappear;
No one would notice, no one would care.
Why was I born? Why was I left alone? Where do I fit in?
So many unanswered questions.
The emptiness which has filled my soul;
Leaves me shattered, torn, and scared.

For me, I can hardly wait;
Beyond life there is a valley where my soul aches to be.
The valley of death surely awaits me.

Sharon M. Jipson

Simple Kindness

Would you do me a favor, dear stranger or friend?
Would you do something nice before this day comes to an end?
Would you hold open a door for someone you don't know,
Or give to some poor children the price of a show?
Would you buy a sandwich for a poor man who needs food?
Would you try to cheer a friend who seems in a foul mood?
Would you smile at a stranger as you pass on the street
And not look away or down at your feet?
Would you stop at a nursing home and ask if there's one
Who could be cheered by a visit when your day is done?
Would you pick up a piece of rubbish left carelessly behind
Or offer to read a story to one who is blind?
If you see a chance to be nice, would you please not shirk,
Because if you don't...you'll be doing God's work.

Barbara Patton

Oklahoma Rain

I watch in horror as the drama unfolds.
Deep in the heart of the country, the shocking story is told.
I live so far away, how could something like this happen today?
I watch the TV screen, in the background, I hear a child scream.
I see her sweet, little innocent face all covered with streaks of
    blood, not just a trace.
These images I see releases my emotions like a storm whirling
across
    the Oklahoma prairie.
Tears fill my eyes, tears for you, I begin to cry.
I didn't know a single one, it wasn't my mother, daughter, father or
    son to whom this destruction was done.
Tears of sadness and grief, tears of anger, shock and disbelief.
Tears for you, I can't stop crying.
I watch the fireman with the dead child he is holding, the look on
    his face tells the entire story that is unfolding.
All I feel is shock and dismay, my heart is full of sadness and
pain.
I try to keep my anger at bay as tears of sadness fall away.
Tears for you do I cry, tears for you, the ones who died.
For those who survived, more tears do I cry, for you, the nightmare
    will never end, nightmares of loved ones who didn't make it
through.
All my tears, all my tears are for you.

Susan M. Smith

May Sarton

For all of us to death we must succumb
Death makes our bodies completely numb
We must think of the joys of living while we're here
Not of the inevitable with our eyes with a tear

May, as long as you can think and write
Since early life, your words were right
You must not say, "I'll write no more."
You have lived long, — you know the score

There have been many a word you have had
For some reason you thought they were sad
There must be some you did not publish
Thinking some might judge them outlandish

Even if you do not have any words kept
Words have come to you while you have slept
Then one word starts you to think
Who knows what you'll find in a kitchen sink?

That next poem will come to you, oh sensitive soul
Do not depress those words,—let them flow
It might be a simple as the word, "Bowl"
Let others enjoy that word into verses grow.

Bill Ruzenski

The Great Blizzard Of '96

Snow - soft, white, silent,
Clothing the gardens in billowing robes,
Transforming mundane objects into fantasy figures:
Trash bins hooded like an outer space Klan;
And summer's table an inverted kettle-drum,
Or Swan Lake ballerina poised on slender legs.

Neighbors checking on neighbors:
Three handsome young brothers shovelling - thrice - the snow
From driveway and path, with cheerful chat and easy strength.

Like Shakespeare's, birds sit brooding in the snow,
Feathers fluffed against the cold,
Vying with squirrels for hidden seeds,
'Til a new-scattered feast provides enough to share.

To northern folks our plight is small -
They're used to many times as much and cope each year.
But milder winters are our lot, so this large fall
Has caused disruption to a normal life.

Despite it all, admire the beauty, cheer the change, and
Think up tales of dire events with which to entertain (or bore)
In years to come our bedtime-story-seeking progeny!

Winifred M. S. Anthony

Too Close To The Fire

Today I lost a friend,
a very close partner,
a friendship I built myself.
When I spoke to my intimate, it would
cackle back to me.
I watched it leap with joy,
I witnessed it flourishing,
Occasionally it would shimmer and radiate.
It was very peaceful and serene,
responsive to my touch,
It is dying now, slowly perishing,
my lonesome tears help put it out.
I will never have a friend again as warm
hearted and magnificent
as my fire.

Susan Gest

That The Heart May Sing...

Intricacies of science, of mind,
Of a thousand mysteries entwined,
Unravel themselves pretentiously
As human gifts of things to be —
Because of rights from God divined.

But then the world is heir to ills
Of fear and greed and crime that chills
The very marrow of one's bones.
Material gifts are worthless stones
Without the peace that love instills.

Let every living being implore
His brother and sister forevermore
To share God's blessings and rejoice
Together in one swelling voice —
That the heart may sing...perchance to soar,
   Perchance to soar...

Charles Veal

Words To My Father

Oh Father, hear my lucid words,
For they are meant only for you.
And if you listen with your heart,
You'll know this declaration is true.

Time, which we have spent with each other,
Has been seldom, if not only rare.
Though the wind has carried me afar,
My roots stay embedded with you there.

Thus, each day a I gaze into the mirror,
Behold! The face of the one man I call dad.
I can ponder over those moments we've shared,
The sweetest recollections in life that I've had.

And Father, as I stare at my reflection.
Looking obscurely into your eyes of green.
Tenderly, I utter the words "I Love You",
Hoping you'll hear them each night as you dream.

Karen Shahidi

Rodeo John

At seventeen I left school enlisted in the
Marine Corps and went to prepare for
Vietnam, so home sick all the time I was there,
but no one ever knew.

In our bunker once when I looked up,
I seen this big snake crawling by.
The snake kept going and going, how long is this thing.
As it kept going will I ever see the tail go by.

But how glad I am its crawling by
instead of coming down to look me in the eye.
I thought when I get home, if I ever do
a bucking horse in the Rodeo I will ride.

When home, I was told practice on a bale of hay
how cool, that is just what I will do.
The 4th of July was here, I signed up and drew the horse
I was to ride, Kemo Sobie was his name, I will never forget.

He came out of the shoot with a jump and a roar
around and around I went, up and down, then on the ground
all bent and bruised, I will never do that again, I said.
There is no comparison riding a bucking horse to a bale of hay.

Nellie M. Brand

A Spring Night

The scent of roses in the air,
The lovely face of a lady fair,
The handsomeness of her gentlemen friend,
And sounds of music all to tend,
To remind you of a night in spring,
When birds did chirp and coo and sing,
And love found you and your heart's delight,
All on that wonderful "Spring Night",
You gazed into his amber eyes,
So clear so bright so very wise,
Yet warm and gentle were they too,
As he whispered softly "I Love You",
Always now in the month of May,
You look back nostalgically to that day,
When your loving husband was that beau,
And the love found then did blossom and grow,
To the mature, feeling love that it is today,
Loving; more tender in every way.

Flossie Pyle

The Vols

They give their all to answer the call
  and some may never come back.
They do their job without a thought
  of what lies there across the track.

Some leave their jobs and rush to the scene.
  There are others who jump out of bed.
No thought is given to "should I go".
  The object is full speed ahead.

They risk their lives to save a life.
  How fast the adrenalin flows.
These are the men at the head of the line
  Ever ready to man the hose.

They will climb the ladder a rescue to make
  Never knowing what they may find.
They will brave the flame and call out a name
  in the hope they have left none behind.

When their work is done
  they will take their rest.
They can walk the road and stand real tall.
  They can take their place with the best.

  J. B. Hansen

Summer In Paradise

Like sparkling jewels put on display,
The sunlight glistens on the sea today.

A gentle wind caresses my hair.
The weather is warm, the day is fair.

Waters too cool in which to wade,
The sandy beach provides no shade.

Seashells wash upon the shore,
Treasures to take home and store.

Sea gulls glide on winds above,
A perfect day to share my love.

Tourists tanning upon the beach.
Time stands still, tomorrow is out of reach.

Windsurfers catching the wind in their sail.
A child at waters edge digs sand with his pail.

Laughter and goodwill definitely abound.
Pleasant gentle fog horns make their lonely sound.

A day at the beach on the West Coast,
With sunshine and water as the gracious host.

Oh, how I hate to return to the desert heat.
For summer in paradise is very hard to beat.

  Paula K. Cowan

Turn

A quarter turn, a half turn,
  Toward the new century.
See it in big or subtle ways -
  In bridges, streets, construction and attitudes;
Different stages of development,
  Laws - good or bad.

A quarter turn, a half turn,
  Toward the new century.
Changes of forever - some different, some not;
  Some you live with - like it or not.
A turn - first sharp, then nothing;
  Then a quarter and a half and not.

  B. Miles Jackson

Let It Be Known

There's a creature that lurks somewhere within,
A being we'd rather not know.
It emerges with unforgivable fury
Onto others, vicious words it may throw.

In some, it may rise up quite quickly,
And in others it may brew for a while;
But it can be a vindictive villain,
Bringing one grief instead of a smile.

Sometimes it stays with us for many a day,
Maybe even several months or a year,
Showing off its abusive nature,
And intimidates anyone who comes near.

Most have learned to control it,
But for a moment it might rise and appear,
Not wishing it to stay on the surface,
Takes a strong will to make it disappear.

Though this creature is one we care not to admit,
For its actions we really mistrust.
It is known quite simply as "anger,"
And it resides in each one of us.

  Anita J. French

To Chose...It's My Choice

I would rather feel the warmth of memories...than feel nothing
For I have felt nothing for too long.
I would rather know that I have someone that loves me...
Even if that is the love of a friend, than die alone.
I have free will...
When I chose to love, that is my choice,
With that comes the risk and the responsibilities of the choice.
If I feel pain, then...maybe I will grow
If I feel joy maybe, then I can find happiness
If I feel nothing, then I am nothing;
I would rather chose the risk, than remain nothing

  John R. Breault

My Friend, George

My friend, George, had a sweetheart. Carol Ann was her name.
She was only seventeen. He also was the same.
They talked of marriage. He gave her his graduation ring.
They also spoke about the future and the happiness it would bring.

One day he waited for her to spend the afternoon.
Just the two of them together, that lovely day in June.
But, their love was interrupted. A note was sent to him that day.
It was from her mother. This is what she had to say:
"Carol Ann isn't coming...or ever will again.
We are taking her away, as far from you as we can.
Because her future does not fit in our plan
With someone we feel is unworthy of our Carol Ann."

It was while she was away, she took sick and died.
When he heard about it, he just cried and cried and cried.
Now she's up in heaven, where all the angels go.
And he's here crying, down on earth below.
"We were so in love," he told me. "Why couldn't they let us be?
If only they didn't interfere, she'd still be here with me.
I'll never forget her. To me, she's more than just a memory.
She'll be with me always, walking alongside of me."

  Mary Anne (Prokop) Barczak

I Am

I am an artistic person.
I wonder if I will ever be better.
I hear the sounds of my picture.
I see what I am down inside me.
I want to draw everything there is.
I am an artistic person.

I pretend I am the greatest of all.
I feel wonderful in every way.
I touch the moist paint.
I worry I may get teased.
I cry when I get all touchy inside.
I am an artistic person.

I understand the little ones who try, try and try.
I say I will teach you.
I dream of being very, very famous.
I try to do my best in all ways.
I hope I will draw, paint and create.
I am an artistic person.

Daniella Olson

Sonnet of a Sunset

At dusk the shadows dominate the land.
The only light comes from the distant sun.
The sky explodes of color bright and grand.
While the sun looks back at what it has done.
Vibrant shades of gold and orange appear
As if God sent the earth a heavenly gift.
The sky once blue is red and seems to sear.
And clouds once white are golden peaceful drifts.
The flaming sun is bold and bright and vain
As it escapes below the horizon.
Yet it kisses the sky to end its game
With one last golden kiss as night arises.
    The golden gift from the sun now expires.
    But dusk again will put the sky on fire.

Christine Judith Deschler

Love in Denial

Love is denial, though it may take a while
It is well worth the wait
As I slowly walk another mile

Love in reserve
Is it love in denial?
Or is it love with a different style

Love can have you confused,
When you don't know what path
To choose. (Should I stay or should I go?)

Your love is in reserve
For which the time is it wait.
Which is the time well deserve.
To who's time it is
    It is the time
        Still unheard.

Laurence Brzozowski

Angels

They speak with a whisper, a smile they bear
In dreams you think you see them, a message they always share
It's questions that you ask, you wait for a reply
A kiss on your cheek, eyes turned towards the sky
Bathed in bright light, it warms your heart and soul
Guidance is what's given, what really is my role
Like branches of a tree, many paths that you may take
Some good, some bad, decisions you have to make
Believe in those little whispers always at your side
Not to answer questions, they're only there to guide

Joseph Cristanus

Loves And Lies

The loves and lies of life ease time's passage
With sadness and joy; allowing them to glide
Past each other, and boredom, avoiding both
But occasionally touching the heart of another.
Fleeting, in passing the Love can last forever,
Or never...and the Lies bring Lovers closer.
Sometimes painfully, awakening hidden knowledge
Or love.
At any rate then, Things not better left unsaid,
Or undone, are Not.
Thanks to the Loves and Lies of Life.

Bruce D. Tefft

Mother Nature's Tears

Listen and you may hear with your heart as well as your ears;
Feel what I am saying, these words I have for you;
I give you rain to wash away your pain and fears;
To grow strong and endure life's obstacles to;

Just like my trees that give you shade;
The grass that stretches like a blanket to rest upon;
Or the flowers that give you sweet fragrance in May;
All these things, to give you peace and keep you calm;

I am Mother Nature, and my rain are my tears;
That slowly falls from the sky when you are sad;
Because you are lonely and ache from within my Dear;
So stand strong and don't give in, for it's okay to get mad;

Let me cry for you, when you cannot cry yourself;
For I am with you, should it be today or even tomorrow;
So I may gently wash away your sadness that I have felt;
And to try and eliminate all of your sorrow;

But you only need to listen and you shall hear;
My voice echoing through my tear drops with love;
As a reminder that there is nothing to fear;
Because I'm always watching you from above.

Vivian Zaret

Passion

The moons shimmering light bounces off
your beauty to show satisfaction!
The sun drops dead because you're a knockout!
The stars shine brighter as they look
down upon your refinement! The planets
rotate faster for your style! The
meadow's hills roll more before your
bloom! The leaves crunch more for your
delicate feet! The birds croon louder
just because of your pulchritude! The
river is swift around the twists and
turns again because you're so exquisite!
Mother Nature is jealous of your beau!
That's having the world wrapped around
a single finger! Like passion.

Kristen Karakostas

The Will

A family is born
    and lives and grows together

They go through life believing
    this happy state will last forever.
But passage of the years
    comes the time that brings the tears
And families lose fathers and their mothers,
Then a will is decreed
    and some in their greed
Turn against their sisters and their brothers!

Frank W. Jacoutot

Leave A Clear Print

We are but thumb prints on vista of life.
We make our many circles and swirls a glee,
Leaving permanent grooves out of our strife,
Forever etched on life's canvas of greed.

Like old fossils, our minute smears reside
Hidden beneath refuge, compost, solid clay,
Waiting years for our dynasty of pride
While viewed and valued on some future day.

To leave unique prints of our daily swirls,
Assuring life-line threads to days of old,
Press hard, leave your clear prints for future worlds
'Cause history is more precious than gold.

Becky J. Richardson

Expressions of Life

With thoughts of you, I wake a new,
for each morning brings your kiss in a dream.

Touching my heart as I reach your way,
passion for you throughout my day.

Expressions of life each day with you,
expressions of life to carry us through.

Loving the moments to the seconds we spend,
embracing each feeling so it will never end.

Our affections so warm like rays of sun,
speak our emotions with love and fun.

Expressions of life each day with you,
expressions of life to carry us through.

Happiness adorns us with a sincere like peace,
and set us a table to enjoy the feast.

You are the plethora of my joy,
and you are the reason for my joy.

Expressions of life each day with you,
expressions of life forever a new.

Gene Spraggins

September Day

The days of Summer are long gone
and Fall has emerged from its shadow.

Leaves go from variations of green to
vibrant orange, brown and yellow.

A rustling sound accompanies each step taken
and the breeze blows hints of a brutal winter.

The grayness of the clouds sets the mood for a lazy
day and the broken branches and naked trees send
subtle reminders that death is unavoidable.

Still, I am impelled by life's beauty and
choose to live on, anticipating the outcome.

Roberta Curry

A Good Bye

Were you an angel sent from above,
or a devil from below?
You came into my life high intentions,
You left with every piece of my soul.
A kiss on the lips,
A whisper good bye,
I will love you forever,
So hear my cry.
When I told you I'd love you till the day I die,
I just want you to know, I did not lie.

Charles Eberhart

The Greatest Story Ever Told

I called upon my Lord, and my Lord called upon me.
My Lord decided that he'd die, and thus He set me free.
I asked my Lord why He needed in order to succeed.
My Lord answered, Salvation's all you need.

So, why do we wander 'round, Lost and hopelessly confused,
When Jesus offers us a peace, that all are free to use?
I often ask myself these things, and great it is to know,
That Jesus gave us everything, In Heaven, above and below.

Now, if you ponder why I sing of a great and mighty world,
Just sit right back, and you will hear The Greatest Story Ever Told.
A story of a man so dear, that He gave His life for us.
A man, who without a tear, Died on a dogwood cross.

He died for sins.
That He didn't do,
Sins that were committed,
By me, and by you.

Not a bone of His body was broken,
Not a drop of His love was lost,
But His spirit was given up,
That we might be saved by His loss.

Paula Jucene Helphenstine

To Whom It May Concern

To whom it my concern,
I just turned fifteen.

I may not reach the day,
I have my sweet sixteen.

That mean old man he hurt me,
he touched me and he played.

How could I have stopped him,
my body he'd invade.

He gave me something awful,
something terrible and so mean.

I never told anyone,
but who could have seen.

To whom it may concern,
my body's not the same.

I feel so very different, only he is to blame.

Now my life is shortening, and they still don't have a cure.

I take it one day at a time, but it's still so unsure.

To whom it may concern, I just turned fifteen.
I may not reach the day, I have my sweet sixteen.

E. Rodriguez

I Knew You Were Leaving

I knew you were leaving,
Never wanted to say good-bye.
My heart wept openly,
Yet not a tear filled my eyes.
Some days I was very angry,
But wanted no regrets.
Never wanted you to leave me,
Yet knew it was for the best.
Why do things happen?
The reason seemed so unclear.
People say they understand,
but those are only just words.
Time is supposed to make it all right,
Only moments seemed to pass.
Changing the way it should be, maybe not,
There was a reason.
I knew you were leaving...

Holly Faunce

Mother

Mother means, a strong soldier that stayed on the battle fields
until God waved the flag of victory.

She fought a good fight, she wore the whole armor of God at all
times. Her loins were girded with the truth, she wore the breast
plate of righteousness.

Her feet were shodded with the preparation of the gospel for
peace. She was surrounded with the shield of faith. Mama
wore the helmet of salvation as she meditated on the sword of the
Spirit which was God's Holy Word.

Being a woman of God, a mother, a friend and a fighter until the
very end.

Evangelist Carrie Vaughan

Mirrors

You see your reflections and
all your beauty don't be afraid
because you're a cutey.
Although you may think you're
ugly but you're not, just take
a look and you won't be shocked.
If you forget to do your
hair and you have a comb, and
a brush look at the mirror and fix it up.
Going to dinner or on a date
need your compact to see how
much make-up is on your face.
You're in your car and you hear
a beep, just look in your
rearview mirror and take
a peek. Just look at you as
pretty as you can be. The
mirror can help you and me.

Nkese Nyanibo

I Think I'll Bug My Mom Today

Nothing to do, no one can play,
I think I'll bug my mom today.

"Mom where are you? I found some new bait."
"I'm in the bathroom. Please can't it wait?"

"But I want you to see, can I come in with you?"
"No, I don't need any help. I know what to do!"

"It'll just take a sec... I need you to see."
I knocked on the door as loud as could be.

Mom opened the door, I showed her my bait.
She screamed very loud then started to faint.

I caught Mom in time and helped her sit on the floor.
Then I leaped the chair and ran out the door.

Nothing to do, no one can play,
I think I'll bug my mom today.

"Mom will you read me a book before we eat?"
She sat on the couch and curled up her feet.

Mom looked at me then gave me a hug.
She told me she loved reading to her "little bug."

If that's all it takes to get her to play
I think I'll bug my mom every day!

Rhonda J. Bjelland

Deep Within Myself

No one really understands,
What creeps through my complex brain,
The smallest things are the biggest demands,
Even the fresh Spring Rain.

No one really knows what hides,
Deep within my thoughts,
Even the ocean with its changing tides,
Can't exchange what isn't bought.

For when I ask for a simple chance,
Don't think I'm leading you astray,
For something joyous that makes me prance,
Is your handsome face in the sun of a new day.

Alaina Nelson

Heritage

My father left to me
No wealth of gold, nor precious stones,
No bank account, no stocks, nor bonds;
No house, nor land, in this world of strife.

Wealth untold, a precious legacy,
I will treasure always, in memory,
The example of a Christian life
My father left to me.

Willette Caudle McGuire

Walking In The Night

Will you walk with me tonight?
We'll walk beneath the holy light.
I fear though if I take you on this trip,
your voice will flow and stars will dip.

Tonight I promise you we'll look above,
and I'll show you all the things I love.
The imprint of your name so high,
will stay with me until I die.

The stars will twinkle and heavens burst,
feigns your love, an unquenchable thirst.
To see you standing against the sand,
just makes me want to be your man.

I'll throw myself against the wind,
which forfeits all I have to win.
I love you so and to see you cry,
would make a tear fall from my eye.

I'd hate to see you all alone,
we'll combine our dreams and make a home.
We'll take our time and set things right,
oh please, oh please...will you walk with me tonight?

Michael Daniel Osip II

In Gratitude

The freshness of the rose bud at its peak
Which blooms into splendor by the end of a week
A baby bird with its beak open wide
Awaiting its mother to fill the inside
The shedding of a plant leaf that's gone past its prime
Routinely replaced by a new one in time
Such is the way the life cycle goes.
Unseen, however, lie the heavier blows but
With each sign of beauty and the starting of life
One also is grateful regardless of strife
To be part of existence in this very busy place -
In that which is know as the human race

Gloria Simpson

Only Mine Once

Everyday it's worth getting up for. I struggle to get through the day. I'm tried and sleepy but, when I see you everything is forgotten The wonderful and passionate moments we had together are treasured in my heart forever. My love for you is deeper than any ocean in the world. Your smile brightness my day. Your lips are soft like the petal of a rose. Your kisses are so passionate and hot like the lava of a volcano.

I think about you day and night and wonder if you're thinking of me. I wondered if you meant it when you said "I Love You" but when you held me, looked at me, kissed me in that way you made me feel like a queen. There's nothing in the world I wouldn't do for you. Nothing or no one could get in the way of my for you. Now that you're gone I don't think I could love anyone else like I loved you.

Jemberdy Guzman

Release Me

Release me from this pressure,
    take me from this place.
They leave me without words,
    tears fall down my face.
Nothing left to feel, nothing left to hide; they see no wrong,
    ignore the tears, they hide behind their pride.
My heart can no longer beat for love, living or for fate;
    all those feelings I once had,
    now have turned to hate.
Life is not worth living when all I do is hurt,
    and once again, death an option,
    to which I might revert.
The pain too strong to hold inside, nothing I can do;
    they're blind and do not understand,
    how can I get through?
Knowing my mistakes, replacing them with fear,
    down my face so close to death, falls another tear.

Cyn

The World Is Sad

There's so much sadness, in this world,
Badness, too there is no clue, as to why
it is like this!

I'd be remiss, if I thought, things,
will get better, I can only say,
right to the letter, things are sad!

How can you lift, one's morale, Pal,
When there is no incentive, about things,
in general. The situation seems hopeless,
And yet I feel, I could cope, with less,
if, I didn't want more! So I humbly
implore, people, to look out for each other, more.

This would be a much nicer world,
Give it a twirl, and you'll see what I
mean, if you change your scene, and selfish ways.

The world is so sad, so bad people
Are disgruntled in despair if everyone
Did their share, of giving, to the living.
There would be more joy, more mirth,
here, on our blessed earth!

Marion Solitaire

Dream To Dream

Two ball gloves under the arm and a smile in the sun.
Standing in the back yard, waiting for the one.
The one that sparks his heart and feeds his dream.
The love of his lifetime in a memory in the making.

Toys and joys launching from the corner of the room.
Wonderboy searching for the ball shaped like the moon.
He glances out at Dad, waiting patiently and serene.
The love of his lifetime in a memory in the making.

Floating through the air like a vision in disguise.
Joy, fear, laughter, and tears carry as it flies.
He dreams of hope and happiness for his love that stands afar.
The enchantment develops in a memory of the heart.

Proud and secure, he asks of Mantle and the greats.
In awe of the knowledge, Wonderboy listens without debate.
He realizes the true hero is the man protecting his star.
The enchantment develops in a memory of the heart.

Dusk settles in, the toss has come to a close.
Dreams are forever molded within the depths of their souls.
Arm in arm they walk, best friends for the taking.
The love of their lifetime in a memory in the making.

Gregory S. Edmundson

Ode To The Commode

What a gas, what a joy,
What an absolute thrill,
When I opened that door,
I let out a grand shrill.

For it was an outhouse,
And I was prepared to see...
A sad stinky place to sit and pee.

But this was Bearpaw Campground and I was alone,
And I never expected to see such a throne.

It was pristine white with paper to match,
And an extra roll and a latch that latched.
And I could hardly keep my shrill to a hush,
When I realize that this was a throne you could flush!

Now being a lady and not to excited,
About sitting over a hole where the whole camp united,
I skipped off to dinner with no fear of eating
For I could look forward to our next meeting,

So I hold up my glass and toast to the champ,
Who installed the commode in Bearpaw Camp!

Lauri Fraser Graham

Untitled

Above the silver waters my shadow grows
Descending it closes around my sphere
Moving towards the center, hidden in the spinning ring of eternity
They whispered the truth, but God, let me dream so that I can see you
    again.
The fire threads that cage me extend from smooth seeds of blur that
reflect an inner lie, an inner fear. My bleeding hand reaches to grab
the next block, mounted on a stairway that spirals into a cloud one
shade of gray head down, but now aware I focus on my shaking, feeble
hands as they slowly join and the magic glows.
I was whole and free, expanding accelerating into a thick multicolored
swirl of space, pulsing with vibrations of pyramid ecstasy. Spine
arched, I would fly through odd but lumps of concentrated beauty me
with heavy waves of heightened pleasure.
All the wonderful silver balls washed past the fuzzy velvet wall
perfectly into their symmetric nests, securing a spike of faith in my
    cleansed self.
Melting into the healing fingers of the light, I felt satisfaction,
like a pure infant that wanted and waited to be nurtured.

I stop sucking on your silver lips and I smile and so do you.

Jason Ruscil

My Father, My Love, My Abuser

My Father, my protector, should be,
How dare he, use and abuse me.
Someone, I should love and trust,
Used my body, to satisfy lust.

Physical, emotional, and sexual pain,
My little body, accepting the blame.
Daddy dearest, what did I do?
To deserve the pain, I got from you?

No one heard me scream and yell, I lived daily in my little hell.
Family secrets, were all about, why can't I stand up and shout?

All I wanted from you, dear Dad,
Is the love and trust, I never had.
I prayed to God, almost every night,
To take me to heaven, and save my life.

The prayer, I prayed, never came,
That little child grew up in shame.
All the years, I accepted the blame,
A survivor of abuse, I became.

Learning with my counselors help, to take old memories off the shelf.
Now I'm working on my life, finally, how to take care of self.

Valerie J. Le Mieux

A Diamond

A warm sunset, glittering like silhouette
As it retires behind the horizon's wall.
Crystal-sparkling beauty, replicating God's glory
Forms an image on the eye...
And dazzles as lightning illuminates, the darkest crevice of the sky!

Not a mirage infatuating the mind,
But an antidote replenishing wounded tentacles of my anatomy.
A hope seasoning doubts, refreshing troubled hearts,
Reforming souls; eliciting the values it imparts.

A refined image escorting the dawn of day,
Condescending with character that culminates all virtues.
An infinite love, a disposition divine,
Clad with a personality unique...
Warming all perimeters of my flesh... It is my sweet diamond
Monique!

Daniel Lazare

My Son

Should I have stayed and not gone away
Would I have then not lost my son
the question comes again
And there's no answer none.
If I had stayed would it have stopped
the fate that lay before him
Would God have left him here for me
mortal, mine, so I could hold his hand
eat with him, cool his brow
when with fever he'd be overcome.
Why, my son had only just begun
at twenty-three his steps into the world,
into this play-ground made by man,
and God's, where mountains, rivers
trees and birds stretched open arms,
but no, He had in mind another land,
incomparable by far.
He took his hand and led him there.
Of His plan I was unaware.

I wish I'd stayed so you'd have
had me there with you, my son.

Nalini Dias-Jayasinha

An Awakening!!

I had a sad awakening, today.
A friend that I loved dearly, passed away.
I was reminded no one's here to stay.
We're here for our brief moment, then away!

Now this has been the order from time's passed.
We're told our life is like a blade of grass.
We bloom, we flourish, will the beauty last?
Oh no, our time is gone in just a flash.

We needs be careful what we do and say.
"Oh, I have lots of time", you may say.
Only what's done for Christ will really pay.
Our only promise is just for today.

How very fragile is the thread of life!
Our chance to do what's right is once not twice.
But if we follow closely after Christ.
He will lead us to eternal life!

Gene Key

This Promise

Sleeping in the summer night, all is quiet now...
In my mind I hear these words, I know this voice, somehow.
"Peace on Earth"... I hear within, "Love all men just the same."
Who is that talking to my soul? Please, won't you say your name?

"It doesn't matter who I am, just listen to my song,
I put you on this Planet Earth, to live and get along.
I planted trees to bear such fruit, for everyone to share
I gave you water, clean to drink, and a heart, with which to care."

I heard this voice begin to quake, as I tossed and turned in bed...
This voice was more than just a dream, passing through my head.
When I awoke, I had a quest, bestowed upon my heart...
To heal this dying planet... Now I'll go and do my part.

I'll share my food with strangers, who haven't any bread...
I'll apologize for hurtful words, that I may have said.
As thoughts like this passed through my mind, and plans began to form,
I heard this voice in a wakened state, as thunder from a storm

"I sent a message to your heart, when you were fast asleep,
and now accept this Promise, that I intend to keep.
As turmoil spreads throughout the land, and all seems so despair,
hold fast to the hope within your heart, and know that I'll be there."

Polly J. Schultz

The Wondering Birds

A whistling echoes over the mountain,
The chill of the wind rushes through the air,
Racing towards me for it's not a sin,
As wet spectacles of rain come and tear.

Birds fly in the opposite direction,
To a warmer place above the dull color,
They desert in a pack, and seem to run,
Holding on the back of their new mother.

Their longing journey is almost complete,
Their tiredness can soon be forgotten,
They can lay back and put up their sore feet,
And forget the things that made their brain swim.

No more whispers I once thought were so loud,
Beneath all the warmth, coldness still remains,
Brightness of things I mistakenly found,
Was not as true to me as my old fame.

Stephanie Gettis

Time

Time ticks away,
without a care in the world.
Not knowing that it will continue to do so for ever.
Unlike us,
it goes on for eternity.
It never fails to go by slowly,
when we want it to go by fast.
Or fast when we want it to go by slow.
It seems there is never enough time,
yet time is endless, it is us that are not.
I envy time.
It never has to love or get a broken heart.
Time never dies, or mourns.
But yet, time is not living and we are.
Without time,
we would not be.
But time has no needs, and always will be.

Sonja Armenta

Learning

Reading, writing, thinking, or singing A to Z,
what we learn is what we use as far as we can see.

In day or night or in daze we always use our mind,
collecting thoughts we cannot lose or never leave behind.

Like life, like living, looking up, or reaching for the sky,
grasp all that the senses take; never pass them by.

To tell a story of a picture of a life that's long,
What we learn in memories, we'll find them in a song.

Randal R. Rossow

Maybe Someday

Maybe someday - when I am dead and buried,
You will know exactly how I feel.
You will read what I have written
With pen, and lots of will.

When you hear my thoughts on paper,
Know one thing for sure:
I would rather have said these things to you,
Than wished that you were here.

Be happy though, without me.
Accomplish all you may.
Know that you are very special,
And we will meet again, someday.

I had hoped to know you better,
To share your dreams; your hopes.
But just one thing - remember,
Killing is no joke...

I did not want to hurt you,
And so I let you go. You are better off
Without me;
Even though I love you so.

Monica Larson

Life

As you walk through the dark streets of hell,
You look around and find yourself all alone.
Trapped between the gages; of lust and love
Bound between faith and futility;
Twisted 'round and 'round in a life that isn't yours;
Living a lie that you know nothing about.
Staring towards the future,
Not knowing if you're going to die tomorrow or seek sorrow.
Keeping feelings that will only cause pain,
Looking back at nothing but shame.

Carrie Ferrell

Your Best

Arise, refreshed of body and mind.
Look to the day with anticipation,
and, with strength, go forth and find.

Head high and shoulders back,
with pride of self apparent,
do what needs to be done, do not slack.

Falter not, take your stand,
and looking to the future...
take the world in your hands.

Strive hard for things yearned.
Work with your whole being.
Possess only what you've earned.

How quickly your journey thru life will cease,
but you'll look back with pride,
and you'll know sweet peace.

You'll do it right - you'll stand the test,
always with honor,
you'll do your best.

Carolyn Cartwright

Emily: Of the Deepest Dye

She was of the: Deepest Dye
Profoundly tall, one side scorched
Her spirit energizing, electrifying
Teaching, reaching, transcending

I must have her for my friend
Words spoken, split, divided,
Chopped apart, unequal
Breathing in, exhaling, sharing space,
Air alike, pairing off, not alike

Unwanted opinions, cruel images painted,
Scattered about, prejudice, judging
Minds ignorant, depleted, rot abound
Must we suffer for the division,
Of humanity at the Tower of Babel

Finely we are split apart, never
will I forget, our short lived friend ship
A harvest of innocents, bewildered,
By the division of the naked eye
Just because she was,
An African of the Deepest Dye

Rosie Hutsell

Our House

Our house, our house, no our home!
Treasured pets, once they roamed,
Birthday parties, Christmas cheer,
Flowers flourished, birds nested here.
Happy moments filled our hearts
Never thinking we would part.

Once well kept, neat and clean,
Timeless, timeless, so it seemed.
Weeds, weeds, creeping in
Here they come. Here again,
Once plucked as they appeared,
Stealthily, slithering does anyone care?
More, more everywhere!

Trees, trees planted small,
Towering, towering growing tall.
Insects, insects savoring bark,
Slithering, sliding, making their mark.
Withering, withering, time marches on.
Where, oh where, have the caretakers gone?

Diana J. Weigel

A Valley

There was a valley all green and gold
With reds and yellows and colors untold
Where birds sang and animals played
It was a heavenly place upon which to gaze

With crystal clear waters that flowed from the hills
Down into the valleys and through the woods
The rivers and streams abounding with fish
Provided the food where the wildlife lived

Then along came man with his civilized ways
And said, "Here we shall live for many days."
But greed and hatred became the way
Now nothing lives and nothing plays

Is it too late to mend our ways
To restore the land as in our forefathers days
So that future generations can proudly say
Now here we can live and here we can play

Margaret Sheridan

Goodbye My Friends, Aids Wins Again

My friend I've known you for so many years
We've cried, we've laughed, we're shared our fears
My deepest regret, has come true once again
I've lost another very special friend.
It seems I don't care, but I truly do
I pray that our Lord takes goods care of you
I pray that your pain, was little, or none
I pray for the life, you've just began
God Bless you friend, May I thank you too
for being that friend, among very few
It's hard for me to say, what I've needed to say
But I love you friend, in my own
special way.

Rose Mary Dozier

Are You Ready

Are you ready to meet my saviour
and to share in His wonderful grace,
Are you ready for Him to prepare your heart
and to talk with you face to face.

He's waiting for you Dear friend of mine
and can handle you every need
He is your saviour so good and kind
and from your Burdones, you can be freed.

I know of this love He has for you
and I know of its wonderful power,
It gives you strength in a special way
and will comfort your heart in its weakest hour.

This love for God can be so real
if you will give your heart to him,
and peace of mind will come at last
when you trust alone in Him, my friend.

Alice L. Jordan

Untitled

My love for you never will wilt like a rose.
My love for you will rise like the sun.
My love for you will not end like a story book does.
My love for you will continue on forever.
But your love for me will wilt like a rose.
And will set like the sun.
Your love for me has stopped.
And so my heart has stopped too.

Melissa Sue Parks

Winter Etchings

Vapor spires, and reappearing many miles
Below into a mirrored, polished, jeweled lagoon
Of endless, frozen beauty of a silent clinic
Decorative statue of pristine magnificent splendor.
Minutiae rivers depart the frozen fountainhead,
Winding, probing, groveling, their gushing
Splinters of frigid, swirling, waters endless
Searching for new channels to harbor their wealth
Of torrential currents seeking to absorbed the frozen
Land in their search to the cradle of their birth,
The wide, deep, blue, tear drops of God which
Cries for the mortal souls of man.
Into this pool, a crystal jewel, weeping for
His children's return to the home of their abode.

M. K. Baumberger

Lung Cancer

This monster kills you,
This monster makes you suffer,
This monster takes away the ones we love,
And this monster is born from smoking,
But this monster would not be born if you would
    not smoke.

Brittney Dyche

Much More

Try to take what we have learned
To a better place and time you've earned.

Where things are not always good
But always doing the best you could.

We will always remember our experiences here
So let's all try not to give up dear.

Always soar like the eagle flies
Try not to dwell on lies.

Earth is enclosed in a coat of chaos
It continues to devour the earth like a blanket of moss.

It will try to suffocate your inner self
This moss will diffuse beyond the highest shelf.

There is no where one can truely be hidden
So be very careful that it doesn't harden.

Try not to be disappointed over what takes place
If we are patient, it's amazing what is in this space.

Always remember as we walk through the hands of time
Never once ever looking behind is a crime.

Always securing the roots in mother earth
Letting our branches always reaching for the sky's worth.

Pamela Waller

"Mother-In-Law"

Mother-in-laws are here to stay,
no matter be what may,
without them there would be,
no husband or wife per say.
Son's and daughter's are not married to them, I see,
Why all the squabble between them?
Treat each other with respect at last,
be happier, healthier, bury the past,
Mother-in-laws are here to stay, hold fast.

Joyce M. Watkins-Weight

Black Beauty

Unfamiliar, mysterious, and strong,
when at first this man appeared.

Curiosity, desire, and concern,
left only absence of fear.

Assertive, passionate, and powerful,
intrigue overcame resistance.

With his alluring smile, tenderness, and touch,
all that remained was want and persistence.

It became undeniably clear,
in the most enticing fashion.

With his charm, sincerity, and wisdom,
there is now an infinite attraction.

Forever in my heart will stay,
this unrelenting sense of duty.

To respect, admire, and honor this love,
He is the ultimate in Black Beauty.

Kimberly M. Johnson

I Know A Man...

I know a man who will always be wiser than me.
He lives each day as if it were his last
Ever supportive, ever kind, ever gentle, ever humble, ever loving.
He is always there when I need him.
I always smile when I look upon his face.
In his eyes, I can see that he cares about me.
I care about him too.
I know a man who I can always look up to.
This man lives a very happy life
With a big, supportive family and ever caring friends.
He is loved by all who come in contact with him.
When other people meet him, they feel at home with him.
They see him as a father or as a best friend.
I am grateful that this man is my grandfather.

Jason Aloysious Wong

A Stormy Night

Alone in a house on a stormy night, everything's dark but one
    burning light.
The wind is howling, the storm rages on, the shutters are creaking
where hinges are gone.

There's shuffling and scraping out on the porch, the light goes out,
    you look for a torch.
And while you are fumbling around in the dark, the lightning gives
off but one tiny spark.

The house is lit up but for only a moment, you look outside, was
that a movement?
But how could this be, it made no sound, and there are no neighbors
for miles around.

The dog's in the kitchen, he's safe and sound, he's safe from the
horrors which lurk around. Then a crash, a tinkle of glass, whatever
it is has gotten in at last.

You hear your dog howl, then yelp in pain, you know that death has
made a gain. You open the door and flee into the night, what keeps
you going is an unknown fright. You keep on running till you think
you'll drop, you look around and then you stop.

Your house is in flames, it's all like a dream, but then you hear
that unearthly scream. It came from the house, then that is all, you
run again until you fall. The firemen say it was struck by
lightning, but you know it was something even more frightening.

Shirley Colino

I Tried ...

I tried to be the best daughter,
Some say I failed,
But today I feel I was a great daughter.

I tried to be the best wife,
Some say I failed,
But today I know I was, it was other's mistakes.

I tried to be he best of friend,
Some say I failed,
But today that friendship has survived and is closer
    than ever.

I tried to be the best mother,
Some say I failed,
But regardless, today I have raised two sons, single-handedly
    and they have turned out good, not perfect.

After trying so hard to be the best for everyone in my
    life but me,
I've decided that I was, and am the best at being one thing,

I'm Me........

Joy L. Hill

Fear

Fear is the darkness, evil, and the night.
Fear of the unknown can rule people's lives.
Ignorance feeds doubt and shadows cause fright.
Suspicion stabs hearts like venomous knives
Any mortal man's mind can be clouded.
If dead things don't stay where they are buried.
Fear, you'll stop thinking, your soul will be shrouded
In dark gloomy mist, your heart will be carried
Away by a demonic skeletal hand.
Past other lost souls to the pit of despair,
Down to Hades where all good things are banned.
If fear is in your heart, it will stay there.
So if death's icy grip comes close, comes to near.
Be sure, my friend, that you don't run in fear.

Colin Henry

Life Assay

I cry out in anguish -
Needing to be heard.
But only deaf ears receive my words.
Bouncing off walls, they echo of pain.
Turmoil and confusion seem never to end.
Why always disappointment?
Illusion again, again,...again.
I must retreat within myself.
Only I understand.
Felicity slips through my grasp -
Like the sands of time.
A shadow can not be caught -
Can never be mine.
Lest despondency destroy my soul -
Courage nascent - takes control.
I want to scream - I catch my breath.
Resistance brings reprieve.
I bend.

Betty B. Holmes

Linda Lee

I fell in love with Linda Lee
As we went strolling by the sea.
The waves were rippling o'er the sand,
As we walked slowly hand in hand.

I love my Linda Lee
She is as sweet as she can be.
That is why I love my Linda Lee,
Because she is as sweet as she can be.

As the moon appeared up above,
We talked about our blooming love.
That some day we would find a way,
To finally set our wedding day.

Many moons have passed away,
Since, we set our wedding day.
Now, we are as happy as we can be,
As, we settled down by the sea.

We find that time goes very fast.
As we now have some thing that will last.
We had to buy a card of safety pins,
As we were blessed with a pair of twins.

Leonard Sorenson

Soldier Of God

We knew him, an oh how we loved him,
From the young up to the very old.
We'll cherish his memory forever,
Because he was as good as gold.

His presence made our lives happier.
He was a friend to all men.
He brought our dear Lord to us
And after each prayer, he'd say an Amen.

Yes, he's passed away but not forgotten.
His memory still lives on,
In the hearts of all faithful christians,
Who believe there's a world just beyond.

We should not weep, for our beloved priest is happy.
He nestles close to our dear Lord's breast.
For surely one so good as he, is in heaven.
Our "Soldier of God", is at eternal rest.

Theresa Fish

The Wind And I

When I was small, age two or three
    The wind began to play with me.
It sang a song into my ear -
    "Come here, come here, my little dear."
Its breath was scented like a rose.
    It made me laugh, tickled my nose.

And then right along as I grew
    The wind and I found things to do.
I would run like a little deer,
    And the wind would sing, "I'm here, here,"
And blow and blow about my hair.
    The wind and I made quite a pair.

Now I am old and not quite spry.
    Still I love the wind from the sky.
I like to walk, but I must rest.
    The lovely wind comes from the west
And sings to me, "I'll help you more,"
    Then blows me gently to my door.

Sarah Omanson

'My Poetry - A True Story'

I have loved poetry for as long as I can remember,
the words just come to me as if I were a writer.
It started when I was young, reading was a challenge I could not
refuse, some teachers would bark at me - saying things others might
call abuse. But that did not stop me - I had a talent you see,
my book was always with me, I did not need a key.
I won ribbons and trophies as the years passed on by,
then one day I came home, looked out back, and began to cry.
The large storehouse had been torn down and thrashed,
my ribbons, my trophies, all my books had been trashed!
For the first time in life I really knew the word "sad",
I looked at mom, who just shrugged, then I hated my dad.
How could he do such a terrible, hurtful deed —
without even asking what it was I might need?
My mind was frozen - I couldn't remember my poetry,
my first works were lost, I have a terrible memory.
I didn't care about ribbons, trophies or any such thing,
I could only stand there, hating dad, and just crying, crying.
I wanted my poetry and all I had was none, it took many years to
realize what was done - was done. Well, now I am older, mom and
dad died knowing my love, and poetry is my anchor, my words with
which to move, for only to myself do I need to approve.

Lelia Patterson

To My Valentine On Her Birthday

Happy Birthday to my wife,
    My friend and lover, the joy of my life.
You fill my thoughts, night and day,
    With wonderful memories of the way
We shared all the things that came along
    And made my love for you grow strong.

You're always there for me, and so,
    When sorrow strikes me, you make it go.
You make me happy all the time,
    So I attempted to make this rhyme,
Tell you just how much I love you,
    It's not nearly enough, but it'll have to do.

John W. Olson

Hidden Beauty

Hidden in an emerald garden
Beneath a canopy of leaves
Lies a sleeping beauty
Among the branches of the tree
Inside her woven cottage
Primping for her trip
Dawning a cloak of colors
Shades of orange, yellow
And the hue of red brick
Oh, how majestic she will look
Like a queen in a royal parade
The butterfly ascends from her home of silk
Like some magical houdinistic trick.

Margaret Galli

Early Fall

When you wake up in the morning and the mist is in the air
There's a hint of cool and crispness and the day seems not too fair
As you're looking out the window cross the foggy water blue
Leaves' colors begin to turn into a mesh that's bright and new
Oranges, purples, yellows and browns intermingled
with the green of summer's crowns
New joys and creative desires somehow begin to call
And we know with all these changes we face a New Year's Early Fall.

Mary Elsie Moses

Unnoticed Whispers

Sinking deeper into the darkness
of a secret so horrendous,
never daring to reveal
the secret that could kill.

Frantic screams can't be felt
as the fatal blows are being dealt,
silent whispers echo through the night
as cries of anguish dare not tell their plight.

Twilight wails a still song
while never revealing what is wrong,
whimpers and sobs are finally seen
alas much too late, we feel the final scream.

Debbie Powell-Everett

To the Class of '66

Time is slow sometimes but fast when you look back to where we
were. Children are grown and we focus on a new direction not just
basic survival. Not an easy task but a necessary one. New
goals-retirement-new found freedom from responsibility self
awareness.
Maybe the best has come because now we can be comfortable with the
person inside. Not worrying what people may think but truly glad
that you are who you are. Very unique. Maybe that is what comes
from age. Do you think?

Barbara J. Huser

My Two Sons

We were settin' in two straight backs,
Near the circle city mall.
Waitin' for the brass to come along and
Dedicate the wall.
Us gold star folk we had our place, for we
Were honored guest.
So son and I just set there feelin' humble
Like the rest.
I saw two vet's in a warm embrace, and both
Of them were cryin'.
Don't matter what your color, when the
Bullets start to flyin'.
The dignitaries are speakin now, they talk
A lot bout God.
He's the only one can help you when you're
Layin' neath the sod.
The time has passed, I say to son, let's
Go, it's getting late.
As I gently rub my hand, cross my other son's name,
It's on panel seven, line twenty eight.

John D. Hickman

"The Woods"

Walking through the woods one may day,
I saw a blue bird up ahead a ways.
He was beautiful. I'd have to say.
The grass was plush and green.
Oh, what a lovely scene (this valley of green)
I laid down on a carpet of grass.
How I wish that this could last.
There's nothing like the peaceful bliss,
when you're here there's nothing you miss.
The sky's so blue, the sunshines bright,
I think I'll stay right through the night.
A breeze is blowing, keeping it cool
all this peace is quite a lure.
Now when you're feeling down and out
concentrate hard and it'll come about.
Close your eyes and pretend you're there
it's peace on earth with not a care!

Wanda Webb

The Forlorn Renewed

We have never made it to the pound
So, how were all our animals found?

Our mixed breed dog was hit while running with another
So my daughter brought the other home wanting to be his mother

The black and brown mutt, Sudar, appeared to have been beaten
So it took us some time to get him to eatin'

A yellow lab, Patience, brought home by my brother
Now he has moved out and we have another

They both understand to 'shake' left or 'shake' right
And sometimes cause trouble when they bark and bite

When they run and romp in the backyard together
You are sure they are going to kill each other

A back door held open in the middle of winter
To coax in a black cat, Misty, who was looking thinner

My husband knowing I'd never let him live it down
Brings home Charcoal, a gray, black-striped kitten hanging around

From a litter of five, came a runt golden and white
Sudar cared for Little Guy, so they act a lot alike

A bird named Beaky about to have her third owner
I decided to take her in and stop the turnover

Cathy A. Stevens

Her Tears

Her eyes, they cry
I do not know why
What is it that makes her so sad?
The way that she acts,
The way that she feels
Why can't she just be glad?
Is it because she's missing something in her life?
Or is it because she can't handle the strife?
She cries too often, too hard, too loud
Shouldn't I help her somehow?
But I think it just might be too late,
What can anyone do now.

Beth Beswick

The Presence of Death

I sensed the storm coming; yet I wasn't prepared.
The rain plummet down and I became scared.
The wind blew and the lightning blazed the blackening sky,
And the cracking clamor of thunder filled the air.

I couldn't move and I knew all too well why,
The presence of death was standing nearby.
In the distance I heard my brother moan.
I called out to him, but he never replied.

I didn't want to leave him all alone,
Laying amidst the ash and the stones.
I muster up courage from deep down inside,
And walked into the valley of the dry bones.

I was still standing after the storm subsided.
My brother died and my heart tried to deny it.
When a storm rages there's not much one can do,
Except hold on tight and ride it through.

Sheliah Hackett Jackson

Crossroads

Life is a journey my friend
When it begins you know it ends
But you know you have to go
Crawl fall yet walk and grow

Life is a journey just as you travel in road
We start from here destined to the heavenly abode
It has straight paths also crooked ones
left and rights, bridges in tons
But the most difficult of 'em all is the Crossroads
We have to make our choice and accept the load

Life is a journey my friend
Enjoy it while it lasts
Wrack your brains, hands, legs
But leave a lasting cast

For thousands who are following you in the path of peace
Leave a mark behind where the Crossroads is.

Aruna Kannan

Goodnight

A mother gently holds
Her sleepy baby close
And lovingly just kissed
The one who means most.

Back and forth, the rocking chair goes.
The baby stirs and clings tightly to its mother.
As the mother stands, the baby knows,
It is time for bed, and no time other.

Slowly down the hall,
The tired mother creeps,
To lay her baby down,
And sing to it while it peacefully sleeps.

A song from when she was young,
To her baby sang she,
Until at last she sang no more,
And walked out sadly.

Now alone the mother rocks,
But knowing it won't last,
Because in her heart she knows,
Babies grow up too fast.

Megan Hammond

God

God is good
God is love
He sends us his blessings from heaven above.
He sees our needs
He feels our pain
He showers us with love like the falling rain
He knows of our weakness
He knows of our doubt
Still, He never gives up
He never runs out
He is always there to show us the way
To help us and guide us each and every day
He's there in the good
He's there in the bad
He's there in the happy and the sad
So whatever you do
Don't forget to say thank you to God above
for His merciful love.

Elizabeth Nichols

lil' birdy

lil' birdy, please don't cry
someday... is yours to fly
never know in your heart to fear
and keep all anxiety far from here.

lil' birdy, don't you fear
everything is made for you here
you are a great one indeed
and I share it all with you, please!

lil' birdy, don't look down
on a great platform, the ground
giving a horizon for us to view
but more than that... it's just for YOU.

lil' birdy, I made all of this
providing everything you'd ever need
Partake of my fruits from this tree
Know always, for you, they're free.

lil' birdy, please don't cry
for all I've provided, I don't know why
you won't take it, all for free
always know lil' birdy, that you are me.

Timothy A. Gettig

I Am

I am Megan Flowers
I wonder if the world will never be the same
I hear my self-conscious telling me to behave
I see everything the way I want it to be
I want nothing but the best for my family and friends
I am Megan Flowers

I pretend to be nothing and nobody but myself
I believe that everybody should be themselves
I touch my heart and pull out my true feelings
I feel like I owe something to someone
I worry that I the world is mistreated
I cry when I hear an ambulance or a fire truck siren
I am Megan Flowers

I understand that life isn't always fair
I say that life is sometimes fair
I dream that everyone and everything will be treated the same
I hope that someday my dream will come true
I am Megan Flowers.

Megan Flowers

The Secret Within

Love me, she cried, with desperation that stunned them
Left them helpless, then apathetic that their love wasn't enough
To ease her vicious pain or halt her from slowly drawing away
They loved but from a distance and shared her tears of utter despair

Love me, she demanded, and he responded as best he could
But always she waited for more with eyes shrouded with the doubt
That kept him at a distance while she cried over her aloneness
Until the silence and the questions transformed her into a memory

Love me, she begged, never expecting after so long she'd get a reply
But he smiled at her in amusement, raining love when it suited him
Awed and grateful for the glimmer that left her longing for more
She stood helpless in the abyss when he left her without explanation

Love me, she wished, her words floating in the solitude
Spinning, drifting, then forming a novel and exciting idea
Drawing her at last to the one person who'd gone unasked
Love me, she invited, to the mirrored image as she smiled

Patricia K. Eberhart

Reflections In My Window

"To dream" is a wonderful thing (authors propose to say).
But "to awake" proves that a fallacy in another way.

Looking into the reflection on my window pane,
I'm invited to wander thru a path of sugar cane.
And as the sun reflects its warm,
I view distant clouds without the harm.

However, as a painter I could fill spaces there,
But the scene changes - like life leading somewhere.
There are those pointed leaves upon the tall spring tree.
There are shadows, as on pavement, beckoning "come here" to me.

So it is "in awakening" (I learn) we are invited to share,
To discover life's meaning with breath, and love, and care.

Genevieve L. Ford

Take Me to the Mountains

Dedicated to Kirk Inberg
Take me to the mountains,
I've gone there since I was a child.
Challenge and destiny, changeless yet changing,
The wonder of all things wild.

I'm there with you in the mountains,
In the meadow where the lupine grows,
With a chipmunk clown who makes you laugh,
And the rainbow's flash on the river flow.

On the trail with pine tree voices,
Whispering secrets of ageless wisdom.
The grey of granite, the glaciers of white,
I'm with you there in the mountains.

Take me to the mountains,
Where the stars shine so close and bright,
As your campfire softly glows,
Think of me tonight.

Take me to the mountains,
That's where I want to be.
When you behold them in all their beauty,
Take time to remember me.

Judy Inberg

My Soul Is Taken

Though I carry my burdens with a heavy stride
On this day the Lord is my guide,
For I have no worries after this day
Because the Lord has lead them all away,
My soul is taken.

Don't cry, Don't weep
For the Lord is the shepherd of all his sheep,
He has lead me to the Promised Land
For this is only God's glorious plan,
My soul is taken.

So this is where I will be
way up in heaven,
Thank you God,
My soul is taken.

Kelli Matthews

Ghost's Notions

The fields are now sown for me to reap,
and once again my bargains keep.
For as the night does conjure me,
I hide in wait upon bended knee.
To spring forth cruelly with snares of wine,
and unfurl lucidity upon every mind.
For the night is now at hand and all clocks wound,
and in these last hours true freedom is found.
From both our memories and what will be known.
For there is no reprisal for one of our own.
Keeping in limbo all final tallies,
and leaping and plunging in minds as if alleys.
For I lack the reverence and bar the cool,
to entice with pleasures the blundering fool.
Only horror and torture devices benign.
I call my markings or tell- tale signs.
Screaming and laughing and itching of feet,
these are the memories that each one will eat.
Leaving at last my once pitted soul,
to wallow and writhe upon the streets of gold.

Croley Loyd

Heartache

I miss you more than anyone knows,
as each day passes, my emptiness grows.
The tears in my eyes I can wipe away,
but the ache in my heart will always stay.

No one knows the grief that I bear,
when I look for you and you're not there.
You left me suddenly your thoughts unknown,
but you left memories I'm proud to own.

We are far apart, but I love you still,
there's a space in my heart only you can fill.
Some may forget you; now that you're gone,
but I won't, no matter how long.

I have memories no one can steal,
but separation is a heartache
that will never heal.

Rosalind Marshall

Timeless Train

There's a train traveling the nation
Filled with souls of strange fixation
Some versed in obscenity with no tomorrow
Some with mercies steeped in sorrow

It's on the track, clickity clack, clickity clack

Here a pious judge, a lonely spinster, a wobbling drunk
A glib politician, a gambling minister, a gapping punk
Odd and foreboding are some of the others
Waiting to catch the lap of expectant mothers

Clickity clack, clickity clack, clickity clack

Those on the trail of drowning drugs
With demons loosed in jeering thugs
In the isles are tripping youngsters
Weaving in pattern are preying monsters

Clickity clack, clickity clack, clickity clack

Back in the caboose is trailing death
Betting on souls and their last breath
Where is the train of this traveling nation
It's at the depoe and your next station

Clickity clack, clickity clack, clickity clack

Shirley Fielding

Picture of My Youth

As I gaze into the picture of the child
I use to be, shady glimpses of memories whirl
before my eyes. The revelation of my beginning
seems like generations have swept by. Holding the
portrait of the babe, could this really be me,
so young and unstable, like a tender leaf falling
off a tree, or as age elapse with time, such as a
child shedding its youth, lost in the memories of my mind.
was it so very long ago that I was an infant beautiful,
and so adorable! Where did the babe go, did time
vanish or could it be I never let go, or maybe
I've just grown, did I journey back into time
to recapture a fleeting moment so precious, and eternally divine,
because the innocence of my youth, will never ever die.

Carolyn Jeffries

My Dreams

As my head touches my pillow, and my mind starts to dream,
My spirits are lifted high to the brightest moonbeam.
Because that's where I sit with you holding me tight.
I relax and unwind for these feelings seem right.
You touch my face slightly with your soft fingertips,
You bend down to kiss me with sweet subtle lips.
You tilt my head slightly so your whisper reaches my ear,
You say with true emotion, "I love you and I'll always be here".
I've never been so happy, never felt so content.
I don't wonder if your words are real, I know that they're meant.
So as my dreams continue I fall deeper in love.
And when I wake each morning, I look to the heavens above,
And I pray to my angel to make my dreams come true;
So each night as I sleep I'll be lying beside you.

Michelle J. Evans

Mariposa

Dedicated to Linda's daughter.

Mariposa, mariposa, how beautiful
When you fly,
Are you looking for a mariposa guy?
I am just asking for I'm only a caterpillar
You see. But I could be so much more
If I knew you loved me.
So please stay awhile and flutter
about. For if you do, I'll know you
love me. And I'll surely come out.
We'll fly away together, me and you
Not as one mariposa and a caterpillar but
two.

Tim Boadway

Eva... a Glimpse of Sunlight

From Out the Shadows of a Viennese Wood

Smooth olive annularity, crescents, half moons, dual
satellites. Osteology above the neck. Black satin and
lace, staccato trills and wild strawberries. Avocados from
seed to visual prime... miniscule orange trees from expectorated
seed in an earthen terra cotta pot. A green leaf or three
or four? The old time new time voyager notices the sun filtering
in on the ochre walls. Perhaps they should have been painted
white? Time passes and moves on as the chin chin chinaman
strokes the ivory white whisps of a Manchurian Beard and
A french chime strikes softly on a late afternoon.

Berkeley California... an afternoon visit with a college friend
deep in Mathematical exercises as the writer took a break from her
studies of the aberrant mind.

Pat Brown

Movie in the Sky

Lying in a hammock is a delight
    On a lazy day in the summer's heat.
Clouds that make pictures are a sight,
    To wonder what they portray is a treat.

Racing horses with flying manes and tails,
    Change into playful kittens and dogs.
Boats come into view with billowing sails,
    On a lily pad are a trio of frogs.

Here comes the crocodiles with open jaws,
    They turn into a dragon breathing fire.
A lobster with antennae and open claws,
    And a clown walking a high wire.

The hunch back of Notre Dame comes into view,
    Ladies in hoop skirts and long curly hair.
It's like a Rose Bowl Parade it's true.
    After a stress filled day it's only fair,
To lie in a hammock and enjoy,
    The movie in the sky.

Virginia J. Brady

Impatience Is Not Gracious

Impatience jeopardizes sound reason and rhyme
Impatience wastes your time
Impatience fosters ill emotion
Oftentimes stirs up commotion!

Impatience is your enemy
Impatience churns anxiety
It lashes out unlovingly
with unkind locomotion!

It can cause you to slap a young child in the face when a
whack would be better in some other place!

Impatience kills devotion!

So if you can entertain the notion
Make a motion to scratch negative exposure
Keep your composure
Stop! Don't hit! Think!

"Impatience is not gracious!"

Rosemarie Caluori

The Northern Lights

The stars are brightly shining up above,
The moon is full and whitely bright tonight,
I shall be waiting soon, as Mourning Dove,
To greet the glorious Northern heavenly light.
They streak across the peaceful depths of sky,
They seem as beacons of an early flight.
I've watched this view with interest of eye,
From whence they'd come to give this glorious sight.
The Valkyries from afar bring nigh,
An ever unforgotten starry trail.
The crystal hues suspended ever high,
Light up the darkness as a silver sail.
The lights that shine sometimes are called "Great Wind,"
With brightness soft, no fear of growing dim.

Vernon E. Vidden

301

Friends

I met someone not long ago,
I've grown to love and cherish so.
Our friendship has grown quite rapidly,
You've brought lots of joy to the whole family.
My heart was hoping you'd be here forever,
But love has sparked and you must be together.
My tears flow freely and my heart is aching,
For the time is coming soon a departure you'll be making.
The memories we've made bring a smile to my face,
You could make me laugh just any place.
I want you to know just how great it's been,
No matter where you go, I'll always be your friend.

Libbie Windover

Inside-Out

If only one could share his thoughts
    For everyone to hear;
Then many misunderstandings
    Would truly disappear.

We hide so many inner feelings:
    Some good, some bad;
Until we create a situation
    That makes us very sad.

Why not try a different approach
    Honesty to all who want to hear,
And that would go a long way
    In making communication so clear!

So open up and banish fear
    Be courageous and share your inmost desires,
Putting an end to this senseless void
    And offer wisdom that truly inspires!

Grant A. Gentz

Recipe of Eternity

(1994)

When you are born you have an empty shopping bag. As you go through life the things you value and seek out are put into this bag. If you spend your time on pettiness, jealousy or cruelty these things will also be placed in your bag. The grocery bag that you carry though life will be filled with the things you spent your time seeking out during your life. When you move on to your afterlife you will sup off the feast made from the ingredients in your bag.

If during your life you spent time on hurting rather than loving, you will hurt in your afterlife. If you valued possessions and not people you will be surrounded by material objects and yet be alone. You will determine the richness of the feast that you will sup for eternity; determining your own fate to heaven or hell. Every kind word, every warm smile you give will add to the richness of your feast. Every life that is better for having known you, every friend who you value, will add to the richness and flavor of your feast. Every decision you make is an ingredient for your own recipe of eternity.

Bryan L. Rosen

The Meaning of Life

The meaning of life is like a star.
It's so far...far....away.
No one can grasp it,
Even though it is right in front of them.
Some people don't know it's there,
Some people just don't care.
When I think about it,
I know it's there,
My problem is I don't know where.
The meaning of life is like a star,
It's so far ... far... away,
And no one can grasp it.

Rob Eberhardt

Spring In Massachusetts - 1980

Someone built a woodland spring many,
Many years ago.
Ringed with the farmer's rocks and
Ancient moss, it flows brightly, clearly on;
Sending a gurgling brook winding through
The oak forest.
One warm day we rediscovered it and, for
A few moments, felt at peace in this
Topsy-turvy world.
Overhead two nesting owls protested
Mildly at the unaccustomed intrusion.
Nearby, the April sun shone through
The tree slits and nudged the flowers
On the forest floor to come awake.
It's spring! It's spring! It's spring!
Cried a titmouse high in an oak tree.

Henry J. Adams

The Rosary In My Pocket

There is a Rosary in my pocket
which I lovingly pray,
leading me to Jesus
and teaching me His way.

As I finger each bead,
I ponder His love and His life
with all the joys, sorrows and strife.
What is mine compared to His, I wonder?
And trustingly say, "Mother, take over!"

Mary, then teaches me her loving way
and leads me to know her Son more today.
She helps me trust His plan for my life
and accept with love the pain and the strife.

To the Rosary in my pocket
I have been faithful and true.
Lovingly fingering each bead, each decade,
learning the truth it contains
to live my life for Jesus
and to be true to His Holy Name.

Alma J. Lum

One Mistake

Because of one mistake
A lot of hardship you had to take
In spite of all the pain
You did your best to obtain
Sanity, Peace of mind,
and the will power to be kind.

You found the courage to make a call
and took the risk that changed it all.
You are now beginning a whole new life
With a precious girl and a wife
Life has really been putting you to the test
I am extremely glad things are changing for the best.

You are my brother
Better than any other
Deserving the best
more than all the rest.
Congratulations on this very special day
Wishing you the best in every possible way!

Shelly D. Garrison

What Is Love

Love is not bought, altho it cost everything, yet is priceless
Love is a rarity seldom found, but many times is within one grasp
And maybe had only for the asking.
Love is a priceless gift yet, it cost heaven, God's only son.
The jewel of great price.
Love is found in the eyes of a child.
When she looks at her mother and says I trust you.
My life is in your hands to mold and keep secure.
Love is in a forgiving heart of a mother
When she can weep over her wayward children
After they have broken her heart
Love is giving of ones self sacrificial
Wanting nothing in return but to be loved.
Love is a heart that doesn't look for self
but loves to serve others.
What is love? Love is honesty, truthful and
always caring. Always trusting and faithful.
I found love when I met Christ
He is our true love.

Mae Lingold

A Perfect Creation

A baby is a just cause for celebration;
A little person, it's a perfect creation!
A miniature example of God's success;
A masterpiece, as such, one must have to confess.
A bundle of joy, no gift can compare;
In triumphs, and in defeats, a parent can share.
An angel, full of innocence, completely pure;
They'll become what you help make them, you can be sure.
With hard work, good morals, you'll show them the way;
They are worth the effort, almost all will say.
They are your tiny piece of immortality;
Be happy and proud of your prosperity!

Rebecca J. Gervais

Love is Blind, Love is Strange

Love is blind, love is strange.
It is also kind, warm, and unforgiving touch.
Two people sharing apart of the other.
Reaching into a feeling of understanding, and caring.
Warm as the summer breeze.
Two souls which has to meet.
Belonging to each other.
As the stars and the universe.
Strong as the wind blows.
A love that will always grow.
As deep as the ocean and sea.
A true love that will always be.

Mona Clark

Success

Success can be defined in many, different ways,
to some, it is spectacular, to others, it's a phase.
It can be defined "large", like a single person helping all,
or with many helping one, none of their's can be defined as
"small."
It can be created by one person's hard work and dedication,
or another person doing his best with determination,
to create success, some use amounts of skill with compassion,
while others just operate within a typical fashion,
but for those who cannot even find one,
just look back at what you have done,
a success may just arise,
and maybe you will be greatly surprised.

Derek Fox

"Spring Is Coming"

Earth joyfully already welcomes spring.
From lethargy waken up, washed by rain,
Her veins swelled with pulsating water,
Soon adorn all land with new plants again.

Returns dozing energy of life,
Fauna and flora discards covering
Which sheltered them from winter colds,
Spring sun clasps them tenderly
And cuddles with motherly love and warmth.

Soon, starts flowing awakened stream
Bringing water to thirsty plants and soil,
Whole flora will burst with light green,
Colorful flowers will brighten meadows and fields.

Birds return with whole gamma of trills,
Beautiful butterflies dancing in the sun,
And swarms of insects resound all around,
Buzzing, humming, chirping and singing,
Springtime feasts nature own serenade.

Anna Olechowska-Moskwa

Real Friendships

Value your friendships near; value your friendships far.
Nothing is as valuable as true friendships are.

Friendships of all kinds are tested day in and day out.
Till proven they are true beyond a shadow of doubt.

A friendship can never be bought; can never be sold.
If you're lucky to own one you need never be told.

Friendships exist forever; friendships disappear.
The loss of a friendship is an underlying fear.

Through our own folly or through plain ignorance
from the start some friendships haven't a chance.

Some friendships need to be amply nourished to grow.
Still, will prove lasting no matter how slow.

Others blossom and grow without a second thought,
rekindling these friendships need never be sought.

Be wise and treat dearly the friendships you possess.
Give the care each are due; your devotion do confess.

Don't hesitate to voice the gratitude you feel.
Of all the intangibles on earth, a friendship is most real.

Lois Lilian McCoy Wegner

The Dream

I dreamed I climbed the mountain, and I met the old man there.
Standing in his flowing robe, with his long white hair.

He looked like an older Jesus, and we sat and talked awhile.
As I recall the words he said, I just can't help but smile.

He said a wise man told me, or was it just a dream?
Things ain't always what they seem, not always what they seem.

He said I dreamed I climbed the mountain, and I met the old man there.
Standing in his flowing robe, with this long white hair.

He looked like an older Jesus, and we set and talked awhile.
As I recall the words he said, I just can't help but smile.

He said a wise man told me, or was it just a dream?
Things ain't always what they seem, not always what they seem.

Well about that time I woke up, lying in my bed.
A smile crossed my lips, as I remembered what he'd said.

He said a wise man told me, or was it just a dream?
Things ain't always what they seem, not always what they seem.

Was it real or just a dream? Things ain't always what they seem,
no not always what they seem.

Barney Greenwood

Our Lives

The fabric of life to behold!
Intertwined between you and me.
With a gift of one more day
We cherish with care.

We hope to spend it well
to gain simple pleasures
Gently hearing the sounds
of laughing children

With rain drops falling
gently on their heads.
As they play and chatter
Among the trees.
And cooling breezes.

Reflecting through this fabric
For a serene return of love.
Memories of childhood,
Always at my mother's knee.

Love, patience, fear
to comfort us all
We all gathered around to walk in faith and love.

Sophia E. Conley

My Big Oak Tree

When I die, please bury me.
Underneath my, big oak tree.

So I can rest in peace,
comfortably in a shade.
Hearing the ants feast,
in a marching parade.

To hear tapity tap, from a dancing lizard.
And the caterpillars clap, and an audience is heard.

I will be entertained,
and death is the only fee.
The pretty birds are to blame,
for loving to sing for free.

And to hear that pretty cricket, playing her violin.
I don't have to buy a ticket, she just lets me in.

She always lets me see,
for I cheer at her.
Everyone is talented underneath this tree,
my oak cemetery theater.

Juan P. Perez Dad

Listen......

I love you, beyond all words, beyond all feeling, beyond all time.
I love you more than eternity can endure.
I know for I created eternity.....
I love you far more than the longing in a lost child's cry,
Echoing in My heart forever,
And My heart longs to comfort you....My lost child.
I love you with a patience, that has waited for you since the
 beginning of time.
Sincerity that can only accept....
That the choice between truth and a lie is your own.
Passion....that sent My only Son to His death, and the gates of hell,
To bear your pain to relieve your suffering.
The unique miracle of all creation speaks of My love, My care for you,
If you will listen.....
My love caresses your senses on a soft spring morning.
Shimmers across the water on a moonlit night.
Whispers through the trees on the voice of the wind.
Sings to you from snow-crested mountains.
Thunders through dark, yawning caverns.
The earth is filled with the everlasting sound of it....
Listen.....I love you.

Deborah Backes

Sea of Cowboy Hats

Dedicated to the person who never lost hope,
I love you Ricky McGowan.

If only you could look out your window,
Than you'd see us your friends
There 24 hours waiting for you to wake,
From the road it looked like a
Gang but it was a sea of cowboys
Pulling for our dear friend
We camped out there at U.C. Davis
Waiting for the news,
Many sat an' stared up at
Your window as I did we
Played songs such as "The Dance"
And "I Didn't Know My Own Strength"
Then the day came when you
Woke but you could not walk or
Talk you had to learn it all
Again but we were friends in a sea of cowboy hats

Jennifer Combs

Freedom

So many people say I'm different, that I'm just not the same,
So I'm all alone in this world, just the opposite of fame.
Sometimes I long to dissolve into the ground,
To disappear into the night where I couldn't be found.
I don't understand why it had to be,
That they say I can't fit in, no reason I can see.
Though I'm not prosperous and rich in every thing I do,
Should I be treated like a slave even though I'm just like you.
I have dreams and goals like everyone I know,
Like I had wishes when I was little, wishing I would grow.
I know I look different, just outside its true,
But inside, you'll realize we're the same, me and you.
I've talked to preachers and judges and they just don't agree,
And I yelled, "This is inequity, why can't I just be free."
All the time I wonder what the real difference is in you and me,
But the real question is whether I will ever be set free.

Mallory Gabard

A Dear Brother

Yes, dear brother, I remember today,
when as a youth you'd run and play.
Life was new and worries few,
and, oh the love we had for you!
So soon you grew to be a man,
with chores to do; a life to span.
A job to find; a look ahead;
you were up to the task; and on you sped.
Your country called, your answer gave,
you sailed to North Africa; to Russia away.
You also sailed the Pacific blue.
But listen, Brother, last night as I slept,
a most beautiful vision before me crept.
I was looking outside, it was summertime!
The sun how it shone, children's play sublime.
The old homestead, a vision divine!
But how only memory floods my soul.
Yet I am richer than of old for,
Oh, the pearl and the gold
your love hath left in trust with me.

Hobart Eaton

No Face

What's wrong with me, I'd like to know?
Am I just a nothing? A comedy show?
I turn around to see the stares.
I wonder why I get such glares
My eyes start to water, my head starts to spin.
I try to think back, when did this all begin?
It was that part of my life where nothing went right.
I thought I was over this.
I thought I had long since seen the light.
I still have that feeling deep inside
it's a part of me that will not hide.
I grow so tired of the life that I live.
Is there something unaccomplished,
could there be something I didn't give.
I've given it all, I pray every night.
"Please let me someday be able to give up this fight".
Do I even know what I'm fighting for.
Am I being selfish, do I just want more?
I need love is that too much to ask?
Do I have the strength to tear off this mask?

Michelle Wilson

"Too Close To Home"

The reason for this red ribbon I bear:
For the crimes of others, we pay the cost;
For the silent tear drops that we all share,
In remembrance of those six 'neath the frost.
We know not what's gained, only what we've lost.
Too young a heart made to too old an eye
By lives and loves forever to us lost.
So I hope you'll grasp when I say that I.....
Well, forgive me, my heart, but I can cry.

Hope D. Throckmorton

Life?

What is life?
Is there a purpose for this whole charade?
Is there an end to this twisty, bumpy road?
Is there ever a straight, paved, easy highway,
instead of this never ending, dirt path?
Why are we here? What is going on?
Is this a game?
O, please get me off this runaway trail!
If there is a purpose for us all being on
this dirt road, please let me know before
the path turns into a Dead end.

Sarah Beth Brochu

If There Is A God

If there is a God, why are children hungry and poor?
If there is a God, why are children often abused?
If there is a God, why are children crippled and lame?
If there is a God, why are the children always hurt?
If there is a God, why do some live in poverty?
If there is a God, why are some disabled and maimed?
If there is a God, why do adults suffer hunger?
If there is a God, why are the elderly abused?
If there is a God, why must the elderly suffer?
If there is a God, why has our society failed?
If there is a God, why do bad things outnumber good?
If there is a God, why does malevolence abound?
If there is a God, why do the lawless gangs run free?
If there is a God, why is the Mafia untouched?
If there is a God, why Narcotics? Why abortion?
There most certainly is a God, He's alive and well.
God created a perfect world, it was man who fell.
Man was given his own free will, disobeyed God's plan,
Who can help us, forgive our sin? No one but God can.

David R. Clukie

Nature's Reflections

In sparkling sky-dyed waters where migrant sea turtle roam,
An ancient land of enchanting castles and exotic gardens lies
Encircled by misty shoreline breakers, delicately veiled in foam,
While Neptune's etched sea shells whisper ocean lullabies.

Near palm tree silhouettes float elegant lotus blossoms serene,
As nature's composition and Oriental architecture complement
On an artistic landscape and brilliant seascape of aquamarine,
The recollection of which may stimulate creative sentiment.

In days of yore skillful divers discovered snow-white pearls,
Cultivated in conjunction with a powerful sculptress sea,
Yet within a drop of water, a universe reflection whirls
Eclipsing natural treasures portrayed in poetic melody.

Where the Inland Sea and Pacific Ocean convergence intersect,
When the deep tidal flow of full moon currents has begun,
The sea, gradually falling five feet to ocean elevation, reflects
Cosmic patterns in its whirlpools at the birthplace of the sun.

Carolyn K. King

"Daddy"

"Ouch Daddy,
I've skint my knee.
Please kiss it,
And make it better for me."

Anytime I needed you,
You'd lift me off my feet.
One hug from you was all it took,
To make my life complete.

Your hands that seemed so strong to me,
They were the solution when I could not see.
You'd lift me high above the crowd,
Because you were my daddy I was so proud.

All my life,
I've looked up to you.
You hung each and every star,
Including the moon.

Looking out my window,
I think of you each day.
And how I'll always be your little girl,
No matter from how far away.

Danielle Coleman

Finding Me!

Shed no tears for me,
I am not alone
Don't you see them by my side?
They hold me up when I grow weak, their strong silent
smiles give me encouragement.

I need not demand
anything from them because
They give so freely.
They offer a sense of self, a type of renewing
that never withers or grows stale.

It's unlike that feeling from before.
An isolated, cold hand trying to offer direction?
They have depth, vintage, an airy
Karma that holds me still when I shake.

I used to crave love and
acceptance. I used to
want what was not mine.
Now they have taught me what is of value.
something that will never pale
over time...Myself!!!

Camille Linton

In Love With Love

How green and inviting is the golf course
   and how stately all the surrounding trees
Intoxicating the fragrance of the garden
   how gentle the caress of a loving breeze.

How pretty and cloudless is the sky
   and mysterious the far off hills
How busy at work the honey bees
   and beautiful, songs of Whippoorwills.

How tranquil and lovely the snow capped mountains
   and serene the valleys below
Now and then one sees a flighty hummingbird
   and at night the fireflies aglow.

How blue-green is the ocean
   and sandy the beaches where people go
How starlight and twinkling are the nighttimes
   and how bright the moon that glows.

One might say life is near perfect
   like the world in heaven above
A song expressed by emotions
   when one is in love with love.

William Henry Jones

Love

Love is more than a four letter word
   it's feeling and emotions:
   that are free as a bird,
   it catches you at your most
   vulnerable stage.

When you're wrecked, and full
   of rage,

It steps in, and takes control;
   of your mind, body and soul.
   Leaving you helpless to its hold,

   You see, the word love is very bold
   drawing you physically, and emotionally
   into its fold.

So never say it won't happen;
   to you falling so deep in love
   until you don't know what to do?

   Because it happened to me, you see,
   bitten by the four letters so small,
   but yet so powerful called,
Love.

Robin McGee

A Birthday Poem of Love

   A fathers love, a fathers joy
a visit at work from wife daughter and little boy.
On this day my birthday has come with love in my heart anticipating
fun. The long ride home seems nothing at
all when I hear the voice of my loved ones give me a call.
My wife with hair of beauty and fire her eyes of blue
my one desire. My daughter is sweet
as the honey from the tree, I always enjoy
the play time with me. My son is becoming quite a little man I love
the time we spend anytime that we can.
A family with love is like a strong mountain top,
it weathers with time but cannot be stopped,
like the rushing river's in the valley deep and wide
the love in my family will always be side by side.
I love my family with all my heart, as we walk through life
until we part, and when the day comes when I must leave,
they always will know they have my love to believe.
like the rushing rivers, the valley's wide, the wind blows through the
trees, a bird at your side, love it is deep, love it is wide, without
love we would wither up and die.

Todd Fancett

Without a Choice

Dedicated in memory of the children: without a choice.
You didn't know where it happened, your mind wasn't sure.
Your body had a need, there seemed no cure.
An hour of pain for a moment of pleasure,
from the disease of the world your ounce was measured.

But you had no money, so how could you pay?
You didn't care, had to "get fixed" and on your way.
In payment I was conceived, and in the same I was lost.
Mommy ran up the bill, but I paid the cost!

I remember your face, pretty...but with eyes dark and lonely.
I was needing something too, but not for you to hold me.
A thirty minute life and I was no more,
for you see, I too craved the "glass pipe and all its glore."

You gave your dreams with one hand,
why take mine with the other?
You just wanted to get high, I just wanted a mother!
The dream you gave up was a career, a home, and things of nice.
The dream you took from me was but one precious thing ...
Called Life!

Gregory Keith Ballenger

Arlington

White markers line the rolling hills of green;
Each monument illuminates a grave.
Around those countless stones of death is seen
The flag these brave men fought and died to save.
Beneath the sod the soldiers rest at last;
The sounds of war no longer fill their ears.
Their peace is won from terrors of the past,
The terrors that they fought despite their fears.
Above those dead a flame burns without end,
A spark affirming dreams yet heaven-sent,
A longing wish for freedom that transcends
The valor of a mortal president.
The sacrifice they made to an ideal
Commands us all to watch with the same zeal.

David Oyama

Love

From the bottom of my heart
I see the elegance of your quietness
Engaging your innocence
As an angle imaginary.

In my daily,
I wouldn't dream of going
Without your scent
Your exotic aroma coming
From surface of your shining hair
As spring's winds in your hair.

As a pigeon,
I would like to be freely
Just by being near
To discover what comes into ...
Even, travelling oceans,
Treading sands in islands, my dreamlands,
Whatever, I always see your heart
As my nestle
Whose gentle love is shown
By yours special smiles and glances.

Domingos Ramos

306

Desperately Needing You

As I sit watching the horses play in the open fields. And the birds
gliding in the sky. With the wind blowing gently thru the trees. I
wonder why am I here alone without you. Each night I lay in bed I
hold and squeeze my pillow pretending it's you. My heart aches for
you so badly that the pain just rushes thru my entire body. My eyes
won't stop crying and the tears won't stop falling. Although there
was a good reason for all of this. It's only making me stronger each
day. For each day that I am away from you, my love grows deeper by
the minute. For I love you very much and this I will never give
up. Because you are the only one I want in my life. And as long
as I or you may live and walk on this earth. I will love you like I
have never loved anyone before.

Ricardo Losano

Flying

A rushing, rippling water sound
All else is still except for an occasional breeze
Nothing but country and hills filled with trees
Surround this valley that the river runs down
There is no one around and I'm miles from town
As I raise to the air a fly on a line
And work it to water to see what I'll find

Two O'clock, Ten O'clock, Two O'clock, Ten
As I move with a rhythm again and again
The weight of my line lifts the fly further out
As I spot guide my fly in hope of rising a trout
Again and again, and with the right hatch
If I work the right pocket I'll hook a great catch
And lose all other thoughts in this competitive match

Yes, again and again at this endless old game
Yes, over and over; yet, never the same
Just me and nature so calm and serene
No traces of human kind in thoughts to be seen
year after year in excitement I Fly
Relaxing from life as time passes me by

Dennis Wheeler

Me

I am the sum of all my former "me's,"
Over the years, so many changing "me's", each one a little bit
different from the one before.

All running together in endless change,
Yet linked by memory and feeling -

No one 'me' quite like another; but remembrance holding
together all the changing molecules of human growth and learning.

Forming and reforming in endless cycles a new and yet unchanged
pattern of life, streaming thru Time, sometimes slowly, sometimes
faster than the Soul would wish - hopefully leading
to a more perfect ending than could be dreamed of.

So I live, and love, and learn, and join the flowing throng
of human beings assigned to Life on planet Earth, for one
small minuscule of Everlasting time.

Hoping one's presence in some small fashion has made a positive
mark along the way to improve the total sum of Life.

Virginia Tomlin

Whom Do We Mourn?

Whom do we mourn?
Surely not the dead
Who have finally reached their goal!
Were we to live two life times through
Yet would such glory to us be denied.
'Tis the living then we mourn
Seeking, striving, yearning
Each his separate path
To some uncertain destiny
Some thousand days away.

Those left behind in a sea of tears,
Weep for yourselves.
His eyes are bright with the joy of returning
To whence he came.
The circle is complete
And the real meaning of life is just beginning.
How do I know?
Look to your soul
'Twas ever there.

Henrietta Toner

Be Who God Made You

Have you ever thought about yesterday?
Or today when you had no fun?
Or maybe talked to a boy and thought what you said was dumb.
You think about tomorrow and what lies ahead,
you wish you didn't have to go to school
so you could sleep late in bed.
You wake up in the morning not knowing what to do,
you get up saying some words your mother wouldn't approve.
You look in the mirror to see your cute face,
but because it doesn't look like a models
you think it's a disgrace.
You go to school criticizing yourself
wishing you aren't who you are.
You wish you were some famous movie star.
You drive yourself insane thinking how you hate your name.
But God doesn't care who you are,
He loves everyone the same
Remember to always be yourself and never be a fake,
Cause God made you who you are
and He never makes a mistake.

Allison Ward

Going Toward the Light

We go toward a light at birth.
The same thing happens at the time of death.
One light guides us to life on earth.
The other light guides us to a life after death.

While being born it seems like a dark tunnel we pass through,
Until we see a bright light at the end of the birth canal.
It's the same in death, everything is dark at first,
Then there's a bright light which leads us to a life eternal.

Isn't it a wonderful conception,
These two spiritual happenings
Being guided by a bright light.
One man made, the other of God's making.

It's sad some of us don't follow a spiritual light from birth,
Where we begin life with an innocence so pure,
To the light after death
Which leads us to heavens door.

If we don't start following Christ's teachings,
We might end up in eternal darkness with Lucifer,
Instead of following the bright light to heaven
To be with God our Father.

Dolly Braida

My Closest Friend

We left me on the 31st of March 1996,
all my feelings they did mix.
You left me alone and hurt,
even before I found out you did more than flirt.
I really want you back,
that's the true fact.
You want me as a friend only,
like "my little pony."
Even though you hurt me, I can forgive,
as long as being hurt I don't have to relieve.
Maybe, someday, we can start again,
no matter what you'll always be my friend!
I'll never force you into love,
'cause by my side is the white dove.
Someday, if you choose, you can bring
your heart back to me,
I'll heal it, and make it better, with out one plea.
Even if you don't, you'll always have a special place in my heart,
'cause of that well remain friends, and never part!

Melanie A. Gibbons

The Special Gift

It was, as I recall, a most pristine moment
When my woeful heart was free of torment
Soothed by the peacefulness emanated from you
Mesmerized by your peeks of azure blue

Humbled at the base of your majestic grandeur
I heard the voice of Jesus— my Savior
Drawing ever so near, yearning only to hear
What soon was audible and crystal clear

He wanted to tell me and completely reveal
A simple truth— undeniably real
Not materialistic, vast fortunes, or fame
Of no personal sacrifice or shame

Unselfishly given so I would always see
This gift of beauty— entirely free
Oh, my Grand Tetons, in all your loving splendor
Hermetically sealed in my heart forever

Annette Stuckey

To My Mother

I can always talk to you,
No matter what my problem is,
I can count on you to be there,
'Cause you're the best friend that there is,

I couldn't ask for more from you,
You give me all you've got,
You're there for me when I need you,
Whether you have the time or not,

I hope that you can count on me
The way I can count on you,
I hope that I can be your friend,
And care the way you do,

I hope someday we'll stop arguing,
And really get along,
I'm just trying so hard to get things right,
And trying not to get them wrong,

So I hope you can believe me,
When I say you're the best mother that could be,
I'm glad that you're my mother,
And you can count on me.

Elizabeth Gilbert

Late Bloomer

Oh late bloomer what shyness
    conceals your creative exposure?
Do you know solitude and difference
    makes one lose ones composure?
Oh late bloomer if only you could take a deep breath
    and remain adequately quaint.
Listen to your souls interior
    calling you of your restraint.
Oh late bloomer with your talent
    hidden so within you.
Ten, twenty years,
    and it all begins to debut.
Oh late bloomer the skills you have are many
    and too symbolic to express.
God given ability was held from others
    as a treasurer for future success.
Oh late bloomer you are not late,
    just reserved in being mystical.
Like the pearly gates of heaven,
    it is all clearly metaphysical.

John T. Davis Jr.

Fractured

Hearts, minds spirits, fractured, faith in leaders, gone.
United people shocked, lucid only where their world is considered.
Senseless starvation, beatings, murder, no end in sight.
Men holding signs, "Will work for food".... denotes disgust,
a cowering, spiritless, repelling feeling for blameless leaders.
All considerations, studying, calculating, cannot attain a viable
    solution.
Society abandons the horror with closed eyes and hearts.
Cars for homes, cardboard boxes for shelter.
Parents, children, in line for a possible hot meal in a rich country
we call home.
Knowing...those who have less, give more while those with plenty,
do not care or share.
Acquiescing, a partial answer, give until it hurts, only then,
will ascertain a minimal amount of suffering which will permeate
the earthly circumspect being.
The fracture, a paradox, should never have reach such proportions,
a phenomenon of eventuality in itself.
A paradigm in which a fortunate parent will have no choice but to
explain to his/her child.
Action is at hand for one day it will be all who seek refuge,
in a cardboard box.

Cindy Green

"Can't Understand Why Some People Don't Like Me"

I like the rain upon my face.
I like a child's tender embrace.
I like to hear a symphony.
Can't understand why some people don't like me.

I like to walk along the shore.
I like to hear the ocean's roar.
I like to pick an apple tree.
Can't understand why some people don't like me.

When will the world be a friendly world.
When will the tears run dry.
When will they end this unrest and turmoil.
When can we walk with heads up high.

I like the scent of sweet perfume.
I like to see flowers in bloom.
I like to live in harmony.
Can't understand why some people don't like me.

Ralph Montello

Untitled

I almost drowned in the waters of insecurity
  floated with no direction. I could not see.

Swam in a wave of violence
  felt the salty fear of my own sins wash over me.

Kneeled on a rocky bed of stone cold love
  endured as it bit into me.

Bleed and cried as you promised
  never again. It would not be.

Fought through my own emotional undertows
  sucking at my sanity.

Kneeled up on my own
  braved the new cold air from my old familiar sea.

Crawled through it all to recovery
  Inch by Inch, Meter by Meter I crawled out of that world and upon

  a beach of recovery.

Standing strong in the face of it all
  seeing, feeling knowing, accepting, approving all of me, both the
  warm dry land and that old familiar sea.

   Tamela A. Fish

The Middle Child

I've come with two wrappers instead of one
I am the daughter you craved, not the son
I've been crushed and mangled by that complex system
But my desires and quests have accompanied wisdom
I've got warning labels down my back
They've been there since I've been packed
My warranty runs out when I leave home
This garbage bag feels Ok when not alone
Although my clothing is intriguing
It's really my soul that you are eating
I'm damaged goods, that's what I am
The leftest ruled by Uncle Sam
I feel the pain when I inhale
I am a shiny product-inside I'm stale
I've been shipped through postal systems
I sometimes win, I sometimes fail
(And you wouldn't believe what they do to your mail)

   Kimberly Marie Carlson

Balls Out

Some things you just don't forget like childhood phone numbers, where friends, light years later, still pick up, and you, one thousand miles away, explaining Santa Fe is New Mexico, still wishing you were there, inside the musty ten, watching game shows, then going out to play some catch at 17404 Longfellow Street;

Where Hanzel the Dachshund ruled the grass triangle that divided the streets, the Bermuda of Hazel Crest, forcing kids to think twice about pedaling through, and, now, only having to deal with the occasional lost souls who roll down their windows to ask for directions;

And, if, no, when the ball got away and started rolling down the street, you'd throw your mitts at it and nine times out of ten wouldn't stop it. Your fault, you'd fetch; his, he'd go.

That's just the way it was. He was the catcher and you were the pitcher, but then one day you went private and he went public. He went out for the football team, you learned a foreign language.

"Howya say it again?" He'd ask. And you'd tell him. But things were never quite the same, despite all the Spanish-uttered f***s.

Still, some things you just don't forget, like how you became blood brothers with valiant pricks of thumb, and how, despite all errors of circumstance and all passed balls of chance, balls out; you were best friends, and would always be, because you still had your memories, of playing catch outside of 17404 Longfellow Street.

   Tom Ragan

Ode To The Honeysuckle

Oh most unpretentious vine, no status seeker thou!
You hide the pigsty from our view, at noontide shade the cow.
Our faithful dog finds cool content in dust beneath your bower
And strangers passing by the gate take refuge from a shower.
The hummingbird drinks deeply from the nectar in your stone
And we lean to pick your blossoms as you twine around our door.
You offer many favors, but even more than these,
You bless us all with sweet perfume on summer's gentle breeze.

   Gerry Luther

Prom Night "Chicken"

Driving home to their children
in the dark of the night,
All at once it was upon them,
a terrifying sight.
Two cars racing down the highway,
side by side.
They knew for a certainty,
they would collide.
They pulled onto the shoulder
in a great, swift swerve.
But it was too late, a head-on collision
happened on the curve.
Five lives were taken
that deadly night in June.
A ghastly sight, in the glowing
light of the moon.
A prom night game of "Chicken"
left three children orphaned.
There is no way ever,
that blow can be softened.

   Marie E. Martinez

Life

Life, is but a collection;
Of memories and recollection;

Of all the good times;
And nursery rhymes;

Filled, with the sounds of joy;
With the arrival, of a new baby boy,

Or a new baby girl;
To give you a whirl!

A teary eye;
When you shared a cry;

Or the sound of laughter;
That lasted, well after;

The smiles were gone;
With approaching dawn;

Of which, some were good and some were bad;
Some were happy and some were sad;

Of those who lived and those who died;
Oh, how I cried and cried;

But most of all, I'm glad;
For the chance at life, that I had!

   Robert E. Filip

A Whisper In The Night

They now just hold each other, with nothing left to say,
For a madman's bomb had just taken their only child away.

They are both now members of a broken-hearted clan,
They are the tortured victims of the inhumanity of man.

As he watched her restless slumber, he asked the question why?:
Why must it be the innocent children, that always have to die.

Now two broken hearts, with souls that are filled with pain,
Must bear the pain together or both will go insane.

He feels he must protect her from the demons of the night.
So he holds her while she sleeps and prays for the coming of the light.

Then he tells her that he loves her and everything will be alright.
As he touches her with a soft caress and a whisper in the night.

James W. Duncan

Rainbows

For JC

In my life there is rain:
  it is the tests and trials that come to me
  that block my vision of the sunlight
  and make me forget that the rain washes all things clean.
In my life there is rain:
  it is the tear drops welling up in my eyes, rolling down my
cheeks.

In my life there is sunlight:
  it is the light in my heart from Jesus, my Savior
  that warms my life and dries up the rain
  and brings out the beauty in the storms.
In my life there is sunlight:
  His name is Jesus; He's my best friend.

Today I saw a rainbow, God's promise of everlasting love.
Looking up to where the sun shines through the rain,
I see a rainbow in my life.
It is you....

Lynn Martin

"Side By Side"

  Side by side we both lie, it seems so
strange you and I!!!
  I know this feeling that we both feel must be
love for we both know it's truly - real!!!
  Many things happen in mysterious ways, but
this beats all and I know it's not a fantasy!
  It's really real!
For years we loved, we laughed and we've cried
as friends.
Sometimes even side by side...
I love you and you love me!
I finally found true love,
Something I thought I would never get to see.
  You finally found true love, God knows,
who would have ever thought your true love
ended up - simply Me!

Rose Dawson

Forever Momma's Baby

Oh gentle babe, you little sleepy head,
  Whose tiny curls caress a tired shoulder,
Softly stroking your fevered brow,
  It's Momma, forever rocking... rocking.

Someday you'll be big and strong,
  Someday you will marry!
Will you remember then, sweet baby dear,
  Your Momma, forever rocking you close to her heart.

Jennie C. Kowalski

Speed

He never refused long chains of Lucky Strikes!
Black coffee pours down a spout through his
cup! Surgical instruments, pens and papers,
time the march of death! Swollen ruins of time:
Catch the imageries of rotten-wallpaper-paste!
His poetry lines the attic! F**k every goddamned
tear of success! Time is but brief! Inside, he
dies of cancer! Brittle concludes! Blows to
oblivion: Does heaven wait? Yes, it's a Prussic
Acid Jar! Screw and unscrew the cap! Bitter almonds
are razor sharp! The few decide! Search his closets!
The son-of-a-bitch is gone! Between the immediate
sheets, are scars of Cobra Toxin!

Thomas R. Shoemake

Love Through Gentle Eyes

Love can involve a gentle touch
so why do we fall in love so much.
Love can be such a fuss but,
you must make that choice and don't
deny us.

How do we love thee, should we
travel by car, plane, or just wait by
the sea.
Is love found in your gentle eyes,
or maybe that love is just a moment
in disguise.
Do you see it in your mind, or
does it tingle when you're intertwined.

We dream about love everyday and
hoping to meet that special person when we pray.

Let's take a walk down the road
we all know, and it's just possible you will
find and show your love can grow.

Stuart Rosman

To Be

Somewhere in time, I am.
I wonder tho,
about this space, this place.
Where am I to go...to be.

A journey tis never a journey
lest it ends...and begins.
The selfless search is the search for self.
But who really know this.

The eagle flaps its wings
and flight embodies its grace.
But what of the journey...
has it begun....or ended.

Each breath bears witness
to a new moment, a new journey.
Each dream dazzles the viewer
as does a new beginning...to a new searcher.

But for those who have spread their wings:
New beginnings are never seen nor ended.
And the joy of being is the gift
So flap those wings...and be...just Be!

Kurt Casper

Night Stalkers

Here's a tale of something scary
The night is spooky and very dreary
Up the block, you hear dogs barking
On the streets, you see thugs walking
It's best to stay inside your house
But watch out for that mutated mouse
Knock! Knock!
Your girlfriend's at the door
Who cares, she's ugly
She looks like a boar!
What's that you hear outside your window?
"It's a vampire!" You scream. "It's time to go!"
But hold up a minute, you're running way too slow
The vampire grabs you and bites your neck
And you think to yourself, "Oh what the heck!"
You're turning into a vampire, and that's the end of that!
Unpleasant Night!

Kimani Chesterfield

Wisdom's Price

I am growing older
aged with each oncoming day.
The rose tint in my glasses
has dimmed to a cloudy grey.

Could this be Wisdom
who now beats upon my door?
And if I choose to open it,
will I be disillusioned even more?

Fearful questions smother me -
Will I be as bitter as they?
No, my writing saves my soul.
I will pay Wisdom another way.

So, I now polish my glasses
and, for a while, my conscience feels safer.
My smiles reflect a tranquil mind,
but, oh, the bitterness of my paper.

Lee Bradfield

My Mother and Me

On the day of my birth
So many people welcomed me to earth

With my tiny hands and tiny feet
She was the first I just had to meet

Her hair was long, thick and black
Her beauty had nothing to lack

She had just given me my life
She was my father's wife

She kept me close to her side
I knew from her, nothing could hide

She had a busy schedule to keep
That didn't include much sleep

She always had a smile and a song to sing
In her life I was the most important thing

With a kiss to start the day
Good morning is what she'd always say

In such a little time so fast I grew
Years went by how fast they flew

I'm glad God chose my mother for me
She is exactly what I thought she'd be

Nancy Carol Chatlas

Goodbye, My Friend

God in his mercy gave us a light,
It brightened our lives and warmed our hearts;
But God in his wisdom saw fit to take her
It was time to say farewell and let her soul depart.

Now she is crowned with the love of God,
The one she served with faith and love;
Now she is crowned with the love she left behind,
She lives in the presence of God, in her home above,

Farewell, dear friend, there's no more pain,
Your work is done, there's no more strife.
Your loving thoughts and caring deeds live on and on,
There is no death, there is eternal life.

Nelle Edgin

Sunrise Sunset

Sunrise, sunset;
Can't you see what it means to me?
The wonder,
The beauty,
The splendor of it all for everyone to see.
No matter who you are,
Where you are from, or
Where you are at right now,
God made it for all to see and adore.

Sunrise, sunset;
Can't you see what it means to me?
The beauty of its golden colors and the magic of it all,
Seems to send your mind soaring about every little thing.
It's for everyone to see,
God made it to keep us all living in perfect harmony.

Sunrise, sunset;
Can you see what it all means to me now?

Janie Kovalak

Upon Some Dark Night

Upon some dark night, many ages hence,
When youth and I are but a memory,
If life, for life, seems meager recompense
And brings each painful day new injury,
Take this forgotten poem from where it lies
On paper yellowed by the passing years,
And let its peace illuminate your eyes
Which now, perhaps, are brimmed with silent tears.
Know that my love for you can not be swayed
By baser elements of Fate or Time,
And that my love, thought vast, is scarce conveyed
Within the confines of this simple rhyme.
For if you wish to be with such as I,
I will return, though Hell itself deny.

Loren Higbee

Mama's Flower Garden

Butterflies and bumblebees in the bright sunshine
Caressed the flowers in my grandmother's garden.
They kissed each blossom on the morning glory vine
While the roses blushed deep red in Mama's garden.

Four o'clocks and fireflies awoke at evening time,
And as the pink hibiscus folded up for sleep,
Wee golden lanterns about the garden did shine
While the crickets chirped love songs in the twilight deep.

The bachelor buttons looked on with shy bashful grins
And stood crimson-faced on either side of the walk
While the dahlias and poppies were hugged by the wind
And a chorus of tree frogs croaked idle night talk.

Francine Swann

Equal

Life moves ever at a steady pace.
It never slows down, it never waits.
We need not grasp always for the gold ring.
It's about more than just money,
about more than the right of passage.
Life is about all the struggles
together, and the victories as one race
(the human race).
One is no better than the other.
When God created the first man,
and the first woman.
He made us all come from the same
genealogy tree.
Man's beginning started from there.
I rejoice in the fact that we all
started on common ground, which makes
us all equal in my book!

Katherine L. Bond

Winter's Storms

Like crystal ornaments
The trees, ice-coated,
Bow gracefully 'neath the weight,
Their limbs sweeping the ground.
The sizzle of the frozen mush
As tires revolve on the highway
And the pinging of ice pellets
As they graze the automobile
(Contrasting the warm interior)
Make us grateful for our cozy cocoon,
Transporting us in safety
On our perilous passage.
The emission of the heater's warmth
And the radio's soft, sonorous music
Lull us momentarily
Into a sense of security.
But outside the car's coated windows
Are stalled, sometimes abandoned, automobiles
And flashing lights of emergency vehicles.
How treacherous winter's storms!

Peggy Pullen

It's All in the Name

Can someone clear this up for me,
And kindly set me straight?
What is a "Super Bowl" anyway,
A serving dish that over-ate?
And then I have a question
Concerning a "forward pass,"
Should I warn my daughter about boys
Who try to do things like that?
Now I know all about a "punt,"
I'm not as dumb as I look.
It's some kind of flat-bottomed boat;
I found it in a Webster's book.
What it has to do with football
I really wouldn't attempt to say.
If grown men want to play ball in a boat,
I guess I couldn't stop them anyway.
But finally, what bothers me most
Is something I really want to know;
Can someone please enlighten me
On exactly how to cook "couch potato?"

Crystal Daves

Paper Doll Dreams

I once lived in a glass house made of gingerbread
The opaque walls imprisoned furniture layered in hypocrisy
I kept my face and dreams in a jar by the door
Every morning I put on my mask and hid those dreams
But one day, tired of fighting with surreptitious innuendos
I peeled away the mask and spoke the
                              truth...
Foundations shook
Lies that glued walls together dripped like sour
milk
Corrosive mold eroded marble windows
I smiled briefly
And blew kisses to the tissue people (A.K.A. My family and
friends)
—They fell like feather bricks—
Too genuine for their insincere sincerity to bear
a Huge Wind has crumbled my fragile origami world
Scattered the Paper Dolls containing my dreams
Deported me and my corrupt Truth

Annie Lee

The Bottom Line

Focused, calculable, measurable freedom.
The final accounting of our love.
Love that liberates us from fear, guilt, the past.
We have been incarcerated in prisons of our own making,
and the making of others.
Haunted by the hurts of the past, and the promises of the future.
Afraid to be ourselves...to accept ourselves.
We long for approval.
Constantly adjusting our lives to ensure the flow.
No More...
The bottom line is...
The essence of our freedom.
The awesome inner silence.
Our Love
The final accounting.
It covers all dimensions of time.
Our love is the bottom line.

Dianne S. Mahaffey

U.S. One Now

Turbins turning...the gear begins to slip,
and as another sun, faithfully sets,
I watch as the structure yawns with fatigue,
the purpose being lost within the wheel as it turns.

All, forsaking the other for one,
with one being nothing in a quotient now mute.
Re-arranging and changing the numbers to fit.
For the sake of the justification of now;
with now being nothing, again as in one,
missing the mark just to get the job done.

Watching the faces as they turn away,
in houses of Polly and Saline so fragile.
To ask them if they understand right from wrong,
is asking to rip away all they've become.

The bird understanding, the water, the sky,
the mountain, the planet, the spirit, the eye.
The souls of two million stand looking in shame,
what once was a reason, is re-born a game...
Where all that is, loses, and the wheel spins true,
and I look away, for a day, just like you.

John S. Mortensen

Costa Rica

Bugs and bites with certain stitches
Mountains valleys controlled by witches
Sink beneath the sea again open the mind to new inventions
Think of the creator, waves are the indicator
Eat and breathe the things of nature
Ask yourself who's the cator
The wind whispers chords of caution
Rain pours down with violent motion
Sand stings the feet with invisible blasts
Smell brings sweet memory of lands in the past
Watch the people the way they dance
The local girls - I'll take that chance
Songs to sing with friends of true
Green are the jungles, oceans of blue
Rivers to cross, roads to be found
Reptiles and animals always abound
Rocks and trees and shells all sizes
Amazing what travel realizes

Kenney Joe Jensen

An Impression

His strokes were thick
With a heavy, burdened brush
Considered as the master
He was fascinated with light
Yet could never quite get it right

To mix a color - unpardonable sin!
The eye was to prepare
And formulate the image
Beauty to the beholder
Changed as he got older

But in our day
He's known for fathering
A movement not yet equaled
And for his originality we find
Claude Monet was perhaps, partially blind.

Cory Moss

The Forbidden Dance

"Can I have this dance? Whispers the darkness.
And the night drapes his ebony sheets
over me.
The blackness floats on a sea of silent stillness, and I am
Lost
in pseudo-reverie.

Soon I am drawn into the shadows
By the beguiling hand of
temptation.
Soon I am swaying amidst swirling shades of gray,
Within a cloak
of the night's own creation.

Then I am sighing with the wind
and dancing through moonbeams,
Iridescent.
And when the night creeps stealthily away
I am ready at last to grace the dawn
with my presence.

M. C. Caballero

Popcorn! Popcorn! Popcorn!

Another fun night in my car. And off we go! The kids crammed in the back seat. Here we are again at the Burger King drive through, just another stop before we get home. And there's that funky guy with the long hair who forgot to give us a straw.... What a slacker! And he asks us in a far-out voice "hey man...are you dead heads? You know what I'm sayin'?" There's really only two responses we can say to that, and here they are: "Hey man Jerry's dead," I say. And my sister says "No! But we've been stalked by a few." And off we go into the wild blue wonder, up into the sky... And, well, anyway... On the highway as the cars pile up in front of us and behind, all caught in the web of construction, I wonder if anyone has any...Popcorn! And so I ask in my loud voice— "Does anyone have any Popcorn?" And there's no reply except the hot-buttered burp from the car in front of us. I don't think anyone heard me, except for the kids. And so I lean out a little farther and ask again— "Doesn't anyone have any Popcorn?" And there's still no reply. So we decide Not to see this scene again, after all it's just another interstate 25 B-rated horror flick with no popcorn.

Natalie Beck

Autumn Promise

In autumn's light, golden yellow touched with red,
Playing in and out among the dogwood leaves,
There is a promise - something said.
I can't remember - some words, misshapen,
Their meaning lost or yet unborn,
But speaking still of happiness.

The golden light is tempting,
Yet somehow, still, I fear I'll find that promise
Like a dead bird upon the ground
I'd rather not have seen.

The leaves are stirred and beauty beckons more.
O, Promise, are you waiting there for me,
By faith, to take you up and make you whole again
And thereby fill my cup?

No,- too many times I've looked in vain
Behind the wind, beneath the rain.
Go, Autumn Sun, that knows how to bring
Gold from the dying trees;
Leave my harried world to winter and to peace;
Maybe I'll search again in the spring.

Lurlie Wiseman Allen

Not As Before

All the feelings and emotions
I used to feel
Are gone.
There are others in out lives now
But they will never mean as much.
You were special
And still are.
For you see
Other feelings for you fill me now.
I love you
Not as before
But in another very special way.
I can confide in you
Trust you
And care for you
As I can no other.
I know your insecurities and fears
As you know mine.
Your happiness is extremely important to me.
For I love you as a friend.

Jo Dell Hill

The Promise

Take my hand, and come with me.
I will lead you to paradise,
with your hand in mind.
We'll need no words to surmise,
the beauty that surrounds and binds.
To you, this is my promise.
Come with me, and stay by my side.
My love I give, forever.
All I ask in return is for your love to abide.
I will love you and leave you never.
In the cool of the brook that passes,
we will listen to the sweet rhapsody of life.
The fragrance of flowers will greet us,
as we walk hand in hand.
To you this is my promise.
This is the Lord's promise to humanity.

Jean B. Cloud

Waiting

To watch the sunrise in the morning.
Our weather to change without warning.
Looking for the smile of your child.
Seeing him walk his very first mile.
Hoping to keep the love in his eyes.
Knowing that I might win a prize.
Waiting for him to say I'm sorry.
Knowing that life is our cross we carry.
Sorrows, joy, there is still time to tarry,
and help others to be cheery.
Waiting. Waiting.

Winifred Hilda Vlasak

From My Dreams I Bring

From my dreams I bring the rain
    falling from the dark and erie sky.
I bring the sorrow of my cry
    as it slides down the road.
I follow it as it goes farther and farther
    away.
I see the birds down drinking my tears
    while I roam sorrowing home.

Joseph Mecum

Emerald Owl

As the golden sun lays down to rest,
An owl stirs from her little nest,
Preparing for an ecstatic ride,
She loves to find all those who hide.

Soaring throughout the mystical skies,
The moon begins to emerge and rise,
And darkness is soon gleaming with stars,
The tiny sparkles never afar.

She possesses gentle, twin emerald eyes,
Gracefulness and strength that never dies,
Head set proudly above her shoulders,
Beauty always radiates from her.

She is a strong and well-known symbol,
And even sometimes quick and nimble,
She is a voice, a harmonic chime,
Knowledge and wisdom as old as time.

Olivia Kim Bullard

Shadows of You

What happened to the days of wine and roses,
those barefoot walks that scattered morning dew;
lyric poems steeped in summer sunsets?
All I see are shadows of you.

The nonchalance of youth withers, dwindles,
replaced with ancient lullabies for two.
Intervals of anger rend tranquility
leaving just the shadows of you.

This solitary path, tho' not my choosing,
becomes a necessary measure to pursue
lost dignity, integrity. For now I'll be content
to dwell among the shadows of you.

Connie Hess

Troubled Teens

Our teens are doing drugs and hanging in the mall.
They're vandalizing property and drinking alcohol.
Their dress is inappropriate, their language is profane,
Their attitudes indifferent, their behavior inhumane.

Spending time on schoolwork or with family is not cool.
They're being charged with stealing and weapons in the school.
More teens are smoking cigarettes and having casual sex.
The adolescent, growing-up years have now become complex.

It's time that all we parents rise up and take a stand.
The future of our troubled teens lies within our hands.
The schools and city programs cannot turn the tide alone.
The foundation of a child's life is built within the home.

Linda Vermett

Drive Through The Mountains

Inspired by the Beauty of the Mountains

As we drive through the mountains what beauty we see!
Wishing our true friends were here with me.
Up, up we go, soon we'll reach the top.
We almost feel the touch of God, our hearts almost stop.

Down we descend, and wonder what's below,
When right at the roadsides the wildflowers grow!
With brilliant colors; yellows, blues and reds everywhere,
Again we feel the presence, that God was there.

We continue onward, a trout stream appears!!
Trout of rainbow colors swim upstream and show no fears.
We look further upstream where boulder rocks rest!!
And see sparkles of garnets in rocks they nest.

When the sun warms the earth and the warm winds blow,
I know "God's hands" spread this beauty a glow!
As we drive on further, gardens sprouting everywhere,
A silent prayer of "Thank you God" for putting them there.

So our trip through the mountains we dearly enjoyed,
So often missed by many a man, woman and boy.

Agnes F. Voght

Guns Are No Fun

As we wonder in the years to
come will we have love for every one.
Why must we carry a gun to hurt someone.
If you think gun's is fun.
Try thinking back what guns have done.
There's no doubt we all have fear.
Think what will happen in the next New Year.
Think before you carry a gun
because shooting someone is no fun.

Betty Ann Pierson

The Realization of Reality

The intractable trap,
Expectations too high,
In one's eye, one is king,
Is not the personal best good enough?
Is not 24-7 enough?
As one lives on, one can see
Life is more than who you are.
More than how hard you try,
More than just faith,
More than desire,
More than you or I or anyone else will ever grasp.
Life is as fickle as a daisy blowing in the wind,
To believe in catching breaks is naive, a fatal flaw.
People are as thin as paper, they speak a hollow language,
Words and trust have become insignificant.
What is right is wrong, and what is wrong is right.
Success is elusive.
Challenge after challenge, hurdle after hurdle,
No one is left standing.

Michael Maltese

Country Chores

The sun is setting in the west,
its soft glow encircles like a vest.
Daddy reminds us of evening chores,
as he putters in and out of squeaky barn doors.
I hurry down the country lane
as I find the light beginning to wane;
Sweet honeysuckle, buttercup, and hedge tickle my senses
as I scurry past shadowy country fences.
The cow bells tinkle happily on the evening air,
their rumps I switch and yell with flair,
as homeward we go, daddy's waiting there.
Milk pails brimming with warm, bubbly foam,
mark a day of country chores lovingly done.

Geneva F. Rainey

My Dream

I do not ask for much in life that this world counts as gain;
I do not have a love of money to cause me grief and pain.
I do not wish for mansions; or dream of silver and gold;
I do not care for popularity; or desire high offices to hold.
I find no joy in possession of art treasures, so rare;
I'm sure I'd be unhappy if I were a millionaire.

May I have joy in service; what more is there to ask
Than having deep satisfaction coming from a well-done task?
May I have time to look around and the beauty of nature see;
And I hope for someone close to share my dreams along with me.
At evening when the sun sets and it is time I go to rest,
My heart filled with peace because I know I've done my best.

Others may find joy in riches and owning property and land;
They may want to hold offices and have dreams built on sand.
Without these things to treasure I would not shed a tear
My heart longs for other things; they are what I hold as dear.
I do not want the heartache of owning a lot of things;
I know I'd be happier with what my dream brings.

Betty Daniel Pack

From A. S. Pushkin

If the life says you lie
Don't be angry, do not cry.
On dejection day be calm!
Trust the merry day will come.
  A dream of the future lives in heart,
  The present is so tiresome:
  Whole is instant, whole gets past,
  And will be nice, when it had gone.

Yefim Bilov

Aging

When confined to a Wheelchair or to a bed,
There's time to reflect on the life we have led.
Friends and Family have fallen by the side
Never to be seen or heard again.
We become painfully aware of the finality of death.
Nature provides us with a Brain, it comes without instructions,
It can be used for Good or for Evil.
Our Brain tells us the difference between Happiness and Pleasure.
Pleasures can be bought, they all have a price,
Are they Happiness? We must think twice.
Our Parents gave us life, Good Fortune, a good Wife
The Children we looked forward to with great Love
Are now full grown, from their lips we hear of the job we have done.
If proud of their upbringing they return our Love....
This is our reward!
Our stay on this Earth has been worthwhile.

Sidney Taiz

A Lament

I'm a lonesome cowboy
And I follow the Rodeo
When I come to Town
Bright-eyed kids gather 'round
Ropin', ridin', and Bulldogin too
They want to know.....
All the things about a Rodeo.
I tell them how it's done
And all the prizes I've won,
They touch my fancy Shirt
And ask how many times I've been hurt.
When they leave to go home
I feel lonely
Never had kids of my own.
I can't Rope, I can't even Ride
My fancy Pants never touched a hide.
I hope I don't see those great little guys
My Specialty is.......
Hamburgers, Hot Dogs, and French Fries.

Sidney Taiz

My Friend, My Foe

In the years that have past and years left to come
I realize that you are my only one.
This one that I speak of, this one that I share
Is my other half for whom I love and care.
She creates such emotions of grief and tears
She is the only one who listens, not hears.
I can't live with her, I can't live without
Who is the person I am speaking about?
Could it be a friend, could it be a lost lover
Could it be an acquaintance or even my mother.
She is my sister — my friend, my foe
All she need do is call and I'll immediately go.
I love her with all my heart, soul and breathe
I will love her always — in life and in death.
Our bond is strong and our feelings are rare
And sometimes our likeness make us hard to bare.
I will love you always and that you already knew
See, I'm grateful that God blessed me with you.

Deborah C. Hill

Since You Came Along

I was lonely, angry, and depressed,
My life had become a total mess.
Then you came along,
And now it seems nothing can go wrong.
You're sensitive, caring, funny, and sweet.
You're everything I will ever need.
When I look into your bright, blue eyes.
It seems as though all my troubles are far, far behind,
And then I stop and think,
and I realize you actually care for me,
For once I have someone of my own,
And now I want my feelings to be known,
You are the best thing that's ever happened to me.
You've been locked in my heart and I've thrown away the key.

Danielle Richards

Touch

Reaching hands up high to the sky,
  Feeling the wind as it rushes by.

Cuddling a baby as it touches your hand,
  Heart beating loudly to the beat of the band.

Touching the lives of those in our care,
  Watching them change and become more aware.

The touch of the skin on a wrinkled face,
  Realizing age is running the race.

Fingers sliding across cold thin ice,
  Like the chill of the bones on a winter's night.

This touching and feeling as life goes on,
  Is a miracle and happiness that carries us on.

Barbara Hatten

Special Lady

She was very feminine, very beautiful both
physically and emotionally. She had a heart
of gold. She was intelligent, and full of
life. She fulfilled her life the way she
always wanted to. All her dreams came true,
except for one. She didn't have the joy to
raise her last child, but she left some of
her traits in her. So even though she
couldn't be there to raise her, she gave her
something very special, a heart, beauty,
strength and life. It has been thirteen years
since her death, but until this day she shines
in my heart. I like to think that she is my
guardian angel. I hope she is happy in her
new life, and I hope she will get wings like
an angel should. That is what she is to me a
bright guardian angel, that will never be
forgotten.

Rosa Di Stefano

A Smile

A smile is the color of a sudden ray of sunshine peering
through a dark window.

It sounds like birds chirping to wake-up the forest.

It tastes like a touch of heaven mixed with a colorful
rainbow.

It looks like a rainbow breaking through darkness to get
to light.

Most of all, a smile makes you feel like your in a protective
shield of happiness that nobody can break.

Brigette Kozlowski

A Special Kind Of Love

Like climbing the tallest mountain in the world
Or like coasting down a hill
This is a special kind of love
Between a special mother and son
When you are coasting down a hill
You may get a bill and have to pay the price
Then a little latter you will go up the hill
And try to do the best you can
You may not think the love is always there
But sometimes it hides under the rocks and stones
As you're climbing to the top
But always shared between them is
A special kind of love!

James F. Roy

Dream Exaltation

My embellished thoughts gave way to dreams,
Images were dubious, but not what they seemed.
Little children appeared, so innocent and sweet,
They seemed un-afraid, as they sat at her feet.
Her musical voice whispered, soft as a sigh,
"Come home with me, I'll teach you to fly."
"You shall suffer no more my precious ones,
we'll float on the clouds, and dance on the sun."
But first, you must kiss Mommy and Daddy good-bye,
and watch over them from the glorious sky."
The children stared in awe as she closer grew,
Her arms wrapped them in love, and suddenly I knew.
The serenity of her smile was unlike no other,
as she Illuminated love from the heart of a mother.
"I'm so happy here child, I've plenty to do,
exalting little lambs, and watching over you."
Touched by the spirit, she possessed power and grace,
goodness and purity radiated her face.
A heavenly light streamed down from above,
Endowed by wings was my Mother; an Angel of love!

Arlienshia Shaffer

Cinderella

I was Cinderella for a day when you came and rescued me.
You noticed my eyes and you could see.
There was no fancy carriage or slipper of glass.
You were the guy they called low class.
In my mind I knew we shared a world so cool and sweet.
Too bad you hid behind your feelings and began to cheat.
A hole in my heart.
And I didn't know where to start.
Children involved it became insane.
And I could leave with love to gain.
Now years later it doesn't matter.
Because my life is no longer yours to shatter

Dreama Szutenbach

Whisper of Night

Out my window, the clouds I gaze
dew drops of crystal, beyond the haze.

Green hills flowing, like the stream above,
A bird is nesting its precious love.
Heaven in each wild flower
grew a crisp, steady shower.
The waters sparkling, like a golden jewel.
a breeze of life, fresh and cool.
Valleys of green, lie below
Caressed by mountains tops,
Sprinkled with snow.
The silvery moon lays down its head,
As all of nature goes to bed.

Cara Combee

My Thinking Place

My thinking place is a moss strewn rock
So I go there quite often.
To listen to the whispering of the trees
as they sing their song so softly,
To feel the gentle breeze
as it rustles through my hair,
And to hear the gentle tinkle of the creek
as it flows on to somewhere.
To ponder, yes to think
  of life's great questions,
To sit for awhile in this peaceful decor.
Trying to find the right answers,
Of the why's, the don'ts and if I could's
That keep coming and going forever.
But after awhile I get up and
Toss them to wash down the creek
For another day.

Christopher G. Sivley

Winding Trail

I was walking through the woods along the winding trail.
I was heavy laden, seeking peace of mind;
Trees so tall, grass so green;
Birds were singing in the trees.
While I was walking-crying I called upon the Lord.
He came to me in a gentle breeze.
I looked up through the trees.
The sun was shining at me.
The warmth of the sun gave me peace of mind.
The gentle breeze made me feel at ease.
Joy and contentment were in the trees.
As I was walking-crying along the winding trail.
I left my burdens, my heartaches, and cares;
Along the trail for Jesus to bare.

Pat Brandon

The Deafening Silence

The TV is on and so is the radio but
still the silence is deafening.
Being alone in this house with them gone
is relaxing but also exhausting.
The sounds of my children still
echo through my head.
  As the sky grows darker
the silence gets louder, every
noise in the house is amplified,
a mosquito buzzes through and
in this silence sounds like a freight
train.
  In just a few hours the silence
will be broken and the children
will be home and the most wonderful
sounds in the world can be heard:
Laughing, arguing, crying and loving.

K. Musgrove

Ladies and Gentlemen, Presenting....

The person each day that kindness opens the door
Their personality interaction portrays high rapport
No scale can measure her neighborly love for others by any score

Within a group her compassion comes in like a big tiger roar
Her habits others watch, study, and actively explore
A Higher Influence above the knowledge of man within her heart gives her more
Daily peace than the person who is earthly hard core.

Bobby Branum

Dreams

Little boy, what's on your mind?
What are you building in the sand?
I'm building a castle, you'll never find,
To live in and be a superman.

I want to be strong and learn to fly
Above all building and farm land
I'll see the danger from the sky
And fight the evil with my own hands.

I'll help everybody who needs help
I'll be a hero in people's eyes
I'll build a big house for those, who can't
Afford even their own lunch.

Maybe one day I'll save a girl
Drowning in a storming sea
We'll fall in love and I'll marry her
She'll spend the rest of her life with me.

Too bad, that right now I'm just a boy
But we all have our little dreams
Maybe one day they will come true
You have to believe in it.

Anna Pikina

The Black Book

The Black Book, a book so big it's unable to hold.
It holds the history of our ancestors who were once rulers of Africa.
It tells of our ancestors who were once slaves, the strong Harriet
Tubman who freed so many slaves.

The book which tells of our freedom fighters who fought so
hard to get rid of segregation, to make America a better nation. It
tells of Emmit Till a fourteen year old boy who was killed,
just for telling a white woman bye-bye baby.
Those white men who killed him had to be crazy.
It tells of Rosa Parks who sat in the front of a bus, a white
man wanted her seat and she surely put up a fuss.

I'm tired of reading about the white man in all these books
I have. If I don't learn my history how can I be a better man. If
I don't learn my history I might as well be dead. That's what
they're trying to do, bury us alive. If I don't learn my history I
won't survive. Education is the door, your history is the key.
Learn about your history and then you can be free.

The Black Book, full of stories untold. If America was really free,
the history books would be full of people just like you and me.

Sharese N. Jackson

Centenarian Lady

She lies there, white as marble, still and cold,
Her latest breath, her last, I've just been told.
A century of life, now at its end,
Begun when other values were the trend,
Hard work and basic honesty the rules,
Strive hard for education. Use the tools
That God has given us. Cherish life.
She was a kindly, good, and loyal wife,
A wise and loving mother for us three,
Though we rebelled and sought to disagree.
Through many disappointments, hurt, and sorrow,
With never-failing faith, she faced tomorrow.
She taught us courage, how to be a friend,
The value of a dollar, how to spend,
To save for rainy days, bound to occur,
For sickness comes to all, even to her.
She gave to others, all she could afford.
She's now at peace, her well-deserved reward.

Mary K. Rodgers

My Mother

When I consider the years of our past,
    I feel a love that will always last.
Your helping, caring through the years
    Has calmed our worries and stilled our fears
Great grandmother, grandma, mother and wife
    These are the roles that framed your life.

Your church, your family, and your neighbors
    Have benefited from your life long labors.
Your visits, your gifts, your telephone call,
    Have lifted the spirits of us all.
The example of a life of faith and hope
    Has shown us a way to live and cope

Bless you mother for your strength and love
Leading us with faith towards above
        Gloria Smith Hickson

My, Purpose In Mind

The road is long, my stay is short,
I must make the best of my time
Not to be rule, not to be cruel
But to keep my, purpose in mind
The way is sometimes dark
The sun shine too bright for my eyesight
But I'll find a way in darkness
I'll make a way in the night
So when the morning comes
A better person I'll be
So after all my work is done,
I'll will, live in peace
The call of my people
The color of my skin,
Is no reason why I should sin.
I must travel the road
I must not yield, but only make
The best of my time while I am here.
        Phyllis Malone

Only A Dream...

On an evening cold and lonely
I closed my eyes to sleep;
And there it was, your perfect face
that completely engulfed my dreams.

I reached, and you were waiting
with your arms extended out;
Waiting to surround me
and turn my life about.

So I tempted faith and trusted you
and put your hand in mine;
And together we traveled to a peaceful place
that together, we only could find.

The sun was on fire, the sky crystal blue
life seemed unbelievably sweet;
and before we kissed and fell in love
I awakened with only a dream.
        Jacquelyn L. Bajack

Tangerine

If I promised, if I swore, if I could be the apple you adore, would
you, could you, love me once more?

Remember Bunny Rabbit or Tangerine, echoes in my ears of sweet
sentiments which still remain. Why have you forgotten the sunny
days and held onto the pain?

Was it so long ago words whispered so silent only a heart could hear.
I want to touch your hand and let you know, it's too dark, it's cold,
I will have to let go.

I cherish our time together for no sword could cut the memory from my
heart. The wound which I endure is the cut from the knife that tore us apart.

Rose petals upon the water dance in my mind. It is not what you
treasure anyone it is what you left behind.

Dreams full of deceit bring you close to me, slow dances in my mind,
only you're not there. Yesterday has gone it is the past that you care.

The ice around your heart still remains. I remember warmer days, only
even the sun can not scratch the surface with her rays.

If I could be the apple, a mirror of you, if I could reflect from
your view, would you say what you mean? The tears are warm on my
face, because I know I am a tangerine.
        Lori Henderson

Going to War

I strain to look through swollen eyes, and I see much to my surprise
the teary eyes of fathers and mothers, wives and children, sisters and Brothers.
But I just stand here all alone, and watch the waves of those unknown.
For no one came to watch me go, to fight the war and keep prices low.
No one came to say good bye, I must be strong, I cannot cry.
Five thousand men will leave today, for our return we hope and pray.
I feel so cold and so alone, please someone miss me when I'm gone.
We're going to war against Iraq, not knowing when we will be back.
We'll fight all through the night so long, we'll fight real hard,
we'll fight real strong.
We'll fight by day in the blazing sun, we'll fight until the war is won.
Some of our own will surely die, who cares if one of them is I?
I sit and wonder as my tears burn, will you be there if I return?
        Ralph W. Hayward

Teenage Parents

They came to us, one at a time, a year or two apart. The greatest
gifts we would ever receive; six became the total count. The joy and
surprise we had with each one, the moment they were put in our care;
but we were too young and immature, for the responsibility we now shared.

We thought we were given playmates, only we were expected to protect,
nor did we realize until later years, the hard work not to neglect.
So many things could and did go wrong, as they learned to walk, walk,
talk and fall; we smilingly watched all their challenges, for we knew
these would make them strong.

After a few, wouldn't it get easier? So we took it all in stride, yet
their individuality they displayed; in all a different trait to be
tried. Each one, sometimes struggling, in their private lives, in our
hearts we felt their pain; our concern not always rightly applied.

Did we do our best to guide them? It's up to them to say. They took
all our teachings (some good and some bad) as examples we conveyed.
We could have made it much easier, if, there had been a rule book to
follow, but where could we find one? Now we know, our experienced
knowledge.

Now we wonder, did we succeed, in giving them a comfortable life? We
are aware, we could have done more, if not for all the strife. But to
hear them complain, is very rare, for they knew what was there all the
while; two parents who loved them and accepted their faults; in return
they accepted ours!
        Shirley Bragg Farley

Lincoln

At first look, the man appeared lean and hollow
His physical outline, cast a long and thin shadow

Physically, the man stood like a giant among the people of his time
Mentally, his thoughts and words were of a sincere and brilliant mind

Self-taught, he never had the opportunity to attend a college
Being self-educated, he always had a strong thirst...for knowledge

He studied the law, and made his reputation
Little did he know, someday, he would lead a troubled nation

His determination, to keep the states of the North and South...in one Nation
Were disputed and challenged, by those who wished him... death and damnation

A Civil War had demanded his total time ... While in his Presidential term
But he knew that saving the Union, had to be his major concern

Supporters of liberty, freedom and justice... remember his name
For while on this earth as President, he was never given much fame

Through his efforts, democracy and self-government survived in his Nation
Thus preserving... freedom, liberty and justice...for every generation

Lincoln's words have been composed in books, on monuments, and carved in stone
For generations, no doubt, some will pay tribute, by simply writing a poem!

R. David Fordham

Homesick

Wandering upon the battlefield the soldier came across a fresh, empty
grave and he peered down as if he saw his own reflection. As the
fog begins to thicken, the tears begin to grow. Thoughts of the past
he tried to ignore, but failed. He started to remember his family and
how much sorrow, tears, and joy they had to have suffer over the past
year. The young man did not know who he was or where he was. All
he knew was that he was not with his loving family. The soldier began
to deadly grounds again and saw the men that had perished
search from this grave. Men wearing blue or gray uniforms, men that
were his the friends and enemies laid below his feet. He started to
cry for he stood alone. Going back to the past, the young man begins
to make a list of "whats ifs" and decided his pain was more than
could bear. Then, without hesitation, he fell towards the shallow grave.

The next day the field of blood was discovered. The people began to
clean up and count the dead. When they came across the shallow grave
of the dead soldier, they noticed that he was holding something.
It was a note that read:
I'm going home—
I'm going home.

Jennifer Marchal

Pre-Natal Heaven

A silent yell of ecstasy splits my being when I see your form.
    Could this be some fantasy? It's much too weird to truly be the norm.
And love goes on to meet the dawn and wed the past to now.
    New love is old, all tales have told - it is not "if," but "how"?
The pastel heaven of before mated souls forever-more, to bloom.
    Then shuffled them into the chute, separately, their cries to mute
    their doom.
If they but knew present is past, and they would meet again, they'd fast be still.
    What has been will be again, and for eternity remain God's will.
The muted shades of yesterday are merely to prepare the way of death.
    The vivid hues of living, too, also prepare the chosen few with breath.
This breath of life begins the strife of knowing what we seek.
    The search is keen and would not seem intended for the meek.
The agony of life is death, yet dying brings forth untold wealth of Lore,
    And finally we unite the hues - the screaming reds and silent blues of yore.
The heaven that was yesterday, comes again in another way - by dying.
    Souls united in that before are now united from the core - and crying.
No need to moan, and less to groan, that what they've had, they'll miss -
    For it was love, and God above has sealed it with a kiss - of death,
To meet and love again in his pre-natal heaven.

Arnika-Maia Mott

Racists Don't Bow

The eyes are the trust,
    The bow is respect,
        Discipline is the soul,
Racists don't bow.
Fear causes hate,
    Rage means defeat,
        Artists have honor,
Racists don't bow.
Control is necessary.
Discrimination is doubt.
Honor is the bond.
Power is the gift,
    Love, the tree,
        Life is ever-changing,
Racists don't bow.
Art is expression,
    Life imitates Art,
        Pain is to fear,
Racists don't bow.
    Honor Is Everything.

Kent Lankas

Hate

How do I deal?
I don't, can't.
Just hafta wait.
I'm too young.
Too stupid,
too young to know,
If I hurt.
Damn,
hate him.
If I hit,
I get yelled at,
and I cry.
Tears not blood
I want to die.
but pain's too painful.
Of course, I'm too young to know
if I hurt.

Shevaun Brannigan

The End Is Near

All alone when no ones around
When darkness is all that surrounds

Depression will soon begin
Hopefully it will come to an end

Silence is all that you hear
Until the phone begins to ring in your ear

Your hopes are up oh so high
When you begin to sigh

You only end up in fear
When you hear the end is near

When all you can do is cry
Cause you know you will soon fly

Nakiva Singletary

"Feelings"

Feelings of loneliness come over me
  Even on a cloudless summer's day.
Lonely as a ship lost at sea, never
  To find its way.

Safety of solid ground is somewhere
  Beyond the raging cold sea.
It's so near, yet can't be found by a
  Homeless waif as me.

I've tried swimming, but in vain, to
  the safety of the distant shore.
Waves crash over me, so I return to
  the lost vessel once more.

From the distant shore I hear the reassuring
  call of a morning dove.
The message in her song is clear;
  someday you'll find a special love.

    Shirley Henderson

Wonderfully Made

Do you sometimes wonder why
That we have tears so we can cry?
And upon our face there is a nose
A mouth two ears that have arose
How do our voices sing so high
We can be loud or breath a sigh
Our ears can hear a birds sweet song
Our tongues can waggle really long
The air we breath our heart's do beat
Look at those funny toes and feet
The way I am so wonderfully made
At times my mind sharp as a blade
Did I appear out of the blue.
Or was I created by God or who?
I'm glad I have all of these things
We're quite a lot we human beings
We all are different but do agree
That God created you and me.

    Gaye V. Selover

Untitled

Deep within doorway dark,
youth huddle amongst filth;
rabid denizens of stoop and alley
like a rabbit hiding from danger.
They wait for the next fix,
kicked down food or pot;
spare-changing strangers,
funding 40's of Mickey's.
Struggling to escape
street-level squalor,
the squat in abandoned buildings,
avoiding red tape denizens of society
who are on a holy quest,
trying to "save" and "civilize,"
destroying pride, honor, strength.
Doorway denizens become hooked,
left desperate for the next fix
on the government dole.

    Maht Hector

Strength In Faith

Little flower at this hour, show me your strength. I wish I could,
if I could and if I have the strength. You have the strength if you
believe; then your bulbs would bloom in spring. My bulbs would bloom
if strength I could find, til then I'll just wilt and die. Oh please
do not die little friend of mine, for I can help you grow and shine.
Grow an shine invisible friend of mine; oh how I would love to grow
and shine. Then listen to me and you will see how much of a great
friend I am to thee. Oh please help me invisible friend, for
tomorrow is spring and I will surely die, if tonight I do not find
strength and shine. Dear little friend for I will help, but I am not
as invisible as you think. So rest for now and you will see how
gifted your invisible friend can be. Well night is here and I see
nor hear; for my invisible friend has left me here...alone and frantic
feeling oddness in my bulbs. For the sun will shine and tomorrow I
will be...here...alone...only vines left of me, but rest I shall do,
as my invisible friend said, and I will hold faith and in the morning
I will see; if my friend was really true to thee. Well morning is
here and he I do not see; but the ground is wet and so is thee. For
I have grown and my petals are gold, beautiful gold for the world to
behold...and here alive in spring I shine. Oh thank you invisible
friend of mine.

    Tatina E. Kearse

Dream of Destiny

Once a young girl's life seemed so simple, as a woman, it's crazed and dimpled.
Now of age there is a road to choose, one full of roses sweet as the
  dew, the other needed weeding through and through.
How do I choose, both roads long and winding, one to be destiny the other a dream.
Roses so sweet seem to simple, my choice is to walk in the weeds
  that's plain and clear to me.
My path gets foggy so my eyes open wide, I trip over branches as I plow my way high.
Climbing a mountain round and round I see a light, the heaven I must have found.
Heaven is full of grassy fields with the weeds in-between, the ones I had pulled.
I lie back and ponder over the road not taken, would I have dreams
  made of roses to come true; would my life take a turn for the new.
My walk along the road I choose, only to have aged with time
  as I keep my dreams alive with one rose by my side.

    Julie Morgan

Measure of Time

Time - cannot be measured nor captured in a bottle,
But the simple, undisguised love of one man can cause the fluttering
  flattered heart of one woman
To stand utterly still, breath taken, poignantly suspended, like a
Strong steady hand
To an awaiting airplane throttle,
Taking off in a giddy whirlwind of love, in a rushing flurry of...

Sound - cannot be measured nor captured in a sentiment,
But the heartfelt emotion behind one word can cause the voice of one love
To ring crystal-clear, ever true, never broken, like a loud, hammering heartbeat
To a lover's responsive ear, escalating in a rapid ascension,
With each hovering honey dew kiss, with each tender exchange of....

Breath - cannot be measured nor captured in a fistful,
But the unfathomed miracle behind the first gulp of air from one tiny
  newborn child
Can cause the stirring buried in the most sequestered soul
To suddenly emerge, surprisingly quickly, so sweetly sustained,
Like a lucid pool of warm, molten liquid softly reflected
In the shimmering beauty marking the silent promise of ...

Eternity - for these sacredly locked away treasured capsules of remembrance
Somehow become for mankind, in the long run, the only significant
Measure Of Time.....

    Alexis Renee Steel

Daddy

I can still remember sitting on my daddy's knee
Laughing he would sing silly songs to me

And with his big hands he would lift me up so high,
I felt that my head would surely touch the sky

Then when night time came he would tuck me into bed
leaving nothing showing but a sleepy little head

As I grew older I could easily see all he ever wanted was the very
  best for me
If I ever needed him for anything at all, all I had to do was pick up
  the phone and call

I don't know the reason but it didn't seem right when the Angels came
and took him on a cold October night

The anguish that I felt was so hard to bear
Deep within my heart it will always be there
Everyone said give it time
I tried to put him from my mind
I thought for sure if time would pass this awful ache wouldn't last

Still there's a loneliness in my soul, a hurt so deep it can't be told

Many years have come and gone but I can still hear my daddy's songs
Now I embrace his memory, it brings joy and peace to me.

Ann Thompson

Why

Why can't we let children be children?
Children who play directed by their dreams in noncompetitive solo,
Children who make their own goals through suggestions, not "sign-ups,"
Children who are not pushed into activity but given support for fun things,
Like bicycle riding, watching the stars come out at night, having a pet,
Like getting showered by a garden hose, planting a flower or a vegetable garden,
Why can't we teach without pushing or pulling or making their decisions for them?
Why can't we watch and help children unconsciously grow to a manhood of their
own choice?
Why can't we proceed without being competitive with parents of other children?
Let's just relax and enjoy our children while they are children.

Margaret R. Youngren

The Wall

I never knew the wall before, until I met it face to face.
Along life's journey, I strolled ahead, to reach a goal and a better place.

Solid it was (that unmovable wall), for me the (unstoppable force).
A serious opponent it proved to be, determined to alter my course.

What was this wall, who put it there, and why must it set me down?
No matter, though, this trivial gab, a way to success can always be found.

I'll approach the wall once again, this time a more vigorous try.
I must move on, for I have a mission, that no wall will deny.

But once again it knocked me down, unyielding to my advance.
This wall I now began to deplore was denying me my chance.

I hit it again, and again, and again, and each time it hit back.
My patience now ever growing thin, with each and less persistent attack.

Though the wall itself would not blemish, my spirit and drive began to crack.
If it doesn't tumble with one final nudge, I'll give up and be forced
  to turn back.

The wall held strong, withstanding my assault, and proved to be a superior foe.
I succumbed to frustration and wilted despair, and now the shame began to show.

I guess it was never meant to be, my ascent beyond this certain space.
The wall was there to make that point and keep me in my rightful place.

Now the story here is one that's said, of dreams so swiftly put away.
A weak man's will, too quick to falter from some mere obstacle in his way.

Brad Ball

There Comes A Time

There comes a time that you
remember the past, and are
really not sure it will last.

You see your life through a
looking glass after my sisters
lost their lives.

There comes a time that pain
enters your heart and your
feelings really seem to fall apart.

Remember the past because
that's the place you will be
able to see your loved ones at last.

So, there comes a time somehow
it seems I have found a
way to reach the end of time.

Barbara Koss

On Calvary's Hill

I was not there on Calvary's Hill
The day my savior died
I did not see the rugged cross
His nail pierced hands and side.

I did not see the saddened look
That showed upon his face
As he ascended up the hill
A slowly staggering pace.

I did not see his mother weep
As darkness filled the earth
I did not hear his parting words
Nor hear him say "I thirst."

But I have walked up Calvary's Hill
So many times since then
And I have seen that rugged cross
And pictured Christ as then.

Bertha McQuerry

The Beckoning

No laurels rest upon my head
Yet I'm a man content
Except on rare October nights
And when the moon is spent

I hear a strain so silver sweet
As nebulous as the sea
My senses stir and memories blur
There's one I strive to see

A lissom girl with silken hair
Her face with beauty guised
A smile to break a strong man's heart
And witchery in her eyes

Then on some wondrous awesome night
Star dust will fall on me
She'll reach and take my willing hand
This one who beckons me

Ruth Rutherford

Progress?

The mallard took flight from the sequestered pond
Flying exquisitely across the emerald sky
Its beauty irreplaceable
Its likeness not to be matched by any other

Out of the horizon
A jet screams above him
And he's sucked into the monstrous turbines
Meeting his excruciating death

Yet, one lone feather
Escapes the wanton massacre
And floats ever so slowly
To the ground below

To be found later
By a young boy
Who picks it up
And places it in his hair

With his vivid imagination
He becomes an Indian warrior for the afternoon
Until then feather withers away and is soon discarded
And forgotten along with the memory to which it belonged.

    Tony M. Peppers

The Seasons of Life

Shakespeare once said, "What would be said and lived, will be said and lived again." Life evolving the same, just with different faces. We laugh, we love, we live, we die. How lucky we are to have been given the gift of life. Everyone of us presented our challenges and successes.

Continuing humanity together and separate. All of us here to do something while living, experiencing the human thing. All of us the same, why? Because stripped of status, riches, materials and baskets; we stand with hearts, souls, and minds. Human beings.

God wouldn't have it any different. Understanding, sometimes it's not easy being human.

    Anabel Edwards

Peace By Night

I wake from a peace caused by nothing,
From blank hours of lost emotions.
Tuning in on a world of disco-tech.
Its colors intertwining around our awakeness
Hate and Greed, the parents of violence and
discontentment, having spread their children
through its patterns.

Then when alone with my love, in a vastness
of blue sky and green waters, soothed by the
touch of the sun and breeze, lulled by a choir
of the free creatures. The hours of light
sink again into night.

Now the clash of light against my lids of peace
breaks my night into day.
World problems, with man's confusion are all
through us striving to mingle in black and white

I kneel with God's children in the awesome warmth
of love, feeling the power that can control
forever absorbing all my anxiety, and again
making way for the night.

    Marie Carl

Untitled

The jester cries alone at night
  His jokes no longer seem so bright
Standing there is his room alone
  After his friends have elsewhere gone

The drinks he had are wearing thin
  He thinks - I will not do this again
Tomorrow I will start anew
  There must be something I can do

Another day has now arrived
  Should I thank God that I'm alive
I feel there's something I must lack
  I feel this load upon my back

The sun now spills upon the earth
  Happiness doesn't seem so dearth
Today I'll do the best I can
  The universe at my command

Night has arrived - it seems so soon
  It's time to don my frayed costume
Tonight I'll make the others laugh
  Shall that become my epitaph?

    Beverly Carlisle

Ode to a Physical Therapist

The doorbell rang; in rushed this man,
a physical therapist - is his position.
He came to work on my poor broken bones
that had recently put me out of commission.

He kept coming back week after week,
this big jovial fellow
he worked on my muscles and broken limbs
until it made me bellow.

He pulled and cracked and bent my bones,
I almost had a fit;
and then he had the nerve to say,
"It doesn't hurt me a bit."

He was persistent and worked real hard
on each muscle and each bone;
I knew that he was helping me,
but I was glad when he was gone.

With an arm and a leg all broken up
I thought I would never get well,
but now I'm almost as good as new,
thanks to Ted Kimbrell

    Charles Carnes

Night Changes

It's all in my mind, this isn't my life
It's a nightmare, a dream - it just isn't right.
How did this happen, why to me?
I have to change my destiny.
A whirlwind of emotion spins in my head
Can't hold on much longer, I wish I were dead.
Help me, I'm drowning I'm going insane
Please set me free, don't keep me in this rain.
Leave me alone behind my closed door
I can't stand the pain and confusion anymore
Waves of tears are burning my eyes
The nightmare is over, fears begin to subside
Now I'm awake.
The room is spinning, no way out, no way of winning.
It's not in my mind, this is my life.
Got to find away to make it right..
I'm changing my ways, no need for a fight,
A dream saved my life in the middle of the
night.

    Dawn Bireley-Brodzinski

Time

A measure of Mortality, that's called Time,
Is used by Father to measure our progress.
To help, He gave the gospel with love entwined,
Endowed us with knowledge that Life is our test!

We work and we play, try really hard to learn
The purpose of our existence while we're here.
By obedience to commandments we hope to return
To our heavenly home and loved ones so dear.

How dare one suggest that Life ends with death?
Why is it only now that life started!
Our Father provides, with our very last breath,
Someone to meet us, else the plan is thwarted!

Charles, for our earthly ears, your music is still.
So now you can play for the angels to sing!
In each memory we can hear you at will,
All the melodies you played on our heart strings.

As you left us in sadness, we bid you farewell
And wish you Godspeed as you go on your way.
We love you and miss you, as in spirit you dwell,
May God grant we be with you again some day.

Thelma Jo Parker

Baby Seal

Somewhere in Nova Scotia where the wind chills to the bone.
Frigid water's frozen solid as a mass of granite stone.
A baby seal it lingers, not knowing what's ahead.
For in a matter of some moments, it's going to be dead.
Soft, snow white and furry, with big black tear-filled eyes.
A gentle face that makes one smile, with sounds of baby's cries.
It cuddles in the cold which nature equipped it to take.
As off in the near distance, comes man with club and stake.
The little seal knows no enemy, since God has born it free.
At least that's what it's thinking. "Why should one want to harm me?"
But as the man approaches, the little seal's afraid.
Because a sick sense tells it, soon it's life will start to fade.
Then the man brings down the club, on the little seal's soft skull.
A dizziness occurs as all it's faculties turn dull.
He then unsheathes a knife and starts to strip it's tender skin.
An agony so painful, a deed that's such a sin.
And some woman wears a seal skin coat, displaying it with pride.
Not realizing the pain its caused to the baby seals who've died.
I can only multi-emphasize, yelling as loud, as loud I can.
"If we can't show pity to gentle beasts, how can we be kind to man?"

Edward A. Nicholson

Turkey Talk

Miles I'll have to run, ropes I'll have to jump
So I won't be getting fat, juicy, round and plump
'Cause I don't want folks eatin' my fat legs and wings
Heart, liver, thighs and many other things
And with my head chopped off, this I would kinda hate
So that someone can have me on their dinner plate
My Mom cooked in the oven
My Daddy was there too
But you will never find me
In some old geezers stew
Running all these miles
Has to be my way
Of keeping me off the plate
On Thanksgiving Day
I guess by now you know
I'm a Turkey and you'll see
By stayin' skinny - you won't want
Any part of me.
A Happy Thanksgiving to you, too.

Eugene W. Miller

My Friend

Her hair, is curly and white
Her eyes, are blue and bright

Her teeth, show white as pearls
each time her smile unfurls.

Her skin, is like a peach
I love to keep, within my reach.

Her tender touch, is like a feather.
She is the loveliest wife and mother.

No matter what the problem be
She is always there for me.

Her jokes, her words, her pleasant way
through sweat and toil, each hour of every day.

To hold her close and tenderly kiss
Is something I would really miss.

Yes, my wife, my love, my friend
that I will keep, until the end.

John Consolo

Untitled

It's all around, I cannot see
I cannot hear, I cannot reach
I cannot move it is so deep, is surrounds me
I am submerged in something sweet,
something soft yet firm, something never ending
Although I am imprisoned I am not a hostage
If the door were to open, I would not speak
I would not listen, I wound not move
I'd stand in sorrow
Until the door was closed
I'd lay still as a stone
Though I could be touched
I couldn't feel
Because the door was opened
my soul has disappeared
Until the door is shut, I lie as a corpse
Until my soul reappears

May take an hour, a day, or a year
But the day the door is closed
Is the day your love appears

Nina Marie Herndon

The Struggle

They tied our hands, and left us bare.
They turned their heads, and did not care.
No, not a glance, did they look back,
except to torment, and maybe attack.

We are the sad chapter, in life's longest story.
No prize, no praise, and never the glory.
Though progress was made, but rarely acknowledged.
How long will it be, to make their life's college?

Our path is not set, our future not clear.
Maybe our justice, is finally near.
Yes still tie our hands and leave us bare.
For this is our challenge, and yes we still care.

Mary E. Brown Payne

Rough Winter Day

Walking beneath pastel grey skies
crunching snow beneath my feet.
I struggle through the bone chilling cold
to the small pond behind the orchard.
Tiny dancers of winter wind
twirl in exotic rhythms before my eyes.
Each join together in a ballet
of passion and peril before resting
quietly upon the sleeves of my coat
Though the journey is short
time becomes an enemy to my day
robbing precious seconds
as I struggle to reach my special spot.
The pond is frozen deep with cold
not wasting the brief time at hand.
I lace blades to my feet where I can glide and twirl
with the winter wind.

Michelle Dudensing

Atomic Adventures

Only atoms endure; everything
Else is just a fleeting pattern.
Even stones suffer their own hell, melting
Under the weight of younger rocks.

But atoms remember all their past forms
And trade stories of their hard knocks,
Their gay gatherings and riotous swarms,
Their jobs and bosses - small talk.

Atoms from around the world, from oceans,
From mines and wells, unite to hawk
Themselves from grocery shelves. Promotions
Into human bodies are prized.

The people atoms saunter down the aisle.
Aware of being lionized,
They regally inspect the rank and file.
Whom shall we call to our station?

After a person's atoms are dispersed,
They treasure their brief vacation
And forever tell tales to the unversed
Of love, beauty, wisdom, and woe.

Wayne Comeaux

Is There A Place Called Halfway To Heaven

You know as I sit here all alone
And I keep staring at the old phone
My mind keeps thinking of my dear old dad
Lord I miss him, that makes me so sad
As the hands of the clock gets closer to eleven
Again I ask myself
Is there a place called halfway to heaven?

Oh it's been over five years now
But the year 1991 seems like only yesterday
The thoughts still drift through my mind
Since he passed away
I think of him often.
As the shadows of my childhood slowly
drifts through my mind
The answers I'm looking for where can I find?
Did my daddy give his soul to Jesus our savior
These answers I need to know
These thoughts are constantly on my mind
I keep looking, but still I can not find
Is there a place called halfway to heaven?

Harold O. Brewer

Child of Mine

Beloved child of mine
If only I could have been your eyes, your ears
To have heard, to have seen
I would have gladly
Now I'm left with tears and sorrow

It's all too new to seem real
I keep listening for your voice, your footsteps,
Waiting for the sound—the opening and closing of the door
I can't sleep thinking of all the things I have to tell you
The house echoes its loneliness, cracking and popping long after the
   midnight hour

People talk to me
Recalling all the good things, special things so wonderfully you
My heart aches with cutting pain
The hurt only a mother would know—one like no other
If only I could hold you again, touch you
I loved you so
Did I tell you enough

Eternity beckoned before I was ready for goodbye
Beloved child of mine
Forever Mom

Barbara M. Thomas

Dear Mommie

Dear Mommie, can you hear?
I'm in heaven — have no fear.
I'm so happy with Jesus who loves me, too.
I won't ever have to cry,
To be fed or made dry.
I'm still waiting and longing for you.

Dear Mommie, what a shame,
You had no chance to call my name.
I'm in heaven, where the angels sing.
Oh, how they sing so sweet,
To all the babies round their feet.
But I still miss you more than anything.

Dear Mommie, say a prayer.
I'm in heaven — wish you were here.
I'm so happy, although I heard you cry.
Very soon I'll see your smile,
I'll save my love for you a while.
We'll be together, you and I.

Franklin Kincaid

Mental Art Masters

What is a poet but an artist of the mind?
To create written pictures conceived from sometime,
spreading mental beauty through words for thought.
Thinking of things we've learned, seen or been taught.

It's how we conceive it and what we believe it seems,
for in the minds eye, there's no end to the scenes.
Writing lovely little phrases of powerful poetry.
Signing ones name as to recognize a stamp of notary.

In the world of words, the puzzle is in the playing.
Mixing and matching, running rhyme of what it's saying.
Working long and hard on a piece as if no end to the day.
Writing and rewriting 'til the true meaning can stay.

Yearning completed composure, capturing moments or mood.
Thriving and living on verses as if they were sweet food.
We wine it, we dine it, and flatter it to good time.
Never happy 'til finished with the ending of some rhyme.

Once we've mastered our mystery abounding to great end,
We just wake up another day to start all over again.

Kevin Lacey

The Dilemma Of Life

Is life an illusion?
Where human beings are in total delusion;
Or is it, the vision of an ever better tomorrow!
Which never seems to come.

Is life mere formality?
A place where people worship, Artificial decency.
Or is it about utmost Sincerity.
Which holds up our integrity and human dignity.

Is life just shattered dreams?
Where more dreams are discouraged than encouraged.
Or is it, the perseverance towards one's dreams
Which gives significance to an individual's worth.

Is life just fragmented events at random?
A place of chaos and Mayhem.
Or is it, fragments fused invisibly by the hand of God!
To make sense of the order that lies amidst the chaos.

Is life apathetic, utters ignorance?
Where many dwell in stupendous Arrogance!
Or is it, the brilliance of Knowledge.
That illuminates our life like a new Sunrise!

Saikat Mondaz

Reminders of Love

The stars mingle with the Heavens to dally,
and the earth revolves around the sun.
The mountains dip to meet the valley,
and the dawn embraces a new day as it is spun.
Each mingle in harmony,
as I with thee.

The dew kisses the fragrant flowers,
and glittering rainbows clasp the sky.
Somewhere in the night's darkest hours.
Moonbeams kiss the sea and sigh.
This is how I feel with thee.

Lingering hues of dusk give way to the approach of night.
Playful summer winds caress with a tease.
A damsel in distress is rescued by her shining knight.
A heart's love is released by the man with its keys.
Each reminds of me and thee,
and of a love that is pure and natural,
and like time itself, eternal.

Melissa Syring

Womanhood: A Place of Honor

My vision and my posture,
touch the panoramic scales of the natural world.
I am Mother, Father, Guardian, Protector and Ally.
I am the dwelling place of a Goddess.
I embody dread, harmony, harshness and majesty.
I beckon and overwhelm with my sheer presence.
I am a symbol of the prime axis of my world.
I rage above all my experiences.
I can become Rock-hard, and
unmoved by the storms, and tribulations,
of the happenings on the surface of
my outer world and
our world of illusions.
I am still,
at times...soft ..gentle..and flowing,
embodying unwavering stillness and rootedness,
I encounter the weather of my life
without denial...and honor it with wisdom.

Sotera Ramos

So-So

So many times-so many ways
I never could say what I wanted
My tongue would get tied
And then I would hide
From simple things that I found too frightening
I wouldn't go forward
I couldn't go back
And I knew standing still was no good
I'd get down in the dumps
And feel all of the bumps
And imagine they were there just for me
So I took a step up
To the window above
To see what I'd been missing
It was such a surprise
What I saw with my eyes
Was that nobody else had been listening
So I left it alone, my beginning has grown
Into life which was taken for granted

Fran McEvoy

How Can I Say Goodbye

How can I say Goodbye to someone I care about, admire and
will deeply miss? How will I ever know the wonder of what
you will become in the world? I guess an easy way out of the
sadness I feel would be to say that I'll keep you in my
prayers, although that is true, it does remove me from my remorse.
We have shared so much of our beings and although I came to
teach you...I learned. My meeting you has reaffirmed my
being that Human Nature is good. That mankind in any
circumstance has the capability to choose his/her own
destiny, and that to live with the choices, if incorrect, is
only temporary until we regroup as a being once again and
pursue the self. I wish you well, and, yes, I know you have
the potential to overcome absolutely any hurdle that passes
     your way.
I wish for you, my friend, the pursuit of happiness, and upon
entering the journey of happiness, I hope the trip never
ends. So rather than Goodbye...

R. Steven Miller

The Holy Child

You come to a world that is dark and dreary,
Where people are lost, frightened and weary
Bring back again that star T which shone bright.
Come into our lives, come into our lives,
Oh Child of Light,

You come to a world where much life is unfair.
Children are hungry and cry in despair.
Return again from heaven above.
Come into our hearts, come into our hearts,
Oh Child of Love.

You come to a world of hate and of greed,
Where power and wealth help man to succeed.
May angels again proclaim wars will cease.
Come into our world, come into our world,
Oh Child of Peace. Oh Child of Peace.

Eleanor Gutmann

Autumn Shadows

Beneath the wintery autumn sky
the winds across the valley high
The clouds cast shadows dark and long
reflecting change as season's song

Then just as winter's deep frozen cold
Consumes life's empty chilling hold

A crocus shoots its arm of green
against the grayish barren scene

And life again begins to creep
and shadows run away to sleep
For in the wind the seeds do blow
the sun begins again to glow

New days of sweet and fragrant scents
the past is gone, is done, is spent
And now the earth must stretch so high
and turn its face up to the sky

For now a new time has arisen
which life can use and God has given

Dennis Charles Garberino

Untitled

Who knows how the storm goes?
Rolling over the land disrupting lives
Through the crowd the wind blows
Selecting, wrecking, drives.

Where will the lightning hit?
As one tosses a coin to the ground
His shoulder or his brow lit
Casually, random, found.

And when will our mother freeze
And weigh our heads with snow?
Movement is burdened on hands and knees
Lethargic, constricting, slow.

Do clear skies divide the storm?
Or does she hide to be reborn?
Will this storm go as others past?
Or has she swallowed the sun at last?

Paul Stewart

The Fabulous Fifties

We met at the corner drug store
Where us teens would like to gather.
Some sat to chatter on still more,
While like us, we sat together.

You came riding along with me
In my merry convertible.
Now you cuddle up close to me.
Lover's lane was memorable.

We came to stop on town's main street.
Walking over to corner drug store,
We had a soda fountain treat.
With talk, we knew each other more.

Listen to Nickelodeon,
Singer of fabulous fifties.
Hold hands, and eye contact goes on
With the varying melodies.

Leaving drug store, I went her way.
"Drive me home," she asked of me.
At her parent's home, she did stay.
I spoke to them of her and me.

Arvid Homuth

The Deathless Symphony

I've wandered over every key, yet have not found that symphony,
That deathless song which will enthrall; Ah, Lord, heed Thou my earnest call.
Pray grant these hands mold that refrain, let inspiration touch this brain...
That on the distant seas of time, it will eternally reign sublime.

Then, when some master of the keys expectant throngs is fain to please,
Its stirring chords will reach each soul, as ethereal bells will toll...
And vibrant as the lark's sweet cry arise, then as this singer fly
To Thy bright throne, who patrons song. Take from these chords which
to Thee throng
Thy choice; return them then to me distilled into my symphony...
Which, when it flows from artist's hand, will spread as mist oe'r every land
And mate with all the elements...that when despair its poison vents
Upon some sobbing soul, it will embrace it, sooth and sweetly fill
The aching void, then drift away to live for e'er its deathless day.

Bob Wangler

The Promise of a Black Woman

I am black and I see the future. Although there's much sorrow. I
know deep down the happiness held within. In time of being jobless,
you see the tares of your people that grows among this race.

The other kind sees prejudice, unfairness, discomfort, and altogether
wrong in us. I work hard as other fellow-men. I follow the path of
hopefulness, yet, still I stand against fear.

Sometimes I wonder is it just people, or the race of the races.

They say we're much stronger than our men. Mothers to our children
and country. They say we're head-strong people. Beauty inside, but
bold on the outside.

"Well, they're right." We're good lovers, but the best of friends and
enemies. Even though our men argue with us. They're still somewhat
determined to stand beside us.

I see the future. I see what it contains. It's there it holds up the
B.L.A.C.K.——W.O.M.A.N... We're educated very much in all ways I
see what the future holds today. The Promise Of A Black Woman.....

Cheri Marie Odom

Let's Get Away

Today I was talking to my wife and I said "let's get away",
Some place we can drive to, maybe stay a couple of days.

Maybe find us a little cabin on a stream or on a lake some place,
Slow our life down a bit, move at a slower pace.

Just take a couple shirts, shorts, undies and things,
We could try it for a few days, see what life brings.

She looked at me and said, "Ok, wonder what will our friends say?"
So with our clothing just thrown in the van we were on our way.

We were laughing and joking like a couple kids running away,
We hadn't discussed where we were going or how long we were going
   to stay.

I could hear the tar strips on the highway as they clicked away,
It was time we should get a snack, maybe find a place to stay.

We found a bed and breakfast a few miles off the noisy highway,
It felt good to stretch out weary bones, it had been quite a day.

Our host fixed us some food after we told them what we had done that day,
They said, "No need going back out on that highway, not today."

We stayed a couple of days, we walked the streets, what few that were there,
We found this quaint little chapel, we even stopped in to say a prayer.

We really don't know where this place was, really don't care,
What we do know is that when we needed it, it was there!

George Gurney

You Alone

You alone I long to please.
You alone possess the keys
To my heart, my mind, my very soul.
You alone have made me whole.

It's you alone I long to touch,
To kiss, to hold, to love so much,
To give unselfishly from me
The passion that will set you free.

You alone have made me laugh,
Made me cry, made me sing.
You alone have picked me up
When down and out is where I've been.

You alone are right for me,
You lift me up; you've set me free.
You rescued me from loneliness
To live with you in happiness.

You alone have shown me light
When all was dark, no love in sight.
You have given ecstasy
This... you alone, have offered me.

B. J. Farron

Untitled

Handle with care our fragile
fools gold bodies
Handle with care our faded
glass blown souls
Store our thoughts in
vacant arcane graveyards
Play with zodiacs
dancing in the snow.
Stomachs hate the whiny
cracked-up servant
We all know we play that
part ourselves
Someone broke the sobriety
of the city
At least we know the
weeds are gonna grow

Carrie Peckar

"Confusion"

Life isn't confusion,
Confusion is life.
Where are you going?
Where have you been?
Will you actually get there?
Or are you there.
Can you say, "I love you"?
Or, just that "You care"!
Do you know all the answers?
Who asked the questions?
For better or worse,
Not now, or ever.
Do you feel like you're drowning?
Can you catch your breath?
Relief is your savior,
Or is your savior death?
Life wasn't confusion,
Confusion, was life!

Susann Conklin-Palermo

Forgiven

As laugh turns to tear
And tear turns dust
Upon the face of torment
Washed a smile of purest gold

As a face of fear turns to ponder
And sufferings unknown seem to dwindle
The sun casts a twinkle
To the eyes left to dry in the breeze

As cold lips of ice, quiver no more
And color returns to heal the scars
The thoughts that provoked her
Seem to wash away with the tide

As hands that had once shook
And first that had mangled
A warm touch leaves but a thought
To the fear that had crippled her pride

As soft words from a lover
Soothed her thoughts to a shiver
She gives thanks with kiss and caress
To the one who set her mind to rest

Lee Fischel

God's Concern For All

Thank God for His concern.
Oh sinner! That I am.
God having sent the child.
His only begotten Son.
Born this day for all to behold.
Praise His Holy name!
Give God the honor and the praise!
Hallelujah Jesus!
He lives and He reigns.
Repent and confess.
Jesus the Savior, King of Kings,
Lord of Lords.
Receive the greatest gift of all.
Salvation for all who accept.
Free gift of eternal life.
Engrafted into tree of life;
A branch for evermore.
The living water flows.
My King! My Savior!
Thank you for saving me.

Mother Gertrude Snell

Untitled

By the water
Down the stream
I am lost
Or does it seem
I am drowning
Dying in my shame
Lost in my head
With only myself to blame
Ease my pain
Let me fly
All I really want right now
Is to die
The house is burning
The world is freezing
What are they doing
The government is teasing
Create a world
But let it burn
Every human sucks
No one deserves another turn.

Melissa Resch

Untitled

I miss your smile, and
the laughter that once filled the air.
These happy spaces now
echoing despair.
What was then so
joyful and satisfying
Now lying sick, hopeless,
and dying.
The sun does not
shine here, it too is alone.
It is cold in July
because you are gone.
Half my world shattered,
taken away.
Each passing moment
growing darker grey.
Every waking minute I
continue to pray.
Lord, return my love to stay.

Mary Viveiros

The Dove

Time flies like a bird on its wings,
Bringing death and destruction,
But in its eyes is the hope and
the peace
Of a young world that's dieing.
Its feathers are stained by the
blood of the innocent,
And its wings are washed with the
tears of the strong.
It hears the cries of the dieing
heroes,
And it sings the song of tomorrow's
dawn.

Maria Pitcher

A Beautiful Day

It's a beautiful day to take a walk
Or maybe just sit and talk.

To watch the sun come in the sky
Or see people passing by.

Tell a neighbor that you care
As their troubles they do share.

To watch the children as they play
And to hear what they have to say.

Just to see the trees so brave
And how their branches wave.

To hear the birds as they tweet
Oh, that's a wonderful treat.

If you see someone falling down
Pick them up without a frown.

Tell them they're as an abode
For the ones with a heavy load.

Give everyone a happy smile
It will all be worthwhile.

All of this will make a way
For us to have a beautiful day.

Elizabeth Cothren

To Earth

My friends, when my life ends,
don't keep a sacred plot for me.
Instead, just toss in air my ashes:
Let the winds - free blowing -
ferry me - unknowing - here and there,
as non-polluting dust.

But if I die at sea,
then let me feed, when dead,
the living in that sea
where once my forebears bred.
Toward that ancient debt I'll pay
with flesh and bone
and be recycled thus.

If grieving - carve no stone
recalling me to mind
but let me stay defined
in memory, as ecologically inclined:
Let that the essence be.

Iris Pape

It's A Hallmark

An amber shot of whiskey
A foamy chase of beer
Makes my feelings tipsy
And wishing you were here.

Diane Beck

Some Call It Sleep

Some call it sleep,
Some call it rest.
Some call it life,
Some call it death.

Seasons, they come,
and seasons, they go ...
just why and when,
nobody knows.

Leaves, like they fall,
lives do the same.
Breezes, they blow
the fires of the flame.

Slumber is peaceful,
when it's done best.
Kneel down and pray,
that yours, too, is blessed.

Barry W. Shelton

Jesus Shares

I share with Him my Sorrow,
  He shares with me His Joy!
I share with Him my Trouble,
  He shares with me His Peace!
I share with Him my Unbelief,
  He shares with me His Faith!
I share with Him my Guilt,
  He shares with me His Grace!
I share with Him my Disappointment,
  He shares with me His Hope!
I share with Him my Loneliness,
  He shares with me His Presence!
I share with Him my Fear,
  He shares with me His Comfort!
I share with Him my Sin,
  He shares with me His Forgiveness!

Bobbie Jean Rigney

Images of the Lonesome

Images
of a distant land,
secluded from society.

Mirrors reflecting
a melancholy being,
broad-minded and lonesome.

Alone
in a fantasy world,
full of memories.

Grieving,
living in poverty and deprivation,
speechless and abandoned.

Exclusion
from the prayers of the rich
pierces the heart.

Spectator
concerned about his status in society,
Free?

Shemeka Jones

Child's Dream

Crying with challenge
Crawling without knowledge
Reaching with determination
Running without consideration
Walking with strength
Exploring life's length.

Darlene Banghart

Untitled

Today we give
Our promise
To each other
To keep forever.
In our saddest days,
We will cry with each other.
In our happiest days,
We will laugh with each other.
In our sickest days,
We will hold each other,
In our roughest days,
We will stand by each other.
And we will be as one,
Today...Tomorrow...and
  Always!

Erinn Fisher

My Prince Charming

The pounding of a heartbeat.
A soft lullaby.
When I think of you,
my thoughts turn into a sigh.

I look for you everywhere,
but you're not around.
I call your name in every city,
but I here no sound.

There is a person for everyone,
or so people say.
But where are you my prince charming?
Will you rescue me someday?

Rebecca Newburn

Dawn

My Soul will not carry it.
Burdened thoughts of old age;
  Wrinkles, withering blossoms
  Emaciated bodies, bare branches.

Seasons must revert
And promise themselves
A time of Beauty.

The Brown must rub itself
  Off the Bark, Look inward
  And remember it's Green.

The Symphony must rise and fall
  As when the gentle stroke
First sighed through the woods.

It must all lie in the Beginning,
  Clasped tight
Under the warmth of the Wing,
And love and life
  Dream endlessly,
  Watch incessantly
The Distant glow.

Manjushree S. Kumar

Once in Time ...

Once in time I heard a voice
  "Be still and listen to thy heart"
I dare not stop, 'cause of time
  "Be still and listen to thy soul"
Time was mine to stretch and strain
  "For once be still and listen"
Then time stop I know not why
  "Be still for now and forever"

Bernice James

Silence....

Often I am silent
For I speak with my eyes

Listen when they speak
They say more than I ever could

Listen when they cry
Hear them when they scream

But know when they are silent
They say the most

I often find myself looking away
By doing so, building walls

For when I look into your eyes
You can hear me

If you could only learn to listen...

Heidi Marie Peeples

Soccer Team

We pass
We dribble
We shoot
We miss
They dribble
They pass
They shoot
They score
We lose

Erica Ellis

Sun-Risen Faith

A hint of silver and of pink
  on the eastern horizon's brim.
A spark and then a fiery flame,
  that started out so thin.

An open window, facing east,
  looking on sky so blue.
And on the sill a Bible rests,
  a sign of faith so true.

A Bible touched by Morning's Glory
  at the rising of the sun.
Glinting gold on black leather
  a prayer, "Thy will be done."

Brielle M. Cordingley

Wolves

They run. They jump
They leap, they crawl
They hunt for food
or do nothing at all.
"The wolves" "The wolves"
They're coming here
"The wolves" "The wolves"
They're close and near.
I can hear them creeping
in the woods.
Close the doors and windows.
Hide all the goods.
Wait I can see a light
Look at the wolves
They're trembling with fright
For they see a hunter
Into the night.

Tiffany Horn

Mr. Death

I watched you Mr. Death
In a street peddlers hand
Snowy white pebbles
So much in demand
I bought you Mr. Death
With my money and my mind
With my soul and my family
And trinkets I could find.
I used you Mr. Death
And you used me in return
You taught me how to lie
In the streets how to earn.
I loved you Mr. Death
In an obsessive kind of way
So I stalked you out at night,
And I stalked you in the day
I must leave you Mr. Death
For your charm has lost appeal
Your desire was only to harm me,
Your desire was to kill.

Nora E. Butler

Untitled

A star fell from heaven and landed
in my hand and I crushed it and
ate it and wondered what it was.

When it fell from heaven and came
into my mouth, I put it on my
tongue to taste, but it had no
taste.

Chris Wilke

You'll Never Know

You lived your life in shadows
  hiding behind the lies.
You'll never know that true love
  is the kind that never dies.

You'll never see a rainbow,
  or hear a robin sing.
You'll never dance in moonlight
  or know the joy it brings.

You'll never hear the songs
  that dance upon the wind,
Or know the peace and happiness
  a summer storm can lend.

You'll never know the love
  Of just sitting on the sand
To listen to the ocean
  As it claps its mighty hands.

For peace and love need each other
  like the water needs the land.
Without the one the other
  Is nothing more than sand.

Joy L. Drake

God's Child

God make the heaven's
God made the earth
And God made me
I know what's right and good
Temptations are everywhere
Like sun filtering though the trees
it will find its way to you
God gives you the choice of
making your own decisions,
to overcome temptation to walk away
To smile another day
So if I should leave this world today
I do not fear for I am God's child.

Judy Champlin

Lay Me Down

God is here,
all the time,
the wind blows,
I hear the chime,
loves all around,
the house is filling,
of gentle music,
very willing,
my time is up,
but yours is not,
lead me to,
the place, or spot,
thank you Lord,
for all my life,
I'm very grateful,
to you, tonight.

Caitlin Creitz

My Son

Where is he now
asleep forever.
Does he know
that he's missed,
that his voice
is silenced.
Except in our hearts
where he'll live forever!

Joan Schimoler

Friend

Teach me that which I don't know
Light the path where I must go
Encourage me when I must bend
Throughout my life, remain my friend.

Praise me when I do achieve
Sigh with me when e'er I grieve
When down and out, be there to lend
Throughout my life, remain my friend.

Content will be my short stay here
With thoughts of you so very dear
Peace will rest me at my end
Knowing that I called you friend.

Gladys L. Washington

Untitled

If you fail to do
what has to be done
you fail to achieve
what you have to do
The road to the sun
is one that burns
The more pain
The more pleasure
An extreme
to the intellect mind
A conscious truth
in the lies we breathe
Awaiting salvation in my dreams
as the days drift
Time flies fast
for nothing
A surprise in the night
and you fall asleep
without a dream
without salvation

Steven Tressler

Ode To King

One on the ground
fifteen for the show.
Four with their sticks raised,
ready to go.
Hate in their heart,
blood will flow.

First King Martin
died teaching the truth.
Second King Rodney
lives the victim of hate,
and the L.A. Blues.

Maryters and heroes
laid side by side,
the dead counted fifty
by the end of the night.

Reginal Denny almost
died in plain sight.
History repeated
the city burned bright.

Bobby Lee Gabell

They And I

They killed John F. Kennedy,
By shooting him.
They killed Jesus Christ,
By sacrificing him.
They killed Socrates,
By poisoning him.
They will not kill me,
Because,
I am not insisting to,
Tell the truth.

Divyesh Patel

My Amour

My amour,
You, I do adore.
Oh, how I need you so,
So let us go
Amid the stars
To wish upon a far,
For a time, our eyes closely laid,
Our moist lips tasted
And mingled so softly
With the many wishes
To feel each other close;
You, I have wanted the most.
How can I never share
My thoughts, my heart,
How I care.
Never will we part.
You are forever in my heart,
For I love you more,
Oh, how I adore,
You, my amour.

Melissa Ann Miller

Untitled

Her smile is as a mid-day star
creeping into chambers made bright
as the Dawn when it wrests
from the starry hold of the horizon
casting bold relief upon the soul,
Stepping upwards in silver patches
to retrieve the day from Night.

In return we rested our sight
away over the linen of our faces
not the same as when years before
the leagues of the sky made us dream
Now our words are as clouds
which threaten to cast off beyond
all living Memory into the ranks
    of sleep.

Thomas Fitzgerald

Ode To Dreams

Here by night
Gone by day
Some I wish
Would go away

Some are good
Some are bad
Some I'm happy
I ever had

They can be about anything
From now or then
But when I wake up
They're gone again

BJ Wells

Untitled

Believing my mother to think;
of herself nothing dearer;

Oh! The tears I'd blink;
while looking in the mirror.

As I'm looking at a-face;
that's rather forlorn.

I feel so out of place;
and my heart seems torn.

My life was perfect;
and now I don't know what to do.

Everything ends up a wreck;
even though my intentions are true.

Now I suppose I'll have to wait;
an eternity with no end.

Just so I won't be late;
for my chance to be happy again.

In other words I wish we'd forgive;
each other.

So my mother and I could live;
in happiness with one another.

Rachel Jones

My Strength

You've never done anything
wrong in my eyes,

The perfect being;
the perfect love,

Forever not doing wrong,

You've been my tower of
strength,

The person I lean on taking
my troubles away,

You're my strength in
this world.

Dominique Hall

Youthful Dreams

Kites
scale high
dive deep
bob
in a
wilderness of
blue
chasing downy
figurines
engaged in daring
chivalry — Those
skits of a
youthful
yesterday
engraved
upon hidden
stars
traversing through
the prism of time
undaunted by age.

Linda Kaye Gray

Untitled

My life means so little,
death means much more.
Fighting a never-ending battle,
making the mistakes of people before.

You are there when I need you,
you are so open and warm.
I know I can trust you,
not to do me much harm.

Outside the window,
look down to the floor.
I fell into the shadow,
I don't live anymore.

Please don't feel guilty
Remember you tried,
to make me happy,
each time I cried.

Back to the window,
look down to the floor.
My spirit in the shadow,
will be forevermore.

Rebekah Stark

Song Bird

Way up in the tree top
There sat a lovely bird -
He was busy singing
The sweetest song I've heard.

I watched him for a while
And listened to his song,
Suddenly he saw me there -
And then he was gone.

His song lingered in the air
It brought joy to my heart,
And I saw him later -
As thru the trees he'd dart,

I wondered why this was
When before my eyes I see -
He and his little loving mate
Had build a home in that tree

I slowly walked away
I never meant to disturb,
The lovely song he sang
The "love song" of a bird -

Rose Marie Wilkin

Goodbye

Your eyes a deep reflection,
though I couldn't see.
A piercing tear of blood,
escaped prisoners flee.

Revealing knowledge strikes,
cringing shrill of need.
Parting soul of heaven,
a witches strike of greed.

Carving stone of absence,
dagger kisses flesh.
Father's tale of agony,
blade as sharp as death.

A loss of sorrows glimpse,
I release your heart to who?
My soul shatters in memories,
for I am still in love with you!

Jenni L. Bilodeau

My Angel

A little girl
So very pretty
She shares her M&M's with me -
She's even funny
Her eyes just sparkle
She's a pleasure for me to see.

Blond hair, blue eyes
Energetic as ever
What a unique child God made -
We color and read
We take pictures, too
Special moments never fade.

So grown up
And yet a child
I treasure her tender touch -
She's my angel
And so special
I love her so very much.

She's my granddaughter!
My most precious granddaughter!

Mary Renken Dam

Somewhere Up There

Kevin is in heaven
He was so full of fun
And he loved everyone
And they loved him
People gathered 'round
When he'd play the clown
Children and old folks
Were his favorite, to them
he was like a magnet
He called me "His best girl"
To me, that meant the world
He was taken suddenly, only 33
He was my son, you see

Helen M. Williams

Black Pearl

Sometimes I ponder a pure
black pearl looking clear
past a suppling dose of
grown seasons.
Scouring my shinny
exterior along a
midnight current
down the Mississippi
flow, blessing a Southern
tipsy groove in the
midst of a
backdrop glow. As I turn
abroad in heed from the
distant blackness
so much like my own
I feel at peace
among a noir exposure,
within a pearl kennels
darker shade of soul.

Shauna Davis

Nature's Bouquet Of Beauty

Where skyline meets water
On the horizon beyond;
A painter's soft brush
Conveys nature's infinite bond.

Adrift on the ocean,
Wind master of the sails;
New islands are encountered,
Peaceful uninhabitancy prevails.

A style all its own,
Soaring to new heights above;
The great mechanical bird
Mimics the song of the dove.

As the tide breaks the surf
Upon the forever changing beach;
Merging wave upon wave,
Blending together, all within reach.

When Nature's Bouquet of Beauty,
Most often taken in stride;
Awakens the human emotions,
So a friendship is solidified.

Judith Duren Davis

Coward

When hate strikes down upon thee
strike back!
But no, wait.
Cower in fear like field mice scurrying
into their burrows from the night
owl screeching with the hate for them
which we call hunger.
Run away only to find yourself hating
the choice you made to back
down and not speak up loudly
into the microphone of belief.

Justin B. Smith

Peer Pressure

I never thought it would
happen to me
I thought I was too smart
It only took a couple of friends
That pressured me to start
They got me into drinking beer
and even smoking pot
It got so bad that I can't even stop
My friends have tried to help me
But it just won't work
Day by Day Night by Night
I'm drinking my life away
People have tried to help me
But I think it is too late!

Ashley Watson

In the Station

In the bus station
People are arriving.
Some are going off
Some are left behind.
The sadness
The happiness

Expecting the unexpected
The new for the knowing —
The knowing left behind.
Like a tree - its leaves gone
New ones will soon arrive —
Young, green and shiny.

Martina Alcantar

Truth of a Truth

Flight of the first
Watch the sun burst
Pillows of white cotton
Pollution is rotten
Forever endless blue
World with no clue
Green capped with snow
Corroding planet below
Oceans full of pain
Curtains of acid rain
Don't give up the fight
Radiation lights the night
Forever questful desire
Plunge into the murk and mire
Watch the falling stars
Screaming heard from a far
No more plan of attack
The full moon just cracked
Moment of truth realized
All is gone vaporized.

Voctavio

War

War
Where has the Dreamer gone?
Off to war.
And his Dreams?
He had to lay them aside.
Will he ever Dream his Dreams again?
Only after the War.
Will he win the War?
Only if he returns with new dreams.
When will the War end?
Never.
Then how can he ever return home?
Only when he stops fighting.
Who will survive the War?
No one at all.
What kind of War is it?
No one knows.
Who is the enemy?
He is.

Charles R. Wagner

Angels

Someone touched my life today
An angel it would seem
not the kind with gilded wings
but came to me just the same

I looked upon a star up high
shinning bright as it could be
I thought about you knowing
what a gift had been given me

Angels come in subtle ways
perhaps when I'm not looking
Let things happen as they should
Accept and recognize what's good

If we listen carefully
and open up our hearts
Life can be so beautiful
a new beginning or fresh start

An Angel touched my life today
as strange as that may seem
Will only happen seldomly
to someone as lucky as me

Lady Poets

A Stormy Night

Oh I have seen some emptiness
oh you've seen some emptiness too.
turn between heartbreak, half
turn between smile.
Visions our yesterday.
The darkness that consumes us.
Oh the storm is blowing away.
Darkness fades today. The peace
has come home, the pain has
blown away.
Oh never let us make the same
mistake, yesterday pages has turned
But we laugh in our own way
we learn from our mistakes
we look back to retract the
yesterdays.

Arlie Smith

The Numb

People are all around but,
I feel alone.
Everyone is talking but,
I hear nothing.
I see someone touch me but,
I feel nothing.
I speak but,
No one responds.
Is this what it is,
To be empty.
Oh how scary it is,
To be so alone.
And the only feeling is,
The Numb.

Joseph A. Baldridge Sr.

The Dream

I picked a million leaves yesterday.
They were not very strong.
All but one,
He was strongest of strong.
Greatest of great.
He was one foot long.
One foot thick.
He was red as the reddest rose
Orange as the most orange of suns.
But the most unique thing was.
That he may not have been real,
But he may not have been fantasy,
Because he was only a dream.

Aubrey Bird

Untitled

Friendship is golden,
leaves are green, apples are red,
and the inch worm crawls.

As the great swan travels
down stream on a sunny day,
the fox retreats in fear of
the hounds.

Sweet smelling cherry blossoms
send their scent of baby powder
to the nostrils of the sleeping
bull under the brush of the meadow.

Mother nature has her way
of expressing herself through
the beauty of this earth.

Angela Rainville

The Abandoned Child

My tiny fingers
reached out to touch you
you were not there

My young voice
cried out to you
you were not there

My small arms
stretched out to hold you
you were not there

My soul, my heart, my being,
screamed for your response
you were not there

My tears of despair
tried to dampen your skin
you were not there

The universe became my mother
the earth became my comfort
I searched for you
until my little feet bled
you were not there

Saundra Papritz

Cascades

Crisp, clear liquid
falls endlessly
past the crags and cliffs
of this world.

Water falls.

Beginning to end;
there is no detour
but destructive forces
change terrain.

Water falls.

In this waterfall
of life,
the only thing we can do
is to follow the flow of the water.

Ben Belchak

Not I But God

I want to tell the world
    God will speak
I want to shout it out
    God will speak
My words come out confused
    God will speak
My lips refuse to move
    God will speak

I'm so scared
    God will speak
I don't know what to do
    God will speak
My voice is shaking so
    God will speak
I'll get in the way
    God will speak

Forgive me Lord
    For being weak
I'm ready
    To let you speak

Melody Faircloth

Devils, Angels And Devils

Came demons into the morn;
not seeing the devils horn.
Through fog they flew;
killing the dew.
Then back to hell to adorn.
To hell to adorn.

Came angels into the morn;
never to see God's scorn.
Through mist they flew;
awakening the dew.
Then back to heaven to adorn.
To Heaven to adorn.

Came people to the morn;
not seeing the earths forlorn.
Through darkness they flew;
their foresight askew.
Then back to death to adorn.
To death to adorn.

Gail Reiser

Nature

I watched a flock of mallards there
As they flew across the sky;
One could hear them as their honking,
All in formation as they fly.

Then I wondered how they could know
When to take to wings on high;
Who told them when the spring is near
When back we watch them fly?

I watched a small barn swallow there
Build her nest upon a beam;
To raise her family a rest of straw
Quite clever that would seem.

And I wondered why all nature knows
All the things it needs to do;
For they always do it right on time
Seems as if they always knew.

It just makes one wonder who that is
Who did place a guiding hand;
Over all the nature that we can see
As he works a marvelous plan.

Richard E. Ainsworth

Despair

When people fall for drugs
because they think they are life calmly
and when they experiment
without knowing the results
and they ignore consequences
of that pleasure and euphoria
only is found a pain to be
for the nervous in the brain
had been swallow with the pleasure
When the nervous settle down
left only holes in the brain
and only can be filled up
with more drugs that cause euphoria
and the pure souls only think
that it is not transitory
without knowing that the help
are very close to their hearts
but the addiction they have
doesn't let them see the light
and that love, that is the cure.

Fausto D. Velez

Life Lesson Learned

I think the world would be
　a better place

If we could see it through
　our Creator's face

I face through which man's time
　does not exist

Events that take place are but
　a gentle kiss

The end result of which would
　cease to be

Our thinking that I am the
　only important me
Saundra S. Adams

Things

Sometimes things just happen,
That are way beyond control.
They are triggered by emotion,
And fueled by our soul.

When logic loses meaning,
And with common sense denied,
The only truth is passion,
And a love too great too hide

And, despite the complications,
A romance 'oft will bring,
They seem so unimportant,
Inconsequential things,

That are products of bad timing,
Or heirlooms of the past.
Things that simply happened,
But somehow did not last.

So, we seek some retribution,
For the love we've had, but lost,
And we search until we find it,
No matter what the cost.

Mark Charles Grech

Haven

Out of the back
coming from the
kitchen
the screen and wood
box of wonderful
relaxation
In summer a lazy
sleep in place
to go
the green is liquid
an almost eye
pain
Look out to forest
that can hide
suburbia
A sunday morning paper
coffee with cream
haven

Tom Augustine

The Light

The light...
peeks through,
bright
or dark,
the light..
I see, comes from
you and me,
the light...
shines
even through
the blinds
of others,
the light...
can touch
the light...
can feel
the light's...
brightness
is up to you and me
can you see the light?
Tia Butler

Soul Mates

　If we are destined to
find our soul mates,
　　Then I will have to look
no further,
　　Because I have found my
one true love. In you.
Tracey Allen

Day and Night

By day, a mean momma machine
With house, laundry, children to clean.
Discipline-strictly-enforced zone
All bellowed or shrilled in angry tone!

By night, a quivering mass of guilt
Self-doubt, self-pity hidden by quilt.
Penance-prone promises to keep
Swearing to God before sweet sleep.

Six am: three, two, one-year olds up
Belly kicks, husband yawns, no let-up.

Eleanor Kaimakliotis

Untitled

Just looking into your eyes,
you tell me to stay,
I believe too many lies,
so I turn to walk away.
As you grab my hand you say,
"Please forgive me,
I won't again stray."
I've tried too hard,
to love you more.
You dealt me a blank card,
just so you could score.
I never understood you,
and don't think I will.
You hunted my heart,
for my soul to kill.

Danielle Wysocki

Desire

A fire burns deep within my soul,
The source of which I can't control.
For when e'er the spark is near to me,
It lights a flame near instantly.

At times the blaze consumes my all,
No earthly matter can I recall.
But when the heat subsides somewhat,
I gain control... but all for naught.

Perhaps it is my sweet desire,
To be consumed by such a fire.
The flames of passion scar my flesh,
And leave their mark upon my breast.

It seems that time can not succeed,
In vanquishing the lovely seed.
That lights my spirit and my soul,
And fans the flames beyond control.
James F. Barrall

Haiku

Art in all cultures
and many different colors
hanging over walls.

Swing that mighty sword
how powerful you're showing
coward to us all.

Mamma came to me
but only in my dreaming
only me that way.

Loading up your gun
using up my brainstorm
victory is mine.

Wendy Lynn Casey

Defacement

At first at the sounds of the
rain trickling down upon the
great canopies and the exotic
birds singing above the rain-
forest soothed my slumber.

Suddenly loud noises overcame
me. All but seemed to drift
away as I woke up on a tree
stump that once had been a
lush and majestic tree.

I listened closely hearing
the roar of chain saws as
they cut trough the strong,
Sturdy trees; not caring for
the animals and their homes
of which they destroy.
Devon McConnell

Lion and Star

Go
Like the twelve
Into the wild
Take the creatures
Through the storm
Erase the darkness (and)
Reign

Mike Thompson

Shadow

Shadow, oh shadow
why do you hide?
On a bright sunny day
you're always at my side,
when night time comes
you're no where near.
I'm always looking for
you to appear
do you sleep at night or
do you hide.
When darkness comes, you
are not at my side.
As I go for a walk you
take every stride, step by step
you're still at my side
now darkness has come and
I'm lonely inside
oh shadow oh shadow
where do you hide.

Eva J. Cox

Dedication

I send this dedication
To my two sisters who's dead,
Somebody who'll cheer you up,
When you're sad.

I send this out to them
Cause they'll thank me for it,
And now since they've gone now,
I know I shouldn't ignore it.

One has been gone for three years
The other eighteen years,
And when I write this dedication,
My eyes is filled with tears.

Tiffany I've seen face to face
Cherwana not even a face,
I'm glad they've went to heaven,
To be in a better place.

We'll I'm ending this dedication
And gonna write some more,
Bye Tiffany - Bye Cherwana,
Now my heart is filled with joy.

Lakisha Hamer

Deceased

The brilliant flame did burn;
Burn beneath my heart...
The blinding flame did flicker;
Flicker in my brain...
The ailing flame did dwindle;
Dwindle in my eyes...
The silent flame did die—
Death cold kiss upon my lips
And harden wax the candle drips
Seals my tomb...
My life eternally cease
And torments forever desist.

Amber L. Stuver

To My Friend

Here's to a friend
A friend indeed
Who soothed my soul
In my hour of need
When my heart was broken
And my soul was sore
God sent this friend
To my front door
Now, he is gone
On his journey's end
And I pray that God
Will bless my friend

Justine Bowen Shawk

I Scream Alone

I could sense the fear in the
Women called Mother.
If I should cry really loud do
You think she would hear.
What if I kick and scream with fear.
What could I do to make her see
What could happen if she should
Choose to kill me.
Picture in your mind my Mother
So sweet that my heart has already
Started to beat.
A soul without form is nothing
You see so I hope in your heart
You'll choose to let me be free.

Deborah Demary

The End

All my dreams are melting away
with rage and rain,
Soon I will be left with nothing
but my eternal pain.
I wish I was apart of it all,
But I'm so alone,
So alone.
In the rain, in the cold,
In the dark that holds me so,
We're left to die alone.

Patrick Begay

Snow

Snow, beautiful white snow
you fall so silently;
like a blanket
you lay there quietly.
You make me feel peaceful
and tranquil;
you give me contentment
and goodwill.
Snow, beautiful white snow
you are so clean
and pure too;
why can't people be
as pure as you?

Flo Creech

The Path Ahead

There is a path,
ahead for us.
One with bumps,
and curves, and turns.

The path ahead,
is strange to us.
Unknown and untraveled,
to all, but one.

The path could be,
terrific and rewarding.
Or have a lousy,
crashing end.

The path you choose,
isn't final, retrace your
Steps and try again,
for the path is never,
exactly the same.

Jessica Mills

The Rising Sun's Overture

I fear the sinister night
Just beyond the gentle light
I sense the heavy shadow
Outside the safety of this glow.

But I must venture thence
With lamp the ebon to quench
Trusting; I go not alone
Into the intangible unknown.

Only one step at a time
My lamp lifted to shine
Walk carefully; not run
'Til I reach the Rising Sun.

'Tis the gloom I cannot fathom
Every shadow seems a phantom
Hark! The ominous rumbling
I feel my spirit crumbling.

But darkness cannot endure
The Rising Sun's overture
One day my trek will be o'er
Where the Sun sets nevermore.

Elaine E. Kelso

At Day's End

At day's end my dear, dear
friend is not very far away.
Don't be upset don't be afraid
the day's end is coming soon
my dear, dear friend please
have no fear I will watch
over you. You will not be hurt
or sad. Day's end is coming
soon. So go on your way, and
I'll go on mine. I will see
you again but for now I
must say goodbye

Heather Kendrick

Autumn

Blue eyes, blonde hair
Sweet smiles and laughter
Running through my mind
Memories of you

Small chatter, I'm hungry
Bubble baths, you so pretty
Scrambled up, tossed around
Memories of you

Big hugs from small arms
I love you's that melt the heart
Precious moments unspoken
Memories of you

Small cries from noises in the night
Purple dinosaurs and music
Simple things that spark
Memories of you

Denise M. Ammons Wright

Alone, I Wait

As I wait for her to show
I think, why did I come.
I realize she
Will only leave me
Sitting on her door step, so
Alone, I wait.

As the rage builds inside me
I wonder, will she show,
Or just leave me to wait
On her door step, so,
Alone, I wait.

Furious am I
Still waiting to see
Her beautiful face,
When finally, I realize,
She shall never show, so,
Alone, I wait.

Jacob Williams

Weeping Heart

Exasperated
Heart of mine,

Tears by remembrances
Penetrated,

Torn life
Of mine,

Time, which I can't
to resuscitates,

Life past away
Weeping heart left behind

Arthur Adalbert Albert

Love

Love makes your heart shine
brighter than above,
Love makes you break down and cry
like the rain from the sky
Why is everyone so in love?
And when I am in love will
my heart shine like the light above?
Will I break down and cry when
My heart doesn't lift me high?
Love will I still
be loved when and while
I am above?

Denise West

The Little Things In Life

Too often we don't realize
What we have until it's gone.
Too often we wait too late to say
"I'm sorry, I was wrong"
Sometimes it seems we hurt the ones
We hold dearest to our hearts
And we allow stupid things
To tear our lives apart
Far too many times we let
Unimportant things get in our mind
And by then it's usually too late
To see what made us blind.
So be sure that you let people know
How much they mean to you
Take the time to say the words
Before your time is through
Be sure that you appreciate
Everything you've got
And be thankful for the little things
In life that mean a lot!

Ashley Coston

Mother

Mother, you are the seed that
God once planted
He watered it, he talked to it
And he watched it grow.
It started as a seed, then it grew
Into a green stem,
And then into a beautiful flower
That the sun loves to shine on.
Mother, let the rain, rain for you,
And let the sun shine for you
Because you brought me into this world
And I live for your happiness.
I am your seed that you once planted
Now I hope I flourish like you do.

Jessica Walguarnery

Listen To The Children

Listen to the child.
  Listen to her words,
    Hear what he is saying.
Listen to the child.
  Be open to her worlds,
    Receive what he is sharing.

Listen to the children,
  They have much to give.
Listen to the children,
  They will help us live.

Giles C. Ekola

"My Mom"

My Mom is a computer
An expert at business
She smells as sweet as perfume
She's fast like a rabbit
My Mom is red and black
Bright and dark
Like home lit with candles
She's fun like snow
My Mom is excitement!

Gavin Roche Malm

In Passing

Yesterday seems, so very far away.
I find that it plays in my mind...
A familiar tune.
One, I hold on to this day.
It is hard to vanish loving memories,
Held so dear to the heart,
And with them come many tears.
Of joy and sorrow.
Times spent in agony and defeat.
So many fill my days,
Until I am lost in them.
To my own dismay!

Ofelia Martinez

Silent Tears

I need to find a hollow tree
One I can hide inside.
Where it will just be me
And my foolish pride.

People say it isn't right
I should just face my fears.
But they never sat up at night
And cried silent tears.

When you feel the world's against you
Know you're not alone.
For I'll be there it is true
I don't have a heart of stone.

This is true you know
I'm not telling a lie.
So don't feel low
And left life pass you by.

You will make a difference
As the future nears.
To those who never
Cried silent tears.

Amy D. Dorsey

Dreamer

A cold, windy night
no one was insight
A drop of sound
made my heart pound.

I found myself there
standing all alone
yet I felt presence
under the dim moon

I fell asleep without a problem
yet in my head
I still remember
All my thoughts, all my fears.
I shouldn't worry I know
someone's here.

Denise C. Bernard

True Love

My heart is but a rose,
And his love is my life.
My heart blooms
When he smiles,
My heart grows
With each kiss.
My rose dies,
When his love ends forever.

Shelly Williams

A Man

A man, a husband
Strong in mind and body
Working smart and
Playing hard.

A man, a friend
Demanding of self
Giving with faultless fever
Never looking back.

A man, a father
Outvoted often
Respected always
Loved without restraint.

A man, a grandfather
Filled with pride
Fire in his heart
Life to teach.

A man, his life
A passion for living
His family, his friends
The memories enduring

Nancy L. Chuss

Black Is

Black is the shape of a dark
Empty cavern.
Black is the color of
The deepest part of
The sea.
Black is the color of
The Gumbo in the pot
With shrimp and crab.
Black is the sound of
A soft nothingness.
The color black makes
Me feel at ease.
Black is the color of
The million man march
In Washington D.C.
Black is the color of
A black panther.

Je'anna L. Morton

Sadly Missed

Tony was one,
Of our very best.
Now God has taken him,
To eternal rest.

All of his friends
Will miss him so.
But we know that in time,
We'll have to let go.

He looks down on us,
As we go on our way.
We can see his smile,
In every way.

We will always love him,
And always care.
Deep down in our hearts,
He'll always be there.

Karen Overrein

Day of the Butterflies

Over pansies wet with dew
In the morning light,
From the sky of deepest blue
Come butterflies - all white.

Beds of jonquils, sunny flowers,
Nature's arms enfold,
And like sudden April showers
Brush butterflies - all gold.

In the stillness of the evening
Over tulips dust-pink hue,
Straight from heaven come descending
Butterflies - all blue.

Judith B. May

Sacred Moments

Are they forgotten nights
When we made love
To the morning light
The ways you would say
I love you
for all your ways
There is no wrong you could do
That is how much I love you
yes these are all in the past
life never lets
A good thing last
There was fun and laughter
we had together
Each time I thought it
was getting better
There is no sun
Nor will it shine
My memories will be sacred
Happiness is gone, all
Left behind

Frank L. Niglio

My Love For You

My love for you is like a rose,
  sitting in the sun.
You are the sunshine
  that feeds my love.
I know you are the one.

My love for you is like a storm,
  tumbling into a stream.
You are the water
  that holds my love.
You are the one I dream.

My love for you is like a sword,
  held by a shining knight.
You are my hero
  who saves the day.
I have you in my sight.

My love for you will last forever,
  flying with the dove.
Yet when the wolf cries,
  and our brave hawk dies,
Remember...You are the one I love.

Tricia Zimmerman

One and the Same

We're one and the same
But on a different plane

There must be a reason
For the seasons

Are never quite right
To blend with delight

I can only guess
It must be the rest

Of the work to be done
Before the three can become one

I was told it doesn't matter
What we do for after

All is said and done
He is the one

The author of the story
All to his hope and glory

Althea V. Fonville

Friendship

To whom this may concern;
Time of togetherness at last
we meet.
Here we stand together hand in hand
standing on our own two feet.
No burdens, no boundaries to
keep us apart.
Together forever hand in hand and
heart to heart.

Jason L. Werle

Untitled

The night
envelops the day
and all its joy.
There is a cry from deep within.
Darkness falls about,
a lost child wanders in
the moon light
Sad souls dance in the shadows
playing strange music.

Blackness feeds the child's dreams.
And runs his terror faster
as he becomes their song
in the deepness of
the night.

Debra Deese

Vision of Gold

In memory of my brother Justin Adams.
A windy breeze blows throughout then land;
While the sun shines bright in my eyes.
Water ripples down a mile long stream.
I envision him as a river of gold.
He walks on clouds with eyes of stars,
That twinkle as he blinks.
This is my brother, my other bro;
Who is now an angel of the heavens.

Tina Adams Sotelo

Dreams

If you let go of a dream
And it doesn't come back,
Just carry your dreams
Down a different track.
If it doesn't come back,
Then you will know
Your dreams were too fast
Your steps were too slow.
If you let go of a dream
And it does return,
It was always yours-
A lesson you'll learn.
Nothing in life
Is as though it may seem,
But those who are greatest
Are those who can dream.

Jodi Swanderski

Without You

My heart aches for you
But you have another.
My soul longs for you
But yours not for me.
My arms reach for you
But yet they fall short.
My eyes cry for you
And in their tears
I will drown.
For I am nothing
Without you.

Christine Michelle Boldwin

Untitled

To live each day
completely new,
To greet each sunrise
with yesterday concerns
As distant
As if they'd never been..

This is what I wish for me -
To be free
From the cares of yesterday,
Bringing to this
And all my days
Only the joys
that bless each one,
Only the dreams
come true.

Amanda Joy Pelton

If

If I was to give the love
that you give me, wold you be
happy, would you be free? Would
you take that love and run like
the wind, or would you bottle it
up and drink it like gin?

If I could give you the moon and
the stars would that satisfy the
contents of your heart? Would you
need more, or would you need less?
You could take what you wanted and I
would hope for the best.

If I was to give you all those things
would you be mine, would you be mine?
I would yours till the day I die, just
to see the sparkling in your eye.

Christ Lescher

In the Words of a Child

Children's cries will grow quite,
yet they fear forever more,
the broken trust abuse,
tearing deep to the core.
    The bruises will heal,
the tears dry after awhile,
how can you look at them afterwards,
the saddened eyes of a beaten child.
    Little one's looking up to you,
their only source of guidance,
innocent free of sin,
pure of heart only knowing kindness.
    Children say a tearful "I'm sorry,"
no matter what you've done,
thinking it must be their fault,
to you will they succumb.
    "Please don't hurt me,
you're much bigger and stronger,
I'm too little to fight back,
don't you love me any longer?"

Willey E. Thompson

A Passion of Love

Love is kind and true
there was never a doubt
from the moment I met you
and though we've only just begun
I've had to set you free
for I trust in thee an know
thee trust in me. Life and love
for years too come will always
be ours. You see we are the
seeds that sow from day to day
living life loving an cherishing
each other this day. For we
may be gone tomorrow.
These are the ties that
bind a passion of love.

Ramona Lackey

Love

Love is the purest most
definite emotion that man
can conceive.

It is a gift that should not
be abuse or forsaken.

One should carried this gift
as someone would carried their
newborn child.

Caress and adore this gift,
but never misuse it.

Love is power and it has the
ability to conquer all.

Love is life and life is
love.

Without love, life is dead
and existence is merely an
illusion.

Kanita Terrell

Winds Of Change

The winds of change brought you here
The tears are falling like new rain
The loss of you fills me with fear
I keep walking down this old road
The waves are crashing on the shore
Looking up at the bright, blue sky
I feel like I went through a war
Why didn't you just say goodbye
Trying to keep my inner peace
Just figuring out who I am
Knowing my feelings will soon cease
You know I will not go out like a lamb
My future is really, really bright
I can finally see the sunlight

Stephen Austin

Captain Fantastic

It's not inspiration I feel.
Maybe it's just love.
But that can't be
because he is gay.

Missy wanted him to be our father.
Mom was already married, though,
plus
we didn't know where to find him.
Besides, after the problems with Steve,
he was avoiding men with glasses
altogether.

Rachel Welker

Death

God cried today.
I know because I saw his tears
On the windshield
Through my own.

God cried today,
Not for you,
But for my grief
Which he knows I'll have soon.

Then...

God smiled today.
The sun came out.
The tears went away.

God smiled today
Because he's going to welcome you home.
His precious angel is needed in heaven
And He waits with open arms.

Connie L. Dorscheid

I Am

I am lost
Can you find me?

I am hurt
Can you comfort me?

I am abused
Can you protect me?

I am frightened
Can you hold me?

I am a child
Can you love me?

P.J.

Umbilical

I am tethered
to the earth by
a lifeline of
daisies, roses,
pink azaleas
and sweet, wild rye.

When I am old,
pain-pressed, time-torn,
I shall clasp a
bud, cut the cord,
and joyfully
go to be born.

Carolyn Beard Garrett

Untitled

Pitta, patta,
Down comes the rain,
Soft and hard then soft again.
Making rose branches heavy,
And everything wet.
Sometimes it's hard to forget,
Sitting up at night,
Listening to,
Pitta, patta,
The rain on the roof.

Rachel Edwards

That Special Someone

That special someone
whose eyes gleam with delight.
That special someone
who I think of day and night.

That special someone
who brings a smile to my face.
That special someone
who keeps me running at such pace.

That special someone
who brings joy to my ears.
That special someone
who I wish could always be near.

Kristina Proch

Snow

The snow is just beginning.
The ground is getting white.
Soon houses will be covered,
The trees a lovely sight.

Beautiful, the snow is,
It hides all sorts of things,
Makes everything look lovely,
But that's not all it brings.

For many have no shelter,
No home to keep them warm.
No place to heat a cup of tea,
They can't escape the storm.

So I sit beside my window
And watch the falling snow,
My kitchens warm, the coffee hot
I'm rocking to and fro.

I'm grateful for this comfort,
And if I had a wish
It would be that everyone
Could be as warm as this.

Jean Arcangeli

Rings Out

Echoing laughter rings out around me
Are you there?
Do you hear it, too?

A bubbling jubilation
That echoes off the walls

All around me, everywhere
I do not know
From whence it comes

But does it matter to me, now?
Perhaps not

We'll never know
For the laughter's fading
Do you hear the emerging silence?

Lenora Popa

"Grandparents"

Roses are red, violets are
blue, I am such a lucky girl to
have two grandparents like you.
You live in Florida, I live in
Tennessee but that still doesn't
stop my love for you as you
can plainly see. A grandmother
with a gentle voice and the
softest cheeks, and a grandfather
who knows all there is to know
about fishing, every night before
I go to sleep I just keep
wishing that we were closer
together than a bird and a feather.
You both have been the best
you can be and you'll never know
how much it means to me.
I wanted you both to know I
love you and I know you
love me too!

Mandie Adams

What Is A Friend

A person who is genuine,
Reliable, someone you trust.
A sympathetic listener
Is an absolute must.
They're dependable,
A pillar of strength, a supporting arm.
A reassuring blanket to bring you calm.
They're a breath of fresh air,
With smiles that glow.
Whose reply to a favour
Is never a no.
What is a friend?
Why it's a person like you.
I only hope one day
To be a friend too!

Steve Rowland

Wintry Skies

I saw a crimson slash
Through cool turquoise
Mirrored pink on the snowy crest,

Long ago she said,
"How I love wintry skies"
Now alone I sadly glance on high
And softly whisper, "Mother,
So do I, so do I"

Ethel Howell

Change

I think my hair is getting longer,
I think my bones are becoming stronger.
I need a hair cut,
That's for sure.
But is there really any cure?

For me to be getting taller,
Never any smaller.
Really is quite scary,
My, I am so hairy!

Soon I will not be a child,
But an adult,
So meek and mild!

You see change isn't really that bad,
Just sometimes very, very, sad,
For our parents!
But remember, change is for the best,
And is sort of like a great quest,
For adventure and loveliness.

Kathryn Ann Floro

First Love

Thoughts of leaves and lovers words
it is the winter of my memory
wind and time push you
from my mind

I am forgotten now
as the sun pushes the grey
from the sky
I am a lost moon

My love hurts me because you cannot
know it
Love like the dawning sky,
spreading in a winter morning

The morning is cold,
I see my breath
I wish she could see,
the words of my heart

With words you end our love
with an unnoticeable hand
the moon pushes the sun from the sky
day becomes cold night

Jean-Paul Fabris

John Stephen

Betwixt the rising hours
of the light, so I mourn
your absence.
As each moon rises,
so grows my love for thee.

For by thy side I cannot
stand and lay
I cannot in thy chamber,
til my precarious fate hath been
secured and my privilege
hath once again been granted.

It is then I shall profess
my immortal adoration.
I beseech thee, heed with a
prudent ear for mine heart
is true nor many;
but solely thee.

Be contented, whence forth my soul
shall dwell an element of thine
existence.

Holly L. Hirt

Vulnerability

As she speaks to him,
He envisions her naked.
As she opens her soul to him,
He tears off her blouse.
While she cries for him,
He goes for her belt buckle.
And, as she freezes in fear,
He takes his dive.
She is hurt, she's bleeding.
Both mentally and physically.
As he rolls off of her
He grins and sighs.
The air has stopped circulating and
she suddenly feels faint.
As she slips through consciousness
She can barely hear him say—
This never happened.

Emily Rebecca Kozlow

When

When we were together,
Everything seemed right.
When I was in your arms,
I wanted to stay there all night.
When I was confused,
You made everything make sense.
When I heard your voice,
I was no longer tense.
When I needed your help,
You were always there.
When I no longer believed,
You taught me that life was fair.
When I lost faith in us,
You learned how to cope.
When everything ended,
You still had hope.

Sara Hillman

One Love

My love for all is like a song
Winging up to touch the dawn.
A new and fragmentary joy
To hold, to praise and to enjoy.
Such wonders burst upon me now
Such great unfoldment that I vow
My life shall ever praise thy way
And look to the far distant day
When all shall hold their eyes on Thee
And look with joy on what they see.
A world that's ruled by love alone
To freely live and all condone
A fragile, peaceful, lovely thing
With harmony and hearts to sing.
A joy that runs its own true course
With true acknowledgement of its source
Ah life! How can I wait for this?
I'll send my thoughts out with a wish
Embracing all of God's creation
Into one world, one love, one nation.

Edith Thomas

Where Are the Golden Years?

I wish that we'd go back in
time and do it all again.
The yellow roses, you brought
me, with just that special "Grin,
You loved me then, (as you do now)
But as we grow older, why do the
good times fade and things do"
Bug us so?
Were come thru many miles of joy
and seen the hard times too
I've watched the sparkle in
your eyes, that once were oh, so blue
Turn a little faded now as
time takes more of you.
Wish that we could all go
back to "love's" most precious "time"
but they call that hindsight
and it's not so very kind.

Esther M. Chapman

The Blissful Day

When I saw you on that blissful day
I never thought it would be like this

I thought that maybe a touch
or even something like a kiss

When all of that never happened
I thought that we were doomed
but over the time of all those months
my love for you has bloomed

I was in a state of confusion
and wondered if it were all an illusion

But I realize the way it is
when I look into your eyes

My selfishness is gone
my glory distinguished
I bask in your beauty
to me you are a goddess

My frustration, my anguish
is all swept away
this fire inside me would not burn
if not for that blissful day!

James Carter

Earth

This earth is nothing but
wasted no taste in what
life has to offer,

This earth is a terrible thing,
all that you hear is an
abusive ring.

This earth is months, dates,
and times, all we hear of
today is crimes.

This earth is life, birth,
and death.

Lisa Leenheer

Bionic Flowers

Man. Woman.
One attracting the other.
Woman. Man.
One needs one
Need one another.

Yonder. A field.
One flower too many.
Shades. Fragrance.
Delicate shield.
Weeds. Thorns. Wind.
Storm. Sea.

If men can be
The great pretenders
Women can be
Bionic flowers.

Mary Anne P. Gaston

An Exile's Song:

Died of a Broken Heart

It's been a while since e'er I saw you
It's been a while since I was home
But don't you fear because I love you
When I lay my head down
I know I'll be home again some day

It's been all of seven years
It's taken all my innocent ways
But I can still see your colors
When I lay my head down
I know I'll be home again some day

It's been all of seventeen years
It's taken all my blonde hair
But I can still hear your music
When I lay my head down
I know I'll be home again some day

It's been all of twenty seven years
It's taken all my breath away
But I can still smell your flowers
When I lay my head down
I know I'm home today

Rosaleen Crowley

The Cross

Look at the cross
Watch him die
Hold back the tears
Try not to cry
As nails go straight through his hands
Cry down towards the God-given sands
Now watch the nails go through his feet
Try not to scream at every awful beat
Why did they have to call him a liar
He was only here to fill their desire
He loved us, but why
Why did he have to die
He forgave our mistake
Yet got a heartbreak
They laughed and joked
Just then as he choked
He died just for our sin
But God made him rise again.

Lynette R. Frazier

Wish

I wish I could fly,
I wish I could fly,
and soar on my wing,
in a big sunny sky.

I'd fly over the planes,
and over the seas,
over the mountains,
and over the breeze.

I'd fly over the highway,
right past a bird,
I'd fly and be happy,
and not say a word.

Loren Carney

Passion

Slowly sipping of the wine,
    He turned to me and said,
Oh my dear, I think tis time,
    We ought to be in bed.

The evening cloaked us gently warm,
    Dipped fingers in the wine,
I shyly turned to him and said,
    But first we ought to dine.

We dined, sublime in evening's light
    And partook a bit more wine
Gently then, his glance intense,
    He signaled his intent.

Yet languidly my every sense
    Responded to his whim
And, slowly closed the blinds to night
    Responding thence to him.

Gerri Fusco

Cancer

Cancer came, cancer stayed,
Cancer grew, cancer confused,
Cancer mad, cancer sad,
Cancer surgery, cancer treated,
Cancer happy, cancer hope,
Cancer radiation, cancer check up.
Cancer comes back all over the place.
The head, lungs, throat, and spine.
Cancer stayed, cancer confused,
Cancer mad, cancer sad,
Cancer hope.
This time there wasn't hope.
Cancer had won.

Beth Bergman

Moonstruck Memories

Sometime in April,
    Maybe somewhere in June,
I found myself gazing at the moon.

In a star-filled sky
    that filled my eyes,
Memories came in, to enchant my mind.

I thought of all that had happened,
    and all that would come,
But could not come to release myself
    from the events so soon gone.

It was then that I noticed
    the tears down my cheek,
That said more to me
    than words could ever speak.

Tanja Schelenz

Sadness

To never hear a newborn baby
Cry... a miscarriage is the reason
why.... tears that flow from the
eye... don't console the reason why.

To lift a neglected blind baby
by surprise... looking into blank
spots...where there should be eyes...
holding her tightly to apologize.

To seek fortune thought major crime...
the results of a young person's wasted
mind... to see your child laying in the
street... from a gun that did repeat.

To a certain degree with all man's
technology... it's something you can't
explain.... death is a natural thing...
so share the closeness while you can.

For death is certain for every man.

Phillip Lockhart

Relationships

A relationship is like a flower
The seedlings are the helpful deeds,
    that two people so gladly do.
And love and laughter are the showers,
    that strengthen and renew.
The roots are the cherished memories,
    of good times in the past
And the buds are tender promises,
    that relationships joys will last.
A relationship is where bright new
    dreams can start.
And it only blossoms in the heart.

Crysta Carrier

Remembrance

Today I walked down a lonely road
Not knowing what I'd find
As I stopped to rest upon a stump
These thoughts of you came to mind

My youthful days have long been cast
My memories are short and few
But what I remember most of all
Are the days I spent with you

I hope and pray that when I'm gone
You'll think of me as a friend
For that's the way I think of you
And will until the end

So please be my friend today
Not wait until tomorrow
For nothing beats the time that's lost
But trouble and of sorrow

Irene Dimeglio

The Window

Looking out the window,
As far as I can see.
Looking out the window,
I see someone looking back at me.

Looking in the window,
As nosey as can be.
Looking in the window,
Someone's looking out at me.

Annie Sawyer

The Final Battle

It is dark and dreary
This night is so weary
I stare out into the abyss
Outside my window
I listen as the winds hiss
This night as I wait
For the final battle
It is growing late
I hear the rattle
My eyes draw to a side
My head tilts to my shoulder
My eyes grow wide
As I stare at the window
The winds leak in
The cold takes over...

Nauman Ali

Talking About the Weather

    Like the veins of God they
rip through the sky,
a flash! And then gone in
a blink of an eye,
then a rumble, followed by a
tumble!
Oh those sounds make me feel
so humble,
the sweeping rains that follow,
clearing my senses and cleansing
my soul,
the cool breeze blowing that
tells me it'll be better tomorrow.

Robert Sousa

A Music Box

A music box
cherished by two
destined lovers.
A music box that plays of
undying love,
undying devotion.
A music box
granted by the heavens above,
destined to play forever,
for lovers who love,
for dreamers who dream.
A music box
cherished by two
destined lovers,
destined to love forever,
like the forever playing of
a music box
granted by the heavens above.

Jennifer Cory

Regrets

I am dust in the wind
The only thing left is fragments
of my imagination.
Here today memories tomorrow of
A time long ago, no man dare
Tread alone for thoughts of success
Will mold you like stone
Don't let your dreams be your
Weaver of lost youth!

Sandra Lee Lund

340

Only I Know Me

Tell me what I'm feeling,
Tell me what I dream,
Tell me I'm just acting,
Tell me how I seem.
Tell me who I hate,
Tell me who I like,
Tell me how I rate,
Tell me you are right.
Tell me who I am,
Tell me how I look,
Tell me all you can,
Read me like a book.
Then I'll tell you something,
Although you won't agree,
Only I know what I'm thinking,
Only I know me.

Arianna Dae Ronchini

Stray Dog

I looked at her today
But you know she wasn't in there
Her mind had taken her astray
And now I'll bet ya,
That she's left herself
Wide open
For evil, to make its play
she doesn't even know it
but her face will start to show it
She's looking like easy pray
Stray dog:
get your stuff together
Cause you're going to have to
make your move
Stray Dog:
Get it together
Else you're gonna loose

Marty Anderson

"Solitude"

Solitude
Within silence
Her naked night time
She is everywhere
Like the warm wind upon my face
Surrounding me
She caresses me
With delights
Like the sweetest smell
With nights summer air
I turn to look
Within smile
And freeze still
She's nowhere
Love found
Dancing naked away
Into night
She leaves me alone
By myself

Joseph D. La Tour Jr.

Color Me Dead

Purple pretty
  (the sky at sundown)
Prickly gray silence
  (the air between our words)
Locked up blue
  (the past that haunts us)
Razor red
  (the pain that lingers)
Silencing brown
  (the earthen graveyard)
Crystal clear
(the tears that drown us)

Cathrine Hamby

Memories

Hey! You! Come here!
A word to share!
It speaks the truth,
Here and everywhere.

It joins our thoughts,
Our lives and such.
It's not very long,
Just about this much.

The lives of those friends
Who are no longer here,
We speak of them
Perhaps twice a year.

It tells our stories
For all to know,
Of births and deaths
And how we grow.

It is a word
So close to me.
Think very hard now,
You just may see.

Robert C. Van Der Griend

In the Mind of the Beholder

Beauty, what that word implies
As it issues from the tongue,
Embraced by all that stuns the eyes
And by every song that's sung.

All the odors sweet that please us
And the flavors keen that tempt,
Or the softness that can stir us
Of the sensual touch that's dreamt.

But before we bow the knee
To give thanks for what gives cheer;
It's not all those things we see
Or touch, or taste, or smell, or hear:

For those are but gems that fly
Through the mighty panorama,
Caught in the beholder's eye,
Portrayed in his directed drama.

Beauty then the will dispenses
By each soul of every kind,
Filtered finely through the senses,
And emanating from the mind.

Henry M. Ditman

The Snow

Up, up and away
we go!!
To the sky
over the ground floor!!
Will we know,
or will we see the snow...

We don't know
We don't know
We don't know...

But we hope the
sky will stand
still long enough
for us to land and see...

Yes we know
Yes we know
Yes we know...

How beautiful the snow,
from up here we
can see the ground floor...

Oh how beautiful the snow!

Cynthia Y. Randle Jackson

O Leader Of Hosts

O teacher of hosts,
Lest we forget.
O leader of hosts,
You test the mind.
  Life's ABC's
  Swings go up and down,
  Life's merry round.
  O leader of hosts,
  Gates can open
  Life's ABC's
Like worthless paper wads,
Past folds of time.
O leader of hosts,
Do preserve us
  Life's ABC's,
  Success is the crown;
  Stumble, don't fall.
  O leader of hosts,
  Teacher, guiding friend
  Of Life's ABC's

Dorothea Kampfe

I'll Always Love Him

I want to be with him
I love him so
hoping he loves me
I feel better
thinking of him
I think about him
all the time
I long to be with him
I hope he wants to be with me
I hope he feels
Like I do
about him
I miss him so
can't express
how I feel
tried to tell him
hope he feels the same
I guess I'll never know
oh well
I'll always love him, forever.

Rebecca Anne Sires

Boogie Man

Boogie man this,
boogie man that,
Here he comes
all big and fat.
Run, run, run,
as fast as you can
I bet I hit him
with a trash can.
Still running away
Watching his belly sway
What can I say
He's just that way!
All big and fat
Like a big old cat!

Sarah Slaughter

The Valley

As I stood looking down over the valley
From my place high on the hill.
I saw all of God's beauty around me
So peaceful calm and still

The sun made little reflections
From the cars in the valley below
The wind brought the leaves downward
And set things all aglow.

As I turn to leave the hilltop
One more glance I give to the scene
Leaving all of God's beauty behind me
So peaceful, calm and serene.

Marie Shalonis

Sunsets

The sun of your
lives may have set,
but it keeps on
shining in the next,
bigger and brighter
than before.
You came into this
world with pain
and left with the
same feeling.
Those left behind only
see darkness.
The light is only in
their memories.
Show them the
light so they might
live again.
As you shall also.

Bonnie Bair

Theft In the Mist!

Awaken my mind from
where you are.
Lying asleep in a place
where it doesn't belong.
Stolen innocence held
and kept new butt torn
butt torn.
  Aware!!!

Kathleen A. Boyd

Memories

Along the smallest trickling stream
Beneath an old oak tree
I stopped to rest, to meditate
And you were there with me
atop a hill, not far away
I looked and chanced to see
The fading of a rainbow
And you were there with me
I caught the sound of laughter
From a heart so full of glee
I saw you then, because your face
Lives in my memory
I was alone beneath the tree
and only I could see
The better times and other days
When you were there with me

Bonnie J. Baker

Naomi Davis

Needing a love now more than ever
A crush long gone now and forever
Often I wished things were not so
My love inside only left to grow
Insane? Thanks, but I know

Doodling came pictures of thou
A divine babe I thought out
Vanquished life had left me nothing but
  a lonely soul
Indecent emotion has lead me down to
  a lonesome road
Shedding tears as I make these all flow

Mike Chang

Metaphor

  Happiness lies on the hill
  Can I reach and find a way?
  I stand, watching and wondering
  Can I make that Climb today?

Mind's Eye

  'Tis a wonder to behold
  What has become of me?
  There is music in my mind
  And what is true.
  Can I kill the fool too.

Hey Girl!

  Hey! Girl! Hey!
  Can you put your measurement
  On display
  Can you squeeze-eez-eez-eez into
  That dress or jean?
  How dare they be to tight
  And not fit
  Go girl! Get on with it
  And hit those hips.

Clarice Alexander

Unlasting Love

Love is very warm
When it's fresh and new
But love can fade away
Like the morning dew
It can bring sorrow
Scarring the heart through
Love can turn cold
And become untrue.

Lisa Rohn

The Flight

When I'm busily engaged
In doing household chores,
My mind goes a wandering
In and out the doors —
And round about the weeks,
Days, months and years,
Dredging up all sorts
Of thoughts — happiness and tears.
I pen such inspired stories,
(Mentally of course)
Of truth and wit and myth
From many a scattered source.
So I desert the labors
Of keeping home intact,
And flee to my writing nook,
To set down these gems, in fact.
Alas, as soon as I am poised,
Posterior in place,
With pen and paper assembled —
Thoughts go without a trace!!!

Ruth J. Wason

Mirrors of the Soul

It's said your eyes
are the mirrors of your soul
When I look in yours
the loneliness unfolds
So much you have to say
if only you'd let go
I offer you my hand to hold
no strings to bind your soul
and offer you the comfort
that only two can know
you see I've found
looking in your eyes
has been a reflection of my own
what a story they have told

Linda Clark

Andrea

God gave me many grandsons
And each one of them is fun
But when it came to granddaughters
He only gave me one.

Won't tell you that she's pretty
Or say that she is smart
There's something in the way she smiles
That gets me in the heart.

I love my many grandsons
And need them like the sun
But I cherish that granddaughter
Cause he only gave me one.

Margaret Kritikos

My Birthday

I like my birthday,
It's on February 27th
It was my 8th
But I wish it was my eleventh

We played with guns,
But they were only fake.
We broke the "Pinata",
And we had some cake

No more of my party,
I say bye to my friends
I go to sleep,
And that's when the party ends.

Jordi A. Navarrette

342

Dad

As Father's Day comes to rest
Reflect upon those days at best
Sometimes seems so long ago
Other times the pain does show

A sudden glimpse at garden gate
A voice that slightly dissipates
Feet that creak the aging floor
A boylike grin, the kitchen door

Little known and lesser spoke
Now and then a witty joke
The strength of steel he did portray
At times I wished, a man of clay

So as this day comes to arrive
I ponder back on both our lives
And raise a glass to which to say
I miss you Dad, this Father's Day

James F. Hackman

Ghost Mountain Wolves

Golden eyes
Swift through shadows
One dark one light
Drifting somewhere between

Snow that drifted on the breeze
Their presence felt more than known
Turn to look and they were gone
Nothing but wind snow and trees

My soul had been captured
Drifting on quiet feet
Seeing through golden eyes
Slipping back into the shadows
Dark and light

Garry Thompson

Friends

They're like a light in a window
on a cold dark night.
A warm refuge where you're
always welcomed.
A treasure that is beyond compare
whose value and worth grows and
increases with each and everyday.

They are delicate flowers rare and
exquisite to look on.
Rare jewels whose worth simply
cannot be measured.
So very special friends are
they're rare, beautiful
whose price and worth are beyond
the absolute purest of gold
wonderful exquisite rare treasures.

Ruth A. Stafford

Ruin

Beauty inches forward
from this mess I'm calling life,
Inches forward slowly
under this drug
    under this drug
        under this drug
and I've learned to hate you at last,
Beauty

Esther Cervantes

A Savior's Love

The stripes on His back
were worn without shame;
His love for a lost world
was being proclaimed.

A lowly crown of thorns
adorned His holy head;
Spilling forth infinite love
as righteous blood was shed.

The burden of lost souls
spurred Him forward;
Mounting that lonely cross
becoming Savior and Lord.

Undying love nailed Him
to that old tree;
Rectifying sin through Him
that a world could be set free.

Cheryl Elliott

"What Will I Do?"

What will I do
When you're no longer here;
Where will I go
Who will care?

Who will I talk to
A hundred times a day;
Who will be there
To show me the way.

When I'll need a hug
Or a shoulder to cry on;
Who will I confide in
Who will I rely on.

How will I manage
When our time comes to an end;
How will I go on
Without my very best friend.

Kandi M. Siegel

Grandma Mary

This is for Mary
A Mother of three
so talented and wise
though she couldn't even read.

Her life was not easy
Many times it was hard
But thru pain and thru suffering
she kept faith in the Lord.

Though now she is gone
We will always remember
that morning she left us
In the month of November.

Mary knew one day
that she'd pass from this life
And like a blink of her eye
She'd meet Jesus Christ.

Along with her Saviour
her husband would be there
to greet her with a kiss
And say I missed you, my dear.

Jackie K. Akin

New Beginning

There's a cup of coffee
setting on the countertop;
Steam rises in riverlets
toward the ceiling...

You always liked your coffee black-
just like the colour of your heart...

I'll let it stay
until the smoky tines disappear;
I'll wait until it's as cold
as your calculating soul...

Then I'll carry the cup
to your shallow grave,
and pour the darkness over you;
I'll stand there and laugh
right along with the angels,
and thank God for the courage
to break you.

Dawn M. Potter

Chimes of Time

If you listen
    you will hear;
The happy chimes
    of yesteryear.
Fifty years of yesteryears,
When you shared your laughs
    and fought your fears.
Watching children born
    and grown.
Giving them love,
    and love returned.
Sharing sorrows
    as well as joys;
Nurturing all things,
    in spite of foils.
But through it all,
    you did survive.
To live and love,
    as days pass by;
To hear, the chimes of tomorrow.

Erna D. Vasios

Brown Eyes

Your big brown eyes
that are forever shining,
remind me of my love for you.

The pleading eyes
that once looked out at me
from the small cage,
begging for adoption.

The eyes that see everything
that show your love
and your pain.

The brownness that, though tired,
watches over the small family
in which they are most loved.

The wishful eyes
that know freedom,
yet long for love.

And falling snowflakes
will never again be seen
without a window to protect
those quiet, brown eyes.

Laura Brown

"Life Is A Gift Of Love"

We went through some troubled
times in our teen years some
had a hard time they quit
   school or got into an accident.
Bad things happen, but we
need to be on the bright side
   of life also.
Sometimes we all have a fear of
   getting out of bed, and being
afraid something bad will
happen. Even if it does
just say hey, I faced my fear.
   Life is sometimes a struggle
or perhaps a pain. But
   always remember life is
a gift of love.
Dead ends may occur, but
we can turn them around
and make them better.

   Kimberly A. Bakanec

A Sunny Awakening

The morning sun is rising
The birds are in the trees
As I look from out my window
There's a cool refreshing breeze.

Who, but God above
Can make this picture real?
Guardian of all that's great
He makes you truly feel

As the day starts within
Your heart does truly say
"Guide me Lord and Master
To do my Best Today

Take my outstretched hands
Keep my mind so clear
Guide me in your footsteps
This is my prayer-sincere."

   Louise L. J. Davis

The Accident

Into my life
The darkness came
I broke my neck
I'll never be the same

From the jaws of life
To the helicopter flite
to Iowa City
to save my life

When I woke up
you could plainly see
I was
In total misery

They'd put a halo
upon my head
and I was lying
flat in bed

For two long weeks
They kept me there
And never once
washed my hair

   Marion Spicer

Weird Emotions

My dreams are all I care,
But some dreams are a scare.

My feelings are a sort of weird,
Though they have not appeared.

My shadow is a stray,
Though it moves every way.

My heart is tearing apart,
Though my past is in the dark.

The times I use to pray.
Things still go my way.

The times I use to try
Everything turned dry.

Everything is going alright
I wonder how I got through life.

   Maria Luisa Martorillas

Grandmother

Tired, wrinkled hands
Reach out to me -
Trembling, shaking
   My heart is breaking.

Her eyes are aged with wisdom
Her hair has turned to gray
The pain and hurt of years since gone
Time couldn't wash away.

Do you know who you are?
Do you remember me -
And all the times you made me laugh
When I was only three?

I'll hold you in my heart always
They'll never be another
Who could ever take your place
My dear, sweet, kind grandmother.

   Barbara Rebert Little

Shattered

The tinkling of the glass,
The mirror hits the floor,
Pieces of another life,
That is now no more.

The pieces cut their feet,
As they try to walk across,
Trying to find their way again,
But finding that they're lost,

Another life yet broken,
Because of simple things,
Shattered shards of glass,
Hit like bells rings.

   Kimberly D. Pearson

Two Hearts

Two hearts united
beating as one
each beat a word of love
a love so strong
to last forever
this kind of love
I will give to you
a love strong enough
to last forever
and one more day
on into eternity

   Donald Beeler

Untitled

When I look in his deep blue eyes
It reminds me of a blue lake
With his eyes sparkling and glittering
He walks over to me and speaks

His voice is deep and smooth
He speaks in a friendly tone
I think I could just melt
Melt away and never be seen

He asks me to dance
I gladly say "yes"
I am so happy
I feel like flying

We dance the night away
With no care in the world
I want to stay in his arms forever
And he says I can

   Letha-Joy Howard

Distance

The stars that I see,
   seem smaller than me
As I am observing them
   from below
They tell me 'tis not true,
   but that distance has
distorted my view
   and that the stars are much
larger than me
Though finite I am
   and infinite is near
as I travel with our sun,
   our nearest star

   B. H. Marcroft

Always

I always though you'd be there
to hold me in the night
to gently soothe my cares away
and turn what's wrong to right

I always thought you'd be there
I guess my thoughts were wrong
and always seems to end too soon
so goes the familiar song

I always thought you'd be there
although it fell apart
and each has gone our separate way
you'll always have my heart

   Cynthia L. Bradley

Obsession

Every time
I close my eyes,
I see you look at me.

So perfect,
In my mind, are you,
I fear you'll always be.

With me
Everywhere I go,
For everything I do.

A longing wish,
A captive heart,
Forever wanting you.

   Kelly Thompson

Untitled

Aged, Hunched, Teabags, Slow, Careful, Gray, Blue.
When you have lived a wonderful, terribly exciting life.
Have mingled with the jet set of Washington.
Worked on interesting medical research.
Made a difference somehow in society.
Love life, adored living, moving, balancing, caring.
Gathering all the wisdom from all the years of lessons and experience.
Along the path you have given from your soul or maybe just from

Your heart.
Now eighty, lonely, left with the memories that people half listen to.
To walk,takes the effort if once took to do a week of work.
You've made it to your destination, the table.

No one on the other side.
And I watch you from behind.
Cherylann Bartello

Just Another Morning In The Burbs

Another day, another dollar,
hurry, press down dad's white collar.
The clock radios are all ringing,
is that a rock group I hear singing?
The toast and tarts are popping,
the floor could use some mopping.
There's a glob of jelly on the fridge,
and don't forget, we're hosting Bridge.
Come on, it's my turn in the shower,
this milk is old, it's even sour!
What's that jackhammer noise out in the street,
how's baby Jane to stay asleep?
The school bus is in sight,
kids, grab your lunch and please don't fight.
A kiss for dad, he's out the door,
three meetings today, or maybe four.
Mom struggles with the laundry, it weighs a ton,
yet it's eight a.m. — and her day has just begun!
Dorothy Lingg

The Holy Family

My Father pours His eyes in mine
His wine warms the winds of my soul
Father sees me, a ruby in the dew
I see it too, I am made whole.

My Mother turns to Him, bends to Him
Mouth upon His mouth, heart upon His heart
Her beauty is the art of endless gifting
The arc of golden Love between them, lifting.

And with the tend'rest of smiles She beckons me
And offers out from Eternity
Her Truth, a vessel filled with tones and bones
And herbs and oils and stones and sacred geometries
Moonsongsilver! Moonsongsilver!

This is the day.
This is the day I take my place
Amidst His glowing and Her knowing
In Grace.
This is my place. This is my place.
This, the Holy Family
My Father, my Mother, and me.
Ellen Roos

The Walking Hormones

The walking Hormones, live in a world of their own.
When asked to do chores,
They simply laugh and close their bedroom door.

Be prepared for any type of clothes.
The kind that sags from head to toe.

You know what kind of food is hip.
Hamburgers, cokes and chips.

Let's talk a minute about hairstyles.
Colors that are short and funky, is this my child?

Listening to rap with Vanilla Ice and M. C. Hammer,
would drive any sane parent to the slammer.

If you think, I am exaggerating! Look at the specimen
My daughter is dating.

Mom, "Isn't he cute in his black leather suit?"
Am I seeing clear?
There is a chain strung from his nose to his ear.

Oh well, I must learn to survive,
If I want to come out of this situation alive.

Because honey, when I am dead and gone,
There will be another generation of walking Hormones.
Audrey Jandran

Firefighter Macho

This group of guys claim fair and decent.
My feeling is, the fair is recent.
The other part, I have no doubt,
Was in their being - sure to come out.

The idea of fair, regarding women,
Was surely not at all a given.
After all, it seems to me,
Fair to women cannot Macho be.

It's just that they aspire to lead.
Along the way, they had to read
The theory of human relations
Is what you study to lead nations.

Their nation is the world of pumps,
Hoses, ladders - and old grumps
Who said a woman is weak and feeble,
Hire her, it's like a needle
Stuck somewhere it should not be,
You won't be able to be free
Of those nagging, painful little pricks
Caused by the species with no dicks.
Julie Ann Llorente

In Answer To A Voice; The Wood Duck Speaks

I track the tangled wood of the marshes bed.
Along empyrean paths of infrared
I wing the azure maps of the welkins light.
I am rapture dressed in feathered flight.
A voice issues from the earth under
The dark cloud scrubbed skies.
A voice racing like piercing thunder,
It's sounding multiplies;
Arises from the brambled woods beyond
This fragile spangle of emerald pond
Sings in the swamp cold mud
Hums in the heated blood
Emanates from heaven's crystalinity
Calls it's chant from some savage divinity
It tunes into each ear
The stuff of life is here!
Janice Takata

What Is A Father

A father can be a very special
person in your heart.
A father can be so dear,
you don't want to be apart.
A father can be someone to
suddenly come into your life,
And when you're frustrated and
confused he gives you wonderful advice.
A father eventually becomes a
grandfather, which makes his life complete.
Then you know you filled his life
with joy and happiness, which
makes you feel really neat.
So when you're feeling down and
you don't know what to do, then
just call your father, he will take care of you.
A father doesn't have to be the
one who helped conceive you.
A father can be your father when
all he says is, I Love You!

Pam Smith

In the Eyes of a Teacher

In the beginning my head was down
And my eye could only see
What I myself could believe in.
But a person of great heart,
Never gave up on me.
All though there were things
That this special lady could not solve
In the eyes of this teacher,
She saw many things.
But to every eye there's a trick
Not despiteful,
But helpful
The sadness of the word that was spoken,
Could only be in shame
That I had no one to turn to
On this cool March day.
So as in every eye,
You see something special in anything and anyone
And to find that it was all
In the eyes of a teacher.

David Lloyd

Key To My Heart

I had closed the door upon my heart
And wouldn't let anyone in.
I had trusted and loved only to be hurt.
But that would never happen again.

I had locked the door and tossed the key
As hard and as far as I could.
Love would never enter there again,
My heart was closed for good.

Then you came into my life
And made me change my mind.
Just when I thought that tiny key
Was impossible to find.

That's when you held out your hand
And proved to me I was wrong.
Inside your palm was the key to my heart
You had it all along.

Amanda Plunkert

'Till We Meet Again

Today I watched the icicles melt
Gently dropping outside to the earth
Mother nature was quietly weeping
On this day of my dear Father's birth

In this memory I lit a lone candle
And I sang his song up to the sky
Then the tears started falling so softly
Matching those on my window outside

How he loved sitting silent in native
And he passed that gift right down to me
We'd bask in the warmth of the sunlight
Watching birds come to feed from the trees

Oh what joy he taught me how to feel
With his quiet and most gentle way
How blessed I was to have his love
And I cherish that gift even day

His spirit now flies with the highest
Those who lived life with love and with grace
He helped to land man on the moon
Now he's free to soar off into space

Judy Woodward

The Kiss

It was a moment she had waited her whole life for and it was
about to happen.
She closed her eyes and waited.
Finally, she would be able to know what it was like to be like
everyone else.
They knew what it felt like, and had done it many times before.
But this was a first for her and she knew that it would change her
life forever.
She could feel her palms; they were sweaty.
She was so nervous and it was the waiting that was killing her.
A deep rush of excitement filled her body, her heart pounded, and
her cheeks began to flush as something soft touched her.
It was happening, and she couldn't believe it.
Then, just as it seemed like she was floating on air, it ended, and
the moment she had waited her life for had come and gone and was
forgotten like all the rest.

Tami Hallman

A Memory In Lavender

"Oh mother, how pretty!", I exclaim in my pleasure
as I gaze on this beautiful, lavender treasure.
She replies in a voice low, sweet and sad,
"It's the dress that I wore when I married your dad."

And I see the face of a lovely, young girl
her hair, burnished copper, in ringlet and curl.
Wide blue-gray eyes, creamy skin smooth as silk.
Soft smiling lips showing teeth white as milk.

And the face of a young man glowing with pride,
for the girl on his arm, as he makes her his bride.
A portrait preserved, like a rose that is pressed,
wrapped in the folds of a lavender dress.

The trunk has since vanished, I know not to what place,
lost in our travels, disappeared without trace.
Taking with it the relics of a time long ago,
leaving but ghosts in a lengthening shadow.

Now and again, in my fond reveries,
I revisit the trunk and its treasures.
When I open the matchbox, I so well remember,
I'm carried away on a billowing cloud of pale lavender.

Lydia E. Morang

Presence

I was there when you cried and nursed your sorrow.
I was there when you were happy and I rejoiced.
I was there when you were hungry and offered you food,
   restoring your life anew.
I was there when you were afraid and restored your faith.
I was there in your darkest hour, holding your hand,
   carrying you over the abyss.
I was there when you were naked and I clothed you with hope.
I was there in your imprisonment and visited your spirit,
   upholding your soul.
I was there when you suffered and were hurting,
   bringing healing wings to bind your hurts and fears.
I was there when you were alone,
   being your constant friend and perpetual comforter.
I was there at your birth, blessing your beginning.
I was there at your death, bridging your journey home.
I am the Alpha and Omega,
   he who believes in Me shall inherit Eternal Life.
I am, was, and will be there.
My name is Jesus.

Marilyn J. Clemens

Faith and Fascination

Life is such a wonder.
Why oh' why do I ponder,
on the fascination
of God's imagination?

To have created life,
husband and wife,
emotions and feelings
in all earthly dealings.

How could he know,
what feelings show?
Why love plays such a roll
and hate takes a such a toll?

So many questions to ask,
it must be quite a task.
To be watching from afar,
knowing this is only one star.

To believe or not believe,
hoping that the faith will never leave.
Knowing you will always have a helping hand,
when you find on your own two feet it is hard to stand.

Vikki Palazzari

Frustrated Fisherman

Little fishy in the brook,
Saw a man with a pole and hook.
Said "You silly man you want to play,
I will steal your worm away."

He took the bait and away he swam,
Back to his family by the damn.
Told his Mother with a smile,
"The man's up the river just a mile."

Brothers and sisters you want to come,
Oh what fun we'll have some,
We'll tease the man with the pole and hook,
Teach him to fish in our little brook.

So they went back up and swam around,
Laughing and teasing never making a sound.
Frustrated the fisherman went home with a frown,
But the Fishes were Happy and went back to their Damn...

Wanda Gail Hough

No Glory

A man of average age and height
Sends a sphere soaring into flight.
The shot is good and then floats right.
The ball goes long, the man yells, "Bite!"

He evaluates his shot for a while.
What's wrong with my swing, my stance my style?
It seems he missed the hole by a mile.
A frown on his face, no chance of a smile.

Jason Smith is his given name.
He's like many seeking fortune and fame.
Neither of these will come to him through this game.
For his stance and his style will forever be the same.

A new set of clubs is what Jason bought.
A single decent game is all that he sought.
But this decent game will come to him not.
For golf gives no glory to tempers that are hot!

Stephen Kit Coffeen

Who Will Wait

i came tonight to say good-bye...
i came alone but, we are all together...i stand and wait

small talk and laughter... hugs and tears... overdue reunions...
the moments turn to memories... the line grows longer...
i stand and wait

six thousand seconds now since i came... i wonder why
...The Spirit is here, his contributions to life abound...
still.. i stand and wait... now, not to say good-bye

i open to embrace... there are no words... all have been spoken...
eyes meet... thoughts touch... hearts enfold... the love is
overwhelming... so many yet, that stand and wait...

his life an inspiration... i leave with more comfort than was
possible to give!

i go today to comfort those she left behind...
i go with others but, we are alone...no need to stand and wait.

those remaining are pleasantly withdrawn...
their comfort is in no more earthly pain
...my pain is seeing no heavenly comfort.

i ponder on two lives spent... what of this life I am living
and think now of my leaving... those I will have passed....
will others come and be together...will any stand and wait?

Ginger K. Silver

Fingerprints

Fingerprints here - fingerprints there
   Fingerprints everywhere.
Was it really so
   Or did it seem as though
They could not be cleaned away?

Clay, paints, mud - all left in fingerprints -
   How often have I missed them since.
For now that our walls are clean,
   No patterns on them seen,
We miss them, I can truly say.

Jay, Sandy and Judy are grown
   With darling families of their own.
And now I see their walls adorned
   With fingerprints no longer scorned.
For what the picture, makes joyous every day.

Jeanette Becker

The Chair

The chair is a double recliner
The chair we shared was divided
Like us, it was half of a whole
The chair is still here, though worn from years of use
It is still here mostly because I still can't bare to
Part with it, and it still hurts to see anyone else sit in it.
So it has been replaced in our favorite sitting place
By a new sofa recliner
When I need to feel close to you
I still go and sit in our chair in the next room
I don't know what I expect to happen
It can't bring you back to me
But maybe it helps to keep my memories
Of you more alive
Although the chair has been replaced
Your place in the chair hasn't been
Nor have you been replaced in my heart

Shirley Bundridge

I Am Death

Of all my faces you never know which one you'll see,
No matter who you are you belong to me.
I can show mercy or I can bring pain,
I am the one first known as Cain.
As it was in the beginning, it still is today,
I have but one job, that is to slay.
I can never love my heart is of stone,
You better tread lightly you're never alone.
For I am always watching, you best beware,
The slightest slip up and I'll be right there.
I am the monkey on your back forever,
You cannot escape me despite your endeavor.
I can choose whomever, day or night,
When I want you, I got you, no need to fight.
Who can save you from my grip? None,
Whether you're full of sin or an innocent one.
To me it does not matter, it's all the same,
For misery and sorrow I am to blame.
I am death, my name sends shivers down the spine.
Sooner or later you will be mine.

Agueybanai Rivera

Forever

When I first looked into your eyes,
  I could see the fear, the worry, and the pain.
You hid it well
  though I could sense the confusion.
You tried so hard not to let anyone know your hurt,
  but I knew it
  and I felt it.
Now your eyes are closed
  forever to the world
  no longer open to the pain
  no one can see the hurt now.
And as I look in the mirror,
  I see your eyes
  looking back at me.
I see the fear, the worry, and the pain.
Full of darkness,
  forever.

Gena Yingling

Mother

How did you survive all that pain?
It almost killed me just to watch you
Curl up and get so old, so fast

Soon you were a shell in the chair,
with that one light, books as your company,
pain as your friend

Inside yourself,
no one touched you

Papa and I talked about what would happen
if you never made it back to us

We talked about what might happen in
the green-white disinfectant hospital
the smell scared me, I was scared for you

Now, you manage to smile
through the lines that pain left on your face
you are shrunken, withered
and I do not tell you enough "I love you",
or how I admire you

I admire you for being brave, for surviving, not for yourself,
but for us, the needy ones, who wouldn't; couldn't let you go

Kirsten Power

"The Elephants Upstairs"

Some elephants moved in upstairs from me.
I hear the pounding thud of each footfall.
They trumpet every morning in the hall.
Banana peels where they ought not to be,
They make me slip most inconveniently.
The cracks begin to lengthen in my wall,
As they rehearse for their next costume ball.
A ceiling tile just landed in my tea!

I think I'll have a talk with my new freres,
And tell those pachyderms a thing or two.
I'll knock and say "I've had it up to here,"
"Be quiet, or I'll call the cops on you!"
That should work, but if perchance I hear
Them once more, why, I'm calling up the zoo!

Thomas J. Tobin

Brother Curtis And The Gate

A song in his heart.
A smile on his face.
He waved at people.
As he stood by the gate.

He told one and all.
Of his love for the Lord.
And when Curt was around.
Nobody got bored.

He sang for the birds.
The squirrels, and the trees.
He even sang his song for me.

Now the gate where he stands.
Are all made of pearl.
And the songs that he sings.
Are not of this world.

This sweet simple man. That we all know,
Is walking now on streets of pure gold.

He went to the garden alone. But when he entered the gate.
There his family did wait.
Now he's no longer alone.

Patricia Browning

Deep Reverie

I lay there unmoving, my head on his arm
Time passing as life had, our memories so warm.
In closeness and stillness, the wind in my hair,
Our own piece of Eden, no worry, no care.
We shared many thoughts, no need to be spoken,
I, content with his presence, eternal, unbroken.

I awoke to awareness of wild nestlings apeep,
My love still beside me in my reverie so deep.
I lay there in limbo still sensing his nearness,
Reliving our lives, our love and his dearness.
Unwillingly I roused to reality....alone,
Realizing I had dreamt on his cold, bare gravestone.

Bertie D. Conn

My Husband

We've been together since that day long ago
When you said I love you and I want you to know
You're my choice for my wife
And from this day forward, I give you my life
To share with me all the days ahead
Forsaking all others there's nothing to dread.
And so we were married, my lover and me
With small golden bands for all to see
That we were united in love, evermore
For love was our beacon, and you were the door
To days full of happiness (though times we were sad)
We remembered our vows and the good times we had
And we steered through all the waters of life
You, as my husband, and me, as your wife.
So we ask the Lord for His Help from above
To be together with all of our love
All the days of our lives, with you in my heart
Always together till death us do part.

Joan M. Morgan

Lucky Me

On a summer day as a child I used to lie
On my back in the shade of a tree and look up at the sky.
I'd see animals, people and things all passing by
Made of soft fluffy clouds.
I'd say to my sister, "I see an elephant up there, do you?"
Well it looked like an elephant until the wind blew...
Now it's just a fluffy cloud.
Then sometimes at night before going to bed,
What was that poem we said?
Star light, star bright, first star I see tonight...
Then all the millions of twinkling stars came out of their hiding
    place
Until the whole world was covered with a dome of sparkling lace.
Oh the things we'd imagine...the pondering that the night sky brings.
Where did God come from...where is he now...do the Angels really have
    Years have passed and it's been a while
Since I was that fun-loving country child.
But there are still fluffy white clouds and millions of twinkling
    stars.
They are still up there in the sky
Do children still know of their beauty and fun...
Or, are they as lucky as I.

Joyce Knight

Remember Mama

   Please remember mama and all the times we shared.
Whenever you needed a special friend, you knew that
I was there. Please remember the good times, the
laughing and the love, and honey please remember
mama's watching from above.
   Sweet heart please remember all the tender growing
years from formula to teddy bears, mama was with
you and mama cares. Baby please remember
through the good times and the bad, that mama's always
with you and never wants you to be sad. So in the
times ahead of you, do everything you can to remember
mama loves you as you grow into a man.
   Sweetheart don't think of me as lying in the
ground, know that I'm in heaven now, but that I'm
still around. Someday you will marry, and have a
special love. Honey please remember mama's
watching from above. Even though your heart is
breaking cause your mama's gone away. Baby
please remember we'll be together again
some day.

Cindy Anderson

Something To Think About

During the hard times in life we always ask "why me",
    But do we ever remember there are people who are worse off
    than us?
We face many decisions in life,
    But do we think of who we may hurt if we make the wrong
    one?
Sometimes we choose to join the crowd when they are making fun
of someone,
    But do we ever put ourselves in the other persons shoes?
We may sometimes give in to peer pressure,
    But do we ever think about what will happen to us is we do?

In life we have to learn to look at both sides of a situation,
    For then we are not only being fair to ourselves, but to
    everyone.
We have to learn to think before we do,
    So that we may save someone's feelings.
We also have to realize this,
    We are not the only person who counts: everyone does.

Betsy St. John

A Sweet, Sweet Dream

There is a place among the trees,
With gumdrops floating in the breeze.
Lollipops sticking around everywhere,
The odor of chocolates fills the air.
I see huge nut filled candy bars.,
There are marshmallows not too far.
Jelly beans stuck on long red stalks,
Peanut brittle line streets or walks.
Sodas and milk shakes run like a brook,
Will you just stop and take a good look.
Peppermint trunks are on all of the trees,
Taffy on their branches swings like leaves.
An ice cream mountain looking oh so slick,
There are nuts sliding down towards the bricks.
They are licorice, instead of black,
forming a long line like a railroad track.
Candy, ice cream, goodies are everywhere,
On the ground, on the trees, and in the air.
All of these sweet would make anyone sick.
I hope I am dreaming, please wake me quick.

Blondelia Morris

Jeannie Immortalized

Into my life, as if out of a dream you came,
Giving me determination, and new inspirations,
Which I never would have had,
Had I not met you.

You can never leave me, Jeannie;
Not my mind, not my heart.

The smell of loveliness you personify
Reminds me of flowers in Nigeria and Nairobi.
Your physical touch gives off a natural high.
Your eyes fill my mind with reminiscences
Of the sun setting, amidst a background
Of golden hue.

You boil my blood with the intensity
Of your consuming, smokeless flame,
When you touch me.

You can never leave me;
You can never go away, Jeannie.

John Wilcox

My Parent's Lesson On Life

Looking back to when I was a child,
    remembering that painful sigh,
Every time your eyes became clouded,
    when I asked those questions why.

"Daddy, why do you cry?"
    "Mommy, why are you so sad?"
"Have I done something wrong?"
    "Am I being bad?"

Wrapping your arms around me,
    replacing every bad feeling with good,
Throughout each day you strived,
    until your lesson was understood.

"Our promise today and always,
    from you we shall never part,
But, one day we must leave you in body,
    to remain forever in your heart."

Your life's lesson became so clear,
    that I need share time and love freely each day,
For when once you give them to others,
    they can never be taken away!

Debra Kay Buschkoetter

War's Never Ending Battle

I look upon someone's face-is it friend or foe
Am I in another time, another place from long ago?
The restless nights with sweat streaming down my face
Praying I'd get out of this God forsaken place.

There's an emptiness and constant gnawing in my soul
As I see the explosive lights and hear the thunder roll
Of distant fire and feel the earth tremble with each fired round,
My body motionless, crouched upon the cold damp ground

I can feel my heart beating fast and hard from fear
While my senses warn me the enemy is near.
It was kill or be killed, for war destroys
And those that were killed were still only boys.

I try to block out the painful memories of this barren place
And the look of horror on my buddies blood soaked face.
I fought in a war many years since past,
But the war within me rages fast.

Suddenly, I hear the roar of choppers overhead
Thank God! I'm safe, - I jump - out of bed
To look upon my wife's face - is it friend or foe
Am I in another time, another place from long ago?

Sandra May Bradshaw

Swinging Free

Three brave, brown leaves
Hanging on the branch
Swinging and swaying
In the wind of cold December.

They were there in the green of Spring
The warmth of summer
And the gold of fall
As I remember.

When all those that I have companioned are gone
And I am left with one or two others
Will I hang in there to my native vine
As firm and strong and free?
Swinging in the wind of cold December.

Roberta McLean

Life Wishes

If I could wish a life for you, its path would be so smooth.
No sharp edged rocks to stumble on, no thorny hedge to block
your view.

A wondrous walk so straight and true, through sparkling
yellows and calming blues.

But your life is not mine to make, and this road not mine,
but yours to take.

When it twists and turns and narrows, you must choose which
way to go.

Use your heart, your mind, your soul.....
    for out of these spin dreams and goals.

Katherine M. Littrell

I Am; The Birds of the Lake and Shore Speak

I am the measured motion of
The avenues of the wind's highways.
I am of the rainbowed heads of
Storm fronts and lightning slashed skyways.
I ride the squall of the dimpled waters
As easily as sleepers stretch out in summer's hammocks.
I am ease from the crowded city's din
Of trains, ells, sirens and delivery trucks.
I am multitudes of wings
To frame the clouds with feathered nations.
I am of the intellect
Of each season's grace and occupations.
I am *that* voice; that tremolo
On the summer lake that softly floats to ground.
I am *that* voice that calls you;
That sews itself into your soul with threads of sound.
I am *that* dance of dark and light
Upon your beachheads of reflected sun.
I am *that* insistent energy
Of new dreams and climates begun!

Janice Takata

Alone

Something inside me is hungry for life
and cutting at me like the blade of a knife.
I'm stifled inside with no way out,
and I can't stop my heart from filling with doubt.
I want to stand on a mountain and yell with all my might,
life is worth living, but there's no one in sight.
Someone to talk to, just one on my side,
who'll understand what I'm feeling and know the size of my pride.
The room is so full and talk has left my throat dry,
yet no one has heard me and I can't understand why.

Laura Pylman

Freedom's Song

Tiny sparrow on the wing....
Freedom is the song you sing!
You know nothing of constraints...of mental prisons and human pain...
This must be why your song is joy!

To have no limits...
High or low...
Flying so freely as you go...
No heavy heart or hidden tears, no sad regrets or captive fears...
This must be why your song is joy!

If I could be a tiny bird...
With endless space before me...
I'd fly and leave it all behind...
My mind, my heart and memory!
Like you, I'd know a solitude, as I soared on freedom's wing...
And far above the pain below, my song of joy I'd sing!
S. J. Tanquary

Why Not?

I have created a steeple from this and that
Selfishly, I lock the door
Life is confusing for the fact I mismatch
Now, state of mind seems poor
Still, trying to do for others is a difficult task
I'm a psychic, insecure
A budge toward the thick clear line is all I ask
A tap through a make believe (door)
A shove up off the cold (floor)
A space where I may truly breathe
An attempt that is ever so bold
Why not?
Kevin Jenkins

Welcome Rain

An umbrella of clouds drift overhead,
protecting from sun the dry lake bed.

So long without rain no water is found,
only large cracks in the sunbaked ground.

Clouds darken and a breeze welcome by all,
hoping soon the rain should fall.

Small puffs of dust from first drops rise,
while thunder echoes across the skies.

So welcome the rain, could there be a chance,
that the God's understood the drum and the dance.
Dennis Elliott

The Mother Sea

Remembering the velvet nights. The
nights we fell upon our berths and
spoke but a few words. We fell
forward into the space where darkness
engulfs and dreams rush forth.

In those few moments before the dark,
we felt the gentle rolling. We rocked
slowly from side to side and were lulled.

Within the undulating swell, the
delicate tongue of sleep lapped upon
our senses, and we folded and
enfolded and become swaddled babes
within a watery womb.
Susan Vail

The End

My heart lies shattered
On the cold and damp ground
I lie beside it in sullen darkness
Tasting the pain of death's fatal touch
In the deepest pit of my soul
I can't go on anymore

Pulled down further
Into a dark abyss
In the end will I survive?
As thAnd I can no longer breath
In the end will death call on me?

Life has no meaning anymore
Lost in hopelessness, filled with despair
Death seeks me out, stealing all I love
Leaving me to suffer
With no strength to go on living
I wait for the end
Nikki Craig

Love of My Life

I see you in my mind.
You are one of my best friends,
So it makes it even harder to show my love for you.
Every time I pick up the phone,
And dial your number I spaz.
Maybe I feel this way because you're so kind,
But when I see you my heart glows.
I hope you feel this way too.
I am so afraid you'll just say no.
You make me spin like I am "Taz."
I love you so much it puts me in a bind.
When I think of you my eyes shine.
I just wish I could tell you;
I miss the warm sent of your favorite cologne.
If I tried to tell you I know I will only spaz.
You, you are my every breath.
You are the love of my life.
Alisha K. Degase

I Shall Speak

I shall speak of Eagles, soaring upward,
Symbols of this nation.

Oceans roaring, in and out
With the tides never ending motion.
Bubbling brooks, sparkling Lakes
Mountains stretching high above
Puffy white clouds, topped by snow peaks
Shrouded by misty fog, that surrounds it.

I shall speak of a Deer
Running over the field of tall grass,
Tail bobbing, up and down
As he runs, in fear of man
Finding a place of seclusion.

I shall fly by plane, to a strange land
Stare in awe, through a window
At the white clouds and blue sky
While a golden sun in sinking.

I shall express, feeling of joy and tears
Create with words a picture
for others, to see, In poetry.
Ruth Merolillo

Walls, Windows and Bed

Walls, hard cold and uncaring seeing my weeping and my daring
life is so undawn, with its light daring to morn;
life and the pursuit of happiness; I laugh in its face
for they are for the rich in mind and spirit, I do be witch
walls, windows, and bed; to those, goes to those that are dead;
does make a prison and its keeper; to the meek I think it goes deeper;
it causes them to grow weaker and meeker
walls, you hide light and friendship, that once was or can never be,
windows you hide nature and air; that can grow to be
so, bed are you my new prison, coffin, and keeper,
For will you be my death, your words still go unsaid,
I say you will be no more, until-my last baited breath, for you I
    give no
comfort; for you I give no pain. Walls, windows and bed, for you I do
not blame, nor do I tame; for my sorrow and shame are only mine to
blame, because death I will tame, so now I am ready for fortune and
fame, Death beware; for I am coming to tame, your fire and your flame.
Death beware; because I will soon be there. And finally to
you — walls, windows and bed; listen to my words about to be said:
"You Are No Longer My Prison, Coffin Or Keeper."
For Death I have tamed; I have returned, to you; to do the same.

Tavia M. Rich

The Darkest Night

The clouds cast shadows on the sunset sky
To prepare the world for the next dark night
To ride the skies and tell us lies
To push us down with all its might

The trees cast shadows on a sunrise field
Just to make us aware that the darkness is there
To push away all the believers and
To tell them that they better beware

And she runs everywhere for cover
As she sky climbs high above her
She can run but she can't hide
The darkness will find a way to her mind

The world finds its way through the darkest night
Just to feel the pain of another lost fight
And she tells the world everything's fine
But still she can't say what's on her mind

Tyler J. Bankes

Her Chanson

Where am I?
I cannot recall
I'm most certainly not where it seems I am
The lovely song surrounds us and soaks us
Her head rests softly against mine
As I hold her beautiful form perhaps too tightly
We sway slowly
Almost as if pulled by no resolve of our own
But by a superior one
My face is solemn
For my thoughts aren't considering the world around me
My senses have been dismissed by my heart
Where was I?
A place greater than I have known

Alex Cummings

Ode To My Love

If you leave me behind-
I will forever be on your mind.
You'll always be on my mind
    and all the wonderful, kind
    things you've done for me.
Never unselfish, always to be
    the greatest love always to me.
I put you through so many pains
Awaiting our day of profitable gain.
We stayed together for years
We did our share of shedding tears
But no one told us what to do
We did our best to keep from being blue.
All my thanks to you -
    for remaining true.
I did what I could do -
    hoping it would be enough for you.
You stayed by my side as we vowed till we die.
Nothing greater than how I feel for you
Honest dear - "I do love you!".

Sandy Doherty

The Girl

The time I'm without her
I mourn in sadness,
I swim in the tears of the sorrows of pain

The time I'm with her
I treasure the time we spend together,
I forget the shyness I hold in myself,
    And come out into the open

When I'm with her in the coldness of the night,
I come close to her heart which beats against mine
    And warms me up like an open fire

When it's dark and I look into her eyes,
I see two blue sapphires shining in the moonlight

As we are walking down the sidewalk and turn to her house,
I whisper softly into her ear,
"I love you".

Chris Ivers

Deep In Our Hearts Your Memory Is Kept

God saw you were getting tired.
And a cure was not to be.
So he put his arms around you
And whispered come to me.
With tearful eyes we watched you, mother.
And saw you pass away.
Although we loved you dearly,
We could not make you stay.
Your loving heart stopped beating,
As you laid there at rest.
God broke our heart to prove to us
He only takes the best.
It has been a year since our Lord
And savior called you home,
Leaving a void that cannot be filled.
Your friends and family love and miss you.
May you find peace in the shadow of a loving God.
Dough Boy still sits and waits for you by the window.
Please protect us.
There is still much more to come.

Evelyn Tallman

Autumn's Artwork

There's beauty in an autumn morn; its colors red and gold.
The sunlight is a work of art; with secrets yet untold.
There's beauty in an autumn day; when flowers shyly nod.
They drop their petals one by one upon the waiting sod.
There's beauty in an autumn eve; when sunlight shadows fall,
Upon the brown and yellow leaves e'er winter comes to call.
There's beauty in an autumn night; the moon a silvery glow,
With promise of a frosty bite when autumn turns to go!

Helen F. Roberson

Missing You

Tonight I am alone,
my shadow by my side.
Lying in my empty bed
sitting in my empty room imagining I
was with you.
Now, walking alone
I was once by your side.
Your love kept me warm on the coldest
winter night.
I hear your voice in silence and see your
reflection in black.
Telling only the tears on my pillow at night.
How bad I want you back.

Corrine Bruder

Life

You were there in the midst of my turmoil.
You were there when I planted my soil.
You were there when I shed a tear, a cry.
You were there to drive away each care, each sigh.
You were there listening to every word I say.
You were there to pave my way.
You were there when I reached from either side of the distant
shores.
You were there when I could bear no more.
You were there when the echoes bound to a joyful sound.
You were there, I could endue the calm of your presence, it
surrounds.
You were there in my peace and serenity.
And surely you will be there for me through eternity.
And for that I thank thee, for Life.

Janice Brooks

The Roots of Darkness

Flowers for her wrist, the petals are her hair.
Her glowing, radiant beauty is suspended in the air.

The roses mark her gentleness; so delicate, so fair.
The stems now reach into her soul to sip from gifts so rare.

The flower draws the melted light that drips upon the pair.
The seeds will bond the new life with a kiss that will not tear.

She smiles a smile that will not fail; the heart, it beats this prayer,
while inside out she turns about, without one bit a care.

The stem has reached that poison layer that fills the bitter core.
It gulps a ghastly selfish drop which tastes sweet - nevermore.

The flower breathes that broken grace and coughs a silent roar.
It takes part its gentleness, turns black - falls to the floor.

And she, a smile to carry on lives on without a care.
The flower gently pulls her back - the stem she swiftly tears.

David Moore

My Senses

Hearing this voice, I am lulled into silence.
I cannot quite make out her words
I want to embrace his sounds
If I could only hold her voice

Seeing this smile, I forget my fears.
I don't know just why
But I am calm and I am at peace
If I could only touch his expression

Smelling this sweetness, I am high.
I don't ever want to come down I long to kiss him slowly
If I could only touch his sweetness

Tasting this love, I am satiated.
I'll never be hungry again
Help me to recall the flavor if only I could touch him love

There is one derelict sense; it is touch
It is the only sense we cannot distort
It is the sense whose distortion suggest the vulnerability of an alliance
It is though my hands are tied and my fingers are numb I cannot feel
and I have no ally.

Keri Fiscella

Sunrise In Paradise

Darkness, thick like amber, stirred by restless winds
as branches sway, mourners of the lost light.
Then sounds are stilled, ever more suppressed
save for washing waves upon protesting sand.

Try, and fail, to perceive the shift,
to catch the darkness yield to light.
One blink betrays, the black waves blue,
the horizon forms, sounds return.

The arrival of the arc of the sun,
its first golden ray stabbing the eye,
replenishing the soul with hope, and wonder,
in a distinguishable flash of glory.

As the giver of life rises to paint
the ocean with a rippling mirror of itself,
and sound converts to the quality of day,
the observer is silent, and satisfied.

Mark Durbin

My Sister's Eyes

Her eyes saw only shadows, shapes, and forms
No real features could she see
No color of hair or shade of skin
When my sister looked at me.

She couldn't see the way I looked
What the world saw, she never saw.
She looked at me thru blind eyes full of love
And that was what mattered, after all.

When I walked into a room, she knew my step
And although her eyes were too dimmed to see
Her face would light up like morning sun.
Her heart always told her, it was me.

And though she never clearly saw my face
She truly loved me from the very start
My sister couldn't see me with her eyes
But she always, always saw me with her heart.

Louetta Young

Untitled

Angels of the heavenly love,
we miss your beautwith grief we say goodbye,
with love we wish you happiness in
your world above,
thy love reaches your heavenly boundaries,
rainbows, flowers, kindred thoughts,
I wish, with hope to meet
again at heaven's gates.

Mallory Taylor

Somewhere

Somewhere the sun is shining
  Somewhere clouds dissipate -
Somewhere's a silver lining
  Where love over rides all hate.

Somewhere's all joy and laughter.
  Somewhere there'll be no more tears.
Somewhere there's some thing to help you...
  Banish all troubles and fear.

Somewhere seems so evasive
  But somewhere seems to impart
That somewhere abides within us
  Cause somewhere is in your heart.

Helen C. Hughes

This Day in May

This day in May I got a surprise.
As I walked through a meadow not a lawn.
It was early, not long after, sunrise;
The display was something to look upon.

For spring had broken out all over,
God had resurrected life anew,
The gross was greener even the clover,
With the trees and flowers in full view.

God taught me something that day,
We can learn if we open our eyes and look;
Do not pass by and go on our way;
We do not learn everything out of a book.
But we do learn and should from the Bible.
It is God's word and what we should do and be
If we listen and accept it we will be reliable.
It will teach us the right way to do and be.

When God sent His son He gave us the Light;
He healed the blind and opened deaf ears
To accept and believe is what is right.
And he will restore us and take away our fears.

Clarence Livermore

Illusion

The raven has crowed as far as we hear,
But this today we shall not fear.
In this life that has no bounds
Have we cast our shadows down.

When shall we awaken to the truths that we hold;
And speak that which we all were once told.
The moment has come my fellow beings
To take a stand against that which is seen.

The day is not long when we shall know
That which our hearts truly do show.
The time has come and long over do
To share that which is truly you.

Karla Davenport-Gratzol

Untitled

Where Kingdoms great were born
And ocean blue till there,
I have seen the man who conquers nothing but rage
Nothing is real but it hurts.
Some loved, some left
Sons and daughters of faraway lands
Whispering in the quiet green grass
Bringing the joy of a morning rose
Followed by simple rain,
Fine young life walking away
Do not forsake me for I am ahead of my voice
The voice in my head,
The one that keeps my head down.
I'm tempted by the world,
Dancing around me like chariots of fire,
Burning my soul through my desires
Many fears are born in loneliness
Many more are waiting for me.
Wicked man am I.

Eugene Muncan

When We Met

When we met, my fears faded away;
My emptiness was fulfilled.

When we met, my eyes saw into the future;
My ears heard only your laughter.

When we met, my mind came to a stop;
Absorbing your thoughts of hope.

When we met, the loneliness was chased away;
Friendship entered my life.

When we met, my dreams became realities;
My sadness turned to joy.

When we met, my heart was full of pain;
Then healing took place that day.

Thank you for being a part of my world;
A special moment, when we met.

Sue Ellen Walden

Reflective Reflections

During my adolescence
I had a longing —
To dwell in a place
Where our mother held you so dear

Looking back on reflective, reflections
Revolve in a cyclical, cycle
Carousel like
A mirage of an image
I once wanted to imitate
As a woman today
Looking back realistically at
Reflective, reflection is
A journey into an abyss
Where the pendulum swings
Transparency evolves
Self discovery emerges

Anna Gilmore

I Am

The eye of the Hubble scans the past.
Events appear as here and now.
Far in the future we see at last!
What new stars are born today?
Who will see them aeons from now?
The beginning of time or the end of eternity..
Meaningless words to mark a sequence...
No beginning, no end, no time in between...
We live for now; we live forever.
Unchanging I am through a surreal world.

Paul A. Williams

Crime

As I watch the light snowflakes drifting past the window
In the dead silence of the lonely room,
I wish...
As I sit in an uncomfortable chair
With the lights dimmed and fear filling the air,
I hope.....
As I think of the wrong that I had done
And the unknown consequence that I will face,
I pray.....
My crime, a few minutes of uncontrolled pleasure.
My consequence, my whole life depending on one word
Coming out of the mouth of an educated man dressed fully in white.
As I sit in a room the doctor, looking directly into my eyes,
I know.

Stephanie Trathen

Carousel

White, black, yellow, painted faces
powdered glare, artificial sneer
hamburgers, coca cola
sex from birth till death, gang - hold up at the bank
the headlines scream: Drugs, prisons are full, guns at the school

America, America - mechanical carousel

Cliches: Rich men, poor men
tops over heaven, bottom below hell
gold arks and illusory nests, food stamps for starving cats
fortune is not blind, Themis undid her eyes
bon-tone and perfect lies, total corruption of morals

America, America - magnetic field

Pretty, padded, powdered, perky
fridas, lindas, cassies, robins, michelles, hussies
in porsches carry their silicon-porno-body (vibrator in the trunk)
prey on divorced men
with shopoholic syndrom shop, shop, shop...until they drop

America, America - an old myth

Weronika Arent

Eternal Damnation

As darkness approaches and falls,
His hypnotic voice calls.
Terrifyingly beautiful he is now in sight,
The hunter of mortals, king of the night.
With his illusive stare she dares to chance,
She goes to him as if in a trance.
He smells her mortality and reaches for her hand,
Unbeknownst to her who thinks he is man.
As he tilts her neck her hair dangles and hangs,
The moonlight shows the glint of his fangs.
The blood flows, her heart beat fades;
She is now dead only a lifeless body remains.
The dark angel's thirst has been fed,
He will forever roam as the living undead.

Tracy Caine Romano

Ask An Angel

Her steps are heavy, as she maneuvered toward the front of the
bus, Her feet are red and swollen, from the 14 hour shifts,
she works because she must.

Her skin, is black as midnight, as she emerges into the light
of the moon, Her face shines with oil and weariness, her only
thought, that she'll be home soon.

Her travel is hampered, by the massive weight she carries around,
She hears the sirens in the distance, but the direction, isn't found.

Slowly, she labors to the corner, her apartment is mid-way down
the street, The flashing lights come out of the darkness, as
her heart, seems to skip a beat.

As she slowly approaches to the scene, her heart clamped hot
by fear, a policeman, walking toward her, he's speaking, but
through her panic, she cannot hear.

He gently leads her to a boy, who lay bleeding and dying in
the night, "He's a good boy", she said of her son, not fully
comprehending the sight.

She eases herself to the pavement, She cradles his head in her
hands, His eyes flicker open for one last time, It's answers,
he demands.

"Why me Mama," were his last words, and as her son is laying
there dead, Her tears mingled, with the oil on her face,
"Ask an Angel," was all she said...

Sherry Keown

The Kingdom

There's a kingdom that I know of in a very distant land,
Where the trees can reach the heavens with a gesture that is grand.

There's a dragon in the shadows singing such a lovely tune.
She is singing to the heavens of the coming of the moon.

And the heavens start rejoicing, making stars that shine so bright,
And the moon begins its rising with the magic of the light.

And the moon starts off her magic with a pretty lullaby,
Putting all the land to resting, so you hear the kingdom sigh.

There is not a noise around here as the moon is in the sky.
Streams and rivers stop their flowing as the moon is standing by.

Dreams take over at this hour, some appease and some cause fright,
And the spirits get to walking, they are such a lovely sight.

Flowing here and drifting there, dancing in the vacant light.
Not a soul denies her grandeur, yes, the moon is such delight.

Then the stars lose all their glitter and the moon starts her descend,
For the sun will soon be rising, morning's just around the bend.

Yes, I hear the trumpet sounding the announcing of the dawn.
Yes, I feel the wind is stirring and the land is newly drawn.
Flowers wake up as if smiling, pink and yellow, blue and green,
Stretching miles and miles beyond us, farthest any eyes have seen.

Yolanda Sherman

Darkness

Intense darkness found deep within,
Pulling at the heart and reeking of sin,
Preying on the weak and blind,
Motivating self-delusion and seducing the mind,
Morbid as the night on Hallow's Eve.
Disguised in appearance trying to deceive,
It dwells in the shadows slowly invading the light,
Trespassing on innocence leaving no goodness in sight,
Engulfed in the obscurity beyond the point of return,
Snared by the profound power there's nowhere to turn.

Amy Swain

355

Third Time Survivors

The water poured from the sky one night.
It seemed to have no end.
The creek began to win the fight
And with the land it did mend.

Instead of water falling down,
Up from the ground it rose,
A siren was heard in a small town -
With terror all hearts froze.

The angry creek began to war
With all that was near.
Each witnessed the water's roar
And soon began to fear.

For many hours the waters flowedAnd crushed the small town.
Then once more the earth showed
from beneath the waters that drowned.

Although the damage was very great-
The town of Hyndman obtained a lore.
By not dodging their terrible fate
They survived twice and now once more!

Ryan Pensyl

Untitled

As sure as the stars will continue
    to shine...I'll love you

As sure as the sky's will open up
    and the rain will come fluttering down
    upon us...I'll need you

Like the intensity of a caged animal
awaiting to run free...I'll want you

Like a favorite photograph forever lost...
I'll miss you

As sure as the sun will rise at dawn
then set again at dusk...
I'll always care.

Like the perfect song at just the
right moment...
Please tell me you feel the same...

Raeann Saari

The Children of Nature

Carry my spirit away, great Wind.
Away, you Gales to the Rainbow's end.
Fly me through Clouds away from this Earth;
Nestled in your arms like a child at birth.

Cleanse my heart with your sweet, gentle Rain
And let fall to Earth my sorrow and pain.
Place a glow amidst these apathetic eyes,
That I may see truth in a world of lies.

Shine down, you Stars, so warm and so bright,
And lessen my fears in the dead of Night.
Sing, Nightingale, a melodic tune,
And soothe the waking of a drowsy Moon.

Blow gentle breeze, through Forests of green;
Humming a lullaby, soft and serene.
Awaken my slumber, oh break of Dawn;
Help me to greet the Day with a song.

Smile, oh morning Sun, upon my head.
Erase the traces of tears once shed.
Children of Nature, strengthen my soul
That I may cherish Life and all it holds.

Donna Jones

The Big Red Bull

He lies there motionless - the independent young man
who never wanted to be dependent;
And now He is - as He waits to be fed, to be bathed, to be dressed;
As He has done - since He was catapulted from the back
of The Big Red Bull.
The hours, the days, the weeks, the months go by -
frequently spent in hospitals;
He hears the cries of his little ones -
but can't hold them in his arms;
His wife or his parents set them on his bed - to kiss their Daddy;
His little boy - once his shadow - is now Grandpa's shadow;
His little girl has learned to crawl - and to walk -
without his helping hands.
He dreamed of becoming World Champion;
Then He would have the ranch, the cattle,
the horses of which He dreamed;
Before He met The Big Red Bull - that shattered his dreams.
Now He hopes to ride a horse in the rain again when - He is better;
He hopes to hunt and fish again - when He is better;
He hopes to drive a car with his family beside him again -
when He is better.
He may never realize the pain and the grief of his parents -
each time they look upon Him;
He may never realize the agony and the sacrifice of his parents -
as they tenderly care for his needs - night and day.
A life of their own is no longer possible - their health fails;
They have no choice but no care for this child they love - how long?
There's no relief.
Seven seconds changed these lives forever - when he was brought down
by The Big Red Bull.

Dee Roberts

Light of My Life

The love you gave me was oh so vast,
and through eternity. I hope it lasts.
Your smile, your eyes, all engraved in my head.
Thoughts of you I think of at night in my bed.
When will you come back? I sit and wait
For my heart to you is an open gate.
The sound of your voice makes my heart skip a beat.
Waiting for the day when once again we will meet.
When I think of you a tear comes to my eye,
Hating the day that I said goodbye.
Thinking about you every waking minute.
Even my dreams have you scattered in it.
A photograph of you brings memories to mind.
Hoping your new world will treat you kind.
Until the day that you return.
And the light of my life will once again burn.

Sarah Schaffner

In Memory Of Barbara Treece

Barbara is my sister. God was picking
flowers when he picked Barbara.
Oh how we all miss her. Sometimes I
want to go see her, then remember Barbara
is not here with us anymore.
Barbara wanted to live so much, if only
I could have taken her place that day.
I would have been glad too. Barbara had
lot's of friends and she is missed by all.
Barbara know that she was dying.
But with grief, sadness, and sorrow, she
kept it all to herself. Now Barbara has no
more pain and sorrow for she is
walking with God. She loved and cared for
others. Her life was giving and loving
every person she met and ask for nothing
in return. Barbara, when God picked you
He got the prettiest flower of all.
Barbara I miss you and I love you sister.

Patricia Colquitt

Lesbos

We stand together joined
by our souls, hearts, hips
questioning eyes, gossiping tongues
leading players
in some fictional work of closet fantasies
cast in the roles in our eight grade year
the script changing
as boston and kansas
made it a touring company
but the fantasy remained
without motives
just the bond of two woman
finding comfort in each others minds
taunted by strange rumors
which they secretly desire to pursue
unsure of their own emotions they point in our direction
closed minds don't hear so we don't argue
we know
but directions direct their own vision
so we supply the script

    Abbie Lee

At Least

Down the backside of the wind, up from the floor,
Cool wind flows around the trees like a stream.
Trees like legs, Head like world
World forgotten in her eyes. World left spinning cold and hard and
dry but still
Spinning. At least.

How did it all come to this and grief and why
Where did the space enfold the spark first?
How then and now do they forget?

Here the Heroes fight and bleed and die
Here where the witches keep and clean and fly...

And the damsel face was like stone, but it still moved.
Cool wind flows like water.

She walks into the dream space to remember.
Half of life and real as grass, but quiet when it is unpresent - transparent
like jellyfish.
Turn! Face away. Damsel ears hear the echo of the earth and substance.
I will remember for you. At last.

    Alias Lyonn

The Brain Versus Brawn

A pen and pencil are fabulous inventions,
They are the most important tools in existence,
Especially when used properly by people,
With common sense to accomplish good.

These implements are more powerful than any weapon,
That mankind has now or ever will devise,
For this one article alone can bring about,
More good than any riot or demonstration ever has.

However, people fail to take advantage of this tool,
By casting votes, writing letters or signing petitions,
As a simple and peaceful way of accomplishing a goal,
Because there is no fame and publicity to be had.

Neither can innocent peoples property be damaged,
Nor can their rights to move about freely be hindered,
Because this is the perfect setting for open murders,
Robbery, assault and arson without fear of retribution.

Which are scare tactics that are not available by using,
An envelope, sheet of paper, pencil and postage stamp,
Nor is there any thrill in taxing the mighty brain,
When the brawn can so easily be flaunted to create fear.

    Clyde J. Barton Jr.

Everyday Is Father's Day

Once a year we honor our dad's;
which one day to me is very sad.
  We should show them we do care;
to be there for him when he wants to share.
  Like when he wants to share the memories
you both had.
  Like the one when you was just a small
lad.
  Yes, there are times when he fills lonely
and blue;
  So he'll pick up the phone and he'll call you.
  Just to hear you voice will make
him happy,
  As you say to him. "I love you Pappy."
  As I know I'm lucky to have been
blessed.
  With no other "Dad" because you're
the best!
  To me everyday is "Father's Day",
and I wouldn't want it any other way!

    Debbie Markley

Love Lives On

They came one day and slaughtered a century tree,
  loaded its firewood,
  dragged away its branches,
  replaced the stump with dirt and sod.
The only remnant of that majestic oak
  was a clump of leaves
  hiding under a nearby shrub
  to whisper that greatness once stood here.

Not so, with our loved ones,
  they too have stood tall along their fellows,
  walked and worked and played
  and faced the winds of the seasons.
But, they have also lived
  and that love lives
  and we share it
  forever present

    N. Clifton Howard

The Quilters

There's a group of ladies in our church,
  And "The Quilters" is their name;
They come armed with thread and needles,
  And have won both praise and fame.
They work on quilts, both large and small,
  with time out for a snack or dinner;
The quilts come off this "assembly line",
  And each looks like a "first-prize Winner".
Some quilts are flowered, some are blue
  Some with patterns of gold or red;
But when they're finished with stitches so fine
  They'll look beautiful on somebody's bed.
I won't mention names, just the "quilters" they'll be,
  For each has so well done her part;
With her needle and thread and stitches so fine,
  That have come from her hand and her heart.
Blessings on our "Willing helpers",
  And with the setting of the sun;
May they hear the Master's voice, say,
  "Enter thou, well done!"

    Ruth A. Eastlick

357

Shallow Tears

Something changed with my son the other day
You see he told me he is gay.
And God forgive me, but for a moment it felt like someone died.
    And I cried.

I threw a glass, it shattered. Like my dreams, torn and tattered.
Future visions I'll never see, no child of his on my knee.
    I cried.

I wanted to hold him, hug him to my heart
Let him know he and I would never part
But my arms were still, they wouldn't ascend
My emotions felt dead, would these tears never end.
I cried.

He turned to leave, a tear in his eye
He reached out his hand as he said good-bye.
I thought of the love through all the years
Shadowed now by all the fears.
I cried.

He looked at me like never before
And I grew a lifetime before he reached the door.
I rose and extended my arms he needed his mother, he needed my calm.
Unconditional love was now mine to give
A mother to child for as long as we live
and I cried no more.

    Pamela Corbin

The Red Rose

Red is the rose when its beauty is fresh
Red is the blood 'fore it turns cold from death.
Red is the passion burning in the soul,
Red is the fire burning out of control.

Black is the night when passion grows old,
Black is the ash when fires burn cold.
Black is the mind when it's filled with lies.
Black is the heart when the red rose dies.

    Jillian A. Walker

All My Heart

As I sit here alone,
    I try to think of what I did to make things go so wrong.

And I try to call you on the phone,
    but all I hear is a dial tone.

And I don't want our relationship to go to waste,
    so I think we need to talk face to face.

And at this point I have no doubt,
    so I really hope we can work this out.

And I don't want our relationship to fall apart,
    because I love you with "All my heart."

    Hope Ann Platz

Starlight

One little star to light our way,
One little star, when we go home to stay.
Dimming in the daylight, but twinkling in the dark
With angels to guide us and show us our mark.
One little star - that will forever be
Shining in the sky for you and me!
That one little sparkle will never go out
If we believe in Jesus and don't have a doubt;
So if we are good and earn that "Starry" place
We will greet our father in "His Heavenly Place!"

    Shirley Naymik

What Love Can Do?

Love never hurts, it protects
Never saddens, causes laughter
Understands and feels
Love is not weary, but peaceful.

Works on weakness to produce strength
Love never hates, it likes and adores
Love thinks it is hard to accept negatively,
but waits to hear the truth.

Love is graceful, divine, honored and respectful
Love can come into action
Goes places where no other can
Love stimulates to achieve to one's fullest
Love upholds its friends through needed time the most
Love stops even death that others sometimes may not see
Love is great, powerful, causes positivity, growth and unity

    Iris Murray

Eleven Years

Kisses soft upon my face
    -Enter in love's warm embrace
Summer rains in the afternoon
    Silver beams flow from the moon
and surround us...

In a garden entwined we walk alone
    To a cottage made of mortar and stone
My glass house shattered by a whispered vow
    A smile, a caress, into a bough... of roses
To set me free...

Eleven times you called my name
    Eleven times you tried in vain
Until you found me alone and waiting
    For only you and your love
Forevermore...

    Angela Bailey

Christmas Treasures

I sit me down beside the fire
To watch the embers glow
To remember and think about
Our christmases of long ago

Remembering, remembering past Christmases
Of little faces all aglow
The New Mexico sun, of races run
Making footprints in the snow

The day we would put up the tree
Is one I will always remember
The memories of the bright farolitos
Still light those past Decembers

I sit here and think about
The times that have already past
The years have flown like thistle down
How did they pass so fast

So mom and dad these memories you gave to me
How can I ever weigh or measure
Because of you they will always be
My own private treasure

    Lela Ford

Spring Comes To America

Almost imperceptibly the days
Have lengthened and the sky has grown more blue.
Unclipped forsythia tangles in a blaze
Of gold; bright jonquils shine, and crocus too,
Amidst the paler shades of blooming trees:
The pinks and whites of apple, cherry, pear,
And darker redbud in the pastel seas
Of tossing blossomed limbs so lately bare.
Grass reborn spreads its imperial jade
In carpets envied by a monarch's throne.
And birds from dawn to dusk sing out their hearts.
And in each town some space is found or made
For that sure sign that winter's truly flown:
With that first pitch, at last the summer starts.

Karen Davis

A Brighter Light'll Shine Someday

It once was a flame.
How I wish things could be the same.
For you, it was only a spark.
So, now I'm in the dark,
But, I've seen that heavenly light in your eyes;
As beautiful as summer skies.
A brighter light'll shine someday.

We were like a magnet come alive.
With you gone, I wonder how I'll survive.
Our lips were locked in an eternal embrace,
And never have I seen a more beautiful face.
So tempting, I thought, perhaps, you were a devil in disguise.
Until I gazed again into those big, blue eyes,
I hope to meet those heaven-sent eyes again.

Just look around.
Don't turn your eyes to the ground.
'Cause if you just look, you will see
That everyone's soul shines.
And, if you're in the dark, perhaps you're blessed,
'Cause you'll better see the light of God in the end.

Jeanne Marie Frances Young

Our Cat

We have a black and white cat
Who is so completely relaxed,
Her name is "Boots or Pal"
and since she has no tail, she's a manx.

She moved with us down south
and now is out of the cold,
we really love her so much
we hope she'll never grow old.

We know there's one thing she doesn't like
and that is thunder and lightning,
she slinks down the hall on her belly
because she is so frightened.

We really dread the coming day
when she no longer will be here,
every little thing she has ever done
has always been so dear!

Ethel P. James

P. O. W.

Oh, it's been such a long, long time, since I've seen my old friends.
  And, this cold and lonely place...I just want to see them again.

How the time it drags by, the minutes last for hours, it seems,
  And the clanging of the cell door, shatters my reality escaped
  dreams.

Waiting, hoping, for some chance to leave, as the thoughts
  race in my head...
  even though they just lie to me, I cherish each word that's said.

But, that door, will open, I know. And I'll walk that hallway soon.
  Will it be more torture this time? Or, that last walk towards my
  doom?

Why don't they get it over with? Line me up and blow me away.
  The suspense is killing me, pardon this old cliche.

Oh, I wanna be with my old friends, the folks I love the most.
  But, all I have is precious memories, and those too, will end.

How it's tearing my insides apart. The pain, the tears, that flow.
  I need to be free!! Miles - just disappear!
  To see them, once more! Before I go!

John Tabor

The Balance

Sullen sun has slipped behind blackened walls
owl and coyote screaming their calls
Desert fox moves slyly from his den
and deadly snake looks to strike again

Smooth quick rattler moves his venomous head
spotting cautious prey and killing her dead
Hawk glides powerfully across darkened sky
benigned pack rat labeled to die

Bobcat stalks through warm night air
to feed the family of his lair
Quiet green lizard traps small innocent prey
wild coyotes feast until day

The night feels bane and beautiful still
all looks so quiet gazing up at the hill
Desert sands blow gracefully across this place
scorching all tracks with nearly a trace

In this balance of beauty nature stages
her might
So violently revealed on this calm
desert night.

Michael Reiter

The Garden Tomb

When first I saw the Garden Tomb
My heart was hurt as I recalled
His beaten body, scourged and torn
Those hands that healed with boring holes
His face abloodied with the thorns.

But gentle hands His body bore
To that rich grave as prophets told
And wrapped Him in spices and the cloth
His burial clothes, His earthly shroud.

Then as the mighty stone was rolled
Dark darkness filled His last abode
But light as love o'er comes the black
Of evil, so He rose, that we

Because He died that way
Might strive with love to keep abay
The evil of that frightful day
And cleanse our hearts to live
With Him forever.

Janice Judd

Forever and Always

I love you so much,
You're a part of my life.
You take care of me,
When my world is full of strife.

You love me,
Even though I have no wealth.
You help me up,
When I can't do it myself.

When I have a hard decision to make,
You help me make it.
When I feel as if the world is against me,
You help me take it.

My feelings for you,
Can never be described.
Even though to talk to my heart,
I have tried.

But there is one thing you must know.
I'll love you,
Forever and always!

Andrea Henry

You

I turn to you as mankind greets the dawn
With eye uplifted and the brow of hope
For night, uncertainty and pain are gone
And days new light finds firmness in my grope.

I turn from falseness to sincerity,
From weakness to the stronghold I have found.
My mind has turned its foot with clarity —
My heart will turn with slower foot but sound.

I cannot vouch for speech from out my mouth
But there is strength behind my feeble words.
My heart in darkness flies to your warm south
As desolation brings the flight of birds.

Peggy Turman

A Touch Of Magic

All is lost to those who still slumber
Beneath piles of coverlets,
The beauty of this moment,
This early frosty morn.

Such a magnificent creation,
This mysterious white blanket,
Like a quick swish of an artist brush
Is no more...

Lost is the joy in watching the sunrise
Just above the crystal-white mountains.
Lost is the tranquility viewing distant church steeples
Along-side quaint little house-tops on translucent glass hills.

The sparkling frost seems to make everything magical.
Gray smoke ascends from tall chimneys,
Everything seems clean and pure,
Steam dances from the mouth of a dog.

Glistening-white embraces rows of evergreens
As a rabbit races across a barren-white field.
Safe inside a house, hands raise a cup of hot coffee to the lips
As eyes peer outside and a soul is quiet and still...

Charlotte Ann England

Miracles Come To Mind

The stillness is broken, as I anxiously await,
Suddenly my deliverance comes, a long prepared for date.
Miracles come to mind with the sound of a robust cry,
Hearing he is healthy, with relief emit a sigh.

I reach out and hold this small child, feel its helplessness,
The dependence on me for its wants and needs too many to express.
Miracles come to mind as I touch this new born child,
Feel the softness of his skin and sense his manner mild.

Perfect is he in every way with such beauty to behold,
Who can imagine a gift so great designed from a flawless mold.
Miracles come to mind as our eyes met face to face,
A vision of lifelong oneness and love nothing can replace.

A soft kiss upon the cheek shares all I have to say.
The greatest gift, the power of life, is given to me this day.
Miracles come to mind as I taste this kiss of my affection,
Savoring this sweet time, a sense will later become reflection.

Linda Baker

My Dad

There's a wonderful man
I'd love for you to meet...
He's a unique person and... Oh so sweet.
Is 5'6" but... To me stands tall,
Just loves buttered popcorn and watchin' football.

He works hard, yet it never shows on his face,
Is always gentle and full of grace.
Whether he's trimmin' the hedges or mowin' the grass...
He bears some special touch of class.

Poor thing can't make it through a day without a sneeze...
He's allergic to the pollen that falls from the trees.

Yep, this man taught me to swim, ride a bike and even blow my nose,
Share with my kin, and then squirt 'em with a water hose.

Too bad we're all grown out of our childish ways,
But there will always be memories of the good old days.

I'm sure if you knew this wonderful man like I do,
You'd want to tell everyone else, too.

Thanks to the good Lord above, I'm proud and glad,
To introduce you to my very own Dad!...

Emily Conner Reid

Spring Magic

Spring is a time for warmth and caring,
A time for holding hands.
Spring is a time for love and sharing,
A time to give life a chance.

I love spring in all its changing phases
And to watch the children play.
I love to see their smiling faces,
Enjoying a beautiful spring day.

I watch the kites soar as high as a bird
And the children holding the strings smile,
All the cares in the world seem absurd
As I look into the face of a small child.

I love the spring in all its glory,
The magical effect it has on everyone.
The life it brings as nature
  begins its story,
Around which a web of aura is spun.

Faith S. Arthur

360

No Partition

It was a law broken, two human fools who did not heed to the Lord's
   rules
They let a person who works for cash, destroy what they had.
Forward of a person, clothed in a robe, who granted the
wish of these two souls, now sorrow is what they face, due to a
foolish separation in God's place!
If one unites with another, the doom will strike Not from a wood
   bench,
but from all His might. Why be a moron, reconcile your problems,
let no money hungry man grant you sorrow

    Curtis Tillmon

Whither-So Ever

Three roads lead out; which one will be my way?
   I came on one but was not satisfied.
The past fades in the distance of the day,
   and evening knows the pain I have inside.
What lies ahead has always lain behind,
   its difference only in death's secrecy.

There is no vale of happiness to find,
   none differ in their lack of hope for me.
All earthly roads have only turns and miles,
   for 'here' or 'there' is all the same you see,
No travel worth the effort and the trials,
   there is no road where you could wait for me.
The far horizon touches on the sky....
   another way exists no one can see.
I view my choices as no choice at all
   if in Elysian fields you wait for me!

    Lucy M. Voller

The Moments

The only thing greater than yourself is the moment
The feelings of love can all be told in a moment
Life as we know can be lost in a moment
At school I study long and hard
And I do look forward to graduation
But it's the handshake and the thanks that is
all given in a moment
As I look around at my world
I began to feel joy
And I do understand
We all were given life
In just a moment

    John Norris Smith

It's Not Fair

It's not fair that he was taken from us,
I was only twelve and they were still young too.
It's not fair that he had no choice in leaving,
no one was prepared for this saddened loss.
It's not fair that he isn't here for our achievements,
he would have been proud of all of us.
It's not fair that when I talk to him, he can't talk back,
I would have loved to hear his advice.
It's not fair that it is getting harder to remember him,
I know we will never forget him though.

    Clarissa Powell

Untitled

When the water runs dry
When the air is clear
My love for you will be there

As strong as the wind
As clear as the water
Our love will shine as bright as the sun
The sun burns skin
As your love burns my heart

My heart is strong
My mind is clear
My love for you is so dear

It will never die
It will always shine
As long as you are by my side

So love me tender
And love me true
Then I will always love you

    Alisha Pignato

For the Love

(1990)

We cruise the lake and gaze at the sky,
wondering why our loved ones had to die.
In sharing our grief, our love and our hope,
we manage to march on and even cope!
Some days are good and some are bad.
We might be happy or even sad.
Our loved ones are gone and we hurt and blue;
but the "Love of Christi" is pulling us through.
Shortly we'll dock and be on our way.
Tomorrow will bring us another day.
A time to remember the good and the bed,
and thanking God for the times that we've had.

    Tee Barbour

Miracle of the Visitation

The power of the Goddess has overcome me.
I feel the spirit taking a breath of sweet ecstasy.
What is this I see, a new child God has given me...
What wonders you have done for me, I kept
Your truth inside of me, a babe so helpless and clinging to
me, that someday would render back to his mother great
dignity, James the best has kindly just blest me.
A child with soul and spirit that I protect with every ounce
of strength, the Goddess Mary, has infused in me. Just
the gift of faith I prayed for has overtaken me. I am so
surprised, it has shaken me, I am so thankful, and full of
simplicity, why? I ask, when I could be sad, of the work
ahead of me. Oh, Mary, the Goddess whispers to me. It
is your completing this task I give you that will bring
you both to me. You have willing graciously
accepted the wonderful part of you, and you were right,
the hand of God will always guide you.
Find joy in God your savior.

    Mary Davis Hight

The Residual Family Tree

Quicksilver teeth gnaw the boughs
The cradles crash with a clamor
On the blood-trodden path of crosses
No one, not nature, neither is there
Only remnants of shells, a soul's prison
Eyes defunct staring at what was once innocence
But now - only perpetual opaqueness.

    Maria E. Rodrigue

Fly Away

Beautiful Bird, as I open the cage door,
The ache gets heavier in my heart.
Even before you're this tiny wish, how could I have not realized,
That never were you mine from the start.

As you fly towards the never-ending sky,
To live your life finally happy and free,
Forever these eyes will search for you,
For together was all I wanted us to be.

Someday in your solitary flight,
A soul-mate you may find who'll make you happy.
And as you both soar towards the height of heights,
I may become just a distant memory.

As life continues its journey,
And as the sky without fail changes from black to blue,
Maybe one day, just one day you'll look down only to find,
Even in death I'm waiting for you.

Dorothy Prarthna Prasad

Hearts

Hearts share one beat
They share beats of love and beats of hate
Hearts are filled with many emotions
Both of sad and happy emotions
My heart beats for your love
Its every big or little beat
means something from you
There are many beats which
show my love for you
But there's one thing for
sure, the beats of our
hearts will last eternally together

Aimee Jerome

The Love That Lived Within

Now that I am finally grown
    and able to make it on my own,
I remember all the days at home
    and the love that lived within.

Both of you were always there
    ready to sacrifice, love and care,
Willing to discipline, eager to share
    the love that lived within.

And when my days were darkest blue
    and I needed a hand to pull me through,
Both of you were there, with "two,"
    to keep the love that lived within.

Dear God, I pray that I might be
    just half the parent you gave me;
To guide my children, as did these,
    for the love that lives within.

Brenda K. White

"Jacqueline"

She graced a nation and intrigued,
She wove a myth that we believed;
She walked in beauty and with grace,
We breathlessly waited for a glimpse of her face.
That breathless voice remained a mystery,
To go on intriguing throughout history.
A nation tried to face tomorrow,
While a widow suffered an aching sorrow.
We crowned her regally like a queen,
This mystical legend named Jacqueline.

Amanda Marlatt

It Is God's Great Gift

It is God's gift he come from love and two Angels one right and
    one wrong
We learn the present by investigating the past.
And the great Future is only a repeat of the Past.
The mind, the largest of all to understand and does control man.
Memory the greatest individual Book in the world.
Make it large, well organized, and full to the last page-
Or it can be small, thin, empty and blank to open at all.
Some where along the way, we were looking for peace with ourselves.
Not by mistakes we made, or problems we couldn't solve.
Nor the good things, we couldn't hang on to very long at a time.
It was a good life? Or was it not?
Never stop thinking the positive.
Negatives thoughts can only destroy you.
The days get longer - the nights get darker and
Depression slips in like a thief in the night.
Thought travel back instead of next day or day after —
Then suddenly you find you are alone - all alone;
You finally close the door, and drift away.

Marcia Whalen

My Angels

My heart cries out to you, Oh Lord, I pray.
Be thou my Comforter throughout the day.
And at evening when I lay my head to rest,
Around my bed, six angels I request.
One to wipe away my tears,
One to take away my fears.
One to mend my broken heart.
For my Love and I are now apart.
One to spread o'er me its golden wings.
In glorious voice, they began to sing.
Praises to our Heavenly King.
I listened well, then heard them say.
"Our Lord does hear you, as you pray".
"He walks beside you all the way."
"He counts the tears you have shed".
Kneeling, I pray, beside my bed.
Numbered, recorded all my tears in the Book
When it's time for His will to be done,
He'll soften the hearts with the tears He did store.
True Love returns, will be doubled and more.

Doris C. Korelc

Dare To Dream, Dare To Live

In this world of strife there are many
people who are in despair and live seemingly
hopeless lives.

Let my life be one that changes people's
lives from sadness to gladness.

We all need to look at God's fantastic
creation and then look at ourselves and realize
we are a part of it and accept his invitation.

He invites us to a glorious new lifestyle
one for which we will give him much adoration.

Instead of being in a prison of discontent
where pressures mount, let us live a life
that will really count!

We can with God's help win life's victory
race and then in the next life we will see
God's face and all will be joy forever.

Richard S. Collins

Reading My Bible

When I sit down to read my Bible
After my day's work is through
I read 'bout a dear Saviour
Who died for me and you
Who suffered on the cross
With nails through his feet and hands
Trying to save all the sinners
in this wild and weak land
He even prayed for the sinners
when they pierced him in the side
While they gambled for his
purple robe just be for he died
He prayed, "O God forgive them
for they know not what they do
please bring them up to heaven to be with me and you."
They rolled away the stone when the darkness came all around
The angels came down from heaven and rolled away his stone
To free him again so he could sit up on his throne
So when it seem like your burden is so heavy and hard to bear
just look up to Jesus and thank God he is there

Dottie Riley

A Day in the Life of the Lord

I've gone away, what the hell have I done
I've gone away, I've left everyone.
I've hurt my family, I've hurt my wife
I've hurt myself, what's left in life.

I could end it all, that's a choice you know
I've lived forty years, with nothing to show.
So run real fast, yes run right now
You can decide later, the when, where and how.

Whoa, where are you headed son, said this voice from above
Who is that speaking, is it someone I love?
Yes my son, it called down
I can help you, to rid your frown.

Just ask for my help, for you I'll be near
You are one of my children, one very dear.
What do I do sweet Lord, when all has seemed lost?
Is life really worth living, and at what cost?

The choice is yours, he said to me
I died on the cross, so you could be free.
I see what you mean Lord, my life does have worth
As it did forty years ago, on the day of my birth.

Lawrence Calhoun

Magical Praises for the Secret Rainbow

Ummm, umm, um... the five black women shout,
as they beat their feet to the sound of the drums.
They dance in a circle,
waving their hands in the warm summer air.
Women wearing a bright array of colors;
that represents the colors of their heritage.
The rainbow brings wealth and happiness,
in which they are praying for.
Round and round they go,
waving back and forth with their hands.
Louder and louder beat the drums.
Faster and faster they spin.
Suddenly there is silence, complete silence,
Nothing can be heard for miles and miles around.
Then the sky became cooler and darker.
Darker and darker until a huge, bright rainbow appeared.
As before the women started the dance,
waving, spinning and praising.
There in front of them was their rainbow,
the product of their dreams.

Diana Seib

I Am

Petals of love divinely unfold, a sound of life, a
vision told, a song in motion so ever old, I am...

The lover, the loved, they play their part but I am
love from the ageless start. In my being love takes it
flight into darkness and back to light.

For you my love and I are one, the lover, the loved,
the love, I am...

Lauren L. Branscome

The Dream

Why oh why can I not touch the sky?
No matter how high I fly, it's just too high.
And why oh why can I not touch the bottom of the sea?
No matter how deep I swim, it's just too deep for me.
I dream of the day I will fly so high and swim so deep
That the memories I'll have will be mine to keep.
So now I lay me down, close my eyes and dream my dream,
For in my mind it's always real and I can do whatever I feel.
But when the sun rises and I awake,
The night is gone and all I have is the truth to take.
That all I can do now is wait
As my dream melts and my memories are free to take.
Now that all my memories are gone and my heart has melted to a
    puddle,
I wait for the night to come and the darkness to cover the earth
In hopes that I might dream my dream once again.

Allison Kirk

Band Of Brothers

It has often been said and written by others,
    That the U.S. Marines are a Band of Brothers,
Forged together, in peace or war,
    Semper Fidelis to Country and Corps.
Today we honor one of our own,
    His sacrifice helped keep us free,
He fought on far off battlefields,
    And he did this for you and for me.
Now we have come to pay our respects,
    And to show just how much we care,
To a U.S. Marine who has answered the call,
    This is a time we all now share.
One day, we all will meet once more,
    Look each other in the eye,
And say, "welcome aboard Marine",
    Well done! And...Semper Fi!

Boyce Clark

The Woman

The woman standing near me.
I look at her with eyes that possible say it all.
Staring, wishing, admiring, adoring, lusting, loving.
The hair of this woman. Straight and flowing and diving. Oh, the
hair of this woman is black with a little dark maroon in it.
The woman's legs are long and thin.
This woman is perfect.
She is looking up. I am frozen in awe of her beauty.
She is unique.
She has tigh-fit black pants on and a black leather jacket.
This woman looks very feminine, but open. Oh, how I long for her.
Okay, so you can hug and kiss and hold me now.
Her neck is so perfect. It meets her face with such grace.
The woman's eyes are mysterious.
Her black shoes and hands in her pockets excite me.
No, no, oh no please! Please don't leave! But I love you! Do you
    love me?!
She's gone. Or, have I gone? In my head she stays forever, in my
    view she doesn't.

Rhea Taylor

Mrs. Harte

Mrs. Harte is nice. She doesn't like mice.
She likes to skate on ice.
She was born in June. She likes to dance to a tune.
But does she want to go to the moon?
Mrs. Harte likes to get hugged. But she doesn't like to get bugged.
So she sips out of her mug.
Mrs. Harte likes to go to the shore. So she doesn't get bored.
And she walks till she gets sore.
Mrs. Harte likes to sit under an oak. So she doesn't get soaked.
And drink her coke.
Mrs. Harte likes to dance. When she goes to France.
And sometimes she'll prance.
Mrs. Harte likes to shop. Till she drops.
Sometimes sucking on a pop.
But most of all she's my teacher and I think I'll keep her.

Michelle Banom

One Soul's Lamentation

Trapped - under the impression that only the rich
fulfilled their dreams,
I left mine far behind.

Unaware - a safe - secure path I did take.
Subsequently,
releasing - the golden ring of life.

Within - an emptiness - an unauthentic feel -
did rise.
What could I do - but hide?

The Dreams? To my surprise! They lived, they nagged,
they screamed!
Within my deafened ear.

Till I stood fixed - I heard them not.
And that - my friend - brought sorrow
to my being.

Alas - I knew no life was this, for one as strong as I.
No genuine goodwill rest here,
just one - poor soul - to die.

Anayansi Ricketts

The Hand

It's dark and cold
and I'm all alone.

I'm getting old and gray and right now
I'm just yearning for someone to hold my hand.

Please don't laugh and walk away,
please try and understand.

I just want to still feel as though I'm still
a man (woman).

I've lost a lot and I just need a little touch.

If you'll just hold my hand, it'll mean so
much.

It's like newborn baby fingers as they
frantically search, trying to connect.

I'm here searching in the dark and I'm not
feeling nothing yet.

So please try not to hurry and don't give me
a pill.

I just need a hand from someone who cares
enough to make me feel.

Denise Isaac-Tolliver

Legacy To My Children

Today I started my journey
I must take it all alone
At the end is a promise God gave me
That some day I could come home

I'm leaving my loved one's behind me
with a message and my love
To be given to you when you need me
on the wings of a snow white dove

If you see a tear in someone eye's
please hold them close for a while
And given them something I gave you
A beautiful shining smile

I'll always be there for you
in every rainbow and beautiful cloud
Always remember my darling's
You made my life so happy an you made me very proud.

Dortha P. Whitaker

Sincere From The Heart

A soft and warm sincere smile;
The touch of your hand so meek, so mild,
Our eyes how they glisten,
Our ears as we listen;
To the sweet sounds of birds so sincere;
Making sweet romance as we do, my dear!

My mind it wonders, and puzzled so long;
To understand why our loves so strong;
We kiss, we mingle, touch and caress,
To understand our love, it has to be best;
We argue and quarrel, without any doubts;
But yet no one, can ever figure us out.

We say things wrong, then say things right;
But after the kiss, we make love all night;
Our minds are befuddled, we don't understand;
Why I am the woman, yes! You are the man.
But all this time, we cared from the start.
And our love has grown, sincere from the heart!
So here's to the image, our hearts know not pain;
The love we have, shall always remain.

Karen A. Guyton

Grandma's Junk Drawer

When I go to Grandma's house
There's nothing I like more,
Then take lots and lots of time
And look in her junk drawer.

You can't imagine what's in there
She doesn't throw anything away,
Bet I know what she's thinking -
It might come in handy some day.

There's bolts and pliers and an old toy car
A marble that's broken in two,
There's a ruler that's used for a spanking stick
And Grandma means business too!

She must of emptied out Grandpa's pockets
And dumped it all in the drawer,
Cause whenever you need to fix anything
Just go and look some more.

And I know as I grow older
And am learning to explore,
I'll never forget the time I spent
Going thru Grandma's old junk drawer.

Cora L. Abels

I Was There

I came to you at a time when you had no one to cling on.
When you needed someone to care, "I was there."
You had someone else's child to bare and through it all, I was there.
There were nights when you had frightful dreams that sent you in a
   dreadful scare.
When you reached out you noticed, "I was there."
There were holidays that meant nothing til I came.
Because of you the promise was broken to my Lord.
Now I'm faced with the burden of disgrace, never to bring honor to
   my name.
You said, our downfall was due to voodoo on a stick.
Til this day, I thank you for the one year that I got to play dear ole
   St. Nick.
In years to come for you, life itself will be hard an unfair.
Just remember! Everytime you needed me, "I was there."

Terrence Carter

Little Angel

Just yesterday you were here playing with the other children.
You were so happy and gay, but God called and took you away.
You want get to play with your toys with the other little girls and
boys, but you possess more precious things up there playing in the
   angels band.
Little angel, I Put your toys away this morning as I wipe the tears
   from my eyes,
although I know you are there in paradise, I wonder why you had to go.
For we miss you so!
As I think of the blessed Saviour's love who sent down His
   heavenly dove,
I know He needed another rose bud to bloom in His little children
   garden.
I will always remember each night when you knelt beside your little
bed to say "now lay me down to sleep". You would put your little
arms around me and whisper "I love you so sweet."
These things we cannot understand, and we wait until we meet you in
heaven and shake your little hand.

Nadine Loden

Life and Love

Living is experiencing life, all not part.
Love is a feeling that's in your heart.
Being here is not what it's all about;
It is being alive within and without.

Barbara L. Moore

Auntie Anne

As a young girl
I loved to be near her
She smelled sweet and heady
Her purse jam-packed
With tortoise shell glasses, elegant lipstick
She wore spike heels
Played tennis
Went to shows and drank Manhattans.

At eighty-one
She still smells sweetly
Make-up fresh and jaunty
Sporting a new perm, she sparkles
Though she has trouble walking too far

At thirty-five
I have tasted lightly of life's adverse conditions
Touched sadness, and in my lanky frame
I am still confident.
In her lined face I see my clear eyes
In her pained walk
I will knock down any wall.

Marianne M. Lamont

The Key

I have found a place on earth or so it seems to be
This sacred place touch not the ground
It lies inside of me
It is a place, when fear's upon me
To find peace and happiness
It took me many years to know and understand
That God is always with me and where my choices lie
For I have total proof that God is on my side
Satan has no hold on me hard as he may try
I believe in God, completely, there is no doubt, you see
I do not tempt the devil nor dare he try to me
God has kept His promises to give me all I need
To help me through this testing ground
To fight off Satan's greed
The Veil doth have a rent in it through which I can see
I know who holds the keys to this promised land
I am positive I hold one in my hand
Satan cannot stand its fire, He knows it means his end
One foot have I on the other side
The other barely touching ground

Marjorie Jean Hall

Abortion's Requiem

It is not what was destroyed.
It is what was lost.
It is not the fetus treated wantonly.
It is the body that cannot be held.
It is not the blood abandoned.
It is the incapability of the soul to blend.
It is not the forgetting of what you knew.
It is that you will never see what is forgotten.
(The running feet toward nothing's joy,
Will never be defined as girl or boy.)
Abortion is war's evil cloud.
Obliterating justice!
Leaving an eternal shroud.

Joseph F. Sauer

Softly Moans

Wind, thru lofty trees, gently moans
and high above me an eagle screams
as I search a stream for stepping stones
lest the silence erupt with my groans
for ice within the water gleams.

Wind, across a green meadow, moans
passing by rocks scattered like thrones
the litter of long ago flowing streams
which moved those silent, huge stones.

Saw three horses, one black and two roans,
which were eating meadow grass by reams
oblivious to the wind's haunting moans
uncaring of its varied, eerie tones.

Now, to me, it does and truly seems
as tho a person could move those stones
to wind up weary to his bones
but be able to build a house of dreams
and live in comfort where soft wind moans.

I often ponder over those huge stones.

Everett W. Snow

Stolen Moments

Lying on the bank of a slow moving stream
My head in your lap, being teased by a dream
Soft, loving fingers gently caressing my brow
Overhead, squirrels and blossoms leap from the bough
The soft cool grass beneath as we lay
No hurry, no rush, no cares - no, not this day
The love that we share may well last forever
But not this moment, not this day; we both know better
Savoring your kiss, the sweet taste of your lips
Our breasts pressed together, bodies joined at the hips
We groan, we clutch, a glorious moment we share
That which matters most now, the delicate scent of your hair
We dress slowly, quietly; our time now is through
We retreat to our homes to start another day anew
Apart, but together, our minds meld as one
Our hearts count the days 'till the next meeting comes

Steven Keesling

My Calico Girl

She was a lovely lady all dressed up her calico gown and always was so clever in everything she found.

She loved, she played, she visited but always returned home to be with us her family.

She enjoyed life to the fullest and everything was to be looked after. She had a special place, actually there were two and she proudly wore her calico colors always. At times she would stop and spend time with my son and me but not too long. Then she returned to her special place and stayed there to rest.

Now she has a new special place and never more to leave, for she's with God for all eternity.

Rest now, lovely Mandy and we will be with you some day. My Calico Girl is now at peace and knows we will love her always.

May you find peace and happiness with Misty Blue, Sheba, Bud Pansy and Bootsie. God bless you, my beautiful Calico Girl.

Ellen M. Wardrop

Wrong Again

I see a Van Gogh on the wall,
and I think "That's the most beautiful thing I've ever seen."
Then I see the swelling colors of the fall foliage,
and I think "Wrong again."

I see red streaks across the evening sky,
and I think "That's the most beautiful thing I've ever seen."
Then I see roses blooming in the spring,
and I think "Wrong again."

I see the stars shining in the clear night sky,
and I think "That's the most beautiful thing I've ever seen."
Then I see the golden moon on a summer night,
and I think "Wrong again."

I see a sunrise over a grove of oaks,
and I think "That's the most beautiful thing I've ever seen."
Then I look into your dark brown eyes,
and I think "Wrong again, but never again."

Gary Lehman

End of the Day

When the end of the day comes,
Are you all fractions or are you all sums?

When you fill your bowl at supper time,
Are you all lemons or are you all limes?

When you sit down for that twilight drink,
Are the colors: brown, gray or shades of pink?

When the moon rises in the eastern sky,
Are you really you or are you living a lie?

B. Vitelli

No Where

They run seeking the freedom of safety,
From evil to the unknown, a child did flee.
Alone in the darkness of despair,
No one to give a care.
Dark strangers fake to become friends,
Strangers who will bring a means to their end.
Tired and hungry, reaching for anyone,
Beatings and violation, their payment for false freedom.
Into nowhere they were hurled,
The streets became their unwanted world.
In shadowed doorways, they work a living,
Forced by hunger, not willfully giving.
To the bitter night they fall prey,
Helpless to ill takers they lay.
Found by no one, frozen in the night,
They died, without a fight.
The butchered innocence of a child,
Never again to smile.
In the freedom of safety, forever they sleep,
The Lord their souls to keep.

Janet Lea Morjoseph

Journey Back

I'm loosing my mind.
Where is my soul?
When ever did I let go?
I'm letting things go to waste, like my mind.
Where is it?
I'm losing time.
Like watching sand run through my hands hitting the ground.
You can see what's happening, but can't hear the sound.
Where do I start, when it seems like the end?
Where do I go, when I'm lost around the bend?
What do you say, when the word is on the tip of your tongue?
Who will believe you, when only you know what you've done?
You're struggling within your soul.
Your mind is in a mental trap.
You're trying and trying to find a way out.
Walking into a deja-vu, thinking when, and about or who.
You just can't place the time.
You want to find peace of mind.

Amanda Patterson

Walk the Tall Wind

What was it?
Who saw it?
Who heard it?
Who felt it?

It was the foreible characterized by mental and physical power of all mankind.
It was as man saw life, as it passed away into the quite vigil of death as the bells tolled of his begin and end.
It was the mark of all souls as they walk the tall wind of time.
It was the great artist as he painted the life of man soul.
The soul of man heard the tall wind, as the voices of time cried out with fear, hate, love and laughter.
As the tall wind of life carried the life of man some say it was man dream unseen.
It could have been a virgin vision of life yet to come.

Edith Borbas

366

Arabella

There once was a doll named Arabella
She lived with us - so we knew her well
Her embroidered nose and button eyes
Made her look so very wise

Her body was of sheeting stout
With cotton stuffed to puff her out
A wig of yarn topped her head
Sort of brown, with a tinge of red

She tumbled down stairs so many times
To tell them all would take many rhymes
Hugged or thrown - she couldn't care less
Sometimes ended up quite a mess

A scrubbing with a brush she took
To help her keep a nice clean look
One time her face had to be remade
When out in the rain all night she stayed

There's still a pattern and wool for the hair
But the urge to make one just isn't there
Arabella may have been just a name
Yet no other doll would be quite the same

Marie Hanson Ellingson

A Cleansing Breath

A beam of light upon my face,
A ray of joy challenging my past.
Carving out its own crescent,
Through the mountain my choices have made...

A thousand white doves,
Sailing through a cloudy sky.
Their broad wings...
A moon beam, shining through the dust of life.

The only sound for miles...
The tide's white crest massaging the ever trodden sand.
The beaches calming heart beat,
Knows not the havoc of every day life.

A breath from heaven,
Relieves the claustrophobia of carbon copy days.
Showering the fragrance of tropical flowers,
Down to the fingertips of life.

A lightning bolt of energy,
Shatters all dimension of feelings previously known;
While grains of sand sift past the rough surface of my hands.
A cleaning breath...

Jennifer Roizen

Ebony's Dream

A strange occurrence in the midnight hour, the peking-poo lying
asleep. I could see his little legs moving in motion like he
was running toward something. In Ebony's dream he seems like he
was running toward something or perhaps he was chasing after
another dog or cat. Whatever it was he seems like he was excited
about something or someone and he was experiencing a happy dream.
Ebony heard the sound of a car coming down the Cumberland Height
Road. He whined and yelped. Ebony suddenly rose from his sleep.
He saw me standing there and he ran toward me; wagging his tail
with so much enthusiasm. I had to squat down to pick him up and as
I did he whined and yelped just like before, he woke up from his
dream. He hugged my neck. I believe I was in Ebony's Dream.

Valerie D. Keesee

Oh, No!

There's a little grey mouse
That works in my house

Most of the time he goes where I ask
And does for me the most menial task

But, there are times he refuses to go
For reasons that I certainly never will know

All of his work goes straight to the trash
Doesn't this seem to you to be overly rash?

To top off this tremendous frustration
My "Mac" simply smiles through the whole operation.

Donna Henn

The Dream

"What?—"
I sat up in bed,
Eyes aching for light...
Fighting for some glimpse of sight.

The dream was startling
Enough to wake me.
I turn my head in the black soup of night,
The thickness so murky it reminds of a past time's blight.

I feel a longing,
I'm not sure for what.
Something I've never had before, yet I long for it.
The quest of my life: I'll know when I find it.

The murkiness pushes me down
Like a depression.
I heave a heavy sigh, feeling the sweat roll down my temple
And neck, and soaking my shirt.

Again I lie in bed,
Uneasily remembering the fiction in my head.
I turn on my side
And sleep with the ominous bog that lives in my room at night...

Peter Amaral

Why?

Why did you leave I ask myself?
When I yell your name, you turn and walk away.
When I touch your shoulder I feel you shudder,
and when I ask you why you left me, you say "don't"
When you see big tears rolling down my cheeks and my
body shaking violently, you look away disgusted.
Then you walk away leaving me along in the cold and dark.
Asking myself, why did you leave?, And all I know
is that you left without even saying "goodbye"

Andrea Therkelsen

Time On My Hands

Time on my hands and what shall I do?
Bake some bread or make some stew/

Shall I read a book about love and war?
Or shall I lie on the couch a little while more?

The clock's ticking on and nothing's been done.
Shall I practice the piano just for fun?

Shall I give to the world and move mountains so high?
Will I hear every unheard baby's cry?

Shall I give smile to the sad and bread to the poor?
Or will I line on the couch a little while more?

Candy McClure

The Cross

My cross is made of special wood
He was nailed on me so very long ago
His agony made my splinters stand on end
My cross is made of special wood
His hands, they will not mend
I wished he would not go
My cross is made of special wood
He was nailed on me so very long ago.

Clea Peterson

A Kiss for You

Bright red and wet
Soft, tender, and warm
Puckered from lemon sunshine dew
Our friend's and family's hearts forlorn
We leave a kiss for you.

Mellowed bursts of energy
Caught by sea and grass
In the best places
We toss your body's ashes
And leave a kiss for you.

Planted on the waves of life's sorrows
Swirled by the wind
Shaken by the storm
We beg for forgiveness
And understand why you were born;

Dig too deep for comfort
Shallow in our understandings
Think of our many blessings
And then we know why
We leave a kiss for you.

Linda Cummings

Twilight With You

Softly the sun lies down to rest,
A wistful breeze is sweetly whispering thru the
Magnolia tree, kissing the air; as if wishing us all the best!
Stop! Oh golden time twixt the elderly day and
The infant night!
For the glorious power above has made music with
nature, orchestrating it in a brilliant, harmonious rhyme!
We played on, pass the afternoon's blistering fever;
Now our reward has come forth; the sky's soft cooling glow.
Somewhere wedged in the deep blades of green my
Ball is lost. Not to worry though, for I circle the
Moment with my eyes, I feel the loss; is at no cost!
Thy bones some day destined to decay,
Beneath this inspiring portrait; forever will they lay.
One wish I plead! here not deteriorate my
Memory too; of this magical hour shared
In the twilight with you.

Anthony DiRossi

Watching Everything Slip Away...

Watching everything that was stable in my life slip away
I realize that I should have held on
tighter.
Watching it slip away
Falling through my finger tips.
I try to grab on to what I can of what is left of
my
pathetic life.
But there is nothing
to hold on to.
And now as I grab on I start to fall with it
I should have stabilized my future
so I could live in it.

Kiera Evans

All of Me

All my life searching for the one to share,
the space within my heart,
to stand right by my side.

Then you came to me,
shining as the morning sun.
You gave your love to me,
and I knew you were the one.
The one to share my life,
to make all the wrong so right,
to live as one for all eternity,
you and me.

I'm giving you all of me,
because you gave me all of you.
I'll love you forever,
for my love is so strong.

I'm giving you all of me,
because you gave me all of you.
We'll stand together,
and our love will always carry on.

Donovan Clift

Chains

Chaining up my creativity
They stopped my brain from thinking
I lashed out at the material barrier
Hurting my oppressors with my fists and my feet
They chained me to a wall and taught me to be weak
Being too young to know the feelings enveloped me
My difference in intellect made me hated
They lashed out at me I refused to fight back
Authority says it's my fault
I move on
I move on

The beatings more frequent
My body and mind, they suffer
Deterioration in my physical form
I am dying...slowly

Mash Figaro

Tiny Hand Carved Boat

Twas a small hand-carved hardwood boat
Sometimes stirs my thoughts.
I went to other shores
Where deep down, within
A lasting friendship dwells;
Twas encouraged, Robert lent the boat
To myself, I traveled outdoors.
Winds came, helped move others.
I smiled and followed uncle to do chores.

Gone out in the world, a boat placed offshore,
Unsettled in time, swept briskly along.
Trusting, I face a world of troubled souls.
I push on, with God the boat pilot
Who waits patiently for me, a maker strong.
Still His child, I make that boat a favorite.
Unforgotten, it really was a fine carved toy
Given by someone dear to their little boy.
Which became, to me, a friendly spirit.
In retrospect, this always reminds my heart
I loved it then and now, to have been a part.

Mary Louise Anderson

A Night In February

In the vault of heaven
embroidered with stars, a wandering moon
arrayed in shimmering white
girded and belted with a garland of lilies,
stooped to kiss a little star.

A night in February
In the silence of that room, I embrace my love,
now so quiet, so at peace, remembering;
he had been the fulfillment of all my dreams.
A night in February, likened to a dried seed
our love did flourish and grow,
enveloping us both with rapture,
so elegant, so supreme
and, oh, so esthetically pure,

A night in February in this, my longing heart,
forever you shall remain,
effused with celestial mystery
likened to those heavenly stars.
Yes, we shall meet again,
together, we shall kiss that little star.

Joseph Sicignano

Painter's View

When the mind is stronger than the body.
The mind could overcome anything.

Vincent Van Horn was not a person of his time
He was smarter than most and had manners quite fine
He lived in a shelter cause his parents were dead
And there he did nothing, except paint all in red.

As a man his paintings awakened with colors
Giving his creations applause's from others.
Then one dark storming night, the worse fate came to be
Starring at the ceiling, he could no longer see.

Enraged with madness cause his real dreams could not start
Alone in a tower, he suffered for his art
Then one day he decided to paint once again
For long days and nights he was obsessed with no end.

His last painting, "Vision," was his doorway to fame
all who looked upon it could understand its name
Vincent soon after had died in his sleep at night
He was able to follow his dreams without sight.

Nakisha Chanel Leon

February

Warmth. February quest.
Again the stars reign as I am drawn to the heat of our closet orb.
Traveling beyond the gray. Stealing the vitality and brilliance the
sun offers. Escaping the realities of the winter.
Momentarily, as it is these same realities which summons me home.

The heart. Buried treasure.
Buried by my own beliefs.
Its value often discounted unless in the possession of another.
I am forced to listen to the cadence.
The drummer marches alone.

Friends provide warmth robbed by the wind.
Their presence is my gift.
Their loyalty protects the treasure within.
Distancing me from the threats of the external light.
I must challenge my perceptions.

I am alone. The silence is broken by the cadence
I am alone. Isolation is a choice.
I am alone. The winter cover shades my view.
I feel the warmth of the spring sun.
I must challenge my perceptions.

Mark C. Kelley

First Love

She told me of Loving then showed me the "how,"
My Life, then, was never the same.
She taught me to Love and I think of her now,
But I cannot remember her name.
She was blonde, she was tall, Lady Eve all in all,
And we played by her rules of the game,
To Love and then Leave... now it's hard to believe
That I've somehow forgotten her name.

Ed Reimers

To You This I Pray...

Dear Lord watch over someone who right now is far away.
Keep him safe with your protection, to you this I pray.

What I've found in him is rare, and for me it's all so new.
Since I can't be there with him, my only hope is you.

If and when he gets lonely, or even a little scared.
Remind him of who's waiting, and how much she really cares.

He's so brave in what he does, he has courage beyond belief.
And knowing your watching over him, gives that extra sense of
relief.

At night when all is quiet, and he stares into the sky.
Let peace enter his heart, as he thinks of him and I.

I'm always with him in spirit, but I need a helping hand.
Incase he ever may need you, please be his Footprints in the Sand.

If he needs help, please carry him to see another day.
Guide him, protect him, take care of him, to you this I pray.

Pamela K. Hubbard

Colors Bright

Colors bright, darkness and light, tiny
birds taking flight,
Bricks and steal, and love that is real.
Clouds and crowds, and summer's beyond
the sunset,
Playing games and friendly names, the
younger ones are the same,
Gates leading to bright new days, through
cold and damp caves.
Lakes with boats that go so far,
Airplanes flying through the air
would you be so good to cave,
Through the day time, would have
us free a new star.

P. Sulpietro

Tale of an Oak

It was not long ago a place I have not know
Aimlessly I strolled no cares no concerns
The sun bore down no breeze to cool
In the distance the greatness of an oak stood tall and proud
I pondered its loveliness as I drew near
Below its massive frame its strength I could feel
How did you survive all alone in this field so grew
Within the stillness her leaves began to sing
Never alone am I, for God has placed me right
In this field so full of life, the birds have shelter to raise
   their young
The squirrels and deer eat the fruit I yield and lay by my side
So I am as you, never alone as you now can see
It is by faith that I survive in this field of green
For God has nourished me and never left my side
So be as I stand tall and proud keep your faith in God he is only a
breath away many will come in your field so empty and bare
Fill them with love, happiness and spirit of song
Never again will you walk alone, remember the oak, it is so full of life.

Daniel Parente

My Tribute to Arsie

Once in a while a calf will be born into a herd,
That will grow into that one in a million cow of stories you have
    heard.
Arsie was born in my arms on a sunny October 1985 day,
She was tall, with colors of black, red and white, over 90 pounds she
    did weigh.
As time went by and Arsie grew older,
She outgrew the Jerseys, but never acted any bolder.
When it came time for Arsie to be in the milk line,
I called her my gentle giant, for she never was in a hurry, but,
    always taking her time.
She could milk with the best and was a mother to all,
from baby calves, cats, dogs, even the goat and pigs, to her it didn't
    matter how small.
Arsie was with the herd for ten and a half years,
in good times as well as bad she was always near.
This past winter was hard on old Arsie for she had trouble getting up,
Never kept her tied, she always was loose, but, with the ice and cold,
    the winter was just too rough.
It was a sad day in April of 96 when I had to load her up,
for she was more than a cow, but a friend, and like one of my kids
    that I led on the truck.
Arsie is gone, but she still lives on, in her daughter, nieces, and
    now her son.
Valentino is a baby now but will be a breeding bull in the next year,
and if I am lucky he will produce babies like his mom, Arsie, so she
    will always be near.
        Patty Nichols

American Pie Reprise

We were singin' bye, bye Miss American Pie
in front of the trailer just Andy and I,
him sippin' Bush, me a Pibb

'cuz after one year of treatment the keg was dry
and all I had was a caffeine high
and memories of socials and Tina

by my side singin' this'll be the day that I die.
But we didn't die, just tried and tried
to get drunk in the fields tippin' cows.

Now the good ol' boys are drinkin' whiskey and rye
not in dark pastures hidden under night skies
but in Eddie's Lounge and A-Go-Go

while guys like me and Andy, workin' nine to five,
decided to let the 'glory days' die
for new trucks, a dog, and a loan.

So we went on singin' bye, bye Miss American Pie,
forgettin' the time and the day that we'd die,
just lookin' at stars, feelin' nothin'.
        Elizabeth M. Vondrak

Batbabe's Verse

Frolicking, frisking, demon-eyed sight,
my plotting, planning, sly hunter at night;

Relaxed, free-willed, lazy—a bit,
daytime is heavenly for my cat, I admit;

Precious, rare, my perfect cat is,
through the eyes of the beholders, mine and his;

Your actions and thoughts, oh dear cat of mine,
are worth more than treasures of any kind;

I will cherish you and love you until the end of time,
oh precious, perfect, dear cat of mine.
        Angela Ragsdale

Parallels Between My Mother And Mother Earth

If in God's dictionary I could look,
I'd find the word Mother in this wonderful book.
The words I'd read would be gentle and kind,
For when he created Mother he had these thoughts in mind:
Mother/Mother Earth
Provider of:
shelter, food, clothing, warmth
Giver Of:
Life, beauty, laughter, pleasure
A beautiful and wondrous thing, not to be taken for granted,
neglected or ignored.

So when I hear a gentle rain falling from the sky,
It brings to mind my mother's voice in a soothing lullaby.
And when I feel the summer sun shining upon my face,
I am gently reminded of my mother's warm embrace.
And when I look up in the sky and see the starry night,
The vastness of my mother's love is a beacon of brilliant light.

My mother and Mother Earth, two of God's most beautiful creations.
        Nancy Williams

Blue Monday Blue

I am an everyday guy, or so I thought, no-one ever called me a slob.
Like everyone else, I used to complain about having to go to my job.
The job I have isn't all that tough, I just didn't want to go in.
Then one day I met a homeless man, he said his name was Ben.

He said, I had a good job once and I used to complain like you.
For me going to work was an energy drain and something I didn't want
to do. Until one day I went in, and my boss said to me, Ben, I have
a pink slip here for you. On that day it was raining, and I'd just
stopped complaining, about it being A Blue Monday Blue.

When I first got the news, I was shocked and confused. My plans for
a good life were gone. My wife was pregnant, we had three kids
already, and I'd just bought a brand new home. With bills a mile
high and my life yakking at me, my plans all went down the tube. I
didn't like my job until that horrible day when I found I had no job
to lose. My wife divorced me and took all the kids, and said not to
call her honey. She said, she didn't need a man that was broke, the
minute I ran out of money.

So a word to the wise, when your job opens the doors, if standing
outside were I you, I'd prepare for that day when somebody could
say, "You no longer have a job to go to."

Since talking to Ben, I wake up each day and jump out of bed like a
missile. Now when you see me, I got a smile on my face, and I go
skipping to work with a whistle.
        Harold H. Carlock

Unspoken Word

You left us all with an unspoken word,
A word that can never be heard,
My heart cries out for you day after day,
I can't imagine why God took you this way.
I never thought I'd live life without you.
And still today I wish none of this were true.
You left us all with so much to say,
Things that weren't said when you left us that day.
We hold you very tight in our hearts
Even though we're lifetimes apart
If you can hear or see us so high,
Know that we love you and want to say goodbye!
        Julie Davidson

My Rays of Golden Light

Softly, like gold streams, from the harboring tide I shine, flowing
quietly, and slowly where I reside,
Fully alive, free, and fragile, like the hand of a gusty wind
blowing through a woman's dress, grasping, reaching, embracing as
to dance under the naked, clear, calm, and blue sky,

Morning dew, petals and purple poppies, gather at my request,
friends, with which I discuss matters during the day, quietly with
joy and laughter, each of us enjoys the golden "Rays Of Light."

Echoing to aid me with my rise, calling me, forming me, like songs
from neighboring children, growing while singing at play,

Yellow in crowded masses, we stand firm,
Like tiny towns on a huddled map,
birds flock like seagulls on a journey to nearby sunset, as a
tiny baby's hand opens up, both greet me and run astray,

Butterflies zoom across the periphery of my meaning, gliding while
destined with delight to reach an unknown place of comfort, leaving
me, the sunflower to gaze upon lovely and warm "Rays Of Light"

"Rays of beautiful golden light" on a clear day,
My beautiful, and cherished "rays of golden light."

Lolita Oliver

A Grandmother's Day

You wake in the morning and crawl out of bed,
You stumble around with a muddled-up head.
You head for the kitchen for a cup of the brew.
If it weren't for coffee, Oh! What would we do?
Put bread in the toaster, take a sip of orange juice,
then look around you, and think, "What's the use?"
The phone starts to ring, you laboriously walk,
to answer its call, and with someone to talk.
Then over the wire, you hear a little voice say,
"Grandma, we're coming to see you today."
You now see the sun, that's been shining so bright.
The clouds in your head have all taken flight.
Instead of a shuffle, you walk with a spring.
Instead of grumbling, you now want to sing.
How quickly things change, as from night into day.
Because on the phone, you heard a little voice say,
"Grandma, we're coming to see you today."

Corene Wagner

Untitled

Darkness fills the lonely room,
A splinter of light seeps
through the boards,
The stench of death hangs in the air,
Fog, surrounds her from head to foot,
She stands in this rat infested place
In the back of the room lies the silhouette of
someone she once loved,
Grief has passed over her,
Hope is useless,
She prays that sanity keep her,
As she stares at the darkness,
She turns to leave,
She whispers his name,
It seems as though even
the corpse is ignoring her,
He never did listen, she goes to exit,
knows she must go on existing,
And feels guilty, because this time her
love was not reason enough.

Tara Eshelman

Love Untold

When the sounds pound
and my world comes crashing down
I reach for him and hold on
he comforts me, he soothes my pain
he feeds me desires needed to live
gives me pleasure internal, external
he who needs me he who wants me
I who want him, need him, love him
he who takes me down on silk covered beds painted with
    colorful petals of mid-born roses
hot candle wax surrounding empty glasses of red wine
steamy oil mixing with the scent of sweaty love
pleasurable pain
    guilty love
    lovers forbidden who meet in secret
hope fulfilled and dreams conquered
in a room where desires become reality
for he is my desire he is my dream
he is my lover
in our love untold.

Brandi Coleman

Precious Son

Dear Lord, you have given me
Something more precious than a diamond or a pearl.

No one could have given me
a better gift - a baby boy, not a girl.

You can't replace him with any toy
because my little boy is a bundle of joy.

When he cries, I comfort him,
not a holler, not a whim.

Dim the lights way down low,
rock-a-bye my little guy.

Hush-a-bye, don't you cry,
while I sing you a lullaby.
Goodnight my son, sleep tight.
Thank you, Lord, for what you have done.
Thank you, Lord, for my precious son!

Bethany Wise

Gingham's Iron Thread

She stands there,
this gingham-proud anachronism
in sprawling worlds of voice mail and microchip,
core-confident of her importance as she kneads,
old lullabies rising from her heart,
old virtue oozing from her soul
like pure water through cracked porcelain.

Innocent of purpose, stalwart belief in
love's tender grace is her only buttress,
for she offers nary a concern
about agenda bridges
or mountains of knowledge to climb.
Neither does she realize the sanctity
of this cohesive posture,
this quiet, vulcanizing sense of self.

It is iron thread, covertly exalting her spirit
while she shapes dough
and fantasizes about golden loaves.

Rosemary Cacolice Brown

A Time to Die

If I had my way
I'd die on a day like today
Sun filtering the trees
A breeze in the leaves
The air warm and thin

It is gentle on my skin
My spirit is at peace
Few years left on my lease
I've made a few marks
On accomplishment charts
Why wait until I am ill
To lie in bed in pain
For years and turn life into tears?
I could say farewell in this heavenly state
I'll come back again as I have before
So let my body rest.

I'd like to die on a day like today
I wish it were possible
I wish there was a way!

Margery H. Cory

Alone

On an ocean coast I see the waves hitting the rocks,
sometimes roughly.
I feel a misty spray upon my face.
It's a gloomy day - gray, blue and black - all at once,
yet separately.
I hear many voices thru the winds of my past,
uncaring, unknowing, humiliating,
leaving me empty and alone.

I remember the screaming,
within the silence of my solitude.
The voices die down just as all the people had died.
On a soft whispering breeze they reappear,
tears fall, the salt stings,
they're gone and I'm still here - alone.

The cold ground enters and climbs throughout my body,
uncontrollable shivers take over.
An old man whispered to me,
  "Someone's walking over your grave"
I wonder who it is?
I trembled, turned and walked away - alone.

John W. Larson

A Doctor's Prayer

I ask for help each morning
  As I start the newborn day.
To give me strength to do my best
  And be not afraid to pray.
I ask for temperance with compassion
  As I go about my work.
Each day unfolds new suffering
  And fearful problems always lurk.
There is anguish, fear or pain
  On almost every face I see
Demanding everything within me
  To allay their misery.
It may just take reassurance
  Plus some medical advice,
Or it might need drastic surgery
  And it's a life, there is no price.
Comes the dusk and then the darkness
  Will this night be blessed with rest?
I raise my eyes, then bow my head
  In silent prayer - have I done my best?

Frank T. O'Brien M.D.

Gone Forever

Because of your absence no one knows why,
we just listen, try to understand, and cry.
  We don't want to let go, we're all
refusing, we wish you weren't the one we're loosing.
  You never did anything wrong, nothing
deceiving, and because of your kindness
you stopped breathing.
  Your love was like a dove, it soared freely
in the sky. Even though you're gone visually, you'll
always be inside.
  Now we can look outside as God lets
down the rain, we can cry loud or soft to ease
the pain.
  We've remembered everything you've done in the
past, you weren't the first to go and won't be the last.
  Everyone must go sometime, somehow I just
wish you didn't have to go now.
  But now you're gone and never forgotten,
in our hearts you'll always stay, always
be remembered and never fade away.

Melinda Marie Ortiz

Cyberspace

The rush of information flowing
a vast sea of data beyond the horizon
intoxicating the mind
tantalizing and stimulating the brain

Technology and biology intermingled
together in harmony, melding as one, unity

Flashy and decadent, spatial and geometric
universe of energy and Ram
soaring above cities of knowledge
clusters of bytes as datascape

Limitless boundaries beyond the mind's eye
brilliant streaking highways of input
racing across the matrix, infinity unfolding

Profound silence resounding throughout
muted commotion flooding the mind
delighting the consciousness
captivating the soul

Interfaced directly with world of technology
surrounded, engulfed in its enormity
awestruck by its flawless splendor, ultimate freedom

Lewis W. Schlossberg

Indian Sorrow

The buffalo and deer now run so few
Along the plains and forests fresh with dew.
The land of their father sight with grief.
Warriors mourn the loss of a chief.
How brave his spirit enduring such.
Traditions of forefathers losing touch.
Tears of sorrow flow from the waterfall.
Crying for the native Indian call.
Will the little red children see a bright day,
With fighting, bloodshed and tears put away?

The sacred lads of warriors brave,
Wrestled away only memories save?
The barbarous lies of many white men.
Echo with anger around the mountain.
Injustice tars at my heart with a knife.
Removal of lands and a way of life.
The heartaches and pain carried round with care.
In the kindred spirits of the wold and bear.
Will the little red children see a bright day,
Dignity restored with freedom to pray?

Toni Stearns

A Dedication to My Son

Jonathan,
A year has passed since that day in May
God sent you to Heaven

You will always be in our hearts my youngest son

On your birthday, we blow out the candles on your cake
dreaming of what you could have been

So young to die, but we can't ask God why
He has a reason for everything that we can't understand

You were there when our Lord reached out his hand

The sweet memories of your childhood
run wild through our minds

To remind us how precious life can be

I will always be your mother,
I held you in my arms after you were born
I held you in my arms when you died

You can't imagine the tears I have cried
from the depths of my heart, until I am worn

We want to remember you with joy and pride
We know God is at your side

We love you and miss you
Rhonda Branson

Tree Of Life

The tree of life is love you know
These are the elements that make it grow.
It starts as a seedling but with patience and care.
All of a sudden...a young sprout is there.
Encouragement is the strong roots below
That nurtures it along and helps it to grow.
Understanding, like the rain and warming sun
Nourishes the trunk that's already begun.
Virtues, humor and honor are there
Respectfully branching, out everywhere.
The budding leaves of knowledge, Yes indeed!
Are the results of all you have given the seed.
The blossoming morals and wisdom you see
Is a child of love, as sturdy as a tree.

Frances M. Norcross

God Intended Me To Die

I get off the floor
And shut the door
I give it a lite
It's my very last night
I sit in the corner scared and in fright
Why'd he have to go
If only he would know
Of the love I gave
And I wish God to save his soul
I want no more pain
But I'll have to quit the game
I'll pull the gun up to my head
And blow myself away
But there's no need to cry
God intended me to die

Stephanie Teague

Memories

Lonely in this dark gloomy room
— as I gaze intently at the wall
My mind travels through rapturous and somber past
— and — I realize how years have gone swiftly by.

My mind recalls the good times
The times I spent with my friends,
friends that were —
Warm hearted, good willed, and loving.

I remember the time
The time of fear,
fear of —
Monsters, darkness, and death.

I call back to the moment
The moment I graduated,
graduated with —
Honor, respect, and dignity.

The commemoration of these memories,
Memories filled with sorrow and contentment
Shall stay with me —
Throughout life and eternity.
Uzma Bhatti

A Miracle Happens

In times of trouble,
full of worries,
fear is something
that seems to double.
Every minute feels like an hour!
Every day a lifetime of gloom and doom!
Just then the Good Lord
gives you the power
to make it through.
A miracle happens
and boom:
Mountains of pain turn into mole hills of dust,
and the limitless problems
that cause the never ending depression
are no longer a must!
Rosie Conti

Old Golfer

"How am I?" Oh golfer friend
Have to say, I'm on the mend
But just in case - turns ill my fate
Here's my Riopan and Trisalicylate
There's my Nitro, Dristan - what can I say?
There's even a tube of my ole friend, Ben Gay
I always did, my needs foresee
I even carry my Doc with me
Golfing's fun - be it light or dark
When with my partner, Doctor Clark
We hit tree trunks and tear off the bark
We drive, chip and putt, me and Doc. Clark
And when he asks: "How are you today?"
It's all the above that I always say
Getting older is not such a lark
But I have my pills and the good Doc. Clark
Spiro Thomas Chelemedos

Simple Lament

Today is the day to say our goodbyes.
To remember your laughter, your smile, your eyes.

Today is the day to stop and reflect,
The wonderful memories, lest we never forget.

The family gatherings, the Christmas-time fun
You were the center for all of us; my own shining sun.

You watched us grow up and always stood by
You laughed when we laughed; cried when we cried.

You touched us in ways we can never repay,
And now that you're gone, in our hearts you will stay.

Mother, Grandmother, Teacher and Friend
A symbol of strength right to the end.

So on this sad day, while we are all still together
I want you to know through this storm we will weather.

Our lives will go on, just as you knew
Only now there's a place that is empty without you.

So we'll cry a few tears and then say goodbye
And know that you're resting above in the sky.

Watch over and guide us in your own special way
And know how truly loved you are...each and every day.

Kim Rafferty

The Drinker

The drinker is a thinker, all alone
No one knows what happens when he goes home
Everyone thinks he is the life of the party
But he lays awake in the midnight hour saying he's sorry
for the wrong he has done
For the drinking, driving and the abuse of the women he's
preyed upon
He has mental anguish for what goes on
He has everything and knows nothing because he is in
denial
Because of this stupid, want to be cool, fake lifestyle
But, if you think he is just one you're wrong
Because the old school taught the new school through
ancestral genes
Do you know, do you know, do you know what I mean
things are not what they seem
He tries to quit and there is nothing more sobering
Do you know, do you know, do you know what I mean
things are not what they seem

Joseph L. McCrary Jr.

Target

A sparkle in her eye glistens as the illumination targets her.
A gunshot is heard from behind.
The target is still, overwhelmed...
She thinks.
"Run...run," she tells herself.
Locking up as though there were chains surrounding her body, she
stands motionless.
The whirling bullet strikes her with raging fear.
Her heart takes a hard pound.
It breaks, unfastening the pain, anger, and frustration.
The clock stops ticking... time's up!

Amulya Pasupuleti

Identity

Snow falling softly
A powdery mist sprinkled from the heavens
A child at play feels the moist gentle touch
As an angel's kiss
And feeling a oneness complete
With the infinite
The child resumes his play.
Christ, this is Christmas.

Avonale Stephenson

The Lady and the Garden

Majestic mountain in radiant gown
spiritual garden terra cotta and brown
their beauty and strength eternally bound,
mere human endeavor doth falter.

With words or brush who scarce can know
the boundless beauty through ages old
the vast endurance and endless show,
through the portals of passing seasons.

By sacred decree in heaven's plan
the grandest wedding in all the land
majestic lady and spiritual man,
camels kiss in celebration.

Human spirit in finite end
to death's invite doth not befriend
there stands a testament of eternal plan,
the Lady and the Garden.

Gary R. Ellenberger

Nationless People

Nation of many people
Divided we stand
United we fall

Unlimited cultures
Flags of many places
All under one insignia
Divided we stand
United we fall

Racism is the key
To all hate crimes
Love for unity is not in the air
Divided we stand
United we fall

Blood on the streets
Bullets whizzing by my head
Hate is at our gate
Divided we stand
United we fall

The world is never going to be one United Nation

Andrew T. Brickey

My Friend?

I don't want it to end like this,
we were suppose to enjoy years and nights of enjoyable bliss.
You make me hurt and quiet to all,
as you play and toy...Damn your gall!
What happens to a love that suddenly turns sour,
as we stare and gaze into a vase of dead flowers,
Our love is dead like the flowers on the table,
Can I love again,... I don't know if I'm able.
Secrets and lies have torn us apart,
while your wicked ways have broken my heart.
It's sad to think of this as an end,
but I'm hoping you will live in peace,...
My Friend?

Tracy D. Trent-Hall

Aftermath

hey hey Mother of Nature, changing as I
I wonder if I conform to you
or do you follow my lead?
rain pounds, softens, cleanses
the Earth discovers itself all over again
as do I

Did you look into my eyes?

did you see the water?

Did you look into the water?

did you see my eyes?

No

You never even tried
the
pure
white
flame

tapped but alone
a monogamous virgin
can I be the focus?
I've waited so long ....
Ross Neely

The Two of Us

We've been together twenty-seven years; The Two of Us.
Our love has stood the test of time, through thick and
thin. The Two of Us. I still see you at Valentines
to be that girl of seventeen as I once saw you those
many years ago. We've raised a family with our love
entwined together. The Two of Us. Life at times
has been hard to bear but love for one another has
seen us through. The future, if there be one, belongs
to us because nothing can separate our hearts from
each other. I love you today more than all those
yesterdays. I wish only for you happiness and
brighter tomorrows and for us many more years
together with a love that only grows deeper and
stronger for The Two of Us.
Haskell Dale Hamilton

A Child of Love

The hardest thing in all these years,
Of all the poems I've tried to write,
Was finding words, while fighting tears,
To express the love for my child of light.

How do you run with a butterfly?
Or count all the wild flowers on a hill?
Capture the love in a lullaby?
Or tell the dancing wind to still?

How do you bottle the morning sun?
Or hold onto the rolling sea?
Jump over the rainbow, just for fun?
Or define eternity?

Such gentle peace and joy within,
A child so full of love and grace,
When thoughts of broken dreams begin,
I simply look upon your face.

No, I cannot find the words to start,
Confined by lines of black and white.
I pray you'll know when we're apart,
You are the poem I cannot write.
Bonny Dunlap Smith

Road of Loneliness

As I walk down this long, lonely road,
Emptiness, loneliness, and sorrow, fills my heart,
my body, my soul,
my soul roams endlessly,
Through the darkness of the night sky,
Forever wondering, and questioning, the reason "Why?",
Does true love, true happiness,
Come from deep within the heart and soul,
Or, is it something that comes and goes,
Like the passing of time, itself,
Do the dreams, the moments, and the memories shared,
Fade away more, each, and everyday,
Or, will they last forever,
Like the stars, the heavens,
And the universe, themselves,
A vision, of what once was,
A lifetime, of what, may have been
Roger Jenks

Snow

The snow that falls it's lovely to see
As it covers the ground and blankets the trees,
The branches are spread and bending low
As if bowing to this beautiful snow,
It's awesome to see it glitters like gold
It twinkles like stars this lovely snow,
Such joy it gives for all to see,
The snow that falls and blankets the trees,
No matter how big the size or shapes
As it falls from the sky no noise it makes
This fluffy white stuff we call snow.
Helen Shelton Keith

Suicide

Both of our lives were hard
With our own choice to stay alive
Living in this hateful world
We thought you would survive

We were best friends forever
And both of us swore
That we would live and die
Until we could live no more

I noticed you were slipping
Down the line of life
Until you cut the rope
With a sadly wounded knife

We were supposed to stay together
But how could I have been so wrong
To let you make me think
You'd keep your promise and stay long?

It makes me think how much you loved me
To go and take away your breath
Now who am I to meet at the crossroad
On the boundary of life and death?
Sara Guerrero

Hi God

Hi God. All of a sudden, for I don't
know how long, you were there and then all
of a sudden you weren't. It was so good to say
the least to see you there. So good that I'm
writing about it thanks to you of course.

I'll always remember it. I'll always
be happy with you and long for you too.
So please excuse me but hi God and thank
you for giving this to me too.
Carolyn Irene Schauguard

"God's Miracles"

As I awaken each day, and start to pray,
I see God's creation all over the nation.
It takes you away to a beautiful day,
When all our cares will be wiped away.
It makes us so thankful to God.
And to realize he is the wheel and the cog.
He takes all our burdens on his shoulders of love.
He hears all our prayers from heaven above.
I love him and harken to his voice so
sweet, and pray each day in heaven I will meet.
He is such a great God so honest and true.
I want to go to heaven, how about you?
To live here on earth in heartache
and pain, and die and go to hell is simply insane.
So follow Gods footsteps and always
pray, and I will meet you in heaven
some beautiful day.

Murle Allen

The Jury

The line of scrimmage,
the struggle for rights and fairness and equality,
the appeal to a higher power for justice,
for a gain that cannot be undone,
in the contest between good and evil,
the game is won.

The lines of battle formed,
the struggle is begun,
the men of blue, the red blood, white faces,
unwavering in what must be done,
for freedom can only be true
when it is for all or none,
and when the process due
cannot be disrupted by just one,
for what due process was given
to those who came before,
who laid their lives down
at such a cost,
this time around,
the game was lost.

Geoffrey L. Hitchon

Hats!

I love hats!
Because they are so charming;
They tell about a person,
Whose head they are adorning.

My, what a variety of hats there are,
Bright ones, floppy ones,
Distinguished and tall -
Velvet, denim, silk, or straw.

Why! Hats bring out the acting in us humans;
They can reveal a person's dreams,
Their work, their hobbies, and their schemes -
Courage, rebellion, kindness and care
Can also be told by the hats that we wear.

A hat tells a story;
It can be joyful, sad or funny,
Next time you see a hat -
Remember this...
I wonder - what's it saying?

Martha Frost

The Death Of The Mountain

Asleep in the clouds on a nice sunny day,
Dreaming of wild flowers by the bay,
Suddenly a pain came to his member,
Awaken him from his peaceful slumber.

His poor body throbbed with pains,
Thundering anger covered the plains,
Once animals lived in his timbers,
Now his sides are void of members.

His scarred body made the base,
For bloody tears to come down his face,
No more life left on his sides,
His dreams went out with the tides.

On-Kay Wong

You and Me

People laugh
And people yell
Do they think it makes things swell
My feelings hurt
On the verge of tears
I've dealt with this through all my years
What can I do
To change these things
I know we are all human beings
But why do we laugh at others pain
Doing this we have nothing to gain
Our selfish pride
Makes us think we are right
But then we feel guilty late at night
This torture might stop
If only we could start to see
The stories inside you and me

Sara Baughman

Dark Chapters

Here I teeter on a thread
My pain, so lonesome, I cannot shed
As I pen in ink, the dark chasm, I'm on the brink
Back and forth I sway
Could I but return to a better day
Here I balance on thine thread
This lonesome pain I cannot shed
To know this, alone I bear,
fills my heart with dread
Would that I were strong,
so lonesome, I would be not long
Deep, Dark Despair
Out of the dark, I gasp for air
My soul is rending....., with pain un-ending
from this mortal being....., of the deep, un-seeing
I am a creature of the night,
Never again to shine so bright
My heart once burning like a flame,
Is now a cold pit....., of guilt, and shame.

Robert Bain

Storm

Thunder rumbles through the mountains,
It shakes the forest shade.
Lightning strikes with a vengeance,
It sets the trees ablaze.
The rain rips through the night,
It pounds the cold hard earth.
"Beware!" The wind screams as it passes.
"Watch out!" Cries the thunder boom'n 'round.
"Too late!" Sighs the lightning as it strikes a tree,
"She has taken an old life to make way for a new,
Wise Mother Nature."

Adair Marie Hill

Requiem to Joe

To Joseph Stanley Stoner who died of pneumonia at age 26 — 1938
I dreamed last night you were alive
And teaching yet at the one-room school
Where I attended as a child.
I passed that school each day
To catch the high school bus.
'Twas then in '34 you noticed me
Trudging along that country road.
We fell in love and planned a home,
But God called you to his home instead,
Tearing me apart in grief.

You took one half of me along with you;
The other half was left behind
To walk on in faith, not sight,
Without you by my side.
But the guiding hand I held to then
Still guides me in these golden years.
I still recall your parting words:
"We are not divided, dear, just separated."
Time draws us closer now when halves will join
And we'll both be home together.

Isabelle Reddick-Rodgers

The Answer

There is something special about you and I.
How come we didn't get together sooner?
I don't know why.

I'm sure glad the old Nova didn't start that night.
Because, since then everything in my life has been so right.

I had prayed many times for someone like you.
My prayer has been answered; this I know is true.

I wondered what took so long, as I prayed each day and night.
But later I learned that God's timing is always right.

He has a plan for us already figured out.
This I believe in my heart and have no doubt.

Everything feels so right with us; I feel no wrong.
I've been waiting on you my whole life long.

What we feel together, you just can't get anywhere.
Just stick around, and let me show you how much I care.

James Tucker

Shadows of the Light

From that time from dusk to dawn,
    when it appears that dreams,
    are single faucets that pour out life,
    replaying it, it seems.

In the form of joyful melodies,
    that play throughout the night,
    my dreams are but shadows,
    reflecting the living light.

During this time when I'm at rest,
    when twirling thoughts abridge the day,
    acting out their own opinions,
    unsure of what we'll say.

Unsure of whether we'll awake,
    in sleepy smiles of delight,
    or whether we'll rise cold and shaken,
    as victims of the night.

But when the dawn breaks the spell,
    my dreams will await the night,
    the time when they can return,
    as shadows of the light.

Kristin Keating

Finding Out

Maybe in a year or two
I'll find out whom I am
And find out what I want to be
I'll find out if I can

I'll weigh the things that I do best
Against those that I can't do
I'll speak against things that I think are false
And speak for those that I hold true

I'll alter all my lifetime plans
Or see them to the end
I'll cast out all my enemies
And draw close the ones that I call friend

So maybe in a year or two
Or maybe three or four
I'll find our where I'm coming from
And where I'm headed for

Theron Max Miller II

The Bluebird

The bluebird, standing there on the window ledge,
twittering in the smooth breeze.
Its song as sweet and soft as a toddlers kiss.

I start humming a tune of my favorite song.
He stops and listens to me,
turning his body and showing me his bright eyes.

I take him in my hands being very gentle with the little thing.
He Pecks at my palm as if he is looking for something.
I put him down on my pillow and give him some bread
to nibble on.

He feels the breeze coming from the window hitting his wing,
he looks at me bewildered then looks at the slightly open window.
I take him in my hands and brush his soft feathers against my face.
Then I let him go.
He swoops down to his nest and looks back at me with his
mysterious eyes.
Then he flies away.

Valerie Bitici

Teddy

In my closet full of creatures
you're my favorite one
I call you "Angel,"
'cause that's what you are.

You've shared my happy times
I've soaked you with my tears
and when I'm angry, well,
I'm sorry, but you make a good punching bag.

You calm me when I'm afraid,
though silently.
I can confide in you;
you'd never tell a soul.

I can use you for a pillow
when mine just won't do.
You accompany me to sleep overs,
you're the perfect guest.

We've been together through the years
and, though sometimes I put you aside,
I'll always come back.
You'll be my best friend forever.

Stefanie Caloia

If I Never Went Through

If I never went through the valleys and trials
I would never be so strong to smile.

If I never went through the sadness and pain
I would never cry out for His name.

If I never went through the weakness I may feel,
I would never seek the Lord for I know His strength is real.

If I never went through the urging to carry on
I would never have made it through this long.

Donnette Lee Schumacher

The Awakening

Life here on the planet is not without its ups and downs;
Like the masks of the theater, one smiles, the other frowns.
It's so easy in our humanness to get caught in the trap,
Of thinking we are lost souls who don't know where we're at.

We must trust that the heart is the center of our feelings;
The logical mind is limited to floors, walls, and ceilings.
Infinity of space and time hide out when we are born;
We've forgotten we are spiritual beings here in human form.

We each have our contract written in the stars;
We only think our deals are made in restaurants and bars!
Each of us has been around a time, or two or three;
The time has come when many are soon to be set free.

Beware of the barrenness of a busy life;
Of cheating on ourselves, our husband or our wife.
We are always on the run, doing this and seeing that;
Only by listening to the silence can we know where we are at.

Love in its purest form leaves no room for fear;
Do not shake your head when there's a ringing in your ear.
Consider that the source is sending you a wake-up call;
Take a giant leap of faith, you won't stumble, you won't fall.

Ann Kennedy

My Hands Are Made For

My hands are made for grabbing,
To bring the ones I love so near:
My hands are made for working,
So that I can provide for the family I must rear:
My hands are made for searching,
So that I can find out what is true and real:
My hands are made for teaching,
So my children will know what is real:
My hands are made for helping,
So that I can dry another's tears:
My hands are made for clapping,
To be a part of those that cheer:
My hands are made for holding,
So that I can caress my love so dear:
My hands are made for praying,
So that the Lord will come and be near—

Benjamin E. Thompkins Jr.

Circus

Circus of eyes.
Blood in a wading pool.
Sinking in the breeze.
Thoughts race by me like thunder clouds rolling in to meet the storm.
Words compile in my mouth.
None of which will ever be spoken in any form.
Bicycles in the street.
Air escaping from the tries.
Mixing in with my breath of discomfort.

Dawn Rogers

Hearts

Home is where the heart is, so it goes.
My home travels with me from California
To Colorado, from husband and friends to
Family and friends.

I always hate to leave and am
Always so anxious to go. For, you
See, my heart is split in two.
Confusion reins over my emotions.

Some parents follow their children
From town to town. Children need
their own space at times and
Parents must respect child space.

Never take for granted a child's love
They need respect and may repay
You with resentment.
Such a complicated game.

Elaine Parker-Courtier

A Quiet Moment

The surf beats at the sand
We sit, we talk, we dance in the moonlight
The tiny sandpipers flit to and fro
Chasing the water in an ongoing back and forth ballet

You tell me your secrets, your inner-most thoughts
I listen, I comfort, I reassure too
I hold you so close and I tenderly say
Nothing matters my dear except the love that we feel

Know that my love for you always will be
Lasting and faithful and always so true

The tide's coming in now it's time to move on
To another small corner of God's beautiful earth
Where we'll talk and we'll dance
And we'll whisper sweet things

We'll walk in the sand to an ongoing song
The song of our love which grows stronger each day
A love that was given by God up above
A love that endures, this is all that I pray

Jacqueline M. Carfi

Fatherless

Yeah, I grew up fatherless.
My mother's hugs warmed my heart, because my father wasn't there to
    hold me.
I watched my mother struggle and learned responsibility.
My father was too busy leading the carefree life.
My uncles gave me my first taste of independence.
My father gave me my first taste of abandonment.
Blessed by God I am creative.
And you better believe when I acted up my mother lit me up.
She had to be the disciplinarian because I grew up fatherless.
Feeling every tear that fell from my mother's eyes
as she cried herself to sleep, made me compassionate.
Over hearing her complain about the wrong that men do,
made me a romantic.
Thanks to the guidance of my grandmother I am considerate,
open minded and dependable.
She had to be my mentor because I grew up fatherless.
And thanks to the love, grace, and mercy of God.
I am at peace with myself.
My son will be all these things and more.
He will become a man with his father by his side.

A. D. Kennedy

A Message

Emptiness, a creation of one's own fear, Scared to
be loved, Scared to be held dear.
Lower the walls that guard the little child, Cast
away all painful thoughts that behind your eyes
run wild.
The past is a closed book with scriptures already
read, The future is a Web of dreams conjured in
your head.
All will come true, With strength and
perseverance, Keep in mind you are cheating
yourself, If standing with independence.
Reach out, Open your gateway, Release the agony
that clutches your spirit, Angels reach out with
arms extended far, But silhouettes
of demons are all you saw.

Sean Stanley

Missing A Close Friend

It's been many years since I've seen your face
Or held your hand as we said grace
Or played on the sewer or on the swing
And pretended to be a queen or a king.

These are fond memories of which I see clear
And hold at my heart so close and so dear
And continue to remember as I grow up fast
I think of these things as I remember the past.

Now we've grown older and moved up in the world
From pigtails and ponytails to hair that is curled
No more playing on playgrounds and fighting with boys
We gave up that stuff along with our toys.

We've talked on the phone about what's going on
From boys we are dating to those that have gone
I miss all the games that we used to play
And fighting and making up all in one day.

We've stayed together for many years
Through laughter and heartbreaks and so many tears
And now that we have grown apart
You and our friendship shall stay in my heart.

Barbara Ann Bynaker

To My Sister, Elisa

We grew up in a happy home, you and I.
Our wonderful parents taught us on Jehovah to rely.
They taught us to get along with one another.
Despite the minor faults of the other.

As sisters, we did almost everything together;
I had hoped that it could last forever.
Life's road still did have its many bends,
Yet, through them all you were my best friend.

I often wondered who you would eventually marry.
I can't tell you how happy I am that it turned out to be Terry.
I couldn't imagine you marrying any other;
I'm so honored to have him as my brother.

And on this, your special day,
I'm happier for you both than words could ever say.
I always knew you'd be the most beautiful bride,
As you and Terry stand side by side.

So as you start your life together,
I wish you both happiness forever.
Thank you for being the best sister anyone could ask for.
No one person could I possibly love more.

Katrina Shuler

A Nurse

A nurse sometimes, is a terrible fool.
Who tries very hard to follow the rule
Of the place where she works eight hours a day.
Literally running her feet off, for not much pay.
But, oh the rewards, when she hears someone say,
"God bless you my dear, when you came in today,
My heart turned to gladness, and just for a while,
I forgot the pain in the joy of your smile."
When this comes from a patient that is wracked with pain
Then, she knows they are happy to see her again.
She forgets her own worries,
And with a song in her heart,
Goes on with a job she has loved from the start.

Mabel Zigan

The Feeling Of A Calalily

Opened up to the world,
I let the sun fill me up,
Starting at the top,
It flows through me
Down my stem and into my roots
The running water beside me
feels cool and refreshing
It brushes by my tips
as it pounds against the soil
But the best enjoyment is
Swaying in the wind
As it breezes by,
It sends a chill down my stem
All my friends and I gently
Wave from side to side,
Letting the wind control all our movements
Careless to which way the wind blows us

Hollie Randall

The Color of Scarlet

I lay asleep and dreamed last night that I was wide awake.
I traveled forward into time across a vast mistake.
I saw a scarlet bird, in flight, against a scarlet sky.
I knew I knew that scarlet bird, that scarlet bird was I.

I few o'er scarlet mountain tops. I saw the scarlet snow.
I soared on scarlet wings of time where scarlet lay below.
I rode the scarlet winds of death above a scarlet sea.
I saw a scarlet cloud adrift. The scarlet cloud was me.

I heard the scarlet screams of death invade a scarlet land.
I watched the scarlet cloud I was, become a scarlet band.
I looked and a saw a scarlet child upon a scarlet bed.
I saw she wore a scarlet shroud. The scarlet child was dead.

I lay awake and pray today that dreams do not come true.
I fall into a scarlet sleep. A scarlet dream review.
I live a hundred-thousand years without a single birth.
I dream I am atomic waste. I kill God's child called earth.

Carl P. Henry

The Beggar

There's a man on the corner, he's a ragged old soul
his years on the street have taken their toll.
He leans on the lamp post and scratches his head
what is he thinking? "Am I better off dead?"
He looks to the crowd with a hand outstretched,
"Go away go away you tired old wretch."
So slowly he turns as they pass by,
the look in his eyes, to see a grown man cry.
A prince now a pauper?
Destiny or design?
A wretch on the corner?
No, a man gone a wry.

Tara McCarthy

Spring Delights

Fragrant air that scintillates the senses
A freshness belonging only to this time of new life and growth
Sounds of nature take on an exciting pitch
as creation emerges from places of winter hibernation.

Severe, brusque winds calmed into mild, gentle breezes
Kaleidoscope of rich colors where-
cold, dark barrenness lay just days before.

To experience the season with all the senses is to birth in our
hearts an energy of spirit and promise.

As we witness the transformations all around us.
we see once again, the Creator's signature on the covenant of life.
And we rejoice in this cycle of rejuvenation for the soul.

Patricia A. Harrow

Problem Child

You know mom and dad,
I really don't get you.
You treat me like I'm nothing
but dirt under your shoe.
I'm the child you're supposed to love,
not something you're ashamed of.

I do my best to be what I
should be in your eyes,
but according to you I fail,
and then you turn into someone
I don't even recognize.

Because of you I feel
like I have no life.
Every time I try to talk to you,
it feels like the third World War or strife.
To you, my ways make me a bad daughter,
So, how can I smile,
When I'm just your problem child?

Angela Vinsh

"It Reminds Me Of You"

While searching through a field of daisies, I look
To find one special one.

There's so many alike, thousands encountering,
Soaking the sun.

I reach out to touch the petals so soft, to
Smell the fragrance of one;
One different, one true... A little daisy that
Reminds me of you.

While taking it home to put it in a vase; I handle
It gentle as though it were your face.

It stands for a meaning so bright and so true, I
Water it often, and I smile, because it reminds me of you.

When the time comes to watch it wilt... I hold my
Head down, but not in guilt.

Thank you God for the time I had...

Now I lay down my daisy for someone else who's sad.
Take good care of it I pray...
It's different, it's true, and it reminds me of you.

Donna Roberson

Friendship

Friendship is a very powerful thing,
That makes your heart want to sing.
Hold on to friendship, for if it goes by,
war will break through, and peace will die.
Friendship is something special from the heart,
not something you get from a shopping cart.
Hold on to friendship, for if it does go,
Then love and happiness, no one shall know.
Friendship is a true dedication of love,
That could've only been created high above.
Hold on to friendship, for if it passes on,
Then we wouldn't be friends, and smiles are gone.
Friendship is well worth keeping around,
as long as you have it, there's no need to frown.
Hold on to friendship, for it is quite grand,
and is well-known all across the land.

Heather Donham

The Rites Of Venus

Moonlit night filled with sunbeam smiles,
Brought together from across the miles.
Starry eyes at one another gaze.
Two young lovers, dancing in delight.

Shot by Cupid's well-aimed arrow,
They reach and feel that eternal flow.
Having no choice, they sweetly embrace.
Two young lovers, dancing in delight.

Soaring higher and ever higher,
They taste of love's eternal fire.
Bond of moonlight, sealed by dawn.
Two young lovers, dancing in delight.

Pamela R. Morr

The Serpent

As I am denied an unfelt emotion by an unseen man,
As I see the people around me moving on while I am still right here,
As I notice the things around me changing while I remain behind,
I feel the cold serpent of Loneliness crawl up my spine.
As its icy claws clutch my heart and slowly still its beatings,
As its arctic tail encircles my throat and slowly blocks its breathing
My mind screams out in pain and terror and slowly realize I am all
    alone.
And I come to the conclusion, that unless someone happens by
    to save me from
myself, that very soon the Serpent will prevail and I ...
    And I will surely die.

David Good

I Am What I Am

I am what I am.
I wonder why the sky is blue.
I hear my parents say "I love you."
I see people.
I want what I want.

I pretend that I am the best Archaeologist
I feel the love of my parents.
I touch the grassy field.
I worry about the seventh grade.
I cry when my Mom and Dad get mad at me.

I am what I am.
I understand that my family loves me.
I say "all men are created equal."
I dream of a nice world.
I try my best,
I hope I got good grades.
I am what I am.

Jacob Potter

Change the World

The earth is tattered, torn, and tired,
Much of it's creatures have expired.
They've gone away, no more to roam,
They've left, for now they have no home.
No more trees for beautiful birds,
No more fields for buffalo herds.
No clean water for fish and fowl,
No more forests for wolves to howl.
Where have all these treasures gone to?
The answer lies within the Blue.
The Blue sky that has been tainted,
And the Blue waters that have been painted
With smoggy gas and toxic waste,
We've done the polluting, we've made no haste
To poison the water and stain the sky,
And now we must change before more creatures die.
Remember recycling and utilize its purpose,
Because now we know it's up to us.
The planet's life shouldn't be rearranged,
So now we must change the world we've changed.

Jason Cline

Homeless Brother

The lives and cries of the homeless seen through my eyes...
They don't lie! They have nothing to Hide! They have no money to
    buy...
They sleep in boxes, or under a bridge.
They'd feed you the last bite out of what they call a fridge!
They'd give you their shirt even though they live in dirt.
The squaller of the maze! Each day is haze!
The days go past and they don't see... for one days the same as the
    other for the homeless brother!
They care and love each other, for them there is no other.
They run for cover from the wind and the rain, some cry in pain!
    To some begging is a main
They try to show they care and extend an arm.
    To those who don't know, they show alarm!
        They mean no harm!
    To the homeless brother, a brother is a brother even if you
        have a house for cover.
So lend a hand... he's only a man!
For love is like no other than that of a
    Homeless brother!

Sandra Porcaro

Grandma's Rose

Today I passed the old home place and something there stood
out beside a house weathered by age and time, a rose bush budding out.
My mind went racing to a wonderful place in time remembering
when the tattered bush was just a tiny vine.
Like every Grandma she was kind and full of grace, with a
heavenly glow of an angel that shown about her face.
Running about her yard one day out of the corner of my eye
was a soft red beautiful rosebush lifting towards the sky.
That day when Grandma took me home we placed a starter in the
ground I could feel the love within her heart showing all
around. "Grandma are you sure this vine will become a tree"?
"From tiny things come great wonders" is what she said to me.
I watched it through the summer I watched it through the fall
and when the harsh winter came I covered it with straw.
Then, one day when springtime came I went outside without a
doubt and there upon my rosebush a single bud was out.
They say the Master gathers flowers for his bouquet and
I believe my Grandma's a rose in his array.

Kathy Bryant

No One To Look At My Face

I lived for him; he was my entire life.
I feel a bitter emptiness from within.

The hurt is overwhelming and the sadness exhausting.
I feel angry; sometimes I feel cheated.
I'm cold inside; my existence is numb.

There is no one to help me now; no one to hold me now.
And there is no one to look at my face.

There is an empty space in my house.
I see his strong hands, I feel his gentle touch.
I hear his hearty laugh, I miss his loving face.

He was my friend and a friend to many.
He put people at ease; he made them laugh.

He was my chauffeur and an errand boy.
He was a business partner and a teacher.
He was a handyman. He could fix anything.

Simple things made him feel best.
We had so many plans. He had dreams for his children.

I will find it difficult to live without him.
He gave me eleven parts to hold on to,
But now, there is no one to look at my face.

Joann K. Roberts

No Answer

What's the cow see when she looks at me?
Would she eat me if she had the chance?
Where would she be if she were free?
What lies within that glance?

Who is this man? What does he want
with me, my friends, my kind?
Why does he heard, and hurt, and hunt?
What lurks within his mind?

Does this cow feel? Is her pain real?
Does she miss her newborn son?
How does she deal with a fate I seal?
No help from anyone.

When will I get to graze again
among the ones I love?
When will I get to gaze again
at the blue sky up above?

Is it possible the papa bull
grieves with a mournful moo?
These lots, so full. These blades, so dull.
My God, what did I do?

Chad Muse

Million Man March

Wake up Black Man. Arise
It's time to claim the prize
Of dignity; of pride
With hands held out - open wide.
Reach out; no clinched fists
No anger, no blame
No head bowed in shame
Stand up. Stand up tall
Answer freedom's call
Go forward; don't look back
No white, no black.
Love yourself, love life
Be kind to your children, loyal to your wife.
The time has come, black man, arise
Join the March and gain the prize.

J. P. Pope

There I Was

Without the bald head, there I was.
Without the belly, there I was.
Without the flat feet, there I was.
Without the fuzz on my chin, there I was.
There I was in the land of honey, milk and cream.
But alas it was all just a lovely dream.

Charles L. Walker

Untitled

You say that your heart is in pieces lying at your feet,
surrounded by created darkness, you cry out to the stranger
being just a mere image left in the distance.
The strangers voice echoes through you; "walk my friend,
for the light is ahead of you, this door must close for you
cannot go on if it lies open."
  You fall to your knees, your chin sinks into your chest;
hopelessly you reply, "but what about my heart?"
The strangers voice grows further but you can almost hear
clearer; "Stand Up my friend, for what lies next to you
is but an image to what your feeling, don't be as blind as a
man who cannot see, for the doors ahead of you are a way in
not out, this is meant, so please, let me close this one as you
have closed many behind you, so I can too grow, and I shall
meet you in the next doorway where you will not only hear me,
but see me."

Cindy R. Evans

Reflections Of Yesterday

As you walk along the beach at night
You see the moon shining on the tide,
A young couple walking hand in hand
Smiling and laughing as they cross the sand.
The moon illuminates them against the tide,
As you recall times, which have slipped away,
leaving you only, reflections of yesterday.
A happy dog with a wagging tail
followed by a man who's old and frail,
chasing the tide the dog runs fast
bringing you memories from the past,
oh, how time has slipped away,
leaving only, reflections of yesterday.
The dog is confronted by a child with a ball
you watch closely as they meet
recalling times that used to be,
you watch the child smile
as they begin to play,
leaving you only, reflections of yesterday...

Tom Saal

An Education

I watched the young readied for school -
High school and college, these kids are no fool.
I wish I could, just one more time -
Walk the campus, stand in line.
Carry books, gossip and go to class -
With computers and shakespeare both hard to pass.
Meet people in my section and lab -
Purchase equipment, supplies, run a tab
Find teachers, students, surroundings all new -
Sit near a boy, have feelings of youth, when love is due.
Borrow a pencil I don't need, pretend to be busy so I read
To dream again of this boy, a picnic a walk, just us two.
School would lend me all of this -
Memories and dreams, feelings of bliss.
If I were a teen just one more time -
I would collect my honors, stand in line.
Be a good student. Make them proud -
No drugs, no babies, no sleeping around
To be perfect as I vowed.

Ruby Stewart

The Soft Boiled Egg

A Love Story
Each day I rise on the dot of six that little egg to fix
Some morning jumbo, large or extra large
Always an egg — I hate eggs.
They always have a shell that grates my teeth.
He loves eggs, "just right" and so
Each day I rise on the dot of six that little egg to fix.
With the coffee hot, the toast all crunchy
I call up to my honey bunchy — it's ready!
I hate eggs. When dropped they splatter
With such abandon and slither 'cross the floor
And through the slots of spatulas and so
Each day I rise on the dot of six that little egg to fix.
Forget the shells that grate and slime that slithers.
He loves eggs "just right" and so
I am learning to love them, too.

Marie B. Forget

Untitled

And I said, if you see my hand shaking,
    well then, the story's over.
But, if you see my hand steady,
    then the story has just begun.
And he said, what in the hell does that mean?
And I said, I don't know,
    I just like how it sounds.
And he said, you're insane.
And so I smiled

Jill Schneider

America

America with its music, its laughter, its fun,
America with its people, and work to be done,
America with its riches and future so grand,
In all the wide world, this is the land.

America and free men are synonymous signs.
America has bled for these signs in past times.
America is young but has shown the world
Democracy will fight to keep its flag unfurled.

America has freedoms as basic as breath.
Freedom of worship, and from threat of death,
Freedom from want and freedom of speech.
Where else can we find these; you I beseech?

America with its wounded and its sadness of war,
America with its heartache and memory sore,
America with its tragedy and political strife
Still stands supreme as the way of Life.

Who is America? Why of course you and me.
So let us go to our tasks and try to see
That of all the earth that is under the sun,
Thank God for America, there is only one.

Gilbert Hoffmeister

Confused

Lost confused and dazed
It's like trying to find my way around a
great maze
It's not knowing when to say I love you
or when to say I'm seared
It's so lonely and scary in that great big out there
being lost is bad but being alone is worse
because then your heart is as
sad upset and frustrated
as you are confused because
you can't find your way out
and know one can come in!

Aubrey Hulse

Untitled

One more pretty face turned away,
One more fragile heart ripped apart.
Is this all I am to you?
All I ever was?
Tonight as I sit and think of what you meant to me,
I realize how little I meant to you.
Did you ever love me as you said you did?
Or was that a game too?
I would do anything to make you love me again,
But I can only wait so long, I'll not wait forever.
It's not fair,
when time's all I have left.
I love you as much as I always have,
Why pick me to torture and slowly kill?
All I ever did was love you,
Now all our dreams are finished.

Sara Piepkow

Dreams

Dreams are made from the calling of the nightingale,
   the gentle bird that sets any wandering soul to rest.
My soul yearns for its peaceful song;
   it can bring peace; it can bring happiness;
   it can bring inspiration; it can bring curiosity;
My heart and soul cry out for the broken dreamers.

Dreams are like a gentle flowing stream.
They bring serenity to a raging man;
   they stir up anger and jealousy that is none but beneficial;
   they bring a woman hope and joy and love.
They bring the impossible to reality.

Dreams are dying every day.
Without a vessel dreams wither like ashes.
We must keep dreams alive in all of us;
   let them guide us through our dark journey called life.
Never forget your dreams, for without a dream all is lost.

Paul Johnson

Fifty

Just as a messenger
who runs full-speed ahead to deliver urgent information,
breathes a sigh of relief and satisfaction
upon reaching the destination,
the long-awaited birthday is here.

All those born in 1946 join me,
the first of the baby boomers,
flower children of the 60's,
hopeful, anxious, restless,
resisting adulthood, looking younger than we are.

Now
This is what 50 looks like
This is what 50 feels like
full of energy like surging water cresting a waterfall,
a sense of wisdom growing out of the turmoil,
dynamic as we lead the next generation,
constantly looking ahead with excited anticipation.

Still wanting to do our own thing
Still wanting this to be a better planet
Still hoping that we can make a difference.

Rosemary Henderson

Mortality

He sits there listening
I watch from the corner
Not facing him directly
I'm forced to face his mortality
When I cannot face my own
A gaunt figure in the room
As opposed to my own flesh
Which is over filled
Why is this happening to him
I watch his decline over months
Yet he lives like there is no tomorrow
For him there may not be
My friend is dying before my eyes
Unknowingly teaching me to live in his decline
I've yet to listen
Did he know this would happen
Or was he living life in blissful ignorance
Not heeding the price he might pay

Wade Johnson

Betrayed

Not a golden band, but a cheap metal ring,
Rusted by my tears,
And ruined by the touch of tempting felines
In heat and reared wild like papillons in the wind.

Maybe domestic bores men. Spooked by soapy water
That cleans and brings fresh living,
Like flowers amongst debris.
They hide and play with what's black, tight, dirty, and cheap.

Gluttons of the fruits and juices,
That give sweetness to the skin,
That too ferments into a curse of constant thirst,
And loneliness.

Perhaps I am the one to blame
For loving blindly — forgiving over and over again.
For thinking he thought of me
And put me on a pedestal, like I did him.

Despite the tears, the pain, the patience I shed for him,
Like autumn leaves desperately waiting for spring,
He never felt my love.
Instead he hid into the night and betrayed me once again.

Joanne Martin

"I Do Not Understand"

I do not understand
Why there are so many homeless people
Why people have to live in fear of their life
Why there is world hunger and no one helps.

But most of all
I do not understand
Why there is war between countries
And they seem to want to fight with each other
Instead of compromising
Fighting doesn't help any
But instead, it just takes innocent lives.

What I understand most is peace.
No one tries to hurt or kill others
And people get along with everyone else
There are no enemies
Just friends.

Ginger Anderson

The Legacy of Hope

Hope is a living thing, seeking solace for all that's lost,
and wending its way, though tempest tossed.
It spreads its wings to challenge ruthless foes -
death, anguish, and despair, pain and unyielding sorrows.
Hope laughs at misery and scorns melancholy.
It bids us to disregard all our former folly,
and despite incredible odds, it sends us to reclaim our prize,
the dream others believed we could not begin to realize.
Hope dares us to vanquish tyranny and holocausts with the weapons of
our mind, and undaunted, we commence anew, a finer world to find.

Yvonne Schmidtman

Life's Twists and Turns

Sometimes life is like a roller coaster ride;
Or a package wrapped in colorful paper,
With a surprise inside;

With a thrill, it goes to the very top of the track;
And without warning,
It comes swiftly, twisting, and turning back.

You are so happy you can hardly stand the ride;
Then suddenly there is a sadness,
That you just can not hide.

Why can't life be simple like the track,
And always take the straight,
And narrow way back?

Bridget Cloud

The Sky

As you look in the sky you can see the moon smiling at you.
The sky brightly colored blue. Cold air falling on
you as the sun sets. The sky slightly turning pink and
purple. You can see the trees reaching to the sky, and
hear the birds whistling. There sits a little helpless
bird flapping its wings frantically. You don't think
the newborn robin will make it. All of a sudden he soars
up into the sky. You know for sure you heard it say
"thank you."

You go inside but can't wait to see what nature has
to tell tomorrow!

Artesia Moon

Will O' The Wisp

What's left behind cannot be gathered
although the moon and stars play tricks
I have seen but could not hold
the will o' the wisp

I've seen a goddess clothed in light
my true desire was to be with her there
to possess her till dawn comes stealing
the stars from morning air

What I sought was pristine beauty
that first eternal kiss
but few and far are the bogs and woodlands
that hold
the will o' the wisp

Charles D. Harvey

Declaring My Love For You

You are my sun, when my days are filled with dark gray clouds,
You give me strength and hope when my heart aches with doubts.

You are my energy, lifting my spirits beyond the sky, you give me the
hope to become the person I desire, never to give up and just die.

You are my rainbow, dispursing the brilliant array of colors,
You give me the passion I need and as one we are destined lovers.

You are my life, breathing your love and humor into my lungs,
You give me the courage to never give up, and my heart praises you
as the song of life has been sung.

You stand by my side in the shadows,
Allowing me to reach my goals, my hopes, and my dreams,
running wildly against the winds through the stormy meadows.

You have supported my childish dreams of success, allowing me to
become a lover of fantasy, through you, I release my tight rein on
life and become a woman full of ecstasy.

Perilous adventures and pleasant thoughts stir my blood,
But, as always, it is You, who collides with my world
with a passion as strong and fierce as a flood.

My dreams accepts the woman I long to be, while reality scorns the
woman I am, and in the end, you love me, for not what I want to be,
  but because you love me.

Rilla M. Edwards

Desire

I desire a woman.
A woman who with every touch of her breath my life is new.
A woman who captures my imagination.
A woman that possesses every beauty that nature has to offer.
A woman that is sexy, but not out of reach.
A woman who is real in every sense.
A woman who knows how to be a friend, and a lover.
A woman who knows when to touch you.
A woman who knows how to touch you with her eyes, her smile.
I desire a woman.
A woman with skin as soft as silk.
A woman that I can lie down with and forget about the world.
A woman who lets me escape me.
A woman who lets me realize who I am, not what I am not.
A woman whose smile lights up the midnight sky.
A woman I can play with wherever we are.
A woman I can be intimate with at any moment.
A woman that does the word love justice.
I don't desire this woman.
She is in my arms right now.

Brian Sapp

Starting Over Again

She sits by the sea shore. Listening to the sound of waves.
Wondering what went wrong with her life she had?
Once she was young and beautiful and full of dreams.
Now she's in her forties and all her dreams had shattered.

She sits by the sea shore. Listening to the sound of waves.
Wondering will she love again? Her body is ready;
Her heart is broken. Not healed as of yet. She knows it's
not time yet, not yet!

She sits by the sea shore. Listening to the sound of waves.
Wondering what to do next? She knows she has to let go
of the past. She knows it's not easy to let go, its never easy!

She sits by the seashore. Listening to the sound of waves.
Nothing but peace around her. She wonders what will
become of her? She knows she must be strong.
To carry on, to live a new life!

Maria Haslam

A Message To My Dad

Dad I know we almost touched;
but in your dreams we played so much.

You held and kissed me through the night;
it was no dream, it felt so right.

I knew your thoughts throughout the day;
so don't be angry this I pray.

Our hearts and minds have always been united;
just ask "Mom", she was so delighted.

So please be strong, and don't you cry;
I can only tell you, God knows why!

So give Mom a kiss and hold her tight;
I'll always be there day and night;

Dad please understand, I felt no pain;
when darkness passed;
the light then came.

   I love you Dad
    Your son,
     Andrew
   Bernard Skiles

Untitled

The breeze whispers through my screen
telling tales it's heard or seen.
Still everything lays
hidden in haze until the days very first rays
cut through the dark.

The glittering star cover
continues to hover, and I desire to be
soaring over the sea of summer's new yield
in each dewy field.

I'll dance over the wheat, all nice and neat.
Delicately tiptoe,
along each fence row, and swim through the trees
with incredible ease.

The breeze so sweet would tickle my feet.
I could travel afar and kiss the stars.
With the moon be friends, even though he tends
to be a little on the quiet side.

Now I float back to bed, sweet visions in my head,
and surrender to sleep with memories to keep.

In the hazy nights of June I live not yet but soon.
   Catherine Clouse

Do You Know Your Worth

Have any one of you
found your place
in this universe...

Can you face each day
With the joy of life
The excitement of living...

Do you stand tall
And gaze at the clouds
Knowing each one is yours...
  by declaration of the king.

Are you aware that you have a
ninety-nine year lease on the stars...
And the pink slip to every wave on the ocean...

You can homestead the milky way...
And farm the forests of your mind.
Look closely now, there's gold in your memories...
And certainly there's silver in your dreams.

   Barbara Santino

Two Peaches

There were two peaches on a tree,
one was you and one was me.
We ripened there so round and fair,
we glistened in the morning air.
We dangled, bouncing in the wind,
we grew so close, God called us friends.

Time and seasons came around.
Not being picked, we hit the ground.
We fell and lightly hit the earth,
the seed inside cried for rebirth.
Upon the earth, our beings fair,
were fading into earth and air.

Birds soaring by, they saw us there,
the fruit was gone, the seeds were bare.
They plucked us up and carried high
the waiting life we had inside.
Oh, bury us close that we might grow
once again a friend to know.

No longer peaches then we'll be,
We'll bear much fruit, we'll be the trees.
   Janita Black

The New Season

Without a rhyme or reason
We learn of a new season
Sprinkled from the wings of a dove
Settled by the eyes of love
It's not winter, spring, summer, nor fall
It's a season that tops them all
The name of this season everyone knows
But somehow it bothers me so
I know it should be candy sweet
And oh so hard to beat
But it's unfair to name
The season played as a game
It's the vows you make
The icing on the cake
Nobody can take this away
For this is a game he or she does play
It is a easy simple deed
Something you and I both need
Tell this to your nephew and niece
This new season is Peace
   Stephanie Chapple

What Could I Do?

They always fight,
I lay in my room pretending I don't hear,
Everything will be better tomorrow...

He wants a divorce but she wants to work it out,
I know the truth,
She knows there is another woman too,
Please don't cry mom...

He leaves one night with his clothes,
She can't eat and always cries,
I just hug her and say it is alright...

The divorce is final,
He lives in motels and she tries to move on,
He comes to see me once a week,
I don't think he loves me anymore,
I am sorry dad...

I try to be strong for her,
I wonder if he cares,
Does he cry too...

Life goes on,
What could I do?
   Erin Otto

Moon Beams

As I watch the moon play its beams on the water,
Your face comes to mind and that's all that matters.
The wind blows on so strong and cold,
Which makes me feel all the more lonely and old.
A question comes to mind,
How can you be so blind?
Our love was so strong,
How could it be so wrong?
You look at me with eyes full of hate and grief,
From where I don't know it was conceived.
But I look at the moon play on the water,
And realize my heart, soul, and beliefs are shattered.

Brandy Donatiello

Pride

I see you up there without a clue,
I wish they had not chosen you.
You stand there looking lost and confused,
I know today you're just being used.
A stand-in for the one who's gone.
Everything you do is wrong.
They sit and laugh at the things you say,
And you just wish you could run away.
I sit and watch the things you do,
My heart is reaching out for you.
I start to stand, then sit again,
I wouldn't know where I should begin.
No, that's not the reason I know inside,
I won't get up because of pride.

Stephanie Zufelt

Grandma

Someone to turn to, to run to, to talk to.
Always a caring friend, always there until the end.
Forever a shoulder to cry on, Forever my best friend.
Never putting me down, Never embarrassing me.
Caring of all my thoughts, Caring of all my faults.
Till the fish forget to swim,
Till the swan forgets to look pretty
Till all the stars fall from the sky,
Till the day the world dies,
You will always be my grandma.
You shall live a full life,
And you'll always be my papa's wife.
And I love you with all my heart!!!!!!

Kimberley Gentry

Untitled

We met in an odd sort of way;
We talked to each other almost everyday;
Something happened between me and you,
Oh...I only wish you felt it too.
There isn't a day that goes by;
That I don't even think to sigh;
oh, we live so far away;
I wish we could be together
someday.
You are so kind to me;
If only you could see;
How much I really love you;
And it really wish you felt that way
too.

Daniella Houston

Freedom

Why haven't I found the right one,
with whom I can go out and have even,
with whom I can kiss and talk and be me,
with whom I can spread my wings and be free.

You think you're that one with whom I can be,
with whom I can talk and kiss and be tree,
But with you I just can't seem to fly,
up in the sky blue and high.

Sometimes I ask myself why I'm still living,
Why I'm still loving and caring and giving,
But I'm stuck in this hole so deep in the ground,
And I'll still be stuck here when eternity sounds.

I have to spread my wings and fly,
Up in the sky so blue and high.

When drifting to sleep I think of this place,
And realize I'm only one of our race,
They won't miss me when I die,
when I spread my wings and begin to fly.

Brook Bolander

The Redwoods

Infinity,
    The trees reaching out
    Touching and becoming a part of us,
    Continuing upward forever,
    Sharing themselves with Earth and Heaven.

Giants,
    Stronger than the Earth they grow out of,
    Forever reminding us of our fragility,
    Also reminding us of our strength
    And telling us to draw from it.

Beauty,
    That we can see and feel
    Like rain on a sunshiny morning,
    Dew on a flower petal, or a smile on a child's face.

God,
    Creating and loving the trees
    Almost as much as we do.
    Showing us a piece of eternity in the trees,
    Showing us part of His strength,
    Strength, which like the Redwood trees, will go on forever.

Sharon M. Fore

And A Big Man Falls

Now I know what makes a big man small
strutting around so proud and tall
with minds that are so very small
smaller than the puddles in the street
all the while stepping on the little man's feet

Now I'm a little man and it hurts when the blows come raining down
but once my momma told me that what goes around comes around
so here I sit waiting for that day to come
when I am respected and known as someone

And the big man will fall
won't stand quite so tall
he'll feel like he died inside
when someone hurts his pride
by stepping on his feet

All these years I've tried to do my best
tried to keep up with the rest
but no matter what I do
as far as you're concerned I'll never be an equal to you
so strut around so proud and tall
for one day the big man will fall

Jalmar C. Bell

Dispense With Love

Dispense with love,
With fear and frustration,
With acts heroic and ridiculous.

Dispense with love,
Forego tears and disappointment
And agitation of hands,
Forego pain and anguish, sacrifice and gains.

Dispense with love
In bedroom, in foxhole,
In whorehouse, in gay bar,
In tunnel, in village,
In dead-end streets and on the beach -
In all the clandestine places we go to meet.

What did I know of the ravages of love, What did I know?

Dispense with love! Dispense with love!
Dispense with love!

Charles R. Croghan Jr.

Hope

The time is 1933
When Jew's, as I had, to flee.
Wearing stars for identification,
Hitler's powers ran throughout the nation.

Hitler's philosophy was genocide,
A Jew cried, a Jew died.
When times got tough and we had to hide,
Certain Germans were on our side.

If Jew's were captured we began the road to Hell.
Concentration Camps began to swell
Torturous souls was our fate,
Adolf Hitler we did hate.

Hope was here but hope has gone,
Day by day the hours linger on.
Lives are tortured everyday,
The only hope that's left is to pray.

My life is back to normal once again,
Except for the memories I have of way back when.
Times got tough but we made it through,
Without hope we wouldn't have known what to do.

Laci Jones

The Breeze Flows Aimlessly On

When the day begins to fade,
  and mist dost fill the air -
When shadows creep onto the earth,
  and the sky dost turn an eerie black,
When whispered words and silent thoughts
  wander aimlessly on the breeze.

When I hear the voice echo in the night,
  and it takes me back to happy days-
When we were brave and free
  and we had not yet tasted loneliness,
When our thoughts were one,
  and our goals followed one path.

When our friendship was unblemished,
  before we found our tragic flaw -
When the clouds slowly move,
  and I see again the moon,
When in the moon new hope is found,
  and the breeze flows aimlessly on.

Christine Empey

The Last Mile

Life is full of learning
Throughout our years of trials
Sometimes it may be bitter
But oh how sweet to see your smiles

Your eyes can say I love you
Your actions tell a tot
I've always known you're very special
Even when you were a little lot

In the years of growing
I see you've come very far
Although I, within myself knowing
You are one of God's brightest stars

You have known some sorrow
You have had your share of tears
But let us always look for tomorrow
And believe God will take away your fears.

Sometimes life is a hard teacher
But don't ever lose your smile
for I am a firm believer
you will travel the last mile.

Jackie Jeffrey

The Journey

Knowing when you see the sunset
there will be a sunrise.
That's faith.

Knowing that when you sit on a chair
it will hold you up.
That's faith.

Knowing when you see a rainbow
it has rained somewhere.
That's faith.

Feeling a soft breeze
and calling it wind.
That's faith.

Feeling warmth in your heart
and calling it love.
That's faith.

Feeling certain and not knowing why
that the bad news is ok.
That's faith.

Life's a fantastic adventure, a journey
full of faith.

Melody Kaufman

In Darkness

In darkness
You are alone
You feel a chill
A coldness
Space expands endlessly in all directions
The air is clean
Alien
Objects move
Voice are heard
From your past
And your daydreams.

Angela Jones

The Dedication of a Mother

My mom has been there for me since birth.
The very reason why I exist on Earth.
My mother is responsible for my first breath,
with the price of her almost certain death.

She is a person always full of love,
because I'm the child she takes care of.
My mom expresses her tender care,
especially since she has always been there.

She's kind, nice, funny and dependable,
that is a parent who is indispensable.
In time of need, she is always reliable. I think of her as a role
   model.
My mom is a friend who works to get ahead.
She keeps food on my plate and a roof over my head.

Mothers are people who can't be replaced.
Because without them there would be no human race.
I owe my mom a lot of respect, even though, that is what they
   should expect.
My mom supports me with attention and praise,
without her, life would be nothing more than a phase.
This poem is not just another piece of art,
because it comes straight from the heart.

   David Francis Crow

Epitaph

To the human race,
So innocent in its youth;
Always striving to understand the unknown;
Never really controlling the power
Of the things that they learned.
So full of pride,
Thinking they could handle anything,
Yet so insecure;
Grasping at easy explanations
And superstitions.
They really didn't think
That their own creations
Would be their destruction.

   Roger Alan Range

Give Me Her Pain!

My second-born, another girl, blue eyes and hair of gold
What has life in store for her as I see her world unfold
Tonsils out and broken bones, the usual childhood ills
I never thought this child of mine would soon be popping pills

I shared her music and her songs, and watched her dance on toes
How could my little girl be plagued with oh so many woes
Pain in knees and in her head, surgeries that weren't the fix
How does she handle all this weight, it's like a ton of bricks

She laughs, she cries, she's up, she's down, what is this seasaw life?
Why is a child of innocence born under such a strife?
Why doesn't her pain diminish or just get up and leave?
What a terrible nightmare our complex bodies can weave

I would give up my life gladly if it would make her well
Will my angel ever be freed from her personal hell
I stand in the shadows and watch her trying to stay sane
Oh Lord, I beseech you, make her whole and give me her pain!

   Felicity Huff

Love Scale

Give me the thrill of your hand on mine
And the look that brings us close.
Let me respond to your soothing voice
And your silence that tells me the most.
Offer your love for me to take
And the freedom that opens up.
Replenish the hope that seems to dissolve
When life runs over its cup.
Inspire me by your every move
And the little and big surprises
Announce your love again and again
With the message in many sizes.
Joust with me as you've learned to do
And convince me it's my idea.
Enter into our fantasy world
Where it's painless and life is clear.
And after you've done all of these things
Place them on the scale of love
Now place my love on the other end
And watch yours rise above.

   Ronn Munro

Silence On the Battlefield

Shattered in a hollow of darkness, were two human souls.
Suddenly words became scarce,
Afflicting deep wounds on every molecule
That once made a chemistry, so perfect as this.
Interludes of quivered and broken voices, of two loved ones
Punctuated the continuous melody of the air.
'Twas a battle of soul verses flesh!
If this is what lover's combat,
Then love truly is a harsh and bloody battle field.
Life sent forth a cruel and brutal blow
That wrenched friendship apart.
Unfair to those who cherish and delight.
In dignity of the flesh and human character.
What makes men to pride and relish in Satin and velvet flesh,
And forget the virtues of the soul?
A heart mutilated and torn
A mind entangled and revolting against the tyranny of the flesh.
The knight in shinning armour stood still and gazed.
In a sad and melancholic voice she began to sing
And in her soliloquy felt a loveless, damned abortive thing!

   Cheryl Uhde

My "Babies"

I planted their seeds and watched them grow
Keeping them out of harm's way and from being mowed.

Their colors are so bright and amazing
From afar, I can see the neighborhood kids gazing
As they truly enjoy what I see
I have to say I am proud of my "Babies"

I go to my window more than 10 times a day
To see my flowers sway in the wind
As I watch and watch, they seem to
Say, come on and let's play.

Soon after their colors fade and their blooms fall.
Ever so softly I hear their call
We'll be back next year to play some more.

   Ingrid M. Chambers

388

A Father's Hope

I will never understand why the Lord took our baby away.
In all of our lives, it was one of our darkest days.
When so many people throw their babies away
and so many people keep their children at bay.
The Lord took our baby away.
But somehow I know our daughter is happy and free
and sitting on my grandmother's knee.
God must have needed her, to take her so soon
because if she could have stayed, we would have given her the moon.
One day we will see her in Heaven, and she will say,
"Please don't feel so sad.
I know you would have loved me, and I you, Mom and Dad".

John M. Sandberg

Laycie

She loves without measure,
  Her love will never end.
No matter what they do to her
  She'll always be their friend.

She may not be included
  In all the games they play;
As she watches from the sidelines,
  She loves them anyway.

Her love is like my Lord's,
  So innocent, so true.
Even when you have forgotten them
  They have not forgotten you.

When her loved ones have all left her
  This is when she cries.
When her presence has escaped their minds
  Her little heart just dies.

In her I see more clearly
  What my Saviour does go through
'Cause if you turn your back on Him
  His heart will cry out, too.

Angel Peters

The Red Tricycle

My father kept a snapshot of me
in his wallet. Faded, wrinkled,
worn with the wearing,
it kept me forever his child.

Face framed by a white angora hat,
I sit astride my red, balloon-tired tricycle,
ready to ride around the world,
follow a bus route, or drive down
to my grandparents' farm.
Feet perched on the pedals,
hands grasping the bars,
I smile in eager expectation of life on the road.

Far back beyond the sidewalk,
standing by the porch,
my mother watches me
undertake the journeys of childhood.
She gave the picture to me when my father died.

I, a white-haired woman,
recall its safekeeping
and treasure it still.

Reinette Seaman

Paradise

As I walked along the fields today,
  The clover smelled like new cut hay.

Was that a Cuckoo I heard sing?
  Far away he has his fling.
He swiftly flies from the west
  To push little birds out of their nests.

The meadows are adorned with flowers,
  Pollinating bees by the hours.

Wild roses trail along a hedge,
  A snake slithers downs the ledge.

Heat comes up from the ground
  No breeze stirs upon its mound.
I take a path that leads to home
  And leave this paradise alone.

Hazel Hallmark

Seattle Washington - Albuquerque New Mexico

Good by to Seattle,
My last farewell to you.

You have been my loving home,
For many a day or two.

I leave with lots of memories,
Many good and some are sad,

But I will always remember,
All the good life I have had.

It's time for moving forward,
To the next stage in my life,

And with no regrets or sorrow,
I look forward to my plight.

Welcome to New Mexico,
The land of sand and scent.

Where one can see for miles and miles,
Which was the Lord's intent.

Our skies are clear, the breeze is brisk,
and there's no lack of sun.

So open your heart to an enchanted place,
For having lots of fun.

Milford Richey

Living On the Streets

As the snow flows on a winter's day.
As the light of the moon shines away.
As I looked up at the stars wondering
will I make it today,
will I survive this awful stage of hell.
Living on the streets I hunger with
fright, starving is the worst thing in life.
But I must live, and to live is to
survive the awful streets I must fight.
This is my way of life for me it's different each day.
I do different things to stay alive.
I've learned a lot about people and the way they are.
The way they treat you like you don't exist.
But you must beg and plead for food or money.
To get this way is self destruction to your own self.
To be a bum is the worst, to have
nothing is the hardest, to be something is special.
For I am something and I am special.
Understanding me would be nice for
someone to take the time to notice that I am human.

Elizabeth Walker

Utopia

We live in a world with no peace,
No harmony.
And love is only a distant dream,
A memory.
Religion or race, color or face.
It's all the same when we close our eyes.
No hatred when we realize.

Danielle Erkoboni

Can't Do You Harm, Just Keep Your Eyes On Me

I once had a dream that I can't forget of a massive snake That Was.
It had the biggest head I'd ever seen and a body many times as
large.

The black beady eyes and split tongue to match hissed each time
I moved. I stood there so afraid to breathe I thought it'd see my
chest move. I heard a voice from overhead say "grab the snake don't
be afraid," just keep your eyes on me.

Don't be afraid did I hear the voice say? For, I was too afraid to
move.

Then the voice became flesh and grabbed the snake That Was
he pushed it's head to the earth it ate dirt from the ground.

Then the flesh said take a hold this snake can't do you harm.
I grabbed a hold, held on tight it ate dirt from the ground.

I turned to the voice that became flesh to show my great delight but
in a twinkle it was gone had taken another flight.
Afraid again, I let it go. I thought my pillar was gone.

Then I heard the voice say:
"Grab the snake don't be afraid, This Snake Can't Do You Harm."

John W. Stephens

The Glorious Sun

Through the clouds on that rainy day
I saw the hope of a distant ray
A piece of the sun and great beauty untold
A purpose so renown, and a greatness it would always hold
And though the rain was streaming down
I could still see the sun's victorious crown
For in a few minutes that passed away
The sun was back and there to stay
And it lit up my house with a remarkable light
But soon it mellowed out and along came the night
Up sprang the stars with their silvery glow
And too came the moon, it's greatness to show
But I was so tired I fell right asleep
And inside my dreams the light I tried vainly to keep
And I awoke with a feeling that my soul would ignite
I awoke looking at the sun, and it's glorious light

Robert Lane

Words Not Spoken Yet

Well babe, you saw me weak,
Fear in my soul, tears on my cheek,
This key I give to you to hold,
It unlocks my heart once sold,
Your touch I long for each day,
And without hesitance I wait to say,
"I love You", but cannot muster the nerve,
To utter these the most all powerful of words,
How would you react, what would you say,
If I kissed you and spoke this way,
Would you laugh, would you start to cry,
Or would you just sort of wonder, "why?"
In my dreams you bow and smile,
Then raise your head innocent as child,
"I love You too", you whisper soft and intent,
It's only then I feel what you meant.

David K. Good

About You

What am I thinking about
I'm thinking about your voice
how it turns me on each time I hear you speak
what am I thinking about
I'm thinking about what you look like
wanting to see your body to touch every inch
what am I thinking about
I'm thinking about your lips
wanting to kiss them feel them upon mine
what am I thinking about
I'm thinking about you
what we will do if we ever get together
what am I thinking about
I'm thinking about making love to you
pleasing your every desire then holding all night
what am I thinking about
I'm thinking about you
thinking about you
About you

Naomi Woods

From Storm to Calm

From my window I gaze out on the landscape...
  vibrant, rain-sated, a brilliant green...
The sky deeply blue, filled with giant fluffs
  of cotton-soft clouds.
White now, they look too heavy and unreal
  to be floating
In air smelling so pungent, sweet and fresh
  (as I pull it eagerly into my lungs)
From the recent red-yellow-green rainbow arc
  of cascading water and sunlight
That I marvel and wonder at Nature's ability
  to change in just a few short moments
From stormy harshness to such soul-satisfying
  beauty and welcome calm.

Betty L. Weaver

My Love

  You're a memory that could never fade away,
You're that voice inside my head day by day.
  You're the twinkle in the stars,
You're in my dreams but so very far.
  You'd always say we'd never part,
You always said that from the start.
  You'd surprise me in so many ways,
You'd say some things you needed not to say.
  You'd take my hand when I was feeling weak,
You'd give me love I was meaning to seek.
  You were by my side through good and bad,
You were my smile when I was sad,
  When I wished for things that soon came true,
It was all because the good in you.

Charlene Elizabeth Bryant

A Touch of Memories

I walk the path of memories
that now rest in the recesses of time
yet alone in the mind and heart.

I reach out to touch the face of those
I loved but they no longer abide with me.

The seasons have touched me
and I respond to their call
Birds have left their nest to venture on

I arise to each day with faith and
expectation to what Planet Earth
has contrived for me.

Joseph F. Savoni

Ode to Dear Mom

This is a paean to a mother who is dear;
This is a poem that should make her cheer;
It is about a mother so merry;
Who is bright and pretty as a "peri".
Children often take mothers for granted;
But moms can never be supplanted.
A hug or a kiss or a smile is what counts;
That is enough to make a mother bounce;
She is not in need of gift or presents;
All she wants is the child's presence.
Memories are what we truly cherish;
The love and feelings should never perish.
On this Mother's Day so special and cheery;
A mother mustn't have to cook and weary;
She should be taken out to dine;
And why not-she can even have a little wine.
So on this day, so happy and gay,
Please, please lead us the way!
A thousand times I pray and say,
"Oh, dear Mom, Happy Mother's Day!"

Ajay Malaviya

The Three Month Plan

Another "fat" summer, and she was depressed,
just couldn't go out, have fun or get dressed.
She vowed that she'd start to exercise daily,
and cut down on doughnuts, bagels and bialy's.
"By New Year's," she cried, "I could look so appealing,
I'll wear skin tight jeans, and tops so revealing ..."
She dug out her tapes, Richard Simmons and Little,
and diligently worked on her big butt and middle.
Three days later she stepped on her digital scale,
1/2 of a pound gone, "That's great! I won't fail!"
Then Halloween came, Trick or Treaters were few,
Leftover candy, now what could she do?
The days were just flying, Thanksgiving came soon
and seconds of stuffing made its way to her spoon.
"Oh, what can I do now? Christmas is near,
but I still have a month ..." (The beginning of fear).
'Twas the night before Christmas, and reality hit,
She went through her closet, and "Shit!" nothing fit.
"Well I guess it's too late to lose 50 pounds,
I'll hide from the camera, and ignore people's frowns."
New Years was next, with its laughter and glitter,
and she found herself being her skinny friend's sitter.
"Aha," she declared, a New Resolution,
"I've three months 'til Spring, I must find a solution."
And out came the tapes, and Slim Fast's new flavor,
A new self-help book was a real life saver.
Then Valentine's candy (partaken alone)
Then chocolate bunnies, a sigh and a moan.
"Now why did I do this? Summer's coming too soon,
I see by my calendar, next month is June."
"Well by August," she said, "when I take my vacation,
I'll lose so much weight, I will be a sensation!"
Another "fat" summer, and she was depressed ....

M. Barone

The Sun's Gift

Only darkness can hide
The ghost following close behind.
He is secure in sunlight's groove,
Enabling him to trap my every move.
He shares my happiness, my fear;
A firm affection he stands, not a tear.
Sunset arrives as he fades away,
His reoccurring death announces the end of the day.

Allison Busch

The Planet of Love

MANY LIVES, MANY MASTERS
Each one equals less disasters.
The sun, the moon and stars above
Create the blue print for the planet of love.

The life you were born to live
Is the eternal process of learning to give.
Magic, numbers, birthdays and signs,
Each life you created hence the beginning of time.

GOING WITHIN you will see,
The master inside of you and me.
Intuition guides of if we'd just LET IT BE.
Discern your ILLUSIONS, ENGAGE IN THE FLOW and freedom's a
guarantee.

Buddha, Jesus and St. Germain
Different cultures and dates, their message is the same.
Freud and Cayce say that life is but a dream...
Ironically enough people still think God is mean.

Acupuncture and pyramids date back to so long ago,
THE WAY OF THE PEACEFUL WARRIOR is apparently the way to go.
So don't be weak and let your ego put on the show.
Have no fear and every year you'll SAY YES TO LIFE instead of no.

Dayna Colell

To My Dear Daughter Libby Claire

Where did I come from?
I came from a City founded by Gedyminus
Associated with its land, fauna and flora
Above all dear to my heart is a small station
That in Lithuanian language "Jashunai" is called

There before my eyes, the first time the world appeared
There I felt warmth of mothers and fathers arms
There beloved sisters little brother hugged and kissed
There in starlight nights thoughts flew the milky way

Not yet is the end of my modest tirade
Sense began with a tale now by verse extolled
Where did I come from and how stormy seas brought me to this shore
My thoughts of-ten flow to baby clime

And though I live on the other half of the globe
Far in distance spread by oceanic shores
I cherish deep in my soul that remote call of my fancy
The land of early dreams the cradle of my youth.

Ira Senzon

Sand Burial

He is sixty five. Gray. Vigorous.
He wears a suit. Three piece. Gray like his hair.
His two bronze skinned grandchildren flock about him.
He is lying on his back, smiling. They are shoveling sand on him,
Burying him in his suit. The surf is sneaking towards them
As they pat the soft sand so hard he can't budge.
The boys are all giggles.

"Grampa is buried," they sing.
They are dancing. Waves are forming, waves with frothy foam.
He is covered with white sand. All but his head.
His skin is pale. He is no longer smiling.

"Grampa is buried," they say,
They stop dancing and press
Their mouths near his lips. Buried. In his best suit.
The sun is setting. Fiery orange and red.

"Grampa is buried." They cry.
"It will not be the last time," he whispers.
Waves crash on the shore.
The foam tries to swallow them.

Christopher W. Coffee

Sometimes

Sometimes
I dream —
and when I dream, it is of lovely
places. Places where there is peace;
air so clean, it is pure. A breeze so
soft, it is like silk on your face.

The places I go in my dreams —
are beautiful and pure. There are no
worries, there is only peace and serenity —

My paradise is without flow —
It has no beginning, and I'm certain
there is no end.

When I go to these places
in my slumber, it pleases me; for
I know that when I arrive in my
paradise I'll meet you there —

J. A. Stark

Untitled

Sometimes you wonder why it happens.
Other times you wonder how it happens.
Then some times you wonder what causes it.
Nobody really knows the answer except God.
    He has all the answers.
He needs not to explain himself.
He has a reason for everything he does.
God does what is best for the person.
If he takes your best friend away.
    He has a reason.
If he takes your family away,
    He has a reason.
You may get angry at God for what he does,
He knows the right thing to do.
Don't get mad at God
Just understand, it's the best for you or the person.
But don't say goodbye
Because God's will, will bring you back together.

Toby Ashbaugh

Christmas...Vietnam

The battle was furious, and struck in the head
A G.I. Is left lying in the field with the dead.
All through the night, he's unable to move
While the memories pass as a parade in review,
Of a cold winters day on a snow covered hill,
Of a lonely nights call of a lone whip-e-will,
Of a mother and father who gave him their love
Of a sister that died and has gone up above,
Of his brother who was crippled in world war 2,
Of a sweetheart that vowed, I'll always love you.
Of the Baby Jesus, born to Mary this day,
With no place to sleep, but in a manger of hay.
The sounds of a choir still singing His praise,
Reminding him of his own childhood days.
Regaining his strength, he struggles to his knees,
When suddenly, from out of the trees,
A sniper fires, it hits with a thud.....
He Falls....Dead....Face In The Mud....

Rachel C. Anderson

Moms

Moms are special sometimes mean,
They make you look so very clean.
    They dress you up from head to toe,
And in your hair they clip a big fat bow.
    They are there for you every day,
And you never want to move away.
    They love you so from their dearest
heart,
And soon you'll never want to part.
    They care for you when you're sick,
They tell your dog to give you a lick.
    They tuck you neatly in your bed,
And say have sweet dreams all
through your head!

Melissa Losey

The Local Fast Food Restaurant

She is African-American. I am "All-American."
She has two children. Unmarried.
Dare I judge or condemn?
Her son makes straight "A"s, I was surprised to see.
In my ignorance, it had not occurred to me.
What do I have she has not?
Opportunity. "Family Ties." A degree.
No! A religion that has given me these.
I let it rest, but down the line
I saw many here of the "less-sophisticated kind."
A different, young mother with boy friends too many for a child to see
My heart yearned to teach morality.
In each face was humility, unaffected.
No big strive for a grand career,
Only to raise the one's they hold dear.
"Give a cup of cold water in my name's sake."
A christian plea. Educate and set them free.
"By the wayside." Jesus said Crudehomes and public places.
We may learn and grow from such faces.
Talk gently, as a friend; break the conservative within.

Amy Kretsinger

Nature

What is nature
Is it a snake slithering through the tall grass
Is it the crowing of a rooster in the early morn
Is it the roar of a tiger as he hunts for his meal
Is it the buzzing sound of an annoying bee
Or is it all the animals in the world?

Is it the smell of flowers in the springtime
Is it the odor of fresh cut grass in the summer
Is it the fear of freezing on a cold winter night
Is it all of the colors in the world on an autumn afternoon
Or is it the sight of a rainbow after a storm?

Could it be that nature is all of the above
More than we can smell
More than we can hear
More than we can see
More than we can touch
Or is it much more than any of us will ever know?

Diana M. Schulz

Peace In The Evening

As the moon rises the sun goes down.
Nothing is left except the sound,
the sound of birds chirping and chattering,
the sound of frogs blurping and splashing.

As the sky with its colors of red, purple, and
orange... Blend together dusk is down unlike
the morn.

Danielle Wilder

392

My Future In Your Eyes

I've fallen many times before for many different guys, but then
there was You, and I could forsee, my future in your eyes. A
loving man to come my way is more than I had dreamed. No one
else dared touch my heart, or thought it always seemed. A
special feeling was truly there the first time our eyes met.
A thrill I'll always hold with me, and learn to treasure yet.
For you I hold a special place within my once empty heart.
With each beat repeating my love for you, in hopes we never
part. I see in you all happiness, someone I can adore. You're
everything I hoped you'd be, the one I've been searching for.

Sandra M. Barthlein

One Heart Complete

Their eyes meet
their souls embrace
no words are needed
they share the same spirit
two halves made whole
one heart complete
joined by a bond that exceeds even their own desires
created for one another from the dawn of creation
a work of art from the master builder
no one can separate this union
not death, not distance, not the destruction of the universe
they are joined by the divine
they share the same spirit
two halves made whole
one heart complete

Kristy Hoch

Friendship

Some things cause a person, to choose another for a friend,
That person chooses also, "Without both", a friendship ends.
In a way it's kind of funny, the way you find a friend.
I meet them nearly everywhere, I love the cheer they send.
The depth of friendship varies, sometimes it's very light.
There're others, deep and full of life, that vanish over night.
In all, they have a likeness, they are thoughts, that we can keep.
There are friends that pass by quickly,
    some, friends, disturb our sleep.
Our friends, are of our choosing, they have given, in their way.
So, sharing in that friendship, means a lot to me each day.
My friends are caring people, not built by sex or greed.
Still they are the ones I look to, to fill my every need —

Frank F. Faherty

The Log Entry

...so we took up our pens

to draft the extension
of ideas which seem to hover
from the ethereal ages
and given to those elected by choice.
We threw back our heads and stretched

to cogitate and relax:
avant-garde writings
or traditional lay
of meter attention and their days of air-mail
or haiku, perhaps, and free verse submissions -
poems invited and sent
for the scrutiny of judges.
...and we laid down our pens
in eclectic repose

to rest the point structures
and patently typed.
We fist-rubbed our eyes plainly
from cerebral exhaustion...
a relative task on crushed wood and straw.

Byron Sanders

Light for a Gambler

I can see you
I can feel you
I think that if I find you
I'll be in a better place.
You give me inspiration
You give me thrills that take
Me higher than this quiet
Unknowing plateau that I and everyone live.
I can't find you
I only feel your pain
You leave me in a world of doubt
Worse than if I ever gave you much thought.
You give me fear.
You give me despair.
You give me the emptiness that this
Patterned world seems to be drawn to.
The worst part about you is I know you
But if I can reach a level to give
You an honest challenge, then I
Am accomplished and you have no dark.

Greg Wohrle

Memories

Memories are beautiful things
They last to the longest day.
They never wear out
They never get last and can never be given away.

My memories are the days I fed
my chicken and ducks, pluck the
feathers and syringe the hairs;
Fed my horse and rode him;
The days I took care of a racoon,
who ate eggs, chicken and bread,
and took him for walks.

My memories are when we went
to the park, on rides, played ski
ball, ate cotton candy, candied apples and french fries.

Memories are picking flowers and
taking them home to mom, doing
my chores, going to the store and
paying bills for mom and dad.

Memories are when my husband and I went fishing,
to the flea markets through all kinds of weather.

M. Sperling

Temperature Change

It is awfully cold tonight.
Since the sun has gone to rest,
It seems the chill in the air
Carries a sting that pierces my breast.
There is a coldness that makes my heart ache;
It fills this room with emptiness
And makes the light seem dull.
I think it is because you are away.

The days are long and I feel weary.
The chores seem heavy to do.
The reason for living becomes unclear.
It must be because you are not here.

Food tastes bland and unappealing.
I forget it is time to eat or sleep.
It is a shame life should become so dreary,
But I'm quite sure it's because you're not here.

The phone just rang. Oh, you are coming home,
You will be here tomorrow!
I'll sleep warm wrapped snugly in hope.
Away with the cold and the sorrow!

Norma Elder Moreland

The Mask

The mask is worn by everyone not meant to be seen through.
It covers up the real face that's feeling sad, or blue.
The mask can be a great disguise when you're feeling down,
But, the sadness seen within one's eyes clearly shows the frown.

The circus has a painted face the clown that looks so gay.
Who, through his blunders, makes us laugh
At his carefree, funny way.
The smile drawn upon his face for everyone to see
Hides the frown that lies below for love that cannot be.

The lady dons her make-up one shade at a time
To hide what worry's gave her, the wrinkle, and the line.
The color put upon her lips makes a lovely smile indeed,
But, look into her sad blue eyes, you'll see the woman's need.

The tiny child comes into life
His eyes flowing with tears.
Not knowing yet, nor does he care
To cover up his fears.
Through comfort, love, and guidance
He learns to stand upon
His own two feet, then wear the mask life forces us to don.

Bruce Courtier

My Crush

I walked into the room
And saw you sitting there.

You had the most perfect smile,
And the most beautiful brown eyes.

I didn't know what to do
I was in love.
You probably didn't know
I exist.

I wanted to get to know you,
But I saw you were already taken.

I have to admit she was very beautiful.
I knew I could never compete with her,

I was hoping that you saw me,
But you probably didn't notice my staring.

I guess all I can do now is wish
Because you are my crush, and I'll
never have a chance.

Shanean Jones

My Friend...I Can Not Reach You

My life is no perfect illustration...
But my friends still know I care...
My friend I can not reach you...your lifestyle is there...
Your lifestyle so corse, so hard, and so entwined...
My friend I can not reach you, you are yours and no longer mine...
Your lifestyle it is you and your friendship it is yours.
My friend I can not reach you, you have locked all the doors...
Your lifestyle holds the key away from your friend...
My friend I can not reach you, your heart will not bend...
Your lifestyle not your heart controls you now...
My friend I can not reach you, I just don't know how...
Your lifestyle it will reach you and teach you somehow...
My friend I can not reach you, I'll just pray for you now.

Barb Swartz

"My Best Friend"

My best friend is someone I know well,
and all of her secrets, I'll never tell.
When I need her, she's always there,
and about her, deeply I care.
If there's a problem, on her you may depend,
because over backwards, she'll always bend.
Always willingly to help,
she knew exactly how I felt.
Her best quality is her big heart,
and she and I are never apart.
Lending a hand whenever I fall,
never judges people because of their flaws.
Always has a shoulder on which to cry,
and making people believe they can reach the sky.
For people, she never tries to impress,
no one can tell her than others she's less.
All our dilemmas together we face.
And she's the one I'd never replace.
Even her nature seems to be free,
and my best friend has always been me.

Rhonda Martin

Dandelion Dew

Within the dandelion dew of dream catchers
A wondrous web of warmth surrounds us
For within the Lord of Lotus flowers
We are free to fail...to succeed...to begin anew
There we can know all pure peace
And be one with each and all
For we have always been one breath...one being
One world...one vision
Breathing with passionate purpose
All pure potential is ours to experience...
The quiet essence of a purple rose petal in motion
A split second, soulful timing transcending
Where there is no sound, only open heart
For within this wondrous world of warmth
We are all one heartbeat one breath

Gloria Federwitz

An Agnostic Man

"Save for me, my stellar friend,
this final wish — so near the end.
Keep it safe within your aura,
for a thousand years beyond tomorrow.

Time has nearly passed me by,
grant one last dream before I die.
'T is I who hold the secret key,
fulfilling hopes of eternity.

Seasons of all have come and gone,
blackness surrounds long after dawn.
Give to me a thousand years more.
Keep me from death — lest time be over."

Dieing wish of an old, old man,
unnamed, soft-spoken, modesty grand.
Entrusted thoughts to a single star,
(beware the powers of who you are).

With a final eclipse, all had ended,
last of all, the star he befriended.
Take away that last flicker of light,
'T was Father Time who died that night.

Brenda A. Kulpepper

Just Look and See

Just look and see
    and you will know
peace, beauty and honesty ...

Just look and see
    and you will experience
solitude and tranquillity ...

Just look and see
    the smiles of understanding
and compassion that flows within ...

Just look and see
    past the exterior, noise and chaos ...
the ultimate fantasy
    a fulfillment of happiness ...

You look, yet you don't see,
    you know only the vision of sight,
but, see and you will discover the
    miracle of insight.

O. G. Bazzell

How Am I?

What is I?
Is it the pounding of the heart?
The slowing down of the walk?
The heaviness in the limbs?
Or is it the feeling of the heart
And the wide dimensions of the mind?
Is it the tumblings rumblings of the laughter
That empties and refills barrels of energy?
The outstretch of the arms
To envelope children - friends - neighbors - a stranger seeking
help?
The pounding changes to throbbing
The heaviness of the arms
Envelope another in soft streams of love.
How am I?
Eager for
Another touch.

Bella Scheckner

Past the Pain

When you see past the pain
Life opens and light becomes your way
So comforting this light that guides your weary soul
Go slow
Breath free
Receive
Love surrounds you
Just look and you will see
Lighter and lighter you begin to feel
Forgiveness has set you free!
Is that so simple it is hard to see?
Then why is changing so hard for me?

Naomi Lynch

Sweet Dreams

Wicked dreams, violent screams
A delinquent hidden in the subconscious
Filled with rage and fury
A nocturnal prowler, corrupt thoughts
Of fire and death settle in, what will you do?
Accept this invitation to our celebration, our
Gathering, or run, hide, pleasant thoughts coincide,
Escape, wake up! Too late, the dream is over!
The screams have ended! Did you have a
Good night's sleep? Next time, sweet dreams!

Eric Matthew Sealey

Life

A poem, someone asked me for a poem.
I thought how can you explain in few words the beautyness or
    sadness of this life?
How can you explain the great feeling of a sky full of stars.
The peace in your soul when you're seeing the sunset.
How, when in a flower you can see the power of life.
How can you explain all the pain in your heart with a death of a
    child, a short life that had few days, to enjoy the beautyness of
    this world, but to long to know about death.
How can you get words to explain every emotion of your life.
I just can say live your life the best as you can enjoy every minute
of your life the last one and if you want to know about miracles look
inside yourself and you'll see the most great miracle "life" and you
won't need words to know about poetry, you'll feel it.

Jessica Ocampo

April Star

My April star shines above
But faraway and cold
Your arms are near enough to touch
Your love to far to hold
The April star now shining bright,
lights up a memory of love we shared,
forever young with me
The April star makes love live on,
the love I have for you. If the love I have for you,
should go, I'll see a night, the moon above burns bright.
My April star so far away what causes love to die,
the star then fades, as if to say there is no reason why,
and then once more each April star shines brighter then before,
to keep alive a memory of a love that is no more.

Rhonda Adams

Nature's Cry

The rustling of water, down the stream,
Is a pleasant sound to hear;
As water gurgles down the rocks,
It whispers melody in the ear!

The rustling of leaves, as the wind blows by,
The blooming of flowers in spring;
The bees' melodious buzzing sound,
And butterflies with gauged wings!

The forest full of birds and beasts,
And crystal lakes in the glade;
Yes! This is the beautiful Nature-
The Nature which the dear God made.

God made this beautiful Nature,
With one thought in His mind;
That its beauty would not be destroyed,
And we would be gentle and kind.

But we are not abiding His wishes,
So we must all in haste:
Stop Destroying Nature's "God-Given Beauty",
And Not Let It Go To Waste!

Neeti Nagpal

Seasonal Gossip

The squirrel told the chipmunk
And the old raccoon,
The bee told the grasshopper
Not a day too soon;
The butterfly sighed to the heart of a rose,
A marigold nodded (Do you think she knows?)
Someone passed on to the meadow mice
Whispers of snow—rumors of ice.

Martha Crabtree

Reflections

The reflections in the lake mirror my thoughts
  of tall, slender, pine trees
  and flames shimmering on the water.

In the twilight shadows a squirrel
  runs through the tall grass
  to his nest in the tree.

A spider's web glistens in the rays
  of the late afternoon sun
  as he waits for a tasty fly.

A caterpillar crawls from his cocoon
  and slowly unfurls his wings
  then waits for strength to flutter away.

The water splashes as a fish catches his evening meal
  and a bird flies into a tree
  to rest for the night.

All the sights and sounds of nature
  surround my senses.
How can one not believe in God?
    Karen Weldy

A Child Cries

Within that very little child,
Lies a heart meek and mild.
The things that child has suffered through,
not knowing how or what to do.
Her tiny heart has been broken,
within words unsaid, to be unspoken.

She reaches out with a gentle touch.
To find someone that loves her very much.
She tries to run away from the pain,
but as an adult, it comes back again.
Now, she sees she's not insane,
it wasn't her fault, she's not to blame!

At last the past, is all behind her,
no longer there, no constant reminder.
    Rhonda Lane

Birthday Wishes For A Scot

I wish for you the Faith of your heather
  that grows from your craggy hillside;
The Constancy of your ocean
  with its in and out-going tide;
The Courage of the men who brave and braved
  those waters wild and deep;
The Hope and Patience of those awaiting them
  that loving wives and bairns keep.
I wish for you the Joy of a morn
  with the mist o'er your land
And the Peace of the shepherd boy
  with his well-protected band;
The Wisdom to know real happiness
  that comes from your simplest things
Like seeing the rainbow, feeling the breeze
  and hearing the meadowlark sing.
These are my Birthday Wishes for you,
  not money or material things;
Love, Good Health, and Happiness...
  all touched by the angels' wings.
    Mary Eilene Hamilton

Treason Of The Axe

When the blindman hears the color of the rising day
I see his fields and know he wields
Death's prism casting ray

The bitterness he feels for you is not born of reason
But the axe you used in acts
Against him you did treason

You chopped his life, around the world the missing pieces scattered
And those nations ate these rations
Left his poor soul tattered

Shreds of dust among the desert are what's left of him
Can you blame this missing name
To call the Cherubim?

And now he has this prism ray to use against you, dear
Through you it shows how evil grows
Within your soul of fear

And so the justice is completed for your acts of treason
And it's my fare, so you I tear
With this axe of reason
    Scott Nelson

Untitled

The day we became friends I knew,
We'd be best friends until the sky was no longer blue

We'll be best friends for ever and ever,
Because we have so much fun when we're together

I can share anything and everything with you,
And when I'm down you always know what to do

My most deep darkest secrets are only heard by your ears,
And I don't have to be embarrassed if I ever want to shed a tear

The friendship we have is closer than many others,
And it will stay that way even when we become mothers

I wrote this poem to let you know,
That the friendship we have will never go

Now it seems like I'm rattling on,
So my last line will be ABC-ya I'm gone.
    Kelly Whitfill

The Opposites of Life

Angels are happy; devils are mad.
Good people are nice; mean people are bad.

Checks are paper; credit is plastic
Life is good; a death is drastic.

Typing is good; writing is bad.
Dresses are for Mom; pants are for Dad.

Pickles are sour; chocolates are sweet.
Fingers are for hands; toes are for feet.

Fighting is bad; Peace is good.
Frown is a will; smile is a could.

Erasers are rubber; pencils are wood.
Move is a must; still is a should.
    Nicholas Clark

Yellow Sunsuit

I walk the beach alone now
looking for little footprints washed away
knowing they are forever gone
as you are.
There are other children romping
building sand castles along the shore
splashing small feet in the white surf
knowing no fear.

The seascape is dotted with red shovels and pails
yellow sunsuits, blue and white shorts
dimpled fingers digging in the wet sand
for a shell treasure.
Your wiggly toes no longer make a print
the yellow sunsuit, pocket full of sand,
lies folded in a dark chest.
Tears fall silently.

Anna Dollins

Possible Transformations

I see now that I am 15
A part of me I have to set free

It is the part that is me.
I have to think before I say,
If I don't want a man to stay.

The part of me that loves to
with fire, will have to stop
so I can get hired.

The part of me that loves to
drive straight pin through my
hands and feet. That is the
other part of me I have to beat.

I now see I have to change
more than ever. But whatever.
Maybe it will happen and maybe it won't.

Meredith McMullen

Pink or Blue, a Battle with Infertility

All those needles taken in vain,
All the sickness and the pain.
To our surprise it worked one day.
We prayed our happiness was here to stay.
We loved this baby with all our heart,
but then you decided it was time to part.
With very few memories left to spare,
we can feel our hearts begin to tear.
We hope you understand in our dismay,
we want to know why you took our baby away.
Our prayers were not answered.
Our dreams only shattered.
We only hope someday,
Please, not too far away
make our dreams come true,
and give us a baby dressed in pink or blue.

Priscilla Frost

To A Loved One

She stands apart,
Hallowed by her earthy deeds,
Tall, noble, blessed with beauty and allure,
Brimming with generosity, honesty, mercy, what only God decrees.
How can we capture her in words that will endure?
Look to the Latin for linguistic access
To form the perfect phrase.
"Dea Certe"—translated it proclaims
"Assuredly a Goddess,"
A semantic crown to wear in endless days.

Alfred C. Roller

Meadowsweet

I wandered by a riverside,
Where meadows meet a clear blue sky,
With thoughts of my homeland far away,
And its lush green meadows where children play,
With flowers growing brightly, waving in the breeze,
Where you can run and laugh as you please,
With raindrops on petals making droplets of dew,
In that lovely meadow that I once knew.

It lingers on in my memory,
As these precious dreams grow old with me,
But my spirit is light as I dream of that place,
And it dances with joy and sings with delight,
As I wander by this river so bright,
With thoughts of my homeland far away,
And the lovely meadow where I used to play,
Where church bells ring and the meadow lark sings,
As it builds its nest in the sweet scent of spring.

Sylvia Johnston

I Wonder ...

There are so many things that I wonder,
So many things that I always ponder.

Like how the stars always shine so brightly,
Or how little baskets are woven so tightly.
Or how small cottages are kept so neat,
How to take a place on the County Seat.

How a tiny bird can fly so high,
To get lost in the clouds of the deep blue sky.

How does the night turn into day?
Does a horse like eating hay?

Or how do storms come about in the day?
Why do dreams sometimes seem to float away?

Why do leaves change color at the beginning of fall?
Why did Cinderella want to go to the ball?

What does sushi taste like?
How does a person make a bike?

Why do pesky flies always want to stay,
And pretty butterflies always fly away?

All of these things I like to ponder.
All of these things I really wonder.

Kelli Marie Mackey

Our Garden

Attention needed in every niche,
a job or a joy, we're not sure which!
Planting, weeding, watering, feeding—
envision our garden with beauty exceeding!
Sow the seed then nurture to flower—
this landscape changes by the hour!
Fill small dishes with plenty of seed.
Watch shy squirrels and chipmunks feed.
Singing bird visit, butterflies dart
above the flora and then depart.
Over red blooms humming birds hover,
sip a bit, then dash for cover!
Never mind, they'll all come back
brightening the scenery as they snack.
Tired at sunset we feel content—
our garden well worth the energy spent!

Patricia H. Tyson

Colors of Jesus

Aqua is the color of the tree that Jesus sat under.
Brown is the color of the cross that Jesus
was nailed on. Why did they do that? I wonder.
Cranberry is the color of Jesus over flowing blood.
Daffodils are the colors of Jesus light
that shone brightly.

Evergreen is the color of an everlasting
tree that will never die.
Fruits are the colors of you and I.
Glass is the color of shine that our heart
will have when we ask God for help.
Health is the color of a bright system.
Intelligence is the color of the Bible which
has knowledge, when some people read it.
They remember how He died.
And Jesus is the color of righteousness,
salvation, forgiveness, and love.

Jennifer Vassel

Untitled

Spring has sprung, and the grass has risen, Today is the
first day of your new life as it is...
Memories of yesterday will slowly fade, Tears of sadness
will wash them away. Let go of the sad times as well as the good.

Look for your ray of sunshine in the mist of the tears. God
gave her to you for a purpose you see. She will bring you
happiness, understand and love. Today is your new life
let the memories fade.

Only one memory shall remain!!! Name, mention it I shall not.
For you know her to well....Build your new life around her,
more important no one should be.

Time will pass, grieve will go, memories fade, happiness
grow. Love is there even though he has gone. The love of
a Mother and Child he can not take away. Look for tomorrow,
grow from today.

I admire you for your strength, though it may seem small
to you now. This strength you have has shown greatly
Never let go of that strength, for it shall help
you survive.

Today is your new life......

Jo Ann Carney

After the Soccer Game

The nets are down
The crowd has flown
The stands are empty
The players gone and all is silence now

On empty field
With challenged health
A lonesome boy makes labored touches to move his ball

In his mind
He's strong and tall
He drives his foot and boots the ball

The nets are up
His shot does soar
The stands are full
He hears the roar
His imaginary game goes on and all is music now

Philip J. Scrofani

Our Ransom Paid

A tough time getting there
Not knowing how, when or where.
Seems as if we danced with the devil,
Trying to get on our feet and on the level.
Like being in the eye of the storm, the cyclone roared.
Mountains came crumbling down causing desert waves,
Then a quieting sound.
From above - someone sent an angel.
"Our Ransom Paid"
We were swooped out on the wings of the wind
And faith colour us gold. Then appeared. . .
A glorious light and a country rainbow.

Ruth Yates

To My Daughter

The night before your birthday
I got a call from you
When we finally finished talking
Thought I'd write a poem too.

You made two people happy
Just thirty seven years ago today
When we drove down to Cincy
And brought you home to stay

Trials and tribulations
Yes we had some to bear
But the good things always
Topped the bad as we soon learned to care

No girl's father ever cared more
For his child than did your dad
Your mother loved you just as much
But couldn't show it and felt so sad

You've grown up now
And have turned out to be
A wonderful person
As everyone can see

Kathryn Gladden

A Clock

A clock
measures time.
Predictable and punctual,
Never-ending and relentless.
Nothing can stop its forward march.
Echoing our anger, fears and resolve,
a clock ticks loudly.
Reflective of our meek and tender thoughts,
a clock ticks quietly.
Sharing our contemplative mood in the
glow of an afternoon fire,
a clock ticks slowly.
Sensing our haste to catch a bus,
a clock ticks quickly.
In measuring the indomitable force of time,
a clock measures us.

Sara Friesen

Collage (A Collection Of Good Ones)

Crazy they tell me. Insane. If I'm really
crazy, why do they complain? Stupidity
racks my brain. They all agree, I'm insane.
I cry and no one cares. Can't deal with all your
dares. The pain is here to stay. It is mine,
this hell I've made. God can't save me, I'm
so afraid. I am ashamed of the choices I've made.
The world above me, one day shall fall, I have
the strength, I'll kill them all.

CeCe Brooks

L-i-f-e

When I'm under a starlit sky,
I dream of white comets flying by.

The black spots on the moon, make me wonder why
There is such a private sky.

The green grass that I so comfortably lay on,
Feels so much better when I'm peaceful and alone.

The planets unspoken for, have a unique difference I'm looking for.

The aliens flying in their ufo's,
Are going where nobody knows.

Now that there's no sky to see,
I can still feel it signaling to me.

Now that there's nothing to hear,
I can't tell you what's far or near.

Now that there's nothing to smell, it's hard to tell what's in the air.

Now I tell you there's nothing to feel,
I can truly say I have nothing to heal.

Now there's nothing in my life,
Now there's nothing to worry about, not even a lovely wife.

I have nothing to give, nothing to say
I wish I could live another sweet day.

Jacob Powell

Daybreak

The sun rises slowly far off in the distance, giving
    off a beautiful light that brightens the sky.
The day bursts into a joyous chorus as the birds begin to sing.
They fly about telling each other that a new day has begun.
It is a time to be free, a time to enjoy the gifts
    so graciously given to us.
The bright colors of the flowers blend to make a
    glorious prism of beauty.
They say, "come and see us, smell the fragrance
    and be still for a while longer."
The trees blow gently from the wind, whispering
    the affections of the Lord.
He says, "Come spend a little time with me and
    tell me what is on your mind. For I care about
    you and long to be with you."
So I take the time, and a deep peace like a
    flowing stream fills my soul.
Yes, it's the beginning of another day, a chance
    to live and to reach toward the sky, for God
    has prepared it for us to enjoy.

Noelle L. Schlegel

Untitled

Your love for him is great, he doesn't know how great.
He loves you so dearly, he'll listen to everything your heart
desires to speak about.

He lives through your eyes and becomes a part of your daily
activities.

He has cloth you with a blanket of love since the moment he
laid eyes on you. Until you rest in peace he will always protect
your love.

His tender touch is warm and kind, this is what makes you
love him much greater.

He is a prince.
He has become the person your heart so desperately needed.
He loves you completely and you enjoy loving him in return.
He has promised that if you let go and give him all of you;
He will catch you and never let you fall!

Rebeca Galiano

"The Best Things In Life Are Free"

So often heard and oh so true..."Best Things in Life are Free"
And things we take for granted.....especially Liberty.
Remembering too, great happenings like the miracle of birth
When You and I were welcomed.....arriving on this Earth.
And now we count our blessings for the privileges abound
Enjoying God's great treasures so many are around;
The Clouds, the Stars, the Moon and Sun
With special beauty in each one;
The Wind, the Sea, the shimmering Trees
Bring happiness with balmy breeze;
The roaring of the Waterfall sends music to our ears
The trickling of the Meadow Brook helps ease our human fears;
The mighty Mountains capped with Snow
The Sun cast on them all aglow
The myriad Forests filled with Love
From Antelope to cooing Dove
This puzzle of life's mystery we do not understand
But know that we are safely held by God's Almighty Hand.

Betty Ann MacPhetridge

A Rose Everlasting

Art thou a rose; a rose I hold
For you my love, my beloved wife

The kiss of dew; dewdrop so sweet
I hold this rose; this rose everlasting

Remembering you; loving you so much
So delicate and soft; scattered rose petals

Thy day was given; to bloom for all
Cherished and warm; your lips deep red

Touching the sky; colors ever flowing
Arriving alas; the warmth of night

While lying on a bed; full of rose petals
I hand you this rose; this rose my love

Peace and beauty; love fills the air
Silhouettes of our bodies; united as one

We masquerade the night; 'til the early dawn
We wake up together; in each other's arms

We reach a new day; our love is even stronger
Because of the rose; that I'd given to you.

Diana F. King

We Are To Touch The Soul

I've come to believe that you and I
were meant for the business of healing.
Some may say, how bold, how dare,
How dare we think that we have a magic touch,
a soothing glance, a healing hand.
We've been quiet, not knowing that we
were sent on an errand of love, through the pain,
ridicule, and denial that we have endured.
Much more are we to endure as we
are being called to stand among the masses.
Sometimes with just a smile.
We are to speak out for the voice
who can't lift its head to speak.
We are to walk with those
who feel they can walk no more.
We are to feel the whip crack as a broken body falls.
We are to touch the soul
of those who have lost their dream
We are to, with love, encircle those
those who feel no love surrounds them.

Philip Matosich

Untitled

It seems like only yesterday,
Since my loved one went away.
I remember the hour and time of day,
In my memory it will stay.

It was so hard to see him go,
But he is in a better place I know
Weariness, suffering, pain all gone,
For now he is forever home.

I said goodby through many tears,
And kissed the one I love so dear,
Then thanked the Lord for all the years.
Happy years I recall, thank you Lord for them all.

God knows my heart is lonely today
Remembering the time you went away.
So he gave me a dream to comfort my heart,
You were here, we were not apart.
As long as I live, you will be in my heart.

Margaret Kibodeaux

I Breathed in Fire Burnt Out the Light

the Dear Lord Came Down And ...

I dream of Heaven
I dream of Earth
I always wonder if they're what it's worth
Worth the pain life has brought me
Worth the torture that they just can't see.
When my life will end is it heaven or hell?
The path is so confusing I just can't tell.
Who's right or wrong, which path to choose
They say "stick with one path, and you just can't loose."
I tumbled down no one heard my cry
All I wanted to do was curl up and die.
So I breathed in the fire
And burned out the light
It was then when the
Lord came down, and
kissed me good night.

Leslie Felarca

Intercourse By Teardrop

Surprise proposal gift arranged. Engagement promises exchanged.
A diamond causes hand to jewelry. Eyes neon: "Love you truly."
Eyeshine designs into droplet.
   I begin to feel what her eyes can't conceal.
Few have ever really felt
   when God commands an eye to melt.
Emotions in motion without fear;
   the sexual act through her tear.
A tear sperms to slide the eye, free upon her cheek;
   my male heart to seek.
Small bows and packages made of water,
   to honor me, the ring I've bought her.
Droplets trace, like liquid lace,
   the velvet vessel of her face.
Her tears catch my eye, senses soak, and stain impart,
   to pulsate pathways to my heart.
Spiritual seeds, seeping through sensation,
   sperm within my heart their perfect impregnation.
Seeds at rest, a'bedding now, each tiny token,
   soon to birth as wedding vow, never to be broken.

Russ Hansen

"Juniata"

I picked her up, and I fell in love
She fit in my hand, just like a glove
Giving her food, keeping her wet
Even a visit to the family vet

Although water was her greatest demand
A long walk was quite grand
Across the meadow to climb or slide
Just to find a place to hide

Hibernation won't be no trouble
And her size is almost double
She's quite contented with her home
It's doubtful she would ever roam

She has made me happy, from the start
And slowly managed to steal my heart
Looking and listening, when I call her name
This "Turtle" will never be the same!!

Joan Hower

My Own Way

I could not live the way they said,
I only wanted to choose my way,
And they would not let me.
They said I was wrong to want my freedom.
They said their way was the only way.
I did not agree with them,
So I decided to find my own way.
I am leaving them far behind, and I am finding my own way.
And though they will not admit it,
Many others have done the same.
Now I search for those who have left before,
And I will join them when I find them.
I will have my freedom, one way or another.
I will not live without it.
I have lived under the iron hand of tyranny,
And I will never live there again.
I have grabbed onto freedom with both hands,
And I will never let go.
I see a camp fire in the distance,
And in it, I see a future for me, my own way.

Brenda Kay Hale

Appreciation

There's a throbbing in the air tonight,
Like a generator shooting electric pulses into the sky.
It's thick and dull and pounds within my ears.
I thought of you more than I would have liked today.

But now it's gone.
Turned off, I suppose, by the same one that started it up in the
   First place,
Having satisfied their need for its provisions.
The silence, now, is more complete.

Faded roses hang upside down from a tiny nail on my wall,
A gift from someone longed forgotten.
Their color's grayer now, their fragrance much diminished,
But seeing them reminds me of spring and sunshine and scented
breezes.

You asked me once, not long ago,
Why I kept withered dead things in my room.
Morbid, you said.
Perhaps.

I find myself wishing you had stayed,
But console myself with
The beauty of dead roses and
A silence more complete.

Kristen Burr

A Dream Come True

Unbound and unknighted across the ions of time
As if endowed for a purpose
A part of a grand design
I'm leaving the threshold of my world,
Into this majestic pageant of life
Lured by a strange fascination
    returning to you for light.

I have a reaffirmation
As silently we descend
Slowly thru Gods, vistas
Ultimately to win.

Silently——so hushed
As closer we come to thee
And - there you are, I see you now
My "Pearl" in the South China Sea.

Lorene Key

Mom

Moms are always there whenever things are right or wrong.
Holding out her hands to you that are tender, yet very strong!

She would move a mountain for you if she could, Or reach you a
    star from the sky.
She is always there with that undying love. To know her, you need
    not ask why.

Yet, we take our Moms for granted, and forget them until time of need.
But need not worry, she'll be there, and in you she'll believe.

Moms come in assorted packages, some big, some small, some short,
    some tall.
There's also a variety of colors, black, white, and all the others.

But no matter the color, the shape or the size, even if they're
    young or old,
You'd best believe that all our Moms to us have hearts of pure gold.

So Mom, I'm thinking of you as I write this, and in my heart is all
the love anyone's heart could possibly hold.
For in my eyes there could never be another Mom
That's definitely fourteen-karat gold!

Nan M. Hamler

The Rainbow

Oh! How magnificent as it appears.
Your eyes will be full of tears.
The colors so bright.
Will make your heart delight.
Red, orange, and yellow;
How sweet and mellow.
Green and blue will sing a tune.
Purple and white
What a lovely sight!
The name of the tune is in key "G"
"God Almighty", whom you can clearly see.
Behold the rainbow!
It is a picture of pleasure
Which reveals beauty.
All the colors total seven,
And you will find your soul in heaven.
The angels are now singing.
There shall be eleven.
The song is familiar.
It was your well being!

Gilbert F. Heiney

Untitled

Images and visions of you are all so beautiful.
Long hours on the phone, and good conversation.
I was hoping I was all you desired.
But now to me it seems as with me you are tired.
I thought your love, sex and money was all needed.
What I need the most you won't give me.
You have had my mind, my soul, and my body.
What I want you to give now is your time and some harmony.
Your friendship is what I most treasure.
But you just want me as your lover.
I wish I can let you go, but you have a strong grip on me
and won't let go.
Time after time I find my self puzzled.
I don't understand why won't you come see me?
Why have you stop calling me? Do you really love me?
Slowly, slowly, and slowly our relationship is diminishing.
We can't turn back the clock.
Today is to late to say sorry. Maybe one day I will forgive you.
Tomorrow you may never find, see, hear, touch, me again.
Nothing Last Forever!!

Anika Gia Labossiere

Untitled

Do you ever really get
    through another person's mask?

Do you ever get a true answer
    to the questions that you ask?

How do you know that one is sincere
    in the gifts that he gives?

And is his apparent lifestyle
    the one that he really lives?

"Would you like to go to dinner?" "yes"
    But would he really rather be home?

When you're spending time together,
    Is he wishing he were alone?

You think the shield he wears
    is lifted when you're around,

But then you find, there's a different kind,
    of shield, on him to be found.

When you finally realize,
    There's a piece you shall never see,

You look in the mirror and discover,
    That masked person, too, is me.

Kristie Hoff

Fall Mountain Memories

Into the calm of the mountain morning,
the sparkling dew falls, clinging to the colored leaves.
Golden rays of sunshine dance on the rivers waters,
falling quickly to the rocks, like waves of the seas.
In this gorge of chimney rocks, and through the hollows just below,
Sunday music fills the mountain air,
from a little church there I know.
Here high in these mountains, quiet in this lofty place,
Within my reach, I can touch the magic of creation,
and know my grasp is safe.
Memories of the times long ago,
Spent in the shades of the mountain oaks.
Fast forward, flooding our minds of times we shall never see again.
Permanent scenes, etched forever in living dreams,
Even as the shades of time draw closer, even near,
No one can take or even alter, the memories we hold here.
Where deep into these rocks and mountains, in timeless chimes,
Still ring of soft and peaceful rest,
as the multiple shades of colors, wall the distant crest.
I shall return again to fill my soul, when the fall is at its best.

H. Quinton Chapman Jr.

To Baby, With Love

To us you are a miracle
That God has blessed us with,
He must have been here listening
When we made this special wish.

We know that you can't hear us yet, but only if you could,
You would know how much we love you
Just as parents should.

Right now you are a challenge
A baby on the way, but one thing we can promise you
Is to love you more each day.

The day that you will join us
Will be a special one indeed,
We can't wait to take care of you
Trying to fulfill your every need.

What happens now is up to us
And God will help us out,
Because love and happiness is all we ask
And that's what you're about.

So just remember all the love, and hope we have in you,
For nothing can come close to compare, to a baby so pure and true.

Nicole McGee

The Answer

I have been dreading another Christmas without you there
filled with sadness, self pity, and despair.

Guilty of not being able to find the time to do
the things I would like in memory of you.

I asked myself Have I failed to do what I can?
and the answer I received in the garden does stand.

For a rose has bloomed so delicate, pure, and white.
as if to say please don't worry I'm alright.

Roses are not supposed to bloom in winter snow
but I guess it is just your way of letting us know.

That you are with us each step of life's way
and from one anothers Heart we shall never stray.

James Edward Young

Untitled

Time is precious, while enjoying your little infant
childhood life. Their little fingers, gentle touch
your firm hands putting all their fear behind. When
you strolling through the parks and sidewalks ever-one
takes and peek. Smile are large, from young to old,
Cameras are flashing at the little ones, and they
are wondering why so much fuss. Remember that the
days are number, and before long they off on their
own. So enjoy their little tears and messes now,
before you realize it will be. January, February,
March that the little one will be in the house.
April and May their little fingers will be helping
you with planting. June, July and August, they off
playing in the pool and drinking Kool-aid. By
September and October, they off playing in the leaves.
Then comes November, December around, they watching
the little snow fakes fall to the ground. Before you
know the season has change and so have they.

Thomas Martin Besmehn

You Will Always Be There

You give me freshness,
when I need it.

You also mess up my hair
when I run to school,
But you also give me life
Everyday and every night.

You are always there
to dry my eyes when I cry
and you're always there to listen to my whines.

That's why I write to you,
wishing that you will always be there.
I know that you won't leave me without your tender loving care.

So I will go away.
Thanking you.

For always being there.

Even though at times
it seem I don't notice,
that your love grows towards me.
But I'm asleep.

I need help to awakened from my deep sleep.

Edna Ruiz

Eternity

Sails are blowing in the wind,
storm clouds threaten,
sea and horizon entwined:
eternity...

The jungle whispers,
birds are chirping,
lions and panthers taking a rest:
eternity...

The thunder rolls,
the sky is a fireworks,
the forest comes alive at night:
eternity...

High out of the mountains
a waterfall ripples,
the crystal clear lake untouched by men:
eternity...

Dessert winds caress the soul,
a lonely coyote howling away.
Footprints today, gone tomorrow:
eternity...

Ursula Dow

Survival

The sun has now risen, another new day,
The future now brighter in every way.
A new chance to begin my life over again,
And make all much better than it has been.
Greet every day as if it were the last,
Charge towards the future, forget the past.
What has happened is over and shall never return,
New horizons emerge, eager to learn.
I am the force behind all I endeavor,
No matter what obstacles I may have to weather.
With no one to count on, no others alive,
I am the strong one and I will survive.

Janette Barranger

The Visitors

Late at night - when the house is quiet,
and the wind goes rustling about;
I sit in my chair - dreaming there,
hearing the children shout.
The sound is faint and rather quaint —
for it's traveled for you, see.
It's the sound of children, now grown up
   coming back to me.

Kay Gallo

Untitled

Darkness overcomes my sleep-laden eyes.
Fingers slowly caressing my lone brow.
Follicles rotating counter-clockwise,
Dialing in my grey-colored mind. Wow
He who is neither black nor white soon dies.

Darkness overcomes my sleep-laden eyes.
Pressure shoots beams of red light from my mind
To the small back eyelids of these black skies.
Time taken away in spite. He is kind.
I need this time in a world of black lies.

Thoughts rushing from the hearts to the heavens
Up the bright light to the white heart of one.
Tears rolling down a facade of sevens
Wondering when it's okay to be done.

Andrew H. Carlson

The Land Of The Free

See them embark on the freeways of the land
In Car Cocoons.
Lone, wrapped in a tense isolation
Trapped in mindless rumination
Four lanes with one direction
Speeding forward to separate destinations.

See them disembark from the freeways of the land
Male and female.
Hidden behind a bright facade of animation
Covering their sense of desperation
When entering the grey gulf of active participation
Driving ever onward to greater stress and frustration.

See them embark once more on the freeways of the land,
In Car Cocoons.
Lone, caught in a grave transformation
From pointless actions to tedious distractions
Trapped in mindless calculations
Four lanes with one direction
Moving backwards to separate destinations.

Marie A. Paulson

My Place

Salient sparrows sang so sweetly there.
The sky, so blue, gave sapphires envy.
I romped around with out one single care.
While burning pinon's scent gave seren'ty.

The ground, sometimes capped with lazy gold haze,
had little green clover growing with might.
The endless horizon upon which I'd gaze;
majestic mountains that proved quite a sight.

This place which does seem like heaven, is not.
I really do wonder which is the best:
This place or heaven, both are a great lot.
In grouping, they are apart from the rest.

My place and me are quite far apart,
But it will always be kept in my heart.

Darien Clary

Angels

Angels are sent by God above, to be your very own.
Heaven's soldiers sent with love, to safely bring you home.

Hidden from the sight of man, where no one can see.
Yet be assured they are there, keeping you company.

As you travel life's winding road, not sure of its direction.
You'll feel them tugging at your heart with guidance and protection.

And on the nights you can not sleep, burdened by life's cares.
I pray they brush you with their wings, reminding you they're there.

I hope today, tomorrow and all the days to come,
you will be comforted to know that you are not alone.

Laura Pace

Untitled

Do not pass by this empty husk
For I was young and happy once.
Vibrant in my quest for truth,
I, like you, fought the rules.

With passion did I fight the fight
Proclaiming (living), equal human rights.
Fairness, an illusive treasure,
Battled for in full measure.

Battles won and battles lost,
Then I began to see the cost.
Weary as I was of this,
Hypocrisy was less than bliss.

And so, my passion burnt so low
My soul was charred, there was no glow.
No glow, no ember, darkness fell,
Not feeling is a living hell.

So do not pass this empty husk,
Your youth will warm me in the dusk.
And if my soul should catch afire,
That feeling is my one desire.

Theresa Tucker-McFarland

Intermission

Follow the encompassing spiral outward into space, beyond the stars. Light as a feather, you circle upward through the horizon of another world's sky. Reaching beyond the clouds, far below, you can now see grassy plains decorated with wildflowers, stretching over the gently rolling hills of tomorrow. Soon, you are set down in this field of nowhere and everywhere. The air is dry and sweetly pleasant. This comfortably warm land is filled with soothing scenery. Floating slightly above a mulch pathway, which you are following rapidly, you notice that your attire consists of a flowing toga and white sandals. The path leads upward and over the green hills.
Peering across the declining slope, you envision a small village beyond a crystallized pond. Travelling towards this scene causes no fear to invade your being since you are clear that this place must be the very meaning of life. Knowledge flows through your veins as other toga-donned residents of this intensely loving environment greet you. Now an inner trial takes place.
You have been given the choice of dwelling here in happiness or travelling back from hence you came to uphold tranquility. The latter conquers because you are now empowered with the vitality of true harmony and wholeness. As you turn to begin the voyage of your new day, the frozen pond of Peace crosses your mind once again. Then, the canal of life embraces you.

Stacy M. Haag

Unsaid Understanding

And so without understanding I speak;

I understand,
from the impeachment of my words,
I understand
What you say, but the forgiving
is not said, is unsaid
Sadness from nothing said weeps itself
to sorrow; weeps itself to death
And (but) still nothing is said-
Our beginning numbs itself;
To the end the cry is heard-
but it is not there-
So we die knowing nothing
except for what hasn't been said.
I love you.
(Goodbye?)
I love you.

Charles Kevin Mason

The Lifeguard

I went to the ocean today
And washed my face in the salty spray
As the waves pounded upon the shore,
Seemingly shouting, "Do you want more?"

I walked upon the gleaming white sand,
Sprinkled so freely by God's own hand,
I silently watch children at play
Laughing, carefree, happy, and gay.

Looking out over the beach and sea
A lifeguard lifted his hand to me;
I wonder if he's lonely there,
Perched so high up in the air.

Lois M. White

The Gentle Seduction of a Sage

A sage has shorn the salt he's built
of dirt, of endless mire, unshackled silt.
But, too, he doused his dimples
with consumptive guilt.

His spangled spirit betrayed bewilderment,
quickened, then quailed into demise
and fainted as a vision
daunted by azure skies.

The maudlin moon eclipsed
this vanquished ego stilted by feigned pride,
so now like the moon,
it conferred upon the sun good-byes.

Tomorrow teases and taunts
of seductive though not salacious jaunts
through unsavory but dazzling haunts.

Agony, admiration farm a fusion of rage;
he's caught in cosmic revery
on this a patalous page
in the ongoing saga in the life of this sage.

Audrey J. Saunders

The Ninth Sign

Vigorous, virtuous woman, fresh, natural and pure as the virgin snows.
Introspection, the contemplation of one's own thoughts and sensations.
Romanticist dreamer, day dreaming of her lover and of romancing him
   with lite candles, soft music, wine and captivated fragrances.
Giving her all, for she's warm hearted, devoted, expressive of love
   and capable of great love.
Oh, beware for she is easily offended, taken wrongly, sensitive and
   can become very offensive.
Woman of wisdom, sophistication and earthiness.
Over modesty, a victorianism, keeping things well hidden for she is
   ashamed of emotion.
Moderate, protective of her feelings, she'll meet you only halfway.
Attraction of powers with her glamour, charms and bewitchment. Can
   be very loving and affectionate.
No stopping her flirtatious, cause when she's out shopping, she's the
   shopper of love. Virgo Woman, The Ninth Sign........

Lavita Stallings

First Love

You were my very first true love, though maybe not my last
But you'll always have a special place, in my future was well as my past
The first time my lips ever formed a smile, was when looking into your eyes
And I'm sure you were there to dry my tears, the first time that I ever cried

The first man to ever hold me, and the first man to love me true
Though since then there have been many others, I am positive the first one was you
You have seen me at my very best, and at my worst more times than not
And even when I was in a foul mood, you loved me no matter what

You were there when I got my first broken heart,
To pick up the pieces and make it all better
And it hurt you probably more than it did me
As you helped but my life back together

And though they say there is no love
Like the love of a child and its mother
I just thought I'd tell you
They were wrong for there's truly another

For no matter how much we may argue
When all's said I wonder why did we brother
Because in the years Dad I have come to learn
There's no love like the love of a Father

Francine Corgliano

Monday's Love

All day Monday I daydreamed. All day Monday I thought of and about you. All day Monday...the facade...All day Monday I wept inside. All day Monday I hurt. All day Monday I became fully aware that life is passing very swiftly by. "Get proper food", you said, "To keep healthy." "Get plenty of rest", you also said "to stay strong." But why? For what? For whom? My deep concern for you and the blessed remembrance of sheer intimacy, completely fills my mind so much so that I cannot, I shall not, I dare not think of the apart hours. Yet, I know I must for to prove to you my complete and ultimate faith in doing what is best for you (for us), I do promise to try. For what I want most is to have you remember me without bitterness, without sadness, without sorrow, only tenderness. And often I remember the last thing I said to you about my uncapped well of love that you opened...But now this exploding and gushing well of love with all its pains and frustrations still pours out of and over me. How now I do cap the power? The force? The surge? Will there ever be another time for you to help me? At times like these I cry dry all the tears that may be left and at other times I force my mind to wander. For, the human mind cannot dwell on two different ideas at exactly the same moment. I am still shrouded by a fog, embraced in a sea of despair.
Time would help if you would help, the times I need you.

Francis A. Ciminera

Untitled

Just as time the hands they go in a circle to tell where you stand
and exactly what bestows us in the future. It controls the life of
many and tells who, what, when and where, there is the dare. The dare
of life. Yet to rebellious soul takes over the shy and there the shy
take over the rebellious. All as these hands travel within their
circle watching upon the ground with grass of green then brown. As
she lies safe and sound. So clear the darkest night. Never to carry
fright. Throughout every breath of air. There is where dare. As the
hands they go in a circle.

Paul Richard Barr III

Sitting On a Cloud

Birds singing while sailing in flight, animals scurrying and fluttering at night.
Sounds of thunder, streaks of light, ocean's waving and roaring with might.
Sheets of hail create pounding rain, flash floods charging leaving no remain.
Collapsing avalanches bury all below, freezing cold temperatures, blizzards of snow.
Hurricanes, typhoons, cyclones that go, angry winds hitting not knowing where to blow.
Zooming tornadoes or twisters that spin in mighty tunnels climaxing within.
Winter brings volatile energy with strange powers, silenced only by
    Spring and its sweet flowers.
Tropical rain forests, blankets with green, shades of grey yet to be seen.
Crystal blue waters, patches of brown, dazzling rainbows without sound.
Translucent shadows that can be found, iridescent layers trickled around.
Glimpses of multi-colored speckles resembling confetti sprinkled on the ground.
Glazing lights glittering with blaze, various shapes with luminescent haze.
The sun beating hot with Summer in sight, drenching humid days without coolness at night.
Temperatures rising, blistering heat, smoldering air without relief.
Unexpected panic announcing an earthquake, diminished to silence with the calm of a lake.
The bristling noise of rustling trees captures the embrace of a soothing cool breeze.
Falling leaves with no discretion, relaxing waterfalls that form a better perception.
The waking of Fall comes into sight, followed by Winter's return of a fight.
The continuing cycle of seasons return, dramatizing action with lessons to learn.
Hypnotic visions of a night's dream, come to reality with what can be
    seen by sitting on a cloud.

Norma S. Murray

Death Has No Favorites

When death comes and knocks at the door, you will go with him whether
you're rich or poor.

You may be a person of high position or even lacking in nutrition,
but when he knocks you'll have to go even though he sometimes takes
it slow.

Boast of your riches and boast of your wealth, but when he comes
there is no one there to help.

He takes no bribes and there is no place to hide; he takes the
foolish and those puffed up with pride, leaving behind many teary eyes.

What man wouldn't redeem his soul if he could pay off death in silver
and gold and bless him with riches untold?

Man and beast both are alike because death comes and puts out their lights.
Man sometimes puts up quite a fight, but in the end he's still booked
for the flight.

Once in the grave, man turns back to dust and there is no more need
for him to rush, he can now relax with anymore fuss.

He brought nothing in and he takes nothing out and what some leave
behind make others shout.

It doesn't matter whether you're great or small, it is your destiny
is to meet this fate, and on his calendar for each of us he has set a date.

Queen Shalom

My Kingdom for a Cup of Tea

There's one thing that amazes me,
is how the English love their tea.
The English friends I choose to see
will sit me down and serve me tea.
The English plays appeal to me,
like Upstairs Downstairs whate'er be.
The character in them pleases me,
they act with such reality.
English hostesses, gracious as can be,
will greet her guests affectionately,
exchanging happenings of family,
also the misconduct of their Royalty.
She seats them all most comfortably,
then signals the butler to serve the tea.
Below the stairs maids are busy as can be,
but will take time out to have their tea.
I partake of the brew occasionally.
How much I indulge depends on me.
However, unequivocally, I must agree
the English really love their tea.

Minnie Carter

The Burial

Your little body lay warm as I found you
Innocent eyes forever closed in time
Silence whispers your soul away
Death has darkened your mind
Goodbye sweet creature of happiness
childhood swept away
How I prayed never to return to this place
I had buried your family today
As I rip at the freshly torn earth once more
Your limp body held close to my heart
The blood of my soul swells up in my eyes
Lifting the box for your final depart
Inside lay two little bodies
So peacefully huddled in place
I tuck you in beside them
Together at birth together in grace
Goodnight sweet fragile felines
Too young to have a name
Goodbye sweet creatures of happiness
A white cross is all that remains

Tara Devine

Ode To Poe

As the winking stars flirt with the moon,
    and the tidal ballet begins,
The sapphire sky knows when to swoon,
    as the rapacious night sets in.

Seeking cessation from the anguish,
    midnight cries out for a haven ....
While, in lassitude I languish,
    I think of you ... And the Raven.

As did Annabelle Lee succumb to the sea ....
    and the sepulchral kiss of madness call,
The salacious dream that captivates me —
    did beckon you .... Upon night-fall.

Yes, I hear the beat of your tell-tale heart,
    bearing your pain; forever engraven,
And each swing of the pendulum does impart ....
    thoughts of you .... And the Raven.

Andrea C. Farley

Our Prayer

Our thoughts and prayers are with you
A you lost a loved one today
That God will keep you in his care,
I just what we will pray.
He giveth and he taketh,
Just why, we do not know
That he choose this special one
The one you all loved so.
He's in a better place you see,
Guided by that Gracious hand
Who put us here, and call us home,
To that Great Promised Land
You'll be sad and you miss him
As he enters that Golden Gate
But happiness will greet him
Up where the angel wait
Our Lord has chosen to call him,
To that mansion in the sky,
Someday you'll be together
In that "Sweet bye and bye".

Shirley A. Land

Robin in the Roses

A robin is a pretty thing,
I'm sure we all agree.
But growing roses is my hobby,
And this bird is haunting me.

I feed and water and cultivate,
And my roses do me proud.
But when it comes to spraying,
Then on my horizon there's a cloud.

For the robin visits daily,
My rosebuds moist and wormy.
And in order not to poison him,
From my spraying he deters me.

Now my spraying lacks its constancy,
From the problem this bird imposes.
And my rosebuds are in jeopardy,
From this robin in the roses.

Virginia Miehl

Jesus Is Standing By

When the storms of life beset us
 And the waves are dashing high;
And there seems no one to help us,
 Jesus will be standing by.

He feels our every heart-aches;
 And hears out every sigh;
When we need some-one to comfort,
 He will be standing by.

He's there in times of testing,
 And helps us carry on;
Till in His presence resting
 With all life's battles won.

And when this life is over
 And we are all called on high;
To welcome us to Glory,
 He'll be standing by.

When Heaven's gates are opened,
 He'll bid us enter in;
To live 'n realms of Glory,
 Forever-more with Him.

Clara E. Hooey

Simply Love

It reaches from heart to heart, I go without food because I am so full.
Days and nights how I longed to be with it. In time I knew that I would have it.

Though seas and oceans would separate love from me and I from love.
My need and longing for it would never be quenched.

In one unforgettable evening in a look...a stare, in eyes so full of life, I found it!
But could it be, it caused me, to choose to stand tall and to be strong.

What is the origin of my new found strength? Was it the look, her touch, or was in those eyes piercing so deep into my soul: An expression of what I needed inside.
As I pondered and prayed a voice from within spoke to me and said, "You will find love again." For it will complete you and make you whole.

As I traveled through the portals of time, on a cool and brisk night. I once again found my love, and I shall never let go of love again.

Daniel W. White Jr.

The Pit

Spiraling headlong into the pit of depression. (Hard to breath.)
The sound of laughter haunts my dreams, not the laughter of happiness
... but the vexation of enemies watching my every move... waiting
for me to falter, The comforting of my friends and family seems pale
and quite weak. (It's More Difficult To Breath!!) Work, work is just
a trap, a trap with smooth walls and fine cracks, My fingers are
bloody from attempting the climb... failure. I hear distant laughter
(getting closer) fingers hurt, blood stains my dreams... Dreams become
dark. Nightmares without form. Will becomes weaker and smaller.
(Hard to see now) Blood dries, fingers still hurt, dreams coated in
sticky coagulated plunder.

Life Plundered, Desolate, Lost...

Lance DiBitetto

A Gentle Touch

In my hand lay a flower seed, and I carefully plant it into the ground.
Loving care with a gentle touch it grows upward into the world around.
The beauty of the flower, when it's in bloom, shows on my face.
Every petal and leaf so delicately shaped blows gently in the breeze with grace.
From a seed into a flower this is a wonder to see.
I am pleased and happy this transformation is a part of me.

Adelia Jean Pendleton

"E" Is For Alligator

Mommie, is there an alligator in this shopping mall?
No, there's no alligator in the mall. Not any, Sweet Cher, that I can recall.
Alligators live near wet swampy land. They bask in the
sun, on rocks and the sand. Look, there is a fountain. Look at the
fish. This is a wishing well. Let's make a wish.

Mommie, I want to ride on the alligator.
No Cher, no Cher, there are none in this mall. Not any, Sweet Cher,
not any at all. Gaters are dangerous and scary, too. Never get near
one or he may eat you.
Look, there is a restaurant called a cafe.
Hamburgers are on special for today.

Mommie, can I eat my hamburger on the alligator?
Cher! Cher! I told you more than once before. There are no
alligators in this store!

Mommie looked and she started to grin. It was so funny it made her
thoughts spin. Yes! Yes! The alligator you may ride. Please
watch your step and hang on to the side.
Escalator, Sweet Cher, is the right name.
Big jawed alligators are not the same.

Carol Urguhart

"Love"

Love lingers in the night
like fire flies burning bright.
Two lovers holding tight
not knowing weather it's right.
Love can be deceiving simply
when there's no believing.
The walks in the park
late when it's dark.
The knowing you're alone
the hurt and the pain of
the foolish games
makes you wonder
how many other names.

Shannon McCarty

My Haikus

The trees grow high up
And seem to pierce big white clouds
That float in the sky.

Flowers are blooming
And flourishing in the grass.
More are blossoming.

The rain is pouring
And splashing down on people.
There are big puddles.

Trees can be leafy
And sway in the summer breeze.
That one's bark is rough.

There are some foxes
Barking, running fast and swift.
They have some babies.

Colleen Renee Powers

Withered and Torn

Withered and torn,
I'm tired of fighting.
The light has gone
from my eyes.
Dreams have shattered,
memories have faded,
Time has passed me by.
I wear a crown of wilted flowers
upon my head.
If I had another chance I
would be one of the dead.
Withered and torn,
I'm tired of fighting.
Slowly I die.

Amanda Burchell

Ah, Columbus

Ah, Columbus. Way too late?
Your glory's matched upon your fate?
And so tis now and yet to come
The greatest pitfall of mankind.

Too late one sees the wealth he has
Until the wealth he has no more.

And so into a pit of sureness,
We lose our sense of now awareness
And hence become the inevitable poor.

Ah, Columbus! Way too late?
Just add your name onto the slate,
For it will only be one more.

Pamela J. Ingle

Untitled

Cameras take pictures.
Pictures tell stories.
You take hearts,
and rip 'em apart.

Watches tell time
as time passes by,
you left me gold,
and I wanna know why.

Hearts are broken,
feelings betrayed.
Guys are trouble,
now all I see are
the tears in
the eyes of my heart.

Judith Jamieson

The Day I Can Smile

So far I can't touch you,
Yet so close I can feel it.
No color but I see blue,
On top of everything yet in a pit.
I speak but no sound,
I hear but I hear nothing.
I see only your pictures,
Yet they all seem sad.
I feel like a mixture,
Of years gone bad.
Knowing that you're there,
So far away.
I need you here,
Each and everyday.
But I can wait,
For a little while,
Counting down to the date,
To throw my tears in a pile.
The day I can see my mate,
Is the day I can smile.

Angela Eick

Whispers

The cool, summer soil squishes
Between her toes
Embedding itself
Within the creases of her knee.
Soft, plaid gloves
Protect her hands
From the worm-infested
Darkness she searches.
Pushing aside the dry surface,
It crumbles
Through her clothed fingers.
She is searching
Through death
To discover,
The moist depths
Of earth,
Still housing the remnants
Of past snowfalls,
The perfect spot for conception.

Sarah Stec

River

A swishing sound down the river.
A fish jumping up and down.
Little canoes going by.
Waterfalls passing by.

Lynn Amanda Horowitz

Coffee Daydreams

Our lips touch
and passion wells inside us
like swollen bread.
Human pretzels fold and bend,
baking in the heat beneath our sheets.
We ebb and flow into each other
re-inventing the glove.

Love is how I tolerate
the toilet seat, feet
dangling off the couch
on Saturdays.
Football plays
blasting past my reverence.

Cartoon-like zzzz's snake
around the lump you make sleeping,
while my coffee daydreams
anticipate your awakening.
A moment more to feel you close.
A silent wish
for this love to spill another dose.

Lorise Roon

The Feeling Within

The feeling within
Burns with a fire all its own,
It's like a crashing sensation
Of being torn between
Two forces
And not knowing exactly
What is driving me -
Insanity or Hell.
The feeling haunts me
With a desire to kill
Who ever comes near.
Then, without a warning,
It caresses me
With a touch of an angel
And drains itself from my body
Once again...

Angela L. Allen

What Is Another Word for Love?

I melt in your smile
Wishing and dripping
All the while to feel
Your breath in my ear
Shivering sweet
Magnetic to the heat of you near
Speak your soft thick words
Thoughts I have never heard
Like a chanting love spell
In disguise so much to tell
In your eyes
You are flesh untasted
I am yours to hold
Together we create a story;
yet untold.

R. M. Sanchez

The Flow

Electric head sparks flying
Our past comes back to us on a
Mono filament wire.
We are all numbered and plugged
in with our neighbors
follow the wavy path forward
power up the generator let the
current flow
into the future where we all
must go.

Eva M. Forbes

Summer Daze

Why, oh why, when snow was piled deep
And frozen pipes made me weep
Did I pine just to greet
    July, and its heat!?!
Now, the sweltering air makes me
    Crave that deep freeze—
I would get on my knees
    For a cool summer breeze!!

Araminta Pierce Blowe

A Whisper of a Memory

A whisper of a memory
of the touch of your skin

Will start the fire to
burn within

The deepest, darkest
midnight

You ignite

A spark in the blackness

All the feelings in one second,
that would take years to express

Lori Musselman

Your Love

Wrap me in your love my Lord
Wrap me in your love
I feel the warmth of your presence
When you wrap me in your love

Your love is my protection
From all the hurts that come
I cannot live without your love
You're my protection from above

Wrap me in your love today
And do not let me go
You are my security
The only one I know

Lois Ortega Valverde

Summer

I think summer is a great
season and here is a reason:
There is lots of fun for everyone!
And when it's time for the fourth
of July, we can play games until
we cry! It is time to party and
it is time to have fun, and summer
will be great for everyone!

Kimberly Hinton

Animals

There are so many animals.
A lot of them are mammals.
Some are birds.
They say no words.
Most are insects.
They cannot watch the Mets.
There are amphibians.
And then there are humans.
Some are warm-blooded.
Others are cold-blooded.
We all live in the world.
It looks like colors swirled.
There are so many animals.
A lot of them are mammals.

Amanda Kashnow

The Image

I look, I see an image
And what I see I like
I see my goals get finished
Me getting on with life
I see my self doing good
Better than I ever had
I'm doing what I really should
That makes me very glad
I look back and remember
The bad things that I did
I now think they are stupid
I'm moving toward the bridge
Success, the bridge, I have no doubt
A bridge that's strong and very stout
Leading me to something nice
A new beginning in my life.

Stephen R. Pratt

Balloons

Balloons
They come from all over the world,
in many shapes, sizes and
colors.
Their beauty is evident
for all to see.
They float and bob
bringing laughter and joy
to all who see.
And sadly they are
only here for a
short time.
Like the ones that we love,
the grandparents of our past,
who ultimately soar
magnificently into the
heavens.

Candice Molina

Life

Life
A very precious thing
Most take it for granted
Until we see
How easily it can be taken away
One pill to many
One step too far
It doesn't take much blood
To see how alive we are
One pull of the trigger
One tug on the noose
It really takes too little
To set our spirits loose

Erin Wilcke

Little Black Children

Little black children kneeling
around a bed with a sweet black
mother the protector at the head.
Her hand would never touch you
Your spirit knew it was there
You see her hands was always
together to God in prayer.

Her head thrown back; her neck
would be exposed and the tears
from her eyes ran all down her
cheeks and nose.

What a wonderful way to learn about
Jesus kneeling around a bed with a
sweet black mother the protector
at the head.

Jean G. Ortiz

Love Goes On

Your typical bar —
Six thirty in the afternoon;
The usual regulars,
Plus a few,
Who are strangers.

Perhaps loneliness
Brings a construction worker,
And an over-the-hill blond
Together, for a drink,
Or two — or three.

The lonely have
A scenario all their own.
They've "Been There,"
And "Done That."
There is comfort in being together.

Perhaps that is the answer!
We are nothing, alone,
And everything together;
And maybe your typical bar,
Is where it all begins.

Marhsall Kline

Going Back

Alas, alas
I Must go home
From these Colorado Rockies
Where I stand alone,
Admiring the aspens
So tall and so gold
Planted on the mountainside
By our God, I'm told.

The elk, the bear, the deer—
They all roam free,
But, you know, I've been told
That's the way it should be.

So alas, alas
I will someday come back,
If only in my memories
Where I look up at the sky
And praise my God.
What a lucky person am I.

Becky Hope Palone

A Lost Soul

What am I supposed to do
To keep my heart from loving you?
I know this feeling can't be right
But I think of you both day and night.
I wonder why I love you so
But in my heart I guess I know.
I love you just because you're kind
Your laughter echoes in my mind.
You always treat me with respect
In my mind you are perfect
The way you make me feel
As though our love is truly real.
If our love should ever end
A piece of my heart to you I'd send.
With my heart I give you all my love
And all the stars from above.
Now that I've told you all this
Please be kind and give me a kiss.
This is how my feelings end
A wonderful message I hope to send.

Jason L. Lane

After The Loving

After the loving, then after
the bad hours have past, we
make love and cry as we do,
because after the loving's so true,
we lay and can find our feelings
so blue and thank the Lord for
blessing us like he do, cause
after the loving comes truth.

Patricia Cole

Untitled

I recall a rose -
Delicate petals
Misted in honey light.

The wind sweetly breathes
Shadowy reminders of tomorrow,
Waking me from my trance.

Time blows a cooling storm -
Blue skies now black,
Leaving garden dreams
Behind.

If only the sun
could rob
Winter
Of its
Void.

Adriane A. Moxley

Awake

Emptiness has filled me,
there is nothing left to explore.
All walls are up,
never to fall down.
All shadows seem to follow me.
Staring eyes leave me blind.
I question reality.
The blackness of the night
blinds me.
The stillness scares me.
All life has taken a halt.
Not once,
but twice.
Reality kicks in
only to remind me that
I must awake from my dream.

Danielle L. Balzer

Reflections From the Heart

It's not easy to break that spell.
Returning back from a living hell.
This is the way I see things now.
Coming out of my darkened cloud.
It was a state in which I cried, and
fell upon my deepest pride.
Alone in thoughts but not in prayers.
God forever healed my fears.

Now that I'm back on my two feet.
I want to make sure that life is sweet.
Forever until I die.
God's my witness and my stride,
This is the way that it should be,
happy and a family.
Being together all the time.
In heaven that's just fine...
    with me.

Lisa Michele Chapin

"Balance Of Nature"

Amidst nature's work of art
are creatures large and small.
Butterflies dance to a rhythm
that we don't hear at all.
They flutter and surround
fragrances in the air,
and with discriminate senses
pick flowers for their fare.

Frogs, muted colored, blend
and hide near the water.
They listen to croaking sounds.
They're aware of one another.
They sit beside umbrellas
of fungi growing nearby,
surrounded by the plants
upon whose source they must rely.

Yes, nature has a balance,
a beauty, and a reason.
If we take care and remain aware
for all these there'll be, a season.

Mary Spade

"Grief-Stricken"

A boy - a lifeless black cat
one cold and dreary
winter night
The ground was frozen
blankets of snow
covered the
backyard trail
He carried Petri's limp body
with bare hands
and sobbing
Laid her gently - gently in
the homemade grave.

I said a prayer and threw in
some flowers from
a vase
before we covered her
with loosened earth.

Elma Diel Photikarmbumrung

Utopia

Windstorms lift Sahara's prime
Pyramids surrender Pharaohs time
Eyes entwine Milky Way's view
Hyenas lurk while laughing
Bird of Paradise beauty's baffling
Climbing Mount Everest allures

Bright clouds tantalize mirages
Rain forest leafy camouflages
Lightning strikes Mangroves's bark!
Angel falls down below heaven
Myths mesmerize tall legends
Cheetah bites like frenzied sharks!

Rainbows glow at midnight
Platinum stars enchant sky life
Fairy tales mislead intrigues
Oceans swallow Island seas
Blue moon follows golden sun
Utopia calls the earth turns
Utopia calls the universe stands firm

Patricia Johnson

Winter Sunset

Dried oak leaves dance
Across the crusty snow
The evergreens gaze in snobbish disdain
At denuded dogwoods
Who shiver from the cold
Stark black branches
Crackle in the wind
The setting sun sheds
Its wintry rays
Across the scene
And sighing, goes to sleep.

Evelyn Grant Flynn

Brought Into The Open

I want to reach in my mind.
I want to pull it all out.
I want to lay it on the table
And erase all your doubts.
It's so hard to explain the
Feelings just right
They won't come to order
Nor into the light.
They're strong and they're humble
And they come from the heart,
But the minds explanations
Keep them apart.
It's who you are and who we'll be
That I seek to explain.
And what you mean to me.

Eric Cleveland

Just One Touch

My heart sends my brain to a
different level whenever your
hand touches mine.
You can only imagine what goes
on with the rest of my body.
While I'm fighting to stay
on the ground. You're sending
me higher with every little
word from your lushes lips.
If you could only join me at
this moment and let our eyes connect.
You'd see the love that lives
deep within us.

Jermey McLain

Shiny Armor

The casting line has been out,
and not a nibble in sight.

It's been a long time, and I am
tired of losing time.

Like fishing,
you wait and wait
for the grand daddy of them all,
but you never get the big yank
to crank in for the big score.

The ocean out there is murky,
but here on land
they look jerky.

All those fishes might has well
been toads since they
didn't turned into
my knight in shiny armor.

Marleen Schlottman

Your Anniversary

On special days like these
There are special things to do
Love, Care, Respect and share
That passes through and through

Sometimes you think about the past
Which has so many memorable thoughts
Those laughs, smiles, happy times
Those times that can't be bought

All these years spent together
each so unforgettable
Hopefully there's more to come
Each so unique and so lovable

We thank our Lord, Almighty God
For People just like You
Whenever you say you love me
All my dreams come true!!!

Rachel Ann B. Amposta

Lost

Stumbling on the words
Denying all of the pain
What else is there
For me to gain

I have lost the game
And in it was you
I was doing fine in the beginning
You were too

The understanding
And all of the time
Were lost in the war
To fight away crime

The undying love
So bitter and sweet
Maybe someday
We will again meet

Jill Gaudreau

Today

Today is here and mine to use...
    Tomorrow may not be,
And as the present I would choose
    To task my energy.

The opportunity I hold
    Within my hand today
May prove to be the precious mold
    To shape my future way.

Today is still the only time
    In which to do my work,
And mighty triumphs, and sublime,
    May in its moments lurk.

But even tho the lowly vale
    Of common life is my way,
The only thing that will avail
    Is duty done today.

Marjorie G. Taylor

Yellow

I wish the world were yellow
No blue - no green - no brown.
Just sunny golden yellow
Without a trace of frown.

If all the world were yellow
And darkness never born -
Surrounded all in yellow
No heart could feel forlorn.

But color booms like thunder
Inside a life of tears.
I wake each day to wonder
What could be left to fear.

Hide me from blue and every hue
That cracks the golden glow
Because if not for yellow
I could not find my soul.

Jo Walter

Past... Present.... Future

As I type, time ticks away.
This verse, begun in the past,
Will finish in the future.
The present lasts no longer
Than the tap of each key,
Then recedes into memory.
Yesterday was many key strokes ago.
Tomorrow seems far away,
Like a tree on the horizon
Aside a long, straight highway.
It seems forever to reach,
But goes by in a flash,
In an instant becoming
An experience past.
The past consists of memories,
The future, only fears and dreams.
Only the present is real,
A fleeting moment, it seems,
In which to conquer fears
And convert dreams to memories.

Walter Randolph Johnson

The Straw

He sat on the edge of the bed
With the gun pointed straight
at his head.
He had just buried his beloved,
his wife.
After a lifetime of hardships,
and strife.
The crack, sliced, the gloom of
the room.
The bed turned red.

Don Eckles

Untitled

The fragile line so firmly trod
Balancing its way toward God
Falters, frivols, trips and tears
And knows its help in its despairs

Dorothy Kiely

Ghost Dancer

Shuffling pointed feet, caressed
the shiny floor as
painted eyebrows arched
over smoldering eyes,
beckoning, a wanton invitation.
A subtle, gliding motion
parted the stygian veil,
unclothing the shadowy torso,
a silent seduction.
a spirit aroused,
dancing....
a midnight pirouette
with feather light feet
never touching the floor.
A pale reflection permeates
this dance macabre,
as the gossamer shroud
falls to the floor
in a whisper,
the dancer lost to the dark.

Vijay Steve Persad

The Guitar Player

He crooks his soul
Around his lyre;
His fingers fly
On wings of fire;
His lifeblood pours
On strings of air;
By magic knife
His heart laid bare;
Captive, faster
Yet he plays;
Crimson from his
Fingers flay;
His spirit dances
Overhead...

And finished now,
His song is dead.

Luci Risinger

Spank - Teach and Pray

If I was the president, I'd spank
a congressman or two, and set them
in their easy chairs and teach
them a thing or two. We need
medicare, and social security too.
So lets work together, and be faithful
kind and true. Maybe if Satan gets
arthritis, and has to go to bed, the
good Lord will take over, and we'll
all be far ahead.

Audrey Z. Smith

Battle

I fight to keep me
I fight to remain me
  It's a battle so lonely...
  I think if only
I could learn to conform
I would learn to reform
and perhaps in the doing
I would feel less scorned...

Scorned by the others
who see only black and
    white
and feel so right
with life, lived in black
    and white...
I see only grey and
    no absolutes
for me it's the
    only way...
The only way you see
In my being true to me...

Nancy Stone

Web

I'm stuck in a web of life
A web of anger
A web of hate
A web of love
A web of fate
A web of fear
All together entangled in
What we call life.

Melissa Schmitt

My Knowledge In Time

A thought of mine
My knowledge in time

When I speak
Considered a freak

The instincts in you
Demand to ridicule

The first time you hear
A reason and idea

Disagree you must
An under-breath cuss

To concede that I know
In your mind can't be so

A though of mine
My knowledge in time.

Steven J. Lever

The Playing Field

A distant sound of laughter
Then a cry, a scream, a yell
The children on the playing field
Giving each other hell.

Playing on the rope swing
Pushing each other fast
Each child only thinking of
How long their turn will last

A smaller child is put on the swing
And the others all push him about
The rope swing getting way too high
Then 'let me off!' He shouts.

All afternoon they play these games
They fight and then they laugh
Name calling and ganging up
Dividing them in half.

Then dusk begins to fill the sky
And mom's come to take them away
But they've all had the greatest fun
They'll be back another day!

Helen Young

The Animal In Me

I am a lion moving without
fear,
I pick up the vibrations of
something coming near,
Slowly and steady is how I get
ready,
I stoop down low and close
myself in,
all the action will begin.
A herd of elephants, could it
be?
I can't tell, I can't see,
As I slowly approach and
start to attack,
Something inside is holding
me back,
I walk back to my den,
feeling like I didn't win,
I decided to sit and rest again.

Nicole Bradley

Heavenly Beauty

A crescent moon, one lonely star,
Strugglin' to light up the night,
They search for all the others help,
But there's no more in sight.

The crescent moon soon disappears,
The lonely star shines on,
As if to say, "I'm still here"
Until all my work is done.

Hours pass, the heavens black,
The clouds roll slowly by,
Still wonderin' how this lonely star,
Expects to lighten up the sky.

Morning creeps above the clouds,
The sun comes peeping in,
The lonely star has disappeared,
Till his shift comes up again.

Charlene J. Hatton

Endless Journey

The sun never rises
in my days that have no end
Darkness dwells upon the path
I travel once again

And if the sun should cease to hide
And darkness falls astray
Endless clouds abound my stride
To chase the sun away

From day to day I wander
Weaving dreams I'll never find
This lonesome path I follow
Leads me nowhere but behind

I wonder if I'll ever find
the sun around the bend
But as I still myself with time
my path will have no end

Edwards R. Amorose Jr.

Autumn

Come back summer,
Seems like you just got here
Then the screen doors slams,
And you're gone.

Sheila Cofer

Morning Returns

Staring in the distance,
I know not what I see.
It may have some appearance,
But I know not what it be.

I may not be an ace,
But I bid you reality adieu.
Looking off in space,
I imagine dreams come true.

As I lie and ponder a stare,
The world turns into dreams.
I wonder what is air,
I wonder what all this means.

My imagination is at work,
My inspiration comes from nowhere.
Suddenly there is a jerk,
The light brings forth a glare.

The world comes back into sight,
yellow has taken over black.
It is no longer the night,
Morning has come back.

Kirsten Amlaner

Sleepover

  Playing games til late at night
then starting a pillow fight.
  Just you and your closest friends,
daring each other to lick bookends.
  Listening to music and watching tv,
staying awake until three.
  Sleeping in bags on the floor,
laughing until your stomach is sore.
  Wearing face masks and eating chips,
having dance contests and doing flips.
  Goofy pajamas with pink and plaid,
having more fun than you ever had.

Valerie Wickert

True Love?

Could a true love ever exist
Be-tween two strangers,
Who only met a time or two?
A love in the name of friendship,
Tempered with respect and decency,
Sealed in understanding and honesty?

Rudy M. Wieland

The Waterfalls Of Peace

My days are as my nights
My nights are as my days;
I wallow in the darkness
    that surrounds me.

They say the eyes are the windows
    of the soul;
Dare you look at what I behold!

My spirit is empty, hollow and vain;
My body is dry, weak and ashamed;
My mouth thirsts after the
waterfalls of righteousness;
the cool cascading waterfalls
of peace.

Shall I ever find this mystical
being called peace? Will we
ever be one in the same?

Where do I begin? Will not
one soul show me?

Kristina Gold

God Forbid

    I overheard two people talking
about fear, while waiting at
a grocery checkout line.
    As I left the store the one
phrase that kept coming up in
that conversation was "God Forbid"
    I thought to myself should
I be afraid of crossing over a
bridge or getting on a plane
    looking over a cliff or a tall
building or should I trust that
my Lord put me here on earth
to serve him without the fear
that God would forbid me.

William S. Soto

Take That Chance

When we were both in our teens,
We talked about all our dreams.
As we grew older
We came so much closer.
When you were by my side,
I made believe you were mine.
When we were together,
It couldn't get any better.
Then came the time when we had to say
    goodbye,
But I just left you wondering why.
Now that I'm all alone,
I wish I had you here to hold.
Now that you're away,
I wish I said all I couldn't say.
We could have had a wonderful
    romance,
Had only we weren't afraid to
    take that chance.

Eddie Lopez

Nothingness

4-26-96

She sits alone in the darkness
Nothing is left to be said
She ponders a moment
On what will soon be done
Slowly she raises to her head
The gun
She stole from her dad
"It is done"
And with these last words said
She pulled the trigger
And now she is dead

Gandy GayLee Baker

Dictum

"In hoc signo vinces"
Now I can plunder, persecute,
trample you with impunity
of course,
under the sign of the cross.

Mankind has turned
the cross into a switchblade
religion to oppression
love into hatred
heretic, pagan, barbarian, infidel
by this sign you shall die.

Romulo Habla Estareja

The Country

My heart is in the country
where the sweet wild roses grow.
And the mockingbird's loud melody
brings on the morning glow.
Where mountains meet the deep blue sky
and there's music on the wind.
From birds and bugs and waterfalls
that sound out in deep smooth blends.
The country, ah the country
where deep lush grasses grow!
And trees so tall make a canopy
of shade in the sunlight's glow.
And thoughts give rise to heaven
in praise of God on high.
For giving us such beauty,
so lovely to the eye.

Brenda Johnson

Untitled

Dearest Friend or Foe,
It's awfully nice to know,
That it was my heart —
You've chosen to borrow,
Even though upon the morrow,
We shall perhaps meet sorrow.
Time and distance separate, but,
Caring never comes unpreparate —
These few words I write,
Hoping you think of me —
Once in a while,
And within your heart,
Is hidden a warm smile.

H. T. Piwowar

Symbolic Economy Of Means

(For Lord B.J. in den Bosch)

Reduced, now, to linen fragments,
in the moonlight, cold, white
marble where once he taught
logical students the fact of
assorted pebbles and bones, pieces
of copper, the forgotten message
of trade, and the luxury of
enriched departure which, it has
been learned, cannot be afforded,

Simply a case for grim
interrogations, the empty purse,
invited, confined, running
frayed, a slab upon which the
arrow might rest a subtle phrase.

Baron Joseph A. Uphoff Jr.

Dear Bobbie

What is a sister?
Not only a sister
But my best friend.
She's always with me
Until the end.

Relying on someone
that you can trust,
Not only a necessity
But a must!

She's a saint and a mom,
though sometimes it's tough.
She's always a lady
Gentle and calm.

We'll be there together
Although we're apart.
We're connected forever
From heart to heart..

Sue Sims

A Temple For Your Presence

Make me your vessel, Lord
    Filled with your love.
Help me to pour it forth
    Peaceful as a dove.

Many there are, Lord
    Hurting, here on earth.
Needing your guidance
    Since their day of birth.

Make me your servant, Lord
    Finding lost sheep for you.
Teach me to bring them forth
    In all I say or do.

May I become, Lord
    A temple for your presence.
A home for your Glory
    As a trusting, humble peasant.

Make me your temple, Lord
    To use in your own way.
Filled with your Holy Presence
    Helping those lost, astray.

Peggy Payne Boyle

Emotions

Swirling masses
Jumbling forms,
Beating rhythms
Pulsating storms.
Emotions!

Moving hither
Overriding senses,
Causing hurt and
Building fences.
Emotions!

Here today and
Gone forever,
On the morrow.
Feelings differ.
Emotions!

Dawn A. S. Moser

Untitled

If...
    you could know...
        it's not the things,
        no not the things...

It's...
    sharing of Truth...
        intermingling of perceptions,
        and knowledge,
            without pretense...

I yearn for that from you...
    and if you could see me,
        as I am...
            naked before you,
                uniquely me...
            and wanting you to share
                your naked self with me...

What a celebration that would be...
    and so I wait, and Love you...

Until
    you can Love yourself...

Lynne A. Riedy

A Lone Sailboat

Are you as majestic as you look
Alone on a sea of gray
Almost lost in a misty fog
As you press along your way?

Your silence is breath-taking
From my perch - a seaside deck,
Drifting so silently along
In the distance - a mere speck.

Did you reach your destination
In the mist and fog that day
Or are you still busy searching
Out there beyond the bay?

Sybel Haugen

Mother

Mother
Gentle and sweet
Caring, lovely, helping
Like a graceful rose
Beauty

Robyn Lyon

Me

By myself I think to much, and
by myself I fight the storm.
Within myself I will draw, and
protect myself from the world.
Within myself I must live, and hope
myself, I will always have
to be myself my one real goal.
My one true friend, I'm my only foe
probably end up alone, I know, but,
to the end I'll be, everywhere I go.

Wayne Johnson

Storm

Steel-gray ocean seethes wildly today.
Turbid waves smash against rigid rocks,
Becoming decimated salty spray,
Then flow down stony reefs
Glistening in murky storm light.

Storms pass, though exceeding slow.
New day dawns.
Rosy reflections on blue sea
Welcome exhausted storm waves tenderly,
Like mother soothes her child.

Ocean turns calm and blue at last
Smooth waves sway peacefully
On their way to shore
Where resplendent future waits.

LuRee Harding Sperry

Candy Kisses

Candy kisses taste so sweet
Wet and warm
Like a summer shower of rain
Felt all over

Candy kisses make your
Toes tingle
They make you feel
Loved and needed

Candy kisses are so necessary
Like the breath we breathe
Or the water we drink
Without them life is lonely

Johnnie L. WoodAll

Night

Twilight sneaks upon me,
The sun it melts away,
Leaving but a memory,
Gone another day.
Amber shadows lengthen,
Stretching into night,
Tiny stars and slivered moons
And flowers folded tight.
Crickets' chirps and frogs'
Low sweet baritone
Waft in through my window
Where I sit alone.
I'll not be frightened
Of the dark,
Tis only end of day.
How boring it would be if
The sun forever stayed!

J. A. Claar

Untitled

If I were the wind,
I'd fly through trees,
Talking with butterflies
And dancing with bees.

I would make the water ripple
I'd make the flowers fly.
Then I'd sit back and watch them
Offer themselves to the sky.

I'd fly through the heavens
Then back to the ground
On a cold winter's night
I'd be the only sound.

I would fly to the mountains
where nobody dares,
And play with the tigers
And tease all the bears..

Joelen Elizabeth Kersten

The Beneficial Stream

The stream is high,
    with the winter snow.
In the summer draught,
    it becomes somewhat low.

It's always clear,
    and refreshingly cool.
It descends from the hills,
    in a crisp, little pool.

There are no impurities,
    to ruin its taste.
Neither city fumes,
    nor factory waste.

Its brooks and ponds,
    have quite an effect.
Our homes and our buildings,
    it's sure to protect.

The good it does,
    is surely stunning,
To benefit all,
    its purpose in running.

Cameron P. Parke, Sr.

Snow

All that glitters is not gold...
but for one taste of the sweetness
of the earth I will with pleasure
endure the chill that brings colors
to the leaves and the cold winds
that bring the glittering snow.
I will laugh with the birds come
Spring, and cry with the tears of
the clouds.
I will sit under the Summer night
skies and recall the snow of winter
and her bitter chill.
And for these the changing seasons
there is no sacrifice as great and
wondrous, nor worth as much as
the magic bringing the beauty of
the snow.
And I realize...
that which glitters is indeed far
better than gold.

Barbara L. Wheelihan

Medium - No A Wink Of Sleep

There must be a medium,
So he thinks.
He is unsure of himself.
One dream pulls his right arm,
Another his left.
But reality swipes his feet from
Underneath him.
It is hard to get back up,
But he does.
Only to fall again
And get up again
And fall again.
Floored..he thinks..
There must be a medium.
Something, someone,
To pull him up from the ground.
...and she does.

Vincent Michael Sarnicola

New Hampshire

We don't boast of crowded cities.
Where the people come and go;
We have our share of "Beauty"
I was raised here and I know
When God made the white mountains
Where the "Old Man" still stands,
He put his "Seal" upon them.
You can find it anywhere;
So, when you need a vacation
and a place to stay.
Pack your bag climb aboard,
and visit New Hampshire today.

Katherine Ham

Vision of Love

Love is the most
Talked about,
Dreamt about
Written about
Laughed about
And
Cried about
Human emotion
I used to say,
"I will never
write about
love like
the millions of
other poets
in this
world."
And then,
I loved.

Stacy Walsh

Us

So gentle a soul
In such a determined body.
Chair only a disguise —
You would never guess
The content of the man inside.
Aura of love
Concentrated to a point;
Walking away drops left behind
Only to be pushed harder into the skin.
Reaction of a girl
So sick inside —
Never to be loved;
Never to reveal the truth
Of a past pushed aside.

C. Johnson

The Student

I am a student
So are you.
There are a lot
Of students
In this world too.
I think
I am a good student,
But not that great.
I got suspended
From the bus
When I was eight!

Paul E. Cannon Jr.

People Let You Down

People will let you down
they will not be there
When you need them they
will look at you with a funny
look and put their feet in your
mouth so if you find someone
like that you better put on your
running shoes because they will
walk all over you. People can be
your friend for a litter while
but when your back is turned
they will laugh in your face
But when your luck has run out
your friend is going out the door
so people will put their feet
in their mouth and let you
down. So try to find someone that will
be a real good friend to you.

Suzanne Hall

3:00 Am

Marking time
by unbearable circumstance
crossing every T
dotting every i
keeping meticulous track
of the pain is
kind of like my job
A lost art
like the scribe
of the tribe
tracing the familiar outline
so as to least feel something
each milestone reverberates
with a heart splitting accuracy
living is too close for comfort so
I sit in a darkened room, reviewing
old newsreels, reported
with a slanted viewpoint

Christi M. Post

Happiness

Enjoying good times
smiling at something that
makes you happy.
Winning something that
you'll get to keep for ever.
Getting something
you love and always
dreamed of.
Happiness

Colleen Speight

Waiter-Boy

Sweet waiter-boy doing your job
for me. Carry your shoulders
proudly—no matter their weight.
I know you waiter-boy-I know
you waiter-boy.

Your starched white uniform boxes
me away from you with creases
standing as boundaries that I am
not to cross. I will interfere
sweet male. You know me.

Sweet waiter-boy, my glass is near
empty child. Do you see it?
You should know empty from full.
Do not assume that I do now know
the difference.

I am calling you dear one.
Do not turn away from me.
Bring your pitcher of water and
sit beside me. Pour me some
refreshment and explain yourself.

Christy M. Ikner

Untitled

Rain falls on the
corner street lamp,
like the patter
of a trotting
horse.
Snow covers all
the streets like
a big white fluffy
blanket.
Thunder may be frightening
to some, as little
children hide under
their cozy blankets
waiting to get a
kiss good night
from their loving
parents, Mom and
Dad.

Christine Seminara

Love's Death Lost

I once knew a great man
He died three times in my soul.
But from then on, he was
The greatest man I'd ever known.
I loved him greatly, I loved him dear,
I wanted him to take my dreams
To near, to touch or feel,
But to just hold in my heart
As if he were the pinnacle
Of my soul's desire and fear.

He died twice in my heart,
This great man he was.
We both wanted what we thought
We could never have
Because we were afraid
Of each other's love.

So we both died once,
For mortality's sake
Alone and grim we were,
Holding the key to each others heart.

Shelly Annice Shanks

Of Castles and Violets

Cold towering castles
Glass and steel,
Lighted battlements at which
  I gasp
Noble men and ladies
Strut, silent
Peacock hues at which
  I gape
Sound and smell of demons
Captured, tamed
Willing transports at which
  I grasp.

And behind my heel
Crushed, a tiny violet
A futile struggle of which
  I did not know.

Jacqueline H. Teng

Red and Yellow Tulips

Red and yellow tulips
Reached boldly upward
From frayed green leaves
Their flower
Like cupped hands
Swaying in the Spring wind
Valiantly displaying themselves
Until their struggle is too great
And they yield peacefully
To their destiny
And fade away.

Warren Galli

Myrtle's Turtles

The turtles of Myrtle's jump hurdles
"How, do you ask, is it done?"
Well, to tell you the truth
You'll have to ask Ruth
For she's the ol' tortoise who won

Ruth, the expounder, I've found her
Perhaps she can give you the shake
for Myrtle says Ruth
has forgotten one truth
We turtles belong in the lake

Yes Ruth, you have told us your tale
but we still want to know how you sail
like a horse over beams
when it knows it redeems
carrots, the long ones, in pails

At last I'm here to be truthful
so here it is once and for all
when Myrtle says jump
I lift this old rump
before she can heat up her soup bowl.

Dru Melissa Hixson

For You

My heart is filled with hope
That you'll stay in my arms
And not ever leave me
You keep me from harm
I thank you now
And I thank you then
For all the good times
We have spent
  Together.

Kory E. Newell

Cherished Love

Smell the sweet ocean breeze.
Hear the wind in the trees.
Feel our love blossom and grow.
I shall love you more tomorrow.

Our time together is heaven sent.
I love each and every moment.
Happiness dances in our eyes.
Ahead; nothing but blue skies.

Memories fill my heart with bliss;
the tenderness of our first kiss,
the songs that we danced to,
the lovely things you say and do.

The love we share is very strong.
Together, we cannot go wrong.
I have given you my heart to hold.
I pray our love never grows old.

Melissa Shank

A Heart

There once was a Heart
On a throne next to mine
With Magical features
That are so hard to find
She had beauty and elegance
Full of joy and delight
She emitted fine radiance
And possessed the beauty of flight
The Heart carried wings
The color of Gold
That sparkled in the night
Like the stars bright and bold
But there's emptiness that fills
My Heart on this day
For the heart that I loved
Took flight and flew away

Brian A. C. Williams

You Just Open Your Eyes And See

Why don't you look with your heart?
Are you afraid of the surprise?
You don't see love or desperation,
You watch only with your eyes.

You see a hobo cross the street,
His poor eyes are calling, "Help me."
But seldom would you notice this,
For you just open your eyes and see.

Why is it that you are so depraved?
Do you not hear my constant cries?
Your empathy has forced me to ask you,
Why do you look with only your eyes?

If you give that child a hug and kiss,
Then watch her unwillingly depart.
You will know the inner strength
You get, when seeing with your heart.

Andy Valdez

Rain! Rain!

Rain! Rain! Don't go away
I will take you everyday
You give water to the earth
Which all seeds need
To give birth.

Amber Lee Lassiter

Naptime Blues

The pool is full,
The sandbox is ready,
Where's little Haley?
We miss her already.

The yard is empty,
The toys are in place,
Where's little Haley?
Is she coming to play?

It's so quite, with no one around,
No laughing voices, shouting aloud,
Naptime is lonely,
For all Haley's toys.

Then just two hours later,
The door flies open with a crash,
There's little Haley,
Back for more fun at last!

Teresa Alexander

Our Last Day

To My Late Husband Mark Brown Stovall

It's a little windy, but a warm
November morning. The sun is
really bright, I think to myself
as I sat on the bed watching you
sleep wondering why you have a
smile on your face. Suddenly you
open your eyes and raise upon your
pillow looking at the wall in
front of you. Softly but clearly I
heard you say, come and get me
you never heard me call your
name the tears I shed that day were
all in vain. The words you spoke,
the smile on your face the feeling of
peace in the room keeps me going
on and makes each day with out
you a little easier to bear knowing
that your God and mother had
come for you and you, my love,
are at peace.

Saundra McCraig Stovall

A Tornado

A tornado is near what
should I do, sit and
Watch or run, as
fast as I can.
Go under a bridge,
or into a ditch,
Oh what should
I do it's coming
right towards
me. Help me somebody!
The wind started
to fall, I was hit by a branch
and was knocked out.
The first thing I noticed
I was still alive.

Ashley Welsch

A Last Goodbye

You have waited for this day,
for many years.
But now it has come,
and brought many tears.

The countdown has ended,
today you shall depart.
The year has ended,
with many in your heart.

Your future is now,
it has come so fast.
Your Senior year,
is now in your past.

What is next?,
that is for you to say.
But I do know,
you'll never forget those
    Last Senior Days!

Amy E. Bryant

C'thula!

The blue skies of Rome,
A falling holy empire.
Orgies of the mind,
Dressed in physical attire.
Dreams of sanctuary.
Our absent minds still crave.
Erotic visions in boredom,
A leather bound slave.
A dance with cast down spirits,
A dark and empty grave.
For chaos we scream eternal
His long forgotten name.

Larry D. Anderson

Violent Storm

As lightening streaks across the sky
The vibrant thunder roars,
Tearing the curtains of heaven in two
Baring her hidden doors.

A torrent of rain falls heavily
Spilling the narrow streams,
Eating away the softened earth
As it widens out her seams.

The wind whips up with raging fury
Displaying her terrible wrath,
Violently blowing on her course,
Claiming what's in her path.

Then on it moves to the open sea
Exhausting her wicked force,
Leaving a wake of destruction
As she surrenders to her source.

Louise E. Fogell

Dear God

How I wonder if it might
In the quiet night
I seen you coming
In the bright moon light
My thoughts raced through my head
Dear gold am I dead?
Has my love really come?

Bernie Thurman

Good Dogs

Dogs can sit up, dogs can stand.
Dogs can sometimes shake your hand.

Dogs are docile, dogs are delight,
Dogs are bashful, dogs are bright.

Dogs do dog shows, dogs do tricks.
Dogs catch frisbees.
Dogs fetch sticks.

Dogs are loyal
Dogs defend
Dog are always, man's best friend.

"Bad Dogs"
Dog's jump fences. Dogs give chase.
Dogs lick neighbors in the face.

Dogs like bushes. Dogs like trees,
Dogs like sharing all their fleas.

Dogs chew flowers, dogs dig holes,
Dogs knock over doggy bowls.

Dogs are frisky. Dogs forget.
Dogs are friendly, when they're wet.

Heidi Risley

Memories Never Left Behind

Memories kept in our heart
Remind us of our lives
Our ambitions and our dreams
Were never left behind

When we think of long ago
The world of yesterdays
Our minds cry to the heavens
Asking "why couldn't it just stay?"

Our childhood was full of life
and everlasting love
We'd smile at the sunsets
and gaze at stars above

Now that we are older
We wish a fair a'deau
To childish ways, childish hearts,
and life forever new

Lisa VanNostrand

The Sun Will Shine Again

Today the sunshine may be
hiding behind a big dark cloud
If you look beyond the clouds
there's still sunshine to be found

There's a rough rocky road in
the way of your path
But there are nice green pastures
after you pass over that

I've seen beautiful spring days come,
and I've also seen them go
I've felt the heart of summer,
and I've seen a long winter's snow

Happiness is like sunshine
and sorrow is like rain
We experience them both
We loose and we gain.

Cynthia Freeman

Love Potion Number 10

A stick of red lipstick,
a bottle of cologne.

A boy and a girl,
and a room of their own.

A very sad love song,
and the lights turned
down low.

I won't tell you the rest,
that's all you need to know.

Joanne Moore

Happy Anniversary

We wanted to give you a
    special gift,
To show how much we care
But how we feel is something
    that nothing could compare
You've given each other so much more
Than words could ever say
We see that love grow even stronger
With every passing day.
You may have weathered many storms
You may have shed some tears
But looking back on all you've shared
It's been a great 25 years.

Deborah Vadala

A Vulnerable Moment

This thin coat
    protect me from harm

I feel invincible
    my flesh invisible

Torn and caught
    turning red

Like a petal
    how do I live

Morrow wrapping what makes Life,
    crush ourselves.

Diana M. Henthorn

My Love

I cry when you're there,
I cry when you're away,
I feel lost and gone astray.

When I look at your smiling face,
I feel happy,
and strange,
like I'm in a fairy tale place.

When you hold me tight,
and you pull me near,
suddenly,
I lose all my fears.

When I smile,
you laugh,
when I cry,
you cry,
your love for me,
sometimes,
makes me want to die.

You mean the world to me,
... I love you.

Mindi Grim

And We Remember...

Life is like a rose,

When were young it springs
    to life,
A bud on a stem of green.

As we age,
    it blossoms,
Bringing forth vibrant colors.

When life comes to an end,
    the petals fall off.
Leaving the sweet fragrance,
    of the rose behind.

And we remember...

The soft feel of the petals.
    The lush color of the rose.
And the memories of its fragrance
    are forever etched upon our minds.

Shirley Ashurst

Self Control

Once I had a knot in my shoe,
And it would not come out.
I tried and tried and pulled and pulled
But it would not come out
I got so mad I kicked the door,
And stubbed my little toe,
If only I had learned a little
    bit of self control.
I never liked to brush my teeth,
I wish that I could stop.
I'd have more time for candy bars,
And drinking soda pop.
But soon my teeth would hurt so bad,
From all of those cavities,
I'd better learn some self control
So this won't happen to me.

Jeana Bagno

Confession of Love

You may not see me now
My hurting wounded child
But this I'll have you know
I've been there all the while.

And dark that it may seem.
There is no light of day
But I the Lord of Love
Will guide you on your way! Amen!

Richard Eichhorn

Sea Shell

I walked along the beach one day
And found upon the sand
A sea shell, white and delicate
And heavy in my hand

For one brief moment I stood still
Lost in another time
When you gave me a sea shell
And put your hand in mine

I shook my head and, turning, threw
The shell into the sea
I left them lost beneath the waves —
A shell, a tear, a memory.

Anna Stanford

"A Child's Dream"

A child's dream
    Is full of love,
Some dream they owned
    The whitest dove.

And other children
    Dream and dream,
Of chocolate pie
    With swirls of cream.

The female child
    Dreams of dolls,
That sleep and walk
    But never falls.

Guns and trucks
    And silver toys,
Are major dreams
    Of little boys.

A child's dream
    Is full of peace,
And never shall
    Their dreams decease.

Leza Williamson Johnson

Me

I am the wind,
Fierce and strong.

I am a fight,
Needed and wrong.

I am the sun,
Warm and bright.

I am emotion,
Happy and dark as night.

I am the rain,
Miserable and steady.

I am a cloud,
Floating and ready.

I am a cut,
I hurt and I heal.

I am a flower,
Growing and I feel.

Katlyn Groppi

Silver Linings

Silver linings
And a thousand years old
Like children crying
And the days of old
Nothing more
Nothing bold
Again I'm not
The perfect mold
Just still crying
And close to sold
Cause I've just been told
There is no more
Silver linings
From the days of old
With only one birthday
And time as old
I'll have silver linings
As a thousand years old

J. Pascual Garcia

He Bit The Bullet

As the lead shatters
The cranium another
Life has been lost.

The life for this soul
Is over in its human form, but
Has just returned to its
Own original form.

    Will it be heaven?
    Will it be hell?

No one knows for certain
For the choice has already been
    Decided.

For he who created this being
    Knows where this soul is
    Headed. For this soul is
On a road that no one knows
Where it leads.

Ben Barton

Christmas

Christmas is a time for joy
And not because of every toy.
It is because of Jesus's birth.
He came to save each man on earth.

Kaylynn Reed

Fleeting Thoughts

I put my hand to paper
    to write a little rhyme
The telephone kept ringing
    so I didn't have the time.
Thoughts that had been neatly
    tucked into my busy brain
Fell away and lost themselves
    like gently falling rain.
I thought I could reorganize them
    as the day went on
But to my grief and sadness
    the messages were gone.

Betty J. Mair

This Time I'll Fall In Love

Your heart beats the way
in my dreams of today
close to the flowers of yesterday
and when you touch me
this time I'll fall in love.

I'm yours in my mind
dreaming tonight in time
of the falling maple leaves I find
and then you are there
this time I'll fall in love.

Slowly at your side
your seesaw soul I ride
in the pink pitter patter I slide
I have dreams you see
this time I'll fall in love.

And the world will know
seeing that inward glow
of your spirit as the wind will blow
you're the one that cares
this time I'll fall in love.

Penny Houston

One Last Wish

You just had one beer
Now there's no way you can steer
The car that you drive
which took a life.

You caused a disaster
Not looking forward to here after
There's no way to survive
Only God can save your life.

You don't want to die
So you're wondering why
You took a drink
And didn't think.

Now that you have died
You wish you would've tried
To avoid this drama
Which caused a trauma

Now you're looking back
On all you left behind
You wish there was a button
That just said rewind.

Lindsay Wilkin

The Tide

The tide moves out
and runs along.
It goes about
as if nothing can go wrong.
Sweeping along
until it must turn again,
to go back through
where it has been.
Racing and tumbling
through the sea,
to make its way
back to you and me.
And when the tide feels
the sand beneath
its soft, damp,
and little feet,
the tide knows that
it must begin
its long, long journey
back again.

Elizabeth Darter

Awareness

Hast thou noticed the fields,
The streams and the trees,
The glowing flowers,
The buzzing bees?

Hast thou heard the songs
Of birds on the wing,
The sounds of every living thing?

Hast thou smelled the fragrance
Of a bakery baking bread
Of roses yellow, pink and red?

Hast thou touched a furry kitten
And listened to him purr,
Held him gently not to make him stir?

Hast thou spoken to the Holy one,
And thanked Him for these things?
For when you do He smiles and He sings!

Richard J. Johnson

Super Teen

Super Teen is my kind of magazine.
I like the posters, I like the stars,
But most of all I like my Super Teen.
I like the smiles, I like the contests,
But most of all I like my Super Teen.
I like J.T.T., and I like being me.
So please, don't take my Super Teen!

Sunday Frey

Looking Glass!

I look deeply into your eyes
seeking out your thoughts
Desires! Hopes! Dreams!
Others before me have ventured glances.
Some intrigued! Some repulsed!
None ever telling
what they found.

Are the questions hidden
within the questions you ask?

A brave soul I am
who seeks out the truth
torturing!!
The pain of experience

In your eyes
I see the scars
the injuries inflicted
by the truth
As you cried out in vain
for others to listen
to your questions

Christopher R. Gourley

My Grandfather

I walked along the shore
leaving footprints on my way
and I stopped to watch the ocean
quickly washing them away

I thought of someone close
when I sat upon the sand
and through water warm and salty
I felt a gentle hand

It beckoned me to come
and keep it company
for it was all alone
forever, in the sea

I splashed into the water
an infinite embrace
and through the crystal surface
I saw his loving face

He seemed to say "I love you"
as I stared into his eyes
and for a wishful moment
I was pacified.

Lisa Villarreal

Sara

My heart overflows with love
As I gaze at the purity of your
Beautiful soul reflected in your
Innocent blue eyes.

Sandra Terrell

Land of Dreams

Long ago in the land of dreams
It came to be what I couldn't see
the visions of joy and family
when I was in the land of dreams

I dreamt of all the possibilities
the way things should and ought to be
but thrown in were the
responsibilities
and the dreams got shattered by the
realities
when you leave the land of dreams
your days and nights turn gray
you close your eyes and turn away
but the shattered dreams and pain
remain
but now has come the time at last
when the shattered dreams and pain
have passed
and the visions of love and joy have
cast me back in the land of dreams.

Lacie

Not All Angels Wear Wings

An angel can have
long, shining gold hair;
soft, feathery wings,
and skin soft and fair.

But I know many angels
who don't have these things.
They are loving and giving,
but they never wear wings.

An angel can be
a spiritual being.
What a spectacular sight
for one to be seeing!

But not all angels are the same,
for I know many angels who
help, care, and give,
but are people just like me and you.
Not all angels wear wings.

Elizabeth Ann Reddington

Your Mother

I see the beauty of your Mother
With her gentle voice and hand,
Outstretched to protect you
As now, you try to stand.

I see the smile of your Mother
So kind, sincere and true,
Trying to direct your words
The first you ever knew.

I see the kindness of your Mother
As shown by her deep love,
How she tenderly directs you
In ways ordained by God above.

I see the deeds of your dear Mother
She performs day by day,
I trust she'll be remembered
For these kind acts I pray.

I see you grown to full manhood
Your Mother's job is done,
For the love your Mother gave you
Today you are a faithful Son.

Mary M. Borello

As Time Perishes

Everything is but a
beat of my heart,
It's as quick as a
blink of my eye,
It's only a wisp of wind.
But not you,
You're there to be my friend.
It's hard sometimes I know,
For I - I can be as
cold as the snow.
When everyone else bails,
you friend, never fail.
You're as warm as the sun
as I know it,
You're as wise as the moon is lit.
You, friend, have been there
for me through fears and tears
And that is why I pray
that you will be there
throughout the years.

Dawn Fleming

Clouds

With a wispy shade of white
Covered with a vanishing grey,
Oh, the beautiful sight,
That passes by everyday,
Over the tallest trees,
Tallest mountains, over seas,
To see through a window pane,
Standing out beyond,
All creations,
Taken on all mysterious shapes,
and forms of the living,
Floating above and beyond,
the dark filled sky,
They drift pass the full moon,
To make at ease,
a long and peaceful night,
Quickly passing,
Slowly fading,
So now this sets your heart at ease,
Which the wonderful clouds do please.

Tracy L. Walters

Europe

The day after Salvador Dali died
The wind was blowing from Spain
Vertebral clouds spread across the sky
Mountains dropped their grey light
To the sea.

The day after Salvador Dali died
Was the day before
Claudio was leaving for Athens
To bring a coat, to go to Belgrade
In it.

Marlene M. Royle

Green

Money is green
Turtles are green
Leaves are green
Vines are green
Eyes are green
You are green
But hold your breath
And now you're blue

Katie Rock

Haiku

In the morning mist ....
When all the world is quiet
A sea gull appears.

Gloria A. Easley

Still Life

A shiny pink glass bowl
Blushing apples hide shyness beneath
    sprawling plump grapes
One partly-eaten Mexican platano
    contemplates her fate
Wrinkled wax hugs the body of
    a fading candle
A Communion-white table cloth.

Like your photo, the painting only
    seems real
I touch the canvas gently
Its lifeless beauty mirrors
    my sadness
An anxious tear escapes
But I smile

What if frames held no pictures
    at all?

Lottie Carney

The Trail

There is a world that no one knows,
in which people go to pay,
homage to a different kind,
of normal man they say.

How far is this land,
beyond the road,
the path of a different light,
that shines on the side,
that solves the issue,
of the pain we must all fight.

There will be a signal,
a sign of aid,
an angle of the unknown,
a new form with shade.

This brand of action,
has instilled a spirit,
we must all grow,
with the understanding,
that we all hear,
that we all know.

Rafe Friedman

Spring

The wind blows,
The flowers grow,
The rain it comes,
Springs begun.

The animals are born,
We plant our corn,
The Belgium's graze,
While I sit and gaze.

Now's the time we have our fun,
aren't you glad that
springs begun.

Amy Norsworthy

My Grandfather

My grandfather was a stately man,
As good as good could be.
He was always so much fun,
And loved to play with me.
He looked like Jesus
With a long beard - so neat,
I never saw him angry,
He was so loving and sweet.
I was twelve years old,
When Jesus took Him away
I could not understand then.
And can't this very day.
I know you must have needed him
To make heaven a brighter place,
I forgive you Jesus
But I'll always miss his kindness
    And His heavenly face.

Jennie Fant

An Ode to a Thief of Time

O' Sylvan Nass
Thou thief of time
That I should long to
See thee go
From hither on the
Pasture green
To Yonder Mist
The Ever glow

The hour doth pass
'Tis sure a crime
That linger here
I must, yet know
In vain I wait
For light from thee
Who nary a morsel
Can bestow.

Robert Goldberg

What Is The Key?

What is the key to happiness?
Is it the dreams we all possess?
Is it the smile of someone fair?
Is it in schemes or what we share?

What is the key?
Is there a key?
What is the key to happiness?
Is it the wind-its soft caress?
Is it a voice that floats on air?
Is it a song that makes us care?

How short our lives,
Three score and ten;
We scale the heights,
Then fall again.

What is the key to happiness?
Is it good deeds and then God bless?
What is the key to happiness?
Oh, what is the key?

Theodore G. Twitchell

Love

You were here but now you're
gone. I have only memories left
to help me go on. I never knew
it could hurt this much for just
a few hours of your tender
touch. The yearning I have in
my heart is true, because I
can give my love to no one else
but you. My heart is broken
this is true, but I can only
love one person and that
person is you. I hope someday
you decide that it should
have been I by your side.
They say parting is such
sweet sorrow, I would do
anything to be by your side
tomorrow.

Gerri Casson

Crossroads

Sometimes I wonder,
where do we go from here?
We've been through so much,
through this past year.

I may by gone next year,
but we'll always be together,
no matter how far apart we are,
don't worry, things will get better.

Eventually, we will be together again,
go through more bumpy roads,
but remember just one thing,
we will meet again, at the crossroads.

Nikki Seymour

Untitled

Sing a song of solitude
A pocket full of Poe
A satchel filled with Emerson
And ee cummings - no
Not quite of them, not quite,
But of their dreams, their visions,
Fears that haunted them at night
When up they sat (as I have)
Coffee wired at desks
And of their spirits freely gave
(At least they tried their best)

Yet they were so successful
That I just feel depressed
When with humble, crooked imagery,
I my dreams express.

Tommy Scott

What Do You Feel

Walking hand in hand
you fingers touch
your mind wonders
you wonder what he's thinking
does he like me
does he even care
does he feel what I feel
when he let go to open the door
I let go forever

Margaret A. Pistone

And I Owe It All To You

I know, Mom, I've been
More trouble than I should
I know I hurt your feelings
More than others would

But I know that one day
My dreams will all come true
And I'll tell all my fans
That I owe it all to you

"Cause you brought me into this world
And you can take me out"
As you would sometimes say
When I would fuss and pout

I struggled when I was younger,
All I wanted was a friend
Little did I know that
It was on you I could depend

I've gone through some changes
And can you believe I'm through?
I graduated, Mom
And I owe it all to you

ShaLynn Blair

Untitled

Jumbled
thoughts
inside
a brain
twisted
words
not one
the
same
falling
quickly
too late
to catch
the words
are
gone
no
more
is
said

M. Christine Garrity

Life

Life is such a troubled thing
such a wondrous expedient affair.
Does it possess less the meaning
If but a plant would be its lair.
Should an animal be the scapegoat
when life's troubles come our way.
If we be the master creature
do we have the right to say
    God gives life and he can take it,
For this is the righteous way.
Should we use our means to take it
when alas we cannot make it.
Let us spread the world with joy
using only that we need.
Giving right unto the lesser creatures
and thus forget our human greed.

Theodios Won Knucklebuster

Mother

For as long as I remember,
You were always there for me.
To give me confidence,
To give me support,
To give my life meaning.

For as long as I remember,
You were always the person
I looked up to.
So strong,
So beautiful,
So full of love.

For as long as I remember,
I pray I will always be able to share,
All the love you have filled me with,
For you are everything
A mother should be.

Toni Kesinger Birdsell

The Love of My Life

I never knew I could love so much
and be so afraid,
Hurting deeply inside for the child
I had made.
My son was the most beautifullest
child there could be,
No one could make him smile,
the way he smiled at me.
There were days when he made
me feel good,
Doing all of the crazy things only
he and I understood.
I never tried to blame anyone
because I didn't have the time,
For he was nobody else's sick baby,
only mine.
Now I have no one to take care
of and it cuts like a knife,
I never really wanted to lose
the love of my life.

Tiffany Benefield

Reflections

Saying, seeing, being, doing
Times have come for us to share.
Can we say what really happens,
When so few truly know what's there.

Is there truly one who loves me?
Does this fairy tale come true?
And when it does, will she stay near,
Or run away when love is through?

Peace and hope, and love and life
Are things we all desire.
But can these each exist alone
Without some loss, or pain, or strife?

Our truths create hypocrisies,
For they are what we most avoid.
We bend and bulge, we tint, we tear.
The mirror held is rarely clear.

J. Cawthra Taylor

When Summer Sun
Melts Winter's Snow

As summer's sun melts winter's snow
The time has come for us to know
That seasons, like our moods do change
And we must now, our lives arrange.

Far above and way below,
Our ever changing thoughts do go.
We think of death and think of life,
And all that's good and all our strife
Of all our joys and of our woe,
All of our grief and deep sorrow.

It's time to let the sun shine in,
So winter's dismal chill can't win.
We only reap what we shall sow,
Not what another does bestow.

And when the earth does warm from sun,
Our days of cold and bleak are done.
The time has come for us to know,
That summer sun melts winter's snow.

Harriet N. Feldman

The Divine Original

I am not like you
Though sometimes I long to be.
I have so many faults
And when I look, that's all I see.

But God sees only what He made,
Unique in every way,
With gifts and talents all my own
To use for Him each day.

He desires not a copy
Of someone famous or smart;
He wants someone He can use
So He gave me a willing heart.

He could have made me like you,
Exactly in your mold,
But would I then have any worth
As silver or precious gold.

No, I am not like you
A copy I'll never be.
I am a divine original
Proof of God's ingenuity.

Florence Van Horn

Forgotten Dreams

Now I lay me down to sleep,
But wonder when I wake...
What was in my mind last night?
What dreams did pass me by?
What kind of people did I meet,
Or were there none at all?
What did I say? To whom, and when?
Where did my travels take me?
Was it fun, or did I cry?
There's no one here to tell me.
For I'm the only one that knows
What was in my mind last night,
But it seems that I've forgotten
What my sleeping eyes did see.
My dreams have come and now have gone
Somewhere I do not know.
If only my mind remembered
What my closed eyes do see,
Then dreams would be much clearer,
And I'd be able to answer me.

Erin Steinbrunner

Captured

The silence of the halls
The echoing of the footsteps
The wafting of the music
The beauty of the moment
Captured
The stillness of the air
All that is real
All that is not
To speak would be ruin
An end to the mystery
Empty tables
Empty glasses
Open the books stale from age
Releasing a thousand tales
Regrets and fears
You can almost hear them
Hopes and joys
Almost tangible
All there
Captured

Samantha L. Russell

Untitled

Oh to write words
Powerful words,
painting pictures
that eat at men's souls
oh to write verses
lingering verses,
with meaning
that leave minds searching
oh to write feelings
profound feelings
often thought of,
rarely written down.

Courtney Girdwood

This Anger

This anger is tearing me apart ...
oh no what should I do? I feel
as though my heart is on fire.
It hurts, it frustrating,
but most of all, it's painful.

Everyday I walk around... trapped!
The doors are closed, and there's
no way out... I'm scared, frightened,
and sad.

The anger is a tidal wave... breaking
the dam ... the pressure keeps building
till I can't take anymore!!
Oh no, what do I do?!!

Andrea K. Bailey

Born Too Soon

I never touched your tiny face,
But in my heart it's you I embrace.
I never heard your newborn cry,
Instead I'm asking God "why?"
I never saw your gentle smile,
But you'll always be my little child.

Even though we're worlds apart,
I hold you close within my heart.
I place you now in God's strong arms,
Safe from worry, safe from harms.
And when in heaven again we meet,
Then my child, we'll be complete.

Jule Ann Martin

Dream

I dream of you at day
I dream of you at night
Once before I dream I was
the Sun, shining my warmthness
upon your body
I dream I was the Sea which
washed all the bad memories away
I dream I was the Star which
holds wished and dreams just for you
I dream I was the wind, which
allowed only the gentle breeze
through your lovely hair

I also dream you were a
princess in a deep sleep
and only I with a magic kiss
can bring you to your own
two feet

But what I think is not what
it seems what I felt for you
is not a Dream

Ruong Huynh

Alone

How can I ease the tension?
When the cause is not known.
How can I even mention,
that I'd rather be alone...?
How can I make it work again?
when working takes two,
how can I begin to mend
when all that I am is confused?
How can I listen to you
when you don't hear me?
How can I feel so abused
and still this need this need?
How can I even write
when you don't want to read?
How can I stop this fight
before it starts to bleed?
How can I trust your intentions
when the result is not shown?
How can I even mention
that I'd rather be alone...?

Leslie Duprey

Untitled

She stands alone
the eyes of strangers overlooking
the blemish in their not-so perfect
world. Many a times she tried
to find the key to open
the doors to their society, but
every door she opened led to
the same fear and pain.
And then again, she'd walk
in the shadows of the forgotten.
Why can't they see it?
What blinds them so?
If one only knew.
Until then,
I stand alone.

Kirsten Tourville

For Jeffrey And Donna

May the Lord look down upon you
with peace and joy to give,
And may His blessings be forthcoming
for as long as you both shall live.

May His light shine bright about you
through your love for one another,
And keep you locked within his arms
as husband, wife, friend, lover.

May you walk this path you've chosen
with fairness, trust, and love,
And reap the harvest of life's true joy
through His blessings from above.

God Bless you both.

Marilyn R. Seymour

The Mystical Garden

I glide across the valley of hope,
I swim through the river of faith,
I fly with the eagle of wisdom,
I eat with the animals of hunger,
When I reach the gates of heaven,
I cross the Kingdom of peace,
Finally, I am in the mystical garden.

Megan Seckerson

Untitled

Standing at the edge
I feel a cold wind blow
The leaves rustle
And the moonlight glows

Looking through the veil
Of lies and untruths
I see a world below
That can burn and soothe

The years pass slowly
As the moonlight fades
I fear the dawning of light
As I move to seek shade

The valley looms near
As I descend into its depth
I roam through the fields
Running to catch my breath

Margarita Gomez

The Change Of Seasons

Above and about the world
The mutiny lightning spreads.
In its light and violent threads
The peal of thunders hold.

I hear the voice of the rain,
In forests growth and bloom.
Behind the forest I see a train,
Where many trains have zoomed

I hear the music of the birds
So pure, so sweet and sorrow.
Those sounds are natures words
Will sound and sing tomorrow.

In future I see a summer gaze
And have the natures feelings.
That can be so much more appealing
After the fall and winter days

Michael Kuznetsov

It's About Time

Thank you Lord for your grace
That you gave free to me
Thank you Lord for redeeming
And setting this captive free

Thank you Lord for your love
That will never go away
Thank you Lord for your peace
I get from day to day

Thank you Lord for your mercy
That endures forever
Thank you Lord for life's abundance
You know what? You're so clever

I thought it time to thank you Lord
Because I love you so
I also appreciate you, too
I needed to let you know.

Winifred Britton

Deeper Love

For all the times you've been there,
For all the words you don't say,
My love grows deeper for you,
With each passing day

With warm smiles that welcome,
And hugs that follow too,
With tears of compassion,
My love grows deeper for you

With eyes of understanding,
Gentle touches too,
A few words of encouragement,
My love grows deeper for you

With patient waiting
Kindness follows through,
And loving understanding,
My love grows deeper for you

My love grows deeper
A love that can't be taken away,
My love grows deeper,
And it's there to stay

Jill Nelson

Water Way

A watery mist
Settles upon my eyes,
As the man you once knew
Slowly wilts and dies.

A teardrop rain
Softly cools my devil heart,
Washing over all the pain
To you I impart.

A fearsome flood
Splashes this forlorn soul,
Cleansing its black causeways
Darkened with soot and coal.

A dew resolves
Within my spirit renew'd;
I again redeem myself
As the man you once knew.

A river flows
'Tween our gardens bloom'd together,
And through any storm
We can weather, together, forever.

Christopher Black

In Me

When I was lonely
He was there
He showed me his love
Way beyond compare
He lifted me up
He cleansed my soul
I was torn and broken
He made me whole

My heart is now full
His love overflows
Each person who sees me
Automatically knows
There is something different
Maybe not quite right
I'm odd to some
Maybe weird in their sight

Why so content?
No riches to see
My friend, my dear friend
The richness is in me

Mary Flaherty

Serpent's Savior

Am I the serpent's savior
Hanging on to frightened eyes
Holding souls that want to go
Letting time just pass us by

Knowing that the end is near
Which one of us will cry
Am I the serpent's savior
Possessing love that's gonna die

Am I the serpent's savior
On the pain of love do I thrive
It's getting hard to reach your heart
Do you really want me out of your life

The wall that separates us both
Towers up and through the sky
If dreams are all you're searching for
Then what the hell am I

Am I the serpent's savior

Edward Nixon

He Is Very Cool

He is very cool
But a little bit small
He is there but no one can see him.
Sometimes he appears,
but in a blink of an eye
He is soft as pedals on a rose,
But yet strong as a rock
He is something that everyone
must find out in their life.
Some people say he is like a roof
over their heads.
Or a turn from each mountain.
He is so special that one person
can experience him by themselves.

Heather Shockley

This Beauty Surrounds Their Terror

The sky turns dark
as the sun goes down.
Tears well in their eyes
as stars fill up the sky.

This simple act of nature
brings peace to most.
For many others,
fear is the host.

Oh! Please believe me.
I did not error.
For many,
This beauty surrounds their terror.

Sherry Lynn Pabst

Forever Free

Lost inside my own thoughts
I was a lonely prisoner
All alone in the world
Wandering through the misery
But now I am set free

You gave me life
Allowing me to see
With sweet calmness
Giving me hope
And setting me free

Forever free to live
Free to give
Free to smile
Free to be happy
And free enough to love

I use to be all alone
Insecure and cold
Then you gave me your love
Washing away the hurt

And now, I am forever free.

Julie A. Labbe

The Pier

I think of you, dear
Each day we're apart
Each special moment
Save deep in my heart.
Sweet thoughts of the nights
We spent on the pier
Gentle waves lapping
Dispelling my fears.
You helped me to laugh
When I wanted to cry
Giving me strength
When I felt I could die.
Memories of talks
As we sat on the pier
Your gentle caress
As you dried my tears.
Loneliness left me
As you held me tight
Alone on the pier
On those warm summer nights.

Susanne L. Bergeron

Reflections

Whenever I think of "Old Glory"
My heart fills with wonder and pride
I think of the hard won battles,
of our soldiers, side by side,
We're call Medics and nurses,
where dedication brings praises.

Families suffered and worried too
About those fighting a cause so true,
We pray for the countries abound,
Still struggling for freedom so hard

Now we are her for a purposes
to help those depending on us,
Someday will meet on the
Golden place,
and see her love ones - face to face.

Vivian Johnson Borders

I Dream

I dream of good things,
like warm, soft words
and beautiful mischievous
angels.
I dream of a waterfall
and a lovely blue sky,
I dream of fragrant flowers
zapping colors across
the horizon.
I dream of sharing
thoughts and secrets
and laughing together,
I dream of music, the songs of Spring
and long walks in the park.
I dream of hugs, of love,
of arms holding me tight,
I dream of never being
alone!

Barbara Walters

What I've Lost

Of all the things I've lost
I miss you most of all
The days of sitting by the phone
Waiting for your call

Even my brightest days are dark
Since I can't spend them with you
The precious days we had together
Were entirely too few

When I remember things we used to do
And may never do again
It tears apart my heart and soul
And they may never ever mend

I miss seeing your smiling face
And feeling your gentle touch
They were the highlight of my day
And I miss them very much

They're no words I can say
Or anything I can do
That can fully explain the depth
Of how much I miss you

Jeffrey Glenn Ayers

White Ghosts

White ghosts
Caught in trees
And on barbed wire fences
Billowing,
Bellowing,
Begging me
To surrender.

Theresa Brown

Sun and Moon

As the sun sets,
giving each sun a moon.
As the moon runs for the sun,
giving each land a new morning.
As the land sleeps,
giving each animal energy.
As the earth rotates,
giving each star discovery.
As the parties begin,
giving each person a friend.
As the light beams slowly decrease,
giving each beam a new awakening.

Lydia Laurant

Fog

Soft caressing fingers, drift
O'er hardened gritty skin
As the ocean sighs so softly
And the fog bank settles in.

Touching places in the headlands
Where nobody else has been.
Sighs of pleasure fill the dampness,
Ecstasy? Or just the wind?

Questing tongues and reaching fingers
Breach the crevices and pools,
While the cries of raging hunger
Move the sorriest of fools.

Filling places fraught with danger,
Meeting needs that can't be met.
Pulsing, churning with the current.
Release will come - but oh! Not yet!

Cries of seabirds in the distance,
Storm tossed bodies on the sand.
The fog is lifting, slowly lifting.
Letting go its lovers' hand.

Judy Purkerson

Rain

Rap-tap
Rap-tap goes the rain on my window
pane
Rap-tap
Its rhythm did wonders for very tired
soul
Rap-tap
Rap-tap
It thunders on the roof, and in my head
Rap-tap
Rap-tap
Slowly it fades away....away....
  away....
    Rap.......
      tap.

Catherine E. Marshall

Loosing Time

Where has time gone —
  it steals away so quickly!
We wonder of lost time -
  of persons gone away.

But now, to slow down -
  to feel the passing moments
  and remember what is precious.
As to linger on with love—
  Look inside oneself,
  down that narrow passage,
  leading to one's heart.
A fragile place we protect,
  with timid character.
Always fearful of what love really is -
  To see the truth yet,
  run away from it.
To be so close yet,
  so terribly afraid!
Move On! Move On!
Your Time Has Come.

Cory J. Miner

Loneliness And Solitude

Loneliness and solitude
  now seep from out my soul
Where once was splendor's glory,
  back in the days of old.

In younger years I knew of love
  and innocence possessed
but now in memories long since gone
  have passed to emptiness.

Where have ye gone frail glory
  and dream still left untold.
Departed ye from out my life
  and left my blood run cold.

What life is there within me
  since our parting come?
For if not loved we have no life
  and splendor has no name.

Evelyn Von Hagel

Tornado

"Oh, boy," I yelled to my mom,
"This is really fun!"
Then we run,
Through the forest and thickets,
All to find my cat Jimeny Crickets
"The tornado is coming," Dad yelled
We had no warning
I was left in total despair
The next morning,
My hopes of finding Jimeny Crickets
Turned to air.

Ashlee Elyse Knoll

Alone

Mom, I love you
And I miss you
And what takes you so long?
I miss you!
I wished you were here,
But you weren't.
It's night time.
What takes you so long?
Why don't you come?
I expected you to be here by now,
But you're not!

Chance Logan Smith

Caress The Lyric Gun

Come into the temple, son
You've been away too long
It's time to caress the lyric gun
And bring the world a song.

Up against the wall, creativity
I've waited for you all night
And finally my reward, nativity
My words have taken flight.

I heard the wizard say go
He caused a million doves to fly
Many wise men say they know
Still hungry children cry.

Broken hearts can feel the sun
Inside the answer is locked and loaded
It's time to caress the lyric gun
The grand message must be decoded.

When truth is looking down the muzzle
And still you resolve to be free
Some day peace will solve the puzzle
And the world will have a family tree.

Richard Applegate

Your Life Touched Mine

My life has been enriched
And has been very fine.
This all has happened -
While your life touched mine.

And then you went away;
You found another lover,
Oh! Devastated me
Has gone undercover.

Forcing myself to go;
On without you; to guide
To love and console me -
Smiling - crying inside.

Thelma J. Benner

Pretty Unpretty Girls

  Satan came to rule her world,
He's come to make very pretty
unpretty girls,
  With flashes of lightning and
crashes of thunder he's come
to rule her world from under,
  Have you ever seen the moon in
the early noon, or the sun's hot
light late into the night, this is
the world of very pretty
unpretty girls,
  Walking the streets in jeans
tight at the seams smoking
cocain and full filling all of
satan's dreams.

James Kelly

Strands of Mind

Ever knowing strands of mind,
Quiet until they are heard,
Which truly know all...
Quieter...

Quieter still...
Unless we are wise,
No one will ever know...

Through infinity and
Infinite doubts,
The strands of mind can be heard...
Only if you listen...

Andy Graves

Jumper

I feel that I've been falling
  but just don't seem to care
  it's not so much the quickness
  or the swiftness of the air
For me life's not come easy
  they say I made it so
  deciding that it's come my time
  I've planned my way to go.
Depression has a funny way
  of holding on real tight
  and having no more energy
  I just gave up the fight.
Many times I'd left before
  to take my midnight walk
  this time it will be different
  this time I will not balk
Climbing up the many stairs
  reaching for the top
  I know what I must do now
  before I can be stopped.

Dennis R. Diefendorf

Ricky's Lullaby

Close your eyes
and fall asleep.
Drift off into
a world of dreams.

Close your eyes,
and you will find,
all the joys
that are in your mind.

Close your eyes,
my little lamb,
drift off into wonderland.

Robin Lord

Thanksgiving Prayer
November 25, 1993

Thank you for this house
and all the people in it.
Thank you for this day,
This hour and this minute.
Thank you for the food
that we're about to share
and Thank you Lord for keeping us
in your tender loving care.

Martin J. Gill

My Life Resembles A Little Purple Flower

I am Blinded by the big green blades of grass that tower above me, I
struggle to get the water I need to stay alive, I have to fight for
the love of the sun to make me big and strong, I'm surrounded by other
purple flowers but, I am alone, Ladybugs hover above me, afraid to
land on my soft petals, they try to see me as just one of the flowers,
but I'm different, and they can never forget, I'm a shade lighter than
the rest, so I am constantly stared at, they don't mean to cause me
any harm, but everyday I find myself getting weaker, when the wind
blows, I wish it would carry me away forever, when the rain falls hard
on my leaves, I hope and pray that it will push me back into the
unknowing earth, but as each storm comes and goes, I am still here,
different from the rest, as the sun beats down, the others start to
fade, they begin to look like me, I am no longer different, I now
blend in with the rest, But just as fate would have it, I was taken by
a naive child, I am uprooted from the only place I know and the place
I learned to love and accept, carried beyond the boundaries of my
knowledge, I am frightened by the unknown, carelessly I am discarded
upon rigid rocks that hurt me, my petals have fallen off, and my stem
is wilted with pain, and here I lay, dropped from unconcerned hands,
drowning in a puddle of tears.

Tara Lennon

Emphasis of Love

No way can there be love pronounced, is there a way for it to just go away.
Why have you bewildered me in no way or the other.
Can't I ask for your patience in the stormy clouds.
Clinging on towards the falling rain gives no other way it to repel in the rush.

For I have noticed no more sweet crosby in your face or in your voice.
The dirt I have chosen to become for you.
Only know the sorrow of thy, Lord presents me in his dungeon.
You have turned me into a love slave of thy's shadow.

Roaring bells turn my blood vessels into a chamber of no joy.
Sweeping muffs surround the enlightening of my stomach for when I pass by you.
Can't I regard the follow of your face or the sweet question that I had to replace.
One side badly delegated me for the love of your passion.

One side deliberately fell on me for liking even your hungry reactions.
Day by day the world changes so does the fashion, but day by day I
change along with my own ordinary but humble, loving tradition.
Ignore you why not forget you.
You make me turn like a beast, with the numb peachiness in the outside world.
Rights have there own causes, faults have there own consequences, and
so does our two hearts, which are not confused and are confused?

Mollishree Garg

I Pledge My Vow of Love To You Tonight

'This vow I'm pledging to you tonight is honest, and sincere and true.
I know I'll always love only you. Tonight were pledging our undying
love to each other and heaven above. 'This night will be complete and
full; always everlasting as we stand here together and pledge this
moment forever.

'In our lives we will withstand the wind that will be blowing
against us now and then. I know we'll withstand the storms that come
our way almost each and everyday. Oh and then when I look in your
eyes I see a sparkle and shine that tells me you're all mine. Oh now
I know in my heart, soul, and mind that you're the only one I'll love
forever and all time. Oh I know I'm yours and you're mine. For
when it's raining you are the sunshine in my life, the blue clouds,
in the sky, you are the stars out at night with the full moon shining
exceptionally bright. Tonight as we say our vows of love I know you
feel the same way I do when you kiss my lips and hold me tight.

I believe I'll still feel the same each and everyday; years, from now
when were old and gray and our children have grown up and moved away;
Oh I'll still be loving you and only you always and forever I believe
we'll be together. For on this night I'm pledging more than a vow
I'm pledging my life, my love for our happiness together with you my
love; I'll be always and forever true....

Audrey Meilhammer

The Train

One car, two cars,
　Maybe even ten,
As the train goes fast or slow,
　When did it start,
Well who knows when?

As it rides on the tracks,
　And the horn blows loud and clear,
As we wait and sit in our vehicles,
　What does its destiny hold?
Well no one knows where.

Now the train is gone,
　And soon another will come,
How many cars will it have,
　And how long will it run?

Marina Arlene Zorz

Child Within...

What do you know
　about an innocent mind
The child within
　searching to find,
Mysteries of life
　open and new
Ready to be conquered
　by so few
Questions of why
　looking up to understand
Hearts filled with love
　offering an open hand.
Does the heart change
　as it grows with age
Realizing pain
　to reach the next stage.
Little do we know
　about the child within
Except to love
　and forever begin...

Nancy Baker-Shearer

May 31

I visit places seen before only
in dreams of impassioned love,
but now to see them alone;
how the warm sunlight
leaves but one shadow
on the tall grasses swaying
gently in a summer breeze
and the wind carries thoughts
across the open fields
where solitary footprints wander.
The pain now is part of
the happiness then,
yet nobody knows but I,
shrouded in my darkened world
on this most glorious sunny day.
And so the day fades in the shadows
just like any other day,
but grandiose illusions fill
the empty night where a
lover's eyes ought to have been.

Daniel R. Brunstetter

Introspection: A Personally Guided Tour

The Plexiglas boxes establish the mind.
Our music's hooked all you foxes;
the whole world is blind.

Six metric shapes
show the stages of the mind.
Come on along, let's look inside.

It's icy cold in triangular scenes.
Patterns of silver and gold,
imbedded in protruding green.

In circular patterns there are luxuriant rooms.
The illustrious matter was formed around noon.

The rectangular spine, I'm surprised to find;
Sound rocking us blind on runways of the mind.

A row of three squares piled atop the brain.
Each with new fairs,
exciting the endless game.

Michael J. Haas

We've Done Our Hitch In Hell

I'm sitting here and thinking of the things I left behind
And I have to put on paper what is running through my mind.
We've dug a million ditches and cleared ten miles of ground
A meaner place this side of Hell is waiting to be found.
But there's one consolation — gather closely while I tell
When we die we'll go to heaven,
For we've done our hitch in Hell.

We've built a hundred kitchens for the cooks to stew our beans
We've stood a million guard mounts and we've never acted mean.
We've washed a million mess kits and peeled a million spuds
We've rolled a million blanket rolls and washed the Captain's duds.
The number of parades we've stood is very hard to tell
But we'll not parade in Heaven,
For we've done our hitch in Hell.

When final taps is sounded and we've laid aside life's cares
We'll do our last parade upon those shining golden stairs.
The angels all will welcome us and harps will start to play
We'll draw a million canteen checks and spend them all one day
The Great Commanding General will smile on us and tell
"Take a front seat, soldiers,
You've done your hitch in Hell."

Richard U. Taylor

God's Wonderful Love

If I would only heed my ear
The word of God to truly hear
To follow his word, and watch and pray
So as not to stumble and go astray

I need only heed his daily word
So as not to follow blindly, behind the herd
For they are of this world, and do not see
That they in Christ can be set free

When I arise to morning's warm light
I know who kept me throughout the night
So on I travel and daily I pray
That I will lead no souls astray

The journey is rocky, beset with fears
And often wet by bitter tears
I ask him, Lord, why did you keep me
He answers so that others my love might see

Lois Johnson

June's Twin

Most folks just could not believe
June and her twin were of any kin.
People from miles around would say
Whisper your secret quietly to me.
How do you find the time to systematically
Consistently plan every passing day
As your twin daily wears a hefty grin
Staring jovially into each inquisitive face
Gleefully singing, "planning is like capturing
Time and placing it in a dusty jail."

It was a cool day in the middle of May
When Judy Jocks noticed June Jocks
Holding a bright shimmery goldenrod box.
What's in your box my twin June Jocks?
Judy Jocks, I have lots of bonds and stocks
Locked in this special treasured box.
Judy Jocks turned scarlet red and said;
Today, I'll start carefully planning
My life too, and maybe someday
I'll fill my empty silver box with stocks.

Florence M. Jones

When Love Strikes

A silly adolescent teen, you ask?
Oh, no! Au contraire!
A sophisticate of thirty summers
Who plays games without a care? Wrong again.
A matron of forty, with perhaps the seven-year itch?
Oh, no, she just enjoys playing the wicked witch!
Then we have fifty or sixty or so,
Can one, at that age, still feel a bright glow?
Let's stop at seventy, going past that is not too kind,
And to do so would boggle many a mind.
But facts are facts, a reality,
She never thought ever again would she love,
But love did come, as an easing from pain,
A substitute, that engulfs her, like a gentle summer's rain,
And she hopes that for awhile
This elusive, tender joy will remain.

Kay Vossbrinck Edwards

The Inheritance

Among mother's things was a red stole.
She said her mother made it.
Sometimes on cold, winter evenings
she would let me wear the cherished wrap.
I would pretend I was a princess in a crimson gown.
On cool, spring days she would drape the lace around
her shoulders to enhance a dress of silk.
Her auburn hair would glisten with red reflections.
As she grew older, she would sit in her favorite
chair with the shawl wrapped around her frail body.
The soft cocoon eased her chilling bones.
Her hands would stroke the soft fleece, drifting
in contentment, lost in memories,
One night, in a tranquil moment, she left behind
the crimson glow.
The local thrift store received most of mother's
clothes but I kept her cherished stole.
Sometimes on cold winter evenings I wrap the crocheted
lace around me. In the gossamer reflections of memories
I am a princess again.

Doris Hartsell Brewer

Venturing

For earthlings, who are born—and strive—and die,
(God's brief parenthesis in one eternity)
How comprehend we, who are wrought in Nature's clay,
What it shall be to live forever and for aye?
And though we're all-approving such a boon
From Him who was, and is, our present stay;
Our finite minds, however far they stray,
Are baffled by the certainty of what we scarce presume.
When Christopher assayed to find a distant clime
Beyond the far horizon of man's doubting mind,
Faith it was that filled his venturing sail—
Faith that was greater than all his doubt's travail.
Oh, little bark, on Life's tempestuous sea,
Sail on! Sail on! 'Tis My hand that covereth thee.

Rush T. Morrow

High Point

A raven, or a crow?
Though we lightly raised the question
And truly wished (we thought) to learn the answer,
The bird's raucous, raspy cry was cut in half —
The second half shut out by us, discarded from our
    consciousness —
When our shoulders touched so gently
Atop the craggy prominence amid the ancient spruce and pine.

How small we were, insignificant but to ourselves
As we embraced, unmoving, for a long and tender moment
In that sanctuary of beauty both visible and inferred;
A single, whispered word — it was your name — the sole
    intrusion on the ensuing symphony
That would have swelled the grandest concert hall
Had those thousand violins been real.

No other words were sought or needed
To certify the truth and ardor of that moment,
When breeze-borne clean-scents from your hair
And sentiments delivered through encircling arms
Gave too-brief taste of purest joy.

Neil A. Poppensiek

My Friend Will Be There

When I am alone and want someone to talk to
or just to be around I know
My Friend Will Be There.

If I am bored and need someone to put a
little excitement into my day
I know My Friend Will Be There.

If I am sad or mad and need someone to cheer me up
or calm me down all I have to do is
go to My Friend and He Will Be There.

There are times when I want to talk to My Friend
in the middle of the night all I have
to do is get out of bed, down on my Knees
and say "Dear God, My Friend..." and
talk to him, for He Will Be There.

Niessa Brown

A Peace Of The Future

For years we have drowned in corruption and sin
Through our lies, our crimes, and our dealings within
We have used, we've abused, we have falsely accused
Our honor and pride we have grossly refused
But the time has now come, for we must take a stand
To bring justice and order back into our land
To save mother Earth from our own devastation
And provide for the unborn, our next generation.

Timothy T. Crissinger

Love

On a warm tropical night
two people met, in a friendly atmosphere,
where the setting seemed just right.
As the evening progressed,
A feeling of bonding began.
A feeling of want, a feeling of need,
So strong, there was one thing to do.
Just follow it through.
As the days passed on.
An understanding came into view.
Love was surrounded and blossomed for these two.
Their hearts became one, and life became fun.
But all too soon the fire wore thin,
and love was the question.
There was no doubt.
Was it a feeling, was it a whim.
Or was it love, they fantasized about.
There's no answer here, love is a puzzle.
The answer lies within the two hearts,
broken abandoned and troubled.

Frank Polizzano

Nature's Melody

Who wouldn't stop to watch a sunset?
Stand in silence, amazed in its awe.
If we could all just stop to watch a sunset...
Feel the magic as you pause, Shh in a moment
it will be gone.

In the distance a small echo begins to roar.
You can hear the beginnings of a thunderstorm.
As you stand, you see the lightning, feel the
breeze, watch the clouds form.

Tiny raindrops fall to wash the world anew.
Look into the horizon as the sunshine pushes through.
Out of nowhere budding in the afterglow, what can be
more magical? Rising up from the misty fog the
glistening colors of a rainbow.

How wonderful our world could be,
if we could stop to watch the sunset,
pause to listen to the breeze, or
reach out — to touch a rainbow.

Patricia K. Wright

Elements of God's Elegance

God's elements so full with delight
Like a river of running water
As it flows like a stream

God the highest above all because
of his being...
Fields of nature round about
Embodied in our vision

God's word he left behind to assure
we make the right decisions...
Man in his formation and earth
is his creation
The sun, the moon, the stars
Elements of God's elegance those
who bring any other message
To God it is irrelevant

God's elements so full and pure
Our sins he has endured
Elements of God's elegance - His
word you can relate - God is all
About love and is not the author of hate

Carol E. Hicks

Dancing Shoes

Dancing shoes, all askew,
Some are old and some are new.
There are pink ones and black ones,
and even some white.
None are too big,
but some are quite tight.
Some are for jazz, some for tap.
But ballet ones, go on in a snap.
All these shoes, wherever they go,
Is where you'll find Sarah, Dancing...you know.

Valorie Stinton

Memories

As I grow old, I look back and see,
Those memories, long planted in the heart
Become the ones most missed. Some unions seem to be
Too close, even for death to tear apart.

Those who have lived together through the years,
Have deeply learned to read the other's minds,
Joy and tempers, virtues, frailties and fears,
Cannot be forgotten when one is left behind.

'Tis wrong to bury the past too deeply,
Live it again and again, and understand
That remembering so much, so clearly
Will keep these sweet dreams fresh to your hand.

Andy Ross Marshall

My Father's Love

My dad found a beautiful lady and married for love
And that marriage was blessed from God above.
When I was born I looked into dad's eyes
And I knew God put me with a man who was wise.

For whatever reason that made me cry
Dad would always sing me a lullaby.
Taking care of his family was his heart of gold
And that is why our love for him will always grow.

He took us to church so we would learn about God's word
And this is why our family has stayed in accord.
We honor our fathers once a year
But with love they should be honored everyday of the year.

Linda L. Waymire

A Floral Image

Fate delivered you to my doorstep in the shadow of a
Renaissance man's dream. He told me that our uncanny duality
of being in a sea of oneness was written in the heavens at
the hour of our births.

My feverish awakening brought forth a floral prophecy set in
Paradise, unchallenged by the third eye of a psychic and a
maternal revelation from Nirvana.

How could such great symbolism have come from a flower that
sacrifices conventional petals, leaves, and fragrance for the
privilege of displaying the countenance and nature of amour?

These unusual flowers have always occupied a hidden corner of
my consciousness. Their fragile beauty, resilience, and
promise of rebirth exhibit the telltale qualities of true
love.

... And what will become of us, as we find ourselves
surrounded by fate, prophecy, haunting visions, and the
peculiarly heart-shaped flowers? My silent prayers speak to
appease the Gods in the heavens and the holiest of saints who
possess the powers to seal our destiny and mate our
souls.

Susan M. Tanigawa

Untitled

The friends I've found in lands afar,
are friends indeed to me.
They stood fast when times were hard,
they helped me to be me.

They shared with me their greatest gift,
the one that's hard to give.
They shared with me their love of life,
they helped me learn to live.

And if our prayers are answered,
and I've seen a few come true.
I only hope what I give back,
means half as much to you.

Tom Davis

My Three Ladies

Amor conquers all Things
Never did we imagine to be so happy in
America; in God we trust
Surrounded by two beautiful Oceans
To love and protect for ever and ever
Anastasia and Rachel in America were born
Souls of my wife and I
In this land; happiness you will find
America, Anastasia and Rachel. Indeed; Splendid you are.

Remember to love Thy Father and Mother
Amor conquers; a poet said one's
Courage and love we obtain from our children
Here and forever praise the Lord
Enriches our lives; when we trust in God
Lovely was the day each of them were born

America is still the land of the free.
By Americo Vespucci; America was named
Enlighten by minds from all over the world
Love will save the day.
Oh!; America, Anastasia and Rachel. How beautiful you are!.

J. T. Abelo

The Rivers' Bend

Today I met a special friend,
Who joined me for my morning walk.
He said my child, please walk a little slower today...
    as you reach the Rivers' Bend:
For I know what lies ahead for you and the joys you have sought.

I trusted him...and soon slowed down my pace.
It was peaceful and quiet; as we silently moved along.
    Soon the geese were squawking and the birds began to sing.
I delighted in the gentle breeze as it swept o'er my face.
Breathing deeply, my whole being was then saturated with heavenly
    perfume from the sweet honeysuckles of spring.

My heart was smiling with ecstasy!
It's so strange...I walk the same way day after day,
Yet today it was so different and more meaningful to me.
I wanted to ask my new friend why He had chosen this way:
But as I looked around, He was not there; I did not see Him,
    as I reached the Rivers' Bend.

Lois Howard

Goodbye, Mother

In Mother's eyes the tears do weep,
With emotions strong her features sweep.
A voice too weak to fully express
Her Mother's love and tenderness.
A life so nigh its blessed end,
With her beloved children to attend.
Each wish reprieve from sadness blue
Aroused by slights in truth so few.
But kindness from her eyes does bring
The reprieve each child may truly sing.
Though her death shall break our hearts,
'Tis a better place to which she departs.
Angels patiently wait close at hand
To carry Mother to God's Promised Land.
We will each miss you, Mother Dear,
But God's love soon will be so near.
And in our hearts you shall remain
'Til God brings us to your home again.

Pierre A. Kleff Jr.

Invisible

If I could be Invisible for one whole day,
I would play pranks on people
in every single way.

I would pull their hair...
Kick their chair,
Just let all my spirits fly free.
They'd blame it on someone else,
And never know it was me.

I'd play around...
Act like a clown,
And fire up some rapture.
I'd kick over a chair...
Make the classroom a lair,
And then some people I'd capture.

But wait...that sounds cruel,
Why, I can't break the school rule.
So, I'll just dream and dream,
all the day,
only about good things...
cause that's my way.

Lauri Schleher

Mother

Daddy told us that you had gone away,
To a far off place where you would stay.

We didn't know why you left us there,
Daddy said he guessed you just didn't care.

I waited for weeks for you to come home,
I would've stopped waiting if I had known.

You never would come back to see us,
But we were strong and didn't fuss.

Daddy became our Mommy too,
You hurt us so much, if only you knew.

And then I stopped looking when I was ten,
I knew I would never see you again.

I have only one question to ask if I may,
Just why did you leave on that cold, cold day?

Marcie Stayton

The Phone Call

Waiting by the phone.
Waiting for it to ring.
Wanting, hoping, praying it will be him.
Knowing exactly what you want to say,
but knowing the second you hear his voice,
your mind will go blank.
Seconds, minutes, hours, go by.
Has he forgotten you?
Has he forgotten your number?
Has he found someone new?
The phone rings.
Your heart jumps and begins to beat harder
and faster.
You picked it up and force a soft, quiet
hello, despite
the nervous sickening feeling in your stomach.
You slam the phone down in anger
and give up.
Wrong number.

Kelly Thompson

Untitled

Trust and respect are
something I can give
without cost. It's a way we both can
share and not end up in divorce.
I respect you I give
you my trust I really
really truly love you it is not mere lust.
I respect you, you are my friend and that you
can depend, I respect you, you can trust me even
in times of imagined distrust.
You can trust me when you turn your back,
if you watch me closely you
will find loyalty is something I don't lack.
You can give me respect and be sure to get it back.
You can trust me when you close your eyes because
my hearts not wearing any disguise.
You can also trust me not to tell you lies.
You can get all this and much more if you
just let respect always be your open door.

Andrea D. Shaw

Words

A word is but a quilt of sound in air,
Familiar feel, and well scrunched up and worn,
A quilt of letters, if each one a square
When time has but two parts, the night and morn,
And words have twenty-six, then who's to say
A single word won't justify the day,
And if a crash is silent unless heard,
Then do we really think, unless in words?
I sing an ode to words, the author's day,
Sculpting sounds as inspirations strike,
Daubing clay in endless varied ways,
The self-same lumps form hands or feet alike.
I sing an ode to words, the verbal rays
Which of themselves create the means to praise.

Susan Emerson Strasser

Untitled

Snow falls on bended branch and fallen leaf
on weathered hills and icy creeks.
Snow falls on trodden path of weary feet
on somber brows of those we meet.
Snow falls on worn fence of rusted wire
diluting heat of summer's fire.
Snow falls from heaven's high perch
onto feeble, frigid earth.

Brian S. Lipkin

For a Moment

God has given mankind a clue where Heaven is.
When you listen and hear His voice, He says, "I'll show you the
way."
He gives us a clue where Heaven is, when we see a rainbow after a
    thunderstorm.
For a moment God lets us observe the external planet "Alpha and
Omega"
    where Heaven is.
When we see the dawn of a new day and it's summer, after the
calm of
    a storm.

Paul Laffaty

If Love was Like a Song

If love was like a song
playing on a CD
then if I pressed repeat
would it last 'til eternity?

Would the motion of its rhythm,
the power of its beat,
the passion of its words,
the loudness... ever cease?

Could not our love then dance forever
with our bodies endless motion
pressed together?
Could not our hearts then beat forever
in the endless rhythm
of our passions heat?

If only the song could play forever...
If our love could last...
Could this really come to be?

But if all was in the power of a little button
could not someone come
and turn our world off, into Nothing?

Yolanda Zieba

Mother

Mother, are you listening during the night?
Can you hear my agonized call?
Mother, are you watching me closely
When you see that I've failed and I fall?

Mother, do you silently condemn me
When you know that I have sinned?
Mother, can you hear my voice
Calling out to you on the wind?

Mother, I have spent countless nights
Unable to search and find sleep.
Trying to conceal these hot, scorching tears.
How you hated to see me weep.

Life will always be unpredictable.
It can be bitterly cruel, it's true.
For life selfishly robbed me the chance
Of spending my days close to you.

Mother, I love you, wherever you are.
I close my eyes and you're all I can see.
My voice is strongly calling out to you.
Mother, I only hope you can hear me.

Lisa Scopa

What Is Love?

What is love? Can anyone truly say?
Is it wanting and needing someone in a very special way?
Is it caring about someone to the point of putting that one's wants
    and desires above your own?
Or is it sharing equally the pains and pleasures that can make a
soul
    moan?
For in love, as well as life, there must be pain to recognize
pleasure
    when received,
Just as a newborn babe must cry, when born, so that its birth will
    be believed,
And in my confused and troubled mind I am not sure of what to do,
But I care and in so caring, can it be said that I love you?

Cynthia Smith

Don't Forget the Children

Dedicated to Angie and her brothers.
The children they did nothing wrong
by the family they were left standing alone

With tears in their eyes
like the rain falling from the sky

With pain in their heart
Worse than the pain from the start

They were done wrong by their father and mother
at least they were there for one another

Don't forget the children for they did nothing wrong
It was their parents hand that was strong

They had a mother who beat them
A father who molested them
This was not their fault

Right now they need the family love
to feel that they belong
don't leave them standing alone
Make them know they have a place to call home
Don't Forget the Children for they did nothing wrong

Eva L. Smith

Genesis

He gives us the Earth and we deprive it of life.
He gives us the Heavens and we fill them with pollution.
He gives us the Seas and we fill it with toxic waste.
He gives us Morals and we give Him betrayal.
He gives us Nourishment and we poison it with chemicals.
    He gives us all the Creatures of the world
        and we mistreat them.
    He gives us Life and we give it damnation.
    He gave us His Son and we gave Him death.
And still He gives and gives each and everyday
        to each and everyone.
    How long will he give before He tires?
    The end is near, be ready to receive Him
        when He comes to collect!

Bernadette Cortes

Shattered

A soulless barren horizon is my endless
fate. As I search hopelessly for another, the
pain is my unholy existence.
    Numbly I try to untwist my thoughts.
Shattered is the mirror that reflects my lost
image. Tears are the frozen ice that has
formed my cage of cold. Slipping into an
insane abyss, a raging fire within, a fragile
child waits.

Kelli Berman

430

Wind

Wind a mystery blowing by,
carrying birds across the sky.
Will it bring dust, or rain, or snow?
Where did it come from? Where will it go?

Walter W. White

Not Just Another Day

I just had my 30th birthday
I got an early gift: a head injury
What is a head injury?
No one knows what to say

When ever I ask that question
I feel I get nothing but lying
But I will keep trying
Hey you got another suggestion

Tell me the truth about my injury
Come now be honest with me
I might be slower now but I can still see
Your nonsense answers are making me crazy!

What did this accident take from me
My girlfriend, job, and a degree
But I will come back you'll see
That is if God allows it to be!!!

Troy Lundberg

Nicole

A love never had will never be lost.
The feeling of desire lies within the heart.
I live and dream of a love with you,
In this dream, I might...
nothing lost, but fallen in love.
A sensuous touch deepens my desire.
A favor is drawn from that touch of desire.
You were there for me, but I left you in the dust.

In the meadow, where I sat,
I watched and felt, lived and dreamed,
a moment of time, alone, me and you.
If I knew that you could hold a love for me as I could for you...
Together always, a love true, yet...
It was never meant to be, you and me.
Never a true love, never meant to be.

Steven Kleinman

Retirement - Bah!

Heard said that I am too old,
Don't fit the new modern mold.

Through the years I've upheld my part,
Done everything right from the start.

Never turned anybody away,
Did my job morning, noon, night day.

Do I ever get a second glance,
No sir. Not a chance.

For twenty years never missed a day,
Maybe they are going to let me stay.

I've never done anything wrong
And I am still very strong.

They are moving me around a lot.
Hoping to find me a spot.

Now everything is up in the air.
What do I know, After all I am only a chair.

C. R. Crosthwaite

A Woman's Awakening

There was a woman who was a victim of her culture.
She was poisoned to believe
A good woman obeys her man and accepts her destiny.
She prayed while she was suffering and crying....
"Oh! God, give me strength and show me my path."
She did not know
Eyes can be opened.
Heart can be guided.
Life can be chosen.
Prayers can be heard.
One day her life changed...
She moved to a country called America.
Then, her eyes were able to see.
Her ears were able to hear.
Her heart was able to feel.
Much, much more than before.
She learned, she awoke, she was reborn.
Now, there is a woman who makes choice for her own life.
Who is responsible for her own choices.
Who faces her own challenge with hope, joy and dignity.

Hsiu-Wen Hsu

Heritage

What a surge of passion forth through the cells and out the pores
Drenching so the skin and soul,
A visage and a trait endowed.
Perhaps it's Yorkshire or Yiddish prayer uniting succeeding heirs,
A single thread that knots the time
Holding fast tradition's rhyme.
For constant enceinte woman swells preparing molds of molecules.
A framework of the kinship core,
Fertility accounted for.
Yet it lies within the soul, this yearning for historic hold,
That brings to life this ancient cast
Of our mystifying past.
Snapshots, shutter pressed by time, expose a notion quite sublime:
For relatives of here and late
Remain the models of our make.
A laugh, a talent, or physique though individual's quite unique
Share and speak to each generation
With these, anatomical variations.
Oh, what an honor! May it be
That such of someone lives through me.

Gillian Crisp

I Dream of Castles

I dream of castles in far away lands
   I see the bricks and mortar
Set in place by ancient hands
   I see the weathered boards
And the damage time has wrought
   Yet the castles stand as if caught
In another place and time

I dream of castles in the air
   Built on clouds of joy
With children living there
   I hear their gentle laughter
And see their shining faces
   Exploring all the beautiful places
In a world neither yours nor mine

I dream of castles in the sand
Planned in the mind, brought to life by the hand
   I see the drawbridge and the moat
I see the windows and the doors
   All disappear as the ocean roars
And reclaims its own one more time

Debra L. Rodgers

The Kind Ones

Ages and ages ago they were sent
  To help us with our life.
Never, not ever to cause us
  Pain or grief or strife.
God made us a little lower than they.
  With fabled wings they touch us as we pray.
Lower than they but kindred still
  We need them as we climb this hill.
Ever upward they now lead
  With our tiny mustard seed.
Service is their grand forté.
  From finite time to this our day.

   Mary A. Mayfield

Fornevermore

Did you listen to your words when you said "Forevermore?"
Were you callously indifferent to the impact those words bore?
Did you trivialize their meaning just so you could singly score?
Were our hearts in syncopation - or were you rotten to the core?

Did I know you then or now?; that's the riddle I can't solve!
Must I suffer endless yearning?; or somehow soon resolve
Why your pledge was merely vapor while mine was substance pure,
Did you ever really want me?; was there never true allure?

'Twas my love that was responsive; the quest was yours, recall?
And I didn't succumb quickly; you teased I was slow to fall!
What then stopped your ardor?; and why was I the last to see
That I was there for you when you were no longer there for me?

Love stories should have endings; mysteries be disclosed,
Where are our missing pages?; why am I alone supposed
To settle for "unfinished" when the author's close at hand
Who chose to script my bio; now it's I who must demand.

Can you help pick up the pieces of the heart you broke in two?
If you had shattered china, they'd expect that much of you.
All I ask as you move on is that you heart to heart explain
"Better to have loved and lost" when there is so much pain!

   Jane Hays

The Station

Walking to the station, I was ready to board.
I looked at the platform-when He said, "All aboard.

I felt the train was going; Straight to the Promised Land.
I hoped that I going - into my Father's hand.

I'll have to pass Lord Jesus... whose judgement will seek all
I'll have to please the Savior; to walk my Father's hall.

How many shirts were on my back - when others had so few?
How often did I share my bread... when little would renew?

No matter where I'm going - if not the Promised Land:
I yearned to serve Lord Jesus; His will was my command.

Faith was our salvation that readied souls to part...
With trials and tribulations - we filled our Father's heart.

I know where I am going... straight to that Promised Land.
I know that I am going - into my Father's hand.

I saw the Light and heard my Lord - and boarded right away...
In company with God's Angels... I boarded and will stay.

The Angels took my sufferings... They loaded all my sins.
The Spirit washed my soul in Light - I boarded pure and cleansed.

With faith my journey ended - within my Father's Hand...
Rejoicing now I enter... The Holy Promised Land.

   Cathy McNutt

Nobody Ever Kissed My Mother's Tears

Crying all these years, in love your all alone
Those painful silent tears, true love is not at home
As time goes by you see, no wedding bells or songs
Instead your love is free, and love had come and gone.

Life has been hard for my Mother, not fair
And time did not take away the fears
There are times I feel no one really cares,
Because
Nobody Ever Kissed My Mothers Tears.

   Beth Brown

No Ordinary Guy

He is a guy of many talents,
A perfect lover with a fascinating mind,
He is no doubt, one of a kind,
No ordinary guy is he.

He can mix with the worst of them, and like a flip of a card impress
the best of them.
He will charm you and disarm you
His smile, his touch, his kiss, his spirit bright.
There is no dimming this shinning light.
No ordinary guy is he.

He is patient; he is impatient
He loves you, he doesn't
His thoughts, his desires, his dreams, listen if you dare.
Once you know him, you'll find you truly care,
No ordinary guy is he.

Wherever he may go, wherever he may end
His eyes will sparkle, unclouded and serene.
How his branches will cross with life's road is still uncertain,
But for those a little faith, beware, he'll leave his mark for all,
I swear. No ordinary guy is he.

   Jesse Carter Johnson

"Who" Am I?

Here I lie in this beautiful boat
All covered with everything sweet;
I'm sometimes white and sometimes dark,
But always piled high and so neat.

My boat is fancy with see-through sides,
And a railing that's ruffled and thick;
And on top of me are three huge mounds
I'd really like to lick.

Sometimes I am covered with chocolate
Or strawberries or caramel or jelly;
Then a swish of cream with nuts and a cherry
Are still piled high on my belly.

You still can't guess just "who" I am
And why I lie and not sit?
Well, nothing is better than "who" I am,
I'm a luscious banana split!

   Marguerite Popovich

The Greatest Joys In Life

The greatest joys in life, I have found in my two sons.
Laughing, playing, smiling; having lots of fun.
The day they were born, is the day that joy begun.
They are so very special. They are my chosen ones.

The greatest joys in life, I have found in my two guys.
They are quiet the treasure. They are my grand prize.
They are my stars in the night. They are my sun rise.
They know that I love them, sealed with extra special ties.

   Jeanette Trauth

Untitled

Candy canes, silver lanes, holly berries aglow
Has Santa been here I want to know
The tree with a star on top
Don't touch it Tommy, Stop!

See those snowflakes fall, they are pretty
See them, they're big and small

I want a happy family
A stocking red and green filled with gifts galore
And toys on the floor
A tiny tree for Christmas Eve
To see that reindeer fly
To know Santa is nigh

Kristin Elizabeth Knox

Heat

On the north shore of Kauai in the dead-zero midst of
August is when all you wish is for a few brief moments
Back in the darkness of your December Sierra.
Back where the rewards of hunting wolves and
White stags through a pale snow forest keep
You safe from the infinite murderous winter.
You feel it being carried into the morning by a tornado
Tearing its way across the Joshua Tree desert while the rocks of
The Hidden Valley sear and ignite into flames under your skin.
You can feel it slipping in somewhere between the satin
Sheets and the other naked body sharing one deep-sunken
Bed as the mixing perspiration boils hot and streams gently
Through the curves and crevices of the other's swelling flesh.
It prowls into your blood like a ghost, allying with adrenaline
As you dive from an iron falcon into miles of Earth rushing at you,
Praying that a cocktail of cloth and string will save you.
You become infected by this force of God's sunlight, feeling
The pain, the comfort, the exhaustion, the ecstasy,
The Lazarus-rising of summer's animal viciousness,
The rising... of Heat...

Morgan S. Purdom

Eucalyptus

A gust of wind rustles through the eucalyptus
Sending the leaves dancing and shimmering
Like sequins on an evening gown,
Like the sun glistening on the ripples
Of a lake disturbed by the wind
Brushing her hair in its reflection.

The sound is like crenaline under a full skirt,
Like steam bursting out of a hot iron.
It's white noise, background music in nature's music score,
Aided occasionally by sporadic notes of chime.

Shadows play on the tree trunks.
The willowy boughs sway like swings on rope,
Back and forth the branches bay like nodding giraffes.

The breeze cools my skin and kisses my face.
The wind blows harder now.
And its spirit moves through the trees like a flock of birds
Spooked from their roost and fleeing in haste.
The wind will not end today but it soothes me just the same.

Julene Evans

Before Our Lives First Touched

I first met you playing in cotton candy clouds
    dancing ballet on golden rainbow that traced your beauty
across deep blue skies seared by radiant summer heat

On sandy beaches long ago, I searched for you amidst afternoon
    of hazy, humid, tranquil sun list that hovered over me.
While lost, I wandered upon wet sand castles clutching
    yellow plastic shovels and red tin buckets.

The quiet was shattered by the shrill calls of majestic seagulls,
    gliding along warm shafts of warm sunshine, running
with soft, cool ocean breezes, while crested white waves
    were crawling up to me, whispering your arrival

Your magic touched my life back then, I sensed your
    coming. I craved your soft touches, gentle glances,
and piercing beauty. Sadly, I had to wait until my childhood
    fantasies and dreams had run their course, until
I could love you for all of the lifetimes I have yet to live.

Whenever I walk the boardwalks of life, I still yearn to
    play on the beaches, running against the cool zephyr
thrusted by the pounding waves as the sand is reclaimed by the
    undaunted ocean, just as our lives, too, shall be taken back.

C. B. Kimmins

A Friend

As the darkness turned to light... Learning from mistakes
I've made, life has bestowed on me an entirely new insight...
    Making sure to open my eyes... That I may see things
clear... It was you the only one to have faith enough to stay
near...
    Never once stopped trying to reach the inner me...when
you could have easily walked away...leaving my pointless
existence be...
    You were a part of me from the first moment we met...
you walked into my life being the stranger whom I'd never
forget...
    I believe in trust, love and happiness once again... and
with no one else to thank but you... You truly are a friend.

Susan Volpe Meeg

I Wonder

When I die, will I go to heaven? And
if I get there, will all the things that
meant so much on earth be there.

Will the squirrels still hunt for nuts
and scurry all around.

Will I see my dogs and cats, will all
the birds be there and flowers all in bloom.

Can you take a walk down tree lined
clouds and feel the rain upon your face.

Is there grass in heaven and inland
lakes and fish to catch and sparkling sand.

Does my soul have arms and legs to
travel heaven's way.

These questions stand unanswered and
perhaps I'll never know,

So I'll just stay awhile on earth until
it's time to go.

God willing.

Katherine M. Ratliff

433

Thunderstorms

Why does the rain fall continuously?
Why do the storms never seem to end?
There should be nothing except sunshine and rainbows.
The rain and storms should be dead forever.
All the darkness and dreariness should be over.
There shouldn't be a cloud in the sky.
But no matter what happens, that rain always falls.
That clouds always lingers.
And that storm never ends.
The sunshine pushes them away sometimes
But it never lasts.
And no matter how hard that sunshine pushes, it always fails.
Always.
The feelings of emptiness and loneliness fall with this rain
And are hidden in these clouds.
Laughing an evil laugh.
They've caught yet another soul.
Another soul to drag down into the world of Forbidden Happiness.
To torture with a surrounding happiness that poor soul will
never feel.

Lesley Plugge

Some Days...

There is a dragon in everyone's heart,
a creature that must be overcome.
Whether you face fire breathing monsters or anxious fears,
a slayer of dragons is never done.

There are those who will forever struggle
and seek to find what others have lost.
Be it treasure or fame or heroic deeds,
they will strive to reach it no matter the cost.

Even these seekers must face their hearts
and conquer their dragons in the end.
But no matter how noble the cause or how valiant the fighter,
Some days, the dragon wins.

Ron Williams

Batty Family

I love my Daddy
Even though he drives me Batty
I love my "Batty Daddy."

My mom is also Batty
Just like my Daddy

I call my mom "Batty Matty"
Cause' my daddy is "Batty Daddy"

I am also so Batty
Just like my "Batty Daddy and Batty Matty"
I call myself "Batty Watty"

I Love My Batty Family!

Mia Synodinos

Untitled

I broke out of the box
not knowing what I would find...
Artist? Monk? Mortal man?
I found you
drunk with your own perfume
drowning in the nectar of self
seeing no structure but your own
hearing no sound but your own personal beat...
(I ran
searching for the lid)

Florence Conlon

"Innocence In Pain"

Innocence in pain is about every child all over
the world who must struggle to gain.
It is about the children suffering senselessly when
they should be out playing.
It is about the unfortunate youth who have no place
warm when it rains.
Unless you have witnessed this with your own two eyes,
Or have heard their heartbreaking cries.
Then you know the children need us now so much
in order to survive.
The other sad fact is as I write these words down.
There are children with unfair chances in life
laying to rest in the ground.
So no matter who or what you are whether near or far.
Only in the children's eyes you will find that long lost star.
What I really feel like saying is if you have children.
It would be best not to kill the youth in them.
Because if you do it will not stop like the flow in your veins.
And there is just another young child in need.
Innocence in pain.

Elias Padilla Sr.

In Memory of Our Mother

Our dearest mother was the eldest of nine
A quiet sort of person yet generous, loving and kind.

Hardest of times didn't seem to keep her down
In facing adversity, great strength she often found.

She toiled and labored 'til each day was done
Devoting her life to God, husband, three daughters and a son.

Her physical being grew weary, thus taking its toll
She now has a new body, with God is her soul.

She never won a blue ribbon nor won an award
Today it's as though we can hear her say, "My children, I'm home
    Yes, home with my Lord."

Evelyn E. Cooper

The Hippy

Everyone's a dandelion at age 17:
Pretty but still a weed.
So it's unusual to see a sunflower, in this field of dandelion,
climbing high and stupid against the sky.
The colors are the same, but the brazen lift, that silly height
that sweet, numb smell of wax wings melting,
are part of a choice made not by nature, but by self.

Dandelions become those irresistible
little heads that are victim to the strong breaths of grade schoolers.
We scatter everywhere, carried by the wind, real and unreal,
praying that we take root somewhere.
I wonder if when everyone,
the surly little kid and the skater and the jock and me,
have taken root somewhere,
the sunflower won't still be there,
trying to pull up up up from the earth,
dancing wildly to the wind's cold music as dandelions come and go.
And, when the winter comes and it is solitary in the hard field,
if it wonders how far down its roots can go.
And why they dig still deeper.

David Roth

The Life Of A Survivor

Oh, to the survivors, your strength is admirable.
But your hearts have become like burlap, rough and textured.

Thine eyes that once gleamed and radiated life, seem dull and
dormant.
And the tears have seemed to dry, turn brittle and break.
Thine goodness has become rigid like the stem of a nail
Driven further and further into thine own chest.

And lines around the eyes of the love at heart spread like streams
through a valley carrying pain, tears, and mercy to the harsh,
broken
ground.

Thine heart lays within thy chest and beats a steady rhythm between
each breathe.
And the soul of the weary minded closes its eyes to the world
outside
And fall slumber to the soothing mesmerizing dance.

Kimberly K. Beasley

Above And Beyond

As eagles soar through heavenly skies,
They find homes and prey with very keen eyes.
They see things from a different view,
Most unlike any person could do.
They see the shape of the horizon and all about,
Instead of humans which see heavy traffic and shout.
A bird's eye view is different from ours,
Because they are able to see small budding flowers.
But for that fact any living thing has a different view,
Of many things old and new.
So many things that we grow fond,
We forget to look above and beyond.

Brian C. Lee

Nature, Who Cares

Where green grass grows and where trees spring
Where flowers bloom and birds sing
Where amazing feats happen and bees buzz
Where mantids lay eggs that look like fuzz
Where spring and summer sun greet the dawn
Where mother deer gives birth to baby fawn
Where Fall's red and yellow leaves dance across the ground
Winter trees with branches bare in icy air
It's nature that makes these amazing things happen
And look at us the destroyers of nature
We are like ravenous wolves consuming everything in 'her'
But soon there will be no trees to clear
And the end of nature will be near
That includes humanity too!
And nothing will ever come back anew!
So far the human race isn't extinct, other species are!
Some are endangered with annihilation not quite far!
We must learn our lessons before we meet our fate
We must come to our senses before it's too late!
Let's be humble and not let the world crumble!

Tejasvi Ravilochan

The Silent Fall

It is sad when happiness ends,
Down the road, around the bend.
Beyond the haze of blood and tears,
There is a notion to calm your fears.
In a place inside the soul,
Within a heart of solid gold,
There is a place around the bend,
Where silence falls, and all things end.

LaToya R. Morgan

Give Me

Dear Lord:
Give me Guidance to understand life and all
its reasons why...

Give me strength to succeed and always
want to try...

Give me courage to look upon life the way
it should be...

Give me wisdom that opens my heart nd
sits my soul free...

Give me faith to trust in my fellowman...

So united and together is where we might stand...

Let me life as you intended it to
be..

Filled with love, devotion and every
person born equal and free...

Thank you Lord for a life that has been
full and content...

Guided and built on the love that
you sent...Thank you Jesus

Dawn Beckworth

Life

Life is neither silk or cream,
   but holds infinite dreams.

Life can be very cold,
   yet treasured like the purest of gold.

Life is heaven, life is hell
negativism shall not dwell.

Life has its ups and down.
   Many smiles begin to frown.

Life is sometimes good, sometimes bad
   cherished memories to be had

Life is short, without guarantee,
   so respect it with the utmost to thee.

Mattie Townsend

A Shakespearean Sonnet

You believed that you had finally found
Someone, he, who would take you as you were.
Unique, was the way he formed your name in sound,
Freely and caring, for you were his her.

Carefree days, spent in the sun, perfect bliss.
There were many starry nights, in his eyes.
You surrendered all doubt, all of it amiss.
Wonder of it all, so open it cries.

Yet, as with the seasons, feelings do turn,
Memories are what's left, your heart may break
To re-live them again, for that you yearn,
But stop yourself, for reality's sake.

Hold on to those times, but keep on going,
You were loved, that's all that is worth knowing.

Catherine Shaw

Live In The Present

Forget the past and live in the present hour;
Now is the time to work, the time to fill
The soul with noblest thoughts, the time to will
Heroic deeds, to use whatever dower
Heaven has bestowed, to test your uttermost power.

Now is the time to love, and better still
To serve our loved ones, over passing ill
To use triumphant; the perfect flower
Of life shall come to fruitage; wealth amass
For grandest giving ere the time to be gone.

Be glad today, tomorrow may bring tears;
Be brave today, the darkest night will pass,
And golden rays will usher in the dawns;
Who conquers now shall rule in coming years.

Jennifer Christian

What Kind Of Man

What kind of man altho shedding a tear
at the sight of injustice brutality and fear
caused a noble nation to realize-
that only peaceful resistance could win the prize,

What kind of man altho beaten and jailed,
and denide his right to simply post his bail
would still kneel and pray, within his prison cell,
that the one's who'd jailed him would not burn in hell,

What kind of men who has seen the view,
And know that his life is in danger too,
Would nevertheless carry right on through
Keeping solid faith with what he'd set out to do?

He must be a man of hope, a man of faith, and sweet charity.
A man of the cloth - a man of the - light- of the God of eternity
A man of the just - the truth- and and the Dove
In short - he must be a "King" and a Man of "Love"

Juanita Brit'tain Gist

From the Heart of Knight

There are no words with the descriptive power;
That can bring comprehension to this hour.

Penetrating screams of sorrow assail the atmosphere, and cling like
barnacles on to the tumultuous air.
Will a sound now escape that can convey a thought of care?

Can love ripped from the womb be replace?
I see your smile on every face.

Can my heart embrace the wind?
I think not my friend.

No! I think not.
And yet there are those who would say I should bear my lot.
Some say I should bare my face, and brace; even embrace the wind.

Rose L. Marsh

Untitled

You have stimulated the master organ in my body - the brain
getting my ideas organized for a prize-winning poem is a strain.
Think of all the delicate reactions going on in my head.
All my past experiences my brain has been fed.
What a wonderful machine is this brain of mine.
I hope it produces the winning line.
If it doesn't, it has boggled my mind.
And I will try a contest of another kind.

Hazel Riverside

Time

Time, it waits for no one.
It was yesterday, it is now, it will be tomorrow.
There is no measure for time.
It is neither here nor there.
It is a moment, a minute, a day, a week, a month, a year.
It means everything to everybody.
It can be an appointment, a meeting, a luncheon, or even fun time.
Time waits for no one, it is fast and disappears without you
Realizing it's gone.
Time can be an era, a moment of long ago, or even later.
Time can be saved, spent or used.
It was before, it is now, it is after while, even tomorrow.
It is arranged, it is found, it is lost.
Time, what is it? No one knows for sure, but everyone has it,
Needs it wants it and cannot live without it.
And once it's gone it cannot be recaptured, so don't waste it!

Philomena Rossi

Spontaneous Melody

Sit back and listen to the guitar player,
Playing his harmony to the beat of life.
Watch his fingers rearrange every symbol of rhythm,
As the sound tickles your ears with every move.

Listen to the music, while it lifts up your soul,
As it eases your pulsating mind.
Drums create the beat that imitates your emotions.
Taste the air from which passion is made.

See the birds flying above the deep blue sea.
They inspire the illusion of spirits;
Creating the sounds that fills your emotional void.
But who will stay to watch the angels play?

Images starving for attention,
Awakens you from your greed of fear.
Why should you embrace the darkness
As you did your mothers breast as a child?

Let the vision of children playing,
Enter into your uncertain mind.
Let the sound of music abound in your soul,
And you can die knowing your spirit was free.

Marvin Shawn Ezzell

Just Passing Thru

Bittersweet memories of moments in time
forever lost in shadows of dreams
Never to savor the warmth of good friends
Nor walk thru the field or sit by the streams
or gaze at the sky of deep azure blue
—— I just didn't take time,
I was just passing thru.

Gone was my childhood, days swiftly passed by
like the leaves of a book turned by the wind
And finally stop as by destiny's hand
At some point in time, when again I begin
to remember, but they fade away too
—— I just didn't take time,
I was just passing thru.

So heed some advice from someone who knows
for time could be short and the race nearly run -
Yesterdays gone but tomorrow's still bright
take time to slow down and sit in the sun.
Inhale all the joys that are out there for you.
—— Just forget about time, and 'bout just passing thru.

Clark Beardslee

Evil Personified

A souteneur living on spatchcock dinners
Rearmost in the line of sovereignty
Living a sterile existence in a stercoral squat
Stigmatized in squalor; A man of strychnine wit
He finds sardonic satisfaction in satanic worship
Selfish in his own living sham, yet devoted to the Devil
Set for a sarcophagus in Hell
The sooner, the better

Duncan Mitchell

My On-Line Friend

Some say it is not real
But I know how I feel
Even though I have never seen your face
In my heart you have found a special place
Where dear friends are held high
And I know not why

Whenever we do meet
My heart skips a beat
I feel I can tell you most anything
And be judged fairly like a noble king
From golden days gone by
And I know not why

Diane Foose

Goodbye

I've said hello
I've said goodbye
now I'm leaving you
and don't ask me why
with a wave of my hand
and the kiss I blow to you
I go on my way
to my grave in heaven's ocean blue
I will not forget you
for you are my one and only
but don't despair
because you are not the reason I must go away and be lonely
I would visit you often
but I may not
and that is why I must leave you and get in my coffin
but please do not cry
because I will see you again
but if you must
go ahead for it isn't one of the seven deadly sins

Aaron D. Watson

Our Marine Soldier

Thousands of miles away from home, with thousands
of soldiers. Does he feel alone?
He's like a grain of sand in a desert so vast.
Our young marine becomes a man so fast.
Serving our country, the red, white and blue.
Standing side by side for me and you.
Don't criticize him, don't tell him it's wrong. With
his life on the line he needs to be strong.
Someday he'll come home. I don't know the date.
After the conflict to liberate Kuwait.
If you're not standing beside him, then stand behind
him, give him the strength he needs.
He has a big burden, a big load to carry. Make it
a little lighter, make his day brighter. Support
him and our country.

Betty Jo Tatroe

Night Wind

You whistle through the sideboards of my house.
I brace myself, unaware.

Howling like an injured child
Your voice rises higher, louder
Drowning out the monotonous hum
Of the refrigerator
Creating a chorus with the metal flap
Of the stove vent slapping against the metal plate
And the muscles of my neck and back
Tighten as you rant and rave like an angry father.

Where do you come from?
What do you want?
Why do I fear you?

The walls creak; an echo to the wind
And I sit in this chair
Alone.

Sue Paleafei

Colors

Colors have many different hues,
So let me give you the latest news.

Some cause you to sing the lonesome blues.
While others prompt you to pay your dues.

Some are very, very shiny bright,
But never, never get up tight.

Some are shocking to your sight,
While others make you want to fight.

Some blaze through the morning sky,
Bringing you to a super duper natural high.

Some may make you want to soar and fly,
While others will make you moan and sigh.

Some produce a full faced smile,
Although some say that's not their style.

Some make you think of lots and lots of money,
While others make you just want to kiss your honey.

Some might cause you to be sluggish and lazy,
Even though things have made you very crazy.

So that's the scoops on the colors of your life,
Remember this and you will have less daily strife.

Jamie Lax

I Wonder Where the Spider Sleeps

I wonder where the spider sleeps,
  hidden away in darkened deeps.
When the night moon fills the sky,
  on a thread of silk she'll fly.
A creature of black, the phobic fear.
  Her silence so deadly, that none can hear.
Entangled in web, her frantic prey begs,
  as she covers her victim with eight working legs.
The widow is lonely, she stalks the unknown,
  and disappears at night fall, forever alone.
The haunted walls her cobwebs coat,
  across the threads of silk she floats.

I wonder where the spider sleeps,
  hidden away in darkened deeps.
She fights and she hides, but none really know,
  where she creeps in the night, so frightfully slow.

Lori Ann Crisci

Oh Journey

Oh journey long-to what end be
Say the pondering

Yet with great beauty - empowering strength
Each step might bring

Oh journey long - where shall I go
Say the wandering

Yet with spirit uplifted - goodness and blessing
Each direction contains

Oh journey long - what lies ahead
Say the impaired

Yet with deep passion - the mighty anchor
Each place assured

Oh journey gone - say the forgetful
Of yesterday lost

Yet with Thanksgiving - the healer of souls
Today is a journey of its own

Oh journey be...
Tammy L. Hoffman

Impressionable Night

Rainy nights with starry skies
peacefully black like deadly eyes

A most human nature looks down
releasing a fearful, harmless sound

As lonely children rise like night
and soundful people range and fight

Teaching the small a horrible lesson
to rebel against life's natural succession

And their tears flow like endless rivers
while children sleep in the night that quivers

Look at the beaten children all black and blue
hoping that one lesson will help them through

And maybe it hurts and maybe it'll burn
but one day it will be avenger's turn
Theresa Armetta

"All Alone In Silence"

Alone this day in silence this day;
this day, along I stay.

Sifting through my anguished thoughts;
hearing, angry inner cries.

All alone in silence,
this day, alay I stay.

Melodies, of discordant sounds;
fill my inward sides this day.

Residing all alone this day;
this day of empty sorrows; this day of quiet ways.

Daylight fades, to evening's ways,
my shallow life continues; in its somber, grievous ways.

Evening's twilight soon does fade,
to nightfall's land, of blackened shadows turned.

Sitting, with my inner self;
reflecting, bygone ways; mulling through my inner dreams.

Alone, this cursed night I stay;
to try again, another day!
Fredric Marsh Jr.

That Blues Thing

I've been up so long, yeah it's great to be so high
Life has been a breeze, so it's hard to say goodbye
But it's time to come on down
Yeah I knew it had to end
I should have known I'd be doing that blues thing again

You know the feeling friend, you got your feet on the ground
Then along comes a wind and the sky comes crashing down
Things will get better
But first they're getting worse my friend
Don't matter if you fight it, you got that blues thing again

It's a hard ride like you heard the man say
When you find a dollar bill but the wind blew it away
When a man on the street won't give you the time of day
How you gonna get it on with your life this way?

Things will get better, first they're getting worse my friend
All good things have got to come to an end
You should have known you'd be doing that blues thing again
Dennis A. Eschrich

Dreams of Peace

What is happening to the world we're in?
Everybody is living in sin.
The screams left unheard,
The gunshots ignored,
Little children on the streets,
Oh help us Lord.
Stricken by diseases,
So deadly, so soon,
We need to protect ourselves-
Or we'll be heading for doom,
Put your hand in mine,
Either black or white,
Divided we fall,
Together we unite.
This is our world and our life,
Only we can make a difference.
So stand up strong,
We'll battle any weather -
To keep our world alive forever.
Jacqueline Modica

Meet Me

Meet me 'neath the pear tree at half past eternity,
within the orchard of holy souls, past a sea of clouds;
through the gate of peace and love, where evil's not allowed.
Flowers bloom in sweet perfume and daylight never ends,
this is the favorite meeting place of since past mortal friends.
We'll share some honeysuckle wine while cherubs are at play
for children get their wings you know, soon as they find their way.
Where lush green meadows dotted gold unfold to water crystal clear,
brooks as blue as our Lord's eyes; as calming as His stare.
Bathed in light so pure and white, come with me to the shore
of oceans filled with rainbow fish, where feet can touch the floor.
My Grandmother so dear to me foretold of things to be,
in dreams she had in twilight years; I had no doubts you see.
And by some chance your time should come before I travel on,
just set your watch and I'll set mine and I'll meet you anon.
C. Cooper

Dreaded Memories

There are many things in life
That give a country girl a thrill.
But one thing a Texas rancher dreaded most
Was a broken down old windmill.

Grandpa Reeves said wind, water and breakdowns
Were things that made a rancher old.
While grasshoppers, jack rabbits and Anthrax
Tended to make those ranchers bold.

They learned to dip and vaccinate the cattle,
Had to burn them if they died.
They learned to destroy rattlesnakes and critters
'Til their success spread far and wide.

Without wind they had no water.
Without water, they had no life.
With a contagious disease like Anthrax
Ranch life was work, worry, death and strife.

They put their minds and hands together,
On the Lord they must depend,
To take them through those dreaded times,
Or ranch life would surely end.

Willie Lou Shirley

Aerial Raptures

As the silver sky weeps tears of spring, the seagulls soar in
the breezes. Gliding around in circles, dropping in the down
drafts, then swooping back up again, they fly in beautiful
array. Calling aloud, they urge each other to greater and
greater heights, then folding their wings come crashing down
towards the Earth. At the very last minute, they snap open their
wings and cry out triumphantly, before swinging back up to do it again.
Riding the currents with wavering wings, sliding through the
air in spiraling circles, they gather together in the rain, enjoying
it in a way we never could. The wind tosses them to and fro,
tipping them from side to side and sometimes tossing one out of
the current of air. The gull sinks rapidly, then recovers, flinging
wide his grey wings and strongly beating the air with them until he
rises on an updraft of air. He calls aloud as if laughing at the
trick the wind played on him and taunting it to try again. Then
suddenly losing interest in the game, they fly off, strong wings
pushing against the wind. And just as quickly as they appeared,
they are gone.

Laureen Allen

Blossoming Flower

Blossoming flower
with a scent so sweet
would thou be a rose
with out thorns to cover thee?

Tall nettles why shelter
prickly thistles from a welcome rain
or the sweetness of a shower
and how it clatters that hour on
the blossoming flower

O! How stinging the thumb
was bloody red much tears were
wept from that rose she said

But I think a smile is showing on
cheeks like fine lace from a
gentle kiss and a fatherly embrace to take its place

Dark brown but kind eyes wearing soft hair
and gray he left the garden of splendid mirth with
a smile each vision made such moments
pleasant on mother earth where in the old man
has gone to sleep has gone to rest.

R. Reyes

The Color of Pearl Harbor

Pearl Harbor in the morning
Shimmers in the orange light of sunrise,
The color of ripened papaya.
The gentle breeze
Makes the water ripple
Over a sleeping oyster
Settled in the sand.

Pearl Harbor in the evening
Glitters yellow in the rays of a full Hawaiian moon,
The color of pineapple.
Ka makani hani—the soft winds
Lap the water onto the grassy shore
Leaving it glisten in the starlight.

The color of Pearl Harbor
Lingers in the eyes of those who look upon it,
The color of the fruit of nature.
The breeze speaks of peace,
Speaks to the heart
In a language of the soul.

Keoni Aloha

Addicted Inmate

Here I sit in prison once again
This cycle seem stop never end
At times, I believe, this is where I belong
Because I'm weak to a drug, which I know is wrong
A drug addict in reality is my title
My mother, unforgiven, is my idle
Staying drugs free is so hard for me
I always lose track of reality
Yet, change in what I want so bad
Happiness, peace of mind, no longer sad
But every time I get on the right track
A small obstacle seems to bring me back
To that comfort-zone, when I get high
Immediate gratification, no reason to cry
I hate it, I don't want it anymore
I need help, to get to the inner core
Prison doesn't work for me, an addicted inmate
There must be something else, to help alleviate
The pain, self, mutilation, my low self-esteem
To help me, an addict, reach my destined dream...

Lynn Howard

LunAr Eclipse

It was a rare stare into the LA night
Clear, Sober
O senile sky, how could you forget to hide your
mysteries?

Full moon flocks cumulus sheep across Elysian
fields
Desperate to evade lonely Orion
"There is a crispness in the air unusual to these climes"
Climb climb climb

Lend me your lunar light, just for this night of the full
moon

I have awaited your coming
Withstood the piss-bright day
I deserve these solo, not solar, moments with you Luna

Who are you Earth-dog to deprive me of my rays?
An ugly display of geocentric imperialism
Cast your shadow elsewhere!

Conspirator Sun, breaker of day, and stingy
contributor to the Night's phenomenon

Michael T. Stone

My Friend

I wish my friend, my deepest gratitude.
She who gives me clarity of thought. For we
think alike. She, who knows what I am, and the
magic that makes up my soul, as well as her
own. We share thoughts, feelings, doubts,
concerns and irritations. She as well as I believe
in the fact, not the unrealistic faith of scripture.
We are the ones who search for the unanswered
questions of our surroundings. My friend and I
know how to speak our minds. We are not ruled
by what others think. We go by our own rule.

Kara Stamm

God's Mercy

An angel appeared the day you were
born. A blessing was given, a child
came to form. You're in God's thoughts,
you're in His prayers. But, most of
all he's the one who cares. So let
us rejoice God in his Mercy.
And keep you in good health. Be gone
with all fears. For now we find hope.
The good Lord is kind. We must keep
praying for some peace of mind. Let us be
thankful for good things we have
God hasn't forgotten his child in mind.
And for this he will cherish you always for all time.

Frank Polizzano

My White Dog

I have this white dog with a brown spot
on his head who comes into my room when
I go to bed.
With a circle on his eye - yes, a circle I
said, that matches the spot on the top of
his head.
His back he likes scratched and this I
don't miss cause my bed time reward is a
big slurpy kiss.
I love my white dog with the brown spot
on his head and how he comes into my room
when I go to bed.
He lays by my side after his tummies been
fed, and we fall asleep while I gently rub
his spotted head.

Connie Davis

Mirror On My Mind

Is this what everybody else see
Or is it just me? Oh, maybe it is you
Bringing out what I think I only feel inside
Frustration I try so hard to conceal
Masking the smiles I thought I always have on
I get it! It is the sweat, now a cake of wax
That is giving me this look of hopelessness
Which I don't have to go through life with

Tears, more tears, more hot tears
Real expressions of the feelings inside
Cannot change the expressions outside
Because the wax is not melting, it is me!
But I won't give up, the strong survives
It is a heart, mind and soul thing, I'll circulate
See what's out there for me
I'll emerge from the jungle, a conqueror.

Kunle Tayo

The Night

A certain feeling hits you as your mind begins to
drift;
the stillness of the night air motivates your
spirits' and tends to give you a lift.

Listen to the silence speaking, as if to warn you
not to think out loud;
It makes one's thoughts dig deeper into the mind in
search of a thought for which to be proud.

The roar of your imagination hits an extreme high;
Your dreams seem so real it seems as though you
can reach out and touch the stars as you fly by.
Then almost like the gigantic thrust of a rocket,
you jump to you feet and look into the sky;
Could it be I'm finished? No, it's only the sun
telling the night goody-bye!

Kenneth Smith

To Jane, On Her First Birthday

How can we tell you we love you,
You who came into a strange land
of giants and gibberish,
With no words, but only cries of fear and hunger?
We touched your silken skin and worshipped
all your wonder.
Did this tell you how we loved you?

You enchant with a smile that makes us cry.
We giggle and Da-Da with you in unbridled joy.
You waddle-toddle proudly, then fall down;
We hug and kiss, then hug and kiss again,
And try to let you know - we love you.

Adrienne Cox

Sleepless

It's a mystery
Borne in the dead of night.
Salivating, It hungers for release.
To be free...
Longing to reach out
To its Master.
The one He calls out to
In the darkest hours
As He lies
Sleepless.

It's a mystery
To Her and all others.
He stumbles through His day with Its desires
To be free....
Longing to reach out
But unable.
Trembling with Its strength,
Staring into space,
Still He lay
Sleepless.

Robb Flynn

Autumn

A winding down of summer to a gentler pace,
The frenzied dance of summer almost done.
Like a mother shaking out her apron after supper
to settle in a chair and doze,
Knowing that the day was over, and a resting time was near.
Feeling that tomorrow would bring a crisp, cold wind,
but a warm sun shining on her hair
as she cut still blooming roses, or rested in a chair.
And her memories, like swift, bright leaves
would skitter to the ground and lay there
heaped around her feet.

Emma Jo Fox Ware

The Dentist Chair

While I sit here in the dentist chair...
Looking up at the light, feeling fear.
He's telling me it's gonna be o.k. relax
a little you're much too afraid.

I am trying to tell myself there's nothing
to it, just keep still look up at the light
and everything is gonna be alright.

When here come's this big needle for
my gums, I'd better keep still until
he's done. Oh no the feeling is getting
numb. I am telling you this is no fun.
After that short, I am always sleepy,
I hate the drill it sound so creepy.
So if the dentist is a trip you don't
want to make, take care of your teeth,
for goodness sake. Or you'll live to regret
it, and never forget it,
The Trip The Dentist Chair.

> ***Rita Burts***

Sonnet

Today I talked with one who recently
Had lost his only son - a stalwart lad
With body strong; his mind such training had
As love and sacrifice provide. And he
Had died so soon. A double tragedy
My friend had suffered, for his wife, quite mad
With grief and worn with weeping, did but add
Another care; yet he could say to me,

"With each experience that life has brought
O sorrow deep, catastrophe, or pain,
Upon my aching soul a soothing balm,
Of suffering fashioned and by patience wrought,
Which makes endurance possible has lain.
Companionship with grief brings strength and calm".

> ***Cora Lee Beers Price***

Trust

Dedicated to my guardian angel, Janet

I know how to be perfect, smile at the right moment,
To say what people want to hear, causing everyone to like me.
And in doing so, I live in a safe and acceptable prison,
With walls so thick no one could penetrate them and touch me.
For in touching me, the prison walls would crumble and I would be
   exposed.
The exposure feels like death, but I don't know why.
So, instead, I die a slow and safe death, day by day.
Some part of me wants desperately to live and whispers to try,
   try to trust.
And with that whispered plea, all the warning flags of my
   prison are raised.

You seem so genuine, so honest, so real.
Where is your superficiality and judgment?
I envision trusting you, perhaps opening the prison door a little.
I step out, ready to retreat at the first sign of rejection.
But you, you do not seem to judge me.
Your acceptance makes me wonder if perhaps I am acceptable.
And something inside me begins to bloom, slowly through all the
   fear.
It is a very powerful and grounding thing.
It is the doorway to becoming human, but it is scary and new.
It feels like a glass of water in the desert and I want to drink
   from it.
I think they call it Trust.

> ***Donna Schulze***

World View After Eighty

The more we know the less we understand
We fight and kill and hope for paradise
We scream and wail and tell so many lies
Why can't we make out peace with every land?

So like a giant jigsaw puzzle is our life
One moment all goes well and then comes strife.
This place fits here, this one can find no place.
Yet with persistence will emerge a face.

Why are we born to this great mystery?
To live and die and never know the way.
We wander lost and wondering day by day
And never know the joy of jubilee.

Is there no answer to this inner urge
To self-destruction - thus to purge
Ourselves forever from this place
Yet hope there will arise a perfect race?

> ***Helen E. Tank***

Love Began With A Doll

Love is a doll that we held as a child,
That we rocked as she lay in our arms.
That we dressed, and we walked and we kissed everyday,
And were thrilled by her various charms.

   Love is our most precious possession
   It grows very well in us all.
   But remember, our love for each other
   Began - with our love - for our doll.

She was ours, and we were a mother to her
As our mother was a mother to us.
A doll of our own, but still wanting more dolls,
Over whom we could fondle and fuss.

   So think back to the dolls that you owned as a child,
   And the babies you've loved on your way.
   But remember, the love of your dolls was the start
   Of the love that's within you today!

> ***Rita S. Meyer***

Oxymoron

Like drowning in water - I sink, but I'm free
Like the empty fullness that's inside me.
Like the slender obesity I try to write
Like the quiet noise I hear at night.
Like the naked cover of sin and lies
Like the heart that bellows those silent cries.
Like the future that comes when I'm asleep
Like the comedy in me that makes me weep.
Like the bitter tastelessness of life in motion
Like moments clarity that give me this notion.
Like the sweet sorrow I know too well
Like the boring passion I try to sell.
LIke the quick trudge up the downward hill
Like the pleasant pain that eats my will.
Like the taste of heaven and hell that that haunts
Like the bile of death that no one wants.
Like cursing the good, but helping the bad
Like the living and dying that keeps us
iron - clad.

> ***Loraina Floyd***

Goddess Across the Ravine

Abandoned concrete basement embraces a world in bubbling puddle,
  Where a duck couple nest flanking an ugly snapping turtle.
Reed stalks extend hustling and jostling toward the ravine,
  Nearby a shanty sits for years since its estate was ruined.

Within the glade, beyond the ravine an old mansion stands prudishly,
  Showing off in mossy mansards and ivy art nouveau plaster walls.
Draperies are seldom opened or lights switched on at night,
  Neither presence nor movement of the inhabitant is seen.

Some chilly fall day a young sculptor moved into the shanty,
  Fixing interior to exterior with his dexterous magic hands.
This tiny universe becomes a gorgeous palace and castle for him,
  Who was a war orphan wandering from various foster homes in
Detroit

Ill-matched architectures stand off lining at stream all winter,
  While entire landscapes hibernate under frozen air and snow.
The day spring began, ice storms thrust a huge tree into the mansion,
  Reverberatively a goddess in green velvet jumped out for help.

Her chiseled features in blond hairs, blue eyes, crimson lips,
  Matching milky slim body early in forty captivates him totally.
Fragrant breathing surges this Asian youth's dreamy chemistry,
  Leaves only pathos as the shanty's removal starts within weeks.

Esaku Kondo

Does!

  Does the sky listen late a night?
Does the moon question where it gets it light,
does the stars shine ever so bright?
Are they only there, for lovers delight?
  The wind blows softly through the trees,
does it whisper their secrets to the leaves.
The flowers are such array of colors.
Are they too only for lovers.
  Beautiful sunset, early morning dawn.
The beauty of this world is on a throne.
It is ours to have and to hold.
It is up to us to set our goals.
Will we run, or will we stand still?
The choice is ours, to do as we will.

Ethel Procell Wynn

Window-Pane Scenery

When I need a lift any time of the day
  My little garden just brightens my way
Like a canopy of trees that shades the lane,
  That's the view from my southern window-pane.

A new day's dawning like a faint light beams
  Slowly waking me from my dreams,
And I hear the fluttering wind-blown leaves
  That's when I need the view in the east.

But, often in summer when I need the sight
  Of snowflakes falling on a wintry night
When the winds forbid us to venture forth,
  Then, I turn to the window facing north.

When shadows descend and the sun's gone to bed,
  Gay autumn leaves tell me summer has fled,
That's the time and the view that I like the best
  The scene from my window-pane to the west.

Edna E. Moore

The Time Unspent

Though time has no bounds, it limits all men,
For we live life to its fullest, but yet all life must end.
We take a lot for granted and we know not what we miss,
But if you know not what you have, you know not what it is.
We pass our time intently, only some know where they'll go,
But for the rest of time -- lost minds, they lose touch of their souls.
They try too hard to reach their goals, caring not what's left behind,
So when their past returns for them, the shattered hearts they'll find.
They'll say their past is history, never caring for what they've done,
But deep beneath their silence proves they're not the ones who won.
If we are caught in our own arrogance, we're not willing to admit,
The longer we wait for the other to move, the deeper we fall in the pit.
To understand what life's about, give it all you can,
And in the end what you've not done, is meant to be, it's in the plan.
You learn from what you do, you learn from what you don't,
But when the final song comes 'round, the losers are the ones who
  "won't."
Life is so short, yet life is so long,
You can't make a right if you can't see what's wrong.
You know if your life's been good, if you know what it has meant,
So don't waste your time reliving the past or searching for the time
  unspent.

Clark Layman

Untitled

We laid another love away
We all meet here this day.
God why did you take our love away?
Because she's tired you say.

Yes, of course she is, how did she get that way?
By giving life and love away
Day after weary day.

To give away her love was not work to her;
she laughed and run and gave it here and there.
And now she's gone away.

We gather in this celestial hall
with verily room for all
Because we are just some;
She served along the way.

Catherine M. Pitts

What Happened

What happened to fists being the weapons in fights
To families walking on warm summer nights
To neighbors respecting each others rights
Tell me, what happened, to these?

What happened to peanuts being poured into cokes
To drive-ins and kick can, carrying groceries in pokes
When mules did the plowing, old men told boys jokes
Tell me, what happened, to these?

What happened to Dad's quarter for cutting the grass
For washing his car, for a gallon of gas
Are all of these good things just memories to pass
Tell me, what happened, to these?

What happened to little girls mimicking mom
To pig tails and sea shells, to being safe at her prom
Why have these good things been gotten away from
Tell me, what happened, to these?

What happened, is called progress, does progress deal drugs
Or is it technology, are there technical hugs
Moral parents raise leaders, moral leaders abrade thugs
May we never ask, what happened, to these!

Robert Boyles

Gunship

Out of the sorry red Vietnam sun;
Like listening into a stethoscope,
Its spinning pinwheel blades:
Making the sound of a speeding heartbeat
And rowdy rivers.

The faint murmuring sound:
Getting louder, bolder....
Darting out onto a village below,
Scanning the terrain for black pajamas:
As if on an easter egg hunt.

Unwanted ventilator thru the floor:
Nearly nipped us in the bud...
Irked, we tore along the shore,
And a little digression we took.

The turning sparkle of the rocket's blast,
Gagging the sorry sanguine sunlight:
Where shattered leafless trees turned bright:
A fortified bunker, just in sight.

Joseph Rodrigues Jr.

Like A Long, Lingering Kiss

Life should be a slow dance,
All balance and grace;
Sights, sounds and sensations savored,
Like a long, lingering kiss
That leaves you lethargic,
And slightly dazed.
But we scurry about our business,
And life leaks away from us
A gallon at a time.

Yet you were different,
You truly lived your days,
Saw the beauty in the flowers,
And the hidden melodies of songs unsung.
Your courage carried us over the chasm of your illness
And when it was time to go...
You did so with grace, like a long, lingering kiss
Goodbye.

Deanna M. St. Germain

Dad

You taught me many things, but a girl was I.
Your confidence in me, gave me strength to try...
Your words were sometimes too bold, you didn't
see when I'd cry, for still a little girl was I.
You didn't say a word, when I broke your heart,
but you took my hand and held me, and gave
me fatherly love.
I often felt that I was yours truly,
this I saw in your eyes and I knew the answer surely.
Now my eyes can't see you
and I can't feel the strength of your arms,
yet I see you... with a different sight,
so clear, so clear, so clearly.
And with your arms you're holding me tight,
so near, so near, so nearly.
Dad's little girl am I.

Cynthia J. Brewster

The Violin

I listen to the violinist play,
the sound brings me along on its way.
With gentle fingers guiding the bow
moves me closer, ever so slow.
It paints me a picture so strong,
a picture that can do no wrong.

The overture feisty and steady,
the Andante, calm and ready,
the Allegro, playful and fun,
while the Largo warms like the sun.
I'm enjoying the violin at its best,
I sit back dreaming, as I rest.

Thank God for this music so fine.
It's a glorious song that tastes like wine.
Thank God for the sound that sings.
I close my eyes, I feel like I have wings
and flying to heaven so quietly,
while touching the angels so lovingly.

Liv Elise Leftwich

What Mom Took

Most often when I think of Mom, I like to think of what she's given.
The softness of a loving touch a gentle guide for living.

A nightly tiptoe into my room or an understanding look.
But sometimes when I think of Mom, I think of what she took.

She took the child and taught me how to live my life with pride.
She took my kindergarten tears and held them all inside.

She took the hands that longed to hold this child and not let go.
She'd gently guide me along my way so I could thrive and grow.

She took my heart, when I'd hear her sing.
The music in my memory rings.

She took the time for many things but above all else for listening.

She took the time to clean and cook but never asked thanks...
for all she took.

Sharon Frost

David

My little boy, as I sit here, and watch you at your play
    I wonder, what's ahead for you, in this troubled world today
Every mothers thoughts must be paralleled along with mine
    I want for you a happy life, and every thing that's fine.

Right now, you're shooting birds you see, flying thru my kitchen door
    The tigers and the panthers, are everywhere upon my floor
And now you want your sweater. Slam-bang, there goes the door
    "Sunday". Just three days more my son, you will be four

I watch you as you cup your hands, around your baby mouth
    And call the duck, and birds, and geese as they go flying south
Here they come, get set now, hand on trigger steady
    Shoot at will, those phantom birds, you've bagged the limit already

What fun, this land of make believe
    too soon, you will emerge
I pray, my son, as years go on
    You'll be shooting, still, just birds

Dorothy O. Graham

Don't Be Scared

Let me tell you 'bout the thing that I found last night,
I went down the basement steps and then I took a right.
I took one look around the room and then I saw the creature,
Then I took a closer look and saw his special feature.

A wretched smell filled the room as the monster stood up tall,
then I saw the baby monster curled up in a ball.
Then she said a magic word that made a magic lever,
when she pulled this little thing they disappeared forever.

So if you see a monster too don't forget they're clever,
cause when they say their magic word they'll disappear forever.

Zach Sullivan

Pluperfect Promise

In the twilight of my thoughts
    you lift me up,
    carrying me,
    as if on the wind
But stable to see your truth.

In the darkest hours you swiftly move
    through the pages of my mind.

In this time of fleeting desperation
You flip to the page of enlightenment.
This enlightenment has been buried
in the pages filled with worry.

Enlightenments brought forth through your spirit,
Which you've taught me in your word.
You filled those pages with reassurance and hope,
Promising you'll always be there.

    You lift me up,
from the twilight of my thoughts.

Dawn M. Thomas

The Lonely Path

We've walked the same path, you and I,
And trod the self-same, lonely road.
Not bearing just our burden on the way
But usually bearing part of someone else's load.

The path we travelled seemed always uphill.
It was a most unfruitful lane.
But there we found exquisite happiness and ecstasy,
The happiness turned to exquisite pain.

Yes, we trod the same path, you and I.
We walked in loneliness with no one else in view.
But one day, on that path, I found a kindred soul
And now there's no one else in sight but me and you.

The path seems not so weary nor so steep
With someone else to share the loneliness and pain,
As on this path, we two, as friends will meet
And walk together and our hearts seem light again.

LaVey Adams Alexander

A Lonely Heart

I wait and wait and wait,
But I still hear no reply.
Then I begin to wonder,
And finally I ask why.
I say, "Dear, I love you,"
But there is complete silence all around.
I wait, thinking maybe I just didn't hear,
But then I realize I'm all alone.

Barbara D. Davis

My Mom

As I stare into the
shimmering light
I see nothing not a thing
The light fells cold
it chills my skin
But I am all alone
there's no one not even a soul
Just then the light
turns warm, comforting
A figure comes towards me
I feel loved
She flows to me
Her bright smile
Her gentle voice
A mother is always there for you
She teaches you to expect rainy days to come
But sunshine will always seep through
She also says miracles happen like rainbows too!!

Kayla

To A Stewardess

A stewardess lives above the clouds
Beneath the ever-azure blue.
So intimate she's grown with stars
Mirrored on wing each jewelled hue!

To catch a glimpse as she speeds by
The snow-capped peaks project their gaze.
The clouds below her sail along
Quite unaware of her sweet ways.

William Wayne Nelson

The Greatest Love

Since God created heaven and earth, a love for man was born,
But this love has been abused and often shown scorn.
This love is offered to everyone, no one is left to need.
But many seek their separate ways, God's offer they do not heed.

No greater Gift in all the world, was ever given free,
His love is given to everyone, even you and me.
And when we sin against, the Heavenly Father above,
He never turns His back to us, or takes away His love.

How can anyone, deny a love so strong,
And turn their back on Jesus, and go on doing wrong.
So seek the loving Father, who lives in heaven above,
And claim the Father's promise, of eternal life and love.

Donald D. Bastendorf

The Little Things

It's the little things I miss the most
Like sleeping together you holding me close
The times we shared together alone
Teasing and playing how love was shown
But most of all I miss the words
Told not often but meant as much
Now we are apart as well
Not speaking or touching how real
Love was good while it was here
Gone for now never fear
You will find another as I
For now we will hurt till whomever comes by
I still long for you as long as I can
Hold on to my memories forever I plan
I just tell you now don't ask me why
I'll love forever you goodbye

Karla Smith

The Working Mother

I am the working mother, I feel a lot of woe,
I know I must endure and be steady on the go.
Many days I'm weary, especially when days are dreary,
I want to rest, but I know I must do my best.
Who knows how I feel, am I human or unreal?
I get up tired, and I go to bed the same way,
Oh, God! Help me make it through the day.
Many tears have fallen more than I care to remember,
This has been my plight in life from January to December.
Who wants to emulate me? None as you can plainly see.
I am sometimes my only aid,
What a tremendous 'roe to hoe' I've made.
My children all depend on me, I'm as tired as can be.
But I must continue to persevere.
To be brave without showing any fear —
I am the working mother!!

Fredi Jackson, Ph.D.

Why Does It Make You Cry

Why does it make you cry,
When someone lays down to die?

You know they were doing bad,
But why does it make you feel so sad?

Where they are they're doing better,
But now your eyes are always wetter.

You feel sick for many days,
Your feelings change in many ways.

After feeling bad for a while,
You think about it and smile.

Not because they've gone away,
Because they did not stay another day.

If they did stay here,
They would always shed a tear.

Now you know they're in a better place,
That puts a smile on your face.

Sahara Sara Weems

God, Our Flag and Country

So proudly we stand as the flag waves on high
our hearts almost burning with pride
united we stand, divided we fall,
God and country we defend to keep freedom for all.

Our hearts sing out the words: Of the people
By the people and For the people,
as we gaze upon with awe to this symbol of freedom
Everything round about seems diminished in mist
as we focus our thoughts on this scene.

Many lives have been lost to keep old glory flying,
may they not have been given in vain.

We must show loyalty to God and our country as one
for God's blessings to be showered on us,
if we do,
all else will fall into place,
putting a glow in our hearts and a smile on our face.

Marolyn E. Baker

Portrait of a Hero

The pilgrimage was blessed with the
Presence of a basketball player.
He was tall in stature and was loved by innocent youths.
Of his time he was the best, but was overlooked for a white man.
As a youngster he struggled because of poverty,
But determination was a product of the entire ordeal.
It was said that he signed a contract
Which supported him with the necessities and more.
His wrist contained a Rolex and his hand carried a cellular phone.
His head was hairless but not due to age.
At nights he had his fun and was famous in all town bars.
His wife was left at home and was said she is now bearing fruits.
His money he kept for himself
But a tenth would go to charity in fear of God.
He was not around much on the trip
Perhaps due to his Narcicus like voyages to the men's room.
He had what he asked for when he was a youth
But his friends he left behind to struggle.
Enjoyment came when he would go to the ghettos
Wearing his custom made suit and his smile.

Emanuel Zareh

My World of Hopes and Dreams

Come little girl but wash your tears into the sky.
Where we're going you will no longer want to cry.
It's a place in a far away land, come little girl take my hand.
Don't be afraid like you were before,
step behind that once so called "closed door".
Crying is all you want to do, alone is what you say,
I know what goes on, I watch you every day.
You're becoming a teenager, yes I see,
you want to be comfortable and sometimes free.
Come with me I know who you are.
Let's go look beyond the stars.
Is it so hard to put a smile on your face?
All they have to do is win the race.
The race leading to your heart is what I'm trying to say.
Win it and never throw it away.
You will walk into my world of dreams and beautiful sounds.
That's only if you stop those tears from falling down.
So when ever you want to let out a tear, think of me and I'll appear.
I am always with you under every seasons gleam.
Remember you are always welcome to my world of hopes and dreams.

Courtney Munn

(Taken From) Last Night I Dream...

...Last night I dreamt oh heavenly dream!
That a beam of light was coming down from the heavens
proclaiming what it wanted from the men,
what this world needed most:
it wanted sincere and honest people
from the bottom of their hearts,
men who always give their back to the badness,
loyal men to their duties as the compass is to the North Pole,
men who don't betray, men who don't destroy,
humble and good men with a golden heart
to give love to everybody with their full hands,
men who always stay aside of the justice
Even if the heavens fall down!
I just woke up still feeling
the beautiful emotion of this dream.
But... what did I see on the earth?
The men destroying, betraying,
killing, and still doing the same bad things.
But... I'm a man too!
And I started crying!

Fernando D. Medina

My Sister Bay

Legs closed, eyes open.
Grandma praying.
Mama hoping,
Hoping I don't end up like my sister Bay.

Skirts tight, heels tapping.
Old women gawking.
Old men lapping,
Lapping like dogs in heat when Bay walked the street.

Five kids, four different men.
A night at the club,
In love again.
The next day, she'd give it up to a man without knowing his last name.

Busted lips, swollen eyes.
Her man beat her down.
Enjoyed her cries,
Then promised not to ever raise his fist to her face again.

Legs open, eyes closed.
Dried up blood left a trail from her nose.
Though her face was badly scarred,
We knew the naked body was my sister Bay.

LaJenine T. Wilson

God Is The Answer

This world it is a horrible place.
Is there something against the human race?
The drugs, the rape, the blood and death.
Is there a way? Is there any hope left?
Yes there is. Believe it or not.
There is an answer. His name is God.
Why do we believe to get through the times,
We have to murder, do drugs, and other crimes?
He built the earth as a place to grow,
Not to destroy the grounds we know.
In other lands the children starve,
And we stand here with meat to carve.
If you stopped to think about all the troubles,
You'd find out a lot more than gripes, complaints and grumbles.
We are all God's children and he loves us all.
But we need more to get over the wall.
If we do our part to help our lives
We wouldn't need guns, weapons, and knives.
If you are with me raise your hands.
Shout the Lord's name and praise His land.

Lacey Michelle Holcomb

Mother's Day Poem

You may write a thousand letter's, to the girl that you adore,
And declare in every letter, that you love her more and more.

You may praise her grace and beauty, in every glowing line,
And compare her eye's of azure, to the brightest star that shine.

Now, if I had the pen of Shakespeare, I would use it every day,
In composing written lyric, to my sweetheart far away.

But the letter far more welcome, to an older gentler breast,
Is the letter to my Mother, from her boy whom she loves best.

She well read it very often, when the light's are soft and low,
Sitting in the same old corner, where she held me long ago.

And regardless of its diction, or its spelling, of its style,
All do its compositioning, would provoke a critic smile.

In her sweet and tender fingers, it becomes a work of art,
Stained by the tears of joy and sadness, as she hugs it to her heart.

Yes, The letters of all letters, look where ever you my roam,
Is the letter to my Mother, from her boy away from home.

John Peters

New Diamond Auroras By Love!

Above at twelve everbloom months, top flavor dove-white
kerryberry, a crop saver for all, at new dash rose purple
fashions of sun flame white peaches, may get aurora
clad fun mists of real need by future zeal heed in
aurora genuine diamond greenhouse homes given by a
mankind's keeper rule of instant wealth
to all, not similar duty nations of Cain's born mad
swarm cowers to invent dependent self-destruct tax to
later jilt all justice lead to wars of coy trust and
death to all, unlike any royal birthright wealth giving
beliefs of Able, in a global past era greenhouse made
by clouds of pristine sun filter waters, later crash
froze to thaw past the poles near vast soil beauty
crust tunnel of love, like YHVH jewel-white panacea
love in fruity sensations of new ultra-modern Edenic beauty
sensations inside of the larger hollow Earth having rivers,
no oceans, no streams or earthquakes in a natural seed shape
double world of genius charm hours gifts to
graduate mankind into immortal flesh, of fruit hybrid charm
powers, away from Satan having destroyed two worlds, away
from warm flowers barnyard Earth mad dinosaurs of the
alien mad sun, or Cain's bad run in all ahoy
thrust eras of toy rust, but, under a new
land and sun with an elegant cash pose, like
a jubilee bouquet of pleasures to cherish in, new diamond
aurora by love ...

Aloha E. Grant

Untitled

Sitting all alone
In the dark
Listening to the rain
Fall to the dry ground
Thinking about my past
And of those who walked out of my life
Everyone leaves you at some point in time
But most of them leave for a reason
'Til this day, I have no idea of what the reason is
Was it something that I did
That made you leave me so soon?
I have feeling that others will soon follow in your footsteps
Is there something that I can do to stop it?
I wish that you were here to tell me the answer
But like the others, you walked out of my life
And I now realize that you will never come back

Stephanie Mineo

Untitled

I'm only just beginning to see your trust and love for me.
To see you as vulnerable and as dependent on me as I am you.
To see you as the love of my life.

I've spent so long trying to protect myself against any possible hurt,
That I have blinded myself to the reality of your love.

Forgive me for taking so long to open myself to you—
For being too cautious with my feelings for you,
For being careless and too occupied with life's demands to see
when you're reaching out to me...

Thank you for trusting me with your love!

Paula S. Dowdle

Misjudgement

People are so strange today, they judge your looks and what you
say. They judge you by your length of hair, or judge you by the
clothes you wear. They judge you by your color skin, or judge
you by your next of kin. But me, I judge not class nor pride,
the part that counts is what's inside!

Jimmy Barthlein

446

I Love My Mommy

I love my mommy because she cares,
I love my mommy because she's always there

I love my mommy because she loves me for me,
I love my mommy because she makes me feel free

I love my mommy because she's someone to talk to
All I want to say is, "Mommy I love you."

Sharla Wilson

A Husband's Lament

I don't need a doctor, my wife's a hospital volunteer
She's picked up some medical knowledge from all she hears
When I'm on the golf course and getting ready to putt.
I recall her words as I look down at my gut
For they keep running around in my head
All the helpful things that she's said
Just ditch that cigarette, don't you dare smoke
Don't you care that others around you cough and choke
Stop eating that chocolate bar, it's full of fat
Put away those potato chips, you can't have any of that
So what do I "nosh" on when I'm watching T.V.?
Her healthy advice is sure getting to me
I think of Jack Sprat if you know what I mean
Get rid of the fat, keep your body lean
I know my wife wants the very best for me
Even thought she keeps harping continuously
'Cause if I live longer she's got someone to nag
But just between us, I really love the old hag

Ruth Stalerman

Spoken Words

The limbs reach out in gentle beckoning.
On a single branch, a bird is pecking.
A new found home, but the tree is loyal.
The strong body twists down to the dark soil.

As a gentle wind moves through the branches,
It smiles while it watches his dances.
It softly speaks its wisdom to he,
Trying desperately to make him see.

"Listen," it pleads as he starts to walk away.
Maybe he will return another day.
Will he ever listen to its message?
Will he ever understand or acknowledge?

As hard as it tries, as hard as it might,
It will always shadow the light.

Lisa Edgington

The Gatekeeper

I start each day in search of the truth,
The enlightened spirit that was lost in my youth.
I've struggled without; Lord knows I've struggled within
Never really knowing where to begin.

There have been many detours along the way.
I never realized who had to pay.
My world was blackened by my false belief,
A dark cloud forever with no chance for relief.

As I search within and trust in my soul,
I envision a rainbow as the drums begin to roll.
I have embraced the wisdom, the awareness to know
During the most troubled times exactly where to go.

My heart is the place and it always will be,
The owner of this elusive key, the one that I will always see,
Now I know...
The gatekeeper is me.

Dave Kochenberger

Shh

Shh — do not speak, be very still
Listen to the silent words
Hear the sounds of movement
Shh — listen to what you don't hear

Shh — the baby is in her sleep
Her chest moves with inhale, her mouth curls a grin
New to the world and need of care
Shh - listen to the love of innocence

Shh - the ballerina takes the stage
Her feet are soft - the music is just a glow
Rhythmically a story unfolds
Shh - listen to the magic of dance

Shh - the priest ascends the altar
The host is raised, the wine is blest
With faith and praise we are saved
Shh - listen to the grace of God

Shh — the funeral coach is passing
Sadness and tears walk close behind
Gone from us now, her work is finished
Shh - listen to the peace of death

Dennis J. Dopkins

On An Airplane With A Frequent Flyer

"I was once on a flight to Hawaii and I was waiting in line
for the lavatory. There was always a line for a flight
this long, you know, it seemed the washrooms
were always on demand on a flight this long. So
I finally got into the washroom, you know, and I
looked into the toilet, and someone, well, lost the battle
against a very healthy digestive system and left the
"spoils" in the toilet, stuck. Maybe it didn't want to go
down into the sewage tank where all the other
waste from this long trip went to. Can you imagine
all the stuff this airplane had to carry across the ocean?
Well, anyway, so I saw this stuck in the toilet, and I
went to the washroom, and when I was done it still
wouldn't budge, and so I opened the door and walked out
into the aisle of people waiting to use this cramped
little washroom, and I just wanted to tell them all,
'you know, I didn't do that.' And then it occurred to me
that everyone, when they leave the bathroom on that
plane, will think the exact same thing."

Janet Kuypers

The Last Katydid of Summer

All summer long your evening song has made vibrating chorus
   across the mountain forests.
How irrepressible your ecstatic joy of life and love beneath
   the summer stars!
We listened from the man-made deck, a bit above the valley
   of the ridges,
And felt our very blood grow tyrannous with ancient primal
   passions.
Hearing you, we could not doubt that we would live forever,
Knowing well you would return each summer, always and forever.
Yet, now in gold October, your tribe all fled to destined silence,
You alone linger on, a single voice, still chirping.
My love, my tiny dying ghost of night, lost like a valiant echo
   among the darkened hills,
Is it joy your dying notes encompass, Katy, or a silly sorrow
   for the fate of man,
Who knows he shall not return?

John Craig Stewart

Untitled

In the deepest darkness,
when everything seems to conspire against you,
a new light opens, awakens, parting the darkness.
That ray of light is hope, helping change darkness to a different hue.
If you don't lose it or your will, your despair will change to nightless.

Benjamin Sunde

Untitled

As I sit in my room
Bars in front
Walls of stone
Life passes in front of my eyes
I dream of life beyond these walls of stone
I have eyes but can not see
Dream that I can not dream
So
What should I do

Johnnie P. Clagg

Oh, Hearken Prose

Oh, hearken prose, being present to behold
Beauteous the senses, this arduous amuse
Awake, I beseech thee, the gleam of blissfulness

Bound upon vivid wisdom, oh, delicious is the word
Utmost versed twine, promise and treasure
Transcends worth, brace with virtue, my friends

Petition rays of purifying vigilance, preserved by powers that be
Heavens offering, hearts delight, distant voices ascend
Virgil and Dante, cascade forth with springs from their fountains

Thence, embrace passionate, desire for the prose
Echoes whisper a delicate promise, beloved, celebrate verse
Trumpets resounding, substained, sweet varieties sublime

Inspiration rests restored, upon this fertile heart
Adorn, with valuable things, nurture deeply this sacred art
Stretch, no bounds, proclaim: The purposer is watching

Endless electrifying aim, glows upon this moment
Majestic powers, birth the souls, ultimate cry, "Go for the goal"
Purpose purpose, fulfilled, fulfilled

Patricia Tinoco

Jimmy and Sooky

Jimmy was the boy and Sooky was the girl
They both swam around the Bay in a whirl

They ate those dead things, deed they did
The scum of the Bay - they helped to rid

Sooky laid her babies way down South
The water's salty there - it's called the Mouth

Crabs have hard shells — but they get soft
- (a couple times a year) - they don't do it oft'

What happens is they need a bigger shell
- (a couple times a year) cause they grow like hell

Spring and Summer they stay in shallow water —
Winter they go deep (and South if they wanna)

Now, they have to be a fighter with lots o' clout -
- cause waterpeople catch 'em and sell 'em out!

Once they sell 'em people buy 'em by the lot!
Them Jimmy and Sooky end up in a Pot!!!

Beverley Covert

Untitled

When the cage is opened, I'll still know how to fly!
I'll catch the wind to play and dance across the sky.

Oh, yes! I know I will. My heart was never penned.
In one long burst of joy, up! Through the door, ascend.

Yes, stretch my eager wings, long fettered and unused.
So long (but nevermore) locked up, disdained, abused.

It's better far to risk in winging high and free
Than stay within a cage in scant security.

Heart, polish up your song. Our freedom time is near.
Remove that plaintive tune and simply leave it here.

Nancy Cohn

A True Mistake

I see my friend lying there, her face so ghostly white.
The doctors say it's not too good, she may not get through the night.
What were we possibly thinking, when we decided to drive drunk?
Better to have stayed, shared a two person bunk.
Better to have passed out, with a hangover the next day.
Than to be in this stuffy hospital, worrying over you this way.
The doctors say pull the plug, because you'll never make it.
I run, where I don't know, my poor heart just can't take it.
Now I stand over your grave, trying to stop the tears.
"Friends to the very end," our motto for all these years.
I whisper "I miss you", as the tears continue to fall.
It hurts so much to read the headline "Teenager Lost To Alcohol"

Maria Mills

Song of Four Seasons

Drizzly raindrops I am in spring,
With tenderness filled to the brim.
Am I lingering with willows full of dream,
Or, with the silent breeze flirting?

Summer night, I whisper, is me,
With my heart always vexed alone.
Is it because dawn comes too soon,
Or, because the sun sets too late to the sea?

Autumn leaves I'm supposed to be,
Have fallen into the mist of sorrow.
Must I surrender to the crystal water flow,
Or, adhere to the crimson maple tree?

I am earth in winter, I declare,
Forever enslaved by unending toil.
Should I freely melt into spring soil,
Or, just remain settled, with care?

Mamie Huo

Last Leaf

The frisky autumn winds at play
Swirled round the leaf and seemed to say,
Seek admiration while you may
Before your colors fade away.
Do not cling to oak tree bare.
Join your comrades; take to air.

While North winds howled their fiercest song,
This lone leaf hung the winter long.
Spring must not find it, sere and old,
Among the young buds, green and gold.
Oh, March winds carry it to earth
Beneath the tree which gave it birth.

Memory Lane

Samaritan Woman Revisited

All alone at my empty well
you came to visit me in Samaria last night.
No holy visitation in an ancient Middle East,
you were an angel who boldly braved the Samaria
that sits in the middle of me...

Your gentle eyes put me at ease
and I dared to draw you close.
The warming wisdom that searched my soul
shrank not as I approached.
So I lifted my leg to show you my wound
"Will you nurse it so I can walk?"

Then I cut a cloth, the fabric of dreams
to dip in your wisdom's bowl
soaked through with kindness, clothed by your hand
you washed it clear over my soul.

Proof of His presence, for a doubter named Thomas,
"Let me finger the Master's wound."
Would I be convinced if I touched Christ's side
or did He through you
touch my wounded pride?

  Denise M. Rowe

Looking for Self

I found myself looking for myself in strange and awkward ways.
At first I started out scouring for hidden emotions and beguiling
  traits hoping to unlock deep dark untold secrets.
Like a Bosnian refugee, I felt at times a victim and at times a
  predator.
Soon, I taught myself the importance of discovering virtues over vile.
Suddenly it seems there is lots more to learn, much more than I ever
  imagined, now that the focus is right.
Now, the quest to learn about myself is proceeding as a deep
  self-searching introspection; an examination of feelings,
  emotions, and conceptualization.
The "objective me" is the researcher, methodically probing the
  "subjective me" for interesting modes of patterns and behaviors.
The "objective me" feels like the archaeologist, digging
  for "good" finds. The "subjective me" is constantly
experiencing a sort of catharsis and rejuvenation, all at the time.
Myself emerges, each time a little more informed about myself...

  Maggie Gray

Reflections

Guns erupt! There goes another child
My my, our cities gone wild.

Is everyone blind! Can't anyone see?
Some things gone wrong with our future to be.

Are they to blame? I think not.
We used to teach something different.
We must have forgot.

Though blames not the answer,
Nor question to pain.
It's how can we change it,
To total gain.

Sweet sweet child, rest in peace.
Sorry you had to die in our streets.

  Jody Robertson

Untitled

I want to scream to the sky, and whisper to a budding rose.
I want to run and never stop. I want to be alone, alone with
the sun and the sky. I want to converse with the rustling of
the leaves and blow with the gusting of the wind. I want to
stand tall with the trees. And when nightfall comes, I want
to glow with the full moon, twinkle with the radiant stars
and fly with the night owl. I want to cry with Mother Nature
and stop the ticking of father time and spend the rest of
eternity one with nature.

  Megan Williamson

The Touch of a Lover

The touch of a lover
Caressing my soul.
Sends my spirit reeling
To ecstasy unknown.

But if lack of this
Experience leaves you to guess.
It sounds so grand
Delusional at best.

For you who do not know
Of what I speak.
The hand of a lover
Only touched your cheek.

Dedicated to Jan Hebert: Who Never Knew
  How Much She Meant.
My Fear of Love Kept Me Silent.

  Gene Fitz

When Black People Died

Father of nine
Went somewhere to hide

Mother of five
Committed suicide

Fourteen-year-old boy
Shot over pride

Thirteen-year-old girl
Went on a joyride
Discovered in a trash bin
Her brain fried.

Farrakhan attempted to stem the bloody tide
He had a million different reasons
No one else tried.

Politicians will set you free
Sorry, they lied

Welfare recipient
Your benefit's been denied

All the black gone, the reason:
GENOCIDE.

  David L. Terry

Eternity

A trillion stars dot heaven's sky, as diamonds in the air.
Their radiance a golden white, each holds a pauper's prayer.
Crystal sparkling spaciousness all my eyes can see.
Light years of new beginnings, with instants that are free.
I wish that I could travel, to each one to view its core.
The inner pulse of its domain, the glory of its lore.
New hope that is projected, from a power that's to be.
Life's secret of existence, concealed in barren sea.
Locked evidence of mystery, of God's far reaching hand.
Blind openings to comprehend, all though I understand,
A trillion stars dot heaven's sky, are only what I see.
Beyond that there are trillions more.

  Edward A. Nicholson

Counseling

Dedicated to G.L.B.

He's sitting there, he's looking at me
I wonder, wonder, what does he see?

He's smiling at me, reaching out
I hide, I look away, I go inside

Uncomfortable...Embarrassed...
He's still looking at me
Doesn't he know there is nothing to see?
A nobody, a me!

I have needs to be met, but, not by him
The needs that I feel
Must be filled from within

He can take notes, use me as he pleases
How do I feel? The inside of me freezes

Does he know who I am?
Sitting here so smugly
While I sit across, feeling so ugly

Is he still looking?
Does he care how I feel? Why?

Why is he looking? What can he see?
Help! Help! I can't find me.

    Cynthia Colella

Atlantis

So close, yet so far away
A conch shell screams
For the distant ocean.

Digging deep, deep within thyself
The exploration begins
For the strength to break down
This wall of sand
To find thy own way.

Follow the stars to thy heart
To discover the hidden key
To let me out and set thy free
From this lost destiny.

Thy begin to journey, into the vast Atlantic
As thy skin scrapes the barnacles of fear away
I call to the spirits, blinded by a rising sun
To guide thyself and release thy inner being.

Come ride with the dolphin
Fly with the sea gull and sing with the whales
To keep thyself afloat
In these times of changing tides.

    Cheryl J. Field

The Best Embrace

She must have been at home in Lakeland Village.
Thick glasses, slanted eyes, a mongoloid.
The wind was ripping at our hair, at every thistle
And every other thing on the plains.
"Do you want a hug?" I nodded `yes'.
As if between trains whistling North
And whistling South,
We held each other; we held ourselves.
It was the finest hug.
Amid entangled relations, I savor
Its simplicity.
It is as good now as it was then.

    Inge Ferrari

A Call To Mama

I called my Mama late last night
    to ask how she has been,
I've missed her much throughout the years
    and wish we could walk together again.
We chatted about the good old days
    and all the things she used to do,
About the times we put our heads together
    and all the special secrets that we knew.
We talked of all the dreams we had
    of many gardens planted so long ago,
Spoke of all the loving stitches she made
    on my new dress that she hand-sewed.
My Mama went away a few years ago
    but, it seems she's near me everyday,
I've walked and talked with her in my heart
    and I know my life will be okay.
Mama left here and lives in Heaven now
    but, we visit every now and then,
It's so nice to know I don't need a phone
    when I want to talk to her again.

    Eileen Caszatt

Questions

If Jesus came to earth today
What would I do, what would I say
Would I believe that it was he
Or just a dream, a fantasy...

I'd like to know so many things
What songs the angel chorus sings.
Is heaven such a wondrous place
Or a mirage, in outer space.

How do we live among our brothers
And how to cope with other colors.
I think he'd have two words to say
One would be "love", the other "pray".

And so I knew that it was he
the man who walked that day with me,
and then he threw me for a loss
he said, "my friend, pick up my cross"...

    Darlene E. Rogers

A Gang Is Not So Bad

Some goals seems unreachable
due to our color or background
drugs, prostitution and joining a gang
is the avenue we often found

Some obstacles seems unmovable
therefore, we retreat toward the back door
fighting one another with gun and knives
by declaring life is a war

The battle of survival in our neighborhood
have turned many of us cold
we cheat, steal and lie in wait
until the fame of wealth and riches unfold

But if we really took the time
to look what we have become
joining gang is not so bad
at least we all can be one

For it took the Hispanic to discover American
and the Indians to cultivate this land of the free
The black to build and the White to industrialized
But it takes (a gang) all men to unite to bring liberty

    Donna McFadden

Reflections In The Night

A gentle wind stirs the night. The moon resides
Beside the clouds. Trees silhouetted in the foreground
Off-set by the prism-like sunset.
Unpainted picket fences surround the rustic estate.
A natural spring trickles through the shallow stream bed.
Trout are feasting on the hatch, as I hear a soft splash.
I walk along the bank to gaze upon this festive dance.
Frogs sing their merry song, as I walk further upstream.
Slowly I step into the reservoir to soothe my troubled mind.
Before I took this walk-about I needed to unwind; reflecting
Upon the sights and sounds I've encountered to better grasp
How far I've come. Though I know I've got a long way to go, I
Feel my optimism begin to grow.
I must be going now, I regret I have to leave, but I conceive
What I believe to be a feeling of happiness.
I must return now to my empty nest, lest it be no longer mine.
Time and its constraints are catching up with me, it's grown
So dark now I strain my eyes to see. But I carry a light inside
My soul to guide me through the murk as I lurk homeward.
I reach my humble chariot and commence to sojourn home.

John Carter Bennett

"The Pastor And The Good Neighbor"

I shed many sad tears this past weeks;
over the death of two people, I chance to meet.
Although, not very close to me, they were my friend;
I've seen and talked to them, for years!
It seems like just yesterday we met;
How did 25 years, or so, go by so fast?
We'd say, "Hello! Have a nice day!"
Sometimes saying, "Happy Holiday! I'll pray on that!"
Often we'd talk over the fence, being neighborly.
Frequently fellowshipping in church or snacking ice cream.
No more will I see their happy, smiling face;
Their suffering has ended and ours just begun.
I see sad, tear-laden family members now,
Trying to cope with the loss of their loved relative.
Consoling words seem empty and inadequate.
I'll miss you more than I can say;
Your family will be in my prayers, everyday.
Shalom, neighbor! God Bless, Pastor!
I'll try to meet you in Heaven, some day.

Leona A. Knoll

Dreams

Dreams of today, for tomorrow not lost.
Life is a dream, a dream we each must fulfill.
Dreams of happiness hide deep inside each of us,
So deep they are hard to find.

Wonders to live and to fulfill,
We must each find.
Only here a short time, which passes quicker
    than the speed of light,
We each must reach out, grab our dream, hold tight.

Life is like a dream, full of dreams only a few
    of us will reach, due to the obstacle of our life.
Each day we are cut short of our dreams.
We must all pull together, stand as one link in a chain,
one link is broken, the chain is weak.
To make our dreams come into prospective
We must all hold a link to the chain and a key to
release our dreams.

The key to our dreams is only held by one,
The Supreme Being who holds the key to all links.
Open our hearts and let the key be turned into dreams.

Shane Dale

Friendship...

Friendship is the best thing that you and I
share. Whenever I need a shoulder to cry on
or someone to share all my hopes and fears, I
know you'll always be there! Some days can be
rough on you, but no matter what happens,
you know I'll always be there to pull you
through. You remind me of a sweet little dove,
always caring, quiet and full of love. You must
have been sent, from the angels above! When
I look in the mirror, all I see is myself,
looking back at me. Always looking around, not
saying a word, because I had no one to
talk to. You and I have a friendship that won't
ever die. No one could separate it, not even if
they tried. So just remember this... Through
every struggle and strife, we're friends that can
not be apart. As long as we live, we've got each
other. You just always remember that. We
are friends for life, that no one could take
away. Just you and I!!!

Angelia Fisher

You and I

I may have brown hair, you may not.
I may have blue eyes, you may not.
You may have designer clothes, I may not.
Don't judge me by my cover,
Open me up and you'll see
I am your brother.

Whether were a different color,
or from a different place,
You don't judge people
By our language or our face.
If everybody learned
To be each other's friend.
Racism then, would
Come to and end.

Friendship comes in all different kinds,
Open up your hearts and minds.
We come from different worlds and countries,
Some are poor and some with luxuries.
Unity comes from opening your hand,
And holding each other's from land to land.

Kelly L. Wuori

The Powers That Be

There was a time, not long ago, most of my life you see
I dared not make a single move, fear of the powers that be

The powers were not of the Lord or of heavenly things
I feared the truth and opinions of other human beings

As time goes by and lessons learned it's easier to see
That they have been afraid, almost as much as me

I thought by now I'd know so much, knowledge vast and wide
The only knowledge that I have is that I hold inside.

Trust yourself, God is within, you've heard those words before
But it is life's lessons that open up the door.

The time has come, in each our lives, where we must believe
That destiny dwells inside our hearts and we can achieve

There is no need to be afraid, and even if you are
Remember you are not alone, He's never very far

Look deep inside your heart, trust in what you see
That is where the truth lies, Trust the Powers that Be

Julia M. Alvarez

Easter What Does It Mean To You?

Colored eggs to be hid in the tall grass,
Little girls in white pinafores and pink ruffles,
Little boys with bow ties and long pants...

Or could it just mean the six hours on a Friday
that Christianity was born?

For one's darkest failures
that Friday means Forgiveness.

For the heart that burns with futility
that Friday means Purpose.

For the soul looking into the side of life
that is darkest known as death,
that Friday means Deliverance.

And that is like a spring breeze on Easter Sunday.

God gave His very best on the Altar of the Cross,
His Son Jesus Christ,
so that we might have those things:

Forgiveness, Purpose and Deliverance.

How blessed we are to have had those six hours on that one Friday,
to be able to see what God has prepared
For those who love and believe in Him.

Marion Darling

Daisy

She loves me, she loves me not,
Do the petals only fall to rot?
Does it matter the truth in this?
Will love ever again truly exist?
The daisy, its symbol of simpleness,
Its wild, untamed beauty so lifeless.
Yet contains so much pride in its bloom,
The victim of an inescapable doom.
Too soon die from time's own wrath,
A fall it must take on life's chosen path.
But it begins anew if given the chance,
To shine again and possibly enhance,
The beauty it can call its own,
That cannot be produced by itself alone.
And so the petals begin to fall again,
They are like tears if you really listen...

Jeremy Goff

God's Gifts

God gave us the mountains, the valleys and seas...
He gave us hot Summer months, and the cooling Autumn breeze...
God gave us Winter's snow, with its blanket of white...
And the seeds that will flower thru Springtime's delight.

God gave us the trees, extending high towards the sky...
A haven for birds as they fly by...
God gave us the fields and meadows nearby...
He gave us the rain, to replenish when dry.

God gave us the rainbow, colors warm and bright....
He gave us blue skies with fluffy clouds of white...
God gave us the sun, bringing warmth from above...
He gave us the moon to enhance our love.

All this God gave us, to sing life's song...
He gave us our loved ones, to guide us and help us along...
He's given us endurance and the strength to overcome...
All those unexpected things in life that seem to come undone.

He's given us a loving heart, bringing tears of joy and sorrow..
He's instilled in us the faith we need to carry on each
tomorrow...
He has given us countless blessings, to brighten our way...
And always—God gives us—the gift of a "now day."

Anna Rose Maertzig

Scented Forever...

Fate might have had a reason
For lending us only a piece of time
Just a wink to know and to share
Each other's dreams and aspirations
Though it transpired this way
I didn't regret being scented
With the fragrances of your soul
'Cause with each smile and tap
You had whole heartedly shaped with me
Be it the slightest stroke
Or concern left undivulged, yet deeply felt
Restored the redness of my heart
So if there's one greatest thing
That ought to linger in the distant scene
It is your sweetly scented memories
Swarming in my atmosphere
You who had let me taste
The sweetness of a friendship
That has grown deep as the ocean.

Alice D. Aquino

Nocturnal Studies

Syrup words run heavy, slow
Black soldiers in white fields, immovable at guard
Sentences slip through the sift of consciousness
as hours take flight.

Blurred digital numbers mark, through the numbing dust
minutes shot down.
Time impends in the late hour silence

Pages stretch, infinite
Light, bleak... and harsh, scorches cold
Cutting white pallid flesh; before weary eyes, the
Text runs together, a clot of black blood.

Narcotic steam arises from the coffee
as caffeine runs its course,
Frazzled nerves poisoned from their slumber.

Alice Lieu

If You Were...

If you were to get married once more
Would I be the one you'd be looking for?
The one you'd always adore
the one you'd love for evermore

If you were to be married yet another time
Would I be the one who'd make your heart chime?
The one with whom you'd share
the one for whom you'd really care

If you were to get married sometime near
Would I be the one you'd call dear
the one you'd always cherish
the one to fulfill your every wish

If you were to be married once again
Would I be the one that you'd want then
the one you'd want for your wife
the one you'd treasure all your life

Marda Rowe

Mother

I know my mother walks with Jesus
In that distant, promised land,
Where she and her many friends
March along with the heavenly band.

Soon we shall all meet again
With the angels in the sky,
Where we will join our Saviour
Nevermore, will we have to die.

We will know the Prince of Peace
By the nail-scars in his hands and feet,
And his thorn-pierced forehead
Yet, moreover, never once did he retreat.

We'll have a new name in glory
That only we shall know,
Old things have passed away
The promises of God, have made it so.

Our dear mother may set a table
With food of a heavenly savoring,
And we shall ever be blessed
With the presence of Jesus our King.

Arlie E. Ashe

Animated People

Animated people
Living in their space
Singing songs of death
Finding empty souls with no place
We hear their voices in our brains
Planting a seed of inspiration
Twisting our thoughts towards hate
They've become a hateful crowd
They want us to follow
As we listen to their song
We become slaves to them
Our bodies do their bidding
We are toys for them to play with
They become Gods as we bow to them
They may not be smart
But to us they are superior
They control us we do their will
More and more will come
More and more will die
More souls to be lost and no one will care why...

Christine Edson

What Is Fear?

Stop and listen, outside the pane
As rain taps gently, calling.
You'll hear someone, from whom we hide in fright
Outside when water's falling.

"Who's there?" I cry, in lonely fear
Of nothing I can name.
Perhaps the hard, rhythmical beat
Is what drives me insane.

Or is it the Darkness, a child's game,
That was "just a state of mind?"
Is this every person dreads,
That the someone hides behinds?

But what do we fear? Is it a thing
That we can see or touch?
Or an apparition that we almost grasp,
Then lose in a windy gush?

There are a thousand ways to harm us, kill us,
Yet terror drives these things.
We've nothing to fear but Fear itself,
And our fellow human beings.

Christine Rollins

Love Hurts

Our love is a flower that blooms in the sun,
It's deeper than the deepest rivers that run,
But you have to go away,
So you're letting me go,
These memories we had together,
Are easily thrown away by you,
You never told me you love me,
You never cared for me,
And that's what hurts the most.

Love hurts when the love you thought was there slowly vanishes,
How could you hurt me like that?
The love is gone,
and I see you've found a new one,
I have no one to care for,
No one to share my love with,
Why is it so easy for you to find someone new?
Is this how I should feel?
Lonesome and filled with sorrow?
No, it should be you, the one to take the blame,
You should be filled with shame, for leaving me to find another.

Florence Vianzon

My Mother

You may have, more than, one father in life,
but only, one mother, and her you should love.
To me, it's like a special ordination, sent by God,
with his, blessing from above.
A woman, your mother, who carries you, in her
womb, for nine months, is one of a kind.
Her love, and your love for her, is very special,
and should be, of one mind.
My love, my God, yes even my life, was given by,
my mother.
So if there, is any one, that I should truly love,
besides God, it's her, and none other.

For every mother, that was here, is here, or
will be here.

Myron Rudel

A SuperSonic Boom

All male, with manly features is this selection,
A creamy dark chocolate, is his complexion.

With bold sexy big eyes, covered with brows,
A negro nose and juicy lips that produce growls.

Power forward biceps, maneuvered with skills,
Hand not to palm, but fingers to bring forth chills.

Oh, what awesome display of versatility,
Smooth moves, legs of spring converting to jump-a-bility!

Such new found maturity to implement his game,
Champion or not, there's no need to be ashamed.

Yes, he's all that and one monster dunk says he's no wimp,
It could only be one Sonic, of course it's Shawn Kemp!

Rita D. Knox

On Passing Steel Mills In Indiana

If you must pass the steel mills
Coated black in all their grime,
Their gracious billows of the white, white steam
Can raise your soul in time.

And when the slag is dumped at night
Against the inky blackness,
There's a glow of firery red and orange,
As if 'twas beaut'y madness.

Virginia Wootten

Anne

In Green Gables far from sea,
I met a girl who talked like me.
She was kind and sweet,
I'm glad to meet.
Friends forever,
we're always together.
Enemies may be easy to find,
but friends like us take some time.
Such nice flowers in the garden,
give me powers that allow me pardon.
The day is tough but nice and pretty.
I am quite rough but my sites a pity;
long red hair,
freckles on the side.
It is not fair,
It's a thing I must hide.

Fariha Esmail

Jesus

Jesus said love one another
he didn't mean only your
sister, your brother.
Your neighbor, enemy, all
mankind is what this dear man had in mind.
Treat others as you would
have them treat you.
Don't slander or judge them
I beg of you.
Love God with all your
heart and soul, and watch a
different life unfold.
Do all the things
Jesus said to do,
and God will be watching
over you.

Mabel Lodge

Life

I like everything you see
Life means that much to me.

I like to hear the robins sing
A baby's smile lights up everything.

Basking in the sun, as it shines is bright
And the stars and moon glowing at night.

When I see a rainbow in the sky
I always make a wish as it passes by.

My wish is that everything would forever be
Life means that much to me

Bettie Thomas

Moment

Don't look for the insight
Of an almighty hand in your dreams,
Nor adorn with laurel
The insipid mixture of existence.
   That's simply not the point.

Ephemeral beauty is, alas,
But the moment
When the yelling light
Rushes straight into the day
   Makes real sense, it's just worth it.

George Vassilev

Diesel

A myriad of mouths mumble as people move almost mechanically from one
motion to the next.
The red cap seeming to take flight as he moves amongst them:
Some wearing business suits of the shiniest dark gray,
Some wearing blue dungarees and backpacks,
Even some wearing tiny shorts while they hold onto an older hand.

It's time to get Diesel

Outside this rectangular box of confusion, the "Roman Redeye" stands
on rusted steel rollers;
Ash-silver cars bustling with internal commotion preparing to receive
another load.

It's time to get Diesel

Furiously the platform fills with frantic free agents fighting each
other to be first before the final call.
The chain of cars disappearing into the sunset:
As I hear the clanging of the wheels on the track,
As I hear conversations becoming nothing but faint whispers,
Even as I hear the "hoot—hooooooooot" of the whistle, humming its
first song into the falling light.

No time left of get Diesel

Cheryl J. Smith

Soothed Pain

If you would ever leave me, the stars would no more shine. If you
would ever go away, you'd never more be mine. My lonely heart
could not withstand the emptiness that would be, for loving you and
having you near means everything to me. He came to me when least I
knew that a love could be both lasting and true. My feelings at first
were friendly at best, but now he is loved far more than the rest.
He breaths in his soul a love for me that I will cherish until I die.
He is my love and I'll always pray that he never says goodbye. I hold
him near and think to myself what makes him want to stay, with harsh
and bitter feelings of life I burden on his shoulders each day.
complaints and resentments are all too many, loving words are all too
few. My love seems yet so far and unyielding, if only he really knew.
My feelings are real and will learn to be shown, with time it can be
proved. My love for him will last and grow into one which all pain
will be soothed.

Sandra Francine Murden

Challenging the Season Spring to Fall

Depending on where we live, the seasons commonly known,
summer, winter, spring and fall, we're certainly aware of them all.
I'm changing a spring day in May, to the season... "Fall"!
Bear with me a little while, and I'll tell you all.

The perennials with their tiny buds were already sprouting.
I envisioned open mouths of off springs from aviary friends.
As ever year past, I proceeded my chores as a dutiful gardener,
to prune, clip and separate, and try to make amends.

As I jumped upon a spade to split an over grown devil,
I discovered it was quite unwilling and had a mind of its own!
A conspiracy, there had to be, between that spade and plant,
for my body dove back, "No nestea plunge"...but a fall upon my tailbone.

Landing on some rocks, they had no sympathy. A mere little bush
my head lay in, comforted and cushioned me. I thought I heard it
cry. Have I lost my mind? Instead it was an ambulance, to carry
my little behind!

Horizontally I lay on rocks, so calloused and so cold. Even the sky
had turned on me, in shades of grey and darker. Swirling
thoughtlessly in so few seconds, as black engulfed me like a magic marker.

Medically termed a "Doughnut", I sit upon this foam. Not custard
filled nor sprinkles on it, I find it difficult, writing this poem!

Dottie Maick-Race

Love Is Life

Love is believing, love is giving; love is as strong as, death is not living.
Love is not an act, but love is a fact; Love saves, Love heals, Love
builds, Love seals!
Love is you caring, love is true sharing; love is deciding, you want
to love someone.
Love is receiving, when someone's part of you; you can't live without
them, when this love is true.
Love is to miss your love, when they are not around; love wishes the
best for the person who is loved.
Love is believing, when mind is not caring; love can deceive you, if
it comes from Satan.
Love is believing, love is giving; love is as strong as, death is not living.
Love is in your act, yet love is a fact; Love saves, Love heals, Love
builds, Love seals!
God is Love.

Kent Sergio

Greta Garbo

The shrink who went mad, jumping to the ceiling with a Ziploc bag.
All to catch a rat with the face of Greta Garbo.

He broke for lunch. Throwing the Ziploc bag on his desk next to a
smoking gun.

Lunch with a bullet. He thought that he was dead. He jumped into a
river. Or was it a mirror? Shattering the dream that came to an end
in a meadowy glen. Or was it an alley filled with Greta Garbo faced
crawling rats.

He yelled with fright. Grabbing an ink pen and stabbed a sheet of
paper, that bled to death with a thousand bits of glass.

Back at his office screaming at the top of his lungs for
Mellville's "Bartleby" to leave his office at once. Pointing to a
dead fly in the window sill.

He heard a voice ring inside his head. He looked to the floor covered
with scurrying Greta Garbo madfaced rats. He grabbed the smoking
gun and shot with a Bang ...

He awoke in a room, looked about and saw white robed Angels floating
in clouds. He smiled, he was in heaven. Or was it the insane asylum?

Eric Craft

Just Like My Mom

As far back as anyone can remember, she was always loving and strong;
And the daughter knew that one day, she was going to be just like
her mom. Mom stayed home while the kids went to school, and told them
to learn all that they could; she said that they should be whatever
they wanted, and they always knew that they would. Mom encouraged
them at whatever they tried, and always had a smile for them whenever
they failed; she was always cheering at them from the sidelines,
whether it rained, or snowed, or hailed. Mom always took their side,
even though to others it appeared they were wrong;
She was angry if she found out they lied, but she never stayed angry
too much or too long. Mom grinned when they had their first dates,
and tried to make them feel right at home; She always told them to be
quite at ease, and would never leave them in a room all alone.
Mom glowed when her children walked down the aisle, two sons and
finally a daughter; She took pride in the grown her child wore, a
beautiful dress she alone had bought her. Mom was pleased they all
appeared so happy, as they started the lives of their own;
She felt she raised them to be decent and caring, and was always
available for advice over the phone. Mom took great joy in their
accomplishment, for she always knew they would succeed;
She welcomed all of the grandchildren, because her family was her only
need. Mom cherished the call from her daughter, who spoke in a voice
low and calm; "Someone just complimented me today, they said I was
just like my mom."

Kristine M. Whitty

Shadows

A dark alley, a single street light
whispers in the night
A petrified boy sitting alone
in pain and suffering, hear a slight moan
A ripped shirt and dirty jeans
out of school doesn't know what addict means
A bruised heart, arm and face
left alone no one got on his case
A cry from hunger, begs for money
cries now at what he once thought funny
kicked out of his house, regrets every word
wants his mommy and prays to his Lord.

Serli Karanfiloglu

Our Flag

Stands for freedom and must be perfect and above... All
    Waving and flowing...a glorious sight....
    Showing were number One.....
    And always ready to take up the cause.....
    For our men and women, who take this Oath.....
    Putting their lives on the line....
    And always ready to uphold!
Our flag is our symbol...
    "Let freedom ring"
    Join together as we all sing.....
    America Land of the Free and the Brave.....
    We fight to the end.....
    Always wanting to win.....

S. L. Kent

Waiting

I have so much inside me,
and so much to give.
All I need is that
"special someone"
to spend time with.
I lie in bed at night wondering
who he could be?
I wish I could look into the future
and be able to see.
I wonder what he'll be like?
I wonder if he'll like me?
I feel like there are so many pages
in my book of life,
that need to be filled.
I guess I'll just have to wait,
to see what the train of life
brings to me at the end of the tracks.
But, until then,
my dreams will be of my
"knight in shining armor", hope and love.

Lisa M. Jarnagin

In The Blink of Divine Eyes

In the blink of Divine eyes
So breathes the soul of life
A heavy pillow gives rise to morning sun
Relenting to the cycle of evening shade
As blood rushes through our veins
So passes the days of life
With the dawn of birth comes the eve of life
In the blink of Divine eyes

P. C. McKinnon

Let Me In

Knocking at your heart's door, I patiently wait,
To hear a sound, to hear acknowledgment but there is none.
I know you are there, Let me in....

Your heart has been locked for oh so long.
You fear turning the key, allowing me in.
There are no surprises, I wear no masks.
I know you are there, Let me in....

Allow yourself these feeling, this pleasure.
I'm not here to destroy you, only for you to grow.
I'm not here to take from you, only to give all you need.
I know you are there, Let me in....

You have so much to give, in feelings and emotions.
You are like a budding flower, ready to burst open,
Ready to receive the suns rays.
Turn the key and allow me in...

Allow us to grow together, allow us this precious gift.
Allow yourself to experience,
Allow yourself to receive,
Open the door to your heart....

Let me in...

Rusty Harrod

Loving You

I look at all the things you've given to me
And I think to myself-how can this be?
I thought that I would always be blue,
but now I'm not since I got you.
I thank all my stars above,
that I got you here to love.

It's you that I feel so dear
and the one I always want to be near.
It's because of your loving eyes,
That I melt completely inside.
It's the way I feel when I'm with you
and you're the one I don't want to lose

I love it when you hold me tight,
even if it may be day or night.
It was once your hand upon my knee
and that's still where I wish it to be.
But now it's the kiss from your soft lips to mine
that sends the greatest chill up my spine.

When the words "I Love You" are said to me
I wish you knew how wonderful I want this to be.

Suzanne D. Adams

Homeless

Why do you watch me with frightened eyes?
You dare to judge me with your lies.
Do I threaten your American dream?
Cause you can't hear my soul scream.

This is my bench, my sneakers, my place.
You think you know me, but you can't see my face.

Drink from my cup, take a walk in my shoes,
Live in my world, try payin' my dues.
This is my share of what you've given me.
Can you live with your guilt, for what I've come to be?

I sleep in this park and dream in this space.
You think you know me, but you won't see my face.

You can't see past the filth and the grime,
When did being lost become a crime?
I'll keep tryin' till I take my last breath,
But it's a hard life, livin' out this death.

I live in this park, hopeless dream space.
You don't want to know me, I could wear your face.

Michael B. Kirkpatrick

Garden of My Heart

Every year, I have a little garden:
It's where thoughts, are only grown you see.
Yes mine, are mostly all of you dear,
And I hope, that yours may be of me.

You are often, in that precious garden,
Oh to share, just one thought or so.
Yes that garden, lies within my heart now,
And it's where, only friends may go.

Oh I'll see, you there perhaps tomorrow,
When thoughts, and dreams will all come true,
And prayers, will then be also answered,
In that garden, when I think of you.

There are times, when we all feel so lonely.
And the days, just so long seem to be,
That's the time, to visit in my garden,
And collect, a few good thoughts with me.

Yes each year, my garden's growing larger,
Oh it rains, when only teardrops start;
So stop and share, a thought or two with me dear,
While you're in, the garden of my heart.

Nelson D. Bartlett

From Night's Hybernation To Day's Resurrection

The lunar surface's blotches penetrated their glow
Through the black atmosphere

Animated collages blended
Floating on and immersing under sleep's flow

The morning's dawn dust beams
Shone their rays of brightness

Howard Falk

Heaven Is...

As a child, I'd often wonder that heaven was like.
Was it eating ice cream in summer, or just riding my bike?
Maybe it was during summer vacation, swimming at the shore.
Or during a heavy snow storm, and me praying for more.

As a young man, my idea of heaven did certainly change.
It was now driving a car, or a hot date I would arrange.

I'm now an adult, and realize my views of heaven were all wrong
The search for that someone special has just taken so long.
Because I've finally found you, heaven is so plain to see.
It's when you look in my eyes and say you love me.

Edward T. Jefferys

The Almighty God

Lord, I admire a dark blue sky enlighten
by stars and the moon.
In the sun rays I am thinking about You.
The scent of flowers sweets my day and
every drop of rain brings me Thy name.
Your love travels faster than a light.
When the second stops the first still runs.
Today, I am also looking after You.
In one voice with an ocean, earth and
stars I praise the inconceivable
Mercy of God.
Please, let me hear the angel choir
on crossing the rainbow bridge.
Folded in mist I will be bowing to the
Creator's throne and He will welcome me
with open arms.

Krystyna Alina Dabrowska

Elusive Diet

I think I'll start my diet today,
To melt my fatty flesh away.
I will start as of this very morn,
Soon all of my tight clothes can be worn.

At breakfast I have some juice and toast.
My diet plans seem but an empty boast,
So I think I'll put it off to dinner.
A few more hours won't make me thinner.

At dinner I eat bland squash and lean meat.
My stomach roars loudly at this feat,
So I have roast pork for pick me upper,
For after all there still is supper.

At supper I gaze at thin veal chop,
Spinach in the cooker I sadly plop.
Coffee less cream by my hand does lie.
Thoughts of a square meal near makes me die.

With sweep of my arm the tables laid bare,
Cheese fries and thick steak put out with care.
Ice cream and pie are topped with whipped cream,
Diet fades away like a wild old dream.

Theodore L. De Marco

To Be Or Not To Be

When God decided to take her, our family fell apart.
I couldn't believe our love, could leave a broken heart.

I'll never forget that day, how long I cried and cried,
Now she's gone - I'm nothing, without her by my side.

The laughter and joy we had, is now put forth to crumble,
As I am too confused, without her I will stumble.

I ask Dear God to listen and try to understand,
I only wish to see her and grasp her tender hand.

To inform her I am grateful for all that she had done,
To mention I am lonely, but want no other one.

If one was to replace her, I'd see a great disaster,
No one could make it easy, to find the love I'm after.

Nancy Q. Mangene

The Human Race

Love is all we need to make us believe
Peace is all we dream to make us feel
Only two goals to reach, so simple to achieve
That will bring us joy, harmony, and happiness to give

Love is in our hearts from the moment life stars
Peace is in our minds and souls, as a big compromise
Wars and crime is not what we want
But yesterday and today is all we got

Whites, and blacks, yellows and browns
Our own rainbow the planet has
Multiple shadows, shapes, and bright
That distinguishes the faces one by one

Human race: who understands the way you behave?
Would not be easy the way I said?
Love and respect each other all over and anywhere
Here and there, tomorrow, today, to preserve life and Earth.

Our love should cross cities, countries, continents
mountains, trees, rivers, lakes and fountains
Only respect, talks and understanding
should fulfill the planet, today, tomorrow, always...

Sylvia Benzaquen

Dedicated To: My Mother

My proudness of you has forever been known.
Even though it's not always shown.
You've done a wonderful job raising your
children. I couldn't trade you, you're
one in a million.
Although times have been tough.
You've always been there, never once rough.
Sometimes I think we're all alone,
I look, around and realize no one's gone.
I see the harsh world today.
I turn to you, and make it all go away.
Thank you for making the sacrifice,
Having us, ignoring the bad advice.

Leslie Doster

Still Bound: Dead Future

Proud civilized in their own right—taken from their homes with no
chance to fight. Bound and gagged, stolen in the night!

You are not waiting for a bus—standing on that corner.
You are not a doctor waiting for an emergency to save a life.
You are the community's biggest enemy; you are society's greatest fear.
Why? You stand on that corner waiting to poison.
You pretend you're important in search of false fortune.
Your simple vanity is an insult to humanity!
You kill without conscience—believing in counterfeit power.
Unknowing the real—it gets to the point where you don't even care.
Until it hits home then you wish someone would be there.
At one time it was thought that we had no sense—we were beat and
lynched—made to pay a consequence.
We've struggled through the years to get this far today.
Why take lives and throw them away?
Throw away forever the shackles and chains.
Violence and drugs are not gains.
Education's the key that opens all doors.
It's time to stand up and give your lives more.
Be the people we all came from—the kings and queens we were
made from.

Waltine B. Yandel

The Tree

The beauty of a tree
Only a just few can see
What lies inside the bark
Comes directly from the heart
You can see how it grows
When weather is hot or very cold
Oh, what beauty is in the trees
When spring blossoms on the leaves
Summer brings on the heat
While others sit beneath the tree to eat
The fall brings another beauty to all
As the leaves change colors and began to fall
Winter comes with cold wind and snow
And the bark keeps the heart from getting cold
To hold the beauty of the trees
For all of us just to see.

Mary Ellen Stevens

A Gift To A Friend

Not of pity or self servitude
Nor what marks obsessive love
Not for winning points or gain of power
Nor to orchestrate "expected" ends

Kind graciousness and gentle giving
From our deeply rooted parts
Earth looks upon with knowing eyes
Brings forth peace to your friend's heart

Gina Armstrong

457

Untitled

This narrow road is dark and long.
But I do not feel as though I was wrong.
Many times I put a smile on my face.
Knowing deep in my heart there was a hollow place.
I would cry in the dark so no one could see
That is the light love was hurting me.
The make up hid the bruises and scars but not the pain.
Tonight I ended it all - I'll never be hurt again
Now I must disappear from this life - this place.
He is gone forever - he will never again bruise this heart or face.

Latichia Higgins

My Wish For You

You will make mistakes and so
From them you can make plans and grow.

I wish for you a life that's happy and free
One in which you can be the best you can be.

May learning and growing always be part of your life
There will be hardships and there will be strife.

But after a storm the sun will shine
Always keep faith and hope in your mind.

We were put here on earth to do for others - good
So give it your best and try like you should.

A quitter will never find winning in his or her game
So never give up and you can have fame.

Be thankful for nature and stars in the skies above
Notice how other human beings and friends show their love.

Let's move onward and strive toward peace
Be kind to yourself and let worries decrease.

Be Proud To Be You
   And Do What You Believe
Just Do Your Best
   And You Will Achieve!

Sharon Lee Kelley

Untitled

I dream of a life
A solitary life
A life on the road.
Is this what I want?
Emptiness of space
Infinity of time.
Or is this what I want?
To be unattached.
A woman with no husband, no child, no friends
No things.
A woman with no concerns, no connections
An illusion of freedom.
I'll need; car, booster cables, scotch tape, needles, binoculars,
buttons, tissues, pants, 1 straw hat, gloves, down jacket, bathing
suit, make up, belt, tea bags, 1 skirt, sandals, sneakers, 1 cotton
sweater, 1 wool sweater, camera, candles, short sleeve shirt, meds,
pillows, blankets, flashlight, insect repellent, scarf, socks,
travelers checks, credit card, driver's licence, sunglasses, soap,
toothbrush, underwear, tooth paste, nice dress, mousse, hair dryer, a
baseball bat or a gun.

Jacqueline Lichtenberg

One of the Bunch

On a wall a bed of arrowheads gently rests in peace,
framed boldly in hunter green wood,
each arrowhead is placed on caressing clouds of cotton,
they zoom in on each other as if under attack by the enemy center
rock who speaks of destroying the galaxy,
and all in it,
each of 41 arrowheads are different,
in shape and personality,
some are long and big,
some short but lethal,
others are sharp enough to cut through brick,
with the ease of a swan dive into a deep dark sea of chlorinated water,
and yet some look as harmless as a newly born baby at play,
and all rough as the artic ice,
and all as important to a complete piece of art,
as a pound of gold is to a poor man.

Nicole Rhames

A Talk With Time

O time, tell me where have you gone,
Do others only have you alone.
O time, you are like a river that is running fast,
Like a season that is going past.

O time, you are here you say,
Up until my dying day.
O time, you are like a wind that has blown,
Like a bird that has flown alone.

O time, you say farewell to thee,
As you take away my soul from me.
O time, you are like a song that has been sung,
Like a name that is here and is carried on.

Deborah R. Breedwell

If There Was No Tomorrow

Have you ever sat in wonder underneath
a maple tree?
And looked at everything around you that
others don't bother to see.
A bird in flight, a bee on a flower.
The wind with all its freedom, a midsummer shower
The sound of thunder, the tapping of rain.
The tears of a friend whose heart aches with pain.
How fast grass grows in the summer
How slowly it grows when it's cold
A child chasing a butterfly
The young eyes in a loved one growing old
Have you ever taken time to notice anything
during your oh so busy day
To notice the sweet things around you
As you hurried on your way.
What if tomorrow never gets here,
And today is all but gone.
Would you wish you had noticed
Life's simple gifts all along?

Tina Baker

A Heritage

'Way down south in Stone Mountain, Georgia —
Is where home is red, clay hills and southern pine trees
Smoke from burning firewood and cool spring rains -
The fragrance of magnolias and petunias in the hot noon sun
And the lazy droning of a bumble bee around the blossoms
The tang of wild strawberries
The sweetness of honeysuckle

The Southern is very proud of his heritage and culture.
The quiet elegance
The warm graciousness of hospitality.

Louise B. Robertson

The Richer

Of the jewels and the diamonds embarked onto me,
the sound of a whisper would just make me flee.
To the east to the west to a little birds nest,
is the sound of a cry begging me to rest!

Lauren Hickman

Tears For Stephen

Although your ashes have been scattered,
returned these many years unto the dust
while I, like a stranger, here have tarried
your soul abides in quiet Trust

On some glorious and transcendent day
more enduring than this virtual stuff
face to face we'll stand re-united
within that brilliant realm above

Holy seemed our laughter in those fleeting days
like water from our hands they seeped away
the songs upon our lips still linger on
'tho Night hath closed your eyes to light of day

Laughter lifts the heart a little while
but sorrow elevates the very soul
and so eternal, vital love of friend
hath not allowed this death to take its toll

Robert Adams Mattes

America

Oh where could I go, if it wasn't for you?
What place on Earth, could I call home?
What other place could bring out the love,
Humbleness, and pride in me?

Oh my beautiful flag, rippling so high and
Stately in the wind-looking up to you, my
Heart swells with pride-you belong to me,
My America, to all of us, who have watched
Since birth.

The trials, the wars, trouble and fear on the
Home front. So many years, you stand alone,
The best-I love you, America, I'm so glad
You have always been, my home sweet home.

Willie-Dean Bartlett

The Good Path

Cast your troubles upon the shore.
Imagine them floating away,
For all your troubles
Are not so bad.
They could be gone in a day.

For what you think is what you are.
Your heart knows what to do.
'Tis easier said than done, my friend,
But have faith.
Think all things a-new.

Our world is always and ever a-changin'.
Each day a new light is born.
All your thoughts do
Come from within.
Your life n'er has to be torn.

'Tween all the good and all the bad,
These choices your mind must make.
Be still! Shhh...
Listen to your heart—
The good path, you always can take.

Danielle Gerard

Mom

There are nine of us you see
Not five or four or three

There are nine of us to love
Mom always called us her gifts from above

Nine pairs of hands reaching
Nine minds open to the teaching

Nine mouths calling, calling
Knees to kiss after falling

Give me this, give me that
"Mom, she has my hat"

Always wanting, forever needing
There to soothe the hurt and the bleeding

Woman of strength you have gone
But how do we carry on?

And so we must carry on.

Michele M. Herman

Our Son

It seems like only yesterday
    You were just a little boy.
You made our home so happy
    You brought us so much joy.

We have shared your laughter.
    We have shared your tears.
We have watched you grow up
    through all these years.

Tomorrow you'll be leaving
    Your future has begun.
No matter where life takes you
    We're proud of you, our son.

I guess we will soon get over
    the thought of you being gone.
Our home will be so lonesome.
    You're leaving us all alone.

Son we're going to miss you. It makes our hearts so sad.
To know that you are going away you're the only son we had.

We wish for you much happiness and a life time a success.
Never forget how much you're loved. Good bye son, God bless.

Shirley Shrader

As It Snows

I can't help but stare out the window,
While I listen to the same old songs.
I know it's my choice to be sad an alone,
But it's not my choice that you're gone.

We loved through all the seasons,
But it was the Winter when you married me.
Now the snow sends a chill through my heart,
As it brings back painful memories.

The angry words we said to each other,
All the tears that we both cried.
How could something that started out so good,
In the end be a lie?

I search my heart to find the right answers,
I send a prayer to the Lord up above.
To give me the strength and the courage,
To someday forgive the one that I love.

As it snows I find myself missing,
The beginning that lead to the end.
As it snows I find myself remembering,
What I thought I'd never think about again.

Diana L. Stephens

Lights

Oh, How times flies,
You take your first step and
   the next moment you are being laid to rest.
What happened in between?
Where did you go... What did you see....
   Who captured your heart...
Whose life did you change...
   And most of all, did you matter?
Your existence is not in vain.
For within each moment that your heart beats and
   your light shines,
Trust that you are sharing your magic with all that crosses your path.
For you are a miracle.
Embrace the time that is given,
   for it is yours, to have and to hold,
   to burn so bright, illuminating all that is near.
For when you are gone,
   you will be remembered for the light that is still shining
in the hearts of all those that remain.

   Gregory William Zarian

Scattered Stardust

It's all around, the smell, the sound, the gut feeling
Can you feel the sensation?,
Do you sense the tears in the air?,
Only man can stop the tears and the hunger
The wars
Birds can fly and soar
There are no empty rooms
Ahhh, bring your passion unto me
I will embrace your love
As the world crumbles
We will shine and sparkle as the stars above
Shelter and food
The children will sing
And the angels will scatter the stardust
Hope
Hope we shall bring

   Deborah D'Elia

Untitled

You cannot hide your sweetness
From me, for I've encountered
If before you became fearful.
Don't be. Show it again. It is
The real you. The rest is protective armor.

Don't be afraid to love
Me back. It's scare-y,
But if I can do it,
You can do it, too!

Sharing my feelings
Is what I love to do.
Won't you share yours
With me?

   Emily Loube

Please Let There Be Peace On Earth

I wish I could live in a World so peaceful and pure
where there was no violence
and aids had a cure
where not one child had to cry a single tear of fear.
And everyone would listen and lend an ear.
So just think no one would have to live in fear.
If people would pitch-in and help out around here.

   Kristen Winges

Remembering Cara

We wonder...
You touched down like a feather, lingered awhile.
Such a frail, helpless, little being.
Yet, we were shaken as by an earthquake
Stirring feelings deep down in our souls,
Overwhelming grief.
Such a wisp of a child
To bring about such a torrent of emotion.
Your wee, small hand touched us lightly
But we were marked indelibly by your presence.
So you will live forever in our hearts,
Our own dear precious angel.
We love you, Cara.

   Rica Antoine

A Moment's Passing

There is a moment, that I hold dear.
It's in my heart and everywhere.

My backward glance, of days gone past.
I wish the time was meant to last.

A small hand, a big hand to tightly hold.
A slow walk, down a country road.

What my biggest treasure and a memory stored.
Is of a father and a daughter that his wife bore.

The meeting of the hands to touch.
My heart it swells to this memory lost.

A quiet
A lasting
A moment's passing.
Deep within my heart.

   Ellen Heinlein

My Friend "Joe"

My friend "Joe", isn't here today,
His young life was taken away.

My heart feels sad for his father and mother,
his sisters, their families, his younger brother,
for all his friends gathered here today not
knowing why it happened this way.

But as for me, all I can say,
is no one can take my memories away.
Memories of a dark eyed lad,
He was the brother I never had.

Memories of our younger days,
When we were boys in a summer's haze.
Waiting for the fish to bite, or
Laughing and talking thru the night.

Memories of a snowy day,
tracking deer, or just at play.
It mattered not, what we did, you see,
He was my friend and will always be,
Part of my life and part of me.

   Dimitros Milo Chalop

C & O Canal: Pennyfield Lock

Recall the newborn beavers bleating
And the bold bullfrog bellowing.
Recall the haunting smell of honeysuckle
With the sun setting over bright water.
Recall, Recall, Recall, Recall
The echo's of the soft summer night.

   Caroline Tobia

Same Sky

We are all under the same big sky,
so why do we fight? Why do we lie?
Why do we hate and never get along?
Why do we think it's the other one's wrong?
Why do we kill? Why do we steal?
Why do some people go without meals?
Why can't we accept people and they accept us?
Have we forgotten the word they call trust?
World peace it will take time,
but we have one thing in common
We Are All Under The Same Big Sky.

Jessica Black

Why?

When upon natural man I think;
I am found to ponder and wonder why;
with all of heaven's beauty his eye could drink,
God created lowly man as the love of his eye?

When from the very beginning, disobedient.
First was Eve, then Adam freely willing.
Both offered a choice; Both malcontent.
In search of greater knowledge;
generations to come, they were killing.

Oh! How God's heart must have been breaking;
to pass judgement upon a most precious creation.
To know the future toil of Adam's every moment waking,
and at the very end, death his destination.

The God of wisdom knows that for man to be perfect;
A choice must be made; Good or bad, we make it.
Good, a heavenly relationship with a savior kind.
Bad, a constant search for earthly pleasures to fill our mind.

Arron D. Lance Sr.

A Time for God

This precious gift of time, no one can ever hoard
For it travels on and on, with only one accord,
To narrow the span of time, of that long awaited day
When time no longer rules, our ever changing way.

Take time for opportunities, God gives you today
Or they may be lost forever, they never come to stay,
God has a special purpose, for all the time He gives
It must be used for others, it's the reason why we live.

There is a time for laughter, and a time for caring
A time for fellowship, and a time for sharing,
A time for messages of God's greatest love
A time for praise and prayer in His name above.

Take time to study His Word, do not push it aside
Take time to find His peace, and in His love abide
He said, "I will be with you," let Him hold your hand
Then reach out the other, to help your fellowman.

Reach out to give support and praise, a hug or a smile
To understand, or shed a tear, and listen for awhile,
A time for God is being there, when a friend has a need
The love and time God gives to you, give, as you received.

Verona Duchrow

November

Thanksgiving turkeys are lurking around.
They're everywhere and they weigh only a pound
My turkey is dreading this Thanksgiving day
Because all of my family will be eating away
The turkeys are running and running and running,
They wish they could stop Thanksgiving from coming
   Oh well!

Kristen Savage

Morbid Truth

Through the dark deceptions of the world no one can love
a sad soul. The souls of many all confuse, the nature of those are
abused. The crimes of the heart are misled while their bodies are
completely dead. The anger of one is self-induced, the pride of
another is hidden by the truth. The blood of the damned is taken.
The mind and body of the weak has been broken. From the depths
   of the
universe everyone tries to tell you what to do. No one listens when
you scream that you are through. Only time will tell when your
   being
rest in hell. Your final resting place is determined by your fate.
So if you care you may make it there, if you wait you will seal
your fate. Times can be changed but first your life must be
rearranged. Your travels will be long, your wealth will be gone.
Time to take a look and read your life like a book. Your madness
has approached. Your life is just a joke. You cry every night for
happiness and to do what is right. You take too long to figure out
that your life has just been taken out.

Paul W. Gorman Jr.

Divorce

The morning sun shines and another day passes, another day
unlike all the others.

One minute they are together, the next they are not.
What happened to these souls that once were connected.

A child sits and wonders; is it my fault: What have I done?

Daddy looks so sad, mommy looks so angry.
I touch my brother's hand and say it will be alright, but will
it...

Will I ever wake to see them both by my side, I believe not.
When birthdays come.
   When holidays pass,
      When my baby is born I will still asks
   Where will I go - Mommy or Daddy's

Luciann Grossman

Give Me A Rose

If I could have a rose today,
Happiness would come my way.

If I could have a rose tomorrow,
It would give joy, and bring less sorrow.

If I could have a rose this week,
I'd feel all the love, I'd seek.

If I could have a rose this month,
I'd feel more closeness, and less confront.

If I could have a rose this year,
I'd feel more strength, and have less fear.

If I could have a rose and it may have a thorn.
I'd thank you Lord, for the day I was born.

If I could have a rose this day,
And not just when I pass away.

Just one rose from a flower bed,
I will take it now, not just when I'm dead.

So give me one rose, it will lighten my strife,
For one little rose, will add to my life.

Matt J. Chlebanowski Sr.

Guardian Angel

I know not what your name is;
But I know you were sent
To this world to watch over me.
And that you have seen things
That I have yet to see.
I feel your presence when
I'm feeling lonely and
I sit crying.
It's as if I feel a soft touch on my shoulder
And a gentle voice saying;
Please do not give up,
You have to keep trying.
Then I feel a peace and calm
Descend over me.
And the sadness just fades away.
And once again I thank God
For my Guardian Angel.
Because with his love and your guidance,
I'll have the courage
To face a new day.

Paula Tilson Wiseman

"Just Reminiscing"

I remember when the two of you came to visit me,
And we would sit till break of dawn,
Talking about our childhood days
I still can hear their voices clear,
Laughing at the things we did.
How I made them help with the chores,
"That's right they said, you're our second 'mom.
I never will forget those short sweet weeks,
Those happy weeks we spent together
The bond between us became more stronger,
It was more than love between three sisters,
Now you're both gone, gone forever,
And my heart is all but breaking,
Lord give me the strength to bear this pain,
I loved them dearly, but you loved them more.
So Lord, don't ever let me stop reminiscing of...
All the good times we shared together,
Only let me...just remember.

Catherine Louise Stokes

Child of Ra

Oh! Purveyer of the darkest nights recesses;
with softly padded feet.
Oh! Vigilant guardian of the Temple Basht;
exulting in glory equal to that of the rulers of Thebes or Luxor.
The very scrouge of the specie of rodentia;
as unscrutable as the ancient Nile.
Even in your demise your sychophants pay homage
to your undiminished glory.
For only you rival Ra in your willfulness and majesty;
for only at dusk does he leave his dominion of the sky.
Then in repose he reclines behind your mystic and
unfathomable portals; until the birth of dawn.
Oh! Ra brilliant and illuminated disc shinning
as the eternal sovereign of the celestial.

Richard C. Ditsch

Like

The ink flows from my pen
Like time flows through my life.

The pedals on a rose fall
Like men who fall in war.

Salt fills an open wound
Like love fills an open heart.

A caterpillar becomes a butterfly
Like a boy becomes a man.

A sound enters the ear
Like a thought enters the brain.

Chicken pox scars the body
Like violence scars the heart.

Love can be kind
Like hate can be cruel.

With all these things alike, yet different,
Why can't we accept differences,
As we do likes.

Stephanie Solorio

My Grandmother

My grandmother was God's servant.
She was Reliable and always had Answers
and made you feel Needed.
She was Dependable and
always Made time for Others.
She was a Teacher and a Helper.
She was always there with an Encouraging word
and a Radiant smile.

Janice Parker

A Special Place To Me

This special place is very near to me.
It's easy to get to as you will see.
You don't have to take a bus, a plane, or even drive.
Just close your eyes and it'll come alive.
It's a place where dragons roam and spaceships soar.
It's a place where dreams come true.
Great stories come from here,
And songs that move the heart and soul.
Best friends are made and lost in the blink of an eye.
Monsters lurk and wizards fly.
Rockets roar into space,
And cops give robbers a lengthy chase.
Cars and aircraft do amazing things.
Cowboys and Indians roam the plains.
Beautiful women look their best,
And tear your heart from your chest.
If you haven't figured it out yet,
Then this place you've never met.

Timothy James Mummey

Heartstrings

The house seems so empty, now the children have grown,
It's hard to believe that they're out on their own.
The myriad of questions in my mind had begun,
Did we do all we could for our daughter and son?
The sadness o'erwhelms me, as I glance at their beds,
Where as little ones they slept, at peace,
Resting their heads.
During the silence, I suddenly felt
The warmth of an arm slipping 'round by my belt.
Such a kind tender look in my beloved's blue eyes,
Brought me back to my senses, I then realized,
How blessed we have been to have shared just in part,
Of those wonderful lives, that remain in my heart.

Georgia Hughes

Grandma's Soliloquey

I looked in the mirror, and quickly turned out the light!
For the face looking back at me was such an awful sight!
That face was all wrinkled, like a dried up old prune!
And my voice is all crackled, and way out of tune.
Then I looked at my hair and saw what had happened there!
It was shabby, and scraggily, and in need of repair!
Then I considered my body ... so old ... and flabby in spots,
With muscles so scroungy ... that they don't work like they ought!
Old age has come quickly it sure seems to me,
And "Dear Lord!" what a sight I have now come to be!
My mind is all jumbled and scattered about,
My voice is all mingled with cackles and shouts!
When I get up toward, I wobble along ...
And my joints are all loosened and not very strong.
But when I look back where my "get up" has been ...
I can see where that long journey has been full to the brim!
I remember ... and remember ... what happened here and there,
And I'm happy, so happy that I went everywhere.
So as I amble along ... towards my journey's end,
I'm happy and cheerful as I view where my life's been.

Catherine G. Curtis

Without Faith

Life's little temptations...
They will keep us in the game
Shifting through the ashes.
And dancing in the flames.
We'll keep on playing until we run out of time.

These little games...
With our hearts and our mind.
There are no winners.
'Cause there is no way to win.
And the losers, they are buried and forgotten once again

Life's little plays...
We're all doomed to lose.
It's written in the sky.
They say the stars don't lie.
We don't play to win, we just play not to die.

Jessica Sicking

Father's Day

The third sunday in June is father's day
Who is a father
How tall does he stand
Before his wife an children
As a family man

For support, guidance and protection
He is someone for you to look to
From childhood to adult life
As you work to find a place.
In this complex and dangerous world

The home with a christian father
Is built on solid rock
He gives you love an affection
And guides you to your place in life
He is there with a helping when the going gets rough.

All a father hopes to see
Is love on the faces of his family
When he returns home
After a hard day, in this competitive world
To relax and enjoy his family as every father should

Edgar Kleckley

Letting Go

The time is here and the time has come,
To say goodbye to that loved one and,
Let them go where they can be taken
  care of,
And given what they need, but don't ramp,
And rave because someday we'll be with,
  them again.

Judi Riggs

The Scholar

"Come quick! Come quick!" The scholar shouted out.
What bit of research had he just found out?
'Nay 'twas not to be,
As we rushed to see,
Not in library

But in the garden where he pointed out
A magnificent wine hollyhock tree!

Georgette M. Moraud

Minnesota Memories

They traveled from the Netherlands
  early in the 1900's.
My grandfather was one of them,
  settling down to farm in Minnesota.

They carved out a life for themselves,
  those times now called "the good old days".
They themselves though weren't aware
  they were living them back then.

The 50's found us traveling
  from Illinois to Minnesota each summer
visiting relatives on the farms.
  Now suddenly it's the 90's.

As adults we travel to those places
  where years ago memories were formed,
longing for a re-enactment of those "good old days".
  Familiar places remain, but family members have vanished.

Only a handful of graves remain now
  in a remote cemetery in Minnesota,
the only clue to the existence
  of the original brave travelers.

Jean Case

"Letting Go"

My spirit longs to be free
and flow with positive energy
to sparkle with a warm glow.

My soul, being the core of me,
feels lost on an arctic sea
drifting along without direction.
Searching endless for the guidance
needed to let go, learn, grow, and go on.

Strength to stand the pain 'til the end,
believing time is essential for healing and
having faith in my heart for forgiving.

Christi Lynne

A Mother's Concern

As the new day is breaking
Thoughts stampede through my mind
Will I live 'til tomorrow?
What roads will I find?

I hear a soft whimper
From the crib across the room
As my son grows older
Will he face a world of doom?

Mothers abandon their children
It's heard most everyday
Innocent lives are being lost
Outside where they play

Prejudice, pollution —
Gangs , drugs, and violence invade our schools
Brother against brother
No one plays by the rules

Things "of the world"
More frightening each day
Protect and guide my dear Nathan... always
To Thee Lord, I pray.

Victoria G. Lopez-Gomez

Deep In My Heart

Have you ever wondered where a teardrop begins?
    Well, you're wrong if you close your eyes.
It first has to start, deep in your heart,
    before you begin to cry.
For you must be in touch with your feelings,
    before you say, "I understand".
If you are numb, and can't feel your fingers,
    How can you see "God's, master plan"?
We all have our crossest's and hardships to bear,
    Dad said, "Life is like a book".
Only until, our final page,
    Will we know, if we had what it took.
Life is filled with so many experiences,
    We awake, each day a surprise.
And each night, our feelings, are put to sleep!
    New ones night, arrive with the mornings sunrise
Now, getting back to that teardrops,
    And, wondering "when", was the first time I cried?
Well, that tear had to start, down deep in my heart
    The morning my father died!

Peter Globuschutz

Chapter Forty-One

Birthdays are truly special no matter what our age
It marks the passing of a year, not just "another day"

Last year when you turned forty, you struggled silently
Your thoughts reflected on your past and what the future might be

Another year has come and gone, the time went racing by
As I observed, the year went well, your dreams are on the rise

I consider you a special friend and with that thought in mind
I wrote these words to tell you, a friend like you is hard to find

The gift of friendship is a present I give to you each day
It's a gift that is forever, it will never go away

Since I am so much older, I feel compelled to say
The years go by so quickly, find happiness in every day

I feel that life is like a book, that wisdom comes with age
Each year represents a chapter, each day is a new page

People say life begins at forty, I believe it's forty-one
It takes a year to realize that your book is far from done

Gloria Davis

Life's Riddle

Life to some people, is a riddle most profound
With uncertainty lurking at every intersection;
Others find their way, with an ear to the ground
And an inner compass to point out the direction.

Some delight in riddles that stir up the mind
And add to their pleasure with bright gems of wisdom;
But, then there are others who seem to be blind
To truths that can hide in their droll symbolism.

Which came first, chicken or egg? Let's consider
The serious implications that hide in this riddle.
There are rare gems of wisdom beginning to glitter,
When we dig for those gems that are artfully hidden.

The egg cannot hatch into a new baby chick,
Unless a rooster has performed its most vital part.
Could life have evolved from the "Big Bang's" kick,
Without a finger on the trigger at the start?

I reap a goodly harvest from my garden every year,
But it doesn't evolve without my brawn and my head.
Could the clock work of the heavens, and our earths atmosphere
Have begun and evolved from an infertile egg?

Gordon L. Alden

My Gift

A son was born to me one day
A gift from God
A gift for most of my life I prayed
I loved him so
I caressed and kissed his brow
I made him warm when he was cold
But one day my son was gone
Then I knew,
My gift from God was just a loan
God wanted him back to live in His home
But Lord, it's so hard to understand
This son you gave me, to let go of his hand
Although I know he's happy there
I'll always remember
The love that we shared
And please Lord
Help me not to forget
To thank you each day
For the son that you sent

Trena J. Chamness

Heavenly Bouquet

God has made a Heavenly Bouquet
We each are a different flower
He gathers us all together
At a special hour

God loves and takes care of us
Giving each His special care
To be a part of His precious arrangement
That's what makes us so rare

So we all will be His beautiful work
Fragrancing His Heaven
Thanking God for the wonderful gift
That He's so graciously given

Tanya L. Smith

Untitled

What kind of person would I be, if I could let out all the anger?
If I could tightly close my eyes, to let the worries all slip by?
If I could stop crying...just for a moment?
If I were stronger? Prettier? Healthier?
It is said that these things make us who we are.
Without them I would be nothing. So, why am I nothing with them?
Every day I think, worry, pray. Where does it get me?
I want to be something else. Desperately. But where would last
   get me?
Uncertainty, pain, all that is what I am. I have not contributed.
The world will not remember me, the martyr, the patriot, a saint,
   an aspiration.
I am nothing, I have done nothing, myself and my existence are
   worthless, futile, if you will.
Maybe I'll get better, maybe I'll change. Although, probably not.
So in my confusion, despair, and distraughtedness, I have left
something. Although it's not large, not expensive,
It's a gift from the heart, my heart. It's non-refundable.
It is just these silly, sappy, words.
Please put them to good use.

Krystal Mathews

Untitled

Keep in touch is what we say, when friends
Part and go away.
Too busy-too tired-got bills to pay,
Maybe I will call you another day.
Saw your name in the paper,
You became parents today, maybe I will
Congratulate you another day.
Years have passed, getting gray.
Saw your name in the paper:
You died today.
Keep in touch is what we say
When friends part and go away.

Rita A. Clark

The Rain

The rain it falls so hard outside,
brings back memories I'd soon rather hide.
Memories of words said in anger or in pain,
Words to a sad song with a sorrowful refrain.
Once told to me at the age of five...
When I didn't know what it meant not to be alive.
Gone away to a special place was a loved one forever,
Where one day much later on, I too would endeavor.
Though no rain fell at the time for me,
Tears were shed when I was old enough to see.

The rain brings other memories to mind, of the trials in life I've
   left behind.
It symbolizes the release of tears, I've expelled in all of my 21
   years.
It also reminds me of lonely days, sharing with a friend the wait
for sun rays. Watching the rain together with a friend,
We'd talk awhile, help each other's pain to end.
The harder it falls the more I hope, that with future problems
   I will be able to cope.

Because after the rain falls and dampens the ground,
The sun is waiting to come around.
And after the bad times of life subside,
The good memories return, and the bad ones will hide.

Samantha Graber

For You

Let me hold you and share
Share my arms and my heart
For I love you

Smile at me and let me know
Know you love me too
For I need you

Let me comfort you by listening
Listening to your thoughts and problems
For I care

Confide in me and let me feel
Feel the power of your dreams
For I believe in you

Let me kiss you and touch
Touch the man I love, you
For I want you

Finally, look at me, my eyes, and realize
Realize the depth of my devotion
For I adore you
Let me, always.

Myra Middleton

Envy

This life is a dream inside of a dream
I only can see what will never be seen
I am envy and hatred personified

I've never told you anything
You've never truly known me
I hold inside my rage
I've absorbed the hate you've shown me
Try to read my mind and you'd be horrified

There's nothing more I want from life
But freedom from my shame
I died a little more each time
I tried to play the game
Grasping for control as I went
Winding through the spiral
It dawned on me; to die would be
The road to true survival

Doug Layne

The Plotters

No matter what their heritage, theirs the common goal
Nobly into troubled lands they go, their leader at the head
Young men and women who believe their country.
In peacetime they soldier to bring dignity to foreign soil.
At the behest of those in charge, they leave their homes
Callow and confused
Each mind beleaguered by the risk of death
This wonderful potpourri of backgrounds.
Their families proud of their stalwarts ways
Fashioned by maneuvers and commands — a new protocol.
And we who wait salute the recruits, proud and strong
Pride and patriotism imbue the American and the Defender.
While these youth away on alien soil
Daily comply with their country's fiats
The stealthy and the predators plot to undo these noble gestures
Only to destroy the unsuspecting brave and those they love.

Alice Ishkanian

Maggies' Green Thumb

On the walk from her bus stop one too hot evening,
Maggie picked up a little flower someone had thrown away.
It was mostly gone from being long neglected...abandoned,
to unrelenting sun, without protection of shade, but then...
Maggie Had A Green Thumb

Rushing home, she put it on the sill of her window in water,
and hoped, with attention, in time it would be okay.
Maggie had never seen this kind of flower,
but prayed she could keep it alive. She would try, because...
Maggie Had A Green Thumb

Over the years, though often contrary, the flower grew to be strong.
Maggie always knew when it needed extra nurturing, but of course...
She Had A Green Thumb

Maggie looked on with pride, as her flower took a husband today.
From the aisle, when seeing her face I smiled, and whispered...
"Thank You"..... for taking me home that day.

She never said she was special, but God laid me on a path to be found,
by the woman all her friends know as Maggie...
but to me, she has always been Mom.

Consiwella R. Ray

God's Gift

A gift from God was mother dear.
    I think of her while toiling here.
When I used to sit upon her knee,
    I learned the songs she sang to me

The word of God she taught me then,
    Will go with me unto the end.
The songs and prayers I hear them yet.
    The tender words of love I'll never forget.

I write these words in memory of you.
    For I find these words so very true.
The pattern you left, the example you gave,
    Will guide and help, my soul to save.

Anna Lee Blincoe

16 Angels

16 Angels in the sky, 16 Angels flying high.

Life for them was much too short,
And now the rest is left to sort.

Why the babies on this day?
What did this man take away?

Was it the next star Laker?
Or the next peacemaker?

The world will never know
What it was they had to show.

We cry and cry
While yet inside a piece of us slowly dies.

Why the babies in the school?
Why was that man so very cruel?

Time won't heal what he took away,
To the parents what do we say?

On this day our hearts all broke,
As the hopes and dreams went up in smoke.

16 Angels in the sky, because 16 children had to die.

16 Angels flying high, as we all look up and say good-bye.

Sweet babies, fly away, and forget the way you left us today.

Stephanie Joachim

Life's Garden

I walked in my garden one early morn;
    smelled the flowers and touched a thorn.
The scent of the flowers was pure and sweet
    but the pain from the thorn went very deep.

Life is like a
    garden of flowers;
filled with beauty and with pain,
    with sunshine and with rain.

The winds and rain batter and bend
    until it seems there is no end.
Then the sun comes out and warms our souls
    as God's love reaches down and makes us whole.

The sun, the rain, the love, the pain
    all are stepping-stones to the day
when God will take us by the hand
    and lead us to his Gloryland.

Eileen C. Moulton

New York City From Bayswater

Barges and boats under bridges glide,
Planes, birds and 'copters streak 'mid domed view,
Brown crescent dump above grass and bay tide,
Ducks in rows sail glass water silver blue;
Yon horizon skyscrapers and domes grow,
Windows like computer chips of red gold,
Etched against Manhattan orange skies glow,
Crimson sunset tints clouds: Images unfold.

Twilight descends, phantom darkness advances,
Garish day fades, buildings silhouettes turning;
Dark water ringed with jewel lights dances,
Spaced blue ceiling with stars dimly burning.
Zephyrs lull airport noise in mellow Fall,
Man mars, Nature heals, God creates it all.

June P. Williams-Philp

Within Our Hearts

To love, is to love that which lets your mate
        grow and shine
To love, one need not touch
        only share one's spirit
Love is not limited to space
        except that of the heart
I do not love what I see or hear
        only that which my heart feels
I can make love with a touch, a look, a call,
        a card or even a letter
The distance between us matters not
        if we are within our hearts
So I need not hear you, see you, smell you
        or feel you to love
To love, is to know that of you that none can grasp
        yet you touch only me with
For love has no time and we are timeless
        we are each, we are one, we are ourself
We are that part that exists only within the other
        within our hearts

Wayne Lindsay

Petals of Yellow Rose

Glistening tear drops of dew,
    dripping off a rose pedal of gold.
        Could only remind me of you.
Not tears of pain or sadness,
    for that could just never be true.
From your eyes could only drip happiness,
    As if they were petals of a yellow rose too.

Jeff Chichester

The Odyssey of Hellenism In America

(American Melting Pot)

In Astoria, New York and in Toronto,
I met the children of Odysseus;
they were struggling to retain
their Hellenic identity,
amidst the Scyllas and the Charybdes
of the New World.

In Tarpon Springs, Florida and in Chicago,
I met the grandchildren of Odysseus;
they were aware of their Hellenic roots,
but they had named their children,
Gus and Katie, instead of
Kostas and Katina.

In Ithaca, New York and in Athens, Georgia,
I met the great grandchildren of Odysseus;
very few of them were willing to carry on
the Odyssey of Hellenism in America;
most of them did not resemble Odysseus
and did not share his longing for Ithaki.

        Kriton K. Hatzios

The Desert That Did Not Belong To Anything

"This is no place for green grass, This is no place for wars,
Mother Earth sends each jackrabbit to jump high each spring,
Each snake to crawl over her, This place is not all green.....

        This is for hawks that fly swiftly in the air,
We share this land with the wise hawks with sharp eyes,
With snakes that crawls, Lizards that pray, And high jumping
jackrabbits.
Look at this land and look at the animals. This is not ours.

        This space is filled with a lot of hot red sand.
The coyote howls to celebrate each happy night.
Every hill and mountain stretches to touch the sky.

        Mother Earth sends many children here.
The children stretch for berries in the cactus,
But they do not take all of it.

We live on this land but we do not own it.
Either do the animals own it.
The Earth belongs to itself and we belong to it.
So does the hawks, snakes, lizards, jackrabbits, and mountains.

        So give it thanks everyday.
We are in a hot desert but we will never abandon it!

        Kent Lee

Depression To A New Sunrise

As I look out into the night I wonder will I be alright
Will I finally see the light
It's constantly moving out of sight
Maybe I am just at fright, continuing though to keep up the fight
As I look out into the deep, dark sky
I see a horizon forming with my eyes
I wonder for what's to be in store
Behind another closed door
I hold onto this moment until it passes by
Cause, I'll always remember saying "Hello"
And I'll never forget the memories as I'm letting go
When the time comes for saying "Goodbye"
So, as I close my eyes I am remembering
You I will miss and here is a kiss
The sun will begin to rise and shine and I will grow wise
No need for anymore sighs
You can stop the tears and conquer your fears
Just dry your eyes and remember you tried
You can fly high like an eagle way up in the sky so high
Reaching a new sunrise.

        Amy P. Kaufman

Seasons

Spring is the best time of the year
When the new growth first appears
It's like you are born anew
In all the wondrous hue.

Summer is the time to play
Getting a tan, making hay
Vacations are the main topic
While the sun shines all day.
And the moon glows at night.

Fall brings you beautiful color
There's no way to describe
The way the leaves change
You almost believe they are painted.

Winter is the season to celebrate
Getting ready to ski and ice skate.
Partying, Thanksgiving, and Christmas cheer
All in all makes for a wonderful year

        Mary F. Hoagland

Plea

Just give up your grey bitter ghosts of the past
Come and lie in my lap.
I'll message your mind with the spirit of peace
The kiss of forgiveness.

Let go the memories of anger and pain
Let your body relax.
I will stroke your soul and lead your endless thoughts
Into sleep-like freedom.

Retribution and rage only feed on themselves
Turning inward to kill.
Life will lose much of its soft loving sweetness
And gain no peace within.

So give up your grey bitter ghosts of all time
Come and sit by my side.
Smile and forget and go on with your life
In contentment and joy.

        Kay Janda

Meant to Be

The Lord brought us together
because He knew what was in our heart

With our selfishness and anguish
we tore ourselves apart

Waking up, one day we realized
we couldn't make it on our own

So, we prayed Lord Jesus
Please don't leave us alone

Give us strength and guidance to make us see
That this love we have for each other
was truly meant to be

He gave us this vision that was clear as day
That if we put our trust in Him
He will make a way

This vision we saw was as real as you and me
Two people living together very happily

Those two people are happy, as you can see
For the Lord brought us together
and it was meant to be.

        Burnadette K. Jones

Visions Form the Subconscious

In a dream
I was a tiger,
fierce, cunning, powerful
I ruled the land around me,
but I learned that power
isn't everything in life.
I left my subjects in fear,
not knowing how to suppress
the anger burning inside of me.
I yearned to become one of the common people,
but I instead instilled hate
of their leader
upon them.

Brian G. Spence

Performance of a Ruse

The puppet dances amid the strings,
his body swaying to and fro.
A strong hand allows his fluid movements
time to develop into a rhythmic show.
The puppet's stance reflects his status.
He is bent over playing a role
void of his wooden form.
While performing on stage various props are placed into his
    grooved hands.
As the items pass by he always tries to hold onto the cutting
    weapons.
The rigidity of his framework allows the marionette no strength.
The puppet tries to hack and slash
while he has the opportunity during the show,
but his efforts enter into futility.
The ceremony finished and puppet weeps splinters.
He is then hung next to his kin
and sits prone in a dark coffin until the next show.

Denos Myrmingos

Gulf-View

Looking out at the wild blue yonder,
Seagulls briskly ponder,
Listening to the fainting sounds of ships,
While the wind fiercely whips,
As bits of sand sparkles to the touch,
We walked through it - that we love so much,
Clouds swiftly moving a - flow,
As the sun shines a twinkling glow,
Waves beginning to rumble on by,
As it matches the deep blue sky,
Then darkness closes in on you,
But you'll always remember the exquisite Gulf-View.

Susan Kay Genusa Guillory

Untitled

It will dance in beams of moonlight,
And soar with the birds in flight.

It will race with the wind when it blows,
And fall gently to earth with the snow.

It will sing with the sound of wind chimes,
And bloom with the flowers in springtime.

It will laugh with the children at play,
And shine bright in the light of day.

But until that time can come to be,
My soul is trapped inside of me.

Peggy Tuttle

Rain Song

The desert's colors were of scorched bronze
hills of seared granite
valleys of smoking umber
There had been no rain.
The desert plant's stiff roots
probed crusted sands for moisture.
When the monsoon came
first as gentle rain, then as sky seas
the desert floor became pale green.
Plant roots inquired through wet meadows
to restless pools of water below.
The plant lifted its arms to the rain
leaves of jade appeared
At a branch tip a shell pink flower opened
to sing a soft song of the spheres.
Later in a fall meadow the flower faded and fell.
Its song borne by eternal winds
to a distant desert.

Mildred Hegerle

RUBRIYATTE

Joy, Grief, Beginning and The End
Are all illusion? Which the real?
All Time the answer does defend
Til, forced, from out the Here we steal.

Why think, when thinking may not change
The vast inertia of the scene?
Part of a pattern, we - not to arrange,
But blend our reason to the scheme.

Where to we that you hasten so?
What is it that commands?
And, hastening - know you where you go?
Or, going - what demands?

Why all the fuss and flurry?
What so insistent must attend?
There's time enough for hurry,
And - forever waits The End.

What yesterday was totally unlike Today?
So, for Tomorrow may we see,
The only certainty to be assayed
Tomorrow may, or, my not - be.

Joel Wright

Breaking News

Breaking news the news man said.
They shot President Kennedy announced him dead.
And his assassinator ran away just fled.
In what we've read still we dwell.
Isn't it strange we remember so well?
Every one knows clear as a bell.
What they were doing when Kennedy fell.
Every one has a story to tell.
Breaking news the news man said.
Jackie Kennedy, our first lady is dead.
They say time heals dreariness and dread.
Breaking news the news man said.
There is an auction stuffs going to sell.
Thrilling it is as the auctioneer yells.
And it ended with a ringing bell.
A tear fell as my thoughts strayed.
Our President shot and killed that way.
Our first lady's strength she strongly displayed.
Their place in history will never fade.
Forever a flame glows where they lay.

Margie Knight

Sorrow of My Loss

Two to two
Two minutes left in the game
I was anxious who would reach victory.

Being that along the boards
Boards shook.
Crash, Crash, Crash.

The buzzer went off.
Buzzzz....
Overtime.
Pucks flew like bats
Into our team's net.

I felt like a lighting bolt hit me in the heart.
I was roaring with madness.
My team was walking dead.
I shook hands with the other team.

Robert Hashimoto

From the Eyes of a Patient II

*In memory of Joseph Foy, a young cancer
victim whose spirits were high with Hope.*

Doctor do you hear the words you say
When you speak to me?
Do you tell me words of hope
            Or
Sentences of doom?
Does my diagnosis frighten you
            Or
Do you want it to frighten me?
It may be or may not be the time for me
            Could we wait and see?
It just could be that spirit in me has other plans for thee.
Doctor think when you say your words to me
Before blowing out the last candle of hope.
For in each of us a spirit dwells more powerful than
            you or I can see.
So just before you speak make sure you always leave just
A ray of hope for you, as well as, me.
This hope will make our journey together grow in such a special way.
Please know I'll know the time for me the spirit will tell me so.

Donna Foy Jones R.N.

Miss You My Love

Sometimes I just sit down and cry
Because I still don't understand why,
And sometimes, I guess, the reason I'm sad
Is because the pain in my heart, hurts so bad.

Sometimes for a miracle, I only wish
But those times, I know, I'm only being selfish,
And sometimes a smile, I can't even crack
But I know it's because, I just want you back.

Sometimes a day seems so very long
And sometimes I smile just hearing our song,
Sometimes tears out of nowhere appear
And sometimes I can't believe it's been a year.

Sometimes my heart and soul are at peace,
Because I know you're happy spirit will never cease,
And sometimes I just sit and think for a while
And, most of the time, I just miss your Smile.

Allyson Lavigne

Aids

Sex always seems like fun.
But what happens when you're done?
You can only live your life bye and bye.
Only knowing you're going to die.

What happens after they are gone.
Wondering if you will make it till dawn.
Hoping to see them again.
Thinking what could have been.

Spreading your ashes over your favorite lake.
Your family still in a wake.
People really do care.
Wondering if you shared.

People thought you where bright.
Now you are going toward the light.

Kerry West

U. Of KY. Champions At "The Final 4"

Basketball is the game,
others will tell you the same.
How Delk played the game real good,
he turned out like I knew he would.
    You played your best.
    You stood the test.
Wish Rupp could see you proud,
only the fans were really loud.

College was good for me, 1946 and 7,
I thought I was on my way to heaven.
Boys and girls, we had a good mix,
going to classes about half-past six.
The professors, always on to our tricks,
it was then we got our licks.
I'm no Stephen Collins Foster
But at class time, I made the roster.
We studied hard, you could see results,
they were always taking our pulse.
After retirement and 71,
writing poetry lets me know I won.

Gordon Elston

Mainly Spirit

I saw her coming toward me uncertain
As a feather pushes by puffs of air,
As fragile as a china figurine.
Her steps were made of hope and prayer.

She gave a wispy weeping willow wave.
"Hi!" And then she said,
"I'm going to the corner.
I need a loaf of bread.

"I'm never sure when I go out,
But if I don't return by four
And people go to look for me,
Tell them, I'll be near the store.

"'Tis not so much I need the bread,
The important part is trying,
It builds morale and courage,
Plus values no denying.

"I try to do the best I can
To make the world a better place to trod,
And through it all, 'Tis nice to know
I grasp the hand of God."

Helen E. Schmidt

A Mid Century Pause

When that Satchel proffered his sixth advice
that 'looking back, something might be gaining
he didn't mean me, at my 18, 263rd.
For as I look back, at those numbered snails
I see the first decade, as school bells and pigtails.
The second as discovery and more than just pigtails.
The third as war and marriage - though I did not get
a purple heart, I fear, I did, a bruised and blackened brain.
The fourth dwelt on the arrival of my little girl.
And the fifth, mostly the ITT world of travel and toil.

The numbered snails, all named 'when,' each took
a picture of what they saw as they went by.
As I look out at their oncoming line, shrouded in fog,
I must give out a shout, "slow down snails", I have
much to do before your tail end Charley takes that
last picture, and I finish my last barley.

John Susmuth

The Answer

Oh what splendor this world doth hold
The bright, the beautiful, the strong, the bold
But we always want what's just out of reach
To know, to have, to conquer, to beseech
Blinded by the sparkle of the glitter and gold
Lusting for the prize of treasures untold
Pushing and pulling as we strive to gain more
Desire overrules with a frightening roar
While corruption and greed run rampant and wild
All morality lost by murder of an unborn child
The pace ever quickens as we run life's race
As trouble and sorrow are a part we must face
"But why?" Is the question in our wailing and fuss
As we idly point fingers — with three pointing
back at us.

Lori Blakley

The Small Child

The small child's eyes were filled with tears,
How my dear child did you ever get here.

Strangers looked on as they hurry on by,
Not seeing the tears in the little child's eyes?

The nights were the worst, they lasted forever,
Strangers alone just lurking together.

Another dawn, a brand new day,
The child starts the search for another place to stay.

How many of us pass this child in the dark?
How many of us have this child in our heart?

The child should be playing with family and friends,
but instead the child wonders when life will end.

Take the worries from the little child's eyes,
Hold the child tight so the child never cries!

A small dose of warmth inside us all,
Would change the face of a child so small.

A gentle touch. A word. The warmth of your heart,
Makes the little child smile, A miracle starts.

Rebecca Coons

The Old Rustic Swing

There's an old rustic swing in the garden
Where we swing many happy hours away
That's where we solved all our problems
Swinging on our swing every day.

We listened to the birdies in the trees
We watched the squirrels playing in the grass
We watched the leaves floating in the breeze
And wondering how many tears have passed.

The old rustic swing is there waiting
For loved ones to give comfort to
Some couples are still debating
On how to say the words "I love you."

Rita P. Welch

Life

Life is a trip I cannot explain,
It is filled with happiness and with pain.
There are choices you make each day,
Which you will learn from along the way.
You never know what will be next,
Things just creep up on you like a pest.
Life is also beauty, that you can see,
And everything was created by God, even you and me.
We are all here for a purpose, that I know,
But what that purpose is? I wish I could say so.
So until I find the meaning of life,
Or understand the splash of the evening tide,
The truth I wish to know will hide.

Heather Rizzo

Prayer For Hope

Let me move away from this thing.
  This negative power that holds
  me so tight in its grasp,
  squeezing the life out of me.

Let me move on and away from this
  deterioration and destruction that
  seems to be thriving, by making
  a feast of my heart.

Give me the strength to pull loose from
  its clutches and move with a great
  force above and beyond it.

Put that evil thing in an eternal prison,
  for it cannot be destroyed. Then shield
  me with your love and compassion
  so I may never look back again.

But to move forward is all I ask.
  To be able to feel, give, and
  enjoy love again, and be hopeful.

Kathleen Manning

Christian's Purple Socks

Our precious little Grandson
wears purple socks-
kicks his legs a mile a minute
and adorns his head with light brown locks.
This little body of energy
throughout his daily routine,
shines his darling personality
which is so readily seen.
But those purple socks, stand soooo far out
you would have to see them to believe them.
His feet are so fat and stout,
and when the socks are lost,
we have to retrieve them.

Susanna G. Taubenberger

Sweeter End

Somehow life has been bitter-sweet
with each and every day,
through all the bitter complications I meet,
spirits high,
spooning a smile,
needing sugar when the bitter gets wild,
adding enough sugar bitter leaves a while,
but should bitter return and
have me with a sour cry,
I don't give in
more sugar is the blend,
taking bitter and sour to a sweeter end
accomplishing much with the sugar blend within
drawing me like a customer with a satisfied grin
which is truly the sweeter, sweeter, end
of how bitter-sweet began.

John Winston Jr.

The Spirit of Peace (Excerpt 2)

Wrapping and ribbon!
Bows and tape!
No living soul can escape.
The hustle and bustle! The crowds! The fun!
This is a grand time for everyone!

Knitting fast. Shopping wild.
Cutting and pasting. No time's a'wasting.
Striving to fulfill the hopes of a child.

Those large round eyes...you try to surprise...
The luck of the Irish you'll need to succeed!
Peek in the closet! Shake the box!
Big folk must be clever to out-fox.

The lights are all strung.
Threading popcorn is done.
When did we last have so much fun?
Last Christmas!

Wreaths donning doors. Mistletoe hiding.
Pinecones about. Holly throughout.
There is no time left for anyone to pout.
Only St. Nicholas has this much clout!

Gina Osher

Hello And Goodbye, My Cody

Cody, you were my grandbaby, if only for a little while,
I never saw your eyes and I never saw you smile.
But the love I felt was so deep and so strong,
I know if you'd lived, you could have done no wrong!

I never saw you crawl and I never saw you walk,
We'll never have the chance to just sit and talk.
I never saw you play and I never saw you run,
I never got a chance to see you having fun.

I never heard you laugh, I never heard you speak,
And the reason for this is the answer I seek.
Although it was God's will, I don't understand why,
The most painful thing I've done was tell you 'goodbye.'

Hello and goodbye, almost in the same breath,
Then God took you from us in your early death.
I will love you, my little Cody, until the day that I die,
Then I'll see you in heaven and we'll never say 'goodbye!'

P. J. Kiser

Why

As I look into the sky I wonder why, why, why
You'd ever want to make me cry.
I found shelter in your heart.
I thought our relationship would never part.
What could I have been thinking?
Was it just my heart sinking?
Or was it the way you held me so tight?
Where then left my mind was all fear, all fright
But now I'm out of your life.
And I'm out of your way.
As I'm sitting here miserably weeping away.

Kathleen Velek

The Inevitable

Everyone's life comes to an end,
Young or old we don't want to lose them,
We can't control it because we depend,
on the Lord for guidance and help.
It's loud and clear to understand,
What our life is all about, to do,
Good, love thy neighbor and send,
Forth a good family message,
To go in peace knowing our fence
did mend.

No solitude here just the art
of living

Antonio Mottiorcio

I Remember a Time

I remember a time of climbing
trees.
A time when I asked reality, what
significance does that have to me?
A time when thing's were only imaginative
to see, like the sparkling flutter
of a fairy wing.
Fire flies on an endless flight, accompany
the sandman in the night.
Rainbow's and castle's of pink's and
blue's, high in the sky on a make believe view.

Diane Newton

Life

What's there to prove, by the scars on my wrist?
Or the feelings pronounced, by my mouth or my fist?

The little things we do. Most with no point.
What's to be said, by rolling a joint?

All my tears, do you think you know?
They may not always appear, to be what they show.

So you think you can see, through to the scars on my heart?
But can you feel it, tearing itself apart?

Love is my darkness, not my light.
Alcohol my deadly friend, that gets me through the night.

So what's to prove, from life itself?
Buying off happiness, with all your wealth.

So this I say, with a shortness of breath.
What is to be proven, is a long lonely death.

Josephine Marie Pedone

Joie De Vivre

There is this thing of love and time and death
Let us together seize the issue
We shall write our will on the days like
words on paper tissue
We will do this thing, you and I
All men say that time can fly
but our "joie vivre" can stop the flight
and create beauty in the night
So love me dear with body mind and breath
and I'll return it twofold until the very death

Donald C. Crombie

In Memory Of Mona

I once had a little playmate
    As dear as a sister to me;
We played together on school days;
    We play now in memory.

For God has taken her from us
    To increase the ranks up above
Of those who have faithfully followed
    His word in honor and love.

We miss her. Oh, yes, how we miss her.
    But sorrow is comfort we know
For we shall all be united
    When tasks are complete here below.

So, 'til the time of rejoicing,
    'Til my work here is well done,
I shall play with my playmate in memory
    The dear old games of fun.

Katherine P. Perkins

My Mother's Voice

My mother passed away long ago
still today I miss her so.
She was always there when I was young.
To guide me and keep me from all wrong
now I've aged and grown older
my heart seem to have grown colder.
Sometimes I feel such despair
I feel sometimes that no one cares
sometimes I feel so alone
I heard mother voice saying seek God's throne.
Allow him to calm your storms
and put in your heart a new song.
Allow him to be your friend
he will stay with you until the end.
Let him soothes and comfort your soul
there's no need for your heart to be cold.
Find peace, and happiness in his love.
He's always sending it from above.
I've gone on and left you it's true
but God have always been there for you.

Evelyn Smith

My Flower

My flower is very special to me
in a way that nobody else knows.
My flower always makes me laugh
and hardly ever lets me doze.
My flower also has its problems
cuz the world isn't a perfect place.
My flower I always try to help
cuz I don't like to see her unhappy face.
My flower is a present, I do believe,
from the man who runs things up above.
My flower, she is the one I love.

Scott Truman

Untitled

I must deserve this all he thought, with eyes that were so sad;
The things I've done and what I want, I guess I must be bad.

The shame went deep, down to the core, of such a sweet young child;
The lessons taught, he learned them well, and soon became quite wild.

He took care of the family well, he handled every chore;
They called it independence then, they never knew the score.

They seldom asked where he had been, so he thought they didn't care;
He learned to be silent and distant quite well, and learned he shouldn't share.

Off alone, to a place unknown, he dreamed of being grown;
The things he'd see, the things he'd do, and apply that he'd been shown.

He left home early, just to prove, he could make it on his own;
So off in search of life and love, a place he could call home.

Three wives, two houses, one small child, all did fall in his wake;
The pain, the guilt, the unseen hurt, how much more could he take?

He placed the blame, on everything, out there that he could see;
When finally, with nothing left, he had to look at he.

James Hoffman

Forever In Mind's Eye

There she was a poor old and ragged
Mexican woman with street children
Matches they sold by day
My imagination guessed their fate by night
Beggars not sellers
with desperation in their eyes

The ol' woman pushing her wears
upward my way had transparent eyes
that told a story of the heart
With sad eyes a twist of the head
She begged softly "oh please...please!"

Turning away to the colorful sights
of town momentarily I could see
Matches still at the end of her extended arms
Finally in defeat gathering her flock
And vanishing as quickly as they appeared
....Now to live in my heart forever

Roderick Dhu Gray

Passage of the Dead

Form of spirit contact as old as life itself flesh and death abreast power and ancient wisdom a passage to the dead which has been and is eternal the mystic oracle outdates its foe religion
    Simple board of words to most explained unholy to speak unto the dead for this you'll lose your soul it must be of the devil if the sheep don't understand so much is labeled evil dogma fear has blinded man. With a feeling so intense the dead see from within you as one you let them speak to the form they've left forsaken they watch us all they envy our wasted breath lost within the void abyss to grace the living is an honor
    The fears of man have expelled the sacred board living out their meek and feeble faith they burn it in their churches spit upon its wood they do not understand it real life they never could
    As I look upon its surface it truly is a gift silently I beckon I call the ancient presence speak to me this night in oath I keep your wisdom journey through my mind as one we share the visions transcender of flesh life I respect for all you've said your existence carries on with me it shall not end until I walk the path greeting you in death I always shall keep open the passage of the dead.

Thomas A. Beasley

The Color of Peace

Look at me, you see the color of peace in my face
No frowns, no grief, no disgrace in my face

After years of horror and pain
Some how I managed to remain sane

I kept my dignity and increased my strength
If I had not, surely I would have went.

Peace of mind, body, and soul
Is only achieved by the bold

Show the boldness of you
And achieve the holdness of you.

The color of peace is not blue
Just your true color, shining through
And that is the true color of you.

Trilbia D. Coe

Friends

I'm so glad that you're my friend,
I know you'll be there till the end,
Through ups and downs,
Through thick and thin.
They make you smile and pick you up,
They make you happy like a baby pup.
Friends are there when you need to cry,
They don't ever ask you "Why?",
They just hold you as time goes by.
These are the ones you tell secrets to,
Because you know they're between me and you.
You can call them up in the middle of the night,
When you and your parents have had a fight.
They will listen, then give advice,
Of how to make a sacrifice.
Yes, friends do tend to fight,
But they only last about a night.
You'll hug and make up the very next day,
Because friends are here to stay.

Brandon Beau Austin

Memories

I'm blue over you so blue over you;
I miss you since you've gone;
The days are so drear, the nights, so long;
I miss you since you've gone.

The day that we met I'll never forget;
The love we once knew.
And though you have gone,
Still the memories linger on;
I'm blue oh! So blue over you.

The years that we shared;
   through laughter and tears;
The joy we once knew.
They are all in the past;
   for you've gone home at last.
I miss you since you've gone.

Someday we will meet up there,
   in heaven so fair;
Our love we will renew.
Although you have gone, still the memories linger on.
I'm blue; oh! So blue over you.

Marian E. Brown

The Moment

A spring day dawns.
Wet glistening diamonds variegate the emerald field.
In the doorway of the woods lay a small stone;
used yesterday to rescue a boomerang captive in a tree.
On the stone perch a cold twig
partly damp with splendid frost:
Rows of tiny soldiers, stand frozen,
undisturbed in time, proud before the battle;
Yet, delicate for the moment-just seconds before demise.
Soon the sun gleams, rays reaching, stretching
in all directions like tentacles,
Radiant beams conquer the frosty twig.
Gradually, the army dissipates, the tiny frozen soldiers die.
Tranquil poetic beauty transforms into
Droplets of plasma descending aimlessly;
finally, disappearing before touching the stone.

The day has been born and everything is dry.
In the doorway of the woods lay a stone.
On the stone perch a twig that must have fallen from a tree.
Perhaps today, the boy will rescue his boomerang.

Lyn Ora

Thoughts On The New Brave Breed

This new, acknowledged breed,
draped in solemn,
unsmiling black,
Troop out of the shade
of the tree of knowledge.

In retrospection, theirs was a ritual
consumption of the anatomy
of the tree's verity,
In futurity, theirs is but an unspeakable
fictive piece of mystery.

Thus inward the black-gossamered junglette
walk they, the bath-freshed infants,
searching, challenging,
As the breeders of this new brave breed
contemplate in fear and in trust.

Such is the commencement of their exodus
for they shall inherit a sequence
of the theatry of mankind.
Shall we them bouquets of praises greet
or put above their heads anonymous wreaths?

Joseph Uysetuan

Looking For You

Give me a helping hand,
because I love you so much
I want to feel your touch with mine
and live forever in your arms.
Your body is better than anything
and the best of everything.
Your love is so sweet and fine
it's what I want to treasure most of all.
Without you to make the light shine
and to give life,
there can be no love to give
to a lonely soul.
I wish and I wonder day by day
when I'll have you
and we walk through life together.

Ronald P. Farrell

The Fountain of Youth

Standing in the still of the basement
Overwhelmed by the stale smell of a lost youth
All that remains are dusty boxes on shelves shaky from age
Never opened since the day they were put there
Wondering where the time went
Those carefree days never to be found again
Until he unpacked those boxes so carefully put away
Retracing his steps down memory lane
Reminiscing
Recognizing the pleasant times fifty years past
Then brought back to reality, his arthritic joints reminding him
his untroubled days are forever gone
replaced with lonesome months
filled with pain and misery
brought about by aging
Waiting till that one moment
at the end of the road
where his worry free days will begin again
and
A less traveled road emerges as the familiar grounds of life
crumbles.

Larina Pun

Trust

I'd like to believe you when you say you love me,
yet it's hard to believe in something you can't see.
Just like the angels in heaven and God up above,
you can't just open your eyes and see love.
I have heard this line from many before,
not long after, lies and deception hit the floor.
My heart has been broken from believing these lies,
I have to expect to be the one that cries.
When, again, I find myself at that forbidden door,
I tell myself to be careful, I've been there before.
I try hard to believe the words that you say,
but my heart only knows how to be foolish and always turns away.
If I could let someone love me, if I only knew how,
things would be different, I wouldn't be here now,
waiting and wondering if it's all true,
could you possibly love me as much as I love you?

Jennifer M. Harbour

Little White House

Oh so many times I have come home to that little white
House with roses on the fence-

Mother and Dad there to greet me with warmth and with
Love I know that God was looking down, watching from
Above, that little white house with roses on the fence-

The years have come and gone and the frailties of life
Have taken them home-gone from that little white house
With roses on the fence-

So precious are the memories as I travel life's thin thread,
Of all the golden moments I spent there with mother and dad-
At that little white house with roses on the fence.

Patricia Coffey-McDonald

I Sing Each Moment of You

I sing each moment of you.
I sing between your breath and your heartbeat.
I sing in your mid-step and in the reach of your hand.

My song touches the sweetness
of the newborn skin behind you knee
as if my tongue draws its notes on your flesh.

Miriam Moses

Virgin Mary

Running from all the dreams that originate from emotional distress,
She hides in a shadow and stays here to think
Many years of confused thoughts of who she really is
A Virgin Mary she once had been
Alone in this dark secluded place is where she speaks
Speaks of things that all of us wish to hear
Frustrated for she cannot escape those dreams
Of the horrid things that she once did

An extending hand of purity shows her forgiveness
Restoring all of her strength
Now that she can forget about her sins
A new life is where she will begin
No more confused thoughts of who she really is
She will become that Virgin Mary she once had been

Gilb Gilbert Jr.

Los Alamos

On the way to the Mayan village
Where parrots nested and flew multicolored
In the thin clear light of dawn,
Gigantic jeweled hummingbirds with blue throats
Sipped nectar from flaming shrubs
Along a sparkling stream.
Indian children with chunks of turquoise
Skimmed rocky paths to higher plateaus.
The singing quail, attuned to life, kept hidden
But the music lured me still higher
To clumps of yellow blooming cacti
Unbelievably alive with orioles
That matched the sun.
Tropical jays with crested heads
Winged directly above the path.
I stared in secret wonder at "Aduana"
Long tailed with rosy breast,
Bright eyes transmitting knowledge
That our rare meeting was the pinnacle of this day.

Rene LaRue

Blue

Blue moon
I'll see you soon.
In the night,
I'll see your light.
And from below I see your glow
But it will be seen very low.
In the sky we finally meet
with a joy of happy greet.
the moon shines
in silver lines.
It makes me smile
for running a mile.
The moon is as cold as ice
when you seem so nice.
The man on the moon
Sings a happy tune.
And then when the moon shines
I'll make you mine.
I'll be on the moon waiting for you
so tell me my love will I be seeing you soon.

Raquel Velasquez

But I Thought....

Even though it was a wicked night,
I still had no fright,
There was someone else with me in that room,
And she is good with the broom,
She keeps terror out,
Of course she must be stout,
She quickly got into action,
I felt so bad cause she gave dad a scratching.

Andrew J. Tappert

I Wonder

I look up at the deep blue sky,
It seems oh so very high.
I imagine I was soaring like a big black bird,
Singing so I would be heard.
To the tallest building I would soar,
It would be like opening a new door.
Every step I would take would be like flying over a
beautiful lake.
Even if there is no fear,
There is one reason I hate up here.
For there is no one to love and care not even a big grizzly bear.
So I shall land back down to Earth,
To a new nation I will give birth.

Beth Underwood

Waterfall

'O mist-veiled maiden, sparkling waterfall,
Could I but float down cavern walls with thee,
Then echo to the world thy splashing glee,
I'd paint thy glorious trail on castle walls
In every kingdom - so that folk might love
Thy slender stream in beauty's glorious tint
More brilliant still o'er moss and thirsty flint
That blend in filmy trend from heights above;
Alas, I'm no creator of my fate:
For I'm ordained to dwell in mortal shell
Of flesh: a prisoner I - within a cell
Called life: ne'er shall I be thy sylvan mate;
O cataract! O elfin rainbow blush -
Dance with the Muses through the twilight hush!

Raymond Clement Thomas

A Sonnet to the Hollyhock

It thrives and grows against the sunny wall,
That hollyhock that I have learned to adore,
The blooms, so red, appear on spikes so tall,
Just like they did outside my mother's door.

We learned to use those products of the dirt,
For things which Mother Nature never planned,
A bud for a head and a blossom for a skirt,
A tiny sprig to make an arm and hand.

But now I pick those blooms that last and last,
And bring them in the house for days on end,
Of sitting brightly in the snifter glass,
Where I can see and share them with a friend.

Grow on, oh hollyhock, and spread that joy,
That I have cherished since I was a boy.

Eugene A. Murdock

A Portrait of Me

Diana, the dragon lady, the crazy wolf,
Or Tanya, quiet, a loner, completely alone.
"Who is the lady with the waist length hair?"
"My child, how you've grown!"

They think I've grown into an adult.
They don't see the child that wants to live.
So I isolate myself,
So I can't receive or give.

It's safer that way.
I can't be hurt, I can't feel.
I live in my own world
Where nothing is real.

My eyes see the world
But let the world see me.
The shifting colors
Set my emotions free.

Tanya L. Christian

The Wounds Within

The wounds within are
bleeding out haunting memories,
aching in the naked face of painful truths,
burning in the searing sting of harsh realities,
oozing in the ugliness of seething resentment.

Healing begins as the wounds within are
soothed in acceptance and understanding,
eased by salves of nurturing touch,
cleansed by pure waters of compassion,
bandaged by the willingness to forgive,
healed by choice and the freedom of letting go.

...Remaining...
the patchwork of scars which testify
yes, it happened.
But there is a time for moving on,
and the wounds within no longer bleed.

Catherine M. Canning

Music: The Voice Of Life

Music is expressing emotions
the cleansing of the soul.
To rejoice in happiness
while praising his name.

Music is expressing emotions
understanding and dealing with pain.
Quiet moment rocking in the old wooden chair
while listening to rain drops tap on the windowpane.

Music is expressing emotions
The relaxation of the soul
as the body reacts to the beat,
the snapping of fingers
movement of feet.

Music is
Music was
Music will always be
the voice
Of life

Bakari Haynes

And You Were There

I said my prayers; what will be, will be;
When I awaken and hope to see you next to me.
The room is cold, there is a mask on my face.
I am counting backwards-99-98...
With eyes barely open, I saw surgeons gathering.
"How did it go?" "Great! No Complications!"
It's over! I'm alive! I fell asleep again,
But woke up once more to voices commanding;
"I'm pulling out a tube; lift up your back";
I followed the orders as well as I could but all was black,
"Squeeze my hand," a familiar voice - with warmth and happiness!
I touched your hand and you were there;
Now I can rest.

Judie L. Miller

I Feel Like Dancing

I feel like dancing with time
building bridges so wide.
With space enough of life to last forever.
Timeless is my guide.

So often we use forever like stepping stones.
Feeling lost becoming alone.

Forever forms formation of silence
a plausible peace inside.
Tracing the birth of me, planting
life as watching a robin, dotting
a nest of need

I feel like dancing to the laughter of truth.
I am seeing a mountain with no end.

Blades of grass, softly blowing in the wind.
Trees standing tall, I feel like
dancing with them.

Laughter enters into time, and forever never bends.

Patsy Cruz

Philosophically Incorrect

Cut loose this reign that straight jackets my brain
Tie together severed thoughts
To create conscious thinking
Illiterate to conventional wisdom
Freedom of prescribed theories
Able to express my virgin thoughts
Without interference of common knowledge

Rid myself of an entirely analytical mind,
A thought process without the use of a heart
Piece together these separate words
To become common lines
Symmetrically out of place
Standing on one foot I feel balance
Mesmerizing,
Hypnotic,
Comatose state
In touch with reality

Erik Raske

I Was Once Worn By Someone So Dear

I was once worn by someone so dear,
through loving memory will always be here.
So when you hug me up close to you,
just remember,
he loved you too.

Christopher George

Open Window

Outside the open window
The sun rises, mysterious Gods assemble.
Leaves scrape with morning dew.
My elbows got dirty climbing out the open window.

The spiritual morning of the plains.
The highway clings to the night.
Scattered reminders of morning cry out in relief.
Wet grass and the grey skies await the sun.
All this awaits outside the open window.
Poems wattle through the dark's confusing mist,
outside the open window.

Last night cries, the tears of unborn shelter.
Suffered for unspeakable tears.
Stealing battered hopes fresh out on the shelf.

This night ended, and loneliness arrived with the sun.
Bringing knowledge from last night's confusion.
All this was captured outside the open window.

Steve Bradford

Tainted Rose

Standing underneath the moonlit sky,
I broke down to my knees and began to cry.
A tear dropped from my cheek to the ground,
Into a puddle of fears, making no sound.
As I wept, the puddle grew,
Clouded by tears and the new fallen dew.
No one was there to see me cry,
No one was there to watch me die.

As my life withered away,
The sun started to rise and begin the new day.
I melted into my puddle of tears,
Unfulfilled dreams, memories of fear.
Out of the ground, where the puddle once was,
Grew one single rose, my life and my blood.

Bryan Hays

Morning

Dusk comes,
Everything has an ethereal appearance as the earth waits to be
enclosed in the arms of night. Rest comes,
For all the inhabitants of this great planet
From the tiniest insect burrowed in its hole,
to the bison of greatest might.

For man, this time of sustaining means complete rest —
renewal of the mind-regeneration of the soul —
Enlightening of the spirit, whose nightly trek ends at the feet of
God, receiving there some secret instruction, forever his to hold.

Kept inside, quietly, till at some future time and place —
This instruction becomes wisdom from within the heart - a beautiful
gift of grace.

Day comes,
Rays of glorious light burst forth from the heavens to end the night.
And, we can be sure this rest we've known
Is nothing to the rest we'll have when we go home.

Morning, whose light will never end.
Together forever with family and friends;
Songs of praise will be our prayer, when morning comes, over there.

Marica Gahan

My Native Land

Things may be different in this changing world
Since heaven's winds "Old Glory" unfurled;
Her colors a beautiful glorious sight
Some things may be wrong, but most things are right.

There is freedom to worship in this Godly land
For moral integrity with honor we stand;
Our churches the torch of salvation ignite
Some things may be wrong, but must things are right.

As Liberty's statue still beams with each wave
The symbol of hope for the free and the brave;
My land of courage of freedom and might
Some things may be wrong, but most things are right.

When my journey is finished and my race has been run
And I wait to hear that blessed well done;
The star spangled banner enriching my flight
I'll thank God for my country, where most things were right.

Lloyd Brownback

Mississippi

Mississippi is the place to be.
Mississippians are kind, friendly, and believe in family
The people here are nice and sweet.
They will try to help you in an heartbeat.
Some of them will go a country mile.
To say hello, wave, or just give you a smile.
They believe in religion, working, and education.
In church and school they love participation.
If it's beaches you like, then go to the coast for a rest.
If it's home cooking you like, Newton County has the best.
In Jackson we have a great zoo, with animals to see.
In Jackson there's also a TV station called WLBT.
Or go to Meridian there's a park, for a picnic or kids to play.
They also have a TV station called WTOK.
There's all kinds of different things in Mississippi.
I found it to be a good place to raise a family.
So don't believe anything you hear or what people say.
Come check us out yourself someday.

Regina W. Mapp

China Doll

China Doll, China Doll
Why are you so alone?
China Doll, China Doll
stands like stone.

China Doll, China Doll
Why are your feelings secured with a lock?
China Doll, China Doll
stands like a rock.

China Doll, China Doll
Can you take it anymore?
China Doll, China Doll
falls to the floor.

China Doll, China Doll
Is it the words he releases?
China Doll, China Doll
shatters to pieces.

Abby Ahmad

Emotions

The struggle of life you face day to day,
Makes me ask the question, will mine be Okay?
The times ahead are rough at best,
As I travel forward to seek my quest.
Questions arise, answers I seek,
Emotions tearing at me, leaving me weak.
Tomorrow seems gray, today makes me lonely,
Making me long for my one and only.
Troubles are present, from decisions of the past,
Making me wonder how long my sanity will last.
Usually, I'm strong and can battle the best,
For now, I'm defeated and feel I should rest.
Time will march on, my strength will return,
Looking back on my troubles, the bridges I will burn.
Emotions stirred crazy, through I will survive,
And in the near future, I intent to thrive.
Solving the problems that arise one by one,
Then to my amazement, my worries will be gone.

Rebecca Kelley

A Boyhood Memory

He watched the grey gull he had shot
with his new air rifle
Hobble away from the milk-soaked bread
he'd guiltily prepared
After his mother had quietly made him
feel rotten
Because he'd broken his birthday promise
Never to shoot at any living thing.
For days he held his reluctant captive
very carefully
As he fed it with increasing success
on bread, milk and finally meat
The day he released his patient,
the bird shook itself
preened its grey feathers,
stretched its wings and flew
into the sea wind, free.
And, young as he was, he knew
the sharp pain
of rejection.

Marshall Jamison

"Is It Lasting Too Long?"

In loving memory of my Dad
You heard being shouted from across the room.
I'll pick up the broken pieces, you go get the broom.
All books aren't for coloring in and lipsticks aren't crayons.
That was easy to rebuild, but, it used more pieces when it ran.
Mom's good china consisted of eight different dinner plates.
Boots without blades aren't still considered skates.
Don't staple it, a safety pin won't pop.
A jar becomes a vase, when it has a broken top.
Teaspoons are used for stirring, not to set off caps.
Jumping on the beds are not very restful naps.
Yes, furniture needs polishing, but Fantastic is for the sink.
The next time you shave the dog don't hide it with my mink.
Toys are not hammers, stop forcing it to fit.
Don't plug that in there! Zzzziiiitttt!
"Is it lasting too long?"
You heard being shouted from across the room.

Carol Ann Finnigan

The Longing Heart ...

As I gazed at you from afar
You appeared a shining star;
Love, at last, had found my heart
I wished that we would never part.

I saw your soul; you never knew
I saw it more clearly than you wanted me to;
Your distance I feared; it scared me so
I longed for the day you wouldn't let go.

I had wished a thousands times before,
And now I wished even more;
Someday you and I, we would be free
Forever in love, the way it should be.

Now I see my dreams; they were in vain,
And I sense the never ending pain;
So for now, my love, I must move on,
My dreams of yesterday, all but gone.

Someday, my dear, you might realize,
What a wonderful thing has passed you by;
But for this day, you must know,
I only wanted to love you so.

Kim Reed

Untitled

I want to soar into the air, and leave behind all my pain
and despair.
I'll feel at ease up above looking down, never feeling the
pain that's always around.
The thick night air will hold me in a warm embrace, all my
loneliness and sorrow will be gone with no trace.
I'll soar with the birds then dive deep into the sea, the
cold dark water will enfold me.
Now the sorrow is flooding into my head. There's no more
comfort in a warm bed.
Mothers kiss doesn't heal the pain, much less take it away.
Alone I always face the next day.
A thick night blanket pulled over my head doesn't protect
me from my fears and dreads.
Only time will swallow up all my tears, all my problems, and
all my fears.
I feel comfort knowing I can put this pain to an end, I'm
the only one who can help myself, I'm my only true friend.

Allison Rice

My Love To You

Deep in the trenches of my soul
where sadness likes to dwell
tis where I've found this love for him
that I've come to know so well.

And if he ever knew that I
hath come to care so much
why indeed I do believe
that I'd long to feel his touch.

For love it likes to hurt me
merely break my heart in two
no mending could not heal it
nor could it be put back together by you.

Well I guess it's different in the way
the a secret fills my heart
and if I do not let him know
we'll always be apart.

I know you'll think I'm crazy
but there's nothing I can do
this pain has begun to hurt to much
so I confess my love to you.

Amie Robbins

Little Red Rose

Little red rose on thorny stem,
  Like a big bright ruby - priceless gem,
What unseen mystical power hath God
  Allowed you to take from a little dirt clod?

And up through your little green stem so straight
  A soft petaled, sweet fragrant bud create?
In life you oft play a leading role
  Oh little red rose - you must have a soul.

You visit the sick and help them get well,
  Or comfort the mourners at the tolling bell,
Or sit on your rose bed to mother's delight,
  Bringing joy and good cheer to all that's in sight.

And though your thorns hurt when picked by a dater.
  The hurt is endured for your beauty's much greater.
Oh little red rose with thorny stem,
  What is your great power - your priceless gem?

Dale A. McAllister

The Answer

When life's troubles get you down
Upon your face you wear a frown.
Woe is me! Is your cry.
Can't get any where, don't know why.
There's no one you can trust,
Your hopes and dreams turn to dust.
Joy and love from you flees,
Beaten down to your knees!
Now is the time to lift your eyes.
God loves you and hears your cries!
With peace, forgiveness and saving grace,
Your troubles He'll erase!
Self pity you've no need of.
The answer is in God's love!

Shirley J. Payne

The Dream

Come on in here little one
I see your world's turned upside down
What on earth's been goin' on here
since I've been gone?

They don't seem to understand you, do they...
when you say what's deep inside
when you hear the tunes, and dream the dreams
They can't feel, in fact they Hide!

The world's had many like us
some say "artist" some say "weird"
But we dream the dreams, and we build the world
And at times are even feared!

Some few of us get wealthy
Some reach fame once they've gone home
Don't you worry 'bout it either way
Just "make up" another poem

"Happened just the other day"
You know I heard my own heart sing
"said times and trouble dead ahead"
Find what happiness love brings

John B. Richardson

All We Hold Dear

With the meadows still brown from March's solemn dress
Warmed by April's stubborn rules, I confess
Only the sudden freedom of sod and budding trees,
That horses will prance about in April's cool breeze.
The signs of April appear one by one, a delight to see
Each comes alive, like the sapling Butternut tree,
While large flocks of geese fly north in the morning light
Flying in formation, they create a welcoming sight.
Their honking cries echo in the cool morning air
To make their journey safely, seems to be their only care.
Other birds will follow quickly to April's beckoning call
By instinct they too remember, the journey south last fall.
As the bees and butterflies emerge to April's early flowers,
Roosters crow loudly, from their fence post tower.
County folks become excited by April's sudden beauty,
As always, Mother Nature brings to life which is her yearly duty.
But Spring will pass quickly, Summer will appear
The human population will again rejoice, in all we hold dear.

Elsie M. Westrick

Caduceus

The rags are bitter.
The sap merely prolongs my agony.
The sky grows dark.
Sweat and blood cloud my vision.
Are you among those casting lots for my garments?
Inverted on the tree of life hang I.
Letters stream from my lips.
The meaning is unclear.
Awaiting the mercy of the lance.
The fate of the world.

The serpent on the staff.

George E. Schmauch Jr.

A Child's Game (In Another Time Frame)

It came to my mind just the other day, about a game we as kid's
would play

It seems to me, it is played by much of humanity today, even if it
leads them in a very wrong way

It now seems to me, as though most people play this game, even if
we don't call it by the old original name

It didn't make any sense to me, in those long ago days, why anyone
would want to follow in another person's ways

Whether what the leader did, was right or it was wrong, you just
came and followed right along

I guess you could also call it, following the sheep, even if it lead
you into a wrong and dangerous leap

The rules of the game were, to follow the leader you see, regardless
of where, or to what, he was to lead thee

As a child, I guess even then somehow I knew, to follow my own heart,
and to myself be true

Follow the leader, back then was just a child's game, today it seems
to have become a way of life for many - In another time frame.

Jeannette Klee

One Little Word

If I could touch just one little heart,
I would say a prayer and then I would start.
"Please Dear Lord let me shine for you,
Bless me and guide me in all that I do."
Some days have trials that we must endure,
But with you beside me I will make it for sure.
Then there are days filled with joy and with love,
We must not forget to thank God up above.
I go on my way trying to do the best that I can,
Remembering I must hold on to His hand.
When I see people so sad and forlorn,
I hope they have someone so they're not alone.
Trying to touch them with a kind word and smile,
I ask God to bless them so they'll be fine in awhile.
Only God knows all of our insecurities,
He will listen and love you if you only ask please.
For when I leave this world someday,
I hope you'll remember just to pray.
If there are times I ever cross your mind,
Just remember me with love and for being a little kind.

Marty Rae Royer

Tomorrow Is Another Day

Here it comes the night
   I am so tired of putting up a fight
Another day has passed on by
   I don't even have the energy to cry
The pain is still here, it hasn't gone
   Can I make it to another dawn
Oh how hard it is, when all that's left is pride
So many emotions at war within side
Love and trust, hate and anger
   take the battle field
Confusion in the middle
   has my fate been sealed
Is my life a joke or is it destiny?!?
For what's in the future I cannot see
I don't understand everything I feel
it's all so much, it can't be real
Yet I will be strong and protect my self esteem
Things can't be as bad as what they seem
So take a breath, hope and pray
After all tomorrow is another day

Tammy L. Bortel

Fly By Night

The full moon is now high in the night
Each star in heaven is blazing just right
Low Glistening clouds cover the earth as snow
As far the eye can see this brilliant ocean flows

Voices in the air fade to whispers this night
The roar of our engines are now only sight
Peace and wonder fills my soul and sight
It absorbs me completely in its great light

It is time for reflection on man's ongoing plight
And to wonder how I fit into God's universal sight
When my final check ride is due for review
I hope and pray that I have everything right

The cockpit lights from below my sight
Reflect a ghost just to my right
No word is spoken but we are content to gaze
At God's gift to pilots who fly by night

Wes Parks

A Tribute to Teachers

You wake - up feeling tired and dreary
feeling oh so leary
traffic has you worn and weary
another day, oh so bleary

At work preparing for today's events
wondering how the day will be spent
good, bad, uhh so-so another day spent

We arrive wondering too
how the day will be spent and with who
good, bad, uhh so-so another day we won't know

Our day may be filled with joy, laughter with joy, laughter,
smiles,
    and hugs
Our day may be filled with a few tears and shoves
One thing for sure that we do know
Our school is filled with friends and love

Our moms are gone, tho for a short while
our teachers greet us with a smile
with hands that hug and words of love
you remind us of a mother's love
Happy Mothers's Day Teacher!!!!!!!!!!!

  Rae S. Graves

A Mist Like Velvet

A mist like velvet falls about my eyes,
Veiling just enough radiance only compared by the sun,
How can I express something so beyond words,
When fog must shroud my eyes from pure truth,
Phantom gloves spring upon my hand when I reach out,
Covering the searing touch of passion,
Leaving only gentle softness and five trails of cool,
Loving fire upon my palm,
No words, No pictures,
For there is comparison,
Someday perhaps I will find cause and strength,
To wrench from these unworthy eyes the veil that for so long has
held back blinding light,
Tear from fingers that ache gloves I did not request,
To at last make known and know myself,
What it is to look upon pure beauty,
And to touch for but a moment,
Before passion's inferno consumes imperfect flesh,
To reach out a lone fingertip and caress love.

  Scott Bell

What Is A Mother?

What is a mother?
  She's someone who tried to see to it that you never
    needed or wanted anything as you grew.

What is a mother?
  She's there in your times of trouble, sorrow
    and joy to see you through.

What is a mother?
  She's that one person who always just knows
    what you need when you're blue.

What is a mother?
  She's the one who stands by your side and
    agrees no matter what you do.

What is a mother?
  She's the one that you don't tell often enough that you
    love and appreciate her you just assumed she knew.

What is a mother?
  I'm not really sure but I'm so very glad
    that my mother is you!!!

  Laurie King

Bald Mountain Baptist Church

When we built our Fellowship Hall
We had faith in God that we could get it done

We have had our ups and downs in life
Our ups were mighty few
Our downs it seemed were many
But we always managed to pull through

When bad spells seemed to hit us
And the road was hard to trod
We always pulled together
And put our faith in God.

But we all stuck together
Like "peas within a Pod"
We buckled down and won because
We put our faith in God.

  Guyva Nanney

Solitude

Walking through the trees
  alone in the pine woods
  sunlight sprinkles the path.

An open meadow beckons
  birds sing, bees are pollinating
  a fairyland of flowers.

The path narrows, squirrels
  chatter away, a rabbit darts.

The canyon walls are closing in,
  there is little sunlight.

The path descends slowly to a quiet
  stream transporting leaves of deciduous
  trees from the edge of the meadow.

In the sand there are deer
  tracks, a doe and a fawn.

It is getting late. I turn back
  for there are many things to do.

But there is a harmony in nature, a
  subtle rhythm both wild and peaceful
  that soothes the troubled heart and mind.

  Carl H. H. Baumann

Bible Gift

Matthew is where you should look
When you first receive this book.
For in the Old Testament Jesus is concealed,
In the new He is very much revealed.

There is an awesome story on these pages
Which have been told through out the ages
God's word is truth to one and all
So we might walk instead of fall.

Reach out to Him in thought or word
For no matter which your cries are heard
He wants to reach each and every heart
But to save your soul we each must play a part

We have to ask Him into our heart
For that's the only way to start
That's not to say we won't stumble or fall
The Lord is faithful and just to help us all.

  Cheryl L. Guthrie

Is This Love?

When we first met we knew it was love.
Something Heaven sent, a gift from above.
We shared our hearts through our eyes.
The past was behind us so we shared our lives.
The odds were against us but we knew we were right.
So we fell in love that very first night.

It's all over now but the crying.
It's so hard to face the pain, hurt and lying.
Whoever said, "if you love someone, turn them loose",
Must have never had someone as special as you.
Your happiness is everything to me,
I just wish you could see.
So we could fall in love again...
Like that very first night.

If this is love why does it hurt so bad?
I opened my heart to you,
Shared my fears, my dreams and my tears.
You took it all and left me with nothing.
If this is love,
Why does it hurt so bad?

Jay A. Waalk

To Rose Buds

Moma used to tell us all about the rose buds
How they must be treated gentle on the vine
How early in the spring they bloom so pretty
But they won't bud unless the sun be gains to shine
If we're not gentle when we touch the tender rose buds
The pretty flower made by God's design
It will tare and come apart so easy
We must be gentle with the rose buds on the vine
Little children like the rose buds are so tender
They must be treated gentle all the time
Or they will hurt and come apart so easy
And they won't bloom to pretty flowers on the vine
So we must treat the little children like the rose buds
We must treat them gentle and so kind

We must give to them the light that comes from heaven
So they will bloom to pretty flowers on the vine
Because they're pretty made by God's design
Yes little children are made by God's design

Doris Gardner Chandler

The Stranger

The Stranger,
With his raspy voice,
Comes to me when I dream.
With a lighted torch,
He leads me to far off places.
The Stranger,
With his black coat,
Has no name or identity.
With his knowledge,
He can tell what I think.
The Stranger,
With his forceful touch,
And peaceful heart,
Creates new life in the young,
And puts the old to rest.
With his own hands he keeps the cycle steady,
And he shall remain a stranger,
As long as we dwell on Earth.

Susan Tanski

Memories

What will our children think of,
When thinking when they were small,
Will it be love, hot meals and laughter?
And morning sun and smiles for all?

Will it be frowns and sharp words
No hugs, no kisses, just you get on your way?
No prayer, no praise to God above?
No thanksgiving in any way.

Children and grown ups need that love,
To get ready for life as they should,
To thank God for this wonderful day.
And start the day as best they could.

I hope my boys remember the good things,
Not when we were hurrying and scurrying around,
That school was a joy to all,
And the praise of God a happy sound.

I never thought of my self as a maker of memories,
We all provide memories for our loved ones, so dear,
Memories of a warm hearth and home,
A place we could relax in and not live in fear.

Sylvia M. Croan

Children

Children are a wonderful thing.
Oh what happiness and joy they bring.

The little girls are cute and sweet.
They lift their daddy's off their feet.

Boys are their mother's pride.
For their love they do not hide.

Having siblings is a wonderful way to grow.
You learn to love one another you know.

Remember....children are what they live.
So teach them well in all you give.

Mary Lou Martinkovic

Pappy

I think of you often as the day goes by,
I wonder how you are doing and if everything's alright,
Things aren't good and I know they won't get better,
I guess that's why they say - when it's your time it doesn't matter,
I know you're going to go soon, but I'm still going to miss you with
  all my heart,
While you're up in heaven you'll hear my tears fall each night that
  we're apart,
You are my Grandpa and that will never change,
I'll always remember you and all our little games,
As you lay there in your hospital bed and slowly fade,
I sit with a tear in my eye and remember the good old days,
I will take care of Grandma and your little dog too,
Don't forget, when it's my time, I'll be sure to come find you,
We lived through our good times and our bad times too,
So I won't mope cuz that's not what you would want me to do,
So as you fade away, remember there's always a part of you that
  will stay.

Sandy McClurg

For Sake of Children

Here we are, us two, standing face to face.
Wondering how to make it through of what seems to be a pointless case.
Five years ago we vowed to each other and God above,
through holy matrimony our spirits are one in love.
I hope before we make regrets in the future of what we could've and
should've done that we remember most importantly our love is one in blood.

Valerie T. Allison

A Heart Betrayed

He promised her loved and security;
To be his number one priority.
Her heart danced inside her with plans and dreams;
Just the thought of his promises, vanished all her inferiorities.

Finally the day arrived;
Into life's realities, they dived...
Love? Security? His number 1????
Suddenly replaced by responsibility, necessities;
Demands for his time.

Her disillusioned heart, refused to dream or dance;
She forced herself to get up;
but lived most of her day in a sad trance.

The day came, when he walked out and left her;
She cried, "Why couldn't he have stayed?"
But if he had, she would never have known,
what it meant to be;
A heart betrayed.

Theresa Elkins

Suicide

It's a long way down, isn't it?
Oh well.
Soon it will all be over...
Whoa... steady.
Don't want to fall just yet!
Wait until a crowd gathers.
There, that's more like it...
Always liked being the center of attention, anyway.
1... 2... 3... jump!
See, it's not so bad.
Stop worrying!
But wait...
What if I don't die?
What if I become a cripple?
What will happen to my family, my friends...
My dreams?
What was so wrong with my life anyway?
Maybe this wasn't such a good idea...
But it's too late now...
Soon it will all be over...

Kelli Gagnon

A Place By The Sea

A place by the sea is all I ask
   To walk the shoreline, my only task.
The waves flowing gently over my feet
   Making each step a meaningful treat.

A place by the sea diffuses one's choices
   As the sounds of the ocean, sea gulls and muted voices
Surround one's being with splendors untold
   As the wonders of the sea magnificently unfold.

The richness of life is spent on the beach
   Where the cares of the world are left out of one's reach.
It's a place of content for the weary worn
   A place for unconditional love to be born.

The senses are stirred at the waters edge
   The sound of the surf, as it hits the rock ledge
The feel of the sand surrounding one's being;
   It elevates the soul to joys unforeseen.

The ocean makes one feel humble, yet so complete
   It's God's haven of love and holy retreat.
A place by the sea is all I endeavor
   To share with others forever and ever.

Elaine M. Freeman

What's It All About?

There's something big that's coming down
And when it happens there'll be no sound.
But, happen it will you can rest assured
You'll know it then by deed and word.

Our rate of change has opened wide
A rate so fast that it will collide
With all we know or, think we know,
Making us long for days that were slow.

But, we can't help but wonder aloud
Why this has happened and what it's about.
And wonder, it seems, is all we can do.
No action seems possible and that is so true.

We've reached that all-important stage
By which historians will define our age.
But, we haven't the slightest hint or clue
Which possible future we'll pursue.

In the meantime we'll just sit around
While it's happening this thing profound.

Richard Eldredge

A Poem Was Born

"It was Easter Monday ... that special day ...
and in a hospital bed I lay ...
with both legs in casts; I felt such pain ...
it was hard to even think of my name ...
But God in His infinite love ...
looked down upon me from above ...
and blessed me in such a miraculous way ...
I've never been the same; since that day ...
I felt peace and contentment as I've never known
as my Lord and saviour ... claimed me for His own
With the wind softly blowing through the windows across
I knew in my heart that my life was not lost
The sounds were so majestic ... I listened in awe ...
as I felt inspiration enter my soul ...
I started to praise my father above
for saving my life ... and for sending me love ...
and for this bright new day ...I could not mourn...
and suddenly ... a poem was born ...."

Sandra E. Hanna

On Eagle's Wings

On the wings of an eagle our country shall rise and soar.
Above all other nations she'll be great forevermore.
For no matter what we might do or what we might say,
There's nothing like our country, the good old U.S.A.

Her compassion is unequal and is scattered roundabout.
Many nations know her strength - her ideals - her very thoughts.
As we look around about us and all our blessings see
I for one am glad America is here for you and me.

She's been through so many trials, tribulations, days of drought,
But she stands for all the good that our God has always taught.
And when our flag we see, flying bravely, flying free,
There's a stirring in our hearts for what it represents — what it can
and what it will be.

This is our nation - this our country - this the land so many seek
Will forever stand firm and steady and be a beacon for the lowly and
   the meek.
Thank you, God, for having given us this nation in which we live and
breathe, for, oh, so many things.
May we always find that everlasting shelter beneath her eagle's wings.

Peggy Guthrie

The Wind May Blow Tomorrow

No fee or price does the sand demand
for a couple to walk upon its land
Woman and man walking hand in hand
leaving scars on the face of this once-perfect sand.
   -But the wind may blow tomorrow.

All the toils in life a tree might feel
in time the tree may mend and heal
Holding strong with a steadfast will
on a quiet day the tree stands still.
   -But the wind may blow tomorrow.

A child plays alone in an empty park
hears the beautiful song of a meadowlark
Not wanting to leave before it turns dark
writes his name in the dirt and the Earth is marked.
   -But the wind may blow tomorrow.

The sun beats down on a desolate land
God touches the Earth with a mighty hand
But not to scold or reprimand
only for us to understand.
   - The wind may blow tomorrow.
   Allison Hart

Horns, Chain and a Tail" Appendages of Mental Illness

Are you able to see my horns and tail?
Looking somehow demented when you view my face?
Or am I so cleaver in my masquerade;
So that only whispers and files, the source convey?

This 'tail' forever trailing; not easy to conceal
Someone's always lurking; the details to reveal
Augmenting curiosity, suspicion, and close review
Vigilant, unrelenting perspective; predetermined, it's true

Opinions, beliefs, need only to be declared by one
A single individual provides a mind set; now the image of many
Reluctant to doubt; concepts established firmly as truth
Seemingly hesitant to discern; to analyze for themselves

A chain this becomes, with each link reinforced
Not a thought of being objective, putting past events aside
New determinations added, more links; all former close in mind
The tail, it grows longer as "labels," these horns, my heart pierce
   deep inside

This tail continually lengthens, horns impale, and links choke
For the tremendous many with kindred experiences,
Will agree it's futile to be free; wounds made deeper each day
Other ailments, reports and records filed away; but mental illness - a
   bonafide "Keeper"
   Susan E. Rogina

I See You (My Son) In A Rose

The roots have taken hold and formed a strong base,
Just as your footsteps you walk with confidence and grace.
The stems they sprout tender, but sturdy and strong.
Like a baby, a boy, a man, a daddy before long.
Upon these stems the thorns will grow,
Reminding us of the pain and sorrow, we all somehow will know.
The buds will pop out to express its birth,
Showing difference between us here on earth.
And when the buds open the way a rose can,
I can see how you've grown to a wonderful man.
When ever I look at a rose, I can see your face,
The morning dew upon its petals, are like tears upon your face,
And when the dew is wiped away, a smile soon takes its place.
When the petals begin to open it lets me see how you have grown,
Strong proud and confident, standing on your own
As the petals fall and fade away,
I see yet a new difference, you will make today
   Dolores J. Melton

I Don't Listen to the Words of Songs Anymore

I don't listen to the words of songs anymore.
They cause my broken heart to ache.

Songs of love
Songs of promises unkept
Songs that bring a vision of you

Only to be swept away by the bittersweet melody.

I don't listen to the words of songs anymore.

The radio is on and the notes of music begin.
The melody harkens to my soul to remember.
Words are being sung
I cannot hear.

My tears fall in remembrance and with a smile on my
lips, I turn away from my memories.

No, I don't listen to the words of songs anymore.
   D. L. W. B.

Phoebe, I Hear You

Phoebe flew away,
One sad day last May.
I miss her so,
Why did she have to go!

She would jump to Robert's lap,
Never to mine,
Not even one time.

Sweet little creature,
So black with bits of white,
Each day a new adventure,
Free spirit of the night.

Phoebe, I hear you calling me,
In sunshine and in shadow,
A tiny sob, a kind of mew,
A faltering step; I know it is you.

But no little visitor on the path to the house,
And no looking about for that tiny gray mouse,
No eager face peering in my doorway,

Now all so quiet, all so still,
But I hear you, Phoebe, and I always, always will.
   Helyn Granoff

My Gift to You

As the sun shines its warmth upon your face,
I see a glowing smile of charismatic charm.
Your sense of humor and stylish wit brings laughter
to my heart and joyous tears to my eyes.
Deep within ones self there is a curious place
no other has ever dared to explore.
If there lies darkness, I will conquer it and watch
it illuminate from all its hidden corners.
I search for the secret that hides within the shadow of
your soul, for there I will find the answer that portrays your
self-image.
I care enough to offer a gift so true that no other
in this Universe can touch it but only you.
From within my heart I give to you a friendship that
embraces more than the precious gift of love.
I know what I perceive is true and hope that nothing will
ever break the bond that we will always share.
Please accept my gift and never let it go,
for the love in our friendship will always continue to grow.
   Mary K. Mills

Her Answer

She was only twenty-six years old
It shouldn't have been her time to go
Instead of asking for help
She took it upon herself
She was strong, that was her way
How she got so far away
Who's too say
She was so full of hurt and pain
No one could heal
Not even her husband and her three little girls
She had so much to live for
But her fate, she felt was made
Her mind couldn't of been swayed
We loved her then
We love her now
It'll get easier someday, somehow
For she will be a part of our family from now into eternity

Sharon Hutcheson

Cosmic Picnic

Let's soar among the moon and stars
and have a starlit lunch on Mars.
Gliding with our satin wings
let's weave a chain with Saturn's rings.
We'll catch a star to shine its ray
while coasting on the Milky Way.
We'll flag the fastest meteorite
sailing through the endless night.
Back at earth, we'll realize
the stars are still within our eyes.
The enchantment of the moon
will play its mystic, lilting tune
within our hearts to mesmerize—
release us from our earthly ties
We'll leave our troubles here behind
assured that we will never find
a limit to our galaxy—

We're everything we want to be.

Magda Lynn Seymour

Dream of a Key

Can you see the buffalo, running in your heart?
Can you see the stars, drifting in the dark?
Can you see the meadows, blowing in the wind?
Can you see me, trying to get in?
Give me a key, so I can go see.
This is my dream, can't you see?
This is what's calling for me.
So give me the key so I can spread my wings.
I want to leave so I can be free.
Free from all the worries that's ahead of me.
Please, I want the key,
so I can turn this dream into a reality.

David G. Shaw Jr.

Dancing Among the Stars

Dreams are the things of reality,
flying high through the pale blue sky,
or swiftly swimming through the deep blue seas,
each one is a piece of our hearts,
that no other is meant to see,
each one is a piece of our hope,
that someday we will succeed,
every dream is a piece of a puzzle
that makes up who we are,
our dreams are the future we want
that is dancing among the stars.

Chad A. Chaffin

The Sun Catcher

The store was so festive and Christmas was nigh
When a little house sun catcher caught my eye.
"Oh, Santa Claus' House" I said to myself
As I took that purchase from the shelf.

Suddenly I was alone in a crowd store
And I was brought back to the years before
When a string of lights on the tree was strung
When my brother and sister and I were young.

On that string was a special light
That we hoped would always be so bright.
'Twas Santa Claus's house with roof of snow
That had for me a special glow.

But then one Christmas it ceased to burn
And how my saddened heart would yearn
For my favorite light on the Christmas tree
To again to twinkling down at me.

Now the Sun Catcher hangs on the tree up high
And it winks at me as I go by.
Santa Claus's House is back on the tree
Warming my heart with a sweet memory.

Maurelia Kennedy

Loosed, and Set Free

You have set me free of all my sins.
Now, I have been born again.
I said that I would give my all to you,
But that doesn't seem to be enough.
Lord, I know that the road I must take is going to be rough,
And times are going to get mighty tough.
I won't dwell on the pain that I will endure,
Because I believe that you will see me through,
All the hurt and pain that this world may trouble me with.
You have done so many great things for me.
Until now, this moment, I didn't know what part you played in my life.
I didn't know how to open up to you,
To let you tell me the right things to do.
You have allowed a great change to come over me;
You washed, cleansed, loosed, and set me free.

Andrea Fails

Child's Eyes

Birds fly so high to touch the sky,
Wind on the wings of a butterfly.
While in the wild,
You may see things as a child.
When you see things in this way,
All as new as a bright new day
You may see things as I do,
Mind and thoughts are always new.
Light a fire to keep warm, from the light all life is born.
The sun, one big ball of flame,
That keeps all life living the same.
Just one of three things all life needs,
In order to survive in a world, destroyed by greed.
.The second simply is easy to see,
You need the life that breaths from a tree.
If man keeps destroying trees today,
Tomorrow no place for children to play.
Trees the only life that's here,
That lives so we may breath clean air.
Third, their future not so clear.

Shane Hicks

Untitled

A wind song peal's through silence of night
and the nightingale's ballad sets shadows to flight
A cemetery dancer is silhouetted in a flame
deaths necromancer is inside of insane
skeleton's of a doomed soul sways
Asunder within the breeze.
Fallen angels seek redemption on their knees.
With broken wings and bearing sin
A melody sings the screaming wind ride thy dream, ripe thy dream.
Asleep forever, so lonely and cola - this tomb
never to be told, my doom.
Destiny fears the hand's of fate. My own damn
prison I create... I hate.... See the shadows
hear them bleed!? The drip-drop sound
of a rhythmical seed.
Dance fool dance like a mime for your life
and chance time to yield his knife
Purgatory will greet you, greedy but warm
in darkness we'll cause you no harm.

Carl A. Mahane

Stars of Liberty

Beyond the ocean to the West,
I see the banner of liberty rest,
Stained with the blood of men so true,
This gleaming flag of red, white and blue.

Over mountain, prairie and rushing streams,
The gentle murmur of memories beam,
With spirit of men of bygone years,
The undaunted courage of pioneers.

American sons for liberty fought,
Shed their blood at freedom's court
This blessed land of commonwealth,
Keep it safe from tyrants' stealth.

Silvery stars that shine so bright
Will beckon men to freedom's fight,
The vanquished of this tired world,
Lift up their brow with hopes unfurled.

So proudly flies this flag of stars,
Born of men with dreams unmarred,
Honor and glory to freemen all,
By grace of God will never fall.

John C. Robinson

Passages

As we pass thru the various
stages and transitions with in our lives
we may often times find ourselves
confused and uncertain of the possible outcomes.
We seem to become weighted down
by the unforeseen struggles we must face
making it so difficult to see
the end or resolution which lies ahead.
Fears and doubts seem to weaken
our grasp on life, leaving us lost
in the darkness of the unknown
ever searching for the light of clarity.
Yet inevitably each phase each transition
finds the darkness beginning to fade away
as the light of clarity shines
soothing our fears and calming our doubts.
Then with a light relieving sigh
we look back on that passing phase
Smile, and whisper ever so softly
Thank you for allowing me to grow!

Kathleen J. Barry

The Beauty of the Nights

I lay me down once on my Roof Patio one night.
All lonely, and depressed and troubled.
Glazing at the skies above me, with the
Creeping sound of different creatures.
Shooting stars befall the earth
Heavens bright with the full moon and
The glittering stars afar, has for once enchanted my heart.
Magically and astonished, with the sigh of relief
He's acquit my affliction. Converted the
heart of hope, and live.
How beautiful, can the nights really be
No intention of any harm, with the
cool breeze playing on my soft face
The soothing feeling caressing me truly,
A gentle hum of the Peace and Contentment
made me lost in wonder, and clear of mind.
Assured me of that rest, and secureness of my life,
Never to ever fear again, of that wonderful gifted night.
O Beautiful, beautiful feeling of the nights
Who could ever think what could ease your mind.

Diane Miller

Summer Rainbows

It's that beautiful summer sky..
Like blue raspberries
I dare to try...
Freshly squeezed home made orange tropicana....
To wash down my yellow banana...
Ruby red cherries
How sweet the summer berries..
Dark green rhines
Of sweet red watermelon..
The perfect scenario of heaven...
The perfect summer rainbow...
There are sweet little secrets
In our green crowded garden...
They do grow...
So the next time
You look into that beautiful summer sky
With your fruitful eyes...
Take a bite of that summer rainbow
In your garden
Just below..

Saundra Diamante

Scars

We bury the scars,
the cuts too deep, deep, deep.
They dance on our heads,
when we sleep, sleep, sleep.

Some we wear on our faces
when we turn our heads in shame, shame, shame.
Some we plant in our voices
when we blame, blame, blame.

We bury the scars
less we get caught, caught, caught,
just being human,
pretending that we're not, not, not...

Diana L. Counter

Why...

Why are we dictated to by society at large?
Why are we judged by the corporate swine?
Why do people fear what they don't understand?
Why are we killing one another?
Why do humans murder because their blood is different?
Why must we set other cities on fire from the sky?
Why must a ten-year-old boy use a rifle to defend his home?
Why must we feed our unborn children substances that will never
give them a chance?
Why must a family starve to death?
Why must people use explosives to express their views?
Why do we kill animals merely for the price of their hides?
Why is money so important?
Why is our country doing only what we thought others did?
Why must a family of four die for their wallets and jewelry?
Why do some feel that it is not twice as brave to simply walk away?
Why are the odd and artistic scoffed at by the norm of society?
Why does man take out physical frustration on wife and kid?
Why is all I want to know, just tell me why.

James Anthony Lawson

The Picture

It needs no caption
The tall fireman, holding the tiny still figure
tenderly in his arms
a look of desperation, sadness, futility
The tiny one who would never again smile, cry, love...

Was this her destiny?
To be brought to this moment in time
to the arms of this stranger who was
destined to be in this spot at this time.

My heart was touched as a deep sadness enveloped
me and I knew I would never forget this picture
which will be forever embedded in my soul.

Lola Stouffer

Trout Fishing In West Virginia

We live up in these hills,
And fish the water still.
We catch a lot of trout,
Which we like to brag about.
Fishing these waters that glisten and gleam,
Watching our bait as it floats down the stream.
A nobler fish you'll never find.
The glorious trout even challenges your mind.
Searching the riffles, still spots, and cover,
The grand daddy of them all we're hoping to discover.
Now there's a nibble, a sharp pull, a bite,
You set the hook and the fish starts to fight.
The trout makes his move and you counter your weight,
By now he is wishing he hadn't took the bait.
With the fish on the bank, now he is caught,
It gives you a feeling that can not be bought.

Eric Stovall

The Mill

Through the broken window the sun filtered down
On strands of unused thread that draped over the looms,
Like a spider web not mended, am eerie sight.
Now there is a frost of lint that covers them
The hum...of ancient looms lay silent
No sound of chit-chat from the workers that had so tediously performed.
Idle, this mill was the hubbub of industry in Iva
Next to it was a restaurant "Pa's Kitchen" assuming that was its name,
With all too few customers now.
May have served chitlins, ham hocks with collard greens, black-eyed peas
corn bread with honey, coffee with chicory and peach cobbler.
The owner succumbed to grief as he closed the mill and shut the doors.

Ruth C. Huber

What To Do?

A sunken ship I may find
or a treasure of some kind
Maybe I'll solve an ancient mystery
or maybe I'll make history
I just might decide to buy Aruba
and then of course, I'd learn how to scuba
Twenty mountains I may climb
or maybe I'll go back in time
I could find a cure for AIDS
I could stop a terrorist raid
I may learn how to fly
or learn to bake a cherry pie
Through the jungles I may roam
or I may write another poem
There's so much that I can do
the things I can't are but a few

Alison Szetela

Love Again

I've been hurt so many times before
That I thought I could never
love any one anymore
But when I found you I
wondered if it could be true
That I could love anybody
again, and if so it definitely would be you.
And fall in love with you is
just what I did
It's more than a crush held by a kid
And it is the true thing without a doubt
A burning flame in my heart
that makes me want to shout.
"I love you" from every mountain top in sight
And I wont stop loving you without a fight
If this gives you any idea of
how much I care for you
Then, Sergio, you know I'll always be true
Because I love you!!!

Amanda Mercer

Aceldama

If I were an angel, I'd name a star for you
a shimmering, glowing sparkle just like the twinkle
in your eyes
eyes, that looked through me, pierced my heart
with spears of eternal devotion...

Now here you are, one of thousands
resting in one small corner of this vast place
but one, or one thousand, it matters not
this field holds one too many....

With your last fearful gasp you became as one
with those other souls residing in that other field
it hurts to draw breath, here.....where you stood
and valiantly gave your country one more hero...

One more hero, to be tossed in a box and forgotten
here...where the smell of death lingers
and ghosts of those preceding perform their ritual dance
to welcome one more warrior home....

Here...where weeds resembling feathered lances
stand guard across a southern wall
that vibrates with the unfulfilled spirit
of severed love...

Deanna Hines

I Am

I am a person who cares about what is said about me.
I wonder what I ever did to deserve it?
I hear people saying things that aren't true.
I see people look at people like they don't exist.
I want it all to end, but it won't.
I am a person who cares about what is said about me.

I pretend that it never happens.
I feel like I'm all alone.
It touches a part of me that can't take it anymore.
I worry about the things that are going to be said the next
day when I get out of bed.
I cry thinking my life is almost gone when someone very
special is leaving home.
I am a person who cares about what is said about me.

I understand that it always happens to someone.
I say why me
I dream that I can start all over.
I try to let it all by, but it seems to stick with me all the time
I hope the nightmares end.
I am a person who cares about what is said about me.

Valerie Blanton

Cabin in the Pines

I never dream of castles that will crumble down in time,
just a little 'ole log cabin nestled deep within the pines.

All surrounding areas I'd add beauty with my touch,
just to make you happy, the man I love so much.

The atmosphere that I would weave, like spiders do their web,
would encircle you, my darling, with nary thought nor dread.

I'd smother you with kisses and hugs not just a few,
just to see you happy, would be my daily due.

The kitchen in my cabin, with savory smells subdue,
all the tantalizing ardor for my hungry man, just you.

In the parlor near the fireplace, gold red embers steal the night,
I could cuddle oh-so-closely, within your arms that hold me tight.

Then we'd wander off to dreamland after all our needs were met,
dreaming of a great tomorrow, some new challenges we've set.

I can smell the scented roses, see the honeysuckle twine
all around an open window of my cabin in the pines.

Sometimes I think that I'm not dreaming and your dreams are just
like mine, always sharing, always caring, in our cabin the pines.

Emma Noon Reed

Springtime and Flowers

The glorious panorama of springtime has arrived at long last,
And winter with its record snow is now a memory of the past.
Mother Earth had awakened the inhabitants of her vast domain.
In this region, they complied with all the rules of her reign.

I observed them emerge, one by one, each variety in its own time.
First the Crocus, in raiment of brilliant colors in their prime.
Springtime was now a stage for flowers with changing presentations;
Some ground level, flowering trees, and bushes in many variations.

It has been a beauty pageant for God's most exquisite creation.
Flowers must have been created for us and earth's beautification.
What a splendid feast for the eyes and pure joy for the soul!
They also provide enjoyment when displayed in a vase or a bowl.

How sad it is to watch them wilt and, ever so slowly, fade away.
They will, however, rise from the dust and bloom again another day.
For, most surely, there will be another winter followed by spring.
The panorama will be repeated, and once again the birds will sing.

Anne Sibowski

Stay

In Loving Memory of My Uncle

Understanding the death of someone you love,
Is harder than explaining the good Lord above.

When we found out he was dying,
I didn't believe them, I thought they were lying.

There are no words to describe how all of this became,
No one compares to him, no one is the same.

He is a husband, a brother, an uncle, a father,
Don't try to outdo him, don't even bother.

One of these days, the Lord will take him away,
While in the hospital bed, his beautiful body lay.

It's hard to believe that such a man can die,
While all of his family stays close by.

I love him with all my heart and soul,
But sooner or later, time will take its toll.

He's a very great man, who did nothing wrong,
And he's just glad he's lasted this long.

I'll miss him, I care for him, and I want him to stay,
But I know soon, Lord will take him away.

Take care of him, Lord, he's a good man.
But while he's alive, I'll do all that I possibly can.

Dusti Dawn Duckworth

No Title Necessary

A burnout that has not yet began to burn
As it take a killer to kill a killer
And if the sun makes a wrong turn
The moon is to become the earth's pillar

A thirst for the taste of blood
A longing hunger for justification
The simple thought thick as mud
An answer without explanation

To be cut by a blade of grass
Or scratched by the dove's feather
Not to see through the crystal glass
And January is very warm weather

Aside from man versing self
The soul must confront the demon
Having the answer but the world is deaf
Wasted like sterile semen

A giggly laugh
An unsureness of the intention
Accept the whole but only take half
Confusion is a doomed invention

Stan Knight

Life's Decisions

I don't wanna die.
I haven't even lived yet.
I was gonna do great things; maybe a doctor, a farmer
who'd feed a hungry nation or maybe just simply your son
or daughter.

You must of have wanted me, I mean if you didn't, I would
have never been conceived. Now, I hear your voice late at night in
between your tears, I hear you saying, "I must
slaughter my embryonic creation."

Is your world so cruel that you wish me not life!
Or do you wish me not to be a part of your life?

My existence weighs in the balance of your decision.
"Please I don't wanna die....."

Kristy S. Cousins

"Walking In Monica's Shoes"

I am walking in Monica's shoes.
She gave me both of her's to use.
It must have been my happiest day
In my heart, I wanted to pray -
When I took my first two steps.
those where followed by many more footsteps.
I wondered how I would ever know,
Whether or not it could be so -
That my fondest dream was to come true.
It was He, the master, only who really knew,

Each day was a new beginning, each day, fulfilling
As I began my journey toward recovering
How does one begin opening a door that was locked -
upon dark and frightening secrets the mind had blocked.
Looking out from my hospital window that cold, bleak, rainy day
I did wonder if I would ever walk again some day.
I was given such a small measure of hope to build on
Still, there was an inner faith, helping me face a new dawn.
It took many months of therapy to step out of my wheelchair.
By the grace of God I did team work and Monica's shoes of
   matching pair.

Norma Jean Walli

Super-Nova

I have three stars in my universe, not just only one

And although all three are burning bright,
   one dazzles like the sun.

So often times I polish two, and
   one it seems I neglect

But a diamond so bright that shines both day
and night, mere polish would have ill effect.

For she is my oldest and brightest star, this
   super-nova of mine

And if her sister is the rainbow, this one
   surely is sunshine

For you can't have a rainbow without the
   sun, who's rays illuminate

And guide the rainbow, and everyone, who
   follow her light to heaven's gate!

Charles Anthony Simons

Very Simple

We seek the answers but know not when
Or how they might derive
Logic, pain, simple sense
Plane reasons why we are alive

An illusion, a dream, a negative thought
All aspects of the mind
A baffled maze in which we get caught
The end, some never find

Crazy, retarded, mentally insane
Call me whatever you might
Master, master, please explain
For terror is the night

B and E the verb spells be
Which is something we always do
Stop, think, and try to see
How this applies to you

Your day has come, what you've always feared
Now think, of the verb applied
Now I ask do you think I'm weird
Just because you have died.

Jim Beverly

Tears For Harvey

Tears for Harvey let me shed.
Tears for Harvey now that he's dead.

Little old man, unhappy, alone,
Bitter and hurt, God said, "Come Home".

Never again will he plead for our touch,
A cup of water, A smile, An arm for a crutch.

A listening ear, A watchful eye,
A little caring as we pass by.

Tears for Harvey let me shed.
Tears for Harvey before he's dead.

Lord show me your Harvey's, and let me be,
An instrument through which they can see thee.

Tears for Harvey let me shed.
Tears for Harvey before he's dead.

How many Harveys have I passed by,
not seeing, nor caring until they die.

Caril Favors Stanfield

About Him

It's hard to tell what I fell for at first
His handsome smile, or his raven hair,
His fair manner, in kindness well-versed,
Each little thing receives his quiet care.
My heart leaps when my eyes meet his gaze
I long to hear the music of his voice.
Unlike other loves, all based on praise,
I love him because of my own choice.
It's hard to name just one thing I admire
It's like to naming one star in the sky
Now his love for mine I doth desire
I swear to love him until I die.
If he'll be mine, I'll be his catch,
For only Heaven can make such a match.

Annie VanderMeer

Mom

In the darkness,
hers is the light that shines bright.
In the cold,
hers are the arms that keep me warm.
In the summer,
hers is the voice that keeps company.
In joy,
hers is the buoyancy for which it is caused.

Through many tears,
hers are the tears that fall with mine.
In my weakness,
hers is the strength that I draw upon.

She is strong.
She is my light.
She is my heart.
She is the bearer of me.
She is my leader.

I follow and give to her
all of my love.

Tara Bonebrake

Too Easy

Here's your pistol,
painted lunatic silver,
handmade by welders,
of steel and sterling war

Here's your holster,
a fine leather home,
smooth as transparent lace,
with night soaking up a blue sky.

Here's your bullet,
spit-shined with the flag,
gold-tipped in suicide shame,
it spins alone in the first chamber.

Here's your destiny,
self-written on a Sunday,
your ink-stained finger curls the trigger...
I am silenced by the echo.

Jason Tomey

Take It To Heart

I once felt love in a young girls eyes. More beautiful
    that the words I know can describe, that feeling
        brought me to the other side.
    Where she left me sitting lonely.

For many moons in love I sat staring into some sadistic
    game that we seem to call our lives.

Slowly an answer came to me. It said that love had
    set me free from a demon that swallows souls;
Not allowing them to feel from the time they're
    one day old.

Now as I see our Planet's surface proceed to slowly
    mold, I feel sadness in my youth that makes me
        feel old.

While all of us carefree people work towards the
    common goal,

I wonder, is this life or does Satan have our souls?
    If we can ever be in love,
        I will never give up hope.

Zack Tall

My Heart Belongs to You

My heart belongs to you my sweet dear.
Thinking of anyone but you will make me;
    tear.
You are my support, my love, my life.
Everything I do circles around you
I want to explain how and why and;
    for how long, but all I know is
    we belong.
Please my dear please I love you and;
    probably will forever.
We belong.
The shyness I have for you shall be;
    flattering too!
Well my dear. I must bid you adu.
My heart still belongs to you!

Heidi Manders

The Devil Within

The two animals stared at each other with hate in their eyes.
Each one trying to decide who was going to strike first.
Would it be the giraffe?
Or would it be the horse?
A snake stared at them with a devious look as if taking
pleasure in the events.
It seemed to be stuck between the rough land and calm light.

The inhabitants of both areas were also watching the events.
But with different views.
As the sun rises,
A shadow falls. One on the calm lake.
Another on the rough, rocky land.
Both reflections seen in completely different eyes of the
various inhabitants.
A KKK member on the rough land sees the snake's shadow as a
regular person.
But another man sees through the snake's deception

How much longer will it take for everyone to see the truth?
There is not much time left.
The horse is about to lunge at the giraffe.

David Medina

Disparate Things

Atrocity is truly emperor
In your eyes; I can see
Your dark views and your tortured soul
and your thoughts, murky as mud
As I slip in the tape
That triggers off all what is — and isn't

The New Dawn Fading without your knowing
An unquiet disorder,
Candidate for that stupid club
Once it was tied around your neck
May 18/80, your death day
Now you Remember Nothing
Of wife and child, union despoiled
Though Nothing lost, no love lost

No happiness there was then, isn't anything now
Others create a shadow play of you

Holocaust/Death/Destruction/Nihil
Hopelessness/Isolation/Torn Asunder

An Exhibition no longer available

(when will the madness end?)

Dennis Solis

Dream Flights

Crystal spirit I know that you're there,
Flowing and glowing with such care...
Have you come to watch, or merely to seek?
A cosmic friend, or me,... so to speak.

Crystal spirit I have missed you so...
Mystic wonder of so many years ago.
In dream flights you remember me,
When love was young, and we were free.

Magic is in the air this spiritual season,
Mysteries beyond all my reason...
Romantic themes from so many scenes,
Are one with the other, within my dreams.

Comic friends they come and they go,
They bring their love within the flow.
Crystal spectrum of colors gone by
Oh love, oh life,... why can't I fly?

E. R. Janney

Love From A Spider's View

While weaving a web from ceiling to floor,
Miz Spider spied a handsome, young, male by the door.

She waved one long arm, and then she waved two,
As beauteous, single, females, best do!

She showed him she could spin a fine web,
And off to his corner, she gracefully sped.

"It's really a pleasure to share a fine luncheon,
When you have something crispy and crunchy to munch on".

So they ate a huge fly, she'd recently caught.
Then she went on with her life, as her mother had taught.

"When you're done with your mate, and no more do need him,
Get rid of him, dear, or you'll just have to feed him.

She hugged him and kissed him, then bit him twice.
She wrapped him in silk, 'til the package looked nice.

She'd invited him for dinner, but now lacking a host,
She'd serve him for breakfast, with green tea and toast!

Winifred Williamson-Ater

Strawberries, Strawberries

Strawberries, strawberries
I buy them by the pound.
Just cut the little stem out
And swish the water 'round.

They have lotsa seeds on them
But I don't care a bit.
Once I thought I'd take them off
And for hours I did sit.

I planted those seeds and waited patiently.
I looked out the window and what did I see?
Oh my goodness! Oh my gracious!
It was bigger than a tree!

The seeds are gonna stay on this big fruit
Since I've found more important things to do.
I'll stem it and swish it and eat it all up.
...Wouldn't you?

Kathleen Erickson

A Wife

A wife to me is all she could ever be.
What more could a man ask for. She is
There when times are hard, she is there
When times are Good. Together we share
The times they call life.

The "W" is for wonderful; the "I" is for
Important; the "F" is for friend; and the
"E" is for-Ever.

These four letters, give me the reason
for life. For life without a wife would
be no more, for I love her so. She devotes
her time to being a mother; she devotes
her time to being a friend; all in all
only Jeralyn can do what a wife does best!

"She Is My Best Friend"
Your Ever-Loving Husband

Chuck D. Curcio Jr.

Jimmy's Song

There is a mountain, so very high
Where the grass is green and the trees so tall
Where the birds sing and fly — don't you see why?
Don't you see why the sky is blue
and the birds do fly?

there is a river, it's long and wide and
runs so deep, do you see why?

I'm singing this song to tell you why. There's been
so much trouble and killing in this old world,
I know it's coming to an end soon.
Hear my words, hear my pleas — There is
a way to leave this world with no
trouble on one's mind,
Just turn to the Lord, He'll watch over you
And love you true
He'll show you the way to heaven's gates
Where your soul will be blessed and
free forevermore, don't you see?

Pray dear one, pray for soon will come that day,
Don't you see?

James A. Bruce

Friendship

Friendship is a fragile thing;
Like a bird with a broken wing.
The wing cannot be used to soar;
Because the feeling is not there anymore.

Friendship is a state of mind;
Around which our frail emotions wind.
Friends seem to know when help is needed;
And will let them know it will not go unheeded.

Friendship will not tarnish because of time and space;
It will grow and flourish in any case.
Friends are in tune and know when to call;
Just when a friend has dropped the ball.

Even the strong will come into harm's way;
And it will cause a friend to say,
I'm here to help in your time of need
And count on me to do the noble deed.

Life is not a smooth path that leads to an end;
It is full of problems that it wants to send;
So even though distance leaves them apart;
True friendship is there because it comes from the heart.

Stephen P. Matava

The Possum

The Possum may be one of the ugliest
creatures on Earth,
But if it had not been for that car or
truck - she would have given Birth.

For Three Days she sit on the side of
the road and no one could understand why,
But as I pulled up beside her,
I stayed and watched her cry.

There lay before her was a baby possum
on the rocks, as tears came pouring down,
yes even a possum can have pain
as they watch their young die upon the ground.

Suddenly as I gazed at this small
creature that most have no concern for,
It made me realize that all
Humans should start caring more.

Kriston Fegans

Satan Is A Poor Man

He has no power of his own,
his total possession is a loan.
He starts early on people at birth,
destroying minds so he can rule on earth.
He doesn't care about race, color or creed,
he's using us all to feed his greed.
He has no hands to sell drugs,
he's using our boys and girls.
He has no feet to walk around,
he's using men and women all over town.
He has no mouth to tell a lie,
our politicians, on them he can rely.
He wants to destroy homes, churches and schools,
his desire is that we all be illiterate fools.
A will to live, make decisions and understand,
are great gifts from God to man;
Now it's time to take a stand,
and stop being driven by that poor man.

Dorthey L. King

Restless Spirit

Traveling lonely highways late at night
Is a restless spirit soaring in flight
He's searching for something, which to him is unknown
And until he finds it he can never go home
Walking in life's footsteps with sorrow and regret
Hoping to find what he has not yet
Many miles this spirit will roam
Confused, unhappy and all alone
Not knowing what's in front of him
or caring what's left behind
Filling his emptiness weighs heavily on his mind
Oh! Restless Spirit can't you see
Just giving yourself to Jesus
Will make you whole and complete

Tressa A. Hendrix

Mother

I went to your bedroom and you were not there,
I looked at your clothes and sat in your chair.

I whispered softly, I love you so,
Oh why, oh why did you have to go?

I held the picture of you in the golden frame,
My eyes filled with tears; my heart felt the pain.

The fragrance you wore seemed to fill the room,
Lovely and sweet, as flowers in bloom.

Like a kaleidoscope turning colors and shapes;
The memories of you, my mind did create,

Painting a picture so beautiful and true,
No one ever had a mother as precious as you.

Exhausted from grieving I fell to my knees;
I looked up to heaven and cried, "God help me, please!"

A calm filled my soul like a soft summer breeze,
As you reached out your hand, your voice comforted me.

The words that you spoke were gentle and clear,
Pearls of wisdom I needed to hear.

"Trust me, my child, it's all for the best.
Your mother is with me; she's found perfect rest."

Sharon Kramer

"By Me"

What would I give to clasp your hand,
Your happy face to see.
To hear your soft gentle voice,
To see your smiling face,
As in the days that use to be.
In my heart, memories linger.
Always tender, fond and true.
There's not a day that passes,
That I've not thought of you.
Oh, loved one dear to me.
In my heart sweet memories cling to your name.
I loved you then, and still love you just the same.
Dear loved one of mine; you are not forgotten,
even though we are apart.
You will always be with me,
As you've been in the past and present.
For even if it, is just in my heart;
And fondest of memories.
For you will be always "loved"
By Me!!!

Lyle Traxler

A Tribute to a Special Grandpa

Even though you're gone from here, I know you are not
far. For I feel the hugs you gave to me, and the pat
upon my hair. You knew how I was feeling when I
didn't say a word, for you knew my disability was
something hard to share.

You always boosted my ego and made me smile so wide,
you always made me feel special like a glowing ember
inside.

So when I'm feeling lonely, I know just what to do,
I will say a little prayer from me to you.

I will look up at heaven and see your smiling face and
wish that I was there with you to hug my blues away.

Karen Koish

The Ride

Life is filled with so many hardships,
so many twists and turns.
At times it seems to flow smoothly
and at times it seems to stop.
In the end it becomes much like a roller coaster.
The good times being those up-hill climbs,
while the bad times are all down hill.
But once you hit the bottom,
You begin to realize how much you've been through.
So much pain and suffering,
and so little of happiness.
It all seems so useless to stay on,
that when the ride slows, you're tempted to just jump off.
But then you really think about it,
and you decide to stay on the ride
Looking forward to the good times,
and knowing that there'll be bad ones.
But in the end, it all just becomes a ride
and you become another rider.

Corie Stueber

The Worrier

It seems to me you worry to much about what could possibly be.
Relax, enjoy, don't pick things apart, sit back, wait, listen and see!!

No magic is fun once you know how it's done, take things one step at a time.

Have faith in yourself, it's best for your health, not to mention
your peace of mind.

Mary Wheeler

I Lay My Head Upon A Dream

I lay my head upon a dream
each night before I go to sleep.
I wish that I will dream a dream
of magical things and mystery.
I escape to dreamland each night
as my mind plays tricks on me.
I think of all these things each night
as I lay my head upon a dream.

Alexis Oustinoff

The Beginning of the End

It's there.
From our birth to our death, it's there.
It will creep slowly and cautiously at first,
But it will grow rapidly if nurtured and cared for.
It was here in the beginning.
It caught and spread like a fire over dry leaves.
It has caused wars, pain, and suffering.
It's here now.
Where prejudice is it's there also.
It shall always be here.
It's our worst enemy.
It's the beginning of the end.

Darcy Kramer

An Afterthought

One little friggin finger on the trigger
One last second in thought
Another moments notice
Somebodies having a yard sale

My afterbirth is reborn
Fragmented seeds of my youth
Lounge together in afterthought
Left to mate and be consumed

One more moments notice
Another dismal scene
I'm left dried and insecure
I am still waiting...for my rebirth

David Wilson

Friends

Our friends can't be bought
Although money is tough
Our friends can't be sold
No amount is enough.

We all travel in circles
Or so I've been told
But no amount of money can buy
A circle friends when we are getting old.

This verse I have written
As no harm is intended
We pray that our friends
Will never be offended.

We live each day
As if there is no tomorrow
We thank God each day
As if today — is tomorrow.

When Jesus comes back
To claim this old Earth
May we still be with friends
At our Rebirth.

Arnold Eugene Bradley

A Vision of You

Tell me have you ever gone for a stroll on a chilly Autumn eve
And stopped for a brief moment in time on the shore of a wooded stream
Caught your breath, tried to stay warm, looked down at the water below
Staring back at your reflection surrounded by the moon's majestic glow

And soon you moved on because the night air had caused your teeth to chatter
You forgot that little stream as your mind wandered to far more important matters
Never realizing what a precious gift you had given to that special little stream
To catch a glimpse of you in the moonlight is more than any mere mortal could dream

Too many things left unnoticed in these busy, rush-rush days
Things like flowers blooming, children playing, the gentleness of blue-jays
'Tis a shame true beauty is fading into a long lost forgotten art
But forever I will hold a vision of you immersed in moonglow deep
within my heart.

J. Craver

Just A Man

You are just a man, flesh and blood I have watched your eyes, with
tears ready to flood
They looked to you a though you had some special power
As though you could erase a lifetime of problems in less than an hour
Your heart is breaking, wanting to make all of the wrongs right
Taking on the devil as though he was just your personal fight
He has taken your friends, made family and loved ones stray
You want to personally grab him and choke him but you alone can only pray

You are just a man being guided from above
Trying to change a world of sickness into a place where we can all know love
Into a place where a Satan has no power, where he can't cause hate and despair
But you are just a man, you need the Lord and the mortal man of earth to care

Don't ever stop doing the work that you do
You have been chosen for His work to be done through
There have to be days when you wonder if you can even make a dent
You may be just a man, but your words are heaven sent...

Luwonna Rae Gates

"Pop, Do You Have The Time?"

"Pop, do you have the time, can we go outside to play?"
"In a minute, son" I'd answer, then I'd sit him down and say,

"There is nothing you will ever need that my money cannot buy,
So when my time seems precious little, son, you know the reason why."

Well today he finally caught me, made me sit and hear his plea.
I share his words with you, my friends, as it's much too late for me:

"Through the years I watched you closely, Pop, and loved you from afar;
To me you were so perfect, Pop, on the surface not a scar."

"I'd look around me, as you asked, and see the things I had.
But in the final tally, Pop, they only left me sad."

"Yes, I had the best and finest things that your money could ever buy.
But therein lay the problem, Pop, now you know the reason why."

"I would rather have had a worn-out glove, and a second-hand bike, not new,
If I could just have a minute, Pop, to share them both with you."

My son went on to tell me how the pain became too deep;
Of the many nights he'd think of me and cry himself to sleep.

They found him in my study where, I learned, he'd often play.
Pretending I was with him when, in fact, I was away.

The note he left I clutch in hand as he lies before me still.
He ended it, "I love you, Pop, always did and always will."

Claude V. Weir Jr.

The God Send

One day I looked toward Heaven and asked God for my friend God
searched through all His angels and wondered who He'd send. He
thought about my personality and all the pain I'd had, and He picked
you out of the group and questioned why you looked so sad. He told
you "Child, I am sending you but remember this is not for a short
while. I need you to take away her pain and continue daily to make
her smile." You turned away from the Lord and let your tears fall
upon the ground. He lifted your chin and stared deep into your eyes
and whispered, "What is with this frown?" You said, "Lord, I've been
watching this young lady for a very, very long time... To me, she is
the image of everything wonderful, genuine, and divine.. I've sat
here patiently wondering why for her you never chose me and why did
you send the others that hurt her and never tried to make her happy?
The Lord stared at you and slightly exhaled and said, "I can't believe
this sir... She chose all the others herself, I never sent them to
her... Because I knew the day would come when she would put all her faith
in me... Then I could send the man that I chose for her, who would
love her for eternity... And the reason I had never picked you out of all
the rest, I was waiting for her to ask me for her friend because I
knew you would love her best."

Cindy Brown

Deeper Water

Why is it that the obvious is often overlooked?
Someone gives you wealth and you continually mistook
It for a gift from them and that is all.

Look deeper below the surface into what could lie beneath
Pull out the possibilities and mixtures and make yourself a wreath
That is the circle of which all things repeatedly come together.

You may insist on digging in regular soil and pulling out an ordinary rock
All which is already learned to you could easily be a crock
—Misinterpretation is scarcely discovered because you are
unaccustomed to imagining.

You can be more than all those others that just float at the top
It might appear that they look down and mock
You but you are not sinking just as they are not unstable.

They can say that you're too deep and you can say that they're too shallow
But why not get away from the usual reactions and resist the urge to follow
Because lack of deviation will never take you any deeper.

Frances Wade

Justice

One day, in a little town called America, a little boy grew up
with the idea that dreams could come true; dreams of success, for
me for you. The hope of this dream to stay alive is not for the weak
but the strong inside. You see it appears to me, maybe you, that
often ideas do run askew. But before the prize of success comes to
you, the cost of the prize is paid by a few.

You see in this land there's misery, there's all kinds of wars due to
brutality. Violence like thunder comes like the wind; blowing and
thrashing causing the halls of justice to withhold their duty, while
destruction has been witnessed from miles away. People cling
helplessly from remnants of decay. Is this an act of God to show the
sign of the times, or is this a constant picture of a corrupted mind.

The beauty that brings the story to light is that God only knows the
real and true plight. The wonder of this mystery that is so real is
that you and me people fail to feel. Until this decay spreads so
near, no more an ideal but truly hits hard in your village still. If
we want to make a difference let's first change indifference.
Violence in the name of justice has no real friend unless the justice
is a means to an end. Why do I feel, because my little town dreams of
hope and success need to see the open arms of just due process. How
do I feel, like a prisoner of war, waiting for justice to settle this score.

Arthur P. Colbert

"How Sweet It Is"

How sweet it is to see the day break.
To see the birds flying by
And chirping their happy songs.

Then comes the sun in all its glory,
Sending light and warmth over the land
And into the lives of every one.

Oh look at the butterflies as they adoringly
flit among the flowers
As if to say, I love you"

How sweet it is, to hear the hum of
Bees in the noon day sun.
As they cling to the orange blossoms in full bloom.

Then comes dusk, the close of day,
And the blue skies touched with pink and gray.
See the far horizon, and the waves that
roll from sea to shore, who could ask for more?

If we could stand at the window of life
And look out on the world with love.
Then we would know "How Sweet It Is".

Vernetta Foote

He Is Killing Someone Special

There is pain in his eyes but he will try not to cry
There is pain in his heart but will he
destroy his work of art
Why might it be death when you deserve a breath
He says I'm sorry but this is his glory
He is killing while others are willing
I feel like crying but that's not surprising
The questions I ask are never answered during his task
Why is he killing? When others are willing
He thinks he's just done his work of art
Why am I crying? Am I dying?
This person is so special but he is harsh
Why is he killing? When others are willing
Why am I crying? Maybe because someone special is dying
I fear I have lost someone special because
he is killing, while others are willing

Chari Guinta

The Last Child's Prayer

Now I lay me down to sleep,
I pray the Lord my dreams to keep,
As I lie safe in bed,
Let no nightmares go through my head,
Let the faces of the ones I love come through,
The ones I miss who are now with you,
Let them watch over me as I grow,
And let their spirit touch my soul,
And as I wake for another day,
Let them guide me along the way...
Amen

Nikki Goodman

Jackie

Never saw too much of you.
But the pain, yes we felt it too.
A love we shared that had to die,
To bring the world closer, Jackie even you and I.
How long we remember, how soon we forget.
The love we shared I have no regrets.
You were a lady in the eye of the storm.
You tried to keep us, out of the reach of harm.
You were so beautiful and yet so, so strong!
And so I say thank you, for America In God We Trust
That now you are an angel, like you were to all of us.

Ernest F. Simons Jr.

Prisoner

I am free and yet I'm cornered
In a house upon a street,
Held captive by the laws of life
Listen to the trampling feet.

People madly milling somewhere
Blindly driving - walking by,
Searching for unconquered tomorrows
Under smog be ridden sky.

Where is the joy of springtime flowers
Rain that use to smell so sweet,
Turn me loose and let me wander
From this house upon a street.

Let the world again be peaceful
People unafraid and true,
Plant a meadow - walk a pathway
Where now the traffic scurries thru.

Just a dream for I am cornered
Listen to the trampling feet,
I am free yet held a hostage
In a house...upon a street.

Shirley Shraver Coombs

This Feeling Is Real

You ask me to change
it's not that easy you see.
From this day forward
how could we be. You give me
love and take it back, but
my heart you gave no slack.
I have fallen for you and
you turn me away, I'm
begging and pleading for you to
please stay. My tears have
already fallen, but you my dear
your heart seems to be stallen.
My body has felt so much
pain, my mind has gone
insane. I just don't know
what to do anymore, my heart
was broken and tore. You could
never see how I feel but I
know this feeling for you is real.

Angelia James

'Tis So Special

'Tis so special to look
into your eyes.
'Tis like a day under
sunny skies.
'Tis so special to feel
your tender kiss.
Special like a romantic
bliss.
'Tis so special to see
you smile.
'Tis worth waiting
all the while.
'Tis so special to have
you in my life.
'Tis even more special
that I will be your
wife.

Judy Early

Howard

I love you, my dear
Please understand
Why I can never come around

I can't see you like this,
And I'm dying inside...
When I remember your pain

So I'll close my eyes...
And imagine your face,
Warm and smiling again

I know that you're always with me
Right here in my heart
But I can't always touch you
You may be here now
But what about tomorrow

I may not be very strong
But you'll never have to worry
You'll always be carried...
Right here in my heart.

Jennifer Lynn VanVekoven

Matt

Hair like a raven,
eyes, gleaming in moonlight;
How I wish he'd kissed me,
that cool spring night.

We talked till morning,
till the sun threatened to rise.
bright, brilliant, beautiful,
in the Eastern sky

The animals on the hill,
were barely heard.
My heart wouldn't still,
I remember every word.

There we laid,
and watched the stars,
their pulsing rhythm,
matching the one in my heart.

Angel Plumley

Apologize

I will not apologize,
for being me,

I have always been
just what you
see,

If I could change
who would
I be?

Someone different,
or just
plain me!

Barbara Lapinski

Clear Vision

Sparkling stream, as I gaze in
My reflection is sharp and clear
Carry for me this guilt and sin
Ease my pain and fear

Within your soothing soft embrace
I've placed my burden and doubt
The sun at last shines upon my face
Sparkling stream, as I gaze out

Janice Roach

Poem for Karen

I see a woman on a beach
teaching her girl child
sand castles
the waves will come to steal
but she is wise
and knows the water's way
and so they play rebuild, rebuild
until the tide goes out
and they win
the game

Shirly Turney

There Is No Way

There is no way to get you
out of my mind
I love only you because you
are one of a kind

You seem to be the love
for me you see
Do you feel the same
Please tell me you agree

There is no way to ever let
you go my love
There is only you everyone knows
even the heavens above.

Somehow you love only me
I can feel that you care

That is why there is no way
to end this love affair

Marilyn Barker Bates

God's Paradise

I opened my eyes, unsure of
where I had gone.
It was almost as if I'd been
lifted by love.
There was no sense of fear
around me, for I left it behind.
There was no pain, sorrow, or
hurt, and I never knew it could
be like this.
I rose up so high, I felt like a
bird skimming the clouds.
I looked down upon the world,
Unhappy of what it became.
It was at that moment I knew
where I had gone to.
It was "God's Paradise!"

Michelle Rubino

Untitled

It is the strong, confident tree
That willingly bends
If even slightly
To reach the wondrous
warmth of the sun.
Yet below
Dwarfed in the cold shadows
Stands a smaller tree
Stubbornly refusing to bend
Selfishly proclaiming
That it should not have to bend
That the sun should come to it
Yet inwardly
The tree does not bend
Because it's afraid it might break

Holly C. Radley

494

Destiny

Destiny is what happens when
  tomorrow becomes today.
Life's surprise after our
  plans are made.

A new note in our melody
  of life.
The unplanned chapter in
  our book of life.

Neither all bad nor good,
  just different.
Hope defends destiny while
  faith defies it.

We hope for the best but have
  faith to deal with the worst.
Destiny hides in the shadows of
  tomorrow, visible in the
  light of yesterday.

Gate keeper for some, jailer for
  others, we decide which.

  C. Terry Shipp

Untitled

Springtime, and the tree comes
  in to blossom.
Lush foliage shades the weary
  traveler as he rests beneath
  the massive boughs.
Gentle rains keep the leaves
  fresh and full of life.

Autumn, and the times change
  with the wind.
The winds are as harsh as
  cutting words.
Life seeps out of the limbs
  as the leaves fall to
  the ground.

  Susan Harmon

Untitled

To you and yours
  Who are still here, we pray.
God has been close to you this day.

You have felt His Presence,
  Almost seen His Hand,
As He led your loved one
  To His Eternal Land.

Yet, God's Everlasting Love
  Is with you still,
Though it is hard to submit
  To His Will.

May He give you His Love,
  His Joy, and His Peace
Until from your earthly mission
  He would you, also release.

  Helen Bamesberger Ruff

Untitled

He soars through
The sky
But scarcely above
The earth
Carrying a wreath
Entwined
Caught between
Here and the more divine
Circling worlds
Of light and life
And love.

  Lyn Marshall

Not Just A Pretty Rhyme

Together we can make it through,
being a teen and seeing the truth.

One on one fighting is never a
way, only people get hurt and someone
has to pay.

Day by day with that's right and
that's wrong, wondering if hearing
those words will last very long.

I want to grow up with no violence
around, to walk down a sidewalk
anywhere in this town.

We wonder how long we will live,
but being afraid of what may happen
is something you can not give.

Love and peace is nice to have,
nothing to rave about or even be glad.

When life comes down to a single
minute of time, I did not write this
to look pretty and rhyme.

  Claudia Tanner

A Dove

Tears fall freely from wounds
Yet not healed.
As crystals shatter from a world
So shielded.
The image I saw in the mirrors
Now gone.
Yet still I lay frail and weak
Like a fawn.
A pensive thought, a wandering
Expression.
The tides of autumn follow
My depression.
Soon I will escape, no more pain
Or cries.
The dove of life falls, then slowly
She dies.

  Kimberly Smith

Untitled

Be healthy, be happy,
  Be sure, be wise.
Be careful, be loving,
  But look in my eyes.
Tell me you love me,
  But don't shed a tear.
Then I will know,
  You love me my dear.

  James E. Bright Jr.

I've Been Thinking

I've been thinking
When the time comes for me to die
Don't light any candles
Or mourn for me.

Because my life
Has been full of experience
And has been its own reward
So I'm content.

There are those
Who have done great things
Like ended war, and brought about peace
It's those whose memory should remain.

  Jon F. Dewey

Memories

As I walk down these empty halls
I hear the loneliness call
A memory that last
As sounds of the past fall like rain
Although the pain is dear
My heart so sincere
As I say good-bye
I sometimes wonder why
You went away
Never to see another day

  Jodie Roberts

A Mother's Love

A mother's love is hard to find
but harder still to lose
even when you throw it out
it's not for you to chose.

For a mother's love is endless
no matter what you do
it's always unconditional
it's there to see you through.

A mother's love can give you space
when you need to roam
but still can be the life line
that's there to guide you home.

A mother's loves a treasure
that is given from the start,
always there for when you need it
tucked safe within your heart.

So remember all you children
there are angels up above,
that forever keep you cradled
within your mother's love.

  Stacey J. Tipton

Winter Wonders

Winter snow everywhere
Gray clouds in the air.
Ice cones hanging down almost
touching the winter ground.

Blue haze everywhere.
There clench of thirst saying
winters here.
Snow flakes being formed by
something you've seen before.

  Venus M. Smith

A Christmas Poem

I am asleep on the ground,
then I hear a very loud sound.
Where did it come from?
I look and look,
what did I see?
Santa Claus, smiling at me!

Adam J. Valdes

Loneliness Is...

No one to care with
No one to share with
No one to talk with
No one to laugh with
No one to cry with
No one to love with
No one to listen
No one

I yearn for someone to talk to.
Someone to share, to care,
to laugh, to cry, to love with.
To listen to the silence with.
There is no one.

Karen E. Rodman

Flying

What is this lightness?
Now I'm rising,
Floating upward
Earth below—

Firmly planted,
Long and strongly,
Earthly rooted,
Flying free?

How can this be?
I don't know trees
that rise and fly.
I don't know birds
with roots to ground them.

Even so, I know it's true,
Else how could I
be soaring high
to destiny.

Flying—
Feel the wind?
My tree top heart is free.

Barbara Baron

Untitled

Jesus is free, Jesus is free,
Jesus come and live in me;
Jesus make me pure and whole,
Jesus always keep my soul.

Jesus, please, teach me to be
More like you and be free;
Let my spirit sing for thee
For, my Lord, I love Thee.

I'm thankful that You are free
I'm thankful for Calvary.
Jesus is free, oh Jesus is free,
Jesus is free.

Marie B. Smallwood

Beautiful Earth

Flower are beautiful
  in the Spring
Grass looks wonderful
  when it's green
Birds flying around in the mourning
  with that sweet sound
I wake up and just want to sing
The Sky is blue
there is no limit
The earth is round
Just right for everyone in it
All of these beautiful things
came from God above
So we should thank him everyday
to live in this world of love.

Vivian Bright

"Forget"

I want to forget you,
I want you to leave.
I want you to forget me,
I don't want your nonsense memories.

Don't want to be confused,
Don't want to be in pain.
Don't want to be with you,
You only think of mind games.

Please forget me,
Please leave me be.
Please get away from me,
Your mind games mean nothing to me.

I want to forget you,
I want you to leave.
I want you to forget me,
You're just a nonsense memory.

Lisa A. Renner

Regarding An Apple

Apple, you remind me of
an oversized cherry.

Your slick skin feels like
a river of cool silk.

A brown star shining brightly
against a pale yellow sky
is what your seeds are.

Apple, when I bite into you,
it sounds like someone's boot
crunching on dead leaves.

My teeth leave tracks that look like
lonesome footprints tracking the snow.

Apple, I remember seeing you
on top of a pyramid,
waiting to be eaten.

Laura Chan

Silence

When the silence comes
The words begin
In the silence in knowledge
Without it is death
Oblivious to the obvious
One knows all
With your eyes closed
You can see everything

Scot G. Schaumburg

Sister

Your blood is that of my mothers
But our blood is not the same
You have the blood of another
And you're carrying his name.

You are too young to understand
But maybe so am I
There are differences between us
About that, I cannot lie.

"Half" is what they call us
But "half" is jut a word,
So I won't make a fuss
Because it's so absurd.

"Half" isn't what I feel
"Half" isn't what I think
When I hold you in my arms
My heart could never sink.

Because "half" will never be true
And in your infant mind you know,
Love has no name as "half" or "step"
Please remember this as you grow.

Julie M. McLean

Every Thing

I've spent my life working for every
thing that I own.
But if you look deep down inside
my heart, you'll find that I'm
really sad and alone.
Every thing that I own, don't mean
a thing to me, with out you I
don't have anything.
I've spent a life time living alone.
My heart has been broken many
times down the road.
But when I met you I found
everything.
You fill the emptiness in my life.
You gave me feelings back in my heart,
I just want you to know I'll give
up everything that I own
just for you, and you alone.

Mark W. Greenawalt

A Summer Night

The drops have come
cleansing all below.
The smell so sweet
and so forgiving
Shards of light fill the sky
lighting the world below.
The clouds do part
the storm is gone.
Night is falling and
all is calm.
Colors join across the peaks
long enough for all to see,
Fading as the sun goes down.
The clouds still remain-
shades of pinks, reds,
and purples fill the air.
All is forgotten,
all is well.
Nothing unusual just a
spout of summer's rain.

Jerusha Friedrich

So Full Of Life

Relieving the days of attractiveness.
A time where the sun grabs your heart
and breeze strengthens its life.
A time where your body is fulfilled
with a shine that the sun provides
and the breeze enforcing confidence to
your shape.
Becoming aroused by the suns heat,
its feeling of strength in protection
of the cold.
The caressing lips of a breeze
on your body, Loving and
Feeding you.
Making you feel so full of Life.

Angelique Marie Solis

My Search

Doing Damage
to myself
for selfish reasons.
Making the most of
when love is gone...
yet I desire
a sense of inner peace.
But still...
during my search
for the perfect
relationship
I find that
Harsh Reality
takes a permanent
place in my life.
Is it fear of commitment?
No-but there is no
perfect relationship
to philosophize about.

Donna Hamilton

Reflections

Sunrises become sunsets and
The years go slipping by.
The days blend into friendships
That can stand the test of time.

The seasons are a reminder
That things will always change.
But as the seasons unfold each year
One thing will stay the same.

The joys, the laughs, the sorrows too.
We have shared them all together.
I wish for you upon this day
The Happiest Birthday every!

Cheryl A. Benton

My First Car

It was surely a wond'rous sight
It filled my being with pure delight
A convertible that was tan
And only one year old - oh man!
My 1940 Ford V-8
Made it easy to get a date
My gal and I would take a trip
Put down the top and let-er-rip!
I spit and polished it, til it shone
My competition could only groan
Then along came Tojo with his perdition
Bringing an end to this submission.

Harold Goldstein

Shadows Unspoken

For the child in me
Before innocence lost
Who gave of self wholly
Yet to understand the cost
Who slowly slipped away
As anger raged with past
For the wrongs done in trust
Forgiveness becomes the task
There's a picture of parents
Very small and I see
Who only learned what was taught
Unable to set shadows free
With a glimpse of the past
The heart begins to mend
Again I see the child in me
And heartaches that burned end

Christine Daniels

It

It stems from:
the Diva playing early
on Saturday morning.
From Dickens to Ginsberg,
from gastronomy, hyperbole.
Lattes and two long jokes

Your laughter washing my face
each time I
look up from my hands.
And crow's feet narrow
your attentive eyes.

It stems from, and concludes
as the crow flies
to let the osprey take it place.

Beth J. Schnur

I'm Not Alone

My cross is not too heavy,
  My road is not too rough
Because God walks beside me,
  And to know that is enough—
And though I get so lonely,
  I know I am not alone.
For the Lord God is my Father;
  And He loves me as His own—
So though I'm tired and weary;
  And I wish my race was run
God will only terminate it—
  When my work on earth is done.
So let me stop complaining.
  About my load of care.
For God will always lighten it—
  When it gets too much to bear.
And if He does not ease my load,
  He will give me strength to bear it-
For God is Love and Mercy—
  He's always near to share it.

Faye Ryan

Time

I tick away in minutes
I tick away in years
I steal away a lifetime
And still I shed no tears.

People sometimes hate me
Because I waste away
They blame me for my quickness
And wish that I might stay.

Valory Waligoski

Untitled

A
  broken
    wing
takes time
  to mend,
and
  so tenderly
the Lord
  shall tend
to binding - up
  with boundless grace
Your broken heart
  shall he embrace
till,
  as that wing
shall he restore
  in greater strength
than was before
  your heart's ability to soar
upon His Holy Breath.

David E. Ryan

I'm Drought

Flick the salt into my eyes
and maybe I can see again
prick the needles into my flesh
and maybe I can feel again
demand mercy from the waters
and ask them to let go
I'm in the drought of circumstance
and no one will let go
I cannot see the blackbirds
who slam into my windows
they flutter down into the dirt
and die into themselves
they tremble in such pain and loss
and spasms in their legs to thrust
dying in the grass they hate
staring into the sky they loved
wondering just why it never rained
knowing it was me who tried.

S

Marijuana Dreams

Marijuana dreams,
Invading my head?
"It's helping me think,"
That's what I said

Promises empty,
The ones I couldn't keep,
I lie to my loved ones,
For affects not too cheap

I awaken one day,
With marijuana dreams
With opium sobbs,
And Heroin tears

I hide in the shadows
With my new best friends
My marijuana dreams,
We're friends till the end...

Rafael Montanez

Vessel

A she who never was
Afraid quickens
A full-length mirror
Reflecting her
Belly fragments

Quinn Saunders

Peace On Earth

When I look at this world
I don't like what I see.
I see people getting killed
Right in front of me.
In the battle of peace
We can't take a side.
In the battle of life
We have to have pride.
If we all get together
This world would better.
No more gangs, no more guns
Then the violence will be done.
When I do my part to help this place,
There's a big smile on my face.
When I look at this world
I don't like what I see.
For us all to get along
Peace is the key.

Mikaela M. Thompson

Love

Love requires sharing,
Sharing requires struggle,
Struggle requires faith,
Faith requires relationships,
relationships require togetherness,
togetherness requires marriage,
marriage requires a lifetime,
a lifetime requires true feelings,
true feelings requires your heart,
your heart requires loving,
loving requires broken hearts,
broken hearts require crying,
crying requires hating,
hating requires danger,
danger requires hurting,
hurting requires not trusting,
not trusting requires not loving,
not loving requires breaking up,
breaking up requires being in love.

Amy Hedrick

Lord I Am Not Able

Lord I am not able
    To walk the narrow way
Without you here beside me
    Each and every day

Lord I am not able
    To speak words you'd have me say
Lest I seek your guidance
    And to you humbly pray

Lord I am not able
    To show others your true love
Except I follow in your path
    That leads to heaven above

Lord I am not able
    To accomplish anything
Unless each hour that passes
    My sin to you I bring.

Janet Lee

Friend

Outside myself
in a circle of time
you touched me
in a
slow,
warm,
dangling, forever

We meet now only above clouds
in kisses
resting forever,
in time.
upside down.

Diane Ketelle

Embracing Limbo

I seem to be in limbo.
Am embracing it.
Did not choose this feeling
but there's a strong need for
Nothingness

I seem to be in limbo.
Am embracing it
because I'm tired, weary
or hurt and pain
and somehow yearn for
Oblivion

I seem to be in limbo.
Am embracing it
but know it's unacceptable
So shall fight to regain
the agonies and ecstasies of life
and somehow rise out of
this Nothingness state.

Denise Sternberg

Devil in the Wind

Loud,
strong,
death defying,
horrendous,
gigantic, dangerous,
whirling, whipping,
gloomy, vast,
devastating,
black, whistling,
windy, thunderous,

Fast, flying, frightening, tornado,
wild, whirling wind,
is destructive and tremendous
dirty, loud storms
sounds like a train,
threatening weather
massive violent,
overpowering,
twirling, twisters
are very evil

Natalie Grein

A Question, An Answer, An Eternity

If from your hands I somehow slip
like sand betwixt your fingertips
would you travel realms unknown
in quest of me, the world to roam
as years make you a broken man
a noble heart with hollowed hand.
If from my side you chose to stray
like sunlight at the edge of day
I would search the dusk of night
and cry your name in dawning's light
until my pulse was beating low
still onward would I push to go.
But if quite by dismal chance
these hands of mine, from your grasp
must be torn by unkind fate
and foredoom us to separate,
be doubtless, love, and own no fear
there is no doubt or question here
in death we two shall one day lie,
but our love will never with us die.

J.T. Hunt

The Sixth Child

"I love you the best."
He whispered softly to me.
"Promise not to tell."
The words I heard him say.

In life I was so careful,
yet prideful of his caring.
The knowledge ever present,
the promise yet so bearing.

Then life came crashing down.
The sorry words were spoken.
The secret I revealed.
The promise kept, then broken.

"He loved me the best.
He told me so one day."
Then heard my words repeated,
again, again, again — to ten.

He made us feel so special,
that dad who whispered to us.
"I love you the best.
Promise not to tell."

Paulette A. Skolarus

Survive

The devil's tongue makes its mark.
Wounds unseen upon this skin,
And indifferent pit bull he can be.

Basking in acts of kindness,
Can the wounds be healed?
A loving person he can be.

The anger of the pit bull,
And the softness of a purring lion,
Will the devils hold he broken?

Lifted by love and understanding,
Trashed by words of indifference.
Is one to survive the turmoil?

Can all scars be healed?
Save what we thought was there?
Is not the lion King?

Yet some things never change.
For indifference rules his day,
And one must go his way.
Peace, peace at last!

Rodger Junk

Untitled

Why all the search
Why all the rush
Can't anyone see
We can't comprehend much
Still the wheels turn
And energetically we fly
I hear all the noise
But it's still quiet inside

Does anyone really know I'm here
Or am I the one who's blind
Is life happening all because of me
Or something special I have to find
Sometimes I wonder
But then again we all do
In the end nothing matters
Only the beauty of you.

Linda Nelson

I'm Like A Butterfly

It's summer and it's a hot day.
Sit against a tree,
And close your eyes.
Do this only in my park,
where it's very green,
and water runs quietly down stream.
Sit against my tree.
Listen to the birds.
Hear the insects crawl up the tree
and on the ground.
An occasional plane go by.
Then in a still quiet.
A warm wind blows me by.
The dust of my wings
brushed your face
soft as a smooth song never played,
on the wind, you would only hear it,
and as you will only feel it.
And me, I'm like a butterfly
free as the wind.

Tracyne Hines

Toast

Lift your glass
Let's drink a toast
To the years
We lived the most

Lift your glass
Recall yesterday
When we were young
And hard at play

When we loved
When we laughed
When we danced
Yes, lift your glass!

Let's drink a toast
To yesterday
And all the ghosts
Along the way!

DeLee Davis

Birds

I am a bird
I flap my wings to get to my nest
My daddy brings me worms to eat
I rest

Nicole Wagner

Untitled

Special people
Special place
Special thoughts
Remembering them can help
    make your days better
I sometimes wonder how they work.

They can cheer you up
    make you laugh
Warm your heart, or make you cry.

Your life would seem empty
    without them.

Your days would seem lonely.

Memories are the Special
    part of your Heart.

They are warm
    they are the lights that burn
        inside

That no one
    can take away from you!

Nancy Monreal

Untitled

Bells chimed a soft release
Alone in a three sided cell
The light falling
The little girl disappeared
Into the angled
Shadows of the walls
The whisperings of the
Departing
Intruded on the
Ecclesiastical silence
Like muffled prayers
Suddenly, she saw the painting
Through the painter's eyes.
She fought, but too late.
She shook,
And the tears came -
Bells broke the trance.

Kerri Horgan

The Calming Balm of Gilead

Exhausting all life's panaceas
and still imbued with doubts.
Seeking a balm to cure all ills,
Searching....
within....
without....

When in despair and desperation
Gilead's balm I found.
No longer am I harried,
harassed...
confused...
or bound....

The calm the Balm of Gilead
has brought me yet today,
Flows freely to each soul in doubt
To sustain
and aid....
always....

Susan Forrester Casper

Jesus Is Coming

His coming is for told by the
saints of old, through Daniel,
Ezekiel, James and Paul. His
house shall rise, above the sky,
over the mountains and through
the rye. His voice shall sound
with a shouts of joy, echoing
throughout the lands. The
trumpet shall blast for one
last time, for heavens doors
opens wide, there Jesus stands
clothed in white for the
gathering in the sky. We shall
be changed in a twinkling of an eye,
the trumpet shall sound,
the dead shall rise, cause his
victory has been won. Sweet
paradise is where we'll be, serving
the master forever and ever.

Martha Miller

Saturday Smile

If the birds sang this morning
    I didn't hear them.

If there were people in the mall
    I didn't see them.

The "Big Boy" is whining
    I think I know why.

The lake is violent with whitecaps
    They are grinning at me.

It's storming outside,
    But the Oak trees don't care.

They're waving at me.
    We're making a poem.

Five o'clock anywhere
    Won't be fun today.

It's Saturday morning
    Today you are gone.

The house doesn't seem empty
    But nobody's here.

If I am alone
    Then why am I smiling?

Linda Beal Cloud

What Is Purple?

Purple is a plum
Shining in the sun
or, the shape
of grapes
on drapes.
Purple is violet flowers
in showers
of rain.
Purple is bruises
people get on cruises.
Purple is jelly
in your belly
sometimes ladies even purple
their finger nails
with pales of purple

Jessica Frances Weiss

The Bel Aire Pancake House

When it comes to breakfast,
It's always a treat
To go to "Bel Aire",
Where we love to eat.

The food at their restaurant
Is quite a delight,
Their eggs are so tasty
And the bacon's just right

They have pancakes and waffles
That are cooked golden brown,
They're light and delicious
And the best to be found.

You may have been to some places
That boast of foods fine,
And traveled to towns
Where you may had to dine.

But here at the "Bel Aire",
You don't have to look far,
For they have the best food
And deserve "The Gold Star."

Jack A. Feldman

Hampton Court

Now speaks the clock in Henry's tower,
The palace stirs in sleep.
What memories are in these walls?
What secrets does it keep?
Jane and Catherine are you there?
I hear the rustle of your gowns
Trailing and sweeping down the stair,
Or is it just the whispering
Of those who would wear your crowns?
Silent in the moonlight
The towers and turrets stand,
Waiting some royal signal
Or Henry's voice is command.
No Wolsey treads the cloistered yard;
No Henry dines in state.
Only the scream of swooping gulls
And the bested who patiently wait-
Wait for the ages to come into light,
As orion swings over the courtyard
The clock speaks again in the night.

Gertrude M. Taylor

Solos

Resign this evening
    to evergreen solos.
A bullfrog's frozen voice
    will not join
    to add its bass,
Nor will soprano duet
    be heard
    from cricket and katydid.
Two pillars, the ash and oak,
    stand in concrete silence,
    while their instruments lay
    rusted at their feet.
We'll hear only the pine
    hit a melancholy chord
    as the chill wind
    strums its boughs.

James B. Brown

Heartbreak

I find myself by the phone,
Waiting for his call,
I hope he will contact me soon,
But the phone won't ring at all.

I sit in the dark for hours,
Not allowing myself to cry,
You wanted no more to do with me,
But I hope that it was a lie.

Finally, I just give up,
Going to bed with a broken heart,
I cry myself to sleep tonight,
And dream we didn't part.

I long to have your arms around me,
As we talk of the future and past,
But I must have been a fool,
To think that we could last.

But how could it have gone so quickly?
I'm not sure that was fair,
Yet, I find myself wondering...
Was our love even there?

Dana Blair

Lonely

Lonely as I am
One only knows
No one to help me
Expecting someone will,
Lost forever
Yet longing to be found.

Melissa Simon

My Friend

I love my friend
    like a sister,

I respect my friend
    like my father,

I cherish my friend
    like my mother,

I stand up for my friend
    like a brother

I love my friend
    like a sister.

Melissa Strickland

Steps of Living

Majestic swirling colors
Invade my mind
As my universe is altered by the Ether.
The Ether is the wall between
Incredible brilliance
And complete chaos.
The only path through this wall
Is the achievement of excellence
In all things.
To reach this goal you must surpass
All in front.
The only way to make your own footsteps
Is to follow in others.

Michael McDuffie

True Love

Love is truth and understanding,
never binding or demanding.
Seldom taking, always giving.
Sharing trials of daily living.
Comforting and softly calming,
never hurting, never harming.
Enduring, growing, ever steady.
A helping hand that's always ready.
Completely trusting, silent knowing.
A guiding light that's ever glowing.
Hand in hand, together serving
A Heavenly Father all deserving.

Ruth A. Kavanaugh

A Will To Live

Let me count the ways for
what you mean to me, more
than the rising sun each
day gracing life in harmony.

Higher than the stars that
shine, much deeper than the sea.
So much taller than the highest
leaf, that clings onto its tree.

Much vaster than a mountain
range, that graces heaven's sky,
gives me reason to a acknowledge
you, and not to question why.

For no greater gift would ever
be or more than I could
see what has given me the
will to live my life and destiny.

Jennifer Skala

Simple Ring

Sometimes she will sit and wonder
    where the love had to go,
Did it all die for him
    that she does not know.
The love was misplaced
    it was pushed away,
With hopes of being found
    Somewhere else, some other day.
The two people forgot
    of the words they shared,
The times they spent together
    the way they once cared.
Everything now is gone
    they are no longer whole,
They went their separate ways
    no longer one soul.
The love no longer lives
    the heart will no longer sing,
All that is left of lost love
    is a simple ring.

Janet G. Tuck

Hours of Summer

Fields of flowers
Trees like towers
How we cherished those summer hours
A shady spot
Not too hot
With winters grip long forgot
A time to laze while animals graze
To hold a hand
And just feel grand.

A. Vancheri

I Wonder If...

I wonder if that puff of cloud
Is really just a bed,
A ball of misty cotton spun
To rest an angels head.

And if that flow of molten dawn,
With all its fiery light,
Is just that same old yesterday
That went away last night.

I wonder if the surging waves
That purge our island's shore
Are just the plain old drops of rain
That fell the night before.

And if that hue of crystal blue
So deep, and way up high,
Is just the shadow of the sea
That people call the sky.

I wonder if I wonder long
Of things that seem to be,
If all the answers that I seek
Will somehow come to me.

Stanley G. Perry

The Robe

Teddy Toad had a robe that didn't
fit at all.
So he went to the home of
Freddy the frog, and said,
I won't ever go to the ball,
because this robe, doesn't
fit at all.
But, Freddy the fog jumped with
glee.
For the robe fit him to a T.
So sad eyed Teddy Toad hopped down the
road... and jumped into the pond.
So my friends... disappeared and
no one saw him since!
I'm proud to say, Freddy Frog
was the happiest of them all.

Nethelia Osgood

The Rhyme

A rhyme is a friend
To play with
On a day when there is rain.

A rhyme is a friend
To say with
When rain drops streak the pane.

To play with rhymes
Is lots of fun
For two or three
Or just for one.

It helps me learn;
It tickles my ear.
A rhyme is good
To play and hear.

A rhyme is something
To make you smile
And with a rhyme
You can run a mile
And leave sad thoughts
Behind you.

Robert B. Aukerman

Society Of Contradiction

The abused child tells,
    then the advocate denies
Drugs aren't deadly
    while the cancer patient dies.
We say that we accept,
    but discriminate
There are people we love
    whom sometimes we hate.
Out to save the world
    and committing our crimes
Saying poetry's a petty game
    are those who've got their lines.
We're always gonna care
    but the real love is done
The most blatant slam is losing
    when you think the battle's won.

Jessica Ann Lishinski

Full Circle

As we move from the
Crush of love into
The rush of our living,
Somewhere another love dies,
And in the whirling circle
Of our spinning the shadow of
The beginning and the end
Rhymes edge to edge in time;

For at myriad moments of
Dying, launched out of that
First dark sea, moving flesh
Through flesh, another love is born
Away from lovers love split instant
And spent breath, before light
Breaks on sightless eyes,
We haul the shroud shadow
That spreads inexorably toward death.

Arthur E. Carney

Dreaming Mama

What does mama dream about
    as she lays there in her bed?
As she pulls the soft sheets over her
    What is going through her head?

Sweet dreams my mama tells me
    When it's very late at night,
I wish the same for her
    as she leaves and says good night.

How I long for the morning
    to see mama once more,
Like the shells wait for the ocean
    to come and meet the shore.

I wonder what the sparkling night's
    dreams will soon bring,
I hope mama will hear
    the beautiful church bells ring.

Oh Lord, please watch over her
    Laying peaceful there at night.
Why, what does mama dream about
    as I go to turn off the light?

Daniela Caschera

Clue No. 1

A crazyhouse,
blowing east as I flow west,
and we touch...
Oh how warm, warm, warm
are the hands of those we love.

V. Lambert

Grandson

There's a little guy I know,
I think the whole world of,
And when he came into my life,
He brought the meaning of love.

Right now he's just a baby boy,
But he'll be a man someday,
And I'll teach him everything I can
To help him on his way.

If I'm the cause of his laughter,
And not the reason for tears,
I pray that's what he remembers,
Throughout all his years.

When he wraps his arms around me,
And smiles and kisses me,
I thank the Lord for this joy,
My Grandson, Zachery.

John W. Ramsey

My Friend

As I awake in the morning
To start a new day.
I gather my thoughts
and begin to pray.
I pray for my family and
friends near and far,
To guide and protect them
wherever they are.
I ask God for wisdom
and guidance thru the day,
To help, find the lost
who have gone astray,
Then with a smile on my face
and love in my heart.
I try to please God by
doing my part.
And as the long day comes
to an end,
I praise and thanks God
for being my friend

Julia V. Dahlgreen

Teacher's Term

The weary ruffled, rumbled way
Often lonely, frayed nerves arise
Sleep robs us of day to come
Anticipated end of hallowed halls
School days near dusk to close
Rapping, tapping, happy feet
Flipping, clipping, snipping sheets
Old ones, young ones, all the same
Working through the years refrain
Searching, reaching, teaching all
Keeping records towards the fall
Weathered, weary soldiers march
Onward through the embattled ground
Summer's beginning school year ending

Bob Cook

Mountain Streams

Swirling
Hurling
Whirling
Down
Down
Up around
Over the sand bar
Over the pebbles
Over the boulders
On a hot summer day
Birds diving over
Screams of song
Holding on tight
Holding on tight
Around the bend
Down
Down
Rushing
Rushing
Crushing a cool mountain stream.

Winifred Holland

Thank You Lord

I thank you Lord;
For all you've done.
For your guidance and your care.
I thank you Lord;
When in need of a friend,
For you always being there.
I thank you Lord
For finding me worthy
For all the blessings
You've sent my way.
I thank you Lord, for everything
In Jesus name I pray.

Nancy Killinger

Wake

Peace comes while you sleep
Sets in while you dream
No need to worry
You are taken care of
Walk into the light of
Your dreams surprised
Let your subconscious state
Take you where it may
It will be good, without a doubt
And when you wake, worry
Not that you don't remember
It was good
Your sleep was peaceful

Cornelius J. Dougherty

My Children

The light in my eye
The beat in my heart
The breath that I breathe
  My children
The tear in my eye
The ache in my chest
The lump in my throat
  My children
The joy to my parents
The knot that binds us
The jewels from heaven
  My children

Melissa Benscoter

Heart's Desire

Oh, how I love thee
  I want you
and I need you
  to be with you forever.

To touch you
  is to feel you,
to hold you
  and see you smile.

To be with you
  is to hear you, smell you,
to see you laugh
  and to see your smile.

Oh, how I need thee
  my hearts desire,
without you I'm incomplete
  only emptiness inside.

Stay with me
  give me happiness,
be with me
  always by my side.

Jimmy James Tatum

Blessings

Years ago, when I was born.
On a cold and snowy January morn.
Little did I know what was in store.
Would I wind up with less or more.
The years, have flown
Four sons have grown to manhood.
I've been blessed.
Of all the mothers in the world
They've made me the happiest.

Florence C. Cocco

A Vision

Sometimes I have a vision
In poetry and awe
A gift to put on paper
Of life and what I saw;
Sometimes I wonder about me
If there's someone from the past
A poet from the prior
Controlling my pen and cast.
I hold the pen in my hand
Its movement is its own
I give the paper to it
The will is of its own;
Sometimes of when I'm writing
I know not from whence it came
The pen just keeps on moving
Results are all the same.
If there really is a power
That controls my thoughts and hand
I feel it is a pleasure
To write-read and understand.

J. Edward Koch

Highway 18-A

Highway 18-A
Be alert children
Highway
Signing Ends

Sarah Decker

Less

Shadows;
  Flicker across ceilings,
  Dance along walls,
Hide in corners,
Cloud thoughts,
  Father insecurity,
    Nurture doubt,
  Follow your path,
Mock your steps,
  Distort your image...
    Flash!
  What's left?
A frightened child,
  A suffocating shroud,
  A man less proud,
    As shadows fall loud
On deaf fears.

Camille L. Harris

God's Footstool

Earth...creation's error?
Dwellers making mischief,
setting in motion
  satellites,
  missiles,
  arms of destruction.
They trample on justice,
  ignore the widow,
  shock the innocent,
  take life,
  extort money.
Why...
God's footstool earth
rolls on in space...
  a mistake?
Yet, a Redeemer came
to crimson the earth,
to change the hearts
of earth dwellers.

Elizabeth Parente

Love Is...

Love is new
Love is old
Love is happy
Love is cold
Love is blind
Love can see
Love is you
Love is me

Joanne L. Jordan

Reflections

No more can I the blue sky see.
Or see a bird fly in a tree.
Or see the rainbow in the sky.
For now, hereaft' am I of sight.
And though I try, with all my might
my senses I cannot renew.
But I thank God, I still have you!!!

Dominic F. Sicari

Yesterday, Today, Tomorrow

Our todays bear ripples
of past tears in the pond
that is my life.

Yet, your strength is the soil
that absorbs those tears
and produces the beauty of greenery
that is the smiles and dreams
of our tomorrows.

Terresa M. Baglin-Lyda

Eyes

The soul's inner window,
the tell-all of human feelings.
Showing sadness,
fear and glee.
Looking in them you see every thought
be it doubt,
love or passion.
The mouth say with words and shows
with action
but your eyes tell me more...
Tell me of the loneliness you feel
the points you wonder
They tell me what your true
desires and needs are
They let me see
and love
the real you.

Melissa J. Robinson

Tornado

The Tornado comes
in with a lions roar.

He goes for his prey
and goes back for
more nothing to show,
that he was there
except for the remains
of his prey.

Melissa Sharp

Land By The Rio Grande

Howdy Pardner! How's it goin'?
Kick those boots off, if you will.
Then sit down and travel with me
Where the quail are runnin'...still.

In the shadow of Mt. Franklin
At three thousand feet or so,
In the land of commancheros
Where the big ol' tumblers blow.

When you're thirsty, well,
There's water in cool clear banks
Where big rock basins swell
Above the desert at Hueco Tanks.

Once an ocean—now a desert—
You can surf the sands so white;
You just keep a bedroll handy,
Or you'll freeze out there at night.

When at last we are at rest
Beside the mighty Rio Grande,
You best thank the Lord Almighty—
All this was blessed by his own hand.

Mark Reginald Rogers

"A Bit Of Heaven And Earth"

The cumulous clouds floating in the sky
The flowers gracing the earth
The sunshine and the raindrops that
Always came at the right time
And my breakfast on the patio -
Almost seems more than I deserve.
Thank you Lord

T. S. Austin

Lightening Bug

Flash, blink, disappear.
Where did you go?
I know you are near!

Buzzing, fanning, riding the wind.
Are you afraid
When your light goes dim?

Magical, whimsical, little dot.
For a second I see you,
and then I can not.

Judy Hensley Bryson

Hopelessly Devoted

Like the break of day you came to be.
And through you emitted the rays,
That illuminated my being.
You exposed me;
So I walked in your shadow.

Like magnet to steel,
I was mesmerized by
Your effervescent charm.
It awoke something in me.
And I, too, came, to be.

Like a rose you blossomed,
You flowered, you perished.
You ceased to exist.
Then like the setting sun
I disappeared into the darkness.
And I, too, was no more.

Toni Tennent

To Be Different

To be different is a
   hard task.

Because nobody asked
   me if I wanted to be.

It's hard to be different
   when you're in a crowd

To have people stare
   and even point

The hardest thing to handle
   about being different is
      that you can't live it down

Wherever you go,
   whatever you do
      people always stare at you.

Chrissie Cluney

Changing Life

Poems from the heart
Speak feelings from the soul

My better half in life
You always made me whole.

I always felt at home
In the warmth of your hold.

Even apart it seemed to be
Of passions left untold.

So another year of sharing
Like changing leaves of Fall.

The bright colors of our life
Endless seeds we share with all.

Richard Schultz

Happiness Is

Real happiness is
One place to be
A roof over it
And enough to eat

A healthy body
Peace of mind
One Gods worry
No other kind

To get some love
And give it too
Without the love
Life will not do

No warriors spoil
But clothed feet
To till the soil
That's all we need

Rainer W. Raumer

Ocean

Glittery sparkles highlight
the bouncing of the ocean's intentions.
The water...

Like emotion:
fluid and endless.
an infinite sea of rage
longing for the opportunity
to ravage and destroy lands.

A heartless, mindless beast
that lies dormant...
   ...flowing...
searching the world over
for the soul it lacks.

Swells of guilt
repenting for medieval crimes,
longing for forgiveness.

Waves...
silently teetering its
blue, limitless mass
into dream.

Sherwin Tolentino

Question

If living is a vale of tears,
 A thorn-lined, weary way,
Why don't we weep when kids are born
 And if they die be gay?

If heaven is a place of joy,
 Rewarding all who come,
Should death not spawn a merry wake
 Of trumpet, dance and drum?

Why, then, the parting tribal rite
 In tears and glum array?
Why are the signs and symbols such,
 If truth is what we say?

Art Buck

Wars Downside

A war can make you weep,
like Weeping Willow trees.
The blood will make you sigh.
The dead will make you cry,
the smoke rises, the bombs fall.
Wars downside has made its call.
The families cry for the dead
who have died.
The men and women sigh and sigh,
while all the children cry and cry.
War has naught but a horrible downside!

Rachel Buckle

Divine Intervention

In the fields of home
There came a vision clear
I heard a voice, I heard a name.
The springtime of the year.

Oh, my poet, Lord, and friend
Above the crest
Of the stars and of the wind
Above the fields of home.

The poet spoke
The vision through
Conveying convictions
Inspiring intentions
Concerning the fields of home.

Divine intervention
Peace of mind
Exhortations
In the fields of home.

Nathan A. Ely

Day Dreams

As I gaze out of my window
I see in my minds eye
Another scene, another clime
Not this cold and frosty sky.

I see the the sparkling beaches
As they stretch beyond my door
I hear the restless ocean
As it slaps upon the shore.

I feel the soft sea breezes
As they caress my face
My senses are enchanted
By the beauty of the place.

I dream of many a happy time
A time of fun and play
But suddenly the scene is gone
And it's just a winter's day.

Marie D. Walklet

Why'd You Leave?

Daddy, Daddy why'd you leave me?
Daddy, Daddy do you believe me?
Since you're up in heaven in the
sky above,
I just want to tell you I miss
your love.

Daddy, Daddy why'd you go?
Daddy, Daddy I miss you so?
When it's my day to walk down
that isle,
You won't be there to compliment
my style

Daddy, Daddy is your spirit here?
Daddy, Daddy is it near?
Getting awarded for my achievements
while hoping to make you proud,
Sometimes I'll ask out loud,
Daddy, Daddy why'd you
leave me?

Letitia Richie

Left Behind

The imprint of your head on the pillow
Was all you left behind
On it lays the rose you left
With the note that you had signed

The words were scribbled frantically
Or a crumbled piece of paper
And a drop of blood had run down it
From the thorn that pricked your finger

Your message was unmistakable
How could you leave me in this way
With nothing more than memories
Of you on our wedding day

The memories and that note
Is all that I could save
The rose is dead and wilted
And it still lays on your grave

Kathy G. S. Morin

A Boy's Plea

As dawn starts to
brake, across the
westerns skies

a small boy stands
alone to whisper
so quiet, no one
can hear

Lord, am I to be alone
must I lose my momma;
poppa, and sister to
a dreaded disease
called AIDS!

Please, o' please, if
they all must die
then grant me this!
That I too will
get this, this awful
disease and go with them

Cloamae Suiters

Sea Wash

Fragments from the sea
Glisten in beaded scallops:
Footprints disappear.

Doris Mayer

Sunrise

To look upon a sun rise
On a bright mid summer morn
Is like unto a baby's cry
The moment it is born

The blue of the mornings glory
Create a rapture in the sky.
To create a lasting memory
A masterpiece for today, gone by

The promise of tomorrow
Like love for the new born child
Lies only in this sunrise
Such a beauty undefiled

Grace Wallis

A Rose

I am the flower
Who came from the heaven
They wrapped me up
In a blanket
And they put me in
The mail box
I was so teeney weeney
In a flower
I fell off the flower
I grew bigger and bigger
And soon I became
A rose

Catherine J. Tolan

Waiting

Love lingered on while shadows
 veiled the brightness of your smile,
And days passed slowly —
 weighing heavily in despair.
But as dawn breaks through the
 veil of darkness,
Your sweet voice embraces my heart
 so that the very facet of my being
 blossoms with a feeling only you
 can reveal.

Dorothy H. Long

Discontent

I can no longer sit and watch
The water, winds and sun contend
Outside my window. Birds attack
My lethargy and lightly rend
The once protective veil of sweet
Content, with song. The droney plane
In Sunday afternoon research
Ignores my upturned eyes. The pain
Increases! Why must I pour out
My life in watching while the rest
Exult? Are up and doing — free
And going — blest in lively quest?

Audrey Botz

Plurals

If the plural of mouse
Is not mouses,
But mice.
And the plural of louse
Is not louses,
But lice.
It seems to follow to make
All things seem equal and right,
The plural of house
Shouldn't be houses,
You've guessed it — Hice

Frances Emmons

Gotta Fly

Cannot silence my smiles.
Cannot hold back my tears-
Gotta live by my dreams,
Gotta conquer my fears.

My emotions must reign,
Through sunshine or rain-
I have peace in my love,
I have lessons from pain.

Make the chills go away,
Let my wings soar up high-
Feel the sweet joy of day,
And the peace of the night.

Come and warm my soul,
Gotta let my dreams sing-
Feel the summer's warm glow,
Through the rebirth of spring.

Cannot live without love.
Cannot die without fight-
Gotta dance in the sun,
Gotta fly in the night...

Leon C. Boff

Summertime

Summertime! That is the time
To eat strawberries, to can cherries,
(How is that for a rhyme?)
To golf, to garden, to swim,
(Surely, that takes vim,)
To hike, to play tennis, to bike,
(That's done by even a little tyke,)
To travel, to fly, to mountain climb,
(Such would be sublime)
To picnic, to camp, to canoe,
(Right healthful things to do!)
To mow the lawn, to pull the weeds,
(Someone must think of good deeds,)
To only play would be a crime.
So hats off to summertime!

Neva G. Fach

Evening's Events

Dust settles
Sounds diminish
Movement falters as
Light and dark switch places
The moon replaces the sun
Dark shadows alter the view
Mere secrets become dreams
Restless minds seek peace
Day's flame goes out
Night lingers.

Rebecca Taylor

Shimmer

I lit a candle as I fell.
I found a brand new dawn.
I lit a candle as I fell,
And learned where my love had gone.
Its fire burns brighter than any before
Needing to be lit more and more.
Its light is warm but so is hell.
I lit a candle as I fell.
I lit the sky when I talked to me.
I kissed a frog. I climbed a tree.
I gave my eyes so I could see
Why my life is so empty.
I carry a cross. I carry it today.
I gave my shoes to the month of May.
I walk no farther than I did yesterday.
I lit a candle to light my way.
I lit a candle as I fell.
I'll light a candle in this hell.
I'll light a torch of holy art.
I'll light a fire in your heart.

Gerrad Gentzel

Money, Money, Money
(Beneath The Sun)

Money, money, money,
Multiplies like bun-nies,
All you need is a "pair" to lay,
To start you on your merry way,
It buys us things,
And love and power,
Just a little or a lot,
But would you sell your Soul —
Only to pay a heavy toll?
For the fun and the run
To grab your place
    Beneath the sun?

Ah-h-h! It's a greedy dream..
Would you sell-sell-sell?
I know I could,
Of course... I would,
I wonder if I should?
Money, money, money
Gimme, gimme, gimme,
Money!

M. Schutt-Gallagher

The Rose

Ah, the rose
    The blood red rose.
Who tells the story
    Of the many those;
That have lived to love
    And be loved by one.

Oh that scarlet flower
    That tells the tale
Of passion lost
    Or romance fell.

With its prickling thorns
    That scar the heart
Lending lamenting inspiration
    To this lyrical art.

Keri Calloway

The Song Leader

In Memory of Everette Sterling Kipp

Sing the golden song
Sing it, Sing it, Everette
All throughout Eternity

For with your last breath
    of precious life
God took charge with his Angels
To pave the glorious pathway
For the great Song Leader

You left us with your sweet
    and caring way
And a warm smile and laughter
    that touched the heart

Sing it, Sing it, Everette
    for us
When we're on the Glory road —
And there we'll meet you someday —
Heaven smiles now
For the great Song Leader has arrived

Susan Smeltzer

Sleepy Fisherman

You're going to fish; you get up early,
    In fact, it's way before dawn,
And on the way to your place to fish,
    You just yawn and yawn and yawn.
You reach your spot; you start to fish,
    You think of the fish to keep,
You get comfortable; you settle down,
    And pretty soon you're fast asleep.

Bill Parkstone

Someone

My blood crushes
My body and life
When I see her
My heart beats
only for her,
She is the elaborate
sweet diamond
inside me, my
words are repulsive
to her, yet she loves
my more each day
I give her my heart
in return for her
    Love
hoping we will
stay hand and hand
    forever

Harry Eelman

Teacher's Roundup

I wake up in the morning,
The sun just comin' up.
And just like Tootles in his book,
I want to smell the buttercups.
I know that work awaits me,
My heart says "Hey! Why toil?
Your bike is tuned and ready,
just pawin' at the soil".
I pack my gear and head her out,
But wait—just who are we foolin'
My roundup's at the bottom of the hill,
Just waitin' for their schoolin'.

Hilda Gaw Payne

Contentment

There's biscuits in the oven
Fried chicken in the pan
Friendly faces beamin'
On a real contented man

Don't have what folks call riches
Ain't got a tropic tan
But the sun shines while I fishes
On a real contented man

Bet there's plenty fellows wishin'
As world affairs they plan
They could quit and start a bein'
Just a real contented man.

Vera Louise Anderson

My Calls of Lust

The wheels on the bus go round
While I watch your hands move
The wheels on the bus go round
and round on the paved road
While I try to talk to you
The wheels continue to move
But you don't hear
You don't hear what I have to say
I strain my vocal cords
Until my voice is heard no more
No one heard me say
What I had to say
No one heard me say
Dustin I like you
Not one person heard my calls of lust

Jessica Vibber

Summerlin

Sun touched mountains shine bold
Amber, yellow, bronze and gold
Gazing way up in the sky
Colors change as time goes by
Clouds all sizes colors and shapes
Disappear without a trace
Looking up enlightens me
Warm golden tones to set you free
The sun set on the mountains face
Oh what divine beauty from God's grace
Take this moment in your life
and cherish it with all your might
The sun disappears and all is dark
As I sit in this lonely park
And so it's time to close my eyes
To wake and find a new surprise
of my home place called Summerlin
Where beauty lies forever within

Teri Thomason

Little Frog

Little frog in a tree
Sitting happy as can be
Climbing, croaking in the night
Seems to give some a fright
Splash in water like a fool
But to you it is real cool
To frogs flies are a treat
But to us they are not neat
We hunt them down to be our pets
Once we have them there are regrets
Outside they hide away
In hopes no one will disturb their play
And in all I'm trying to say
Please just let them have their way

Ashleigh Williams

Life

Life is a gift the quality of
That gift is made by all who
impact that life.

Lisa Dillon

Hold On

Do I vow to speak no more,
For wrath has passed over these lips.
Do I share not for what's been gained,
In fear that I give in mistrust.
Do I lock myself away,
Not knowing who I am.
Do I give up my faith in God,
For what I think I am.
I say not, to all.
May you humble me Lord,
To get down on bended knees;
And thank you God my Father,
For showing me the help I need.
Give me the faith to know,
When you cut down my tree;
That I will grab onto your roots
And when I grow
This time around,
My blossoms will be of Thee.

Donna G. King

Sweetheart

I thought that maybe you would like
to know, that someone's thoughts go
where you go. That someone never can
forget, the hours we spent since first
we met. That life is richer, sweeter
far, due to the sweetheart that you
are, and now my constant prayer
will be, that God will keep you
safe for me.

Vivian Warren

Sovereign

Can you see the glory
of man's rebirth
In towering monuments
and a heaven here on earth

Do you know that
freedom's in sight
For the man who
lives by individual right

Beyond the rage
and hatred of old
man has turned
his spirit to gold

A temple has been erected
to the strengthening reign
of an intransigent mind
and reason, the pillars that bind

So the fires rage on
in a breathless sky
for the man who is sovereign
none can deny

Mark D. Yeskis

The Light's On In Heaven

Last night I saw Jesus,
    I looked into his face.
I wondered why he had come
    To this painful place.
He came through a tunnel
    Of beautiful light
To calm my daddy's pain,
    His suffering and fright.
Jesus reached down and touched him,
    And to my surprise,
Daddy looked up and smiled
    And said, "I tried".
Then with a flash,
    The light got bright again.
And they were both gone
    Through the tunnel that brought him.
We will all miss him
    For a long time, you see,
Because he was the kind of man
    We would all like to be.

Mary A. Batytes

The Christmas Rose

In a manger long ago
in the stillness of the night,
a child was born to save the world
a child of love and light.

As Mary and her husband
gazed upon his face,
they knew that he was sent by God
to save the human race.

For all the pain and joy to come
to save the world below,
silent tears from all three
fell to mingle in the snow.

As the tears melted through
and soaked into the sand,
a rose as red as blood grew up
and reached out to touch his hand.

With his touch the flower's color
changed to brilliant white,
to teach that there is always hope
as day does follow night.

June M. Wescott

Black Monday

Black Monday
stoned dazed in pain
my hole I stay,
I'm a creep plays
never see day break
never want to see the day,
dead to the world,
I stay
Every day is black Monday!
I stone out the pain
but they come back as demons!
Another take on that LSD!!!!!
A trip to terror,
I screamed!
So I take another hit on that LSD!
It blackens to a dark dim
it's another black trip, and.
Every day is a black Monday!

Joshua D. Hiebert

The Darkened Mist

For me, the mist was never parting
My hope was never ever starting
No light would ever be shining
No one could hear, oh hear my crying
No visitors came to take my place
A saddened look marked my face

The darkened mist seemed never to part
A shadow deep fell upon my heart
A guide I needed to set me free
One who was here and knew me
But no one was there to show the way
I was alone, my friends turned away

But oh behold, what do I spy?
Looking, a tear escapes my eye
A person bearing a sword of light
To cut away my endless night
A friend with friendship to spare
Helping me from my burden to bear

James Stuart

Timeless Time

Time is timeless
Like waves to ebb and flow
To touch the earth and then return
To where we do not know.

You and I are placed on earth
A moment in God's time
To seek and find from our birth
His gift from knowledge - vine.

To fill our hearts and very souls
With the bread of life He gives
To let Him gently take control
Where His seed of wisdom lives.

This is a temporary place
A place for us to fill
To see if we fit in His grace
Of matchless love and will.

For waves that beat upon the shore
Never linger long
For they retreat to sing once more
His wondrous, timeless song.

Adlain R. Culver

My Wife

My wife is my life
My wife is my love
Her hair so beautiful
Her eyes like a dove

My wife has been with me
Through thick and through thin
And hopefully someday
I'll be with her again

I've tried so many ways
To run my own life
I'd never made it
Without my loving wife

So with these thoughts
so fresh in my mind
I'll thank you Lord
For sparing your time.

Fred E. Jones Sr.

My Deliverer

In my night of desperation
it seems I can't go on.
I lift my eyes to Jesus
he helps me see the dawn.
I am weak from faithful praying,
the way I cannot see.
With groans and words unspoken,
the spirit speaks for me.
On knees I bow before him,
he knows my every need.
I whisper "are you listening?"
And the spirit intercedes.
A new strength overwhelms me,
as tears roll down my face.
Christ is my deliverer,
he fills me with his grace.

L. Audrey Merrill

Spring

Spring is in the air,
As I breathe its greenery,
Months of new beginnings,
Between Mother Nature and me.

The trees have given birth,
To the buds upon their limbs,
The ground has new grown seedlings,
Ready to begin.

I walk with Mother Nature,
Ready to explore,
An ever changing world,
Waiting outside my front door.

When life delivers hardships,
Smell the roses along the way,
Cause as one knows, above it all -
Be grateful for each new day.

Thank you Mother Nature,
For the beauty that you share,
For life should be to live and see,
Not to sit and stare!

Pam Miedl

Life's Cup

The old man walked along the road
his face toward the west
stopping now at a grassy spot
his weary legs to rest

His thoughts went back to his boyhood
when along this same road he had run
his barefeet flying o'er the ground
his red cheeks kissed by the sun

How slowly those days had passed
the small boy growing up
how swiftly now they seemed to fly
how shallow was life's cup

His back was bent, his hair was gray,
how dim now were his eyes.
his lips moved slowly as if to pray
as his soul skipped through the skies.

Wanda Fannin

To My Sons

Pondering my mortality
I look at you and see
The spirit that enlivens you
Was once a part of me.

You are my immortality
Through you I cannot die
This world that I will leave one day
I'll see yet through your eyes.

My love will not go from you
The hope, the faith, the tears.
But keep their place within you
To warm you through your years.

Gone but not forgotten
The memory that persists
The force that death can't conquer
The love that time resists.

Janette B. Marks

Walking Friends

I have a friend who walks with me.
We meet most everyday.
We walk and talk and laugh a lot,
And pass the time away.
We've made some friends while walking,
And we sometimes stop to chat.
We take some friendly kidding,
But we're getting used to that.
We speak on many subjects,
From poetry to news,
And sometimes of our childhood,
Or anything we choose.
Sometimes we sit upon a bench,
We like to take a rest,
Then we continue walking
As the sun sinks in the west.
Soon we reach our parting place,
It's time we say good-night,
We'll meet again tomorrow
If God turns on His light.

Nancy L. Goode

America

Turn on the television.
What do you see?
It's all over the newscasts.
Deceit and hatred are reality.

Children are being laid to rest
As an entire nation cries,
While a child without any parents
Sadly questions why.

How do we end the terror
That we must face everyday?
Who gives one person the right
To take so much away?

Can we stop the hatred?
Will we ever win the war?
Or will we just die trying
To even the score?

If America is so beautiful
And the land is for the free,
Why must we live in fear
Of humanity?

Chris Scopa

I'm Waiting

Here I sit, my arms clutched
around my legs, my chin resting
on my knees.
  I'm waiting.
It feels like I'm on top of
the world, though it's just a
hill with some trees.
  I'm waiting.
The feeling of being out so late,
no! It's out so early, just
doing something different
and fun.
  I'm waiting.
Oh! It's 6:00 am; there it is
big, bright and beautiful,
the sun.

Mary Berger

The Twining Woodbine

The Woodbine twines around the door
of the shack that I lived in.
The tumbling walls once held the lore
of frames with old oil paintings.

The fireplace still is standing there.
All the rocks are falling out.
The woodbine's pushing through the gaps
and shoving them about.

The walkway that led to the door
is overgrown with weeds.
It still remains to show the way,
betwixt the rows of trees.

Nostalgia overcomes the mind
of all memoirs before.
The reaching shoots of Woodbine still
are twining around the door.

Glen Bowles

A Lesson of Life

I'm out of school at last
Graduation, the magic word-hurray's!
Away from this dreary past
On to new places, the world awaits!

So many years I've anticipated
Getting away from all ties
Into the real world-awaited
To meet new people-different, alive!

My work days are over at last
Retirement, the magic word - hurray's!
Away from this dreary past
Back to old places, home awaits!

So many years I've anticipated
Coming home-my days to spend
Familiar faces awaited
To welcome me home - friends!

Thelma Porter

Clouds

Clouds so high,
Up in the sky,
Far, far, far,
So far away,
They look like
So many different things,
I wish I could reach
Up and pull one down.

Amanda White

Love

If I could be a thing
Unconsciously viewed by you,
But necessary, as a door
That you pass through;

Or maybe I could be a book
You leaf through
With a thoughtless look;

Or maybe just a window pane
Through which you gaze
At snow or rain.

I'd be most anything you say
If I could see you every day.

Rebecca E. Pfizenmayer

I'll Keep You Always

Walk beside me darling,
I will live for you.

Walk beside me darling,
I will breath for you.

I will search for happiness,
Then share its warmth with you.

A love so strong as are love;
is shared by very few.

Judy Gardner

Why

Why are we here
If only to see

Why are we here
If only to walk

Why are we here
If only to talk

Why are we here
To bring life to this world

Why are we here
To love each other

Why are we here
To bring cultures together

Why are we here
To search for the answer

Why are we here
To leave with the answer

What if there is no answer
Why not...World Peace

Roberta Welch

(Realm of Life Itself)

The strength that lies within
  the realm of life itself
Bears out the weight of all fatigue
Keeps ruin from coming in to sight
Keeps cold from coming in the night
Keeps us from even worse plights
Of savage hunger and ruinous pain
Or nothing but death would remain
And hell would always come again
But of all passions life does ensconce.
Heaven only comes just once
To beat off death and fight the night
To bring love to set all things right

Frances H. Green

"Sparkle"

I tried to take small steps,
So my son could keep in stride.

I tried to live a life,
To give him a name with pride.

I have no fame or fortune,
To help him down life's road.

But there are more important things,
Than that that's made of gold.

Man's soul is the glitter,
To our God up on high.

A son is the sparkle,
In a proud daddy's eye.

Now when my life is over,
And all the joy's been had,

I hope he'll truly say,
I'm glad he was my dad.

Perry R. Tharp

Giving

Though Life is precious,
  its crooks and turns,
are always a matter,
  of personal concern.

We try to look ahead,
  prepare for tomorrow,
avoid if we can,
  what gives us only sorrow.

If we succeed,
  Life is thought worthwhile,
though our mode of living,
  is not the grand style.

Most of us settle,
  for the basics of living,
the solid comforts of home,
  which are always giving.

Luke N. Baxter

Love Is...

Love is you. Love is me.
Love is all we want it to be.
Love is trust. Love is real.
Love is always there to heal.
Love is hope. Love is true.
Love is knowing I'm here for you.
Love is learning. Love is all,
Love is there when you take a fall.
Love is comfort and self-esteem.
Love is knowing love's all you need.
Love is sharing. Love is wealth.
Love is power and all you've felt.
Love is precious. Love is gold.
Love is priceless it can't be sold.
Love is happiness. Love is life.
Love is taking one day at a time.
Love is wanting to be loved.
Love is knowing love is enough.
Love is one. Love is whole.
Love is ever so much more.

Marina Rios

A Winter Kitten

Peeking, peeking
the almond eyes
are seeking shelter.
A gust of freezing
wind sends a whisker
and patch of fur
billowing.
He is beckoning me,
"come out",
drawing attention
with a longing look
in his eyes.
He is a feline pharaoh
capturing us all
with his spirit.

Carolyn Ramsden

"Prisoners Of Darkness"

Prisoners of Darkness
talk to me, tell me
of your pain and misery!

Tell me of your life of Crimes
that sent you to this insane
bed of hell to do your time—

Where there's Drugs
and no Corporation, all tolerated
by a sick administration!

Prisoners of Darkness
talk to me. Tell me of the alcohol
that flows so freely—

Tell me about the Warden
who sees it all but turns her face
to the walls!

Tell me about the Sex
between the Guards and Inmates,
about their love than turns to hate—

Oh! Prisoners of Darkness
talk-to-me!

Patsy Y. Leavenworth

Reflections of a Caregiver

This little lady whose
Weathered life's storms
Falls ever so weakly into
Any one's arms

Her smile so precious
Her touch so sweet
The eyes of an angel
A baby at sleep

Now look at the faces
You encounter today
And ponder the future!
Unknown, wouldn't you say

Except for the watch
Of a powerful eye
And a grace so merciful
Here lies you and I

Betty F. Hester

The Strength That Lies Within

(The Sister Darkness)

Then falls the darkness
Of a moonless night
A woman journeys on
In brilliant blindness
Carrying her burdens and joys
In her heart
And protecting
The evil cloak of darkness
From harming her soul

Many think her
Delicate and fragile
Demanding protection
And forbid her to venture
Into night's bleak blackness

Her simple asylum
Her escape from the burning light
Darkness softly
Wraps around her
Guarding this sister
In comfort and enrage

Debra Cady-Kleinschmidt

Perceptions

Sailboats sailing, some boats failing
To catch the wind in stride;
And in the sun some others run
To chase the oceans tide.

The docile whale shows his tail
To all who want to see;
The gulls that fly, they glide and try
To show us what is free.

So why can't I, a simple guy,
perceive this way of life?
Why must it be so solitary...
And never-ending strife?

For to survive, I'll dare to strive
To be the world itself.
I'll fight for life without the strife
Not sit up on the shelf!

Laurence M. Burke

A Proud Old House

I often wonder —
   Is it standing — still —
That proud old house
   upon the hill —

The flowing creek —
My favorite place
   for hide and seek.

Each time I stroll
   down Memory Lane,
I know that soon I'll see —
   A proud old house
   upon the hill,
      that means so much,
      to me

Mary E. Sterling

A Mothers Wish

Be patient
As I try out my wings
There's no much to learn
So many little things

being a mother
Is no easy task
Be patient my children
That's all that I ask

The love I feel for you
None can compare
With life so hard
It's the only thing that's fair

Be patient my children
For I've much to learn
Love me, guide me
That's all I yearn

I'll hold your hand
As you go through life's trials
With you I'll walk life's miles

Lisa Copley

Because I Love You

I love you like a brother
I love you like a friend
Whenever I need you
You are right around the bend

You know me better than anyone
You know me better then me
Whenever I am blinded
You teach me how to see

You know how I feel
Better then I
You comfort me when I am lonely
You hold me when I cry

You know what I need
By the look on my face
An encouraging word
Or a gentle embrace

I have but one fear
That our time will soon be through
And the only reason it scares me
Is because I Love You!

Jessica Anderson

When the Swallow Decamped

When the swallow decamped
There was no other attempt
There was no thought of return
But to fly far and away
Behind the bower an acacia has bloomed
And the gardener never saw her
With her thought of the rain
In the loneliness of wind
She had her dream...
There was a voice
A call of nothing
And no gardener, ever
Looked behind the bower, never...
And the acacia
In the hands of wind
And the loneliness of her dream
Was forgotten...
And the swallow
Decamped her memory
To the forgotten city.

Annahita Mahdavi

Dana

Little does my lover know
Just how much I love her, so
Perhaps, tonight, God will deem
To send me to her in a dream.

I will take her in my fierce embrace
And shower kisses upon her face,
Then hold her 'til the dream is done
At break of day, when comes the sun.

And perchance upon the morrow morn,
She'll find love in her bosom born:
A love for me inside her heart,
As mine, tonight, I do impart.

Please, dear God, grant this request!
Feel the passion in my chest!
Let me love her in a dream,
And let it to her as Truth seem!

Daniel Kevin Scott

"In Memory Of Mother"

Mothers shouldn't be
    the first to die.
They're here when we laugh,
They're here when we cry.
There is never a time
    when they're not in need,
And whatever the crisis
They are there indeed.
The hand of a mother
Is a comforting thing,
But, we never think
    of the sorrow we bring.
A tower of strength, a statue
    so tall,
No thought of herself,
But time for us all.
So, God, in His wisdom,
    knowing it all,
We'll lay her to rest
At His beck and call.

Elsie St. Martin

Eclipse

Give me back that kinder world
where doors were left
unlocked.

Where neighbors, lended time and
care unhurried by the clock

Where children laughed yelled and
cried at their outdoor games.

Hide-go-seek and statues until,
parents called our names.

Where Mom was there to tend a
scrape wipe away a tear.

She'd fill the place with yummy
smells and love throughout
the year.

Where dreams and hopes were
close, as summer stars.
No limits no walls no bars.

Evil will out if it could
Don't let the bad eclipse the good.

Alice Reynolds

Untitled

A life time of hope
a life time of dreams
flushed down the toilet
don't know what they mean
the hope of the dawn
the newness of day
what does it mean?
Say what you say
the hopes and the dreams
after school they are through
they mean nothing - nothing
not even to you.
Where did they go
when brushed to the side
why can't I find them?
Why must they hide?
I feel the tears crying
And I feel the heart long
for those days when my life
was all but a song.

Kate Harrop

Mine

If I can dream of life,
Can I live in a dream?
At least until - it
Is rejoined with its real,
Then the I becomes who
For whoever was there.

Life though so cruel can still
Dream a dream of real-
ity where my thoughts are
real yet real thoughts by those
Who live for real are still
there, just the same as mine.

Still I want to know if
Real thoughts live on and can.
Are we dead yet? This is
still faulty mine, but then
Mine self I don't live for.

Sean Reilly

You're the Coolest

You're so perfect,
You have the greatest talents.
You never think negative,
Your priorities are balanced.

There's not a flaw in anything you do,
And you know how to follow your dreams.
You're not afraid to do what it takes,
No matter how hard it seems.

You always make me laugh,
Because you are so funny.
When it seems like a gloomy day,
You always make it sunny.

You're an awesome person,
And my heart goes out to you.
I'll be there one hundred percent,
In everything you do.

Virginia Anthony

Open!

The wind, the sea, the plea
it's like the answer to a key.
It's like a cup of tea with me
you flee to be free.

Lacey Ann Richards

Hearts

Hearts of stone, all alone,
Hearts of fire, irk and ire;
Many a dove knows not love,
Many a child, life not mild;
Souls feel pain, eyes cry rain,
Ego pride, dead inside.

Hearts so warm, cannot harm,
Hearts of love, rise above;
Skin not bruised, child not used,
Sun doth shine, life divine;
Friends that care, love to share,
Heart can cope, ray of hope.

Blake D. Schindler

Everything Is You

Your touch, the walk, your smile,
your talk, caressed with
softening passion. Love, lust,
your soothing embrace.
Making any and everyone
long for your powerful
body, your magnificent eyes,
your tongue soothing
touch. Your tuff outside,
softened by disguise.

Nolie MacDonald

Free

The shadow of death is
buried deep inside.

My soul is free, like a
eagle souring in the sky.

The truth is out there
some nights I stare deep
into the sky.
Wondering why it had to be me.

It haunts me sometimes
but now I show no fear.

For I am strong and better
than fear. Though sometimes
it might be near.

I pray and keep strong
knowing that I'll prove it wrong.

I've come a long way
and I'll get better each day.

For they are proud can't you see
there's no more mask on me
so it's better that I am free.

Junie Smith

I Wish... Parallel Poem

I wish I had two million dollars
I wish I had a dog with fifty dollars
I wish I had my very own zoo
I wish it had lions and tigers and
even bears too
I wish I had all of wet seals clothes
I wish I had Eckerds, Rave, Mc'D
Teen Angel, and Moe's
I wish that when I grow up
I will sell lemonade
in little orange cups.

Ariela Friedman

How Far

How far is the sky?
How high does it go?
I wish I could float away

Out over the ocean
Past starlight and dusk
Into another day

Of sorrowless tears
And intimate love
And lives that never grow gray

But alas, I am doomed
The world's perilous gloom
Has banished tomorrow away

And so I remain
Enveloped in pain
Faced with the torture, I stay

Locked in my life
Of ongoing strife
The concept of horror I pray.

Oriyah Yoran

From A Distant View I See Him

I look down the hill,
And I see him.
So close,
But yet he knows not that
I see him.

He is handsome,
But yet He
Knows it not.

He smiles, and my heart
Beats faster.
Yet I am afraid to
Show it.

He looks at me, and I
Melt within his gaze.
Yet he knows nothing.

Oh, for him to know.
Yet he might suspect.

I look down to gaze
Upon him. Yet he has
Vanished.

Jill M. Darden

My Pet Tornado

I had a pet Tornado,
Chained up to the fence,
He just sat there,
Like an elephant's rest.
One day, I saw him,
Break his rusty, old chains,
He got away,
And raced through the plains.
The people shouted, "Go away!"
But he wouldn't budge.
They gave him fruits and ice cream,
But still, he ate the fudge.
He tore down the people's houses,
And ripped them apart.
Finally I found him,
Destroying playful parks.
Using my destroyer,
I zapped him with a loud zap,
And a little bit of Tornado,
Landed in my lap.

Leah and Trevor Dahmer

The Death of Day, the Birth of Night

The birth of night,
Happens at the death of day,
When the sun sinks down,
Down to lay.

Brilliant stars appear,
Then a silver moon,
The night draws the world,
Into her cocoon.

In peaceful slumber,
All deeply sleep,
In moonlights
   and starlights
Keep.

Then comes the birth of day,
Gold and silver,
   in every way.

The night blanket is then shed,
For day is so clear,
Night is over,
Day is here.

Elizabeth Hammond

Forever's Touch

Beyond our world's hateful ways,
There's a beauty existing in itself;
And once you have seen it,
You can not turn away.
A light falls upon you
That will never go dark
Its beams warm the coldness
Which the outside world has brought.
You are uplifted on its wings
Soaring through the heavens,
And the soul begins to tremble
In all of its beauty and grace.
The doors of happiness
Are bound to close on your heart;
And there is not room enough
For the evil outside of its world.
They are cast away like shadows
The beauty surpasses them
Leaving a place in the soul
That has been touched forever.

Michele Dammeyer

"Heaven"

Heaven might be beautiful
Beautiful Angels are floating
birds fly across the sky and
heaven
Heaven, heaven, heaven!
Oh Lord, why is heaven
so beautiful?!
Angels are flying around
The golden sun is up in
heaven
The angels play their music
their favorite music is
classical!
I can tell that heaven is -
beautiful!!!

Ashlee Holland

Echoes

Echoes that carry your name,
through my mind and soul.
Flowing voices that can only be heard,
by my aching heart,
yearning for your love to enter,
that sacred place,
in my being,
that has been empty,
since the moment,
you closed the doors,
to my undying devotion.

Jivelle I. Callender

Sister

Sister's on a journey
But she knows not where
And we all judge and wonder.
Take it like a big girl
And get a tat too!
Shave your head
Then go to bed
With someone you don't know.
Miles stretch behind us
Switching roles
Big sister, little sister.
Where are we now?
Bad dad
Made you mad.
Sister's on a journey
And she don't know where.
Pretend you don't care.

But I love you!

J. S. Bozeman

Heaven And Hell

SoIn this hell we call life,
With all of its pains, its sorrows,
Its grief, and its strife.

It seems like forever,
That I have struggled against fate.
I have fought so hard,
To cope with my anger and hate.

So many times I lose myself,
Amongst a sea of sorrow and tears.
I think of how long I have to go,
Before I conquer all my pain and fears.

And now I realize,
That heaven is still very far.
But in the end I know,
Heaven is knowing who you are!

Gabriel Sison

Secret of Life

   I see you in my mind but I
don't know what I see.
   I hear you in my heart but I
don't know what I hear.
   I feel you in my soul but I don't
know what I feel.
      You're what keeps me all one part.
You're what keeps us all going all day
   and all night.
I wish I knew what you were
   So I'd know the secret of life.

Megan K. Morehead

What Yellow Is, Perhaps

Yellow is Kool-aid,
on a humid summer day,
yellow is a swing,
on which you slowly sway.
Yellow is a love letter,
crinkled up and old.
And now (but not too often),
it's sour and repulsive mold.
Book marks, slug bugs,
Pencils, shawls
sleeping pills, lakers
even signs on shopping malls.
Yellow is polite,
easy going, and clean.
Definitely trustworthy,
Never cruel or mean.
Yellow is the color,
when you swim a lot of laps.
That's what yellow is,
What yellow is, perhaps.

Ashley Sullivan

The Canoe

Rhythmic row and vessel glide
metal frame to wood and hide.

Gray and short to dark and long
skin of white to brown and firm.

Vessel noises to drumming change
ancestral calls the frequent sound.

Mind resists the need to rest
as refuge calls for calm to give.

Why resist peace of ancient life
and cling to pain of current race.

I long for days of simpler times
to ease the grip of mind and chest.

Mark Sylvester

The Comforter

An angle by my bedside
A companion in the day
Since you left me months ago
The Lord has always stayed
He dries my tears, takes my fears
Holds my hand when no ones near
The comforter comes day by day
Supplies my needs along the way
Holds my hand and pulls me near
This comforter, I hold so dear
The nights are cold, the days are long
With him to guide, I can't go wrong
No matter what life holds for me
By my side he'll always be
Attention from his loving hand
Strength from him my soul demands
He gave his life upon the cross
To lose my soul he'd count it a loss
I must go on for him you see,
I can't do less, he died for me

Shonda Stokes

The Love Once Known

Of purest love
    That I once known
Deep in my heart
    Its memory remains
Scattered dreams
    I now possess
Love once known
    My heart confess

How I miss thou
    The love in life
Secret of Success
    To be without
    To be without
So long it has been
    So empty life's
    Been without

Emotional ties
    And I travel on...

John Gian

Prayers

I prayed for blessings
And the Lord answered my prayers
With challenges.

I prayed for wisdom
And the Lord answered my prayers
With experience.

I prayed for strength
And the Lord answered my prayers
With trials.

And now the prayer of my heart
Is thanksgiving
For through my
Challenges,
Experiences,
And trials,
I have received
Strength, and
Wisdom
And most of all
Great blessings.

Florene D. Henderson

Truly Love

Sincerely love first appear,
When a man and a woman,
looks at each one
and guessing never tear apart.
The magic of true love
in this world is everywhere,
no other feeling is so great
for all of us to feel nice.
Experiment in so many ways,
wherever we may be...
Like twinkling stars at nite,
Flowers in colors bright,
Thing that money can't buy,
Sunny days through darkest night
Petals danced early to the ground,
The begin, the end, the light;
These are but few of endless,
Wonders feelings of honest love.
I am glad that god has given me,
The love of truly love.

Juan A. Paredes

"Cradle Carriage"

That innumerable part of me
passing underneath
I am crossing
I am planting my feet one on one
I am crafting
I am pushing my soles upstream

That innumerable part of us
passing through
we are crossing
we are planting our feet two on two
we are crafting
we are pushing our soles upstream

There's a brightness out there
underneath and through
that we must cross
plant our feet
craft our position
and push ourselves against a current
mush like the space between us

Eric C. Villines

Generations

The movement of time
Through the ages rings
Of good and of bad
And of changes he brings.

Time reveals contrasts,
Through pictures and thoughts,
In days remembered,
People, places now lost.

Pictures of women,
Generations past,
They provide us all
With memories that last.

We knew them one time;
We were together.
We all remember
That time gone forever.

They live in us all,
Though they are not here.
In our hearts and souls
They live on and are near.

Barbara Glass

No. 5 In Pining Sequence

Ars gratia artis
is as impossible as
kindness gratia kindness is.

Ulterior motive,
Double objective,
Two birds with one stone,
How else can we own
up to our deeds,
serve another's needs,
without knowing the recipients
of our sincere beneficence,
even the deaf and the blind
will perceive us as kind?

Does being conscious
and desirous
of avoiding it
make you legitimate?

John R. Quinn

Silence

Television on. Radio loud.
Puffs of smoke. Gulps of beer.
Belt hitting. Smell of fear.
Sad eyes. No crying allowed.

Silence.

Breathing shallow. Head splitting.
Bed creaking. People screaming.
Face slapped. Tears streaming.
Dark corner. Child sitting.

Silence.

Lonely. Scared. Dark.
Hollering. Doors slamming.
Hand burning. Fire flaming.
Pain. Shaking. Dog bark.

Silence.

Sirens whaling. People running.
Dark closet. Someone shoving.
Pure hatred. No loving.
Gun shooting. Bullets stunning.
Silence.

Holly Furman-Hanrahan

Needs of a Child

Mother, Mother
My life is in a mess
Indeed I'm trying my very best
It's tuff I must confess

Mother, Mother
I miss your words
Words of wisdom
Left Unheard

Mother, Mother
Reach out to me
Mother, Mother
Give me hope I can see

Lamar Yulee

Jock

Macho and big is his walk
Tough and cool is his talk

His mighty mask is never down
In fear the real him might be found

Succeeding in sports is his grove
To the world he has to prove

Working hard to make the grade
In the spotlight he must not fade

His feeling are rarely shown
Which makes him feel all alone

Inside his mask he has to hide
When real happiness is found inside

Sara Rutherford

Shadowman

Inside is the little person,
The one who knows everything.
A wretched child
Trapped in a wretched adult,
Who wanders the nights
In search of the deepest shadow,
The quietest silence,
The least resistance.
The animal without compassion,
The illness with no reprieve.

And yet comes the softness,
The need and the yearning
To be more than a predator,
The hot excitement of being the prey,
The eager heartbeat,
The molten sheen
On the surface of the skin,
Devoured in the end.

Bernie Shwayder

Untitled

When first she saw the tiny, soft face,
And touched the silken head,
And laid her cheek upon the place,
A sword would make its bed,
Did she cry a little?

When He grasped her finger with His infant hand,
Which a nail would someday pierce,
Did her eyes fill up and overflow, and bathed His
Check with tears?

When she warmed this lovely child next to her virgin heart,
Did she foresee this flesh, so fragrant and sweet,
Bleeding, broken and torn apart,
While she lay crumpled at His dying feet?
Did then she cry?

Or was this joy of mother with Son so great,
That this short-lived possession was worth,
The tears, the sorrow, the fearful fate,
Now dimmed by His joyous birth.

Christine Borders

Addiction

Insanity.
A moment of reality rushes through you
Only long enough to escape once again
into the distorted truth
of who you are, and where you've been,
only you can't recall.
Escape from the past and present,
only temporarily,
'till the incessant pain rushes in
and bludgeons your mind.
Once translucent thoughts become incomprehensible.
Strung out, scared and helpless
you cry once again.
Denial and falseness become you.
Your identity is gone, to where is unclear.
Manifested in words and actions
that you know weren't yours.
Live to use and use to live.
Just for today,
And hope that tomorrow won't come.

Sena J. Larabee

Untitled

Until the crystal blue appears
upon horizon's tender brow
and gulls of white and ebony
begin their ancient morning call,
Until the sand appears as dry
as all Sahara's ever known
and waves of blissful tenderness
begin to rush the great unknown,
Until the morning star is gone
my love, so everlasting been,
this night will last forever on
and never cease to come again.

Joani Durandette

The Metamorphosis

Change, people change, change their hair from blond to brunette
to redhead, from straight to curly, from long to short
Change their clothes, change their minds
Change for a dollar minster-don't take any wooden nickels
Change from happy to sad, change from good to best to baaaaaad
Change occurs as quickly and as quietly as milk turning sour
Change their jobs-more money please, change their wife
Change their life—to—death—to life
Every ending is a new beginning, change from democratic to republican
Vote for me I'll set you free, change their face from young to old
Change their religion, I want a new God, change their race,
we got some new slaves, the rich become the poor,
winter turns to spring, snow turns to rain
Love melts into pain, change their sex—o—no—o—yes
The names have been changed to protect the innocent
The game still remains the same, changing horses in the middle
of the stream, papa got a brand new bag, what's hip today,
tomorrow may be passe', don't change up on me now, take me with u,
can't teach an old dog new tricks, because that's the way of time,
everything must change, nothing remains the same

W. King

To My Beloved Father/Grandfather — Husband

Daddy, at my first you scare me so but somehow you never let go
You gave love, love, limitless love

Daddy, you withheld the rod and spoiled the child, you preferred a
Yes, you love, love, loved all the while

Daddy, you were the one that was Always there
With love, love, love without fear

Daddy, love is a word we ignored in the past but now I say at last
I love, love you above all cost

Daddy, time is the length we can't predict
So continue to love, enjoy, relax — don't quit

We must forget the unchangeable past 'cause God gave us the task
To love and care for each other — don't ask

Daddy, Maw and I will always be by your side; we'll all be your guide
Because we love, love, love you without pride

Janet Gordon-Small

Interstate Indian, Looking For His Horse

I am the Indian chasing my horse over the next hill.

Until the streetlights come on, for then I find myself
Caught up in an overwhelming liaison
With a jealous, impossibly gorgeous moon.

The moon she leaves me wailing for my raisin-eyed Pocahontas.
In my song which becomes my breath, which is only my ache,
I am sending an acoustic transmission at the top of my voice.

Oh how it must stagger up to the moon, drunk on her radiance,
Pleading for broadcast onto the never-ending station of pop-song
Sunrises, onto the other side of night.

Frustrated and foolish I jump on the king-sized mattress
Of the interstate, waiting for an answer from the moon,

Throwing little Indian boy tantrums, for I know my transmission
Will fade away before it can climb to my raisin-eyed Pocahontas.

She won't turn on the station from the other side of day,
To hear the wail of an Anglo-Saxon Indian along the freeway.

I bask on hands and knees in front of the impossibly gorgeous moon,
Wondering how very possible we are.

And I am just over the next hill,

Looking once again for my horse.

Matthew Todd Meldrum

Blurry And Washed Away By The Rain

I like to think of her.
A life and words in the margin,
atmosphere of living on the edge,
about to fall off
this is no pretty pink umbrella holding lady
on a tightrope in a gaily patterned
tent, but a women on a thin line
holding on to the remnants
of a life. She once was famous
she once was rich. Drink took the fame,
husband, the money.
Balance is all important,
those who say it couldn't get any worse
lie.
She could lose her signed picture
"To Patti, Love——". She can't read
the signature. It's been washed away by the rain.
The picture is blurry, but it reminds her of what
she once was, and with it, though she has nothing else,
she is happy.

M. Samuels-Kalow

The Fly That I Killed

It was just an ordinary housefly that I killed!
    Poor little creature, I didn't give it any quarter:
So small and full of life - I thought, should it be stilled?
    Came to my mind, as it lay on its side: "Martyr!"

I stooped and looked at it, and felt a little queer!
    I gently moved the fly, and could plainly see it now.
I blew my breath upon it, and my heart with that fly did stir!
    I alone was to blame - somehow, I wanted God to know!

They say, "a fly carries germs"- a finer use I'm sure he deserves!
    But I didn't choose to see, I did away with the fly to be.
Well - there's a hell they tell me, that awaits the bad such as I
    None worse than I will they find; for I gave hell to a fly!

Stephen Fetchko

Untitled

I am your brother; I look just like you
I know who you are and you know who I am too.

There's just one difference between you and me
You are healthy, but I have HIV

Don't back off, and don't shy away
I have HIV, not full blown AIDS

I know I'm different, I have a disease
I'm asking for kindness, so give it to me please

We've been friends for so long, don't let this come between us now

I know that this is hard to handle
Trust me, I know, but I've come to terms with it somehow

Don't look at me strange, questioning why

There are times when I ask myself the same question,
then break down and cry

Times are hard for me right now without a friend
wondering what will happen to me in the end

So please, tell me you'll stick with me til I'm gone
I don't think I can handle this all alone

So be my friend, til the end and hold my hand, where I stand
Remember me always and smile, even if just for a little while.

Glendora M. Ratcliff

Those Blooming Flowers

The happy little crocus gives a friendly glow,
    Dressed in different colors, they pop up in the snow,
The daffy little daffodils come up in the spring,
    Wearing gowns of yellow, they do their own thing.
Dandelion seeds are blown by the breezes,
    That's why he comes up wherever he pleases.
Daisies don't tell, and violets are shy,
    If flowers could talk, I'd ask them "Why?"
Pansy faces smile when the weather is hot.
    The mums say, "oh! My dear, forget me not!"
Sweet peas and ivy all climb a fence.
    They don't get anywhere - that doesn't make much sense.
Fields of poppies and clover, and sunflowers, too
    Lift up their heads in the early morning's dew.
Gardens of flowers, blooming by the dozens -
    Tulips, aster, roses, - they're all second cousins.
Poinsettias for Christmas - make a great gift
    by the tree with bright packages - give everyone a lift.
So pick a bouquet of those blooming flowers.
    They'll bring much pleasure, for many happy hours.

Margaret Thornton

The Order of Things

The women gathered hovering like so many hens.
Each watching the other with a trace of suspicion.
The air was dense with the intensity
of each woman's thoughts.
I wonder if she likes me?
Slowly the women separated
selecting one group or another.
The selection was most deliberate
and left no question.
Tall, short, brown, yellow,
slim, heavy, blonde, red.
The separation was profound
almost deafening in its expression.

But what is this in the corner?
A group of women awkwardly
moving toward each other.
Small, tall, thin, black, white
How dare they upset
the order of things?

Jackie Booker

The Seventh Madrigal

Wooden flute tempo, lithe lute high on air,
A Queen, Oh; Faire Lady, ... How art thou faire?
Gallery of Minstrels, attending the Queen,
The fairest; Dear Lady, None the world e'er I seen.
\Magic winds flowing, yon harp do I hear?
Gaily drums singing, lending an ear, ...
Oh; Dear Faire Maiden, dance out to the Fair,
Come; My Queen Lady, sweet lady, follow me there.
\Violas' crying, ... a crystal tear carousel, ...
Come; My Queen Lady, for I hear the bell,
Thine own gong of divinity, tis' a beauteous thing,
Tabor drum hear me, ... Farewell to the King.
\My Tabard is torn, a worn peasant I be, ...
Yet the music of the night sets me free,
No Shillings no favor, not but penitence fer me,
Yet in yer arms Lady, I fly high above you sea.
\The carousel closes, the magic night ends too soon,
Yet I hear still; a crescendo of laughter, ...
fore'er dancing within the heart of the Madrigals' tune, ...
To unsheath my heart & sing to my Queen, 'neath the magical moon.

Thomas Weddle

Raindrops and Elephants

The rain,
that nemesis of sun lovers,
spat its fury in staccato insistence
at my window, rain as cold
as a heart never warmed by love.
\Wind-driven, bringing its promise,
it cast defiance with each gelid drop.
I held my breath at this
audacious riot.
\Violets beneath my window
filled their cups and savored the quaff,
while peonies
too coy to spurn the intrusion,
hung their heads at the daring onslaught.
\Then suddenly as it had begun,
the storm turned a disdainful sweep
of its tail like an elephant's pirouette
and went rumbling east
over the hills.

Goldie Hagedorn

January

Shadow star, crescent moon
Angel's song, heading home
Swift warm wind caresses snow
And line by line your kisses melt
Wet against my soul.

Shadow star, crescent moon
Rebel heart, crimson breath
Foaming bitter bled by sighs, and
The last low crackling sheet of ice
Breaks wild against my skin.

Shadow star, crescent moon
Crested sky, winter light
Rain falls whisper sweet on lies
As wolf cries linger on the ground
Lying hard across my mind.

Yolonda L. Young

Definition of "A Friend"

A friend is someone unique,
a person to talk you,
someone you can always trust.

The future looks bleak,
a friend will hold your hand,
won't let you stumble in the dark.

Like a beacon in the night
a friend will guide you,
take you to a safe harbor.

Your deepest secrets,
your darkest thoughts,
a friend will understand.

Oceans and mountains apart
your heart reaches out,
a friend will hear you calling.

A friend will care forever,
a friend is like a pillar.
Friendship is love.

Belle Alexander

A Child's Elegy

You were
And I came because you were.
Now, here am I
Because you were.
And so, here still are you
Because I am.

In me you are alive and well.
All about your life does dwell.
Life is more than touch
Or breath
With this truth, then.
How your death?

David Glaser

The Men In My Life

The men in my life stand tall and strong. They've helped me
whether I was right or wrong.
They've shown me love each day of the year. Helped me to
understand when my mind wasn't clear.
Fought for me in life tough battles. Taught me how to stand tall in the saddle.
Taught me how to ride my very fist bike. Even took me on my very first hike.
Wiped my tears and encouraged me. Made me steadfast although I wanted to flee.
They made me hold my head up high. Even when I felt as though I would die.
The circle of love I'm surrounded by. I'll truly cherish 'till the day I die.
The tender side of the men I know. Have made me flourish and helped me to grow.
You've all been my knights in shinning armor. Guru, Orion, Adonis
have played an important part in my karma.
I give thanks to the Lord for sending me these three special men: a
jaybird, a lion, a scorpion, to watch over me: a wren.
They are always there whenever I need them. My father, my brother, my lover/friend.
So I've etched these few lines on this eternal parchment. To let
the men in my life know exactly how much to me they've meant.

Michelle G. Birt

BIOGRAPHIES

AARONSON, RUSSELL
[b.] May 5, 1953, Brooklyn, NY; [p.] Edwin and Harriet Aaronson; [ch.] Olivia Kate Aaroson; [ed.] Kings Point Country Day School CCNY (Queensborough/Hunter) Swedish Institute of Massage; [occ.] Massage Therapist; [memb.] American Massage Therapy Assoc. Life Savers Take a bigger Role (selection committee); [oth. writ.] Several poems currently unpublished. I participate in poetry recitals through out the Northeast Corridor.; [pers.] Inspirational influences: Nature and intimate relationships. Structural influences: T.S. Eliot. The music will save the world, awake and sing the language of love.; [a.] New York City, NY

ABELO, J. T.
[pen.] Tiofilo Guerrero; [b.] May 27, 1961, Venezuela; [p.] Alfredo Teodoro, Iris Graciela; [m.] Mirian Josefina Rodriguez, March 31, 1984; [ch.] Anastasia and Alexandria; [ed.] Lisandro Alvarado High School, Temple University; [occ.] Salesman; [memb.] The Good Pastor Church; [hon.] Golden Heart Award; Editor's Choice Award; [oth. writ.] Bedtime story of Fred the Bilingual Dog and short poems to my loved ones; Latin, Italian, English and Spanish; [pers.] To know and not to do, is not to know; furthermore to always have confidence in the Lord our God and yourself to succeed. Every person demands: Effort, heart and practice. Every knowledge comes by these THREE.; [a.] Oakland, CA

ACHENBAUGH, BRIAN FORREST
[b.] June 21, 1973, Glasgow, Scotland; [p.] Myrna Allen, Dennis and Teresa Achenbaugh; [ed.] Jackson High School, Ocean County College; [occ.] Was Student and Retail/Hardware Clerk; [memb.] Jackson H.S. Track and Cross Country Team, Ski Club; [hon.] Varsity Letters in Track and Cross Country; [oth. writ.] None published; [pers.] Brian was killed by a drunk driver January 5, 1996. Brian loved the outdoors - camping - skiino and fishing. His philosophy was seize the moment "Carpe Diem."; [a.] Jackson, NJ

ACKER, JAMIE
[b.] December 30, 1983, Adrian, MI; [p.] Dean and Shawn Acker; [ed.] Currently in 7th grade at Addison Middle School; [memb.] Peerlistering, Student Council, Our Savior Lutheran Church; [oth. writ.] Story on my sister, she is disabled other poems.; [pers.] I write poems or stories when I am feeling sad or after someone dies or leaves.; [a.] Addison, MI

ADAM, SANDRA MARIE DAVIES
[b.] January 23, 1938, Salt Lake City, UT; [p.] Mr. and Mrs. Bryan and Edna Davies; [m.] Mr. Milton Franz Adam, August 9, 1960; [ch.] Cristal and Joy Adam; [ed.] AA - Liberal Arts; [occ.] Music Teaching - Ceramics Oil Painting; [memb.] MTNA, LDS, Music Director and Choir Member; [hon.] Poetry published in Pencilings East High School, Salt Lake City, Utah; [oth. writ.] Poetry and prose.; [a.] Fullerton, CA

ADAMS, JANET FAYE
[b.] May 14, 1949, Mt. Vernon, IN; [p.] Darrel R. Allen and Lucille Allen; [ch.] Greg Pinkard - Keri Lea Adams; [ed.] Carmi Township High School, Franklin Pierce College, SUNY - Potsdam, NY; [occ.] Student - SUNY - Potsdam, NY; [hon.] Dean's List - Franklin Pierce College; [oth. writ.] First published poem.; [a.] Massena, NY

ADAMS, LINDA LOU
[b.] July 15, 1946, Washington, DC; [p.] Percy and Leona Lowery; [m.] Glenn Douglas Adams, November 9, 1985; [ch.] Lynn, Dawn, John, Tammy, Bobbi and Shelly; [ed.] Duval High; [occ.] Office Assistant III for the Caroline Counseling Center; [memb.] Diabetic's Association; [oth. writ.] Tender Moments, Destiny To Be, Little Boy Lost, Your Touch, Love's Depth, My Darling; [pers.] I have been influenced in writing poems by my husband as I love him very much and most of the poems I write are for him.; [a.] Denton, MD

ADAMS, MICHAEL DEAN
[b.] June 13, 1963, Woodland, CA; [p.] Gerald Adams, Judith Schuman; [ed.] I was not able to finish High School because of my Cystic Fibrosis. 1987 to 1988 I was able to attend College in England.; [occ.] Disabled - on waiting list for Double Lung Transplant. U.C.L.A.; [hon.] This is a great honor!; [pers.] I have been greatly influenced by my grandfather, Jack Knight, my uncle Byard McHugh, and the Poet Dylan Thomas.; [a.] Upland, CA

ADAMS, RHONDA
[b.] December 1, 1956, Portland, OR; [p.] Charles and Lois Adams; [ch.] Damien Joseph; [ed.] Gresham High School, currently enrolled in Portland State University; [occ.] Student of Criminal Justice; [hon.] Several poems I've had published in several local newspaper; [oth. writ.] Several other poems I've never had published; [pers.] I strive to reflect the quality of mankind, I am currently influenced by poets such as Elizabeth, Barrett, Browning Robert Frost, Ernest Hemmingway.; [a.] Portland, OR

AINSWORTH, RICHARD E.
[pen.] Richard E. Ainsworth; [b.] July 2, 1929, Norwich, CT; [p.] Selvester and Florence Ainsworth; [m.] Crystalia Ainsworth, April 7, 1991; [ch.] Three; [ed.] 14 years and hold a Nursing License - State of Connecticut; [occ.] Operate as Owner/Manager Dick's Vacuum Shop, Winslow, Maine, also owner of apartment buildings.; [memb.] (VIP) Club Member, National Corporation, Church Member, Apartment ASSO Member; [hon.] Have several awards from a National Corporation (retired now), also American Heart Association Award, 1975.; [oth. writ.] I am presently completing a book of Spiritual Poetry, and have hope for its publication. I also have an interest in song writing, and have written many songs over the years.; [pers.] "At the touch of love everyone becomes a poet" wrote Plato nearly 2400 years ago. Love can turn ordinary people into poets as one attempts to clarify the great mysteries of the love of God and of man.; [a.] Winslow, ME

AKIU, DARLENE K.
[pen.] Darlene K. Akiu; [b.] June 11, 1971, Maui, HI; [p.] Daniel and Carolyn Akiu; [m.] Lyon Keoke Alizna; [ch.] Lyric Kamalani Alizna-Akin; [ed.] Henry Perrine Baldwin High School; [occ.] Housewife; [oth. writ.] Several other poems.; [pers.] This poem is dedicated to Kukuiokalani Theodore Kalalau, Dale Edward Tavares and Lyon Keoke Alizna.; [a.] Sunland, CA

ALBERT, THAIS
[pen.] Thais Albert; [b.] August 26, 1980, Malibu, CA; [p.] Kate and Edward Albert; [ed.] Still in High School (11th Grade); [occ.] Currently a Student, Aspiring to be a writer and singer.; [hon.] Won the 1994 International Arabian Horse, Association (I.A.H.A) Youth Essay contest on "If My Arabian Worse could Talk."; [oth. writ.] In the process of finishing my 1st novel, called "The House Of Seven Stories, and finding a publisher for a collection of illustrated children's poetry.; [pers.] Even as a child, before I could even write, I put stories together using illustrations. There was never any a question in my mind as to what I wanted to be when that was I grew up: I would be a writer: a given.; [a.] Malibu, CA

ALBRECHT, KRISTIN M.
[b.] March 13, 1987, Moline, IL; [p.] Carl and Diane Albrecht; [ed.] I am in the fourth grade at Seton Catholic School School in Moline, IL.; [pers.] I love writing about my dreams and thoughts. I have been greatly influenced by my 3rd grade teacher Mrs. Sheila Zack.

ALCALA, ARTHUR
[b.] 1969; [pers.] The poetry I write serves one purpose. That is to express my deepest feelings to the woman I love. Nothing is more important than love to me. Her name is Rita, she is star number twenty five.; [a.] Corona, CA

ALDEN, GORDON
Alden, Gordon L.
[b.] August 8, 1910; [p.] Chester & Myrtle Miser; [m.] Irene E. Alden, June 16, 1941; [ch.] Glen, Leigh, Larry, Raymond & Jean; [ed.] Salutatorian - Turton S. Dak. High School, Metropolitan Bible School - 2 yrs., Gorham Maine State Teachers College - 3 yrs.; [occ.] Retired, Serious Gardener, (Poet?); [memb.] Christian Civic League of Maine, Eagles Club - Crystal Cathedral Ministriess, International Society of Poets; [pers.] In my latter years, poetry has been a medium requiring me to put my long past in perspective and to determine my thoughts of present and future, in order to enunciate and weave them into our beautiful English language to my personal satisfaction. I tend to be serious minded.; [a.] Brunswick, Maine

ALEXANDER, BELLE
[pen.] Belle Alexander; [b.] May 10, 1952, Hamburg, Germany; [m.] Adam Alexander, November 11, 1975; [ed.] B.A. Psychology, Interamerican university of Puerto Rico; [occ.] Tour Operator; [oth. writ.] Poems, sports and special event reporter for daily famous newspaper. Travel reports.; [pers.] Do not waste thoughts on things you cannot change.; [a.] Jacksonville, FL

ALI, NAUMAN
[b.] April 26, 1983, New York; [p.] Asma Ali, Liaquat Ali; [ed.] 8th grade; [occ.] Student; [hon.] Two awards in Science Projects.

ALLEN, JESSE L.
[b.] November 22, 1949, Kentucky; [p.] Betty and Marvin Brown; [m.] Sue Allen, July 10, 1970; [ch.] Richard Allen; [ed.] Shepherdsville High School, Indian River Community College; [occ.] Police Officer; [pers.] My poems are meant to be felt, thoughts or people stir emotions - there emotions stir my pen. I guess all things need stirring sometime.; [a.] Vero Beach, FL

ALLEN, LAUREEN
[b.] August 18, 1969, Flushing, NY; [p.] Carole A. and Robert A.; [ed.] Annville - Cleona High, PA; [memb.] Hyde Park Baptist Church; [oth. writ.] Unpublished poetry and verses.; [pers.] My poems and verses are a reflection of me, my view of our world, my experiences and my feelings. I strive to express these reflections in a vivid and tangible manner so you can perceive the world through my eyes and my heart.; [a.] Bangall, NY

ALLEN, LURLIE W.
[b.] September 13, 1926, Murfreesboro, TN; [p.] Sallie Moon and John D. Wiseman; [m.] Frank Morgan Allen, July 26, 1949; [ch.] Melinda A. Borbely, Beth A. Berngartt, Patti Allen; [ed.] Central High School, Murfreesboro University - '44, B.S. Middle Tennessee State University - '48, M.A. Georgia Southern University - '82; [occ.] Retired - English Faculty Brewton - Parker College - Mt. Vernon, GA; [memb.] Mensa, DAR, Life Member of PTA and UMW (United Methodist Women), Tiger United Meth. Church; [hon.] Outstanding Regents' Award - DAR, Who's Who American Colleges and Universities 1948, American Legion Auxiliary Essay Contest Tenn. State Winner; [oth. writ.] Poems (a few) published in Mensa Publication and "Miscellany" - GA Southern Literary Magazine, article in "Progressive Farmer" magazine Devotional

Material for church groups.; [pers.] Fulfillment for me has been in discovering my real self and my unique God given talents and abilities and being faithful there unto in everyday living as well as in creative and professional endeavors.; [a.] Tiger, GA

ALLENBACH, R. GEORJEAN
[pen.] Georjean Allenbach; [b.] July 11, 1944, Cincinnati, OH; [p.] R. George Allenbach, Jean Allenbach; [ed.] Galion High, Metropolitan State College, Denver, CO, Bachelors Degree Nursing, Science, graduate Philadelphia Paralegal Institute; [memb.] Member of the Evangelical Lutheran Sisterhood of Mary, Abiding Savior Lutheran Church Phx. AZ; [oth. writ.] Various unpublished poems and songs and messages on biblical studies; [pers.] I strive to reflect the loving kindness of our Lord Jesus Christ. I have been greatly influenced by the divinely inspired writings of holy scripture.; [a.] Phoenix, AZ

ALLISON, ELAYNE
[pen.] Laney Allison; [b.] November 19, 1952, Colorado; [p.] Robert and Clara Potter; [m.] Skip Allison, November 9, 1979; [ch.] Scott, Cherie, Barbara, Isaac; [ed.] Belton High, Belton, MO, Longulew Community College, Devry Technology, Kansas City Business College; [occ.] Administrative Assistant; [memb.] North Spring United Methodist Church, Blue Springs, MO, MUMC - Midland United Methodist Cursillo; [hon.] Honor roll, Belton High, Achievement of Excellence - National Coordinator for Employment; [oth. writ.] A collection of poems never published; [pers.] God has shown me that life is not just a matter of personal survival, lust life is a spiritual evolution, with spiritual responsibilities, and unconditional love. He has given me ideals in they are the goals that direct my life.; [a.] Independence, MO

ALTENHOFEN, RALEIGH
[pen.] Raleigh Altenhofen; [b.] January 2, 1978, Iowa City, IA; [p.] Lavon David and Claudia Altenhofen; [ed.] Grade school at Keota Elementary, 7-12 at Keota High School; [occ.] Soon to be a student a Arizona State University; [pers.] "To thyn ownself be true."; [a.] Chandler, AZ

AMALFITANO, WENDY
[pen.] Wendy E. Gruber; [b.] March 20, 1942, New Jersey; [p.] Jeff and Tilda Gruber; [ch.] Danny, Lori, Lucas and Rachel; [occ.] Lighting Designer; [memb.] P.E.T.A. (Animal Rights Organizations); [oth. writ.] (A lifetime of) writing songs for musicians short stories and poems.; [pers.] Listen to your inner voice, and never, ever stop growing. The child written about in my poem is now happily at home, with me - I have thought her not to be afraid of your inner value.; [a.] Congers, NY

AMLANER, KIRSTEN
[b.] February 11, 1980, Oxford, England; [p.] Beo and Dr. Charles Amlaner; [ed.] I am a Junior in High School; [occ.] I am currently a Student at Indiana Academy; [memb.] I play the violin in the Terre Haute Symphony Orchestra, and I also play the Piano; [hon.] President's Education Awards Program for Outstanding Academic Achievement, Dean's List; [pers.] The rhyming poem is the essence of all poetry. I want to continue to keep this lyrical form of poetry alive.; [a.] Terre Haute, IN

AMMONS-WRIGHT, DENISE M.
[b.] May 29, 1966, Rochester, NY; [p.] John Draper and Connie Shutt; [m.] William J. Wright, November 5, 1989; [ch.] Christopher, Aaron; [occ.] Receptionist for A-1 Emergency Mobile; [oth. writ.] My Little One, And My Baby...; [pers.] Look into your own heart, before you judge the hearts of your fellow man.; [a.] Colorado Springs, CO

AMOROSE JR., EDWARD
[b.] February 24, 1970, Philadelphia; [p.] Marie and Edward Sr.; [ed.] Currently working in The Radiation Oncology Dept. at Allegheny University Hospital in Philadelphia, Student; [occ.] Office Clerk; [oth. writ.] All songs and oems that I've written are kept in my own personal collection. None have ever been published, with the exception of my high school and grade school newspapers.; [pers.] To me, writing is the greatest way to openly express one's deepest emotions. To "grasp" the emotions at that very moment, and to express them in your own creative and particular way, is the essence.; [a.] Philadelphia, PA

AMPOSTA, RACHEL ANN B.
[b.] November 19, 1984, Fairfield, CA; [p.] Romeo G. and Raquel B. Amposta; [ed.] 7th Grade Student; [occ.] Student; [pers.] In my poems I try to describe the truth in my heart and soul, trying to prove that love does conquer all. I have been greatly influenced by my family and friends power and will to keep on going to do what I do best.; [a.] Fairfield, CA

AMSTUTZ, KARLEY
[b.] June 30, 1962, Battle Creek, MI; [p.] Jerry Lee Amstutz and Jacqualyn Lee Amstutz; [m.] Jamie Renee, August 31, 1997; [ch.] Jason Kyle

ANDERSON, ADELINE
[b.] January 11, 1916, Billings, MT; [p.] Clarence and Florence Pierson; [m.] Everett W. Anderson, December 31, 1938; [ch.] Paul Anderson and Kristin Anderson; [ed.] High School, various Classes in Art, Sewing Piano and Organ; [occ.] Retired, Housewife; [pers.] I write poems, humorous or other wise, limericks for my own amusement with feelings about the ecological condition of our earth.; [a.] Bellingham, WA

ANDERSON, DIANNE M.
[pen.] Virgo; [b.] September 5, 1951, Rochester, NY; [p.] Louise Waters and James F. Anderson; [ed.] Gates Chili H.S., Monroe Community College; [occ.] Self Employed; [memb.] Habitat For Community; [oth. writ.] Personal poems, not yet published; [pers.] No better a legacy than to leave the world a little poetry.; [a.] Rochester, NY

ANDERSON, GINGER
[pen.] Ginger Anderson; [b.] October 11, 1979, Fulton, KY; [p.] Tom and Laura Anderson; [ed.] Graves County High School - currently 11th grade, currently ranked 6th out of 321 (eleventh grade students); [occ.] High School; [memb.] Graves County High School Band, French Club, Academic Team, Winter Team, Winter guard, Future Problem Solving, Interact; [hon.] Valedictorian of 8th grade class, earned 3 superiors in the state music competition, 1st place in State French Competition, Treasurer of Interact, Freshman band member of the year; [pers.] I would like to thank my parents for all the support they have given me - I love you, Mom and Dad.; [a.] Mayfield, KY

ANDERSON, K. RENEE
[pen.] Lady Poets; [b.] January 19, 1954, Louisville, KY; [p.] C. D. and Bonnie Johnston; [m.] Mark S. Anderson, July 9, 1983; [ch.] Nick and Amber; [ed.] Coon Rapids Sr. High, Vocational School; [occ.] Mortgage Loan Processor at Summit Mortgage; [oth. writ.] Written many poems on my own experiences writing from my heart, beliefs, and inspirations; [pers.] Those that matter seldom mind, those that mind seldom matter.; [a.] New Hope, MN

ANDERSON, PRISCILLA
[b.] February 3, 1940, Saxa Pahaw, NC; [p.] Margaret C. and William E. Buff; [m.] James H. Anderson, March 2, 191; [ch.] Jimmy, Kevin, Buff, Cathy, Rob,

Karen, Sue, Dave and Jen; [ed.] Walter Williams High School, Burlington, NC - O'Shea's Business School, Red Bank, NJ, Brook dale Community College Trinton Falls NJ; [occ.] Housewife; [hon.] Special Editors Award; [oth. writ.] I was thrilled to receive the special editor's award in where Dawn Lingers for my poem "Untitled" this is another pleasure to have my poem published

ANDERSON, RACHEL C.
[b.] February 7, 1933, Rural, Freeport; [p.] Rudolph M., Esther A. Bertini; [m.] Carlos S. Anderson (Deceased), December 23, 1963; [ch.] Four boys, Four girls; [ed.] Eleventh grade only; [occ.] Cook, Housekeeper, Goat herd; [memb.] Only one, of the only race of people not protected by any law. The white race; [oth. writ.] Nothing published; [pers.] The love of life, and the beauty of God's creation is my inspiration. The glorious wonder in nature is so inspiring, like a soul rending, musical composition, it can nearly break your heart; [a.] Freeport, OH

ANDERSON, ROSE DYESS
[pen.] Rose Dyess Anderson; [b.] December 24, 1941, Laurel, MS; [p.] Mildred and Lamar Dyess; [m.] Rushel Talmadge Anderson Jr., May 13, 1965; [ch.] Joel Alan Anderson; [ed.] B.A. Degree, William Carey College, Hattiesburg Mississippi; [occ.] Elementary School Teacher; [memb.] Alpha Delta Kappa Teacher's Sorority, Covington Road Church of Christ, and Magnolia Bible College Associates; [hon.] Nominated for: Teacher of the Year at Northside Primary School (1994-1995), Teacher Hall of Fame with Mississippi University for Women (1994-1995) and Disney Teacher of the Year (1995-1996).; [oth. writ.] I write and design a youth page in the Magnolia Messenger, a religious publication.; [pers.] Life is truly what one makes it and beauty can be found anywhere if one looks for it with poetic eyes.; [a.] Natchez, MS

ANDREWS, BRIAN
[pen.] The Admirer Gunga Dim; [ed.] UHS Graduate; [occ.] Electrician; [memb.] National Pond Society; [hon.] Long Driving Champion, Scandinavian Star.; [oth. writ.] This is my 1st poem ever. I am shacked and honored to have it published; [pers.] Any one can write poetry, we all live it every day. The trick is putting it on paper. Thank you Susan; [a.] Venice, FL

ANDREWS, MRS. ZOLA
[b.] August 26, 1908, Iuka, IL; [p.] Rev. Albert and Myrtle Millican; [m.] H. Eugene (Deceased), August 30, 1931; [ed.] High School Graduate special training in Medical Technology and X-Ray, registered in both.; [occ.] Retired now. Owned and operated my own Medical Laboratory.; [memb.] Pi Epsilon, Pi Sorority, American Cancer Society, Christian Church, AARP, Danville Boat Club.; [hon.] Given a life membership in Pi Epsilon Pi Sorority - and the Danville Boat Club.; [oth. writ.] I have written poetry all my adult life but never submitted any before. My father before me did likewise.; [pers.] I love nature and appreciate all her works around me. And I believe in God!; [a.] Danville, IL

ANSARA, AURORA
[b.] August 4, El Paso, TX; [p.] Kathy Ansara and Deeb Ansara; [ed.] Pebble Hills Elementary, Indian Ridge Middle; [occ.] Student; [hon.] All Region Mixed Choir, Tenth Chair; [pers.] I want to dedicate this to David Leroy Zang, my grampa.; [a.] El Paso, TX

ANTHONY, VIRGINIA
[pen.] Budia Chipper; [b.] December 26, 1981, Norfolk, VA; [p.] Ernest and Stella Anthony; [ed.] Currently a Sophomore attending Bishop Kenny High School in Jacksonville, Florida; [oth. writ.] As a hobby, I have

written thirty-one other unpublished poems in hopes to make my own poetry book.; [pers.] I would like to thank a close friend of mine in which this poem is dedicated to, Garrett Cotnev. Yes Garrett, "You're the Coolest."; [a.] Jacksonville, FL

ANTLSPERGER, ALICE
[pen.] Alice Antlsperger; [b.] July 4, 1925, Chicago, IL; [p.] Thomas Dwyer, Mary Dwyer; [m.] George Antlsperger, August 31, 1946; [ch.] Mary, Judy, Barbara, Patty, Theresa; [ed.] Visitation H.S., Chicago, IL., Institute of Children's Literature, Redding Ridge, CT; [occ.] Retired 1994, Former occupation Religious Ed., Coordinator, Holy Name, Wilmot, WI; [memb.] Various Church and Prayer Groups; [oth. writ.] Articles published in Chicago newspaper. Personal poems for family and friends (unpublished).; [pers.] My main focus in life has been my family. The personal poetry I write for my husband, daughters, and thirteen grandchildren reflects the love I have for them. They are my inspiration.; [a.] Paddock Lake, Salem, WI

ARENDER, CINDY
[b.] March 30, 1961, Taylorsville, MS; [p.] Plez and Jewel Atwood; [m.] Jimmy Arender, January 16, 1981; [ch.] Alisha, Andrea and Allison; [ed.] Taylorsville, High School; [occ.] Store Manager; [memb.] Member of Raleigh First Baptist Church; [hon.] Who Who's Among American High School Students; [oth. writ.] Several poems have been printed in church bulletin's.; [pers.] I thank God everyday for what he has given us. He gave each of us a talent, if we choose not to use it, it maybe be taken away.; [a.] Raleigh, MS

ARENT, WERONIKA
[pen.] Autumn Flower; [b.] January 25, Poland; [p.] Jozefa and Jozef Krupski; [m.] Marek Arent, August 27, Chicago; [ch.] D. Anna, S. Jreneusz Babiak; [ed.] In fine arts and advertising - study in Poland; [occ.] Display decorator and specialist for advertising; [memb.] International Society of Poets and The National Arbor Day Foundation; [hon.] In first golden bookstore poetry contest, and editor's choice award, in The National Library of Poetry contest; [oth. writ.] Many poems published in local magazines. A book titled "God or Devil?", "Creator of America" with very personal experience and observation working for years - with Jewish families in U.S.A.; [pers.] Dekalog - life guide post impressed by the smartest "book" ever - particular by the two kings - (David and Solomon); [a.] Chicago, IL

ARMSTEAD, GARY
[b.] August 8, 1968, Chicago, IL; [p.] Patricia Armstead, James Sims; [m.] Norfariza Armstead, November 7, 1994; [ch.] Norcora, Norsheriza; [ed.] Dwight D. Eisenhower H.S., Currently attending University of MN; [occ.] I-ON Mill Operator (Computer Disc Drives) Seagate Technology; [hon.] Dean's List; [oth. writ.] Various poems on a variety of topics. I'm currently working on a short story.; [pers.] Knowledge is freedom, ignorance is slavery, regardless the route an individual has to take, Education is the equator of all men.; [a.] Saint Paul, MN

ARONSON, JAMMY
[pen.] Jammy Aronson; [b.] January 15, 1908, Chicago, IL; [p.] Morris and Anne Smith; [m.] 1928; [ch.] 1; [ed.] High school graduate; [occ.] Retired; [oth. writ.] Sandman, music and lyrics, published, poems published in Miami 'Reporter'

ARTECA, PINKY DENISE
[pen.] Pinky; [b.] July 29, 1951, Montecristy, Dominican Republic; [p.] Augusto and Denise Mena; [m.] Richard, May 14, 1983; [ch.] Jan-Marie, Ricardo and Joseph; [ed.] Grammar High School, Hunter College, La Guardia Comm. College; [occ.] Executive Legal

Secretary; [pers.] My writings come from personal experiences in my life. All the people that I love and have loved are in my emotions. I have read books from Kahlil Gribran, Emely Dickinson, E.E. Cummings and the Bible.; [a.] Kew Gardens, NY

ARTHUR, JOAN
[b.] Trinidad, West Indies; [p.] Albert and Iona Samuel; [m.] Mervyn Arthur; [ch.] Donnadale, Natalie Phillipa and Noel; [oth. writ.] Poems which I keep for myself, or send to friends in Greeting Cards.; [pers.] Life, and the human person make my thoughts flow.; [a.] New York, NY

ARTL, CARRIE
[b.] April 5, 1975, Cleveland, OH; [p.] Gerard Artl, Martha Artl; [ed.] East Technical High School; [memb.] Whale Adoption Project Moody Blues Fan Club; [hon.] Grade 12 Academic Top ten, National Honor Society; [oth. writ.] Short Fiction Story 3092 Published in the Plain Dealer; [a.] Cleveland, OH

ASAY, LYNLEY FENWICK
[pen.] Lynley Fenwick, Danilyn Chaise; [b.] September 2, 1969, El Dorado, AR; [p.] Dick and Peggy Fenwick; [m.] Kenneth C. Asay, June 5, 1996; [ch.] Jessica Spencer; [ed.] BM - Methodist College 1994, currently an MSA student at Central Michigan University; [occ.] Assistant Registrar - Methodist College; [memb.] Alpha Chi, Gamma Beta Phi, Tau Beta Sigma, Sigma Alpha Iota, Who's Who in College and Univ's.; [hon.] Summa Cum Laude Graduate of Methodist College. OCSA 1991 (Outstanding College Students of America); [oth. writ.] Several journal articles and poems.; [pers.] It has been my experience that we live from moment to moment, and in those moments we are changed, moved, saved... Life is what happens to us in between them.; [a.] Fayetteville, NC

ASHBAUCHER, ROZELLA D.
[b.] October 5, 1907, Herrin, IL; [p.] Mont and Reola Dillard; [m.] Lovin F. Ashbaucher, August 18, 1963; [ed.] Southern Brothers Business College, University of Miami at Coral Gables, FL., AB, '32; [occ.] I was a Secretary, Teacher and Mgr. of my properties. Retired and live in John Knox Village of Central Florida.; [memb.] Delta Zeta Sorority, Martha Ch. of O.E.S., Central Christian Church of Coral Gables, FL, First Christian Church in DeLand, FL; [hon.] Scholarship student of Ruth Bryan Owen Rhode to U. of Miami, (She corresponded with me till she died.) (She was the daughter of William Jennings Bryan).; [oth. writ.] "Poems" for a small private newspaper years ago. I always longed for time to write. Now its poetry for me.

ASHBAUGH, TONY
[pen.] Lynn Ash/Tobalina; [b.] July 4, 1971, Shepherdsville, KY; [p.] Gayle Benkert, Stephen Ashbaugh; [ed.] Bullitt East High School - 1990, Cumberland College, Williamsburg KY, 1994; [occ.] Customer Service, Publisher's Printing Co Lebanon Jct KY; [memb.] Bullitt County YMCA; [pers.] I would like to dedicate this to my grandfather who passed away Oct. 25, 1995. I miss you and I love you!; [a.] Lebanon Junction, KY

AUGUSTINE, TOM
[b.] January 8, 1950, Landover, MD; [p.] John L., Lucille S. Augustine; [m.] Barbara M. Augustine, September 20, 1972; [ch.] Kyle Andrew, Brandon Thomas; [ed.] Bladensburg High School, Prince Georges Community College; [occ.] Patent Researcher; [pers.] Poetry is like memories and feeling frozen in time. By writing it down you get live each moment over and over. We are all poets on the inside. Some of us just went it on the outside and happen to write it down.; [a.] Lake Ridge, VA

AUKERMAN, ROBERT B.
[b.] April 16, 1939, Cincinnati, OH; [p.] Charles R. and Louise H. Aukerman; [m.] Cecelia; [ch.] Judy, Arlene, Robert, Grandchildren: Douglas, Melissa, Marie, Samuel and A.J.; [pers.] My mother gave me verses and rhyming words when I was a child to teach me and to keep me busy. They are keeping me learning and busy still. Thanks, Mom.; [a.] Littleton, CO

AUSTIN, BREANNE
[b.] May 1, 1981, Saint Augustine, FL; [p.] Donald and Sheila Austin; [ed.] Currently enrolled as a Sophomore at Allen D. Nease High School; [occ.] Student; [hon.] A, B Honor Roll, English Awards, Volunteer at the St. Johns County Public Library; [oth. writ.] A few short stories and other poems. None have been published.; [pers.] I believe that no matter who you are you are special and should always be yourself, and try your hardest to reach your goals.; [a.] Saint Augustine, FL

AUSTIN, MRS. T. S.
[pen.] Mati K. (Austin); [b.] June 24, 1910, Hamburg, AR; [p.] Mr. and Mrs. William Edward King (Deceased); [m.] Thomas Sedell Austin Sr. (Deceased), August 11, 1935; [ch.] San T. S. A. Jr., Jacqueline A. Helmes; [ed.] High School, Blue Mountain College Credits to Elementary Teachers - 5 years - Special Course in book-keeping, short hand and typing - and penmanship; [occ.] Monogramming - 28 yrs.; [pers.] This grate I've always loved by Williams Faulker I decline to accept the end of Mar., I believe that man will not merely endure. "He Will Prevail" - He will prevail because he has a sound and a spirit capable of compassion and sacrifice and endurance.; [a.] Meridian, MS

AUSTIN, STEPHEN
[b.] January 27, 1978, Fresno, CA; [p.] Charlie and Mildred Austin; [ed.] Mendota High, Currently attending California State University-Fresno; [occ.] Student at California State University - Fresno; [a.] Fresno, CA; [hon.] All-American Scholar, Who's Who Among High School Students.] Golden State Scholar C SF Top Ten; [pers.] My poetry is influenced by the romantic period of poetry; [a.] Firebaugh, CA

AUSTIN III, ALFREDO A.
[b.] October 20, 1984, Hampton, VA; [p.] Alfredo Austin Jr., Sheila Austin; [ed.] 7th Grade, Lake Riviera Middle School; [occ.] Student; [hon.] Honor Student of Month - April 1996, Poetry Writing Award (Lake Riviera), Poem selected and published in the Anthology of Poetry by Young Americans; [a.] Brick, NJ

AYE, DARRYL GABLE
[pen.] Darryl Gable Aye; [b.] March 11, 1961, New York, NY; [p.] Burl Aye, Anna Aye; [ed.] Germain School of Photography; [occ.] Music Management and Production; [pers.] I strive to turn dreams into reality; [a.] New York, NY

AYERS, JEFFREY GLENN
[b.] July 19, 1974, Pontiac, MI; [p.] Nancy Ayers, Lewis Ayers; [oth. writ.] Previously published in of Sunshine and Daydreams, Memories of Tomorrow, Whispers at Dusk, and Into the Unknown; [pers.] This poem is for and about anyone who has lost someone they loved, either through circumstance or their own doing.; [a.] Los Angeles, CA

BACK, WILLIAM D.
[pen.] William Back; [b.] March 20, 1942, Huntington West, VA; [p.] Mr. and Mrs. James S. Back; [m.] Lynn D. Back, May 4, 1996; [ch.] William F. Back, Brian K. Back, Melissa M., Betty K. Czajkowski, James D. Back; [ed.] Jacksonville University, Rollins College, Stetson University, Florida State Fire College and Mid Florida Tech.; [occ.] Master Electrician/Electronics

Technician; [memb.] Star Trek Fan Club, working with Hospice the Comforter, Heart Association, Cancer Society, Crippled children and children with Aids; [hon.] Admiral of Star Trek Fan Club of Central Florida, special recognition for unselfish work done for Fan Club by Paramount Pictures, Master's Degree in Electrical, Association Degree in Electronics, Paramedic for Astronauts; [oth. writ.] Father's Love, the old farm house, my lady, my grown up son. I have written several poems about love, adventure, and personal outlook on life. Also, about beauty of nature.; [pers.] I believe in helping and working with all who are in need. I have been influenced in my writing by wife, children, nature and the good of mankind.; [a.] Orlando, FL

BAETZ, JUANITA
[b.] March 23, 1937, Beaver Dam, WI; [p.] Robert and Esther Berger; [m.] Ralph M. Baetz, September 1, 1956; [ch.] Susan, Randy, Steve and Jim; [ed.] Hartford Union High School, Hartford, WIS graduate; [occ.] Retired from farming; [memb.] Herman Consolidated School PTO former President Peace Lutheran Church; [pers.] My philosophy is expressed in my poem.; [a.] Iron Ridge, WI

BAGLIN-LYDA, TERRESA
[b.] June 6, 1966, Tampa, FL; [p.] James E. and Mary F. Baglin; [m.] Divorced; [ch.] Taylor Nicole Lyda; [ed.] Greenbrier West High School, West Virginia University, Concord College; [occ.] Full-time Student, Concord - College - Business Administration; [memb.] Student Member of the West Virginia Society of CPA's Southern Chapter and Chapter Assistant; [hon.] Dean's List; [oth. writ.] No other writings published. I Do, However, Have My Own Personal Collection; [pers.] Experience, good and bad, will bring forth great things if all opportunities are seized. I thank the people I have encountered in my life thus far for my experiences. I look forward one day to bring about great things.; [a.] Rainelle, WV

BAILEY, ANDREA
[b.] January 8, 1975, Fort Carson, CO; [p.] Clifford Bailey, Vivian Bailey; [ed.] Copperas Cove H.S., Copperas Cove, TX, Central Texas College, Killeen, TX; [occ.] Advertising Student; [oth. writ.] Unpublished poems; [pers.] My poetry comes from the heart... they are my true feelings. Nothing made up.

BAILEY, IRBY C.
[pen.] Irby Cleve Bailey; [b.] February 26, 1952, Greenwood, MS; [p.] Mr. and Mrs. Cleve H. Bailey Jr.; [m.] Ovida L. Bailey, Febrauny 11, 1972; [ch.] Belinda, Irby Jr., Shannon, Chasity; [ed.] High School; [occ.] Printer at Pennaco Hosiery, Grenada, MS; [pers.] My wife Ovida is my inspiration to write poetry, she's the love of my life. Life is what you make of it, Good, bad, happy or sad.

BAIN, ROBERT
[b.] June 6, 1967, Port Angeles, WA; [p.] Robert Bain, Irma Jean Bain; [ed.] Port Angeles Senior High, Peninsula Community College; [occ.] Undergraduate Student of Engineering; [memb.] World Wildlife Fund Organization; [pers.] Often, I write of the malevolent enervations of Humankind, and its propensity for proliferating iniquities upon Mother Nature. I extricate myself from such brooding moments with the admonition of a Buddhist priest, "Be a light unto yourself."; [a.] Port Angeles, WA

BALDWIN, CHRISTINE
[b.] July 14, 1978, Everett, WA; [p.] Ron and Darla Baldwin; [ed.] Meadowdale High School; [hon.] Varsity Track, Varsity Cross Country; [oth. writ.] Several unpublished poems.; [a.] Edmonds, WA

BALL, BRADLEY ALAN
[b.] April 27, 1954, Houston, TX; [p.] Mr. and Mrs. B. W. Ball; [m.] Karen Ball, July 8, 1980; [ed.] BS/ Elementary Education from Arkansas Tech University, Honor Grad. - Van Buren High School; [occ.] 5th Gr. Teacher - Van Buren Middle School; [memb.] Ark. Educational Association (AEA), Crawford County Art Association; [oth. writ.] (2) unpublished books "Ernie's World", "A Rope for the Hangman".; [a.] Van Buren, AR

BALL, MAGGIE LASHAE
[b.] November 3, 1983, Memphis, TN; [p.] Norma Williams; [ed.] I have education up to the 7th grade. Walker Elem. Oakshire Elem, Hollywood Elem., Spring Hill, Sunny Hill, Treasvant (JH); [memb.] Olympia Sales Club, and The Band.; [hon.] Honor Roll, Principal list. Student of the Month, Science Achievement Award, Citizenship Award, Personal Success Award, High TCAP Scores, and Good Conduct.; [oth. writ.] School writing contests. Class poems, local newspapers; [pers.] I like to give people something to believe in when I write my poems. I like to let them know that if you want to do something or get something you can.; [a.] Memphis, IN

BARONE, MAUREEN A.
[b.] January 1, 1955, Chicago; [p.] Shirley Ferraro, Henry Ferraro Jr.; [ch.] Carmen Frank II; [ed.] Eisenhower H.S.; [occ.] Manufacturing Planner, Free Lance Artist/Writer; [memb.] St. William Parish, Rosary College Parents Club; [pers.] "If all you think about is creating then you are on artist".; [a.] Chicago, IL

BARR III, PAUL RICHARD
[b.] December 16, 1973, Pottstown; [ed.] Owen J. Roberts High School, Indiana University of P.A.; [occ.] Concrete Construction, Laborer; [memb.] Making a living; [hon.] Rewarded at the end of the road; [oth. writ.] Consider as a peaceful, constructive hobby.; [pers.] Mother Earth a just mother. Everyday Birth awaiting another.; [a.] Pottstown, PA

BARTELLO, CHERYLANN
[pen.] Cheri; [b.] December 23, 1960, Philadelphia, PA; [p.] C. R. Bartello, Mary Ann Franco; [ed.] Atlantic Community College, Academy of Culinary Arts; [occ.] Food Service Industry; [memb.] ACC Alumni Association; [hon.] ACA, Gold Medal Graduate, Dean's List, Recipient - of Francis M. Zaberer, Scholarship; [pers.] If you have a dream, then you must have a goal. If you reach your goal then you'll live your dream!; [a.] Ocean City, NJ

BARTON, BEN
[b.] August 29, 1977, Houlton, ME; [p.] David and Lydia Barton; [ed.] Graduated from Hodgdon High School, Hodgdon Maine in June 1996

BASAK-MAY, DAWN
[b.] July 22, 1948, Easton, PA; [p.] Richard and Amelia Basak; [m.] November 10, 1973; [ch.] Deana Marie and Frederick E. IV; [ed.] Notre Dame High School and Northampton Area Community College, Empire Beauty School; [occ.] Cosmetology Teacher and Owner of Dawn's Country Club Road Salon; [memb.] Miss PA Scholarship Pageant Easton Holiday Committee/Secretary Bethlehem Vo-Tech Advisory Committee Lehigh Valley Cosmetology Asso/Membership Chairman; [hon.] Phi Theta Kappa National Honor Society, Dale Carnegie Awards (3); [oth. writ.] Article for NACC College Paper and won contest for naming a company newsletter. Enjoy creating poems for special occasion cards to give to friends and family. They await them.; [pers.] How exciting to be included in the color of thought publication. Thank you for consideration.; [a.] Easton, PA

BEARD, NADINE FAITHE
[b.] Chicago, IL; [p.] Thelma Smith; [ch.] Deborah, Patricia, Rodney, Gregory; [ed.] Dusable High School, Cortez Business College, Harold Washington Jr. College; [occ.] Police Clerk; [memb.] Dusable Umbrella Alumni, Inc. Board Member Committee Chairperson, Dusable Alumni Reunion Committee (High School); [hon.] Union Counselor; [oth. writ.] Free Lance unpublished poems; [pers.] Life and its complex situations, inspires my thoughts thru verse.; [a.] Chicago, IL

BEASLEY, KIMBERLY KAYE
[b.] September 14, 1970, Huntsville, AL; [ed.] Bob Jones High Faulkner University, Bachelors of Business Administration; [occ.] Contract Specialist, Vista Technologies Inc.; [memb.] National Contract Management Association, Highlands Baptist Church; [pers.] This poem is dedicated to all the "Survivors" in which I have been so fortunate to be around and to have transpired into one myself. I have found by now that everything happens for a reason whether it brings triumph or pain. And so, for you, those who have brought flowers and you who have brought stories - I thank you. For I am truly blessed for those that have brought my fears all those loving souls who whispered my fears away.; [a.] Huntsville, AL

BEASLEY, THOMAS A.
[b.] September 3, 1977, Youngstown, OH; [ch.] Two; [ed.] Mostly self thought "Having little to no parental help and putting an end to my governmental systematic brain washing at an early age! Educated myself.; [occ.] I am of the summoned: A local East Dayton Ohio "Metal Band" in which I play the drums and write lyrics.; [memb.] I honor myself with accomplishment and my biggest award would be knowing that I prevail on a self thought path; [oth. writ.] I have many other poems written and have many more to come. I'm also bringing forth a book that will contain some of my poetry although it's not based upon poetry.; [pers.] Look upon the mirror does it reflect thyself "can you dictate thy desention upon a numbered shelf "Can you proclaim your mighty when you transcend another reign "controlled within the abyss of minds thy mirror reflects shame.; [a.] Miamisburg, OH

BEAUDRY JR., ARMAND G.
[b.] July 20, 1962, Providence, RI; [m.] Erin P. Beaudry, September 1, 1995; [ch.] Jeremy, Chris, Laura, Rebecca; [ed.] Smith Field High Devry Tech; [occ.] Firefighter/ EMT-C Smithfield Fire Dept; [memb.] AFL-CIO, IAFF Local 2050; [pers.] My family is my inspiration, but I have to credit most of my inspiration to my lovely wife Erin.; [a.] Smithfield, RI

BECK, STEPHANIE R.
[b.] June 30, 1977, WV; [p.] Marilyn and Dwight David; [ed.] Graduated in 1995 from Petersburg High School. Currently a Sophomore at Fairmont State College; [memb.] Member of the Petersburg Chapter of the National Honor Society; [hon.] Poem has been published in '94-95 high school yearbook and also in the literary Magazine of PHS for the same year. Been selected to the Dean's List of Fairmont State College each semester; [pers.] I wrote "The Torch of Life" for my high school's National Honor Society Induction Ceremony. It reflects my belief that everyone in this world makes a difference to someone.; [a.] Lahmansville, WV

BECKWORTH, DAWN
[b.] September 3, San Francisco; [p.] Mary De Santis and Donald Mendoza; [m.] Michael Wetzstein; [ch.] Igena and Donnie Beckworth; [ed.] Peidmont Hills High, Merced Community College; [occ.] Collection

Representative; [hon.] Honor Roll, Dean's List, President's List; [oth. writ.] This is my first poem that I have ever submitted for publication. I have written poetry since Jr. High.; [a.] San Jose, CA

BEECHEM, MARIAN F.
[pen.] MB; [b.] January 24, 1921, NY, NY; [p.] Deceased, Albert and Marie Krug; [m.] Deceased, James F. Beechem (Retired Army Finance), September 21, 1950; [ch.] Sam Ryan Jr., Loretta Derocher, Joan Krauss; [ed.] Business College, Ladywood High School - Indpls, IN; [occ.] Retired from Air Force Accounting and Finance Center - Denver, Co. Retired - Secretary and Homemaker; [memb.] NARFE National Assn of Retired Federal Employees, Beta Sigma Phi Sorority - Kansas City, Holy Cross Church - Green Bay, WI. Formerly Queen of Peace Church Aurora, Co.; [hon.] Federal Civil Service (15 years), Beta Sigma Phi - 49 years (1947 to 1996); [oth. writ.] "Something that Changed My Life Forever" (Santa Barbara, CA), Elder Hostel - Writing Program 1992. By Cork Millner, author "Write from the Start" writes plays wine books, travel pieces and celebrity profiles - "The Art of Interviewing"; [pers.] Do the best I can to help others in need/ have faith/believe that best in others.; [a.] Green Bay, WI

BEELEN, KRISTEN M.
[b.] April 27, 1981, Holland, MI; [p.] Catherine Top and Richard Beelen; [ed.] Currently attending Hamilton High School, Sophomore Year; [occ.] Student/Writer/ Actress/Musician; [hon.] Several Theater, Music and Academic Awards, Sports awards as well; [oth. writ.] Personal portfolio; [pers.] My hope is to keep my writing honest about life. I write through my experiences.; [a.] Hamilton, MID

BELL, SCOTT C.
[b.] March 26, 1981, Oak Park, IL; [p.] Charles E. Bell, Doris R. Bell; [ed.] Lake Forest High School; [occ.] High School Student; [oth. writ.] Nite writer's literary arts journal; [pers.] Dedicated to Reed, the inspiration for this piece and to so many of my dreams.; [a.] Lake Forest, IL

BENNETT, GRETCHEN E.
[b.] March 19, 1975, Long Branch, NJ; [p.] Gwen and Dale Bennett; [ed.] Monmouth Regional H.S., Brookdale - (Criminal Justice); [occ.] Dispatcher - Eatontown Police Department; [memb.] Eatontown First Aid, Eatontown Fire Department, New Jersey State First Aid Council, Saint James Episcopal Church; [hon.] "Rookie of the Year" High School Softball "1990" - "Outstanding Senior Athlete, 1993" - Leadership Awards Basketball/Softball 1993, Future Business Leader of America - 1992; [oth. writ.] Family is forever, consequences, trials of life, death - right or wrong, and several untitled. All never published.; [pers.] "A true man is not one who gloats when victorious, but one who always remembers to shake hands with the loser when done." Gretchen Bennett.; [a.] Eatontown, NJ

BENZAQUEN, SYLVIA
[pen.] Sylvia Benzaquen; [b.] August 27, 1952, North Africa; [p.] Olga and Jacob; [m.] Divorced; [ch.] Sady Benzaquen; [ed.] 1973 - Intensive English as a second Language. Michigan University at Venezuelan-American Center, Caracas, Venezuela, 1971-71 - General Under-Graduate Studies, Haifa University, Haifa, Israel, 1973-77 - Licensed in Mass Communication, Specialized in Audio-Visual Production, Radio-Television and Cinematography, Catholic University Andres Bello, Caracas, Venezuela, 1983-84 - Intensive Hebrew course for professionals, Yad Eliyahu, Tel Aviv, Israel; [occ.] Free Lance Journalist and Writer, Correspondent in New York City of Newspaper Nuevo Mundo Ispraelita; [hon.] 1983, Order of Saint Vincent, Annual

Award Presented in France to one outstanding Journalist from around the world. Trip sponsored by all producers of Champagne in France; [oth. writ.] Articles: El Diario de Caracas, Revista Momento, Revista Variedades, Revista Taxi Guia, Book: Una Vida, Un Paisaje, Un Pincel, Biography of Amparo Rojas, Venezuelan Painter; [pers.] "Life is too short enjoy every second of it."; [a.] Flushing, NY

BENZOR, LAURA KAY
[pen.] Smilely; [b.] January 27, 1975, Arizona; [p.] Richard, Angela Coughlin; [m.] Luis F. Benzor, December 19, 1995; [ch.] Christopher, Shereta Hogan; [hon.] Trophy for 1st place Essay Writing Contest for the "Color's of Life."; [oth. writ.] Essay for "Color's of Life". And a dictionary for "Slang Words of Today". Both for Eisenhower High School.; [pers.] My writings are based on experiences about myself and family members. "They all come from the heart."; [a.] Glendale, AZ

BERGMAN, BETH
[b.] November 22, 1980, Fond du Lac; [p.] Dan and Barb Bergman; [ed.] Presently high school student; [occ.] Student; [memb.] Church youth group, Sunday School teacher, dancing, newspaper staff, year book committee and forensics; [oth. writ.] Other poetry and journaling.; [pers.] I find comfort in expressing my thoughts through writing.; [a.] Fond du Lac, WI

BERTA, VICTOR
[b.] November 28, 1938, Rock Springs, WY; [p.] George and Cora Berta; [ed.] BS, MS Physics University of Wyoming; [occ.] Retired after 31 yrs. at the Idaho National Engineering Laboratory; [memb.] American Association for the Advancement of Science (AAAS), American Institute of Physics (AIP), Nature Conservancy, Wilderness Society, National Parks and Conservation Association, National Wildlife, International Wildlife; [hon.] Sigma Pi Sigma (Physics Honor Society) 3 Patents; [oth. writ.] Forty-two technical publications.; [a.] Rock Springs, WY

BESMEHN, THOMAS MARTIN
[b.] August 6, 1955, Brainerd, MN; [p.] Richard and Lois Besmehn; [m.] Jeannie R. Besmehn, May 27, 1989; [ch.] Matthew; [ed.] Writing at the Brainerd Central Lake College at night time; [occ.] Self Employed; [hon.] Auto Body and Welding; [pers.] To my son (Matthew Thomas Besmehn) and my beautiful wife Jeannie and Aunt Lou Harding, and all my teachers throughout the years. The St. Francis School and Brainerd Central Lakes College.

BEVERLY, JIM
[b.] November 18, 1960, Jacksonville, FL; [p.] Bill Leishman, Jane Leishman; [m.] Leticia A. Beverly, February 18, 1988; [ch.] James M. Beverly II; [ed.] Englewood Sr. High, NMSU; [occ.] Photographer; [memb.] Smithsonian Institute; [pers.] Having attempted something once is not enough, do not afraid to fail or dream again. Never give up, never ever give up.; [a.] Chaparral, NM

BHUSHAN, NISHITH
[b.] August 2, 1963, Deoband, India; [p.] Mr. Bharat Bhushan, Ravi Bhushan; [ed.] M.S. EE Colorado State, Florida State, UDC (B.S. in EE); [occ.] Programmer analyst, ING Capital Holdings, NY, NY; [oth. writ.] Just Beginning, Rest Is unpublished as yet.; [a.] Somerset, NJ

BIBEAU, JACQUI
[pen.] Jac Lee; [b.] April 29, 1954, Jerome, ID; [p.] Mary Jo and Leon Walker; [m.] Douglas Bibeau, August 14, 1976; [ch.] Megan LaMachia; [ed.] A.A. in Com Science with a business option; [memb.] Member

of St. Cabrini Alter Society, Lector at Church; [a.] Balsom Lake, WI

BILOV, YEFIM
[pen.] Yefim Bilov; [b.] February 1, 1922, Odessa, USSR; [p.] Solomon Bilov, Ida Bilova; [m.] Elila Bilova, July 14, 1948; [ch.] Natalia Bilova; [ed.] High School, Kiev, USSR, Kiev and Uralsky Polytekchnic Institutes, USSR, ME; [occ.] I'm senior citizen; [memb.] MSME; [hon.] Ph.D.M.E., Kiev Polytekchnic Institute; [oth. writ.] Several youthful poems in local students newspapers. In total, over hundred books, brochures and articles on mechanical in-plant equipment, machine-tools, tools and related fields.; [pers.] "...All men are created equal...they are endowed by their Creator with certain unalienable right...life, liberty and the pursuit of happiness." (The Declaration of Independence).; [a.] Baltimore, MD

BIRT, MICHELLE G.
[pen.] "Migy"; [b.] March 25, 1954, NY; [p.] Thomas E. and Margaret (Deceased); [m.] Griffin Calvin L. ("Lenny") Birt, June 9, 1976; [ch.] Melika Ashanna Birt, Grandson: Malik Nashiem Taylor; [ed.] Prospect Heights High School B'lkyn, NY Graduated 6/72 Betty Owens Secretarial School B'klyn, NY Graduated 2/91; [occ.] Receptionist/Word Processor in Aviation Engineering; [memb.] Founder of "The Manny Hanny's" a theatre group (B'klyn, NY). Former Girl Scout Ass't Troup Leader (B'klyn, NY); [hon.] Recipient of the Nat'l Library of Poetry's 1996 Editor's Choice Award; [oth. writ.] "Sisterhood" published in "A Muse To Follow", "The Little King" published in "Best Poems of the 90's"; [pers.] If I can reach people through my poetry, then I have accomplished my goal.; [a.] Stone Mountain, GA

BIXBY, ALICE REYNOLDS
[pen.] Alice Reynolds; [b.] November 18, 1947, Terrytown, NY; [p.] Edward and Ethel Reynolds; [ch.] Clarissa, Tammy and Bonnie Jean; [ed.] Pittsfield High, Massachusetts Hollister Jr. College Lenox Mass.; [occ.] Self Employed Crafts, Home Care; [oth. writ.] Many unpublished poems I have written in the last 25 years.; [pers.] In my poems I try to capture a mood or a feeling about events in time, I have been influenced by frost, Dickenson Emily.; [a.] Holly Hill, FL

BJELLAND, RHONDA J.
[b.] July 26, 1960, Grinnell, IA; [p.] Eldon and Kathy Thompson; [m.] Tim Bjelland, August 27, 1983; [ch.] Kale Marie; [ed.] Grinnell - Newburg High School, Central College, University of Northern Iowa; [occ.] Kindergarten Teacher and Coach, East Marshall Elementary, Laurel, IA; [memb.] ISEA, NEA; [oth. writ.] Two articles published in local paper. I am currently a student.; [a.] Laurel, IA

BLACK, CHRISTOPHER
[b.] October 12, 1975, Oklahoma City, OK; [p.] Rex Owen Black and Cynthia Eva Black; [m.] Carrie Black, May 18, 1996; [ed.] Graduate of Northeast High '94, currently enrolled at Okla. City Univ.; [occ.] Student, Bank Teller; [memb.] Phi Mu Alpha Sinfonia Fraternity, OCU Bass Ensemble, OCU Orchestra; [hon.] Dean's Honor Roll (OCU), National Merit Commended Scholer; [a.] Oklahoma City, OK

BLACKWELL, BERNICE G.
[b.] March 28, 1934, New York City; [p.] Germaine Moore, Percival Moore (Deceased; [ch.] Lisa Blackwell, Pamela Blackwell, Seri; [ed.] York College of City University of NY (BS in Community Health Education), Bellevue School of Nursing (Nursing Certificate); [occ.] Registered Professional Nurse; [memb.] York College Alumni Association, New York State Nurse's Association; [hon.] Vera B. Douthit Memorial

Award, New York State Legistures Nurse of Distinction Award, Dean's List; [oth. writ.] "34th Street", "In Memoriam"; [pers.] Life's challenging experiences have been an influencing factor in my writings.; [a.] New York, NY

BLACKWELL, WANDA
[pen.] Wanda Long-Blackwell; [b.] August 13, 1952, Scottsboro, AL; [p.] Mrs. Elizabeth Long (W.O. Long-deceased); [m.] Richard O. Blackwell, October 10, 1976; [ch.] Richmond Orion Blackwell 16, Katy Elizabeth Blackwell 12; [ed.] Attended College - Chattanooga State Bridgeport Schools 1 - 12; [occ.] Homemaker formerly Bookkeeper of 7 Auto Parts Inc. Blackwell Self Employed Board of Directors - Jackson Co., Al., American Heart Assoc. 1992- 1995, American Indian Parent Committee, Jackson County, Mount Carmel Missionary Baptist Church, Southern Association Accreditation Committee - 1993 - 1996, Drama Club; [oth. writ.] Many writings, nothing published. I write for self - satisfaction.; [pers.] To me, life experiences are so important. There is so much to pass on for others to enjoy and reflect back on. We must not lose our simple memories for they are so rich.; [a.] Bridgeport, AL

BLAIR, TREVOR
[pen.] Trevor Blair; [b.] October 3, 1986, Denver, CO; [p.] Nicki Blair; [occ.] Student; [pers.] This poem was written in 3rd grade. My poem was written from my heart.

BOCHORZ, LAWRENCE L.
[b.] March 13, 1948, Chicago, IL; [p.] Louis Bochorz and Elsie Bochorz; [occ.] Registered Respiratory Therapist; [memb.] American Association of Respiratory Care, Harley Owners Group, Milwaukee, WI; [hon.] Diamond Homer Trophy, Famous Poets Society; [oth. writ.] Several articles for local newspaper. Poems and short stories printed in grade school anthology; [pers.] Dream your dreams, reality has no limitations.; [a.] Chicago, IL

BOLANDER, BROOK
[b.] September 11, 1980, Berkley, CA; [p.] Noela Harrison, Tom Bolander; [ed.] 3rd Year High School; [occ.] Student; [hon.] 3rd in English and Math's competition, sport (Hockey and Tennis) awards.; [oth. writ.] Several poems which I entered in another competition about two months ago, and two other poems and entered in this competition.; [pers.] I go after the motto "Answer the bell and come out on top". Although at the same time I make the most out of life and I always manage to have lost of fun.; [a.] Orting, WA

BOND, KATHERINE L.
[pen.] Kay Bond; [b.] June 7, 1949, Sardis, MS; [p.] Emma M. Clerk and William T. Coble; [m.] John R. Bond IV, July 27, 1969; [ch.] Sonia O'Neal and Tasha Bond; [ed.] Graduate of Joliet West High, some College: Northern Illinois University and Joliet Junior College (both incomplete); [occ.] Medical Transcriptionist; [memb.] The National Authors Registry, International Society of Authors and Artists, Poets Guild, and the National Poets Association, International Biographical Association; [hon.] (5) Editors Choice Awards thru National Library of Poetry and ISP, (4) Achievement of Merit Awards thru Creative Arts and Science Ent., International Poet of Merit 1995 and 1996 thru National Library of Poetry and ISP, President's Award for Literary Excellence thru Iliad Press, Editors Preference Award of Excellence, and Diamond Homer Trophy thru Famous Poets Society, Honorable Mention thru Cartlon Press, Who's Who in New Poets Spring 1996, Editors Preference Award of Excellence for June of 1996 through Creative Arts and Science Enterprises; [oth. writ.] Lord, The Rapture, Her Fight Our Reward,

An Epitaph, Not Yet!, Maryjo, Immortal Man and Seasoned, And Many Others.; [pers.] God and prayer makes it all possible. Proverbs 3:6 - in all thy ways acknowledge him, and he shall direct thy paths.; [a.] Joliet, IL

BOOKER, JACKIE L.
[pen.] Kali; [b.] August 1, 1938, Portland, OR; [ed.] AA Degree; [occ.] Private Investigator; [hon.] Awards of Merit - World of Poetry Silver Poet 1990 - World of Poetry; [oth. writ.] Several poems published by the World of Poetry.; [pers.] I look through your eyes and see how you perceive the world. My writing is my perception of your perception.; [a.] Las Vegas, NV

BORGER, GERALDINE
[b.] September 2, 1942, Clarence, PA; [p.] Mr. and Mrs. Frank J. Waxmunsky Sr.; [m.] Stanley W. Borger, September 19, 1964; [ch.] Vonda, Beth Ann, Doyle, LeAnn; [ed.] Graduate of Bald Eagle Area High School, Wingate, Undergraduate student at Penn State Univ./ attended classes at Centre County Voc. Tech., Pleasant Gap, PA; [occ.] Housewife; [memb.] Mountaintop Ambulance Club; [hon.] Cub Scout Den Mother Award, School Newspaper Editorial Award, School Library Award, Past President and V. Pres. of Snow Shoe PTO, Church of School Teacher, Asst. Pianist, Member of Official Board of CMA Church in Snow Shoe, PA; [oth. writ.] Several poems to be published in hard back books for various publishers. Some poems published in various Church bulletins and local Church news letter, also one in a trucking magazine.; [pers.] You will note the love of God and the joy of nature coming through in most of my poetry and writings. My parents and family have been very influential in writings.; [a.] Snow Shoe, PA

BOROWSKA-RZUCIDLO, ZOTIA
[pen.] Sota Kurylo; [b.] May 13, 1929, Poland; [p.] Ludwika, Joseph; [m.] Widow; [ed.] M. Sci., Ph. D., Polytech. University, Gdansk, Poland; [occ.] Professor, Rockerfeller Univ., New York, NY; [memb.] Am. - Soc. Biol. a Molecular Biol., The Internat'l. Soc. of Poets Polish Inst. of Art a Sci. in America; [hon.] "Who is Who in the World", Who is Who in the East of Am.", Internatl. Soc. of Poets, semifinalist in the 1996 Poets Contest; [oth. writ.] Over 60 articles in professional journals and books poems published in "Across the World" and "Spirit of Age" published by the Nat'l. Library of Poets, (1996) writes poetry and short stories in English and Polish; [pers.] Interest in biological resource, music, literature, paintings. Influenced by romantic a contemporary music and literature. My research and writing is conducted in spirit of "Pro Beno Humani Generis"; [a.] New York, NY

BOS, HANS
[b.] March 17, 1946, Laren (N.H), The Netherlands; [p.] Wieger and Betty Bos; [ed.] Indonesia, The Netherlands, Switzerland, Spain, USA; [occ.] Store Manager; [a.] Terre Haute, IN

BOTTS, BEVERLY
[pen.] Beverly Botts; [b.] September 13, 1955, Glasgow, KY; [p.] Lawrence and Louise Botts; [ch.] 1 daughter Hannah Mai Yan Botts; [ed.] Glasgow High School, Norton Infirmary School of Nursing; [occ.] RN Corporate Infusion Nurse Educator at Caretenders Health Corp.; [memb.] St. Francis of Rome Church Intravenous Nurses Society; [pers.] This is thy first writing, which was written after I returned from China, my daughter was adopted in China.; [a.] Glasgow, KY

BOUCHER, ELIZABETH ANNE
[pen.] Anne Porter Boucher; [b.] February 24, 1915, Fall River, MA; [p.] Elizabeth Rose, Joseph Lawrence; [m.] George Porter, May 27, 1939, Marcel Boucher,

November 24, 1974 (both died); [ch.] Patricia, Elizabeth, Marilyn; [ed.] Fifteen years of the St. Roses School of Boston Chelsea - Mass. Part of Boston.; [occ.] Retired from Unirayd in Prov. G.M. - Framingham; [memb.] I got my best Fiance about my friendships, I song with a Quartet and I sang with my big bunch of singers. I traveled a lot (Europe-Harvard); [hon.] International Woman of the year (Twice) National Woman of the year. (International Society of Poets), 20th Century awards for Achievement. International Who's Who. I have my Wall covered by Plaques, I can't mention them all; [oth. writ.] My life story and my mothers - My Dad and all his relatives way back to years and years ago.; [pers.] I am a very lucky woman to have National Library of Poetry on my side. I have an honored Society placing my poems. I thank you for having my poems put in a book of good value.; [a.] Blackstone, MA

BOWDEN, JESSIE
[b.] September 17, 1956, Denver, CO; [p.] John and Jo Ann Wade; [ch.] Laura, Jo Ann, Dina, John Wade; [ed.] High School, and College Graduate; [occ.] Sub. Teacher - Woodland School Dist.; [memb.] VFW Aux Member 5843 Meeker, Colorado; [pers.] I wrote this poem in May 1995 and put music to it and sang it to my Grandma just before she passed away on July 12, 1995. That was my very special gift to her. One of Love!; [a.] Ralston, OK

BOWLES, GLEN
[pen.] Glen Bowles; [b.] April 1, 1917, Ignacio, CO; [p.] Jesse Bowles, Anna Bowles; [m.] Rose Frazier (February 1924, now deceased 1969), 1943; [ch.] Marlene, Jesse Kim; [ed.] Elementary (graduated 8th grade), Cooking School Army 1943; [occ.] Retired; [memb.] VFW, American Legion, Klamath Basin Senior Citizens; [hon.] Only honored by the praise and the publishing of my poetry each month in the "Today's Senior" section of the local Herald and News in Klamath Falls, OR, and self published books.; [oth. writ.] Four books published (locally) titled, "Poetry of Life and Seasons", "Of Times and Rhymes", "A Personal Touch of Life", "A Big Bag of Wind", all published locally and sold here. Poetry published in "Today's Seniors"; [pers.] My goal is to give people something to enjoy. A smile. A touch of eternity full of love and laughter. One of my main influences would be Longfellow, Helen Steiner Rice and other of their type and style.; [a.] Klamath Falls, OR

BOYKIN JR., MARION
[b.] March 22, 1949, Muskogee, OK; [p.] Marion Boykin Sr. and Loraine; [ch.] Lydia Teresa Boykin; [ed.] High School Vacaville California, University of Utah, SLC, Northeastern State University, OK, Small Business Management, Muskogee OK; [occ.] Poetry and career change; [memb.] NSU Alumni Association, International Society of Poets; [hon.] Athletic Scholarship, Univ. of Utah, S.L.C. Business Certificate, Med. Northeastern State University, OK; [oth. writ.] "The Nature Of Man" published by Famous Poets Society, Famous Poems of the Twentieth Century Winter 1996. "Faith" published by The National Library of Poetry.; [pers.] I want to write words that are inspirational.; [a.] Checotah, OK

BOZEMAN, JILL SIMMONS
[pen.] J. Bozeman, J. Simmons Bozeman; [b.] September 12, 1972, Texas; [m.] Wade Cooper Bozeman, July 15, 1995; [ed.] Tulsa Junior College and Northwestern State U. of Louisiana; [occ.] Writer and Artist; [memb.] Midnight Society of Wilde Poets, Nat'l League of Profuse Smokers, American Automobile Association; [hon.] Presidents honor roll; [oth. writ.] Fairy tales for the advanced child, "Fat Cat", "Sister Revisited", "Ode to a Dullard, etc..."; [pers.] One may say the poet creates

poetry with his tool, the pen, but in truth the poet is the tool of poetry and the pen is simply an invention of necessity.; [a.] Fort Polk, LA

BRADLEY, CYNTHIA L.
[b.] May 29, 1953, Coronado, CA; [p.] Richard H. Bradley, Doris E. Bradley; [ed.] Great Mills High School, St. Mary's College of Maryland; [occ.] Medical Illustrator/Graphic Designer - Juris Corp., Orlando; [memb.] Honorary member - Hospice of Central, FL, Volunteer - Greater Seminole Lasertoma, Volunteer - Orlando Juvenile Diabetes; [hon.] JC Roden Queen - St. Mary's Co. MD, Winner Media Charity Race Seminole Harness Raceway, FL, Volunteer Award U.F.W. Lady's Auxiliary, 2nd Place Canoe River Run, Altamonte Springs, FL; [oth. writ.] Various articles and illustrations for equestrian publications; [pers.] Never be afraid to venture forth, we all falter momentarily but our achievements will last a lifetime.; [a.] Orlando, FL

BRADLEY, NICOLE
[pen.] Nikki; [b.] December 18, 1984, Alexandra Hospital; [p.] William and Maria Bradley; [hon.] I am currently an honor roll student at Woodbridge Middle School. I also won 1st place in the Springswood Elementary Safety Patrol Essay "1995" were I was also an honor roll student.; [pers.] I want to thank my parents and my teachers, Miss Keiser for all their support.; [a.] Woodbridge, VA

BRADSHAW, SANDRA R.
[pen.] Sandee May; [b.] November 1, Austin, TX; [p.] Mr. and Mrs. Raymond Reither; [m.] Henry Franklin Bradshaw; [ch.] Kimberly and Crystal; [ed.] Lanier High, Austin Comm. College, St. Edwards University, Lon Morris College, University of Texas; [occ.] Freelance writer; [memb.] National Assoc. of Legal Assistants, Capitol Area Paralegal Assoc.; [oth. writ.] Reflections in Poetry, Tear Drops From Heaven, Echoes of the Past, Lupus - My Long Journey, From Denial To Acceptance, Pop's Wicked Ways, Gypsy Curse, Soldier Boy.; [pers.] My poems and stories are based on true life experiences. The poem "War's Never Ending Battle" and the book "Soldier Boy" are dedicated to my husband and all other Vietnam Veterans. God Bless All Of You.; [a.] Round Rock, TX

BRADY, LISA
[pen.] Mary Jane; [b.] August 2, 1980, Durham, NC; [p.] Mom-Pam Gunn, Stepfather - Wilson Gunn, Dad - Jody Brady, Stepmother - Candy Brady; [ed.] High School Sophomore (10th grade); [memb.] Junior Beta Club, (7th grade) '93; [hon.] John's Hopkins Talent Search (7th grade) 43; [oth. writ.] "If Humans Had No Eyes" (published in school literary magazine); [pers.] My poetry is a physical manifestation of my soul.; [a.] Roanoke, VA

BRADY, VIRGINIA J.
[pen.] Virginia J. Brady; [b.] November 8, 1924, New Canaan, CT; [p.] Anthony and Margaret Savatsky; [m.] Peter R. Brady M.D., April 22, 1946; [ch.] Virginia, Patricia, Peter, Margo and Katheryn; [ed.] New Canaan High School, Kings County School of Nursing; [occ.] Retired; [memb.] KCSN Alumni Assoc., U.S Army Nurse Cadet Corp, St. Mary's Church Scholarship Donor, International Society Poets, Horticultural Society; [hon.] Three Editors choice award 1995-96; [oth. writ.] Poems published the National Library of Poetry, poems written for bereavement groups also for Local Senior Citizen group and for Public Middle School poetry classes; [pers.] I try to write simply about emotions and controversial issues that we face in life that both adults and children can relate to and enjoy.; [a.] New Monmouth, NJ

BRAIDA, DOLLY
[pen.] Dolly; [b.] April 17, 1937, San Francisco, CA; [p.] Ive and Louise Dougherty; [m.] Arthur Braida, August 25, 1962; [ch.] 2 sons - Ive and Eric, 1 daughter - Katie, 6 grandchildren; [ed.] High School and Business school; [occ.] Homemaker and Poet, go into schools to talk to students; [memb.] International Society of Poets, Madonna's Ladies Group at our Church - AMO AIDS Ministry Outreach; [hon.] 8 Editor Awards, 4 Merit Awards, my collection of poetry past the Calif. Board of Education; [oth. writ.] Collection of poetry called "From Sad Beginnings To Happy Endings" published in 9 anthology plus in the Best of 95, 96 and the 90's. Been asked to be recorded 6 times. A column in The Christ Paper.; [pers.] Through my writing I want to help change the hate, prejudice and violence in the world. I hope to do this by reading my poetry to our young people and adult groups and talk with them.; [a.] Windsor, CA

BRANSON, RHONDA
[b.] February 14, 1958, Alexandria, LA; [ch.] James Branson; [ed.] Bolton High School - Class of 76 LSU - Alexandria 1988-89, currently enrolled in a Correspondence School for Medical and Legal Transcription; [occ.] Homemaker; [memb.] Organ Donation and Transplants Northside Baptist Church - Pineville, LA; [pers.] This poem is my special gift to my son Jonathan on his 15th birthday. I wanted him to know we have not forgotten him, and that he will always be in our thoughts and prayers until we meet him in Heaven.; [a.] Pineville, LA

BRASKIE, AMELIA DE FANT
[pen.] Amelia De Fant Braskie; [b.] June 10, 1907, Taio (Val'Dinon), Austria; [p.] Cirillo De Fant and Louise Franch De Fant; [m.] Walter S. Braskie, October 27, 1934; [ch.] Jean L. Bartos and Eileen D. Kuntz; [ed.] 8 yrs. in Austrian Schools, 4 yrs. in American Schools; [occ.] Retired; [memb.] Tirolesi Alpini of Hazleton, PA, (I was founder of Club 3/19/68); [hon.] Honored by Club Members for many years of service.; [oth. writ.] Several unpublished poems and short stories.; [pers.] I am afraid to do evil, but not afraid to enter where there is evil. I helped prisoners in the Eastern Penitentiary, Phila., PA. I appeared in front of parole board and helped a man get out, after 30 yrs., because he stole a loaf of bread. There is so much good to do, if one takes the time to do it.; [a.] Conyngham, PA

BRASSEAUX, DAVID M.
[b.] February 21, 1980, Lafayette, LA; [p.] Carl and Glenda Brasseaux; [ed.] Currently a junior at Lafayette High School; [occ.] Student; [pers.] In life I've learned to reap the fruits of the vine, then walk away, leaving the weeds behind.; [a.] Lafayette, LA

BRAVO, PATRICIA R.
[b.] April 18, 1961, Burlington, VT; [p.] Raul and Nancy (Chilean); [m.] 1981-1989; [ch.] Santiago 13, and Mariano 11, Wechsler; [ed.] Master in Psychology (Pontifice Catholic University Chile); [occ.] Studying a Doctoral Program in Organizational Consultancy Psychology; [memb.] "Gil Project: A project of Love, Art, and Erotism". (Santiago - Chile); [oth. writ.] Writer of Dissemination articles in the field of Human Empowermnet: "Ya" Magazine, El Mercurio (Chilean newspaper). Illustrator in "De Familia y Terapias": Journal of the Family Therapy Institute, Chile.; [pers.] For me, health is awareness of love's presence, a feeling of inner peace that comes from total relinquishment of judgement. I believe in the energy of Love as the essential existential fact. Love is our ultimate reality and our purpose on earth, it is a radical outlook.; [a.] Orinda, CA

BRAYDA, BEVERLY
[pen.] Beverly Parrish Brayda; [b.] March 29, 1934, Chicago, IL; [p.] John and Omah Parrish (Deceased); [m.] William Brayda, November 25, 1987; [ch.] Six living, 2 deceased; [ed.] Graduated Baxter Seminary, Baxter Tennessee 1952; [occ.] Retired Waitress; [memb.] AARP; [oth. writ.] I've written 60 children's stories, many poems, A Journal Of My Ancestors, My Life, never tried to submit any for publication.; [pers.] I am saved! Try to be a soldier working for the Lord! Happily married to my soul mate, 2 sister (Best friends), 1 brother (Church of Christ) pastor, 6 living children, 13 grandchildren.; [a.] Palatine, IL

BRAZELL, SEAN
[b.] June 21, 1981, Los Angeles; [p.] Diana Brazell, Troy Brazell; [ed.] James Madison Memorial High School; [occ.] Student; [oth. writ.] Nothing else published, but many poems written.; [pers.] I believe that we all die, so we should enjoy what we have now and live for the day.; [a.] Madison, WI

BREEDWELL, DEBORAH R.
[b.] May 27, 1965, Arab, AL; [p.] William Ralph and Lutrecia Rasco; [m.] Danny Ray Breedwell, December 3, 1982; [ch.] Cassie Danielle and Tia Marae Breedwell; [ed.] Fairview High, Wallace State College; [occ.] Cosmetologist; [memb.] Lakeview Church; [hon.] Dean's List; [oth. writ.] Although I haven't yet had any other work published. It is my dream to do so. I have written a book, that hopefully in the future, will be published.; [pers.] We all express our individual thoughts and feelings in our own way. By putting writing on paper, I can let my mind travel, releasing my thoughts and feelings, in words, on paper.; [a.] Baileyton, AL

BRESLAVER, ARTHUR S.
[pen.] A. S. Breslaver; [b.] December 21, 1926, NY; [ed.] N.Y.C. School System New York University; [occ.] Retired, formerly a journalist who worked for more than 30 years in Europe; [pers.] Hail Multiplicity, Love Diversity.; [a.] New York, NY

BREWSTER, CYNTHIA
[b.] October 25, 1959, Clinton, SC; [p.] Shealy and Lillie Johnson; [pers.] In cherished memories of my "Dad".

BRIDGES, NANCY RHAMY
[b.] Wooster, OH; [p.] Alvin E. (Deceased) and Esther Johnson Rhamy, Stepfather Walter Simmons (Deceased); [m.] Robert H. Bridges Jr., May 20, 1989; [ch.] Ronald L. Miller, Steven C. Miller and Jill M. Miller Trippe; [occ.] Local Government Soc'y, and part-time beauty consultant; [oth. writ.] I have a collection of poems I have written through the years (unpublished.); [pers.] My poetry casts glimpses of both happy and sad experiences that have touched my life through, the years. I especially enjoy composing poems that are amusing, and filled with thought for their readers. My friends have been an inspiration to me.; [a.] Sierra Vista, AZ

BRIGHAM, SHIRLEY
[pen.] Shirley Conway Brigham; [b.] September 3, 1932, Amherstburg, ON; [p.] Lionel and Annie Conway; [m.] Aldrich Brigham, July 28, 1956; [ch.] Douglas, Marilee and Brian; [ed.] Graduate of High School, Graduate of General Amherst, Amherstburg, Ontario, Canada; [occ.] Homemaker; [memb.] Member Saint Paul A.M.E. Church; [hon.] Graduate of General Amherst High School, Received The International Poet of Merit Award, Graduate of General Amherst High School Amherstburg, Ontario, Canada; [oth. writ.] Grandchildren, Precious Time, Keeping Marriage Alive, Forgiveness and Cheerfulness.; [pers.] I love writing Poetry. Thanks to God for the Divine Inspiration.

Hoping the readers enjoy it as I do.; [a.] Detroit, MI

BRIGHT JR., JAMES EDWARD
[b.] June 11, 1963, Lebanon, OR; [p.] James E. Sr. and Sandra Bright; [ch.] Zacharia James Bright (12); [ed.] High School/Payette Sr High/May 1981 - Treasure Valley Con. College 1982-83. John Robert Powers, 1983-86; [occ.] Disabled; [hon.] Three years Advance Degree in Modeling Drama Scholarship in 1981; [oth. writ.] Other poems; [pers.] Hitch your wagon to a star keep your seat and there you are. Jesus never fails.; [a.] Vancouver, WA

BRITTON, WINIFRED
[pen.] Windy Britton; [b.] May 17, 1938, Detroit, MI; [p.] William and Naomi Madison; [m.] Henry Rankin, Edward Britton (Both Deceased), June 28, 1956, December 17, 1979; [ch.] La Rita Rankin, Felicia King; [ed.] High School Graduate, Northern High School Detroit, Michigan; [occ.] Homemaker; [oth. writ.] (Memb.) Whole Life Mintries of Augusta, Ga. Dr. Sandra G. Kennedy is the Pastor. She had a book of poems published that I have written. I have several poems unpublished. Daughters of Zion Ministries enter a poem each month in their National News Letter.; [pers.] I believe, before the world ever was, God chose me to come into this world, for such a time as this to share my relationship with Him and His relationships with me to others. I give all the Glory and Honor, yes the Credit To My Lord, Jesus Christ.; [a.] Hephzibah, GA

BRODZINSKI, DAWN BIRELEY
[b.] July 25, 1971, Chester, PA; [p.] Doris S. Bireley and L. Richard Bireley; [m.] Michael W. Brodzinski, October 26, 1991; [ed.] Academy Park H.S.; [pers.] My poetry is about my innermost thoughts and feelings. I believe that writing in any form can help people understand themselves better.; [a.] Sharon Hill, PA

BROOKS, CORTNEY
[pen.] Cece; [b.] October 1926, Montgomery, AL; [p.] Tim Kinney and Deborah Caulder; [m.] Domestic partner - Jessie Hooper; [memb.] Human Rights Campaign; [oth. writ.] Published in Copperhill Quarterly; [pers.] I believe that every person can over come any and all obstacles, with love and patience.; [a.] Prattville, AL

BROOKS, KATHLEEN SHULER
[pen.] Kat; [b.] September 7, 1945, Swain Co, NC; [p.] Vernol and Bonnie Shuler; [m.] Linton L. Brooks I, October 18, 1976; [ch.] Four married daughters and one son at home; [ed.] High School and some college classes; [occ.] Care Giver to Elderly and Notary Public; [oth. writ.] Many published and unpublished poems. Unpublished songs, (Country and gospel) children's short stories and poems.; [pers.] My desire is that my poems touch and help others. To me it is a way to talk to people. They may enjoy reading the words of a poem when, otherwise, they may never hear what is said.; [a.] Whittier, NC

BROOKSHIRE, DOROTHY W.
[pen.] Whitehawk; [b.] September 15, 1949, Lenoir, NC; [p.] Wayne and Louneta White; [m.] Jack A. Brookshire Sr., July 1, 1989; [ch.] LaWanda Faye Brown; [ed.] Happy Valley High, CCC and TI (I); [occ.] Teacher Assistant Exceptional Children (Retired Due to Disability); [memb.] Wordweaver's Writing Club, Fibromyalgia/Chronic Fatigue Support Group; [hon.] Teacher Assistant of the Year 94-95, several Bus Driving Awards; [oth. writ.] Local School Superintendent used one of my poems for county meeting as did a School Principal. Short story published by, Hometown Memories Publishing Co. My newsletter is published by the Morganton FMS/CFS Support Group; [pers.] I try to structure my writing so it can be used for learning

about our environment. I also draw from real life situations for some of my poetry, in-order to help those who are faced incurable illnesses or high stress situations to learn positive coping skills. God never gives us futile gifts.

BROWN, CYNTHIA DUNN
[pen.] Cindy; [b.] June 11, 1966, Ashdown, AR; [p.] Roy C. and Gully J. Dunn; [m.] Divorced; [ed.] B.A. Communications, Minor: Criminal Justice; [occ.] Mortgage Loan Counselor Navy Federal Credit Union, Vienna, VA; [memb.] Washington Hospital Center Mentor Program; [hon.] Good Conduct: U.S. Navy Reserves; [oth. writ.] Local newspaper published two of my poems. Many short stories and inspirational papers written for church programs.; [pers.] Writing is my escape from every day activities. I can become anyone or anything in my writings and I love it. I plan to write a book of short stories and poems ultimate goal.; [a.] Lorton, VA

BROWN, JACOB JEREMY
[b.] April 21, 1965, Denison, TX; [p.] Jimmie and Fiffie Brown; [m.] Robin LeAnna Brown, April 17, 1992; [pers.] Written in remembrance of my wife whom I truly love, I hope she finds what she wants in life, if you truly someone you can't try to keep them with you, for true love is selfless and non possessive, if they return that love then they will be with you by choice. Maybe we all need to learn to walk lightly through life.; [a.] Tulsa, OK

BROWN, LAURA
[b.] April 11, 1983, Livingston, NJ; [p.] William and Deborah Brown; [ed.] Entering grade 8 in September 1996 at Montclair Kimberley Academy, Montclair, NJ; [occ.] Student; [oth. writ.] Miscellaneous poetry and other stories, fiction.; [pers.] I wrote this poem for my wonderful, brown eyed dog, Frisky, who has the ability to make the worst things seem better.; [a.] Little Falls, NJ

BROWN, PAT
[b.] July 16, 1931, Philadelphia, PA; [ed.] B.A. in psychology, San Francisco State University; [occ.] Retired teacher city and county of Napa Valley California School districts. At present a literary tutor, Napa County Library Literacy Program; [memb.] San Francisco State Alumni Association; Congree of Racial Equality — CORE; St. Thomas Quinas Catholic Parish; American Civil Liberties Union; Democratic Caucus, Napa, California; Service Employees Services Association; [hon.] 1995 Award of Achievement and 1996 Diamond Homer Award of Achievement — Famous Poets Institute; [pers.] My college friend, Eva, lost her family in Vienna to the death camp of Auschwitz in World War II and for me she is a very special person. As the Good Book says, "God's greatest gift to man is love."; [a.] Napa Valley, CA

BROWN, SHAKIARA
[pen.] SKB; [b.] July 23, 1976, Philadelphia; [p.] Adrienne Brown; [ed.] William Penn High (Phila) Presently Kutztown University; [occ.] Secondary Education Student; [memb.] Black student Union President, Triumph Baptist Church, Kutztown Gospel Choir; [hon.] The Jarrah Scholarship, Delta Sigma Theta Scholarship; [oth. writ.] Some short stories unpublished, as well as several other poems and raps. I have also written a few songs mostly R and B.; [pers.] Writing is the second love in my life, the first is God for it is the who gives me the strength and wisdom to write the way I do.; [a.] Philadelphia, PA

BROWNING, PATRICIA LORENE
[b.] March 15, 1948, Clint Wood, VA; [p.] Charles and Martha Stewart; [m.] Chester Howard Browning, April 22, 1981; [ch.] Tammy, Tina, Kenny, Ronda, Mary and Chester; [ed.] Woodson High School, CNA, Northern Virginia Community College; [occ.] Nursing Assist. Mary Washington Hospital Home Health; [memb.] Spot Sylvania Church of God; [hon.] Golden poet Award 1988, 89, 90; [oth. writ.] Fly free, Daddy, A Phone Call To Moma, Comfort One Another, Still Small Voice, The Rose, ect......; [pers.] I can do all things through Christ who strengths me.; [a.] Spotsylvania, VI

BRUMBAUGH, JAMIE LYNN
[pen.] Christina-Tracey Rainbird; [b.] January 31, 1984, Altoona, PA; [p.] Sharon Lehman and Bob Brumbaugh; [ed.] 7th grade (Richland Middle School); [memb.] Belmont United Methodist Youth Fellowship; [hon.] John Hopkins Academic Award; [a.] Johnstown, PA

BRYANT, CHARLENE E.
[b.] July 24, 1981, Charlotte, NC; [p.] John Bryant and Kim Ballard; [ed.] Concord High School; [occ.] Student at Concord High School; [a.] Concord, NC

BUCK, ELIZABETH MENCHACA
[b.] April 4, 1954, San Antonio, TX; [p.] Carlos and Velia Menchaca; [m.] Wynn Alex Buck, June 15, 1996; [ed.] University of Texas at El Paso, B.A. 1995; [occ.] Teacher, Secondary and Elementary Education; [memb.] Democratic Party, St. Charles Borromeo Catholic Church; [hon.] Outstanding Teenager of America; [oth. writ.] Personal collection of poetry and prose.; [pers.] The mysteries of life are my main focus, as well as the goodness of all individuals under all circumstances.; [a.] Albuquerque, NM

BUMGARNER, LESLEE
[pen.] Lee Garner; [b.] January 1, 1982, San Antonio, TX; [p.] William Brent Bumgarner, Juanita Lopez Bumgarner; [occ.] High School Student 9th grade; [hon.] Track Trophy, YMCCA Cheerleading Trophy, Fitness Certificate, Fitness Patch, Language Arts Award, Scholarship Award for Improvement, Student of the Month, Perfect Attendance; [oth. writ.] My artwork was displayed at Wilkes Art Gallery.; [pers.] I write what I feel I was influenced by my inner spirit.; [a.] N. Wilkesboro, NC

BURGOS, LYBIA E.
[b.] February 9, 1943, Ecuador; [p.] Pedro Estrella, Maria Estrella; [m.] Armando Burgos, February 16, 1972; [ch.] Sandra Burgos; [ed.] RN and OB/Gyn Nurse Practitioner Philadelphia School of Medicine of Pennsylvania University Journalism at Panama University; [occ.] Director of Special Medical Services at Planned Parenthood of New York City Inc.; [memb.] National Assoc. of Nurse Practitioners in Reproductive Health Assoc. of Reproductive Health Professionals American Society for Colpos copy and Cervical Pathology; [hon.] Planned Parenthood of NYC "Woman of Achievement Award," "The Miriam Manisoff" award of the (Philadelphia) for contribution of the Nurse Practitioner role (National Award) local town poem contest. High School Portoviejo - Ecuador 1958; [oth. writ.] "Panama Star" 1964-1966 "Sunday Supplement" publications of poems. Ecuador "Diario Manabita" publication of poems 1960-62; [pers.] I believe in a world with hopes and dreams. In a human race without colors. I believe in true love at all ages, in caring for others, but most of all in the free expression of our thoughts and feelings.; [a.] Jersey City, NJ

BURKE, MARY KAREN
[b.] September 25, 1938, Minneapolis; [p.] Lea and Marie Schultenover; [ch.] Maura, Michael, Liz, Judi; [ed.] BS Nursing Carlowe College Pittsburgh; [occ.] RN - Certified Alcohol and Substance Abuse Counselor; [memb.] Hudson Valley Writers Assoc., International Woman's Writing Guild.; [oth. writ.] Non published: Short Story, Trilogy of The Pearls - Friday at Shelly's, Play Reunion Single songs - a tradition Bornola, poetry published Birthday - Gannett News.; [pers.] Life is an adventure it's never to late to accomplish goals as long as you are breathing and after that... Who knows?.

BURMEISTER, PAMELA
[b.] March 2, 1949, Evanston, WY; [p.] Bernice Holmes, Herman Hunter; [m.] Mark Burmeister, March 10, 1973; [ch.] Mathew Mark, Michael Shawn; [ed.] 1967 High School Graduate - Evanston, Wyoming; [occ.] Homemaker; [memb.] Peninsula Grave, Brethern Church; [pers.] This poem is dedicated to my mother, "Bea", to Joann Jaillet, Dawn Murphy, my family and to God from whom all blessings flow!; [a.] Soldotna, AK

BURNHAM, KENNETH W.
[pen.] Serious Illyprose; [b.] April 19, 1950, Phil., PA; [p.] Russell O. and Shirley J. Burnham; [m.] Divorced; [ch.] Jacob Daniel and Karena Anne Burnham; [ed.] Grad No Kingstown Senior High and currently, 46 years living with a birth defect that has made me a student of human nature.; [occ.] Medically retired; [memb.] Human (Humane) Race); [hon.] Survived and enjoying life with a full heart and sound mind; [oth. writ.] "Truth and Sillyness" (a collection currently working to be published) "Serious Illyprose Inside and Out" is underway short stories musing. Trying my hand at a screen play script; [pers.] Sometimes I'm serious I. or maybe S. Illyprose or it could be as S.I. a bear for life. What sorrow do we see in this progress, I only ever, it gets far worse, enter, if in your heart be love and care all ye others go elsewhere; [a.] Shannock, RI

BURRELL, BLANCHE A.
[b.] June 26, 1923, Attala Co., MS; [p.] Edna Criswell and James Rufus Abels; [m.] Hal Eugene Burrell (Deceased), October 19, 1938; [ch.] Six; [ed.] BS degree college of Education, Elementary Education, MS State University; [occ.] Retired; [memb.] Sneasha United Methodist Church, Auxiliary Veterans of Foreign Wars, Auxiliary American Legion, United Daughters of the Confederacy, MS Retired Teachers Association, MS Forestry Association, Kappa Delta Phi, Lady Landowners Association, and Reading Club; [hon.] Certificate of honor for having taught Sunday School for over forty years. Graduated with "Distinction" December 19, 1975. Winnie Davis and Jefferson Davis Medals for outstanding historical work on Civil War era; [oth. writ.] A collection of poems - short stories.; [pers.] I am inspired and blessed by the love of God for me, by my loving family and by the wonderful world of nature around me. I try always to live by the Golden Rule. Some of my favorite poets wrote in the Romantic and Victorian ages.; [a.] Goodman, MS

BURRIS, T. EDWARD
[b.] September 21, 1929, Sutherland Springs, TX; [p.] Albert Burris, Elizabeth Burris; [m.] Michele Burris, December 31, 1981; [ch.] Mark, Peter, Rosemary, John, Laura; [ed.] Austin High School, University of Texas; [occ.] President and CEO, Housing Management Services, Inc.; [memb.] Habitat for Humanity, Institute of Real Estate Management, Greater Dallas Association of Realtors; [pers.] I try very hard to exhibit kindness and good-will toward all those with whom I come in contact.; [a.] Heath, TX

BURTS, MRS. RITA
[pen.] Maynell; [b.] May 15, 1949, Westchester, White Plains, NY; [p.] Robert and Slonia Portee; [m.] David L. Burts, March 9, 1971; [ch.] Treena 24, Jerron 21, Shauna 18 and Sonia 17; [ed.] High School Graduate, Six Months Business School, expectance in the Institute of Children's Literature.; [occ.] Casual Clerk at the United States Post Office, when they lay off; [memb.] I do Nurse Aid, Internal Light Church, 149 East Third Street, Mt. Vernon, N.Y., 10550; [oth. writ.] A manuscript of poems, in the process of being copy written.; [pers.] I love to write spiritual things, and to spend time with children to see them happy, and I care about Elderly people.

BUSCH, ALLISON MARIE
[b.] February 1, 1977, Aiken County, SC; [p.] Betty Busch, and the late Richard Busch; [ed.] High School Diploma, Sophomore USC, Columbia, SC Engineering Major; [occ.] Full time Student; [memb.] Grace Presbyterian Church PCA, Army ROTC, Pi Mu Epsilon (Math Club), Society for Women Engineers, SC Writers Worshop; [hon.] 2nd Place - The Mike Snow Poetry Memorial Award (1995); [oth. writ.] Poetry "Kaleidoscope" school magazine.; [a.] Aiken, SC

BUSCHKOETTER, DEBRA
[b.] March 15, 1958, Jasper, IN; [p.] Jerome and Imelda Kiefer; [m.] Bernard Frank Buschkoetter, October 22, 1977; [ch.] Bernard Frank Buschkoetter III; [ed.] Jasper High School; [occ.] Independent Distributor, New Image International (Housewife/Mother); [oth. writ.] None as of this date; [pers.] "May this poem honor my mother and father forever!"; [a.] Huntingburg, IN

BUTRUM, JENNIFER LYNN
[b.] November 12, 1976, Beech Grove, IN; [p.] John and Jamie Butrum; [ed.] 1 year of college majored in Poetry reading; [occ.] Waitress; [oth. writ.] I have a poem "Friendship" published in my senior year book.; [pers.] Strive to reach your goals, never give up without giving yourself a chance to succeed.; [a.] Greenwood, IN

BYNAKER, BARBARA
[b.] June 11, 1976, Fairfax, VA; [p.] Robert A. Bynaker and Sharon V. Bynaker; [ed.] Graduated High School - Centreville High School Class of 1994; [occ.] Data Entry Supervisor; [hon.] MVP of Softball Tourn. 1988; [oth. writ.] I have wrote many poems and short stories, but none have ever been published.; [pers.] Most of my poems are only written so I can express my feelings, I only started sharing with others when I took a creative writing class in High School.; [a.] Manassas Park, VA

BYRAM, ELIZABETH NYE
[b.] Irrelevant, Worcester, MA; [p.] Nancy Nye, Joseph G. Byram; [ed.] University of CT, Boston Univ. - English major Art Students League - painting and drawing persons school of design NYC. and school of visual arts - photography and dark room technique; [occ.] Photographer; [memb.] ASPP - American Society of Picture Professionals, now, NAFE (National Association of Female Executives); [hon.] 1996 Photo Award - Hunter Museum of America AA Chattanooga TN 1993 - Museum of the City of New York acquires 8 b and w photos for their permanent collection. 1992 - Marine Art Award from the sea Heritage Foundation NYC. 1991 - Best in show in Photography Three River Arts Festival - Carnegie Institute of Pittsburgh, PA etc.; [oth. writ.] Selected exhibitions (juried, group) (unpublished) 1996 - Lexington Art League, Lexington KY, Glym Art Gallery, St. Simons Island, Georgia, Ghost Fleet Gallery, Rags Head NC "Imaging NJ Johnson and Johnson, Monmout Museum, etc. N.J.; [pers.] My work reflects a belief that we can "all get along together" I seek at joyous, compassionate exchanges between people of all races and creeds; [a.] New York City, NY

CABALLERO, MARIA CECILIA D.
[pen.] MC Caballero; [b.] June 26, 1978, New York City; [p.] Cecilia D. Caballero; [ed.] High School - Convent of the Sacred Heart, Class of 1996 - NY, NY College - Wesleyan University, Class of 2000 - Middletown, CT; [occ.] Student; [hon.] High School - Salutatorian, Class of '96, Academic Excellence, Elsbeth Kroeber Biological Science Award, Bausch and Lomb Award (in recognition of outstanding academic achievement, good character and superior promise in the field of science), Music Award, Dance Award, Forensics Awards, Hon. Mention - Scholastic Writing Award, Campus Ministry Award.; [oth. writ.] Short stories, published in Convent of the Sacred Heart Literary Magazine and Anthology 1995 of New England Young Writer's Conference, poetry published in CSH Literary Magazine.; [pers.] I want to create works of beauty whose meanings transcend all visual boundaries, ageless works whose messages will be shorted across the generations. I want my words to resound within the confines of opens minds and feeling hearts, a lasting impression upon the psychic of those who open themselves to understand.; [a.] New York City, NY

CACCAMISE, VIRGINIA HUNTER
[b.] January 14, 1926, Leesburg, FL; [p.] Ethel and Julian Hunter; [m.] Sam Caccamise, June 5, 1944; [ch.] Jo Ellen, Don and Clint; [occ.] Retired Medical Assistant; [pers.] Life-long resident of Florida. This poem tells the story of my early childhood, tranquil, wonderful! Five o'clock in Leesburg, the Old Mill Whistle still blows.; [a.] Leesburg, FL

CAIN, TYSON
[pen.] Tyson Cain; [b.] December 22, 1975, St. Joseph, MO; [occ.] Student at Saint Olaf College, Northfield, MN

CALLENDER, JIVELLE I.
[pen.] Jivelle Callender; [b.] February 8, 1977, Panama City, Panama; [p.] Roan and Teddy Callender; [ed.] High School, Currently a dance Education Major at Goucher College in Baltimore; [occ.] Student; [pers.] "There is no reason in life to stop dreaming, because can become a reality."

CAMPBELL, CHIQUITA
[b.] January 15, 1982; [p.] Emma and Hardy Campbell; [hon.] President's Education Award, Beta Club, Junior Historical Society Achievement Award. Outstanding SCMS Band Student, Certificate of Musical Achievement, Superior Achievement in NEJF, Accelerated Reader, Outstanding writing student, SCMS band directors Award; [pers.] Giving glory to God I'd like to thank my family especially my mother who is my back bone and my everything and also to my church family, all who have influenced me greatly.; [a.] Georgetown, KY

CAMPBELL, KRISTINA
[b.] December 29, 1978, Bryan, TX; [p.] Betty Campbell; [ed.] Student; [occ.] Worker, McDonald Restaurant; [hon.] Super Scientist Award, Inane Innorvous Invention Award, Honor Roll Award, Special Science Fair Award, Academic Bronze Medal Award, Certificate of Achievement from B.P.D. for D.A.R.E., program, Outstanding School Service Award, 4-time Citizenship Award.; [oth. writ.] A publication of a poem in the book Recollection of Yesterday by the National Library of Poetry.; [pers.] I try to express myself creatively in my poetry and express love as much as possible. I thank my mother, Betty Campbell, a published writer also, for motivating and inspiring me.; [a.] Bryan, TX

CAMPBELL, SERENA
[pen.] Beanie; [b.] February 23, 1986, Oakland, AR; [p.] Bill and Julie Campbell; [ed.] Currently 5th Grade; [pers.] For my Mom's friend Andy who died of AIDS, and all the Cool girls out there who don't always feel so cool.; [a.] Pleasant Hill, CA

CAPODIECI, ADAM
[b.] February 23, 1978; [p.] Marie and Gene Capodieci; [ed.] Regent's Graduate of High School and now a College Freshman. (High School name Sochem); [occ.] Student at College Dowling - N.Y.; [memb.] Dowling College Baseball team as a staring Catcher; [hon.] 4 Yr. member at my High School for being on the Baseball Team and Art Honor Society at my H.S.; [oth. writ.] Several poems but never attempted to have them published.; [pers.] Most of my writings are sudden thoughts or feelings that come into my head. This particular poem is a more personal and more to my own life.; [a.] Ronkonkoma, NY

CARDONA, EMILY A.
[b.] June 21, 1985, Queens, NY; [p.] George L. Cardona, Lillian Vega; [ch.] Brother - Matthew; [occ.] Student - 6th grade; [a.] Ozone Park, NY

CARFI, JACQUELINE M.
[b.] August 6, 1964, Sewickley, PA; [p.] Donald and Patricia Martin; [m.] Marc S. Carfi, August 5, 1995; [ch.] David Harvey Gibson; [ed.] Moon High, Parkway West Technical School, Bradford School of Business, Courses at Robert Morris College; [occ.] Accounting Manager/Systems Administrator; [oth. writ.] Many poems written for wedding and anniversary programs, newsletters, and church bulletins.; [pers.] I have been greatly influenced by poets Alfred Tennyson and Lydia Baxter, by my relationships with my family and friends and the special love we share has been the true inspiration for my writing.; [a.] Peekskill, NY

CARLISLE, BEVERLY J.
[pen.] Beverly Jane Turner; [b.] June 19, 1941, Cincinnati, OH; [p.] Valles Turner, Della L. Turner; [m.] Frank L. Carlisle, July 15, 1975; [ed.] Community College of Southern Nevada; [occ.] Signmaker; [hon.] Phi Theta Kappa; [pers.] I try to communicate what I believe I observe in those around me, and also in myself. I hope someday I shall be able to communicate through music.; [a.] Las Vegas, NV

CARLSON, JENNI
[pen.] Jenyfyr Locksley; [b.] June 20, 1977, Spokane, WA; [ed.] Northridge High School, currently attending Norwich University; [occ.] Student; [memb.] National Forensics League, Pegasus Players, Arnold Air Society, Norwich University Corps of Cadets.; [hon.] Girl's State, American Legion Oratorical Voice of Democracy, American Legion Scholastic Excellence Medal, Norwich University Dean's List; [oth. writ.] Poems and speeches in inner visions and dominion literary magazine; [pers.] "I am like a little bird in a cage, vivid, resolute, restless, but a captive. Were I but free..." Charlotte Bronte, Jane Eyre; [a.] Northfield, VT

CARNEY, MRS. LOTTIE
[ed.] Degree in Education; [occ.] Retired Teacher; [pers.] A deep reflection of brutality turned positive.

CARPENTER, LAURIE J.
[pen.] Laurie J. Carpenter or Nape Wastewin; [b.] April 6, 1954, Janesville, WI; [p.] Dee Westphal and Dick Carpenter; [m.] (Single) Divorced; [ch.] Charity Shannon, Nicole Sheree, Ryan Christopher, Briana Elizabeth; [ed.] Parker Senior High - Janesville Wis. University of Wassau. Wis - Everett Community College - Everett Washi - Childrens Literature Institute; [occ.] Fine Artist/Writer specializing in Native American

Culture and Daycare Empl. my (Business Name Earthen Treasures); [memb.] NMAI (National Museum of American Indian) The Nature Conservancy and Prairie Restoration/St. Joseph's School for Native American Children/ Southwest Indian Foundation; [hon.] Art Scholarship University of Wassau, Wis./golden poet of the year/ Life time Adopter of American Bison on Prairies/A financial supporter for St. Joseph's Indian School (Award forward); [oth. writ.] Have had several poems published in Books. I am now writing a children's Native American Book titled "The little dream catcher that could". My illustrator is James Keip of Madison, Wis. Also a book of poety is being started.; [pers.] My goal through my writing is to help children to understand and appreciate the Native American Culture to learn to apply their positive lessons and spirit in their own lives. To walk in harmony with the Earth and it's Animals. To be humble, respective and loving to all.; [a.] Fort Myers, FL

CARR, SANDRA LEE
[pen.] Sandra Palmer Carr; [b.] January 21, 1946, San Francisco; [p.] Donald and Mary Jo Palmer; [m.] Charles Richard Carr, March 14, 1970; [ch.] Craig and Boyd (two son); [ed.] Attended Hawthorne High School, Palmdale High School Graduated 1963, 1 year at Pacific Christian College, Long Beach, CA (now in Fullerton) Additional Courses at Jr. College; [occ.] Homemaker, Freelance Writer; [memb.] Christian Writer's Fellowship of Orange County, CA; [oth. writ.] Poetic Tributes Monologues with a Christian message poetry, published in Standard Devotional, published in the upper room; [pers.] My greatest desire is to bring hope and healing to hurting people, and in the process, to honor God.; [a.] Huntington Beach, CA

CARTER, CHESLEY JOANNE
[pen.] Joanne Chesley Carter; [b.] July 8, 1953, Georgetown, DC; [p.] Mr. Francis and Mrs. Mabel Chesley (Mother Deceased); [m.] Eli J. Carter; [ch.] Brad and Jennifer; [ed.] B.S. from Virginia State University M. Ed. from U.N.C. Charlotte Ed. D. Candidate UNC Chapel Hill; [occ.] Educator/Meida Producer Durham, NC; [memb.] NBCDI Nat'l Black Child Development Institute, NBLIC National Black Leadership Initiative or Cancer, PTA, ASCD Assoc. for Supervision and Curriculum Development other community and professional afflictions; [oth. writ.] Unpublished collection titled Unspoken Sentiments, academic publications (in journals); [pers.] The window to the heart and soul is in the pen, and until we've had the opportunity to gaze through this window, we do not really know one's humanity.; [a.] Durham, NC

CARTER, JAMES E.
[b.] March 15, 1980, Corvallis, OR; [p.] Ken and Ester Carter; [ed.] High School - I am presently a Junior - 11th grade; [occ.] Student; [hon.] Eagle Scout Candidate; [oth. writ.] Vast collection of personal writings; [pers.] I write poetry to express my inner thoughts, my feelings, myself. My writings are influenced by my environment today. Music influences my poetic thoughts; [a.] Apple Valley, CA

CARTER, ROBIN VICTORIA
[b.] July 4, 1967, Front Royal, VA; [p.] Walden Carter and Evelyn Carter; [ed.] MPA Degree from NC State Univ., BS in Rehab. Services from Virginia Commonwealth Univ., HS diploma from Fauquier High School, Warrenton, VA; [occ.] Administrative Assistant, Raleigh, NC; [oth. writ.] Various pieces on the Black experience, The Christian experience, love and children and family.; [pers.] I am thankful to God for imparting this gift to me, for parents who have nurtured the gift and for the words of Langston Hughes "Hold fast to dreams for if dreams die, life is a broken winged that cannot

fly."; [a.] Raleigh, NC

CARTER, TERRENCE
[b.] March 9, 1967, Elmer, NJ; [p.] Ernestine, Fredrick Carter Jr.; [ch.] Terrence Carter Jr.; [ed.] Arthur P. Schalick H.S., Infantry Combat Training; [occ.] Depall Operator, Clement Pappas Seabrook, NJ; [oth. writ.] Forever My Love, When My Bury Me, My Friend, also in the works a book entitled "The Infallible Choice."; [pers.] There is no greater pleasure than proving your own self worth.; [a.] Millville, NJ

CASALE, ROBERT C.
[b.] December 19, New York; [p.] Anna and Charles Casale; [ch.] Donna and Robert Charles II; [ed.] Clemson University, South Carolina; [occ.] Architect; [memb.] Past Grand Knight of Knights of Columbus, American Legion, Past Commander of Disabled American Veterans, BPOE Elks Longe #2766 Sons of Italy; [oth. writ.] Two poems publishes: "Searching" and "Earth Dawn" writing a novel Semi-fiction recently completed a short story (fiction); [pers.] My writings help me express my inner feelings about love, life and people, who came in and out of my life. I sincerely hope my friends and loved ones could read and share my poetry in order to somehow touch their lives.; [a.] Palm Bay, FL

CASE, JEAN VAN ALTVORST
[b.] April 20, 1948, Moline, IL; [p.] Henry Van Altvorst and Annie Van Altvorst; [ch.] John Henry and Tara Ann; [ed.] Alleman High School; [occ.] Office Associate; [pers.] If you feel deeply about something, express it in some form of writing.; [a.] Moline, IL

CASEY, TANYA M.
[b.] February 3, 1976, McAllen, TX; [p.] David and Rae Casey and (mother) Pamela Ady; [ed.] Attended MacArthur High School... I am currently enrolled in San Antonio College, and will soon transfer to U.T.S.A. to graduate with an English degree and emphasis on writing; [occ.] I currently work for a plant nursery called Milberger's Nursery; [memb.] I am a lover of animals and a member of the National Wildlife Federation and the Humane Society of the United States; [hon.] I have obtained a Texas Certified Nursery Professional Certificate which brings me closer to the plants I work with.; [oth. writ.] I have thirteen volumes of my personal hand-written poetry which have only been viewed by close friends and family. I have various poems published in school papers and books.; [pers.] My writings are purely influenced by the earth, as our mother, and by the through my flesh from mankind and humanity, itself.; [a.] San Antonio, TX

CASPER, KURT
[b.] July 5, 1951, Hackensack, NJ; [p.] Gustav and Jean Casper; [m.] Andrea L. Curtis, June 12, 1994; [ch.] Noah Ben Or; [ed.] Ridgewood High, N.Y. Maritime, Bethany College, W.V.; [occ.] Building Contractor, Asheville, NC; [oth. writ.] Local Newspaper editorials and comments, 2 books "in the works"; [pers.] The study of self is Mankind's only road of peace - to truly know oneself is to know the gift of creation. In this gift lies the understanding, the fulfillment of love and peace.; [a.] Asheville, NC

CASTELLION, DEE
[b.] February 21, 1942, California; [p.] Gladys and R.B. Scott; [m.] Bob Castellion, August 22, 1964; [ch.] Dana Marie Alsup; [ed.] High School; [occ.] Housewife, part time Clerk; [pers.] I love doing family research and learned about my great, great grandfather. Who this poem is about.; [a.] McAlester, OK

CASTILLE, CHADRICK JAMES
[pen.] Chad Castille; [b.] May 31, 1979, New Iberia, LA; [p.] James Castille and Sue Castille; [ed.] New Iberia Senior High; [occ.] High School Graduate; [pers.] My poems come from my heart and each one tells a story about how I felt at a certain time in my life. And some influence of my poems have come from listing and understanding Cajun French music, my heritage; [a.] New Iberia, LA

CASZATT, EILEEN
[b.] July 15, 1944, Kittanning, PA; [p.] Paul Anderson and Alice M. Anderson (Deceased); [m.] Clayton L. Caszatt, October 26, 1991; [ch.] Tasha (my dog) and Gorby (my cat); [ed.] Kittanning High School and Shenango, Valley Business Institute; [occ.] Retired from Medical Field due to a back injury.; [memb.] Dear Neighbor Volunteer for the American Heart Association for the past 3 years. Distinguished Member of the International Society of Poets; [oth. writ.] This is my third poem to be published in forthcoming anthologies. I am also currently working on Part II of a book containing poems of love and hope that I will try to get published in the near future.; [pers.] I hope some of the love I feel in my heart touches another heart or soul through my poetry. Keep the love of God in your heart and you can become anything you want to be, go anywhere you want to go and if you touch hearts along the way, you are a millionaire!; [a.] Sharpsville, PA

CHAMNESS, TRENA J.
[b.] April 27, 1955, Kalamazoo, MI; [m.] Reubin Chamness, February 28, 1970; [ch.] Michael and Matthew (two sons); [occ.] Specialist in Behavioral Modification of Adolescents; [memb.] Member of S.A.I.N. (Sex Abuse Intervention Network) also Foster Parent Association (Florida); [oth. writ.] Multiple poems enjoyed by relatives and friends, this was my first submitted for publishing, written for a friend for the loss of her 12 year old son; [pers.] I strive for my poetry to reflect upon feelings and events of everyday people, to capture life's emotions.; [a.] Spring Hill, FL

CHAN, LAURA
[b.] May 12, 1986, Bryan, TX; [p.] Paul Chan, Elaine Chan; [ed.] 5th grade, Apex Elementary; [occ.] 5th grade student; [a.] Apex, NC

CHANDLER, DORIS GARDNER
[b.] March 25, 1933, Ringold Co., IA; [p.] Daisy and Ray Gardner; [ch.] Three; [ed.] 8th Grade; [oth. writ.] I've always loved poetry since a child. Thought I'd try my hand at it. Was happy when it turned out like it did.; [a.] Springfield, MO

CHANG, CHRISTOPHER WEI FNG
[pen.] C. W. Chang; [b.] October 14, 1979, Trenton, NJ; [p.] Patricia E. Chang, Dr. Wei Hua Chang; [ed.] Hillsborough High; [occ.] Student; [memb.] Interact, Rotary Club, X-C Team; [hon.] Honor Student; [oth. writ.] Poems in Explorer Magazine; [pers.] I write poetry in order to reflect my thoughts and feelings.; [a.] Neshanic Station, NJ

CHAPIN, LISA MICHELE
[b.] November 21, 1973, Fort Atkinson; [p.] Thomas and Luann Chapin; [ed.] Fort Atkinson High School, Final year at Madison Area Technical College in the Associate Degree Child Care Program; [occ.] Day-Care Teacher at Fort Atkinson Memorial Health Services, Kids Konnection; [memb.] Fort Atkinson, WI - Bethany Evangelical Lutheran Church - Wisconsin Right to Life; [hon.] Madison Area Technical College - Deans List; [pers.] To live each day one at a time.; [a.] Fort Atkinson, WI

CHARLSON, MAY
[b.] November 6, 1928, Los Angeles, CA; [m.] Widow; [ch.] David, Leslie, Joanna, Rhonda, Jay, Daleen; [ed.] John Marshall High Gavelan City College; [occ.] Retired; [hon.] Deans list; [oth. writ.] Short stories (suspense), Children's Stories, many poems nothing published at yet.; [pers.] My writings are thoughts that spring from my heart. They express love, happiness, and appreciation for all things in life. My joy is to share these thoughts. My hope is to touch hearts and to bring smiles.; [a.] Lakeside, CA

CHELEMEDOS, MARY HENRY
[b.] September 2, 1926, Baileyville, KS; [p.] Leo Henry and Agnes Henry; [m.] Spiro T. Chelemedos, August 8, 1970; [ed.] Baileyville High School, San Diego College for Women, John F. Kennedy University of Orinda, CA; [occ.] Spiritual Counselor; [memb.] J.F.K. Alumni; [hon.] I was a Benedictine Nun from 1943-1966 I was an "A" student in a Master's, Degree in Consciousness studies.; [pers.] When my niece, Jean Holthaus, who has written a book about Therapy through poetry, was graduating with her M.A. I wanted to surprise her with a gift a poem most dear to her heart! So I wrote of my experiences which I lovingly encourage every person on earth to allow themselves to experience, also!; [oth. writ.] Composed 18 or more plays for elementary schools, (but never published) (never tried).; [a.] Benicia, CA

CHELEMEDOS, SPIRO THOMAS
[b.] August 25, 1923, Richmond, CA; [p.] Gerasemos and Stamo Chelemedos; [m.] Mary Henry Chelemedos, August 8, 1970; [ch.] 1 - Deceased boy; [ed.] High School plus Trade Schools, Night University - Soil Mech., Surveying and Planning; [occ.] Retired Construction Inspector for State of Calif.; [memb.] Past Member of Mira Vista Golf and Country Club many years. Also Benicia Golf Assc.; [hon.] Retired Enlisted Active and Reserve Military 25 years 1943 to 1968 served New Guinea, New Britain, Biak, and Philippines World War II also through Korea and Vietnam Wars received a few awards and honors.; [oth. writ.] None except 14 articles were published in the Contra Coast times newspaper readers forum.; [pers.] Always love your family respect, be kind to all if they should pass away. Not you no regrets you'll ever recall.; [a.] Benicia, CA

CHEN, MICHAEL E.
[b.] April 25, 1975, Wilmington, DE; [p.] Karl and Virginia Chen; [ed.] William Penn High School c/o 93 Rutgers University; [occ.] Student; [memb.] National Eagle Scout Association, National Honor Society, St. Marks United Methodist Church; [hon.] Eagle Scout Award, God and Country Award; [pers.] I enjoy life for what each day brings me. Never expecting too much, nor settling for too little, I make the best of what I have.; [a.] Bear, DE

CHENEY, GERTRUDE
[pen.] Bette Cheney; [b.] May 6, 1922, Ormond Beach, FL; [p.] William Hope Fagen, Ruth Seabloom; [m.] Raymond Stoddard Cheney (Deceased), December 21, 1968; [ed.] B.S. Tulane University Sacramento State, U.S.C., U.C.L.A.; [occ.] Retired Teacher; [memb.] Local Clubs; [oth. writ.] Widow's songs, local songs.; [pers.] Writing and singing songs very therapeutic!; [a.] La Quinta, CA

CHESTERFIELD, KIMANI A.
[b.] September 22, 1983, St. Thomas, VI; [p.] Noreen Faulkner, Avery Chesterfield; [ed.] 8th Grade Student as of 9/96; [pers.] Thanks to my 7th Grade Teacher Sherdan McGill and my mother Noreen Faulkner for encouraging me to write - even when I wanted to stop. Special thanks to my grandparents, Catherine and Everard Faulkner and Enid De Castro.; [a.] Corona, NY

CHILDRESS, KAREN FLANAGAN
[pen.] Karen Flanagan Childress; [b.] August 3, 1961, Cullman, AL; [p.] Jim and Myra Flanagan; [m.] Billy L. Childress, June 29, 1992; [ch.] Shawna and Brandi Tressler; [ed.] E.M.T. - Wallace College, Secretarial - Wallace College, Hanceville, AL; [occ.] Electronic Technician Rapair, Inc. Madison, AL; [memb.] United Way; [pers.] It is my desire to bring hope to a hurting world thru Jesus Christ.; [a.] Decatur, AL

CHIRONNO, JOHN
[pen.] John J. Chironno; [b.] August 26, 1921, NYC; [p.] Joseph Chironno and Antionet Chironno; [m.] Clara Stella Chironno, August 14, 1948; [ch.] Antionet Chironno and Elizabeth Chironno; [ed.] Manuel Training High School, Bklyn Technical High School, Todt Ship Repair Yard, Marine Machinist School; [occ.] Retired New York City Transit Authority; [memb.] Order Sons of Italy, Constantino Brumidi Lodge 2211, Past Member Loyal Order of Moose American Legion, Retire Association Transport Workers Union NYC Transit Auth.; [hon.] Commendation and Job Meritorious Awards, Certificates New York City Transit Authority; [oth. writ.] National Library of Poetry my poems accepted for their anthology books. I'm a Woman, The Lost Art of Peer Elder Counsel, Are Now All Poets In A Sense, Life's Living Romance; [pers.] The penner creates a mental relaxation to relieve some of the stress in this highly competitive existence that we now live in.; [a.] West Babylon, NY

CHLEBANOWSKI SR., MATT J.
[b.] March 15, 1936, Chicago, IL; [p.] Stanley and Clara Chlebanowski; [m.] Barbara Rogers, August 13, 1960; [ch.] Kenneth, Marlene, Matt Jr. Thomas; [ed.] St Joseph Catholic Elementary Sch., Chicago Farragut High, Chgo, IL Hadley School for the blind, Winnetka, IL; [oth. writ.] I see one manager farewell to our friend love thy neighbor greetings from the grandparents I thank you Lord; [pers.] Interested in writing poetry from High School. Words of encouragement, from family and friends, to express my poetic talent; [a.] Downers Grove, IL

CHONG, LILYLILINOEK
[pen.] Lilinoe; [b.] June 2, 1908, Waipio, HI; [p.] Sentaro and Mary Kawashima; [m.] David K. Chong, August 26, 1926; [ch.] Two boys and six girls; [ed.] Just 9th Grade; [occ.] Housewife; [memb.] Belong to Senior Club, in my village, and the Church of Jesus Christ of Latter-Day Saint; [hon.] Only from church and senior club; [oth. writ.] Compose a song of Waipio Valley in "Hawaiian"; [pers.] I write when inspired, and pray for guidance. I look at the beauty, and memories and the influence of the people, that live and cherish their heritage.; [a.] Honokaa, HI

CHRISTENSEN, LACIE L.
[pen.] Lacie; [b.] October 19, 1960, Cedar Falls, IA; [p.] Dennis and Bonnie Johnson; [m.] Alan Christensen, December 14, 1991; [ch.] 2 - Tony and Shane; [ed.] High School, Licensed Barber, Police Science; [occ.] A T.C.B.Y. Yogurt Shop, Assistant Manager; [hon.] High Honors in School, Poet of Merit, Hair Stylist of the Year in 1982.; [oth. writ.] Days Gone By, Lover's Lane, Life, Harvest Moon, Friendship, My Two Boys, Do You?, Time, Sunshine, Ocean Currents and many more.; [pers.] Live life to the fullest. As my son Tony always says, "Life is like an ice cream cone, eat it too fast, you get a headache, east it too slow and you get a cone full of milk."; [a.] Cedar Falls, IA

CHRISTENSEN, LIBBY JACOBS
[b.] August 29, 1953, Rantoul, IL; [p.] Donald G. Jacobs, Mary L. Jacobs; [m.] Robert W. Christensen, March 4, 1978; [ch.] Nicholas Mycroft; [ed.] Transylvania University, University of Vienna, Vanderbilt University; [occ.] College Instructor, Chapman College, City Colleges of Chicago, University of Maryland at Air Force Bases in U.S.A. and overseas.; [memb.] Malmstrom AFB Officer's Spouses Club, Great Falls Quilt Guild; [hon.] Junior Woman of the Year, Holleian Academic Honorary, Lampas Leadership Honorary Society, Who's Who on College Campuses 1974, Vanderbilt MAT Fellowship; [oth. writ.] No Stress Essay Tests, Pointers to Improve Performance; Two photos selected for publication in Photographer Forum's Best of Photography Annual, 1985 and 1989. Several photos published in Domesday Project Videodisc Encyclopedia 1986.; [pers.] I have usually worked with photography or fabric, but creation in any medium is challenging, exciting, and personally rewarding.; [a.] Great Falls, MT

CHRISTESON, WAYNE
[b.] March 24, 1948; [m.] Anne; [ed.] B.A. Vanderbilt University with honors, J.D. University of Tennessee; [occ.] Formerly a trial attorney practicing civil and poverty law, now disabled because of clinical depression.; [pers.] This poem was written while I was hospitalized at the Menninger Clinic in Topeka, Kansas, being treated for acute depression.; [a.] Leiper's Fork, TN

CHRISTOPHER III, WILLIAM J.
[b.] September 23, 1975, Wilmington, DE; [p.] William J. Jr. and Patricia; [ed.] Salesianum High School, University of Delaware; [occ.] Student; [pers.] Life is too short to be scared.; [a.] Wilmington, DE

CINNAMO, JAMES
[b.] March 7, 1975, Bronx, NY; [p.] Vincent Cinnamo, Ellen Cinnamo; [ed.] Cardinal Spellman High School. Iona College; [occ.] Student at Iona College in New Rochelle; [memb.] Pi Lambda Theta Education Honor Society; [hon.] Dean's List; [pers.] "God is my strength and power, and He makes my way perfect." I have always tried my best to live the word of God and reflect it in all I do. Thank you to my family for their unending support and love. "For with God, nothing will be impossible."; [a.] Bronx, NY

CLAAR, JACQUALYN
[pen.] J. A. Claar; [b.] March 6, 1950, La Mesa, CA; [ch.] 3 Daughters, 4 Grandchildren; [ed.] Mt. Miguel High School Spring Valley, CA, City College, San Diego, CA; [occ.] Office Manager for a Plumbing Company; [hon.] 4th Place Scholastic Magazines Short Story competition with story "I'll Just Watch" began my writing career in 1964; [oth. writ.] Poem "The Old House Across the Street" published in November 1993 Issue of the Oak, Literary Magazine.; [pers.] I write from the heart, all my poems and stories are based on my life experiences.; [a.] Spring Valley, CA

CLAFLIN, DONALD L.
[pen.] Donald L. Claflin; [b.] April 19, 1936, Duluth, MN; [p.] George and Pearl Claflin; [m.] Alberta Jane Claflin, October 14, 1965; [ch.] 8; [ed.] Grade School Bryant Duluth Lincoln Jr. High Duluth Minnesota Received GED in 1982 TST Boces Ithaca New York; [occ.] School Bus Driver Dryden Central Schools; [memb.] Dryden Assembly of God National Education Ass.; [hon.] Several poems have been used on WLNL Light House Ministries, AM 1000 Horse Heads New York. They have also used several poems in local News paper. (Dryden Tidbits); [oth. writ.] I started writing on December 23, 1991 and have averaged One Hundred (100) a year since then.; [pers.] My ultimate goal would

be to touch the hearts and mind of others, bringing peace and comfort into there lives.; [a.] Freeville, NY

CLAGG, JOHNNIE PAUL
[b.] March 2, 1972, Columbus, OH; [p.] Nancy, John Clagg; [ed.] 11th Grade; [occ.] Prison; [pers.] If I can say one thing it would be "go to school, get a small job, marry someone you love, have kids, live life with a smile and be good."; [a.] Columbus, OH

CLARK, EARL BOYCE
[pen.] Earl Clark/Boyce Clark; [b.] February 24, 1927, Salt Lake City, UT; [p.] Alonzo and Ruth Clark (Redman); [m.] Charlotte Lou (Lumbert), March 4, 1950; [ch.] Michael, Dennis, Diane; [ed.] O'Dea H.S. (Sea), Seattle Univ, '48-'49; [occ.] Retired; [memb.] 1st Marine Div. Assoc., Marine Corps Assoc., marine Corps Hist. Society, Disabled American Veterans, Leather Neck Honor Guard; [hon.] Citizen of the year, WA State (Honorary) Young Life Award; [oth. writ.] Remember Me, Marine You Die, Marine Graduation USMC, The Empty Chair, The Forgotten War, Forever Young, Valentine Day, Veterans Day, Marines Remembered, Chosin Reservoir, The Red White and Blue, etc.; [pers.] As you'll note, most of my poetry centers around marines and the copps, some exceptions are poems about my children several poems pub. in Leatherneck Magazine.; [a.] Edmonds, WA

CLARK, LINDA
[pen.] Linda Clark; [b.] September 11, 1953, New London, CT; [p.] Mr. and Mrs. James Rebold; [ch.] Tamara and Cody Clark; [ed.] B.A. in Criminal Justice; [occ.] Ordance Equipment Mechanic; [memb.] IBEW Local #574 Union Safety Steward; [hon.] Numerous work performance awards, and beneficial suggestion awards; [oth. writ.] Shadows Of The Night (poem), Mamas Beware Raise Your Children Right (poem), Foolish Pride (song), all are unpublished.; [pers.] Stand up for yourself with integrity and you'll never have to look back.; [a.] Port Orchard, WA

CLARK, MONA
[b.] December 7, 1957, Huntington, WV; [p.] Clara and Charley Chaffin; [ch.] Dennis McPherson; [ed.] PBI Oxford, MCI Computer, Pontiac Central High School Pontiac, MI; [occ.] Writing; [hon.] 4.0 ave certificate awards at Ponti Business Institute of Oxford. Also honor roll certificates from MCI (Michigan Computer Institute).; [oth. writ.] "Space and Time", "Heaven", "Happiness and Peace", "Inspiration of Love', "True Love", "Hemispheres of Time"; [pers.] I strive and base all my poems on my own feelings, and how I see things. As to my accomplishments, I write mostly love poems.; [a.] Saginaw, MI

CLARY, DARIEN
[b.] September 11, 1979, Albuquerque, NM; [p.] James H. Clary and Karen Clary; [ed.] Junior at Austin High School; [memb.] National Forensics League (Debate), Austin High School Soccer Team, "Amigos" Volunteer in Oaxaca, Mexico, (1996), St. David's Hospital Volunteer; [hon.] Two time Austin City Science Fair Finalist, National Junior Honor Society (1991-1994); [oth. writ.] Several poems published in "A Touch of Class" poetry compilation; [pers.] Judge yourself by your own standards, not someone else's.; [a.] Austin, TX

CLAY, KRISTINA MARIE
[pen.] K. M. Clay; [b.] December 6, 1973, Ogden, UT; [p.] June and Burt Clay; [m.] Todd Outten, November 16, 1996; [ed.] Bachelor's of Art in English Education; [occ.] Bar Manager - Aspiring, Author; [memb.] National Honor Society; [hon.] Numerous Scholastic, writing, and Speecer Awards graduated Valedictorian DHS; [oth. writ.] One novel in the works. Two other published poems - one in the 1996 issue of a Muse To

Follow and one in The Best of the Best of 1996; [pers.] I told my Mom she is the next Erma Bombeck, she told me I'm the next me - she's right. I also wan to say I love you Todd.; [a.] Tucson, AZ

CLAYTON, MARY
[pen.] Consentia; [b.] October 13, 1937, AL; [p.] Mr. and Mrs. Prewitt; [m.] Lewis Clayton, May 24, 1960; [ch.] Two Boy and Girl; [ed.] 12th Grade Computer Basic Prog.; [occ.] House Wife; [oth. writ.] Poems stories Articles can speak in a unknown tongues songs; [pers.] Wish knew what words I was speaking. I've seen space ships in air. I like to write.; [a.] Birmingham, AL

CLAYTOR, JENNIFER
[pen.] Josea Clayton; [b.] March 27, 1988, Shelby, NC; [p.] Dr. and Mrs. John W. Claytor Jr.; [ed.] Student in 3rd grade; [memb.] Brownies, Tennis, Church Choir, Piano Student; [hon.] Citizenship Award, French Merits, Poems/published in Newspaper; [oth. writ.] Poems "Telephone", "Dinosaur Baseball", "Wizard Came To Visit", Stories "Our Tennis Group Falls In Love", "Surfin' James", "States Stories"; [pers.] I like to write poems and stories because I like to feel apart of my writings; [a.] Shelby, NC

CLEMENS, MARILYN J.
[pen.] Marilyn J. Clemens; [b.] December 11, 1945, Springfield, MO; [p.] Anna and J. E. Ramsey; [ch.] Three; [ed.] 15; [occ.] Nurse, retired; [memb.] St. Agnes Catholic Church; [oth. writ.] Published in newspapers church publications, employment newspaper; [pers.] To promote the love of God to all; [a.] Springfield, MO

CLINE, ANNE
[b.] May 6, 1975, Indianapolis, IN; [p.] Charles and Darlyn Cline; [m.] David MacDougal (Fiance); [ch.] Joshua Owen; [ed.] MA Phlebotomist, Institute of Childrens Literature; [occ.] Medical, Photographer, Writer and Musician; [oth. writ.] Currently working on several pieces with intent to publish.; [pers.] I am aspiring to become a published author for juveniles one day adult literature. I receive much inspiration from music, namely the Beatles.; [a.] Sacramento, CA

CLOUD, JEAN B.
[b.] April 17, 1930, Delaware County, OK; [p.] Jonah Blossom and Cora Starr Blossom; [m.] Dan Cloud Sr., October 6, 1922-December 20, 1985, December 24, 1956; [ch.] Deanise, Laura and Dan Jr.; [ed.] Delaware County Elementary, Jay Public High School, Jay, OK, Haskell Jr. College - Lawrence, KA, Los Angeles City College - Los Angeles, Brailk Institute; [occ.] Retiree - Office Personnel; [memb.] Seventh-Day Adv., Bible Study; [hon.] School Volunteer, Bible Study, Incentive for working, raising a granddaughter and attending school; [oth. writ.] Process of writing a biography. Short Stories, poems.; [pers.] Take one day at a time and see the beauty and good in everything.; [a.] Los Angeles, CA

CLOUD, LINDA BEAL
[pen.] Linda Beal; [b.] December 4, Jay, FL; [p.] Charles R. and Agnes D. Beal; [m.] Robert V. Cloud (Deceased), August 15, 1959; [ed.] B.A., Mississippi College, 1959, M.ED. University of South Florida, 1976, Ed. S. Nova University, 1982, Post Graduate Study, Walden University, 1983; [occ.] Retired Secondary School Teacher; [memb.] President, Cloud Aero Services, Inc. Babson Park, FL, Charter member Lake Wales Little Theatre, Inc., AAUW, Babson Park Woman's Club, Sassy Singers, Southeastern Peruvian Horse Club, Florida Sport Horse Club, Babson Park Community Church Krewe of Pegasus, Defenders of Crooked Lake, Human Society of the U.S.; [hon.] Equine Ring announcer EL. State Fair, 1987-88, Judge

local and National Poetry and essay contests, Teacher of the year Fort Meade High School, Recipient Best Actress Award Lake Wales Little Theatre, Inc., 1978-79.; [oth. writ.] Multiple scripts for theatrical, educational, and private entertainment presentations, scripts for Peruvian Horse Exhibitions "Custom" poetry and "Fairy Tales" for private affairs, personal writings, especially poetry for all types of "greeting card" occasions, Articles published in Horse and Pony, and Caballo magazines. Contributions to professional publications.; [pers.] My greatest thrills are attributed to helping teenage writing students begin to know themselves, come out from themselves, expand their minds and experiences, and ultimately creating wondrous combinations of words in writing. And, saying it in writing is such a "forever" thing - scary and awesome!; [a.] Babson Park, FL

CLUNEY, CHRISSIE
[b.] December 15, 1979; [p.] Bill and Mary Ann Cluney; [ed.] Sophomore at Clifton High School; [memb.] International Order of the Rainbow for Girls; [hon.] Distinguished Achievement Award from High School; [oth. writ.] I wrote a autobiography, and a sci-fi novelette.; [pers.] The only thing to fear is fear itself, or one that my friend gave me, words are lethal, choose them carefully.; [a.] Clifton, NJ

CLUXTON, RITA
[b.] November 1, 1963, Paris, IL; [p.] Melvin and Ida Cluxton; [ed.] Paris High; [occ.] Citizen's National Bank; [memb.] United Pentecostal Church; [hon.] National Honor Society, Conqueror of the Year; [oth. writ.] Numerous songs, young children's stories; [pers.] I have found Philippians 4:13 to be true. "I can do all things through Christ which strengthened me."; [a.] Paris, IL

COBRINIK, LAURA
[b.] July 4, 1958; [p.] Ralph and Rena; [ed.] Associates Degree - Lasell Jr. College, Newton, Mass. 1981; [occ.] Full-time Student was a Library Assistant for 14 years; [oth. writ.] "Red, White, and Blue", in Full 1996 issue of Feelings. "A Wedding Dream" to be published in Dream International Quarterly, and "A June Garden" accepted by Night Roses.; [pers.] Never say, "I can't. You can always do anything as long as you put your mind to it!; [a.] Denville, NJ

COKUSLU, LYNDA M.
[b.] June 11, 1956, Atlanta, GA; [p.] Yvonne and J. Adair McCord; [m.] Fethi Cokuslu, August 24, 1986; [ch.] Sasha, Sedef and Samantha; [ed.] Bryman Medical Assistant School, Georgia State Univ.; [occ.] Movie Rental Shop; [memb.] Traveler's Protective Assn., First Speech to include Women in Organization, Learning Disabilities Assn.; [hon.] Award by National Songwriters Assn., Certificate of Merit; [oth. writ.] An unpublished collection of poetry and some children's books about my travels to Turkey and the Middle East.; [pers.] I have devoted my life to official international efforts for peace. For a number of years a novel has been slowly written about my experiences. Perhaps, someday it will be completed.; [a.] Haperville, GA

COLBERT, ARTHUR P.
[b.] April 27, 1966, Detroit, MI; [p.] Anna and Arthur Colbert; [ed.] Graduate of S.U.N.Y. (Albany, N.Y.) Sociology PJA Paralegal Certificate in upper Darby, PA; [occ.] Caseworker (Social Work); [memb.] A and A Fraternity Inc.; [hon.] Appeared on various talk shows such as dateline, Bet, Lisa Givens, Mark Walberg Good Morning Amer. and Peter Jennings. Also featured in people magazine. The topic was police brutality.; [oth. writ.] "Character", "Race"; [pers.] Have the character to achieve despite the obstacles presented.; [a.] Detroit, MI

COLES, CAROL
[oth. writ.] Lisa Mistress, Extraodinaire; [pers.] Life is the last gateway to our eternal soul.; [a.] Oakland, CA

COLLINS, DUANE
[b.] October 2, 1971, Coldwater, MI; [p.] Arthur Collins, Christine Collins; [m.] Shirley Collins, December 2, 1995; [ed.] Hastings High School, Career Training Specialist, U.S. Army Trained as health care Specialist; [occ.] Certified Nursing Assistant; [memb.] American Red Cross Disaster Team; [pers.] I believe the world would be a much happier place if more people would smile more despite any and all problems; [a.] Bristow, OK

COLLINS, RICHARD S.
[b.] August 6, 1947, Englewood, NJ; [p.] Frances D. Collins; [ed.] Amherst High; [occ.] Shipping Clerk, Tri Tech; [memb.] Northminster Presbyterian Church, Virginia Baptist Hospital Volunteer Multiple Sclerosis and Muscular Dystrophy Societies; [oth. writ.] Articles written for Church Newsletter and Devotions and family and friends.; [pers.] I try to bring out the best in people and help them to realize that they are a special gift from God.; [a.] Lynchburg, VA

COLLINS, STEPHEN
[pen.] Heavenly Father - Col; [b.] May 14, 1965, Yeadon, PA; [p.] John and Jo-Anne Collins; [ed.] Highland High (Auto Mechanics) presently educating myself on a wide variety of subjects on interests, particularly - Religion; [occ.] Carpenter, also possess other trades, not a Jack of all trades - yet; [memb.] Philadelphia Church of God; [hon.] Various swimming honors and awards, from age 6 to 18; [oth. writ.] Many other poems of various topics, long and short. Numerous lyrics for songs especially "Makin' Money" a rap song, that I believe will be a "Smash Hit" like no other - once released.; [pers.] I live for the end, when righteousness rules eternally, and oppression on mankind through breed and power is destroyed forever, whereas Peace, Love and Happiness will be The New Way of Life.; [a.] Port Saint Lucie, FL

COMBS, MELISSA NICOLE
[b.] January 21, 1974, Royal Oak, MI; [p.] William and Linda Davidson; [m.] Robert Lynwood Combs Jr., July 13, 1996; [ch.] Autumn Nicole, Jordan Anthony; [ed.] Berkley High, Macomb Community College (currently enrolled); [occ.] Mother; [pers.] My husband and children are my whole world. Everything good I do is influenced by my love for them.; [a.] Warren, MI

CONDON, EVELYN ANNE
[pen.] E. Anne Smith, Evelyn Smith; [b.] July 5, 1933, Biloxi, MS; [p.] Elmer and Marguerite Smith; [m.] Deceased; [ch.] Walter E. Condon, Eileen M. McConn, Carol Anne Bacchuber, Laurence Condon, Janet M. Mulcair; [ed.] High School Grad.; [occ.] Retired Food Service Supervisor and Restaurant Manager; [memb.] Associate of Mercy, Local Church Related Organizations and Local Volunteer Organizations; [oth. writ.] Editor-in-chief, High School Newspaper "The Rostrum" columnist (with Byline) for weekly "West Haven Town Crier." Editor and publisher of "The New England Mercy Connection," a newsletter for Mercy Associates.; [pers.] In writing, especially poetry, a much better sense of my inner self is usually awakened.; [a.] Middletown, CT

CONSOLO, JOHN
[pen.] Johnnie; [b.] April 23, 1917, Schonostady, NY; [p.] Michael and Lucy Consolo; [m.] Marguerite E. Hart Consolo, May 30, 1942; [ch.] Lois, Michael, Nancy, John, Mary, Susan, Christine; [ed.] Schenectady High School; [occ.] Retired Printer; [memb.] American Association of Retired Persons; [oth. writ.] "The Gifts

of God Gave" published in Mist of Enchantment by the National Library of Poetry.; [pers.] Please feel free to use any part of the enclosed publication from a local newspaper. Thank you John!; [a.] Rensselaer, NY

CONVERSE, CLETIS H.
[pen.] Cletis H. Converse; [b.] November 24, 1926, At home; [p.] Naomi Van Tries-Revey, Edward Revey; [m.] Divorced; [ch.] Debra Buy; [ed.] High school - Diploma from The Institute of Children's Literature, West Redding, Connecticut; [occ.] Retired; [memb.] Ladies Auxiliary (Fraternal Order of Eagles), American Lung Association; [hon.] Diploma from the Institute of Children's Literature; Writing for children and teenagers course; [oth. writ.] Other poems published in newspapers. Ten childhood stories written for Diploma; other poems written and not published — in a book for my family when I leave this earth; [pers.] I have written many children's short stories due to my childhood days. Growing up on the farm, was a very exciting time for me. Many new experiences came up each day. I grew up being outside with my Dad.; Our experiences are well worth reading about. [a.] Lawrence, KS

COOK, CAROLYN GRESHAM
[b.] January 9, 1944, Bernice, LA; [p.] Lewis David and Estelle Spencer Gresham; [m.] February 21, 1964; [ch.] Andy, Stephanie and Robert Cook; [ed.] Two-year Associate Business Degree, Louisiana Tech University, Rustin, Louisiana; [occ.] Owner-Operator Cook's Seafood, El Dorado, Ar; [memb.] Union Grove Baptist Church, Lillie, LA. International Society of Poets; [hon.] Poets of Merit, International Society of Poets; [oth. writ.] Several poems published in local newspapers, two poems published in the National Anthology of High School Poems, one poem published by the American Poetry Society, and one poem published by the Poetry Guild; [pers.] All of the praise and glory for my writing goes to my precious Heavenly Father; [a.] Lillie, LA

COOK, CRYSTAL R.
[b.] June 21, 1970, Anchorage, AK; [p.] Gary Wilson, Irene Wilson; [m.] Daniel Cook, January 10, 1995; [ch.] Wilson D. C. Cook, Matthew Taylor Cook; [ed.] Chugiak High, Institute of Children's Literature; [occ.] Homemaker; [oth. writ.] I have an extensive collection of poetry and children's stories I hope to one day see published.; [pers.] I try my very best to walk through this life with dignity and grace and always be the best I can be. I write to give glory to God and perhaps touch the hearts of others. My inspiration and strength come from my faith in God, my children and family. For them I hope to keep alive the message of faith, hope and love always.; [a.] Chugiak, AK

COOK, ROBERT W.
[pen.] RWC; [b.] November 7, 1942, Camden, NJ; [p.] Marie and Harry Cook; [m.] Patricia, August 28, 1967; [ed.] Cherry Hill High School West, Morgan University, Rowan College; [occ.] Physical Education Teacher; [memb.] Phi Delta Kappan Hainesport Education Association, National Education Association, New Jersey Education Association; [hon.] Governor's Award for Excellence in Education, Who's Who Among America's Teachers Induction into the Hall of Fame, High School Athletics; [oth. writ.] Recipes published in local newspapers.; [pers.] Every human being is priceless and has unique God given talents. It is inherently my desire to encourage others to strive toward the discovery of those talents.; [a.] Cherry Hill, NJ

COOPER, EVELYN
[b.] February 22, 1931, Spartanburg Co., Lyman, SC; [p.] Theron and Lila Mae Ellison; [m.] Curtis J. Cooper, July 2, 1949; [ch.] Deborah Darlene Cooper; [ed.] Holly Springs High School Graduate; [occ.] Self em-

ployed, "Evelyn's Collectibles"; [oth. writ.] Poems to my mother and friends.; [pers.] Being the youngest daughter, I have always been greatly influenced through life by my dearest mother, thus writing poems to her on birthdays which she adored. I would have felt an injustice to her if I had not written this poems "In Memory Of Our Mother."; [a.] Lyman, SC

CORBIN, CINDY
[b.] November 17, 1981, Manassas, VA; [p.] Mary Labounty, John Labounty (Step Dad), Ira Corbin (Dad); [ed.] Fred M. Lynn Middle School 6-87, Lake View High School 9th; [occ.] Student; [memb.] ROTC; [pers.] Smile 4-Ever; [a.] San Angelo, TX

CORBIN, PAMELA
[pen.] P. L. Corbin; [b.] June 6, 1950, Augusta, ME; [p.] Russell and Gloria Hall; [m.] Vernon Corbin, November 16, 1968; [ch.] 2 boys ages 24 and 27; [ed.] High school Grad, Certificate Nursing Asst. Grad. I will be attending our Local University as a Freshman Starting; [occ.] Small Business Owner, doing Canvas Work, Bags - Boat Tops etc.; [memb.] National Audubon Society, National Arbor Day Foundation, St. Josephs Church; [hon.] Mary Jane Small Scholarship from our Local Adult Ed. Program. I received it at my C.N.A. graduation and I am using it to help finance my college education. I am majoring in Social Services, Protective Rights for the Elderly.; [oth. writ.] Many other poems - none ever published; [pers.] I write poetry from my heart. I try to "Tell A Story" that may help others understand a situation or maybe just help them smile.; [a.] Gardiner, ME

CORGLIANO, FRANCINE
[pen.] Frankie Layne; [b.] November 21, 1964, Philadelphia, PA; [p.] Sam J. Corgliano; [ed.] Business Major; [occ.] Executive Secretary; [oth. writ.] You, Do It Now, Take A Look, Do It Now; [pers.] We never realized how valuable life is until we're faced with losing it. We never realize how strong love is until someones love shows us. We never realize how closely life and love are linked until the two become one. On December 7, 1995, I received a triple transplant. I would like to thank my father for being my hope and strength when I had none. I would like to thank him for helping me find the love of life, when I had lost it. I would also like to thank God for giving me this great Dad for giving me a little more time to enjoy life and Him.

CORRADINO, R. J.
[b.] July 20, 1979, Hammonton, NJ; [p.] Randy and Holly Corradino; [ed.] Currently a senior at Holy Spirit High School, Absecon, NJ; [occ.] Student; [hon.] Who's Who Among American High School Students 1994-95 and 1995-96, U.S. Achievement Academy All American Scholar award; [oth. writ.] Several poems and stories currently unpublished; [pers.] I try to expose the inhumanities that we far too often accept as simply a part of life.; [a.] Absecon, NJ

COULTER, JAMES
[b.] March 26, 1977, Vineland, NJ; [p.] Phillip Coulter Sr. and Anna Cerasuolo; [ed.] Millville Senior High School, Lessing Secondary School, Schiverin, Germany; [occ.] College Student; [memb.] National Honor Society, German National Honor Society - Delta Epsilon Phi; [hon.] U.S. Congress, Bundestag Youth Exchange Scholarship, The German - American Society Award, President Education Award, Soroptimist International Award; [oth. writ.] Many unpublished free-verse poems and Petcarchan sonnets including a new split-Petcarchan sonnet style, several poems published in "Prospectus Literary Magazine".; [pers.] I don't know why I write. Maybe to preserve memories I have or perhaps to preserve myself after I'm gone. I've been

greatly, influenced by the people of Mecklenburg, Germany.; [a.] Millville, NJ

COUP, JASON
[b.] January 22, 1983, Watsontown, PA; [p.] Randall Coup and Sharen Coup; [ed.] Junior High; [occ.] Student; [memb.] Milton YMCA; [hon.] President's Award for Educational Excellence; [pers.] Life is only so long, but the written word lasts forever.; [a.] Milton, PA

COURTNEY, LORI L.
[b.] December 25, 1964, New Lexington, OH; [p.] David and Linda Slatzer; [m.] Divorced, December 5, 1987; [ch.] 2 boys Devin and Eric Courtney; [ed.] Castle Rock High School, Portland State College; [occ.] Radiology Asst. II; [memb.] American Cancer Society Board, Co-Chair for 24 hr Relay for Life, Cowitz Youth Baseball Leg.; [hon.] Several Cup Awards from work for outstanding jobs. Several write ups for patient care by going out of my way for other people.; [oth. writ.] Several poems some put on the news letter at work. Several poems for friends and family.; [pers.] I feel that with in all of us there is the determination to strive for a better tomorrow. As for me I believe that you can only be the person you let yourself be. So with faith in yourself, and by giving just a little of each other only them we will know just what our most important legacy was made from. And it gives us a gentle reminder of how it came to pass.; [a.] Kelso, WA

COUSINS, KRISTY S.
[b.] December 25, 1971, Zenia; [p.] Eileen and Virgil Spicer; [m.] Herbert (Rusty) Cousins, September 18, 1993; [ch.] Lynsey, Erin and Alyssa; [ed.] H.S. Degree; [occ.] Specification Analyst; [oth. writ.] Various poems.; [a.] Huber Heights, OH

COVERT, BEVERLY BALE
[pen.] Beverly Covert; [b.] September 2, 1945, Boston; [p.] Robert Bale and Dorothy Sain; [ch.] Vanessa Duchman and Scotsmith; [ed.] University of MD; [occ.] Administrative - Legislative for local Gov't; [memb.] All Saints Episcopal Church, BPOE, American Legion; [hon.] Dean's List; [oth. writ.] Not yet published; [pers.] The most beautiful philosophy is "Desiderata" supposedly written by Max Eh'rmane. I whole heartedly agree! And I've learned to appreciate all of God's creations; [a.] Edgewater, MD

COWAN, PAULA K.
[pen.] Paula K. Cowan; [b.] December 13, 1944, Bellefontaine, OH; [p.] Paul Jacob Shoemaker, Mary E. Shoemaker; [ed.] West Phoenix High School, Phoenix College, Lamson Business College, Institute of Childrens Literature; [occ.] Retired Accounting Clerk; [memb.] Copra C14 of Phoenix Retirees Assoc. AARP Member International Society of Poems; [oth. writ.] Over 200 poems children picture books; [pers.] I hope to heighten the interest in poetry to the average man, woman and child; [a.] Phoenix, AZ

COWAN, RUTH A.
[b.] September 24, 1934, Deer River, MN; [p.] John Nevins Spencer and Aili Helen (Maki) Spencer; [m.] Gary Ray Cowan, April 27, 1991; [ch.] Jean Mann, John Hegle, Juliane Ghazi, Janet Hegle, James Hegle; [ed.] B.A. in Cultural Anthropology, The Evergreen State College; [occ.] Voice Teacher, Singer, Musical Theater and Concert production; [memb.] Washington State Music Teacher's Assoc., Phi Theta Kappa, The Masterworks Ensemble; [hon.] Award of Merit, North Dakota State Bar Assoc., Phi Theta Kappa Scholastic Award, Toastmasters Intl. contest speaker and judge; [oth. writ.] "Daughter Of The North" historical novel, unpublished, "Finish-American Immigrants of the 19th and 20th Century", monograph, "Finnish-Americans of the Pacific Northwest", monograph.; [pers.] I write

from the heart. Creative poetry furnishes a window for my reader to look inside and share intimate feelings.; [a.] Lacey, WA

CRAIG, TIMOTHY F.
[pen.] Timmy; [b.] December 20, 1981, Norwich, CT; [p.] John and Jean Craig; [ed.] Preston Grammar School; [occ.] High School Student; [hon.] Knights of Columbus Brotherhood Award; [pers.] I dedicate my poem "I'll Be There" to Samantha Howard. I love you more than words of a poem can ever express.; [a.] Preston, CT

CREECH, FLORENCE
[pen.] Flo; [b.] February 15, 1944, Louisville, KY; [p.] Deceased; [m.] Separated; [ch.] Crystal King, Larry Gordon Creech; [ed.] College (still going) student Eastern Kentucky University Law Enforcement; [occ.] Home Maker; [oth. writ.] I have a lot of poems, but none published. I have never given publication a thought.; [pers.] I write poems for pass time, but I have to be in the mood. All my poems that I write are from my own personal thoughts, feelings and emotions. I have to feel it to write it. Almost all my poems are about love, pain and heartbreak.; [a.] Hazard, KY

CRENSHAW, VANESSA
[b.] July 3, 1956, Philadelphia; [p.] Gladys M. Crenshaw, Northia McClain; [ed.] High School Graduate, currently enrolled at Community College of Philadelphia in education with plans to attend a 4 year college; [occ.] Class room Assistant in Special Education Simon Gratz High Phila., PA; [memb.] Currently a volunteer member at the Clef Club of Jazz and performing arts in Philadelphia; [hon.] First Place Award for Black History month in 1995 at Simon Gratz High School in Philadelphia also honorable mention in 1993; [oth. writ.] I have a book of unpublished poems and songs that I have written through the years.; [pers.] All praise due to God. To invasion your dreams and plan your goals is to actualize them. My favorite poet: Conte Cullen Somber Emotions - in memory of Carl Humphry.; [a.] Philadelphia, PA

CRIBBS, SHIRLEY
[pen.] Shirley Cribbs; [b.] September 13, 1950, Indiana, PA; [p.] George, LaRue Patterson; [m.] Lester Cribbs, July 14, 1990; [ch.] Three daughters; [ed.] High School graduate, general source of study; [occ.] Homemaker; [memb.] Junior Girls Scout Leader for several years; [oth. writ.] I have at least 50 other poetic works yet unpublished.; [pers.] Prior to my retirement I have also been a cook for 9 years and a home health aide for 6 years.; [a.] Commodore, PA

CRIQUI, WILLIAM R.
[b.] December 30, 1944, Montclair, NJ; [p.] Francis and Florence Criqui; [m.] Donna L. Criqui; [ch.] Ricky David, Scott David, William Edward and Julianna; [ed.] High School and One Year of College; [occ.] Welder Planner for GP4 Nuclear; [memb.] The Community of the Crucified One Br. Louis-John Criqui, Rev. William R. Criqui; [oth. writ.] Poems "New Life", "Watch" and "Temple Of The Body", etc. None of our poems have been published; [pers.] To serve our Lord and saviour Jesus Christ and all his children is our life and our love.; [a.] Barnegat, NJ

CRISCI, LORI ANN
[pen.] Alexandra Scott; [b.] June 1, 1972, San Francisco, CA; [p.] Paul A. Crisci, Janis L. Crisci; [m.] (Fiance) Nathan T. Fall, Engaged to be married January 11, 1997; [ed.] Vintage High School, Napa, CA; [occ.] Sign Fabrication and Design, Sign Factory, Amer. Canyon, CA.; [hon.] Vintage High School's Academic Achievement Award, and Certificate of Merit and excellence in Composition/American Literature; [oth. writ.] Personal Poems and Short Stories that have never

been published.; [a.] American Canyon, CA

CRISTANUS, JOSEPH E.
[b.] June 7, 1955, Chicago, IL; [occ.] Paramedic; [a.] Chicago, IL

CROTHERS, MARYLOU
[b.] August 20, 1932, Marquette, MI; [p.] James and Adeline Hudson; [m.] Walter Crothers, December 21, 1970; [ch.] Judy, James, Peter, Holly; [ed.] H.S. Grad; [occ.] Retired; [memb.] Marquette County Human Soc.; [hon.] National Wild Life Federation, Backyard Wildlife Habitat Program; [oth. writ.] Poem, a four letter word; [pers.] Worked 29 years as a Elementary Secretary.; [a.] Marquette, MI

CROW, DAVID F.
[pen.] Joey L.; [b.] February 18, 1980, Media, PA; [p.] Thomas F. Crow, Barbara J. Crow; [ed.] Academy Park High School Junior, Sharon Hill, PA; [occ.] Pisano's Sandwich Shop (Stock); [memb.] Grace Reformed Episcopal Church (Usher), Who's Who Among High School Students, High School Newspaper and Yearbook; [hon.] Two time Who's Who award winner, Perfect attendance award, Honor roll award, Indiana University of PA (I.U.P.), Journalism Workshop 1996 Summer Honors Program; [pers.] I believe that my best writings derive from experiences in life.; [a.] Glenolden, PA

CROWLEY, ROSALEEN
[b.] June 25, 1958, Cork, Ireland; [p.] Cornelius and Margaret Sheehan; [m.] Brendan, September 11, 1983; [ch.] Kenneth William, James Timothy; [ed.] Bachelor of Arts, Diploma in Education, Dip. in Hospital services and Administration, Associate Diploma in Speech and Drama; [occ.] Founder of Relocation and Cultural Training Services, LLC; [memb.] Association of International Women Ave, Friends of the American Pianists Association, Member Entrepreneur's Alliance of Indiana, Inc. member, Indiana Employee Relocation Alliance; [oth. writ.] Several unfinished projects.; [pers.] Leaving behind family and friends is one of the hardest things and have ever done, but moving to another culture and making new friends has its own rewards.; [a.] Carmel, IN

CRUM, BRIAN
[b.] October 25, 1983, Shelby, OH; [p.] Dan Crum, Debbie Crum; [ed.] I am a 7th grader at the Shelby Middle School; [memb.] First Lutheran Church at Selby, 5th Year Boy Scout; [pers.] I write my poems of situations around me. I just change the details.; [a.] Shelby, OH

CRUZ, PATSY IZURA
[pen.] Izura Wade; [b.] October 14, 1936, Oakland, CA; [p.] Deceased; [m.] Robert E. Cruz, October 28, 1978; [ch.] Seven, 4 boys and 3 girls; [ed.] High School Merritt College - "Activity Director" - for the elderly, Camp Counsel - A.M.C. and Chabot College 1960; [occ.] Activity Dir - for the Elderly and Rehabilitation - Social Service; [memb.] Y.W.C.A. - Volunteer for Rehabilitation Unit - Recreational Therapy of Activity - Eastern Star; [hon.] Golden Poet - 1992, Trophy from World of Poetry 11-15-1990 - Honorable Mention - in Appreciation Award of Merritt Certificate - for poem Change Honorary Charter Membership - 1993, International Society of Poets - "World of Poetry" Material for a song,at at New York convention, "No Matter Where You Go, I'll Be There Growing Old" - 1991, Eddie Lou Cole world of Poetry; [oth. writ.] Martin Luther King "No Time Did I See" Sammy Davis Jr. "Yes I Can't" and "I Remember Momma" local campus news paper - Berkely and Hayward Calif. 1970 Oakland Past Poetry Contest - 1971 title "Don't Judge Me."; [pers.] I did it my way what is a women and what

has she got virtue and that means a lot - self indulging a spirit to write, I found a song and did it my way, now what need is, someone to know, I am a writer to exhale my soul. I have a torch, burning to, who is this women! A virtue of many I did it my way!; [a.] San Leandro, CA

CUMMINGS, FELICIA
[b.] April 21, 1979, Baldwin, GA; [p.] Louise Curry and Willie Cummings; [ed.] Wilco Senior High, 12th Grade; [hon.] Golden Poet Award (World of Poetry), Three Band Trophies, Place in School Science Fair, 3rd in District Science Fair; [oth. writ.] Poems that have been published in books (World of Poetry) - God the Master, The Feeling of Love, (National Library...) - Abuse of the World; [pers.] Being a teenager I do not possess power. When I write I can kill, love, hate, and save with my words. Writing gives your everlasting power. Power of the heart and power of soul; [a.] Irwinton, GA

CUMMINGS, WILMA FAYE
[b.] July 2, 1945, North Little Rock, AR; [p.] Herman and Ida Mae Fulmer; [m.] Kenneth Cummings, November 17, 1969; [ch.] Terrell, Michael, Angela, Tanya; [ed.] Sylvan Hills High; [occ.] Housewife; [memb.] Liberty Fellowship Church Liberty Gospel Singers Group; [hon.] Bible course award typing award; [oth. writ.] Poetry - songs; [a.] North Little Rock, AR

CUNDIFF, DYLAN
[b.] April 8, 1976, Houston, TX; [occ.] Student and Southwest Texas State University; [pers.] I try to wrote what I feel about the world and how depressing it is. That is what I try to reflect. "The path of righteousness and seldom found. The path of destruction is wide and found by fools."; [a.] New Braunfels, TX

CURTIS, CATHERINE G.
[b.] July 17, 1917, Portland, OR; [p.] Drucilla and Earl Sweek; [m.] Deceased, February 13, 1936; [ch.] Carolyn and Robert; [ed.] D.C., N.D. Th. D, L.P.N. Associate in Physical Therapy; [occ.] Retired; [memb.] Athletics National Research Foundation 1964; [hon.] California State Board 1962 Basic Science Certificate State of Arizona #6443 Editors Choir Award 1996; [oth. writ.] Religious Articles poems in your books for National Library of Poetry.; [pers.] I believe in the Lord Jesus Christ in the Holy Scriptures. I have been in the mission fields in Guatemala and Mexico and I believe in the soon return of our Lord and Saviour and hope to be ready when it comes.; [a.] Bangor, CA

DAHLGREEN, JULIA
[b.] April 4, 1920, Elderburg, MD; [p.] George and Estella Glover; [m.] John C. Dahlgreen Jr., March 24, 1940; [ch.] Jack, Judy, Dolores; [ed.] Grade school, High school Catonsville Community College; [occ.] Retired from Sears, as Appliance Sales Person; [memb.] Christian Women Club in Home Bible Study Grace Lutheran Church Swallwood Home Makers; [hon.] President of Homemakers Top Sales for Sears Chosen to Model Clothes; [oth. writ.] I strive to bring others to the Lord thru my poems husband deceased.

DALOMBA, JEANINE SUZANNE
[pen.] Susie; [b.] September 10, 1958, Brooklyn, NY; [p.] Pascal and Maria Del Carmen Dalomba; [ed.] H. S. Mater Christi, College - 6 months only, Queensborough Community College and 6 months of College in Madrid Spain studying in Completense De Madrid; [occ.] Retired Police officer from New York City - South Bronx almost 13 years on the force; [memb.] Retired due to a line of duty and disability, taking: Tap lessons, French Lessons, Sculpture Classes; [oth. writ.] Poem came about because I was engaged for 5 years Don and I broke up 3 months before our marriage date. It's been

over 7 years, it's time to forget and move on. I can't seem to do that though it would be a good idea if I did. I compare other men to him.; [pers.] You're never too old to try something you always wanted to do. Don't spend all your days working then waiting till your old and retired to enjoy the simple pleasures of life. Get away, take vacations, live a peaceful life. Don't complicate your life with too many materialistic things, it will only cause you headaches and stress. Live by and within the law. Don't harp on what could have been and let it ruin your life. Take chances, enjoy life-live!; [a.] Palm Coast, FL

DAMPIER, GLORIA
[pen.] Gloria Fields-Dampier; [b.] January 24, 1963, Camdenton, MO; [p.] Stuart and Dola Newell; [m.] Jeffory Dampier, March 16, 1985; [ch.] Bobbie, Frankie, Magnum; [ed.] Climax Springs High, Southwest Baptist University Sedelia State College; [oth. writ.] Payment Due, Divine Advice, Mother Angel, You Only Had To Ask, Lesson's Not Learned; [pers.] I like to make people look deep into their souls and reflect on life's lessons.; [a.] Tunas, MO

DANIEL, JASON RICHARD
[pen.] Jason, Jaycin; [b.] October 12, 1979, Goldsboro; [p.] Richard and Glenda Daniel; [ed.] I was in public school until January of 7th grade. I am now in the 12th grade and have been home schooled since Jan. of 7th grade; [oth. writ.] "Angel Eyes...Mystery Skies", "Look", "Where I Walked I Now Fly", "Freedom Aborted", "The Scent Of Flowers", "Desire", "Looking Glass", "Train Of Faith", "The Promise", etc.; [pers.] I started writing poetry in May of 1996. It was at this time when Jesus Christ revealed to me the talent in which He'd given me. None of my poetry comes from my own thoughts. I write according to how God speaks to me in phases of my life. All glory to God!; [a.] Fremont, NC

DANIEL SR., CARTER LEE
[pen.] Capt. Dan; [b.] April 3, 1949, Wash., DC; [p.] Helen and Junior; [m.] Terry, November 5, 1982; [ch.] Tammy, Helen, Carter Jr. and Crystal; [ed.] Oxon Hill High School, Lincoln Tech Automotive School; [occ.] Head Web Offset Press Person Government Printing Office; [memb.] American Legion, Thai-American Assos., I.S.P.; [hon.] Suggestion and performance awards at work, A.F. good conduct medal, Vietnam service medal, Republic of Vietnam commendation medal; [oth. writ.] Life is short, published writing Gifts of Red, and many other poems still not published many over 20 yrs old.; [pers.] Influenced at an early age, by God's gift to all of us, mother nature try to express my deep inner feeling and views of how I perceive life.; [a.] Laurel, MD

DANKNICH, ALIZABETH ASPEN
[pen.] Alizzy; [b.] May 24, 1983, Denver; [p.] Tammy and Kevin Danknich; [ed.] Allendale Elementary, Drake Junior High School; [hon.] National Junior Honors Society and the Distinguished Dragon award; [oth. writ.] 1993 Anthology of poetry by young Americans.; [pers.] I hope this is the beginning of a wonderful life of poetry for me.; [a.] Arvada, CO

DAPPOLLONE, CHRISTINA
[pen.] C. McGovern; [b.] January 27, 1977, West Phila., PA; [p.] Thomas and Carmelina Dappollone; [ed.] Springfield High School, PA., Ursinus College PA; [occ.] Student, Junior at Ursinus; [memb.] Upsilon Phi Delta, Dean's List, National Honour Society, Literary Society of Ursinus; [hon.] Dean's List, Ursinus College Whitian Prize, Lantern Poetry Award; [oth. writ.] Published in local newspapers, Ursinus College Literary Magazine "The Lantern"; [pers.] For me, writing is a process by which the culmination of words becomes the expression of emotions that all people can

relate to, revel in, and rely upon.; [a.] Springfield, PA

DAVEY, JESSICA
[b.] April 20, 1975, Rockland, ME; [p.] Donald Davey, Laurinda Davey; [ed.] Medomak Valley High School, Eastern Nazarene College; [occ.] College Student; [pers.] If one person thinks about what I have written I will have been successful.; [a.] Quincy, MA

DAVIS, BARBARA DAVIS
[b.] November 20, 1968, Pineville, LA; [p.] Mack Sr. and Joycie Davis; [m.] Michael Wayne Davis, May 21, 1994; [ed.] B.S. in Medical Technology from Northeast Louisiana University in Monroe, La., High School Diploma from Bolton High School in Alexandria, La.; [occ.] Medical Technologist at St. Frances Cabrini Hospital; [hon.] National Honors Society, Dean's List; [a.] Alexandria, LA

DAVIS, BRENDA W.
[b.] August 19, 1942, Spruce Pine, NC; [p.] Millie and Albert Ward; [m.] Robert H. Davis, April 5, 1974; [ch.] Molly M. Davis Summers, and John J. Fry (by previous marriage); [ed.] 12th grade, graduate at Harris High School, in Spruce Pine, N.C., (Milchell Cty.); [occ.] Drexel Heritage, Furnishings - Morganton, NC; [hon.] "Teen" Magazine - published one of my writings on "Suicide" 1958-59; [oth. writ.] I have been writing poetry since 1956, and never entered a National Poetry Contest until 1996. I also write in journals, and love photography.; [pers.] The purpose of my writings is to "paint" a picture, with words, so others can "see", the beauty of nature. And to give reverence to Gods' creativity in all things.; [a.] Morganton, NC

DAVIS, GLORIA
[b.] September 26, 1947, Corpus Christi, TX; [p.] Bill and Ruby Johns; [m.] Robert H. Davis Jr., June 26, 1970; [ch.] Lisa Delaine, Leslie DeAnn; [oth. writ.] I began writing in 1993, have written several poems but had never shared them with anyone other than friends and family. Chapter forty-one is my first published work.; [pers.] My poetry is an expression of love and friendship to the special people in my life.; [a.] Franklin, TX

DAVIS, SHAUNA RENEE
[b.] December 29, 1980, Oakland, CA; [p.] Claudell Marie Preston Davis, Ellis Arnell Davis; [ed.] I am going to the 9th grade in the fall; [occ.] Student; [pers.] The degree of writing I express is exactly where the soul rises and descends. I have been influenced by primarily African American writers.; [a.] Oakland, CA

DEAN, MARY AMANDA
[pen.] Amanda Dean; [b.] March 27, 1964, Milford, DE; [p.] Harry and Cora Bell O'Connor; [m.] Robert Charles Dean Jr., April 19, 1986; [ch.] Jana Nicole, Jeffrey Ryan, Juli Marie; [ed.] High School Graduate Colonel Richardson High School; [occ.] Self-employed Child Educator; [memb.] St. Lukes United Methodist Church, Denton Elementary PTA Treasurer, Girl Scout Leader, Elizabeth Circle Member; [pers.] My poems were inspired by my Dad who died of Cancer. By putting my thoughts into words it helps to personally Express my feelings. My family and God are the most important things in my life.; [a.] Denton, MD

DEBOLT, AURELIA
[pen.] "Eagle"; [b.] July 4, 1943, Los Angeles, CA; [p.] Richard C., Barbara W. Beaudry; [m.] Harold Fredrick DeBolt, September 28, 1962; [ch.] Richard Charles, Catherine Victoria; [ed.] University of Maryland, Kaiserslautern American High School (Germany), Queen Anne High, Seattle, WA; [occ.] Writer, Entrepreneur; [memb.] Charter member Freedom's Foundation, Governor's Mansion Foundation, Olympia Opera Guild, Washington Athletic Club, Olympia Yacht Club - Past President Women's Group, Olympia Country and Golf Club, Sierra Club, League of Women Voters; [hon.] 1st of five non-Chamber of Commerce women members of The National Accreditation Committee (Kentucky, 1975), Environmental Protection and Improvements Commission 1976, Order of Bacchus (only woman at that time) German Wine Brotherhood, and Title: Princess Aurelia I von Kaiserslautern for life, Kaiserslautern, Germany; [oth. writ.] "A trip through The Past," Gettysburg PA, (Book) A Different Drummer - "I am," "Together" - Squaw Talk vol. xx no6, 1983, Travel Host Magazine articles 1978, Poetry published in local newspapers, United Way Pamphlet, "How To" etiquette book (Organizational guide), Novel in Progress.; [pers.] Poetry is the music of the Soul. To create it, one plugs into the Energy of the Universe. I strive to see Truth and have been motivated by the great Poets of our time.; [a.] Olympia, WA

DELPH, TONYA M.
[b.] July 23, 1975, Harlan, KY; [p.] Dianna Delph and Grant Delph; [ed.] Plymouth South High, International Air Academy; [occ.] Order Entry Clerk, Secretary, American Frozen Foods, Plymouth, MA; [hon.] 2nd price in Beauty Pageant - 2nd place in MADD Poster Contest; [oth. writ.] I have over 200 poems since 1987, but this is the first time I've ever entered one in anything.; [pers.] I enjoy showing my feelings for life and love through the beauty of nature, my father, a songwriter for himself, was my greatest influence for my poetry.; [a.] Plymouth, MA

DEMOTT, STEVE
[pen.] Steve DeMott; [b.] June 12, 1949, Rigby, ID; [p.] Dick and Norma DeMott; [ch.] Richard, Keylee, Cody, Daniel; [ed.] Bonneville High, Idaho State Univ.; [occ.] Freelance cowboy; [memb.] Idaho Farm Bureau, Idaho Jr. Rodeo A Assn., Idaho High School Rodeo Assn., Gold Prospector's Assn. of America, Idaho Trapper's Assn., Bonneville Chariot Racing Assn.; [oth. writ.] Poetry published in "Western Horseman" magazine and some writings for local newspapers.; [pers.] Though my writing tends to run the gaunt from philosophical to political, I try to reflect the values and ideals that made this country and the west a great place to live.; [a.] Idaho Falls, ID

DENNIS, JOYCE C.
[pen.] Joyce C. Dennis; [b.] August 8, 1953, Charleston, SC; [p.] Mrs. Ruby A. and Willie Hampton Sr.; [m.] Mr. Larry Dennis, August 8, 1981; [ch.] Larry Dennis II, Lauren Hampton Dennis; [ed.] Registered Nurse; [occ.] R.N.; [memb.] American Nurses Association; [hon.] Valedictorian in 6th grade National Honor Society 9th grade President Line Alpha Kappa Alpha Sorority Inc. President Young Baptist Training Union for 5 years member of Lovely Hill Baptist Church since 1977; [pers.] I am not perfect I have always been strong for others now I must be strong for me.

DESCHLER, CHRISTINE
[b.] July 19, 1978, S. Nassau Hospital Oceanside, NY; [p.] Judith and James; [ed.] Graduated from Sacred Heart Academy in Hempstead currently attending The Hartt School, University of Hartford; [occ.] Student - majoring in flute performance and music, ed.; [memb.] Long Island Flute Club, New York Flute Club, National Flute Association, MENC; [hon.] 1994 All-state wind Ensemble, Long Island Flute Club Competition Ivy Jacobson Memorial Prize 1995, All-Eastern Band, LIFC Irma Miller Memorial Prize, All-state Symphony Orchestra, 1996 LIFC Irma Miller Memorial Prize (all these awards are flute performance); [oth. writ.] Poems printed in school magazines; [pers.] Poetry is communication through imagination. This gives me the freedom to express my mind.; [a.] Lynbrook, NY

DESHA, JOSH
[b.] October 2, 1978, Jacksonville, IL; [p.] Teri Gordon, Bruce DeSha; [ed.] Graduated Calvary Academy High School in Springfield, IL. Currently a freshman at Lincoln Land Community College; [memb.] National Honor Society; [oth. writ.] Two personal compitations of short stories, poems and philosophical statements.; [pers.] Most of my early poetry dealt with suicide, but the more recent poems deal with finding the light in life rather than the darkness.; [a.] Springfield, IL

DEXTER, AMANDA
[b.] May 3, 1979, Portland, OR; [p.] Robert and Cheryl Dexter; [ed.] High school student at Woodrow Wilson High in Portland, OR; [occ.] Unemployed; [memb.] Students for Environmental Action, Wilson High Thespians; [hon.] Presidential Academic Fitness Award; [oth. writ.] None published; [pers.] I use my writing to find the beauty in that which not all would find beautiful.; [a.] Portland, OR

DIAMANTE, SAUNDRA
[b.] January 12, 1959, Baltimore, MD; [p.] Lt. Cmdr. Stanley A. Taylor, RoseMarie Taylor; [m.] Gil P. Diamante, October 25, 1985; [ch.] Gil Jr., Robert, Timothy, Ariel and Athena; [ed.] Graduate from Serverna Park High in 1977. In 1980, I received my FFC Ridio License.; [occ.] Homemaker; [memb.] Member of the I.S. of Poets; [hon.] I have two Editor's Choice Award from I.S. of P. Also, two merit plaque award.; [oth. writ.] "The Balance" in "A Sea of Treasures", "September" in "Spirit of Age", "I Too, Once was a Child" in "Tapestry of Thoughts", "A Bit of X-Mas Cheer" in "Carving in Stone", "Happy Valentine's Day" in "The Rippling Waters", "Promises of Spring" in "Lyrical Heritage", "A Moment of Bliss" in "Poets of the 90's"; [pers.] When in doubt, put yourself in check...; [a.] Daly City, CA

DINKINS, TIMOTHY RAYMOND
[pen.] Tim Dinkins; [b.] September 2, 1927, Bradley, AR; [p.] Clifton Dinkins, F. A. Dinkins; [m.] Gladys M. Teague, December 2, 1945; [ch.] Rodney, Dolores, Raymond, Hazel, Effie; [ed.] Cox Elementary Fouke High, Bradley High; [occ.] Retired; [memb.] B.M.I. Landmark U.P.C.I., International Society of Poets; [hon.] Desoto Nursing Home Desoto TX. Nominated for award by country music Asso., National Library of Poetry; [oth. writ.] It's All In A life time. Cattin' Tonight. A Father's Letter To Santa. The Rose Parade. Mary Sailor in Alaska. Heaven Is Only Knee High. Willow Waltz, A Witness To Your Crown.; [pers.] I do my best to put truth in life, in my writing. Inspired by the late Hank Williams Sr.; [a.] Texarkana, TX

DITSCH, RICHARD C.
[b.] April 2, 1938, Louisiana, KY; [p.] Sarah and R. E. Ditsch; [m.] Ann Erice, August 7, 1982; [ed.] M.A.R.; [occ.] Pianist in church; [memb.] U.S. Chess Federation, Dale Carnegie Graduate, Clinical Hynotherapists, American Association Christian Counselors (Charter); [hon.] American Association Family Counselors, Notary, Licensed, ordained and bowded minister; [oth. writ.] the bewitching hook child of RA, the princess and the frog, Artur is Rex, Fence, Circuses and Carnivals, the Eagle, the Hobo, Carilion; [pers.] My writing has been influenced by POE, Longfellow, Melville, Spenser, pope, shakespere, raliegh, scott, keats; [a.] Louisville, KY

DOBENSKY, SARAH L.
[b.] February 6, 1963, Meriden, CT; [p.] Sarah Soucy and Frank Gavrish; [m.] Richard J. Dobensky, August 29, 1987; [ch.] Richie Jerome, Sara Lyn, Eric Joseph; [ed.] Rham High, Middlesex College; [occ.] Paralegal

- E.R. Secretary, VMMC, Meriden, CT; [hon.] Dean's List; [pers.] Through the goodness of mankind I feel that we may all be joined in the wondrous circle of Life for eternity.; [a.] Meriden, CT

DONAHUE, PEGGY J.
[pen.] P. J.; [b.] June 19, 1941, Flint, MI; [p.] James and Marie Combs; [m.] Ronald R. Donahue, December 16, 1961; [ch.] Kimberly and Karon; [ed.] Flushing High School; [occ.] HW; [hon.] Editor's Choice Award (The National Library of Poetry); [oth. writ.] Lifescape of poems "My Secret Garden" (last year in "The Voice Within"; [pers.] Most of my writing is from what I've experienced or seen in my lifetime.; [a.] Palm Harbor, FL

DOPKINS, DENNIS J.
[b.] April 24, 1944, Janesville, WI; [p.] Henry and Sylvia Dopkins; [m.] Sandra Ruth Dopkins, January 18, 1975; [ch.] Kevin, Shannon and Scott; [memb.] Janesville Little Theatre; [oth. writ.] "The Crumbling Curb", "She"; [a.] Janesville, WI

DOSORETZ, LIZY
[b.] December 28, 1979, Boston, MA; [ed.] Attending a private school. Canterbury School; [occ.] Student; [hon.] Editor's Choice Award for a poem I wrote; [oth. writ.] "Love That Hurts" A Muse To Follow, poems in school magazine; a poem in Choate Roasmary Hall School Magazine; [pers.] I write to show people different perspectives and pertaining to life's questions. We are all on a mission to live happily, maybe my writing will help.

DOW, URSULA
[b.] June 2, 1948, Germany; [m.] Willy Dow, February 5, 1978; [ed.] Degree in Business Admin., AA in Psychology from Inter-American University of Puerto Rico; [occ.] Airline Supervisor, Translator for German; [memb.] Jacksonville Table Tennis Club; [hon.] Numerous Table Tennis trophies; [oth. writ.] Sports reports and special events coverage for a German daily newspaper. Published several poems.; [pers.] Poetry writing is a great recreational tool.; [a.] Jacksonville, FL

DOWDLE, PAULA S.
[b.] Asheville, NC; [p.] John and Frances Shelton; [m.] Ed Dowdle, October 24, 1981; [ch.] Ashley Michelle and Zebulon Edward; [occ.] Program Support Asst., V.A. Medical Ctr. Asheville, NC; [memb.] Merrimon Ave. Baptist Church; [pers.] I encourage everyone to share life by becoming an organ, blood, bone morrow or platelet donor. There are countless people dying needlessly because of the lack of donors.; [a.] Asheville, NC

DOWNS, JAY WARREN
[pen.] Matthew Lovell Downarian, Sterling S. Silverpeace; [b.] September 6, 1936, Reading, PA; [p.] Paul S. and Ethel A. Downs; [m.] Divorced, January 25, 1959; [ch.] Patrick Jay, Brian Scott, Michael Allen, Kevin Glenn, Denise Ann, Kathleen Lynn; [ed.] Reading Sr. High, Univ. of Wisconsin; [occ.] Commercial Transportation Director ARCO Industries Inc., Milwaukee, WI; [memb.] International Brotherhood of Teamsters, American Trucking Assoc., WI Trucking Assoc., National Safety Council, National Assoc. on Transportation Safety, American Fellowship, Minister, Alliance Church, Milwaukee, WI; [hon.] National Safety Council, American Trucking, Assoc., Teamster Union/Local 200, State of Pennsylvania Carnagie Hero Award, Univ. of Wisconsin-Literature, Milwaukee Writers Club; [oth. writ.] Published/Associate Editor of Christian Light, Reaching out Words from within, Numerous, Articles Essays, Poems and Short Stories Pub.; [pers.] I am committed to making a worldwide contribution in literature one poem and one person at a time. As a youth

I was influenced by the great classics, they are responsible for the accomplishment I enjoy today - Thanks, Dad!; [a.] Milwaukee, WI

DOWTY, KIMBERLY J.
[pen.] Felicite Vaillancourt; [b.] February 23, 1976, Seoul, Korea; [m.] Ronald A. Dowty, April 4, 1994; [oth. writ.] I have several other poems, and short stories published on the internet.; [pers.] I greatly admire Edgar Allen Poe. I adore all of his literary accomplishments, especially his poetry, if not for him, I may have never found my calling.; [a.] Fayetteville, AR

DUBOIS, DENIS P.
[b.] December 27, 1941, Saratoga Springs, NY; [p.] Wallace and Blanche Dubois; [m.] Kay Stewart; [ch.] Nicole and Paul; [ed.] H.S. and Bkg Night School Courses; [occ.] Semi retired formerly Int'l Banker; [memb.] Knights of Colombus; [oth. writ.] None published; [a.] San Francisco, CA

DUCHARME, SANDRA
[b.] February 25, 1949, Webster, MA; [p.] Shirley and Andrew Masley; [m.] Roger, June 10, 1972; [ch.] Joseph Scott, Jason Todd; [ed.] Worcester Hahnemann Hospital School of Nursing Chaffey College; [occ.] R.N. City of Hope Duarte, CA; [memb.] Oncology Nurse Certified California Nurse Association Oncology Nurse Association; [pers.] The poem reflects the concern and compassion of families torn apart by catastrophic illness and the desire for the patient and family to share inner fears; [a.] Fontana, CA

DUCHROW, VERONA
[b.] September 6, 1922, Plymouth, WI; [p.] Harvey and Maleda Schulz; [m.] Arnold Duchrow, June 5, 1943; [ch.] Richard and Linda; [ed.] Plymouth High; [occ.] Retired; [memb.] Zion Lutheran Church, Missouri Synod Mission for the Blind; [hon.] Community Service Award for 20 years working for the Blind - 45 years teaching in Sunday school; [oth. writ.] Several poems published local newspaper; [pers.] The love you receive should be shared with others.; [a.] Plymouth, WI

DUKES, SHANDI
[b.] August 14, 1981, Greenville, KY; [p.] Randy Dukes, Teresa Dukes; [ed.] Muhlenberg North High School; [occ.] Student, 10th grade; [memb.] Band, North Stars Spirit Club; [hon.] Band 2 Solo Awards, 2 ensemble awards, 2 All-District Awards, Most Outstanding Band Member; [oth. writ.] None published; [pers.] I spend most of my tine in school and band. And in my spare time I write stories and poems. I write my best writing's when I'm sad or when I'm feeling down.; [a.] Bremen, KY

DUNAGAN, CHARLENE
[b.] November 18, 1929, Chickasha, OK; [p.] S. Doman, Evelyn Doman; [m.] Bobby J. Dunagan, December 18, 1948; [ch.] Susan, Thomas, Robin, Steven, and five grandchildren; [ed.] Capital Hill High, Texas University; [occ.] Homemaker; [hon.] Honor Society; [pers.] This poem came to me while meditating. Having Parkinsons disease diagnosed seventeen years, "Night Travel" has been special for me. I hope it finds a place in the hearts of the people who read it.; [a.] Albuquerque, NM

DUNCAN, JAMES W.
[b.] November 13, 1936, Port Angeles, WA; [p.] William Duncan, Elanore Duncan; [m.] Christine Duncan, January 20, 1976; [ch.] Cathy, Deborah, Brandon; [ed.] Mapicton High School; [occ.] Telecommunications; [memb.] International Society of Poets; [hon.] NLP Editors Award; [oth. writ.] Local Newspapers - 3 Anthologies; [pers.] I write about life - both the good and bad; [a.] Chandler, OK

DUNLAP, ROBERT
[b.] February 17, 1952, Lafayette, IN; [ed.] Graduate of Purdue University, 1974 double degree in Fine Arts and Interior Design; [occ.] Artist/Painter; [hon.] Bausch and Lomb Science Award, President's Academic Award, Hoosier Scholar, Grand Prize Winner of the Ethulhu Writing Competition; [oth. writ.] Skin (Short Stories), The Minister's Tale, (Short Story), The Red Basin (Short Story), Nitocris (A Novel in Progress), others poems and essays, some unpublished; [pers.] I like to use painterly description to create a heavy mood and atmosphere about the subject. I have been largely influenced by Poe and H. P. Love Craft.; [a.] Battle Ground, IN

DUNN, KAREN
[pen.] Karen Dunn, Katerina Dunne; [b.] November 5, 1970, Lowell, MA; [p.] James and Mary Scanlon; [m.] John Dunn, April 22, 1995; [ch.] James John Dunn; [ed.] BS - U. Mass-Lowell - Mgmt.; [occ.] Technical Recruiter; [memb.] NAFE, NEHRA; [hon.] Beta Gama Sigma, Sigma Iota Epsilon, Magna Cum Laude, The "Dean's List"; [pers.] I believe that we should accept all challenges however difficult or hard they seem to be. For if we're not challenged we don't give ourselves the chance to set ourselves free.; [a.] Dracut, MA

DUQUET, DON
[pen.] Don Duquet; [b.] January 10, 1913, Brassua, ME; [p.] Antoine Duquet, Elise Pomerleau; [m.] Fabiola Vashon, December 14, 1979; [ch.] Hazel; [ed.] Educated in Canada at East Angus and Iberville; [occ.] Retired; [memb.] Member National School, Los Angeles, CA; [hon.] Few honors and awards relating to my work in engineering and mechanics; [oth. writ.] My Life 1, 2, 3 and 4, Biography and Autobiography.; [pers.] Would like to leave something that can be imitated and remembered as a good person.; [a.] Winslow, ME

DYE, RUSSELL R.
[b.] March 21, 1933, Indianapolis, IN; [p.] Rector and Dorothy Dye (Deceased); [m.] Betty J. Dye, May 5, 1990; [ed.] One and half years Indiana University, took up Acting I and Acting II; [occ.] Screen writing-Pending "No Greater Love", Working on second screenplay; [memb.] Rock Club-Springfield, Oregon-Moose-American Legion, Writer's Digest Book Club; [oth. writ.] More unpublished poems; [pers.] There are some people out there that shouldn't get involved by getting accustomed in using other people so much in a wrong sense to benefit themselves financially, and etc., by taking advantage of people's weakspot to the point that the other person may become so blind to see what is actually happening, like for example, "Coming in between a married couple from a prior friendship, relationship, and etc." One way for a villain or a hero to get a woman on your side is to tell her your troubles what another woman did to you"!; [a.] Eugene, OR

EASTLICK, RUTH A.
[b.] December 12, 1915, Grant County, WI; [p.] Arthur and Hazel Geyer; [m.] (Deceased) Cecil Eastlick, September 30, 1939; [ch.] 2 boys - 1 girl; [ed.] Cuba City High School, B.S. Degree from U.W. Platteville, Wis. Teacher College - Platteville; [occ.] Retired Teacher; [memb.] V.F.W. Auxiliary - Retired Teachers, Girl Scouts of Am. (Leader), Alumni - U.W. Platteville, Wis., U. Methodist Church - Women's Society; [hon.] I've won many small contests or jingle contest. Just for fun - won 2 bicycles, 2 radios, 25 gift certificate, etc.; [oth. writ.] Wrote a biography of a prominent person for Historical Society at Potosi, Wis. It won 2nd and was put in Historical Society files.; [pers.] I wrote my first poem when I was 9 years old going to a one-room Rural School. I just write for fun. Usually when the spirit moves me.; [a.] Cuba City, WI

EASTO, NANCY
[b.] July 11, 1941, Racine, WI; [p.] Val and Eleanor Chuilicek; [m.] Herbert Joseph Easto, September 2, 1993 just 3 years; [ch.] Forest R. Mapes IV; [ed.] St. Catherine's High, Triton College; [occ.] Retired Nurse due to MS disability; [memb.] Charter Member St. Edward's Perpetual Help Rosary Makers; [oth. writ.] Non-published novice.; [pers.] In all things, thank God. He turns evil into good for those that love Him.; [a.] Hebron, IN

EATON, BETTY MAE
[pen.] Betty Mae Eaton; [b.] July 8, 1935, Indianapolis, IN; [p.] John W. and Dorothy Fishback; [m.] Charles H. Eaton, November 19, 1977; [ch.] Cynthia Ann Smith, Mark Allen Smith and Penny Jo Shumaker; [ed.] 1-8 School #2 City and Freshman, Junior Tech High School City; [occ.] Cashier and Clerk at 43 Roselyn Bakery 10th and Post Rd. City; [memb.] OES 465 Beechgrove Ind. International Society of Poets. Prayer Power Club. Was Chaplin in OES. "I've been interviewed on the Radio Station in NY City"; [hon.] Poems published in Treasured Poems of America Sparrowgrass Poetry Forum Inc. Poems in a capsule to be opened 10-1-2091 Pegasus Time Capsule World of Poetry Who's Who in Poetry Golden Poet Awards, Editor's Choice Awards. Honorable Mentions Awards; [oth. writ.] The Time is Now, Family Tree, Moma's Hands, Colors, Chase Away the Blues, I am a Poet, My Son, A Woman's Place is in the Home, and several others in the Library of Congress; [pers.] I write from real life, to make a point and to make others feel like they count, and are important to me. Life it's self is a poem, you only have to look at it through my eyes. I want someone to know I've been here, when I'm gone, to know I tried.; [a.] Indianapolis, IN

EBANKS, AMANDA LEE
[b.] September 23, 1981, Grand Cayman; [p.] Susan Parker Ebanks; [ed.] Wheeler High School; [occ.] Student at Wheeler High School in Marietta, Georgia; [memb.] National Honor Society, Student Leadership, Key Club, Yearbook Staff and on school newspaper.; [hon.] Celebration of champions, Citizenship Award, Civic Orientation, National Junior Beta Club, State Society Colonial Dames XVII Century, Kaleidoscope 96 of Nations.; [oth. writ.] "The Monster Chaser", "To My Maggie", "Princess World", "Friendship", "Natures Way", "My Brother", "When I'm all alone", "Live Easy, Die Hard", "Oh What Happened?", and "Horrible May Day."; [pers.] I try to see what others are blind to. I look for the truth in everything that I write about. I started writing in 5th grade. My mother, my best friend, James Stinchcomb and my grandmother, Joann Moore, inspire me.; [a.] Marietta, GA

EDWARDS, ANGELA MARIE
[b.] October 10, 1979, Indianapolis, IN; [p.] Waymon and Beverly Edwards; [ed.] St. Matthew Catholic Grade School, Cathedral High School; [occ.] Student - Junior, Cathedral High School; [memb.] "Pride of the Irish" Symphonic Band, Plays flute and piccolo; [oth. writ.] Several poems published in Poetic Licence, Cathedral High School Literary magazine; [pers.] As I am drifting off to sleep, beautiful words and phrases come to me, but grasping these things isn't easy.; [a.] Indianapolis, IN

EFFINGER, CAROLINE VON BONNIE MATZKE
[pen.] Caroline Von Bonnie Effinger; [b.] August 27, 1935, Dayton, OH; [p.] Karl F. Matzke, Jeanette Tarr Matzke Rebert; [m.] John Bernard Effinger, August 28, 1954; [ch.] Bonnie, John, Peggy, Glen, Brian, Suzanne and Genevieve; [ed.] 8 yrs. private piano study West High School, Rochester NY, Rochester Business Institute; [occ.] Vocalist, Choral Director, retired piano teacher, retired landscape gardner; [memb.] Twenty-seven years member of the Greece Choral Society -

Greece NY, 13 yrs. member of director of the Treble Clefs, Our Lady of Victory - St. Joseph's Church Prshnr., Irondequoit Senior Co-ed Softball Lge.; [hon.] Winner of several solo auditions, several art awards (but too long ago), Town Harvest Queen - (also too long ago); [oth. writ.] A series of 5 children's books Auto-biography, Two novels (underway) many poems, essays and letters all unpublished. (Never tried); [pers.] It's a world full of a lot of great stuff, and I'm going to try as much if it as I can, and be as good at it as I can.; [a.] Rochester, NY

EGAN, DOTTIE
[pen.] Dottie Egan; [b.] November 16, 1925, Middlesex, NJ; [p.] Patrick and Helen Egan; [m.] Divorced; [ch.] Kathleen Gargiulo and Maureen Roschel, Grandson Sean Aziz; [ed.] Graduated Bound Brook NJ, High School night classes in several schools 1943; [occ.] Semi retired Banker; [memb.] Bound Brook High Honor Society, distinguished Member ISP; [hon.] Sales Awards in Banking Editor's Choice Award for Poem Courage; [oth. writ.] "Courage" Shadows And Light "God Bless My Daddy" Where Dawn Lingers "My Daughters" Best Poems of '90s "Christmas Eve" Whispers At Dusk; [pers.] The power of prayer, and my two daughters and grandson have influenced my life. Prayers give me courage to face each day!!; [a.] Lighthouse Point, FL

ELLIOTT, CHERYL
[b.] July 21, 1943, Seminole, OK; [p.] L. R. and Eva Norvelle; [m.] John A. Elliott, July 28, 1962; [ch.] Timothy D., John L. and Craig A.; [ed.] Stonewall High, A few classes at Moore-Norman Votech and Oklahoma, Oklahoma City Community College; [occ.] Church Secretary; [memb.] First Free Will Baptist Church, Women Nationally Active for Christ; [hon.] Secretary of the Year 1995; [oth. writ.] A few poems published in church newsletter and bulletins.; [pers.] I strive to share the love of my Savior with His children. I have been influenced by the more modern poets mostly the romantics and also by many christian writers.; [a.] Oklahoma City, OK

ELSTON, JOSEPH GORDON
[b.] January 16, 1925, Stanford, KY; [p.] Charles B. Elston (Father), Josephine P. Carpenter (Mother); [m.] Christine Robson, March 2, 1956; [ch.] Joseph G. Elston Jr.; [ed.] 4 year Certificate Interior Design 1948-52, Memphis Academy of Arts, 690 Adams Ave., Memphis, TN; [occ.] Memphis Pink Palace Museum Preparatory 1957-91 Retired; [memb.] Dixon Gallery and Gardens, 4339 Park Ave. Memphis, TN, 38117; [oth. writ.] My Father Taught Me The Alphabet, ABCD Goldfish?, LMNO Goldfish, SMR!; [pers.] It's so much fun to enjoy a hobby!; [a.] Memphis, TN

ELY, NATHAN A.
[pen.] A. Tad Pole; [b.] June 28, 1927, Carlsbad, NM; [p.] Jasper K. Ely, Lucinda Mae; [m.] Jessica Rayola G. Ely, June 26, 1959; [ch.] Ty, David, Terri, Lucinda; [ed.] B.S. Elementary Education B.Y.U. Provo, Utah; [occ.] Self employed Care Car Shuttle Service; [memb.] V.F.W. life member, National Teachers Association; [hon.] Member Order of Arrow, Medal US Army of Occupation 63rd Battalion 7th Army Germany, 5 yr pin Pacific Power Company; [oth. writ.] Local paper, school events, Institute of Children's Literature; [pers.] Poems are prayers sent out on paper wings.; [a.] Crescent City, CA

EMERSON, PAUL
[b.] July 17, 1966, Chicago, IL; [p.] Paul Emerson Sr., and Carolyn Emerson; [m.] Christina Craft-Emerson, January 6, 1990; [ch.] Steven Craft, Richard Craft, Patrick Craft; [ed.] Farragut High, Community College of the Air Force, Pellissippi State Technical Commu-

nity College, will attend the University of Tennessee in 1998.; [occ.] Student/Freelance Writer; [hon.] Air Force Outstanding Unit Award, Air Reserve Forces Meritorious Services Medal, Air Force Longevity Services Award Ribbon; [oth. writ.] Magazine articles. I am currently working on my first novel.; [pers.] I believe that poetry should do more than excite the mind, it should also move the spirit from the depths of despair to the heights of ecstasy.; [a.] Knoxville, TN

ESCHRICH, DENNIS A.
[pen.] Ann Ominous; [b.] April 30, 1957, Johnstown, PA; [p.] Oscar and Eva Eschrich; [m.] Catherine; [ch.] Daughter, Erin Melissa; [occ.] Meteorologist; [oth. writ.] Several poems published.; [pers.] Every time I write, I hope for something fresh and new. Will collaborate with serious musicians.; [a.] White Sands, NM

ESTAREJA, ROMULO H.
[pen.] Romy, Ronnie H. Estareja; [b.] October 10, 1939, Casiguran, Sorsogon, Philippines; [p.] Domingo Estareja, Presentacion Estareja; [m.] Milagros H. Estareja, February 14, 1964; [ch.] Casiguran High School; [ed.] Nurse - Therapist; [oth. writ.] Other poems and essays all unpublished, original; [pers.] To share beauty, goodness, a glimpse of reality in moments of truth and to reflect the resiliency and courage of the human spirit to uplift.

EVANS, BERNADINE AYERS
[b.] July 12, 1923, Grantsville, WV; [p.] Bernard H. and Sue Ferrell Ayers; [m.] Deceased, July 5, 1945; [ch.] Bernard L. Reed; [ed.] Calhoun High School 1944. Institute of Practical Nursing in Chicago, IL 1962.; [occ.] Homemaking; [memb.] 50 year American Legion Auxiliary #82. Grantsville Life Member of Knotts Memorial Church. Grantsville CCHS Alumni; [hon.] American legion Auxiliary Poppy Girl, Ground Observer Corp.; [oth. writ.] I worked at Patterson Airfield in Dayton, Ohio. My hobbies are writing sermon's, Peace letter's of poetry.; [pers.] Other Writings Of Poetry Life, Prepare, A Good Name, When, My Friend, Thinking Of You, Seed Of Love and God Cares etc.; [a.] Grantsville, WV

EVANS, BOB NANCE
[pen.] VietNam Era (Bard of BaGi); [b.] February 15, 1941, Post, TX; [p.] Mr. J. B. Evans and Mina Nance Evans Staniforth; [m.] Beverly R. Evans, December 31, 1993; [ch.] 5 m and 4 grand-children; [ed.] Graduated from Hale Center High School in Hale Center, Texas 1959 Retired military officer, vietnam veteran...published in Camp BaGi newletter in 1967-68; [occ.] Insurance Agent; [hon.] Bronze Star for Meritorious Service, Vietnamese Tech Service Honor Metal..Past President of Alamogordo New Mexico Chamber of Commerce; [oth. writ.] "Tularosa Jack" published in Travel Host Magazine. "Cowboy Tales, poems and Prayers, I have lived or Dreamed. (Or just plain made up)" Copywrite but un-published....; [pers.] "There is no subject that cannot be addressed in poetry, sometimes it's just hard to figure out the zip code..."

EVANS, CINDY R.
[pen.] Cindy R. Evans; [b.] September 6, 1965, Ohio; [p.] Becky Edwards and Paul Vestal; [ed.] Lemon Bay High School, Englewood Florida, Daytona Beach Community College; [occ.] CAD Operator; [pers.] Life's experiences sometimes leaves a person in an emotional spin, and its hard to express how your feeling. Poems have a way of letting all that out.; [a.] Fort Myers, FL

EVANS, KIERA
[b.] June 24, Chicago, IL; [p.] Drs. Mark and Wendy Evans; [ed.] Attending Roeper School for the Gifted (High School) in Birmingham, MI; [occ.] Student; [memb.] Bass player in local band "Insomnia"; [hon.]

3rd place in the state for "Go Ask Alice" forensics multiple. Won on December 16, 1995; [pers.] It has always been my dream to see my poetry published. Thank you so much for giving me this chance to see my dream come true.; [a.] West Bloomfield, MI

EVANS, MICHELLE J.
[b.] June 18, 1974, Leicestershire, Great Britain; [p.] Nigel J. Evans; [ed.] 2nd Year College Student at Queensborough Can.; [occ.] Server; [memb.] Deans List at Q.C.C.; [oth. writ.] "Lost Love" song - won award at country music Hall of Fame in Nashville Tennessee.; [pers.] Writing has taught me one very valuable lesson - not to doubt myself. I sincerely hope it will do the same for others because self-doubt is the surest way of never accomplishing any of the dreams that lie deep inside the heart.; [a.] Hempstead, NY

EVELYN, HEATHER
[a.] Las Vegas, NV

EZZELL, MARVIN SHAWN
[pen.] Shawn Ezzell; [b.] July 5, 1980, Kings Mountain, NC; [p.] Mary Jane Ezzell, Marvin Earl Ezzell; [ed.] Maiden High School, Maiden, North Carolina; [oth. writ.] Several poems and songs in my own personal journal.; [pers.] Who is to say what is right from wrong, when it is a sin itself to judge and condemn. My influences are Jim Morrison, Edgar Allen Poe, John Lennon, Jimi Hendrix, and all of the world's people and their mixed emotions.; [a.] Newton, NC

FABIANO, DEANNA LOUISE
[pen.] DeAnna Louise Fabiano; [b.] January 17, 1985, Kenosha, WI; [p.] Jacqueline and Antonio Fabiano; [ed.] Mount Carmel, Cordelia Harvey Elementary; [occ.] Student, Kenosha, WI, Harvey Elementary; [memb.] "Just say no", choir, Scamps Gymnastics, Christians Youth Council, Kenosha Area Soccer League, Math Team, Mt. Carmel; [hon.] Reflections, Young Author's Program, Presidential Physical Fitness Award, Student Art Exhibit Track and Field Award, "Just Say No" member, choir award, Honor Roll KUSD Science Fair, Soccer, Basketball and Gymnastics Awards; [oth. writ.] Literature award for reflections, finalist for Young Author's Project, two Poetry Books for school, other different poetry for enjoyment.; [pers.] I let my imagination fly to different heights, so I can create out-of-this world literature. When I write, it's almost like I'm in a whole different world describing what's around me. I'm highly encouraged by my talented mother, whom I luckily take after.; [a.] Kenosha, WI

FABRIS, JEAN-PAUL
[b.] September 24, 1974, Sommerville, NJ; [p.] Dr. Alfonso Fabris, Polly Fabris; [ed.] St. Leos Elementary - Fairfax, VA, Paul VI HS Fairfax, Virginia, Loyola College, Baltimore Md, US Army ROTC, Airborne. Major: History. Minor: Asian Studies; [occ.] Senior at Loyola College Baltimore Md. Cadet US Army; [memb.] Vice President, International Honor Society. History. Phi-Alpha-Theta, Loyola College, Supreme Court Justice. Association of the US Army; [hon.] American Veterans of WWII - award for diligence, Loyola College - Military Science awards; [a.] Oakton, VA

FACTOR, BETTYROSE
[pen.] Bettyrose Factor; [b.] March 31, NYC, NY; [p.] Deceased; [m.] Deceased, December 21, 1947; [ch.] Three daughters; [ed.] B.S./Educ., Central Conn. State Univ. - New Britain, CT. M.A. St. Joseph College - Hartford, CT; [occ.] Ass't. Prof. of English Lynn University - Boca Raton, FL; [memb.] For Approximately Five Years on Standards Comm. at Lynn. Three years on Appeals Comm. at Lynn; [hon.] Certificate of Merit for Freshman Mentoring Honorable Mention from "New Voices in Poetry" for my poems "Widow's Weeds" and

"Widow"; [oth. writ.] Four other poems, "Widow", "Illness", "Guess What", "Gone"; [pers.] "Widow's Weeds" was composed at 3:30 A.M. when, not being able to sleep, the realization came to me that we (spouseless) women are totally "Alone" and "Abandoned" by society. A "Fifth Wheel" in the scheme of things; [a.] Delray Beach, FL

FALK, HOWARD
[pen.] H. S. Falk; [b.] April 24, 1964, Pomona, CA; [p.] Martin and Marcia Falk; [ed.] Lane Community College: Intro. To Creative Writing, Comedy Literature, and Intro. To Drawing; [hon.] National Library of Poetry's Editor's Choice Award of 1995; [oth. writ.] 'Rainbow Universe' and 'Music Notation Garden'.; [pers.] Now if I can just persuade someone to be as interested in publishing my original music composition manuscripts and humor monologues, routines, scenes, and sketches as the National Library of Poetry has been persuaded to publish a bit of my poetry.; [a.] Eugene, OR

FANCETT, TODD STEPHEN
[b.] July 8, 1965, Lansing; [p.] Gary and Becky; [m.] Pamela, August 28, 1987; [ch.] Shelly and James; [ed.] High School diploma, 3 years Military Service, lumber inspection school, Memphis, Tennessee; [occ.] Lumber Inspector; [memb.] American Legion, Cycle Conservation Club; [hon.] Good conduct medal, Overseas service ribbon, Army service ribbon, expert badge M-16 rifle, expert badge hand grenade, Army lapel button, Parachutist badge, Air assault badge, Aircraft crewman badge, Army achievement medal, National Hardwood Lumber Association Diploma; [oth. writ.] Several personal poems to friends and family.; [pers.] I write special poems from within to get a smile or even a grin. The feelings that I have inside I flow with a pen and just let it glide.; [a.] Fenwick, MI

FANNIN, WANDA
[b.] June 24, 1928, Walsh, KY; [p.] John and Lula Belle Phillips; [m.] Irving Fannin, March 18, 1944; [ch.] 5 children, 10 grandchildren, 8 great-grandchildren; [ed.] Attended McKell High School in Greenys County, KY; [memb.] Ladies Auxiliary of American Legion, Alben Barkley Club, New Bethleham Methodists Church; [oth. writ.] Many of my other writings are being passed on thru my children, grandchildren and great-grandchildren.; [pers.] My abilities to write poetry and spin a tale have been passed to me by my Indian-Sotch/Irish parents; [a.] South Shore, KY

FARLEY, SHIRLEY
[pen.] Shirley Bragg Farley; [b.] February 2, 1938, Columbus, OH; [p.] Harold and Esther Bragg; [m.] Allen L. Farley, April 19, 1953; [ch.] David, Brent, Bruce, Vanessa, Valencia and Kimberly; [ed.] Associates degree in Humanities Mount Vernon Nazarene College, Mount Vernon, Ohio; [occ.] Former Business Owner, Clerk now pursuing writing; [memb.] Nazarene first Church in Coshocton, OH Former Coshocton Rotarian; [hon.] My greatest Honor: Grandchildren, children and husband, Sales Awards in Business; [oth. writ.] Memories, unpublished, a short story for youth, a novel, a variety of poems and a cookbook.; [pers.] Families which are struggling to make ends meet, are very much the basis of my writings. Yet hard work does not prevent happiness from happening. I try to elaborate on the good times with a sense of Nostalgia. Encouraging the young is my objective.; [a.] Coshocton, OH

FARRELL, RONALD
[ed.] College Art Inst. of Pittsburgh Mjr - Photography; [occ.] Manager - Photography Studio; [memb.] Church of Scientology, Citizens Commissions on Human Rights; [oth. writ.] Untitled, there are many things...; [pers.] I write from my feelings and usually without the use of

rhymes.; [a.] Vero Beach, FL

FARUQUI, SABEEN
[b.] April 2, 1982, Baton Rouge, LA; [p.] Dr. Shaista and Shaban Faruqui; [ed.] Episcopal High School, (Currently attending as a freshman); [memb.] Key Club, French Club, Mu Alpha Theta, Science Club, and Headmasters Senate; [hon.] Head of Schools List, Headmasters Senate, Knight Award in Volleyball, French Merit Award, Math Merit Award, and National Recognition for Science and Merit; [pers.] My goal in life is to be an ear, nose, and throat specialist - hopefully I'll get there.; [a.] Baton Rouge, LA

FAYE, DARCI CAITLIN
[b.] February 10, 1989, Presque Isle, ME; [p.] David and Barbara Faye; [ed.] Cathy Everett's Nursery School, Hilltop Pre-school, Kindergarten and 1st Grade; [occ.] 2nd Grade Student; [memb.] Northern Lights Dance Company, Denise Green's Gymnastics School; [hon.] Pre-teen Maine Jr 1996, Jr. Miss Maine Star 1996, America's Pride 1996, Maine's Miss Hospitality National Pre-teen Petite 1995, Overall Sportswear Winner National Pre-teen Petite 1995, Community Service Winner Pre-Teen Maine Scholarship and Recognition Program 1996; [oth. writ.] Poem published in "Poetic Voices of America" fall 1995. "Dare to Discover" PTA Reflections Book 1995. I wrote this poem when I was 4 years old about my friend moving away from my nursery school.; [pers.] To be happy and successful, you don't need to have the fame. So when they announce the winner, it should be a real thrill. For if you don't win the title remember... one of your best friend will.; [a.] Caribou, ME

FEDERWITZ, GLORIA
[pen.] Gloria; [b.] January 26, 1950, Marshfield, WI; [p.] Willy and Jeri (Deceased) Federwitz; [ed.] Currently adding and completing on a associate polarity practice therapist; [occ.] Artist, Author, Workshop director; [memb.] Wis Women's Entrepreneurs Institute of Noetic Sciences Association of Humanistic Psychology Marshfield Area Chamber of Commerce and Industry; [hon.] 1996 inspirational volunteer of the year for GEM productions; [oth. writ.] A journey of sacred spirals published 1995. A sacred window to my soul published 1996; [pers.] As a tender of healing wholeness I work with creative communication and artistic abundance seeking to discover and reveal the inspirational presence within all of us; [a.] Marshfield, WI

FEGANS, KRISTON
[pen.] Special K; [b.] April 13, 1982, Little Rock, AR; [p.] Micheal and Marie Fegans; [ed.] I am in the 8th grade; [hon.] I received my highest honor when I accepted Yahweh as my Heavenly Father and Yahshua as my personal savior; [oth. writ.] I am 14 years of age and I have two younger sisters ages 12 and 13. It is very hard being the oldest; [pers.] I consider the meaning of a family "when there are two parents in the home, a mom and a dad to give all the love they can possibly give.; [a.] Tucker, AR

FELDMAN, HARRIET N.
[b.] May 2, 1947, New York; [p.] Belle and Solomon Steinman; [m.] Barry Feldman, March 28, 1970; [ed.] B.A. Brooklyn College, M.S. Long Island University; [occ.] Retired English Teacher; [pers.] What greater pleasure can someone gain than to write for him/herself? It is a release for all the sorrow and woes we bare in our lives as well as the expression of sheer joy and happiness which can be viewed and reviewed over and over again!; [a.] Southampton, NY

FELS, VIOLA M.
[pen.] Mazie; [b.] July 5, 1942, Georgia; [p.] Frances Duffey; [m.] Raymond J. Fels, February 7, 1959; [ch.] Lorena M, Dorothy M, Verna M, Karen M; [ed.] High School Equov; [occ.] Housewife; [memb.] Immaculate Concpt. Church Published in "Where Dawn Lingers the National Library of Poetry; [hon.] The homes of being Ray's wife; [oth. writ.] "The Train Whistle", "Christmas", "Why", "Thank You", "Words" "Myself", "Easter Lilly"; [pers.] A word of thanks to "The National Library of Poetry" for publishing my poems. It is a great persons honor and a most satisfactory experience.; [a.] O'Fallon, MO

FERDINAND, ANGELINE
[b.] May 26, 1982, Worcester, MA; [p.] Denise Ferdinand, Benson Ferdinand; [ed.] Current student of Holy Name High School; [pers.] The poet is the priest of the invisible.; [a.] Leicester, MA

FERRIGINA, DOLORES
[pen.] Dolores Ferrigina; [b.] New York; [occ.] Working woman; [pers.] Thrilled that you selected this poem.

FICHTNER, PAULA SUTTER
[b.] August 13, 1935, NJ; [p.] Milton, Marie Sutter; [m.] Edward G. Fichtner, March 26, 1958; [ed.] B.A. Bryn Mawr, M.A. Indiana Univ., Ph.D. Univ of Pennsylvania; [occ.] Professor of History, Brooklyn College; [memb.] American Historical Assn.; [hon.] American Academy of Religion Award for Excellence; [a.] Brooklyn, NY

FIELDS, LAVERNE H.
[b.] November 21, 1969, Elmhurst, IL; [p.] Maynard and Barbara Reed; [m.] Arthur E. (Gene) Fields, January 12, 1991; [ch.] Barbara Louise (Louie) Fields; [ed.] Spanishburg High - 1987, 1 yr. of Information Processing at Mercer Co. Vocational Technical Center - 1987; [occ.] Homemaker, Mother; [memb.] National Honor Society - 1987; [hon.] Young Author's Day - 1987, Young Writer's Week - 1987, USA English Award - 1985, 86, 87; [oth. writ.] Several poems published in local poem compilations.; [pers.] "Your dreams and desires determine your destination."; [a.] Princeton, WV

FIELDS, PAUL ANTHONY
[pen.] Paul Anthony Fields; [b.] October 1, 1958, Pensacola, FL; [p.] Charlie W. Fields Sr., Jessie M. Fields; [ed.] 12th grade with the Escambia Country Florida, Homebound Tutoring Program; [occ.] Freelance Writer; [hon.] Won I've six poetry Awards from The World of Poetry, including the Golden Poet Award for 1989, 1990, and 1991. I also won an award in 1988 for the poem The Wisdom Of Life, from The World of Poetry; [oth. writ.] In 1991 I had my first poem published by the N.L.O.P in a book entitled Windows On The World. I've been published 8 times in newspapers and Books. I have a novel and a book of poetry I want to have published.; [pers.] I want to be the kind of writer that will make you smile, laugh, and cry, but most of all I want to make you stop and think.; [a.] Pensacola, FL

FISCHEL, LEE J.
[pen.] Odes, L-roy; [b.] September 12, 1976, Denver, CO; [oth. writ.] "What A Dream", "Rain Kissed Rose"; [pers.] There are many things in this world alone that do no even begin to compare to the beauty of the ones we love.; [a.] Westminster, CO

FISHER, ERINN F.
[b.] December 3, 1970, Richmond, CA; [p.] Mary Ellen Manney and John West; [m.] Jason Fisher, April 1, 1995; [ch.] Trevor Charles; [ed.] Central Valley High, College of Siskiyous; [occ.] Mommy and wife; [oth.

writ.] I have many other poems I have written and also a couple of short stories. But to date this is my only piece of work published; [pers.] It has been a life's dream come true, to have a piece of my work published.; [a.] Klamath River, CA

FISHER, PAUL ARTHUR
[b.] April 12, 1974, Ogdensburg, NY; [p.] Linda Lou Fisher; [ed.] Heuvelton High School, and Canton College of Technology; [occ.] Reading and working; [memb.] A member of the Science Fiction Book Club; [oth. writ.] This would be my first writing piece; [pers.] I try to free the mind of its physical attributes and let the imagination run wild. My influence would be Terry good kind in how he makes the characters a part of you.; [a.] Garner, NC

FISK, BENJAMIN
[b.] February 21, 1978, Cincinnati, OH; [p.] Patricia and Michael Fisk; [ed.] Campbell County High; [occ.] Full time Student at University of Louisville; [pers.] My clear view of the world and its ways makes up for my lack of experience. My belief in God and his power greatly influences my writing.; [a.] Louisville, KY

FITE, MARILOU
[b.] July 5, 1959, Peoria, IL; [p.] Vernadean and Alfred Mendenhall; [m.] Baxter B. Fite III, May 24, 1980; [ch.] Amanda Fite, Nathaniel Fite; [ed.] Illinois Central College, Methodist Medical Center of Illinois School of Nursing; [occ.] Registered Nurse; [memb.] First Free Methodist Church of Peoria; [oth. writ.] Poems for the church, friends and family.; [pers.] I believe that my ability to write poetry is a God given gift. I strive to serve God by using my poetry to encourage and uplift others.; [a.] Penria, IL

FITZ, GENE
[b.] June 10, 1954, Philadelphia, PA; [p.] F. E. and F. A. Fitz; [ed.] Working on a Masters Degree from the School of Hard Knocks; [occ.] Iron Worker; [pers.] Dedicated to Jan Hebert, who never knew how much she meant. My fear of love kept me silent.; [a.] Vancouver, WA

FLOWERS, MEGAN
[pen.] Megan Flowers; [b.] September 16; [p.] Sherrie Flowers; [ed.] Student; [occ.] Soccer Club and Rainbow; [a.] Eagle, ID

FODOR, KAY
[b.] Pulaski, VA; [m.] Charles Fodor; [ch.] Gregory Fodor and Kevin Fodor, Grandchildren - Kylie Fodor and Blake Fodor; [ed.] Graduated from Perth Amboy High; [occ.] Retail: Lord and Taylor Freehold, NJ; [hon.] 2 poems published in local newspaper "The News Tribune"; [oth. writ.] "The Beach", "Was It Yesterday"; [pers.] As a writer "I take the prin from my heart put it on paper - and dry my tears."; [a.] Freehold, NJ

FOGARTY, COLLEEN C.
[b.] May 2, 1946, Wisner, NE; [p.] Patrick Jr. and Bly McGill; [m.] James D. Fogarty, December 28, 1968; [ch.] Tess, Erin, Adam, Ben; [ed.] Wisner High School, St. Joseph's School of Nrsg. attending Graceland Outreach Curriculum; [occ.] Staff Nurse in a post Anesthesia care unit; [memb.] Omaha Press Club Cast member. Nursing Organizations; [oth. writ.] "Murder in the Nunny", A dinner play with lines assigned to each quest attending the dinner party. "Smiles of Starch and Stone", in a Muse To Follow; [pers.] When life seems complicated and complex simplify and isolate with paper and pen; [a.] Omaha, NE

FONTENOT, MAUDRIE
[pen.] Maudrie; [b.] January 22, 1947, Lake Charles, LA; [p.] Rollis Fontenot, Mellar Fontenot; [m.] Divorced, May 29, 1965; [ch.] Melody, Sheryl, Chanson and Miel; [ed.] Green Oaks High School, Shreveport-Bossier Vocational Tech. School, Aurora Community College, Pitkins Technical School; [occ.] Accounting Clerk; [memb.] The Nature Conservancy Smithsonian Institution; [oth. writ.] Written poems for years, entered contests recently, my short fiction stories were considered a couple times but were never published; [pers.] In each person's life, their thoughts and feelings, how they respond to life's cares, whether happy or sad, transform into forever changing poems and stories, uniquely different as each individual.; [a.] Aurora, CO

FONVILLE, ALTHEA VICTORIA
[pen.] Alicia Stanford; [b.] April 29, 1952, Pittsburgh, PA; [p.] Levi and Pansy Fonville; [m.] Robert G. Flipping Jr.; [ed.] Gladston High Dickinson College; [occ.] Freelance writer, Homemaker Offer Personal Tutorial Services; [memb.] Cornerstone Television of PA CBN member, other religious affiliations, Humane Society; [pers.] I strive to live under God's influence and to help others do so at all times!; [a.] Pittsburgh, PA

FORD, DIANNE
[pen.] Alora Lee Ennaid; [b.] August 18, 1962, Winston County, MS; [p.] Anthony and Sandra Clark; [ch.] William C. Ford; [memb.] Crystal Ridge Baptist Church; [oth. writ.] A collection of personal poetry.; [pers.] If you believe in God and believe in yourself, everything else will fall into place.; [a.] Louisville, MS

FORD, GENEVIEVE L.
[b.] March 9, Cheyenne, WY; [m.] Robert D. Ford; [ed.] (ERTI Communications, Univ. of George Washington, Washington, D.C. - Economics, Foreign Service Institute, Washington, D.C. - French, Portland State University, Research for International Clearinghouse, Portland State University, Yale Mandarin Language Studies, PPAI CAS degrees in industry, Who's Who in Executives and Professionals: 1995-1996 edition; [occ.] Certified Advertising Specialist; [memb.] Member, PPAI (Industry Int'l), Tigard and Beaverton, Oregon Chambers of Commerce, Beta Sigma Phi Int'l, Portland Sales and Marketing Executives; [hon.] Note above: Who's Who in Executives and Professionals: 1995-1996 edition. Portland Council Woman of the Year, Beta Sigma Phi: 1994-1995; [oth. writ.] "The Legend of The Pink Coyote" Copywriter March 17, 1995.; [a.] Portland, OR

FORDHAM, R. DAVID
[pen.] R. David Fordham; [b.] August 9, 1943, Baltimore, MD; [p.] C. Robert and Frances Fallon Fordham; [m.] Doris Schriefer Fordham, July 5, 1975; [ch.] R. Benjamin and M. Anne Fordham; [ed.] Glen Burnie Sr. High, University of Maryland, Strayer Business College, University of Baltimore College of Liberal Arts and School of Law; [occ.] Maryland Attorney; [memb.] National District Attorneys Assn. Maryland State Attorneys Assn., Anne Arundel County Bar Assn., International Society of Poets; [oth. writ.] Poetry Anthologies: Beneath the Harvest Moon - "Christmas Memories", Best Poems of the '90's "Nature's Spirit", Memories of Tomorrow "The Old House", Admist the Splendor "The Game".; [pers.] Write a poem it's great for the mind! Along with Sir Thomas More, Abraham Lincoln should be included as a patron saint of the legal profession.; [a.] Arnold, MD

FORREST, PENNY
[pen.] Penelope Weatherly; [b.] January 4, 1944, Huntsville, AL; [p.] Josephine D. Williams and James E. Weatherly; [m.] Steven K. Forrest, June 20, 1964; [ch.] Wendy F. Bryan, Kelan A. Forrest; [ed.] University of

Ala. School of Nursing - 2 years - S.R. Batlor High School; [occ.] Babysit Grandchildren, (2 boys) and Writing (retired Allergy Nurse); [memb.] Chilton Civic Chorale, Thorsby Baptist Church; [hon.] National Honor Society; [oth. writ.] None published at this time.; [pers.] I am inspired by nature, love, human relationships, music, art and children. Being able to express myself through poetry is my happiest achievement.; [a.] Thorsby, AL

FORTUNATE, AGNES
[b.] March 3, 1916, Ohio; [p.] John and Georgia Hemler (Deceased); [m.] Herman Fortunate (Deceased), June 18, 1938; [ch.] 2 Boys - 5 girls; [ed.] Went back to school in 1976 (College) and graduated in 1986; [occ.] Retired, Homemaker

FOSTER, M. SEAN
[b.] November 9, 1983, Lynchburg, VA; [p.] Maynard and Rayetta Foster; [ed.] 8th Grade Student at Altavista Middle School; [occ.] Student; [a.] Altavista, VA

FOUCAULT, MARY
Foucault, Mary Francis Faith
[b.] March 23, 1951, Everett, WA; [p.] Both passed away; [ch.] one daughter - Chas; [ed.] High School; [memb.] Registered lifetime member of Songwriters Club of America; [hon.] A Award from NCA Records and Jeff Roberts Publishing Company, Hollywod Song Jubilee and National Library of Poetry; [oth. writ.] Published in my legacy Pet Gazette, The Advocate, Night Roses, The Acorn for Children, Poetry of the Poeple, Poetry Break, Peckerwood, The Carring Connection, plus others; [pers.] Writing poems or songs opens up a whole new world, I like to share this new world with others, so they to can enjoy.; [a.] Seattle, WA

FRALEY, MEGAN
[pen.] Allison Stevens; [b.] November 28, 1980, Vancover, WA; [p.] Daniel Fraley and Barbara Ryan; [ed.] Fruit Valley Elementary Jason Lee Middle School, and currently attending Fort Vancover High School; [occ.] Daycare Provider; [memb.] S.T.A.N.D. Student taking, a new, direction and Prama Club; [hon.] Honor Roll several times most expressive actress; [oth. writ.] Two published poems and many others that are unpublished and quite a few stories.; [pers.] I think life is just one big adventure and you should never take anything for granted and most of all don't let fear control your life just have fun as Megan's mother I wish to include her work as a tutor with 3rd grade students in a behavioral school. Megan also does child care for her 4 yr. old autistic niece.; [a.] Vancover, WA

FRANKLIN, MABEL EDITH
[pen.] May; [b.] February 14, Lebanon, VA; [m.] Elmer Ewing Franklin (Deceased), December 19; [ed.] Lebanon High, Lebanon, VA; [occ.] Retired; [memb.] Right to life TN, Member Republican National Committee TN, Republican Party, Sullivan County Humane Society, Bristol Humane Society, National Rife Association, I am a Distinguished Member of The International Society of Poeters; [hon.] Editor's Choice Award, from The National Library of Poetry, Presidential Achievement Award from President Ronald Reagan, Seven Awards for Outstanding Service in Recognition of Achievement; [oth. writ.] Poems published in Kingsport Times - New's, Reporter for Newsletter at my Employment, and have sixty poems written, want to get published soon, I want some of my pictures in my poem book.; [pers.] I established the Elmer Ewing Franklin Memorial Scholarship Fund at King College in Bristol TN. I am striving to get the Elmer Ewing Franklin Center or museum at King College in Bristol TN. Or Walter State UN. in Morristown, TN.; [a.] Kingsport, TN

FRAZIER, LYNETTE
[b.] August 19, 1983, Madrid, Spain; [p.] David and Janet Frazier; [ed.] 6 yrs Wares Ferry Elementary 2 yrs Literary Arts Baldwin Jr. High; [occ.] 8th Grade Student; [memb.] Member of Youth Group, Drama Teams and Puppet Team of Frazer United Methodist Church; [hon.] City Scholar of the week, Runner-up Patrol Girl of the Year, Honor Student; [oth. writ.] Other poems published in Tapestry, school's literary arts magazine; [pers.] If everyone smiled, life might seem easier.; [a.] Montgomery, AL

FREEMAN, CYNTHIA HUNTER
[b.] December 4, 1953, Asheboro, NC; [p.] Mary Evelyn Latham, Tommy Lee Hunter Sr.; [m.] Divorced; [ch.] Aaron Nicholas Freeman and Rosanna Faith Freeman; [ed.] Quit Half-way Threw 9th grade was going for my G.E.D. at MCC in 1992 but didn't finish.; [occ.] Hosiery; [oth. writ.] Young One, Truck Driving Mystery. Both of these poems where printed in a magazine, made by student's at MCC called: U Wharrie Trials, Four New Angels In Heaven, was printed in the Montgomery Hearld; [pers.] I have been writing poems since I was eight years old, I have a whole book of poems that I have wrote. My dream is to get my own book published.; [a.] Troy, NC

FREEMAN, PERRY ALAN
[pen.] Peregrine Allen; [b.] October 19, 1956, Fort Chaffee, AR; [p.] Cecil and Mary Freeman; [m.] Kimberly Kay Freeman, February 3, 1984; [pers.] To attempt to explore, and to reveal the excellence or ill of Man's Nature.; [a.] Big Cabin, OK

FRENCH, ANITA J.
[b.] November 23, 1942, York, ME; [p.] Barbara Greene and Richard Wiggin; [m.] Terry M. French, July 5, 1963; [ch.] Eric McArthur, Brian Scott and Teri Lee; [ed.] York High School; [occ.] House wife; [memb.] National Arbor Day Foundation; [oth. writ.] Have written many poem's - one published - "Let It Be Angels" - ("Walk Through Paradise" - The National Library of Poetry). Presently working on a children's book.; [pers.] The idea for this most recent poem, "Let It Be Known", came from the realization of knowing that someone, somewhere in the world, each and every hour of the day or night is being abused by a sometimes uncontrollable emotion - "Anger".; [a.] Canastota, NY

FREY, SUNDAY
[pen.] Siss; [b.] March 30, 1986, Greenfield, IN; [p.] Jeff and Mary Frey; [ed.] 5th Grade; [occ.] Student; [memb.] Fitness and Fun too (Gymnastics); [hon.] 2nd place, Art Contest at School and Trophy for Gymnastics; [pers.] I say, trust in God he'll help you through life, because life is hard and he cares.; [a.] New Palestine, IN

FRIES, MARISA
[b.] June 16, 1982, New York, NY; [p.] Robin and Richard Fries; [ed.] Ridge Street School, Blind Brook Middle/High School; [occ.] Student; [memb.] Blind Brook Tennis Team, Rye Community Synagogue; [hon.] Daniel Speare Robinson Award, Accelerated Math Award; [pers.] I would like thank my English teacher, Mr. Del Shortliffe, for helping me to improve my writing. I would also like to thank my mom, Robin, my dad, Richard, and my brother, David, for always inspiring me and supporting me in everything I do. My favorite sport is tennis and I also love writing poetry.; [a.] Rye Brook, NY

FRITZ, ROBERT KARL
[pen.] Rob Fritz; [b.] May 4, 1975, Parma, OH; [ed.] Student, Tiffon University, Junior Year; [pers.] Be original.; [a.] Brecksville, OH

FROST, SHARON T.
[b.] October 3, 1938, Norfolk, NE; [p.] Ambrose and Delora Karella; [m.] Donald W. Frost, June 9, 1956; [ch.] Steven, Michael, Theresa, Tamara, Patricia, 13 grandchildren 1 great grand children; [ed.] High School, 2 yrs. Cosmetology; [occ.] Retired; [memb.] Beta Sigma Phi Sorority VFW Auxiliary; [hon.] In 1991 I won the chicken cooking contest for Alaska - went on to Nationals in Little Rock Arkansas and finaled in the Top 10 of the nation.; [pers.] Often times we feel warm thoughts about others, but we don't take time to tell them. I wrote this poem to honor my mother, Delora Karella, for her 85th birthday through writing my feelings in this poem it helped me to show my mother just how much I love her.; [a.] Houston, AK

FULLER, BARBARA
[b.] April 30, 1959, Frostburg, MD; [p.] Rosemary and Ervin Harris; [m.] W. A. Fuller, October 8, 1988; [ch.] One daughter; [ed.] BA, JD degrees; [occ.] Attorney; [memb.] Washington State Bar Assoc.; [pers.] "Can you play for me the song of childhood?" "I'm sure I once knew it by heart."; [a.] Kirkland, WA

FULLER, NORMAN E.
[b.] June 18, 1932, Bridgeport, CT; [m.] Doris, June 30, 1956; [ch.] Betsy, Barbara, Bruce, Bill, Beverlee; [ed.] DMD - Tufts Dental School 1956, High School - Bridgton Academy, Maine; [occ.] Dentist; [memb.] American Dental Assoc., Benevolent Protective Order of Elks Freemasonry; [oth. writ.] Many poems unpublished; [pers.] "O wud some power the giftie gee us to see ourselves as others see us; [a.] New Haven, CT

FULLER-DE LEON, LORI
[b.] June 13, 1963, Tacoma, WA; [p.] Albert and Deanna Fuller; [m.] Ramon De Leon Sr., October 11, 1988; [ch.] Ramon, Alicia and Gabriel; [ed.] Attended Biola University, Salem Academy (high school), Western Oregon State College, Advanced Individual Training for U.S. Army, senior student at WOSC: English major/History minor; [occ.] Student and Homemaker; [memb.] Sigma Tau Delta International English Honor Society, attend 1st Baptist Church; [hon.] 1981 Who's Who Among American High School Students, overseas service ribbon, army service ribbon; [oth. writ.] Unpublished, poetry, a children's book, working on a book entitled - A Journal of Fear and Hope (from true Accounts as recorded in my journals); [pers.] I am very thankful to God for this opportunity to be published. As my great grandfather always said, "You've got to reach for the stars!" Since I was a child, I have always loved the manger scene and Christmas as this poem reflects.; [a.] Salem, OR

FUSCHETTI, DANIELLE
[b.] December 9, 1987, Long Branch, NJ; [p.] Mike and Laurie Fuschetti; [ed.] 2nd Grade; [occ.] Student; [memb.] YMCA Swim Team; [hon.] Quest, straight A+s, Lead Roles in plays; [oth. writ.] Various poems and short stories.; [pers.] Thanks to my family and my teacher, Mrs. Belena, who inspired me to start writing poetry.; [a.] Tinton Falls, NJ

GABARD, MALLORY PAIGE
[b.] September 24, 1983, Nashville, TN; [p.] Cindy and Joseph Gabard; [ed.] Currently enrolled in 7th grade in Forrest School; [memb.] Junior Beta Club, Junior Student Council; [hon.] Highest reading award in 6th grade; [pers.] Although I am only 12 years old I feel that if you can put life into words age is just a number. I think one's real age life inside your heart, only to reveal with words, so everyone knows what lies beneath your soul.; [a.] Chapel Hill, TN

GAFNEY, LOUVENIA MAGEE
[b.] March 22, 1942, NC; [p.] James and Louvenia Walden Magee; [m.] Divorced; [ch.] Wilda and Willie; [ed.] Eliz. City State U. - NC (BS) GWU - Wash., DC (MA and Ed.D); [occ.] Retired Teacher; [memb.] Phi Delta Kappa, Alpha Kappa Alpha, Israel Baptist Church; [hon.] 1993 DC Teacher of the Year, Tapestry Grant, Coca Cola Grant, Geraldine Dodge Foundation Grant, many others; [oth. writ.] "Remembering The Dreams And The Dreams," "Teachers On Teaching," "Insights Into Successful Practice".; [pers.] I like to write on a variety of "People Related" topics. Writing allows me to let my voice be heard in places that I may never go.; [a.] Upper Marlboro, MD

GAGNON, KELLI
[b.] September 16, 1968, Logan, WV; [p.] Cynthia and Thomas Gagnon; [ed.] Charleston Catholic High School; [occ.] Student; [pers.] Despite the pessimistic mood of my poem, I'm actually optimistic. I wrote it down because it just came to me and seemed to be the makings of a good poem; [a.] Logan, WV

GALLO, KAY ANGELA BAFFI
[pen.] Addie; [b.] March 4, 1925, Clarksburg, WV; [p.] Michaele and Victoria Baffi; [m.] Richard Neal Gallo, May 11, 1970; [ch.] Richard Darner, Patrick Darner, Victoria Darner; [ed.] 1944 - High School Graduate, Roosevelt Wilson, Clarksburg, West Virginia, 1 Year Machine Shop School (During the war years); [occ.] Homemaker; [memb.] Jehovah's Witnesses Organization; [oth. writ.] Several poems and short stories. The Outside Brick Oven, Ti's the Season, There was Love in the House on the Hill.; [pers.] Learn how to attain and keep a close relationship with your Creator-Jehovah God.; [a.] Grants Pass, OR

GANNONE JR., JAMES P.
[b.] December 23, 1967, Philadelphia, PA; [p.] James and Louise; [ed.] St. John Neumann H.S. - St. Martins College; [occ.] Accountant - Day and Zimmermann Inc. Phila PA; [hon.] U.S. Air Force Achievement Medal; [oth. writ.] Poems, musical lyrics, children's books and short stories working towards publication.; [pers.] Poetry is the way I like to express my feelings with what is happening in our world today.; [a.] Philadelphia, PA

GARBERINO, DENNIS
[pen.] Dennis Charles; [b.] February 21, 1956, Saddle Brook, NJ; [p.] Charles Garberino and Dolores Meritai Garberino; [ed.] Saddle Brook and Ramapo regional High of Franklin Lakes, NJ; Fairleigh Dickinson University of Teaneck New Jersey and Wroxton, England, B.S. in Business Administration and Marketing; [occ.] Purchasing, Business Administrator. Past owner of Floral Business; [memb.] N.A.P.M. National Assoc. of Purchasing Managers, A.M.A. American Managers Assoc.; Literary Society of Fairleigh Dickinson University; Distinguished Member of International Society of Poets; [hon.] Dean's List and Academic Honors from Fairleigh Dickinson University; civic letter of accomplishment for writings from local government. Alumni Club of Fairleigh Dickinson University; Poet of Merit and Editor's Choice Award — National Library of Poetry and International Society of Poets; [oth. writ.] Paper: Morality in the Work-Place; Paper: Ethical, Moral and Social Responsibilities of Corporations; Published poems: Autumn Shadows, Grandma's House, Cybernetic PC, A Distant Time Ago..., (National Library of Poetry); [pers.] "Writing for me has become an old friend that I will carry with me to old age." Special thanks to my friends Dee and Chuck, I couldn't have done it without you.; [a.] Saddle Brook, NJ

GARDNER, JUDY
[pen.] JMG; [b.] March 1, 1961, Kentucky; [p.] Kenny and Joyce Helm; [m.] Bill Gardner, March 4, 1995; [ch.] Cody and Hollie; [ed.] J-town graduate; [occ.] For self and Caselton; [memb.] Voluntary (Eng) Clean up Earth ect...; [hon.] Only previous jobs, "Waggner High", poetry put in book at school years ago.; [oth. writ.] For self, never tried to publish my writings of diarys, poems short storys, ect!...; [pers.] I think speaking from the heart along with experience is where its at. Also "keeping your eyes and mind open!"; [a.] Louis, KY

GARRETT, CAROLYN BEARD
[b.] March 20, 1922, Catawba County, NC; [p.] Robert F. and Elizabeth Baker Beard; [m.] Franklin T. Garrett, June 15, 1945; [ch.] Robert Thomas and Franklin Trent; [ed.] B.A. - Music Education Longwood College; [occ.] Retired; [oth. writ.] Poems - "Walnut Leaves", "Ballet de November", "Disconsolate", published locally.; [pers.] My poems reflect my love of nature.; [a.] Annandale, VA

GARRISON, SHELLY DIANE
[b.] August 16, 1978, Oklahoma City, OK; [p.] Garry and Regina Garrison; [ed.] Chatfield Senior High School, Freshman at Colorado State University; [occ.] Student, File Clerk for Levine Investments; [hon.] Colorado State University Cheerleader; [pers.] Take risks and strive with determination and courage to obtain your goals. It is always possible to have a brighter tomorrow.; [a.] Littleton, CO

GENTZ, GRANT A.
[b.] May 17, 1934, Marinette, WI; [p.] Arthur and Ida Gentz; [m.] Marlene, August 1, 1959; [ed.] B.S.E. Martin Luther College, New Ulm, MN, M.S.U. of Wisconsin Madison, Educational Administration; [occ.] Director of Development, Medical Center Foundation; [memb.] Wels - Religious AHP - Assoc. of Health Care Philanthropy Rotary International, Elementary School Administrator and Teacher - 30 years. Church Organist; [pers.] "All to the Glory of the Trivue God".; [a.] Reedsburg, WI

GENTZEL, GERRAD
[b.] March 18, 1978, Commerce, GA; [p.] Joesaph and Maryann Gentzel; [ed.] Jefferson High School, 11th grade education; [occ.] Student; [memb.] Jefferson High School Marching Band; [hon.] Award of Excellence in the field of art, Awarded by Jefferson High School, 3rd place in the Kiwanis Art contest on a 10th grade level, most improved drummer for the 1996, Red coat drum camp, Eagle Scout; [oth. writ.] Several songs and poems, none ever published; [pers.] People have lived for so long and wished for so much knowledge that there is no mystery left in life. I miss the days when the moon was a goddess and the son of God.; [a.] Jefferson, GA

GERLACH, HEATHER S.
[pen.] Pandora James Manson; [b.] September 10, 1979, Altoona, PA; [p.] Stan and Denise Gerlach; [ed.] Altoona Area High School; [occ.] Senior in High School; [memb.] Reach, Under Construction Theatre Company; [hon.] Who's Who Among American High School Students; [oth. writ.] Several poems, none published; [pers.] I'd like to say thanks and I love you to Nathan, my inspiration. And to my mother and father for all they've done for me.; [a.] Altoona, PA

GETTIG, TIMOTHY A.
[pen.] TG; [b.] October 27, 1959, Panama City, FL; [p.] Ronald E. Gettig, JoAnne Green; [m.] Janice M. Gettig, March 9, 1979; [ed.] Graduate from Perrysburg High School, 1978, in Perrysburg, Ohio. Graduated from Michael J. Owens Technical College, January, 1984, in Perrysburg, Ohio, with an Associate Degree in Applied Business in Computer Programming, with a Major in Computer Programming; [occ.] I run my own Computer Consulting and Programming Business. I Engineer Networks and Program many Practical Business Applications, I also sell Advertising, as an Internet Consultant to Businesses wanting to Advertise in the Imall on the Internet; [memb.] I've been Awarded, "Distinguished Membership," by the International Society of Poets; [hon.] My poem, Thoughts Of A Seed..., appeared on the nationally syndicated radio show, Poetry Today, with Florence Henderson, on 1/14/96, heard throughout the U.S., Canada, and the Caribbean. I've, also received Editor's Choice Award for, Thoughts Of A Seed..., from the National Library of Poetry's 1995 North American Open Poetry Contest. Nominated, one of the Best Poets of the Year for 1996, by the International Society of Poets, and visited their 1996 symposium and convention in Washington, D.C. Asked by the National Library of Poetry to include another poem of mine in their upcoming anthology, Best Poems of the '90's. I am proud to have my poem, Just Me!?, published in this special edition.; [oth. writ.] My poem, Thoughts Of A Seed..., was published mid-year, 1996, by the NLP, in The Voice Within. My poem, Sights (Perception), is scheduled to be published, Winter 1996, in an anthology entitled, Daybreak on the Land. My poem, You're my Butterfly, is scheduled for publication, Winter, 1996, by the NLP in Morning Star; [pers.] As I make my way along life's path, searching for what it is I want, many times, usually more than not, I come across another of God's wonders. Surprised I am not, awed by your miracles, I am.; [a.] Margate, FL

GILBERT, PAMELA SUE POTTER
[b.] June 24, 1956, Fort Campbell, KY; [p.] Jurrien J. Potter/Gwen L. Terrell; [m.] Alvin Gilbert, January 18, 1991; [ch.] Christie Lynn Fugate, grandchild Courtney Nichole Wright; [ed.] GED (1991) Owsley County, KY, Associate of Arts (1995) Lees College, Jackson, KY; [occ.] Housewife, part-time Assistant Secretary for Industrial Education and Technology at Morehead State University, I am also a full-time non-traditional student currently working on a Bachelor of Arts Degree; [memb.] Non-Traditional Eagles Society ('95-Present), Societas Pro Legibus: Pre-Law Society ('95-Present), Students for Social Justice ('95-Present), Chi Alpha Christian Fellowship ('95-Present), Phi Theta Kappa Honor Society ('94-Present), Breakthrough Ministries ('93-Present); [hon.] Dean's List ('93-94), Who's Who Among Students in American Jr. Colleges ('95), Recognition Awards for Phi Theta Kappa, Student Government Association and Commuters and Non-Traditional Students Organization ('95), Humanities Division Award ('95), Editor's Choice Award ('96); [oth. writ.] Wrote some poems and short stories which are published in "Musings: The Lees College Journal of Arts and Letters" (1993-94 and 1994-95). The following have been published this year (1996) by "The National Library of Poetry": "Halloween Fright" in Where Dawn Lingers, "In Loving Memory" in Best Poems of the 90's, this poem will also be in Lyrical Heritage.; [pers.] Hopefully this will be "Food for thought" as Professor Lowdermilk would say!!; [a.] Booneville, KY

GILL, MARTIN J.
[b.] November 4, 1954, Marlborough, MA; [p.] William E. Gill and Virginia M.; [m.] Nancy M. Gill, May 25, 1986; [ch.] James, Katherine and Charlotte; [ed.] Marlborough High School; [occ.] Customer Service Representative, Marlborough Savings Bank Marlborough, MA; [memb.] Boy Scouts of America; [a.] Marlborough, MA

GILLAND, JEREMY SHANE
[b.] December 2, 1982, Greenville, TN; [p.] Cindy and Tim Gilland; [ed.] 8th Grade Student at Towering Oaks Christian School; [occ.] Student; [memb.] Student Council T.D.L.S., Central Christian Church, 4H, School Safety Patrol; [hon.] Honor Student with Scholastic Awards, Certificates of Merit in Science, History, Math, Reading, Certificate and Excellent rating from the ACSI South East Region Creative Writing Festival; [oth. writ.] "Life" a poem which received a ribbon of excellence in 1993 from a creative writing festival. 1996 Poem also received a Ribbon of Excellence from the Assoc. of Christian Schools; [a.] Greenville, TN

GIRON, CONSUELO
[pen.] Consuelo; [b.] January 25, 1955, Pueblo, CO; [p.] Elicia Giron; [ed.] AS degree; [occ.] U.S. Army; [oth. writ.] Book called My Indian Lover.; [pers.] My idea of life is writing someones else's dreams.; [a.] Denver, CO

GIRTY, JOANN
[b.] March 19, 1940, Delano, CA; [p.] Elmer and Eunice Pitts; [m.] Widowed; [ch.] Six - 4 boys and 2 girls, 10 grandchildren; [ed.] Sallisaw High, Carl Albert Jr. College; [occ.] Disabled; [memb.] Strength for Living Support Group, Pine Tree Baptist Church, Cherokee Nation; [hon.] I have the honor of being a child of God.; [oth. writ.] I have written many poems, songs, and one story, none published.; [pers.] Thanks be to God, the source of my inspiration.; [a.] Sallisaw, OK

GLADDEN, KATHRYN C.
[pen.] Kay; [b.] June 19, 1909, Reedsville, WV; [m.] Kenneth Gladden (Ken), 1929; [ch.] 2; [ed.] School - parents, 1 teacher high school and football coach and wife teacher of grade schools (Kay); [occ.] Retired

GLASER, CHAYA TZIVIA
[pen.] Morgan Alexandra; [b.] March 23, 1982, San Diego, CA; [p.] Don and Dr. Carol Glaser; [occ.] Student entering high school; [pers.] My goal in writing is to find ordinary objects or aspects in life, and write about them. Then people might look at obvious things from a new perspective. I believe that writing is one of the most important things to have in life.; [a.] Teaneck, NJ

GLASER, DAVID
[b.] September 29, 1919, Brooklyn, NY; [p.] Samuel, Jennie; [m.] Mildred, February 19, 1944; [ch.] Susan, Sherry; [ed.] Thomas Jefferson High School Graduate 1936, Art Student League (Scholar) NY School of Industrial Art, New York School Contemporary Art, Brooklyn Museum Art School, Behring Institute 1954, Teacher Center Island Jewish School. Freeport New York 1959; [occ.] Artist, Sculptor - Fine Art, writing New Age graphic experimentation owner, studio concepts; [memb.] Allied Artists of America, Freeport Art Museum and Conservation, AVC, ACW, Amnesty Int'l, Wildness Soc, World Jewish Cong. Greenpeace, American Museum Nat'l History; [hon.] First poem published 1934 National human review, Nassau County poetry award 198, Art Students League Scholar 1936, Grand prize redesign Levitt Home 1967, Numerous graphic awards, Monadnock Mills, Vet Soc. of American Artists, Desi-Grand prize, 3-man show Heckscher Music Huntington 1964, Shows National Arts Club New York 1959, Art Directions 1959, ACA Galleries 1960, Hofstra U., Adelphi U., Nassau Community Call, Pres. Allied Artists of America 1985 exh. Wantagh Levittown, Civilian Conservation Corps 1936 Artist (Adirondacks); [oth. writ.] "My Mother Died Dancing Book 1970, Catoonist, Editor, Publisher AUS" giggyrandom" 1993-4 orientations (USArmy) writings North Pacific 1945, numerous essay on human condition. Inventor: Mosaic reproduction 1948-50 artists, writer 1945 Bearing

Breeze" Aleutians; [pers.] To question to wonder, to accept all possibilities and to explore whenever possible and to accept so called "failure" as a "given" side road to discovery. "To tune in" to the inner universal self and express what is received back in the song of words or the visual. To go "against the grain" Insecurity expressed positively moves me more deeply toward the full potential.; [a.] Wantagh, NY

GLEASON, LINDSAY SHARON
[pen.] Sabrina; [b.] December 27, 1982, Goshen, NY; [p.] Lauren and Michael Gleason; [ed.] 8th grade student in Monroe Woodbury Jr. High School; [occ.] Student; [memb.] Marlins Jr. Varsity Swim Team, Drama Club; [hon.] All County Chorus, I sang for Senator Larkin, Honor Student, Track and Field Meadilist, I have been in the Art Show many times. Been in several plays in the past year or two; [a.] Monroe, NY

GOLDFARB, JUDITH
Goldfarb, Judith Lynne
[pen.] Judith Lynne; [b.] September 23, 1950. Brooklyn, NY; [p.] Victor Goldfarb (d), Eve Goldfarb; [m.] Significant "Other" - Leonard Birnbaum; [ed.] Lafayette H.S., Kingsboro College; [occ.] Executive Assistant, Jewish National Fund, Rockville Centre, NY; [memb.] National Abortion Rights Action League (NARAL), Simon Wiesenthal Center, National Holocaust Museum; [oth. writ.] Many poems, songs, short stories, children's stories, one novel - BATTLESCARS; [pers.] I get a tremendous sense of accomplishment from writing, and I especially enjoy sharing my work with friends and family members. When I pull out the manuscript of my novel, I feel like I'm visiting with old friends.; [a.] New York, NY

GOLDING, SARAH
[b.] April 9, 1981, Greenfield, MA; [p.] Mr. and Mrs. William Golding; [occ.] Student at Mahar Regional High School (10th grade); [memb.] Student Council at Mahar Peer Mediator; [a.] Wendell, MA

GOLDMAN, JARED IAN
[pers.] God has placed in each soul a spirit to lead us upon the illumined path. Yet many seek life from without, unaware that it is within them.

GOLDMAN III, EDWARD
[pen.] Knightmer; [b.] November 2, 1962, Marion, AL; [p.] Edward and Shirley Goldman; [ch.] Aaron and Rebecca Goldman; [ed.] University of New Orleans; [occ.] Lieutenant for Jefferson Parish Fire Dept., Sysop; [memb.] International Ryukyu, Kempo Karate Assoc., American Mensa; [hon.] 3rd and Second degree Black Belts, several Leadership Certificates, Who's Who Among Am. H.S. Students; [oth. writ.] Stories, fairy tales, articles and other poetry have been published locally and electronically around the world. On the Internet. Many of his stories are still held on private collections.; [pers.] Thank you, Kimberly Jones, for showing me a way. A moment spent at peace may spawn a life lived in happiness.; [a.] Jefferson, LA

GOMEZ, VICTORIA GRACE LOPEZ
[b.] July 6, 1967, San Jose, CA; [p.] Phillip Sena, Sarah L. Chavira-Sena; [m.] Rodney Gomez, September 19, 1992; [ch.] Nathan David Gomez; [ed.] Cajon High School, United Health Careers Institute, San Bernardino Valley College; [occ.] Housewife and mother; [oth. writ.] An article featured in Inland Empire Magazine; [pers.] Although I do not have extensive experience in writing it truly is my passion. My writings reflects my deepest thoughts and feelings. I attribute my talent, if any to the presence and guidance of God and Jesus Christ in my life.; [a.] San Bernardino, CA

GORMAN JR., PAUL W.
[b.] January 4, 1924, Greenville, SC; [p.] C. L. and Gail Hallman; [ed.] Hunter Huss High School; [occ.] Attendant for Handicapped Grandfather.; [pers.] The truth of all that is said is of one that can not be explained.; [a.] Gastonia, NC

GRACE, CORRINE
[b.] January 11, 1979, Iowa City, IA; [p.] Kevin Grace and Tara Grace; [ed.] Dubuque Senior High School; [occ.] D.C. Worker, Kendall/Hunt Publishing; [memb.] Spanish Club, Sierra Society; [oth. writ.] A selected few poems printed in school writing newspapers and several other writings in a personal collection.; [pers.] I attempt to bring out what is hidden beneath, deep in the soul and in the back of the mind in my writings. I've always looked up to Dr. Seuss and am influenced by music and photography.; [a.] Dubuque, IA

GRAHAM, DOROTHY O.
[b.] May 5, 1919, San Diego, CA; [p.] Alf B. Rude, Marjorie Rude; [m.] George A. Graham, March 19, 1943; [ch.] Carolee, David Bruce (Deceased); [ed.] Ventura High School (12th Gr.), Parent Education Scholarships, from local P.T.A. and California State Brd. Ed., San Francisco U. and U. of California Berkeley; [occ.] Volunteer Swim Instructor Ventura, California, Y.M.C.A.; [memb.] Board Member, Ventura Unified School Dist. Educational Foundation. Chairman of the A.W. McConnell Scholarship Committee. Member Cpl. David Bruce Graham Scholarship Committee; [hon.] City of Ventura Chamber of Commerce, 1st Mayor Charles Petit Award. Ventura YMCA Outstanding Service award, Outstanding Service Award, Ventura Schools for fund raising effort for its const., Ventura High School swim. pool, named "The Graham Pool"; [oth. writ.] Programs for P.T.A., and other organizations. Many personal poems, written for special people, family members and special occasions and events; [pers.] I write my poetry for personal pleasures and to make other people happy on special occasions, and to send a message of love and friendship. I try to make all of my poetry positive.; [a.] Oxnard, CA

GRALIKER, MARY
[pen.] "Graeme"; [b.] November 16, 1927, Indiana; [ch.] 5 grown children; [occ.] Retired; [memb.] ISP 1995-1996; [oth. writ.] Published poems - "Autumn" - Rainbow's End, "Wind" - Lyrical Heritage, "Mary" - The Best Poems of the 90's; [pers.] Hobby - primarily oil painting. Constantly try to maximize the joys of each day.; [a.] Jacksonville, FL

GRANOFF, HELYN E.
[b.] September 7, 1929, Prescott, PA; [p.] Charles and Lizzie (Shaak) Mengel; [m.] Robert L. Granoff; [ch.] Dr. David W. Granoff (Physician); [ed.] Lebanon County Schools, attended Lebanon Valley and Ursinus Colleges.; [memb.] The Questers - Perkiomensahl Chapter; [hon.] First Prize for an Essay on Physicians (a Satirical piece) Edited and Compiled a monthly claims Bulletin for an Insurance Company, study paper and dolls for the questers.; [pers.] I believe words can be a powerful force, capable of influencing change. The English poets, Keats, Blake and Tennyson Lake touch my sensibilities most, Edgar Allan Poe continues to fascinate.

GRAVES, ANDY
[b.] January 22, 1981, Tampa, FL; [p.] John and Diane Graves; [occ.] Full-time Student, King High School, Tampa, FL; [pers.] I do not think that poetry should come with experience, but with heart, feeling, and freedom. Age does not matter.; [a.] Tampa,, FL

GRAVES, RAE S.
[b.] July 12, 1962, Enid, OK; [p.] Mrs. Maudell Graves; [ed.] B.S. in Deaf Education Elementary. Worked with Mentally Retarded, Artistic, deaf and downs Syndrome children. Children are the source/seed of life. Give them love!; [occ.] Asst. Director - (9 yrs.) St. Michael's Child Deve. Dept.; [memb.] Zeta Phi Beta Sorority; [pers.] Do all that is in the thine heart, for God is with thee.

GRAY, CLINT
[b.] April 26, 1974, Ottumwa, IA; [p.] Richard and Tula Gray; [ed.] Eddyville High School, Indian Hills Comm. College; [memb.] Distinguished Member of the International Society of Poets; [hon.] I am honored to be involved in the worldly come back of poetry, and awarded when reading the poems and hearing the music of the masterful Leonard Cohen; [oth. writ.] Arranging many of my poems for possible publication, first poem "Violet," was published in the National Library of Poetry anthology, "Beneath the Harvest Moon."; [pers.] The young poet will now raise his mighty, sword-like pen to emblazon a mind-melting wow on an exhausted world craving a "Fresh Set of Clothes."; [a.] Ottumwa, IA

GREENAWALT, MARK WAYNE
[b.] April 29, 1963, Everett, PA; [p.] Velma and Arnold Greenawalt; [ed.] Niagara Falls High, Bryan Adult Center, John Cassablaca Creative Artists; [occ.] Scapes Landscaping, Sterling, VA. Market America Independent Distributors; [hon.] Total quality management. John Casablancas Modeling; [oth. writ.] King James Holy Bible; [pers.] To do good in life, to help out others. I reflect on a of people. I try to influence others.; [a.] Knoxville, MD

GREENWOOD JR., BOB
[b.] July 14, 1950, Emporia, KS; [p.] Robert Greenwood and Dunnice Greenwood; [ch.] Taylor Ann; [ed.] B.S., Social Work; [occ.] Child Support Specialist, State of Kansas; [memb.] Kansas Association of Public Employees, Democratic Party; [hon.] Alpha Kappa Delta; [oth. writ.] Have had several poems published in a local newspaper and have one published in our state employees association newsletter.; [pers.] I'm convinced that my mission in life is to help others. I believe my poems reflect this.; [a.] Independence, KS

GRIFFIN, SHANNON
[b.] November 8, 1971, Gadsden, AL; [p.] Marie and Larry Cole; [m.] Shane Griffin, April 20, 1996; [ch.] Kristii and NaKira; [ed.] High School; [occ.] Poultry Worker; [oth. writ.] I have several poems yet unpublished.; [pers.] I always write from the heart. My goal is to touch the hearts of those who read my writing; [a.] Boaz, AL

GRIGGS, SANDRA
[b.] July 24, 1948, Fort Knox, KY; [p.] Edwin E. and Lorine Ochs; [m.] Divorced; [ch.] Stacy Brian and Kelly Ryan; [ed.] LaRue County High Hodgenville, KY; [occ.] Food Service Mgmt; [hon.] Lifetime Member Ky, PTA; [pers.] My writing reflects my inter feelings and emotions that run the gambit from love to anger...to the joy of the river running wild.; [a.] Louisville, KY

GROGAN, NANABAH C. DODGE
[pen.] Nanabah Chee Dodge; [b.] April 3, 1945, Wheatfields, AZ; [p.] Betoni Tsosie and Zonnie Begay, (Poster Parents) Adee B. Dodge and Veah B.; [m.] George M. Grogan, September 27, 1975; [ch.] Navida C. Grogan; [ed.] Santa Fe, NM. (Acequia Madrew Ele. Sch.) Lavaland, Alb., NM. Ele. Sch. Sedona, Ariz. Tempe. Arizona. Scottsdale Academy of Arts and Science, Scottsdale, Ariz; [occ.] Grandmother and writing of family genealogy. Housewife and homemaker; [memb.] NAIWA (North American Indian Women's Association) with New Mexico Chapter as Membership Director 9 yrs; [hon.] Council on Interracial Books For Children Awards (Literary). "Morning Arrow", by Lothrop, Lee and Shepard Co. New York; [oth. writ.] Poems Arizona Republic Newspaper, Articles in Rocky Mountain in "Whose Who". The Navajo Times newspaper. Red Rock newspaper, Sedona, Ariz.; [pers.] I am a Navajo Indian or Navite American born into a rainbow of knowledge. I've been writing since a child...there is so much to tell and I am living it.; [a.] Albuquerque, NM

GROSS, CHRISTOPHER
[pen.] Chris Gross; [b.] July 11, 1965, East Orange, NJ; [p.] Mr. and Mrs. Robert J. Gross; [ed.] Bloomsburg University; [occ.] Sales and Retail; [pers.] I just try to live one day and one hour at a time. I try not to look back because it won't be coming back.; [a.] Union Beach, NJ

GROSSMAN, LUCIANN V.
[pen.] Luci; [b.] October 4, 1966, Bronx, NY; [p.] Irma Gentile, William Smith; [m.] Lawrence Grossman, September 16, 1990; [ed.] Lehman High School, A.A.S. Business Administration Word Processing, A.A.S. Monroe College; [occ.] Health Intern Middle School 180; [hon.] Dean's List; [pers.] Writing is away of letting the world know what my heart feels.; [a.] New York, NY

GUILLORY, SUSAN KAY GENUSA
[pen.] Susie Q.; [b.] May 2, 1964, Baton Rouge, LA; [p.] Gluriatt and Camello B. Genusa Sr.; [m.] Leonard Guillory, June 27, 1981; [ch.] Princess Ann Guillory (Baby dog); [ed.] Graduate of Portallen High School in LA, Diploma in writer course (writers institute) Diploma from (I.C.S.) in photography Course; [occ.] Secretary and Office person in our own Mechanic Shop (L and S.); [memb.] Arthritis Foundation) Animal Human Society, Humane Society; [hon.] Graduated with Honors, won 2 Golden Poets Award Trophies, won Merit Certificate Awards, Golden Poet Certificate; [oth. writ.] Several poems published in anthologist, magazine; [pers.] I have always loved to write poetry since a child. I love to write poetry from my heart. I love to write song lyrics, greeting card and I love photography. I strive to write from my feelings in my heart.; [a.] Lakeland, LA

GUINTA, CHARI LYNN
[pen.] Ri Ri; [b.] August 23, 1983, Guam; [p.] Dana A. and Stephanie C. Guinta; [hon.] Member of "National Junior Honor Society"; [pers.] I wrote this poem when my great grandfather, Sy Greenberg,, Was ILL. I wish to dedicate it to him.; [a.] Dayton, OH

GUTHERY, DEAN L.
[pen.] Slim Chance Foralaff; [b.] January 24, 1927, Whitebead, OK; [p.] Carl and Gussie Guthery; [m.] Nelda Guthery, May 26, 1957; [ch.] Rek, Jolene, and Dean Brandon; [ed.] One year College; [occ.] Retired Entertain Children and Cowboy Gathering's; [memb.] Rodeo Cowboy's Association Cowboy Poetry Gatherings; [hon.] Nothing to bragg about.; [oth. writ.] 175 poems-none published Book (manuscript unfinished - 207 pages) Western Historical Fiction and a few songs.; [pers.] Life long student of human nature, both humor and pathos after active lifetime as ranch cowboy and rodeo cowboy I'm surprised to be writing about it.; [a.] Flagstaff, AZ

GUTHRIE, CHERYL L.
[b.] January 14, 1947, Franklin, PA; [p.] Mr. and Mrs. Robert I. Bean; [ch.] Dawn Marie, Jackie Lynn; [ed.] Lakeview High School Stoneboro, PA; [occ.] Sewer and much more for Sharon Fitness Products Sharon. PA "Weight Lifting Equipment"; [memb.] My church miracle valley assembly; [pers.] Jesus is alive! Praise the Lord!

GUTHRIE, MRS. PEGGY
[pen.] Peggy Guthrie; [b.] November 23, 1923, College Station, TX; [p.] Mr. and Mrs. L. D. Trevino; [m.] Mr. Jimmy Guthrie, April 7, 1946; [ch.] Sandi and Pam Guthrie; [ed.] A and M Consolidated Elementary, A and M Consolidated High School, Texas Women's University, Texas A and M at College Station and East Texas State U. at Commerce; [occ.] Retired Spanish Teacher; [memb.] Littleton Hite Bible Club, United Methodist Women - Esther Circle, Co Ministry Board, Couples Class Sunday Star, Texas Retired Teachers of Lamar Co.; [hon.] Voted Outstanding Teacher in 1967.; [oth. writ.] Several poems accepted by the National Library of Poetry and Northeast Texas Paris Sulphur Spring District books and pamphlets.; [pers.] My belief in God keeps me going and am only trying to put back what God has given me and my family.; [a.] Paris, TX

GUZMAN, MARY
[b.] June 10, 1927, NYC; [p.] Fela Pagan and Adrian Reyes; [m.] Widowed - Juan Guzman, November 30, 1948; [ch.] Three daughters; [ed.] Taken many college courses, never a degree. Read mostly Biographies; [occ.] Retired have small Cottage Business in Natural Foods and Herbs; [memb.] Literacy Vol. of America, Bi-Ligual Tutor. Am member of the church of Jesus Christ of L.D.S. Play a mean game of Scrabble; [oth. writ.] Recently wrote a children's story titled "The Worm And The Tree". I've written many poems but not send them anywhere's didn't think anyone would be inter. The people said they are great.; [pers.] The greatest achievement I feel I've had has been the raising of my children alone. They have reached great hight's. Oldest has masters in Ed. next is a Civil Engineer, and my Baby is an Attorney.; [a.] Cobles Hill, NY

GWATHMEY, BETTE
Bette wrote her first poem at age eleven when her brother signed up as a pilot in World War II. she and her husband Owen, a retired physician, live on their 500 acre farm, the meadow, near Richmond, Virginia. They have four children and seven grandchildren.

HAAS, MICHAEL J.
[b.] January 3, 1955, Chicago, IL; [p.] Norbert H. Haas, Jeanne M. Long; [m.] Norma (Vazquez) Haas, April 4, 1981; [ch.] Norma Erika, Michael Joseph; [occ.] Midwest Area Manager for an International Marine Surveying Organization; [oth. writ.] Various articles for a local community newspaper/periodical.; [pers.] I maintain an open focal point, however, my poetic influences stem from Wm. Blake and Jim Morrison. I feel the entire world must revel in the Arts, in it's truest forms, and set forth with positive influences in order to build a better tomorrow.; [a.] Chicago, IL

HALE, BRENDA KAY
[b.] July 29, 1980, San Antonio, TX; [p.] Betty Blankenship; [ed.] Devine High School; [occ.] Student at Devine High School; [memb.] Planetary Society, National Honor Society; [hon.] Editor's Choice Award for poem entitled "Exile"; [oth. writ.] "Exile" in Where Dawn Lingers, "My Legacy" in Lyrical Heritages, and "Child of Darkness" in Crossings; [pers.] I strive to relate five themes in my work: Peace, hope, love, harmony, and happiness. These five simple and basic themes are, I believe, the cure for mankind's ails. Always and forever, BKH; [a.] Devine, TX

HALILI, LUANA
[b.] May 22, 1980; [p.] Salvatore Briganti, Suada Briganti; [ed.] Christ the King, Regional High School; [occ.] Student; [oth. writ.] Several poems published in my High School's yearly book.; [pers.] My poetry is

based on reality and the situations and harships that have occurred during my life.; [a.] Elmhurst, NY

HALL, JEAN
Hall, Jean I.
[b.] August 31, 1921, Astoria, OR; [p.] Lawrence & Ivy Jackson; [m.] Clyde Thomas Hall, November 8, 1943; [ch.] Laurence Clyde & Julie Ann; [ed.] Astoria High, Bachelor of Musoc, Willamette U., Salem, OR; [occ.] Music Dir. Institute of Mentalphysics, Joshua Tree, CA., retired private piano teacher and sub. public school teacher; [memb.] Hi Desert layhouse Guild, Joshua Tree, CA, P.E.O., Sierra Club, Church Universal and Triumphant; [hon.] Summa Cum Laude, W.U. '43; [oth. writ.] "What I have learned as a Substitute Teacher", Many unpublished songs and poems; [pers.] My goal: To express the oneness of all life, the God within, and the eternality of existence.; [a.] Yucca Valley, CA

HALL, JESSICA ANN
[b.] June 2, 1981, Wilmington; [p.] Deborah Hall; [ed.] Student of Arthur P. Schalick High School; [memb.] 4-H, E.C.S.J., American Heart Association; [hon.] Honor Roll, Grand Champion Equitation, (4-H); [pers.] I wrote this poem in memory of my first horse, diamond, who was put to sleep on December 22, 1993. I had many different feelings and emotions, so I decided to put my thoughts on paper.; [a.] Pittsgrove, NJ

HALLEY, ANNE
[b.] August 23, 1957, Stockton, CA; [p.] Edmund Paul Halley Jr., Sally Popenoe; [m.] Divorced; [ch.] Michael Aaron Craycraft; [ed.] Tomales High School, UC Davis, College of Marin; [occ.] Antique Oriental Carpet and Textile Dealer and Consultant, Student; [memb.] Board Member, Textile Arts Council, MH De Young Memorial Museum, Textile Museum, International Hajji Bava Society, San Francisco Bay Area Rug Society, Alpha Gamma Sigma Honor Society, President - San Anselmo Baseball Assn.; [hon.] Valedictorian, Tomales High California Scholarship Federation; [oth. writ.] Reports published in local newspapers, co-produced exhibitions and catalogues - Baluch Prayer Rugs, Karai Rugs from Turbot e-Heydarieh.; [pers.] I honor the child within, children everywhere and the joy and innocence of childhood.; [a.] San Anselmo, CA

HALLMARK, HAZEL
[pen.] Hazel Hallmark; [b.] June 8, 1921, England; [p.] Mr. and Mrs. Frederick Rippard; [m.] C. K. Hallmark, 1963; [ch.] 2 Sons (David and Daniel), 1 daughter (Teresa) Moench; [ed.] English Schools, Great Britain; [occ.] Housewife; [memb.] Grange, Quilter's Guild; [hon.] Served in WWII in England and received some awards. Was a barrage balloon operator and served from 1940-1945.; [oth. writ.] Several poems as yet not published; [pers.] Have always love poetry and reading and am reminiscent of my childhood days when I ran through the woods and the green, green fields of England.; [a.] Oroville, CA

HAMBY, CATHERINE
[b.] April 20, 1979, Gastonia, NC; [p.] Renee Hamby and Richard Hamby; [ed.] Senior in High School, Ashbrook High Graduate in 1997; [hon.] Who's Who of American High School Students; [pers.] Dreams are not only meant for dreaming, they are meant to do as well. We can all do anything that we have dreamed of.; [a.] Gastonia, NC

HAMER, LAKISHA
[pen.] Sharri; [b.] December 24, 1984, Nashville, TN; [p.] Johnnie and Constance Hamer; [ed.] 6th grade

HAMILTON, HASKELL DALE
[pen.] Dale; [b.] February 7, 1945, Sparta, TN; [p.] James and Johnnie Hamilton; [m.] Cheryl Anne Hamilton, September 13, 1963; [ch.] James Dale, Kelly Jeanine; [ed.] Tennessee Preparatory School, Volunteer State Community College, Metro General Hospital Radiology Program; [occ.] Radiographic Technologist at Summit Medical Center, Nashville, TN; [memb.] AARP; [hon.] Salutatorian, Civitan Key, John L. Hill Medal; [pers.] I have only written two love sonnets or poems for my wife.; [a.] Goodlettsville, TN

HAMILTON, MARY EILENE
[pen.] Mary Eilene; [b.] November 6, 1932, Upton, WY; [p.] Leo E. McDowell and Johanna Roach McDowell; [m.] James McDougall Hamilton, November 6, 1957; [ch.] James Melvin, Ian and Jean Michelle; [ed.] Oregon City High, MarylHurst College, Grossmont College; [occ.] Homemaker, Artist, Calligrapher; [memb.] Marylhurst Alumnae, St. Mary's Roman Catholic Church; [hon.] Magnum Cum Laude, Gold Key Award for Fine Arts, Dean's List, B.A.; [oth. writ.] Poems and musings for self and others, two stories for my grand children (illustrated).; [pers.] I endeavor to share thoughts of the soul, which I prefer to as "Whispers of Love".; [a.] Escondido, CA

HAMLER, NAN MARIE
[b.] July 20, 1941, Washington, DC; [p.] Raymond and L. Belle Dank; [m.] James R. Hamler, June 16, 1983; [ch.] Stanley Allen Covington, Dolores Ellen Covington; [ed.] King George High School; [occ.] Clerk, United States Post Office, Merrifield, VA; [memb.] Women of the Moose; [pers.] My writings are mainly on a personal note as the one written in this book. "Mom" was written for my 'Mom' on mothers day 1980 so I want to dedicate this to her, my late and dearly loved and missed Mom, Belle Dank.; [a.] Dale City, VA

HAMM, DIANE
[pen.] Jackie; [b.] July 23, 1966, Yamato, Japan; [p.] Gary Hamm, Kaoru Ishikawa; [m.] Jacob Gubran, May 10, 1997; [occ.] Servicer Account Manager, RFC, Universal City; [oth. writ.] Large Collection of poems spanning several years; [pers.] My poetry helps me to express who am I am, where I have been, and how I hope to be.; [a.] Valencia, CA

HAMM, KEVIN
[b.] May 27, 1962, Pittsburgh, PA; [p.] George Hamm, Katherine Hamm; [m.] Arlynnette Hamm, August 6, 1988; [ed.] Penn Hills High in Pittsburgh PA, Morehouse College in Atlanta GA; [occ.] A grip for Motion Pictures Commercials and Videos; [memb.] IATSE Local 479 for Film Technicians; [pers.] I hope to live my life as a light for others.

HANNA, SANDRA E.
[b.] October 30, 1934, Woodbury, NJ; [p.] Raymond A. and Helene L. Sharpe; [m.] John W. Hanna, November 22, 1952; [ch.] John W., Jr. David G., Linda G, and Nancy E.; [ed.] Collingswood High School, Collingswood, NJ; [memb.] Stratford United Methodist Church; [oth. writ.] "Wind Song", "The Power Of Prayer", "God's Healing Grace", "Who Was He", "As I Go My Way", "A Poem for the New Year".; [pers.] I have been inspired to write Poetry, to share it with others. It is my prayer that all who read my poems will be Blessed by them...; [a.] Stratford, NJ

HANNAH, KAREN RENEE
[pen.] KH; [b.] January 4, 1977, Santa Maria, CA; [p.] George and Roxanne Hannah; [ed.] High School Graduate at Ernest Righehi High, completed 1st year at Allan Hancock Community College (currently enrolled for fall 96:) will transfer to Cal Poly State University; [occ.] College Student, am working towards a B.A. in English

goals: To become an English College Professor; [hon.] Harvest Magazine - (short story); [oth. writ.] Poetry published in High School newspaper, short stories.; [pers.] Whatever words of poetry from my fingertips, they are bound to the hearts of those I love most, my family and friends. As I write for myself, I only hope to reveal honest, original thoughts-ones that are timeless enough to live by.; [a.] Santa Maria, CA

HANSEN, J. BERG
[b.] August 27, 1916, Brooklyn, NY; [p.] Julius Hansen and Karna Hansen; [m.] Valerie R. Hansen, July 28, 1960; [ch.] Jon Hansen and 5 stepchildren; [ed.] Hofstra University, Hempstead, NY; [occ.] Retired - formerly Salesman; [memb.] Church of the Redeemer (Episc.), Pastoral Care Committee; [oth. writ.] Monthly poetry submission to the church Parish Post. Published in local community paper The Village Mill.; [pers.] My writings express Hope, Faith, and Consideration; [a.] Midlothian, VA

HARBOUR, JENNIFER
[b.] June 11, 1980, Laconia; [p.] Michael and Marsha Harbour; [ed.] Junior in High School; [occ.] Sales Associate; [oth. writ.] I have never had any of my poems published, but I have written many others.; [pers.] I was inspired to write, because I have a hard time expressing my feelings, so I do it through my writing.

HARKINS, TIM
[b.] November 3, 1953, Birmingham, AL; [p.] James B. and Martha Harkins; [m.] Lillian, August 3, 1985; [ed.] BS from Regents College of New York; [occ.] Technical Writer; [memb.] Retired from U.S. Navy, Oct. '95; [a.] Colonial Beach, VA

HARRINGTON, JERRY LYNN
[pen.] Jerylyn Harrington; [b.] June 14, 1946, Levelland, TX; [p.] A. O. Harrington, Maurine Hellen Harrington; [ed.] Holliday High School, Midwestern University; [occ.] Customer Service Representative, Sitel Corp.; [oth. writ.] Molly Lantrie, Legend Of, The Mystery of The Uobe, The City of The Guardian, Guilt By Association.; [pers.] Life is better, the second time around.; [a.] San Angelo, TX

HARRIS, BILLY E.
[b.] July 8, 1948, Carthage, MS; [p.] Mary and Wrenshaw Harris; [ed.] Grad. American Institute of Applied Science, Cert. Foren Science Police Science Institute, Cert. Gen. Law Enforcement/Conservation and Foresty Black School of Law, Cert. Paralegel; [occ.] Retired Correction Officer Paralegel/Legel Asst.; [hon.] Silver and Bronz Star Medal from the 82nd AirBorne Division in 1968-69 Vietnam; [pers.] I believe that the degree of loyalty one has for someone or something is measured by the loyalty that one has for one's left. Only out of loyalty to oneself can on be loyal to others or other things. Only against, loyalty for oneself can we measure true loyalty for others or other things.; [a.] Lompoc, CA

HARRIS, CAMILLE L.
[b.] July 9, 1971, Pittsburgh; [p.] William H. and Carol D. Harris; [ed.] Penn State Univ. Asso., Degree in Humanities; [occ.] Amored Car Bank Teller; [memb.] ASPLA, Running Story for Am. Indian Children; [hon.] Editors Chief for Nat'l. Lib. of Poetry 1996; [pers.] Bloated? Release...Ann! Allow for an even flow. Vaja Con Dios, Amigos.; [a.] Pittsburgh, PA

HARRIS, SHARON R.
[b.] January 12, 1967, Oklahoma; [p.] Alfred and Euleta Evans; [m.] Lonnie Harris; [ed.] Sarah, Lonnie Jr., Tabitha and Tawny; [oth. writ.] Various poems and co-written some songs; [pers.] With an abiding faith in God and love of family there is nothing that can't be

accomplished. I have been influenced by: Henry David Thoreau and Ralph Waldo Emerson.; [a.] Aurora, MO

HART, FREDA M.
[b.] December 25, 1939, Woodbine Camden County, GA; [p.] Mr. and Mrs. Charles Lenward Miller Sr.; [m.] George L. Hart (Deceased), May 29, 1975; [ch.] Debra Anne Woods and Cynthia Louise Gainey; [ed.] Completed High School - GED; [occ.] Housewife; [oth. writ.] Yes - none published.; [pers.] Inspired-through my parents-both died of tumors - While staying and attending to them. Mother recently passed away.; [a.] Waverly, GA

HARTMANN, BETH A.
[pen.] Allison Hart; [b.] February 7, 1972, Franklin, IN; [p.] Charles and Vickie Caplinger; [m.] Robert M. Hartmann, December 30, 1994; [ch.] Michael and Michelle; [ed.] Indiana Business College; [occ.] Editor; [hon.] Nominated and accepted by the International Who's Who Among Business Professionals; [pers.] My work is a direct reflection of my emotions. Poetry and art as well as other forms of writing and speech are my release.; [a.] Round Rock, TX

HARVEY, CHARLES D.
[b.] May 14, 1961, Waukesha, WI; [ed.] H.S. Two Harbors MN, Colleges, Northern Arizona University 1980-1981, B.A. History, University of Minnesota, Duluth 1985; [occ.] Sgt. Army Reserves, Work with Disabled, Developmentally Disabled; [pers.] Try to illicit a strong statement through imagery and meter either in rhyme or prose; [a.] Hermantown, MN

HASLAM, MARIA
[b.] April 7, 1953, Poland; [p.] Aniela Janik, Joseph Janik; [ch.] Carey, Kimberly, Marci; [ed.] Poland and Paier College of Art; [occ.] Interior Design Consultant; [hon.] Honorary Award for Designing Floor Plan for Hospital's Day Care Center; [pers.] To create you're never too old, never too young. Creativity comes within your soul.; [a.] Wethersfield, CT

HATHAWAY, TODD EMMETT
[b.] June 26, 1969, Johnson City, NY; [ed.] Seton Catholic Central High School, Broome Community College, U.S. Army, NY Police Academy; [occ.] Law Enforcement/Helicopter Pilot; [pers.] Give God the highest praise for even the smallest pleasure. I dedicate this to Grandma, a truly priceless treasure.; [a.] Oswego, NY

HATZIOS, KRITON K.
[b.] August 6, 1949, Florina, Greece; [p.] Kleanthis Hatzios, Adamantia Hatzios; [m.] Maria K. Hatzios, September 8, 1979; [ch.] Adamantia Hatzios, Stavroula Hatios; [ed.] B.S., Aristoleian University, Thessaloniki, Greece, MS., Michigan State Univ. Ph.D. Michigan State University; [occ.] Professor of Plant Physiology Virginia Tech, Blacksburg, VA 24060; [memb.] American Chemical Society, American Soc. of Plant Physiologists American Association of the Advancement of Science Weed Science Society, Hellenic Soc. Paideia; [hon.] Fellow Award and Outstanding Research Award by the Weed Science Society of America Gamma Sigma Delta, Sigma Xi; [oth. writ.] Two Science Books, 110 scientific articles. Three Collections of poetry written in Greek My poems have been published in Greek newspapers and magazines; [pers.] I like to write poems that are short in length, but large in meaning I write both on personal as well as common sense things, I feel satisfied when other people appreciate the message of my poems.; [a.] Blacksburg, VA

HAYES, DEBRA
[b.] March 1, 1954, Taylor, PA; [p.] Claire and Leon Hendrickson; [m.] Donald M. Hayes, September 24, 1977; [ch.] Nicole, Donald Jr.; [memb.] Writer's Digest Magazine, Children's Writer Newsletter; [a.] W. Windsor, NY

HAYNIE, MATTHEW
[b.] April 1, 1983, Darlington, SC; [p.] Wayne Haynie, Pat Haynie; [ed.] Darlington Junior High; [occ.] Student; [memb.] Boy Scouts of America Epworth Methodist Church Darlington Jr. High Band; [hon.] Beta Club, National Jr. Honor Society; [oth. writ.] Several Children's books, A Book of Poems.; [pers.] I enjoy writing poetry and playing the guitar and the trumpet.; [a.] Darlington, SC

HEATON-SCISCO, GLORIA K.
[pen.] Gloria K. Heaton; [b.] January 23, 1932, Pottstown, PA; [p.] Bob and Viola Everingham; [m.] John R. Scisco, February 27, 1993; [ch.] Pamela D. Anderson and Melanie S. Watson (Twins), Brenda K. Miller; [ed.] High School: Elkton, MD, Monrovia-Arcadia-Duarte, CA and Bridgeton, NJ Rollins College, Florida; [occ.] Reflexologist, West Des Moines, IA; [memb.] Mensa, Unity Church, Huna Research, Associated Bodywork and Massage Professionals International Council of Reflexologists, Reflexologist Ass'n of America, Nevada Ass'n of Reflexologists, Iowa Ass'n of Reflexologist Organization of Wisconsin; [oth. writ.] I've had poems published in High School and College publications, also in Adult Children of Alcoholics, Mensa and Iowa poetry books.; [pers.] Since every happening that I thought was so terrible at the time has always had such a marvelous outcome later I do believe that we are watched over, greatly loved and are always being nudged towards our highest potential. Relax and live in joy and peace.; [a.] West Des Moines, IA

HEAVRIN, BRANDIE L.
[b.] September 13, 1983; [p.] Lora Abad, Eric Heavrin; [ed.] I'm only in 7th grade; [hon.] One for writing it 3, 4, 5, 6 grade!; [oth. writ.] These are not published, scary stories, poems, like the weather. The four seasons of the year and a class book!; [pers.] I am only 12 almost 13 years old. I love music and love to write stories, poems, and songs. I am happy to have a poem of mine being published.; [a.] Palisade, CO

HENDERSON, DANA MARIE
[b.] September 11, 1982, Blytheville, AR; [p.] Barbara Semple, Lori Boesen; [ed.] Blythville West Jr. High School; [occ.] Student; [hon.] Honor Roll Student (Principals) A/B average, 1st place in Bird Art Contest for Hummingbird, Art Piece in Display at Asle, in Jonesboro, Arkansas; [pers.] I didn't think I could get anywhere in this contest by my grandmother convinced me too. I was very surprised when I got the letter. You never know what you can do until you try.; [a.] Blytheville, AR

HENDERSON, EARL E.
[b.] August 26, 1902, Durango, TX; [p.] Archibald Calderon and Marguerite Guffey Henderson; [m.] Rena Richey Henderson, June 27, 1929; [ch.] Earl Edwin Henderson Jr., Sandra Jean. Henderson Andrick, and Martha Elair Henderson Hug; [ed.] Graduated from Mart H.S., Mart, TX; [occ.] Retired Horticulturist; [memb.] Masonic Order; [pers.] In my ninety-four years of experience, I have found this quotation from the Book of Proverbs to be out of the realm of human frailties and into the realm of absolute truth: "Trust in the Lord with all thine heart, and lean not unto thine own understanding. In all thy ways acknowledge him, and he shall direct thy paths".; [a.] Berryville, VA

HENDERSON, FLORENE
[b.] September 27, 1939, Cedar City, UT; [p.] J. Harvey Davenport and Florence Campbell Davenport; [m.] Gerald V. Henderson (Deceased), June 7, 1958; [ch.] Kimberlee, Mark, Debra, Jerri Anne, Heather and William; [ed.] HS: Santa Monica High School, (Walnut, CA - 1977) A.S.D. Mt. San Antonio College, BSN Weber State University, Ogden, UT, 1992. (At the age of 52); [occ.] Registered Nurse, since 1980, work in 9-Bed ICU/CCU and Life Flight Nurse, Dixie Reg. Med. Ctr.; [memb.] A.N.A., A.A.C.N., Church of Jesus Christ of Latter-day Saints; [hon.] Writing Contests at Weber State University, 1992 winning essay, "My most memorable experience in nursing 'We love you, blue granny'"; [oth. writ.] As noted, I love writing, but have never had anything published, I write poetry, prose, short stories, and have just finished my late husband's life history.; [pers.] I love life and nature and have a deep spiritual connection with both. The older I get, the more clearly I see things and I quite often will write down my feelings.; [a.] Saint George, UT

HENDRICK, LAURENCE
[pen.] Larry; [b.] September 25, 1960, Oak Ridge, TN; [p.] Roger G. Sr. and Emma Hendrick; [ch.] Adam G. Hendrick; [ed.] Tullahoma High Trade School; [occ.] Painter; [memb.] Faith Lutheran Church U.S. Veteran; [oth. writ.] Wrote for Church Bulletin and Personal poems; [pers.] I write what I feel from my heart.] My greatest inspirations are from those around me.; [a.] Tullahoma, TN

HENDRIX, TRESSA A.
[b.] December 26, 1956, Beebe, AR; [p.] Clinton Hunter and Anna Griffen; [m.] Edward R. Hendrix, June 4, 1984; [ch.] Randall, Edward R. Jr. and Jessica; [ed.] 29 semester hrs. Pre-Nursing, 50 of hrs. Early Childhood Ed. courses and currently enrolled in the Child Development Associate Program at Foothills Tech Institute, Searcy, AR 72143. CNA at Central AR Hosp.; [hon.] Letter from College President for maintaining a 4.0 GPA for Fall 1992, Certificate for Exceptional Performance Award for School Years 1990/91 and from Dept. of Defense Dep. Schools; [oth. writ.] 1. From Daze to Fear, 2. Division of Hearts, 3. Faded Dreams, 4. A Sister's Love, 5. Treasured Memories, 6. Alpha and Omega; [pers.] Writing is a God given gift for me and I will utilize this gift when inspired. Everyone has a special talent given to them from God. Find it and utilize it at his will.; [a.] Searcy, AR

HENRY, CARL PATRICK
[pen.] Capathen; [b.] October 21, 1921, Rulo, NE; [p.] Carl and Jennie (Love Joy) Henry; [m.] Lenore (Donnahue) Henry, November 27, 1946; [ch.] Two girls, three boys; [ed.] College; [occ.] Retired; [memb.] YMCA; [hon.] Silver Star, (two) Purdle Hearts; [oth. writ.] 1. Book - Glimpse In Thought And Rhyme, 2. Book - Stuff And Junk, 3. Book - A Christmas Collection, 4. Book - Journey Out Of Darkness; [pers.] "TGIF" - To be a beast and free with only instinct for a guide, or perhaps a bird in flight above some lonely cape....would seem better than to be in marble halls, entrapped, forever seeking Friday for escape.; [a.] Seattle, WA

HENRY, JOHN R.
[b.] November 12, 1923, Jasper Co., MS; [p.] John A. and Jewell Estelle Henry; [m.] Alice E. Henry, July 14, 1946; [ch.] Leisa R., Mercer and Lorna D. Henry; [ed.] AA, BS, Miss. State U.; [occ.] Retired from USDA after 35 years; [memb.] Pres. Windmore Writers Chapter of VA. Writers Club, Windmore Writers Branch of Windmore Foundation for Arts, Soil and Water Conservation Society, National Assn. of retired Federal Employees, Rapidan Habit for Humanity; [hon.] Eight High Performance Awards from USDA, Fellow Award

from Soil and Water Cons. Society, Superior Service Award, USDA, distinguished Service Award from Lake of the Woods Property Owners Assn.; [oth. writ.] Published in two magazines and 14 newspapers. Published in two anthologies: A delicate balance by NL of P and Touching the Heart by Windmore Writers.; [pers.] Creative writing is my best teacher. I love my teacher.; [a.] Locust Grove, VA

HENTHORN, DIANA M.
[b.] February 22, 1967, Kansas City, MO; [p.] Judy Bungart Henthorn and David Henthorn; [ed.] Nicholls State University, Thibodaux, LA; [occ.] Polish Arabian Horse Groomer; [pers.] For father not to feel disappointment in having only daughters.; [a.] Mukilteo, WA

HERARD, TIFFANY WILLOUGHBY
[b.] December 12, 1973, Bronx, NY; [p.] Barbara Willoughby; [ed.] Cranbrook Kingswood Upperschool, B.A. Cornell University, M.A., Candidate University of California, Santa Barbara; [occ.] Graduate student, University of California, Santa Barbara; [memb.] Delta Upsilon Lambda Rho, Second Baptist Church Choir, Black Graduate Student Association; [hon.] Detroit Korean Association, Metro Student of the Year 1991, Cornell University American Indian Program Award 1993, American Political Science Association Minority follow 1995-96; [oth. writ.] Cranbrook Kingswood Gaullimaufry, Cornell University Umoja Sasa, Cornell University WATU.; [pers.] We have more power to do good than all those who intend to do evil against us. We must only take authority and go where God sends us.; [a.] Santa Barbara, CA

HERNANDEZ, PHYLLIS ANNE
[pen.] "Boma", "Pinky"; [b.] September 1, 1948, Livermore, CA; [p.] Albert DeHerrera, Phyllis Gonzalez-DeHerrera; [m.] Hurlie Edward Neikirk, September 14, 1990; [ch.] Thea and Belia Hernandez; [ed.] AA Hmm Serv/Soc Welfare Columbia Coll 84. American River Coll: Sacramento, CA. 87 Lrng. Dsbts. Task Force 87 - SAC - State Univ Edctnal Equity Prog. Rep: Coll. Brds. Coll. Schrship Serv. Regntv 89. Patton State Hospital B.S., 1994 Sac State Univ. Sal. CA.; [occ.] Recreational Therapist at Patton State Hospital/Loma Limda Behavior Medical Center; [memb.] Internship Committee RT/CTRS, Youth Education Motivation Program 1994 Friends of Victoria, National Association of Forensic Counselors CA. Board of Recreation and Park Certification National Council for Therapeutic Recreation Certification; [hon.] Therapeutic Recreation Specialist 1995, Certified Criminal Justice Specialist 1996; [oth. writ.] Patton Bulletin 1994 to present The National Dean's List 13th Ed. Vol. II 1989-90 Maagizo Winter 1989.; [pers.] "Never give up until you drink from the gold cup and it belongs to you". Never take no for an answer if you believe in your self".; [a.] Yucaipa, CA

HERNANDEZ, RAQUEL
[b.] September 18, 1973, Elmhurst, NY; [p.] Francine and Arthur Hernandez; [ed.] Newtown High School Laguardia Comm. College, Queensborough Comm. College; [occ.] District Secretary; [memb.] American Blood Donor Association, LIC Gospel Church; [hon.] Science Honors Award; [oth. writ.] Freelance (unpublished); [pers.] Poetry is movement in the realms of thought, science and creativity intertwined. Let it cradle your mind and hug your spirits with picturesque light and pleasures of unseen skys.; [a.] LIC, NY

HERNDON, NINA MARIE
[b.] June 1975, Kansas City, MO; [p.] Linda DeGraffenceid, Maurice Herndon; [ed.] Quince Orchard High School, Gaithersburg, MD, Montgomery College, Rockville, Townson State Univ. Towson, MD.;

[hon.] Towson State Univ. Dean's List; [a.] Gaithersburg, MD

HERRING, CAROLYN
[pen.] Carolyn Herring; [b.] April 22, 1945, Roswell, NM; [p.] Fred Fondy, Martha Fondy; [m.] Leon, June 15, 1963; [ch.] John Christopher, Blaze Alan; [ed.] Roswell High, Southwestern Business College, TSTI College, Abilene, TX; [occ.] Operate a local restaurant with husband; [hon.] I continue to enjoy singing and sharing what I have written as the doors open, at many churches and civic gatherings.; [oth. writ.] I have written songs and poems for over twenty years. Most of the time they are about someone in life, or to encourage someone who needs to have his spirits lifted.; [pers.] I believe that we have all been given talents by the Lord, and should use them as best we can, to make a difference in others' lives.; [a.] Haskell, TX

HERRMANN, RACHEL
[b.] March 17, 1985, New York City; [p.] Marilyn and Richard Herrmann; [ed.] PS 158-Bayard Taylor, Wagner MS 167; [occ.] Student; [memb.] 92nd St Y Flying Dolphin Swim Team; [oth. writ.] Pillow and the Stuffed Dog, Horses Are Different.; [a.] New York City, NY

HIATT, ROSEANN M.
[pen.] Roxie Perdue; [b.] August 3, 1958, Sasebo, Japan; [p.] James Marshall, Etsuko Marshall; [m.] Scott A. Hiatt, August 25, 1995; [ch.] Tomiko Rose, Melissa Olivia, Britney Jean; [ed.] Maryvale High, Phoenix College; [occ.] Waitress, Muncie IN, LPN Phx Arizona; [memb.] American Cancer Society; [hon.] St. Joseph Hospital Outstanding Nursing Award, Phx, Arizona; [oth. writ.] Several poems published in church bulletins, and high school paper. Wrote a play for our youth group Foothill Park Baptist Church. Azusa, Calif.; [pers.] I enjoy writing and bringing joy, happiness and smiles to others. I have been greatly influenced by author Dean Koontz and the book of counted sorrows.; [a.] Gaston, IN

HICKS, BETH M.
[b.] July 27, 1967, Pleasanton, TX; [p.] Sara and Howard Hicks; [ed.] Devine High School, West Texas State Univ and Stephen F. Austin State Univ.; [occ.] S.F.A.S.U. Student working on a Psychology Masters; [memb.] United Way; [pers.] Only regret the things you don't do in life. Everything else you learn from. Open your eyes, mind, heart and ears to listen and see the opportunity for you.; [a.] Nacogdoches, TX

HICKS, CAROL E.
[pen.] Carol E. Gilbert Hicks; [b.] August 6, 1951, Indianapolis, IN; [p.] Helen and William Gilbert; [ch.] Grandchildren: Kenneth Hicks and Brittany Hicks; [ed.] Medical Profession, Graduate of Aristotle Medical and Dental School and Shortridge High School; [memb.] ADA - American Dental Association; [oth. writ.] "Perfect Peace", "God's Work Is Never Done", "Relax Your Mind", "Elements Of God's Elegance", "Peace And Tranquility"; [pers.] Attends Grace Apostolic Church, inspiration aroused from previous choir, participations etc. Other poems published with the National Library of Poetry entered Religious poem contest, published with famous Poet Society etc.; [a.] Indianapolis, IN

HICKSON, GLORIA
[b.] February 20, 1927, Sandusky, OH; [p.] William R. and Edrie E. Smith; [m.] D. James Hickson, M.D., August 28, 1948; [ch.] Holly Beth, Amy Blanche, Sarah Dean, David James Jr.; [ed.] A.B. Mount Union College, Alliance, Ohio, 1949; [occ.] Director Social Services Agency (retired); [memb.] Pi Gamma Mu, First United Methodist Church, Albuquerque, N.M.;

[a.] Albuquerque, NM

HIGGINS, BEATRICE BROWN
[pen.] Bebe Higgins; [b.] December 21, 1922, Duncan, OK; [p.] Golda and Ernest Brown; [m.] Malcolm H. Higgins, June 29, 1945; [ch.] Lynne, Chris, Dave; [ed.] B.S. from Oklahoma University graduate classes in creative writing - West Valley College Los Gatos, CA.; [occ.] Writer, Poet, Housewife, Mother, Grandmother; [memb.] Assistance League, San Jose Monday Poetry Group, San Jose Monday Study Group, San Jose Almaden Swim and Racquet club.; [oth. writ.] Poems published poetry books, 5 anthologies. Essays and vignettes published in news papers in California and Oklahoma.; [pers.] Most of my poetry and prose deals with human interest stories of family, friends, ancestors. Also slice of life humorous anecdotes about my children and our pets.; [a.] San Jose, CA

HILL, JODELL R.
[pen.] Jo Hill, JoDell, Smith, Rervee Hill; [b.] April 3, 1970, Medina, OH; [p.] Linda and Andy Anderson; [ed.] Graduated 1988 from Highland High School; [occ.] Lab. Tech.; [memb.] Rainforest Rescue, National Poets Society; [oth. writ.] Published in the following anthologies: The Rainbows End, Beyond The Stars, Best Poems of 1996, The Voice Within, Best Poems of the 90's, Day Break On The Land, Journey of the Mind, The Garden of Life and East of the Sunrise.; [pers.] So many of us get caught up in the chaos of life, we need to remember to find the time to remember and enjoy the simple things in life.; [a.] Elyria, OH

HILLEY, CATHERINE MARIE
[b.] September 18, 1961, Washington, DC; [p.] Mr. and Mrs. Dean A. Hilley; [ed.] High School Diploma June 1979 3 yrs. of College 2 yrs. at PFCC and one year at UMES; [occ.] Unemployed worked as cashier and waitress and music teacher; [memb.] Was a member of MENC and the greenbelt band and grace brethren church; [hon.] Certificates of awards for performing with the greenbelt concert band I have two a certificate of admission to U.M.E.S. work study scholarship; [oth. writ.] Written in college and school also a song writer who has entered competitions and received certificates and official notices that my work was received and accepted; [pers.] I would like to keep writing and receive compliments and awards on subjects that interest me and other people. For someone to admire you that is as talented as the members of The National Library of Poetry is an honor in itself; [a.] Fort Washington, MD

HILTON, KASEY B.
[b.] December 18, 1981, Woodbridge, VA; [p.] Larry and Susan Hilton; [a.] Woodbridge, VA

HODULICH, LAURA
[b.] May 28, 1984, Falls Church, VA; [p.] Patty and David Hodulich; [ed.] 6th grade student, Sangster Elementary School; [hon.] First Place in Reflections Literary Contest ('93-'94 school year)

HOERNIG, LAUREN
[b.] May 17, 1982, Munster, IN; [p.] Victor and Vicki Hoernig; [ed.] Still attending High School at Lowell High; [occ.] Student; [memb.] Drama Club - Choir; [oth. writ.] I keep a personal collection of other poems I write as they come to me.; [a.] Lowell, IN

HOFF, KRISTIE
[b.] October 28, 1972, Anchorage, AK; [p.] Marvin and Connie Maze; [m.] Peter Hoff; [ch.] Michael and Steven Hoff

HOFFMAN, JILL
[pen.] Jillian; [b.] June 15, 1960, Philadelphia, PA; [oth. writ.] Several poems published in various local newspapers. Letters of opinion printed in editorial section of local newspapers, etc.; [pers.] My poems are based on the human heart. Families in conflict, selfishness, prejudice and hate. I would like to try and bring people together rather than separate and divide. In todays world obsessed by fear it helps me to bear every day trials and annoyances, gently and calmly, because I feel there can be no inward peace or happiness without some faith in life's goodness. The things that I hope my poetry can be good for. I hope my poems will brighten somebodies day and touch the heart. So here I go - "an unknown poet who is about to shoot an arrow into the air.

HOFFMAN, TAMMY LAYNE
[b.] November 29, 1963, Pensacola, FL; [p.] Lane F. Hoffman and Mary Spear-Thomas; [ed.] Degree in Applied Electronics Technology, currently working toward a BA in English at Alabama State University; [occ.] Pari-Mutuel Manager; [oth. writ.] A collection of short stories, essays, and poetry that have yet to be shared with the public.; [pers.] To judge mankind for their weight, their race, or the clothes they wear is a verdict that cunningly robs the mind and utterly strips the essence of human value ... debasing self as well.; [a.] Montgomery, AL

HOLMAN, RUBY KRATZER
[b.] September 5, 1930, Newton, KA; [p.] William Kratzer, Mary Kratzer; [m.] Clenard Holman (Deceased), March 21, 1957; [ch.] Robin, Roi, Sherri, Kim; [ed.] Newton High, Metropolitan Business School in Los Angeles, CA, and Los Angeles City College, Los Angeles, CA; [occ.] Retired Medical Secretary from Kasier Foundation Hospital in Los Angeles, CA; [memb.] Christian Chapel of Walnut, Walnut, CA; [hon.] Famous Poet Society for my poem, "Children of the Street"; [oth. writ.] "Beginning", not yet published. "Sparkling Gold", in progress.; [pers.] My mother was my mentor, and although she was never published. She too, was a writer. She still remains my inspiration, and God is my direction.; [a.] Walnut, CA

HOLMGREN, CHRISTINE
[pen.] A. J. Morrison; [b.] June 19, 1971, Ishpeming, MT; [p.] Paul and Lorrie Holmgren; [ed.] Ishpeming High, Northern Michigan Univ., Children's Inst. Literature; [occ.] Medical Records Clerk, Marquette Gen. Hosp.; [hon.] A special Publishing Degree from Inst. Children's Lit.; [oth. writ.] Currently trying to get into print: short stories. This is the first poem I submitted; [pers.] I believe you need to write of the feeling(s) inside of yourself in order to make a strong, meaningful piece — and any feeling is worth a line of writing, because somewhere, someone is going to feel what you did and find comfort in your words. To me, that is the most important meaning in writing — sharing a thought, idea, feeling, or action.; [a.] Marquette, MI

HOLT, JACK
[pen.] J. Neal Holt; [b.] February 10, 1928, Eden, NC; [p.] Charles and Lillian Holt; [m.] Joyce, August 19, 1985; [ed.] Elon College (BA Degree); [occ.] Retired; [oth. writ.] Free lance - feature articles for newspapers and magazines.; [a.] Jacksonville, FL

HOMUTH, ARVID
[b.] February 13, 1929, Jamestown, ND; [p.] Arnold and Clara (Guenther) Homuth; [m.] Mary (Dakutak) Homuth, AK., May 9, 1959; [ed.] Printing (Jr. College) North Dakota State College of Science, Wahpeton, N.D. 58075, B.A. Degree (Sr. College) Valley city State University Valley City, N.D. 58072; [occ.] Retired now but work part time at Elburn Herald Newspa-

per; [memb.] Offer me memberships; [hon.] Editor's Choice Award, The National Library of Poetry, Owings Mills, MD 21117, 1993 - Award of Recognition, famous poet for 1995, Hollywoods famous poets society, Hollywood, CA 90028; [oth. writ.] 1994 "Spring Ahead" (8 lines) in the Elburn Herald, 1995 "When The Temperature Starts to Rise" (20 lines), unpublished, "My White Haired Daddy", 1995, Hollywood's famous Poets Society.; [pers.] My poetry comes from rhythm of music and experience from life never forgot.; [a.] Elburn, IL

HONG, JUNG JA
[pen.] Catherine Park; [b.] Korea; [ed.] Ewha Women's University, Seoul, Korea - BA in French Literary Diploma in Nursing, M.A.S. from New School for Social Research; [occ.] Nurse (Registered); [oth. writ.] Essays on human interests and children's stories waiting to be published.; [pers.] I write to further understanding and Harmony among all man kind.; [a.] Oakland, NJ

HOPHINE, BWOSINDE
[pen.] Ababio B. Ababio; [b.] December 30, 1963, Vienya; Eunice Moraa and Elias Osinde; [ed.] BS Chemistry; [occ.] Analytical Chemist; [oth. writ.] The Petals of a Cross — novel in the works; My Friend the Wind — collection of poems; The Bonds that Bind Us — an autobiography — to be completed in '96; [pers.] I will take with both hands whatever life dishes and make use of it to the fullest.; [a.] Kansas City, MO

HOUGH, WANDA GAIL
[pen.] Wanda Gail Hough; [b.] November 24, 1951, Opp, AL; [p.] Maureen Williams and Henry Boles; [m.] Stanley Patrick, September 24; [ch.] Susan Faye Morrow and 4 wonderful grandchildren; [ed.] I attended school in Plant City Florida where I grew up; [occ.] I am currently wife and homemaker gives me which plenty of time for writing; [oth. writ.] The tree, A Tribute to Moma, The Vow, Special Love, True Friends and many others.; [pers.] I started writing poetry in the 2nd grad. I enjoy writing and reading poetry my friends and family are very encouraging and I thank God for them. Most of my poems are written for specific people or reasons of love. Some are dedicated to my wonderful grandchildren, Josh, Brent, Breawnna and Bryce. Frustrated fisherman, of thoughts are for my husband and Father in Law.; [a.] East Moline, IL

HOUK, RACHEL A.
[b.] October 29, 1974, Oak Lawn, IL; [p.] Raymond and Adrienne Houk; [ed.] Victor J. Andrew High School, Moraine Valley Comm. College; [occ.] Transportation Coordinator; [oth. writ.] Several Poems and short stories not yet published.; [a.] Tinley Park, IL

HOUK, RYAN P.
[pen.] R. Patrick Houk; [b.] September 18, 1979, Canton, OH; [p.] Catherine A. and William D. Ekleberry; [ed.] Senior in High School planning on attending a Fine Arts College in the fall of 1997; [occ.] Student; [memb.] Outstanding English and Arts Student '96, President St. Pauls Lutheran Church Youth Group, Peer Leadership Committee, Drama Club; [hon.] Who's Who of American High School Students 1996, Regional Winner of Midwestern Division High School Writer Short Story Contest '95-'96, Winner of Literary Essay Contest Sponsored by WTUZ. Senior Editor of Trajah Torch; [oth. writ.] Various essays, short stories, and poems including short story "Where the Butterflies Go," published in High School writer and Hospice Newsletter.; [pers.] Everything I write has some auto-biographical quality to it. I feel anyone has the ability to write. The story has always been there, it just needs someone to write it down.; [a.] Bolivar, OH

HOUSEL, JENIFER
[b.] July 15, 1984, Hemet, CA; [p.] Steve and Kathy Housel; [ed.] 7th Grade; [pers.] I want people to enjoy my poems as well as I do. I've loved reading all sorts of poems most of my life even though I'm still young. They've influenced me to write; [a.] Bolivar, MO

HOWARD, JUSTIN
[b.] June 30, 1974, Philadelphia, PA; [p.] Robert and Margie Howard; [ed.] Pocono Mountain High School, East Stroodsburg University; [occ.] Student studying to become on elementary school teacher; [pers.] This poem was written for and is dedicated to my one true love and found soul mate, spirit diamantis.; [a.] Tannersville, PA

HOWARD, N. CLIFTON
[pen.] Cliff Howard; [b.] July 6, 1930, Whiteville, KY; [p.] John and Elve Howard; [m.] Joan E. Howard, February 5, 1971; [ch.] Mary, Doug, Angela; [ed.] BA, MA, Rank I in Education minor in Social Work, major in History; [occ.] Retired Counselor for hospital program, Historical Presentation as Abe Lincoln; [memb.] Teacher, Apprentice Auctioneer, Realtor, Association of Abraham Lincoln Presenters; [hon.] Honor as a Military Chaplain, honor as volunteer worker at Lincoln's Birthplace State Park; [oth. writ.] Articles for Hi Time magazine; [pers.] People need help in learning to love.; [a.] Frankfort, KY

HOWELL, ETHEL
[b.] February 12, 1912, Siakiyou County, CA; [p.] Deceased; [m.] Deceased, 1936; [ch.] One daughter; [ed.] (Teachers College) Southern Oregon College; [occ.] Retired from teaching

HUMES, CYNDI
[pen.] Cyn; [b.] October 2, 1978, Hayward, CA; [p.] Charlotte Wachtel; [ed.] St. John's Elementary, Arroyo High School; [occ.] Unemployed graduated this year June 1996; [hon.] Scholarship to Heard Business College; [pers.] I have been influence by the downfalls of society and life itself. Not everything is as it seems.; [a.] San Lorenzo, CA

HUMPHREY, OWEN EVERETT
[b.] October 25, 1920, Wautoma, WI; [p.] Marion and Flora Humphrey; [m.] Billye Cox (Deceased), April 6, 1946; [ch.] Reba (Humphrey) Rick, Ivye Humphrey; [ed.] Wautoma H.S., B.S., Univ. of Wis., Whitewater, M.S. Univ. of Ark., Fayetteville, Ed. Spec. Univ. of Ill., Champaign; [occ.] Retired School Teacher/Administrator; [memb.] Association for Supervision and Curriculum Development (Hon.), National Education Association (Life), Phi Delta Kappa, Kappa Delta Pi, Collinsville Area Theatrical Society, International Society of Poets (Life).; [hon.] Phi Delta Kappa Service Key, 1984, Creativity Recognition Award, 1972, George H. Reavis Associate Award (PDK), 1991, Granite City Area Council PTA Award, 1979, Military Service Awards (Bronze Star, 4 ETO Battle Stars), Biog. sketches: Dict. of Intern. biog., Who's Who in Amer. Educ., Who's Who in Midwest, Who's Who in World, Who's Who in America, Two Thousand Men of Achievement, Dreative and Successful Personalities of the World.; [oth. writ.] Poems published in several anthologies of the National Library of Poetry, Famous Poems of Today. Articles in various IASCD Newsletters, contributor to Illinois School Research, author of The Greening of Gateway East, A History of PDK Chapter 1097.; [pers.] At age 75, my time is largely filled with writing poetry and performing in a local theater group.; [a.] Granite City, IL

HUNTER, CYNTHIA L.
[pen.] Cyndie Hunter; [b.] April 30, 1964, Hot Springs, AZ; [p.] Dwight E. and Leigh E. Hunter; [ed.] Mansfield High, Belmont Univ., Texas Hair Designers; [occ.]

Hair Stylist, Singer, Songwriter; [memb.] Sigma Alpha Iota, Music Fraternity; [hon.] Dean's List; [oth. writ.] 1st published work but has a diverse collection of poems and songs.; [pers.] I write from a personal place and from the heart, letting my emotion guide my pen, making my work often very intimate and unique.; [a.] Nashville, TN

HUNTER, LORI ANN
[b.] April 24, 1960; [m.] Allen Hunter, August 17, 1985; [ch.] Hanna Rose and Lacy Marie; [ed.] High School, Graduated from a course in childrens writing from - The Institute of Childrens Literature; [occ.] Housewife and Mother

HUNTER, MICHAEL W.
[pen.] Miwah; [b.] Memphis, TN; [ed.] BA in Accounting, Memphis State University; [oth. writ.] None published at this time.; [pers.] There is always something you can do to help someone else.; [a.] Birmingham, AL

HUO, XINGHUA
[pen.] Mamie; [b.] Shanghai, China; [ed.] Tongji University; [oth. writ.] Several poems and articles published in newspapers and magazines; [pers.] To simplify life.; [a.] Las Vegas, NV

HUTCHESON, SHARON J.
[b.] November 30, 1975, El Dorado, IL; [p.] Roy Hutcheson and Peggy Jones; [ch.] Clifford Hockensmith; [occ.] Sales Clerk; [oth. writ.] Baby Girl Brittany, Joy Ride In The Snow; [pers.] This poem is dedicated to my sister-in-law Crystal of ten years. She committed suicide March 3, 1996. She lefted a husband and three daughters behind, 9 years, 4 years and 3 years of age. I want to dedicate this in her memory.; [a.] McLeansboro, IL

HYRE, KERRY FAITH ANN-MARIE
[b.] November 29, 1973, Kingston, Jamaica, West Indies; [p.] Vassel and Beryl Hyre; [ed.] St. Mary all age school, (Jamaica, West Indies), The Queen's School (J.W.I), Vocational Foundation, Inc., New York, NY.; [occ.] Word Processor; [memb.] The New York Public Library; [hon.] Junior Achievement in Business, Attendance/Punctuality Expert Vocational Skills, High Achiever.; [oth. writ.] A book compiled of poems and short stories.; [pers.] We all are our own Ambassadors and when we represent ourselves we must exercise our roles to the fullest of our potentials.; [a.] Bronx, NY

INBERG, JUDY
September 6, 1938, Charlotte, N. Carolina; [p.] Harold James & Lillian Rush; [m.] Richard Inberg, 1960; [ch.] Eric, Kirk, Mary, Ellen, & Lee Ann; [ed.] B.A. Elem Education; [occ.] Special Education Teacher; [memb.] Council for Exceptional children, National Education Association, PEO, Wyoming Wildlife Association, Sierra Club, Nature Conservancy; [pers.] One of our sons, Kirk Inberg was killed in a plane crash while tracking a wounded Grzzley Bear in the mountains of Wyoming. Kirk was a Wildlife-Biologist & Game Warden for the Wyo. Game and Fish Dept. He loved all things in nature but had a special place in his heart for Grizzley Bears. He loved the mountains & I wrote this poem in his memory.; [a.] Riverton, WY

JACKSON, BARBARA BENICE MILES
[b.] June 24, 1948, Fort Worth, TX; [p.] C. B. Miles and Maybelle Dugen Miles; [m.] Divorced; [ch.] Tracy Danyell Jackson; [ed.] I.M. Tevell, Class of 1966; [occ.] Head Start, Day Care Association of Ft. Worth and Tarrant County; [memb.] Carter Metropolitan CME, Church; [hon.] State Employee of the year 1990, Usher of the Year for Carter Metropolitan Church; [oth. writ.] Poetry - Atmospheric Conditions, Renewal, Go Your Way, Ancient of Days, Silent Voices, A Sign, Void of

Times, Be Sure Answer, Keep, Time Chanesurs Time, House on Southcrest Lester and see, Verses, Death Comes at Good Will, How Can it Be? The Whole Smith, Point to Remember; [pers.] In great times of sorry and sadness, look up and know.; [a.] Forth Worth, TX

JACKSON, CYNTHIA RANDLE
[b.] February 6, 1959, Brenham, TX; [p.] Mary Graves and Randle Burton; [ch.] Joshua Jeremiah Jackson; [ed.] Brenham High School, AA Degree - Blinn College, BA Degree - North Texas State Univ., Honorary Doctorate Degree - Mt. Zion Bible Institute; [occ.] Business Owner - Errands for U; [memb.] PTO - Local Member, Delta Psi Omega Drama Honorary Soc.; [hon.] Exceptional Co-op Billing Award (Radio, Radio Goal Busters Award, Radio Quota Awards (Sales); [oth. writ.] Many advertising campaigns newspaper articles, radio news reports; [pers.] I feel we were all put on this earth for a specific reason. If we strive to find what that reason is then life will have meaning and in return you will have Peace.; [a.] Bryan, TX

JACKSON, EARNESTINE
[pen.] E. Jackson and/or Crystal; [b.] April 5, Chicago, IL; [p.] Robert and Lucille Jackson; [occ.] Administrative Assistant; [hon.] Golden Poet Award 1990 - Editor's Choice Award - 1996; [oth. writ.] Family, Green and Mother; [pers.] I like to write about everyday events and have currently written 3 novels and 3 short stories.; [a.] Chicago, IL

JACKSON, SHARESE N.
[pen.] Resse Cup, Tweety Bird, Ms. Short; [b.] December 28, 1978, Alliance, OH; [p.] Mary McDonald; [ed.] 12 Grader; [memb.] Church Trustee, School Choir, Student Government, Step Team (Ladies with Class; [hon.] Senior Class President (c/o 1997), selected for Who's Who of America's High School Students; [oth. writ.] I've written several poems but none of them have been published before; [pers.] All things are possible if you believe and trust in God. Through my poems I can express my feelings, I can be who or what ever I want to be, there is no limit; [a.] Carol City, FL

JACKSON, SHELIAH ANN
[b.] Chicago, IL; [p.] Mtrtis Hackett, Walter Hackett Sr.; [m.] Calvin Jackson, March 30, 1983; [ch.] Rashaun Erik; [ed.] Paul L. Dunbar H.S. Governors State University, MA in English (97) (Paul Lawrence Dunbar H.S.); [occ.] Market Research; [memb.] Creative Writers Workshop National Council of Negro Women, St. Paul C.M.E. Church; [hon.] Creative Writing Award, Dean's List; [oth. writ.] Short stories published in local newspapers, magazines; [pers.] My favorite poet is Robert Frost.] I greatly admire how he reflects nature and life in his poetry.] My short stories and poems also deal with the experiences of life; [a.] Richton Park, IL

JACOUTOT, FRANK
[b.] June 14, 1930, New York City, NY; [p.] Frank and Helen Jacoutot; [m.] Amelia Jacoutot, September 3, 1949; [ch.] Susan and Bruce; [ed.] High School; [pers.] Loved ones should be remembered for the good things they gave us is life not fought over for the things they leave behind.; [a.] New York, NY

JAIMESON, JO
[b.] January 28, 1963, Redwood City, CA; [ed.] Elementary and Special Education, Communications and Psychology, Sign Language and Spanish - Brigham Young University, University of Utah, Weber State University; [occ.] Diversity Trainer for American Express, Sign Language Interpreter; [memb.] Word Weavers, International Society of Poetry, Sparrowgrass Poetry Forum, Member of Church of Jesus Christ of Latter Day Saints; [oth. writ.] Published in The New Era, The

Ensign, other National Library of Poetry anthologies and Sparrowgrass Poetry Forum anthologies.; [pers.] I rely heavily on spiritual inspiration and the beauty of nature for my poems. I like to capture moments of time, feelings, and symbolism that can have a lasting effect on my life.; [a.] Orem, UT

JAMES, ETHEL P.
[b.] February 2, 1935, Williamson, NY; [p.] John and Jessie Plyter; [m.] David E. James, April 21, 1962; [ch.] 2 - 1 Boy 31 years - 1 girl 33 years; [ed.] High School Completed; [occ.] Retired; [memb.] First Cumberland Presbyterian Church; [oth. writ.] Yet to be published; [pers.] This cat has been the joy of our lives. He came to us after one had got her and our hearts were still broken.

JAMES, WESLEY
[b.] May 26, 1971, Delta, CO; [p.] Carl James, Judith James; [ed.] Delta High, University of Maryland, Colorado School of Mines; [occ.] Student/Programmer; [hon.] Air Force Meritorious Achievement, Southwest Asia Service Medal, National Defense Medal, Dean's List; [pers.] Romance and chivalry are far from dead. They live on in the hearts and deeds of every poet and every person who reads those words.; [a.] Golden, CO

JANDA, KAY
[b.] February 14, 1942, Cedar Rapids, IA; [p.] Gen Gatto; [ch.] Diane Elizabeth and David Alan; [ed.] Washington Sr. High, Janda North. VA. Comm. College, Sterling Virginia, Cedar Rapids Business Coll.; [occ.] Checker, Bishops Buffet Ced. Rapids, IA; [oth. writ.] Prose, Poetry "The Aher", "Shadow of Greatness", Pigments of the Imagination" Washington High Lit. Pub. The Quill approx 1959-60. First Pub. Approx age 9 - short story local "Gazette".; [pers.] My writings reflect the events, surroundings and emotional state of my life. I'm currently working with my daughter to compile, illustrate and bind my children's poems, lyrics and one short story. This will be for my 2 year old Grandson Alan.; [a.] Cedar Rapids, IA

JEFFERSON, JEANETTE H.
[pen.] J. Harris Jefferson; [b.] January 9, 1943, Charleston, MO; [p.] The Late Alfred Harris and Mrs. Josie Noe Harris; [m.] John L. Jefferson, December 20, 1969; [ch.] Cynthia M., Lynette P., Kevin L. Jefferson, Grandchildren- Kai Latmegan Jefferson, Amber Troupe; [ed.] A.S. Nursing - RN; [occ.] Retired disabled 1993 Univ. of Missouri, Hospital after 30 yrs. Nursing U.M. St. Paul AME Church; [memb.] Frederick Douglas Coalition, ISP American Heart Association, MO., Writers Guild AHA, MO Div Boone Co. Stroke Club.; [hon.] NLP - Outstanding Achievement in Poetry award 1994, 95, 96, Honors - pending publications, The poetry Guild, Famous Poets Society Pub. by NLP several times.; [oth. writ.] Save The Children, Hate Is A Deadly Disease That We Can Cure, Measuring The Cup Within, They Learned It From Us, We Can Affect Change, The Essence Of Me, Mirthless Parody, Memorial TWA Flight 800; [pers.] I am a stroke survivor, a retired disabled RN. It is my sincere desire to write something that will be meaningful to my fellow mother then my living will not be in vain. I also aspire to be a poet for health, education political and social change, my favorite poet. Maya Angelou. I feel blessed despite my side paralysis. I am healing more everyday. My father keeps me strong.; [a.] Columbia, MO

JEFFREY, LINDA L.
[pen.] Johnnie L. Woodall; [b.] September 5, 1955, Idebell, OK; [p.] Jerry E. Newsom & Johnnie L. Steaveson; [m.] Divorced; [ch.] I have 3 children; [ed.] 12th & 1 year college; [occ.] Disabled; [hon.] High School & College; [oth. writ.] The Woodie Book of Prose and Poetry (Unpublished); [a.] Wakita, OK

JEFFRIES, CAROLYN D.
[oth. writ.] Several more poems, and book will be published in the very near future.; [pers.] I give all honor and praise to the almighty God that created the heaven and earth. Special thanks to my sister Lavon who believed in me, and I also give thanks to a few friends that encourage me.; [a.] Chicago, IL

JERMYN, DEBRA C.
[b.] June 28, 1962, Bronx, NY; [m.] Keith J. Jermyn, July 20, 1985; [ch.] Jade Ashley, Jasmine Lynora; [ed.] Hialeah High School, University of South Florida, Tampa, State University of New York at Rochester; [occ.] Independent Fine Jewelry Representative, Freelance artist; [hon.] Semi-finalist in the 1996 North American Open Poetry Contest; [oth. writ.] Soon to be published in a self-help recovery book which I also illustrated.; [pers.] My writings and paintings are to hopefully inspire others towards introspection and the recognition of the human spirit to triumph over adversity. My passion is to bring awareness to people of the devastating effects of childhood abuse and to help end it.; [a.] Woodway, TX

JIPSON, SHARON M.
[b.] November 7, 1957, Wilmington, DC; [p.] Ella Mae Grose and Carl Grose; [ch.] Maria Lynn and Timothy Warren; [ed.] Christiana High School, Goldey Beacom College; [occ.] Administrative Assistant; [memb.] Professional Secretaries, Int'l President, Layhawk Chp. National Legal Secretaries Association; [a.] Lawrence, KS

JOHNSON, CATHERINE
[pen.] Seajay; [b.] August 27, 1978, Cincinnati; [p.] Chris and Carol Johnson; [ed.] Winton Woods High School - '97; [occ.] Student, Editor of the School Newspaper; [pers.] I use a lot of symbolism in my poetry. You may have to read it a few times before you understand its meaning.

JOHNSON, ERWIN
[b.] May 20, 1925, Roscommon County, MI; [p.] Flay and Emma Johnson; [m.] Mildred Jean (Deceased), January 25, 1958; [ed.] Elementary, Eighth Grade; [occ.] Retired as Factory Worker and Licensed Minister; [memb.] Victory Church; [hon.] Eternal Life through Christ; [oth. writ.] The Only Hope, A Tribute To Mother, God's Perfect Gift, My Wife The Bum, God's Answer Two Roads, The Road That Leads To Nowhere; [pers.] Trust in the Lord not on your own understanding.; [a.] Grand Rapids, MI

JOHNSON, JAMES
[b.] November 27, 1959, Philadelphia; [p.] Robert and Mary Johnson; [m.] Elizabeth Johnson, November 12, 1993; [ch.] Joshua and Jessica; [ed.] Delhaas High; [occ.] Printer; [oth. writ.] One book - The Education of a Honky."; [pers.] The big influences on my writing are three MS Melville, Menken and Henry Miller. They helped verify what I always felt, that literature is life and vice versa, every thought and experience can be turned to accent. The literary life is the best life.; [a.] Chelmsford, MA

JOHNSON, JANICE A.
[b.] January 11, 1950, Boston, MA; [p.] Margaret and Clarence Davidson; [m.] Paul Johnson, September 12, 1980; [ed.] Jamaica Plain High School; [occ.] Housewife; [oth. writ.] Although I have other writings this was the first and only one I had ever submitted to anyone.; [pers.] This was not only a very personal subject, it was one I hope will help others to face their fears, and know they can win!; [a.] Brockton, MA

JOHNSON, LUVENIA
[pen.] Williams; [b.] October 24, 1938, Savannah, GA; [p.] Ernest and The Late Daisy Williams; [m.] The Late Elton Johnson, December 12, 1958; [ch.] The Late Gwendolyn Johnson, Katrina McCann, Dennis Marion Johnson, Andre McCann; [ed.] Have Home High School, ICS School of Correspondence - Day Care Certificate; [occ.] National Church Mother of Christian Way Holiness Unto the Lord; [memb.] Christian Way Holiness Unto the Lord; [hon.] Reach out Prison Ministry, Youth Dept of St. John COGIC; [pers.] "Always remember when all else has failed, God was then, is now, and always will be your friend. So try him now not later."; [a.] Atlanta, GA

JOHNSON, PENNY
[pen.] Penny Johnson; [b.] July 1, 1940, Danville, KY; [p.] Irene Sebastian and Buforo Carr; [m.] William Evan Johnson, July 15, 1958; [ch.] Buddy Johnson and Robbie Johnson; [ed.] Famous writers school graduate - 1967 - Newspaper Institute America - grad. NY. 1969; [occ.] Freelance writer; [memb.] International Society of Poets - International Order of Merit - Member Order International Fellowship Peale Center Christian Living; [hon.] Golden - Ruby - Emerald Poet - Semi-Finalist North American Poetry open - honorary Doctor of Letters, London England - Who's Who in poetry - woman of the year, A.B.I. - Woman of the Year International Biographic Centre - Cambridge, England; [oth. writ.] "Awesome", "The Balance of Nature", "The Best Choice", "My Husband, My Sons", "Fall's Fabulous Gifts", "Sensational Season", "Surprise", "The Symbol", "The Purpose of Poet"; [pers.] Poetry makes the world a lovely place, promotes understanding - makes us sad makes us happy - uplifts us - who can do without it?; [a.] Lexington, KY

JOHNSON, TAMMY L.
[pen.] Lyn Ora; [b.] December 17, 1957; [p.] Rohalia Johnson, Dorothy Saltus-Johnson; [m.] Albert Johnson Jr., July 13, 1980; [ch.] Stephanie Maria and Jason Gerard; [ed.] Eisensenhower Senior High School, Cameron University in Lawton, OK.; [hon.] 1st Runner Up Miss Lawton; [pers.] I have been encouraged to write both poetry and children's short stories by my husband Albert and initially by my mother-in-law Josephine L. Johnson.; [a.] Lawton, OK

JOHNSON, VICTORIA
[pen.] Tori Lite; [b.] December 10, 1952, Alexandria, LA; [p.] Waiter and Phyllis Simmons; [m.] Deceased; [ch.] Jeneen, Andria and Michael; [ed.] ACHS - Roselle, NJ WWA SVRS - Westfield, NJ, The New School NY, NY; [occ.] Sr. Clerk, Typist; [memb.] American Heart Assoc.; [oth. writ.] Presently writing a novel and here written songs.; [pers.] Give me a topic I'll give you a poem to: Tear Smile or Smurk; [a.] Rahway, NJ

JOHNSON-WHITED, SHELLY
[b.] February 5, 1963, Marion, IN; [p.] Bernie and Sally Johnson; [m.] Scott, August 5, 1989; [ch.] Taylor-Marie (2), Christopher (5), Justin (11), Jason (17); [ed.] Marion High School, Ball State University (BS) 1986, Ball State Univ. (MA) 1987; [occ.] Special Ed. Teacher, Hamilton Southeastern Middle School Fishers, In.; [memb.] National Honor Society, International Behaviorology Assoc. CEC; [hon.] Dean's List (BSU) Stephen Bufton Memorial Award; [oth. writ.] Poetry published in "Of Moonlight And Wishes", Several articles for local newspapers, Developed The Add Connection, a newsletter for parents of Add children.; [pers.] I try to write material that is upbeat and relaxing. In hopes of, one day developing a series of children's books. I have been greatly influenced and encourage by my parents.; [a.] Noblesville, IN

JOLLY, FRANCES
[b.] May 29, 1937, Kentucky; [p.] Joe and Maude Walkup; [m.] Dead, June 13, 1952; [ch.] Seven girls; [ed.] 4th; [occ.] Retired; [hon.] Won third prize playing French harp at the good old days in Cave City, KY that was in the year 1989; [oth. writ.] I've written a story about my self in 1955 I sent it to the true story magazine in New York I received a check for twenty five dollars.; [pers.] I play an electric organ I play by ear. I cannot read music. I really like music and writing.; [a.] Glasgow, KY

JONES, DALE
[pen.] Dale Jones; [b.] October 9, 1979, Bossier City, LA; [p.] Roger Jones and Velicia Hubbard; [ed.] St. Stephens Episcopal School, Austin, TX; [occ.] Student; [pers.] We exist only to ourselves.; [a.] Nacogdoches, TX

JONES, ELIZABETH A.
[pen.] E. Jones; [b.] February 16, 1984, Phelps County; [p.] Ray Jones and Joelle Jones; [ed.] I am up to the 7th grade and I am a straight "A" student; [a.] Dixon, MO

JONES, LACI LEE
[b.] September 12, 1982, Lufkin, TX; [p.] Michael and Judy Jones; [ed.] Currently a Freshman at Corrigan-Camden High School in Corrigan Texas; [memb.] Kyssed Club, High School Band, Corrigan FFA, Varsity Cheerleader, Freshman Class Reporter; [hon.] Have had an "A" average for 8 years, Member of the USA received academic recognition for Tasp Scores.

JONES, TIFFANY
[pen.] Tiffy; [b.] March 4, 1983, Baltimore, MD; [p.] John Jones, Mattie Jones; [ed.] Hamilton Middle School 8th Grade; [occ.] Student; [memb.] Inner Harbor Church of God; [hon.] Student Achievement Award, Academic Excellence Upton School, Outstanding Achievement Roll, Honor Roll; [oth. writ.] Other poems and short stories.; [pers.] When I write I try to express my inner thoughts and feelings to put on paper so other people can maybe understand what I see in life.; [a.] Baltimore, MD

JONES, WILLIAM H.
[pen.] Captain J, Bill Jones, William Henry Jones, W. H. Jones; [b.] April 1, 1924, Black Diamond, WA; [p.] Helenor Jones - Father Deceased; [m.] Barbara A. Jones, May 17, 1960; [ch.] Robert Jeffery Jones, Denise Lynn Williams; [ed.] B.A. San Diego State Naval School of Hospital Administration; [occ.] Captain, U.S. Navy (Ret.); [memb.] Federal Health Care Executives, Fleet Reserve Association, Distinguished Member International Society of Poets; [hon.] Legion of Merit (navy), Numerous Service Medals and awards, Graduated with honors 5 military schools, Advanced from Apprentice Seaman to Captain during Naval career, Editor's Choice Award 1995 (1), Editor's Choice Award 1996 (7); [oth. writ.] Sparrowgrass Poetry Forum Endless Thought, Am I Worthy, Treasured Poems of America - April 1996, In His Wisdom We Must Trust, Garden Workshop, Sequins on the Floor, Poetic Voices of America - June 1996, Symphony of the Night, Charlie, Lady of my Dreams, Dearest Mom, Treasured Poems of America - August 1996, A Humble Apology, Customary Places and Faces, To Hell with Diamonds, Man's Best Friend, Dreams I've Had, Poetic Voices of America - October 1996, The Window of His Soul, The Looking Glass, Believer of Deceiver, Chiqui is Her Name, Sweet Pixie, Years of Joy, Treasured Poems of America - December 1996. The National Library of Poetry: Songs Unsung, Beyond the Stars - Fall 1996, Catacombs of the Night, Best Poems of 1996, Stop and Smell the Roses, Spirit of the Age, Home Alone, A Muse to Follow, Devil's Wind, A Tapestry of Thought, Ascent from Hell, Where The Dawn Lingers, No Perfect World,

Through the Hourglass, Please Another Chance, Across the Universe - Summer 1996, Poems Unpublished, Embers, Across the Universe - Fall 1996, Lonely Is the Poet, Lyrical Heritage - Winter 1996, The Hand that Stroked my Brow, Best Poems of 1996 - Fall 1996, Embers, Of Sunshine and Daydreams - August 1996, Lonely is the Poet, Lyrical Heritage, You Were a Good Man Billy Jones, Frost at Midnight - Winter 1996.; [pers.] I believe in personal achievement, inspiring others to fulfill their dreams, at peace with self and others, all with a sense of humor, dedication and perspective.; [a.] Lake San Marcos, CA

JOSEPH, INGE
[b.] November 14, 1920, Germany; [m.] Warner Joseph, December 21, 1940; [ch.] One; [ed.] Elem. and High Schools in Europe. Professionals Schooling in Dental Assisting and travel; [occ.] Part-time travel agent; [memb.] Non-profit fundraising organizations; [hon.] Various for several volunteer organizations work; [a.] Pound Ridge, NY

JUSTICE, PATRICIA JEAN
[pen.] "P.J."; [b.] May 1, 1944, Dover, OH; [p.] Mr. and Mrs. John T. Bair (Deceased); [m.] Gary M. Justice Sr., August 14, 1965; [ch.] Nicholas (married), Toni daughter in law, one granddaughter Gerald, Gary Jr., Bonnie (married) Bob son in law, one grandson and two step grandsons; [ed.] Graduated Dover High School 1962, Business School two years in Baberton, Ohio, Worked at Timken Co in Canton, Ohio; [occ.] New Housewife and Nanny; [memb.] Saint Clements Catholic Church, distinguished Member of the International Society of Poets; [hon.] Won Tuscarawas County Canning and Preservation Contest, Won for the State of "Ohio" too. Won Honorable Mention for Chili Contest. Four H Winfield Willing Workers Club five and ten year pins. A lot of 1st place blue ribbons, all cooking and preservation catagories; [oth. writ.] Published: "A Tribute To My Brother" in the anthology, "A Sea of Treasures" and "A Tribute to Grandpa" in the best poems of 1996; [pers.] I love to reflect on life, all aspects and enjoy reading the poets corner, the books on anthology and magazines and papers where short poems are written.; [a.] Massillon, OH

KABELIS, ALEX
[b.] August 11, 1977; [pers.] Angels cry no mercy for truth yields one word. Inspired by: William Wallace

KALINE, JENNIFER E.
[pen.] Jennifer E. Kaline; [b.] March 29, 1974, Baltimore; [p.] Nancy and Marty Friedl; [m.] Michael S. Kaline, March 24, 1996; [ed.] High School Diploma, and Currently in School (AACC) for Pre-Pharmacy. Hoping to become a pharmacist; [occ.] Pharmacy-Tech.; [memb.] Galiee Lutheran Church; [pers.] I have only written about things, which have greatly effected my life, and the way of view it.; [a.] Pasadena, MD

KAMPFE, DOROTHEA J. L.
[pen.] Dorothea Kampfe; [b.] June 27, 1923, Bertrand, NE; [p.] H. H. and Olivia Ebmeier; [m.] Reuben, May 21, 1994; [ch.] Randall Reuben, Steven James; [ed.] Have Teachers Education, Taught at 2 Bertrand, Nebraska Elementary Schools, (member American Lutheran Church) W.O.C. teachers, Nebraska Teachers World Org. China Teachers, published for Nat'l. Porcelain Artist and Lessons written in Art.; [occ.] Local China Painting and Watercolor Seminars, Teacher in Arts, retired Activity Director 3 years, at Local Nursing Home.; [memb.] Local Porcelain Artists Publications, Pony Express Art Club, Extension Club, Church Volunteer, Local Porcelain Artist Club of World Organization Porcelain Artist; [hon.] I taught at World Snow in Tampa, Florida also at Nebraska Sate Conventions, A Bridge Clubs Members.; [oth. writ.] Lessons in

Art and Porcelain China Painting Magazine.; [pers.] I am an avid reader of Literary Publications and the Cultural Arts, lectures and influenced by instructors of advanced education.; [a.] Gothenburg, NE

KAMPSCHROEDER, HELEN B.
[b.] July 26, 1934, Beloit, KS; [p.] Perry and Mary Spurlock Betz; [m.] Walter G. Kampschroeder Jr., July 4, 1959; [ch.] Karlin Dale, Daryl Walter; [ed.] Three years at University of Kansas (Lawrence) English and Latin, completed NIA (Newspaper Institute of America) writing course over 30 yrs. ago; [occ.] Proofreader of scientific and scholarly journals (Allen Press, Lawrence, KS) (30 years); [memb.] Lawrence Scrabbl Club; [hon.] While a freshman at KU, I won first prize among Hometown Correspondents for news columns I sent to Mitchell County (KS) Newspapers regarding students from that county who were attending the University.; [pers.] I've tried to instill in my sons that - trite as it may be - "the best things in life are free," or nearly so, and that a library card should be considered one of their most prized possessions.; [a.] Lawrence, KS

KANE, MARY
[pen.] May; [b.] June 25, 1960, Brooklyn; [p.] Dolores and Howard Gifford; [m.] Robert aka Bob M. Kane, May 1, 1990; [ch.] Allision, Melissa and Mathew; [ed.] Associated degree in Early Childhood Education. BA in Elementary Special Ed., Brooklyn College; [occ.] Vice President of M.A.R. Optical DBA Eyes on Ave. 'U'; [hon.] Certificate of Acknowledgment of famous poet of 1996 by Famous Poet Society of 1996. By Famous Poet Society for "My Son".; [oth. writ.] "My Love" In Whispers of the Dark, World Art Publishing, Endless Harmony, "Our Wish", feelings Audrey poem "A Haiku", Sparrow Grass "The Night", Poetic Voices of America. Many others and more.; [pers.] Thank you to my family the 'Mouse on the Hill' is for all the "Survivors" I am one. I dedicate my good life and the person I am to my love Bob.; [a.] Brooklyn, NY

KANTER, IRENE L.
[pen.] Irene Kanter; [b.] April 30, 1918, New York City, NY; [p.] Sarah and Max Kupersmith; [m.] Divorced, July 30, 1939; [ch.] Two daughters: Betty Siporick and Jean Ruback, Grandson: Josh Rubach; [ed.] Graduated: Geo. Washington High School, N.Y.C., N.Y. and Graduated Secretarial and Business School, New York City, N.Y.; [occ.] Retired Medical Secretary; [memb.] In my Youth Member of Girl Scouts of America, Later became an Outstanding Scout Leader and Worked to Promote the Organization/Volunteer Unit at Columbia Presbyterian Hospital N.Y.C., N.Y.; [hon.] Member - AARP Two Editors Choice Awards for 1995 and 1996. I was nominated by the International Society of Poets as one of their Poets of the year for 1996. I was to be honored also with two separate special awards at their convention in Aug. 1996. Unfortunately, due to illness at that time, and my golden years of 78, I was unable to attend to receive these awards; [oth. writ.] The National Library of Poetry published and recorded for their sound of poetry, poems: Spring 1995, Christmas, The Five Stages of Life, plus will soon published poem the essence of love. I had four poems published by sparrow grass poetry forum, and numerous ones in seniors today magazine, a local publication serving hudson, bergen, passaic, and essex countless in New Jersey; [pers.] I began writing poetry two years ago, at age 76. I'm inspired by loved for my daughters and grandson, Josh. I strive to be uplifting and give a little pleasure by injecting humor. It can make people smile or laugh through poetry I can express innermost feelings and thoughts reflecting on life, love, family, friends, and the magnificent beauty of nature. But, most of all, poetry affords me the opportunity to make a difference.; [a.] Guttenberg, NJ

KARAKOSTAS, KRISTEN
[b.] December 25, 1985, Washington, DC; [p.] Hillary Kirchman, Frank Karakostas; [ed.] Goshen Elementary School 1-5, Forest Oak Middle School and Kindergarten at Whetstone Elementary; [occ.] Student; [hon.] For Swim Team I received 2 heat winner ribbons, 3 first places, 4 seconds, 1 fifth and 3 personal bests! For 9th grade I received an honorable mention for field day a presidential award for outstanding academic achieved my peers compliments award, an award for completing elementary school, an award for being in the Goshen Chorus, participating in student government, 2 peer Mediation Awards, an advanced band award just for participation, science expo award for participation, participating in the Math Olympiad course, an award for outstanding performance on the morning school broadcast show "A.M. Goshen", an award for completing the Dare Curriculum! For Fourth Grade an award for completing the 4th grade another for being a questioning and motivating learner in Math, another award for service in the student Government an award for completion of Peer Mediating Training. Another award for participating in the Science Eupo, a perfect attendance award! For 3rd grade. An award for a class spelling bee that I made through to the final selection, another award for winning the 3rd grade spelling bee with each final selection for every class with a first place ribbon! Another for being on art helper from the art teacher, another for the student government! An award for participation in the young author's contest! For 2nd grade. An award for a successful completion on the study of Hawaii! Another for being in the Goshen reading olympus. For 1st grade. An award for field day.; [oth. writ.] Poems: Winter, The Icy Wind, The Sun, The Lovebirds Song, Nature, and Flash Boom Patter Patter! There are so many stories I have written paper isn't enough to list them!; [a.] Gathrustburg, MD

KARANDOS, WILLIAM J.
[b.] April 25, 1949, Indianapolis, IN; [p.] George and Rose Karandos; [m.] Deborah C. Karandos, January 28, 1988; [hon.] Veteran Vietnam, US Marine Corp 1968-1970; [pers.] Special love and thanks to my wife Deborah and to the memory of Maj. Joseph C. Bevel USAF. And all who served our country.

KAREEM, RASHAD
[b.] March 10, 1981, Jacksonville, FL; [p.] Dedrea and Stevie Carter, Muhammed Kareem; [ed.] Valley Lutheran High School; [memb.] New Covenant Christian Center Church; [pers.] My desire is to glorify God in my writing, just as he has glorified me with this gift. My goal is to be a vessel God uses to bring salvation to many.; [a.] Saginaw, MI

KASTLER, PAT
[pen.] Patrick Joe; [b.] January 15, 1960, Raton, NM; [p.] Paul and Marlanne Kastler; [m.] Divorced; [ed.] B.S. Civil Engineering from Northern Arizona University (NAU); [occ.] Self Employed doing Computer Design Services; [hon.] Residence Hall Council - Treasure and Vice President NAU; [oth. writ.] "Images" - "Voice Within" - Anthology "Happy Mother's Day" - "Ebbing Tide" - Anthology "Down Mexico" - "Best of 90's poems" - Anthology.; [pers.] This poem was written for all the men devoted to the promise keepers organization, who are striving to be better husbands, fathers, boyfriends and christian men. May God bless our nation, all the promise keepers and all the kind - hearted women in our country.; [a.] Phoenix, AR

KATONA, ROBERT
[pen.] Robert Katona; [b.] March 16, 1947, Athens, OH; [p.] Arthur Katona and Verna Katona; [m.] Jo Bell Katona, 1980; [ch.] Katherine and John; [ed.] Golden High, University of Colorado; [occ.] Artist; [memb.]

North American Falconers Association; [hon.] Society of Illustrators - N.Y., Grolla D'Ora - Italy, On The cutting Edge - N.Y.; [oth. writ.] Feature article Southwest Art; [pers.] A man with imagination has wings - he can fly; [a.] Golden, CO

KATZENBERGER, SHARI LYNN
[b.] July 26, 1984, Great Falls, MT; [p.] Kevin and Virginia; [ed.] Canyon Creek School Billings, MT; [occ.] 7th Grade Student; [memb.] Basket Ball Team Junior High Band; [hon.] Principal List, Honor Roll, Gymnastics Awards Basketball Awards, Montana Fair Ribbons for School Work; [a.] Billings, MT

KAUFMAN, AMY P.
[pen.] A.P.K.; [b.] August 19, 1973, Worcester; [p.] Abee Arlene Kaufman; [ed.] 10th grade dropped out continuous education getting GED then going to college; [occ.] PT work at pet store Ritzworld on Nahck; [hon.] Trophies from playing 6 fun Framingham State champ medal 1st place; [oth. writ.] Poetry; [pers.] I am scared to try for I my fail. Yet there is a chance I may sail. I see not with my eyes but with my heart, my soul, and my mind. I am not blind.; [a.] Framingham, MA

KEARSE, TATINA E.
[pen.] Tee-Tee; [b.] July 19, 1974, Asbury Park, NJ; [p.] Johnnie Mae Kearse; [ed.] Graduated from Sweetwater Union High School; [occ.] Sales Person; [hon.] Authors Merit Award; [oth. writ.] I have written several poems that have never been submitted for publication consideration. I have also written a children's book and adult. (also unpublished).; [pers.] I would like to thank my mom for all the support she gave me growing up and the strength she showed us. I would also like to thank my special friend Chad for his compassion. And my boyfriend Lawrence Lloyd for his encouragement and love.; [a.] Chula Vista, CA

KEATHLEY, MICHELLE D.
[b.] January 30, 1970, Jacksonville, FL; [p.] Alan Brinkley (Father), Linda Kammann (Mother), Mike (Step Father); [m.] Onnie Keathley, December 28, 1992; [ch.] Daniel and Michael Kinser and Onnie Keathley; [ed.] High School Graduate; [occ.] Housewife; [memb.] Boy Scouts of America; [oth. writ.] Several different poems none of which have been published; [pers.] To strive to be the best parent and citizen as I can and continue to write poems this poem is dedicated to my step dad.; [a.] Jacksonville, FL

KEEFE, ROBERT
[pen.] R. Jay; [b.] April 23, 1932, Boston, MA; [p.] Catherine and Frank; [m.] Kay, January 19, 1957; [ch.] Kathy, Maureen, Susan, Karen, Mary Ann, Jenny and Bob; [ed.] Quincy High, Holy Cross College (Quincy, MA), (Worcester, MA); [occ.] Retired, Health Care Worker; [hon.] Dean's List at Holy Cross; [oth. writ.] Articles in local newspapers other poems.; [pers.] Writing good thoughts is a positive influence to develop self-esteem in ourselves and others. They have a lasting quality.; [a.] Vernon Hills, IL

KEITH, BARBARA S.
[b.] Chicago, IL; [p.] Harry E. and Barbara Schaeffer; [m.] Robert B. Keith (Deceased), December 6, 1941; [ch.] Bonnie Lynne; [ed.] High School and P.G Courses; [occ.] Homemaker and volunteer; [memb.] Rockford Writer's Guild; [hon.] World of poetry The National Library of Poetry; [oth. writ.] Poet's Corner Local Newspaper Waterbury Press Rockford Revue; [pers.] All that is has ever been yet to be discovered.; [a.] Rockford, IL

KELLEY, SHARON LEE
[b.] December 4, 1941, Utica, NY; [p.] Lee G. and Vera Byrns; [ed.] New Hartford High 1959, Cortland College (BS) 1963, University of Iowa (MA) 1969, Effective Teaching Workshops, Attending National Conventions, and Continually updating with courses relevant to teaching; [occ.] Physical Education Teacher, Fowler Elementary School, Gouverneur, NY; [memb.] Lifetime member in AAHPERD (American Alliance of Health Physical Education, Recreation and Dance), NYSHAPERD (New York State Association of Health, Physical Education Recreation and Dance) Gouverneur Teachers Association, National Education Association, New York State Teachers Association; [hon.] Outstanding Aquatic Leadership by American Red Cross, 1965, presenter at National AAHPERD Conference, Seattle, Washington 1970, received replication grant to improve fitness in Gouverneur Central Schools, 1979, received mini grant to enhance motor abilities in children, 1979; [oth. writ.] Poems published in school newsletter and poems and speeches written for educators, students and outstanding individuals on various occasions.; [pers.] I believe in the preservation of our natural environment, teaching and learning throughout life a long with the importance of humor sport, play and wellness. I have been greatly influenced by my parents, by Barbara Jensen, Mildred Barnes, Bonnie Bettinger, Lauren Shuman and Abbot Legnard along with students and friends who inspire me in my writing.; [a.] Gouverneur, NY

KELLY, BETTY
[b.] September 4, 1921, Lincoln, NE; [p.] Ludwig M. Larsen and Bessie A. Tyler; [m.] Larry Kelly, August 9, 1947; [ch.] Jo Ann Patrice, Gary Lawrence, Pamela Jean; [ed.] Jackson High School Grad. 1938; University of Nebraska B. Sci. 1943; University of Nebraska MA 1947; [occ.] Housewife; [memb.] Towne Club at University of Nebraska; Faculty at Teachers College Univ. of Nebraska; Senior Citizens Club Los Alamitosa City nearby; [hon.] Had one short story on Christmas in a foreign land published about Dec. 1944 in France during Wars — only published in a small local paper. There were 3 chosen and mine was one of them. I'm only an amateur writer.; [oth. writ.] Society page on daily Nebraska at Univ. of Nebraska Publicity Chairman for Veter-Anns 1946-47 Univ. of Nebraska; Publicity for PTA in Monterey Park, CA at Grandview Elementary School where my children went. Publicity for 5 newspapers for district scouting for both boys and girls.; [pers.] I mostly write poems about my own family to each child on their special occasions. I believe all children can become good citizens and enjoy the world if it is kept safe in years ahead.; [a.] Long Beach, CA

KELLY, DOT HUTCHINSON
[b.] Clover, SC; [p.] Daniel Noah Platt, Margaret Pendleton Platt; [m.] Lawrence J. Kelly, October 8, 1994; [ch.] Karen Hutchinson McRae, R. Eric Hutchinson; [ed.] Education Specialist in Administration 1986, Winthrop University, Rock Hill, SC, Master of Arts in Teaching 1972, Winthrop University, Rock Hill, SC, Bachelor of Science in Elementary Education 1964, Winthrop University, Rock Hill, SC, Rock Hill High School, Rock Hill, SC - Diploma. South Carolina Certification Areas: Elementary Principal, Elementary Teacher, Elementary Supervisor, Media Specialist; [occ.] Temporary Instructor (EDU 449) 8/1995 (present), Winthrop University, Rock Hill, SC - also serve as area Coordinator for Interns. Temporary Instructor (EDU 180) 1/1994 - 4/1995, Winthrop University, Rock Hill, SC. Winthrop Area Coordinator for Interns, fall semester 1993 and 1994, Winthrop University, Rock Hill, SC. Principal 1986-1993, Lesslie Elementary School, Rock Hill, SC. Principal 1979-1986, Finley Road Elementary, Rock Hill, SC. Reme-

dial Math Teacher 1974-1979, Finley Road Elementary, Rock Hill, SC. Sixth-Grade Teacher 1969-1974, Richmond Drive Elementary, Rock Hill, SC. Librarian 1964-1969, Richmond Drive Elementary, Rock Hill, SC. Librarian (for three schools) 1964-1965, Rosewood Elementary, Richmond Drive Elementary and Finley Road Elementary, Rock Hill, SC. Secretary, Home Economics Department 1950-1953, Winthrop University, Rock Hill, SC; [memb.] South Carolina Association of School Administrators, South Carolina Elementary and Middle School Principals, Palmetto Reading Council, Association for Supervision and Curriculum Development, First Presbyterian Church, Rock Hill, SC; [oth. writ.] Poem, Rear View Mirror slated for publication fall, 1996 in of Sunshine and Daydreams. Am currently working on my first fiction book for children; [pers.] Given the interest, imagination, recollections, desire and motivation to write, thoughts and ideas can be organized in a form that provides for great personal satisfaction.; [a.] Rock Hill, SC

KELLY, LOIS J.
[b.] June 18, 1951, St. Albans, NY; [p.] Francis and Adella J. Kelly; [ch.] Sean and Mark Herrick; [ed.] Clifton H.S., Clifton NJ Florida Southern College; [memb.] Assoc. for Gravestone Studies National Museum of the American Indian Fitzwilliam Historical Society, Fitzwilliam Garden Club; [pers.] Appreciate the world around you, listen to nature.; [a.] Fitzwilliam, NH

KENNEDY, ANN
[pen.] Azurite Aura; [b.] December 3, 1947, Terre Haute, IN; [p.] Betty and Bud Brussell; [ed.] Graduate Indiana State University 1969, B.S. Physical Ed. 1970 - American Airlines Flight School; [occ.] Caregiving/Training Horses, Caregiving Dogs and Cats. Living in integrity and joy.; [memb.] Kahilu Theater Jr. Guild, Kamuela, HI; [hon.] 1989 - Travel Director of the years - S.H. Motivation and Travel; [oth. writ.] Small Collection of original poems written in 1996 (non-published).; [pers.] It is my intention to project the light of consciousness and energy from my higher self to fulfill my "contract as an inhabitant on the planet at his time by being in service to humanity, to animals, a nd to Mother Earth.; [a.] Kapaau, HI

KENNEDY, ANTHONY DUANE
[pen.] A. D. Kennedy; [b.] September 2, 1975, Boston, MA; [ed.] Lincoln Sudbury High; [occ.] Cellular Phone Technician; [oth. writ.] Two books of poetry not yet published.; [pers.] It is my belief that you must know God before you can know yourself.; [a.] Roxbury, MA

KENNY, JOSEPHINE M.
[b.] December 12, 1904, Ireland; [m.] Deceased, February 18, 1925; [ch.] Four sons and one daughter; [ed.] Grade school; [occ.] I am 92 and live with my daughter; [hon.] Who's Who In Poetry for 1978 for two winning poems, The Jewel and How Great, these poems will remain a permanent historical record of achievements made in poetry through distribution to the U.S. Library of Congress of Washington D.C. and Libraries and Universities World Wide.; [a.] Brighton, MI

KEOWN, SHERRY
[b.] July 9, 1960, Detroit; [p.] Charles and Helen Weiss; [m.] David, September 22, 1978; [memb.] Aspca, Humane Society, World Wildlife Fund; [oth. writ.] God for a Day, Splashed in Red, Freedom of Horses, Eyes of a Child, Kingdom on the Sea, Halloween; [pers.] Let your mind be your guide. Relax and let the Images flow.; [a.] Warren, MI

KERCHNER, RYAN
[pen.] Ryan David Kerchner; [b.] November 3, 1979, Spring Valley, IL; [p.] Douglas and Deborah Kerchner; [ed.] Currently Senior in High School (Hall High School, in Spring Valley, IL); [occ.] Student; [hon.] Bureau County Young Authors; [pers.] In most of my writing, I try to give an emotion substance as if it were a living breathing creature. I am to make the reader the same emotions written into my writing.; [a.] Dalzell, IL

KERN, LAURA ANN
[b.] February 29, 1960, Walla Walla, WA; [p.] Dale Ross, Toni Ross; [m.] Kenneath M. Kern, May 26, 1986; [ch.] Joseph Andrew Kern; [ed.] Walla Walla High School, Walla Walla, WA; [pers.] As this poem holds a very special meaning to me, I'd like it dedicated to our son, Joseph. You've touched my life so from the day you came home to us from Vietnam, when we adopted you that I was inspired to express my love for you in a poem.; [a.] Walla Walla, WA

KERR, LEANDRA LEE
[pen.] Tweety; [b.] May 5, 1979, Indianapolis; [p.] Wanda K. Kerr, David Lee Kerr; [ed.] Jr. High: Longfellow JH #28 High School: Tech (ATHS) as of now I am still in school and will graduate High School in 1997; [occ.] I have been and will be working at Duffens Optical; [hon.] I have accumulated High honor Roll in the past at school I have been accepted in Who's Who of High School Students in America 1996 and 1993 All-American Scholar Directory.; [oth. writ.] I have written many poems and stories, but as of now none are published. I do plan on trying to publish more.; [pers.] The only other thing I would like to mention is that I am planning on marriage after I graduate to J. F. Workman Jr. and I would like to thank my dad for taking me into entering this contest.; [a.] Indianapolis, IN

KERSTEN, JOELEN ELIZABETH
[b.] August 14, 1979, Livonia, MI; [p.] John Kersten, Helen Krzeminski; [ed.] Erikson Elementary, East Middle School, Canton High School; [occ.] Papa Romano's, Salad Maker; [hon.] Swimming, Flute; [pers.] Poems published in school newsletters.; [a.] Canton, MI

KERSTEN, MARK CHARLES
[b.] August 18, 1986, Livonia, MI; [p.] John Kersten and Helen Krzeminski; [ed.] Erikson Elementary, Bently Elementary; [occ.] Student; [oth. writ.] Poems published in School Newsletters; [pers.] I Love to write poetry and stories.; [a.] Canton, MI

KESTEL, SARAH
[b.] December 14, 1981, Cincinnati, OH; [p.] Martin A. Kestel III and April K. Caudill; [occ.] 9th Grade Student, Princeton High School; [hon.] Finalist in Ohio State Power of the Pen Tournament 1995, Honor Roll, 1996, Presidential Academic Fitness Award, 1994; [pers.] I've written lots of poetry, but none of it was really meant for others. Now that my work is going to be seen by others, my hope is that the love of Jesus Christ will shine through what I have written. 2 Timothy 1:7-8.; [a.] Cincinnati, OH

KEY, CHERYL ANN
[b.] October 15, 1972, Arcadia, FL; [p.] Donald J. and Patricia Ann Key; [ed.] Bachelor of Science Business Administration, Finance from University of Central Florida, Sarasota High School; [pers.] Peace and love; [a.] Sarasota, FL

KIAUSAS, ELIZABETH
[b.] March 13, 1979; [p.] Leonard and Kathleen Kiausas; [pers.] This poem was written in remembrance of my Grandfather, Robert Morrison. I am very proud to not

only let his memory live in my heart, but also on paper for everyone else to share and experience the close relationship the two of us held in our hearts.; [a.] Morris Plains, NJ

KILLINGER, NANCY
[b.] March 5, 1968, Blytheville, AR; [p.] Kenneth McDonald, Carolyn Thurmond; [m.] Frank Killinger, January 1, 1994; [ch.] Zachary McDonald, Amber Killinger, Rachel Killinger; [ed.] G.E.D.; [occ.] Home maker; [pers.] I started writing poems at a early age as a way of expressing my inner thoughts. Poetry has continued in my life to be a inspiration through out the years.; [a.] Parma, MO

KIMBALL, KIMBERLY
[pen.] Kim Kimball; [b.] June 26, 1980, Honolulu, HI; [p.] Philip Kimball, Wha Kimball; [ed.] Clearwater High School (still in school); [oth. writ.] Articles for the terrapin times; [pers.] My poetry consists of strong personal feelings that everyday people face. I enjoy the fact that many are able to relate to my writings. I have been greatly influenced by Walt Whitman, Jim Morrison, my parents and friends.; [a.] Clearwater, FL

KIMMINS, BERNARD
[pen.] C. B. Kimmins; [b.] February 13, 1944, Atlantic City; [p.] Paul and Eileen; [m.] Allison, June 7, 1986; [ch.] Bryn Mirielle (20), Brielle Autumn (6); [ed.] Cardval Dougherty HS Phila., St. Joseph's College, B.S. Phila. Temple V. M.ED and Ph.D. Candidate/ Student Phila.; [occ.] Anti Drug Fighter/Anti Violence Expert and Management Consultant; [memb.] Mantua Against Drugs, Indomitable Spirit, C.B.'s Role Models, National Inter Agency Counter Narcotics Institute San Luis Obispo, Physician for Social Responsibility; [hon.] Nominated for Presidential Medal of Freedom, Nobel Peace Prize '95 and '96, Martin Luther King Drum Major Award. Citations from: Phila. Mayor Ed Rendell U.S. Senators Arlen Spector, Harris Woffard PA, Nominated for President Bush's 1000 pts. of lights Community Service Award from U.S. Congressman Chaka Fattah Common Plea Judge RayFord Means; [oth. writ.] Some 120 other unpublished poems; [pers.] Hope and promise cannot be destroyed by man they lives in the dreams and imaginations of children even if we may have to exchange our lives ensure this truth.; [a.] Philadelphia, PA

KING, DIANA
[b.] September 12, 1974, San Francisco, CA; [p.] Teresa and Robert Wolfgang; [m.] Kenneth King, February 6, 1993; [ch.] Nicole Jonel and Anthony William; [ed.] East Forest High School; [occ.] Amateur Writer and Military house wife; [pers.] I am currently in the process of writing a book. In the mind of a writer is unexplored depths that are written down on paper for the world to enjoy.; [a.] Wichita Falls, TX

KING, LAURIE
[b.] November 15, 1970, Newberg, OR; [p.] Shirley King; [ch.] 2 girls, 10 yr., 3 yr., 1 boy 6 yrs.; [ed.] Taking home school to get diploma; [occ.] Homemaker I just take care of my kids; [oth. writ.] I've never had one published but I've wrote many poems, very few people have got to read them.; [pers.] This is the first time anyone outside my family has read anything I've wrote I hope that it is enjoyed. I wrote this poem for my mom on Mother's Day 1996.; [a.] Corvallis, OR

KING, POET
[b.] July 13, 1952, Washington DC; [ch.] Joseph King; [pers.] To write as free as the birds. To write as free as the wind blows.; [a.] Springfield, MA

KINOSHITA, AYAKO
[b.] May 20, 1969, Kobe in Japan; [p.] Tamiko Kinoshita and Mitsuhisa Kinoshita; [ed.] Communication and Art (P.A.) from Holly Names College, Computer Art and World Wide Web Publishing Certificate from Center for Electric Art in San Francisco; [occ.] Student and Work as a Part Time; [hon.] My life story published in Japanese magazine called "The Diamond Executive"; [oth. writ.] I love to express myself through different medium. Argentine Tango and Salsa are my passion by dancing from my heart. I also kept my poem from 14 years old. Writings has healing effect on my life and problems.; [pers.] Writing was one of a form of Art for me. I wanted to know me and what I was thinking of. I also do design to express my feelings and more. to me, life itself is "Art."; [a.] San Francisco, CA

KINSER, GERALDINE
[occ.] Free-lance Writer, currently writing poetry, songs, greeting cards, children's books and a ghost novel based on fiction with two sequels absolutely suited for actor Timothy Dalton, without question; [hon.] 1986-won beauty contest, Virginia, BBW pageant and best written entry, selected from over 10,000 entries. 1990 Models and Actors Convention, Cols, Ohio. Won best T.V. script for a 40 second commercial, self-acted, entitled, The Hat Back. Took 1st place over 100 contestants; [oth. writ.] Wrote commentaries, narrating fashion shows and seminars; [pers.] Success is having enough guts to go beyond the fork in the middle of the road. Upon this publication of, The Colors of Thought, my daughter, Scarlet Groome also shares the first and last poem she ever wrote entitled, Childhood Memories which is very humorous and we now, have the pleasure of sharing together in publication. Success is having enough guts to go beyond the fork in the middle of the road.; [a.] Millersport, Buckeye Lake, OH

KIRKPATRICK, MICHAEL
[b.] September 14, 1942, St. Louis, MO; [p.] William and Adele Kirkpatrick; [m.] Wendy, September 5, 1981; [ch.] David; [ed.] Archbishop Stepinac HS., White Plains NY; [occ.] Office Professional; [memb.] St. John The Evangelist Parish, White Plains, NY, Coach in the White Plains Youth Soccer Association; [oth. writ.] Numerous unpublished works of prose and poetry; [pers.] Poetry for me is the expression and observation of experiences and feelings. A great therapy for today's lifestyle.; [a.] White Plains, NY

KLEFF JR., PIERRE A.
[b.] October 28, 1942, Washington, DC; [p.] Pierre A. and Mary Emily Kleff; [m.] Rosemarie F. Kleff, March 17, 1973; [ch.] Teresa, Angela, Beth, Michael, Pierre III and Amber; [ed.] Univ. of Dayton BA, Chase College of Law JD; [occ.] Attorney; [memb.] State Bar of Texas, Killeen Junior Livestock Show Ass'n, Reserve Officers Ass'n, American Legion; [hon.] US Army Lt. Colonel (Ret.); [pers.] I am "Jeffersonian Liberal", distrusting big government and retaining an abiding faith in the uniqueness of man.; [a.] Killeen, CA

KLENE, DORIS
[b.] July 30, 1926, England; [p.] Agnes and Henry Lomax; [m.] Ralph Klene (Deceased), April 1, 1945; [ch.] Sandra, Laura, Roger and Robin; [occ.] Retired, Homemaker; [memb.] Several local organizations; [oth. writ.] Several poems and a book on my life in England, titled Past and Present; [pers.] In my poems I try to reflect my feelings and also what has happened in my life.; [a.] Greensburg, IN

KNOLL, LEONA ANN
[pen.] Lee or Lee-Ann; [b.] August 2, 1945, Brooklyn, NY; [p.] Eva Ann (Nee-Anthony) and Edward Oliver Berner; [ch.] Stephanie M. DePalma-Pranin, Susan M. Knapeck, Heather Ann L. Knoll; [ed.] Graduated

Midwood High School, Brooklyn, NY, Insurance and Secretary School, New Jersey; [occ.] Notary Public and Writer; [memb.] National Notary Association; [hon.] Three Editors Choice Awards for Poetry in 1996; [oth. Writ.] Un-named Poem 1993, The Battle For The Mat 1994, Ode To A Problem Child and Write and Reason 1995, Energy Vs Rest and The Mothers day Surprise 1996; [pers.] My friends are my family as the blood related family has gone their own way or has died. When I lose someone to death, especially good, nice people it bothers me. Sometimes we need extended families.; [a.] Vineland, NJ

KNOX, MERITA
[b.] May 31; [p.] Willie James and Mable Knox; [ed.] Andrew Jackson High, Anne Arundel Community College; [oth. writ.] 3 short novels, "No Greater Love", "Soldier of a Higher Power" and "Redefined By Zo"; [pers.] My writings are a true expression of my inner self, it helps me to focus on things that are sincere, valuable and essential, in hopes of reaching to others, to somehow encourage them to express themselves. It keeps me real.; [a.] Odenton, MD

KOCH, SR., JOHN E.
[pen.] J. Edward Koch; [b.] January 30, 1937, Allentown, PA; [p.] John J. and Myrene C. Koch; [m.] Diosa S. Koch, May 2, 1987; [ch.] John E. Jr. and Deanna M. Koch; [ed.] Allentown High School; [occ.] Loss Control Manager K-Mart Corporation; [pers.] I strive with every stroke of the pen to offer life as it was, is and could be. My wish is that readers are able to identify in some way to the readings.; [a.] Allentown, PA

KONTANIS, BEATRICE F.
[pen.] Bea Faye - Bea Kaye; [b.] May 26, 1936, Lawrence, Long Island City, NY; [p.] George and Sophia Facopoulos; [m.] Elias George Kontanis, August 26, 1956; [ch.] Theodore, Tia Louise and Micheal Deceased; [ed.] M.A. Degree - Syracuse Univ. and Columbia Univ - B.A. "English and Art Teacher"; [occ.] Sub-Teaching; [memb.] AHEPA - Daughters of Penelope, Alpha-Beta-Gamma; [hon.] Award from Walt Disney Studios to draw cartoons for films being made for the big screen; [oth. writ.] Many poems some Haiku and unfinished book! Of my life!! Trial and Tribulations.; [pers.] I was devastated by the death of my son and was unable to speak to any one for over a month - as soon as I started talking, I wrote this poems - making me feel that my son was still beside me and would always be!; [a.] Ridge, Long Island City, NY

KORELC, DORIS C.
[pen.] Doris Charlotte; [b.] July 17, 1930, Bay City, MI; [p.] George Andrew; [m.] Divorced from spouse of 30 years; [ch.] Randall Korelc, Annette Toland; [ed.] Zion Lutheran School 8 years - Handy High - Graduated 1948 - Central High; [occ.] Homemaker-Crafts, Quilting, Painting, Cake Decorating; [memb.] Zion Lutheran Church Adult Choir; [oth. writ.] Never submitted any of my writings for publication before now.; [pers.] In my personal experience and love for son and daughter and love for many people, I have hurts and betrayals. Learn from my poems. They tell stories many can benefit from.; [a.] Bay City, MI

KOSS, BARBARA
[b.] May 19, 1956, Paducah, KY; [p.] Clyde and Flora Morgan; [m.] William R. Koss, November 17, 1975; [ch.] Richard Lee and Jeffery Matthew; [occ.] Housewife; [pers.] I wrote "There Comes A Time" from deep inside my heart and it is dedicated to my sisters (Doris Marie Morgan and Ann Morgan Pease).; [a.] Paducah, KY

KRAMER, PAM
[b.] March 7, 1968, Easton, PA; [p.] Walter J. Kramer Jr., Harriet Hanisak; [ch.] "Badge," my Rottweiler; [ed.] Churchman Business School, Moravian College; [occ.] ICD-9-CM Coder, Warren Hospital, Phillipsburg, NJ; [hon.] Dean's List; [pers.] Poetry is emotion in motion...; [a.] Easton, PA

KRITIKOS, MARGARET
[b.] December 21, 1936, Chicago, IL; [p.] Albert and Honorine Van Thyne; [m.] Gus P. Kritikos, May 9, 1958; [ch.] Steve, Mary, Tia, Pete, Al and Marcy; [ed.] St. Philomena Grade, Josephinum High, and Classes at Morton Comm. College; [occ.] Trust Ops. Asst.; [oth. writ.] Yesterday's Heroes In The Rainbow's End; [pers.] I enjoy life and pray that it is a trait that I leave to my children and grandchildren.

KUAN, CECILIA A.
[b.] August 13, 1963, Mexicali, Mexico; [p.] Juan Hernandez Garcia, Agripina Torrecillas Beltran; [m.] Michael Su Kuan, February 25, 1992; [ch.] 2 - Fernando P. Basua Jr., Jennifer Marta Kuan; [ed.] Mexicali College, 1 year Preparatoria, 1 year Elementary School and diploma in Bank Ecomomyst; [occ.] Housewife; [memb.] Saint Marys Church Committee give food to people who are and need every Wensday Outside De Church 11 to 1 PM; [hon.] I have 2 honor for good to people from my church; [oth. writ.] I write for my hard and also for my self. I love to read and also I love life everybody love life.; [pers.] I have been greatly Influenced by my past life and love I have lost and my hard, I always a find my really love, who is the past.; [a.] Stockton, CA

KUHL, JAN EILEEN
[b.] December 10, 1941, Niles, MI; [p.] Carrie and Arthur Kuhl; [ch.] Shelli Zandasrki, Eric Zandarski (Son-in-law); [occ.] Productive Team Manager Bridgman, MI; [oth. writ.] Two short stories and a newspaper article. This is my first poem to be published.; [pers.] I try to show the "Every day" side of life, the goodness and the sorted side of life which is in every one.

KUMAR, MANJUSHREE S.
[b.] September 19, 1953, Bikaner, Raj. India; [p.] Dr. Shivkumar and Mrs. D. K. Shivkumar; [ed.] 1990 - was awarded Ph.D. in English - JNV Univ, Jodhpur, India, 1981 - Masters in English Literature JNV Univ. Jodhpur, India with a gold medal and 1st position in Univ. 1975, Masters in Psychology, 1973 Bachelors in Eng. Lit. Honours, 1969 I.S.C., Loreto Convent, Lucknow, India; [occ.] Independent Scholar and Academic Counselor at Kota Open Univ. Jodhpur; [memb.] Modern Lang. Association of America, New York, American Studies Research (MLA) Center, Hyd India, Indian Society for Commonwealth (ISCS), India, Indian Association for Commonwealth Literature and Language Studies (IACLALS) India; [hon.] Gold Medal for 1st position at Masters English Final exam, Certificates for Academic Excellence in B.A. (Hono part I and II, Certificate of Merit for Editorship of students bulletin, Shield and awards for Debates Music and Elocution contests; [oth. writ.] Academic papers published in the Commonwealth review, Indian Women Novelists - vol. 3, The Literary Criterion, Ph.D Thesis on Paul Scott's, novels published by Umi, Michigan; [pers.] We are all seekers of the ultimate truth. Our action and thought reflect our developmental stage in mind and spirit. Our aim should be to remain in harmony and peace with oneself, others, and finally achieve one is goal; [a.] Jodhpur, Rajasthan, India

LAFFATY, PAUL L.
[b.] Caribow, ME; [p.] Marian Ginn Laffaty and Phillip Laffaty; [ed.] Caribow High School, Caribow, ME; Los Angeles City and State College, Los Angeles; [occ.] Freelance writer, writing a novel; [memb.] Lifetime membership: ISP; [oth. writ.] NLP, the book and sound recordings of poetry, A Far Off Place, Beyond the Rainbows; [pers.] The Oracle 1929 - Colby College, My mother, Marian Louise Giner, Ginny, Anything that is worth doing at all, is worth doing well, my mother. My best friend and my hero; [a.] CA

LAMARRE, JANET E.
[pen.] Jelamarre; [b.] July 29, 1945, Rawlins, WY; [p.] Norman and Merle Stratton; [m.] Albert L. Lamarre, September 1077; [ch.] Debra Lamarre Zimmerman and Meaghan Lamarre; [ed.] Rawlings, Wyoming High School - 1963 The University of Phoenix - 1982; [occ.] Library Assistant; [memb.] AAUW California Association for the Gifted California School Employees Association; [hon.] Graduated with distinction from the University of Phoenix; [oth. writ.] I have written other poems but never submitted them for publication.; [pers.] While under going chemotherapy and radiation treatments for breast cancer I wrote this poem. This expression from within, put into poetic form, was theraputic.; [a.] Pleasanton, CA

LAMOUREUX, GERARD J.
[b.] July 20, 1972, Harvey, IL; [p.] Gerard and Gloria Lamoureux; [ed.] BS in History at Northern Illinois University; [occ.] Drywall Hanger; [oth. writ.] Currently working on receiving publication on my novel, life everlasting: A vampire's autobiography. Several poems published in periodicals and anthologies.; [pers.] I use my life experiences to inspire my writing. It may not always be happy but it's reality.; [a.] Saint Charles, IL

LAMPHERE, MICHAEL
[b.] June 22, 1982, Saint Albans, VT; [p.] Anne and Robert Lamphere; [ed.] Completed 8th grade at MVU; [occ.] Student; [oth. writ.] Personal writings such as stories, poems and songs.; [a.] Swanton, VT

LAMPING, BARBARA
[pen.] A & L; [b.] July 6, 1952, Mount Vernon, IL; [p.] Clarence and Jessie Dobbs; [m.] Leo Lamping, October 27, 1973; [ch.] Kathy, Allen, Robert; [ed.] 2 yrs. of JJC and 3 yrs. of Nursing School of SJMC; [occ.] RN on a Psych Unit; [memb.] INA and Church of the Good Shepherd; [hon.] Many; [oth. writ.] "Jesus" and many other poems and 4 songs yet to be published.; [pers.] I can do all things through Christ who strengthen me.; [a.] Joliet, FL

LANE, JASON
[pen.] Lee Allen; [b.] June 8, 1979, El Paso, TX; [p.] Brenda and Danny Lane; [ed.] GED currently Working on Diploma; [occ.] Autobody; [memb.] In Big Brother Program; [hon.] Two Awards for Art; [oth. writ.] Currently working on a fantasy novel, two poems, Desperate Tears, I Died for Love; [pers.] I wanna to thank my family and my close friend Robert Foland for there help and support through out my life.; [a.] Boulder, CO

LANE, RHONDA LEA
[pen.] Cherry; [b.] August 7, 1958, Salina, KS; [p.] Darrell Williams, Donna Williams; [m.] Divorced; [ch.] Stephanie Lane, Kristy Lane; [ed.] Douglas High School, South Dakota; [occ.] Domestic Engineer; [memb.] Church of Christ; [hon.] I won second place in a writing contest for a love story. I won second place out of 1,000 people; [oth. writ.] I wrote a story called "Ghost Story" I though was good. I have other poems. One poems was put into a bulletin and sent all over California. I also write children's stories and draw

cartoon characters and other drawings to go with the stories.; [pers.] I want people to remember me when I'm gone through my words and my thoughts and what I have contributed to life.; [a.] Merced, CA

LANE, ROBERT
[b.] November 19, 1981, Landstuhl, Germany; [p.] Patrick Lane, Rosemarie Lane; [ed.] I am a sophomore at Rockledge High School; [occ.] Student; [memb.] Protestant Youth Group; [hon.] School Honor Society; [pers.] Writing words on a piece of paper is no great trick but, getting them to express your ultimate feelings is the true mark of a great writer; [a.] Melbourne, FL

LANE, SUSAN PETERSON
[b.] September 3, 1957, Philadelphia, PA; [p.] Leonard Peterson (Deceased), Viola Peterson; [m.] Robert David Lane, September 25, 1982; [ch.] Whitney Ashley; [ed.] West Catholic Girls' High, St. Joseph's University, BA. English 1979, currently pursuing Master's in Education; [occ.] Insurance Underwriter; [memb.] National Teacher's Honor Society; [hon.] Dean's List; [oth. writ.] From the Wasteland of my Heart to the Wisdom of His Ways, Once Upon A Triumph, My Headache, My Heartache, His Healing and When God is Silent Series; [pers.] Sea-First Salvation, then Education with continual/application of both principles and Habakkuk 2 vs 3 for the vision is yet for an appointed time, but at the end it shall speak and not lie. Though it tarry wait for it. It will come to pass.; [a.] Veacon, PA

LARSON, ERIK MATTHEW
[pen.] Kire Nosral, Matt Nosra; [b.] May 3, 1975, Highland Park, IL; [p.] Shirley and Roger Larson; [ed.] College of Lake County, University of North Florida; [occ.] Internal Control Clerk (Auditor), for Six Flags Great America; [memb.] Sigma Chi; [pers.] "A kiss on your lips and one more dream comes true." (Quote from my unpublished poem Dream Beauty). Beauty and love are my keys to unlock my soul.; [a.] Zion, IL

LARSON, JOHN WILLIAM
[b.] October 1, 1957, Oak Park, IL; [p.] John F. and Jacqueline Larson; [ed.] Willow Brook High, Villa Park, IL, Southern Illinois University, Carbondale, IL; [occ.] Area Sales Manager East Moving Systems/Global Van Lines; [oth. writ.] Personal pieces that have not, as yet, been submitted to any publications or contests.; [pers.] My writings come from disappointments in love and life, or as tributes to others. Friendships have been few, loves even less. The world is a lonely place. Amazingly, I have a marvelous sense of humor to see me through. And as an inspiration of hope and promise, I have the music of the Moody Blues. "Music from the head, for the heart."; [a.] Hoffman Estates, IL

LARUE, RENE
[pen.] Renie and Nana; [b.] February 11, Fargo, ND; [p.] Dell and Lillian Willis; [m.] Alton P. Knapp - Deceased, June 1; [ch.] Allan Scott Knapp, Barbara Delle, Timothy John Knapp; [ed.] Many College Courses in Art.; [occ.] Artist (Water Colorist and Oil); [memb.] Smithsonian Audubon Society; [hon.] Painted in Sedona, Arizona for 20 years. Many honors and awards, poems published church bulletins - National Contests also.; [oth. writ.] "The Road Home", "My Little Texas Garden", "Sedona Arizona to Sequin, Texas, "Wildlife Wisdom"; [pers.] "Then shalt thou call, and the Lord shall answer, thou shalt cry and he shall say, Here I am."; [a.] Aliance, NE

LASSITER, AMBER
[b.] May 10, 1988, CA; [p.] Ronald and Mercedes; [ed.] Alta Loma Elementary; [occ.] Student; [hon.] Acta Loma District - Art Fair, Cert. of good conduct, Special Helper award cert. of excellence, Academy Award, Super Citizen awards cert. of Achievements, Library

Award, Special Merit award; [a.] Alta Loma, CA

LATOUR, MELISSA MOON
[b.] July 16, 1962, Denver, CO; [p.] Mr. Dee F. Moon and Mrs. Donna R. Moon; [m.] F. Daniel Latour, August 22, 1987; [ch.] Jennifer Michelle Latour; [ed.] Bachelor of Arts Mass Comm.; [occ.] Part owner Antique and Resale Furniture Store; [memb.] American Diabetes Assoc. Phi Kappa Phi, United Presbyterian Church (USA); [hon.] University of Southwestern Louisiana Honors Graduate, Acadiana Advertising Federation 1995 Scholarship Recipient.; [pers.] To live without writing is to strangle on thinking.; [a.] Lafayette, LA

LATZKE, JO-ANN
[pen.] Random; [b.] August 19, 1978, Waconnia, MN; [p.] Terry Jean Latzke (mother); [ed.] Hutchinson High School, Institute of children's literature, Readers Digest writing school, ICS - Diploma course; [occ.] Chief Prairie House; [memb.] Writer's Digest Book Club, Book-of-the-Month Book Club, Spirital One Book Club, Science Fiction Book Club; [hon.] Editors Choice Award, National Library of Poetry, Outstanding Achievement in the Play "Annie", Silver Lake High School; [oth. writ.] "Under The Night Sky...", pub-in a muse to follow, "Mysteries"- Best Poems of the 90's; [pers.] Each of us can be no more or less than we are. It will be a truly great world when all can live together without hate.; [a.] Hutchinson, MN

LAURANT, LYDIA
[b.] April 27, 1983, Los Angeles; [p.] Hazel and Glendell Laurant; [ed.] Madrona Heights, Orchard Heights, and Marcus Whitman Junior High School; [oth. writ.] Washington, you're my friend, friendship, and money. My favorite is money.; [pers.] I am 13 years old and just completed my 7th grade year. This is one of the most exciting things of my life. And I hope you all enjoy my poem.; [a.] Port Orchard, WA

LAVIGNE, ALLYSON LEE
[b.] March 21, 1974, New Orleans, LA; [p.] Sam Lavigne, Cynthia Lavigne; [ed.] East Ascension High. Louisiana State University - Major: Family, child, and Consumer Sciences; [pers.] This poem is lovingly dedicated in memory to Scott Carpenter, my love and my best friend. For it is he that it is written for.; [a.] Gonzales, LA

LAVIN, MARK
[b.] August 28, 1973, Los Angeles, CA; [p.] Ron and Lynette Lavin; [ed.] Finishing up a Bachelor of Arts degree at UCLA; [occ.] I'm currently circulating petitions for a political organization; [oth. writ.] I've written hundreds of poems and several short stories since Jan. 25 this year, and this here is my first published piece.; [pers.] I find that my best writings, the ones that sing, the ones that really connect with other people are nothing more than humble relics, souvenirs of instants just lived just instants ago.; [a.] Los Angeles, CA

LAWSON, JAMES ANTHONY
[pen.] Jamie Lawson; [b.] December 21, 1975, Fort Myers, FL; [p.] Debbie S. Lawson; [m.] Tatiana Lawson, August 25, 1995; [ed.] Fort Myers High, Fort Myers Florica, Edison Community College Florida; [occ.] Student; [memb.] Seminola Booster Club; [pers.] My favorite poet is John Greenleat Whittien. I owe my writing style to him. I like the reader to think they our in the poem itself.; [a.] Fort Myers, FL

LAZARE, DANIEL
[pen.] Ti-Jean, De Admiral; [b.] October 24, 1967, Dominica; [p.] Stephen J. Caesar, Sylma Lazare; [ed.] A 1985 graduate from High School, named the Dominica Grammar School; [occ.] Painter; [memb.] People Action Theatre (PAT), The Seventh Day Adventist Church;

[oth. writ.] Short Story, Prose, Poems mainly, "A Lamentation" which I hope to submit in next years Poetry Contest. A Lamentation depicts my personal experience in abstract language; [pers.] Speech impediment hinders my eloquence in speech dynamism. Poetry is my channel to express inspired feelings, styled with artistic quality which hynotizes and arrest readers attention, journeying their minds to my world of creative imagination!; [a.] Charlotte Amalie, VI

LEAVENWORTH, PATSY Y.
[pen.] Pitts (Patsy); [b.] January 17, 1942, Joiner, AR; [p.] Tula and Lloyd Rowland (Both Deceased); [m.] Douglas R. Leavenworth, December 22, 1989; [ch.] B.J. Arnold, William, Kathy and 3 step children; [ed.] Dyess High - Dyess, AR, Cochise Community College, Douglas and Sierra Vista, AZ, Phoenix College - Phoenix, AZ; [occ.] Homemaker; [memb.] Disabled American Veterans (DAV), (Cincinnati, OH), Paralyzed Veterans of America of Wilton, New Hampshire; [oth. writ.] Manuscript (550 pages) "Prisoners of Darkness", never been published - lots of poems; [pers.] I would like someday to have my manuscript published also a book of my poems.; [a.] Broken Arrow, OK

LEE, CAROL A.
[b.] January 1, 1949, Chandler, OK; [p.] J. O. Jennings and Thelma Jennings; [m.] James Lee, May 24, 1968; [ch.] Elizabeth Lee, James Lee Jr.; [ed.] Boron High School; [occ.] Homemaker; [memb.] American Diabetes Association, Paradise Chapel; [pers.] Through my poetry I try to image a positive out look on life, even when the way gets rocky and rough.; [a.] Waianae, HI

LEE, JEFFREY L.
[pen.] Jazz; [b.] May 31, 1969, Baltimore, MD; [p.] Rita A. Ckyyou, Matthati A. Ckyyou; [ed.] Forest Park/ Edmondson Westside Skill Center, U.S. Army, and Essex Community College; [occ.] Coordinator of Death Certificates (UMMS), Data Entry Oper.; [memb.] Hero, Frederick Douglas High School Partnership UMMS, Mentor Program, Calvary Baptist church AIDS Committee; [hon.] Urban League Writing Contest "88", Afro-American Newspaper Award (Poet), ATT&T Scholarship, Urban League and UMMS Scholarship, UMMS Partnership/Douglas Frederick mentor Program.; [oth. writ.] Hidden Truth, Modern Slavery, "Lil" Brother, The Need to Understand, To Say A Prayer, Thinking of You, Tears, God, The One and Only, Friendship, Smile, City, Under sieged, and Thanksgiving etc....; [pers.] Through my writing I would like to spread love and peace with a understanding of our purpose on earth. To love each other as "Jesus" loves us all. No matter what race, creed, religions and gender.; [a.] Baltimore, MD

LEE, TANYA
[b.] September 2, 1977, Birmingham, AL; [p.] Gussie Lee and Andrew C. King; [ed.] Ensley Magnet High School; [memb.] Peace and Goodwill Baptist Church, Leadership Class, FHA; [hon.] JROTC, Orchestra, Bible study, Student of the Week, A-B average in history, science and reading; graduated from Ensley Magnet High School in 1996; [pers.] Through many parts of my life I came to a point where I could write and express my true feeling to people. I have been influenced by a lot of famous poets that I look up to as my inspiration as well as people that stood by my side.; [a.] Birmingham, AL

LEFTWICH, LIU ELISE
[b.] March 2, 1925, Norway, IA; [p.] Marie and Oysten Nordsjo; [m.] Richard Leftwich, March 1, 1958; [ch.] 3 Daughters, 2 Granddaughters; [ed.] Business, Home Ec-voice Training (Classical), Voice Norway, London, Rome and New York; [occ.] Homemaker; [memb.] Pound Ridge Com. Church Norwegian Seaman Church Pound Ridge Garden Club; [hon.] Sang for the late King

Olav of Norway Concerts Church Solo's Etc, Several Awards for Flower Arrangements, Diploma from the Institute of Literature; [oth. writ.] Publish Newsletter for my own business, Poems published in Newspapers and the National Library of Poetry!; [pers.] I appreciate the beautiful life-gifts given to me. The gift of Children, Music and Art. Writing Poetry helps me in my search for inner peace, as I walk through life!; [a.] Pound Ridge, NY

LELAND, IRENE
[b.] March 31, 1947, Saint Louis, MO; [p.] Austin Leland and Dorothy Lund Leland; [m.] (Ex) Joseph H. Barzantry; [ch.] Joseph Charles Barzantry (b-70) and Austin Leland Barzantry (b-78); [ed.] Mary Institute, St. Louis - class of '65, Bennett Junior College, Millbrook, N.Y. - '67, A.A.S. - Music and Drama; [occ.] Freelance Commercial Actress; [memb.] National Author's Registry sponsored by Iliad Press - inducted Mar. 8, 1996.; [hon.] Certificate of Merit Awarded for Outstanding Accomplishment in The Writer's Digest 1995 National Self-Publishing Awards - issued June 28, 1996, Certificate of Honorable Mention for Literary Excellence in Winter '96 Iliad Literary Awards; [oth. writ.] The Maze Comes To Life - nonfiction books ('95), On The Right Course - Puzzle/Recipe/Calendar ('93). Also many songs and poems.; [pers.] I believe in truly connecting with oneself and then genuinely connecting with others.... writing is a natural expression and extension of that process.; [a.] Saint Louis, MO

LENNINGTON, LINDA L.
[pen.] Lilana Michilo; [b.] July 18, 1947, OH; [oth. writ.] Sheltered Thoughts, My Heart's Hymn, Fire of Tears, and Angels Surround Them 9n in various anthologies; [pers.] With amazing grace from our heavenly Father, may we all live every day we love, and love every day we live!; [a.] Sunnyvale, CA

LEOPIN, MAK PHILIP
[pen.] Moshe, The Kosher Kowboy; [b.] April 25, 1952, Port Jefferson, NY; [p.] Matthew & Marie Leopin; [m.] Divorced 1994; [ch.] Matthew, Eric, Lance, Adam & Andrew; [ed.] Bachelors Degree in Accounting from the University of Wyoming; [occ.] Accountant and Tax Consultant, Homewood, Alabama; [memb.] Cahaba Heights Baptist Church, Promise Keepers (Men of Integrity); [hon.] Editors Choice Award for poem published in "Far Off Place" by The National Library of Poetry in 1994; [oth. writ.] Book of poems "Love Drops from Heaven", published music album "Praise be the Lord - The God of Israel" produced in 1995 (all original songs).; [pers.] Having a personal relationship with God, the creator of our universe, is the most important accomplishment a person can attain. Surrendering your life to God and studying His word (The Bible) is utmost important in life.; [a.] Homewood, AL

LESCHER, CHRIS
[b.] March 6, 1973, Illinois; [p.] Sandy and Steve Lescher; [ed.] B.S. in Psychology from P.B.A.C. persuing Masters in Criminal Justice At V.T.C.; [occ.] Behavioral Specialist; [pers.] It feels like there is someone else inside me banging on the walls trying to get out.; [a.] Chattanooga, TN

LEVIN, JOSH
[b.] January 13, 1981, Washington, DC; [p.] Steve Levin, Terri Levin; [ed.] Briarcliff High School; [occ.] Student; [hon.] Honor Roll, English Dept Award; [oth. writ.] Other poetry published in school literary magazine, 21st century literary journal.

LEWIS, MARION
[pen.] Mamie L.; [b.] February 27, 1916, Wallingford, VT; [p.] Joseph and Grace (Wade) Wilder; [m.] Winston R. (Stub) Lewis, August 30, 1938; [ch.] Barbara Grace, Richard Seth, Claudia Jean and Joseph Nelson; [ed.] Wallingford, VT grad 1934 St Ann's Hospital, School of Nursing Columbus, Ohio grad 1937 Music and Piano with Mrs Avery Danolds Wallingford, VT; [memb.] Lions Club of America Bowie, AZ First Congregational Church Wallingford, VT Otter Valley Rhythmairs Dance Band over 20 years; [oth. writ.] More poetry, none of which have been published; [pers.] Most of my poems are written for or about our grandchildren. Others have moral guidance, mentally thru verse, striving for a better and happier world for all mankind; [a.] Rutland, VT

LEWIS, RONALD
[pen.] Skate; [b.] February 19, 1941, Boise, ID; [occ.] Retired army surgeon; [oth. writ.] Several published poems; [pers.] A poem should be able to tickle the emotion and/or intellect of anyone who reads it.; [a.] Denver, CO

LICHTENBERG, JACQUELINE
[b.] November 1, 1935, Israel; [p.] Jacques and Elsa Grinstein; [m.] Ben Lichtenberg, December 11, 1957; [ch.] Julie Lichtenberg; [ed.] Educated in France MA Columbia University, NY MSW Hunter College School of Social Work, NY; [occ.] Child and Family Therapist; [memb.] Putney Family Services Board, Putney, VT A Building Alliance, Brattleboro, VT; [pers.] I try to look at life with newness, openness and curiosity. I have been influenced in part by American contemporary poetry; [a.] Putney, VT

LIN, CHIN H.
[pen.] Harobed; [b.] October 15, 1935, Taiwan; [m.] Shu Yuan Hsiao, June 3, 1967; [ed.] MSEE, Georgia Tech; [occ.] Retired, Computer Hobbyist. Museum Volunteer; [memb.] IEEE Computer Society; [pers.] The older I am, the more I believe in what Howard J. Whitman said: "What an individual wants - or thinks he wants - rarely remains constant. At age twenty he is likely to want fame, at thirty-five money, and at fifty peace of mind. Examine yourself, do you want the same things today that you wanted fifteen years ago?"; [a.] New York City, NY

LINCOLN, ROBERT ADAMS
[pen.] Albert Adams; [b.] April 4, 1921, Walton, NY; [p.] Louise Adams and Floyd H. Lincoln; [m.] Catherine Ruth Allen, 1968; [ch.] Leslie Henry and Thomas; [ed.] Yale University, BA; [occ.] Retired from U.S. Foreign Service. Free-lance writing today; [memb.] Diplomatic and Consular Officers, Retired Service Association, U.S. Information Agency Alumni Association (USIAAA); [hon.] Distinguished Honor Award, U.S. Information Agency; [oth. writ.] Regular nonfiction book reviews Richmond (VA) Times-Dispatch. Reviews other newspapers, magazines. Articles Army magazine, I love Cats, Financial Times (London). Special report U.S. Direct Investment in UK (Economist Intelligence Unit, London). Poetry The Sewanee Review, International Herald Tribune (Paris); [a.] McLean, VA

LINDSEY, BERETHA
[pen.] Brown Sugar; [b.] September 9, 1983, Chicago; [p.] Melissa Turner; [ed.] 7th grad in 8th; [occ.] Student; [memb.] Girls and Boys Campfire; [hon.] Science, and Geography; [oth. writ.] Once upon a Disney, Africa and many more poems; [pers.] Treat people the way I like to be treated.; [a.] Lawton, OK

LINTON, CAMILLE
[pen.] Miles-Lyn Forbes; [b.] June 22, 1972, Brooklyn, NY; [p.] Agnes M. and Thomas E. Linton; [ed.] Santa Fe Community College, Gainesville, Florida, Florida International University, North Miami, Florida; [occ.] Executive Assistant, The Ad Team, North Miami, Florida; [hon.] Dean's List; [oth. writ.] Poetry, short stories and sitcom scripts.; [pers.] I do not see myself as writing for personal gain or acknowledgement, instead I see my writings as works for my grandmother who never had the opportunity to do so herself.; [a.] North Miami, FL

LIPKIN, BRIAN S.
[b.] May 5, 1970, New Hartford, NY; [p.] Christine and Stanley Lipkin; [ed.] Utica Senior Academy, Utica College of Syracuse University; [occ.] Medical Technologist, St. Elizabeth Hospital; [memb.] American Society of Clinical Pathologists; [pers.] The greatest influences in my life and writing, have always come from the world of gratitude to my two greatest influences - Jim Morrison and Lou Reed.; [a.] Utica, NY

LITTLE, FRANCIS E.
[pen.] Frank Little; [b.] September 19, 1979, Pensacola, FL; [p.] Dr. and Mrs. Michael E. Little; [ed.] Bishop Dennis J. O'Connell H.S.; [occ.] Student; [memb.] Little Flower Catholic Church Yearbook, School Newspaper; [hon.] 1st Place: Georgetown, Prep Speech Contest, Honor Roll; [a.] Chevy Chase, MD

LIVERMORE, CLARENCE
[pen.] Clarence; [b.] January 8, 1916, Sharon, Mercer County, PA; [p.] Thomas Elliot and Rillian Webster Livermore; [m.] Wilma Morris Livermore, September 5, 1950; [ch.] Edith, Martha; [ed.] Rural #19 4 Grades Schools, #12 Graduated 1933 Hickory High School, 12 Grades Shenanco Businite School, Some Army - 1941-45 Life Underwriting 47-50; [occ.] Retired Letter Carrier, Retired 1980; [memb.] Free Methodist Ch. of N.A., N.A.L.C. Letter Carriers, D.A.V. Life Member Vets; [hon.] Graduate Hickory High School - 1933 SCE Education, Good Conduct Medal, Asiatic Pacific, New Guinea; [oth. writ.] None sent for publication. Have some poems and short stories none published.; [pers.] The Lord has done much for me, I am thankful, also to parents/wife, brother and others dare to be a Daniel don't give up the shine pick up books and go to school.; [a.] New Castle, PA

LODISE, LINDA
[b.] May 4, 1953, Philadelphia, PA; [p.] Antoinette and Joseph Merlino; [m.] Robert, April 17, 1982; [ch.] Christopher and Kimberly; [ed.] St. Maria Goretti H.S.; [occ.] Administrative Asst.; [pers.] I believe that all people are basically good if treated with love, honesty and respect.; [a.] Philadelphia, PA

LOPEZ, LUCITO P.
[pen.] Sir Cito; [b.] February 11, 1973, Philippines; [p.] Dr. Gerardo Lopez, Benicia Lopez; [ed.] Brandon High, Jackson State Univ., Research experiences at Harvard School of Public Health and the University of Mississippi School of Pharmacy; [occ.] Graduate Student in Chemistry, Jackson State University; [memb.] American Association for Artificial Intelligence, Filipino-American Association of Mississippi; [hon.] Phi Kappa Phi, DOW Scholar, Magna Cum Laude, Freshman Chemisty Student of the Year (JSU); [pers.] Poetry is the best way for me to express my love for another. I specialize largely in love poems; [a.] Pearl, MS

LOVELACE, RENEE C.
[pen.] The Lone Poet, Rane; [p.] Deloris and Charles Cattlet; [ch.] Lawrence E. and Elton D. Lovelace; [ed.] University of Kentucky, Human Services Technology, 1979, University of Louisville, Bachelor of Science in

Corrections Administration; [occ.] Corrections, Jefferson County; [hon.] Dean's List, Team Leader-1994, 1993 Bob Ruder Award, Employee of Month 6-5-96, Alumni Ass., University of Louisville, Bob Ruder Award, 1996; [oth. writ.] Several poems published and unpublished. Also writing a novel titled, Rane!; [pers.] Influenced by Dr. Young, English 101 "The Door is open" I have yet to stop writing, for me life is a Book with no sure Ending.; [a.] Louisville, KY

LOWE, MICHAEL JOSEPH
[b.] May 27, 1966, Boston, MA; [p.] Sandra Lowe, Willie Lowe; [ch.] Denisha Lowe (my Princess); [ed.] Copley Square High School, North Adams State College; [occ.] Freelance Writer; [memb.] B.M.U., Black Men United, W.I.M., Wheels in Motion; [oth. writ.] Book of a short stories entitled Black To Love, poem published in anthology entitled Who's Who in New Poets; [pers.] In order for us as a people to get in balance with the earth, we must universally get Black To Love.; [a.] Boston, MA

LUCAS, DAUNITA
[pen.] Daunita O'Neal; [b.] November 13, 1962, Raleigh, NC; [p.] Clyde and Amy O'Neal; [m.] Divorced; [ch.] Diamond Lashay Lucas; [ed.] East Wake High School, Wake Technical College; [pers.] You cannot enrich the lives of others fully until you recognize the treasure within yourself. Until then, a much needed wealth goes untouched.; [a.] Raleigh, NC

LUDDINGTON, BETTY WALLES
[pen.] Betty Luddington; [b.] May 11, 1936, Tampa, FL; [p.] Edward and Ruby Luddington (Deceased); [m.] Robert Morris Schmidt, September 20, 1957, (Divorced) December 1981; [ch.] Irene Losat, Daniel Schmidt; [ed.] Henry B. Plant High School, Tampa FL., USF, Tampa, FL 1980 BA American studies/history, 1982 MA Library Media and Information Studies, 1986 Ed. S Curriculum and Instruction/gifted education; [occ.] Media Specialist, Dowdell Middle School, Tampa, FL; [memb.] HASLMS (Hillsborough Association of School Libary Media Specialist) FTP/NFA/Hillsborough Classroom Teachers Association, Country Music Fan Clubs, Books and Dunn, Diamond Rio, Joe Diffie, Aaron Tippin, ISP (International Society of Poets); [hon.] Phi Alpha Theta Outstanding Student award, Golden Signet award, Who's Who Among students in American Colleges and Universities, Editor's Choice award for outsanding achievement in poetry (1996) Honoraries: Phi Kappa Phi, Kappa Delta Pi, Omicron Delta Kappa, Phi Alpha Theta, Pi Gamma Mu, Honors Council, Honors Convocation and graduate schoolarships ODK Library studies, Alumni Assn.; [oth. writ.] WITAN: A simulation activity for gifted students. "The gifted Child Today", Sept./Oct. 1986. Joe Diffie Fan Club (poems): Diffie Boots", "Diffie Cult Fanfare", "Honky Took Attituder". The Tampa tribune, Dec. 1992: Librarian uses poetry, "I like myself: James Evans" A Voyage to Remember, "Hillbily Knight County Wildflower, "A Tapestry of thoughts", John McEven: Strings Wizard, "Across the Universe, "Sybil Ludington's 1777 Ride" The Best Poems of the '90's, William Benjamin: Educational Leadership, "Recollection of Yesterday, "Sierre Stylings", Wispers at Dusk, Charlene Can, Frost at Midnight, A flower scapes: Mary Vincent Bertrand, Memories of Tomorrow.; [pers.] Inventing a poetic style that flows forward and backwards with accents along the way...making life a poem, a boquet of words that turns each day into something special.; [a.] Tampa, FL

LUTHER, ANNE G.
[pen.] Gerry Luther; [b.] February 20, 1916, Pioneer, LA; [p.] Martha and Leroy Hancock; [m.] Quentin L. Luther, May 31, 1946; [ch.] Michael Ann; [ed.] Kenedy High, evening school at St. Mary's, San Antonio, various courses at St. Louis Junior Colleges; [occ.] Retired from Accounting; [oth. writ.] Several poems, some of which have been published in local news.

LYONS, KATHY
[b.] February 11, 1960, Dallas, TX; [p.] Bert and Vianell Moore; [m.] Divorced; [ch.] Heather, Travis, Patrick, Nicholas, Christopher; [ed.] Aims Community College, Greeley Colo (Dean's List), Paris Jr. College, Paris TX (Deans List); [occ.] Waitress/Cook for Pizza Plaza in Wolfe City; [memb.] First Baptist Church Wolfe City; [hon.] Twice Dean's List; [oth. writ.] Editorials Sulphur Springs News; [pers.] 'Just friends' was written for and dedicated to the love of my life, Doug Brann. This was my first attempt to get a poem recognized and published. Many more will follow it is my dream come true.; [a.] Wolfe City, TX

MACKEY, KELLI MARIE
[pen.] Kelli Marie Mackey; [b.] April 12, 1984, Litchfield, IL; [p.] Kelly and Pam Mackey; [ed.] Beckemeyer School, Hillsboro Jr. High School; [occ.] Jr. High Student, Choir Secretary, Peer Mediator; [memb.] Our Savior's Lutheran Church; [hon.] Letter Award, Education Awards, D.A.R.E. Award, Physical Fitness Awards, Honor's Students Awards; [oth. writ.] "The Circus" in Jack and Jill Magazine; [pers.] Through my writing I hope to show people that anyone can learn to love poetry. I owe a big thanks to my family and friends.; [a.] Hillsboro, IL

MACKIE, RACHEL
[pen.] Rayanne Emme; [b.] October 28, 1981, Scranton; [occ.] Student; [memb.] American Heart Association, School Clubs; [hon.] Valedictorian of 8th grade, Early Bach Medal; [oth. writ.] Songs, poems, 4 books that have not been published; [pers.] You need to have a little rain before you get a rainbow; [a.] Moosic, PA

MACPHETRIDGE, BETTY ANN
[b.] April 3, 1931, LaCrosse, WI; [p.] Dan and Cora Young; [m.] Don MacPhetridge, September 10, 1955; [ed.] 12th Grade plus many development seminars throughout my career.; [occ.] My business training led me to secretarial duties at Trane Co. in LaCrosse, WI where I retired in '88 as a Manufacturing Engineering Assistant; [memb.] 45 Years in PSI (Professional Secretaries International) and am very active in our United Methodist Church; [hon.] Secretary of the Year in PSI; [oth. writ.] Being very involved in crafts I design greeting cards and compose very personal poems to utilize therein. I enjoy coordination parties and always compile the invitation in poetry form. Have written many happy ads for friends that are published in our local paper.; [pers.] Writing poetry, to me, is a neat way of truly expressing oneself and my wish is to inspire hopefuls. My belief in life is to enjoy every moment and to accomplish this it is imperative we care and share. But most of all and a daily priority, we must count our blessings and give thanks!; [a.] Onalaska, WI

MADEJ, DOUGLAS S.
[pen.] Scott Monroe; [b.] March 4, 1971, Amsterdam, NY; [ed.] Galway High School Schenectady County Community College, Fulton-Montgomery Communication Coll.; [occ.] Early Childhood Education Student; [oth. writ.] Poem published in SCCC Rhythms magazine; [pers.] Mom always told me, "This to shall pass", good or bad weather the storm. Depression is just a feeling, what doesn't kill you makes you... Stronger; [a.] Amsterdam, NY

MAHAFFEY, DIANNE S.
[pen.] Dianne Mahaffey; [b.] September 13, 1950, Lynchburg, VA; [p.] Cecil and Ruth Saunders; [m.] William Noah Mahaffey, April 25, 1975; [ch.] Joseph, Randall, Lori and Amanda; [ed.] EC Class High School, Lynchburg General Marsham Lodge School of Professional Nursing, Central VA. Community College, Lynchburg College Old Dominion University; [occ.] Director Hospital Hemodialipis; [memb.] American Nurses Assoc, American Society Post Anesthesia Nurses, American Association of Nephrology Nurses, American Business Womens Assoc., National Association of Female Executives; [hon.] William Thomas Pugh Award for Excellence in Nursing National Honor Society, Dean's List, National Biographical Society, Who's Who in Nursing; [oth. writ.] Short story (children's) "The Littlest Boy with the Biggest name"; [pers.] "Keep your belief in yourself .... always walk into a new journey. You will find it magnificent, spectacular, and beyond your wildest imagining!; [a.] Lynchburg, VA

MAHDAVI, ANNAHITA
[b.] October 17, 1962, Iran; [p.] Mehdi and Mehri Mahdavi; [m.] Mansour Shahriar, October 17, 1988; [ch.] Nirvana Shahriar (3 month's old girl); [ed.] High School Diploma, 3 yrs College; [occ.] Just had a baby so I'm a full time mom now; [hon.] Few awards for the best writings while in school and high school; [oth. writ.] I have written a book about my journeys around the few countries and my adventures in those years. I have written a number of poems.; [pers.] My father Mehdi Mahdavi is a known poet in persian community. I grow up in a poetic environment and I love to be a professional writer and poet one day!; [a.] Venice, CA

MAINES, MATHEW
[b.] February 22, 1979, Clifton Springs; [p.] Ruth and Dennis Maines; [pers.] We're all a part of the largest crux I know of. When all seems hopeless everyone is with you; [a.] Stanley, NY

MAINZ, LAVONNE B. WOODHOUSE
[b.] February 14, 1928, La Crosse, WI; [p.] H. W. Woodhouse, Josephine Woodhouse; [m.] John Mainz, June 2, 1951; [ch.] Karen, Lois, Richard, Robert, Randall; [ed.] Central High School, Writing Classes at W. Wis. Tech. College; [occ.] Artist, Writer; [memb.] LaCrosse Society Arts and Crafts, Western Wis. Art. Assn., Wis. Regional Art Assn.; [hon.] Several State Exhibit Awards for Paintings; [oth. writ.] Several articles have been published in local newspapers, articles in pub. book "Golen Gleanings," children's books with stories and poetry (self illustrated); [pers.] I enjoy writing stories and poems for children.; [a.] Onalaska, WI

MALIK, SAIMA
[b.] May 22, 1981, Canberra, Australia; [p.] Nishat and Sohail Malik; [occ.] Sophomore at James Madison High School; [oth. writ.] No published writings.; [pers.] I believe that writing is the best form of expression because it is free from boundaries of any kind. The power to express ones thoughts need not to be taught or learn, it needs to be found within oneself.; [a.] Vienna, VA

MALM, GAVIN R.
[b.] June 26, 1987, Long Beach, CA; [p.] Charles and Annique Malm; [ed.] Third Grader at Mancano Day School in Albuquerque, NM; [occ.] Third Grader; [pers.] I was eight years old and in the second grade when I wrote the poem. I wrote it because I love "My Mom". My hobby is riding my Go-Cart, collecting medal cars and pictures of cars.; [a.] Albuquerque, NM

MALONE, PHYLLIS E.
[pen.] Phil and Lizzie; [b.] June 3, 1952, Selma, AL; [p.] Mrs. Lovirie Durrah; [ed.] Brantley High University of Portland Oregon, Cambridge University, Cambridge Mass. and Harvard University, Cambridge Mass.; [occ.] Freelance Writer for Oregon Post, Portland, Ore.; [memb.] Columbia Regional Heart Club. The Ameri-

can Songwriter Club; [hon.] "Outstanding Teenager Award", Dean's List, "Outstanding Songwriting Award", Special Promotion and Marketing Award for the song "Aretha" and "Special Recording Award for the song "Make Me Talk It Over"; [oth. writ.] Several poems published in other anthologies. Author of one play, articles for The Boston Times Journal and the author of five songs accepted for recording.; [pers.] I'm the writer who would like to leave behind my words in scarlet flush and gold, to touch everyone's heart in a very special way.; [a.] Montgomery, AL

MANCLAW, RON
[pen.] Mr. Wits; [b.] March 27, 1943, Little Falls, NY; [p.] Homer Edward Manclaw; [m.] Verna Elizabeth Mykel Manclaw, January 29, 1938; [ed.] MBA Syracuse University, BSIE - Utica College of Syracuse University, AAS - Devry Technical Institute, US Navy - Electronics School; [occ.] Management Consultant Computers, Communications, Software; [memb.] Chaplain - Open Door Ministry - A Healing and Prison Ministry - Pompano Beach, Fla Cornerstone Church - Davie, Fla Waterfront Property Owners of Fla, Founder and past Vice President; [hon.] World Who's Who - Top 5000, Elected 1989 (Marquis), Travelers Insurance (Conservco), Humanitarian Recognition Award, Volunteer at Special Sluger/Hugger at Joe Di Maggio Children's Hospital in Pediatric ICU, Surgery and Long Term Terminally ILL - Peds Ward, National Library of Poetry, 1995 Editor's Choice award winner, "My Secret Love Ever More Near"; [per.] "May" - the God of your understanding be ever with you and by Jesus Christ and the Great "Holy" Spirit may you be healed in Soul and Body. May your life matter and be everlasting in heaven.; [a.] Fort Lauderdale, FL

MANDERS, HEIDI
[b.] October 21, 1980, Boscopel, WI; [p.] Kevin and Cathy Manders; [ed.] Seneca High School; [occ.] Student; [hon.] High honors through Jr. High; [pers.] My friends inspired my poems for the most part, but my feelings mainly are what I write.; [a.] Seneca, WI

MANTZOUKA, ELEFTHERIA
[b.] August 3, 1970, Athens, Greece; [p.] Theophanis Mantzouka, Eftichia Mantzouka; [m.] Richard K. Syson, January 1, 1996; [ed.] East Carolina University (ECU), College of South eastern Europe, 35th High School, Athens; [occ.] Graduate student in Maritime History and Nautical Archaeology, ECU; [memb.] Achaelogical Institute of America (AIA), American Association of University Women (AAUW), Institute of Nautical Archaeological (INA); [hon.] Twice "Thomas W. Rivers Study Abroad" Scholar, ECU, Greek Orthodox Archdiocese of North and South America Scholarship; [oth. writ.] A number of publications about care-diving, explorations and underwater archaeology in Greek Scuba-diving and other general interest magazines and periodicals.; [pers.] "There is always a price to be paid in life. Love demands the ultimate: life itself"; [a.] Greenville, NC

MARCROFT, BUD HAROLD
[b.] February 17, 1931, Artesia, CA; [p.] Harold and Ruth Benschneider Marcroft; [ch.] 4 (Vicki, David, Garland and Jonathan); [ed.] BA Degree plus; [occ.] Retired or unemployed; [memb.] Mason, Scottish Rite, York Rite, Shrine, V.F.W., American Legion and many others; [pers.] This is living.; [a.] San Diego, CA

MARIS, ROBERTA BOUSMAN
[pen.] Mari Rober; [b.] August 10, 1923, Santa Monica, CA; [p.] Tracy R. and Lura Bousman; [m.] Deceased, October 27, 1957; [ch.] 5 Daughters; [ed.] 1-6 Woodlawn - Bell Calif., 6-10 Bell High School, 11-12 Eagle Rock, LA City June 21, 1941, 6 months Pasadena City College - WW II, 2 years Yavapai, College,

Cottonwood AZ; [occ.] School bus driver, Laidlaw-contract service, Sedona AZ; [memb.] College of Hardknocks; [hon.] Music - (Piano) Penmanship Board of Control, Creative Writing award Yavapai College, Oil Painting award, Yavapai College; [oth. writ.] "Short stories on Lives of Long Haul Truck Drivers" (mine) Term Papers on Geology.; [pers.] Kind, honest, caring, serious, cheerful, nice to be around. Loving trustworthy, dependable, faithful appreciating or appreciative.

MARKHAM, FRED
[b.] August 18, 1948, Hutchinson, KS; [p.] Fred and May Markham; [ed.] Ph.D. in Mass Communication; [occ.] Song Writer; [memb.] ASCAP, ADAPT, CMA; [hon.] Leadership to service at Wichita University by Omicron Delta Kappa; [oth. writ.] Many national publications, articles, and poetry. Also song writing; [pers.] I am disabled but do not let it interfear with my life activities.; [a.] Hutchinson, KS

MARKS, RITA
[b.] May 31, 1953, San Mateo, CA; [p.] Joseph and Sarah Marks; [ch.] Lazet Howard and Tanesha Howard; [ed.] Canada College, Redwood City, CA - AA degree, College of Notre Dame, Belmont, CA - expect Computer Science degree in 1998; [occ.] Sr. Admin., Asst./Purchasing Agent at Sun Microsystems Inc., in Mountain View, CA; [memb.] Member of Fremont Bible Fellowship Church in Fremont, CA; [hon.] Dean's List - twice, American Business Women's Scholarship - three times, Redwood City Citizen's Scholarship, Canada College Scholarship, Bay Area Urban League Scholarship; [oth. writ.] Self, Rare Bird, Who Was That?, The Love, Life, I Want You, Education, unpublished poems, Slow Down, The Joy You Bring and various others.; [pers.] All the honor, praises, thankfulness, glroy, and my blessings go to God for providing me with the talent to write poetry and to share with others to enjoy. I thank my daughters for their love.; [a.] East Palo Alto, CA

MARQUER, SARAH
[b.] April 30, 1985, San Jose; [p.] Noel Marquer, Marie-Annick Glon; [ed.] Entering sixth grade; [occ.] Student (School), Student in gymnastics; [memb.] Twister Gymnastics Club; [hon.] First Honor; [oth. writ.] This is my first one.; [pers.] I think the only reason why I'm talented at poetry is by all the books I've read. They've influenced me on using descriptive language and wild imagination. I write what I feel.; [a.] Mountain View, CA

MARRANO, FRANCES E.
[pen.] Francine - Fran - Frannie; [b.] December 6, 1934, St. Louis, MO; [p.] Thelma Smercina and Clifford House; [m.] (Deceased) Joseph R. Marrano, December 28, 1952; [ch.] Dr. Rick J. Marrino, Chiara Marrano, Saverio Marrano; [ed.] Coast Guard Auxiliary, Two Year's College, Whittier Adult Business School, Professional Dog Groomer; [occ.] Retired; [memb.] Legal Defence of Animals; [hon.] Special Award Graduated High School at Whittier Adult School in 1983; [oth. writ.] Not shown as yet.; [pers.] In 1985 I started to write a "Groomer's Prayer" but it turned out to be the "Pet Prayer". Too many people neglect their pet.; [a.] Whittier, CA

MARSHALL, MARY J.
[b.] July 27, 1911, Richmond, VA; [p.] Hubert and Ada Templeman; [m.] Alfred Winston Marshall, May 31, 1931; [ch.] Anne, Winston, John; [ed.] BA in History, MA Guidance (School); [occ.] Retired Fairfox Public Schools; [memb.] Strother Society of VA., Fairfox Co. Va. Teachers Assoc. Cherrydale Baptist Church Arlington, VA; [hon.] American Univ. Award for paper on Fauquise white Sulphur Springs, My BA from American Univ., MA from George Washington Univ.; [oth.

writ.] Other poetry stories none published. Also I have written up my testimony as a Christian; [pers.] I am a born again Christian and attend Cherrydale Baptist Church in Arlington, VA. I was raised in a Christian home. My fore bearers came from Gachester England.; [a.] Falls Church, VA

MARSHALL, MELISSA ANNE
[pen.] Missy; [b.] August 23, 1982, Mount Holy, NJ; [p.] Sandra and James Clark; [ed.] T.H.O.M.S., BTHS, age 14; [occ.] A High School Student; [memb.] Key Club, Cheerleading; [oth. writ.] A poem was published in a teen arts book "Please Listen"; [pers.] All my life I have wanted to be a poet I owe it all to my mother, and my seventh grade reading teacher Mrs. Stegmuller.; [a.] Burlington, NJ

MARTIN, DEBORAH
[b.] April 23, 1957, Norfolk, VA; [p.] Joseph and Jane Corbett; [m.] Divorced; [ch.] Michael, Courtney and Caleb; [ed.] Tidewater Christian School. I am currently taking courses to become a Medical Transcriptionist; [occ.] Homemaker; [oth. writ.] Beginning of a Brand New Day, Inbetween, Kaleidoscope, (none yet published); [pers.] I try to make people reflect on their lives and have they done their best. I also enjoy the simple fact that each day is a gift from God.; [a.] Suffolk, VA

MARTIN, JOANNE
[b.] April 25, 1975, Albany, NY; [p.] Camilo and Rosa Martin; [ed.] Carol Morgan (Santo Domingo Dominican Republic), Buchholz High School (Gainesville, FL) and University of Florida (Gainesville, FL); [occ.] Psychology student, French minor; [memb.] President of French Club 1996-7, Treasurer of French Club 1995-6, Pre-professional SVV, organiz. 1993-4; [pers.] Never try to force your own will in life, just go with the flow and things will turn out right.; [a.] Gainesville, FL

MARTIN, LINDA
[pen.] Linda Cobb; [b.] January 15, 1952, Jackson, MS; [p.] Samuel Cobb, Gladys Cobb; [ch.] Nefertira Alysia Martin; [ed.] Wendell Phillips High, Eureka College Chicago State Univ.; [occ.] Educator; [hon.] Chicago State scholarship; [oth. writ.] Children's Story, Romance Short Story; [pers.] Life is precious, moments possessed are intriguing, as time is of the essence. Take heed to savour each while the picking is good.; [a.] Dixmoor, IL

MARTIN, STACY
[b.] December 27, 1970, Smithgrove, KY; [p.] Joyce Martin; [occ.] Factory Work - R. R. Donnelly and Sons Printing Company; [oth. writ.] Wrote several poems in High School and after I got out. I wrote in English class everyday we had to. Mostly for the school teacher he was the best.; [pers.] I try to let myself escape from everyday pressure by writing poems. I have wrote about 75 poems in all. My Senior English teacher influenced me the most. He said I have a natural gift for writing.; [a.] Smithsgrove, KY

MARTINEZ, BOB G.
[b.] June 7, 1949, Las Vegas, NM; [p.] Mrs. Mary Jane Martinez; [m.] Annette E. Martinez, February 10, 1973; [ch.] Lita (Sophomore in College); [ed.] Denver Public School System until 1968, then the School of Hard Knocks up unto this present day; [occ.] Security Department; [memb.] Distinguished, ISP-NLP Colorado Society of Poets, Mile High Poets Society; [hon.] Several Editors' Choice Award (ISP-NLP); [oth. writ.] "Side Tracks", a Personal Compilation of Poems and "My Time To Rhyme", unbroken 302 page Journal of my year from '49 to '94; [pers.] The slightest tinctures upon life's canvas....whether by word or deed, will all be caught...even what's hidden will come to focus...since the heart dictates the colors of thought.; [a.] Denver, CO

MARTINKOVIC, MARY LOU
[b.] May 22, 1952, Jersey City, NJ; [p.] Albert and Ada Dice; [m.] John F. Martinkovic Jr., March 7, 1986; [ch.] Christine and Brian; [ed.] Edison High School, NJ; [occ.] Administrative Assistant to Director of Engineering Frigidane Co, Edison, NJ; [memb.] Ladies Auxiliary Jackson Elks #2744; [hon.] 3 yrs Past President, Ladies Auxiliary; [oth. writ.] Other poems published by "The National Library of Poetry" are "Perhaps Someday" and "Sons"; [a.] Jackson, NJ

MARTINO, JOSEPH
[pen.] Anthony DiBossi; [b.] September 14, 1963, Chicago, IL; [p.] Sam Martino, Patricia Martino; [ed.] 1. St. Joseph Grammar School, 2. Fenwick High School, 3. Dubuque University; [occ.] Actor; [memb.] Screen Actors Guild, Dramatists Guild of America Associate Member; [hon.] Best Defensive player University of Dubuque.; [oth. writ.] 3 Full length theatrical productions produced New York City. 7 One act plays 2 screenplays; [pers.] I write from my heart and hope my writing captures the hearts of others. I am inspired by artists of every nature.; [a.] New York, NY

MASON, DEBORAH LEE
[b.] August 10, 1954, Chicago, IL; [p.] Frank Wesley Weder, Barbara A. Eschenbrenner; [m.] Wade R. Mason, August 12, 1989; [ch.] Carolynn Williamson, Janel Nordyke; [ed.] Steinmetz High, Ippolito's School of Cosmetology, Soderless Wire Jewelry Making; [occ.] Retail Sales; [oth. writ.] Fallen Roses; [pers.] I hold important the expressible depth of humanity, and to radiate the essence of life in my writing.; [a.] Lahoma, OK

MASON, LAURIE
[pen.] Laurie Mason; [b.] November 2, 1947; [p.] Red and Jean Mason; [m.] Divorced, 1991, June 14, 1969; [ch.] Amy Jean Ganim; [ed.] BS from Johnson State University - Vermont, Masters Degree Southern Conn., University Conn and 6th year degree Southern Conn. University; [occ.] Public School Teacher - Grade 2; [memb.] Shelton Education Association, Connecticut Education Association, Connecticut TAWL, The Institute for American Indian Studies, PTO Executive Board of Mohegan School, EMSPAC; [hon.] 1991 Semi-Finalist for Shelton Teacher of the Year, 1995 Winner of Connecticut's "Celebration of Excellence" for series of 3 Parents Workshops, Does a yearly "Poetry Extravaganza" for parents with students; [pers.] I believe or attitudes and perceptions greatly effect our behavior. I see my role as an educator to be the "Guide on the side" rather than the "Rage on the stage". I encourage everyone to follow their dream.; [a.] Southbury, CT

MATSUDA, KAZUE KAY
[pen.] K. Kay Matsuda; [b.] June 27, 1927, Wilmington, CA; [p.] Moichi and Mii Matsuda; [ed.] High School; [occ.] Domestic; [pers.] Japanese American, 5th of 6 children. Father born, Hilo, Hawaii, mother born, Yamaguchiken, Japan. I am an individualist, odd and peculiar, much of my life, alone, poverty and struggle. I always wanted to turn out to be something, so I'm happy to be a poet, also author, and maybe someday, something more I hope people everywhere will benefit by reading what I have written. Another poetry published in book (Today's Best Poems).; [a.] Los Angeles, CA

MAYER, DORIS
[b.] April 9, 1918, Youngstown, OH; [p.] Ruth Margery Ellis and Eugene Simon Mayer; [ch.] Stephen H. Ford Jr., Deborah Helen Ford, Serena Wright Ford; [ed.] Skidmore College (B.A.), George Washington University (Anthropology), Anne Arundel Community College (Paralegal Certificate program); [occ.] Paralegal student, volunteer, Conflict Resolution Center; [memb.]

Unitarian/Universalist Church, Sierra Club, A.C.L.U.; [hon.] Dean's List (Skidmore); [oth. writ.] "Let's Call In The Neighbors", Radio series (15 min.), United Nations Day radio show (30 min.), assorted writings in local newspaper, radio book reviews local stations, "To A Gentle People" (editor, anthology of family poetry); [pers.] The extraordinary richness, complexity, inter-relatedness, conflict, mystery not only in the natural environment but within human beings who attempt to manipulate it - for good or ill.; [a.] Arnold, MD

MAYFIELD, MARY A.
[pen.] Verta (used on painting); [b.] August 31, 1936, Baltimore; [p.] Mary Eleen Blackburn, George Dowerry; [m.] Carl D. Mayfield, July 22, 1956; [ch.] Carl Jr., Hilari, Keith; [ed.] Frederik Douglas - Baltimore Institute of Musical Arts Northern VA Community College; [occ.] Artist - Homemaker; [memb.] UMC - St. Pauls G St. Woodbridge VA, MS Support Group Dale City Fibro my Algia SG of Northern VA; [hon.] First Prize Awards for dance (in the 50's Ballet) Mother and Court of Arms Boy Scouts, Dance Scholarships Picture window painting award - W. Germany; [oth. writ.] Poems and short stories for church - not published - registered at copyright wash DC. Short stories for children in family; [pers.] When one is on one's back look up. There are no real defeats only challenges cry a little, laugh a lot! Judge no one with extreme true harshness. Time is our only possession; [a.] Dumfries, VA

MCALLISTER, DALE ALDER
[b.] September 16, 1925, Prove, UT; [p.] John W. McAllister, Myrl Alder McAllister; [m.] Laura Y. McAllister (present marriage), September 12, 1989; [ch.] 1st Marriage: Earl Craig, Michael Dale, Cindy, Jeffery Scott, Kevin Leo; [ed.] Santa Barbara, Calif. and Manti, Ut. High Schs. Snow College, Brigham Young University. B.A. and M.A. from B.Y.U. Certificate in Library Science. Minor in German. Elementary and Secondary teaching Certificates; [occ.] Retired School teacher - 31 yrs. drive ski busses in the winter and maintain 4 condo's swimming pools in summer; [memb.] Church of Jesus Christ of Latter-day Saints, (Mormon). B.Y.U. Alumni Assoc., A.A.R.P., Universal Campus Credit Union; [hon.] B.A. in music and education B.Y.U. M.A. in Religion and Scripture B.Y.U., Many Misc. bus driving awards. Won B.Y.U. song writing contest and church quartet original song contest. Poem, "Little Red Rose" chosen for publication in "The Colors Of Thought" national publication; [oth. writ.] Several poems, none published. Thesis on the Chronology of the old testament. Many songs, some published, some not. Many arrangements of songs, some published, some not; [pers.] The God, creator, and controller of the universe is the personal Father of all mankind and all men and women can become like him if they want to make the tremendous effort it takes. The basic purpose of life is to live like God and Jesus so that we can achieve the "Fulness Of Joy" that they now have. Everything has both positive and negative possibilities. Maturity is self control. Happiness is having someone to love, work you enjoy doing, and a clear conscience.; [a.] Wallsburg, UT

MCCAGHREN, ANNA
[b.] December 16, 1984, Carroll Co., GA; [p.] Brent and Karen McCaghren; [ed.] 6th grade - Bowdon Elementary; [occ.] Student; [memb.] Bowdon Baptist Church; [hon.] All "A" Student perfect attendance from K-5 thru 5th grade, Woodmen of the World "for Proficiency in American History"; [pers.] In my opinion, you do not have to be a proficient journalist to be a good writer. Some of the best writings have come from the heart.; [a.] Bowdon, GA

MCCARTHY, TARA ANN
[b.] January 27, 1970, Port Chester, NY; [ed.] Harrison High School, La Salle University; [occ.] Special Education Teacher, Bronx, NY; [a.] Purchase, NY

MCCARTY, SHANNON
[b.] June 26, 1978; [p.] Dennis, June McCarty; [ed.] Senior Channelview High; [memb.] ROTC; [hon.] Poem Certificate; [oth. writ.] Other poems.; [pers.] Shannon McCarty born Philadelphia, moved to TX. July 1983. My interest is writing poem, acting I am a senior and plan to go to college.; [a.] Channelview, TX

MCCHRISTIAN, ROBERT E.
[b.] April 4, 1973, Paducah, KY; [p.] Betty Garner, the late James McChristian; [m.] Carmen B. McChristian, June 9, 1995; [ed.] Paducah Tilghman High School; [occ.] Customer Service, Fleming Furniture, Paducah, KY; [memb.] Served U.S. Army 1991-1996; [oth. writ.] Unpublished book of poems and several short stories.; [pers.] I like to write from the very depths of my soul. I strive to display mankind's darkness and the darkness of nature, to enhance our understanding of uncontrollable emotions.; [a.] Paducah, KY

MCCLUNG, ELAINE
[b.] August 19, 1947, Fairmont, WV; [p.] Leon and Eva Sharp; [m.] Keith S. McClung, June 10, 1972; [ch.] John, Alex, Rebecca, Susanne; [ed.] B.A. Elementary Education, M.A. Speech Communications; [occ.] Teacher, Grade 4, Reading, English; [pers.] I believe that everyone can be a writer and has valuable information to share with the world. I try to instill this belief in my students.; [a.] Chester, WV

MCCORMICK, LEONA S.
[b.] February 13, 1924, Oak Hill, WV; [p.] Sparrel H. and Annie T. Stewart; [m.] John W. McCormick; [ch.] John T., Linda L., Phillip D., Janet L.; [occ.] Homemaker; [memb.] Florence Baptist Temple; [oth. writ.] Poems for church gatherings in VA Beach VA Baptist Church, for scrap books for retiring pastors, for sunday school at present address christmas story published in local news paper; [pers.] I wrote love poems in the past and little dittys now I write mostly for the glory of God and for others to enjoy.; [a.] Florence, KY

MCDADE, MIRANDA
[b.] May 31, 1984, Fort Lauderdale, FL; [p.] Brent and Teresa McDade; [ed.] 7th grade student currently "Home Schooling"; [hon.] G.E.M. Award for Gifted Exceptional Math Student of Broward County Florida; [pers.] I enjoy read, writing, and illustrating poems and short stories as an artistic outlet. My favorite poet is Shel Silverstein

MCDONALD, MARLO
[pen.] Sapphire; [b.] March 20, 1979, Corsicana, TX; [p.] Bobby and Yvonne McDonald; [ed.] Barron Elementary, Bowman Middle School, Williams High School, Plano East the best Senior High in Texas; [occ.] Child Growth and Development Care; [memb.] Panther PALS, United Way, American Red Cross Community First Aid and Safety and Community CPR; [hon.] Princess review for Shiloh Baptist Church, Division I in solo and ensemble (3X), perfect attendance, track and field award, attending College a year early due to academic achievements; [oth. writ.] Songs, music, poems, short stories and drama.; [pers.] I strive to inspire and enhance the enjoyment of life through creative writings and songs of true life experiences for the enjoyment of all people.; [a.] Plano, TX

MCDONALD, RUTH
[b.] January 28, Chicago, IL; [ch.] Peggy Porth - Eagle River, Wi.; [occ.] Retired; [hon.] Three Certificate's of Achievement from Billboard Annual Song Contests;

[oth. writ.] Many poems and songs not yet published; [pers.] The romance of life — the beauty of love, be it about people, animals, nature, places, is what moves me to write my songs and poems. It is reinforced daily with the faith of my daughter Peggy, and her believing in me and in what I do. Thank you Peggy.; [a.] Rockford, IL

MCDONNELL, MAUREEN ERIN
[b.] March 5, 1987, Houston, TX; [p.] Chuck and Maggie McDonnell; [ed.] Timberline Elementary Cherry Creek School Dist., Aurora Colorado poem submitted by Deanna Lemieux, 3rd grade teacher; [pers.] Wrote this poem after looking out over the creek and prairie when my new house was being built - age 7, 2nd grade.

MCDUFFIE, MR. ROY
[b.] November 2, 1941, Hazlehurst, CA; [p.] Danilel (Bud) Bud Duffie, Loraine A. Yeomans; [ed.] Jeff Davis High School, Hazlehurst, GA 1960; [occ.] Fiserv; [memb.] Distinguished member the International Society of Poets. New Hope Baptist Church; [oth. writ.] What if published in the through the hourglass, thank God published in the fields of Gold; [pers.] I strive to share the word of God in my poems; [a.] Jacksonville, FL

MCEVOY, FRANCISIS G.
[pen.] Fran McEvoy; [b.] August 7, 1960, Astoria Gen. Hosp., Queens, NY; [p.] Mr & Mrs McEvoy; [m.] I'm not married; [ch.] none for me thanks; [ed.] 1)B.S. Journalism Film C.W. Post (Long Island University) - Minor: Sept. 1995, 2) A.A.S. Communications Media Arts - Suffolk Community College - May 1993; [occ.] Freelance writer and hunting for suitable R/T gig, which I could use, I guess.; [memb.] None-I fail to meet most height requirements except of course Jockeys - which I won't do after that horse on the mountain in P>A> tried chucking me off his back into the trees. It didn't work - almost.; [hon.] S.C.C, Deans List - Phi Theta Kappa, Pi Alpha Sigma, It's certainly an honor..., C.W. Post - Deans list, Cum Laude, Phi Exa, ...and awarded just to be included in the publication...; [oth. writ.] Notes to landlord about where the rent money is and when are 'ya gonna fix that sink in the kitchen?; [pers.] "If you break it - you pay!" So I have a couple of things I really don't want.; [a.] Holbrook, NY

MCGEE JR., DENNIS C.
[pen.] D. McGee; [hon.] Publication in another anthology from the National Library of Poetry; [oth. writ.] Poems edition in college magazines drumboat, calliope and my own zine "Jealous God"; [pers.] Chenish the misery; [a.] Blackwood, NJ

MCGOWAN, JUDY ANN JASMINE
[pen.] A. "Shakespeare" McGowan; [b.] October 22, 1961, New York; [p.] Walter, Evelyn McGowan; [ed.] Associates Degree Southern Nevada Community College, Degree in Casino Gaming-Dealer, Degree in Cosmetology; [occ.] Las Vegas Multi-Game Casino Dealer on L.V. Strip; [memb.] Drug Free Zone Anti Drug Committee, M.L.K, Committee, N.A.A.C.P. Committee, Toast Masters; [hon.] Governors form for anti drug zone certificate; [oth. writ.] 'Tis the Season (questioning our heart's motive vs. the commercialism of the Christmas season, who believe or not and why?, matters of the heart and mind!); [pers.] Mouth Say anything!: People will say one thing but mean another, beware! Always say what you mean and mean what you say! Or II. Procrastination is a killer!; [a.] Las Vegas, NV

MCGOWAN, LARRY L.
[b.] February 4, 1966, Sylvester, GA; [p.] Grover McGowan and Willie Pearl McGowan; [m.] Mary Brown McGowan, March 11, 1986; [ch.] Caitlin Janelle McGowan, Larissa Renae; [ed.] 14 yrs.; [occ.] Staff Sergeant Promotable US Army; [hon.] Expert Infantryman Badge, Air Assault Badge, 3 - Army Commendation Medal 4 - Army Achievement Medals - 4 Good Conduct Medals 1 National Defense medal

MCGUIRE, TAMMY
[b.] December 4, 1964, Kansas City, KS; [p.] Norris A. and Bethel E. Coon; [m.] David McGuire Sr., May 29, 1981; [ch.] Randall McGuire, David McGuire Jr.; [ed.] Turner High School; [occ.] Mother, Wife and Homemaker; [oth. writ.] Several poems not published; [pers.] Life is like a classroom. Live it and learn.; [a.] Kansas City, KS

MCHUGH, ANDREA
[b.] October 4, 1982, Danvers, IL; [p.] Leisa and Bart McHugh; [ed.] Georgetown Middle School; [memb.] Student Council Class Rep.; [hon.] Sports Awards High Honors Academically and Honors; [oth. writ.] "Christmas Eve", "Anne Frank", "Boys in the Pasture", "A World To Be", My Best Friend", Everlasting Friend", Riddle", Grandmother Clair", "Love", etc.; [pers.] I feel Poetry expresses my inner most feeling yet doesn't reveal the actual nature of it meaning.; [a.] Georgetown, MA

MCKENNEY, TABITHA LYNN
[b.] January 7, 1976, Baltimore, MD; [p.] Cheryll Schroeder, Lee McKenney; [ed.] Baltimore School for the Arts High School - Frostburg State - Essex C.C.; [occ.] Sales Manager and Full Time Student; [memb.] National Jr. Honor Society; [hon.] 'Time to Care' Award, Unsung Hero Award; [oth. writ.] Include, First, You Alone, Mind Trap, Forever, and The Gathering; [pers.] My writings are influenced by an intense emotional state that we all seem to travel through at one time or another. Thanks to my mom and my best friends, Shelly McMorris and Cheryl Coto.; [a.] Baltimore, MD

MCMINN, AUNDRA
[b.] March 16, 1962, Fort Oglethorpe, GA; [m.] Thomas McMinn, February 21, 1987; [ch.] Hannah Joy, Moriah Grace; [ed.] G.E.D., also took some classes at Marietta Cobb Votech.; [occ.] Homemaker; [memb.] Hunter Hills Baptist Church; [oth. writ.] I have had several poems printed in church bulletins, newsletters, or edifiers one poem was read over radio, and still others were read to the church congregation in the sanctuary, etc.; [pers.] As a Christian, I am usually inspired by my own personal convictions or experiences. However, I sometimes write about other people's lives and situations, and how I perceive their feelings.; [a.] Kernersville, NC

MCMULLEN, MEREDITH JANE
[pen.] Trouble; [b.] August 18, 1981, Cincinnati, OH; [ed.] 9th Grade I am now going into home Schooling for one year; [occ.] Student; [hon.] Creative Writing; [oth. writ.] Wrote a book in 3rd Grade.; [pers.] "Temper is what gets most of us in trouble. Pride is what keeps us there". I know a lot about trouble because I'm in it all the time.; [a.] Cincinnati, OH

MEDEMA, BETTY
[b.] July 13, 1935, Toronto, SD; [ed.] B.S. Westmar College, LeMars, IA; [occ.] Elementary Teacher, Central Lyon School, Rock Rapids, IA; [memb.] Central Lyon Elementary Education Association, Northwest Iowa Reading Council, Immanuel Lutheran Church, Beta Sigma Phi; [hon.] Valedictorian of H.S. Class, Dean's List, Alpha Chi, Graduated Magna Cum Laude; [oth. writ.] Articles in Iowa Reading Journal, Newspaper articles, Church Christmas programs, many poems.; [pers.] Words are like toys and I experience great joy in "playing" with them. I try to convey this concept to my students and find it exciting to watch them grow as writers.; [a.] Rock Rapids, IA

MEEG, SUSAN VOLPE
[b.] January 5, 1960, Brooklyn, NY; [p.] Joseph and Marie Volpe; [m.] George A. Meeg, October 16, 1993; [ch.] Michael and Joseph Montanino/Jennifer and Michael Meeg; [ed.] Bachelor's in Professional Studies Masters in School Counseling at St. John's University; [occ.] Student/Intern Guidance Counselor; [hon.] Dean's List and induction into the Honor Society; [oth. writ.] Feelings of Living, Because of You, Searching, Grey Skies; [pers.] Don't put off for tomorrow what you can do today... For tomorrow may never come.; [a.] Queens, NY

MEEHL, ERIK R.
[b.] August 10, 1953, Minneapolis, MN; [p.] Paul Meehl, Alyce Meehl; [ed.] Minnehaha Academy, Normandale College; [occ.] Machinist; [hon.] Dean's List, A.A.S. Degree with High Honors, Nominated Phi Theta Kappa; [oth. writ.] Several other poems inspired by the woman of my dreams.; [pers.] The strongest feeling for composing poetry is the pain of love.; [a.] Hopkins, MN

MELDRUM, MATTHEW TODD
[b.] February 3, 1977, Albuquerque, NM; [p.] Gerald and Ann Reid; [ed.] High School Diploma 96B Intelligence Analyst Diploma, U.S. Army Intelligence School; [occ.] Student; [hon.] Awards Finalist Shakespeare Monologue Contest; [oth. writ.] High School play written as a research project; [pers.] I like to write surrealistically but with simple universal message beneath the aesthetic. I'd like to try to blend the line in first-person point of view between character and author

MENDENHALL, JENNE A.
[pen.] Anne Mendenhall; [b.] July 2, 1928, San Diego, CA; [p.] Harry Lloyd McCarty, and Jenne Knapp McCarty; [m.] Robert W. Mendenhall, November 28, 1947; [ch.] Rachel, Mark, Matthew, Peter John, Maria and Robert Jerome; [ed.] San Diego High, UCLA Institute Allende, San Miguel Allende, Gto. Mexico; [occ.] Writer; [memb.] Santa Barbara Bonsai Club, Santa Barbara Art Museum, All Saints Episcopal Church, Bill Downey's Auto Body Shop and Writing Clinic meets weekly in Summerland Church; [hon.] Won a Cup playing Badminton in College; [oth. writ.] Stories, biographical study of three So. Calif. Painters, poem about Silkworms published in 1940 in Jack and Jill Magazine.; [pers.] I write for my own amusement to find out what I think. No limits on subject matter beyond stretching for reality. No high purposes. Wouldn't mind making some money.; [a.] Summerland, CA

MERCER, AMANDA
[b.] January 28, 1981, Kinston, NC; [p.] Pamela Bishop, Peralta Perez; [ed.] East Duplin High School; [occ.] Student; [memb.] Spanish Club, FF A Club; [oth. writ.] Wrote one poem got published in another book but didn't make nothing out of it; [pers.] I write by using how people react on things how they live life and take that into my mind then I write.; [a.] Albertson, NC

MEROLILLO, RUTH ANN
[pen.] Ruth Ann Merolillo; [b.] October 31, 1922, Youngstown, OH; [p.] William and Elizabeth Petulis; [m.] Deceased, October 10, 1981; [ch.] Six children (from previous marriage); [ed.] High School - MRT Training - painting and writing; [occ.] Retired; [memb.] A.A.R.P. Senior citizen Group of Youngstown Ohio-Catholic Church, Retired Insurance Agent - Church Organist Choir; [hon.] Editors Award for Poetry 1995; [oth. writ.] A few short stories working on a novel fifteen poems.; [pers.] Most of my writings began at a Laten life. It's been my way of cotinuing on with things, that keep me happy, busy, and alert.; [a.] Youngstown, OH

MERRILL, DAWN-MARIE
[pen.] Dawn Willis, Dawn Merrill; [b.] September 20, 1971, Lompoc, CA; [p.] Jeff (Cindy) Willis, Janie (Tom) Miller; [m.] Chad Edward Merrill, September 30, 1995; [ed.] Oregon High School, Oregon, IL. Sauk Valley Community College, Dixon, IL.; [occ.] Veterinarian Assistant, Pines Meadow Veterinary Clinic; [memb.] St. Mary's Catholic Church; [hon.] Just honored to have such a wonderful husband, great family, and special friends.; [oth. writ.] Several poems - unpublished.; [pers.] I am greatly influenced by nature and the people around me. "Life" is a wonderful place to be.; [a.] Mount Morris, IL

MESSICK, ERIC D.
[pen.] Q-Tip or Scratch; [b.] December 7, 1980; [p.] John T. and Gretchen Messick; [ed.] Sacred Heart School, Blairs Middle School, Bonner Jr. High, G.W. High School, and my family and friends; [occ.] I work as a phone boy at Domino's Pizza (JTM Pizza Inc.); [memb.] Kim's School of Tae Kwon Do; [hon.] Yellow Belt in Tae Kwon Do, Won a "Questions and Answers" Book in a 3rd grade Reading Contest, Student of the Month for History on July 18, 1995, Honor Roll (sometimes); [oth. writ.] A lot of short essay and poems. "The Demons Within" in 8th grade young authors, nothing ever published though.; [pers.] It is my belief that humans are a "Hypocritical" species. We claim to be the only creature on earth that can reason and make logical rationalizations. But if you look around, we are the only animal that destroys its own habitat with the full knowledge that we are doing so. Even a wolf keeps his own den and clean. (And ignorance is the root of evil.); [a.] Danville, VA

MEYER, LAVANDA ROSE
[b.] March 20, 1949, Decorah, IA; [p.] Rosina and Lawrence Guyer; [m.] James A. Meyer Sr., June 26, 1971; [ch.] James Jr. and Elizabeth; [ed.] North High, West Union, IA., North East Iowa Community College; [occ.] Licensed Practical Nurse; [memb.] Member Immaculate Conception Church, Fairbank, IA; [pers.] In memory of my daughter, Elizabeth, who died in a car accident, May 24, 1992.; [a.] Fairbank, IA

MEYER, RITA S.
[b.] August 20, 1921, Pittsburgh, PA; [p.] Mary and Charles Meyer; [ed.] 3 yrs College - Evening Classes Computer Sciences; [occ.] Retired 1988, Employed Part-time as Accountant, Former Children's Dancing Teacher, owning my own studio for 15 years in Downtown Pittsburgh, teaching part-time for 35 years to go into business world.; [memb.] Order of the Eastern Star - Worthy Matron - Three Separate Terms, Past President, Pgh Chapter, Women In Construction - National Assoc. of Dance Artists - Ladies Of Charity, St. Cyril Of Alexandria Church - Mother Advisor, Faith Assy Intl Order Of The Rainbow For Girls; [hon.] Natl Speech Contest - First Place (Women In Construction), Plaques/Serv Awards - 7 Organizations; [oth. writ.] Wrote poems and articles always, but never pursued it professionally.; [pers.] "Love Began With A Doll" was written for a program when honoring the Worthy Grand Matron of the Grand Chapter of Pa., Sr. Janet S. Harvey. It shows the basis of the love practiced by the Masonic Fraternities and the Order of the Eastern Star in the great charitable work they do all over the world.

MIDDLEBROOK, KING DORTHEY L.
[pen.] Mrs. Russell King, Jr., Lowery Sister; [b.] December 4, 1935, Kentucky; [p.] Mr. Dan Lowery, Mrs. Mary W. Lowery; [m.] Russell King, Jr., August 10, 1992; [ch.] Perry, Charles, Victor and Danie Ruth Middlebrook, 3 step sons - Wayne, Jason and Kevin King; [ed.] Lauderdale High School, Ripley TN., Dyersburg State Community College, Tennessee Technology Center, Newbern, TN.; [occ.] Housewife Sect. Treas, New Jerusalem Temple; [memb.] New Jerusalem Temple Church of God in Christ, Dyersburg, TN., several Committees; [hon.] Public Speaking 1st Place 1938, Drama Performance Lane College, 1940, High School, Salutatorian, Performed on National T.V. 700 Club, 1976, published in 1984 edition of the World Who's Who of Women's Mother of the Year 1990, awarded by the Dyersburg Alumnae Chapter, Delta Sigma Theta Sorority, many other awards and honors; [oth. writ.] (Song) "The Real Meaning Of Christmas Day", several poems written for Easter and Christmas Programs, also dramas for church and programs; [pers.] I was married 35 years to the late Eld. Perry L. Middlebrook, Sr. I am co-founder, of Middle City/New Jerusalem Temple Church of God in Christ. My motto is: "If I can help somebody as I pass this way, my living shall not be in vain.; [a.] Dyersburg, TN

MIEDL, PAM
[pen.] Pam Miedl; [b.] October 17, 1964, Hannibal, MO; [p.] Don and Cheryl Roach; [m.] Jerry Miedl, December 31, 1985; [ch.] Chaise Ryan and Chayne Stevan; [ed.] Wilmington High School, Joliet Jr. College, Moler Hair styling College; [occ.] Mother, Housewife, and Crafter; [memb.] Secretary for the Parent School Organization; [oth. writ.] Heartfelt poem to parent for 25th anniversary, poetic ditties for school organization, news articles and special occasions.; [pers.] Love comes from the heart and life through the eyes, when truly expressed in poetic disguised!; [a.] Morris, IL

MILES, BREANNE
[b.] February 15, 1985, Paducah, KY; [p.] John and Tamela Miles; [ed.] Riverside Elementary, currently a 6th Grader at Hines Middle School; [occ.] Student; [memb.] Northside Church of Christ; [hon.] Odyssey of the Mind, The Newport News PTA, Reflections Contest; [oth. writ.] Story published in local newspaper, poem published in children's anthology of poetry; [pers.] I basically write from the heart and write what I feel. My poetry is all about what I feel inside.; [a.] Newport News, VA

MILETTO, CAITLIN
[b.] February 28, 1929, Pottstown, PA; [p.] Deborah and Louis Miletto; [ed.] Starting 2nd grade at Weatherly Elementary; [memb.] Brownie; [hon.] 1st Place in District Reflections Contest for poem 3rd place in State Reflections Contest for poem; [pers.] I love writing and reading

MILLER, JUDIE LYNN
[b.] June 24, 1964, Philadelphia, PA; [p.] Helen T. Walton, George F. Walton; [m.] Raymund S. Miller, September 22, 1990; [ed.] St. Hubert's High School, EMT/Telemetry - Monitor Technician; [occ.] Monitor Technician; [memb.] International Society of Poets (ISP), Distinguished Member; [hon.] Chapel of four Chaplins, Editor's Choice Award from National Library of Poetry - poems "Mom's Flowers", Book anthology "Rainbow's End"; [oth. writ.] "I've Counted The Flutters Of Butterflies Wings..." self published 1995, "Reversed Luluby" - anthology "Admist The Splendor", "The Promise" - anthology, "Fields Of Gold", "Just Enough Time" - anthology "Best of 90's", "Faith Of A Child", - anthology "Morning Song"; [pers.] Poems are inspired from my personal battle with cancer (1993), and caring for my terminally ill mother (1995), "And You Were There" details my surgery in 1994. This poems is dedicated to those who were at my side after surgery: Ray (husband), Ellen (sister) and Aunt Teresa (who was there because mom was too ill.); [a.] Philadelphia, PA

MILLER, MARTHA
[pen.] Martha Miller; [b.] October 13, 1949, South Bend, IN; [p.] Lloyd Smoot and Rachel Smoot; [m.] Gary D. Miller, August 2, 1969; [ch.] Verlin Miller, Annette, Bentley; [ed.] Jimtown High School Elkhart, Ind; [occ.] Attendant on a School Bus; [memb.] Bayshore Mennonite Church; [oth. writ.] I wrote several other poems, but none published.; [pers.] I just want the "Lord Jesus" to have all honor and glory, for this is His poem not mine. I'm His servant.; [a.] Sarasota, FL

MILLER, R. STEVEN
[b.] May 10, 1960, Doylestown; [p.] Richard and Gladys Miller; [m.] Barbara D. Carlson Miller, May 16, 1992; [ch.] Timothy; [ed.] A.A Business - BCCC, B.S. Business - Delaware Valley College, MBA - Wilkes College; [occ.] Computer System Analyst and Trainer; [oth. writ.] Businessman's Prayer; [pers.] Great is thy faithfulness.; [a.] Doylestown, PA

MILLS, MARY KATHRYN
[pen.] Mari Mills, Xena 58, Mary Loewe-Mills; [b.] July 2, 1958, Wayne, MI; [p.] Audrey Loewe (Deceased) and Mary Mayville (Grandmother); [m.] David R. Mills, October 7, 1977; [ch.] Mari Teresa, Dave, Jeremiah, Chris, Kevin; [ed.] Associates Degree in Science; [occ.] Illustrator - Artist, Medical Record Coder - Accredited Record Technician, Certified Coding Specialist; [memb.] AHIMA - American Health Information Management Association SEMHIMA - Southeastern Michigan Health Information Management Association - I am Vice President of this Organization; [oth. writ.] I am currently illustrating a poetry book. I mostly write poems for my friends as gifts.; [pers.] "The eyes can reflect the mirror image of your soul!" I find myself telling people that "We are in the same boat, just different Lake." "Always seize the day!"; [a.] Garden City, MI

MIRANDA, YNIRIDA
[b.] July 31, 1976, Downey, CA; [p.] Eulogio Miranda, Evangelina Miranda; [ed.] John Glenn H.S.; [occ.] Koliser permanente Hosp. Appt. Clerk; [pers.] I strongly believe that expression is one of the most beautiful gifts in the world; [a.] La Mirada, CA

MITCHELL, ELIZABETH
[pen.] Liz Harding; [b.] July 3, 1953, Spokane, WA; [p.] Charles J. and Helen G. Harding; [ch.] Jessica Anne, Jason Allen, Alan John; [ed.] Shadle Park High School, LaSalle Extension University-Interior Design, Everett Community College; [occ.] Homecare Aide, Sunrise Homecare; [memb.] Bethany Christian Assembly, Bethany Christian Singing Christmas Tree Choir; [hon.] Employee of Month, Stephan Ministries of Month; [oth. writ.] Several poems and short story non-published, three speeches delivered in varies school and community committee.; [pers.] I strive to re fleet the goodness of the Lord in all that I do or say. The inspiration of this poem "Spring Alive" was written at a Street Light after a very trying day this last spring.; [a.] Everett, WA

MITCHELL, JUDY
[b.] April 27, 1958, Elbert Co., GA; [p.] M. J. and Carolyn McMullan; [m.] Don Mitchell, May 11, 1985; [ch.] Ashley Virginia and Harrison Layfield; [ed.] Elbert Co. High, University of Georgia (B.S. in English Education); [occ.] Sales Associate and S.E. Sales Rep. (Women's dresser and better wear.); [memb.] Zeta Tau Alpha Sorority, Junior League of Douglas County, First Presbyterian Church (Choir); [hon.] High School, State 4-H Public Speaking Winner, Chamber of Commerce Girl of the Year, Library Essay contest winner, Honor grad. College Dean's List.; [oth. writ.] Poems and stories published in school and local newspapers, articles for Jr. league newsletters. Currently working

on a children's book.; [pers.] I began writing poems and stories at age 15. My writings start with my deepest emotions and are triggered by waves of joy and heartache.; [a.] Douglasville, GA

MOCZULSKI, CYNTHIA

[b.] August 16, 1961, Flemington, NJ; [m.] Tom Moczulski; [ch.] Laura Louise Moczulski; [ed.] Hunterdon Central High School; [occ.] Planner; [oth. writ.] Several poems to be published in 1997; [pers.] I write primarily about my life experiences and their influence on me emotionally and spiritually.; [a.] Easton, PA

MOJID, RUBABA

[b.] December 7, 1979, Bangladesh; [p.] Dr. M. A. Mojid and Dr. Kanij Fatema; [ed.] 11th Grader in High School; [occ.] Student; [hon.] Placed in the Honor Roll for Creative Writing in "The Fun Times," "Saudi Gazette" in Saudi Arabia, worked and recognized for working in a Saudi Arabian English TV Program for 8 years, most valuable Member of an Organization called United Cultures of Elsik in Houston; [oth. writ.] In the present I have written 22 poems but I didn't think they were good. But now I think I'll start sending them to more competitions; [pers.] I still believe that love and affection exist in this world. Moreover, anything can be conquered through determination and dedication. My writings express the true love of life, success and adventure. I also write to promote peace and harmony.; [a.] Manchester, MO

MONDAL, SAIKAT K.

[pen.] "Shomi", "Scoh"; [b.] May 12, 1969, Calcutta, India; [p.] Mr. Sanat K. Mondal and Mrs. Reba Mondal; [ed.] B.A. from Calvin College, Grand Rapids, Michigan; [occ.] Struggling Artist (Actor) in New York City; [oth. writ.] Poems, essay and journal.; [pers.] In our day to day lives, esp. during moving, we often come across packages, which says "Fragile material inside, please handle with care". Alas! If we truly understood the fragility of human heart, we could not have been so callous and lackadaisical in our ways and attitude.; [a.] New York, NY

MONREAL, NANCY

[b.] July 19, 1953, Los Angeles; [p.] Joseph and Dolores Fracasso; [m.] Frank, March 10, 1973; [ch.] Frank Matthew Monreal; [ed.] Completed H.S. 1971, started College for a career in Social Serv. had to stop due to Mother's illness took care of her 'till she passed away; [occ.] Personnel/Payroll and Benefits Coordinator for Foothill Nursing and Rehab Center; [hon.] I was Valedictorian of my graduating class and was also Editor for our School Year Book; [a.] Temple City, CA

MONTENARO, ANTHONY T.

[b.] November 16, 1966, Amsterdam, NY; [p.] Peter Jr. and Aurora Montenaro; [m.] Kimberly J. Montenaro, June 30, 1990; [ed.] Amsterdam High School; [occ.] Electrician; [memb.] Men's Recreational Volley Ball League; [pers.] I wrote this poem as a one year memoriam of my father Peter L. Montenaro's death. He passed away on April 2, 1995; [a.] Amsterdam, NY

MOON, RIKESHIA

[pen.] Rick Moon; [b.] January 5, 1983, Mercy Hospital; [p.] Rick Moon, Bonnie Myers; [m.] January 5, 1983-1995; [ch.] Five; [ed.] Washington Junior High as in George Washington J.H. Student (Ohio); [memb.] 2nd Baptist, 60 YMCA Boy's Club; [hon.] To all the people who made me to become somebody and become someone and to believe in myself and other's.; [oth. writ.] To have people have strong feelings about what I wrote and to make every paper of poem's I wrote to go in every Wednesday's and Sunday's Newspapers.; [pers.] I strongly hope every one knew about when I was

writing about this poet, if not I was talked about me as in if I were something or someone.; [a.] Hamilton, OH

MOORE, BARBARA

[pen.] Barbara Moore; [b.] December 16, 1952, Dallas, TX; [p.] Billy and Betty Binkley; [m.] Bud Moore, April 8, 1978; [ch.] Son - Christopher S. Moore; [ed.] Red Oak High School, Red Oak, Texas; [occ.] Secretary for the Upshur County District Attorney, Gilmer, Texas; [pers.] I write for pleasure, and I love most poetry. I like to write things that make people feel good.; [a.] Gilmer, TX

MOORE, DAVID

[pen.] David Moore; [b.] November 5, 1973, Raleigh, NC; [p.] Vick Moore, Susan Moore; [ed.] Millbrook High School, North Carolina State University; [occ.] Student; [memb.] NCSU, NROTC, Chi Epsilon, National Rifle Association; [hon.] Chi Epsilon, Dean's List, Marine Corps Association Award, Secretary of the Navy Distinguished Midshipman Graduated Award; [oth. writ.] Several unreleased poems; [pers.] Though sometimes seemingly somber in mood, my poems attempt to inspire the reader to live life to the fullest and grasp his youth. I long for society to retreat from a selfish and power-hungry modern world to a world of beauty and simplicity.; [a.] Raleigh, NC

MOORE, LINDA G.

[b.] December 16, 1946, Wayland Springs, TN; [p.] Grady and Edna Black; [m.] Warren K. Moore, August 1, 1975; [ch.] Michael Cloud, Steven Cloud, Jerry Moore; [ed.] Noblesville High School, Noblesville, Indiana; [occ.] Retired - American National Bank - Noblesville, IN; [memb.] Bethel Missionary Baptist Church; [oth. writ.] Poems published in local paper. I write poems for family and friends on special occasions.; [pers.] My most inner thoughts and feelings are expressed through my poetry. I especially enjoy writing for the people I cherish and love.; [a.] Noblesville, IN

MORANG, LYDIA E.

[p.] Harold O. Carter and Hattie Carter; [m.] Walter H. Morang Jr.; [ch.] Steve, Carole, Chip; [memb.] Distinguished member International Society of Poets; [pers.] "The thing that is hateful to you do not do to your neighbor." - Hillel -; [a.] Bangor, ME

MOREIRA, CHRISTINE

[pen.] "Krystyne"; [b.] September 9, 1975, Fall River, MA; [p.] Dimas and Margarida Moreira; [ch.] Carson Leigh Rego; [ed.] BMC Durfee High School, University of Massachusetts at Dartmouth; [pers.] Sometimes our biggest mistakes turn out to be our greatest achievements.; [a.] Fall River, MA

MOREIRA, ERICK J.

[b.] April 1973, Managua, Nicaragua; [p.] Carlos and Teresa Moreira; [oth. writ.] Forever grateful.; [pers.] Conquer your fears and believe in yourself. Determine your goals and strive to be the best you can be.; [a.] Queens, NY

MORGAN, JULIE L.

[pen.] Julie Morgan; [b.] May 14, 1958, Savannah, GA; [p.] Paul and Joyce Whitely; [m.] Frank S. Morgan, July 25, 1992; [ch.] John P. Morgan; [ed.] Master of Social Work MSW from University of Kentucky Bachelor of Social Work - Morehead State University; [memb.] National Association of Social Workers Since 1995, Social Work Honor Society Since '95 Pi Gamma Mu International Honor Society Since April '95; [pers.] Many thanks to my mom and all those who played a part in reaching my goals and to my husband and son for surviving my college years.; [a.] Morganfield, KY

MORJOSEPH, JANET LEA

[b.] February 8, 1958, Lynwood, CA; [p.] Fred and Yvonne Barber; [m.] Michael Richard Morjoseph, October 4, 1981; [ch.] Julie Lynn, Candace Lea; [ed.] Marina High School, Calif.; [oth. writ.] "Poems In My Life" personal printed book of my writings, non-published.; [pers.] I write poetry as a way to express the thoughts and feelings I can't express in the spoken word.; [a.] Huntington Beach, CA

MORRIS, BLONDELIA

[pen.] Blondelia Morris; [b.] April 12, 1925, Greenville, NC; [p.] George and Hattie Spicor; [m.] Matthew Morris (Deceased), September 30, 1943; [ch.] (4) James, Vernon, Matthew Jr., Anthony; [ed.] 2 yr. Comm. College, Chos. Va. and Norfolk State Univ.; [occ.] Clerks; [memb.] St Pauls CME Church, Usher Board - Missionary Board, Editor on church newspaper, Women in the Arts - Wash. DC; [hon.] Teacher Corp award for training workers. Award for Gov't for Superior Computer word.; [oth. writ.] Short story - Child's Book of Fiction, St Pauls Gazette New for Church; [pers.] Interest in writing stems from more than 18 years of work in elementary schools in the area of reading and math. I want to write a book.; [a.] Norfolk, VA

MORRIS, REBECCA

[b.] November 23, 1979, Stamford, CT; [p.] Kenneth Morris and Candace Morris; [ed.] Senior at Brookfield High; [occ.] Student; [oth. writ.] Several poems published in journals, magazines, anthologies, articles for school newspaper.; [a.] Brookfield, CT

MORTON, JEANNA LOUISE

[pen.] Je'anna Morton; [b.] December 4, 1983, Oakland, CA; [p.] Norman Morton and Kathleen Morton; [ed.] Claremont Middle School; [occ.] Student; [memb.] Local Chess Club; [hon.] The Merit Award, A Poetry contest and met Nikki Giovenni. Martin Luther King Speech Contest, won 2nd Prize Metal. Fleet week Poetry Contest Winner for my school $100 saving bond; [oth. writ.] Poems "I remember Egypt", and "California"; [pers.] First I would like to thanks God, and my mother for being there for me, and I would like to thank my father for everything, and special thanks to my uncle Les Walker, and my play Aunt Gwendolyn Coggs.; [a.] Oakland, CA

MOSES, HASSAN

[pen.] Hassan Moses; [b.] April 1, 1929, Springfield, MA; [p.] Mohamed and Fatima Moses; [m.] Chaheede Moses, April 3, 1960; [ch.] Mary, Jamillia, Kahlil; [ed.] High School, 48 Culinary Apprentice School 69; [occ.] Retired Executive Chef; [memb.] Pres. founder, Society of Lebanese, Folklore Art and Culture, American Culinary Federation, International Association of Amateur Inventors; [oth. writ.] Unpublished book of poem, relating to Civil in Lebanon.; [pers.] I like to write what I see, but mainly how I feel of any situation today and possible solutions.; [a.] Florence, AL

MOSES, MIRIAM

[pen.] Miriam Moses; [b.] August 11, 1950, New York City, NY; [ed.] Bachelor of Arts - Theatre and Communications - Hunter College, NY, M.B.A. - Southern California University; [occ.] Writer, Composer, Lyricist; [memb.] The Dramatist Guild, The Author's League; [hon.] Axe - Houghton Foundation Award - Communications Charles Elson Award - Theatrical Production; [oth. Writ.] Reflections - Musical Theatre, Intimate Friends - Musical Theatre, Eye of the Storm - Musical Theatre, "Survivor - and Pieces of Glass" Short Story, "The Night of the Iguana Hunter" short story various articles for Newspapers and Magazines - Local and National; [pers.] Mine is the life of the passion; [a.] Seattle, WA

MOSHER, MARY ANN
[b.] July 19, 1950, New Britain, CT; [m.] Dennis Mosher, November 22, 1969; [ch.] Desiree, Michele; [ed.] Berlin High School, Hartford Hospital School of Nursing, New Britain Gen. Hospital School of Nursing; [occ.] Nurse; [oth. writ.] An article published in the "Fire's of Kuwait." (My husband and I were hostages in hiding for 130 days in Kuwait); [pers.] While living and working in Russia for over five years we witnessed the struggling rebirth of Mother Russia. Inspiration for my poem came as I watched the workers strive to embrace democracy.; [a.] Bellingham, WA

MOTTIORCIO, ANTONIO
[pen.] Antonio Mattiaccio; [b.] October 16, 1914, Yonkers, NY; [p.] Antoinette (mother), John (father); [m.] Filomena (Deceased December 29, 1992), March 3, 1946; [ch.] Anthony (son), June Ann (daughter); [ed.] Grade School #18 to Ben. Franklin Jr. High to Commerce, High to Saunders Trade and Technical High Graduated 1993; [occ.] Retired Jan 1980, Auto Technician (Mechanic); [memb.] Frank Rea Post 1163, Lady Mt. Carmel Church, Catholic Men's Club, 11:15 a.m. Mass Choir Member, all Yonkers, NY; [hon.] Frank Rea Post 1163 honored me April 28, 1995 with a dinner for doing an excellent job as adjutant (secretary for minutes of a meeting); [oth. writ.] Having written many more poems mostly to my wife Filomena also add subjects; [pers.] I have a strong bond with my wife even though she passed away. I live alone and our 2 children are very goo to me thank God.; [a.] Yonkers, NY

MOTYCKA, ALICE M.
[b.] July 2, 1928, Queens, NY; [p.] Fred and Margaret Schmitz; [ch.] George and Fred Motycka; [ed.] Bachelor of Science in Ed., Framingham St. Teacher's College, MA, Master of Ed., University of ME, Orono, Certified Advance Studies, Univ. of ME, Orono in Language Arts; [occ.] Semi retired, Instructor Univ of ME, Orono ME, Husson College, Bangor; [hon.] 1) Certificate of Appreciation from: The State of Maine, 1978 for Outstanding Contribution to the School Health Ed. Project, 2) Honors and Awards, Special Appreciation from King Alfred's College, Winchester, England, 1983 contribution of 100 hours plus to for The Educational System of England, 3) special Appreciation from The Girl Scouts, 1990; [oth. writ.] Teaching technique as employed by Alice Motychka is discussed and illustrated in the 1996 publication, Talk, Wonder, and Play, Edited by Amy A. McClure and Janice V. Kristo; [pers.] When working with students of any age always employ high expectations, consistent compassion and encouragement. You will be rewarded a thousand times over.; [a.] Penobscot, ME

MUMMEY, TIMOTHY JAMES
[b.] August 1, 1977, Newark, OH; [p.] Timothy L. and Sharon D. Mummey; [ed.] Graduated from Utica High School, Class of 1996; [occ.] Meat Clerk, Kroger Food and Drug; [hon.] Certificate of Merit in writing from Utica High School in 1994; [a.] Newark, OH

MUNRO, RONN
[pen.] Ronn Munro; [b.] May 8, 1933, Camden, NJ; [m.] Linda, August 10, 1974; [ed.] B.S. in Education - Temple University, Phila. PA, M.S. in Education - Temple University, Phila. PA, also attended - U. of Maryalnd F&M College; [occ.] Professional Actor; [memb.] Actor's Equity Assn., Screen Actor's Guild, A.F.T.R.A. (Radio and Television); [oth. writ.] Poems published in A.E.A., Sag newsletters.; [pers.] Giving love comes back to you tenfold.; [a.] Collegeville, PA

MURPHY, JEAN L.
[b.] January 21, 1947, Tacoma, WA; [p.] Margaret Neal and Hilmar Lillehei; [ch.] Lynna Renae Lynch and Allen Daniel Byrd; [occ.] Safeway Checker; [oth. writ.]

First (out of several others) to be published, thank you; [pers.] Learning through words; [a.] Puyallup, WA

MURPHY, JEREMY
[b.] April 8, 1977; [p.] Brenda Murphy, Marty Murphy; [ed.] Mentor High School, Lakeland Community College; [occ.] Dishwasher, La Malfa Center Mentor, OH; [oth. writ.] Never published before; [pers.] I have always enjoyed writing my thoughts, dreams, or interests. This poem is for the dog that I had all man life. She died 2 days after my birthday, but I remember the good times. Memories never die.; [a.] Mentor, OH

MURRAY, IRIS I.
[b.] Monsterrat, WI; [p.] James and Catherine Webbe; [ch.] Carleen, Adina and Raymond Murray; [ed.] J. E. Burke High, Quincy College; [occ.] Nurse, P.A.C.T. Coord. Foster Parent Liaison - DSS - (Department of Social Services); [memb.] Rehoboth Bethel Apos. Church. Missionary, Director of Food Pantry; [hon.] Foster Parent of Year in Boston, MA, June 6, 1993; [oth. writ.] Poem - our Foster Children publish - Dorchester Community News - 1996.; [pers.] I want to touch other lives, in a positive way by writing poems of different experiences I've had.

MURRAY, NORMA SUSAN
[b.] September 25, 1956, Los Angeles; [p.] Angela and Ralph Montellano; [m.] Keith M. Murray, July 4, 1986; [ch.] Jeanine Sarah Kaltenbach, Sarah Melissa Murray; [ed.] Sacred Heart of Jesus Elementary, Sacred Heart High School, East Los Angeles College, Southland College of Legal Careers continuing education through various seminars; [occ.] Legal Secretary, Secretarial Coordinator, Notary Public; [memb.] San Gabrial Valley Legal Secretaries Association, National Notary Association; [hon.] Published poetry, writings, etc.; [oth. writ.] Editor, major law firm of Skadden, Arps, Slate, Meagher and Flom; [pers.] We are what we think! Attitude is everything. We are here to learn lessons. Love is the key.; [a.] Los Angeles, CA

MYHRMAN, AMBER
[b.] April 25, 1982, Phoenix, AZ; [p.] Vicki Myhrman; [ed.] Elementary & Juniou High, Attending Xavier High School as a Freshman 1996-1997; [memb.] Member of the Phoenix Library Teen Council; [oth. writ.] Short story, full length story, many other poems. Currently working on another short story & poems; [pers.] Dreams are the base of reality, just as knowledge is the base of wisdom; [a.] Phoenix, AZ

NAGEL, M. CONSTANCE
[pen.] M. Constance Nagel; [b.] January 19, 1927, Springfield, IL; [p.] Charles Frederick Nagel, Ella Hamilton Nagel; [ed.] Rock Island Senior High, Kansas (Ill) Community High, DePauw University, BA Private Piano and Organ Study; [occ.] Office Associate/State of Ill., Church Organist; [memb.] Peoria Historical Society, Lakeview, Museu, Peoria, American Guild of Organists, Cathedral Church of St. Paul, Peoria, formerly AAUW, Sing—It—Yourself Messiah Committee; [oth. writ.] Verses published in DePauw Alumnus and DePauw Magazine and in other publications, book, a collection of verse to be published in 1997 former editor house organs, include - Decatur (Ill) General Electric daily, Great Central Insurance Company - Peoria, authored articles and newsletters, including those regarding music, wrote documents on sales promotion, hospital area wide planning brochures, and about liturgical music; [pers.] Words are some of my best friends, many of them are a fulfilling uniqueness to passivity, which seems so confining.; [a.] Peoria, IL

NASH, MYRON LEE
[b.] August 1, 1953, Indianapolis, IN; [p.] Jess Mattick, Barbara Mattick; [ed.] Mt. Vernon High School, Vincennes University, Ball State University; [occ.] Television Producer, Walt Disney Studios, Burbank, CA; [memb.] Academy of Television Arts and Science; [oth. writ.] Several non-published works - poems, prose; [pers.] Words have power! I believe a single word can peak the imagination, alter one's thinking and change the course of a life forever. My poems originate from my love for "Words" and are inspired by a combination of real life experience, personal relationships or vicarious longings. Proverbs 25:11; [a.] Los Angeles, CA

NAU, ELIZABETH
[b.] January 12, 1916, Rapid City, SD; [p.] John and Gertrude Schieferstein; [m.] Robert H. Nau, August 15, 1950; [ch.] Son, Dana, 2 Daughters, Diane, Alice; [ed.] Univ. of Oregon, Univ. Illinois, St Paul School of Theology, Military Service: WAVE, WW II; [occ.] Retired: Formerly High School Teacher, University teacher, Ordained Pastor for United Methodist Church; [memb.] Missouri East Conf., United Methodist Church, High School Debate Univ., Oregon Debate team, AAUW; [hon.] Phi Kappa Phi National Scholarship Honorary, Delta Sigma Rho National Speech Honorary, Five awards incl. First place in Forensic Meet, United Methodist Church Pastor of the Year Award, Fort Leonard Wood Army Hospital Chaplain Assistant, (Three Awards for Fort Chaplain Assistant); [oth. writ.] Numerous poems, Religious writings, published, articles on The Shroud of Turin, Dead Sea Scrolls, Oregon Pioneer, Dr. George Atkinsson, Three-Act Drama, "Call Up Rolla Time", "The Lookout Mystery" novel; [pers.] As a child, my Mother often read poetry to me. Also, she taught me to be a caring person and to love God. Outdoor living became a real part of my growing up. These things strengthened the presence of God in my life and His call to become an Ordained pastor. My life has been filled with miracles, witnessing has been made easier through the use of poetry and poetic language.; [a.] Rolla, MO

NAVARRETTE, JORDI A.
[b.] February 27, 1985, New York City; [p.] Ana M. Navarrette; [ed.] J.H.S.; [occ.] Student; [hon.] Certificate of Achievement for Poetry, Math, Computer Sc., Attendance, Good Behavior, "Student of the month"; [pers.] I'm 11 years old and I'm in sixth grade. Last semester I wrote a poem in my school newspaper. I also read one of my poems in my school's Earth Days Celebration. I started writing poems since second grade. I have two brothers and four sisters. I am number four in my family.; [a.] New York, NY

NEEL, ALICIA L.
[b.] November 17, 1956, Indianapolis, IN; [ed.] Herscher H.S., Kankakee Comm. College; [occ.] Factory Worker; [memb.] First Social Brethren Church; [hon.] American Legion School Award, National Honor Society, President's List; [oth. writ.] Unpublished short stories: "A Story of Ebony Black", "Reynold's Story", and "Stolen Happiness" and other poems; [pers.] I believe we are eternal beings, and the older I get, the more exciting life gets. I believe in eternal values (not just family values), and that's what we do we here matters. I wish to dedicate this poem to my psychologist, Dr. Jan M. Lumkes, who has made, and makes life more exciting for me and who believes in me, my writing and all my endeavors.; [a.] Bradley, IL

NEFF, SAMUEL GUNNETT
[b.] September 23, 1914, Frostburg, MD; [p.] Clifford and Edna Neff; [m.] Evelyn Katherine Neff, March 31, 1935; [ch.] Five; [ed.] For the Most Part Self Educated Voracious Reader - had Photographic Memory Special

Interest - History and Politics also Correspondence Course - Penn State; [occ.] PA State Senator - Manager State Workmans Insurance Fund - Owner Operator, Golf Course Nurseryman - Gifted Speaker and Speech Writer; [hon.] Democrat of Distraction Award 1995 in Beaver County PA; [oth. writ.] Spent last 6 years researching and writing book on genealogy as a legacy for his descendants; [pers.] Samuel Neff fought to help minorities, workers and the middle class. He used every means at this disposal when positioned politically to do so. "His Word Was His Bond."; [a.] Ellwood City, PA

NEFF-LEWIS, CHRISTY S.
[pen.] C. S. Neff-Lewis; [b.] January 3, 1969, Lansing, MI; [p.] Maxwell K., Donna J. Malcolm; [m.] Divorced, Widowed; [ch.] James Kelly-Allen Christopher, Anna Kirstyne, Richard Frank all Neffs; [occ.] Writer/Domestic Engineer; [memb.] Alitism Society of MI and Support Group for Families with Special Needs Child (REN); [pers.] My writings/artistry reflect personal travail. These two means of self-expression have proven beneficial in the healing process. Special thanks to Daniel, my brother. I love you.; [a.] Potterville, MI

NELSEN, NORMAN R.
[b.] December 13, 1936, Staten Island, NY; [p.] Bernhard and Gladys Nelsen; [m.] Divorced; [ch.] Ronald Keith Nelsen (Deceased), Katherine Elizabeth Nelsen; [ed.] Princeton University AB 1958, Woodrow Wilson School of Public and International Affairs; [occ.] Retired International Business Executive, Consultant; [memb.] The Presbyterian Church, Basking Ridge, NY, Scholarship Committee, The International Society of Poets; [hon.] Phi Beta Kappa; [oth. writ.] "Revival" in Sea Of Treasures, "Critters Who Aren't Quitters" in Spirit Of The Age, "On Castle Rock Road" in Where Dawn Lingers, "Risky Mission" in Across The Univerce, "Loonacy" in Best Poems of the '90's, "The Tree Tao" in Portraits Of Life, "Murder In The Cathedral" in Day Break On The Land, "Poetic Justice" in Moonlight And Wishes; [pers.] Often I write of the unity and diversity in what God has created and continues to create.; [a.] Basking Ridge, NJ

NELSON, MALINDA
[pen.] Eternal; [b.] August 14, 1978, Edison, NJ; [p.] Vickie Carson, Charles Carson; [ed.] Currently attending Jackson Memorial High School; [memb.] JV Softball Team, Manager of Field Hockey, Layout Editor for Jackson Views '96; [hon.] Athletic Award, High Honor Roll; [oth. writ.] Several poems published in Jackson Views Literary Magazines; [pers.] I hope my poems are enjoyed as much as I love writing them.; [a.] Jackson, NJ

NELSON, SCOTT
[b.] November 18, 1979, Texas; [p.] Bob and Wendy; [ed.] Junior in High School; [hon.] Nothing published, no awards; [oth. writ.] The Book of Purple Dreams, Shards of Shattered Minds (In the making); [pers.] It's better to be loved, than feared.; [a.] Pecos, NM

NELSON, WILLIAM
[pen.] Billy; [b.] October 1, 1924, Arelee, Saskatchewan, Canada; [p.] William and Lena; [m.] Aris Nelson, June 7, 1964; [ch.] Frank, Kevin, Colleen, Eric, Mimi; [ed.] (B.A.) Long Beach State College June 1963, (M.A.) in English at California State College in Los Angeles December 1967; [occ.] Retired After 43 years of teaching; [memb.] British Columbia Teacher's Federation, Canadian Teachers' Federation Seventh-day Adventist Church, British and Foreign Bible Society, American Bible Society, Member of the SonQuest Prison Ministries; [oth. writ.] Study lessons on numerous Bible themes; [pers.] My teaching motto has been the counsel found in King Solomon's inspired Ecclesiastes 9:10 - "Whatsoever thy hand findeth to do, do it with thy

might".; [a.] College Place, WA

NESTOR, NANCY
[b.] March 16, 1938, Kimberly, WV; [p.] Joseph and Ethel Kirk; [m.] Jannes Nestor, June 4, 1988; [ch.] Three: 'Bill' Keyser, Mindy Markley, David Keyser; [ed.] 11th grade Eact test; [occ.] Retired - 17 yrs. with city of Titusville Police Dept.; [memb.] 'Nickerson Family' Life Group; [hon.] 'Organization Values Award' in 1992 from the city of Titusville; [oth. writ.] Explanation - I have never shown my poetry to anyone, I simply keep the poems in a book.; [pers.] I write from my heart and usually about life experiences of my own or others whose lives have touched mine. I am the care giver for my 85 yrs. old mother who is afflicted.; [a.] Mims, FL

NEUREUTHER, EARLENE R.
[b.] April 23, 1979, Peoria, IL; [p.] Aaron and Mary Neureuther; [ed.] High school student at Houlton High; [occ.] Student; [memb.] A class officer for the Junior Class (Secretary); [a.] Houlton, ME

NEVSHEMAL, JOHN
[pen.] John Nevshemal; [b.] October 14, 1935, Milwaukee, WI; [p.] Anthony and Beatrice; [m.] Divorced, November 19, 1966; [ch.] Kris, Tony, Marty, Mike and Joe; [ed.] BS and MS Engineering and Marquette University; [occ.] Chief Engineer, Professor and Consultant; [memb.] Sigma XI (Research) International Society of Poets, Stephen Ministry; [oth. writ.] Several poems (Published) and short stories (Unpublished); [pers.] I explore the inner being, life's relationships, man/woman, de family as the basic unit for human society and love as the goal of all relationships.; [a.] Parker, CO

NGUYEN, TU KHAC
[pen.] John Tu Nguyen; [b.] March 20, 1942, Vietnam; [p.] Thuy V. Nguyen (p), Khi T. Cao (m); [m.] Phin Thi Vu, February 2, 1972; [ch.] Tiep R. Nguyen, Xuan Thi T. Nguyen; [ed.] Bachelor's Degree in Law, Saigon University, VN. Hotel/Restaurant Management Diploma, ICS, Pennsylvania.; [occ.] Houseman at the Portland Hilton Hotel; [memb.] Southeast Asean Vicariate; [oth. writ.] No Democracy in Vietnam. Who has the Right to Die? (Measure 16). Peter Nam, Martyr. (Catholic Digest, May 94) A Few Questions about Religion (Song Magazine, August, 1996); [pers.] I was a writer and a poet for 25 years in Vietnam. I wrote about God's love through the nature and the human being's life. I hope that I will be a writer and a poet in the same my writing in the United States America.; [a.] Portland, OR

NICHOLSON, EDWARD A.
[pen.] Edward A. Nicholson; [b.] October 14, 1936, Glen Cove, NY; [p.] Edward and Annie Nicholson; [m.] Christina, May 21, 1960; [ch.] Kimberly; [ed.] High School Glen Cove College University of Hawaii; [occ.] VP Sales and Marketing American Prime Inc.; [memb.] Reformed church of Locust Valley NY; [oth. writ.] The National Library of Poetry. "Man's True Pride" a muse to follow "Eternity" carvings in stone "Invincible force best poems of 90's "Condensed Beauty" recollections of yesterday "Message of the winding stream" "Memories of Tomorrow" "Winter's Night Wonderland" Whispers at Dusk the Poetry guild "A Walk of Bliss" footsteps in the sand; [pers.] Dear God, If my poetry can make some happy let them be joyful. If it creates sadness let there be reason for the sadness. If it delivers an essential message let them understand - it's meaning. And in a cumulative effort, let us all take heed, contribute solutions. And with thy help strive to make this a better world to live in.; [a.] Paterson, NJ

NIEHART, MICHELLE
[b.] October 25, 1970, Pomona, CA; [m.] Donald Niehart, February 17, 1996; [ch.] First one on way - due Nov. 13, 1996; [ed.] Chaffey High, Saddleback Comm. Coll, SDSU, ICS: Child Day Care Course; [occ.] Home Day Care Owner; [hon.] 4 other poems published in other National Library of Poetry books; [oth. writ.] This is the Day, To Remember Again, Where I Stand, I Promise; [pers.] Always follow your heart. And never give up!; [a.] Santee, CA

NIGLIO SR., FRANK
[pen.] Sonny; [b.] April 24, 1934, Elizabeth, NY; [p.] Helen and John Niglio; [m.] Ludamyla Niglio, August 26, 1996; [ch.] John, Frank, Michelle Niglio and Denise Otoole; [ed.] High School 9th; [occ.] Electrical Contractor; [hon.] Losing it honorable mention; [oth. writ.] Losing It; [pers.] The inspiration for my writings comes from my past loves, mom and dad as well as my children here played a big part in my writings.; [a.] Brick, NJ

NOVOSELETSKAYA, SVETA
[b.] April 26, 1976, Kiev, Ukraine; [p.] Yuliya and Sam Novoseletsky; [ed.] I am currently a Junior at the University of Colorado at Denver majoring in History; [oth. writ.] I have never been published before. My best friend entered my poem without me even knowing about it. But I do have a pretty selection of writings in both English and Russian.; [pers.] When my family moved from former USSR to the USA in August of 1991, there was a great deal of emotions involved in having to deal with the new culture. Much of this is expressed in my poetry as well as the feelings of just being a somebody who is different from the rest.; [a.] Denver, CO

NUGENT, ANGELA
[b.] December 28, 1941, Wuerzburg, Germany; [p.] Jean Buch, Mathilde Buch, Deceased; [m.] Maxim E. Nugent - Deceased, October 6, 1961; [ch.] Robert, Karl, David; [ed.] 7 Years of Grade School, 3 years of Business School; [occ.] Retired Sporting Goods Manager; [oth. writ.] Final Journey pub. in, Tomorrow Never Knows, National Library of Poetry also Pub. in "Best Poems of 1996".; [pers.] I write when I am deeply touched by something or someone.; [a.] Lawton, OK

NUGENT, KARI
[b.] May 16, 1978, Wyandotte, MI; [p.] Larry and Marlene Nugent; [ed.] John F. Kennedy High School, Henry Ford Community College; [occ.] Student, Course of Study Pre-Veterinary Medicine; [hon.] Magna Cum Laude, President's Education Awards Program, H.F.C.C. Honors Program Scholarship, Department Award of Merit, State of Michigan Competitive Scholarship, Language Arts, Social Science, and Business Awards; [a.] Taylor, MI

O'BRAOIN, RIOBART E.
[pen.] Robert E. Breen and R. Patrick O'Bannion; [b.] December 18, 1939, Cohoes, NY; [p.] Norman and Bernadette Breen (Both Deceased); [m.] Divorced, 1987, July 3, 1965; [ch.] Five; [ed.] A.A. Journalism Glendale College Arizona, Troy High School - Troy, NY, Van Schaik Grade School, Cohoes, NY; [occ.] NY State Comptrollers office of unclaimed funds; [memb.] American Legion (U.S.A.F. Vet Nat'l Rifle Association Loyal Order of Moose, Cohoes NY Veterans of Lansingburg, No. Troy NY, CSEA - Union Albany, NY; [hon.] Numerous Silver and Gold Poetry Awards, Including "World of Poetry," since 1980. 1977 Poetry Award - College Literary Magazine, "The Traveler" Glendale Coll. 1st prize. (April 1977); [oth. writ.] Many more over past 45 years (Former Journalist) "A Tear" - memorial poem to Actor David Jansen, Sent to his widow Via Johnny Carson. (you led...) "The Greatest Land - Memorial Poem to Pres. John F. Kennedy.

'Tis Only a Dream - Poem for Irish Freedom.; [pers.] I have been writing poetry since age 12 I am now nearly 57 years of age. There is much ugliness in the world, but much more beauty and love. It is the beauty of sight and sound and love I write about.; [a.] Cohoes, NY

O'NEILL, C. L.
[pen.] Christi Lynne; [b.] March 7, 1963, Jackson, MS; [p.] David Howard Watson Sr. and Gaynell Louise Whyte; [m.] Robert C. O'Neill, July 7, 1989; [ch.] Thomas Brian and Shelley Faye; [ed.] Eisenhower High Texas Tech Correspondence San Jose Community; [occ.] Administrator; [pers.] This first publication has encouraged me and given me a feeling of accomplishment. I look forward to entering another fine piece of art.; [a.] Arnold, CA

O'NEILL, DANIEL
[pen.] "Geronimo Joseph"; [b.] Detroit, MI; [pers.] I write not for benefit or exaltation but to humbly express an inner spirit of creativity which has been animated by the following collection of influences: A proud and iron-willed father, confidence from an ever supportive mum, adventures (and misadventures) with two brothers, an appreciation of two self-assured sisters, a marriage to the love and delight of my life (Cheryl), the mystifying magic and love for my small children, the diverse experiences of my life's path, and being bestowed by God with a feeling of satisfaction when creating with the written word.; [a.] Detroit, MI

O'SHIA, JENNIFER
[b.] July 5, 1957, California; [p.] Louis and Betty Roberson; [m.] Rick O'Shia, December 10, 1978; [ch.] Gabriel Roberson and Dennis O'Shia; [ed.] High School; [occ.] Domestic Engineer; [hon.] Honor Roll, Presidents all American Team.; [oth. writ.] Several non-published poems written to loved ones or for loved ones.; [pers.] Sometimes we wait to long to tell people how we feel. If you can't find the right words, try writing a poem. My mother never saw my poem to her. I hope she's proud wherever she is.; [a.] Antioch, CA

OHMART, PAULINE ROBINSON
[b.] April 14, 1908, Ector, OK; [p.] Thad Cowan, Christine Cowan; [m.] Perry G. Robinson, May 23, 1931; [ch.] Perry M. Robinson, Sand Tyrer; [ed.] Beaver High, NWOSU, BA Post Grad. work, at PU - OSU, WSU etc. (OCC) Elementary School Beaver Orienta, Jr. H. Kingfisher, Altu SCK Longmont, CO, Wichita, KS; [occ.] Retired; [memb.] First United Meth. Church Circle 6, Parkinson S.S. Class, Enid Writers Club, International Training in Communication, Retired Teachers Association; [hon.] I've been honored to be President of the 5 above mentioned Organizations. Member of Nation Honor Society in BHS; [oth. writ.] In my Father's House there are many - (biography) book of poetry, a poem published in Communicator (St. Magazine of ITC). I've published biographies in Country Historical Books.; [pers.] I've always liked biographical reading and writing. I enjoy poetry. At one time writing was not possible because I taught 30 years. Now I have time.; [a.] Enid, OK

OJEDA, JOSEPH T.
[pen.] Tex Ojeda; [b.] March 25, 1950, New York, NY; [p.] Maria Luisa Ayala and Benigno Ojeda Plaza; [ch.] Kenneth B. Ojeda, Lorraine J. Ojeda; [ed.] Queens College, N.Y. New York Institute of Technology - Teacher of Adult Education.; [occ.] Put-practice Clinical/Medical, Hypnologist/Psychologist, Teacher of Adults; [memb.] National Counseling Association, International Association of Counselors and Therapists, American Presidential Task force (Trustee), New York Institute of Technology - State Department NACCE; [hon.] Medial of Merit for Community Involvement by President Ronald Reagan; [pers.] I thank James Baldwin

for inspiring me to open spontaneous. The novelist and essayist, at a crucial time in my college writing career, advised me, "Joseph, trust what you see and write, the effort to write is an effort of love. God speed...", Nowadays, I pursuit to creatively unfold and render the optimal spiritual expression of the word. Blesses to all pioneer writers, now and tomorrow.; [a.] Queens, NY

OLIVER, LOLITA
[b.] September 20, 1962, Atlanta, GA; [p.] James Oliver, Bessie Oliver; [ed.] Franklin County High, Emmanuel College, Georgia State University, Southern Technical Institute; [occ.] Safety and Health Inspector, Maryland - OSHA; [memb.] Toastmasters, American Society of Safety Engineers, Afro American Historical/and Genealogical Society, Inc.; [hon.] Art Award at University of Georgia, Art Symposium; [oth. writ.] Recent submission of article for local newspaper; [pers.] I enjoy focusing on the delicate, and lovely items in nature, and everybody living which are gifts in disguise.; [a.] Silver Spring, MD

OLMEDA, JOHN M.
[b.] January 26, 1983, Santa Monica, CA; [p.] Gregory and Grace Olmeda; [ed.] St. Augustine's School (Parochial); [hon.] Honor Roll 4th-8th Grade, 20 Home Runs Culver City Little League Baseball; [pers.] Will be attending Loyola High School Los Angeles, CA in September '96; [a.] Culver City, CA

OLSON, JOHN W.
[b.] December 27, 1949, Springfield, MO; [p.] Carl I. and Vera R. Olson; [m.] Catherine A. Olson, August 2, 1984; [ch.] Chad V. Glass; [ed.] MSEE; [occ.] Engineer, US DOD; [memb.] IEEE, ACM; [hon.] Army Meritorious Service Medal (2), Meritorious Civilian Service Medal; [pers.] I dedicate this poem to my wife Cathy who inspires me.; [a.] Davidsonville, MD

ORNSTEIN, RANDY B.
[b.] July 20, 1979, North Miami, FL; [p.] Libbie and Morton Ornstein; [ed.] University School, Nova Southeastern, Ft. Laud, FL; [occ.] Student; [memb.] Key Club; [hon.] Who's Who in High School Recipient - Scott Wigley Scholarship 9-12, Cross Country - Honorable Mention - Sun Sentinel Miami Herald - MVP National Honor Society, Honor roll; [oth. writ.] Articles for school newspaper - Sun Beat; [a.] Plantation, FL

ORTIZ, BETTY
[b.] August 5, 1968, Chicago; [p.] Miguel A. Ortiz, Betty Ortiz (Deceased); [m.] Jo DiSalvo, June 20, 1995; [ed.] Lane Tech HS; [occ.] Paramedic; [oth. writ.] Several poems yet unpublished but shared with my friends; [pers.] My writing is a personal runaway for me. I write of memories and special moments with my best friend, Mom. My career gives me great insights that I can never return. And my friends, especially JoAnn, help me grow and express my emotions to never give up on a dream.; [a.] Chicago, IL

OSHER, REGINA LYNN
[pen.] Gina Osher; [b.] February 11, 1951, Topeka, KS; [ed.] El Cerrito High School, El Cerrito California University of Oregon, Eugene, Oregon; [occ.] Employment Counselor, Alameda County Social Services, Oakland, California; [oth. writ.] I have authored approximately 100 poems to date. I have also written four children's stories: "The Legend of Greenhorn", "The Barefoot Boy", "Sky and Cloud Together" and "The Little Plum Tree". I have also written an article: "Journal of a Californian" about my experiences, observations, thoughts and afterthoughts in regard to the October 17, 1989, Bay Area Earthquake. I have taken my first steps toward writing my first novel.; [pers.] I believe that people should be connected by the down-to-

earth aspects of life and I revere Mother Earth. I try to reflect this in my poetry. I try to create poetry that will promote peace on earth and peace of mind and which is timeless and enjoyable to all.; [a.] Almeda, CA

OVERDORF, RICHARD
[b.] August 30, 1931, Johnstown, PA; [p.] Theodore Overdorf, Lillian Rogers; [m.] Jo-Anne Shoaf, December 24, 1964; [ch.] Lori Ashton, David Massimo; [ed.] B.A. Economics, Univ. of Pittsburgh, Computer Learning Center, Anaheim, CA, Certificate in Programming as - 400 current UCI Student in Computer Graphics); [occ.] Investment Advisor and Stock Broker; [memb.] Lutheran Church of the Cross, Screen Actors Guild, American Federation of Radio and Television Artists, American Legion, and Civic Organizations; [oth. writ.] Published last year in the National Library of Poetry's Volume, "Forever And A Day", Love to write lyrics for country music, and radio commentaries on sports.; [pers.] There are many forms of love and many ways of expressing them. May we all have the privilege of feeling and using these gifts from God.; [a.] Laguna Beach, CA

OVERSTREET, ROBBIE LEE
[pen.] R. Lee Overstreet; [b.] February 13, 1947, Port Sulphur, LA; [p.] Robert Bailey and Sophia Marie Hill; [m.] Olen Overstreet, November 18, 1978; [ed.] Bachelor of Science - Bus. Education, Master's Degree - Business Education, 30 hours in Accounting; [occ.] Accountant/Small Bus. Owner; [memb.] Pi Omega Pi Honor Society, Delta Pi Epsilon Honor Society, College Park Baptist Church; [hon.] Pi Omega Pi Honor Society, Delta Pi Epsilon Honor Society; [pers.] I never quit trying to improve myself and find the good in things. I still have many dreams to complete before I depart this world.; [a.] Houston, TX

OWENS, SUSAN C.
[b.] April 25, 1951, Dayton, OH; [m.] Michael L. Owens, October 5, 1985; [ch.] Sean McKown, Larry MagLicco; [pers.] I am a constant writer of poetry and have had two poems published in a local newsletter. I fill my life with ministry work and try to reflect my experiences with those I care for in my writings.; [a.] Gilbert, AZ

OWENS JR., LLOYD
[b.] May 5, 1963, Pasco, WA; [p.] Diana and Lloyd Sr.; [m.] Akiko C. (from Japan), August 26, 1992; [ch.] Maya R. Owens (after Maya Angellou); [ed.] Two years College University of Maryland. High School was Henry Foss Graduated 1981; [occ.] Civil Engineer with the U.S. Air Force; [oth. writ.] I have many writings in my vault, but this (when love turn to dues) was the first that I have the courage to display to the public. I just recently got interested in writing after reading some of Maya Angelou's work.; [pers.] It is said that "A Picture Is Worth A Thousand Words." I hope, someday, that I can take a combination of those words and make a beautiful picture.; [a.] Tacoma, WA

OXMAN, NANCY
[b.] February 8, 1951, Phila., PA; [p.] Joan and Stanley Green; [m.] Steve Oxman, November 26, 1981; [ed.] Springfield High, Penn. State U., Non-fiction Magazine Writing Course with teacher Art Spikel that changed my life desires.; [occ.] "Want-to-be" poet.; [pers.] In a world cold and hard we all need a thing warm and soft. This is why we have poetry!; [a.] Havertown, PA

OZILL, TANJA
[pen.] Aishafoote; [b.] August 8, 1984, Ranliz, Israel; [p.] Rachel and Mike; [ed.] My schools are Mt. View Mid, St. Johns, Manor Woods; [occ.] Work at my pizza store.; [memb.] I go to a health Club.; [hon.] I won a Poetry contest. I was 7 in a writing contest at school;

[oth. writ.] I like writing stories; [pers.] I love my sisters. I would like like to thank my mom, dad, sisters, friends, my uncles, aunts, grandmas, to my heroes to Ram Vidal, Lucy Lawless and Kevin Serbor; [a.] Ellicott, MD

PACE, SAMUEL
[pen.] Samuel Pace; [b.] April 5, 1962, Elgin, IL; [p.] Samuel Pace, Lorraine Pace; [ch.] Joanna Lynn, Stuart Lee, Bradley Samuel; [ed.] Irving Crown High McHenry County College; [occ.] CNC Set-up man; [oth. writ.] Several poems published in local newspapers. Completed short childrens novel "Fableville". Currently working on "Death of an American Factory".; [pers.] Do not allow yourself to be influenced by other writers, rather observe your surroundings and write from your heart. This is the only true form of writing; [a.] Huntley, IL

PACILLI, JASON
[b.] March 22, 1958, Brooklyn, NY; [p.] Sara and Richard Pacilli; [ed.] Bachelor of Fine Arts - School of Visual Arts, Cooper Union, Master of Fine Art - National Academy of Fine Arts; [occ.] Consultant, Sales; [hon.] Dean's List, Master Eagle Graphic Award, Certified Instructor, Level I, II, III, Instructure Sales Senior at Dale Carnegie Institute, many Service at Leadership Awards; [oth. writ.] First time published; [pers.] To reflect the innermost thoughts I emotions that are unspoken. Possibly though the written word, they can be expressed.; [a.] Brooklyn, NY

PACK, BETTY DANIEL
[b.] May 24, 1924, Waverly, OH; [p.] Charlie Daniel & Madge Ball Daniel [m.] Laudie John Pack (deceased 12-18-88), April 25, 1944; [ch.] Melba McDaniel, Wanda Schubmohl (5 grandchildren); [ed.] thru Mifflin High School, Columbus, Ohio; [occ.] Housewife; [memb.] Church of God, Community Bible Study, Ashland, KY, International Society of Poets; [hon.] Editor's Choice Award - The National Library of Poetry; [oth. writ.] poems in anthologies: "Tomorrow's Dream", "Frost at Midnight", "Daybreak on the Land" and "Best Poems of the '90's". I have had a story accepted for publication.; [pers.] "My Dream" was written when I was a teen-ager. I believe I have accomplished many of those goals. I have written numerous poems; most are religious or about nature. I have written several short stories, both fiction and non fiction, for my grandchildren. I am working on my autobiography. It is my desire that my writings be a witness. "I can do all things through Christ who strengtens me." Philippines 4:13 NKJV; [a.] Ashland, KY

PADILLA SR., ELIAS
[b.] September 27, 1971, Los Angeles; [p.] (Grandma) Alicia (Apache) Padilla; [ch.] Elias Jr., Claudya Renee; [ed.] Lincoln High School and Stagg High where I met an English Teacher who pointed me in the right direction; [occ.] Full time father of two beautiful children; [memb.] Proud Member of people like myself who wouldn't give less to someone who needs more if capable of doing so. (If that counts); [hon.] The honor of being awarded Semi Finalist in the 1996 open poetry contest. Also having my poem selected for publication in an anthology. I feel like I already won first place; [oth. writ.] I have written other poems, lyrics for music, some stories and the thoughts that I finally found the words for all of which have not been published; [pers.] Writing books, stories, music or poems is a form of art and should be taken seriously. Never let anyone convince you otherwise. Creativity should be encouraged. People who think differently are people who do not believe in themselves.; [a.] Stockton, CA

PAGE, BERNI
[pen.] Biddi; [b.] Bridgeport, NE; [p.] Alma Cochran, Father - Deceased; [m.] David E. Page; [ed.] Bridgeport High School, Purdue - Grandview, Scottsblaff Jr. College; [occ.] Semi-retired Manager - Caterer - Chef, USPS Rural Letter Carrier; [memb.] Memberships - ILCW; [hon.] Jr. Dramatics Director, World Pork Expo judge, ACF Secretary; [oth. writ.] Short Fiction, Recipes for Cookbooks, poem in Dance On The Horizon.; [pers.] I write to reflect on the inordinate natural beauty of all entities as a part of each other.; [a.] Des Moines, IA

PANFILO, SABRINA
[p.] Amelia and Carlo Panfilo; [ed.] Third Year Student of Journalism at New York University; [pers.] Most of my poetry is written on behalf of all humankind - a nature that suffers from every kind of loss. I believe that we, as individuals, are all unprotected, loss is simply an inevitable pang of the human heart.

PAPADOPOULOS, CHRIS
[b.] August 4, 1981, NY; [p.] Terry and Angela; [ed.] Sophomore Norwalk High School; [a.] Norwalk, CT

PAPE, IRIS M.
[pen.] Iris Pape; [b.] March 5, 1911, China; [p.] Europeans; [ed.] A.A. San Mateo J.C., San Mateo, Calif. 1939, B.A. San Francisco State University, San Francisco, CA; [occ.] Retired since 1973, from Social Work; [memb.] Y.W.C.A., U.S.P.I.R.G., NWPC, AARP; [pers.] During WWII, I was a wac mechanic in the army air corps, so was able to finish college on the G.I. Bill.; [a.] Salem, OR

PAQUET, JUDITH B.
[pen.] Elizabeth McGowan; [b.] March 19, 1944, Wilmington, NC; [ch.] Daniel; [ed.] Registered Nurse plus Degree in Communications/Public Relations; [occ.] Director, Program Development for a Medical Continuing Education Company and principal Laughters Central.; [memb.] Author's Guild (NYC), Toastmasters International, Procrastinator's Club of America, American Association for Therapeutic Humor 1993-94 and 1996-97; [hon.] Listed in: Who's Who in American Nursing, Who's Who International 1990, Who's Who in Advertising 1988-90, Who's Who of American Women 1995-96, Amer. Biog. Instit. - 2,000 Notable American Women 1994; [oth. writ.] Essay - John Natchett-Pubria, Exquisite Corpse, Octogenarian (poem) pub. in 1995, Journal General Intornal Medicine "Stanford's Keep" (novel) unpublished, Many medical and allied health articles Exec. Editor _ Anesthesia Today put by Comed Communication Inc.; [pers.] I enjoy the use of descriptive prose, the flow of poetry, and the life lesson's that are reflected in poetry. Humor drive's my days and lights my nights.; [a.] Clementon, NJ

PARASCHOS, DIONYSIA GARBI
[b.] August 12, 1936, Greece; [p.] Nick-Ageliki Garbis; [m.] September 4, 1974; [ed.] In Greece four years study, Philosophy, Science, Classical Greek, Cosmography. In the USA Cambridge Schools, Rhodes School (Study English) Queens College, Career Brokerage Inc. Dejay School of R.E.; [occ.] Real Estate Broker, Principal Dion Realty Ing. 30-47 86 St. J. Hts. NY; [hon.] Honorary W. Irish Poet, The 4th Annual Irish Poetry Competition, Cyprus The Tragodia Sou, Extraordinary Reviews from Greek and Cyprus Governments, your poems are 2's Solomos and Kalvos, in all Greek Papers articles; [oth. writ.] "Cyprus The Tragodia Sou", 60 poems in Greek Language 1976, and others articles in the papers and magazines also unpublish, a collection of poems 60 in English Language, I wish to published - soon.; [pers.] "Poetry is the desire of the soul to express herself." "My love for peoples express in poems."; [a.] Jackson Hts., NY

PARENTE, DANIEL PAUL
[b.] September 10, 1960, Jersey City, NJ; [p.] Joseph and Snooky Parente; [m.] Carlene Singley, September 17, 1988; [ch.] 4 - Daniel, Nicole, Jeremy and James; [ed.] H.S. GED 1 Year College at University of Southern Miss.; [occ.] Professional Drapery Installer; [memb.] Arbor Day Foundation, Veterans Coalition, Schools for a Drug Free Nation; [oth. writ.] Childrens Stories, Reflections of Thought, Christian Music - Songs; [pers.] Strive for perfection in all I write I try to express a moral of value to reflect on. Proverbs - the pride of parents is their children; [a.] Sumrall, MS

PARENTE SR., ELIZABETH
[pen.] Elizabeth Parente; [b.] March 20, 1917, Cambridge, NY; [p.] Thomas Parente, Mary Parente; [ed.] BM, Georgian Court College, MM, Catholic Univ. of America, Post grad. NY; [occ.] Director of Religion Edn. St. Thomas, The Apostle, Bloomfield, NJ; [memb.] ASCAP - Who's Who in ASCAP, Member of Pastoral Associates of The Archdiocese of Newark; [hon.] Damien Dutton Award 1995, Mother Ninetta Award 1994, Articles about my music achievements in the Congressional Record, Musart Magazine, NJ Music of Arts, TV Guides, The Talent; [oth. writ.] Piano and Vocal Music 14 Published with G. Schimer Inc., Willis Music Co., McLoughlin and Relly Co., Boy State Music Co., Heidi - Operetta for children, Mass in honor of St. Lucy Filippini in English and Italian etc.; [pers.] Whether teaching here at home or in Italy, Ethiopia, Israel and Kuwait, I found the arts to be a powerful creative force transcending national barriers and uniting us in understanding, spirit and truth.; [a.] Pequannock, NJ

PARKER, KEITH W.
[pen.] Keith W. Parker; [b.] January 19, 1961, Jacksonville, FL; [p.] Kenneth and Linda Lee Parker; [m.] Judy M. Parker, March 16, 1991; [ed.] Trinity Christian Academy (High School); [occ.] Mail Room Clerk and Courier at Winn-Dixie Whse.; [pers.] I try to reflect, that which is, and that which should be. For there to be a world with alot less problems.; [a.] Jacksonville, FL

PARKER, THELMA JO
[pen.] (Possible) Thel Griffin; [b.] November 12, 1915, Rogers, TX; [p.] Jordan S. and LaNora Moeller Griffin; [m.] Warren Parker, December 11, 1954; [ch.] Four; [ed.] High School, Bus. College, Music Courses in continuing Education; [occ.] Poet, Housewife; [memb.] ISP; [hon.] Salutatorian, High School Scholarships, Church, Douglas Aircraft as Machinist, Real Estate Salesperson and others; [oth. writ.] Words and Music to "Uh Huh" "Babbling Book" "Leave Me Your Heart," "Welcome Little Angel" working on autobiography, Family History, Greeting cards, etc. not published yet (haven't tried!); [pers.] Last child in Art Institute of Seattle. Now it's my time!; [a.] Placerville, CA

PARRISH, DANIEL WAYNE
[pen.] Sparky; [b.] October 14, 1946, Smithfield, NC; [p.] Doris B. Pittman - (Mother), Melvin H. Pittman (Step Father); [m.] Judy A. Parrish, July 16, 1977; [ed.] High School Grad., 3 years U.S. Army - Vietnam Vet.; [occ.] Rail Road Worker - CSX Transportation; [memb.] Wild Life Action, Inc., National Rifle Asso.; [hon.] Combat Certificate Republic of Vietnam, Bronze Star Medal; [oth. writ.] Several other unpublished poems.; [pers.] I write mostly for relaxation and personal pleasure. I try to reflect my feelings for mankind and nature in my work!; [a.] Florence, SC

PARSONS, CYNTHIA CATHERINE
[pen.] "69 Cyns"; [b.] July 6, 1971, Badkreuznach, Germany; [p.] Robert L. Parsons Sr. and Catherine J. Parsons; [ch.] Chase Christopher Parsons (Nephew), April 22, 1994; [ed.] Spanaway Lake High School; [occ.] Cyn's Rainbow Sicles, Subcontracted through KoolPops, Vendor - Ice Cream Truck Driver; [oth. writ.] Several other poems written, but not seen; [pers.] My writings mostly influenced through experience of life, love and relationships.; [a.] Spanaway, WA

PATORA, DEBORAH
[b.] November 14, 1957, Brooklyn, NY; [p.] Saverio Marino, Virginia Marino; [ch.] Jake; [ed.] State University of New York at New Paltz; [occ.] Equipment Sales Manager, Metropolitan Concessions; [memb.] National Wild Life Federation, World Wild life Fund, Antivivisection Society, Humane Society of The United States; [hon.] Dean's List, Magna Cum Laude; [oth. writ.] Several poems and sonnets: Musical compositions: Trio for Clarinet, Oboe, Bassoon, 3 jazz songs, 12 tone compositions for Piano and Voice.; [pers.] Every individual has the potential for spirituality and psychic ability. Look within yourself.; [a.] La Habra, CA

PATRICK, CHARLENE RODERICK
[pen.] Char; [b.] May 20, 1962, Scottsbluff, NE; [p.] Ben and Rose Roderick - Divorced; [m.] Kent Patrick, September 16, 1989; [ch.] Colton Bryan 5 year's old; [ed.] Winneconne Grade and Middle School, Winneconne High School, U.W. Oshkosh Wisc. College 1 1/2 year's; [occ.] Nursing Assistant; [oth. writ.] I have other poem's but not yet published. I do like to write about drugs and alcohol and try to spread the word on how dangerous the substance is since I'm a recovering alcoholic.; [pers.] The poem's I write, come from my heart, and about the people that I love. Also about the struggles I've dealt with in life which I know other people have had worse. I write on my true feelings.; [a.] Weyauwega, WI

PATRICK, RADONNA J.
[b.] October 3, 1965, Massillon, OH; [p.] Ray and Maxine Clay; [m.] Chance W. Patrick, May 3, 1986; [ch.] Joshua C., Jacob A. and Jarod W.; [ed.] Tuslaw High; [occ.] Wife and Mother; [memb.] Calvary Baptist and Church of Moffitt Heights; [oth. writ.] A journal full of poems that I've written since Jr. High none ever published before.; [pers.] To fully express oneself isn't always easy. It has always been my desire to use my poems to help others understand the depth of their own feelings and begin to express themselves!; [a.] Massillon, OH

PATTON, BARBARA
[pen.] Barb Patton; [b.] April 3, 1937, Pontiac, MI; [m.] Tom, June 30, 1973; [ch.] (Step) Tod, Tondah, Tracy; [ed.] Some College - in Michigan and Illinois; [occ.] (Retired from the Communication Industry) Vocalist with many moods band; [memb.] National Association of Female Executives. Volunteer Guardian Ad Litem (for Abused children) in fort Myers, FL. and serve on the Advisory Committee; [oth. writ.] Wrote humor column for local newspaper, currently working on biographical book about early life of abused child and book of humorous poetry.; [pers.] I love to write story poems, especially those appealing to children. Humor and a love of God are my motivations.; [a.] N. Fort Myers, FL

PAULLIN, ANNE B.
[pen.] Javol; [b.] December 30, 1945, Wauwatosa, WI; [p.] William Poyser, Thelma Poyser; [ch.] Lisa, Debbie, Bart, Michelle; [ed.] Basic; [occ.] Public Relations; [hon.] My children and grandchildren, my vision and my life; [oth. writ.] None published.; [pers.] Just another voice in the ocean of life, the broader the base, the

higher the tower.

PAYNE, HILDA
[pen.] Hilda Gaw, Hilda Harmon, Hilda Gaw Payne; [b.] June 22, 1940, Hilham, TN; [p.] Carlie Gaw, Ola Blown Gaw; [m.] Everly Payne, June 14, 1986; [ch.] Pamela Wells, Jama Landreth, Paul Harmon; [ed.] Anderson High, Anderson Indiana, Tucker Career Center Marion Ind.; [occ.] Pre School Teacher - Heritage Christian School Lodi, NJ; [memb.] Community Baptist Church Garfield NJ, National Library of Poetry, (NRTA) National Retired Teachers Assoc.; [oth. writ.] Beast of Burden, Boy of Beauty, Bird of Flight, If This Child, "Will You Be Called Mother?", "Where is my Beloved?", "Lifted", "Like The Wind" (all published) Clipped Wings (A Widows Prayer) Two year old Scholar; [pers.] I want to glorify Jesus Christ in all my works.; [a.] Garfield, NJ

PAYNE, MARY ELIZABETH
[pen.] Mary Payne; [b.] September 20, 1948, Forest Home, AL; [p.] Mary M. Brown, Elijah Peagler; [m.] Herman Payne Jr., June 16, 1974; [ch.] Herman M. Payne and Chandra M. Payne; [ed.] Nursing School, 2 yrs college (Miami-Dade Com. College), high school Greenville Training; [occ.] Licensed Practical Nurse 20 yrs.; [memb.] Advisory Council member 1978-1990 for the Dept of Child Development Services Dade Co., FL. Greater Bethel African Methodist Episcopal Church.; [hon.] Certificates for the Offices of Secretary and Second Vice Pres. for The Advisory Council and The Dept of Human Resources of Dade Co. Fla. 1983-85. 20 yr Ser. award Service for the Public Health Trust.; [oth. writ.] Several unpublished poems written for family and friends.; [pers.] My writings come from personal experiences and the undying hope that mankind can co-exists in a greater harmony than we have today. I am greatly influenced by Maya Angelou.

PEARSON, DONALD E.
[b.] June 21, 1914, Madison, WI; [ed.] B.S. University of Wisconsin-1936, Ph.D. University of Illinois-1940; [occ.] Chemist, Pittsburgh Plate Glass Co. 1940-42, Technical Aid, U.S. Government Office Scientific and Research 1942-44, Assistant Director OSRD Chicago Operation 1945, Research Chemist Mass. Inst. Technology 1946, Associate Professor Vanderbilt University 1953, Professor Vanderbilt University 1960, Professor Emeritus Vanderbilt University 1979-Present, Research Director Reclamation Services Unlimited Madisonville, Kentucky 1989-Present; [hon.] President, American Chem. Soc. Nashville Section (twice), Merit Award, U.S. Government (War Work), Donald Pearson Award to Senior with Most Outstanding Research (Vanderbilt), Who's Who in the World and in America, member, American Chemical Society; [oth. writ.] Publications: Most significant: 1. J. Am. Chem. Soc., (1949) - Discovery of the Rearrangement of Hydrazones. 2. J. Org. Chem., (1952) - Mechanism of Beckmann Rearrangement and Discovery of Hammett Sigma+ Values. 3. J. Org. Chem., (1963) - Lethargic Reactions (Those which are very slow like wine ripening). 4. J. Org. Chem., (1964) - Discovery of New Methods of Directing Substitution into Aromatic Compounds. Also J. Org. Chem., (1965). Paper 8. 5. J. Med. Chem. (1975) Paper 9. Antimalarials. 6. Chem. Commun., (1974) - Conversion of Methanol to Gasoline. 7. 5th Intern. Symposium of Electron Spin Resonance, 1982. A deuterated and N15 maleimide, the most sensitive probe ever synthesized. Books: With Elderfield "Heterocyclic Chemistry", with Buehler "Survey of Organic Syntheses" Vol. I and II, with Hall "Natural Hazardous Materials Control Training Seminar" for EPA, book in writing "Illustrated Organic Chemistry"; [a.] Nashville, TN

PEARSON, KIMBERLY
[b.] December 25, 1980, Hinesville, GA; [p.] Tom and Cindy Pearson; [ed.] Freedom High School (currently attending); [occ.] Student; [a.] Morganton, NC

PEEPLES, HEIDI MARIE
[pen.] Melancholia; [b.] August 21, 1975, Olympia, WA; [p.] David and Linda Peeples; [ed.] In route to a Bachelors degree in English from Southern California College; [occ.] Administrative Assistant/freelance writer; [memb.] Numerous poetry clubs, sectional Editor for college Newspaper, SCC's exclusive Literate; [hon.] Academic Presidential Scholarships, Young Writers Awards; [oth. writ.] Poetic favorites include: Anthony, Prince of Reserve, The Stories They Tell, Shadows, once a dreamer and many more. Also journalistic articles.; [pers.] If words can stir the heart, inspire the mind, and bring forth questions without judgement, call these words poetry.; [a.] Costa Mesa, CA

PELED, NATALIE TAL
[b.] September 19, 1984, NY; [p.] Hillel and Ruth Peled; [ed.] Abraham Joshua Heschel Middle School; [occ.] Student; [oth. writ.] Several poems written for school and for fun; [a.] New York, NY

PENCE, SHERRY SEE
[pen.] "Sherry"; [b.] September 7, 1958, Hermiston, OR; [p.] Norman and Thelma See; [m.] David Lee Pence; [ch.] David, Jami, Chris, Phillip; [ed.] Privately Tutored in Alternative, and Metaphysical Healing Techniques: Presently Working toward a degree.; [occ.] Full-time student and self employed; [memb.] Member of the, Walla Walla Valley Amateur Radio Club and Amateur Radio Emergency Services; [oth. writ.] "Reflections of Life" a collection of illustrated poetry: Future works - "She Gave Them Daisies", a collection of non-fiction short stories: And "A Different Kind of Love" a special journey.; [pers.] My dream is to share with the world my experiences along my journey of enlightenment, to create a feeling of acknowledgement, validation, peace, joy, love and healing.; [a.] Walla Walla, WA

PENNINGTON, DOLORES H.
[b.] September 9, 1924, New Orleans, LA; [p.] Samuel and Mattie Hammond; [m.] Edward Pennington Sr. (Deceased), January 25, 1945; [ch.] Joanne Pennington Coleman, Edward Pennington Jr.; [ed.] B.S. Dillard University, M.A. Xavier University, Certification as Supervisor of Student Teachers; [occ.] Retired Teacher and Elementary Consultant; [memb.] St. John Baptist Church, Zeta Phi Beta Sorority Inc., Louisiana Teachers Assn.; [hon.] Honored for 20 years of service as Youth Director, Honored as Outstanding Zeta 1977; [oth. writ.] Poems - "A Teacher's Reward" and "Reflection", Children's Book - "From Kriss Kross Korners To Rainbow's End"; [pers.] All children have the ability to achieve.; [a.] New Orleans, LA

PENSYL, RYAN
[pen.] Ryan Pensyl; [b.] September 18, 1979, Cumberland, MD; [p.] Lynn and Carle Pensyl; [ed.] Hyndman Junior - Senior High School; [occ.] Student; [memb.] National Honor Society, National Eagle Scout Assoc. United States Achievement Academy; [hon.] Eagle Scout, American Legion Award; [a.] Hyndman, PA

PEREIRA, MICHAEL A.
[pen.] Mike O'Dan the Snakeman; [b.] November 12, 1944, Boston, MA; [p.] Deceased; [m.] In the process of divorce, December 23, 1989 and November 24, 1990; [ed.] Milton High School graduate. Self-educated in every branch of science and engineering. Self-educated in the sciences and superstitions of the world.; [occ.]

100% disabled veteran; [memb.] American Civil Liberties Union, Amnesty International, Americans United for separation of church and state, Coalition against censorship, fully informed jury association clerics of Azagthoth, Unbaptist Church; [hon.] Wanted for blasphemy in Massachusetts, and a fugitive from the Massachusetts Mental Health System, now living in rural central Maine. I distributed many copies of my prose and poetry but Massachusetts had insufficient evidence to prosecute until it legalized evidence obtained through wire tapping, to be applied in 1992. I absconded that New Year's Eve; [oth. writ.] Absolute proofs that an infinite person, i.e., God, is impossible for example. E-Mc 2 says all is one substance. There can only be motion in closed circuitry in one substance, therefore, any entity must be a closed circuit. An infinite circuit can never close. And all persons are complete. Infinity also means never complete; [pers.] This poem is true. Religions tyranny drove me to discover the truth: there is no God. Therefore, there is no excuse for verbal "decency". Its imposition is religious tyranny. The consequence of the one substance and its exclusively closed circuitry, mentioned above, mechanizes an impersonal law of "Karma" that actions bring reactions that return with equal worth; [a.] Corinna, ME

PERIERA, VIRGIL
[b.] May 1, 1939, Tulare, CA; [p.] Frank and Geneva Periera; [m.] Barbara Periera, August 26, 1988; [ch.] We have 9 between us; [ed.] Hi school Patterson High; [occ.] Disability; [a.] Patterson, CA

PERKINS, PAMELA SHEKINAH
[pen.] Shekinah Perkins; [b.] February 15, 1959, Durham, NC; [p.] Betty Perkins Jones, Palmer L. Perkins Jr.; [ed.] UNC Chapel Hill and New York University, Masters of Arts in Communication; [occ.] Asst. Professor, Dekalb College, Artlanta, GA; [memb.] Speech Communication Association (SCA), Rites of Passage, SCA Black Caucus, Shepherds Chapel; [oth. writ.] Several entertainment articles and poems published in community newspapers, professional writings; [pers.] "The only thing that matters when its all over, is who you have touched and how you touched them."; [a.] Atlanta, GA

PETERS, LANESE HOPE
[pen.] Angel; [b.] May 8, 1977, Natchez, MS; [p.] Huey Peters, Savannah Peters; [ed.] Graduated from Vidalia High School and currently attending Copiah - Lincoln Community College in Natchez, MS; [memb.] Vidalia First Assembly of God; [oth. writ.] The poem "Laycie" is about my six year old niece. She was diagnosed with having cerebral palsy at eight months. One night during prayer. God touched my heart, and from my heart came this poem.; [a.] Vidalia, LA

PETERSON, ERIK PAUL
[pen.] Erik Peterson; [b.] July 8, 1977, Perth Amboy, NJ; [p.] Ruth and Gary Peterson; [ed.] Raritan High School, Ramapo College of New Jersey; [occ.] Student; [memb.] Ramapo Literary Organization; [oth. writ.] Publications in "Alive," re-ramapo literary organizations outlet for writers and artists.; [pers.] The only thing that possibly could change this schameful world, are voices from society make your voices heard!!! My writing is greatly influenced by love of nature and on the other end of the spectrum, angst towards war. Violence and abuse of power by govt. officials.; [a.] Hazlet, NJ

PETITT, KELLY APRIL
[b.] November 24, 1982, Lakewood, NJ; [p.] Juliet and Guy Petitt; [ed.] In 8th grade; [occ.] Student at Russell O. Brackman School; [hon.] Elected to the "Kaps" Kids as problem solvers in her school. "B"-honor roll consistently in Jr. High; [a.] Barnegat, NJ

PETROWSKI, ROSEANN
[pen.] Anna Rose; [b.] February 8, 1949, Cleveland, OH; [p.] Joseph D. Zummo, Ann D. Zummo; [m.] James R. Petrowski (Deceased, March 21, 1995), May 15, 1971; [ed.] One full year of College attended Lakeland Community College; [occ.] General Assembler - Production; [memb.] Eastlake Jr. Women's Club of the General Federation of Women's Club Past President and Past Vice President; [hon.] General Federation of Women's Clubs National Poetry Contest 1st place State District - 2nd place National Golden Poet Award and Silver Poet Award from the World of Poetry Organization; [oth. writ.] Published three individual poems in world of poetry anthology two poems in Eastlake News Views Paper Gen. Fed. of Women's Clubs National and International News Letter.; [pers.] I believe poetry should be likened to art. Whereas the visual artist captures beauty and emotions with oils, coals or pencil, the literary artist does so with words. If a picture is worth a thousand words, then a few words properly and effectively placed are worth a lifetime of pictures.; [a.] Mentor, OH

PETTEYS, RHIANNON
[b.] February 8, 1981, Newport News, VA; [p.] Sheri and Gary Petteys; [ed.] I am currently in the tenth grade, and being taught at home. I have been home, schooled for five years; [occ.] Volunteer at Virginia Living Museum and Williamsburg Regional Library; [pers.] I think poetry is an expression of emotions, without it we only have words.; [a.] Williamsburg, VA

PETTINATO, MICHELLE REBEAUD
[b.] January 24, 1948, Paris, France; [p.] Abel Rebeaud, Paulette Rebeaud; [m.] Steven Pettinato, August 12, 1982; [ed.] Lycee Fransais (high School) Ecole Des Arts Appliques (degree in fashion design), Ecole Des Hautes, Etudes Choreographiques (dance/history of dance/choreography etc...degree); [occ.] Dancer/Dance Teacher, also Restaurant Manager; [memb.] Actor's Equity Association A.S.P.C.A. Vietnam Veterans Association; [hon.] Actually - I attended New York Restaurant School for management and graduated with honors in 1987; [oth. writ.] Personal Christmas Cards by the thousands, in English, and in French letters and poems to my family in French; [pers.] I try to use words to paint, or to create a dance - words are color to my eyes and music to my ears. I also feel that if you can make a statement, using two words rather than ten you master a language.; [a.] New York, NY

PFAFF, ELAINE
[pen.] Elaine Pfaff; [b.] June 13, 1983, Lawton, OK; [p.] Ralph and Marie Pfaff; [ed.] Kuntz Elementary, Bamberg Elementary (Bamberg, Germany) Park Lane Elementary, MacArthur Junior High School; [occ.] Junior High Student; [memb.] National Junior Honor Society; [hon.] 14 Teacher Honor Rolls, 2 Principal Honor Rolls, Reading and Spelling Certificates; [pers.] I like to write poems when I'm outside and alone.; [a.] Lawton, OK

PHILLIPS, CAROLYN
[b.] July 2, 1943, Winston-Salem, NC; [p.] U. G. Davis Jr., Norine Higgins; [m.] Everett Phillips, July 14, 1963; [ch.] Scott, Andy, Amy; [ed.] Mitchell Community College, The Institute of Children's Literature; [occ.] Customer Service Supervisor Hunt Mfg. Co.; [memb.] Wesley Mem. Methodist Church, Phi Beta Lambda Professional Div.; [hon.] Who's Who in American Junior Colleges; [pers.] I would like to dedicate this poem to my husband who has given me love and encouragement through the years, but most of all to God who has given me this talent.; [a.] Statesville, NC

PHILLIPS, DOROTHY O'NEAL
[pen.] Dot Phillips; [b.] May 15, 1925, Alpine, AL; [p.] Tom O'Neal, Mattie O'Neal; [m.] Neal Phillips Sr., December 24, 1943; [ch.] Rebecca Jane, Neal Jr., Robert Lee, Larry Fred; [ed.] Lincoln High; [occ.] Retired from Civil Service (Stenog.); [memb.] Lincoln United Methodist Church, American Cancer Society, NE Al, Al. Assn. for Family and Community Education, Nat'l. Assn. of Ret. Fed. Employees; [hon.] Being Mother of four wonderful children and eleven Grandchildren!; [pers.] I try to point out the blessings of life, as well as the adversities, with a little humor. Note: This poem was written for my husband on our 50th Wedding Anniversary.; [a.] Lincoln, AL

PHILP, JUNE WILLIAMS
[b.] May 19, 1932, Jamaica, W.I.; [m.] Dennis G. Philp, August 8, 1959; [ch.] Kurt, Wayne, Adlin; [ed.] Elementary and private - poetry vital part of school curriculum, Shortwood Teachers College Jam. University of the West Indies, Mills College of Education NY, Hunter grad. College Teachers College, Columbia Un. completed each degree in one year; [occ.] Teacher N.Y. P. School, Lecturer Assisted team from Netherlands to set up special Ed. at Mico Teachers College Jam. WI; [memb.] Van Ministry Community Health Service, Association for Education and Psychological Consultants; [hon.] Won poetry recital Distinction in Math, Science and English Literature; [oth. writ.] Newspaper articles effective in bringing change in Education. Several unpublished articles in Education and Literature - of good commendation.; [pers.] Acted in movie "Builders of the Nation" rejected offer to continue acting to pursue Education. I feel that the good or evil we do to others will have a pyramid effect - therefore do all the good you can, when you can.; [a.] Far Rockaway, NY

PHOTIKARMBUMRUNG, ELMA DIEL
[b.] February 26, Philippines; [p.] Alfredo D. Diel and Concepcion D. Diel; [m.] Sam Photikarmbumrung, October 14; [ch.] Nate, Nick and Neil; [ed.] Dumangas High School, University of the Philippines, Silliman University; [occ.] Part time Lecturer/Ofc. Asst.; [memb.] Presbyterian Women's Association, Silliman Alumnia Association, Dumangasanon of Chicago/Midwest, International Society of Poets (Distinguished Member), Poetry Society of America, N.Y.; [hon.] Class Salutatorian, College Scholar-Academic, Poet of Merit Awards: 1995, 1996, Semi-Finalist, I.S.P. Convention, WA-Hilton 1995, WA Sheraton 1996; [oth. writ.] "It Pays To Be Alone At Times", "The Wanton Trail", "Daydreams '94", "Musings '95", "Alternatives At Daybreak", "Makajawan", "The Awakening '93", "Eternal Fires", "The River Kwai 1996", and "Forbid Me Not"; [pers.] "Writing is where I find my true self, I believe in faith in the Almighty God, this is the foundation on which I raised my family. A strong faith overcomes man's limitations".; [a.] Palatine, IL

PICCIRILLO, CHERYL
[pen.] Cheryl Posada; [b.] September 16, 1954, Tampa, FL; [p.] Shirley and Lee Adair, Joe Posada; [m.] Divorced; [ch.] Christopher, Autumn, Summer, Anthony Piccirillo; [ed.] Hialeah High; [occ.] Career Waitress; [hon.] Awards Associated with The BSA including their highest; [oth. writ.] Several poems written through the years 1st time publication will be for Sparrowgrass Poetry Forum Early 1997.; [pers.] My poetry reflects my life. It's about how I feel about any given situation at the time.; [a.] Fayetteville, NC

PIERSON, MRS. BETTY A.
[b.] May 7, 1947, Brooklyn; [p.] Mrs. Ruth and James Saunders; [m.] Mr. John D. Pierson, August 10, 1980; [ch.] Pat, Pam, Lloyd, Floyd, Leroy, Troy and Joshua; [occ.] Housewife; [hon.] Pratt Institute, The Regional

Education Center for Economic Development, of the Utilities Plastics Company. On May 11, 1990 PN Brooklyn, New York.; [pers.] I'm glad to be in the world of Poetry. I find myself, proud to come to the knowledge of my own mind, to write my own poem. And would love to have it shown to everyone in the world.; [a.] Brooklyn, NY

PINNO, MELISSA
[b.] June 29, 1977, Tarzana, CA; [p.] Doris Pinno and Siegfried Pinno; [ed.] Alemany High School, Sophomore at Cal Poly Luis Obispo; [hon.] 1994 Girls State Candidate, NHS-CSF 4 years, Presidential Award for Academic Excellence, Dean's List, Volunteer Award, Student Council Award for Excellence in Community Service; [oth. writ.] Publications in our High School's Award Winning Literary Magazine - "Reflections"; [pers.] We are on the Path of the Voice of Righteousness. Some of you are different in the eyes of God because of your sins. What do you say? Are you going? Are you going to Heaven? - Noyana Traditional African Folk Song...; [a.] Northridge, CA

PIOTROWSKI, STEPHEN
[b.] September 8, 1975, Yonkers, NY; [p.] Stanley and Gloria Piotrowski; [ed.] Pinelands Regional High School, Richard Stockton College of New Jersey; [occ.] Full Time College Student - Marine Biology Major; [memb.] Alliance For A Living Oceans; [hon.] Adelaide - Hollander Scholarship; [pers.] If poetry is pleasing when one reads or writes it, them its good poetry to them. Poetry is made to recall a metal snapshot of memories and fantasies; [a.] Tuckerton, NJ

PITCHER, MARIA
[pen.] "Star", "Diana", "Renegade"; [b.] July 7, 1980, W. Germany; [p.] Donald and Eileen Pitcher; [ed.] Elementary through eleventh grade; [occ.] High school student and in spare time - freelance writer and artist; [hon.] Honorable mention '96 Ogden Art Festival; [oth. writ.] Several poems, a few short stories and 2 and a half fantasy novels, but none have ever been submitted for publication.; [pers.] I write to escape, to find adventure, and to express my soul.; [a.] Ogden, UT

PITTMAN JR., LIONEL O.
[b.] March 5, 1985, Chicago; [p.] Lionel and Nancy Pittman; [ed.] 6th grade - Robert A Black Magnet School - Chicago Public School System; [occ.] Student; [memb.] Omega Baptist Church; [hon.] Honor Student; [pers.] I would like international peace, and a cleaner environment.; [a.] Chicago, IL

PLANTE, DORIS L.
[pen.] Dorie; [b.] February 1, 1950, Woonsocket, RI; [p.] Philippe Couturier (Deceased), Bernadette Gendron; [m.] Divorced; [ch.] Dennis Henry, Dawn Leona; [ed.] Our Lady Of The Mountains Academy, Community College of Rhode Island, Special Education; [occ.] Machine Operator, Avery Donnison Milford, Massachusetts; [memb.] Volunteer for Special Olympics; [hon.] Certificate of Appreciation St. James at Woonsocket C.C.D. Teacher, Award for Excellence in Recognition of Significant Contribution to Donnision Manufacturing Co. for contributions above and beyond one, normal job responsibilities.; [pers.] I would like to touch the heart and souls of all humanity through my poetry, and give people hope, while living in sometimes a rather cruel world.; [a.] Woonsocket, RI

PLUMLEY, ANGEL
[b.] July 2, 1982, Morehead, KY; [p.] Rita Thompson; [ed.] Rowan County Senior High School; [memb.] Marching Band (Color Guard), FCA (Future Christan Athletes); [hon.] D.A.R.E. Graduate, 3rd place academic award.; [oth. writ.] Several poems written in spare time, in process of writing a novel.; [pers.] A

special thanks goes out to Matt Harper, the basis of my poem, John Walker, who has influenced my poetry writing a great deal (Thanks Bub!) And to my sister, Cheryl and mother, Rita, for being there for me when I needed you the most. (Thanks y' all!!); [a.] Morehead, KY

POHLHAMMER, CHRYSTAL
[b.] September 20, 1983, Cudahy, WI; [p.] Judy Pohlhammer, Joe Pohlhammer; [ed.] Raymond Elementary; [hon.] I won the school Spelling Bee in 5th grade. I had straight as throughout 6th grade. I was in Student Council, Band, and head of the sixth grade yearbook.; [oth. writ.] I was head of the Raymond Elementary, sixth, grade yearbook of '95-'96.; [pers.] I was influenced to write poems by my fourth grade teacher, Mrs. Linda Grise.; [a.] Franksville, WI

POPOVICH, MARGUERITE
[b.] July 10, 1915, Saginaw, MI; [p.] George and Hannah Witt; [m.] Robert Popovich, February 14, 1958; [ed.] Bachelor of Arts, Alma College, Alma, Mich, 1937, Mals-Master of Arts in Library Science, University of MI, Ann Arbor, MI. 1967; [occ.] Retired; [memb.] NEA-R, MEA-R, Kent Co. (MI), Humane Society, Kent Co, Humane Society of the U.S., Delta Rescue of CA., National Humane Education Society, Sils Alumni Society, Univ. of MI; [hon.] Alpha Theta, Alma College, Golden Thistle Award, Alma, taught 43 years in Michigan public schools and for U. of M. 4 years; [oth. writ.] Occasional writings in newspapers, poem "Pig Skin" in the voice within, c. 1996, National Library of Poetry.; [pers.] No matter how hard "The chips" may fall, there is some humor in life for all!; [a.] Grand Rapids, MI

POPPENSIEK, NEIL A.
[pen.] Bill Temple; [b.] June 28, 1945, Teaneck, NJ; [p.] Dr. George Poppensiek, Mrs. Edith Poppensiek; [m.] Danilee, June 19, 1976; [ch.] Michelle, Megan; [ed.] B.A., Gattysburg College, M.S. Ed., Elmira College; [occ.] Resource Teacher; [memb.] U.S. Naval Reserve (Ret.) Adirondack Mountain Club, DeWitt Historical Society, Adirondack Museum; [hon.] Elected to membership in Pi Delta Epsilon, National Journalism Honor Society, 1967. Commander, U.S. Naval Reserve (Retired).; [oth. writ.] Technical articles and one popular history published, first fiction piece now ready for publication.; [a.] Ithaca, NY

PORTER, THELMA
[b.] July 22, 1932, Elm Grove, LA; [p.] D. A. and Hallie Horton; [m.] Aubrey Euell Porter, August 3, 1951; [ch.] Donald, Rick, Vic, Steve; [ed.] Haughton High School, Banking Courses in various places; [occ.] Retired; [memb.] AARP, Red River Baptist Church; [pers.] This is the first poem I've attempted ever, but have written several more since I mailed this one in to you. Thank you for this opportunity.; [a.] Benton, LA

POUNDER, E. DONALDT
[b.] May 12, 1919, Tabglewood TX; [p.] James L. & Marjorie A. Pounder; [m.] Jacqueline, June 18, 1991; [ch.] Donna, Donald, Douglas & Mary; [ed.] Graduate. "Industrial College of the Armed Forces", Attended: George Washington University; [occ.] Retired; [memb.] National Parks and Conservation Association - Chairman Emeritus, Charleston County Parks and Recreation Commission; [hon.] South Carolina Recreation Award, Southern Division (NAUFAC) Employee of Year Award, Realtor of the Year Award; [oth. writ.] "A New Baby, Boy or Girl, Can Change The Whole World"; [pers.] Have a positive mental attitude - "Think Good things and good things will happen."; [a.] Mt. Pleasant, SC

POWELL, AMBER
[pen.] Amber Powell; [b.] January 7, 1971, Oklahoma City, OK; [p.] Daniel and Alice Powell; [ch.] Danny; [ed.] GFD, Central Texas College Majoring in Business; [occ.] Under Guidance of Mr. Carpenter for Field Crew in T.D.C.; [oth. writ.] Although I have written many poems, this is my first to be published; [pers.] My influence to published poetry has come from Zedella Bush, who I love and my never-ending desire to better my life for my son. My higher power, The Daniels, Billy Jackson, my dad, Zee, Danny, this is all for you!; [a.] Amarillo, TX

POWELL, CLARISSA
[b.] August 20, 1980, Richmond, VA; [p.] Ralph Edward and Marianne Powell; [ed.] High School Education; [occ.] Student; [memb.] St. Peters Episcopal Church, High School Year Book Staff, Gymnastics Team; [hon.] Who's who among American High School Students, 2nd year Gymnastics Letterman; [pers.] The poem I selected to be published was dedicated to my father and my entry of this contest was inspired by my Grand mother, Edith McCaul.; [a.] Quinton, VA

POWERS, COLLEEN RENEE
[pen.] Annie Porter; [b.] May 18, 1988, Rockford, IL; [p.] Patrick and Patricia; [ed.] Currently a 3rd grader at Martin Luther King Jr. Elementary School, Rockford, IL; [occ.] Student; [hon.] 2nd grd. award for drug awareness essay, 2nd grd. award for essay on accepting challenges, 2 creative writing awards; [oth. writ.] Colleen writes new material daily: poetry, essays, etc. with illustrations.; [pers.] "So many books - so little time"; [a.] Cherry Valley, IL

PRESSON, ALLEENE
[b.] October 30, 1927, Forth Worth, TX; [m.] James E. Brown, September 10, 1947, Robert E. Lee, June 1, 1996; [ch.] James Allen Brown (Died June 13, 1983), Carolyn Joy Brown; [ed.] Graduated Jr. College 1945 University of Texas at Arlington (then N.T.A.C.), University of Texas at Austin, Macon College, Macon, GA and Giorgia College, Milledgeville. GA; [oth. writ.] Only previously published works were: Texas Sunset by Alleene Presson, age 10, in a Local Newspaper, and part of a Parody on Blue magazine Tail Ply in a camping about 1962.; [pers.] Together we now have four children, six grandchildren, and 2 gr-grandchildren. After living 28 1/2 years in the same house in Warner Robins, GA I moved to a whole new life. Now live in a lovely "new" house on Lake Blackshear, 66 miles south of Warner Robins, but at the moment still commute to work five days a week, Robert is retired, and we are looking forward to the time when I will retire, more or less. Actually I love tax work and would love to continue working during the heavy part of tax season-January through April. We are still working out the kinks. We are Baptists and attend a lovely little church at the Lake-Lakeshore Baptist. We have four dogs and a cat, and Robert loves to work in the yard, and outside everything is lovely. Inside I keep on fighting the mess and hoping for Forth Worth, Texas, my son in New Jersey and my daughter in Elko, GA. I have a Huge wonderful new family that have really taken me in their own, and a whole wonderful new life!

PRICE, CORA LEE BEERS
[b.] November 28, 1908, Janesville, WI; [p.] Clarence Palmer Beers and Cora Giffith Beers; [m.] Griffith Baley Price, June 18, 1940; [ch.] Cora Lee, Griffith B., Jr., Lucy Jean, Edwina Clare, Sallie Diane and Doris Joanne; [ed.] Janesville, WI. High, B.A. Beloit Coll., 1932, M.A. Claremont Coll., 1933, Ph.D, Stanford University, 1940, retired after teaching English, Latin, and other Classical Studies for 26 years (secondary level, 2 years, college level, 24 years; [occ.] Retired

Prof. of Classics, Emerita, University of Kansas, KS.; [memb.] American Classical League, Lawrence Music Club, Sigma Alpha Iota, Pi Lambda Theta, KU Retiree' Club and Univ. Women's Club, Zodiac Lit. Soc., Baptist; [hon.] Phi Beta Kappa, Graduate Fellow, Claremont Coll., 1932-33, several academic prizes during student years, Mortar Board teaching award; [oth. writ.] None published, to date.; [a.] Lawrence, KS

PRIMROSE, OLGA
[b.] April 3, 1919, Overton, NE; [p.] Olaf and Emma Johnson; [m.] Cecil C. Borders (Deceased), January 9, 1988; [ch.] Sharon Buckler, Karen Class; [ed.] High School, taught my to paint, Good at faces, scenery self etc., also, played plane at 5 years old (by ear) still do.; [occ.] Retired; [memb.] United Methodist Church, AARP Health Biothody and Card Party.; [hon.] Won 1st prize the Logo for best Albion Hospital, in 1988, In Swedish American; [oth. writ.] Mostly short poems, won first for "Good Samaritan Center" out of 90 entries. 1995 Printed in Albion News.; [pers.] An interest in Government, trying to help others. Especially 3 sisters in local nursing home. Bring treats, clothes. Love and respect all churches. All kinds and colors people are admired.; [a.] Albion, NE

PRITCHETT, CHRISTOPHER JAMES
[pen.] Wogvebsalantesocruel; [b.] October 8, 1971, Elgin, IL; [p.] Ken and Carole Pritchett; [m.] Jennifer Lynn Saltzgiver, December 15, 1990; [ed.] Valley Lutheran High School St. Chas. IL, University of Maryland (Europe), Elgin Community College (current attendance); [occ.] Welder, General Kinematics Corporation; [memb.] Humane Society, Disabled Veterans; [hon.] Various military awards: 1 Good Conduct medal, 3 Army Achievement medals, Draper award recipient/ participant Letter of Appreciation from CSM Robert C. Braggs; [oth. writ.] Nothing published working on a book Absolute Digression; [pers.] Everything you do comes back to you. I live everyday of my life as if each day were an olympic event. I am an avid climber, cyclist, adventurer, and a master of the Hackey Sack/ Cipa.; [a.] Elgin, IL

PURDY, MARY E.
[pen.] Mary E. Purdy; [b.] October 2, 1960, Los Angeles, CA; [p.] Rev. and Mrs. R. R. Pitts II; [m.] Robert A. Purdy, July 26, 1980; [ch.] Jason R. Purdy (15 yrs.), Leann M. Purdy (13 yrs.); [ed.] Graduate of Redbank Valley High School, Attended Clarion State Univ. Attended Pensacola Junior College; [occ.] Office Supervisor M and I.S. Inc. - Bridgestone La Vergne, TN; [memb.] American Heart Assn. Women's International Bowling Assn. 1st Church of God - Murfreesboro, TN American Cancer Society; [hon.] Employee of the Month - Warners Corp - 2/93; [oth. writ.] Good-by Reed" poem published in Clarion State Univ. news paper; [a.] Murfreesboro, TN

PYLMAN, LAURA
[pen.] Laura Atencio Pylman; [b.] May 31, 1962, Brooklyn, NY; [p.] Dick and Pat Atencio, Ava and Bernie Ramirez; [m.] Dan Pylman, August 14, 1993; [ed.] Port Richmond High School, Staten Island, NY; [occ.] Sales; [memb.] (PETA) People for the Ethic treatment of animals, woman's shelter St. Judes; [oth. writ.] Friend, the words just don't exist,' passion, life his path faith; [pers.] Don't waste today worrying about tomorrow. Surround yourself with good people and just glide. Keep your head above water, and never lose faith.; [a.] Clinton, NY

QUEENER, KELLY
[b.] January 3, 1982, Indianapolis; [p.] Sherry and Steve; [ed.] Under Construction; [occ.] Student; [memb.] Dynamo Football Club, North Central High School Soccer Team; [hon.] Gifted and Talented program,

Washington Township Schools, both in academic and arts; [oth. writ.] Poems published in school newspaper (Crooked Creek Ripple); [pers.] Keep Ever smiling!; [a.] Indianapolis, IN

QUINN, JOHN R.
[b.] October 2, 1961, NYC, NY; [p.] James Quinn, Theresa Piliero; [ed.] Harvard College, Harvard Law School; [occ.] Staff Reporter, The Provincetown Banner; [oth. writ.] Extensive academic writings, including "Lost Language of the Irish gay male: Textualization in Ireland's Law and Literature" in Columbia Human Rights Law Review, articles on Angels in America, William Faulkner's Absalom, Absalom, several poems.; [a.] Provincetown, MA

RAGAN, TOM
[b.] March 10, 1964, Chicago, IL; [p.] Lawrence and Regina Ragan; [ed.] BA from St. John's Univ. in English Literature in 1986; [occ.] Reporter for the Santa Fe bureau of the Albuquerque Journal; [oth. writ.] Newspaper articles, including pieces published in the Los Angeles times.; [pers.] Some of my favorite poetry is spoken by people who aren't even aware they're being poetic. But it doesn't happen often.; [a.] Santa Fe, NM

RAMIREZ, SAN JUANA
[b.] April 19, 1944, Pearsall, TX; [p.] Ysabel and Dominga Ramirez; [m.] Manvel Medina, July 12, 1964; [ch.] Mary, Lucie, Anthony; [ed.] Holy Family - Elementary School - St. Mary High School; [occ.] Housewife - mother and grandmother; [pers.] This being my first writing, I am very happy and overwhelmed to be accepted among others who are more deserving than myself. I have never won any honors or awards but I feel I have given a little of myself in this writing.; [a.] Chicago, IL

RAMOS, CYNTHIA A. N.
[b.] January 18, 1946, Honolulu, HI; [p.] Natural parents or real parents: Joseph Demicola, Eleanor Demicola, adoptive parents: Alexander Burgess, Edith Burgess; [m.] Joseph P. Y. Ramos, March 12, 1962 (Divorced January 3, 1989); [ch.] Jennie J. Joseph Jr., and Alexander J.

RAMOS, DOMINGOS
[pen.] Domingos Ramos; [b.] March 20, 1965, Cape Verde; [p.] Manuel Antunes and Filomena Ramos; [m.] Ana Ramos, January 4, 1989; [ch.] Emanuel, Lolobrigida and Dewonderlo; [ed.] High School, General studies of Culture, Red Cross and Strive-Job readiness; [occ.] Avon and Shaklee Independent Seller.; [memb.] Capeverdean Association of Education and health (board of Direction); [hon.] Avon President's Club, Merit of Recognition, President's Jury of Capeverdean Vocal song and poetry celebrity in USA 1993, winner of General Civil and Notary Services contest 1989, Teacher of Portuguese and French, Radio Correspondent, Juvenile Organization leadership.; [oth. writ.] Brochures to Department of National Culture-Cape Verde, some poems published and exhibited in Radio, Magazines and community celebrities. Song writer, fluent in Capeverdean, Portuguese, French and English.; [pers.] I really share the nature. I tend to preserve the traditional culture and bring it up to the new generation. My pretention in writings, is be in edited, creative, connotative and understandable.; [a.] Boston-Roxbury, MA

RAMOS-FORD, VALERIE
[b.] October 30, 1959, NYC, NY; [m.] Christopher; [ch.] One son and one daughter; [ed.] BA - Allegheny College Ed. M - Harvard University; [occ.] Educational Consultant, Peace Educator; [memb.] Coalition for peace action, center to prevent handgun violence,

NAEYC, ASCD; [hon.] 1995 Activist of the year, coalition for peace action of Princeton.; [oth. writ.] Several articles and chapters also published, primarily in the fields of gifted education and violence prevention for the very young.; [pers.] Write so others may read. Peace.; [a.] Princeton Junction, NJ

RAMSDEN, CAROLYN
[b.] November 18, 1982, Syracuse, NY; [p.] Jack and Anne Ramsden; [ed.] 8th grader at Pi Beta Phi Elementary; [occ.] Student; [memb.] Math Club - Pi Beta Phi Elementary 1995-96 Brain Bowl Team - Chiloquin High School Band Member; [hon.] President's Education Award Outstanding Achievement Selected from school to represent it at Oregon Writing Conference (when I lived there); [oth. writ.] I've had several poems published in Anthologies, newspaper; [a.] Gatlinburg, TN

RATCLIFF, GLENDORA M.
[pen.] Chantae Alexander; [b.] September 28, 1970, Chicago, IL; [p.] Shirley A. and Alex Ratcliff Jr.; [ch.] Breanna C. and Bryan A. Ratcliff; [ed.] Completed High School, (Pershing High, Detroit, MI); [occ.] Sr. Data Entry Operator; [pers.] Although I don't have the disease myself, I would like for my poem to inspire people with the HIV and Aids virus to express their feelings and not be afraid or ashamed to do so.; [a.] Chicago, IL

RAWLINS JR., MATTHEW
[pen.] Fuse Roberson; [b.] April 29, 1951, Darby, PA; [p.] Matthew Rawlins Sr., Rutha M. Rawlins; [ch.] Robert D. T. Adams; [ed.] Darby Twp. High, Quaker City Aero School; [occ.] Research Technician Boeing Helicopters Phila., PA; [memb.] Local Union 92, Assoc. Leader Cub Scouts of America, Philadelphia; [hon.] Athletic Awards - High Sch. Quality and Pride Awards - Boeing Helicopter (North American Open Poetry Contest Award Pending); [oth. writ.] Articles in Local Papers Charitable Advertisements, Local; [pers.] I create a mode of transportation for the minds of readers in a majority of my projects. Once aboard, food for thought is served. For dessert, the satisfaction of digesting an understanding.; [a.] Sharon Hill, PA

REDDINGTON, ELIZABETH
[b.] November 29, 1982, Jersey City, NJ; [p.] Barbara Reddington, Francis Reddington; [ed.] St. Paul Grammar School, now in freshman year at St. Dominic Academy; [memb.] Hooved Animal Humane Society; [hon.] Mayor's Academic Achievement Award, President's Award for Educational Excellence, St. Paul's General Excellence Medal; [pers.] I love to write. My dream is to become a best selling author.; [a.] Jersey City, NJ

REDING, EUNICE ABBY
[b.] January 13, 1916, McKees Rocks, PA; [p.] William Henry Ward and Eunice Ward; [m.] Richard Wallace Reding, August 28, 1937; [ch.] Barbara Ann and Richard William; [ed.] Warren G. Harding Senior High; [occ.] Reading National Library of Poetry Anthologies... Writing; [memb.] St. John United Church of Christ, The National Library of Poetry, Philatelist Society, AARP, American Cancer Society, American Heart Association; [hon.] Poetry printed in The National Library of Poetry Anthologies, Editors Choice Award, Plaque and Membership Pin; [oth. writ.] Invisible Enigma, What's Good What's Not, Reluctant Regrets, Lasting Happiness, Summersaulting Into Fall, Why on Fun day?; [pers.] I endeavor to support The National Library of Poetry ideals, hoping my efforts are worthy to be printed and of interest to others.

REILLY, SEAN P.
[pen.] Patrick; [b.] September 4, 1976, Red Bank, NJ; [ed.] Keansburg High School Brookdale College; [occ.] Student; [oth. writ.] Soon to be published...; [pers.] Though ignorance assists in the pursuit of greatness. Greatness is the assistant in the quest for ignorance. I do not ignore, for I know what it is like to be ignored.; [a.] Keansburg, NJ

REITER, MICHAEL
[b.] March 31, 1953, Ollentown, PA; [p.] Frank and Pauline Reiter; [occ.] Self-Employed; [pers.] Don't let fear stand in the way of your dreams!

REYES, RAQUEL
[b.] September 19, 1980, Englewood, NJ; [p.] Carmen Reyes, Jose Reyes; [ed.] The Academy of the Holy Angels; [occ.] Student; [memb.] St. Michael's Roman Catholic Church, Religious Education Staff in St Michael's Blueprint Literary Paper of the Academy of the Holy Angels' [oth. writ.] A number of works published in a literary paper in school; [pers.] My biggest influence is my family. You guys are all so special to me, I couldn't live without you! [a.] Palisades Park, NJ

REYNOLDS, EMMA L.
[b.] September 17, 1937, Charleston, WV; [occ.] Retired - Bell Atlantic, Self Employed Wood Crafts and Boarding Dogs and Cats; [memb.] WV K-9 Search and Rescue, Kanawha Charleston Humane Assoc., Kanawha Presbyterian Church; [oth. writ.] "Point of View" booklet published by Bell Atlantic, Subject: Mental Health; [pers.] My dream is to have wisdom and love enough to help others find faith and hope in life.; [a.] Charleston, WV

RICHARDS, DANIELLE
[b.] December 4, 1979, Opp, AL; [p.] John H. and Shirley Richards; [ed.] 11th Grade High School Student at Zion Chapel High School in Jack, Alabama; [memb.] Band, FHA, Beta Club, Youth for Christ Club, Basketball Team, Drama Club, Mt. Olive Assembly of God Church Youth; [hon.] District Honor Band (2 yrs.), UAB Honor Band, All-State Band, County Public Speaking 1st Place Winner, was enlisted into the National Honor Roll and was put in the United States Achievement Academy Yearbook the 92-93 year, accepted as a contestant in the America's National Teenager Contest; [pers.] My poem is dedicated to the love life, Bryan Mandella.; [a.] Brundidge, AL

RICHARDSON, BECKY JOHNSON
[b.] August 11, 1940, Newnan, GA; [p.] Elder Charles I. Johnson (Deceased) and Varon Broadwell Johnson; [m.] Divorced; [ch.] Ivy Louise Head; [ed.] Sardis High School, Boaz, Alabama. AA degree from Snead State Junior College, Boaz, Alabama. University of Alabama, Huntsville Campus. George Mason University, Fairfax, Virginia. Many continuing education courses (CE Credits); [occ.] Retired from IBM (for medical reasons) after 23 years in the publication profession. As a hobby, I have a small home-based greeting card business, which provides creative opportunities, both artistic and literary, to keep me challenged. I also use my computer to embellish artwork and to visit on the "net"; [memb.] Toastmasters, International. Multiple Sclerosis organizations (I have MS). The Association for Retarded Citizens (daughter is learning disabled). Sigma Tau Delta sorority (while in college). Drama Club (college). Atlanta Writers Club. Northeast Georgia Writers Club.; [hon.] National Honor Society (high school). Won High School National Spelling Bee (age 13) and placed second in county spelling contest. Dean's List several times (college). Several service awards from IBM. Won several speaking awards in Toastmasters.; [oth. writ.] Poem "Rigidity" published in The Rainbow's End by The National Library of Poetry, 1996. Poem "Friends" published in A Tapestry of Thoughts by The National Library of Poetry, 1996. Poem "For Ivy" accepted for publication in The Best of the 90's by The National Library of Poetry, 1996. Poem "Doorways" accepted for publication in Essence of a Dream by The National Library of Poetry, 1997. Article, "Mistakes are just Wisdom Happening!", accepted for publication in The Light Ahead by The Association for Retarded Citizens, Georgia Division, 1996. Verses and designs for greeting card, using hand-painting as well as computer graphics, which I sell to family and friends.; [pers.] When I need closure to a personal tragedy or trauma, I write a poem that expresses the many emotions I experienced getting through the situation. My favorite one liner is: "Mistakes are just wisdom happening!" My retarded daughter inspired it. She needed a positive viewpoint because she was trying out failing at a particular task.; [a.] Marietta, GA

RICHARDSON, TOM
[b.] January 15, 1947, Los Angeles, CA; [p.] Luther and Helen Richardson; [m.] Raelynn, January 27, 1980; [ch.] Rhonda, Kimberly, Elicia, Adam, Timothy; [ed.] Huntington Park High School, Green River Comm. College, Temple Faye University, I have a degree in human dev.; [occ.] Tool expediter for being aircraft co. reserve police office.; [oth. Writ.] Just To Say I Love You, Dreams, Friendship, and many more love poems.; [pers.] Poetry is only words. But it is how we assemble them that makes the difference. I try to share just a little love with everyone.; [a.] Auburn, WA

ROBERSON, DONNA
[b.] January 26, 1953, Durham, NC; [p.] Jack and Doris Ray; [m.] Bob Roberson, July 7, 1979; [ch.] Tonia Brantley and Jeremy Roberson, one grandchildren- Carley Brantly; [ed.] Durham High School, Technical School; [occ.] I devote myself at home being a good wife, mother, and grandmother.; [memb.] Grove Park Garden Club, Calvary Baptist Church; [oth. writ.] Several poems I've written, if there was a way if you only had time and etc.; [pers.] I have been inspired by my family, and by the beauty of the earth and God's love. The talent I have comes from the heart, and the many surroundings I encounter in life.; [a.] Durham, NC

ROBERTS, DEE
[pen.] Dee Roberts; [b.] July 6, 1931, Florence, AZ; [p.] Oscar T. and M. Ellen Johnson; [m.] Robert H. (Bob) Roberts, July 24, 1948; [ch.] Three children's, four Grandchildren; [ed.] BS in Business Administration NSU, Tahlequah, 1983; [occ.] Retired; [oth. writ.] Columnist for San Miguel Basin Forum, (Weekly newspaper) Nucla, CO, 1990 - 1991); [pers.] "The Big Red Bull" is a narrative of my - then 21 year old - grandson, who was bucked off a bull in a rodeo and instantly paralized from the neck down, February 18, 1995. (Many bones fractured, many infections, 13 surgeries).; [a.] Tahlequah, OK

ROBERTS, SHERRI JO
[b.] February 26, 1964, Syracuse, NY; [p.] Nyla Sweet and Robert LaLone; [ch.] Carol, Phillips, Mike and Tabatha Roberts; [pers.] My children give me the strength to write about my feelings. Thank you guys.

ROBERTSON, SUSANNE
[b.] October 2, 1950, Troy, NY; [p.] Dorothy Catman, Bill Maloney; [m.] Scott W. Robertson, March 10, 1984; [ch.] Two - Paul E. D'Angelo Jr., Ryan S. W. Robertson; [ed.] Elem. Sch. St. Coleman Home - Watervliet NY, High School - Valley Leniral Montgomery, NY, College ethan Allen, Manchester V.T.; [occ.] Adult Family Home Owner Housewife; [hon.] Honor Student N.Y. S. Scholarship Award; [oth. writ.] Poetry for high school newspaper. Poetry published in local newspaper - the throw away child a broken heart; [pers.] this poem is dedicated to all of the children abused at Saint Coleman's Home for Orphans in Wateruliet NY at the hands of the Roman Catholic Nuns.; [a.] Buckley, WA

ROBINSON, EVELYN E.
[pen.] Evelyn Robinson; [b.] November 24, 1925, Bishops Head; [p.] Greensberry Pritchetta Odessa; [m.] Rodney C. Robinson, September 7, 1941; [ch.] Three son, one daughter; [ed.] High School; [occ.] Sea-Food; [memb.] Wingate Church Methodist Women United Home-Makers; [hon.] Special Recognition '94-'96 Talbot County Library - Poetry Contest; [oth. writ.] Annie Oakley Great Women of the County - my Grand Mother two-time winner Maryland - you are beautiful contest; [pers.] As we help someone we help ourselves. To write is to paint a picture with words; [a.] Toddville, MD

ROBISON, DEBBIE RENEE ROSS
[b.] January 7, 1959, Castro Valley, CA; [p.] Lawrence and Edna Ross; [m.] Ronald Paul Robison, February 8, 1986; [ed.] Sunset High School, Hayward, CA 1976, Heald Business College, Hayward, CA graduated 1977; [occ.] Administrative Assistant; [hon.] Honor certificate Business English and Communications - Heald Business College; [pers.] As an incest survivor in recovery, I look each day to God who provides the strength to allow me to share my honest self.; [a.] Hayward, CA

RODGERS, DEBRA L.
[b.] July 26, 1960, Rockford, IL; [p.] Warren Hudson, Evelyn Hudson; [m.] Phillip Rodgers; [ch.] Dustin Rodgers, Courtney Rodgers; [ed.] B.S. in Psychology, Rockford College Presently Working Toward an M.A. in Professional Counseling at Illinois School of Professional Psychology; [a.] Rockford, IL

RODGERS, ISABELLE H. R.
[b.] September 9, 1918, New Castle, PA; [p.] Samuel H. and Mary Forbes Hunt; [m.] Donald M. Reddick (Deceased 1984), August 25, 1941, Thomas A. Rodgers, May 2, 1987; [ch.] Jack C. and Samuel R. Reddick; [ed.] New Castle Business College (1936 graduate), Certificate in Journalism, NYC (Correspondence Course), Graduate Harlansburg High School (1935); [occ.] Retired Secretary, English Dept., Slippery Rock University, Slippery Rock, PA; [memb.] Highland Presbyterian Church, Slippery Rock, PA, Frank P. Cheesman Post American Legion Auxiliary #393; [oth. writ.] Letters for Church Newsletter, Slippery Rock Reporter for Butler Eagle, Butler, PA; [pers.] I strive to make readers think and understand the real basic values in life.; [a.] Slippery Rock, PA

RODRIGUE, MARIA E.
[b.] August 24, 1979, New Iberia, LA; [ed.] Catholic High School; [occ.] Student; [memb.] National Honor Society, Campus Ministry, Mu Alpha Theta Math Club; [hon.] Biology II medal for highest average in class, French I, medal for highest average, English II, medal for Highest average, Serviam Medal for service to school, Gladys Viator Memorial Award for excellence in English; [pers.] A being has not truly lived if he has not failed - he has only survived.; [a.] New Iberia, LA

RODRIGUES JR., JOSEPH O.
[pen.] Joseph Rodrigues Jr.; [b.] July 27, 1943, Honolulu, HI; [p.] Joseph and Sarah Rodrigues Sr.; [m.] Carol Berini Rodrigues, September 16, 1968; [ed.] Balboa High, San Francisco, CA, College of Marin, Kentfield, CA; [occ.] US Army Retired, Investor; [memb.] Paralyzed Veterans of America, Disabled American Veterans, Life Member, Distinguished Member, International Society of Poets; [hon.] 1996 Editor's

Choice Award in Outstanding Achievement in Poetry; [oth. writ.] Several poems published, "Battle Wound" A Tapestry of Thoughts, "Battle-Zone" Fields of Gold, "No Bugles in the Morning" Best Poems of the 90's, "After the Fall" of Moonlight and Wishes; [pers.] Writing poetry is new to me, the words I write are feelings long with held and feebly expressed through my personal life experiences in reflecting the nature of mankind and the horrors of war.; [a.] San Rafael, CA

ROE, STEPHEN W.
[b.] October 26, 1963, Columbus, OH; [p.] Wayne and Norma Roe; [m.] Elizabeth Roe, August 13, 1988; [ch.] Brandon Michael, Kaitlin Elizabeth; [occ.] State Trooper - Ohio Highway Patrol; [pers.] I am inspired by the relationships I have with others.; [a.] Waterford, OH

ROGERS, DARLENE S.
[b.] September 19, 1919, Harvard, IL; [p.] Frank, Minnie Whitehead; [m.] Welford B. Coombs, February 11, 1995, Van W. Rogers (past marriage), October 5, 1942; [ch.] Barbara Sorren, Mary Knop, Harold Rogers, Floyd Rogers, Bonnie Bridger, David Rogers; [ed.] Harvard Community High Grad '38 Harper College Palatine Ad in Nursing '72; [occ.] Retired RN; [memb.] United Methodist Women Loyal Order Moose #1289 Philathea Club; [hon.] Circle of Pearls of United Methodist Women Travelled extensively and Written about many places; [oth. writ.] Poems used in programs I have given for church and other organizations; [pers.] I use my poetry as a means of expression of my personal feelings on many subjects.; [a.] Harvard, IL

ROGERS, DAWN M.
[pen.] DMR; [b.] September 17, 1975, Hobart, IN; [p.] Don and Judy Rogers; [ed.] Graduated High School and currently attending, through homes studies, the writers digest school of Ohio.; [occ.] Bank Teller at the Demotte State Bank; [hon.] Senior year of high school I won a composition award, other than that, my work has been very personal.; [oth. writ.] I have written one novel and three poetry books that I want to get published at one point in my life.; [pers.] I believe writing for me makes feelings and emotions become reality writing is my released. A tribute to my soul in so many words.; [a.] Rensselaer, IN

ROHN, LISA
[b.] December 6, 1978, Beaver Dam, WI; [p.] Roy Rohn, Carol Rohn; [hon.] Honor student; [pers.] I am very pretty, intelligent, and talented. I also have a great personality; [a.] Beaver Dam, WI

ROHN, ROY
[b.] April 8, 1940, Beaver Dam, WI; [p.] Don and Francis Rohn; [m.] Carol Rohn, December 11, 1975; [ch.] Lisa Rohn; [ed.] High School; [occ.] Repair Mechanic, Magician; [hon.] Expert at MI Rifle Flame Thrower, 50 Cal. Machine Gun; [a.] Beaver Dam, WI

ROIZEN, JENNIFER
[pen.] Jenny JR; [b.] August 3, 1981, San Francisco; [p.] Dr. Nancy and Michael Roizen; [ed.] Student at U. of C. Laboratory Schools High School; [occ.] Student and CIT; [memb.] National Library of Poetry; [oth. writ.] Several published poems in books, and on tapes; [pers.] I try to reflect a love for natures pleasures within my writings.; [a.] Chicago, IL

ROLLINS, CHRISTINE
[b.] October 9, 1982, Bryan, TX; [p.] John and Becci Rollins; [ed.] Carroll Middle School; [occ.] Student; [memb.] National Junior Honor Society, "Saints" Soccer Club, Student Council, National Charity League, Carroll Middle School 8th Grade Symphonic Band (Bassoon); [hon.] Membership to the National Junior Honor Society, Academic Recognition in Math and

Reading in the Duke University Talent and Identification Program; [pers.] When the shadow envelopes you, look up and let in the light.; [a.] Southlake, TX

ROMANO, TRACY C.
[b.] July 19, 1977, Kearny, NJ; [p.] Barbara and Gary Romano; [ed.] Riverview High School; [pers.] I have always dreamed of having some of my works published, so this is a wonderful accomplishment for me. I hope my work continues to get noticed.; [a.] Sarasota, FL

ROOS, ELLEN
[b.] August 5, 1948, Saint Louis, MO; [p.] Lawrence K. Roos, Harriet Schneider; [ed.] All but dissertation, Ph.D. is Counseling Psychology; [occ.] Singer, Songwriter; [hon.] Two songs for Humanity Awards. Winner New Music Festival; [pers.] My commission is to put the highest of my spiritual vision into the most accessible artistic forms and to let my living reflect that vision all in service to the Lord of Lords.; [a.] Loveland, CO

ROPER, CLAY
[b.] January 7, 1978, Dallas, TX; [p.] David Roper, Karen Roper; [ed.] High School; [occ.] College Student; [memb.] Treasurer of Local Village Idiot Chapter; [hon.] I am the Finest Swordsman in all of France, National Merit Scholarship Semi-Finalist; [oth. writ.] Nothing published yet.; [pers.] There is beauty in everything, the trick is learning to appreciate it. Life is too short to accept everything you're told.; [a.] Plano, TX

ROSS, LESLIE E.
[pen.] Gloriana, Queen of the Fairies; [b.] August 9, 1946, Chicago, IL; [m.] Divorced; [ch.] Jeffrey Keith and Jeremy Daniel; [ed.] University of Houston; [occ.] Asst. Admin. Officer - Phoenix Employment Relations Board, I also entertain audiences of all ages as "Gloriana, Queen of the Fairies.; [hon.] Best New Character (Gloriana) Arizona Renaissance Festival (1992, Music Award for Outstanding Accomplishment - Wright Jr. College 1968, Dean's List - Wright Jr. College 1968, Music Scholarship U. of HOuston - 1964; [oth. writ.] The Adventures of Clarence The Dragon, Leander and The Fairy, The Fairy and the Honeybee, Reflections of a Fairy queen, A Special Place in Santa's Heart, The Other Side of the Rainbow; [pers.] Into our society rife with violence, Scandal and all manner of abuses, I seek to bring an ancient spark of light which draws to it all who seek escape to a better place - a place where Love, Kindness and Compassion reign supreme, a place where the yearnings of the human heart are answered in full measure.; [a.] Phoenix, AZ

ROSSI, PHILOMENA
[pen.] "Chookie"; [b.] October 6, Latrobe, PA; [p.] Anthony and Viola DePrimio; [m.] Anthony F. Rossi (Deceased, May 5, 1996), July 22, 1950; [ch.] Michael, Jessica, Patrick and Antoinette; [ed.] 2nd year High - quit and had to go to work to help and support family.; [occ.] President of Entertainment Co. "Entertainment Services and Promotions; [hon.] Editor's Choice Award, Outstanding Poetry from National Library of Poetry, Story of Success Printed in Catholic Accent-Newspaper; [oth. writ.] Storybook - "Stories for Children of All Ages", Poetry: Where Would You Go?, Our Steelers There To Stay, I Walk Alone, Do You Remember?, A Seed, With You Eternally, Winter's Grief, Winds, Keys, Do You Hear The Rain, Time, The Special Train, The Mystery of Coffee, 2nd children's story book halfway finished, working on it now.; [pers.] I feel very grateful God has given me a gift I can share with others and I will try my best to do so.; [a.] Greensburg, PA

ROSSOW, RANDAL R.
[pen.] Randal R. Rossow; [b.] September 10, 1959, Reno, NV; [p.] Leo J. and Jacquelyn M. Rossow; [m.] Linda K. Rossow, May 27, 1989; [ch.] Glorianna L. Rossow; [ed.] University of Nevada, Reno (Class of 83); [occ.] School Teacher; [memb.] University of Nevada Symphonic Choir; [pers.] The simple things in life are the most valuable.

ROWE, DENISE M.
[b.] September 26, 1954, Elizabeth, NJ; [p.] A. Charles and Marylou Cocuzza; [m.] Garry W. Rowe, July 8, 1978; [ch.] Two; [ed.] Associates Degree in Computer Programming, B.S. in Bible, M.S.W.; [occ.] Freelance writer; [memb.] Christians for Biblical Equality; [oth. writ.] A number of other pieces I have written have not yet been submitted for publication.; [pers.] It is my deepest desire to communicate, through my writing, the healing grace of God available to us through Jesus Christ and those whose lives exhibit Christ's likeness.; [a.] Holt, MI

ROY, KENNETH MICHAEL
[b.] May 1, 1971, Grosse Pointe; [p.] Kenneth Roy and Helene Roy; [ed.] James Madison College at Michigan State University, BA in International Relations, Wayne State University Law School, Juris Doctor; [occ.] Law Clerk; [memb.] American Bar Association, American Trial Lawyers Association, The Humane Society of the United States, Phi Delta Phi Legal Fraternity, The Detroit Social Club, United States Golf Association, West of West; [hon.] Book Award in Labor Law, Book Award in Sports Law, Jessup Moot Court Team, STAP National Team; [oth. writ.] Megret's Journal, The Book of Conflicting Emotions, the Reuper's Son, the Nightwatchman; [pers.] Generally, humankind strives to be good. In rare instances, it makes an attempt at greatness. Sadly, too often we fail at both. In my writing, I try to explore all the realms in which we exist, making clear to different majorities what they otherwise would never see.; [a.] Royal Oak, MI

ROYLE, MARLENE M.
[b.] November 15, 1963, Buffalo, NY; [ed.] Boston University - Sargent College of Allied Health Professions, 1985; [occ.] Occupational Therapist Registered; [oth. writ.] No publications; [pers.] Impressions from life in Newfoundland, Greece, Israel, and Russia have influenced my writings.; [a.] Northeast Kingdom, VT

ROYSE, BEVERLY
[b.] June 11, 1972, Portsmith, VA; [p.] William and Sharon Logan; [ch.] Gabrielle Royse; [ed.] Willcox Elementary School, Willcox, AZ. Trinity Baptist Elementary, Willcox, AZ. Globe Jr. and High School, Globe, AZ.; [occ.] Sales Representative; [hon.] Editors Choice Award Presented by The National Library of Poetry; [oth. writ.] "Native Blue Morning" published in A Muse to Follow; [pers.] Most of my writing has been inspired by true life feelings combined with fictional characters.; [a.] Casa Grande, AZ

RUBINO, MICHELLE
[b.] August 22, 1979, Boston, MA; [p.] Sheila and Joseph Rubino; [ed.] Braintree High School; [occ.] Student; [memb.] Arthritis Foundation, Easter Seals Society, Save The Children Foundation, World Wildlife Fund; [hon.] Blue w/ Green Stripe Belt Karate, Winner of several Spelling Bees; [oth. writ.] Several poems published in the "Joint Report" Arthritis Newsletter; [pers.] I feel a special bond with under privileged people and all endangered species. I believe we are all a part of "God's Paradise."; [a.] Braintree, MA

RUDEL, MYRON
[pen.] Myge; [b.] December 21, 1933, Stevensville, MI; [p.] Andrew and Katherine Rudel; [ed.] High School; [occ.] Retired; [memb.] V.F.W., D.A.V., Amer. Leg.; [oth. writ.] 20 Religion, 10 natures, 10 animal mostly bugs no nothing of life in common.; [pers.] My writing in the philosophy of mankind with insight into and man's soul, my soul.; [a.] Benton Harbor, MI

RUHF, DOROTHY MARLEY
[b.] July 26, 1924, Wilkes-Barre, PA; [p.] Mabel and Bernard J. Marley; [m.] Carl S. Ruhf (Deceased), February 11, 1954; [ch.] Gary Lee and David Charles; [ed.] Hanover High, International Business Machines Course Plus some Colleges Credits; [occ.] Retired Conrail; [memb.] Bethlehem Charter Chapter American Business Women Association- National ABWA. Past Member Bethlehem Chamber of Commerce; [hon.] ABWA Women of the Year, 1971, Past President and a Member of the National American Business Women Association's Inner Circle, State Advisor, United States Congressional Advisory Board, Recognition from Defence Advisory Board, Distinguished Security Council Foundation Leadership Award; [oth. writ.] None - First Attempt spent time Oil Painting; [pers.] I love people and strive for a better America and World Peace.; [a.] Bethlehem, PA

RYAN, JUDITH
[b.] December 1, 1940, Little Rock, AK; [p.] Raymond and Isabelle Duckworth; [ch.] Robert Debbaut, Linda Smith; [ed.] Woodrow Wilson High School, Long Beach, CA; [occ.] Motivational Speaker in Metaphysics; [oth. writ.] Article on meditation published in Spirit Dancer.; [pers.] I enjoy people and would like to share with them my poetry, stories and philosophy of life by sharing who I am.; [a.] Springfield, MO

SAARI, RAEANN
[b.] February 25, 1971; [p.] Arlene Simpson, Richard Saari; [ed.] Quincy High School, South Coastal Career Development Center; [occ.] Assistant Buyer, G.M. Stop and Shop; [oth. writ.] Currently writing a novel.; [pers.] I'm fortunate in having my sisters Lea and Julie, and niece Christina. Thanks to my mother for Everything. Thanks to true friends old and new.; [a.] Wollaston, MA

SACHDEVA, UMA M.
[b.] July 27, 1981, Philadelphia, PA; [p.] Dr. Ajit and Rajeev Sachdeva; [ed.] The Baldwin School, Bryn Mawr, PA; [occ.] High School Student Freshman at The Baldwin School; [memb.] Various High School Clubs including Student Government and the Literary Magazine; [hon.] Silver Medal in 1995 National Latin Exam, Gold Medal in 1996 National Latin Exam; [oth. writ.] Some unpublished short stories and poems; [pers.] I believe that an ideal poem would discuss a sad or unpleasant feeling, such as loss or regret, in such a way that it could provide comfort to those who experience similar pain without losing the ability to entertain. Its readers.; [a.] Rosemont, PA

SAMPSON SR., DAVID E.
[b.] June 6, 1936, North Bonneville, WA; [p.] Willard and Julia Sampson; [m.] M. Annice Sampson, August 5, 1955; [ch.] Four Sons - David Jr., Anthony, Troy, Gavin; [ed.] Camas High School, Clark College; [occ.] Semi-retired from the Pulp and Paper Industry; [memb.] Zion Lutheran Church, Camas-Washougal Historical Society, Orchard Hills County Club, Camas Social Club, LaCamas Credit Union Supervisory Committee, Friends of the Camas Library; [oth. writ.] Several columns and articles written for the company news letter and many un-published poems and writings; [pers.] In my writing, I try to express my personal experience in life and feelings concerning family, friends and spiritual growth. I hope that those who read them can relate to or feel the communication that is written into the contents.; [a.] Camas, WA

SAMS, PATRICIA A.
[pen.] Pat Bussie; [b.] June 6, 1953, Chicago, IL; [p.] Jolly L. Bussie Sen, Jettie B. Bussie; [m.] Robert E. Sams, June 21, 1976; [ch.] Ericka, Consuela, Tia and Robert Jr.; [ed.] Wendell Phillips High, Bryman College, Albert Enestein Elementary School; [occ.] Medical Assistance, Chicago, FL; [memb.] Zion Pentecostal Church of God in Christ, Chicago, IL, and Organ Donor, (I also play "Jesus" at my church); [hon.] Medical Graduate; [oth. writ.] Vol. I book of poems - Entitled "Remedy Of The World". Contents - 41 poems and working on Vol. II poems. Poem recited at Wedding - Funerals - Church - Schools and Social gatherings.; [pers.] I consider my work to be the extension of my mind on paper, they're my thoughts given to me by a higher being. My poetry, will enlighten you. And help you to become aware. I believe that I have got the gift of poetry.; [a.] Chicago, IL

SANDERS, A. NICOLE
[b.] January 6, 1976, Spokane, WA; [pers.] I believe a good writer on author comes when you write for yourself, not others. It is only then that you are judged by the highest judge of all. Yourself.; [a.] Renton, WA

SANFORD, DEBORAH L.
[pen.] Deborah Manze; [b.] May 12, 1970, Norristown, PA; [p.] Mary Ellen (Lutz) Manze; [m.] Mark A. Sanford, October 14, 1995; [occ.] Secretary, Heyser Landscaping, Norristown, PA; [memb.] All Saints Episcopal Church, Norristown, PA; [oth. writ.] Poem published in The National Library of Poetry Anthology, "Daybreak On The Land"; [a.] Royersford, PA

SAPP, BRIAN CHRISTOPHER
[pen.] Brian Sapp; [b.] April 16, 1975, Birmingham, AL; [p.] James R. and Monica Sapp; [m.] Donna Parrott Sapp, December 17, 1994; [ch.] Logan Christopher Sapp; [ed.] Carrollton High School, Ultrasound Diagnostic School of Atlanta; [occ.] Ultrasound Technician; [memb.] Society for Diagnostic Medical Sonographers; [oth. writ.] An assortment of personal poems that reflect my life.; [pers.] The love of one special person is what every soul desires. My soul desired every aspect of this poem - and thus, my soul is content, my wife Donna is my desire and my constant reminder of God's grace and serenity.; [a.] Carrollton, GA

SARNICOLA, VINCENT M.
[pen.] Vincent Cole; [b.] December 6, 1972, NY; [p.] Andrew and Marie Elena Sarnicola; [ed.] Wantagh High School, Private Acting Classes; [occ.] Warehouse; [pers.] Writing is simply a fantastic release.; [a.] Wantagh, NY

SAWYER, ANNA MARIE
[pen.] Annie Sawyer; [b.] June 9, 1986, Cincinnati, OH; [p.] Jack and Jan Sawyer; [ed.] Attends Milford Schools, was in 4th grade when poem was written; [occ.] Student; [memb.] Christ Presbyterian Church, Children's Church Choir; [hon.] Honor Club of Pleasant Hill Elementary, Enrichment Class at Pleasant Hill, Honor Roll, Spelling Bee Finalist (3rd Place); [oth. writ.] I have written books for Young Author's Day at my school. I wrote Little Lion, Kidnapped, The Monster that Lived on Kay Drive (none published); [pers.] I like poems by Jack Prelutsky, Shel Silverstein, and A. Nonny Mouse. I have a mom, a dad, a brother, and a twin sister.; [a.] Milford, OH

SCHALER, KARISA L.
[b.] November 9, 1981, Redmond, WA; [p.] Margaret Johnston; [ed.] High School Freshman; [occ.] Full Time Student; [memb.] Immanual Lutheran Church; [oth.

writ.] I have written many poems, but I have never been published; [pers.] I write because I want to help people, let them know that they are not alone. When people read my poems, I don't want them to see just a bunch of words. I want them to be able to relate to what I write.; [a.] Lake Stevens, WA

SCHERT, PAUL
[b.] December 21, 1917; [p.] John A. Schert (deceased) [m.] deceased; date of marriage April 30, 1944; [ch.] Paula Parvey, Gregory Schert; [occ.] Retired — 78 yrs. young; [a.] Coon Rapids, MN

SCHINDLER, SUSIE
[b.] March 19, 1980, Kansas City, MO; [p.] Mary Schindler and Rick Schindler; [ed.] St. Thomas Aquinas High School; [memb.] People for the Ethical Treatment of Animals, German Club; [hon.] Principal's Honor Roll ('96); [oth. writ.] Staff writer for school newspaper, The Shield.; [a.] Kansas City, MO

SCHLEGEL, NOELLE L.
[pen.] "Jobeth"; [b.] September 8, 1971, Allentown, PA; [p.] Robert and Janet Schlegel; [ed.] Emmaus High School, 1 year Allentown College, 1 year Lehigh Carbon Community College; [occ.] Cashier; [memb.] Miller Blood Bank; [pers.] I would like to dedicate this poem in gratitude to my best friend Troy Rubright. He encouraged me to chase my dreams and to never give up.; [a.] Allentown, PA

SCHLEHER, LAURI ANNE
[b.] January 1, 1985, Trenton, NJ; [p.] Lois Schleher; [ed.] Dunnellon Middle School 6th grade; [occ.] Student; [hon.] 3rd place Science Fair winner 1994-1995. 1st place Science Fair winner 1995-1996 at Dunnellon Elementary School. Honor roll 1995 and 1996.; [oth. writ.] Letters to Editor Riverland News, Dunnellon, on seat belt safety on school buses.; [pers.] My mom encourages me to write. I prefer poems that are funny and light hearted. Maybe I would like to be a Newspaper reporter or journalist when I'm an adult.; [a.] Dunnellon, FL

SCHLOSSBERG, LEWIS W.
[b.] March 19, 1978, Upper Darby, PA; [p.] Brett A. and Susan P. Schlossberg; [ed.] Akiba Hebrew Academy; [occ.] Student; [memb.] United States Tennis Association, Motorcycle Association; [oth. writ.] Miscellaneous short stories and essays; [pers.] "Those who desire to give up freedom in order to gain security will not have nor do they deserve, either one" Thomas Jefferson; [a.] Bryn Mawr; [Cnty.] PA

SCHMIDTMAN, YVONNE F. M.
[b.] December 16, 1954, Chicago, IL; [p.] LaVerne Baley Allen, Russell Allen; [m.] Daniel Schmidtman, January 19, 1983; [ed.] Graduate of New Buffalo High School, attended Lake Michigan College; [occ.] Office Manager for Amoloc Investigation Services; [memb.] Honorary Lifetime Membership in Delta Psi Omega (A dramatic fraternity); [hon.] CDA in Child Development, Dean's List; [oth. writ.] Poems include "At Sunset", "The Emissary", and "The Man-Eating Goat Adventure". One novel - "The Flayl Master".; [pers.] I believe life to be an on-going series of adventures. We have only to join the fray and hold to our sense of humor!; [a.] Coloma, MI

SCHMITT, MELISSA SUE
[pen.] Melissa Schmitt; [b.] April 15, 1981, Mobile, AL; [p.] Melody J. Schmitt, James D. Schmitt; [ed.] John S. Shaw High School; [occ.] Student, 10th Grade; [memb.] Young American Bowling Alliance; [hon.] Excellence in Academics - Highest GPA Math Skills (9th Grade); [oth. writ.] None published; [pers.] I enjoy art, reading and spending time with friends.; [a.] Mo-

bile, AL

SCHNEIDER, LENORE
[b.] June 8, 1938, Cambridge, MT; [p.] Gertrude Berman, Irving Schneider; [ch.] Neil Jay Yagendorf; [ed.] Brooklyn, (MA) High School, Boston Univ. for Interior Design, U. of Arizona, BFA in Art Education Harvard U., Graduate Courses; [occ.] Interior Designer, Hobby: Photography; [memb.] Artist Member, South Shore Art Center; [pers.] I am an artist whose creations directly reflect the feelings that bubble up from somewhere deep inside me.; [a.] Hingham, MA

SCHNEIDER, SARAH
[b.] October 30, 1980, Greeley, CO; [p.] Jim and Jacque Schneider; [ed.] Now attending Douglas County H.S. (Freshmen) also attended Castle Rock Middle School, Roxborough Elem., and Plum Creek Elem. (All in CO); [occ.] Student; [memb.] Ballet Student for 12 years at Colorado Dance Center, Littleton, CO; [hon.] Outstanding 8th Grader 1994 at Castle Rock H.S., 1994-Metropolitan Mayor's Youth Award; [oth. writ.] Poem in H.S. paper "the Write Issue." Small article in local paper "Castle Chronicle"; [pers.] I express my feelings through my every day experiences and what I see, hear, feel, and wonder about all around me.; [a.] Littleton, CO

SCHOONMAKER, IRELEEN J.
[pen.] Ireleen J. Schoonmaker; [b.] February 10, 1934, Montgomery, NY; [p.] Edna and William McPhillips; [m.] Granville K. Schoonmaker, December 28; [ch.] Five; [ed.] 11 1/2 yrs - also many years of experience in The Hard Knocks of Life; [occ.] House wife; [memb.] Precently, Vice President of our Home Owners Associations Past - Womans Aglow Hostess Chairman. Church Treasurer and Ladies Ministries Treasurer; [hon.] Cheer Leader, Awards for Sports, honor of having The Lead Part in Senior Play.; [oth. writ.] Many poems and devotional writings, I pray one day to put in a book. This is my dream.; [pers.] My life is dedicated to God who gives me the inspiration for everything I write.; [a.] Wallkill, NY

SCHULTZ, CONCEPTION BERNADETTE
[pen.] Bernice Schultz; [b.] April 26, 1958, Honolulu, HI; [p.] John B. Castro, Josephine B. Castro; [ch.] Richard, Sheena, Kristin; [ed.] Star of the Sea High School, University of Hawaii; [occ.] Music Teacher, Holy Family Catholic Academy, Hwl., HI; [oth. writ.] Articles for Parish Church Bulletins; [pers.] It is through my thoughts and creative imagination that I try to reach out and touch the special people in my life. To my children, you have influenced my writing, thank you...I love you.; [a.] Honolulu, HI

SCHULTZ, RICHARD
[b.] November 15, 1951, Libertyville, IL; [p.] Ralph and Luella Schultz; [m.] Diane L. Schultz, November 5, 1971; [ch.] Richard Michael, Jeffrey Robert; [ed.] College of Lake County, National College of Education; [occ.] Business Owner; [oth. writ.] Personal book of poems.; [pers.] I write poems to people close to me so they have something to remember me by.; [a.] Mundelein, IL

SCHULZE, DONNA
[pen.] Jessica Bell; [b.] September 7, 1950, Camden, NJ; [ch.] Chris and Doug Schulze; [ed.] Woodbury H.S., Trenton State College; [occ.] 1st Grade Teacher Martin Luther King, Jr. School Willingboro, NJ; [oth. writ.] Poems previously published in "The Healing News" newspaper and former church magazine.; [pers.] I believe that every experience that comes into our lives, no matter how it may appear on the surface, presents itself to give us the opportunity to heal something in our lives if we are open to allow the healing. In my case the

experience was breast cancer. The greatest gift we can give to others is to be there for them in a loving, nonjudgmental way, loving them as they are so they may become who they are meant to be. My poem is dedicated to my guardian angel Janet who did this for me.; [a.] Marlton, NJ

SCHUTT, M. REICHERT
[pen.] M. Reichert Schutt; [b.] July 23, 1907, North Dakota; [ch.] Four; [ed.] St. John's Hospital, Farog, No. Dakota (R.N.) 1928, Education and American University, Wash., DC, (degree B.A. (R.N.) Nursing/Journalism 1965); [occ.] Retired; [memb.] American Univ. of Women and Eastern Star; [oth. writ.] Nursing/Newspaper Articles; [pers.] One is never too old to be creative.

SCHWARTZ, DIANE
[pen.] Diane Carta; [b.] July 28, 1949, Washington, DC; [p.] Mrs. Michael A. Carta; [m.] Ronald Schwartz, March 31, 1973; [ch.] Michele and Angela; [ed.] Catholic Education and two years Emerson Institute; [occ.] Mother, Mom, Friend, Support line, Protector, Nurse; [memb.] Volunteer in school and Nursing homes, Association of Mirian Helpers; [hon.] My Honors and Awards are from God who blessed me with two wonderful kind daughters who worked extremely hard for higher education and personnel respect for human kind.; [oth. writ.] This is my first, and hope in the future to do more work, in honor of the children of the world. With great humility, hope they may be published.; [pers.] I wrote this poem so whoever may read it will look upon all children, with love and respect for their innocence. And stir their conscience. Dedicated to Katherine.; [a.] Silver Spring, MD

SCHWIESOW, ERIN
[b.] August 5, 1982, Colorado; [p.] Linda and Norm Schwiesow; [occ.] Student; [a.] Woodland Park, CO

SCOTT, KAREN
[b.] April 5, 1979, Oakland City, IN; [p.] Ronald Wright, Julie Scott; [ch.] Chris Scott (brother), Ronetta Wright (sister); [ed.] Lowell Elementary, Brumfield Elementary, Princeton Comm - High School; [occ.] High School Student 11th Grade; [oth. writ.] Poem race published in school paper, also race published in tapestry of thoughts book. Indian dance published in best poems of the 90's, by the National Library of Poetry.; [pers.] I just enjoy writing poetry and stories, I hope that for anyone to read my poetry, will see the world in a more caring and positive way.; [a.] Princeton, IN

SCROFANI, PHILIP
[m.] Susan B. Scrofani, July 13, 1968; [ed.] Ph.D.; [occ.] Clinical Psychologist; [memb.] American Psychological Association; [oth. writ.] Many articles in Psychological journals published one previous poem, 3 act play on inner city youth, novel about the future of the American family (unpublished).

SEALS, CAROL SUE
[b.] October 26, 1941, Louisville, KY; [p.] Joseph and Evelyn Leming; [m.] Earl Y. Seals, October 5, 1963; [ch.] Joey Earl, Scott Shane; [ed.] Completed High School at Berea High - Berea, KY 1960; [occ.] Homemaker; [oth. writ.] I've only used my poems as gifts to the family or to friends. Thank you so much - I'm speechless.; [pers.] I just like to put down on paper, in the shape of a poem, things that have happened to me. Or my family or my personal thoughts. (Sorry, I'm nervous).; [a.] Berea, KY

SEGALL, JO-ANN B.
[pen.] Jo-Ann Segall; [b.] August 26, 1924, Des Moines, IA; [p.] S. Donald Butters, Aileen M. Butters; [m.] Edwin E. Segall, April 29, 1955; [ch.] Jeffrey, Lewis,

Becky; [ed.] HS diploma Theordore Roosevelt High School, Des Moines, Iowa, All but dissertation for Ph.D. in International Law and Relations, Univ of Chicago, MLS Catholic University (1883); [occ.] Head Librarian Sidewall Friends Upper School; [memb.] Foreign Service Women's Association, Lakewood Country Club. Previously Secy/Chair of the school boards of the International Schools in Belgrade, Yugoslavia and Djakarta, Indonesia.; [hon.] Member of Beta Phi Mu, the Library Science Honor Society. I was awarded the Amateur World Championship of 3-gaited horses; [oth. writ.] Poems published in Sidewall Friends Literary Magazines. A couple of letters of the editor of the Washington Post; [pers.] I want Students to know traditional literature which was so beautifully written. I would like to see modern poetry stress rhyme and rhythm. I would like to see also modern writing stress the perfection of God's creation.; [a.] Washington, DC

SEGER, TAMMY JO
[b.] November 8, 1969, Clearfield, PA; [p.] James and Eunice Seger; [ed.] Curwensville Area High School, Curwensville, PA DuBois Business College, DuBois, PA; [occ.] Medical Transcriptionist; [memb.] Tennessee Walking Horse Breeders and Exhibitors Association, Certified Emergency Medical Technician; [pers.] My Love of animals and nature greatly influences all of my writings.; [a.] Grampian, PA

SELBY, CORY
[b.] April 5, 1983, Kirksville, MO; [p.] Jerry and Patricia Selby; [ed.] Presently attend Kirksville Junior High School, Kirksville, MO; [occ.] Jr. High School Student; [hon.] Was chosen to attend the Joseph Baldwin Academy at Northeast Missouri State University; [a.] Kirksville, MO

SELOVER, GAYE V.
[b.] February 21, 1934, Miami, OK; [p.] Jim Padgett/ Faye Landers; [m.] Marion V. Selover Jr., February 14, 1973; [ch.] David E. Reed, Michelle Hall, Michonne Pieksman; [ed.] Payette High School; [occ.] Art Teacher and Stained Glass Instructor; [memb.] Assembly of God Church, T.V. Art, Glass crafters Creations in Glass.; [oth. writ.] Pondering published in "Where Dawn Lingers", Obits, published in "Best Poems of the 90's".; [pers.] My Grand kid's Jason Jeffrey. Nicole, Scott, Patrick, David. Brian and Camille, have kept me in great spirits and laughter. I feel along with my belief in God. They are my personal happiness.; [a.] Payette, ID

SEYMOUR, MARILYN
[b.] June 23, 1941, Elizabeth, NJ; [p.] William and Genevieve Lubischer; [m.] Calvin Seymour, May 21, 1980; [ch.] Thomas, Tracy and John; [ed.] High School (Battin High) Elizabeth, NJ; [oth. writ.] Numerous; [pers.] Try to view the world around you with open eyes, open mind and an open heart.; [a.] Roselle Park, NJ

SHARIFI, HAIDER
[b.] April 26, 1980; [ed.] Long Branch Elementary School; [occ.] High School Student; [oth. writ.] A number of unpublished pieces.; [pers.] My poems, songs are about what I feel of the world. I have been greatly influenced by modern day songwriters.; [a.] Arlington, VA

SHARP, JERRILYN SUE
[b.] July 15, 1957, Kalamazoo; [p.] Jackie and Ron Rohlfs; [ch.] Courtney Maline Sharp; [ed.] Vicksburg High School, Lakeland Medical Academy, California College of Health Science; [occ.] Medical Technologist; [memb.] I.S.C.L.T. (International Society of Clinical Laboratory Technology); [hon.] Graduated from

High School and College with a B+ average.; [oth. writ.] "Too Often"; [pers.] Always follow your heart.; [a.] Greenville, MI

SHAW JR., DAVID G.

[b.] May 7, 1977, Aberdeen, WA; [p.] Jeanne LaRocque and David G. Shaw Sr.; [ed.] 1996 graduate of Northriver School Brooklyn, Wash.; [hon.] Grand Champion in the 1996 Spring Youth Fair - Photography Sr. Division - Centralia, Wa Best of Youth (Photography) Ocean Shores Convention Center, Ocean Shores, Washington, 1996; [oth. writ.] I have written several poems, but have not submitted any prior to this.; [pers.] I have been influenced by the people and scenery of the Turtle Mountain Chippewa Reservation in Belcourt, ND from which I am a member.; [a.] Hoquiam, WA

SHEARER, NANCY BAKER

[pen.] Nancy Baker-Shearer; [b.] March 26, 1956, Charlotte, MI; [p.] Carroll and Louise Baker; [m.] William Shearer, June 16, 1984; [ch.] Josh Duane, Jeremiah Michael; [ed.] Deerfield Bch High School, Art Major; [occ.] Florida Power and Light - Meter Reader/Safety Coordinator, Longaberger Consultant; [hon.] Honor Student with Art Awards.; [oth. writ.] Personal Journal; [pers.] Life's combination of personal tragedies and triumphs have inspired my writings. My two sons, husband, and parents give me unconditional support. Believing, sharing wisdom, and respect from special friends and family, my poems are for you. Thank-you...; [a.] North Port, FL

SHERIDAN, DIANE

[b.] May 22, 1956, Long Branch, NJ; [p.] Nina E. Walzer, John S. Walzer Jr; [m.] Glenn L. Sheridan, January 14, 1990; [ch.] Evan, Gordon, Jacob; [ed.] Marlboro H.S. Marlboro, NJ Kutztown State College, Kutztown PA; [occ.] Construction Operations Coordinator, and Realtor; [memb.] National Association of Realtors, Pennsylvania Association of Realtors, Central Montgomery County Association of Realtors; [pers.] Let's try to get through challenges, look for some humor along the way. And if you care about someone, let them know it. To my sons, I love each of you, always!; [a.] Pottstown, PA

SHERIDAN, MARGARET

[b.] April 30, 1932, Scranton, PA; [p.] Charles and Anna Primich; [m.] Robert Sheridan, March 21, 1951; [ed.] North Scranton High, Center Conn. State University; [occ.] Retired Governmental Accountant; [memb.] Connecticut Songwriters Assoc, National Academy of Songwriters, Connecticut Governmental Accountants; [oth. writ.] Various Songs, A Valley (variation of poem), A Parent's Love, There's More To Love, I Don't Know (a valley and I don't know have been picked up by music publishing companies); [pers.] It is my wish that people of all nations will realize that peace, love, and tolerance of each other is the only way to ensure a place on earth for future generations.; [a.] Kensington, CT

SHERMAN, DELORES

[b.] June 17, 1963, Florida; [m.] Ralph E. Sherman Sr., August 3, 1983; [ch.] Ralph Jr. and Ashley Ann; [occ.] Mother, part-time writer of children's stories; [oth. writ.] The Adventures of Teddy (unpublished); [pers.] My gold's are that all children learn to read. Most of my writing is designed for the young minds. Hoping to encourage their learning.; [a.] Salem, AL

SHERWOOD, DEBRA SUE

[b.] November 9, 1959, Arlington, VA; [p.] James A. and Margie R. Sherwood; [ed.] B.S. Parks and Recreation from George Mason University in Virginia (Fairfax); [occ.] Executive Assistant; [memb.] The Nature conservancy National Parks and Conservation Association, National Audubon Society; [hon.] Schol-

arship 1984 for Riding Instructors Certificate at Morven Park International Equestrian Institute; [oth. writ.] I have written poems for myself and others over the past several years. I have another poem that the Nat. Library of Poetry offered to publish, but I did not submit the paperwork for it, poem was Faith Endures.; [pers.] I write about things that have a profound impact on my life and that touch the deepest most inner core of my emotions and heart. I write about things that stand out in my mind as being issues of mankind or things that are dear to me.; [a.] Sterling, VA

SHIRLEY, WILLIE LOU

[pen.] Willie Lou Shirley; [b.] October 1928, Menard Co, TX; [p.] William J. and Tennie Reeves Bell; [m.] Rev. James T. Shirley (Deceased), December 25, 1938; [ch.] Karl, David, Anne, Sylvia, Rebecca; [ed.] BS degree Elem. Ed. 1938 Specialtist Springfield MO. Howard Payne Univ. Brownward Tex 1 year Southwestern Seminary Fort Worth Tex. Drary College; [occ.] Retired Teacher in special Ed. 26 years Baptist Pastors Wife; [memb.] First Baptist Church St. Chas. Alpha Delta Kappa Chapter Rt. Teachers of MO.; [hon.] Several awards from Husbands Churches, Senior Citizen of year 1989, "Adopted" Grandmother for youth Mission groups of church 1987-90; [oth. writ.] Dreaded memories, Book "Labors of Love" book of "Family History" News publications for hometown and church - "A trip to the Ozarks" Hobo Zero Here", "Quitts", "Peace", "The Rocky Road", "The Syrup Mill", "The Butter Churn"; [pers.] Greatly influence by Ranch Life in early childhood and husband's Ministry. Love to write about people, home, birthday greetings get well cards reflect life in the thirty's in good times and bad.; [a.] Saint Charles, MO

SHOOK, OELIA E. K.

[pen.] Ofelia Martinez; [b.] July 15, 1959, Havana, Cuba; [p.] (CPA) Raudeal Martinez, Ofelia Soto (Art grad.); [m.] Michael K. Shook/self-employed Business Professional, August 9, 1989; [ch.] Tomio, Tsuruko and Joseph Kurosowa Shook; [ed.] St. Lawrence Elementary School/Tampa Catholic High/Sanata Fe, Hillsborough, Central Florida Community Colleges/ Manhattan Beauty School/Division of Vocational Education Horticulture; [occ.] Professional Cosmetologist; [memb.] Distinguished member of the International Society of Poets/American Quarter Horse Association/ The Cat Fanciers' Association/ The American Kennel Club/The American Half Grade Quarter Horse Association.; [hon.] Editor's Choice Award/Volunteer Red CRoss Nurse/National Guild of Piano Players and National Piano Playing Auditions/Carmen Morales School of Ballet and Spanish Dancing with the Castanets/ Intern Teacher at Manhattan Beauty School/Spanish Teacher at New Hope Elementary School Tampa; [oth. writ.] Published poetry in beneath the harvest moon. Published poem in the best poems of the 90's. Published poem in morning song. Poem published in of moonlight and wishes. Published poem in the colors of thought. Personal collections; [pers.] I must give credit to my parents for instilling in me to put God first in my life. The courage to face any adversity, and stand up for what I believe in right. To push myself to the limit. Never settle for anything less than the best I can be. To hope and to dream. That I can do anything in life that I desire, as long as I work hard to achieve that goal and reach it! Never give up. Be kind and thoughtful and compassionate of others less fortunate.; [a.] Ft. White, FL

SHOUSE, JORDAN

[b.] April 20, 1985, Winston-Salem, NC; [p.] Doug Shouse and Ruth Shouse; [ed.] Coth grade Cook middle school; [occ.] Student; [hon.] Art Awards, Science Award, Stevens Center Chorus; [oth. writ.] The Midnight World "Poem" Sherwood Newsletter.; [pers.] I

try to show the beauty of nature and the cycle of life in my poems.; [a.] Winston-Salem, NC

SHRADER, SHIRLEY

[pen.] Shirl Mack; [b.] August 5, 1935, Jenkin Jones, WV; [p.] Jerry and Nora McCroskey; [m.] James D. Shrader, September 4, 1968; [ch.] Deborah, Sue, Randy and Lori; [ed.] High School Graduate; [occ.] House Wife; [oth. writ.] I like to write poetry and short stories in my spare time, but none have been published.; [pers.] Anything worth doing is worth doing well.; [a.] Bluefield, VA

SICARI, DOMINIC F.

[b.] August 1, 1908, New York City; [p.] Carlo and Fara Sicari; [m.] Mildred Sicari, June 19, 1932; [ch.] Aileen, Charles, Robert; [ed.] Newtown H.S. 1927; [occ.] Retired Postal Superintendent; [memb.] NARFE Former Officer, Columbian Association, Holy Name Society, Church Choirs over 70 yrs.; [oth. writ.] Have been writing poetry all my life for the pleasure. Never entered anything for publication.; [pers.] I believe in celibacy while single, faithfulness while married, and always strive to abide to the golden rule.; [a.] Flushing, NY

SIDEBOTTOM, PAUL E.

[pen.] Bud Sidebottom; [b.] September 4, Avoca, IA; [p.] Aaron and Ida Sidebottom; [m.] Maxine (McKenzie) Sidebottom, September 19, 1939; [ch.] Loretta and Nick; [ed.] Shelby Consolidated and Marne Elementary; [occ.] Retired; [oth. writ.] Misc. poems and some newspaper articles, many in local paper, I attempt to write about various subjects - some real some imaginary.; [pers.] Always keep an open mind as the opportunity to learn never ends. Also it pays to listen as opportunity knocks very lightly.; [a.] Deming, NM

SIEMEK, KELLY MICHELE

[b.] July 19, 1977, Baltimore, MD; [p.] Patrick Siemek, Patricia Siemek; [ed.] Northeast Senior High School, University of Maryland at Baltimore County; [occ.] Student; [memb.] Emmanuel Lutheran Church; [hon.] Valedictorian, Delegate Scholarship, Senatorial Scholarship; [pers.] My poetry is a reflection of the unconditional love I feel whenever I look into my mother's eyes. She is my inspiration and makes me feel as though I am truly touched by an angel.; [a.] Pasadena, MD

SILVER, GINGER KELLER

[pen.] Ginger K. Silver; [b.] October 5, 1949, Tallahassee, FL; [p.] Floyd Keller and Marian Poole Keller; [m.] Marshall D. Silver, June 30, 1973; [ch.] Amanda N, Marian M, Mathew D; [ed.] McEvoy High School, Macon Georgia Class of '68; [occ.] God's servant, wife, mother, Nations bank Vice President; [oth. writ.] "Daddy Knows", "Birthday Lament", "Making God Real...A Collection of Children Sermons"; [pers.] I don't know where the saying originated but I find its message motivating. "Our life is a gift from God. What we do with it is our gift to God."; [a.] Lucia, NC

SIMONDS SR., JAMES E.

[pen.] James E. Simonds; [b.] January 19, 1925, Windsor, VT; [p.] Walter E. Simonds, Thelma Boomhower; [m.] Jacqueline G. Simonds, December 21, 1957; [ch.] Shawn C., Kimberly J., James E., Jr., Scott E., Mark J.; [ed.] December 1973, graduate Beal Business College Associate Degrees in Accounting and Business Management; [occ.] U.S.A.F. Retired June 30, 1967, Served 20 years active duty. General Electric Co. 1968-1985; [oth. writ.] Various other poems.; [a.] Bangor, ME

SIMONS, CHARLES ANTHONY
[pen.] Chuck; [b.] March 23, 1954, Oceanside, NY; [p.] (Mother) Filomena, (Father) Charles; [ch.] Christina my Super Nova, my Rainbow Jennifer, my Tornado Matthew; [ed.] Oceanside High School, Burlington County Community College (AS), Community College of the Air Force (AS), Southern Illinois University (BS); [occ.] Just a Truck Driver; [memb.] Southern Illinois University Alumni, National Association for Fathers, Abortion Stops a Beating Heart, Roman Catholic Church; [hon.] "Silver Fox Award", for most supportive parent of my son's little league team! Dean's List: Southern Illinois University, Carbondale, Illinois; [oth. writ.] "The Rainbow", "A Ring in Round", "God are You There", "Imelda's Shoes". These are just a few, they have not been published but have never been submitted. Super Nova was my first time I ever submitted anything! I have been fortunate enough to find 3 rainbows in my life and I am most truly blessed!; [pers.] "You can't have a rainbow without a little rain, and it takes both rain and sunshine to make a rainbow, only fools look for the pot of gold at the end of a rainbow, the wiseman knows his rich just in finding the rainbow!"; [a.] Belleville, IL

SINGKEO, PHETSAMONE
[b.] June 22, 1978, Laos; [p.] Lot Singkeo, Seng Singkeo; [oth. writ.] Thousands more unpublished; [pers.] In loving memory of my dear grandfather, my words in this piece of writing are dedicated to him, Kraw Siriya. We all have our own ambition to pursue and what I am to be, I have a passion to honor my Grandmothers, Seah Siriya, Good Singkeo, Long Singkeo, and my parents, lot and Seng Singkeo for what I am now becoming. I am a man who is in love with writing. I will write, write, and write until I die.; [a.] Seattle, WA

SIRES, REBECCA ANNE
[pen.] Becca, Becky, BAS; [b.] March 18, 1972, Rock County; [p.] Jim and Linda Sires; [ed.] Hadfield Elementary School Waukesha North High School 3 yrs. (10 to 12 grade diploma) for 3 yrs. (4 to 6 grade) Elm Grove Lutheran School for 3 yrs. (1 to 3), Butler Middle School, 1/2 yr. (7 grade), Elm Brook Middle, School 2 1/2 yrs., (7 to 8th grade twice) Horning Middle School, 1 1/2 yrs (8 to 9 graded); [oth. writ.] Writing a book of 200 poems, tempting to have it published. And that I chose for the contest, is from my book I'm writing. I've been writing for 3 yrs.; [pers.] I hope that my poems will reach to peoples hearts. Because they are truly from my heart. I've been writing for years. And now I realize that after this, my life is full words to share with the world; [a.] Waukesha, WI

SKALA, JENNIFER
[b.] July 12, 1977, Chicago, IL; [p.] Thomas Skala and Judy Skala; [ed.] Reavis High School; [occ.] Waitress, Villa Rosa - Italian Restaurant; [oth. writ.] Several poems published in the high school literary magazine.

SKILES, BERNARD
[pen.] Bernie Skiles; [b.] October 11, 1948, Los Angeles, CA; [p.] Alfred and Lucy Skiles; [m.] Teresa A. Skiles, January 23, 1970; [ch.] Bernie, Julie, Nicki, Liz, Steve; [ed.] Bachelor Art - Public Administration - 1979 University of Redlands, CA; [occ.] Senior Investigator Riverside County District Attorney Retired L.A.P.D. Detective4 - 22 1/2 years; [memb.] Calif. Homicide Investigator's Assoc., L.E.I.U., "5" Countries Intelligence Assoc., U.S. Army 1968-70 Vietnam Veteran; [hon.] L.A.P.D. "Police Medal" (Valor), L.A.P.D. Detective of year (NOM) 1989, 25 years Wedding Anniv. (Wife - Teresa); [oth. writ.] Poems to my wife; [pers.] This poems is dedicated to my son Bernie Jr., and his wife Marlene; [a.] Rowland Heights, CA

SKOTNICA, JUDITH A.
[pen.] Judith Simone Skotnica; [b.] June 8, 1941, Buffalo, NY; [p.] Mr. and Mrs. Joseph A. Simone Sr.; [m.] William Skotnica, June 21, 1986; [ch.] 8 Children, 11 Grandchildren; [ed.] Extended Education in the arts, Literature and Computer Science; [occ.] Artist poet and aspiring writer; [memb.] Mythology, Literature and Art Study Workshops of Central California, Poetry Workshops, American Reflex Sympathetic Dytrophy Association (ARSDA); [hon.] Citation of Merit for outstanding performance in the Titan IV space program, editor's Merit Award in Poetry; [oth. writ.] 1. Current in-progress work, auto-biography and poetry. 2. Published: Poetry in the National Library of Poetry's "A Muse To Follow", and "Best Poems of the 90's"; [pers.] Words are food for the human experience, a conduit to personal development, and an expression of our deepest belief; [a.] Morro Bay, CA

SLATER, JESSIE
[b.] February 2, 1984, Saint Vincent's Hospital, Manhattan, NY; [ed.] Student of Museum Junior High School, Yonkers, NY; [occ.] Student; [oth. writ.] Poems, haiku, and short stories (no other works published).; [pers.] I want to show the goodness of God, family, and friendships. Emily Dickinson is a favorite along with Edgar Allen Poe, and O. Henry.

SMALLWOOD, BILLY M.
[pen.] Mike Smallwood; [b.] December 9, 1952, Jasper, AL; [m.] Donna Sue Smallwood, February 21, 1987; [ch.] Tabitha, Brent, Joseph, Adam; [ed.] Cordova High School, Cordova Al., Walker College, Jasper Al.; [occ.] Supervisor, Zartic Inc.; [memb.] Harmony Baptist Church, Jasper Al.; [hon.] Honorable Discharge U.S. Army, Vietnam Era Veteran; [oth. writ.] Songwriter, Country, Rock and Roll, Religious, Christmas for Individual and Holiday events. Positive response from the White House, and President Clinton concerning America Homeless Vietnam Veterans.; [pers.] My dream is to touch the heart, ease the mind, see the tear, hold the ear of not what I gain but what I can share to leave something behind to all people everywhere if it be the Masters will.; [a.] Rome, GA

SMITH, AMANDA
[pen.] Mandy Denise; [b.] October 28, 1982, Pasadena, TX; [p.] Daniel and Marlene Smith; [hon.] National Jr. Honor Society Charter Member — Floresville Middle School; [pers.] If you make a mistake, it's not the end of the world, it isn't your first and won't be your last.; [a.] Floresville, TX

SMITH, CAROLINE CHRISTINE
[b.] July 1, 1938, Chicago, IL; [p.] Arthur and Agnes McAfee; [m.] Jack C. Smith, February 18, 1955; [ch.] Jackie, Shirley and Sandy, (Grandchildren) Robert Reitz, Jason Bell, Jillian Pierce, Ashley Richard, Rachel Richard, Adam Richard; [occ.] Housewife, Mother and Grandmother; [memb.] A.A.R.P. Medic Alert and American Diabetes Assoc.; [hon.] It's been an honor being with the National Library of Poetry; [oth. writ.] 1st poem "My Lords Touch" published in "Beyond The Stars" in 1995 and 2nd poem "A Mother's Prayer" published in "Tapestry Of Thoughts" in 1996; [pers.] I'm dedicating this poem to my 6 beautiful grandchildren, Robert, Jason, Jillian, Ashley, Rachel and Adam, with all my love always; [a.] Osage Beach, MO

SMITH, CHANCE
[b.] April 15, 1990, Tahlequah, OK; [p.] Lanna Smith; [ed.] Kindergarten; [occ.] Student; [a.] Tahlequah, OK

SMITH, DIANNE MARIE
[pen.] Dianne Dellamater-Smith; [b.] December 15, 1945, Saint Johns, MI; [p.] Raymond and Arola Dellamater; [m.] Richard McRee Smith, May 19, 1983;

[ch.] Steven Lee Smith; [ed.] Graduate of Sun Prairie High School, Sun Prairie, Wisconsin, Madison Business College Madison, Wisconsin, and the Institute of Children's Literature, Redding, Connecticut; [occ.] Director's Secretary for the HQ of the Wisconsin Army National Guard, own my own craft business Dippidy Doodads; [memb.] State and National Humane Societies, Association of Crafts and Creative Industries; [hon.] 1) Headed the first word processing center in the National Guard system nationwide. We were the test case — paved the way for computers within the National Guard throughout the country. 2) Obtained a court Reporting degree. Typing speed 125/machine shorthand 200 wpm.; [oth. writ.] A poem on Frankie Avalon in a "16" magazine, a "how-to" article in Crafts and Things and various articles in National Guard newspapers and magazines.; [pers.] My writing brings me self-satisfaction and great happiness. If I can make someone else feel good through my writing, then I am a success.; [a.] Lodi, WI

SMITH, EVELYN
[b.] March 2, 1947, Milton, FL; [p.] Ms. Bessie M. Garrison; [m.] Charles Smith, November 10, 1963; [ch.] Charles, Nathaniel, Martin D.; [ed.] G. E. d. 1 yr PJC Cosmetology Course; [occ.] Cosmetologist; [memb.] Bethlehem Primitive Baptist, Under the leadership of Elder E. Hayes; [oth. writ.] The three children listed above are my biological children. I have seven other children which means a lot to me. Keitha, Ruby, David, Ellis, Alfonso, Tramaine, and Jonathan.; [pers.] My Mother a single mom of four is my inspiration. She's gone but left my sister Addie, and my two Brothers, Curtis and Kennon, a treasure of memories. And my seven grandchildren also inspire me.; [a.] Milton, FL

SMITH, JOHN NORRIS
[b.] December 1, 1954, Little Rock, AR; [p.] Mr. and Mrs. John C. Smith; [m.] Dorothy Ann Smith, October 5, 1975; [ch.] Demetre, Nathaniel, Katherine; [ed.] University of Central Arkansas, 2 years; [occ.] Student Pharmacy Tech, Concorde Career College; [memb.] Disabled American Veterans, American Diabetes Association; [hon.] The Army Commendation Medal, The Army Achievement Medal (1st and 2nd Award); [oth. writ.] "The Leopard" forthcoming anthology...Into the Unknown; [pers.] Life is only a moment and poetry is a joy.; [a.] Aurora, CO

SMITH, JUNIE
[pen.] Junie; [b.] March 6, 1980, Chicago; [p.] John Edwin and June Smith; [ed.] Freshman in Griffin High School Griffin, GA; [occ.] Student; [memb.] Drama Club; [hon.] A-B Honor roll Art Excellence Rewards; [oth. writ.] I continue to write poetry on a weekly basis; [pers.] Writing poetry express my true feelings and make me feel great; [a.] Lawrenceville, GA

SMITH, JUSTIN
[b.] October 1, 1979, Saint Louis, MO; [p.] Jon and Denise Smith; [ed.] Henderson Elementary School, Bornwell Jr. High, 2 years of high school but plan to finish and go on to an art Institute; [memb.] French Club, Art Club, Judge of School's Literary magazine; [hon.] Academic excellence award, perfect attendance award, Who's Who Among American high school students award 2 consecutive years; [oth. writ.] A few poems published by the Iliad Press Co.; [pers.] If it were not for my cousin TJ Gagliono, I would never turned my head towards poetry and other arts so I'd like to thank him at this time. "Death is a familiar face no one wishes to encounter."; [a.] Saint Peters, MO

SMITH, KENNETH EMERSON
[pen.] Ken Smith; [b.] May 28, 1951, Toccoa, GA; [p.] Ralph Emerson and Ruby Cleo Smith; [m.] Mary Glenell Smith, October 25, 1975; [ch.] Mark Thomas, Kevin

Matthew; [ed.] Stephens Co. High School, Dalton Jr. College, Dalton GA, West Georgia College, Carrolton, GA; [occ.] Supervisor, Textile MPG Color Matcher; [oth. writ.] I have several other poems and stories but none published.; [pers.] Quietness combined with solitude can cleanse the mind and give your day a breath of fresh air.; [a.] Toccoa, GA

SMITH, KIMBERLY ANN
[pen.] Kimberly; [b.] February 25, 1981, Omak, WA; [p.] Stephen and Constanza Smith; [ed.] High school sophomore - exchange student to Colombia; [occ.] Student at Omak High School - work part time at cinema; [memb.] O.H.S. International Club, F.H.A. member, O.H.S. Volleyball Team, Our Lady of the Valley Catholic Church, O.H.S. Softball Team; [hon.] Student of the Month - M.S. , MSB Class Representative - Middle School, Science Olympiad, Champion Team members, selected to attend Young Writers of America Conference M.S., ASB School Treasurer - M.S., Most inspirational at Chicago A. Camps, Volleyball player and sophomore class secretary for 96-97; [oth. writ.] A short Christmas story for children published in the local newspaper. A published illustration of a christmas scene.; [pers.] Life is short, time goes fast. Enjoy it while you can.; [a.] Omak, WA

SMITH, MARY JEAN
[pen.] Jean Smith; [b.] May 4, 1952, McGehee, AR; [p.] The Late Nathaniel Richardson; [m.] Missie R. Taylor; [ch.] Melinda, Tiffany, Kesia; [ed.] Graduate Desha High School, May 19, 1970, Attended Capital City Business College; [occ.] Certify Nurse-Aide, AR Dept. of Health In-Home-Service; [memb.] Palestine Missionary Baptist Church, McGehee, AR Pastor Rev. R. L. Cook, Sr. Former Church Clerk, Sunday School Teacher and Program Chairman; [hon.] Christian In-Reach Youth Leadership - Former 4-H Leader; [oth. writ.] My 1st poem selected to be publish title Jesus made me excited.; [pers.] I am the proud grandmother of Jordan Latrell Taylor and Justin Antonio Taylor, The late Stephanie Latrell Taylor. I enjoy writing, reading, cooking, singing and travelling, I love people all people.; [a.] McGehee, AR

SMITH, MICHELLE
[b.] January 21, 1977, Brooklyn, NY; [p.] Margaret Sweet, Michael Smith (Deceased); [m.] (Deceased July 20, 1996); [ed.] Academy of Art College, San Francisco, CA

SMITH, RODNEY SANFORD
[b.] December 4, 1965, Corinth, MS; [p.] Larry and Louise Smith; [ed.] Graduated from Alcorn Central High School in 1984, Attended Northeast Miss. Junior College from 1984, to 1986; [occ.] Industrial Technician and Writer; [memb.] Corinth Evening Lions Club; [oth. writ.] "Twenty - Five Years Without The Lizard King" and "Poetry Fit For A Vampire"; [pers.] I have written poetry since high school days, but began to really enjoy it, and work harder after listening to and reading books about the American Poet of the Sixties, Jim Morrison; [a.] Glen, MS

SNELL, GERTRUDE
[pen.] M-O-M; [b.] February 27, 1943, Newark, NJ; [p.] Clarence Spence, Lucille Spence; [m.] Dewey Hosea Snell Jr. (Divorced July 19, 1969), November 25, 1961; [ch.] Gayle Marie Snell, Lucia Donata Snell, Elger and Claudia Montfort; [ed.] Seven Grandchildren; [occ.] Weequachic High, Newark, NJ Special Course Management/Supervisory Training Oklahoma University Okla. U.S. Postal PEDC Training Courses; [memb.] Missionary - California NJ, Private Geriactric Care Nurse Asst.; [hon.] Faith Temple, C.O.G.I.C. Supt. Joe Scott Jr - Pastor 151 Berry St. Hackensack NJ, Pres. M-O-M, Public Relations, Private Duty Nurse

Assistant and New Jersey Certified Home Health Aide and Mother/Child Care Infant; [oth. writ.] Several non published works; [pers.] I'm an instrument used and inspired by Holy Spirit to be a bridge between God and mankind to give God the honor, the praise and the glory. Thank you Jesus, in Christ's Humble Service.; [a.] Califon, NJ

SNOW, ADRIENNE MARIE
[b.] June 12, 1978, Passiac, NJ; [p.] Guy and Lillian A. Snow; [ed.] Graduate of Ridge High School in Baskilg Ridge, NJ and Hour a freshman at Marywood College Scranton, PA; [memb.] The Somerset Hills Handicapped Riders Auby Hugh O'Brien Youth Leadership Foundation, NJ Commission for the Blind; [hon.] Hugh O'Brien Youth Foundation Selilar, very special Arts of New Jersey Outstanding Performance, All Eastern, ACDA Choir; [oth. writ.] How Long Shall I Wait.; [pers.] Don't let anyone doubt you, or tell you that you are not good enough. For in the end you will be the one with your head up high, and feel proud while they realize they were no better off theme.

SNYDER, CARON WITHERS
[pen.] Caron Withers; [b.] April 17, 1944, Fort Worth, TX; [p.] I. A. and Helen Withers; [ch.] Caron, Chris, Jennie; [ed.] Texas Wesleyan College; [memb.] Prospective membership: Daughters of the American Revolution, United Daughters of the Confederacy, Daughters of the Republic of Texas; [oth. writ.] "Through the Hourglass" poem "The Angel and my Mother; [pers.] Writing allows me to express my deepest grief, my most content joys and all emotions in between these two poles.; [a.] Bedford, TX

SNYDER, EMILY
[b.] September 11, 1984, Saint Louis, MO; [p.] John Snyder, Suzanne Snyder; [ed.] Our Lady of Lourdes Catholic School; [memb.] Washington Swim Team, Speech Club; [hon.] Won 1st place at a school poetry contest, ribbons from Swim Team; [pers.] I have to write for myself.; [a.] Washington, MO

SOMMARIO, LISA
[b.] October 26, 1980, Oak Park, IL; [p.] Frank Sommario, Mary Jo Sommario; [ed.] Immaculate Conception High School, Elmhurst, IL; [occ.] Student; [memb.] Immaculate Conception Christian Service Leader; [hon.] Who's Who Among American High Schools Award; [pers.] I can remember creating poetry on my own during my elementary school years. I find comfort from life's daily pressures as I write my poems.; [a.] Melrose Park, IL

SORENSON, LEONARD L.
[pen.] Len; [b.] April 30, 1913, On a farm; [p.] Gilbert Sorenson and Annie Hansen; [m.] Viola Wallin pass away February 8, 1991, November 25, 1939; [ch.] Sharon Stangler and Colleen Hanson; [ed.] High School; [occ.] I now law RS or any kind of work I can get. I have many kinds of work including bookkeeping at the Little Sauk Co-op. Creamery 16 yrs.

SOWERS, STEVE
[b.] December 22, 1974, Charleroi, PA; [p.] Cindy Sowers; [oth. writ.] My favorite unpublished poems: The End of Night, Together As One, Those Who We Hold Dear, Vision of Love, Shaman of Exile, Night's Kiss, Beautiful Woman II; [pers.] I started writing poetry at an early age. My collection consists of several hundred unpublished poems.; [a.] Monongahela, PA

SPENCER, TAD
[b.] December 7, 1975, Cheyenne, WY; [p.] Dave Spencer, Linda Spencer; [ed.] B.A. Creative Writing and Philosophy University of Denver, graduation 1998; [occ.] Student; [memb.] Formerly with an improvisa-

tional theatre group, presently not affiliated with any organization; [hon.] Multiple Art Awards, Dean's List, several essay awards; [oth. writ.] Je Suis Malade - My first book of poetry, published 1995, my second book is currently in the editing stage. Weekly column in the University of Denver paper, poem in the undergraduate literary magazine.; [pers.] The artist's nature must be a giving me. The artist's purpose is to use his/her talent for creating gifts to give to the world. What I write/ paint/compose is my gift to all of you.; [a.] Denver, CO

SPERLING, MARY LOU
[b.] December 24, 1945, Elmira, NY; [p.] Fred and Mary Beardsley; [m.] Charles Sperling, July 15, 1979; [ch.] Sgt. Fred C. Beardsley; [ed.] Elem - Geo. M. Diven, High - Elmira Free Academy, Nurses Aide - Chemung County Nursing Facility; [occ.] Retired; [oth. writ.] 9 Times - published in World of Poetry.; [pers.] I love to write and always have. I am greatly influenced by poems relating to my life of growing up and my life with my spouse. This is dedicated to my loving husband Chuck.; [a.] Beaumont, TX

SPICER, BEATRICE
[pen.] Bea; [b.] February 6, 1955, Selma, AL; [p.] Dennis and Sallie Starks; [m.] Edward Spicer, June 12, 1993; [ch.] Two girls 7 years old and 16 years old, one boy 5 years old

SPITALERI, JULIE ANN
[pen.] Jules; [b.] October 29, 1968, Santa Clara, CA; [p.] Fred Spitaleri, Yvonne McDonald; [ed.] Santa Teresa High School (San Jose, CA); [oth. writ.] Other poems published in the National Library of Poetry.; [pers.] Thank you Jesus, who inspired me to write a poem that him. Thank you Dad, Mom, Mac, Yvette, Jack Cris, Ricky, Pam and my Grandma Antoinette Spitaleri, Who is also a published poet.; [a.] Fremont, CA

SPITTLER, KAREN KAYE
[pen.] KK; [b.] June 23, 1961, San Bernardino, CA; [p.] Walter Spittler, Mary George; [ch.] John Henry, Adam Michael, Leilani Kaye; [ed.] Cajon High School; [occ.] Bartender, Supervisor, Mom; [hon.] Graduate on Honor Roll; [oth. writ.] Personal poetry; [pers.] I believe that God guides us all to our highest good - I like to write about that. Live, love and be happy.; [a.] Kailua-Kona, HI

STAAT, EMILIE
[b.] January 7, 1982, Columbus, OH; [p.] John and Retha Fitch; [occ.] Student; [hon.] Recognized for achievement in the Young Georgia Authors Writing Contest; [oth. writ.] Published Snow, Dreams and People in the Atlanta Journal Constitution, Lightning in YGAWC, and Quest in "Mists of Enchantment".; [pers.] Writing is an escape from everyday pressures and stress. I pray I write that my reader's obtain as much pleasure and escape as I did.; [a.] Marietta, GA

STAFFORD, RUTH ANN
[b.] January 19, 1967, Stella, MO; [p.] Mae and C. D. Stafford; [ed.] Graduated High School; [occ.] Breakfast Cook; [pers.] Cherish your loved ones and those around. For they are a special and wonderful treasure whose presence grace our lives but for the briefest of moments.; [a.] Neosho, MO

STALLINGS, LAVITA A.
[b.] September 22, 1955, Kansas City, KS; [p.] Louie S. Stallings-Parson; [m.] Divorced; [ch.] Son 21, son 18, and daughter 13; [ed.] 1973 I graduated from Central High School in St. Paul, Minn. I graduated from Donnelly College with a two years degree in Business in 1983. Attended and completed Women's Network in 1993; [occ.] I'm a Security Officer at the K.C. Mo.

Middle School of the Arts; [memb.] I walk the 13 mile March of Dimes Walk America in K.C.Mo. every year; [hon.] I graduated from Donnelly College one of ten top students of my graduating class. I've received several outstanding and special awards in my present occupation; [oth. writ.] I use to write all the time throughout my years but was never encouraged nor had confidence that they were any good. I've been in the process of writing a book on my life for the past two years; [pers.] Reading, hearing and watching all the young talent here in the school of my occupation. Wishing I had this when I was their ages have given me the courage to take the chance of my dreams which is writing a book. Seeing the poetry Contest I took a chance to see if I had any talent. receiving your letter really gave me the confidence I wish I had years ago.; [a.] Kansas City, MO

STANFORD, ANNA
[b.] July 29, 1964, Manila, Philippines; [p.] Antonio F. Pison Jr. and Florencia A. Pison; [m.] Blair Alan Stanford, September 5, 1993; [ed.] Doctor of Veterinary Medicine, University of the Philippines; [oth. writ.] Article for sports Asia. Magazine, article for lifestyle Asia Magazine.; [a.] Long Beach, CA

STANTON, JOY MARIE
[b.] September 20, 1953, Winchester, MA; [p.] Walter and Elaine Stanton; [ed.] Shawsheen Elementary, Andover Jr. and High Schools, Merrimack College (some); [occ.] Insurance Clerk

STAPLES, ELIZABETH
[pen.] Mig Tik'Bota/Elizabeth Miree, Rev. M. Staples; [b.] August 7, 1941, Sprott, AL; [p.] Rev. Mozelle Miree/Ozzie Miree; [m.] Thomas Leroy Staples, July 31, 1976; [ch.] Trazana Hillman/Joseph Staples; [ed.] Aracoma High, W.Va. State College, M.S. Xavier University/Criminal Justice/Corrections; [occ.] Retired Teacher, Retired Social Worker; [memb.] Alpha Kappa Alpha Sorority, Notary Public of Ohio, Licensed Social Worker Ohio Board, Tyree Baptist Church; [hon.] Guest Poet U.S. Air Force Black History Extravaganza/ Brussels Belgium Jan. and Feb. 1992; [oth. writ.] The Poetry of Mrs. Staples c. May 5, 1992; [pers.] Until my soul returns to Heavenly Father, I shall do my best, that is all I can do and all God expects of me.; [a.] Forest Park, OH

STEADHAM, DANIEL G.
[pen.] Cowboy; [b.] November 14, 1951, Atlanta, GA; [p.] Joe Steadham, Frances Snow; [m.] Janet L. Steadham, October 8, 1994; [ed.] High School GED; [occ.] Vocational Instructor Dept. of Corrections Florida, Retired Msgt. USAF; [oth. writ.] Personal poems to friends and family under the pen name Cowboy.; [pers.] All my poems express true meanings. My insight of others and myself provide material for my poems. My poems depict characteristics of my subjects whether good or bad. My personal poems reflect my hopes and dreams.; [a.] Panama City Beach, FL

STEC, SARAH
[pen.] Sarah Stec; [b.] July 6, 1975, Chicago; [p.] James and Rae Stec; [ed.] Providence Catholic High School, New Lenox, IL. The School of The Art Institute of Chicago, Chicago, IL.; [occ.] Graphic Designer; [memb.] AIGA; [oth. writ.] I've had some poems published in the Ink column of my school newspaper. It is a column solely devoted to student's writings.; [pers.] I always keep this quote in mind when I am creating a design or writing a poem: "No great artist ever sees things as they really are. If he did, he would cease to be an artist." - Oscar Wilde.; [a.] Joliet, IL

STEEL, ALEXIS
[b.] July 24, 1970, Jamaica, WI; [p.] Frederick and Jeanette Steel; [m.] Fiance: Anthony Ward Caplan; [ed.] Kwantlen College, I.C.C. Institute of Children's Literature, Vancouver Film School; [occ.] Film Actress, Song/Scriptwriter; [memb.] Screen Actors Guild, America Teacher Cadets, I.S.P., Feed the Children World Mission, U.S. Marine Corps Reserves; [hon.] Nat'l Honor Society Literary Award, Inspirational Teacher Cadet of 1995 award, S.A.G. Editor's Choice Award; [oth. writ.] "When Daddy Comes Home", (I.C.L., 1992), "Bull's-Eye!" (Focus Magazine, 1995), "Hold Your Fire" (Leatherneck Magazine, 1995), various articles/poems for local newspapers and film scripts; [pers.] My poetry focuses on the common threads in human emotion, to touch each individual spirit, to bond each searching soul closer together in the magical, universal tapestry of unconditional love.; [a.] Hollywood, FL

STEPHANI, EDWARD P.
[b.] May 18, 1944, Manitowoc, WI; [p.] Orville Stephani, Lucille Stephani; [ed.] High School Graduate; [oth. writ.] Poetry in local newspaper; [pers.] I am dyslexic. I unscramble my thoughts with pencil and paper. Poetry is a favorite medium. A lifelong ambition is discovering the English Language, and to reflect life's experiences.; [a.] Escanaba, MI

STEPHENS, DIANA
[b.] February 26, 1965, Huntington, WV; [p.] Larry and Mary Stephens; [ed.] High school graduate from Huntington High; [occ.] Sales Management; [hon.] "As It Snows" is my first recognition of my poetry writings; [oth. writ.] None that have been published; [pers.] I am a big believer in expressing one's thoughts and feelings. I have written songs as well as poems, starting at the age of 9 years old. Each poem holds a special place in time and in my heart. Life's experiences have been my greatest influences.; [a.] Huntington, WV

STEPHENSON, AVONALE
[pen.] Abbie; [b.] September 9, 1915, Jerome, PA; [p.] John W. Stephenson and Bessie N. Nelson; [m.] Walter D. Griffith (1), Andrew Siko (2), August 17, 1932, June 12, 1942; [ch.] John Edward, January 7, 1945; [ed.] BA 1942 holds 10 diplomas in subjects such as Management, Supervision and Briefings, Completed courses Industrial College of the Armed Forces, 1968; [occ.] Retired. Perform volunteer service UDT/Seal Museum and St. Lucie Co. Historical Museum. Contributor to local Arts magazine children's stories on a regular basis.; [memb.] Soc. Tech Writers and Eds., US Commission Military History, IEEE, Tech. Pub. Soc. and Tech Illustrators Mgmt Assn. Listed in "The World Who's Who of Women" "International Who's Who of Intellectual and "Community Leaders of Virginia."; [hon.] Numerous awards and Certificates while employed in Dept. of Defense - US Army, plus awards for paintings (selling every painting available for sale upon completion.) Served in the US Army (WAC) 1942-1945. From 1953 - 1980 worked in Defense Industry and US Civil Service as writer/editor (aeronautics and electronica) In same period taught at US Dept. of Agriculture School evenings (ADP Documentation and Writing); [oth. writ.] Numerous articles, regulations, press releases, handbooks, manuals and operating instructions. Managing Ed. Defense Systems Management Journal.; [pers.] Think, seek knowledge, learn and teach but never, to the best of your ability, teach a child anything it will later have to unlearn!; [a.] North Hutchinson Island, FL

STERLING, MARY E.
[b.] Bedford, IN; [ch.] Vernon Jr., Vickey Lynn; [ed.] Bedford High School, Bedford - Indiana; [oth. writ.] Several poems written but only one was published in the local Concord Tribune, Thanksgiving 1994; [pers.] Were it not for the inspiration of my children, this poem would still just be a dream.; [a.] Concord, NC

STEVENS, MARY ELLEN
[pen.] Mary Ellen Stevens; [b.] February 27, 1948, Lake County; [p.] Edward and Elizabeth Deaton; [m.] Billy Stevens, December 6, 1969; [ch.] John Dewayne, Tracy Ellen, Angela Renee; [ed.] Friendship High, Dyersburg State Community College; [occ.] Housewife, Mother, Grandmother; [memb.] Southside Assembly of God; [oth. writ.] Several poems in the State Gazette Paper, Dyersburg Paper; [pers.] I try to reflect the beauty of this earth, and the people in it. I just want people to see and to feel the joy of life that I see.; [a.] Friendship, TN

STEWART, ELAINE DINNALL
[pen.] 'Epiphany'; [b.] Kingston, Jamaica; [occ.] Registered Nurse for over 20 years; [hon.] Diamond Homer Award 1996; [oth. writ.] Over 300 compositions of poetry; [pers.] To honor the positive aspects of the self and reflect with passion the beauty in every moment writes daily!; [a.] Mentone, CA

STEWART, JOHN CRAIG
[b.] Native Alabamian; [ed.] B.A., M.A., University of Alabama. Served four years in WW II in Pacific to rank of major.; [occ.] Retired from Professorship at University of South Alabama, Dept. of English and Chair of Creative Writing; [oth. writ.] Published Works, Four novels, one sold to movies. Over 20 short stories, including publication in Atlantic Monthly and Saturday Evening Post. Two Alabama histories. Numerous articles and essays in anthologies, magazines, and literary periodicals.; [pers.] The value of literature is unlimited in its study of and assessment of the human character and experience. Real literature reflects truth in life, revealed through the quality and beauty of writing.; [a.] Pisgah Forest, NC

STEWART, THERESA C.
[pen.] T. C. Stewart; [b.] October 9, 1954, Lake Hurst, NJ; [p.] Warren Jones, Frances Hargraves; [ch.] Dennis Warren and Miranda Nicole; [ed.] Fairfield High School, MT, O.W.C.C., Niceville, FL; [occ.] Church Secretary, Freelance Designer/Artist/Poet; [memb.] Outreach Ministries Pensacola, FL; [hon.] Dean's List; [oth. writ.] Several poems published in church newsletters.; [pers.] There are many gifts, but none as precious as those that God quickens and draws forth from the darkness of the soul into the light of the spirit. To God be the glory.; [a.] Pensacola, FL

STOELTING, CHRISTINE J.
[pen.] C. J. Stoelting; [b.] July 24, 1983, Niagara Falls, NY; [p.] Claire Knowles, Roy Stoelting; [ed.] Grade 8, Age 13, Edward Town Middle School, Niagara Falls, NY; [occ.] School; [memb.] Honor Society, Middle School Band - Flute; [hon.] Honor Society, Presidential Academic Fitness Award, President's Education Award, Principals Award - ETMS; [oth. writ.] Short stories; [pers.] My future goal is to become a successful doctor.; [a.] Niagara Falls, NY

STOLIKER, KIMBERLY A.
[b.] May 15, 1955, Troy, NY; [p.] Robert and Charlotte Stoliker; [m.] Joseph Jacon; [ch.] Christy Stoliker; [ed.] Waterford Halfmoon High School; [occ.] Computer Operator/Accounting Dept. at Mohawk Paper Mill.; [memb.] Reach to Recovery - American Cancer Society Volunteer, Greater Capital District Coalition for Cancer Survivorship; [oth. writ.] Story in Chicken Soup for

the Surviving Soul Book; [pers.] I strive to help other women with breast cancer to know that there is life after breast cancer and to gain strength and hope from my experience.; [a.] Waterford, NY

STOLLE, MARY
[pen.] Mary Neumayer-Stolle; [b.] July 7, 1954, Philadelphia; [p.] William J. and Elizabeth C. Neumayer; [m.] Warren D. Stolle, December 14, 1972; [ch.] Dawn T. and Warren J. II; [ed.] John W. Hallahan CGHS, Peirce Jr. College; [occ.] Housewife; [memb.] Oxford Circle Jewish Community Center, Oxford Circle Jewish Choir; [oth. writ.] Remnants Of A Tortured Heart, A Moment Of Memory, Two Broken Hearts, Ashley, The Last Encore, An Answer For The Call To Life; [pers.] Never give up on your dreams. Only you can make them come true.; [a.] Philadelphia, PA

STONE, MICHA T.
[b.] August 18, 1965, St. Johnsbury, VT; [ed.] Lyndon Institute, University of Vermont, Pepperdine University, Malibu, CA - MBA; [occ.] Sales Manager; [oth. writ.] Numerous unpublished academic papers, business memoranda and a personal poetry compilation; [pers.] Gratitude to my inspirers - Poe, the Symbolists, Rod Serling and I.D. Morrison; [a.] Orange, CA

STONE, NANCY
[b.] February 1927, Chicago; [p.] Eileen and Francis; [ch.] Janice and Anthony; [ed.] Longwood Acad Xaxier College; [occ.] Tax Consultant; [oth. writ.] Freedom a poem for all freedom both personal and universal.; [pers.] I feel so good when writing I only hope the writing will help someone in a moment of trouble or concern; [a.] Chicago, IL

STORINO, HENRY ENRICO
[oth. writ.] I have a poem and a Biography (pp 717) in your Book "A Muss To Follow". Please use this same biography in "The Colors of Thought"; [pers.] Military: World War II, P38 Fighter Pilot in the Pacific Theater; [a.] Wilsonville, OR

STOUFFER, LOLA SAMANTHA
[b.] October 22, 1927, Terra Alta, WV; [p.] Levi and Mary Robinson Yonker; [m.] Louis E. Stouffer, December 26, 1972; [ch.] Linda, Bonnie, Betsy and James Shaffer; [ed.] Graduate, Terra Alta High School/1944; [occ.] School Secretary, Terra Alta - East Preston School; [memb.] American Points of Light #70; [hon.] American Points of Light #70; [pers.] Be kind and considerate of others, especially children/our children are our future.; [a.] Terra Alta, WV

STRAND, CINDY
[pen.] Mrs. C. Lee White; [b.] May 12, 1953, S.L.C., UT; [p.] Mr. and Mrs. Albert Eric Strand; [m.] Mr. Richard Michael White, October 13, 1973, Divorced 1979; [ed.] University of Utah, Graduate Bellevue, Community College, Bellevue, Washington; [occ.] Computer Information Systems; [memb.] International Society of Poets, High School Latin Club, Kappa Alpha Theta Sorority; [hon.] Poet of Merit medal, International Poet of Merit Award, President's Honor Roll, Dean's Honor Roll, Bellevue Community College; [oth. writ.] "Autumn's Painted Leaves", "One Last Goodbye", "He Strengthens Us To Stand", "If I Were A Tree", "Froggies and Lillyponds", "Embrace of Nite", "What If God's A Cowboy?"; [pers.] Literature can lift us to a higher plane.; [a.] Seattle, WA

STRICKLAND, DOROTHY
[b.] March 1, 1929, Kaufman, CO; [p.] Clyde and Martha Clemmons; [m.] Willie Strickland (Deceased), June 2, 1945; [ch.] Betty Rhodes, Carolyn Tarvin, Wanda Burnett (three daughter); [ed.] High School; [occ.] Retired; [memb.] Wylie Book Club, Blue Bonnet

Chap of Poetry, Society of Tex., Poetry Society of Tex., Nat'l. Poetry Society, First Baptist Church "Silver Chords Choir"; [hon.] Nominee of Hilton Ross Greer Outstanding Award (3 yrs.) 1994-1995-1996 - Winner of Numerous Contests State Councilor P.S.T., Past President of Mockingbird D.C. Hap McKinney, Tex. of P.S.T. (2 times), Founder and 1st Pres. of Blue Bonnet Chap. of P.S.T.; [oth. writ.] Chap books published "Down Memory Lane," "Petals by the Wayside," "The Winding Path," published in poetry society of Tex. "Lucidity," Tex. Game Warden, North Tex. Writers Asso., Baptist Standard, Wyle News, Sandin Corp. National Publ., Texas Game Warden, Sandin Corp. news letter (International), Wylie, Baptist, Wylie News, Mockingbirds Anthology, McKinney, Tex., Lucidity, a poetry quarlerly, Houston, Tex. and Eureka Springs, Ark., North Tex. Writers Asso., "Notions and Potiions", Texas Poetry Society's State Contests.; [pers.] "Poetry is a pallette of words, brushed with color on the canvas of our hearts."; [a.] Wylie, TX

STRICKLAND, MELISSA DANIELLE
[b.] February 21, 1982, Dothan, AL; [p.] Jeffery Strickland and Arlene Strickland; [ed.] Currently attending Abbeville High School, Abbeville, AL; [occ.] Student; [memb.] AHS Marching Band and Concert Band, AMS land 8 grade Beta Club, Historian - AHS Jr. Academy of Science Spanish Club, Prayer Group, Low Brass section leader and 1st Trombone of AMS Band (95-96), First Baptist Church of Abbeville Youth Group, First Baptist Church Puppet Team, Abbeville High School Student Government Association, 2nd Trombone AHS Band; [hon.] 1990 Winner Electric Safety State Calendar Contest, Honor Roll, Jr. Beta Club, Won AMS poetry contest and was submitted for State judging.; [oth. writ.] Other writings include "Thank You", "Grandmothers", and "My Backyard", "My Backyard" won the AMS poetry contest in 96'; [pers.] Most of my poetry is about childhood memories or people who I look up to.; [a.] Abbeville, AL

STRINGER, SHEILA YVONNE LYONS
[pen.] Von; [b.] March 29, 1956, Columbus, OH; [p.] Dr. Charles Lyons Jr. and Mrs. Rosa D. Lyons; [m.] George Lewis Stringer, August 9, 1986; [ch.] Hoping to adopt; [ed.] Graduate of Hampton with BSN in Nursing in 1978; [occ.] Registered Nurse-Staff at UNC and Duke Student Health Services; [memb.] Zeta Phi Beta Sorority; [oth. writ.] Numerous unpublished stories and poems.; [pers.] I write stories and poems about people and things I am passionate about. When God grants you gifts, you must use them to somehow benefit mankind.; [a.] Durham, NC

STUCKEY, ROSANNA
[pen.] Criquet; [b.] October 9, 1967, Iowa; [p.] Herbert and Vickie McClimans; [ch.] Nikki, Micheal, Anthony and Kasi; [occ.] Seal-Pae, BC; [pers.] For anyone who knows me or want's to can find the true me through my writing and my children's eyes. Thanks to Philip my mentor and my best friend Tammy.; [a.] Baytown, TX

STUEBER, CORIE
[b.] August 27, 1977, Long Island, NY; [p.] Pat Stueber, Frank Nesbitt; [ed.] Morgan, Co. High, Georgia College; [occ.] Medical Student; [memb.] American Heart Association, National Wildlife Federation; [oth. writ.] Currently working on a novel; [pers.] I would like to dedicate "The Ride" to the loving memory of Jeremy Schumate. He was my inspiration for this poem.; [a.] Madison, GA

SUCHY, CAROL A.
[b.] September 6, California; [p.] Roy Lavina Juden; [m.] John, April 21, 1972; [ch.] Two sons; [ed.] College ADN; [occ.] RN; [oth. writ.] Poems; [pers.] As we walk their life its our God given duty to uplift others as much

as possible, even though it be a smile, or simple caring act.

SULLIVAN, JOHN D.
[pen.] J. Dennis Sullivan; [b.] October 20, 1961, Catholic Orphanage; [p.] William and Sarah Dittrich; [m.] Cindy Sullivan, June 27, 1992; [ed.] Rhema Bible College, Culinary Institute of America, Oklahoma State University Tech; [occ.] Businessman, Theologian, Writer; [oth. writ.] Autobiography of John Sullivan translated into the Hindi language; [pers.] man is flesh, intellect, and spirit and should strive for excellence in all of these plains; [a.] Tulsa, OK

SUNSHINE, DOROTHY
[pen.] Lumia; [b.] NYC; [p.] Dead; [ch.] One alive; [ed.] H.S.; [occ.] Retired; [oth. writ.] Musical; [pers.] Be happy you are alive, Thank God.; [a.] New York City, NY

SUSMUTH, H. JOHN
[b.] September 21, 1923, Bridgeport, CT; [p.] John Joseph and Felicia S.; [ch.] Dawn Kennedy; [ed.] De La Salle Academy, Toronto, Ont., Northwestern Univ. Evanston, IL, USAAF Cadet Training for Pilot; [occ.] Retired ITT Exec.; [memb.] Sigma Nu Fraternity GB Chapter, West Point Officer's Club, Amateur Radio KC4 ABE, 376th Heavy Bomb. Group Vets. Assoc., ITT Snack and Yak Club; [hon.] Distinguished Flying Cross, Air Medal with 2 Oak Leaf Clusters, various Minor Service Medals; [oth. writ.] Popular Song - "We're Through" A.L.A.S. (Terralae) Picture of the world showing actual land mass shapes, in relation to key lines of Latitude and Longitude.; [pers.] "Once things get started, they tend to get worse."

SWAIN, AMY LYNN
[b.] July 15, 1977, Washington, NC; [p.] David Swain, Vickie Swain; [ed.] New Bern High School Craven Community College University of North Carolina at Greensboro (UNCG); [occ.] Student at UNCG; [hon.] Dean's List Senior Superlative; [pers.] My career goal is to become a professional Interior Designer.; [a.] New Bern, NC

SWAIN, TRACY V.
[b.] December 2, 1956, Philadelphia, PA; [p.] Mr. Clyde Swain and Mrs. Elma Swain; [m.] Mrs. Denise Swain, July 30, 1983; [ch.] (2) Sabriyah, (18) Naiima (12); [ed.] High School Graduate, 2 yrs. at Clarion State College Clarion, PA, currently attending Manna Biblical Institute, Chester, PA; [occ.] United States Postal Service Position, Machine Clerk; [hon.] Ordained as a Deacon 3-28-93. Licensed as a Minister 3-31-96; [oth. writ.] Various other unpublished religious poems; [pers.] My goal is to not only reflect God's presence in our everyday life, but also point out our responsibility to him.; [a.] Newark, DE

SWINEY, WILMA JOYCE
[pen.] Wilma Joyce Swiney; [b.] December 27, 1943, Cookeville, TN; [p.] William L. and Cora E. Long; [m.] Franklin D. Swiney, October 26, 1968; [ch.] Randall Williams and Lisa M. Swiney; [ed.] Stivers High 1961, Miami Jacobs Jr. College; [occ.] Retired from Chrysler Corp; [memb.] Greenview Calvary Tabernague, Democratic Voters League; [hon.] My biggest honors are my husband, children and my precious grandchildren, Savannah Rose Williams and Joshua Scott Williams; [oth. writ.] Gospel poems; [pers.] If I can just touch one person, that makes it all worth while. My inspiration comes from my faith in God and my dreams.; [a.] Huber Heights, OH

SYKES, PATRICIA YORK
[b.] March 4, 1954, Corsicana, TX; [p.] Ethel York (Deceased) and Jody York, (Stepmother) Mary York; [m.] Rickey Sykes, August 24, 1989; [ch.] Gary Sykes (stepson), Devin Garrett, Danielle Garrett; [ed.] Corsicana High School; [occ.] Manager Convince store; [pers.] Writing is my way of relaxing. I enjoy evenings with just my pen and me. Sometimes!

SYLVESTRE, RENEE J.
[pen.] Renee Joy; [b.] September 19, 1975, Woon Hospital; [p.] Kathleen Raymond Sylvestre; [ed.] High School; [occ.] Sales at DEB Department Store; [oth. writ.] Fallacy, Law over, Excumbrance, Kismate, Relegate, Intageos, Striving, Destiny Loneliness, District, Stepping Stars, Covenant etc...; [pers.] We all come from the same place, but who can express there knowledge and soul to prove there point.; [a.] North Smithfield, RI

SZUTENBACH, DREAMA
[b.] August 5, 1954, Bainbridge, MD; [p.] David and Joyce Dishman; [m.] Richard Szutenbach, July 2, 1983; [ch.] Chris, Richard and Bryan; [ed.] St. John's High, some College; [occ.] United States Air Force; [memb.] Air Force Sergeants Association, 700 Club; [pers.] For my sister Diane. No matter how much pain and hurt you go through, there is happiness at the end. I love you Rich! Thank you God!; [a.] Dover, DE

TABB II, RODGER CLAYTON
[b.] March 15, 1970, Philadelphia, PA; [p.] Rofea Tabb, Wanda Tabb; [m.] Majorie Jill Tabb, October 14, 1995; [ch.] Marquise Al. Tabb; [ed.] Cardinal Dougherty H.S., Chowan Jr. College, Bowie State University, West Chester University; [occ.] Songwriter; [hon.] High School and College "All American Basketball Player; [oth. writ.] Article published in the Philadelphia Inquirer; [pers.] Poetry is nothing more than a connection between ones heart and mind, resulting in ones own master piece.; [a.] Sharon Hill, PA

TALLMAN, EVELYN
[b.] November 13, 1922, So. Westerlo, NY; [p.] Mrs. Hazel Mabie; [m.] Deceased, January 23, 1940; [ch.] One; [ed.] Greenville Central High School National Baking School 835 Diversey Parkway Chicago, Illinois; [occ.] Retired and write poetry; [memb.] Social Service with Albany County Social Security Benefits

TANG, TIFFANY
[pen.] Tiff, Tiffy; [b.] January 23, 1987, New York City; [p.] Albert and Nancy; [ed.] 4th Grade; [occ.] Student in Asher Holmes; [hon.] New Jersey Music Teacher Association, 1996 Annual Auditions, Honors Award; [pers.] I enjoy reading animal stories.; [a.] Marlboro, NJ

TANK, HELEN E.
[pen.] Betty Tank; [b.] January 26, 1910, Chatham, NY; [p.] Morton and Stella Tank; [ed.] Chatham High School 1928 Russell Sage College Teachers College MA 1954; [occ.] Retired still writing; [memb.] Fellowship of Reconciliation, Mahck, NY 10960. United Methodist Chatham, NY Alan Deroe Club, Chatham, N.Y.; [oth. writ.] Articles in Chatham N.Y. Courier various times. Asiatic Olympus" in Appalachia a pub. of Appiladian Mt. Club c. 1946. "Pushing My Shadow" a memoir of 1939-45 while in England and Turkey Pub. 1995 Lily Press E Chatham, N.Y.; [pers.] I am a 20th century woman who hates war and believes we must learn to live amicably. I am essentially a diarist attempting to record life as I see it. I have lately found poetry a good way to the pressure of man and memories.; [a.] Shelburne Falls, MA

TANQUARY, SANDRA J.
[pen.] S. J. Swallow; [b.] August 13, 1951, Pueblo, CO; [p.] James and Dorothy Rafferty; [m.] Richard L. Swallow (1st, Divorced 1978), May 4, 1968, Will L. Tanquary (2nd), July 20, 1992; [ch.] Judy Lynn, Richard Lee, Randall Louis; [a.] Northglenn, CO

TARAZI, CRYSTAL CLAYTONIA
[b.] April 8, 1985, Mission Hills, CA; [p.] Farris and Elvia Tarazi; [ed.] Graduated fifth grade in 1996 with a presidential academic award and a 4.0.; [occ.] Background parts in movie and T.V.; [pers.] Writing is a blessing that I am developing through all of the other blessings that God has and continues to provide me with. I plan to utilize all of the blessings I receive to serve humanity.; [a.] Lancaster, CA

TASSONE, GINA
[b.] May 28, 1981, Oklahoma; [p.] Frank and Erline Tassone; [ed.] Sophomore at Edmond North High School; [pers.] Sincerity and kindness are the keys to life. Be the best person that you can be. Only then are your living life to the fullest.; [a.] Edmond, OK

TATUM, JIMMY JAMES
[b.] December 20, 1965, Elizabethtown, NC; [ch.] Jimmy James II, Brandon James; [oth. writ.] Questions Of Understanding, published in The Golden Treasury of Great Poems, publisher and editor John Campbell.; [pers.] Hearts Desire was written for the mother of my children. May it live in our hearts forever.; [a.] Bladenboro, NC

TAYLOR, STEVEN G.
[pen.] Kathy Hemingway Jr., Prince Michael; [b.] October 29, 1957, Louisville, KY; [p.] Harold E. Taylor, G. G. Taylor; [ed.] Completed Three years at Earlham College, I.S.U. Laboratory School (High School), Thornton Elementary; [hon.] Valedictorian of my High School Class I.S.U. Laboratory Class of 1976; [oth. writ.] Have written much but have not published except for a poem published except for a poem entitled "Love" in the anthology Symphonies of The Soul. (Poetry Guild); [pers.] God the father has called me into the High Priesthood through his son, Jesus Christ. He has named me "Michael, the white Horseman"; [a.] Terre Haute, IN

TAYLOR, WHITNEY ROBYN NOHEALANI
[pen.] Whitney Taylor; [b.] August 19, 1985, Wahiawa, HI; [p.] Samantha and Robert M. Taylor Jr.; [ed.] 6th grade (Elementary Home Schooling; [occ.] Student; [memb.] National Wildlife Federation, Green Peace; [hon.] Honor Roll, Music Award, Hoku Award, Traffic Safety Writing Contest Winner; [oth. writ.] Lockness (poem); [pers.] Although I've only written two poems, I enjoy writing very much and it's lots of fun too.; [a.] Mountain View, HI

TAYLOR JR., JAMES U.
[b.] July 28, 1960, Chicago, IL; [p.] Mildred and James Taylor; [ed.] Luther High School North, Wright College; [occ.] Salesman; [memb.] American Legion; [hon.] National Defense service medals, 2 Humanitarian service medals, Armed forces expedittenary medal, Navy Expeditionary medal, 3 good conduct service medals.; [oth. writ.] Several unpublished poems.; [pers.] A big part of what you see, depends on what you're looking for.; [a.] Chicago, IL

TAYO, ADE-KUNLE
[pen.] Hoppy, K.T.; [b.] June 19, 1971, London, England; [p.] Johnson Ademorin and Felicia Adesola Tayo; [ch.] Nebiso Bula (sponsor child); [ed.] Ibadan Grammar School, University of Ibadan, Nigeria; [occ.] Salesman, Script-Writer; [memb.] Independent Features Project, New York; [hon.] Best Graduating Student -

Business Economics, University of Ibadan, Nigeria, 1993 Class; [oth. writ.] Movie - scripts still in development, poems and lyrics.; [pers.] Dream dreams and never give up on them.; [a.] Brooklyn, NY

TEAGUE, ALICE MARIE
[pen.] Alice M. Teague; [b.] November 15, 1949, Muskogee; [p.] Louie Teague (Deceased), Lillian Humphery Teague; [ed.] B.S. Early Childhood Education, B.S. Elementary Education Northeastern State University, Tahlequah Okla. Manual Training High School, Muskogee OK. A writing degree from the Institute of Children's Literature Redding Redge CT; [occ.] Pre-School Teacher; [memb.] Church of Christ; [hon.] Editor's Choice award for a poem chosen for the Sound of Poetry the same poem chosen for the Journey of the Mind National Library of Poetry Associate Membership in the International Society of Poets; [oth. writ.] Rainbow of Love, Journey of the Mind, The National Library of Poetry Did You Thank the Lord, Pathways of Poetry, When Christmas is Here, The National Library of Poetry Best Poems of 1996; [pers.] I believe that God is the source of all that I am are will be.; [a.] Muskogee, OK

TEFFT, DR. BRUCE D.
[b.] December 1, 1951, Biloxi, MS; [p.] Jack D. and Beverly J. Tefft; [m.] Nina Brochart Tefft, October 30, 1995; [ed.] B.A. New College, Sarasota 1972, M.A. Univ. of Denver 1974, J. D. Univ of Denver 1974; [occ.] Retired CIA Officer; [oth. writ.] "One Brief Shining Moment... Czechoslovakia 1968", "Rendezvous At Adobe Walls", "Dimensions Of Insight", "Mindwork And Other Musings"; [pers.] "Regrets? Too few to mention."; [a.] Centreville, VA

TENNENT, TONI
[b.] May 21, 1972, Kingston, Ja; [p.] Trevor Tennent and Veronica Allen; [ed.] Lehman College; [occ.] Language teacher of French and English as a second lang; [hon.] Dean's List; [oth.] A collection of poems to be published in the near future. Several articles published in the local news paper; [pers.] Why walk in someone's footsteps when you can print your own and make a better impression?; [a.] Bronx, NY

TEOLI, LAURA
[pen.] Leperachaun; [b.] July 10, 1979; [p.] Theresa and Emery W. Teoli Jr.; [ed.] High School (Tantasqua - MA) pending (Temescal Canyon - CA); [occ.] Full time student; [memb.] Marching Titans Band, Concert Band, Jazz Band, CSF, Renaissance; [hon.] Spirit Award (Jazz Band '96), Outstanding Ensemble Member ('94), Central Massachusetts District Band ('93), Solo Chair Trumpet ('94), Outstanding Member ('95), Letter in Band (3 yrs.); [oth. writ.] Several poems and stories published in school literary magazines, published in National Poetry Society Anthology Collections.; [pers.] Listen to the shrouded cries of the soul, let the a a bysimmal voice encompass your weary heart, feel the passion of ice... Seek beyond the known into the deep dark reaches of the heart.; [a.] Lake Elsinore, CA

TERAM, JENNIFER
[pen.] J.P. Hunt; [b.] November 28, 1969, Brooklyn; [p.] Zvi Teram, Julie DeMarco; [m.] David Julian Ayuso, December 27, 1991; [ch.] Jacob Ayuso; [occ.] Homemaker; [oth. writ.] The Secret Heart, Volume of Poetry, unpublished still.; [pers.] If it were not for my family's support, I might never have attempted to submit my work. Especially motivating and encouraging is my younger brother, Jonathan Teram, who has always believed in my writing potential.; [a.] Fresh Meadows, NY

TERRELL, KANITA
[b.] January 18, 1975, Detroit, MI; [p.] James and Kmay Terrell; [ed.] I graduated from Edwin Denby High School and presently I attend Wayne State University; [occ.] I am a student a Wayne State University; [pers.] Loving thyself is paramount.; [a.] Detroit, MI

TESS, WAYNE C.
[b.] September 12, 1949, Philadelphia, PA; [p.] Stanley and Claire Tess; [ed.] Moses Lake High School, Moses Lake, Wash. 2 yrs. at Sophia University - Tokyo, Japan; [occ.] (Unemployed) singer/musican/songwriter/writer; [hon.] Camden (NJ) Courier Post Silver Pen Award for Best Letter to the Editor, May 1994; [oth. writ.] Short novel for senior project in High School, numerous songs, poems and letters to the editor.; [pers.] Life has familiarized me with many injustices worth writing about. I also like to keep a humorous, upbeat and healthy outlook.; [a.] Pitman, NJ

THERKELSEN, ANDREA
[pen.] Andrea Therkelsen; [b.] January 25, 1978, England; [p.] Gary Therkelsen and Lora Setter; [ed.] Hopkins High and Invest; [occ.] Housekeeper at Bloomington Marriot; [oth. writ.] Nothing that has been published; [pers.] When I write, I write about the things that are hopping around me.; [a.] Edina, MN

THIELMANN, PIA
[b.] March 23, 1957, Oldenburg, Germany; [ed.] Master of Arts in American Studies, University of Kansas Magister Artium in German literature, University of Hamburg; [occ.] Ph.D. student in American Studies; [memb.] Mid-America American Studies Association Modern Language-Association African Literature Association Mid-America Alliance for African Studies African Studies Association; [hon.] Direct Exchange Scholarship University of Hamburg-University of Kansas Master's Thesis Defense passed With Honors Kansas University Endowment Association International Student Scholarship; [oth. writ.] Book on Marge Piercy, articles on Toni Morrison, Alice Walker, and on the tensions between Black and white feminists.; [a.] Lawrence, KS

THOMAS, BARBARA M.
[pen.] Ann Thomas; [b.] April 3, 1942, Banks County Lula, GA

THOMAS, DAWN MICHAL
[b.] July 31, 1961, San Mateo; [occ.] Dianne Livengood and Bud Brewer; [m.] Richard Allen Thomas, March 25, 1990; [ch.] Michael, Richard, Sarah; [ed.] Leroy Anderson, Fountain Valley High, Golden West College; [occ.] Hair Designer and Homemaker; [memb.] National Right to Life Comm., International Society of Poets, Distinguished Member Christian Coalition, American Family Association; [hon.] "Auspicious Dissension" read into the Congressional record by Robert K. Dornan, (Congressman) with article on July 16, 1996. Appears in Anthology "Best Poems of the 90's"; [oth. writ.] "Dripping with Honey", "Floral Rainbows," "Partial-Birth-Abortion Hearts-Waxed-Cold." "Auspicious Dissension."; [pers.] To touch the lives of others with the love and truths of Jesus Christ, "My Lord and God," and expand the beauty and wisdom of Poetry are my goals!; [a.] Garden Grove, CA

THOMAS, JENNESE R.
[b.] August 23, 1972, Kent, England; [p.] George A. Thomas, Romane R. Thomas; [ed.] Christ Church University Canterbury, Kent, England Major: English Literature (B.A. Hon.); [occ.] English Teacher; [oth. writ.] Several short stories and poems not yet published.; [pers.] I strive to bring out the best qualities in my students. By listening to their need, studying their actions, then guide and encourage their minds; [a.]

Moreno Valley, CA

THOMAS, ROBERT WAYNE
[pen.] Bob Thomas; [b.] July 25, 1954, Philadelphia; [m.] Nancy, June 28, 1975; [ch.] Cathy and Robb; [oth. writ.] Love and Time

THOMASON, TERI ANN
[b.] July 26, 1953, Burbank, CA; [p.] William and Ruth Baker; [ch.] Tiffany Thomason and Jonathan Mosz; [ed.] James Monroe High Pierce College Sawyer Business College; [occ.] Legal Secretary; [oth. writ.] My poems are the enlightenment of the unique Beauty of Nature, the skies of the universe and imagination through a childs eyes. They are delightfully innocent. Future poems will focus on the Beauty of Holidays.; [pers.] I dedicate this poem to my mother and father William H. Baker, Ruth M. Baker - Deceased. With Love Forever; [a.] Las Vegas, NV

THOMPSON, VIRGINIA
[pen.] Gin; [b.] June 5, 1947, Baltimore, MD; [p.] George Schmidt, Norma Schmidt; [m.] Richard Thompson, June 5, 1976; [ch.] Denise LaVardera, Jeana LaVardera; [ed.] Mergen Thaler Voc. Tech. High School; [occ.] Legal Asst.; [oth. writ.] Memories - A Family History Novelette, Poems: The Other, Mindbend, Reflections, What I Used To Be (none published); [pers.] I strive for full understanding and hope to help others to believe, as I do, that the only thing in life worth living and fighting, for is love.; [a.] Baltimore, MD

THOMPSON, WILLEY
[pen.] Dark Man, Pale River, Omega, Xxoxx; [b.] August 19, 1965, Corbin, KY; [p.] Enoch and Wonda Thompson; [m.] Margaret G. Thompson, September 27; [ch.] Logan Enoch Thompson; [ed.] West Newton Christian Academy High School 11/2 years Vincennes University; [occ.] Motorcycle Officer Truck Driver; [hon.] A.C.T. against Drugs sponsored by Mayor Hudnut accomplishment award by 238th Ranger Div. Ft. Harrison D.O.T., AG School, and Sower Support Center and General Wood's; [oth. writ.] Dozen's in a paper in McKee KY. Called the Jackson County sun and a few passages on A.O.L.; [pers.] It's not death if you refuse it J. O'Barr is a genius; [a.] Indianapolis, IN

THOMPSON JR., GEORGE H.
[pen.] "Rity" Thompson; [b.] November 16, 1914, N.O., LA; [p.] Joan Thompson, George; [m.] Guen Thompson; [ed.] (Jr Coll), (BS), (MA); [occ.] Teacher, (Part time); [memb.] A and A Trust Masonic. (Nat) Teachers (ORC); [hon.] "Teacher of the Year" football, track, basket ball; [oth. writ.] Book of poems sending you a copy of my poems; [a.] Tuscaloosa, AL

THORNE, SEAN K.
[b.] April 5, 1980, Pasadena, CA; [p.] Sonja and Philip Thorne; [ed.] Student Kingswood-Oxford Prep School, West Hartford, CT.; [occ.] Full time student; [pers.] Life's bitter sweet memory; [a.] Avon, CT

THORNTON, SERENA G. MILLS
[b.] January 15, 1920, Balto., MD; [p.] Frank and Beatrice Lewis; [m.] John H. Thornton, February 14, 1992; [ed.] High School Grad., took 2 yrs. Business Courses; [occ.] Retired since 1981, Volunteer Recruiter; [memb.] Retired and Senior Volunteer Program, Women, Power, Inc., N.W. Baltimore Corp., Inc. "Ages On Stages" acting ensemble; [hon.] Mayor's Awards for best Poetry (1981-85-86), as Historian of Pimlico (1986) for Community Service (1987-89), Named May 13, 1993 as "Serena G. Mills Day", Senior Citizens Hall of Fame; [oth. writ.] "Books: Poets and Poetry", "Mentor Wisdom", "Women Friends, Men, Friends", "Hoes Hgts", "Landquest", "History of Old Park Hgts" and Old Primlico"; [pers.] People need to get "off their

duffs", assert themselves in the community against grime and to set a positive example for young people.; [a.] Baltimore, MD

THROCKMORTON, HOPE D.
[pen.] Alia Alte Sperate; [b.] May 29, 1979, Parma; [p.] Barbara Attawkins, Dan K. Throckmorton; [ed.] Cloverleaf High School (I am a senior.); [occ.] Student; [memb.] NHS, Tri-M, SADD Drama Club, International Thespian Society; [hon.] Honor Roll, Academic Certificate, Academic Medal; [oth. writ.] I am currently working on my first book. It is entitled Can You Run?; [pers.] I believe it is one of the greatest gifts in the world to be able to look at yourself in the mirror every morning and laugh your head off. Also, I believe if you are going to be honest with one person, it should be yourself.; [a.] Chippewa Lake, OH

THRONE, T.
[b.] June 3, 1954, Kaukauna, WI; [p.] James and Lois Throne; [m.] Maki Fujita, March 17, 1995; [ed.] Theater, Ballet, Pre-Med, Structural Integration, Acupuncture, Cronial Saral Therapy, Neuro Linguistic Programming, Ericksonian Clinical Hypnosis, Feldenkrais, Yoga, Tai Chi, Qi Gung, Trance Dance.; [occ.] Founder and Artistic Director of Throne Dance Theater the Tribe, a Multi-cultural, Internationally Touring, Evolutionary Ballet Ensemble. Through contact with the American State Department and White House's Office of Special Presidential Messages has functional as Ambassadors of Peace through.; [hon.] Culture and Ecological Evolution through Art. This ensemble has received awards from the National Endowment for the Arts and New York State council on the arts.; [oth. writ.] Founder of Body Evolution Systemic process for physical, emotional and spiritual evolution, has also worked as an actor, singer fire breather clown, mime, martial artist, photographer, musician and writer; [pers.] I stand for integrity, health, love, compassion, courage spiritual experiences.; [a.] New York, NY

THURMAN, BERNIE
[b.] November 30, 1981, Fartuna; [p.] Charles Thurman and Janet Branson; [ed.] I will be entering my freshmen year at HHS in Hayfork Cal.; [occ.] Student; [oth. writ.] I have been writing poetry for the past 3 years. I am inspired by the music I listen to and by my inner thoughts.; [pers.] I wish to continue pursuing my dream of one day becoming a great poet.; [a.] Hayfork, CA

TIA, BETTY
[b.] December 16, 1981, Los Angeles, CA; [p.] Iang Tia and Lang Tia; [hon.] 2nd grade Book-a-thon, 3rd grade Book-on-thon, 4th grade Book-a-thon, 6th grade Book-a-thon, Top Student - Math, Perfect of Attendance, Student of the year, Honor Society; [a.] Los Angeles, CA

TINOCO, PATRICIA
[pen.] Renee St. James; [b.] June 1, 1943, Chicago, IL; [p.] John Lane and Helen Lane; [m.] Deceased; [ch.] Sandra Lynn, Christine Ann, Barbara Jean, Marlo Renee; [ed.] Lindblom High; [occ.] Retired - Active in School for daughter Marlo; [memb.] Green Leaf Baptist Church - Calvary Chapel; [oth. writ.] Essays, poems, and short stories for church, school, and friends.; [pers.] Family encouraged me and friends recognized my writing abilities. I enjoy studying poetry and forming, sustaining and delighting this work upon paper. My religion is also a strong influence.; [a.] Whittier, CA

TOLENTINO, SHERWIN
[b.] April 15, 1974, Vigan, Philippines; [p.] Basilio and Nenita Tolentino; [ed.] Radford High School, University of Hawaii at Manoa, University of Maryland at College Park; [occ.] Student Coordinator for Freshman Advising Center (UHM); [memb.] Katipunan,

Timpuyog; [hon.] Phi Eta Sigma, Dean's List (UHM and UMCP), 1995 student Employee of the Year Nominee; [oth. writ.] Several poems for myself, friends and loved ones. (Hopefully one day they will be published.); [pers.] My writing style has been greatly influenced by my friends, who are fellow writers. Much thanks to Charmaine, Charlene and Eddy. Love you Guys.; [a.] Makakilo, HI

TOLSON, FRANCES E.
[b.] September 15, 1913, Licking Co., OH; [p.] H. H. and Mary Hoover; [m.] Melvin L. Tolson (Deceased January 18, 1994), November 8, 1953; [ch.] 1 stepdaughter - (Deceased), 4 grandchildren - 4 great grandchildren; [ed.] Newark High School, Bachelor's Ohio State Un., Master's Art Ed. - Kent State Un.; [occ.] Retired Art Teacher; [memb.] State Retired Teachers, Carroll Co. Retired Teachers; [hon.] Who's Who in American Education, Who's Who in the Arts 1971-1972; [oth. writ.] Christian Life Letters, The Lookout, Free Press Standard, World of Poetry, Christian Evangelist; [pers.] I try to make words bring pictures to the mind of the reader.; [a.] Carrollton, OH

TOMB, MELISSA CELESTE
[b.] January 16, 1974, Des Moines, IA; [p.] M - Cathi Cooke, SF - Cord Cooke, F - Dave Todd; [m.] Jarrod Blaine Tomb, July 2, 1993; [ch.] Ariel Ann-Tomb, Autumn Tayler Tomb; [ed.] Red Mountain High School; [occ.] Secretary and Housewife; [memb.] I was a member of "Club Rif" my high school years, and also my choir club.; [hon.] I have had many art awards in elementary school and in Jr. high school, as well as high school. Was on the honor roll my Jr. high years.; [oth. writ.] A piece called "Alone", which I was motivated to write with the memory of my dear brother Donnie.; [pers.] My life is complete with my family. Without my wonderful husband by my side, and my beautiful daughters life would have no meaning. "Happiness is where the home is." My family is my home.; [a.] Mesa, AZ

TOMBLIN, GARY L.
[b.] April 11, 1962, Sherman, TX; [p.] Georgia E. Harper; [m.] Teresa J. Tomblin, August 21, 1981; [ch.] Jillian, Stacy, Gary II, Andrew; [ed.] Foss High School, Regents College University of New York; [occ.] Aeromedical Evacuation Pilot (Dustoff) U.S. Army; [memb.] Army Aviation Association of America; [pers.] Show compassion, human kind are destroying themselves.

TORGERSON, HARRIS O.
[pen.] Harris O. Torgerson; [b.] July 26, 1918, Slayton, MN; [p.] Mabel Ecklund, Hans O. Torgerson; [m.] Verley Lovene (Dahl) Torgerson, September 16, 1943; [ch.] Richard and Dianne Hunziker, three grandchildren; [ed.] 2 years College - Augustana, College, Sidox Falls J. Dan, August 1941, Graduated AS Naval Aviator, Nas Pensacola, Florida. I served 8 1/2 year as a Naval Aviator; [occ.] Retired; [memb.] Jr. Chamber of Commerce, Rotary Club, Church Choirs - Soloist, "Association of Naval Aviators", Navy League, Life Member "Tailhookers", member Naval Institute, Lutheran Churches; [hon.] Distinguished Flying Cross, 2 Airmedals, Presidential Unit Citation, 4 Combat Area Ribbons; [oth. writ.] Several unpublished poems.; [pers.] My wife and I have been married for 53 years, I wrote this poem on our 45th Anniversary. The Lutheran Church Has been very Important to Our Family.; [a.] Greenwood Village, CO

TORRES, MARIO JOHNNY
[b.] May 27, 1978, Orange; [ed.] Valley High School; [pers.] You can never live with an empty heart!; [a.] Santa Ana, CA

TOWNSEND, MATTIE M.
[b.] August 6, 1956, Parkin, AR; [p.] Tanzy Weaver, Clara Lott; [m.] David, February 6, 1988; [ch.] Raushanah Danielle, Raphael Anton; [ed.] Martin Luther King Jr. High Wayne State University; [occ.] Distribution Clerk, US. PS. Romulus, Michigan; [hon.] Work Performance; [pers.] Seeing Society today, along with personal experiences inspired me to write this poem; [a.] Detroit, MI

TRAVIS JR., CHARLES C.
[b.] October 2, 1924, Lynchburg, VA; [p.] Charles C. Sr., and Mabel P. Travis; [m.] Mildred Lindsay Travis, March 1, 1953; [ch.] Tracy and Jon Travis; [ed.] Hampden - Sydney College, BS, Lynchburg College (50), Grad. Work, Pacific C.; [occ.] (Retired) MGR, Communications, B and W Nuclear Power; [memb.] Phi Kappa Phi, Nat'l Honor Soc., Soc., Technical writers, AM NUC Soc., American Legion, Vet. Foreign Wars, Repb. Natnl CMTE, etc; [hon.] Sr. Honor Soc., LYBG College, awards for tech. writing manuals report style guides, newsletters, etc.; [oth. writ.] Technical writing manuals, report style guides, laboratory manuals, etc., misc. poems related articles pub. in tech. writing soc. publications.; [pers.] Personal philosophy framed by a strong sense of family values and our willingness to sacrifice much for each others success. Emily Dickinson remains a strong influence in my poetic efforts.; [a.] Lynchburg, VA

TRENT-HALL, TRACY D.
[b.] September 27, 1961, Darby Township, PA; [p.] Marlene and Robert Trent; [ed.] Graduate of Darby Township JR/SR High School, Class of 1979; [occ.] An MPLSM Clerk for the U.S. Postal Service, 30th St. Station, I am a Part-time Photographer, Part-time Poetry Writer, Part-time Tractor Trailer Driver, and Full time Believer in dreams and trying to do positive things, I write about Life, and the Reality of Life; [pers.] Thanks Mom for everything! Thanks Chuck for the inspiration.; [a.] Darby, PA

TRUJILLO, MARY D.
[pen.] Diane; [b.] August 11, 1965, Channelview, TX; [p.] Melvin H. and Frankie Likehart; [m.] Victor J. Trujillo, September 10, 1982; [ch.] Adolfo Joe, Jennifer Mae, Cimmerron Julian; [ed.] Madisonville Texas High; [occ.] Administrative Operations Assistant; [pers.] I am an open, outspoken person. I like to express the goodness of my heart in my poems so that it may help others to see the goodness all around us. My inspiration was my Grandmother Velma Mae Likehart, an angel in my eyes.; [a.] Yuma, AZ

TRZECIAK-KERR, M. M.
[ed.] BSJ - Ohio University, MST - Ohio University; [memb.] Society of Professional Journalists C.R.O.W. The Crow Foundation, (B.B.L.); [hon.] Dean's List, Cum Laude, Summa Cum Laude

TUCK, JANET G.
[pen.] Janet G. Tuck; [b.] June 15, 1971, Roxboro, NC; [p.] Melinda Wilkins, Keith Wilkins, and Tony Tuck; [ed.] Person Senior High School, Roxboro, NC; [occ.] Manager of Subway 1808 in Roxboro, NC; [hon.] (1) (Health Assistant Award), (2) Management Training Series for North Carolina Subway Group Inc.; [oth. writ.] First time ever published; [pers.] Dwayne Conner taught me love makes the world go around. Also you have to let go of lost love to find "Heaven" in real love. He's my heaven.; [a.] Roxboro, NC

TUCKER, NANCY
[pen.] Nancy Tucker; [b.] May 9, 1960, Corpus Christi, TX; [p.] Clyde and Pat Stevens; [m.] Weldon Tucker, July 22, 1978; [ch.] Brad Weldon and Chelsea Rhea; [ed.] Nueces Canyon High, Sul Ross State University

(currently enrolled as senior); [occ.] Instructional Aide for Nueces Canyon C.I.S.D.; [memb.] N.C. Booster Club, sponsor for N.C.J.H. Pep Club and cheer leaders, Nueces Canyon Church of Christ, U.I.L. sponsor in poetry interpretation; [hon.] First place poem and short story in Creative Arts Contest at Southwest Texas Junior College, Uvalde, TX, Dean's List, 2nd place poem Creative Arts Contest at SWTJC; [oth. writ.] Several poems published in, school annual, college newspaper, college publication - The Palm's Leaf.; [pers.] My writings are greatly influenced by the happenings in my life and the lives of loved ones. Personal experience as my writings are from my heart.; [a.] Camp Wood, TX

TUCKER, WILLIAM
[b.] January 22, 1928, Warfield, VA; [p.] Alfred and Rose Tucker; [m.] Sarah, September 21, 1965; [ch.] Tonya, Rosa; [occ.] Baker for over 40 years; [oth. writ.] The Four Seaons, The Earth the Rain and Sun, Way Out in the Golden West; [pers.] I William was raised in Virginia and I've always loved nature and the out doors and I love to write about it I also have music to my poems.; [a.] Philadelphia, PA

TUCKER JR., JAMES R.
[b.] December 30, 1966, Nashville, TN; [p.] Linda Bullard; [m.] Julie L. Tucker, August 13, 1995; [ed.] Riverdale High School, Airforce Community College; [occ.] Owner of "Mailboxes and more Inc., Nashville, TN; [memb.] NALC and 4 Branch union, compassion International, 1st Baptist Donelson Church; [hon.] Honorable discharge from the United States Air Force Art Achievement; [oth. writ.] "The Truth"; [pers.] The poems I write come from the love in my heart. I have been greatly influenced by a wonderful mom and a great wife. I'd like to thank God for all my many blessings.; [a.] Nashville, TN

TUNE, CARL
[b.] November 19, 1976, Fort Worth, TX; [p.] Carl and Ivonne Tune; [ed.] Attending The Ohio State University in my Sophomore year.; [occ.] Student/Poet; [pers.] I refuse to title my poems because I believe that titles influence the reader on what to see in the poem. I believe the beauty of art is the diversity other may find in it.; [a.] Cincinnati, OH

TURMAN, MARGARET A.
[pen.] Peggy Turman; [b.] November 22, 1925, Waukegan, IL

TYNAN, CRAIG
[pen.] X, X-man; [b.] December 7, 1969, Schenectady, NY; [p.] Geraldine Brietenstein, Barry Tynan; [ed.] High School CBA College of St. Rose, Albany, NY Deans List; [occ.] Circulation Manager; [memb.] NY Triathlon Club; [hon.] Deans List, St. Rose College, College on a Base Ball Scholarship; [oth. writ.] Many as yet unpublished poems; [pers.] I write to express my thoughts. Creating poetry lets my heart and soul speak to everyone.; [a.] Albany, NY

TYREE, RICHARD DEAN
[pen.] Richard Dean Tyree; [b.] March 7, 1949, Columbus, IN; [m.] Janet Rose, May 14, 1995; [ed.] High School; [occ.] Self employed, singer, song writer; [oth. writ.] Numerous songs.; [pers.] The written word separates man from the beast.; [a.] Columbus, IN

TYSON, PATRICIA
[pen.] Pat Tyson; [b.] March 29, 1930, Greenville, SC; [p.] Mr. and Mrs. R. O. Hudson (Deceased); [m.] Albert W. Tyson Jr., June 12, 1951; [ch.] Galek Tyson Cutler, Laura Lynn Tyson; [ed.] Parker High, Class of '47, Art Courses (Private); [occ.] Retired (Dir. Christian Ed.), (Presbyterian Church (USA)); [memb.] Trinity Presby-

terian Church (Mission Committee, - Education Committee, - Superintendant of the Church School) Murals artists; [hon.] 1) Girls Scout Thanks Badge, 2) Life Membership PTA, Elder (P. Ch. USA), Board Member, Travelers Aid, - Atlanta, GA., Board Member, East Point Child, Development Center, - East Point, GA; [oth. writ.] 1) Church Newsletters, 2) Presbytery Newsletters, 3) A couple of articles and a poem published in "Girls Scout Leader" magazine. (A long time ago!); [pers.] Dear Howard, I thank you for the honor of considering my "Little Poem" for your publication, "The Colors Of Thought". Sincerely, Pat.; [a.] Greenville, SC

UNDERWOOD, BETH
[b.] May 9, Camden, NJ; [p.] Maureen and Harry Underwood; [ed.] Presently 7th Grade; [occ.] Student; [hon.] Honor Roll; [pers.] Beth was 11 years old when she wrote this poem.; [a.] Gloucester, NJ

UPHOFF JR., PROF. JOSEPH A.
[pen.] Joseph A. Uphoff Jr.; [b.] March 15, 1950, Colorado Springs; [p.] Joseph A. and Melva C. Uphoff; [ed.] A.A. Fine Arts, EPCC, B.A. Fine Arts, UCCS, Shodan (Black Belt), TIMA, Dr. Div., ULC, Hon. Dr. Let., IAR, Hon. Prof. Math., ICR, 1993, Nidan (Black Belt), NJI, 1995.; [occ.] Surrealist; [memb.] International Society of Poets, The First United Methodist Church, United States Judo Association, The National Geographic Society, The American Numismatic Association, The Colorado Springs Art Guild. Famous Poet for 1995, FPS, Hollywood, CA, 1995,; [hon.] The Knight of The Year, International Writers and Artists Association, Presidential Sports Award, Bill Clinton, Senator Council Of States for Protection of LIfe, Msgr. Viktor Busa, Diploma of Honor, IAI, Paris, France, Count (San Ciriaco), 1996, Full Accreditation, International Cultural Correspondence Institute, Madras, India, 1996.; [oth. writ.] Theory of Absurdest Drama, 1983-1996..., 1010 Pages, Martial Arts Sets, 1985-1996..., 1217 Pages, Dance Sets And Analytical Labanotation, 1991-1996..., 425 Pages, Chemical and Heterocyclic Geometry, 1995-1996..., 400 Pages.; [pers.] Surrealist Poetry is a collection of ongoing events and relics invoking standards of minimal and necessary regulation, maximal allowable freedom and privacy, reasonable opportunity for expression, mixed media including biography, autobiography, sculpture, painting, fiction, criticism, Mathematics and choreography, and philosophical discussion.; [a.] Colorado Springs, CO

UPSHAW, BONNIE
[b.] January 28, 1968, New Jersey; [p.] Bryce and Mary Biddlecome; [m.] Michael, July 21, 1991; [ch.] Krysta, Courtney and Lauren; [ed.] College Park High, Junior College; [occ.] Nursing; [memb.] Children's Cancer Society; [hon.] Creative Writing; [oth. writ.] Several poems published in bereavement newsletters.; [pers.] All my poems were written to my daughter Courtney, who's now my little angel. She'll always be in my heart and soul.; [a.] Laurel, MD

VAIL, SUSAN
[b.] January 21, 1943, Marshalltown, IA; [p.] Carl Wedgwood, Mary Helen Erickson Wedgwood; [ch.] Kristine Mary, Deanna Lynn, Jennifer Susan; [ed.] Marshalltown High, Collin County Community College, University of Texas at Dallas (BAIS), Amber University (MS); [occ.] Vail and Associates Consulting (Business, Travel, Antiques); [memb.] Society for Human Resources Management, SHRM Consultants Forum; [hon.] Professional in Human Resources Certification, Training and Development Certification.; [oth. writ.] None published. Numerous scholarly items including poetry, short-short stories and research papers. Also

poetry written for personal enjoyment and gifts to friends and family.; [pers.] Insight provides the nourishment needed to live life to its fullest to benefit the soul, and influence others with whom you have contact with even the briefest of contact!; [a.] Plano, TX

VALDES, ADAM J.
[b.] April 18, 1986, Tacoma, WA; [p.] Dan and Corinne Valdes; [occ.] Adam is a 4th grade student University Place Primary; [oth. writ.] This is Adams 1st published work. He wrote this poem at age 9.; [pers.] Adam enjoys sports, especially basketball and baseball. He enjoys reading and of course, writing! He collects Titanic Memorabilia.; [a.] University Place, WA

VALESKIE, GAIL
[b.] May 16, 1953, San Francisco, CA; [p.] John B. and Vera C. Valeskie; [m.] (Divorced) May 21, 1996, May 21, 1983; [ed.] BA and MA and Teacher's Cred. from Lone Mtn. College, SF, CA and U. of Valencia and Music Conservatory, Valencia, Spain; [occ.] Self-employed, Valeskie Data/Word Processing; [memb.] Organist/Music Dir. - Shepherd of The Hills Luth., Amer. Guild of Organists, Amer. Choral Dirs. Assn., Prof. Assn. of Secretarial Sucs.; [hon.] Who's Who of Amer. Women (1993-94, 1995-96), 2000 Notable Women ('90-91), The First 500 (IBC '90), Who's Who Among Bus. and Prof. Women ('89-90), Who's Who Among students in Amer. Colls/Univ. ('73-74), graduated Magna Cum Laude with honors '73.; [oth. writ.] I've set several of my poems to music and have had them performed by the Women in Music, Columbus OH and by several churches in San Francisco.; [pers.] I've been deeply inspired by "Women Who Run With The Wolves" by Pinkola Estes. I strive to encourage all people to discover their life-purpose, to use their innate gifts and talents, and to rise above limitations, whether self-imposed or by others.; [a.] San Francisco, CA

VAN DYKE, BONNIE E.
[pen.] Bonnie Caldwell Van Dyke; [b.] December 26, 1942, Marion Co, TN; [p.] Stanley and Millie Caldwell; [ch.] Garnet Rust, Jo Ellis, Kenneth and Stanley Van Dyke; [ed.] Jasper Elem, Marion Co. High Licensed Practiced Nurse Training at In. State Vocational; [occ.] LPN Assistant pianist at Church; [memb.] New Hope Community Full Gospel Church; [oth. writ.] Several poems published in church newsletter and also local newspaper in AL. Have complete collection of unpublished poems. Also write songs some of which are sung in church.; [pers.] Most of my poems are inspirational and portray how faith in God can bring us through life's crisis. Also, there are a number of light fun poems. Write philosophical ideas in free hand.; [a.] Sequatchie, TN

VANDERMEER, ANNE
[b.] December 16, 1980, West Lafayette, IN; [p.] Mary Ann VanderMeer, Philip VanderMeer; [ed.] Rhodes Jr. High School, Dobson High School; [occ.] Student; [memb.] Baha Youth Group, Girl Scouts, University Presbyterian Church; [hon.] President's award for Excellence, Honorable Mention for Personal Narrative in Mesa Public Schools District Writing Contest, Top 1% in Nation for Global Challenge; [oth. writ.] A collection of poems some short stories, and a novel, all of which I want published, and I'm working on many more.; [pers.] In my fifteen years of living, nothing has been so utterly incredible as the moment when I knew I was in love. Though my poems are very different, I try and blend the Baha belief of 'Unity in Diversity' with my parent's christian teachings to express an almost childlike appreciation for the wonder that is life.; [a.] Mesa, AZ

VASSEL, JENNIFER D.
[b.] March 12, 1987, Los Angeles; [p.] Dennis and Grace; [ed.] Attending Mount Calvary Lutheran Elementary School in 4th Grade Currently; [occ.] Student; [memb.] Sunday School, Drill Team; [hon.] Good Student Award, Certificates for Exceptional Art Work also Writing; [oth. writ.] My own private writings, I kept privately in my scrap book. Several of them I recited on school talent nights; [pers.] I like to express myself through writing and drawing. That's the way I allow others to get to know me.; [a.] Chino Hills, CA

VASSILEV, GEORGE ASSENOV
[b.] May 30, 1975, Sofia, Bulgaria; [p.] Theodora Nestorova, Assen Vassilev; [ed.] "I English Language High School" and "Sofia Music High School", "Sofia University St. Kliment Ohridski" - Philosophy - Sofia - Bulgaria; [occ.] Student; [hon.] 1990 - Third Place - " I National Pop Song Competition" and 3 Top Radio Countdown Songs - in Bulgaria; [oth. writ.] More than 50 poems and song lyrics, two novels and a half, not published yet.; [pers.] The free play of imagination brings harmony to the controversy of mind and soul. Improvise!; [a.] Los Angeles, CA

VAUGHAN, CARRIE
[pen.] Evangelist, Carrie Vaughan; [b.] January 7, 1955, Bentonia, MS; [p.] Mr. and Mrs. Willie D. Vaughan; [ch.] One son, one daughter; [ed.] Gibbs, Ele, Bentonia, MS, Bentonia High, Bentonia, MS, Kennedy King College, IL, American College, Jackson, MS, Wesley's College, Florence, MS; [occ.] Nursing - Caring for the disable, or total care, patients; [memb.] Blair Metropolitan Amez, Church - 100 Women in Faith; [hon.] Plaque, Employee of Month, In home Health, Certificate for classmate of the week at American College, 3.0 average in Evangelism; [oth. writ.] Several poem's and song's done on radio ministry once a week. Own lyric's and music.; [pers.] I believe in sharing, the ability that God has given me with others, I know that true and encouraging words can bless the body, mine, and soul.; [a.] Jackson, MS

VAUGHAN, WENDELL L.
[b.] May 8, 1921, Iberia, MO; [p.] Sam and Mellie Vaughan; [m.] Vivian Vaughan, December 28, 1941; [ch.] Victor and Deborah; [ed.] High School, 4 yrs college, 3 years, post graduate; [occ.] Retired; [pers.] I have sought to write varying subjects meters and styles of poetry; [a.] Lake Wood, CO

VEAL, CHARLES
[ed.] Hughes High - Cincinnati, OH, Univ MD, Univ AK, Cortez Peters Bus College Univ Nebr at Omaha, BGS (Psy), BS (Educ/Art), MS (Reading/Learning Specialist); [occ.] Teacher, K-12, Reading Teacher, Spec Educ Teacher, ESL Teacher; [memb.] Hospital Volunteer, Omaha Literacy Council, Red Cross (10 yrs Recognition Pin Award), AAHPERD, Nebr Rec/Park Assoc, YMCA, Christ Child Society; [hon.] Dean's Honors List, Kappa Delta Pi, Phi Theta Kappa, Regent's Scholarship, Graduate Cum Laude; [oth. writ.] Occasional essays published in newspapers, poems, articles in school papers, various unpublished essays, poems, research articles, critiques and book reviews; [pers.] Having been born with the creative obligation to express ideas and feelings, the writing of poetry fulfills a two-fold destiny: (1) To discover universal truths, and (2) To untangle the problems and complexities sometimes encountered by humankind.; [a.] Omaha, NE

VELEZ, FAUSTO ART A.
[pen.] Velez Abarca; [b.] February 27, 1938, Loja Ec; [p.] Arturo and Beatriz; [m.] Eliza-Candel de Velez, August 22, 1964; [ch.] Four; [ed.] Borja #2 Quito Ecuador Franco Ingles Mexico University Autonoma Mex; [occ.] Tenneco Co L.A. California; [hon.] Some

at work; [oth. writ.] 2 Books some poetry; [pers.] President Kennedy told us:] "Is what you can do for your country". This poem will help people that is intelligent and some smart young boys and girls; [a.] Tustin, CA

VELOTAS, STEVEN GARY
[b.] March 20, 1969, Clark AFB, Philippines; [ed.] Bachelor of Science Aerospace Engineering from United States Naval academy, 1991; [occ.] Naval Flight Officer in E-2C "Hawkeye" (Vaw-126); [memb.] First Lutheran Church of Norfolk Choir and Co-ed Softball; [hon.] Air Medal for work in Bosnia, Shell Back, Engineer-in-Training, Klein Forest High School most likely to succeed 1987, Eagle Scout; [a.] Virginia Beach, VA

VERMA, NARAYAN
[pen.] Vibhakar; [b.] July 1, 1953, India; [p.] Sarla and Baldeo Verma; [m.] Neelam Verma, May 23, 1978; [ch.] Arunima, Ankur, Akshay; [ed.] M.D. (Medicine) also specialized in Neurology and sleep medicine; [occ.] M.D. (Private Practice); [memb.] American College of Physician, American Academy of Neurology; [hon.] Award by W.H.O., National Board Examiner, Science Talent Scholar; [oth. writ.] 740 Research articles in medical journals, 7100 medical publications; [pers.] This is my first attempt at writing poem in English. I have written numerous medical articles in English, however; [a.] Groose Pointe, MI

VERMETT, LINDA
[b.] July 26, 1947, Rockford, IL; [p.] Floyd Beck, Henrietta Beck; [m.] Larry Vermett, July 25, 1970; [ch.] Stacy Lynn, Nicole Alayne; [ed.] Rockford East High, MacMurray College; [pers.] Expressing one's feelings is medicine for the soul.; [a.] Harvard, IL

VICTOR, ANDREW
[b.] November 4, 1934, New York, NY; [p.] Joseph Victor MD, Stella Victor; [m.] Dorothy (Nee Tresselt), December 9, 1955; [ch.] 3 Lisa, Joseph, Jean Victor Linsteadt, 3 grandchildren; [ed.] University of Maryland MS, Swarthmore College BA; [occ.] Retired, part time Consulting Physicist, Victor Technology; [memb.] American Inst. Aeronautics and Astronautics, International Pyrotechnic Society, American Defense Preparedness Assoc.; [oth. writ.] 140 published technical articles in physics, chemistry, and engineering and WWW page. Numerous other unpublished poems. Researcher/writer for San Francisco travel, guide.; [pers.] I use poetry to express deeply felt emotions that pass through my mind as pictures that cannot express in any other way.; [a.] San Rafael, CA

VIDDEN, VERNON E.
[b.] October 14, 1930, Fertile, MN; [p.] Herman & Christine Vidden (Deceased); [m.] Bernice Erna Vidden, June 8, 1958; [ed.] High School graduate. (1949-Fertile, MN) and two years trade school (newspapers since graduations); [occ.] Retired Grand Forks Herald 9ND), nearly 26 years; [memb.] American Legion Post No. 157, East Grand Forks, MN, 35 years member; [hon.] High School Journalism Award, Column entitled "Kidden With Vidden" (1948-19), Retirement plaque Grand Forks (ND) Herald (1969-1995); [pers.] The poetic and profound beauty of earth and sky has been beautifully portrayed through thoughtful and inquistive minds. I believe as we learn more we gain greater knowledge for our benefit.; [a.] East Grand Forks, MN

VILLARREAL, LISA
[b.] July 22, 1974, Durham, NC; [p.] Dr. Alfredo Villarreal-Rios and Michelle Villarreal-Rios; [ed.] Incarnate Word High School, Trinity University; [memb.] Gamma Chi Delta Sorority, Psi Chi Honors Society; [hon.] Phi Beta Kappa, Dean's List, Cum Laude; [pers.]

Writing is a tool I use to better understand myself and others. I strive to explain the complexities of life with simplicity and clarity.; [a.] San Antonio, TX

VIRGIL, DAVISON
[b.] August 16, Thomasville, GA; [p.] Rev. and Mrs. Washington and Lula Bell Virgil; [m.] Georgeanne (Brown) Virgil, August 4; [ch.] Ashley, Whitley, Khalilah, DeVaughn, Sheroyd; [ed.] South Miami Sr. High, Albany State University; [occ.] Environmental Specialist, Oklahoma Dept. of Environmental Quality; [memb.] St. John Baptist Church, Alpha Phi Alpha Fraternity, Oklahoma Society of Environmental Professionals; [hon.] Outstanding Young Men of America, Army Commendation Medal with 3 Oak Leaf Clusters, Army Achievement Medal, National Defense Service Ribbon; [pers.] We are a composite of all the people we have met and known, giving us the power to elevate the good and suppress the bad in mankind.; [a.] Lawton, OK

VITELLI, BRIAN
[b.] July 16, 1956, New Haven, CT; [ed.] Doctor of Veterinary Medicine; [occ.] Veterinarian; [oth. writ.] To dream in color (a poetry book).; [a.] East Haven, CT

WALGUARNERY, JESSICA MARIE
[pen.] Jessie Marie Smith; [b.] July 31, 1975, Clearwater, FL; [p.] Christine Vaccaro Smith; [ed.] Curlew Elm. Palm Harbor Middle Countryside High Anchor Ad. (Priv); [occ.] Hot Flash Holograms and Village Inn; [a.] Tarpon Springs, FL

WALTERS, TRACY LEANN
[pen.] Kat; [b.] January 12, 1983, Kinston, NC; [p.] Sandra Walters; [ed.] 8th Grader at West Craven Middle School; [occ.] Honor Student; [memb.] Beta Club, S.A.D.D. Club, Battle of Books Club; [hon.] Young Authors Award, Honors Award; [oth. writ.] Several winnings from The Craven Crave which my poems where published short story "Unwanted Desire"; [pers.] Poems are like gateways to the past future and present.; [a.] Dover, NC

WALTON, LEWIS E.
[b.] May 15, 1903, Halifax, MA; [p.] Deceased; [m.] Anne L. Walton, June 25, 1927; [ed.] AB Bates College, MA Brown Univ., Ph.D. University of Penna; [occ.] Retired since 1970 from teaching at U. of Miami; [memb.] Phi Beta Kappa; [hon.] Several awards for Newspapers called me "The Grandpa Moses of Verse; [oth. writ.] Poetry and short stories and professional writing.; [pers.] My poetry is the classical type modeled after the poets of the 19th century.; [a.] Woodford, VA

WARD, ERICKA
[b.] August 14, 1983, Detroit, MI; [p.] Hezekiab Reed, Angela Ward; [ed.] Power Middle School (Farmington, Michigan); [occ.] Student; [hon.] Honor Roll, Spelling Bee; [oth. writ.] Many other poems kept in a private poetry notebook.; [pers.] I was influenced by my heart and my feelings and I want to thank God for the talent for me to write those feeling down on paper in my most creative way.; [a.] Farmington, MI

WARE, EMMA JO FOX
[pen.] Jo Ware, Emma Bombeck; [b.] April 25, 1939, Graham, TX; [p.] Alice B. and J. O. Fox Jr. (Both Deceased); [m.] Mickey G. Ware, August 5, 1960; [ch.] Nickey Dean Ware and James Kyle Ware (Deceased); [ed.] M.A. from Midwestern State University in Wichita Falls, Texas May 10, 1986, English Major (with a concentration in creative writing), Minor in Sociology; [occ.] Freelance Writer and Housewife; [memb.] Alpha Kappa Delta (Sociological National Honorary Society), Midwestern State University Ex-Students Association; [hon.] First place in the Essay

Division, Creative Writing, Vinson Literary Awards (MSU) in 1986, Invited to study in England for six weeks (sociology dept) in 1986, Invited to join the Martar Board, a National Honor society for Jr's and Sr's with a G.P.A. of 4.0 or above, wrote the "Dedication" for a family cook book, The Dunagan Family Cook Book; [oth. writ.] Something for Myself, The Brass Bed, As the World Turns, Autumn, Code 99, The Door, Anniversary Dogs are Better than Kids, There's a Dog on My Head, Sunshine Dancer, It was Just a Dog, Stars in My Crown.; [pers.] When my son was killed in an automobile accident in 1979, I turned to writing as a means of comfort and a catharsis. I refer to my writing as "putting my guts on paper". I decided that (writing) this would be the best way to honor my son's memory and go forward with my life, and perhaps leave something of myself prosperity.; [a.] Wichita Falls, TX

WARNECKE, BILL
[pen.] Billy Ray Warnecke; [b.] September 23, 1964, St. Paul, MN; [p.] Bill and Diane Warnecke; [m.] July 4, 1997; [ch.] Bill R. Warnecke, Renee F. Warnecke; [ed.] Salem, Ill Jr. High, didn't graduate 8th grade!; [occ.] Crane opp., Pay Cal Steel, St. Paul, MN; [oth. writ.] Many poems written for personal enjoyment. Never tried publishing any of my poems before.; [pers.] Due to my father dying when I was young, I've always had a hard time expressing my feelings. I find I can express myself through poetry. Now I devote myself to being the best father I can be to Billy and Renee.; [a.] Roseville, MN

WASHINGTON, GLADYS L.
[pen.] H. B. Redlef; [b.] November 13, 1948, Petersburg, VA; [p.] Tyree Felder, Frankie Felder; [m.] Lloyd G. Washington, June 13, 1969; [ch.] Ayse Monae, Tasha Juanita, Ngai Canute-Tyree; [ed.] Frankfurt American High, Frankfurt, west Germany, Kings County School of Nursing St. Joseph's College, Ext degree, Maine.; [occ.] Registered Nurse - D.O.N. Coram Healthcare, Miami, Florida; [memb.] South Florida Society of Healthcare Risk Managers; [oth. writ.] Several other poems, none published. Two books in progress.; [pers.] Poetry writing is a source relaxation and a means of sharing feelings that are not easily expressed otherwise. My inspiration is from every day life. Any talent is from my grandmother and my father. There is poetry in everyone.; [a.] Miramar, FL

WASHINGTON, PENNY L.
[ed.] BA English Literature, West Chester University, West Chester, PA; [occ.] Journalist, Story Teller, Poet, Public Speaker; [oth. writ.] My work as a poet has appeared in a local journal called, The Next Day; [pers.] I strive to honor my African American heritage through my writing. I feel blessed to do the work I do.; [a.] West Chester, PA

WATSON, ASHLEY
[b.] February 5, 1983; [p.] Bob and Sue Watson; [ed.] In the 8th grade; [hon.] Honor Roll Student; [pers.] I am 13 yrs. old. I am in the 8th grade at Dayton Middle School, Dayton, KY. I am an honor roll student who enjoys sports, cheerleading, and writing poetry.; [a.] Dayton, KY

WATSON, JONATHAN CHRISTIAN
[pen.] J. C. Watson; [b.] October 10, 1977, Florida; [pers.] This poem is one of my favorite because it artistically conveys the entire story of he world from creation to the final conclusion. The hope that it (this poem) speaks of is the only real hope for anyone: Jesus Christ. He has stood throughout history for hope to all those who believe.; [a.] Glendale, AZ

WEATHERS, PAULA F.
[b.] August 13, 1946, Hannibal, MO; [p.] Alonzo and Anna Hall; [ch.] Gearald, Crystal, Kyra, and JaNae Weathers; [ed.] Hannibal High - 11th grade; [occ.] I am a Nurse's Assistant at Hannibal Regional Hospital; [memb.] I belong to New Hope Gospel Church. I teach adult women Bible study. I am on the Board of Directors at the Church. I am on 2 committees at the hospital.; [pers.] I believe that we can do all things through Christ. Faith is the most important thing we can hold on to. This is the first time I have written a poem for a contest. I write for my own enjoyment and I wrote some in school. My family and friends told me to give it a try, so I did. Thank God.; [a.] Hannibal, MO

WEATHERSPOON, C. DANNY
[pen.] CDW Spoon; [b.] June 28, 1952, Champaign, IL; [p.] Alvin and Lola Weatherspoon; [m.] Gloria Hayslett Weatherspoon, June 25, 1994; [ch.] Sherry Adams, Kenya and Ebony Weatherspoon; [ed.] High school graduate, Champaign Centennial High, USN, ICA School and Basic Electronics, BS Electrical Engineering U. of Illinois Urbana/Champaign; [occ.] Engineering Specialist, Monsanto Company, Muscatine Iowa; [memb.] "Institute of Electrical and Electronic Engineers IEEE", "International Society for Measurement and Control, ISA", JKA, Japanese Karate Association; [hon.] Martin Luther King Scholarship (out of high school), Honorable Discharge USN, Vietnam Veteran, Special Scholarship to study Meteorology and Space Science U. of Wisconsin; [oth. writ.] None published; [pers.] Gods gifts of love, peace and happiness can be found in and through a poets humble pen.; [a.] Milan, IL

WEEDIN, TRACY KATHLEEN
[pen.] Roo; [b.] August 10, 1977, Seattle, WA; [p.] Garth W. Weedin and Kathleen A. Weedin; [ed.] Liberty High School; [occ.] Customer Service; [oth. writ.] Various other poetry written for Personal enjoyment; [pers.] Poetry for me is a beautiful way to express myself, it brings me innerpeace.] I would like to thank my friend, William, who helped me find myself amongst the chaos of life.; [a.] Renton, WA

WEGNER, LOIS L. MCCOY
[b.] August 27, 1934, Minneapolis, MN; [p.] Buel L. McCoy, Olive McCoy Alberhasky; [m.] Ronald Wegner, May 25, 1973; [ch.] Wesley D. Durow; [occ.] Secretary, Kirkwood Community College, Ag Science, Cedar Rapids IA; [memb.] American Diabetes Association; [pers.] My writing is my way of dealing with and sharing the ups and downs of this wonderful life I have been given.; [a.] Cedar Rapids, IA

WEIGEL, DIANA J.
[pen.] Diana Jean; [b.] August 30, 1945, Torrington, WY; [p.] Alvin Weigel, September 10, 1965; [ch.] Shawnalyn Weigel, Physical Therapist; [ed.] Abraham Lincoln High (Denver, CO), University of Colo. (at Denver, Co. 1 year) Jones Real Estate College MSEC (Supervisory I-II, Denver, CO.) Jefferson County (WordPerfect I) Disability Awareness (City of Lakewood, CO) Proofreading (City of Lakewood, CO) Productivity Point (WP II, Lotus, Golden, Co.); [occ.] Poet/Writer; [memb.] New Life Christian Church The International, Society of Poets 1995 - 1996 Member 1996 Distinguished Member; [hon.] Top Listing Agent Century 21 (October 1981) Commendation (Verification Dept./Cost Efficiency Jan. 1984) Commendation (City of Lkwd, Implement Police Agent New Payroll System, January 1990) Editor's Choice Award Presented By The National Library of Poetry 1996 for "The Flower In My Life" published in The Rainbow's End, 1996 Poet of Merit Award, International Society of Poets, Poetry Convention and Symposium to be published in Best Poems of the '90's Snowflakes (December 16, 1993), To be published in Daybreak On The Land entered in NLP contest May 20, 1996 China Doll (April 16, 1993); [oth. writ.] Unpublished, Rose 1991, Friends March 28, 1993, Diana Who July 10, 1993, Where Am I? September 8, 1994, Twilight July 8, 1995, Cool Cloudy, Grey Day September 7, 1995; [pers.] Life is a breeze through the trees. It can be a web of lies that seems like truth. Seeking and finding a sometimes painful truth, is better than lies that are devastating. Peace comes from Jesus, His truth is eternal.; [a.] Arvada, CO

WEIR, MEREDITH J.
[b.] May 18, 1953, New Jersey; [pers.] I like my poems to reflect my love of nature, and also to share the struggles of this life and my faith in God.; [a.] Lompoc, CA

WEIR JR., CLAUDE V.
[b.] January 22, 1951, New York, NY; [p.] Claude Weir and Doris Stevenson; [m.] Yvette Arsenec, December 6, 1994; [ch.] Jesse Jeremiah Owens; [ed.] Dartmouth College, Harvard Law School; [occ.] Senior Vice President, The Chase Manhattan Bank; [memb.] American Bar Association/NYS Bar Association, NYS Chamber of Commerce-HR Committee, YMCA of Greater of New York-Board of Directors' HR Committee, Bayley-Seton Hospital Advisory Board; [oth. writ.] Several poems written through the years for the pleasure of family and friends.; [pers.] I want my writing to make people reflect on those things that are truly important in life before it is too late to do so.; [a.] New York, NY

WEISS, JESSICA FRANCES
[b.] November 8, 1986, Rock Springs, WY; [p.] Morris and Bernie Weiss; [ed.] 4th Grade at Walnut Elementary School in Rock Springs, Wyoming; [occ.] Elementary School student, piano player, violin player, swimmer, snow Skier; [memb.] Member of Congregation Beth Israel in Rock Springs, Wyoming; [hon.] Straight a honor roll, won first place in non-fiction local young authors contest, and tied for first place in poetry in third grade both in my age group; [oth. writ.] "My School" non-fiction in first grader local young authors contest, and "My Favorite Poems" in third grade in some contest. Neither was published.; [pers.] I like to write something that's not mushy!; [a.] Rock Springs, WY

WELCH, FAYE
[pen.] Granny; [b.] May 31, 1930, Livingston; [p.] Charles and Alma Terry; [m.] Sam G. Welch, January 19, 1952; [ch.] Karen Steve, Diane David; [ed.] McHenry High School Completed Nineth; [occ.] Disability; [oth. writ.] Safety Slogans, Lindale MFG Co.; [pers.] Worked forty five years Peppell MFG Co., Rachel Patches Misty Stephanie Grandchildren Bryan Great grandchild; [a.] Rome, GA

WELCH, JEAN P.
[b.] December 19, 1940, West VA; [p.] James M. and Annie A. Barnett; [m.] John E. Welch, June 5, 1961; [ed.] Jeanna, Kimmi, Scott and Amanda; [occ.] Home Maker; [pers.] I write for my own personal satisfaction, about people, places or things that affect me, this particular poem "How Deep", was revised from a longer version written after learning of the death of Ray Combs. He was a favorite host of mine.

WELCH, ROBERTA
[b.] November 8, Cambridge, MA; [p.] Robert and Anita Butler; [ch.] Harold Welch; [ed.] CRLS High, Bentley College, Newbury College; [occ.] Administrator, Mass. Inst. of Technology, Cambridge, MA; [hon.] Associates Degree, Dean's List; [pers.] My poems reflect the way I feel about the environment and my everyday experiences with people and places.; [a.] Cambridge, MA

WELSCH, ASHLEY
[pen.] Ashley Welsch; [b.] October 2, 1984, Atlantic, IA; [p.] Eugene and Joan Welsch; [ed.] In 6th grade; [occ.] In school; [memb.] 4-H; [pers.] I like writing dramatic poems because they are exciting to me.; [a.] Greenfield, IA

WESLEY, EILEEN
[pen.] E. W. T.; [b.] May 28, 1953, NYC; [p.] Anne, Bill Wesley; [m.] Confidential; [ch.] Two beautiful Carrie and Leonilda Theriault; [ed.] 12 years, plus College Courses Mental Health, Nutrition, Fitness, Legal Assistant, Transcripting Psychiatric Association and Elderly and Young; [occ.] Mental Health Worker American Psychiatric Association; [memb.] National Education Corporation; [hon.] Legal Modeling for hobby sports; [oth. writ.] Not yet!; [pers.] William Shakespeare has always influenced me throughout my life. I always try to judge people or incidents, after looking at both sides of the coin. Taking a look at the good first, then dealing with the bad.; [a.] Bangor, ME

WESSEL, PATRICIA A.
[pen.] Patricia Fanning Avery Bawcum Wessel; [b.] May 11, 1942, Weehawken, NJ; [p.] James J. and Elizabeth C. Fanning Sr.; [m.] James R. Wessel, March 1989; [ch.] Deborah K. Avery O'Mara, Jayson K. Bawcum; [ed.] Graduated from St. Mary's High School 1960 Alb. NM, attended the University of New Mexico, Alb. NM, attended Technical Vocational Institute, Alb. NM; [occ.] Retired Administrative Secretary current occupation Housewife; [memb.] The International Society of Authors and Artists, National Authors Registry, International Society of Poets, Songwriters Club of America; [hon.] 4th place in Captured Moments thru Creative Arts and Sciences, Ent., Honorable Mention from several anthologies Accomplishment of Merit several times thru Editors Choice Awards thru National Library of Poetry; [oth. writ.] Numerous poems in various anthologies by Creative Arts and Sciences, Ent. The National Library of Poetry The Amherst Society, World Art Publishing Best new poems 1996 The Poetry Guild Who's Who in New Poets 1996 JMW Publishing, etc.; [pers.] The two verbs we all must use are care and share to attain peace on human life or allowing people their rights in humane and unchristian. This poem has deep meaning to me. I was not, when writing it trying to be creative and I know it will not win any prize because of any clever presentation. I have been working on this poem for two years in an effort to put the words in what I felt to be the briefest most truthful words, getting the words across in a non-offensive way and without sounding like I was preaching. It is simply an honest, matter of fact, way of achieving peace in my opinion.; [a.] Albuquerque, NM

WESSINGER, LANA
[b.] January 9, 1979, Atlanta, GA; [p.] Randy Wessinger and Laurie Clifton; [ed.] Senior in High School at Rabun Gap Nacoochee School; [memb.] School Organizations: Jane Austin Society, Prefect, Literary Anthology Staff; [hon.] Most Potential Actress, Most Valuable Dancer, Work Ethic Award; [a.] Macon, GA

WEST, DENISE
[b.] July 3, 1981; [p.] Wanita Frost; [ed.] Elementary School Gilbert Augusta ME 1-4, Helen Thompson Gardiner 5, Gardiner Middle School 6-8, Gardiner High 9; [occ.] Student; [memb.] Drama 1995-1996; [hon.] Honor roll all 8th grade year. New England Color Good Camp 1995 1st and second place. 1996 New England Color Guard Camp 1st and second place Science award 1995 grade 7.; [oth. writ.] Jealousy 1996, Perfect 1996, He Drank He Drove 1996, Inno-

cent Until Proven Guilty 1996, Ann's Story 1996; [a.] Gardiner, ME.

WESTERMAN, RENE
[b.] May 16, 1948, Chicago, IL; [p.] Madeleine and Floyd; [m.] Gary Westerman, January 6, 1973; [ch.] Tammy, Terry, Joshua; [ed.] Mount Greenwood Elementary Morgan Park High; [occ.] Homemaker; [oth. writ.] Articles in daily newspapers. The most special one was framed by friends in IL. and is in our home for all to read titled "Remember the Elderly."; [pers.] My inspiration is my love of life and my family; [a.] Chino Valley, AZ

WHALEN, DONNA
[b.] April 10, 1968, Indianapolis, IN; [p.] William and Shirley Smith; [m.] Wayne Roy Whalen Jr.; [ch.] Rilan, Jessica, Allie; [ed.] Casey High, Casey Illinois; [occ.] Home Maker; [pers.] Due to divorce, Jessie somehow lost her Daddy on 7-1-96 Jessie was adopted by a wonderful, loving new Daddy. I love you Jessica Nichole Whalen; [a.] Chatham, IL

WHEELIHAN, BARBARA LYNN
[b.] January 9, 1968, St. Joseph, MI; [p.] Kathleen Joan and Charles McIntosh Wheelihan; [oth. writ.] I write children's stories but as yet have not submitted any for publication.; [pers.] I live on the farm that my great grandfather grew up on; my mother was born in the house I live in. There is a great sense of peace here as well as occasional isolation. I wrote this poem for my mother, to help her remember why that is a beautiful thing.; [a.] Capac, MI

WHITE, JENNA
[b.] January 29, 1981, Oklahoma City, OK; [p.] Mike and Jerry White; [ed.] Presently attending Bryant High School - Plan to go to college in Arkansas, either UCA or V of A Fayettville; [hon.] 1996 Lady Honet Softball, a. State Champions, b. Named best all around, c. all - conference, 1993 - 1996 Dream team Softball, 1993 - 5th in national town., 1994 - 2nd in world town and 3rd in nationals, 1996 - 4th in national town.; [pers.] I enjoy writing about my life. I hope to show my dedication and love for life to many people and hopefully inspire them to be their very best. I'd like to say thanks to all my friends for their love and support.; [a.] Bryant, AR

WHITEMAN, PATRICIA
[b.] May 5, 1945, Salinas, CA; [p.] Hazel and William Horn (Deceased); [m.] William Whiteman (Deceased); [ch.] James Prola - 34 and Lois Prola - 33; [occ.] Disabled; [memb.] Seventh Day Adventist Church; [oth. writ.] "Love Me", "She", The Rippling Waters; [pers.] When I wrote "Beautiful One" I was feeling really Low going through divorce. The Lord brought these thoughts to my mind... I have 7 grandchildren; [a.] Salinas, CA

WICKERT, VALERIE
[b.] May 4, 1981, North Syracuse, NY; [p.] Kenneth and Melitta Wickert; [ed.] Smith Road Elementary, Roxboro Road Middle School, North Syracuse Junior High, Cicero - North Syracuse High School; [occ.] Student; [memb.] St. Margaret's High School Youth Group; [hon.] President's Award for Education, Honor and for Merit Roll, Fay's Drug Quez Show; [oth. writ.] Poetry in school publications; [pers.] Your family will always be there for you, be nice to them. A few good friends are better than a lot of fair weather friends.; [a.] North Syracuse, NY

WIELAND, RUDY M.
[pen.] Rudy M. Wieland; [b.] September 8, 1916, Berlin, Ger.; [p.] Eric and Wally; [m.] Elsa, November 26, 1940; [ch.] Roxana; [ed.] Carrick High School, 12th Grade Carrick, Pittsburg, PA; [occ.] Retired - U.S.

Navy, retired Panama Canal Co., Civil Service; [memb.] Fleet Res. Assoc., U.S. Navy Memorial, DC, VFW, American Legion - U.S.O., Navy League of U.S.A.; [hon.] 20 yrs. in H.S.N. of which 12 yrs. were in the Submarine service. The Awards that over 50 yrs. of marriage, my wife has given to me; [pers.] "Eternity," 'tis said, that anything that has an ending, could verily be the start at a new beginning, so, should we ourselves, pass away, and drift thru the gates of heaven or hell. We let again, our destiny determine, that in truth, what had once begun, in life, has no ending.

WIESNER, EUGENE F.
[pen.] Eugene F. Wiesner; [b.] April 22, 1956, Hays, KS; [p.] Eugene and Helen Wiesner; [m.] Maria P. Wiesner, May 23, 1988; [ch.] Simon D. Wiesner; [ed.] Billings Senior High, Billing Vo-tech for Auto Mechanics, Eastern Montana College - one year; [occ.] Baker; [memb.] St. Patricks Church; [oth. writ.] I wrote "The Hundred Songs" a collection of one hundred poems and "The Hundred Songs Of Fatima" which I received a letter from Pope John Paul II on. My poem "Two Trees" was published in a "Museto Follow."; [pers.] Love your brother as yourself and God with your whole heart.; [a.] Laurel, MT

WILCOX II, WILLIAM S.
[b.] May 17, 1972, Washington, IA; [p.] Robert Wilcox, Charlotte Wilcox; [ed.] Chatfield Senior High, University of Denver; [hon.] Phi Sigma Iota; [oth. writ.] Editorials, poetry and short fiction published on the internet.; [a.] Littleton, CO

WILDER, DANIELLE MARIE
[pen.] Danie; [b.] February 9, 1983, Albuquerque, NM; [p.] Franklin Duane Wilder and Joanna Wilder; [ed.] Educated at Buckeye, AZ, Preschool - 2nd grade most of 3rd at Cherokee Elem. 4th - 8th at St. Joseph Catholic Private School; [occ.] Work for father at Wilder's Home and Garden Center; [memb.] I belong to the Girl Scouts of America G.S.A., the Math counts Program. I also belong to St. Joseph Catholic Church and my 8th grade softball team.; [hon.] 3rd and 2nd place ribbons in School Science fair. Lots of walk America Walking Medals. A certificate of Appreciation from the Optimist Oratorical contest.; [oth. writ.] I don't have any other writings, but I have other artistry, like drawings and paintings. Although I once wrote a speech.; [pers.] I never new I could ever write such a beautiful poem, but as they say you never know what you can do till you try. May my poem inspire millions of people, young and old. - Danielle Wilder; [a.] Muskogee, OK

WILKIN, ROSEMARIE
[b.] May 6, 1910, Clinton Co., OH; [p.] Omer Sheldon - Mary Gilbert Sheldon; [m.] Charles C. Wilkin; [ch.] Seven; [ed.] Blanchester High School Dale Cargone, Christian Educated Experience - life and by reading.; [occ.] Retired Church Work, Sr. Citizens, Writer-artists (Volunteer); [memb.] Berrysville Christian Union Church. DAR, Hillsboro, WCTU. Story telling Sr. Citizens, Hillsboro Columnist for Hillsboro Press Gazette.; [hon.] Award for writing note 1993, CU Church, Sr. Citizens Pool Playing (1996) 1992 Expressing Written Word of Faith National Office Work. Local and County. Active in Sr. Citizens. Teacher in School Past Elder, Missionary, Good cheer person, Historian DAR, Youth leader; [oth. writ.] June 16, 1992, The Christian Union Witness Presented one a Certificate of recognition, for Excellence of expressing there the written word my testimony of faith - in essay contest. "Why I love Christian Union my CU Witness"; [pers.] I hesitate to write - so many things I've done in my life time there I joined not story tellers; [a.] Hillsboro, OH

WILKINSON, LELWIN
[b.] December 1, 1916, Canebeds, AZ; [p.] Joseph T. and Annie W. Wilkinson; [m.] Viva Wilkinson, December 30, 1938; [ch.] Floyd, Bruce, Verl, Alma; [ed.] B.S. Utah State University Logan, UT 1940 - M.A.T. Michigan State University Lansing, Michigan 1961; [occ.] Retired H.S. Science Teacher; [memb.] Alpha Zeta, Lions Club, Optimist Club, National Education Association; [hon.] Biology Teachers of NV Award as Outstanding Biology Teacher Of The Year 1968-69, LV NV Rotary Club Teacher of The Year Award 1966-67, Future Science and Engineering Award 1971; [oth. writ.] "The Rozencrann Treasure", "Kenneth Rink, The Romeo Kid" - Saga Of The Demise Of The Sheep Industry In Utah's Dixie And The Arizona Strip"; [pers.] "He who does the best be can is a Hero". Author Unknown.; [a.] Washington, UT

WILLIAMS, BRIAN A. C.
[pen.] Batyun-We; [b.] July 25, 1962, Washington, DC; [ed.] Calvin Coolidge High, Mary Wash College; [occ.] Systems Engineer; [oth. writ.] Many unpublished poems. Some on local BBS.; [pers.] In between the two points of life and death there is much work to be done.

WILLIAMS, CHERAY T.
[pen.] Cheray T. Williams; [b.] February 14, 1970, Saddlebrook; [p.] Raymond and Theresa Williams; [m.] Casey W. Teeple, September 21, 1996; [ed.] BA William Paterson College, Working toward masters at William Paterson; [occ.] Accounts Receivable Clerk, Freelance writer; [hon.] Dean's List, graduated Magna Cum Laude, Distinguished leadership Award.; [oth. writ.] Extensive news reporting, short stories, play, published and performed locally.; [pers.] Life is full of turning points that can occur within seconds and affect us for years. Through my writing, I try to reflect what the human being experiences during these moments.; [a.] Newton, NJ

WILLIAMS, MRS. MAGGIE NEAL
[b.] September 15, 1927, Tuskegee, AL; [p.] Mr. and Mrs. John Pasture and Maggie Guna Neal; [m.] Mr. James H. Williams II, Deceased; [ch.] James H. III, Emmett D., Frantina R.; [ed.] Tuskegee Institute High, Alabama State University; [occ.] Retired school teacher in Macon and Russell Counties in Alabama; [memb.] In active Member of Zeta Phi Beta Sorority; [oth. writ.] Several poems published in the local newspaper, U.S.A today, and other private publications.; [a.] Tuskegee, AL

WILLIAMS, NANCY
[b.] October 4, 1951, Peoria, IL; [p.] Francis McGuirk, June Haikey; [ch.] Wendy, Adam; [ed.] Manual High School, Methodist Med. Center School of Histotechnology; [occ.] Histotechnologist; [memb.] National Society Histotecnologist, Washington State Histotechnologists; [oth. writ.] Several poems. I have been writing poetry for my family since childhood.; [pers.] I usually write only for my family. I find it easy to write from the heart and I try to express my feelings through my poetry.; [a.] Renton, WA

WILLIAMS, RON
[b.] October 4, 1962, Sandusky, OH; [ed.] Athens High School, Athens, Ohio; [occ.] Computer Tech., Ohio Univ.; [a.] Athens, OH

WILLIAMS, SHELLY
[b.] November 20, 1980, Montclair, CA; [p.] Shirley Jones; [ed.] Rialto High School, Henry Elementary School, Frisbie Middle School; [occ.] High School Student; [hon.] Honor Roll at Frisbie Jr. High, Rialto High School, Frisbie Middle School; [pers.] I am a 15 year old student, when I wrote this I was a 10th grader. I got my inspiration from the play Romeo and Juliet.;

[a.] Rialto, CA

WILLIAMSON, LORANN A.
[pen.] Lorann Adams; [b.] January 17, 1960, Gastonia; [p.] Mr. and Mrs. Willie Greene Adams; [m.] Clarence Edward Williamson, June 18, 1993; [ch.] Amy Michelle Birch (12), Iya Qynaya Williamson (4); [ed.] 1978 Graduate of Hunter Huss High School Gaston College (1 year); [occ.] Machinist Operator; [memb.] I am a member of the Weeding Mary Baptist Church Young Adult Choir; [hon.] Mars Hill Choir Clinic (Recorded 2 albums for school) Award for Passenger Talent show on the "Fun Ship" Fantasy Cruiseship.; [oth. writ.] Poems, short stories, plays, songwriter.; [pers.] I feel that, to know the spirit flowing in the presents of nature, is to know the spirit experienced in the hearts of humans.; [a.] Gastonia, NC

WILLIAMSON, SANDRA
[b.] February 9, 1955, North Carolina; [ed.] Murfreesboro High, NC. St. Peters College; [occ.] Substitute Teacher, Jersey City Board of Education; [pers.] In my poetry, I try to create, a warm and sensitive appreciation of the human spirit within a person. My study of earlier women poets some what propelled me.; [a.] Jersey, NJ

WILMOT, RONNIE
[pen.] Poet; [b.] September 20, 1972, Corvallis, OR; [p.] Richard and Barbara Wilmot; [ed.] B.S., Psychology, University of Oregon Reality; [occ.] Painter; [oth. writ.] None worth mentioning; [pers.] We shall not cease in our exploration and the end of all our exploring will be to arrive where we started and know the plan for the first time.; [a.] Juneau, AK

WILSON, DAVID H.
[b.] July 31, 1963, Clarksburg, WV; [p.] Alpha E. Wilson, Phyllis E. Spera; [ed.] Delaware Technical and Community College; [occ.] Full Time Student; [pers.] My personal rhetoric is my belief in the crossing of social boundaries while imploring goal directed behavior in counteracting social darwinism for the possible reduction of deviant behavior in the hopes of making everyone's social reality a more pleasurable experience.; [a.] Milton, DE

WILSON, JANICE A.
[b.] September 11, 1951, N.Y.C; [m.] Horace C. Wilson, March 4, 1972; [ch.] Zulema and Kenya Wilson; [occ.] Minister of Gospel (Retired Executive Assistant) (Comsat Corp., Bethesda, MD); [oth. writ.] Many poems and inspired writings compiled now is the time to published!; [pers.] Since I was a young girl, I always believed there was power in words. I believe the creative word was spoken before time, and me, who are now in time and eternity, journey through the manifestation of it.; [a.] East Point, GA

WILSON, JENNY MARIE
[b.] April 18, 1979, San Antonio, TX; [p.] Jimmy Lee Wilson, Janet Wilson; [m.] Jeffrey Wayne Dartman (Fiance), End of '97; [ch.] One on the way - Timothy Lee Dartman; [ed.] I am a dropout. But I intend to get diploma and maybe get into college.; [occ.] I am very interested in becoming a Great Poet.; [hon.] I have never received any awards or honors until now. It makes me very excited to be acknowledged by The National Library of Poetry.; [oth. writ.] I have written many other poems. I hope to have them all published one day. Most of my poems are all from my personal experiences. Some are also what I feel.; [pers.] When you have a dream don't give up on it. Just hang on to it and believe and soon you shall reach your goal.; [a.] La Monte, MO

WILSON, MEREDITH M.
[b.] October 26, 1979, Atlantic City; [p.] Kathryn E. Wilson and Martin S. Wilson Sr.; [ed.] Anita Metzger School, Ventnor N.J. Elementary and Middle School, Holy Spirit High School, Absecon N.J.; [occ.] Student, 11th grade; [memb.] Drama Club, Ski Club, Crew, Piano, Guitar and Voice, Art; [hon.] Bill Donelley Poetry Club; [oth. writ.] Short Stories and Poetry (unpublished); [pers.] "I'd rather be a servant worthy of a king than a king unworthy of a servant." Meredith; [a.] Ventnor, NY

WILSON, MICHAEL D.
[b.] March 28, 1959, Philadelphia, PA; [p.] Janie Wilson, Eddie Wilson; [ed.] South Philadelphia High School, Penn State University, Cleveland State University, West Chester University; [memb.] American Society of Composers, Authors and Publishers (ASCAP) 1992-1995; [hon.] High School Honor Student, Deans List, Fall 1981 CGU; [oth. writ.] Unpublished songs, music compositions; [pers.] I'm a modern romantic, love nature. "The best things in life are free." Nature is the dawn of inspiration.; [a.] Philadelphia, PA

WINGES, KRISTEN
[b.] November 11, 1982, Redwood Falls, MN; [p.] Chris and Janet Winges; [ed.] Milbank Elementary, Milbank Middle School; [memb.] Awana, United Methodist Church; [hon.] 1st and 2nd book awards for Awana; [a.] Milbank, SD

WISEMAN, PAULA TILSON
[b.] May 9, 1959, Harriman, TN; [p.] Bill and Mabel Tilson; [m.] Jack Wiseman, September 7, 1984; [ch.] Amber, Zachary, Corbin; [pers.] I hope that my writing will touch or help at least one person if it does then I'm happy.; [a.] Harriman, TN

WITT, CORNELIUS L.
[pen.] Neal L. Witt; [b.] September 7, 1921, Denver, CO; [p.] Laurens and Petronella Witt; [m.] Pearl J. Witt, December 7, 1980; [ch.] Daughter by previous marriage (wife deceased); [ed.] South Denver High School, some College (2 yrs); [occ.] Retired Surety Bond Underwriter and Agent; [memb.] Family Life Church Rancho Message Caly, Past President: Christian Businessmen's, Committee of Los Angeles, Past Chairman Surety Underwriters Club of Southern California; [oth. writ.] Several unpublished poems; [pers.] I am convinced that most people are too preoccupied to appreciate the wonders and delight of Gods creations, both inanimate and animate.; [a.] Cathedral City, CA

WITTMAYER, LAURIE
[pen.] L. Lynne; [b.] October 27, 1949, Mason City, IA; [p.] Wilfer and (late) Blanch Anderson; [m.] Rae Wittmayer, August 12, 1972; [ch.] Daniel age 16, David (Deceased) June 17, 1987 at age 9; [ed.] A.A. Waldorf College (cum laude) '70, B.A. in Special Education '72, Post grad Certification - Multicategorical '90; [occ.] Multicategorical Resource Teacher K-3; [memb.] Evangelical Lutheran Church of America, National Education Association, Iowa State Education Association; [hon.] 1st Prize poetry contest winner for Local Arts Festival in '95 and Prose in '96.; [oth. writ.] Pieces of Me, by L. Lynne, an unpublished collection of Christian reflections of every day events. (Prose and poetry).; [pers.] Looking at life from middle age.; [a.] Washington, IA

WOHRLE, GREGORY DREW
[pen.] Greg Wohrle; [b.] May 15, 1972, West Chester, NY; [p.] Barbara Wohrle and Gary Wohrle; [ed.] Pine Crest High, University of Florida; [occ.] Investment Advisor, Dean Witter; [memb.] Young Philosophers, Pi Kappa Phi; [hon.] Florida Undergraduate Scholars Fund Recipient, Team Debate Novice State Champ, All-State Football Player; [oth. writ.] Being depressed and falling in love with yourself, in hope of the future the reason; [pers.] I believe that we all have love and goodness in us, but some of us have gone through too much pain to be aware of it. Freedom is my ultimate value; [a.] Fort Lauderdale, FL

WONG, JASON ALOYSIOUS
[b.] October 20, 1973, Honolulu; [p.] Mr. Aloysious K. B. Wong, Mrs. Rosemarie Wong; [ed.] B. Ed. with an emphasis in English from University of Hawaii at Manoa, Damien Memorial High School, St. Theresa's School; [occ.] English teacher and Sales Associate; [memb.] NEA, Our Lady of Good Counsel Education Board Member; [oth. writ.] Colors, a poem published in A Muse to Follow anthology; [pers.] All writing is great because writing allows each of us to thing. All writing can be improved to show how we've come to mature. Writing is a means of evaluation and assessment.; [a.] Aiea, HI

WOOD, ERIKA
[b.] June 24, 1980, Pittsfield, MA; [p.] Thomas and Wendy Wood; [ed.] Shelby High School; [occ.] High School Student, Shelby High School, Shelby, NC; [memb.] National Beta Club, Shelby High Drama, and Technical Theatre; [hon.] Finalist in the 1994 Parade Magazine, Young Columbus Essay Contest XXXVIII, Top Honors in National Latin Exam; [oth. writ.] Many poems mainly for pleasure.; [pers.] I don't waste my time thinking of the perfect thing to write. I just give the pen a piece of my mind and it does what it will.; [a.] Shelby, NC

WOOTEN, DOROTHY
[b.] October 3, 1952, NC; [p.] Robert and Ester Stennett; [m.] Andrew Wooten, June 9, 1991; [ch.] Michelle Dean and Angela Dean; [ed.] Gaston College, Dallas, N.C.; [occ.] Secretary and Nursing Assistant II; [memb.] American Heart Association, American Cancer Association and American Diabetes Association.; [hon.] American Red Cross Adult and Children CPR; [pers.] I believe in following your dreams, striving for perfection, and always putting God first. I thank my daughters and my husband for their love and support.; [a.] Dallas, NC

WOOTSON, GERRY L.
[pen.] Gerry L. Wootson; [b.] March 30, 1973, Coco Beach, FL; [p.] Mr. and Mrs. Johnnie and Carrie Wootson; [ed.] North Lenoir High School; [occ.] Student; [memb.] Deeper Life Church Ministries; [hon.] United States Achievement Academy Award for Physical Science in 1988; [oth. writ.] "Without You" published in Unframed Thoughts in 1990. "Outside in the Rain" published in Unframed Thoughts in 1991. "Treasures of Beauty" published in Poetic Voices of America in Spring 1997; [pers.] I hope that whoever reads this can relate to it. Everyone, I believe, has bad their heart broken. If one lets that hurt linger it turns into bitterness. Do not walk around with all this hurt and pain. Let inner healing begin.; [a.] LaGrange, NC

WORGAN, J. M.
[pen.] Jennifer, J. M. Worgan; [b.] November 13, 1951, Greenville, SC; [p.] James J. Worgan Jr. and Joan Worgan; [ed.] Colegio Americano - Mx., Coleman High, WI, California State University, Sacramento - CA, BA Bilingual/Cross Cultural Diversified Studies, Emphasis: Spanish, Univ. of The Pacific CA, Teaching Credential Multiple Subject K-12; [occ.] Bilingual Resource Teacher, Adult Ed Spanish Teacher; [memb.] Association of Mexican American Educators; [hon.] Graduated 2nd in my class in High School, was a member of National Honor Society in High School, First place state wrote Spanish contest Cedar Rapids, Iowa 10th grade; [oth. writ.] The Colors of Mariposa's

Wings, Blues and other Hues, Mournings and Dawns, Flutterbying, four collections of poems.; [pers.] I've been through changes of countries, language, culture, views of God and new divorce and self discovery. The one thing that has not changed is what I was taught as a child-Jesus loves me.; [a.] Porterville, CA

WORK, MEGHAN E.
[b.] May 23, 1975, New London, NH; [p.] Michael Work, Christine Work; [ed.] Kearsarge Regional High, Candidate for Bachelor's of Arts, Cornell University, May 1997; [occ.] Student, Cornell University; [oth. writ.] This is my first published work.; [pers.] I try to address complicated issues using a simple style. My hope is that readers not only enjoy my poetry, but also evaluate their beliefs after reading it.; [a.] Ithaca, NY

WYSOCKI, DANIELLE ROBIN
[pen.] Danielle Robin Wysocki; [b.] April 17, 1982, West Branch, MI; [p.] David and Tammy Kann and Mark and Kelli Wysocki; [ed.] Elementary and Junior high school; [memb.] Mio United Methodist Church; [oth. writ.] Only non-published short stories and poems.; [pers.] Get everything out of life that you can. Always do the best you can in everything you do.; [a.] Mio, MI

YANG, LIS YA-WIN
[b.] February 27, 1974, Taichung, Taiwan; [p.] Cliff Yang, Nami Yang; [ed.] Van Nuts M/S High, UCLA, New York Medical College; [occ.] Medical Student; [memb.] Formosan Presbyterian Church in Los Angeles, National Marrow Donor Program Registry, UCLA Marching Band 1992-1996; [hon.] Good Samaritan Scholarship, UCLA Regents/National Merit/Alumni Scholar, National Science Scholar, Dean's List; [pers.] I am a Christian, Pianist, in-line skater, Ballroom/swing dancer, and soon-to-be physician. I think dogs are wonderful.; [a.] Acton, CA

YARBROUGH III, WM. VESTAL
[b.] February 13, 1969, Tahlequah, OK; [p.] William V. Yarbrough Jr., Kaye F. Wilson; [m.] Jodi R. Walker/Yarbrough, September 28, 1996; [ch.] Cats (3): Sadie, Alfaus and Simon; [ed.] Sisters Elem, Springfield High, Lane Community College; [occ.] Mechanic/Welder/Carpenter/Jack of many trades; [oth. writ.] Numerous unpublished poems and free writings that I would like to have published.; [pers.] "Words must be read as reservedly and deliberately as they were written..." Thoreau; [a.] Federal Way, WA

YESKIS, MARK D.
[b.] June 9, 1972, Brockton, MA; [p.] Gail and Anthony Yeskis; [occ.] Musician, Romantic Composer; [pers.] I am concerned primarily with the great heights that a man can achieve. I believe that life is a constant upward motion and that stagnation is death. I uphold reason, individual rights and capitalism as the means to achieve human greatness.; [a.] Bridgewater, NH

YOUNG, HELEN
[b.] June 27, 1974, England; [p.] Peter and Marian Taylor; [m.] John Young, August 3, 1996; [occ.] Student; [oth. writ.] Poems published in local newspapers and read on the local and national radio stations in England; [pers.] Most of my poems reflect my personal experiences both past and present. Others are based upon mythology and fantasy.; [a.] Drexell Hill, PA

YOUNG, JAMES ED
[b.] July 21, 1948, San Francisco, CA; [m.] Joan Young, June 11, 1976; [ch.] James (Jed) Edward - La Roy Charles; [ed.] Occawa High - Immaculata College; [occ.] Food Service Director; [memb.] The Compassionate Friends of Del Co. - Dietany Managas Asso.; [oth. writ.] Several other writtings to our son Jed who

passed away April 2, 1991; [pers.] I write to owr son in hopes of helping myself, and perhaps others, in working thru the grief of losing a child.; [a.] Drexel Hill, PA

YOUNG, YOLANDA L.
[b.] March 31, 1966, Seattle, WA; [ed.] University of Washington; [occ.] Legal Assistant; [a.] Seattle, WA

ZALL, MARY JANE
[b.] July 31, 1915, Tulare, CA; [p.] Cecil Billing and Gerald Frank Roche; [m.] Sam Zall, April 10, 1937; [ch.] One Son - T. A. Zall; [occ.] Housewife; [oth. writ.] (Anthology) Poetry "My Heart on my Sleeve" by Mary Jane Zall. Children Stories: "Naughty Pugsley", a book of three stories, by Mary Jane Zall, "The Dragons of Borey", Published by Appeal-Democrat, by MJ Zall "The Survivors", by J. Sullivan and MJ Zall. The Historical past of Yuba-Sutter Counties; [pers.] My children stories were written for my grandchild in the hopes he would understand more about friendship and kindness. My poetry was written for my friends, about the simplicity and joy of every day living.; [a.] Marysville, CA

ZARLENGO, MEG
[b.] December 27, 1984, Denver, CO; [p.] Dr. Gerry and Kerry Zarlengo; [ed.] Our Lady of Fatima (Catholic School); [memb.] Girl Scouts, Soccer Team; [pers.] I continue to try to put God and religious meanings in my poems. My grandparents, parents, sister, Katie and two of my favorite teachers, Mrs. Ballentine and Miss Galmish have continuously encourage and inspired me to write poems.; [a.] Lakewood, CO

ZIMMERMAN, TRICIA LYNN
[b.] March 6, 1978, Pottsville, PA; [p.] Robert Allen and Patty Jean Zimmerman; [ed.] Blue Mountain High School; [occ.] Seamstress; [memb.] Red Creek Wildlife Center; [pers.] Love shall last forever in the heart of the believer.; [a.] Cressona, PA

ZIMPFER, DANIEL W.
[b.] October 16, 1968, Rochester, NY; [p.] David and Mary Lou Zimpfer; [ed.] Oakland Mills H.S. (Columbia, MD) and Roosevelt H.S. (Kent, OH). B.S. in Civil Engineering, U. of Minnesota, 1991; [occ.] Civil Engineer; [mem.] Am. Soc. of Engineers; [hon.] Captain, U. of Minnesota Men's Gymnastics Team, 1989-91. Member, U.S.A. National Men's Gymnastics Team, 1988-90, competitions in Eastern Europe Zimbabwe, Olympic Training Center, 1991-92; [pers.] Daniel died in a mountaineering accident at age 26 in 1994. Physical, mental, emotional and spiritual health were all important to him. He loved the out-of-doors: an avid hiker, camper, climber, skier. He wrote this poem on a 7000 mile cross-country cycling trip in 1992, during the height of fall color near his families summer cabin in northern New York. A thoughtful young man, he turned to photography poetry and music to express his appreciation for the wonder of his natural surroundings. He often ruminated about his relationship to God and to the world, and the poem fore tells his own demise.; [a.] Redwood, NY

ZUFELT, STEPHANIE
[b.] December 1, 1980, Logan, UT; [p.] Lee and Connie Zufelt; [ed.] Madison High School; [oth. writ.] Other poems and short stories at home.; [pers.] I like to write poetry because I can express the way I feel and the way I think about things. It's the best way to share my thoughts.; [a.] Rexburg, ID

INDEX